AIR TRANSPORTATION

FOURTEENTH EDITION

Robert M. Kane

KENDALL/HUNT PUBLISHING COMPANY
4050 Westmark Drive   Dubuque, Iowa 52002

Book Team

Chairman and Chief Executive Officer   Mark C. Falb
Vice President, Director of National Book Program   Alfred C. Grisanti
Editorial Development Supervisor   Georgia Botsford
Developmental Editor   Angela Willenbring
Prepress Project Coordinator   Sheri Hosek
Prepress Editor   Carrie Maro
Permissions Editor   Renae Heacock
Cover Design Manager   Jodi Splinter
Cover Designer   Deb Howes
Senior Vice President College Division   Thomas W. Gantz
Vice President and National Field Manager   Brian Johnson
Managing Editor, College Field   Paul Gormley
Associate Editor, College Field   Greg DeRosa

BRIEF CONTENTS

Dedicated to the loving memory of my wife, Georgia,
for her constant love and support.

CONTENTS

PREFACE

This text, *Air Transportation*, has been in continuous publication by the original author since 1967; it is now being used by a third generation of students. The continuous acceptance and use of this textbook may be attributed to the basic purpose determined by the author from the beginning. That purpose was, and continues to be, to provide a text with the needs of the classroom teacher and the students in mind. The author well remembers being a student in classrooms as well as thirty years as a college professor.

The new fourteenth edition of *Air Transportation* continues this basic premise. Obsolete material has been deleted or combined with relevant subject material so as not to be lost entirely, but to be saved as historical information. The current conditions of the industry are discussed along with expectations for the future.

The author does not believe that opinion, speculation, or discussion of current events should enter into this text. Discussion of current issues that influence the air transportation industry should take place in the classroom using the textbook as a basis for such discussion and further study into a more complete study of the various facets of air transportation that are to be found in this comprehensive presentation of the industry.

Robert M. Kane

For I dipped into the future, far as human eye can see
Saw the vision of the world, and all the wonder that would be;
Saw the heavens fill with commerce, argosies of magic sails,
Pilots of the purple twilight, dropping down with costly bales.

From "Locksley Hall" by Tennyson who foresaw air transportation before the advent of the airplane.

The author Bob Kane "turning on final"
(Pilots note: read the instruments)
Photo courtesy of Eric Smith

LIST OF TABLES

LIST OF FIGURES

ACKNOWLEDGEMENTS

Grateful acknowledgments are made to the many individuals who supplied resource material as well as personnel of the following air transportation organizations at the governmental, corporate, and private levels.

- Federal Aviation Administration
- Department of Transportation
- National Transportation Safety Board
- Air Transportation Association of America
- International Air Transport Association
- International Civil Aviation Organization
- Airports Council International
- General Aviation Manufacturers Association
- Aerospace Industries Association
- National Air Transport Association
- The Boeing Company
- Lockheed Martin Corporation
- Airbus Industrie
- Cessna Aircraft Company
- Piper Aircraft Company

A special thank you to Eric Smith, computer wizard, who created the program to run the CD-ROM which is included on the back cover of this text.

Acknowledgment is extended to the students for whom this text is prepared. It is hoped that they will find the subject of air transportation interesting and fascinating.

Features of the Fourteenth Edition

All tables, charts and graphs have been updated with the latest data depicting the various aspects of the air transportation industry.

The CD-Rom located in the back of the book outlines each chapter and provides some additional information. No installation is necessary to use this CD. Simply insert it into the CD drive and it will run automatically. It is suggested that you use the CD-Rom to preview the chapters before reading the textbook.

There are several unique features on the CD.
- The opening page has an audio of a jet aircraft flying by.
- Video clips in Chapter 3 are of several airplanes and Lindbergh's take-off on his famous flight.
- An audio in Chapter 8 is of a control tower in action and illustrates what is heard by pilots.
- Video clips in Chapter 9 show several aircraft crashes.
- An audio in Chapter 27 produces the sound of a Cessna aircraft engine.

ORGANIZATION OF THE TEXT

This air transportation textbook is organized into five separate distinct parts. Each part and the chapters contained therein are complete within themselves to allow for ease of reference and to provide instructors the ability to present the material in whatever order they prefer.

Part One, "Historical and Present Status of Air Transportation" presents an historical review of the industry.

Part Two, "Regulation of Air Transportation" presents the various regulatory agencies that govern the air transportation industry. This Part has been significantly updated to provide current information. Two new chapters have been added: 14. A Review of Non United States Air Carriers and 15. Commercial Space Transportation.

Part Three, "Administration of Air Transportation" has been updated for most of the chapters. A new section in Chapter 16 presents a discussion and an exercise in Managerial Economics.

Part Four, "Aircraft" contains new data about commercial aircraft. Chapter 21 has been completely revised and updated.

Part Five, "General Aviation" has been revised to include the latest statistical information concerning the General Aviation aspects of Air Transportation. Cessna and Piper aircraft companies are featured with new information about Mooney and Raytheon-Beech aircraft companies.

Appendices provide additional material consisting of organizations and membership lists.

Glossary has been updated to include new terminology included in this edition.

Index provides a quick access for locating information throughout the text.

PART 1

HISTORICAL AND PRESENT STATUS OF AIR TRANSPORTATION

Part 1

Brief Overview of Chapters

1. THE IMPORTANCE OF AIR TRANSPORTATION

- Addresses the most important aspects of the air transport industry in terms of economic, social, and political issues and participation of air carriers in the Civil Reserve Air Fleet Program.

2. MAN'S EFFORTS TO FLY

- Reviews the pioneer experiments in flight . . . from fantasy to success with balloons and dirigibles.

3. DEVELOPMENT OF THE AIRPLANE

- Discusses historical development of flyable aircraft from early hang-gliders to controllable flying aircraft.

4. THE BEGINNING OF AIR MAIL AND COMMERCIAL AIR TRANSPORTATION

- Emphasizes the important role that the United States Post Office played in development of commercial aviation.

CHAPTER 1

The Importance of Air Transportation

The airplane, and therefore aviation, is not yet older than some lifetimes. There are millions of Americans living today who were living when the Wrights launched their airplane. It was on December 17, 1903, that Orville Wright left the ground from the sand dunes of Kitty Hawk, North Carolina, in the world's first controllable powered flight. At that moment of take-off he ushered in what has proved to be the greatest period in the history of humankind. The first powered flight covered 120 feet. The progress in air transportation since that day can be summed up in a single comparison: the entire length of that historic flight could be measured off inside the cabin of a modern jetliner and there would still be room to spare.

The history of humankind, as much as we know of it, goes back about two million years. Walking was the only means of transportation during the first one and three-quarter million years; and as transportation has developed, so have humans. In those prehistoric and ancient times knowledge of the world was limited to approximately a ten-mile radius from where one lived, because that was the distance which one was able to travel. The only means of transportation was by foot. Early people had only the customs and language of their tribes—the people with whom they lived and worked. The knowledge of that group of people was all the knowledge that existed in the world as far as they were concerned.

Civilization did not begin to develop to any extent for thousands of years. The various groups or clans of people who lived on the various parts of the earth had no way to communicate with each other. In fact, they did not realize that any people other than themselves even existed.

When humans finally domesticated animals, they used them to ride on their backs, and the limits and knowledge of the world expanded.

Water Transportation. Civilization began to develop and flourish along the inland waterways and the coastal areas of the oceans, and humans invented and learned to use boats for water transportation. This made it possible to find and visit other groups of people. People took the knowledge of other peoples and carried it back to their own people. For about 4,000 years civilization developed along the waterways with the assistance of water transportation. Various groups of humans were then able to communicate with each other. Culture and knowledge, which are the basis of society, were beginning to spread because of available transportation.

Along came the wheel, which is considered one of humans most important inventions. It was first introduced into the Mediterranean area indirectly by the Chinese, according to history. The Romans then carried it into Europe during their years of conquest. The wheel, and the many mechanical refinements which it produced, greatly speeded up our ability to travel.

The Air Age. Over the centuries, invention followed invention until finally just after the turn of the twentieth century the air age came into being as a result of the Wright brothers' flight in 1903. Their first airplane, which was nothing more than an oversized glider upon which an engine had been placed, developed 16 horsepower. The first sustained flight lasted only 12 seconds. The modern jet engines on today's airliners develop many thousands of pounds of thrust horsepower.

The Wright brothers flew in their first airplane at a speed of 31 miles per hour. Some military airplanes fly in excess of 2,000 miles per hour. With the introduction of the supersonic transport, commercial aircraft also are able to attain this speed.

The number of passengers carried by United States certificated airlines in 2000 was 665 million. These passengers traveled 692.5 billion miles. The airlines hold the position as the number one common carrier in the interstate passenger business. Airlines produce 92.1% of all the intercity passenger miles of public passenger transportation in the United States. It was 77% in 1970. Domestic air carrier revenue passenger miles are expected to increase at a 4.3% annual rate and international air carrier revenue passenger miles 6.8% through the year 2012 according to the Federal Aviation Administration forecast data. This rate of increase means that the United States certificated air carriers' number of passengers carried in the year 2012 should be over a trillion.

The air carrier fleet had grown to 5,647 large jet aircraft by 2000. This number is forecasted to increase to 8,503 by the year 2012. The Federal Aviation Administration predicted that load factors on United States air carriers will rise to 80.0% by 2012 compared to the current 79.2%.

After 2000, air carrier traffic is expected to rise steadily. However, the major companies will probably have difficulty earning more than modest profits. They will continue to struggle to reduce costs and deal with competition. Increasing airport delays, threats of recession, new taxes, and rising fuel costs could offset any possible financial gains.

The long awaited rush to acquire new, quiet aircraft began in 1996 and will continue through the year 2012. Regional air carriers will thrive and continue to expand as they acquire more jet-powered aircraft and larger, faster turboprop transports to operate over longer routes.

The Jet Age. Commercial air transportation has barely passed its youth. In relatively few short years the air carriers have developed in a remarkable fashion. This tremendous growth was accelerated by the jet age, which signaled a complete change for the air carrier industry; one which has been marked by a phenomenal change.

A great potential market of air travelers is, therefore, available. Many of these new air travelers will take to the skies in high-speed jets. Surface methods of transportation are rapidly becoming obsolete due to the relatively higher expense to the passenger. Many examples exist today where a dollar for dollar comparison will show that it is cheaper for a traveler to fly or a shipper to send cargo by airline than to use conventional surface means of transportation, to say nothing of the many intangible benefits, such as greater comfort and savings in time.

The hopes and promises for future civilization are in the air. The jet age in the United States promises to make available more jobs with greater security for aviation-minded people. It also means a better way of living for all citizens tomorrow. Through its ever continuing progress, the aviation industry of the United States has become one of the most vital economic forces in our capitalistic system of free enterprise. Commercial air transportation will continue to increase. Aviation in itself is progress, and a sound commercial air transportation industry is essential.

THE IMPORTANCE OF AIR TRANSPORTATION

Probably, the most astounding thing about aviation is that it has become so important in such a short time. It is easy to understand the rapid growth of aviation's influence if we remember that aviation means the air age—the age of the wing—a period of time characterized by air travel and transportation. It is these two facts—that air travel knows few physical obstacles and that it decreases the time of transportation so greatly—that have caused dramatic changes in the course of human events.

It is now possible to travel from coast to coast in less than six hours by commercial aircraft. Military aircraft fly this distance in much less time. It took the pioneers, who expanded our country westward, six months to travel from Independence, Missouri, to San Francisco, California, a distance only half as great. In the days of horse and buggy travel, one who lived on a farm or in a village may have journeyed all day to reach the county seat. Today, by airplane, anyone can reach the nation's capital in a few hours, no matter where they live in the continental United States. One can reach by air any capital of any nation from any airport anywhere in the world more readily than George Washington could reach Philadelphia from Mt. Vernon by stagecoach.

The invention of the airplane wing made it possible to travel through the air and over obstacles, such as mountains, deserts, swamps, and ice caps, which make surface travel slow and costly, if not impossible. Moreover, air transportation is swift beyond the most fanciful imagination of a few generations ago.

> Today, by airplane, anyone can reach the nation's capital in a few hours, no matter where they live in the continental United States.

Today, the greatest tribute that can be paid to commercial aviation is the fact that it is taken so much for granted, particularly in the aspect of safety. Air sickness affected at least half the people who flew in the 1930s; motion was a prime cause, of course, but psychiatrists say that fear was an important element. Air sickness among today's travelers is extremely rare; the smoothness of jetliners plays a major role in reducing such discomfort, and there is a direct correlation with the reduction of fear of flying.

Aviation is important because of the ways it influences everyday living. Everyday, aviation affects our social, economic, and political surroundings. It affects the way all people live and work and it has influenced the nature of relationships with other nations. It enables people to travel with greater ease and to visit countries around the globe. Thus, world leaders can readily assemble in conference.

The importance of commercial air transportation can be summed up in three ways: **economic, social, and political.**

ECONOMIC

It is through their continuous efforts in the public interest that the air carriers of the United States have moved forward. This is the prevailing attitude of the air carriers. The jet equipment program was revolutionary, not only in terms of air carrier effort, but also in terms of the benefits for the nation. Progress made by air carriers in the past two decades has been brought about by constant attention in such areas as safety, operational techniques, and services designed to make flight more pleasant and convenient for the passenger.

A look at the air carrier industry yesterday and today will readily indicate the growth of air transportation. As a result of governmental legislation in 1938, the 23 existing air carriers became an organized industry.

In 1938 less than 300 cities and towns were served by air carriers. That number has increased to 650 cities today, most of which have jet service.

More than 40 U.S. airports handle more flights a year than does London's Heathrow Airport, the world's busiest outside of the United States. (See Table 1.1.)

Table 1.1   Top-20 U.S. Airports—2000

(in thousands)

Passengers (Arriving & Departing)			Cargo Metric Tonnes (Enplaned & Deplaned)		
1	Atlanta	80,171	1	Memphis	2,489
2	Chicago O'Hare	72,136	2	Los Angeles	2,054
3	Los Angeles	68,478	3	Anchorage	1,884
4	Dallas/Ft. Worth	60,687	4	New York Kennedy	1,826
5	San Francisco	41,174	5	Miami	1,642
6	Denver	38,749	6	Louisville	1,520
7	Las Vegas	36,856	7	Chicago O'Hare	1,464
8	Minneapolis/St. Paul	36,688	8	Indianapolis	1,174
9	Phoenix	35,890	9	Newark	1,083
10	Detroit	35,535	10	Dallas/Ft. Worth	905
11	Houston	35,246	11	Atlanta	872
12	Newark	34,195	12	San Francisco	870
13	Miami	33,570	13	Dayton	832
14	New York Kennedy	32,779	14	Oakland	703
15	Orlando	30,823	15	Philadelphia	563
16	St. Louis	30,547	16	Honolulu	482
17	Seattle	28,404	17	Denver	470
18	Boston	27,413	18	Boston	466
19	New York LaGuardia	25,234	19	Ontario	464
20	Philadelphia	24,901	20	Seattle	441

Source: Airports Council International.

In 1938 the newly certificated airlines had little more than 300 airplanes, and these were of the small, twin-engine type, in comparison with today's aircraft, which number 5,647 representing a $70 billion investment. Of today's aircraft, most are jet aircraft. In the early days of the air carriers' passenger carrying business, 5,000 daily seats were available in the United States. Today, over 200,000 seats are available on more than 12,000 daily flights.

In the early 1930s, the beginning airlines had airplanes that flew little more than 100 miles an hour. By 1950 airplanes were capable of flying 300 miles per hour. Today, the jet transport is capable of flying 600 miles per hour. The commercial airliner of the next century is well into the development stage and will carry passengers at almost three times the speed of sound, or in excess of 1,800 miles per hour.

> In 1938 less than 300 cities and towns were served by air carriers.

In 1939, 13,000 airline employees were paid $24 million. In 2000, 679,967 individuals were employed in the airline industry with average pay in wages and benefits of $68,775.00 per employee. (See Table 1.2.)

One outstanding feature of all this increase in growth and better service to the public is that the average fare an airline passenger paid in 1939 was 5.6 cents per mile. Today the average fare is only slightly higher when considering the increased cost of doing business, as well as the increase of other prices which have risen consistently since 1939. (See Table 1.3.)

U.S. airlines carry a majority of the world's air commerce. The industry has grown to a point where transoceanic flights are an everyday occurrence. The continued expansion of both the U.S. and world economies has had a major impact on the demand for aviation services. The financial performance of U.S. and world commercial airlines has also shown remarkable improvement. Based on data compiled by the International Civil Aviation Organization (ICAO), world air carriers (including U.S. airlines) reported cumulative operating losses of $3.8 billion and net losses of $15.9 billion during the 3-year period between 1990 and 1992. However, over the next 4 years, world airlines reported cumulative operating profits totaling $35 billion, $25 billion in the last two years alone. There was also a notable improvement in the carriers' net position in 1995 and 1996, with cumulative net profits totaling $9.5 billion. For world air carriers financial results appear to be positive.

The financial performance of U.S. commercial airlines has, to some extent, mirrored that of its worldwide counterparts, although its financial losses were significantly deeper during the downturn, and its profits significantly greater during the upturn. Between 1990 and 1993, U.S. carriers' cumulative operating losses totaled nearly $5 billion, while its net losses totaled over $11 billion. However, over the last few years, the

Table 1.2 Employment U.S. Scheduled Airlines
(Full-time equivalents)

	1990	2000
Pilots & Copilots	47,131	72,586
Other Flight Personnel	8,904	11,452
Flight Attendants	83,443	113,696
Mechanics	60,952	72,782
Aircraft and Traffic		
Service Personnel	251,187	311,051
Office Employees	43,883	42,096
All Other	50,309	56,304
Total Employment	545,809	679,967
Average Compensation per Employee		
Salaries & Wages	$38,130	$54,813
Benefits & Pensions	6,929	10,172
Payroll Taxes	2,817	3,790
Total Compensation	$47,876	$68,775

Source: Air Transport Association

Table 1.3 Airline Ticket Prices vs. Consumer Prices (1990 = 100)

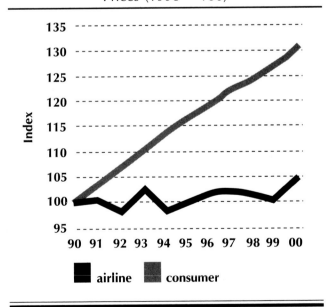

Source: Air Transport Association

industry has reported cumulative operating profits of $7,073 million while its net profits have totaled over $2,638 million.

Entire industries have been changed radically by air transportation; flowers and food, for example. Lettuce picked in California on a Monday can be eaten in a New England home Tuesday night. Lifesaving medicine, emergency replacement parts to prevent major industrial outages, and even valuable horses are some of the thousands of items dependent upon air transportation.

Commercial air transportation is a young industry which has made rapid progress—more rapid progress than a means of transportation has made before. This unprecedented growth in air transportation has not been brought about without obstacles and problems presenting themselves. Air transportation can develop only as far as facilities permit. Aircraft have been developed faster than the facilities upon which they must depend. This is especially true of airports.

The government has recognized the fact that the airlines are like a public utility, and as such the service they offer is said to be in the public interest. This public interest concept includes three basic areas. First is **commerce**—the everyday business of the country. It includes transportation of passengers and air cargo. Second, the airlines' public interest includes the **postal service.** Tons upon tons of letters travel by air, and since 1953 first-class mail, which formerly went by railroad, went by airline. Nine out of every ten intercity first-class letters are carried by the airlines. The third aspect of public interest includes **national defense,** which is discussed later in the chapter.

The Aviation/Aerospace industry is classified into three groups: **manufacturing, air transportation,** and **general aviation.**

Manufacturing

Manufacturing includes all of the research, development, design, construction, fabrication, assembly, and sales of aircraft, engines, parts, accessories, missiles, and spacecraft. It also includes maintenance, modification facilities, and major overhaul.

The United States aircraft manufacturing industry became capable of producing 100,000 units per year during World War II. Employment climbed to over 1.3 million people. After the war ended production dropped to a rate of 6% of its wartime capacity because enough civilian aircraft had been produced to satisfy the need. The industry began to expand again at the start of the Korean War and has grown into one of the most important industries in the United States.

In recent years over half of the federal government's budget had been allocated to national defense, and a large portion of this was directed to the aerospace manufacturing industry. A large percentage of the total sales of aerospace companies is to the federal government.

The United States reduced its military expenditures because of the end of the "cold war" and the breakup of the USSR into the Commonwealth of Independent States. This should result in a shift to the development of products and expenditures of funds for civilian purposes.

Jobs created by this industry call for a wide variety of skills to produce its product. The amount of money spent for research and development in the industry often exceeds that of all other industries.

Civil aircraft sales increased sharply after a modest decline, but sales are projected to increase with commercial transport aircraft being responsible for most of the gain. Large aircraft manufacturers continue to benefit from effects of the Deregulation Act with strong demand for moderate size, fuel efficient aircraft for fleet expansions and replacement needs. There is also a renewed interest by the air carriers in larger aircraft as a means of alleviating the congestion problem at United States airports. The commercial air transport industry represents the strongest segment of the U.S. aerospace industry with a record backlog of orders—foreign orders account for most of the backlog. Narrow-body aircraft orders and deliveries outpace the demand for wide-body aircraft, which reflects the air industry's continuing reliance on schedule frequency to accommodate projected passenger demand.

General aviation aircraft production is increasing. Turbine powered aircraft production is stronger than the single engine piston aircraft production. Manufacture of all types of general aviation aircraft has gone in cycles since World War II. Production increased steadily during the 1970's, reaching a peak in 1978; then general aviation aircraft manufacture declined. The single engine piston aircraft market is the base on which general aviation activity is built. Three quarters of the aircraft in fleet are single-engine piston type. When the single-engine piston market declined, it signaled the slow down of general aviation activity. This condition has changed since builders of general aviation aircraft, like Cessna and Piper, are increasing production.

Commercial Air Transportation

Air Transportation consists of the activities of the commercial air carriers; the routes they fly to serve the public.

Table 1.4   Traffic Growth Rates

revenue passenger
miles (RPMs)

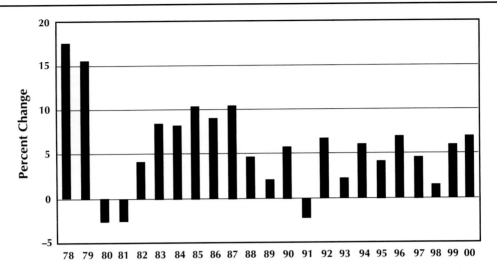

Source: Air Transport Association

October, 1958 brought into being the new era of commercial jet transportation in the United States. Pan American World Airways inaugurated regular scheduled service from New York City to Paris, and later National Airlines inaugurated the first domestic jet service with leased Pan American jets.

The jet era entered a second generation in February 1970 when Pan American World Airways introduced Boeing 747 service between New York and London. The 747 is capable of carrying 420 passengers. The Boeing 707, which Pan American flew in 1958, carried 150 passengers.

The economic effects of the present air transport industry are:

- a shrinkage of distance in terms of time

- an expanded transport capacity of the jet in comparison to propeller-driven aircraft

- an increase in the number of people using air transportation for business and pleasure

- a shift of traffic volume from surface to air

Recession and inflation, the latter highlighted by soaring fuel costs, combined in 1980 to produce an operating loss and a sharp decline in passenger traffic for the nation's major scheduled airlines. (See Table 1.4.)

The Air Transport Association views traffic declines and growing cost pressures with special concern because they impede intensive airline industry capital formation efforts. The capital is needed to acquire the quieter, more fuel-efficient aircraft that will best meet air transport needs in the new century. U.S. airlines have placed orders for billions of dollars worth of new aircraft to take full advantage of improved air transport productivity. (See Table 1.5.)

After a somewhat inauspicious beginning during the first five years of deregulation, the U.S. commercial airline industry's financial fortunes had improved until 1990–1991. The industry's slow start was the result of a number of factors, including airline management's lack of experience in competing in an unregulated market. In defense of airline management, however, the early years of deregulation were by no means the best of times. Starting in 1979, OPEC precipitated the second world oil crisis, with the increase in jet fuel prices severely affecting U.S. airlines. In addition, the U.S. economy went through two economic recessions (1980 and 1982) which, in turn, reduced the demand for air travel. In an effort to stimulate traffic, U.S. airlines resorted to industry-wide fare wars with disastrous financial results.

The U.S. commercial airline industry incurred operating and net losses in three of the first five years of deregulation. During the 5-year period between 1979 and 1983, U.S. carriers posted cumulative operating losses of over $1 billion and cumulative net losses of $967 million. Starting in 1984, however, the industry's financial performance turned around. The industry posted an operating profit in each of the next 5 years, with cumulative operating profits totaling over $10.1 billion over the 5-year period. The industry also earned a net profit in 4 of the 5 years, with a 5-year cumulative net profit of almost $3.2 billion. However, from 1990 through 1994 the industry's losses were $13 billion. In 1994, losses narrowed considerably due to lower fuel prices and the sacrifices airline employees and stockholders made during the industry restructuring. While the air industry's rate of return is still below that of other unregulated industries, it does appear that airline management has learned to adjust to the new economic realities of deregulation and competition. In 2000, net profit was $2,638 million.

Although the industry's overall financial fortunes have improved, not all carriers have shared equally in the financial turnaround. There have been a number of Chapter 11 bankruptcies since deregulation and more would have occurred except that failing carriers merged with or were taken over by other carriers. As profits tend to be concentrated among a relatively few carriers, so do losses. Some of the carriers, although profitable, have managed to post only meager operating profits and oth-

ers have incurred net losses. The large re-equipment programs currently underway in the industry raise the question of how the new aircraft are to be financed. While aircraft leasing arrangements have given the industry room to maneuver, this does not entirely solve the industry's long-term financial problem. The industry's real financial problem is, and will continue to be, the sizable long-term debt currently held by the industry and the revenues that must be generated annually to service the debt. Over the past decade, the industry's long-term debt has almost tripled. With 2,664 aircraft on order and options for hundreds more, the amount of long-term debt held by the industry can only increase.

The weakness in the economies of the world over the past several years has caused the air carrier industry to experience its worst financial year in its history. Two of the oldest and greatest names in the industry, Eastern Airlines and Pan American, ceased operating years ago and others are facing bankruptcy. Three major air carriers—American, Delta, and United—account for more than one half of the total traffic of the industry.

Table 1.5 U.S. Commercial Air Carriers Total Airborne Hours[1]

(in thousands)

Fiscal Year	Large Narrowbody			Large Widebody			Total
	2 Engine	3 Engine	4 Engine	2 Engine	3 Engine	4 Engine	
Historical							
1995	7,649	1,583	312	980	938	558	12,020
1996	8,042	1,504	314	1,021	945	555	12,381
1997	8,430	1,472	293	1,149	940	530	12,814
1998	8,661	1,477	259	1,285	942	511	13,135
1999	9,195	1,385	249	1,489	908	503	13,728
2000E	9,885	1,206	196	1,756	847	504	14,394
Forecast							
2001	10,266	1,025	200	1,902	829	503	14,725
2002	10,756	915	201	2,074	840	506	15,292
2003	11,193	830	201	2,212	840	510	15,786
2004	11,670	739	201	2,385	824	527	16,346
2005	12,094	736	202	2,585	824	543	16,984
2006	12,571	739	202	2,762	806	554	17,634
2007	13,038	744	202	2,953	821	562	18,320
2008	13,659	749	202	3,129	818	570	19,127
2009	14,333	752	202	3,326	835	581	20,029
2010	14,945	755	202	3,548	830	591	20,871
2011	15,579	757	203	3,765	830	605	21,739
2012	16,293	760	203	3,956	860	626	22,698

Source: Form 41, U.S. Department of Transportation
[1] Includes both passenger (excluding regional jets) and cargo aircraft

There have been many organizational structure and operational changes in the air carrier industry since the passage of the Airline Deregulation Act of 1978. A proliferation of low fares resulted in a dramatic increase of passenger traffic. Many communities saw improved air service with increased frequencies through connecting hub airports to multiple destinations. Some air carriers had significant increases in operating profits. Then a downturn in the United States economy occurred at a time when operating costs escalated.

The year 1991 ranks as one of the worst years in the U.S. commercial air carrier industry until 2001 as a result of the terrorist bombings in New York City. First, the U.S. economy entered into a recession in July 1990. This downturn in economic growth had a major impact on travel demand. Secondly, the Iraqi invasion of Kuwait on August 2, 1990, caused jet fuel prices to skyrocket from $0.564 a gallon to $1.092. This cost seriously eroded air carrier profits. Thirdly, the U.S. and Allied Forces began Operation Desert Storm on January 16, 1991. The immediate result was a significant decrease in air travel, especially from the U.S. to Europe and the Middle East, because of fears of terrorism.

When hostilities ended on February 28, 1991, the anticipated recovery in the U.S. economy and air travel failed to occur. The effects of decreased travel demand brought on by the recession and the Gulf War along with the increase in fuel prices, seriously affected an already financially-weakened air carrier industry. This situation cannot and will not remain. The business cycle has moved upward causing an improved U.S. economy. The air carriers emerged more experienced. They will continue their long term gains and service to the public to whom they are dedicated.

The airline industry is, to a certain extent, a victim of its own success. Commercial aviation has grown faster than the airport and airway system in which it operates giving rise to many of the industry's current problems. Twenty-one airports are labeled seriously congested by the Federal Aviation Administration. The agency warns that another 20 may qualify for this dubious distinction if there are no additions to system capacity. According to agency forecasts, large hub airports, which account for virtually all of this congestion, can expect a 28% increase in air traffic and a 70% increase in passenger enplanements by the year 2012. Without offsetting increases in system capacity and efficiency, which will not be easily achieved, the system will be under even more pressure in the future.

Wherever the industry ends up, Congress is certain to have a significant role in the outcome. As keeper of the public trust, Congress deals directly with the full range of technical, institutional, and economic choices expected to play in a long-term solution. The public looks to Congress to solve not only deep-rooted system problems, but also problems of a more immediate, parochial nature involving service, noise, and personal safety. As pressure on the air transportation system increases so will constituent pressure on Congress to provide relief.

Prior to 1978, the airline industry was one of the most regulated of U.S. industries. The Civil Aeronautics Board prescribed airline routes and fares, engaged in consumer regulation, and handled other matters that largely determined the nature of the industry. The only way airlines competed was by the quality of their food and other services.

The Airline Deregulation Act of 1978 (P.L. 95-504) ushered in a new era for the airlines. Airlines now compete essentially as businesses. They are free to succeed and fail like other businesses. The 1978 Act, however, did not completely change the airline industry operating environment. Airports have remained under public control at the state, local, or regional level. The air traffic control system has remained under Federal control. Some consumer regulation and other competitive practices have continued to be subject to Federal oversight, albeit at a diminished level.

Since 1978, Congress has exercised constant oversight of the effects of deregulation. In some instances, such as in 1984 when Congress passed legislation providing for the early sunset of the Civil Aeronautics Board, it has directly affected the course of the industry. More often, however, congressional committees have used their oversight powers to influence administration and industry thinking on such subjects as computer reservation systems.

A few members of Congress have advocated returning the airline industry to its regulated past. Many members have expressed constant concern that the industry remain economically viable and competitive. The recession that began in 1990 along with the effects of the Persian Gulf War had a disturbing impact on the industry. In 1990 the domestic airline industry reported record operating losses and 1991 was not much better. Eastern Airlines, the once self proclaimed "wings of man," and Pan American have disappeared and other air carriers have followed.

The results of the September 11, 2001, hijacking and attack upon the World Trade Center in New York City and the Pentagon in Washington, D.C., had a devastating effect on the air transportation industry. Due to a prior slowdown in the economy of the United States and a slight recession, the air carriers were already in a relatively weak financial position. Because the air transport industry is of such importance to the operation and economy of the country, the federal government provided a direct relief fund. (See Table 1.6.) On September 22nd $15 billion was provided to the industry to help absorb some of the extraordinary losses that they had incurred. A total of $40 billion or more was promised.

Within minutes after two aircraft were crashed into the Twin Towers and one into the Pentagon, all aircraft were ordered to land immediately at the nearest airport. Many thousands of passengers were stranded. Flights were not permitted to resume until a week later and then only on a restricted basis to complete the destination of scheduled flights.

The air carriers drastically reduced air schedules when the public became reluctant to fly. Only 25 to 45 percent of aircraft were filled with passengers, causing load factors to drop to less than 50 percent at a time when 65 percent was necessary to break even.

Within a few weeks, air service was permitted to resume but the industry had lost untold billions of dollars. As many as 100,000 employees were laid off from their jobs.

Boeing Aircraft Company announced a reduction in the number of aircraft to be produced. They also released many thousands of workers.

Never in the history of the United States has such an event occurred. Security at airports and generally throughout the country was greatly increased.

The United States then embarked on an all-out war against terrorism by mobilizing its armed forces. Airline officials estimated that it could take a year or longer for air traffic to recover and the air transport industry to return to normal. Surely the resolve of the public and the industry will overcome whatever disastrous effects terrorism has caused.

Table 1.6   Initial Payments to Air Carriers

Air Carrier Name	Amount
Air Tran Airway	$ 15,125,739
Air Wisconsin Airlines	4,687,931
Alaska Airlines	45,431,677
Allegheny Airlines	1,828,077
America West Airlines	60,281,956
American Airlines	359,419,230
American Trans Air	32,293,436
Atlantic Coast Airlines	5,722,621
Atlantic Southeast Airlines	8,636,852
Big Sky Airlines	253,253
Cape Air	151,254
Chautauqua Airlines	2,834,737
Chicago Express	307,743
Colgan Air	407,277
Comair	10,347,727
Commutair	512,071
Continental Micronesia	9,133,488
Continental Airlines	191,212,249
Continental Express	12,267,855
Delta Air Lines	326,985,791
Eagle Canyon Airlines	238,379
ERA Aviation	204,531
Federal Express Corp.	100,679,072
Florida West Airlines	819
Frontier Airlines	10,118,474
Frontier Flying Service	77,505
Great Lakes Aviation	982,220
Gulfstream Int'l Airlines	496,091
Hawaiian Airlines	18,010,127
Horizon Air	5,031,723
JetBlue Airways	8,395,378
Mesa Airlines	5,775,980
Mesaba Airlines	6,571,704
Midwest Express Airlines	7,530,299
National Airlines	11,030,915
North American Airlines	1,013,794
Northwest Airlines	229,667,738
Pacific Island Aviation	33,954
Piedmont Airlines	2,607,483
Promech	11,539
PSA Airlines	1,260,382
Shuttle American Corp.	291,763
SkyWest Airlines	5,656,835
Southern Air	724,673
Southwest Airlines	144,373,750
Spirit Airlines	10,799,992
Sun Country Airlines	8,207,621
Sunworld International Airlines	563,727
Trans States Airlines	2,323,213
Trans World Airlines	78,047,235
US Airways	159,746,129
United Airlines	390,671,788
United Parcel Service	24,556,636
Vanguard Airlines	4,579,896
Vieques Air Link	4,013
Total	**$2,328,126,342**

By October 1, 2001, the Department of Transportation had paid out $2.3 billion in airline relief act grants. For each carrier, the amount was about half of its estimated total compensation payment, subject to establishing that losses resulted directly from the Federal Aviation Administration September 11th ground stop.

General Aviation

General aviation is broadly defined as all aviation activities except those of the military and commercial air transportation utilizing large aircraft. General aviation aids people in many different ways. For the farmer, general aviation increases crop yields, makes fertilizing more efficient, and reduces the spread of crop disease. For the businessman it means an efficient, productive means of transportation. For the small town it means jobs and new dollars brought in by industry that utilizes community airports.

Diversity is the real significance of general aviation. It has a major role in the transportation system of the nation and is a partner in that system. General aviation and the air carriers together make up the air transportation network of the United States. General aviation consists of 645,539 pilots and a fleet of 219,464 aircraft, of which about 45,000 are used by large and small companies to enhance their business. These operations serve over 5,000 airports, 96% of which are not served by airlines. General aviation aircraft account for 98% of total civil aviation aircraft.

General aviation aircraft fly about thirty-two million hours yearly carrying 130 million passengers over 4 billion miles. General aviation aircraft are used by some 400 law enforcement and government agencies; 65% of commercially applied crop protection; and to transport more than 600,000 patients to hospitals.

Many airports and communities rely partially, and in most cases entirely, on general aviation for air transportation. One of every 3 intercity air passengers travels on a general aviation aircraft. There are many reasons why people fly general aviation aircraft. (See Table 1.7.)

> **The impact of aviation has been felt in all fields of humankind's endeavors.**

Table 1.7 Reasons People Fly
General Aviation Aircraft

Personal	35.6%
Corporate	11.4%
Business	11.3%
Instructional	18.6%
Aerial Application	4.8%
Air Taxi	7.6%
Aerial Observation	3.9%
Public	3.5%
Other	3.3%

Source: Federal Aviation Administration

SOCIAL

The effects of the automobile on our daily habits of living will provide a clue to the far greater changes brought about by air transportation.

A philosopher once said, "Transportation is civilization." He saw many years ago that the civilizations of the world depend upon transportation for their existence. Air transportation has produced significant changes in population trends. The airplane has helped to redistribute populations. Through the use of air transportation, heretofore untouched resources have been developed. This is especially true in South and Central America where the mode of transportation progressed from the ox cart stage directly to the air age. Many internal areas which were virtually inaccessible due to the lack of roads have been developed as a direct result of the use of the airplane.

In the early history of the United States mass movements of people traveled from the east across the western plains using the covered wagon as their means of transportation. The railroad followed the wagon train trails and finally stretched its iron tentacles to the Pacific Coast. Today's air traveler covers this route in a matter of hours in complete comfort.

Air transportation has altered educational concepts: our understanding of geography has changed. No longer is the shortest distance between Chicago and London in a northeasterly direction. By flying over the top of the world, the distance between these two cities is greatly reduced. Likewise, a direct non-stop flight from San Francisco to Tokyo would not be southwestward across the Pacific by way of the Hawaiian Islands. Rather, the shortest distance in miles and time would be a great circle route north from San Francisco over Alaska, and down toward the northern Japanese islands. The measurement is no longer in miles, but in the hours and minutes of time.

It took George Washington half a day to travel between Philadelphia and New York. Today this same half-day travel by commercial jet aircraft would allow a passenger to leave New York, fly to California, and return.

What we take for granted today—the speed, comfort, convenience, reliability, and safety of air travel—was beyond comprehension in the early 1900s. Flying was considered the equivalent of today's science fiction.

Air transportation in the United States reached its present state of development in a relatively short period of time. In recent years aeronautical technological improvements have taken place at an unprecedented rate. The people of the world have realized the advantages of air travel and are using this means of transportation in large numbers. Due to the time saving element of speed alone, air transportation has become invaluable from the standpoint of business and commerce, the postal service, and national defense.

The increasing role of the airlines to the nation is due to several factors, some obvious and some not generally realized or appreciated. Speed and efficiency are prime reasons. Of course, no one has yet to calculate the enormous man-hour savings achieved by the nation's business traveler through use of air transportation, nor the economic benefit from the availability of vastly increased leisure time.

Less visible, but equally vital, is the industry's contribution to fuel efficiency. Although air carriers carry the bulk of public intercity passenger traffic, they consume less than 4% of petroleum fuel used in the United States. In fact, the air carriers have reduced fuel consumption even as they boosted traffic. Since 1973, when the fuel crisis began, passengers flown per gallon of fuel used have increased some 21%.

The air carriers employ thousands of workers. Many thousands of people are employed by companies producing aircraft, engines, spare parts, and other related hardware. Scores of thousands of Americans work at jobs dependent upon commercial aviation—at airports, hotels, motels, restaurants, travel agencies, and public surface transportation businesses such as taxi firms and bus companies. In the average large American city approximately 1 out of every 20 workers is engaged in air transportation or a related job. A study of San Francisco International Airport shows that the economic impact of the airport on the Bay Area amounts to more than two billion dollars annually.

One reason for the success of the scheduled air carrier system is the fact that a person can walk into the office of any scheduled airline or travel agent in any city and buy a ticket that will take him or her to any point served by scheduled airlines throughout the world. The same service is available for freight shipments. The airlines' intercarrier cooperative program for passenger and freight handling is unique among transportation modes.

Air transportation is an example of applied technology. A jetliner contains 4.5 million parts, 100 miles of wiring and 2,000 pieces of tubing. An aircraft is built from 75,000 engineering drawings and requires 12,000 pages of maintenance manuals. Its seats alone cost more than an entire twin-engine airliner of the late 1940s. A single giant airliner costs up to $80 million, 8 times the market value of the whole airline industry in 1938. U.S. airlines provide the best air transportation in the world for the lowest cost; U.S. air fares are priced 50% under European tariffs over similar distances. Today, many airline passengers take advantage of discount fares.

Aviation has become an influence in the life of every citizen of our nation. The magnitude of its effects has increased as new developments in aircraft have progressed. These effects stem from the fact that aircrafts surmount obstacles to surface transportation. To a pilot and his passengers, the hazardous reef, the frozen waste, the precipitous mountain, the jungle, and the desert merely become features of a changing scene lying beneath an aerial pathway. The impact of aviation has been felt in all fields of humankind's endeavors.

POLITICAL

The third aspect of the importance of air transportation and of vital concern to the public is national defense, which encompasses international affairs. Aviation has helped to make our country one of the most powerful nations of the world and to place it in a position of world leadership.

Before aircraft reached their present stage of development, the countries of the Western Hemisphere were protected from outside attack by surface obstacles such as the ice cap over the Arctic area and by the oceans, east and west. If attack comes today, it will be from the skies. Today, defense rests upon air power and diplomacy rather than upon physical barriers.

People must grasp the concept that air power does not belong solely to an arsenal of military weapons. On the contrary, there can be no air power without the civil elements of aerospace manufacturing, air transportation, airports, and industrial and scientific research. Today, however, the strength of the civil element of air power is to a large extent nourished by the needs of military aviation. The result is that they are inseparable; both make the entity of American air power. They share a common objective, the well-being of the nation.

[George Washington said] To be prepared for war is one of the most effectual means of preserving the peace.

These words are as alive today as they were when he spoke them. The concept they illustrate lies at the source of our national defense program. The principle the words express is old; the means we have adopted to preserve the peace is new. Air power is our modern method. Air power is peace power. Until a better way for achieving a lasting peace is discovered, the American people must use—as the principal instrument of defense—air power, the most powerful instrument of peace known today.

The Air Transport Command and the Naval Air Transport Service of World War II helped establish world aviation. They proved air transportation was a vital arm of war. Its remarkable postwar achievement in the Berlin airlift established aviation also as an instrument of national policy in peacetime. Considerable credit for helping to get this force off the ground in time of crisis goes to the airlines. Their equipment, crews, personnel, and organizational experience provided a necessary foundation to build the military air transport organization.

After the war this military operation repaid the airlines with interest. It gave them a complete network of intercontinental airways, ready for long-range air transport operation. It gave them technological knowledge that ordinarily would have taken decades to acquire. Hundreds of C-46 and C-47 aircraft, both twin-engine airplanes, were used to lift tons of cargo over the treacherous Himalaya Mountains. Each operation of these airplanes brought new information. Each flight over the Hump and across an ocean was, in a sense, an experiment, and each flight contributed to a mass of data on airlift performance and efficiency, which in peacetime would have taken several years to accumulate.

War Air Service Program (WASP)

On February 26, 1963, President Kennedy signed Executive Order No. 11090, which redefined the emergency preparedness functions. In preparing this national emergency plan, there are two organizations which play a large role.

The War Air Service Program (WASP) is a program designed to provide for the maintenance of essential civil air routes and services, and to provide for the distribution and redistribution of aircraft among civil air transport carriers after the withdrawal of aircraft allocated to the Civil Reserve Air Fleet.

The Civil Reserve Air Fleet (CRAF) are those air carrier aircraft allocated by the Secretary of Transportation to the Department of Defense to meet essential military needs in the event of an emergency.

The Director of the Office of Emergency Transportation shall advise and assist the president in determining policy for the performance of this order. The "War Air Service Program (WASP) Resource Report" depicts the annual survey of the nation's projected civilian airlift capability in the event of a national emergency. The report concludes that the domestic and international WASP fleets have ample capacity to accommodate the essential passenger and cargo requirements.

Executive orders require the periodic assessment of the availability and airlift capability of commercial aircraft in order to plan for their use in the event of a national emergency. The WASP fleet is composed of commercial aircraft remaining after the Civil Reserve Air Fleet is withdrawn for military use. Even in an emergency, commercial air service would be essential to meet the nation's civilian needs. The entire WASP fleet has an annual requirement of over 7,500 air crews comprising about 20,000 flightdeck personnel.

The WASP program has been inactive for several years. Most of its functions have been incorporated into other government organizations developed in later years.

The Civil Reserve Air Fleet (CRAF)

As air transportation profited from the wartime activities of military air transportation, so today's military forces profit from airline activity. One of the lessons learned for national defense was the importance of commercial air transportation as an essential part of our national security. As a potential military auxiliary of the United States, the airlines are closely tied to military aviation through a plan known as the Civil Reserve Air Fleet (CRAF). This tremendous fleet affords an immediate airlift to supply troops and supplies to any point in the world. The maintenance of this stand-by fleet does not cost the government one cent. It would require millions of dollars to build a fleet of this size for government use and the fleet would stand idle until a national emergency arose. To keep this fleet in ready service would cost the government many more millions of dollars annually.

The Civil Reserve Air Fleet is currently made up of 812 modern jet aircraft; some are modified for military purposes. The total capacity of these aircraft is about 30 million ton-miles per day. Both military and CRAF could carry about 60 million ton-miles a day. All are in commercial operation, but earmarked for military use if needed. Their value has been placed at over $500,000,000. Added to the airlines' annual cost of training crews and maintenance, the value of the Civil Reserve Air Fleet approaches a billion dollars. The CRAF airlift capability expands as new airplanes are added to the fleet.

The CRAF program began with the Korean War in 1950 when the sudden demand to transport troops and equipment could not be met by the military who could only spare 100 aircraft. President Harry S. Truman issued an Executive order in early 1951 which resulted in the establishment of the Civil Reserve Air Fleet. It was patterned after World War II experience and the Berlin Airlift. The new program enlisted the air carrier industry to create a contingency airlift capability for the national emergency.

Airlines that take part in the program offer a list of available aircraft to the military that they are willing to commit to the government. Aircraft usually are long-range jumbo jet aircraft to carry passengers or cargo. The air carrier and the government then sign a contract, usually for a period of one year. This entitles the Air Mobility Command to mobilize the aircraft and crews in the event of a national requirement. Airplanes are assigned to a particular task such as short-haul cargo or long-range troop transporting. They are placed in one of the CRAF stages, either I, II or III, which are designed to enable the government to activate them according to the needs of a particular emergency.

The CRAF has three main segments: international, national and aeromedical evacuation. The international segment is further divided into the long-range and short-range sections and the national segment into the domestic and Alaskan sections. Assignment of aircraft to a segment depends on the nature of the requirement and the performance characteristics needed.

The long-range international section consists of passenger and cargo aircraft capable of transoceanic operations. The role of these aircraft is to augment the Air Mobility Command's (AMC) long-range intertheater C-141s, C-5s and C-17s during periods of increased airlift needs, from minor contingencies up through full national defense emergencies. Medium-sized passenger and cargo aircraft make up the short-range international section supporting near offshore airlift requirements.

The aircraft in the Alaskan section provide airlift within U.S. Pacific Command's area of responsibility. The domestic section is designed to satisfy increased Department of Defense airlift requirements in the U.S. during an emergency.

The aeromedical evacuation segment assists in the evacuation of casualties from operational theaters to hospitals in the continental United States. These aircraft are also used to return medical supplies and medical crews to the theater of operations. Kits containing litter stanchions, litters and other aeromedical equipment are used to con-

> **The Air Force has kits that convert passenger aircraft into flying hospitals.**

vert civil B-767 passenger aircraft into air ambulances.

The airlines contractually pledge aircraft to the various CRAF segments, ready for activation when needed. To provide incentives for civil carriers to commit these aircraft to the CRAF program and to assure the United States of adequate airlift reserves, Air Mobility Command awards peacetime airlift contracts to civilian airlines which offer aircraft to the CRAF. The International Airlift Services contract is the largest of these. Recently the guaranteed portion of the contract was $345 million. Air Mobility Command estimates that throughout the year it will award more than $362 million in additional business that is not guaranteed.

To join CRAF, carriers must maintain minimum long-range international fleet commitment levels (30 percent for passenger and 15 percent for cargo). Aircraft committed must be U.S. registered aircraft capable of overwater operations, at least 3,500 nautical mile range and ten hours per day utilization rate. Carriers must also commit and maintain at least four complete crews for each aircraft. Short-range international section aircraft must be capable of overwater operations and at least a 1,500 nautical mile range. National segment aircraft must be capable of carrying 75 passengers or 32,000 pounds of cargo. Carriers with aircraft too small to be eligible for the CRAF program are issued a certificate of technical ineligibility so they can compete for government airlift business.

Three stages of incremental activation allow for tailoring an airlift force suitable for the contingency at hand. **Stage I** is for minor regional crises, **Stage II** would be used for major regional contingencies and **Stage III** for periods of national mobilization. The Commander in Chief, U.S. Transportation Command (USTRANSCOM), with approval of the Secretary of Defense, is the activation authority for all three stages of CRAF. During a crisis, if Air Mobility Command has a need for additional aircraft, it would request USTRANSCOM to take steps to activate the appropriate CRAF stage. Each stage of the CRAF activation is only used to the extent necessary to provide the amount of civil augmentation airlift needed by the Department of Defense (DOD). When notified of call-up, the carrier response time to have its aircraft ready for a CRAF mission is 24 to 48 hours after the mission is assigned by Air Mobility Command. The air carriers continue to operate and maintain the aircraft with their resources; however, Air Mobility Command controls the aircraft missions.

Safety is the paramount concern, and numerous procedures are in effect to ensure that the air carriers with which Air Mobility Command contracts afford the highest level of safety to the Department of Defense (DOD) passengers. Prior to receiving a contract, DOD carriers must demonstrate that they have provided substantially equivalent and comparable commercial service for one year prior to flying for the Department of Defense. All carriers must be fully certified Federal Aviation Administration carriers and meet the stringent standards of federal aviation regulations pertaining to commercial airlines (Federal Aviation Regulation Part 121).

A Department of Defense survey team, composed of experienced Air Mobility Command pilots and skilled maintenance personnel, performs an on-site inspection of the carriers. This team conducts a comprehensive inspection that includes carrier's aircraft, training facilities, crew qualifications, maintenance procedures and quality control practices to maximize the likelihood that the carrier would safely perform for the Department of Defense. After passing this survey, the carrier is certified as Department of Defense-approved.

Air Mobility Command analysts then continue to monitor the carrier's safety record, operations and maintenance status, contract performance, financial condition and management initiatives, summarizing significant trends in a comprehensive review every six months. In addition to this in-depth review, there are several other surveillance initiatives. These include safety preflight inspections of commercial aircraft by Department of Defense designated inspectors, periodic cockpit observations on operational flights by highly experienced pilots from Air Mobility Command's Air Carrier Survey and Analysis Division, and an increase in the frequency of on-site surveys. These initiatives and the surveys are further supplemented by an open flow of information on all contract carriers between Air Mobility Command and the Federal Aviation Administration through established liaison officers.

The following air carriers are currently members of the Civil Reserve Air Fleet:

Long-Range International Section:

Air Transport International
American International Airways
American Airlines
American Trans Air
Arrow Air
Continental Airlines
Delta Airlines
DHL Airways
Emery Worldwide
Evergreen International
Federal Express Airlines

Fine Airlines
North American Airlines
Northwest Airlines
Polar Air Cargo
Sun Country Airlines
Tower Air
Trans Continental Airlines
United Airlines
United Parcel Service
World Airways

Short-Range International Section:

Alaska Airlines
American Trans Air
DHL Airways
Evergreen International
Express One
Miami Air International
Sun Country Airlines
Sun World
USAir Shuttle

Aeromedical Evacuation Segment:

Delta Airlines
USAir

Domestic Section:

America West Express
Reno Air
Southwest Airlines

Alaskan Section:

Northern Air Cargo
Reeve Aleutian
Lynden Air Cargo

The management of CRAF continue to seek Pentagon and other federal government business which can be added to their structure that will cause an incentive to participate in the CRAF program. Legislative approval has been obtained for a program that will allow carriers to conduct operations from military bases. The airlines will pay for this worthwhile privilege to compensate for inadequate access to airports and saturated commercial transportation infrastructure. Carriers have approval to designate military bases as preplanned weather alternates and for unplanned technical stops. One advantage for this is to be able to list flight plans that will allow them to carry less fuel to meet the Federal Aviation Administration emergency requirements resulting in significant savings.

Commercial airline aircraft committed to serve the CRAF make up more than 90% of the long-range passenger carrying capability of the Air Force and 30% of its cargo capability. If this airline fleet were not available it would be all but impossible to replace it.

The CRAF program is managed by a Memorandum of Understanding (MOU) and Memorandum of Agreement (MOA) between the Department of Defense (DOD) and the Department of Transportation (DOT). The CRAF program itself started as a CRAF plan intended to meet the defense requirements during a formally declared national emergency. The plan was initiated by a joint agreement between the DOD and the Department of Commerce on December 15, 1951. The Secretary of Commerce, under Executive Order 10999, had the responsibility for developing plans for a national program. Upon the establishment of DOT in 1967, the transportation emergency preparedness program was transferred.

The CRAF is a cooperative, voluntary program, which includes the Department of Transportation, the Department of Defense and the United States civil air carrier industry. The air carriers volunteer their participation in the program by contractual arrangements with the Air Mobility Command located at Scott Air Force Base, Illinois.* In return, these air carriers participating in CRAF are given preference to fly commercial peacetime missions for the Department of Defense. This can only be done if the air carrier has suitable aircraft needed for CRAF activation. In addition, any retrofit of the aircraft to meet the AMC requirements are at the expense of the Department of Defense. Often the aircraft are greatly enhanced, especially in retrofitting the passenger aircraft for hauling large size cargo.

The rate paid to the air carriers when they fly for CRAF may vary. In the CRAF operations serving Desert Storm it was 1.75 times the seat mile or cargo mile rate. A fee for a 400 seat passenger aircraft at six cents per seat mile, flying 7,500 miles, times 1.75, would be $315,000. Contracts are renewed from time to time and the rate may be changed when the new contracts are signed. The CRAF program covers situations up to and including a declared national emergency or war, and it includes both passenger and cargo airlift.

CRAF Activation

The first time the Civil Reserve Air Fleet was activated since its inception in 1951 occurred following the Iraqi invasion of Kuwait. The United States quickly mobilized its forces and started the largest airlift in history. Thousands of flights were made carrying thousands of military personnel and millions of tons of equipment to the Persian Gulf. The U.S. Air Force used C-5, C-141 and C-130 military aircraft. Within a few weeks, 95% of the USAF cargo aircraft were flying from the United States and Europe to the Persian Gulf. They soon became over-burdened with the enormity of the transportation needs.

The CRAF was officially activated on August 17, 1990. Two DC-10 aircraft under contract to the Air Mobility Command left Pope Air Force Base, North Carolina, on August 7, 1990. It was loaded with 520 troops of the 82nd Airborne Division bound for Saudi Arabia. Sixteen airlines provided 38 large jet transports in 24 hours with 4 crews with each airplane. (See Table 1.8.)

The civilian air carriers participating in the CRAF eventually used 110 aircraft in support of Operation Desert Shield and Desert Storm. They conducted 5,324 flights of which 2,568 carried personnel and 2,756 carried cargo. Between August 1990 and July 1991 they transported 60% of all personnel, and 25% of the total cargo, to the war zone. Eventually three quarters of a million service men and women, along with their equipment, were transported. In addition to this performance, the U.S. air carriers participating in the CRAF carried 85% of all passengers and 41% of all cargo back to their home bases at the end of the war. Twenty-seven U.S. air carriers made up this immense operation. During the entire operation AMC maintained mission control while the air carriers retained operational control.

CRAF activation is divided into three stages which gives the Air Mobility Command flexibility to put together the force it needs in any crisis. Each stage increases the number of civil aircraft assigned to the airlift needs. While AMC controls the overall mission, each air carrier operates and maintains its aircraft with its own personnel and resources. (See Table 1.9.)

- **Stage I** activates 41 aircraft for military duty and is geared toward minor emergencies.

- **Stage II** is aimed at supporting an airlift emergency and may only be activated by order of the Secretary of Defense. It can add another 149 aircraft to the fleet in Stage I.

- **Stage III** activates the rest of the Civil Reserve Air Fleet which can bring the total to 495 aircraft.

---

*Reorganization of the U.S. Air Force operational commands took place on June 1, 1992. The Military Airlift Command (MAC) became part of the new Air Mobility Command (AMC) which includes airlifters and tankers.

Table 1.8 Civil Reserve Air Fleet U.S. Air Carrier Activity in Desert Shield/Storm (August 7, 1990 to June 30, 1991)

Air Carriers	Flights	
	Passenger	Cargo
Air Transport International	—	156
American Airlines	98	—
American International Airways	—	370
American TransAir	494	—
America West Airlines	39	—
Arrow Air	—	119
Buffalo Airways	—	22
Continental Airlines	91	—
Delta Air Lines	26	—
Eastern Airlines	33	—
Emery Worldwide	—	152
Evergreen International Airlines	—	347
Federal Express	29	576
Flagship Express	—	249
Florida West	—	54
Hawaiian Airlines	263	—
Northwest Airlines	268	117
Pan Am	335	69
Rich International Airways	14	—
Southern Air Transport	—	252
Sun Country Air Lines	30	—
Tower Air	242	1
Trans Continental Airlines	5	—
Trans World Airlines	236	—
United Airlines	177	—
United Parcel Service	—	123
World Airways	188	149
Total U.S. Carriers	**2,568**	**2,756**

Source: U.S. Office of Emergency Transportation

Table 1.9 Civil Reserve Air Fleet 2001 Aircraft Allocation

Air Carrier	Number of Aircraft
Air Transport International	8
Alaska Airlines	36
American Trans Air	56
America West Airlines	19
American Airlines	90
Atlas Air	8
Continental	46
Delta Airlines	81
DHL Airways	5
Emery Worldwide	31
Evergreen	9
Federal Express	92
Gemini Air Cargo	13
Hawaiian Airlines	6
Lynden Air Cargo	3
Miami Air International	8
Midwest Express Airlines	5
North American Airlines	4
Northern Air Cargo	2
Northwest	74
Omni Air Express	4
Pan American Airways	7
Polar Air Cargo	20
Southwest Airlines	44
Spirit Airlines	9
Sun World International	2
Trans World Airlines*	25
US Airways	11
United Airlines	78
United Parcel Service	7
World Airways	9
Total	812

*Merged with American Airlines

The figures are cumulative from one stage to the next. Stage III must be approved by the Secretary of Defense after the president or Congress has declared a national emergency, a state of war or need to support a national security goal. In the Gulf crisis the CRAF did not exceed State II.

As the United States and Allied needs grew and combat appeared imminent, more demand was placed on the U.S. transports. A shortage of long-range strategic lift aircraft prompted an initiation of Stage II on January 17, 1991. Only a small number of Stage II aircraft were actually used, approximately forty widebody cargo aircraft. There was a reluctance to move to Stage II because it had the potential to disrupt the airline industry at the December holiday season.

Each aircraft in the CRAF is categorized into one of seven mission segments. (See Table 1.10.) They are:

- Long Range International Passenger
- Long Range International Cargo
- Short Range International Passenger
- Short Range International Cargo
- Alaskan
- Domestic
- Aeromedical

Each air carrier contractually pledges aircraft to different segments. The aircraft include McDonnell Douglas DC-8, DC-10 and MD-80; Boeing 707, 727, 737, 747, 757 and 767; Lockheed L-1011 and Airbus A310. (See Table 1.11.)

CRAF Performance

The CRAF program performed extremely well. It proved the viability and absolute necessity to have a civil aviation component as part of the nation's mobilization structure. The carriers provided the needed aircraft, which DOT allocates monthly to the program, and DOT, through its Federal Aviation Administration, maintained operational support and assistance by accommodating CRAF movements and requirements throughout the civil air space system. No major problems arose from the civil or military perspective that could have jeopardized CRAF effectiveness. This is not to say that there were not lessons learned during the Desert Storm crisis. These concerns were reviewed and appropriate changes made.

The Pentagon studied the CRAF based on experience in the Persian Gulf War. The initial conclusions indicate that few adjustments were needed. Some cargo air carriers may be reluctant in the future to participate because they lost business when their aircraft were activated. Some passenger air carriers welcomed the additional income because they were experiencing a sharp decline in their international business.

The CRAF has proved to be ready and capable to answer the call to mobilize civilian air carriers, in time of national emergency or declaration of war.

Table 1.10   Civil Reserve Air Fleet (CRAF) Program

Air carrier aircraft assigned to the CRAF in 2001

Aircraft	Type
387	International long range—passenger
205	International long range—cargo
88	International short range—passenger
4	International short range—cargo
4	Alaskan
68	Domestic
56	Aeromedical
812 Total aircraft	

Table 1.11   Office of Emergency Transportation: Civil Reserve Air Fleet (CRAF) Allocation

INTERNATIONAL LONG-RANGE PASSENGER

ILP Segment	AAL	AMT	COA	DAL	HAL	NAO	NWA	OMI	TWA	UAL	WOA	TOTAL
A-300-600ER	10											10
DC-10-10 Series					6			2				8
DC-10-30			6				22	2				30
DC-10-40							21					21
B-747-100							1					1
B-747-200							20					20
B-747-400										16		16
B-757-200ER		13	40			2			13			68
B-767-200ER	18								5	8		31
B-767-300 Series	49			6					4	28		87
B-767-400				6								6
B-777-200	8			7						25		40
L1011 Series		19		5								24
MD-11	5			15							5	25
TOTAL	90	32	46	39	6	2	64	4	22	77	5	387

Table 1.11   Continued

INTERNATIONAL LONG-RANGE CARGO

ILC Segment	ATN	DHL	EIA	EWW	FDX	GCO	GTI	NWA	PAC	UAL	UPS	WOA	TOTAL
DC-8-60 Series	3			1									4
DC-8-62 CB	3												3
DC-8-70 Series	2	2		23									27
DC-10-10C/F				4	39								43
DC-10-30F				3	22	11				1			37
DC-10-30CF												1	1
B-747-100F			5						9		7		21
B-747-200F			4				8	10	8				30
B-747-400F									3				3
L-1011-200F													0
MD-11F/CF					31	2						3	36
TOTAL	8	2	9	31	92	13	8	10	20	1	7	4	205

INTERNATIONAL SHORT-RANGE PASSENGER

ISP Segment	ASA	AMT	BSK	NAO	PAA	SWI	SWG	TOTAL
B-727-200/B		24	8		7	2		41
B-737 Series	24			2				26
MD-80 Series	12						9	21
TOTAL	36	24	8	2	7	2	9	88

INTERNATIONAL SHORT-RANGE CARGO

ISC Segment	DHL	LYC	TOTAL
B-727-100F	3		3
L-100-30		1	1
TOTAL	3	1	4

NATIONAL-ALASKA

AAC Segment	LYC	NAC	TOTAL
DC-6		2	2
L-100-30	2		2
TOTAL	2	2	4

AEROMEDICAL

AERO Segment	DAL	TWA	USA	TOTAL
B-767-200ER			11	11
B-767-300ER	42	3		45
TOTAL	42	3	11	56

NATIONAL-DOMESTIC

DOM Segment	AWE	MEP	SWA	TOTAL
A-319-100	4			4
A-320-200	5			5
B-737-300	10		35	45
B-737-500			9	9
MD-80 Series		5		5
TOTAL	19	5	44	68

CARRIER LEGEND

AAL	American Airlines	MEP	Midwest Express Airlines
AMT	American Trans Air	NAC	Northern Air Cargo
ASA	Alaska Airlines	NOA	North American Airlines
ATN	Air Transport International	NWA	Northwest
AWE	America West Airlines	OAE	Omni Air International
BSK	Miami Air International	PAA	Pan American Airways
COA	Continental	PAC	Polar Air Cargo
DAL	Delta Airlines	RVV	Reeve Aleutian Airways
DHL	DHL Airways	SWA	Southwest
EIA	Evergreen	SWI	Sunworld International
EWW	Emery Worldwide	SWG	Spirit Airlines
FDX	Federal Express	TWA	Trans World
GCO	Gemini Air Cargo	UAL	United Airlines
GTI	Atlas Air	UPS	United Parcel
HAL	Hawaiian Airlines	USA	U.S. Airways
LYC	Lynden Air Cargo	WOA	World

Memorandum of Understanding (MOU)
between
the Department of Defense
and
the Department of Transportation
Concerning
Commercial Aviation Programs

WHEREAS it is the policy of the United States to recognize the importance of the commercial air carrier industry in meeting both peacetime and wartime airlift and associated support for transporting Department of Defense (DoD) personnel and cargo; and

WHEREAS civil air is used to augment military airlift regardless of an activation of the Civil Reserve Air Fleet (CRAF); and

WHEREAS the Secretary of Defense is responsible for both the DoD program for oversight of commercial air safety in the transportation of DoD personnel and the CRAF program for providing augmented airlift and associated support; and

WHEREAS both of these important programs require close coordination with the Department of Transportation (DOT) and the Federal Aviation Administration (FAA) which retains primary oversight of civilian aviation safety; and

Commercial Air Carrier Safety Information

WHEREAS the Secretary of Defense is responsible under Chapter 157 of Title 10, United States Code (U.S.C.), for issues relating to the charter air transportation of members of the Armed Forces, and for the air movement of DoD personnel via commercial airlift in peacetime as well as during contingencies and war; and

WHEREAS the Administrator of the FAA is responsible under Subtitle VII, Part A, of Title 49, U.S.C., (hereafter referred to as "the statute") to ensure that U.S. air carriers remain properly and adequately equipped and able to conduct safe operations in accordance with the rules and regulations applicable to those operations; and

The Civil Reserve Air Fleet Program

WHEREAS it is the policy of the United States to recognize the interdependence of military and civilian airlift and associated support capabilities in meeting national wartime air support requirements, and to promote those national security interests contained within the commercial air carrier industry in order to preserve the industrial mobilization base; and

WHEREAS the Secretary of Transportation is responsible under Executive Order 12656 for developing plans to use civil air transportation resources to meet civil and military needs during national emergencies and defense-oriented situations; and

WHEREAS the Secretary of Defense in accordance with Executive Orders 12656 and 12919 has developed a cooperative plan, entitled the CRAF program, with the civil air carrier industry to augment DoD organic airlift capability and associated support capabilities; and

WHEREAS the CRAF program may be incrementally activated by order of DoD to meet ascending levels of DoD requirements up to and including the most demanding level of requirements based on plans approved by the Joint Staff; and

WHEREAS all the civil air carrier aircraft included in CRAF are contractually committed to support DoD requirements and, for stage III, are allocated to DoD by DOT, pursuant to the Secretary of Transportation's priorities and allocations authority contained in Title I of the Defense Production Act of 1950, as amended (50 U.S.C. App 2061, et seq) and Executive Order 12919, Part II.

NOW, THEREFORE, it is agreed between DoD and DOT as follows:

Section I

1. *DoD Commercial Air Safety Programs:* DoD, represented by the DoD Air Carrier Survey and Analysis Office and DOT, represented by the FAA Flight Standards Service and the Office of the Secretary of Transportation (OST) Air Carrier Fitness Division (OST), shall share aviation safety-related information that assists both agencies in fulfilling their statutory and regulatory responsibilities regarding air carrier fitness and safety. While not all inclusive, each agency agrees to share the types of data and documentation indicated below:

a. DoD shall provide the following information to FAA and where indicated, to OST: Copies of survey reports prepared after each DoD on-site survey of a civil air carrier; access to the DoD Air Carrier Automated Support (ACAS) system data base (OST also); immediate notification of any air carrier being considered for suspension of nonuse by the DoD, and any actual nonuse decision by DoD (OST also); and oral or written feedback on any significant aviation safety issue identified by DoD.

b. FAA shall provide the following information to DoD: Copies of each National Aviation Safety Inspection Program (NASIP) inspection report after an FAA air carrier inspection; access to FAA operations, airworthiness and safety automated data bases; access to FAA's automated System Performance Analysis System (SPAS); International Aviation Safety Assessment reports; Regional Safety Inspection Program information; oral feedback and information from appropriate FAA Flight Standards District Office (FSDO) personnel relative to air carriers undergoing DoD periodic tabletop performance evaluations. Preliminary inspection results will be provided to DoD as soon as reasonably possible after the inspection is completed.

c. DOT and DoD, represented by the offices identified in paragraph 1 above, shall meet at least annually to review and discuss air carrier issues of mutual concern (e.g., safety trends, agency program developments, and information sharing).

d. DoD, represented by the office identified in paragraph 1 above, shall annually meet with and brief the FAA Associate Administrator for Regulation and Certification regarding the results of the DoD Air Carrier Oversight Program.

2. A review committee to include the Deputy Under Secretary of Defense for Logistics, the Deputy Assistant Secretary of Transportation for Aviation and International Affairs, and the FAA Associate Administrator for Regulation and Certification, will meet as required to review the status of this information sharing program.

3. DOT, FAA, and DoD shall independently fund all their respective costs associated with the implementation of this MOU.

4. *Points of Contact*

a. *Department of Defense.* The DoD Air Carrier Survey and Analysis Office will serve as the point of contact for DoD and will implement and administer section I of this MOU for DoD.

b. *Department of Transportation.* The Deputy Assistant Secretary of Transportation for Aviation and International Affairs and the FAA Associate Administrator for Regulation and Certification will serve as the points of contact for the DOT and will implement and administer section I of this MOU for DOT.

Section II

1. *The CRAF is a program:*

a. In which DoD, by contractual arrangement, makes provisions for using aircraft of U.S. civil air carriers, certificated under 14 C.F.R. Part 121, that own or otherwise control such aircraft.

b. Under which DoD, through airlift contracts, allocates normal day-to-day peacetime requirements for civil augmentation based on air carriers' commitments to the CRAF program.

c. Which can be incrementally activated by DoD in response to defense-oriented situations, up to and including a declared national emergency or war, to satisfy DoD airlift requirements.

d. In which DOT allocates committed aircraft to Stage III of the CRAF program to augment the military airlift capability of DoD. Allocations are made in accordance with DoD requirements or as mutually agreed upon by DoD and DOT.

2. All civil air augmentation of DoD airlift, regardless of a CRAF activation, will continue to be governed by the appropriate Federal Aviation Regulations (FAR) applicable to civil aircraft operations and comply with those requirements until such time as DoD requests a deviation to the FARs and FAA, if determining the request appropriate, provides the requested deviation. Pre-approved deviations and exemptions approved by DOT or FAA to facilitate the emergency and expedited movement of U.S. forces or the evacuation of non-essential personnel shall be included in a supplemental agreement pursuant to Section V of this MOU.

3. *The Department of Defense shall:*

a. Determine the number and types of civil aircraft needed to augment military airlift resources in a variety of situations including the most demanding national defense-oriented emergencies.

b. Advise DOT at least annually of the numbers and types of aircraft needed for CRAF Stage III, by segment.

c. Provide timely advice to the Secretary of Transportation when DoD intends to activate CRAF or any portion thereof. United States Transportation Command (USTRANSCOM) will provide information to DOT as needed.

d. Provide access to DOT and FAA, during any activation or contingency, to existing airport surveys, information pertinent to aeronautical infrastructure, and threat information by way of the classified intelligence net.

4. *The Department of Transportation shall:*

a. Develop plans, through the Research and Special Programs Administration, and allocate civil air carrier aircraft to CRAF Stage III based on DoD requirements pursuant to paragraph 3.a. above, after having considered overall DOT administrative and statutory responsibilities. Aircraft shall be allocated to CRAF by manufacturer, model and series, registration number, manufacturer's serial number, owner/operator, and the intended CRAF segment or section of use. DoD shall have priority consideration in any allocation situation.

b. Advise DoD in the event that DOT plans to allocate to CRAF fewer aircraft of any type than the requirement stated by DoD pursuant to paragraph 3.a., and provide the rationale for such reduced allocations.

c. Notify DoD if a particular level of CRAF activation will have a serious adverse impact on the civil air carrier industry's ability to provide essential service.

5. *Allocation Arbitration:* Upon notification by DOT that a particular level of CRAF activation will have a significant adverse impact on the civil air carrier industry's ability, as a whole, to provide essential commercial service, DoD will consult with DOT to identify alternatives or determine ways to minimize impact. DoD requests for additional allocations, following activation of stage III, will be expeditiously considered by DOT; however, priority over other competing interests cannot be guaranteed. Either party to this MOU reserves the right, authorized by Executive Order 12656, to present issues regarding the DOT CRAF allocation or the DoD requirement for the CRAF aircraft to the Director of the Federal Emergency Management Agency (FEMA) for resolution, or if not resolved, to the Assistant to the President for National Security Affairs.

6. *Activation of the CRAF:* The Commander in Chief, United States Transportation Command (USCINCTRANS), with the approval of the Secretary of Defense or the Secretary's designee, may activate any stage of CRAF during national emergencies and defense-oriented situations when approved, USCINCTRANS may activate and deactivate the segments (e.g., international, national, or aeromedical), or sections (e.g., long range international passenger or cargo, short range international passenger or cargo, etc.) within that stage, or in increments, as required.

7. *Points of Contact:*

    a. *Department of Defense:*

        (1) The Deputy Under Secretary of Defense of Logistics will serve as the point of contact in DoD for issues associated with Section II of the MOU.

        (2) USCINCTRANS, as the DoD single manager for DoD common user transportation, will administer and implement the policies set forth in Section II of this MOU for DoD.

    b. *Department of Transportation:*

        (1) The Director of Emergency Transportation, Research and Special Programs Administration, as DOT's principal departmental staff officer for all civil transportation emergency preparedness matters, is the DOT point of contact for all CRAF activities, including allocations to the CRAF, and will implement and administer Section II of this MOU for DOT.

        (2) The Manager, Emergency Operations Staff of the FAA is the operational point of contact for all CRAF activities.

Section III

1. *The Aviation Insurance Program, Established under Chapter 443 of Title 49, U.S.C., is a Program:*

    a. In which the Administrator of the FAA, under a delegation from the Secretary of Transportation, may insure certain aircraft operations where commercial insurance is not available on reasonable terms, and is authorized to respond, evaluate, settle and pay third-party liability claims arising out of an accident or incident insured pursuant to Chapter 443.

    b. In which DoD is required to reimburse DOT for payments made under non-premium insurance policies issued pursuant to Chapter 443 of the statute arising from DoD contracted airlift incidents or accidents.

    c. In which DoD is the primary agency using the non-premium aviation insurance program under Chapter 443 of the statute and DoD has both a national defense and fiscal interest in prompt claims resolution.

    d. In which DoD has a present capability to respond, evaluate, settle and pay third-party liability claims under non-premium insurance issued by the FAA pursuant to Chapter 443. It is an efficient use of government resources for DOT to use the claims personnel resources available within DoD and for DoD to provide those claims resources.

2. *The Department of Defense shall:*

    a. Through USTRANSCOM and its component command contracting officer, submit a timely request to the FAA to activate non-premium aviation insurance coverage, consistent with commercial insurance programs, pursuant to Chapter 443 of the statute when needed for peacetime civil air support and for the CRAF program. DoD and FAA will jointly develop and maintain notification and other coordination procedures to be used in the event of an accident or incident involving an aircraft insured under Chapter 443 of the statute.

    b. Pursuant to the Indemnification Agreement between the Secretary of Defense and the Secretary of Transportation, upon notification by the Department of Transportation of a Chapter 443 non-premium insurance claim pursuant to a DoD contract, the Department of Defense shall transfer funds necessary to pay the claim to the Aviation Insurance Revolving Fund in Accordance with the provisions of 10 U.S.C., section 9514.

    c. Pursuant to the delegation from FAA of third-party claims response authority and the authority to evaluate and settle such claims, the Secretary of Defense shall re-delegate to such claims personnel as he or his designee deems appropriate, the authority to respond, evaluate and settle claims using DoD claims procedures and drawing from funds in the aviation fund established under Chapter 443 of the statute.

    d. The Secretary of Defense or his designee shall notify FAA within 90 days of the execution of this MOU of the Secretary of Defense's designees and re-delegations. DoD will notify FAA within 90 days of any change in designees and re-delegations.

3. *The Federal Aviation Administration shall:*

    a. Assess the availability of commercial insurance coverage when requested for peacetime civil air support and for CRAF activation, and, if unavailable under reasonable terms, provide non-premium aviation insurance coverage pursuant to Chapter 443 of the statute. DoD and FAA will jointly develop and maintain notification and other coordination procedures to be used in the event of an accident or incident involving aircraft insured under Chapter 443 of the statute.

b. Delegate hereby third-party claims response authority and the authority to evaluate and settle such claims for incidents or accidents arising from DoD-contracted airlift insured under Chapter 443 of the statute to the Secretary of Defense, with authority to re-delegate. The Administrator of the FAA further authorizes the Secretary of Defense or his designees to pay such claims using standard DoD claims procedures and drawing from funds in the aviation fund established under Chapter 443 of the statute. Aggregate payments made under this authorization for any one insured accident or incident shall not exceed the amounts agreed to in a Supplemental Agreement pursuant to Section V of this MOU without first obtaining increased funds authority from the Administrator of the FAA, or his designee. The agreed amounts should be adequate to enable payment of the majority of claims which may reasonably be expected in the event of an accident or incident, but in no event shall the agreed amount be less than $5,000,000.

4. *Points of Contact:*

a. *Department of Defense:* USTRANSCOM, or its designated component, shall be the point of contact for DoD on insurance issues.

b. *Department of Transportation:* The FAA Office of Aviation Policy and Plans shall be the point of contact for the DOT.

Section IV

1. In accordance with title 49, U.S.C., section 40105, DOT shall consult with DoD on broad policy goals and individual negotiations, to include international aviation issues affecting the viability of the CRAF program. Consultation will be made through the Assistant Deputy Under Secretary of Defense for Transportation Policy or designee and the Deputy Assistant Secretary of Transportation for Aviation and International Affairs, or designee.

2. In support of the CRAF program and FEMA's disaster response obligations under the Federal Response Plan, DOT can forward air requirements for FEMA to DoD, which will procure the civil airlift through USTRANSCOM and its components.

Section V

1. *Supplemental Agreement:* The Deputy Under Secretary of Defense for Logistics and the DOT Administrator, Research and Special Programs Administration, the Deputy Assistant Secretary of Transportation for Aviation and International Affairs, and the Administrator of the FAA may enter into supplemental memorandum(s) of agreement required to carry out the provisions of Sections II, II, and IV of this MOU.

2. *Amendment:* This MOU may be amended at any time by mutual consent.

3. *Effective Date:* This MOU supersedes the MOUs between the Secretary of Defense and the Secretary of Transportation dated 25 September 1987 and 24 September 1987. It will be effective as of the date of last signature indicated below and shall continue indefinitely, unless amended by mutual agreement or terminated.

4. *Termination:* Either party may terminate this MOU with six months written notice to the other party.

Secretary of Defense
Date: June 10, 1998

Secretary of Transportation
Date: November 10, 1998

CHAPTER 2

Man's Efforts to Fly

Throughout humankind's early years on this earth progress was limited by means of transportation. We progressed successfully through various evolutionary stages and found ourselves capable of covering greater distances. It was always our fondest desire to break away from the bonds of the earth and become airborne. For centuries humans had looked at the birds and envied their freedom of flight. Ages passed while humans enviously watched the birds soaring in seemingly effortless flight. Archaeological findings of civilizations dating back to 3000–4000 B.C. indicate humankind's early interest in flight.

For centuries people had visions of magical powers and other occult devices that would unlock the key to the secrets of flying. Many of these strange ideas were recorded and are available today in historical archives.

The beginning of the story of the earliest known evidence of human efforts to fly goes back to the ancient literature of Greek and Roman mythology. In this world of legend the ways of flight were many.

Apollo's son **Phaethon** rode the skies in a sun chariot. There were winged men of Egypt and the winged bull of Assyria, spoken of in the Bible, who protected the palace of King Sargon in 708 BC. Well remembered is **Sinbad** the Sailor who flew on his bird "Roc." The Arabs had their magical flying carpets. The pre-Christian settlers of the Middle East dreamed of traveling by smoke.

One of the oldest tales is about the Greek mythical character **Icarus**. He was the son of **Daedalus** who was a sculptor, architect, and inventor. When he feared that his nephew Talus would surpass him in originality he threw him from the Acropolis in Athens and fled to Crete. There he built a labyrinth to house the Minotaur for King Minos. The king refused to allow him to leave and put him in prison. Daedalus then constructed wings made of wax feathers for himself and his son Icarus.

They flew away but Icarus flew too close to the sun; his wings melted and he fell to his death into the sea. Daedalus flew on and successfully escaped to live alone in Sicily.

Nike, the winged goddess of victory whose statue appeared on an island in the Aegean Sea in 300 B.C. Hermes, the Greek god called **Mercury** by the Romans, was the winged messenger of the gods. There is the story of the flying horse **Pegasus,** the famous ancestor of our present-day horse, who carried Perseus whenever he chose.

A Persian legend from 1500 B.C. says that **King Kai Ka'us,** who built the tower of Babylon, was tempted by evil spirits to invade the heavenly realm. To his gold and wood throne he had attached four poles. Four large eagles were tied to the poles. The birds, flapped furiously and as the story goes, lifted the throne a short distance before becoming exhausted, causing the king and throne to crash. His fall was taken as a sign that people were not meant to fly. Thereafter the king was known as the Foolish King.

In the Americas, the Incas had their legend of **Ayar Utso,** who grew wings and flew to the sun. From ancient days through the pre-Christian era, until the fifteenth century, a conglomeration of ideas on flying had been presented. All were impossible and none were worthy of fact. Humankind had yet to fly.

In 863, **Bladud,** the King of Britain broke his neck when he attempted to fly using wings of feathers. In Nero's time, Simon the Magician was killed when he attempted to fly in the Roman Forum.

There was a Saracen who, in 1100 B.C.E., in the presence of his emperor, Comnenus, attempted to fly around the Hippodrome of Constantinople. Legend says that he took off clad in a long white robe spread out to catch the breeze. He jumped from a high tower, but the weight of his body dragged him down and he did not survive.

Figure 2.1
Ancient Attempts at Flight

Khensu—a winged hawk head deity of the Egyptians was prominent 1,000 B.C.

Cherubim—the Assyrian winged bull with a human head protected the palace entrance of King Sargon at Khorsabad in 708 B.C.

Icarus—who disobeyed his father; his wings melted when he flew too close to the sun and fell to his death in the sea.

Nike—Victory of Samothrace, a female figure of flight, was erected 306 B.C. on an island in the Aegean Sea.

Mercury—god of commerce was believed to be the winged messenger of the Roman gods.

Pegasus—the flying horse ridden by Perseus of Greek mythology.

Persian king Kai Ka'us—who built the Tower of Babylon in 1500 B.C., is supposed to have flown on a flying throne powered by four eagles.

Eilmer of Malmesbury—is memorialized in a stained glass window in Malmesbury Abbey.

Spain was the scene of an attempted flight about the year 875 when an Andalusian physician named **Abbas ibn-Firnas** ventured to fly. He covered himself with feathers, attached a couple of wings to his body, climbed onto a ledge and flung himself into the air. According to the testimony of several who had witnessed the performance, he flew to a considerable distance as if he had been a bird. However, when the ambitious physician attempted to land like a bird, he crashed heavily to the ground and severely injured his back. With more sympathy than understanding, the account explained that he had crashed because, "not knowing that birds when they alight come down upon their tails, he forgot to provide himself with one."

The lack of a tail was blamed also for the near undoing of an eleventh century English monk named **Eilmer** who was one of the first tower jumpers. In 1065 he fitted himself with wings and leaped from a tower at Malmesbury Abbey. A bewildered medieval historian reported Eilmer "had by some means fastened wings to his hands and feet so that, mistaking fable for truth, he might fly like Daedalus, and collecting the breeze on the summit of a tower, he flew for the distance of several hundred feet." Historians generally agree that Eilmer did achieve some sort of uncontrolled glide. If he man-

aged to cover an eighth of a mile he could credit luck more than skill. Like Abbas ibn-Firnas, he had a rough landing. He fell hard to the ground, broke his legs and was crippled for life. He said that "the cause of his failure was his forgetting to put a tail on the back part." (See Figure 2.1.)

Roger Bacon, the celebrated English philosopher and scientist, who lived from 1214 to 1292 was probably the first person to suggest an apparatus might propel a man through the air. He also was the first to commit to paper any scientific speculation about flight. Bacon, a Franciscan monk, was a prolific writer with a deep interest in natural science, alchemy, and mathematics. Around the year 1250 he wrote a book titled *Of the Marvelous Powers of Art and Nature* in which he sought to demonstrate the superiority of reason over the magical powers claimed by the alchemists of his day. Mankind, he said, was fully capable of building "instruments to fly that would be propelled through the air by flapping, birdlike wings." Furthermore, he said: "It is not necessarily impossible for humans to fly, but it so happens that God did not give them the knowledge of how to do it. It follows, therefore, that anyone who claims that he can fly must have sought the aid of the devil. To attempt to fly is therefore sinful."

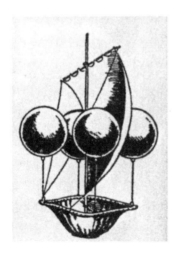
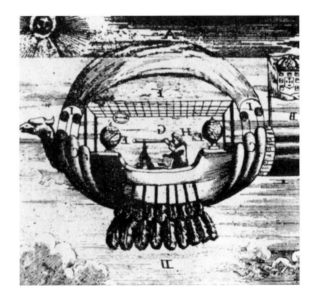

Figure 2.2   Early Flight Machines. (a) Jesuit Francesco de Lana—1670; (b) Friar de Gusman's Passarola, Portugal, 1709.

LEONARDO DA VINCI

We next come to the beginning of the sixteenth century and that incredible genius, Leonardo da Vinci, the prophet of flight and a man of the Renaissance. When he died in 1519 he left his collection of over 5,000 pages of manuscripts and drawings to a friend who never made them public. It was not until the late 1800s that his work received serious notice. By then many of his ideas had been discovered by others. If his work had been known earlier the progress of flight may well have advanced by centuries. (See Figure 2.3.) We can mark da Vinci's work as the turning point in the people's efforts to become airborne. It was da Vinci, a true scientist, mathematician, and scholar, who applied known scientific knowledge to flight theory. From his notebooks we know that he spent years trying to find the solution to the problem of human flight, and that he knew that someday it would come about. (See Figure 2.4.) Da Vinci's invention of the propeller with which he equipped his small helicopter models was a contribution to the ages. Hardly less important was his invention of the principle of the parachute. It was a tent made of linen that would enable a person to throw him or herself down from a great height without sustaining any injury.

Da Vinci is remembered as a genius of the Renaissance who studied the anatomy of birds and their movement. He wrote the first important paper on the mechanism of flight that was the beginning of scientific research. In his treatise of 1505 he said:

There is in man the ability to sustain himself in the air by the flapping of wings. A bird is an instrument working according to mathematical law, which instrument is within the capacity of man to reproduce in all its movements.

Da Vinci constructed a flying machine based on the wing structure of the bat. (See Figure 2.5.) One of his servants supposedly tried to fly it and crashed after a short flight. History will attest to the fact that the bird was indeed man's teacher in the difficult art of flight.

After da Vinci's work there was little aeronautical progress for many years. In the early seventeenth century, **Gaspar Schott,** a physicist, observed that empty egg shells were extremely light and also that dew rose from the grass in the early morning. He reasoned that the way to fly was to get a sufficient number of egg shells filled with dew and be lifted into the sky.

De Lana in 1670 designed a vacuum balloon airship, which could not fly because he did not know about atmospheric pressure on the globes which he proposed to hold it aloft.

In the middle of the seventeenth century, the Italian scientist **Giovanni Borelli** said that it is impossible that man should be able to fly aircraft by using his own strength. He determined that the key to flight was to learn how birds flew, but not try to imitate them. Borelli's theory was disproved August 23, 1977, when a 70-pound aircraft with a 96-foot wingspread flew by man power only. The feat won for its builder, Paul MacCready, $86,000 awarded by the British Aeronautical Society.

A humorous thought of an unknown writer was that a goose is able to fly because of its feathers and that, if enough goose feathers could be used to cover a man, then he also could fly.

In Portugal in the eighteenth century, **Friar Bartholomew de Gusman** invented an airship which was to be lifted by magnets. Bellows were to provide a draft in the event the wind did not blow the craft hard enough.

The Frenchman, **Besnier,** constructed what some regard as the first glider. It was an ornithopter in which he jumped from a garret window and flopped to the ground below; he immediately decided that he was through flying.

In 1742 the **Marquis de Bacqueville** attached paddle-shaped wings to his arms and legs. He sought to fly across the river Seine, but instead dropped into a washerwoman's boat in the river and broke both his legs.

DEVELOPMENT OF THE LIGHTER-THAN-AIR-SHIP

The first successful experiment in air transportation was accomplished with the efforts of two French brothers, **Joseph and Etienne Montgolfier.** (See Figure 2.6.) They lived near Paris and were papermakers. One evening Joseph Montgolfier threw a piece of lightweight paper into the fireplace and saw it go up the chimney. He thought this occurred because the fire produced a lighter-than-air gas, and reasoned that it could be used as lifting power.

The brothers immediately experimented using paper and then a silk bag filled with smoke from fire. The bag rose to the roof. This aroused their interest and

Figure 2.3
Leonardo da Vinci's Sketches

Self portrait of da Vinci made in 1514.

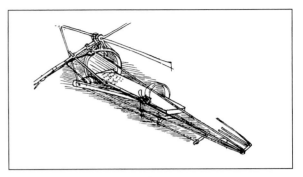

An ornithopter flown in the prone position.

A spring driven helicopter designed by da Vinci.

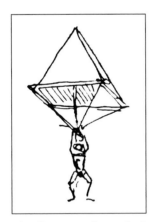

The first parachute design.

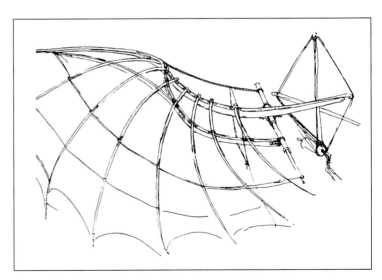

Leonardo da Vinci's wing design.

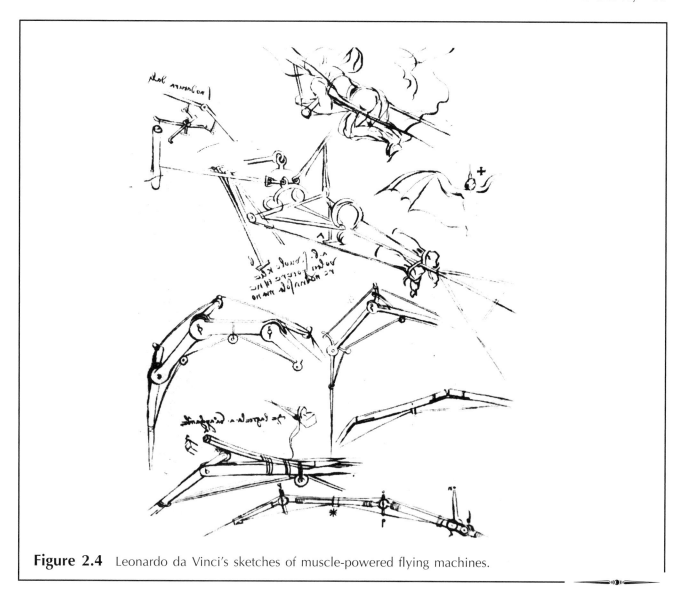

Figure 2.4   Leonardo da Vinci's sketches of muscle-powered flying machines.

spurred them on to making a bigger paper bag which developed into the first balloon. On June 4, 1783, a balloon made its first official public appearance. It was a 31,784 cubic foot envelope made of cotton sewn on paper coated with alum. It held a gondola with burning straw and wool. The balloon ascended to 6,600 feet for ten minutes. It burned when it landed in a nearby field. There were sufficient witnesses to this flight to register the Montgolfiers' discovery with the French Science Academy. Benjamin Franklin saw this along with several thousand others and said, "This is a discovery of great importance which may possibly give a new turn to human affairs."

In an experiment on September 19, 1783, they sent aloft a sheep, a rooster, and a duck which became the first aerial passengers in a man-made machine.

The Montgolfiers' experiments attracted the head of Louis XVI's natural history collection, **Jean de Rozier,** a noted French scientist. He helped the Montgolfiers design and build a balloon large enough to carry a man. On November 21, 1783, de Rozier became the world's first successful test pilot, as well as the first human to accomplish flight in a man-made device, when he ascended to an altitude over 1,000 feet and stayed aloft 23 minutes. A cousin of Louis XVI, Marquis de'Arlandes, accompanied de Rozier on this flight. (See Figure 2.7.)

In June 1785, de Rozier fell to his death when his balloon caught fire in an attempt at crossing the English Channel. In England in 1784, Mrs. Tible became the first woman to fly a balloon.

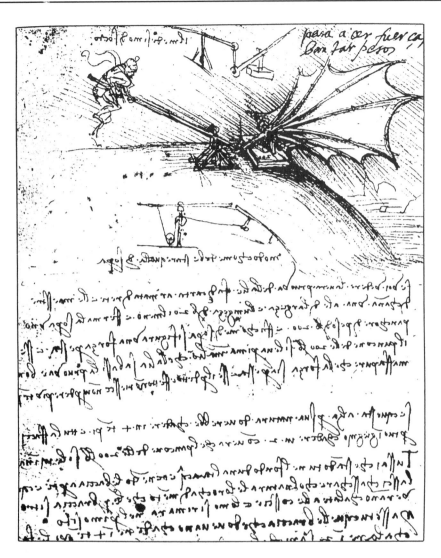

Figure 2.5   Manuscript drawing of flying machine, Leonardo da Vinci (1452–1519).

On December 1, 1783, a coating of dissolved rubber was added by Professor **Jacques Charles** to the silk fabric of the balloon, to make an airtight covering. Charles' balloon was filled with hydrogen, a very flammable gas that is seven times lighter than air. Charles, a chemist, made an ascent from Paris which demonstrated the advantage of hydrogen over the heated air. This flight lasted one hour and forty-five minutes, and the distance traveled was 27 miles.

The first known balloon ascent in the United States took place at Baltimore on June 24, 1784. **Peter Carnes** built a Montgolfier-type balloon. Before launching a thirteen-year-old boy, Edward Warren, who was standing in the crowd asked to make the trip. The boy became the first aerial passenger in the United States.

In England on January 7, 1785, **Jean Pierre Blanchard**, a Frenchman, and **John Jeffries**, a Boston physician who financed the project, made the first balloon flight across the English Channel from Dover to Calais. On January 9, 1793, manned ballooning was only nine years old when Blanchard, who had made 44 flights in Europe, arrived in Philadelphia. President George Washington gave him a letter of passage in case he met difficulty after landing; thousands watched as Blanchard and a companion, a little black dog, ascended in a hydrogen balloon from the Walnut Street prison yard. (See Figure 2.8.) They soared to 5,812 feet and floated 15 miles in 46 minutes before putting down gently near Woodbury, in what is now Deptford, New Jersey. (See Figure 2.9.) The temperature was

Figure 2.6 Joseph and Etienne Montgolfier.

Figure 2.7 Balloon which carried de Rozier and the Marquis de' Arlandes over Paris on November 21, 1783.

To All Whom These Presents Shall Come:

The bearer hereof, Mr. Blanchard a citizen of France, proposing to ascend in a balloon from the city of Philadelphia, at 10 o'clock a.m. this day, to pass in such place as circumstances may render most convenient, these are therefore to recommend to all citizens of United States, and others, that in his passage, descent, return or journeying elsewhere, they oppose no hindrance or molestation to the said Mr. Blanchard; and, that on the contrary, they receive and aid him with that humanity and goodwill which may render honour to their country, and justice to an individual so distinguished by his efforts to establish and advance an art, in order to make it useful to mankind in general.

Figure 2.8 Blanchard's Passport. This passport was given to Jean Pierre Blanchard by President George Washington, dated January 9, 1793.

55°F—"most delightful and quite extraordinary for this season of the year," he wrote.

Blanchard died in 1809 from a heart attack. His second wife, Marie-Madeleine Sophie Armant, was thirty years younger than he. She carried on his work and became well known throughout Europe. She had made her first flight in 1805. She became the first woman to die in a balloon accident in 1819. Her balloon caught fire when it hit rooftops and she fell to the street below.

The earliest use of balloons for military purposes dates back to the French Revolution. On June 26, 1794, two soldiers in a balloon directed artillery fire by using signal flags. Later, Napoleon Bonaparte proposed to send armies via balloons across the English Channel to at-

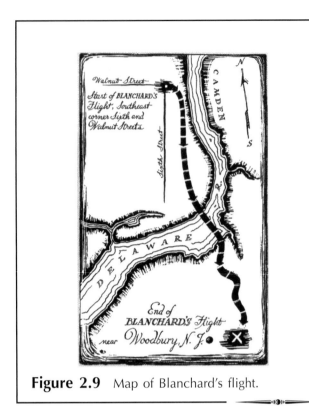

Figure 2.9   Map of Blanchard's flight.

Figure 2.10   Alberto Santos-Dumont.

tack England in 1804. During the U.S. Civil War Abraham Lincoln ordered the use of balloons to observe and map the Confederate positions. Balloons were also used during the Franco-Prussian War in 1870, when letters were sent out of the besieged city of Paris by balloon. Felix Nadar, who organized this service, became involved in the first air battle in history when he encountered a German balloon at 10,000 feet over Paris and had to shoot his way out of the situation. The French balloons were made in the Paris railroad station.

THE DIRIGIBLE

In order to gain control, balloons became elongated with vertical and horizontal planes at the end for directional control. Engines were soon developed for driving power.

The dirigible was the logical outgrowth of the balloon. In 1852 French engineer **Henri Giffard** constructed the first practical steerable balloon of the elongated design. It was 144 feet long and 40 feet in diameter.

Captain Thomas Baldwin made the first parachute jump in America from a balloon in 1887 at San Francisco. He built the first dirigible for the United States Army, as well as the first dirigible balloon in the United States.

Alberto Santos-Dumont, a Brazilian, was among the early builders and pilots of controlled airships. He flew his airships in Paris beginning in September, 1898, and later flew around the Eiffel Tower. He built and flew a total of 14 airships. Santos-Dumont said, "Trying to propel a dirigible balloon through the air is like pushing a candle through a brick wall." (See Figure 2.10.)

History may prove that the balloon was of no real assistance to the development of aviation. In fact, it may even be considered an obstacle to the progress of the airplane, because the balloon's development distracted the direction of research, which could have been devoted to the study of the airplane.

Probably the greatest contributor to lighter-than-air craft was **Ferdinand von Zeppelin.** (See Figure 2.11.) On July 2, 1900, the first rigid airship to fly made history in its 17-minute flight over Lake Constance near Friedrichshafen, Germany. It was the 420 foot LZ-1 designed by Count Ferdinand von Zeppelin. The LZ-1 meant "Luftship Zeppelin One."

Built rigidly with an aluminum framework, inflated with hydrogen gas and propelled by two 16-horsepower engines, the cruising speed of the dirigible was 20 miles per hour.

Count Zeppelin, a retired general of the Prussian Army, made two other test flights in

Figure 2.11 Ferdinand von Zeppelin.

the LZ-1. Although the second flight lasted a full eight minutes, journalists and critics belittled his efforts. Among these critics was a young yachtsman and economist, **Dr. Hugo Eckener.**

Undaunted by this criticism Count Zeppelin designed, experimented, and built three other models. It was the LZ-4 that brought him national acclaim. Successful flights of this lighter-than-air-ship lasting twelve and twenty-four hours converted Dr. Eckener from a skeptic to an admirer.

When the LZ-4 crashed and burned at Echterdingen, the people of Germany arose to the occasion. They subscribed six million marks so that Count Zeppelin could continue developing airships.

In 1908 Count Zeppelin celebrated his seventieth birthday. German cities named streets in his honor. Prince Henry and the Crown Prince clamored for rides in his airship. The Kaiser, in awarding the decoration of the Order of the Eagle, honored Count Zeppelin as the greatest German of the twentieth century.

Dr. Eckener joined Count Zeppelin in 1909 in forming DERLAG, the world's first passenger airline. They built aerodome facilities at Berlin, Dresden, Frankfurt, and Hamburg; they produced such airships as Deutschland, Hansa, Sachsen, Schwaben, and Viktoria-Luise. By 1913 they boasted of a perfect safety record in over 1,600 flights carrying more than 35,000 passengers.

The German navy under Admiral Alfred von Tirpitz ordered its first airship, the L-1 from Count Zeppelin in 1912. The airship was principally used for training purposes, but it was also teamed up with the fleet on scouting missions. A larger model, the L-2, was produced in 1913. Although both ships were casualties, the German Admiralty ordered another ship and placed Peter Strasser in command of the Naval Airship Service.

Zeppelin designed and built airships for the German war machine in World War I. They were used to fly over England and drop bombs from high altitudes. Not until the Allies were able to destroy the Zeppelin manufacturing works was this threat ended.

When World War I began in August 1914, the German Naval Airship Service had only one Zeppelin, the L-3, and no base facilities. These conditions were soon remedied. Construction started on a main base at Nordholz and on two others, one near the Dutch border at Hage and another near the Danish frontier at Tondern. The war stimulated development and 61 airships saw action during the war.

> **Of 125 Zeppelins built by Germany between 1914 and 1918, only six survived the war.**

During the first two years of the war and before England had perfected its defenses, these raiders wrought havoc. The first air raid began the evening of January 19, 1915, when Zeppelins L-3 and L-4 flew over Yarmouth and King's Lynn. Zeppelin raids continued for the next two years doing only sporadic damage. Yet they ultimately forced the Home Defense to tie down 17,341 anti-aircraft troops and 12 R.F.C. squadrons with 110 planes, which were all desperately needed on the Somme.

As the Zeppelins proved vulnerable to bad weather, anti-aircraft fire, and fighter planes, the German High Command turned to long-range bombers. The most damaging raid by Zeppelins occurred on September 8, 1915, when two tons of bombs dropped on London.

Of 125 Zeppelins built by Germany between 1914 and 1918, only six survived the war.

After World War I other nations of the world became interested in dirigibles, no doubt because of impressive use Germany made of them during the war. Great Britian built the R-33 and the R-34. Honors for the first transatlantic crossing went to the R-34 which completed its round trip on July 13, 1919. It took 75 hours for this first crossing. Later both the R-33 and the R-34 were severely damaged during rough weather.

In the early 1920s both England and France built and experimented with dirigibles. Both countries soon became discouraged due to failures. France ceased in 1923 after the Dixmunde disappeared over the Mediterranean and no trace of it was ever found. England continued until 1930 when their R-101 crashed and killed 47 persons.

In 1923 the United States Navy began operating one rigid airship, the *Shenandoah*. It crashed in Ohio in 1925 after breaking into three parts killing fourteen crew members. The *Shenandoah* was built from Germany's World War I design.

Another dirigible arrived at the Lakehurst, New Jersey, Naval Air Station on October 15, 1924. It was the 660-foot ZR-III, the 126th airship built by the Zeppelin Company, and was obtained by the United States as part of Germany's war reparation. It was delivered by Dr. Eckener after a flight of 81 hours from Germany. This airship was later christened *Los Angeles* and used by the United States Navy.

Italy also entered the dirigible field. Umberto Nobile flew the Amundsen-Ellsworth Expedition over the North Pole in the *Norge* on May 12, 1926.

Airship LZ-127, the Graf Zeppelin, crossed over the North Pole on one of its record-making flights. Previously, on the first leg of its round-the-world cruise in August, 1929, the Graf Zeppelin set an unofficial endurance mark of 6,980 miles indirectly from Germany to New Jersey. Eckener was in command, and the Graf Zeppelin carried 25 passengers for the cost of $2,200 each. It also flew from Germany to Rio de Janeiro, Brazil. The Graf Zeppelin crossed the ocean 144 times and flew more than one million miles with no accidents.

The Goodyear Company became the United States builder of airships. They built the *Akron* for the United States Navy in 1932, and the *Macon* in 1933. The *Akron* was designed to be a flying aircraft carrier; it had an internal hangar bay that carried five Sparrow Hawk biplanes. Both of these airships crashed in storms within a year or two after being built. It was believed that the large rigid type of airship was not successful because its structure was inflexible in rough, unstable air. This ended the United States attempts with rigid airships. The *Akron* crashed off the New Jersey coast on April 3,

> **The United States had the monopoly on helium, the only practical non-flammable gas.**

1933, when a storm forced its tail into the water. Of the 76 men aboard, only three survived.

The United States Navy dirigible airship *Macon* was 785 feet long and 144 feet wide. It contained 7.5 million cubic feet of helium that provided a gross lift of 410,000 pounds. It was commissioned in April, 1933 and built for the Navy by the Goodyear Corporation. It was powered by eight 12 cylinder 560 horsepower engines capable of producing a top speed of 85 knots per hour; cruise speed was fifty-five. The *Macon* was a flying aircraft carrier holding five Curtiss F9C-2 Sparrow Hawk fighters that could be launched and recovered on board while the airship was in flight. (See Figure 2.12.)

The *Macon* was lost during bad weather on the evening of February 12, 1935, while returning from maneuvers to its base at Sunnyside Naval Air Station, now Moffett Field. It had been cruising at 1,250 feet when it was hit by a gust of wind that snapped its vertical tail fin and punctured three helium cells in the aft section. The crew fought for thirty-three minutes to regain control but it settled onto the ocean about fifteen miles

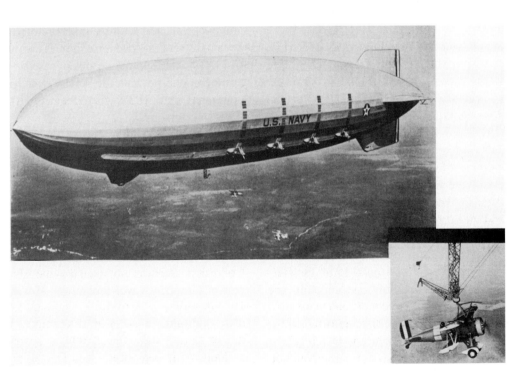

Figure 2.12   The *Macon* with fighter aircraft hook-on.

offshore. Eighty-one of those on board were saved; the two who died could have been saved also had they not panicked and jumped overboard before the airship settled into the water. Commander Wiley, a survivor of the *Akron* disaster, guided the airship to the surface of the ocean. The *Macon* had logged 54 flights and 1,798 hours of flight time before it was lost.

Wreckage of the *Macon* was found June 24, 1990, under 1,500 feet of water in the Pacific Ocean near Monterey, California. Parts of the aircraft may be salvageable.

The English experimented with launching fighter aircraft from the R-33 and R-34 dirigibles while in flight. The United States also was successful in aerial launchings of aircraft from the *Akron* and *Macon*. This idea was known as "skyhook." The purpose was for the airplanes to scout ahead and return to the airship. They were also to serve as defenders to ward off attacking hostile aircraft.

The United States thereafter used lighter-than-airships only of the smaller blimp-type to be used for observation by the Navy.

The Germans made one final supreme effort with the dirigible. This was in the middle 1930s when the world's largest and greatest airship, the *Hindenburg*, was built.

The United States had the monopoly on helium, the only practical nonflammable gas. They refused to provide it to Germany because of fear that the new Nazi government would use it for military use. The *Hindenburg* flew successfully carrying passengers across the North Atlantic to Lakehurst, New Jersey. It was unique in that it provided staterooms, restaurant facilities, smoking lounges, and other extreme comforts. It was the largest airship ever built, being over 800 feet long and 135 feet in diameter. Unfortunately, this giant of the skies exploded and burned while attempting a landing at the Lakehurst, New Jersey, Naval Air Station on the evening of May 6, 1937. (See Figure 2.13.) Of the 97 people aboard when it crashed, 62 miraculously escaped death. Films of the *Hindenburg* crash were not shown in Germany until after World War II.

Eckener built a sister ship of the *Hindenburg*. It was completed in Germany and made forty flights in 1938–1939, however, it was later melted down to make fighter aircraft needed for World War II. However, he would not put it into operation unless he could secure helium. Hitler and the Nazi government did not think the airship had a

Figure 2.13 Explosion and crash of the *Hindenburg,* Lakehurst, New Jersey, May 6, 1937.

> Commercial blimps are seen today over sporting events carrying television cameras and at night displaying lighted advertisements.

place in their war machine, so Eckener and his new dirigible lay useless during World War II. Finally the airship was melted down for the use of its metal.

During World War II the United States Navy used nonrigid airships in convoy operations. Some 170 of them escorted 89,000 ships without loss of a single vessel. It has been estimated that they logged 500,000 hours' flying time and in 1944 were patrolling three million square miles of ocean.

After World War II nonrigid airships were used as units of the Early Warning Squadron. They were the ZPG-2-type built for the United States Navy by Goodyear. One of them, the *Snow Bird*, broke the Graf Zeppelin endurance record when it landed at Key West, Florida, after logging 9,070 miles. Commercial blimps are seen today over sporting events carrying television cameras and at night displaying lighted advertisements.

THE FUTURE OF ZEPPELINS

A serious approach to the redevelopment and use of the Zeppelin has recently taken place. The company in Germany named Le Bourget Deutsche Zeppelin-reederei, built and became the first operator for their designated Zeppelin NT. The company plans to initially conduct revenue flights using the airships for sightseeing tours over Lake Constance where Ferdinand von Zeppelin built and flew his first airship in 1900. The first prototype of the Zeppelin NT (NT for new technology) took part in daily flights at the Paris Air Show in June 2001.

Zeppelinreederei was established by Zeppelin Luftschifftechnik, which developed and built what is now the largest Zeppelin and the only one with rigid internal structure. The manufacturer chose to operate the first three airships itself. Luftschifftechnik president said he wants to prove the three airships operational feasibility and confirm calculated data. He said, "We know we have the best performing Zeppelin but we want to demonstrate that in reality."

Public interest in Germany is overwhelming. Initially the company received more than 2,000 reservations for flights in the Zeppelin NT that seats up to twelve people. A one-hour flight over Lake Constance cost about $300 per seat.

Potential buyers have been placed on a waiting list. The company will decide whether to focus more on building and selling the Zeppelin, or expanding its role as a commercial operator. A final decision depends on the market and how successful operations will result with the first three airships. The company's market studies forecast a demand for 100 to 1000 airships for use in advertising. There is uncertainty as to use of the airship for passenger transportation.

Luftschifftechnik plans to reach a break-even point at 20 to 25 air ships. Its present facility has the capacity to build two and one-half airships per year with an assembly time of eight-and-a-half months per Zeppelin. If successful the company plans to construct a larger version of the Zeppelin NT. The company sees a demand for a thirty-seat airship having a payload of five to six tons. Their present Zeppelin NT has a two-ton payload limitation with a range of 559 miles. It is 246 feet long and 64 feet in diameter and reaches a speed of 125 KPH.

Airships have served a purpose in the effort to fly and they may be used successfully in the future. The idea still persists.

CHAPTER 3

Development of the Airplane

During the years of lighter-than-air ship development, other inventors were experimenting with heavier-than-air craft known as the airplane.

If the studies of da Vinci had not been ignored for so long, then the dream of flight might have been realized centuries ago. From his death in 1519, until the first half of the 1800s, aeronautical progress was attempted by dedicated experimenters. In 1670 the Jesuit priest, **Francesco de Lana,** made an approximate determination of the weight of air at sea level, but he never succeeded in raising his craft using only four light copper spheres to create a vacuum. The Brazilian Jesuit **Laurenco de Gusman** firmly believed in his Passarola but he never succeeded in building anything except a fragile glider. Although Bacqueville, Letur, and De Groof were personally able to test their ornithopters, dozens of others never went beyond the drafting of plans for their fantastic projects. When people finally understood that muscle power alone was not enough to lift a man off the ground and sustain him and the machine in flight, no matter how light it was, they designed plans for the use of the steam engine. Neither the steam engine nor the gunpowder motor, planned by **Pomès** and **De la Pauze,** could offer the correct solution for heavier-than-air flight because the weight of these engines was too great in proportion to the power created.

Humankind owes much to the scientists and dreamers of the last four centuries for having continued to believe, in spite of their failures, that someday people would be able to fly.

No major effort was made in the development of airplanes from 1505, when da Vinci wrote his scientific paper on aircraft, until 1810. At that time an English

> **Humankind owes much to the scientists and dreamers of the last four centuries for having continued to believe, in spite of their failures, that someday people would be able to fly.**

scientist, **Sir George Cayley,** (See Figure 3.1) published a series of articles proposing that a surface could be made to support weight. Cayley is considered the father of British aviation. This was the first scientific thought of what we know today as the airfoil. All successful airplanes have been constructed according to Cayley's principles on the surface of a wing.

GEORGE CAYLEY

In 1842, Cayley designed the Aerial Carriage, (See Figure 3.2) which had rotors, propellers, and a canvas covered fuselage to hold its steam engine. The Smithsonian Institution built a model of this aircraft according to Cayley's plans and found it workable.

Cayley is remembered for writing a collection of "how and how not" into a sensible monograph concerning flying. This approach to flight was based on the principle of mechanics. Not content with telling how not to attempt flight, he pointed the way toward eventual success.

Figure 3.1
Sir George Cayley.

Cayley even foresaw the future development of the engine. He called his engine "an explosion machine," for want of a better name. Cayley was about 55 years ahead of his time, because it was not until 1865 that Lenoir completed the first practical gasoline engine.

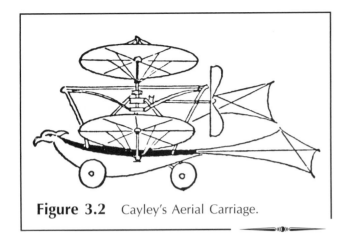

Figure 3.2 Cayley's Aerial Carriage.

Figure 3.3 William Samuel Henson and John Stringfellow.

Sir George Cayley theorized on the problems of aerodynamics and addressed velocity, wing loads, bending movements, and the necessity for combining lightness and strength. He foresaw and wrote about the need for streamlining, and he realized that a cambered or curved wing was necessary for flight, and that a flat wing could never do the job. Cayley was the first to think about the construction of a multiwing airplane.

Cayley said that wings to lift and sustain great weights in the air ought not to be made in one plane but in parallel planes one above the other at a convenient distance. Such an arrangement would reduce the likelihood of damage to a large single wing without sacrificing the required wing surface. He went on to propose wings in the form of a three-decker, each deck being eight or ten feet from the other to give free room for the passage of the air between them. In time, this multiwing idea suggested by Cayley would be adopted by many other aviation pioneers, Wilbur and Orville Wright among them.

His idea for a biplane was used in building a glider which he fitted with horizontal and vertical rudders; these were the beginning of the controls of today's airplane. History does not show that Cayley himself ever attempted a flight, but he wrote of his glider's success.

WILLIAM HENSON AND JOHN STRINGFELLOW

The idea of the airplane was given further thought by two other Englishmen. **John Stringfellow** (See Figure 3.3) was born in 1799 and became very prosperous. His greatest challenge was to build a lightweight steam engine to power an aircraft. **William Samuel Henson** (See Figure 3.3) born in 1812, was an engineer in England's lace-making industry before he embarked on designing aircraft. He also had worked on developing a breech loading cannon, an ice making machine, and had patents for a safety razor and an improved steam engine.

Henson did not follow Cayley's advice for a multiwing but designed a single-wing airplane for his proposed aerial steam carriage. (See Figure 3.4.) Lacking funds to build a prototype, Henson and Stringfellow proceeded with a grand scheme for launching an international airline known as the Aerial Steam Transit Company in 1843. They sold stock valued at £2,000. The intended purpose of this company was to build and operate flying machines. They designed a giant of an airplane. It had a 150-foot wingspan and two six-blade propellers 20 feet across; it was powered by a 30-horsepower steam engine. They attempted to raise funds with massive publicity. Descriptions and illustrations of the proposed craft appeared in such popular journals as *The Illustrated London News* and *L'Illustration of Paris*. Fanciful scenes were reproduced not only in magazines but on souvenir items such as decorative cloths and handkerchiefs, showing the aerial carriage steaming over London, the English Channel, the exotic Plains of Hindustan, the coast of France, the Pyramids, and China.

Claims for the aircraft were so great and the promotion so lavish that interest turned to skepticism and then to ridicule. Potential backers withdrew their support in the face of jeers and laughter. The Aerial Transit Company soon ceased.

Not discouraged, Henson and Stringfellow set out to build and test a scale model of their flying machine, hoping for results impressive enough to attract funds for a full-size aircraft. The experiments seemed promising but support was not forthcoming, and in September, 1846, William Henson appealed to Cayley for help. He wrote, "We therefore apply to you as the 'father of aerial navigation' to ascertain whether you would like to have anything to do in the matter or not."

Cayley's reply was gracious and he must have relished being addressed as the "father of aerial navigation." Cayley said that, while he approved of Henson's zeal, he could spare no money to support his experiments. Of course he would be most gratified if Henson could show some proof of progress in achieving mechanical flight, in which case, Cayley said he "perhaps might be able to aid you in some manner by my experience in connection with other mechanical persons."

In 1847 Henson and Stringfellow conducted final tests with a miniature aircraft that had a 20-foot wingspan and two steam-powered propellers. The model rolled down its inclined launching ramp and executed a brief descending glide, but that was all. It failed to achieve sustained flight.

Because both the model of their airplane and the stock sale were hopeless failures, disheartened Henson gave up the whole business, got married, and emigrated to the United States. Stringfellow continued his work on the problems of flight. He built a steam engine and a new model airplane with a wingspan of ten feet. Some historians call this engine the first practical model capable of successful performance. The glider on which the engine was mounted actually became airborne in a test flight in 1848. It flew a distance of 120 feet and proved to be the first successful power-driven airplane

> The term "aviation" was originated by the Frenchman, La Landelle, about 1863 when he helped found the French "Society of Aviation."

to be flown in free flight; however, no one was aboard the airplane. He was never able to construct a full-size airplane that could be successfully flown. Stringfellow tested an improved Henson model in 1848, but it was no more successful than its predecessor.

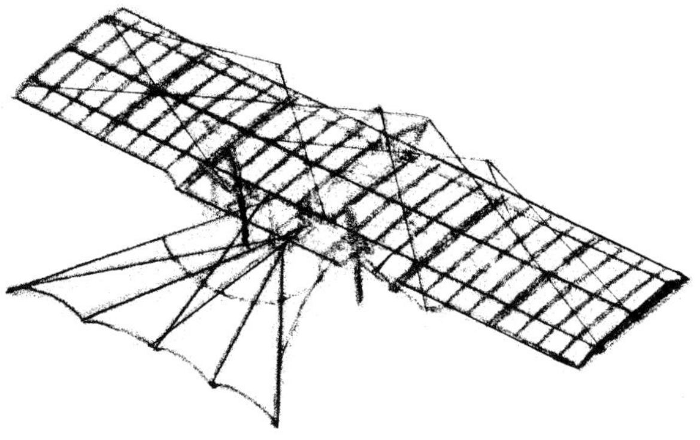

The contribution of the two men was more significant than their failures suggest. Henson's design was logically conceived, if only on paper, and his aerial carriage was a plausible expression of what an airplane should be. The showy publicity brought ridicule to the Aerial Steam Transit Company, but it also called worldwide attention to the pursuit of mechanical flight and fixed the vision of an elegant flying machine upon the public mind. Though the tests with the models were unsatisfactory, they were, nonetheless, a serious attempt to fly a propeller-driven, engine-powered airplane. The concept of the Aerial Steam Carriage was a lasting stimulus to other inquiring minds.

George Cayley, whose enthusiasm for aviation did not diminish by his advancing age, was influenced by the machine. Following his own advice to Henson, Cayley made a major departure from his earlier work and began experimenting with a three-winged glider, which he optimistically dubbed a "flyer." As Cayley described it in his notebooks, the aircraft consisted of a boat-shaped wheeled car with a pilot-operated elevator and rudder; three tiers of wings were affixed atop the car at a dihedral, or shallow V-shaped angle.

By the spring of 1849 this triplane glider had been put through some brief tests, one of them similar to the flight of a kite. Cayley wrote:

> *A boy of about ten years of age was floated off the ground for several yards on descending a hill, and also for about the same space by some persons pulling the apparatus against a very slight breeze by a rope.*

Then came a 1853 ride of a reluctant coachman on board a glider Cayley called the "new flyer." It sailed across a valley in true non-powered flight. It is reasonably certain that the vehicle used was an improved version of the boy-carrying glider. Cayley then spent his time with his very ill wife. After she died he went back to his work. His strength was failing and he died on December 15, 1857, twelve days after his 84th birthday. His only surviving son had the historic flying machine dragged to a barn where it served as a roost for chickens.

Figure 3.4 An 1842 drawing shows the cambered wing structure of Henson's aerial steam carriage.

JEAN-MARIE LE BRIS

Jean-Marie Le Bris, a French sea captain, who conducted aerial experiments in Brittany from 1856 to 1868, was a man not given to understatement. Le Bris did practically nothing to advance aviation, but the mixture of fact and fantasy regarding his experiments have become firmly fixed in the history of aeronautics. Le Bris gained knowledge during his voyages around Cape Horn and the Cape of Good Hope. He watched the graceful flight of large albatrosses and to him this was an insight into the secret of flying. He captured and killed a bird to study the shape and structure of its wings by holding it aloft in the wind. Obviously the air blowing over the wings of the bird caused it to rise slightly due to its shape. Captain Le Bris exclaimed:

I took the wing of the albatross and exposed it to the breeze, and lo in spite of me it drew forward into the wind; notwithstanding my resistance, it tended to rise. Thus I had discovered the secret of the bird! I comprehended the whole mystery of flight.

Abandoning long sea voyages for short runs along the coast of France, Le Bris devoted his time to the construction of a full-sized glider inspired by the albatross (See Figure 3.5). The body of the craft, built to support a pilot, was shaped like a canoe; the narrow arching wings, each 23 feet long, were moved by pulleys and cords, provided a lifting surface of 215 square feet. In 1857 Le Bris tested his device by having it pulled down an incline on a horse-drawn cart and then releasing it against a brisk wind. He succeeded in making a short glide on his first try, but a crash on the second attempt left him with a smashed glider and a broken

Figure 3.5 Jean-Marie Le Bris' "Albatross" on a wagon for transporting.

leg. By 1868 Le Bris had developed a larger version of his glider which made several successful unmanned test flights before it crashed. Nothing more was reported of his aerial activities.

FRANCIS WENHAM

In 1866, at the first meeting of the Aeronautical Society of Great Britain, an address was given by **Francis Herbert Wenham,** (See Figure 3.6) a marine engineer interested in internal-combustion engines. Entitled "Aerial Locomotion," his report was to become an aviation classic like Cayley's articles of 1810. It was based upon his years of carefully studying the flight of birds. He is remembered for having contributed a great deal to the understanding of technical problems which finally led to successful flight.

Figure 3.6 Francis Herbert Wenham.

Wenham had conducted extensive tests with airfoils and airplane models. He advised his fellow enthusiasts that a cambered, or curved, wing was more effective for lift than a flat wing and that the leading edge of the wing, or the front portion, provided most of the lift required for sustained flight. It was obvious, he said, that a long narrow wing would, therefore, exert more lift than a short stubby one. Wenham further concluded, as Cayley had earlier, that several such wings, one above another, would provide the greatest lifting area with the least strain. He also advised that prospective fliers should master the control of unpowered gliders in the air before attempting to leave the ground in powered aircraft.

Wenham had little practical success with his own gliders, which he built with five wings. He advanced aeronautics significantly by building the first wind tunnel for simulating the movement of variously shaped wing models through the air. His apparatus consisted of a long wooden box with a steam-driven fan at one end. And while Wenham himself conceded that his tests were somewhat crude and incomplete, later and more sophisticated versions of his equipment became essential tools in aviation research.

Wenham's work would prove useful to both Octave Chanute and the Wright brothers in the United States.

Figure 3.7 John Stringfellow's steam-powered triplane hanging from the ceiling at the first exhibition in 1868 by Britain's Aeronautical Society.

It had a more immediate influence on John Stringfellow, the Englishman who had been absent from the aeronautical scene since the failure of the single-winged Aerial Steam Carriage model he had built with William Henson in the 1840s. Spurred by Wenham's report to the Aeronautical Society and recalling that Cayley also had recommended multiple wing surfaces for heavy aircraft, Stringfellow resurrected the old aerial carriage as a triplane. Stringfellow showed his new model (See Figure 3.7) at the world's first exhibition of flying machines held in the Crystal Palace in London in 1868, sponsored by the Aeronautical Society.

ALPHONSE PENAUD

In France, the brilliant but tragic **Alphonse Penaud** (See Figure 3.8) was one of the most outstanding airplane experimenters preceding the Wright brothers. He dominated the field of practical aeronautics in the 1870s. Prevented by the disabling hip disease from following his admiral father into the Navy, Penaud applied his training as a marine engineer to aeronautical matters. He built many models and in 1870, when he was only twenty, he discovered the twisted rubber band as a power source for model airplanes. He used his invention in a workable he-

Figure 3.8
Alphonse Penaud.

licopter model which spurred toy makers to produce thousands of rubber band driven helicopter toys. Then he used his creation in his own more sophisticated airplane models.

In 1871 Penaud built what he called the "planophore," a monoplane twenty inches long with tapered dihedral wings, an adjustable tail assembly with dihedral tips and a rear-mounted pusher propeller. The wing and tail design made it much more stable than earlier airplane models. When Penaud demonstrated his planophore before a group of aeronautical enthusiasts in Paris, it flew 131 feet in 11 seconds; the first flight of an inherently stable aircraft.

Penaud's next major achievement came in 1876, when he patented his design for a full-sized amphibious monoplane. It included such forward-looking features as a glass-domed two-seated cockpit, a single control column to operate the elevators and rudder, and a retractable undercarriage with shock absorbers. It weighed over a ton and he calculated that it should fly at a speed of sixty miles an hour providing he could find a powerful enough engine. Penaud was too far ahead of his time. Lack of a lightweight engine stymied his progress and he was unable to raise funds to build his machine or pursue his research. Frustrated, discouraged, criticized for his work, and in failing health he committed suicide at the age of thirty. Later experimenters including **Wilbur** and **Orville Wright** would rank Penaud close to Cayley as one of the most significant 19th century aeronautical thinkers.

Penaud was one of a growing number of scientists and other researchers approaching aviation as an engineering problem that could be solved by good scientific methods. (See Figure 3.9.)

H. F. PHILLIPS

Another experimenter who contributed to the advancement of flying was **H. F. Phillips.** In 1884 he patented a series of curved wings for airplanes. In constructing these he copied the concave underside and the convex upper side of bird wings. He experimented wing models in one of the first wind tunnels.

CLEMENT ADER

Not every experimenter was captivated by the idea of multiple wings, nor did all aeronautical researchers agree with Francis Wenham's conclusion that unpowered gliding would be a useful preparation for attempts at

Figure 3.9
Early Experiments in Flight—1670–1880

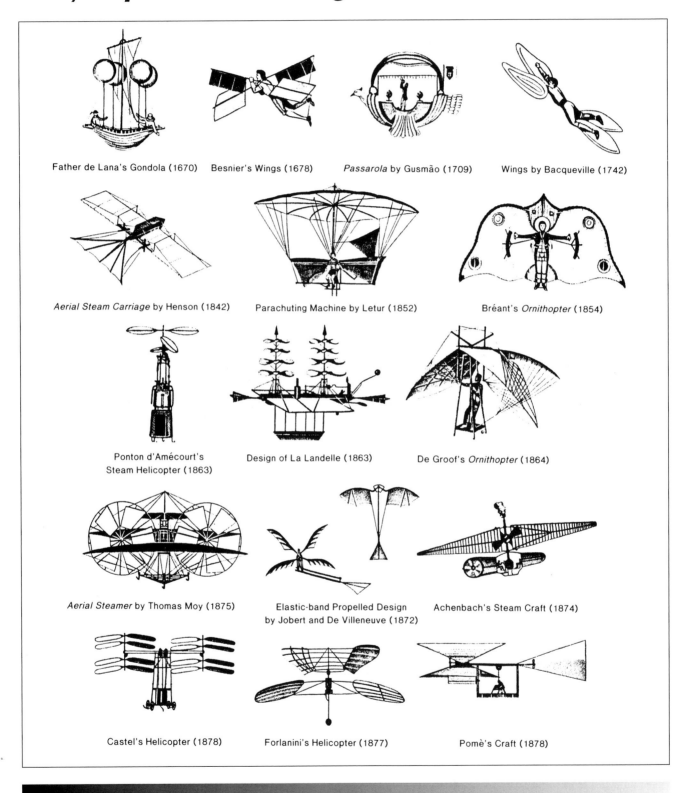

Father de Lana's Gondola (1670)   Besnier's Wings (1678)   *Passarola* by Gusmão (1709)   Wings by Bacqueville (1742)

Aerial Steam Carriage by Henson (1842)   Parachuting Machine by Letur (1852)   Bréant's *Ornithopter* (1854)

Ponton d'Amécourt's
Steam Helicopter (1863)   Design of La Landelle (1863)   De Groof's *Ornithopter* (1864)

Aerial Steamer by Thomas Moy (1875)   Elastic-band Propelled Design
by Jobert and De Villeneuve (1872)   Achenbach's Steam Craft (1874)

Castel's Helicopter (1878)   Forlanini's Helicopter (1877)   Pomè's Craft (1878)

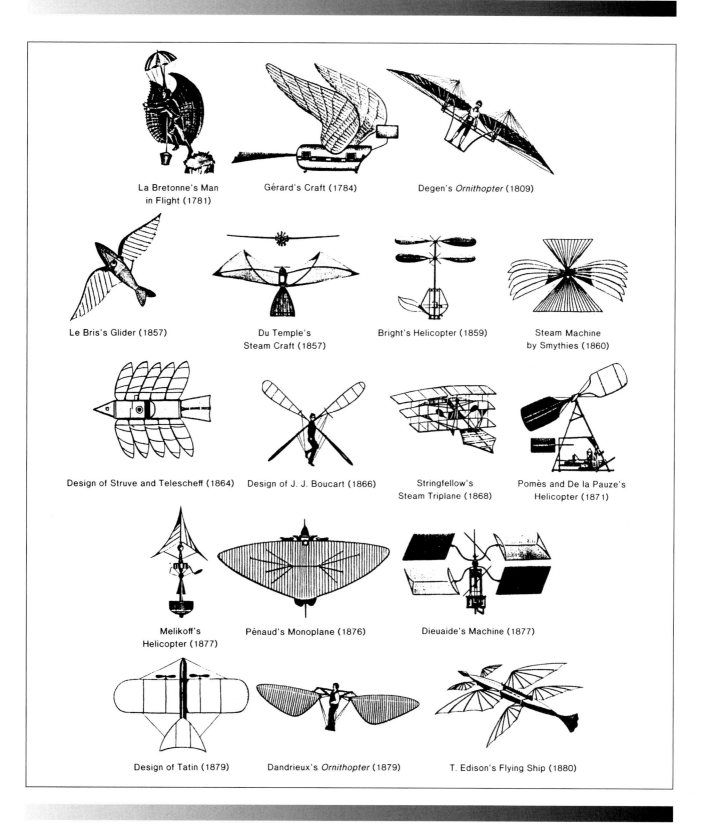

La Bretonne's Man in Flight (1781)

Gérard's Craft (1784)

Degen's *Ornithopter* (1809)

Le Bris's Glider (1857)

Du Temple's Steam Craft (1857)

Bright's Helicopter (1859)

Steam Machine by Smythies (1860)

Design of Struve and Telescheff (1864)

Design of J. J. Boucart (1866)

Stringfellow's Steam Triplane (1868)

Pomès and De la Pauze's Helicopter (1871)

Melikoff's Helicopter (1877)

Pénaud's Monoplane (1876)

Dieuaide's Machine (1877)

Design of Tatin (1879)

Dandrieux's *Ornithopter* (1879)

T. Edison's Flying Ship (1880)

engine-driven flight. There was the Frenchman **Clement Ader** (See Figure 3.10) and the American-born Englishman Sir Hiram Maxim who also believed that successful flying could be achieved simply by attaching a sufficiently powerful engine to a pair of wings.

Figure 3.10
Clement Ader.

Clement Ader, born near Toulouse, France, in 1841 became one of the most controversial figures in aviation history. He spent 25 years and $120,000 in an effort to produce a successful airplane. Many of his early efforts were failures. Ader was a distinguished electrical engineer and inventor who was among the pioneers in the development of the telephone; he also studied the flight of birds and bats. In 1873 he built a bird-shaped aircraft with goose-feather wings. Ader did not try to fly this semi-glider; instead, he tethered his artificial bird to the ground, nosed it into the wind, and lay prone upon it as stiff breezes raised it to the limit of its anchor ropes.

His curiosity about gliding flight now satisfied, Ader began planning for a powered takeoff. By 1882 he had started the laborious construction of his first aircraft and the exceptionally light steam engine that would be its most remarkable feature. In 1886 he built a flying machine with batlike wings powered by a 40 horsepower steam engine turning a four bladed propeller. Its wingspan was 46 feet and the entire structure weighed 440 pounds. The *Eole* crashed on its first test after going 150 feet.

Ader built another airplane in 1891 with a 54 foot wingspan. The *Eole*, or "god of the winds," was finally ready for testing. Resembling a huge bat, it was a monoplane with deeply arched wings that could be moved in four different directions. Its propeller was driven by a 20 horsepower steam engine that brought the craft to a total weight of only 653 pounds including the pilot. In several critical respects the design left much to be desired. The cockpit was located behind the steam boiler which provided almost no forward visibility, and Ader had given little thought to how he might handle the machine if he managed to get it off the ground. The mechanism for controlling the wings was complicated and difficult to operate. There was no elevator or rudder. Ader was brimming with confidence on October 9,

when he transported the *Eole* to an estate at Armainvilliers for testing. Only a few assistants witnessed what happened after Ader wheeled his bat-like aircraft to level ground and slipped into the cockpit. By the inventor's own account "he ran up a full head of steam, sped along the ground and rose to height of about eight inches before touching down and rolling to a halt." The *Eole* had traveled through the air a distance of 165 feet. If Ader's account is true, and there is no reason to doubt it, his aircraft was the first manned airplane to take off from level ground under its own power. Aerodynamically unsound and too heavy for its engine, once airborne the *Eole* was uncontrollable and could not sustain flight. There is some doubt if it flew but it did cause the French government to advance money to Ader.

The French Ministry of War commissioned Ader to build an improved version of the *Eole,* which he named the *Avion III* (See Figure 3.11) with two engines. On October 14, 1897, with military observers watching on a gusty afternoon, he tried to get airborne. The aircraft was caught in a strong wind before its wheels had a chance to leave the ground. Ader shut off the engines but his airplane almost overturned. Too damaged to do more testing and not having gotten the airplane off the ground, the War Ministry stopped their financial support.

Whether Ader had actually flown or not is beside the point. His efforts did spur others onward to further experimentation. He is remembered for successfully mating engines to airframes. His engines were strong enough to give sufficient power for flight.

HIRAM MAXIM

The enormous and highly publicized winged vehicle that **Hiram Maxim** built in the early 1890s was equally incapable of sustained and controlled flight.

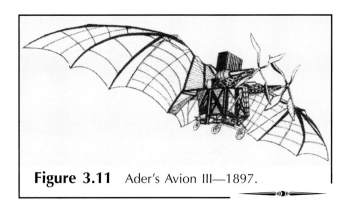

Figure 3.11   Ader's Avion III—1897.

FLIGHTS OF FANCY

Thomas Edison

Thomas A. Edison, a well known experimenter of the late nineteenth century is best known for giving us the light bulb. Most of his work having to do with aeronautics was with propellers although he did design an airplane. In 1903, a few months before the first successful flight of the Wright brothers, Edison said the flying machine is bound to come but it will take some time at the rate we are now progressing. Edison designed a six-winged ornithopter that was to be powered by electrical motors and launched from a large tower. His drawings accompanied a newspaper interview in 1880.

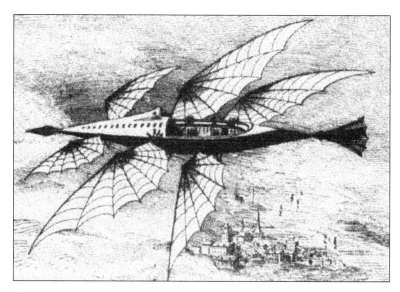

Figure 3.12 Edison's six-winged ornithopter.

Maxim's primary concern was merely to build a flying machine that would lift itself from the ground. His experiments were marginally successful, though Maxim himself conceded that problems of aerial steering and control remained to be solved before practical aviation could be achieved. Maxim had been interested in aeronautics since his boyhood in Maine, where he was born in 1840.

Maxim's youthful interest in aviation resurfaced in the late 1880s when he began to study wing forms and propellers. After proving to his own satisfaction that heavier-than-air flight was possible, he turned his considerable talents to the development of a powerful but lightweight steam engine. In Kent he rented ample room to construct work sheds and a track for testing his proposed aircraft.

In June, 1892, Maxim described the kind of aircraft he had in mind. He said:

It is neither necessary nor practical to imitate the bird too closely; because screw propellers have been found to be very efficient when operated at sufficient speed to produce thrust. Without doubt, the motor is the chief thing to be considered.

Maxim's flying machine reflected his preoccupation with powerful engines. It was an enormous biplane equipped with two 180 horsepower steam engines, (See Figure 3.13) each driving a pusher propeller nearly 18

feet in diameter. The platform for the engines, boiler, and a three-man crew was 40 feet long and eight feet wide; the craft measured about 200 feet from tip to tail and had a 107-foot wingspan. To provide stability, Maxim placed an elevator fore and aft and set the outer wing panels at a dihedral angle. The aircraft had a total lifting surface of 4,000 square feet and weighed an incredible 8,000 pounds, including crew.

Figure 3.13 Hiram Maxim with his 180 horsepower steam engine.

FLIGHTS OF FANCY

Machine Gun Invention

At the age of 24, Maxim became an apprentice at his uncle's engineering works in Fitchburg, Massachusetts. There he gained impressive skills in draftsmanship, wood turning, brass finishing, and coppersmithing. In the early 1870s Maxim moved to New York, where he became chief engineer for one of the nation's first electric utilities. Toward the end of the decade he invented a machine gun and showed it to the United States War and Navy Departments; both agencies found the gun ingenious but impractical and turned it down. When Maxim made a business trip to London in 1881, he found the British War Office considerably more interested in his ideas and he decided to settle in England. Eventually he became a British subject, though he displayed the Stars and Stripes in his home. In 1884 he perfected the 600 rounds-per-minute Maxim machine gun, a devastating weapon that made him rich and famous. The machine gun proved so valuable to the British in military engagements that the inventor eventually was knighted by Queen Victoria.

Maxim built an ingenious two-level track for testing his machine. The lower track, built of heavy steel rails, was the runway, engaged by the four cast-iron wheels of the undercarriage. The upper track, made of 3×9-inch Georgia pine, was intended to keep the ponderous biplane from escaping its test track and lofting into uncontrollable flight. If the machine rose more than a few inches from its runway, a second set of smaller wheels would engage the wooden guardrails and hold the vehicle down.

Delayed by mishaps and breakdowns during test runs in 1892 and early 1893, the Maxim machine in motion was an awesome sight. A journalist, visiting Maxim in 1893, took a ride on the huge biplane. He wrote later about his experience saying:

When full steam was up and the propellers spinning so fast that they seemed to become whirling disks, Maxim shouted, 'let go.' A rope was pulled and the machine shot forward like a railway train with the big propellers whirling, the steam hissing, and the waste pipes puffing and gurgling, it flew over the 1,800 feet of track in much less time than it takes to tell it.

The machine did not actually fly—then or ever. On its final test run on July 31, 1894, Maxim guided the aircraft at high boiler pressure along the track. After covering 600 feet and gaining a speed of 42 miles per hour, the machine lifted from its steel runway and rose until the secondary wheels reached the wooden guardrails. Suddenly, one of the rails snapped. The machine was liberated and briefly floated in the air. When a piece of broken guardrail smashed into a propeller Maxim immediately shut off the steam. His clumsy and uncontrollable flying machine settled to the ground, never to rise again. Maxim had demonstrated that a powerful engine could lift a heavy winged object from the ground. He was too busy with his other affairs to continue his aviation experiments.

Even though he contributed little to aeronautical progress, Maxim's reputation and his experiments helped convince the public that the age of heavier-than-air flight was nearly at hand. He said, "Even under the most unfavorable circumstances, aerial navigation will be an accomplished fact inside of ten years." How prophetic he was; the Wright brothers succeeded in 1903.

OTTO LILIENTHAL

The man we call the father of glider experiments was a German engineer, **Otto Lilienthal** (See Figure 3.14). As a young boy, Otto and his brother, Gustav, played in the meadows near their home where they chased storks they found there. Otto noticed that when the birds were frightened they would take off toward the boys even though this meant flying toward danger. Not until they were off the ground did the birds turn and fly away. Gustav later wrote that "rising against the wind might be easier than with the wind."

From those early days in 1860 until his death in 1896, Otto Lilienthal continued to search for the answer

Figure 3.14
Otto Lilienthal.

to the problem of flying. He and his brother, when in their teens, constructed model airplanes with 6 to 9 feet wingspreads. At first they attempted to fly in calm air, but remembering the storks, they were able to get their small gliders off the ground by turning them into the wind when it blew.

The Franco-Prussian War of 1870 interrupted the Lilienthals' work, but it was quickly resumed when the war ended. From 1871 to 1891 Otto concerned himself with the principles of aerodynamics. He derived many of his principles from the study of birds' flight. He recognized the superiority of a curved wing to the flat type. Otto recognized that nature utilized the advantage of the curved wing, not only in the bird kingdom, but also in the vegetable kingdom, by giving seeds of certain plants little curved wings which enable them to be picked up by the wind to fly along to a fertile spot.

Lilienthal believed that a cambered wing was necessary to obtain successful flight. In his workshop he built test equipment to measure the lift that would be produced by various wing shapes. His experiments demonstrated the superior lifting quality of the curved wing. In 1889 he published his findings in a book entitled *Birdflight as the Basis of Aviation* that became a classic of aeronautical literature. He described his studies of wing structure and the dynamics of bird flight. He included a description of how birds propel themselves by the twisting action of their outer primary feathers. He showed the lift provided by wings at various degrees of camber. Lilienthal's belief in gliding as preliminary to powered flight led him to experimenting with several unpowered craft that were fixed-wing monoplanes (See Figure 3.15). He later experimented with biplane designs. In a report published by the Smithsonian Institution in 1893, he stated that he approached flying one step at a time. In 1894, he constructed an artificial hill not far from his home. Running downhill from the summit and leaping into the wind, he repeatedly achieved glides of 150 feet and more.

Lilienthal then chose a hill near Berlin from where he achieved glides of up to 1,150 feet. Such performances were evidence that man could fly through the air. Lilienthal said that "he came to know the ocean of air; no one can realize how substantial the air is until he feels its supporting power beneath him. It inspires confidence at once." In an article for the Smithsonian Institution's Annual Report for 1893, he cautioned, "that the wind was a treacherous fellow; the man who would fly must proceed cautiously, achieving stability through

> **The man we call the father of glider experiments was a German engineer,** Otto Lilienthal.

the design of his flying machine and by his flight-control system. A flying machine's balance is constantly shifting and stable flight can be maintained only by a constant and arbitrary correction of the position of the center of gravity."

Lilienthal balanced his own craft by throwing his weight around in a series of acrobatic body movements that kept the glider flying on an even keel. A typical flight was described by a reporter for the *Boston Evening Transcript*, who accompanied Lilienthal to the hills of Rhinower one Sunday afternoon in 1896.

Lilienthal was dressed in his usual flying costume of flannel shirt, heavy shoes, snug fitting cap, and knickerbockers with the knees thickly padded in case of a rough landing. With an assistant's help he carried the machine to the top of a hill and took his place in a rectangular frame beneath and between the wings. Lifting the craft from the ground, he grasped a crossbar and rested his forearms on a pair of small cushions that were attached to the main frame. The reporter, armed with a camera, wrote later that he took up a position downhill and waited for Lilienthal, who "faced the wind and stood like an athlete waiting for the starting pistol. Presently the breeze freshened; he took three rapid steps forward and was instantly lifted from the ground, sailing off nearly horizontally from the summit. He went over my head at a terrific pace, at an elevation of about 50 feet, the wind playing wild tunes on the tense cordage of the machine, and was past me before I had time to train the camera on him. Suddenly the apparatus tipped sideways as a gust got under the left wing. For a moment I could see the top of the aeroplane, and then, with a powerful throw of his legs he brought the machine once more on an even keel and sailed away below me across the fields at the bottom, kicking at the tops of the haycocks as he passed over them. When within a foot off the ground he threw his legs forward, and notwithstanding its great velocity the machine stopped instantly, its front turning up, allowing the wind to strike under the wings, and he dropped lightly to the earth."

For those occasions when his descent was not quite so gentle, Lilienthal had incorporated a shock-absorbing device into a glider he built in 1894. Called the prellbugel, or rebound bow, it was a flexible willow hoop fitted in front of the pilot's position to act as a

Otto Lilienthal about to test his first hang type glider in 1891. It had a wing area of 197 square feet and weighed 40 pounds.

Lilienthal made a flight in 1895; he traveled a quarter of a mile and obtained an altitude of 75 feet.

Lilienthal flying his biplane glider near Berlin in 1895.

Figure 3.15   Flights by Lilienthal.

bumper guard upon landing. At least once it saved Lilienthal's life. He wrote of the near-fatal occasion:

During a gliding flight taken from a great height the center of gravity lay too much to the back; at the same time I was unable, owing to fatigue, to draw the upper part of my body again toward the front.

Overloaded in the rear, the machine shot skyward, stalled and then nose-dived toward the earth from a height of more than 60 feet. The prellbugel splintered as it buried itself in the ground, but it absorbed the shock of impact and Lilienthal escaped with minor injuries. His crash landing did not dampen his enthusiasm for future glides.

For all his practical experience, Lilienthal had one misconception. He believed that flapping wings were the answer to aerial locomotion. First in 1893, and again in 1895, he built powered devices with ornithopter features. Each machine was fitted with a lightweight carbonic acid gas engine, producing about two horsepower, that was to make the wing flap and thus drive the craft ahead. The first model was so ineffective that he did not even attempt to fly it; the second malfunctioned during trial runs and did not achieve horizontal flight.

Lilienthal was never able to give these curiously old fashioned machines another test. On August 9, 1896, he took off from a hill in one of his gliders. A sudden gust tossed him upward at a sharp angle. Lilienthal immediately threw his weight forward and tried to bring the nose down. The craft stalled, its left wing dipped sharply and the machine plunged to the ground. This time there was no prellbugel to cushion the impact. Otto Lilienthal who frequently said that many sacrifices would have to be made on the road to manned flight, died the next day of a broken spine.

Otto Lilienthal's flight research had probably taken him about as far as he could go. His concept of wing-flapping propulsion was a blind alley, as was his approach to the problems of stability and control. He crashed because his machine was unstable and controllable only by human strength and agility. These qualities were not adequate for successful sustained flight, nor could they readily be incorporated in a practical flying machine.

Despite his limitations, Lilienthal's influence on aviation was incalculable. He was a fundamental airman, the personification of man in flight. His writings were translated and read throughout the world. Newspaper reporters and magazine writers who had made tentative test flights with his gliders wrote glowing accounts of the wonderful sensation of soaring. Widely distributed photographs of the German flying master in action showed a fascinated public that man could indeed sustain himself in the air on artificial wings. Other aviation enthusiasts studied his work, sought his advice and copied his machines. Perhaps Otto Lilienthal's greatest achievement was to arouse interest in others who continued the advancement of man's effort to develop the airplane.

During his years of experimenting Lilienthal performed a great deal of research into the problems of flying; he also realized that only by actual flying were the real answers to be found. Otto Lilienthal is regarded as one of the greatest pioneers of aviation. He proved the superiority of curved wings over flat wings. He brought the art of gliding to an everyday accepted fact.

PERCY PILCHER

Among those inspired by Lilienthal's example was the Scotsman **Percy Sinclair Pilcher** who was an assistant lecturer in naval architecture and marine engineering at the University of Glasgow when he built his first glider which he named the *Bat* in 1895. The *Bat* was much like the standard Lilienthal monoplane hang glider pictured in the newspapers except that it lacked a horizontal stabilizer. With commendable prudence, Pilcher decided to visit Lilienthal and practice in proven machines before flying his own craft.

Lilienthal generously allowed Pilcher to gain gliding experience with him and made a number of suggestions for improving the *Bat*. Pilcher followed the advice and went on to build other gliders named the *Beetle*, the *Gull* and the *Hawk;* all of increasingly effective design. The *Hawk* (See Figure 3.16), completed in 1896, the year of Lilienthal's death, was a particularly successful hang glider, with cambered wings, a tail unit that hinged upward and a wheeled undercarriage fitted with springs. Using a rope-and-pulley system to launch his craft, Pilcher was able to glide for distances of up to 750 feet.

Pilcher next intended to build a powered version of the *Hawk*, its four-foot propeller driven by a small gasoline engine of about four horsepower. Pilcher planned to take off in this machine by running down a hill; once craft was in the air the propeller would be started, and the machine would fly on or about 30 miles per hour. Pilcher completed his engine in 1899, but experiments with a new triplane glider and attempts to

Figure 3.16 Percy Pilcher, right, ready to fly in his most successful glider, the *Hawk*, 1898.

form a company to promote his machines kept him from completing and testing his powered craft. On September 30 he staged a gliding demonstration for a group of English aeronautical enthusiasts who had assembled on the estate of Lord Braye at Stanford Hall in Leicestershire. The day was damp and dismal and for some reason Pilcher's gliders had been left outdoors for several hours. All were sodden and heavy by flight time, but Pilcher decided to go on with the show. His first launch in the well-tested *Hawk* ended in a premature but gentle landing. On the second try, the waterlogged craft soared to an altitude of about 30 feet; then a soggy bamboo rod in the tail assembly gave way with a snap. The whole tail unit collapsed and the *Hawk* plummeted to the ground. The 33-year-old Percy Pilcher died two days later without regaining consciousness. Two years before his fatal crash, Pilcher had wirtten prophetically that his gliders were mere practice vehicles to be employed only until the advent of engines that could drive an aircraft forward. He said, "Then a person who is used to sailing down a hill with a simple soaring machine will be able to fly with comparative safety." Pilcher's efforts proved that controlled powered airplane flight was possible and soon to be a fact.

That great leap from soaring to powered flight was not destined to be made in Europe. Following the deaths of Lilienthal and Pilcher, the scattered community of European aviation enthusiasts made little progress. The quest for aeronautical progress had already passed to the United States, which had its own source of inspiration and information in the somewhat unlikely person of a sexagenarian bridge builder named **Octave Chanute.**

JOHN J. MONTGOMERY

An American at the turn-of-the-century who did a great deal for the advancement of controllable powered flight, was **John J. Mongomery,** a science professor at Santa Clara College in California. He experimented with gliders at his family ranch near San Diego, California. He named his first craft the *Gull* which he tested in 1884. His feats in the realm of aviation have been called everything from great to doubtful. It is known that in 1893 Montgomery attended the International Conference on Aerial Navigation held in Chicago. His comments at this meeting demonstrated awareness of airflow and pressure on wings. He understood the importance of curved wing surfaces for lift. This subject was not widely known or understood. As early as 1883 Montgomery built a birdlike flying machine with flapping wings (ornithopter). He next constructed three gliders which demonstrated the need for curved wings. He continued his work and research on the problems of balance and control. Montgomery built several man-carrying gliders which were launched from balloons that carried the gliders into the sky and then released them. On one flight on April 29, 1905, his tandem glider called *Santa Clara* was flown by professional parachute jumper Daniel Maloney. A balloon carried the glider upward to 4,000 feet and released it. Maloney flew a controlled flight going eight miles in 20 minutes. He performed spirals and dives and landed at a pre-arranged location. Unfortunately Maloney died in a crash three months later.

Montgomery is remembered for his acrobatic stunts in public. He had a team of three pilots who, beginning in 1905, did some of the earliest aerial stunting. (See Figure 3.17). One of their tricks included a "corkscrew descent and side somersaults." The great San Francisco earthquake of 1906 interrupted Montgomery's experiments for five years. In 1911, while Montgomery was making a flight, a little whirlwind caught his craft and smashed it to the ground. Professor Montgomery landed on his head and, although he did not appear to be hurt, he soon after complained of severe pains and died.

OCTAVE CHANUTE

Throughout the development of the airplane many names appeared, several of whom made important contributions to furthering the reality of the airplane. One such great name immediately preceding the Wright

Figure 3.17 Advertisement for The Montgomery Aeroplane.

Britain. Aeronautics was simply a hobby for Chanute until he reached his middle sixties. Prior to this time his aviation activities were confined to gathering and writing information on the subject. He was chairman of the International Conference on Aerial Navigation in Chicago in 1893. The following year he published a book called *Progress in Flying Machines,* which was a large volume and discussed

Figure 3.18 Octave Chanute.

the history of aviation up to that time. Past the age of 60, after becoming successful and having retired, Chanute seriously began the study of flying. He once said that he was influenced by the work of others. After Lilienthal was successful in man-carrying gliders, Chanute turned his major interest to flying. Whereby Lilienthal tried to control his gliders by shifting his weight, Chanute proposed a mechanism that would control the glider by moving the wings.

In 1896 and 1897 Chanute made over 2,000 gliding flights along the shores of Lake Michigan. (See Figure 3.19). For many of these strenuous experiments the older man had to rely upon the services of younger enthusiastic men. Chanute's earliest airplanes consisted of five and six wings, but after experimentation he eliminated some wings. Chanute introduced to airplane building the civil engineering concept of strut and diagonal wire bracing. The best flight by one of his pilots was 359

brothers was **Octave Chanute** (See Figure 3.18). He was a learned, successful engineer, and his approach to the problems of flight was carried through on a scientific level. Chanute contributed much in the progression of successful flying.

Octave Chanute was born in Paris in 1832 and came to the United States with his parents at the age of six. He was a civil engineer who achieved notoriety and fortune as well as a well-deserved reputation. In 1891 he was chosen to be president of the American Society of Civil Engineers. He had designed the first bridge to span the Missouri River at Kansas City. His name is well remembered for designing and constructing the vast Union Stock Yards in Chicago.

Chanute probably became intrigued with the problems of flight after reading an article written by Alphonse Penaud in his report to the Aeronautical Society of Great

Figure 3.19 In 1896, Chanute poses with the *Katydid.*

feet in 14 seconds. Chanute was convinced that further experiments with gliders would lead to stable controllable aircraft that could be driven by an engine.

Chanute constructed five man-carrying gliders in all and flew them hundreds of feet. He published his findings in the *Journal of Western Society of Engineers* and invited other experiments to improve upon his results. No one accepted the invitation until 1900 when Wilbur Wright wrote to Chanute inquiring about his construction, materials, and experiments on airplanes. Wright, in his letter, said that he had no ideas of his own but could think of no better way to spend his vacation. Chanute was happy to comply with Wilbur's request. This was the beginning of the long road to the Wright brothers' eventual success.

Octave Chanute and the Wright brothers became fast friends and had several interchanges of letters. When the Wright brothers were experimenting with their gliders at Kitty Hawk, North Carolina, in 1903, Chanute was present. However, due to mechanical delays and cold weather, he was not present when the successful flight took place on December 17, 1903. Chanute felt as a proud father to the Wright brothers' experiments and remained interested in their efforts until his death in 1910. Octave Chanute had given the Wright brothers guidance and inspiration. They made true his greatest wish, the hope and belief that the goal of useful airplanes could be reached.

Figure 3.20   Manly and Langley.

SAMUEL P. LANGLEY

Another great scientist known for his aeronautical experimentation was **Samuel P. Langley** (See Figure 3.20), who was a mathematician, astronomer, and physicist. Like Octave Chanute, he enjoyed a wide reputation and notoriety by the time he began experimenting with aircraft in his later years.

After the Civil War he became an assistant at the Harvard Observatory, and in 1866 he became a teacher of mathematics at the United States Naval Academy. For the next 20 years his major concern was astronomy, and by the time he was 52 years old he was recognized for his contributions to that science.

In 1889, Dr. Samuel Langley went to the Smithsonian Institution as its secretary. It was there that he began publishing his aerodynamic findings and was recognized as the country's leading authority on aviation. (Figure 3.21.) Wilbur Wright said that Langley's knowledge and position as the head of such a scientific institution was an influence which further led them to in-

vestigate the possibility of flying. Langley had built some 40 rubber-powered airplane models. He directed experiments using all kinds of engines such as hot air, compressed air, gas, electricity, carbonic acid, and gunpowder. He analyzed the problems of airplane design and construction and studied propellers. He also directed his attention toward airplane stability and control. Because of his duties and responsibilities as head of the Smithsonian Institution he had to rely upon assistants for much of the actual work.

Before Langley could launch a successful airplane he needed a lightweight, high-powered engine. He decided steam had the greatest possibilities and directed a program to perfect a steam engine. Trials for the launching of his aircraft were conducted from a houseboat moored on the Potomac River near Quantico, Virginia. A catapult mechanism was designed to launch the airplane from the top of this houseboat. During 1893 and 1894, because of weather conditions and mechanical problems, not much was accomplished. However, the fifth model was successfully launched, flew 35 feet, and fell into the water after a three-second flight.

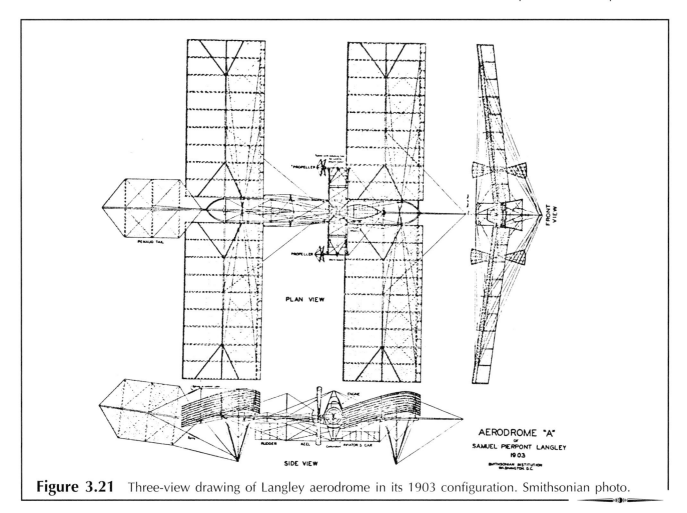

Figure 3.21 Three-view drawing of Langley aerodrome in its 1903 configuration. Smithsonian photo.

The next model Langley built was observed in May 1896 by Dr. Alexander Graham Bell. The model weighed 26 pounds, and flew 3,200 feet attaining a speed of 25 miles per hour. To Langley the flights of these models meant success, and he wrote:

For the first time in the history of the world a device produced by man had actually flown through the air and had preserved its equilibrium without the aid of a guiding human intelligence.

Langley was in his middle sixties and his administrative responsibilities at the Smithsonian Institution grew heavier. During the Spanish-American War, President McKinley asked Dr. Langley to construct a flying machine that could be used as a weapon of war. Langley accepted this mandate on December 12, 1898. He estimated the cost of this work to be $50,000 and stipulated that his work was to be done privately. Langley enlisted the aid of a Cornell University graduate,

Charles Manly (See Figure 3.20), to take charge of the technical aspects of construction. Eventually models were constructed and several successfully flew, but there was always some kind of trouble. Despite several troubles a larger houseboat was made ready for the eventful day when a full-sized airplane would be flown. The houseboat measured 40 × 60 feet and provided living quarters and workshops. Atop the houseboat was a steam catapult for launching the airplane.

The engine to power this new aircraft was not available. The New York manufacturer who had agreed a year earlier to design and build a lightweight engine according to Langley's specifications, was unable to produce the final product. Langley and Manly spent six weeks in Europe searching for an engine manufacturer who could produce an engine of their desired high power and light weight. Wherever they went they were told that it was impossible to construct such an engine—12-horsepower and weighing less than 225 pounds. If it were possible, the European manufacturers would have already constructed one.

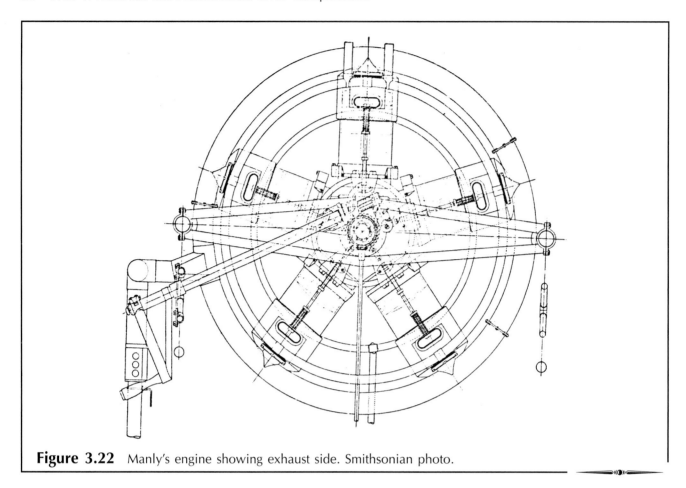

Figure 3.22   Manly's engine showing exhaust side. Smithsonian photo.

Not dismayed by their findings, Langley and Manly returned to America where Manly designed and built a revolutionary five-cylinder radial engine (See Figure 3.22). It weighed 125 pounds, developed 54 horsepower at 850 RPMs and became the forerunner of airplane radial engines. With this new engine the Langley airplane was ready for a flight attempt in the summer of 1903. This airplane, which was designed to carry the first man in controlled flight, had a wingspan of 48 feet and a body 52 feet long which was constructed of steel tubing. The airplane had two pusher propellers powered by Manly's engine. The wings were covered with cotton cloth and the total weight of the airplane was 850 pounds including the pilot. Every effort was used to give the airplane control.

On July 4, 1903, with ground testing complete, the airplane was placed upon the houseboat and moved down the Potomac. Langley had hoped to launch his airplane in private, according to his agreement with the Army. However, the Potomac soon became a haven for boats carrying newspapermen wanting to report the story. For three months the press moved up and down the river waiting for the eventful day. Everything was ready for the historic flight of the big airplane. Manly, who had designed and built the engine was to be the pilot. He wore, in addition to his work clothes, a life preserver, goggles, and tennis shoes on the first attempted flight.

For almost a month bad weather prevented his first effort and finally on October 7, 1903, the trial did come off. Ironically, Langley was not present. He was detained in Washington, D.C. on official business. Shortly after noon the airplane was lifted to the launching platform where Manly climbed aboard and started the engine. George Brown, a newspaperman, wrote for the *Washington Post:*

Manly looked down and smiled. His face hardened as he braced himself for the flight which might mean for him fame or death. Propellers were whirling a thousand times a minute a foot from his head. A man forward fired two skyrockets. A mechanic stooped and cut the cable holding the catapult; there was a roaring, grinding noise and the Langley airplane went off into the Potomac River and disappeared.

October 7, 1903, Langley's "aerodrome" on launching catapult.

The ill-fated take-off.

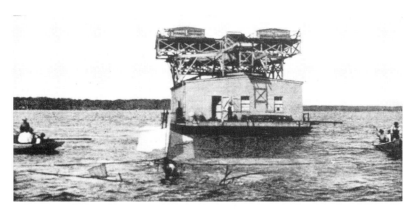

Boats moved to pick up Manly out of the Potomac River.

Figure 3.23   Launching the aerodrome.

COLLAPSE OF THE AIRSHIP.

AIRSHIP FAILS TO FLY

Prof. Langley's Machine Goes
to River Bottom.

PROF. MANLY ABOARD

THE LATTER RESCUED FROM
PERILOUS POSITION.

Test of t   Off the Arsenal

had proved successful it would have had a
free flight up three branches of the stream

Construction of the Airship.

The airship itself is built of slender steel
tubing and wooden supports. It has four
sixty-foot wings, two propellers and a rudder propeller. The wings and their supports are not attached to the machine until
just before the time for the flight, and the
propellers and other detachable parts are
not assembled until after the machine has
been placed on the launching car. To
handle the heavy wings and canvas propellers in a strong wind is out of the question, according to the opinion of the experts in charge of the tests, and the prospect of a test Saturday was dissipated by
a strong wind which began in the morning
and gradually increased in velocity.
Sunday no work was done on the house
boat, but Monday the workmen were on
hand early and started in to prepare for a
test. Ice covered the river, except in the
main channel, and the weather was cold
and biting. P...

Figure 3.24 *"The Washington Star,"*
December 9, 1903.

Except for a good wetting Manly was unhurt; he blamed the failure on incorrect balancing of the aircraft. However, it was later determined that a part of the launching mechanism of the catapult had fouled and pulled the airplane down to disaster. Manly's engine was undamaged and the airplane was repairable. (See Figure 3.23.)

Langley had spent the original $50,000 appropriation from the Army as well as $20,000 provided by the Smithsonian Institution. The airplane was rebuilt and on December 8th, in a last desperate attempt to fly it, something again went wrong. The wings collapsed, and the aircraft again crashed into the river. This time Manly had to fight his way out of the submerged wreckage, and as he did, he bumped his head on a block of ice which was floating in the river—but he was finally picked up and carried to shore. (See Figure 3.24.)

During all these trials the Army had been patient, but had hoped for quick success. The Army was criticized, and Langley became a point of ridicule. In 1906 Dr. Samuel Langley died. It was reported that he was the victim of a broken heart. Langley's accomplishments in the human effort to fly were notable, even though his man-carrying airplane failed. In June 1914, the Langley Aerodome with modifications and fitted with floats was flown from Lake Keuka near Hammondsport, New York by Glenn Curtiss. (See Figure 3.25.) By some it was considered proof that except for malfunction of the launching gear Langley's airplane would have flown in 1903. With equal conviction others said it was a fake operation. This led to controversy which lasted until 1942.

THE WRIGHT BROTHERS

It was on December 17, 1903, at the sand dunes of Kitty Hawk, North Carolina with the wind blowing 27 miles an hour that Orville Wright climbed aboard the flying machine and started along the launching tract. After traveling 40 feet the Flyer lifted into the air where it remained for 12 seconds before coming back to earth a total distance of 120 feet from where it started.

This episode marked the end of the long hardships of trials and errors of several men for the preceding centuries. Success had finally been achieved in an airplane that was flown in controllable powered flight.

Although this marked the point of success in the long progression of inventors and experimenters, it was not the end, but really the beginning. From that time on the airplane developed upon a sound scientific basis to achieve the success that it enjoys today.

How did the Wright brothers (See Figure 3.26) succeed where so many others failed? Earlier that month

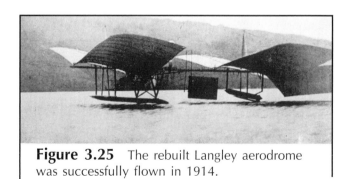

Figure 3.25 The rebuilt Langley aerodrome was successfully flown in 1914.

Wilbur
1867–1912

Orville
1871–1948

Figure 3.26 The Wright Brothers (top). The Wright Flyer (middle). December 17, 1903; the flight the world remembers (bottom).

of December, 1903, Samuel Langley's airplane had failed for the second and final time. This ended 17 years of Langley's effort and more than $70,000 in funds.

Before Langley's failing efforts others had attempted and also failed. Maxim and Ader, who were amply financed, came to grief. Although an engineer and a scientist had attacked the problem of flight, they fell short of the ultimate goal achieved by the Wright brothers. Lilienthal and Pilcher were killed while experimenting with their inventions, and Penaud had committed suicide due to his frustrations and inability to accomplish what the Wright brothers achieved.

It was more than blind luck that led the two young men from Dayton, Ohio, to succeed where others had failed. The Wright brothers were bicycle manufacturers in their own little shop and were not scientists or engineers. In fact, neither of the boys had graduated from high school. This was due to their lack of interest in diplomas rather than a lack of intelligence. They were the sons of a bishop and they developed the habit of reading. It was through their intense interest in reading that they learned of the work of Lilienthal and Chanute and which led them to begin a correspondence with Chanute.

The Wright brothers did not invent the airplane; this is a misconception.

Actually, it was a series of events which led the Wright brothers on the path to succeeding where all others had failed. When they were young boys their father brought home a rubber band-powered flying toy. Being inquisitive mechanics, this toy started them thinking along the avenue which produced the eventual results. They read of Lilienthal's experiences and decided that he was correct in his approach to flying, but that he had not gone far enough when he was killed. They figured that in five years, Lilienthal spent no more than a total of five hours actually gliding in the air.

The Wright brothers decided that if people were ever to fly successfully they would have to learn how to design and build wings, how to devise power for flight, and, most important of all, how to control the machine once it got into the air. Of these three problems the first two had been reasonably worked out by the efforts of others. Although these two were very important problems to overcome, they would be for nothing if the airplane could not be controlled once it became airborne. The Wright brothers devoted their attention to this third problem. The Wright brothers did not invent the airplane; this is a misconception. What they are given credit for is producing a man-carrying airplane which was capable of controlled powered flight.

As boys, the Wright brothers spent their early years building models which they flew as kites. They continually made larger kite models, and each one showed improvement over the previous kites. They eventually produced a large glider whose wing tips could be twisted by the pilot to direct the wind and change the direction of the airplane. These wings were controlled by a wire arrangement down to the pilot's position.

Since the area around Dayton, Ohio was not satisfactory for their flying experiments, they looked for a suitable place. They required an area which had moderate wind currents, hills from which they could launch their gliders, and, most of all, privacy from onlookers who doubtless would ridicule them. After much seeking they chose the sand dunes of unpopulated Kitty Hawk, North Carolina. They went there first in the summer of 1900. Their glider rose into the air where the wind was steady for good gliding, but it did not have much lifting ability. The next year they returned to Kitty Hawk with a new glider which had larger wings, but this one did not operate as they had planned. They decided that, in order to save time and money, they would make changes in their airplane by reproducing these changes on a model. They put the model in a long, open-end box wind tunnel where they were able to see the effect of their design changes. The wind tunnel idea which the Wright brothers conceived is still in use today. In fact, the engineering aerodynamics of jet aircraft and rocket-powered missiles are extensively tested in huge wind tunnels before they are put into full scale-sized production. From their little wind tunnel test the Wright brothers succeeded in building an airplane which they considered to be successful. From the test results of the glider they decided that the time had come to design and begin construction of an aircraft equipped with an engine. (See Figure 3.27.)

On December 14, 1903, the Wrights were still at Kitty Hawk. They had stayed late in the year hoping for eventual success. They agreed to toss a coin to see who would be the one to make the first test. Wilbur won the toss of the coin and made the first try. It was a cold day but the wind was very mild. The Wright Flyer barely got off the ground for two and one-half seconds. Minor damage resulted, and the boys agreed that this flight didn't count as a real flight. Three days later they had completed the minor damage repairs, and it was then Orville's turn to try. This was to be it! Twelve seconds and 120 feet later history had been made!

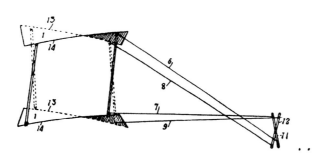

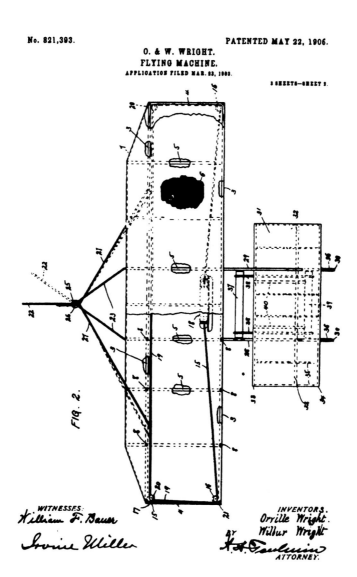

Figure 3.27 These drawings are part of the patent application of Orville and Wilbur Wright for a "flying machine." Filed March 23, 1903, the application pre-dated the first powered flights by nine months. The flying machine patent was granted May 22, 1906, and it won for the Wrights membership in the National Inventors Hall of Fame established at the Patent and Trademark Office of the U.S. Department of Commerce.

Figure 3.28   The Wright cycle shop.

Figure 3.29   Taylor's Engine.

Three additional flights were made that same day with the brothers taking turns at the controls. The best and the last of these flights was made by Wilbur—just under one minute, for a distance of 852 feet.

This successful Wright Flyer had been constructed at their bicycle shop (See Figure 3.28) in Dayton, Ohio, where they had a flourishing repair business going. They had hired a mechanic, Charles Taylor, to work for them in their bicycle business. It was Taylor who built the engine for their first airplane (See Figure 3.29). The crankcase and block were aluminum; the cylinders and pistons were made of cast iron. The engine weighed only 170 pounds but could develop 12 horsepower. It was not a fancy product but it was dependable. The problem of constructing adequate propellers was a big one. They looked to ship builders for assistance, since boats used propellers. They discovered ship propellers were still being built on a trial and error basis. They correctly thought that an airplane propeller in the air would act the same as a ship propeller in the water. Also, they figured the propeller was actually a wing in itself and would behave as such. From these ideas they hand-built their own propellers. The efficiency of the propellers was remarkable and was one of the essential factors leading to the success of their flights.

The Wright brothers were craftsmen and excellent mechanics, and they knew how to fabricate with wood

> **The wind tunnel idea which the Wright brothers conceived is still in use today.**

and metal. They learned how to conduct scientific research like true scientists. They could visualize results of their designs and fit all of this together into a workable result.

The Wright brothers continued their experimentation and by 1905 they had made more than a hundred flights totaling 160 miles. They were soon to become famous, not only in this country, but also in Europe. However, the acceptance of their successful flight did not take place immediately. As a result of their successful flights on December 17th, the Wright brothers sent a telegram to their family at Dayton. The message read:

Success, four flights Thursday morning. All against 21 mile wind. Started from level with engine power alone. Average speed through air 31 miles. Longest 59 seconds. Inform press. Home Christmas. (Signed Orville Wright)

The telegram did not reach the Wright brothers' father until that evening and when it arrived it had gathered errors in transmission. The brothers' sister, Katherine, sent a message to Chanute reporting their success. Their father prepared a brief message for the press. The reporter in the *Journal* office was annoyed over being expected to accept such a story, and nothing about the Wright brothers' success appeared in the newspaper. The headlines were concerned with the stores being filled with Christmas shoppers. When the story was finally printed in the newspaper it was to the extent that the Wright brothers would be returning home for Christmas.

FLIGHTS OF FANCY

Daredevil Pilots

In the early 1900s fliers risked their lives almost daily to set records, to compete for aviation prizes of thousands of dollars, and to learn more about aviation. Many of the biographies of these daredevil pilots end with the words *"killed in an airplane crash."* Many crashes occurred because planes were unreliable, pilots knew little about weather, and they knew little about flying.

A full decade after the Wrights, the noted Harvard astronomer, William Pickering, firmly denounced the idea that the airplane would someday become a major transportation vehicle. He wrote:

The popular mind often pictures gigantic flying machines speeding across the Atlantic, carrying innumerable passengers. It seems safe to say that such ideas must be wholly visionary. Even if such a machine could get across with one or two passengers, it would be prohibitive to any but the capitalist who could own his own yacht.

Pickering was not as pessimistic as Simon Newcomb, a mathematician and scientist. In 1902 he was handed a model of the Wright Flyer (See Figure 3.30) by the two brothers who proposed to build it. They wanted his opinion and he gave it—handing the model back with a smile, he shook his head. "Man will never be able to fly a heavier-than-air machine," Newcomb decreed.

The most famous aviation expert in the United States, 10 years after Kitty Hawk, was asked about the chances of flying across the Atlantic. The expert was dubious.

It is a bare possibility that a one-man machine without a float and favored by a wind of, say, 15 miles an hour, might succeed in getting across the Atlantic. But such an attempt would be the height of folly. When one comes to increase the size of the craft, the possibility rapidly fades away. This is because of the difficulties of carrying sufficient fuel. It will readily be seen, therefore, why the Atlantic flight is out of the question.

That statement was made by none other than Orville Wright.

Wilbur Wright became ill after eating fish at a Boston Hotel. He became feverish and went to bed. His father said he was suffering from typhoidal fever. He died quietly on May 29, 1912.

A Wright military aircraft in flight at Fort Myer in 1908.

Figure 3.30 The Wright Flyer.

Orville died on January 30, 1948, after suffering a heart attack while fixing his doorbell. He was seventy-seven years of age and had lived to see the extent of his efforts.

Those who foresaw the time when mass, long-distance air transportation would become a reality were considered crackpots. For example, Rufus Porter preached the forthcoming glories of commercial flight from the prestigious pages of the *Scientific American* magazine of which he was the editor. In 1850, Porter actually tried to raise money for construction of an aerial ship capable of carrying 150 passengers which would easily carry them to California or London in three or four days.

Yet even as late as 1925, only two years before Charles Lindbergh's New York-Paris feat, Jose Navarro, an aeronautical engineer, proposed an airliner with a wingspan of 185 feet, a 38-man crew, nine engines, a bar on each of several decks, separate dining rooms, sleeping compartments, and electric kitchens. Navarro's goliath would carry at least 150 passengers and the suggested New York-London route, with refueling stops at Newfoundland and Iceland, would take only a day.

Lieutenant Thomas E. Selfridge (1882–1908) of the

> **"Man will never be able to fly a heavier-than-air machine,"
> Newcomb decreed.**

United States Army Signal Corps was the first person killed in an airplane crash (See Figure 3.31). Selfridge had become interested in flying as a member of the Aerial Experiment Association headed by Alexander Graham Bell, the inventor of the telephone. He helped build some of the association's experimental airplanes.

Selfridge was appointed one of the Army officers to judge the military value of the Wright brothers' airplane. In a flight with Orville Wright on September 17, 1908, a propeller broke 75 feet in the air. The plane crashed, killing Selfridge and severely injuring Orville. Selfridge Field, an Air National Guard Base near Mount Clemens, Michigan, was named in his honor in 1917.

Controllable powered aircraft was now a fact; many noted airmen and aircraft developers appeared. After the success of the Wright brothers in 1903 in the United States and that of Santos-Dumont in 1906 in Europe, a revival of interests in heavier-than-air machines took place. History has not recorded all the names of the scientists, engineers, mechanics and geniuses who put all they had into their effort to build aircraft. From 1904 to 1912, hundreds of prototypes appeared. Among some

Figure 3.31 Lt. Thomas E. Selfridge became the first fatality in a crash with Orville Wright on September 17, 1908.

of the most important of these flying machines was the Ellehammer, built by the Dane **Jacob Christian Hanson Ellehammer,** which rivaled the 14-BIS of Santos-Dumont for the title of the first airplane to fly in Europe. On September 12, 1906, his airplane hopped 140 feet. **Henri Fabre's** Hydravion deserves acknowledgment as the first seaplane in the world. On March 29, 1910, it flew almost four miles and made a perfect landing. Other aircraft which should be noted are the Dunne D-5, the first all-wing airplane built by **John William Dunne;** the Muller and the Chiribiri, among the first to be designed and built in Italy; the Cody built by the American expatriate **Samuel Franklin Cody,** who lived in Great Britain, and was the first to fly in that country.

No concrete proof exists that the Givaudan, with drum-shaped wings, the Safety, with looped wings, the Edward, with rhomboidal wings or the Seddon, ever got off the ground. Nevertheless, they did testify to the dedicated commitment to research and stood as objects of study and inspiration for all who endeavored to solve the problems of flight.

The aircrafts that made brief flights were Captain Dorand's Aeroplane, destined for military use; the Koechlin-De Pischoff; the Cygnett II, designed by the American **Alexander Graham Bell** and built by the Aerial Experiment Associa-

> **Lieutenant Thomas E. Selfridge (1882–1908) of the United States Army Signal Corps was the first person killed in an airplane crash.**

> **In 1906 Alexander Graham Bell said: "There are two critical points in every aerial flight; its beginning and its end."**

tion. It seems impossible that this strange aircraft, built like a honeycomb, was able to fly before crashing on frozen Lake Keuka, in New York State in 1909.

Horatio Frederick Phillips' Multiplane flew only a short distance, but the studies he made on wing-surface curvature and later tried to test became very important for the future. Nor did the young Rumanian engineer Henri Coanda's aircraft ever fly though he presented at the second Salon de L'Aeronautique in Paris in 1910. But its design anticipated the advent of the turbine engine. Twenty-five years would pass before others would succeed where Coanda had failed.

Glenn Curtiss (1878–1930) (See Figure 3.32) began racing bicycles as a teenager, which led him to the use of air-cooled engines and, therefore, motorcycles. In 1902 he began helping the balloonist, Tom Baldwin, produce a powered dirigible for the United States Army, and as a result, in 1905, the United States had its first military airship.

Curtiss joined Alexander Graham Bell in his Aerial Experiment Association in 1907, and in 1908 he produced the *June Bug*, which won the very first aviation prize to be offered in the United States. (See Figure 3.33.) Curtiss started the first aircraft factory in the United States where he built and sold his first airplane for profit. This action caused the Wrights to file suit claiming Curtiss infringed upon their patents, thus beginning several years of controversy and court action which was finally won by the Wright brothers.

Curtiss built the first successful seaplane in the United States in 1911 and became the "father of naval aviation." A Curtiss pilot, Eugene Ely, made the first

Figure 3.32 Glenn Curtiss in his *June Bug.*

Figure 3.33 The *June Bug* won the Scientific American prize in 1908.

Figure 3.34
Early Aircraft Designs

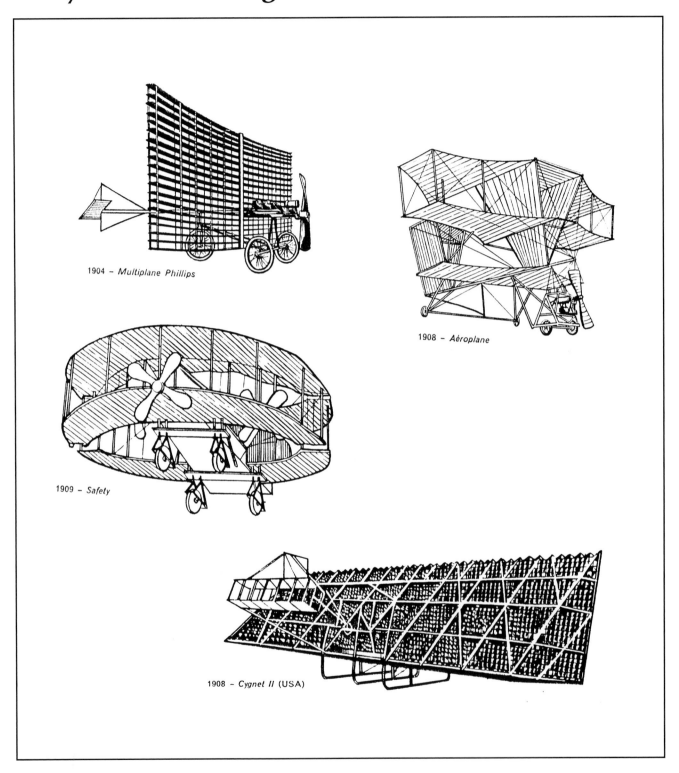

1904 – *Multiplane Phillips*

1908 – *Aéroplane*

1909 – *Safety*

1908 – *Cygnet II* (USA)

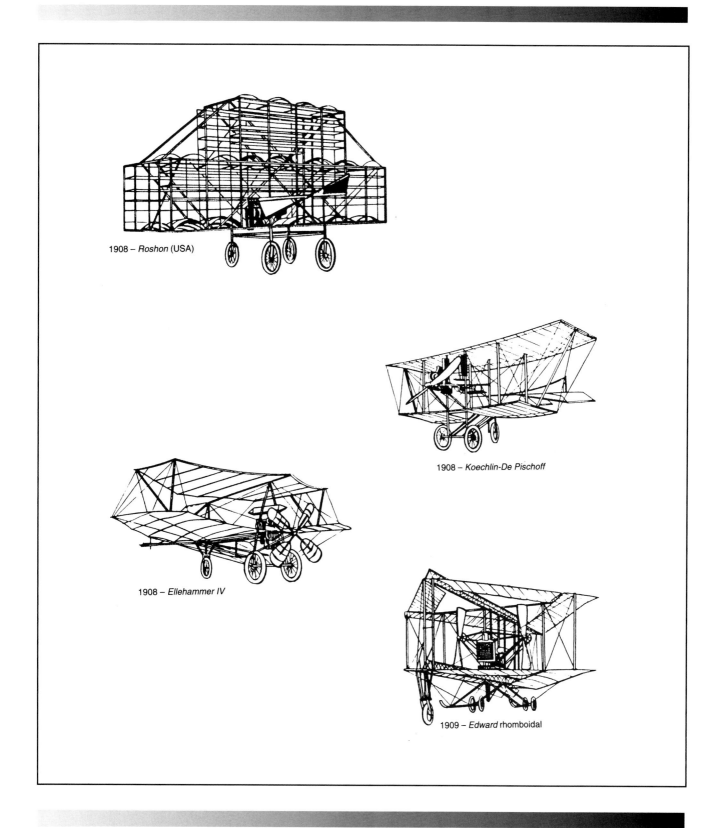

1908 – *Roshon* (USA)

1908 – *Koechlin-De Pischoff*

1908 – *Ellehammer IV*

1909 – *Edward* rhomboidal

Figure 3.34
(Continued)

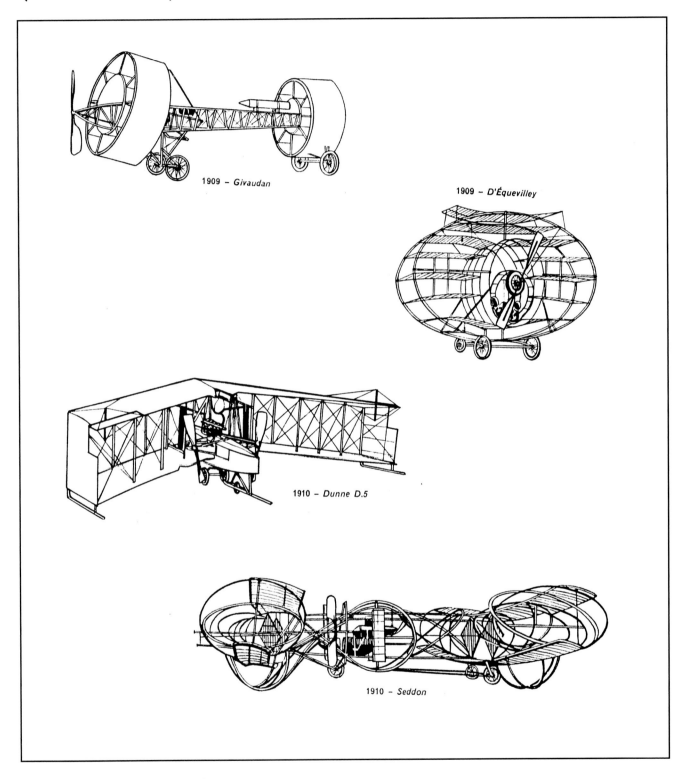

1909 – *Givaudan*

1909 – *D'Équevilley*

1910 – *Dunne D.5*

1910 – *Seddon*

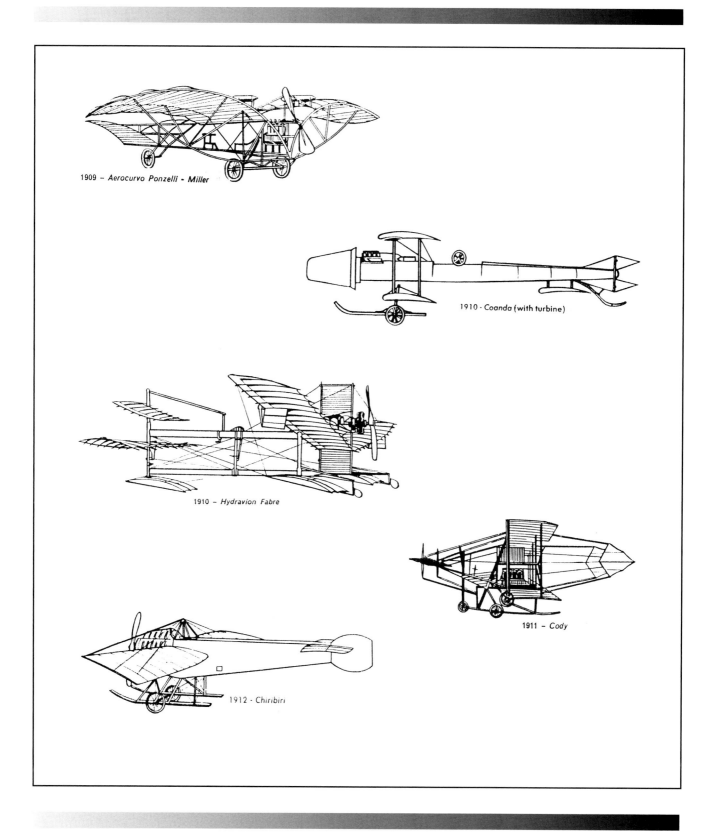

1909 – Aerocurvo Ponzelli - Miller

1910 - Coanda (with turbine)

1910 – Hydravion Fabre

1911 – Cody

1912 - Chiribiri

shipboard take-off doing so from the cruiser *Birmingham* on November 14, 1910. (See Figure 3.35.) Two months later Ely made the first landing on a naval vessel.

Another member of Bell's group, **James A.D. McCurdy,** in August, 1910, received and sent the first radio messages from an airplane over Sheepshead Bay, New York.

In the meantime, flying made great progress in France. **Alberto Santos-Dumont** (1873–1932) (See Figure 3.36), a wealthy Brazilian, made the first airplane flight in France on August 22, 1906. **Louis Bleriot** (1872–1936) made the first international flight in an airplane. He flew across the English Channel from France to England in thirty-seven minutes on July 25, 1909. Bleriot became a prominent airplane manufacturer in France. He was the first to build monoplanes with the engine in the front, a stabilizing tail at the rear, and controls attached to a stick for the pilot. **Henri C. Farman** (1874–1934) made many daring flights, including the first night flight, in 1910. The first altitude flight of over 3,000 feet was made in an Antionette airplane in 1910 by **Hubert Latham** (1833–1912).

In 1910 the Curtiss Exhibition Company was putting on airplane shows and gave the Wright team competition.

On August 2, 1911, **Harriet Quimby** (See Figures 3.37 and 3.38) became the first woman pilot in the United States to obtain a Federation Aeronautique International certificate; it was number 37 and given to her at Mineola, New York. On April 16, 1912, she was the first woman to fly across the English Channel. She was killed later that year when she and a passenger fell out of her airplane while flying 2,000 feet above Boston Harbor.

September 23 through 30, 1911, the first officially approved public service airmail in the United States was flown during the International Aviation Tournament at Garden City, New York. Captain Paul Peck of the United States Army piloted an airplane with Postmaster General Frank Hitchcock carrying the first mail bag. Earle Ovington piloted later flights during the week of airmail service. This effort proved that airmail service was feasible.

Grover Loening, an early aviation pioneer, who later was elected to the Aviation Hall of Fame, received

Figure 3.35   The first flight from a ship, November 10, 1910, was made by a Curtiss pilot, Eugene Ely, at Hampton Roads, VIrginia. The Naval cruiser *Birmingham* was the vessel.

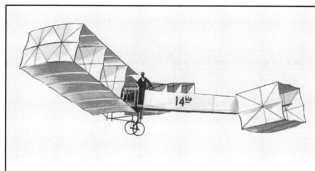

Figure 3.36 Alberto Santos-Dumont, 14 BIS, France 1906. Wings and engine were at the rear of the plane.

Figure 3.38 Wilbur Wright and the first female pilot in America, Harriet Quimby.

the nation's first master's degree in aeronautics in 1910. Orville Wright hired the promising young engineer in 1913 as his assistant and factory manager at Dayton, Ohio. In 1917 Loening formed his own company and built seaplanes for the United States Navy. Later his Air Yacht set many world records. The Loening Amphibian, first flown in 1924, was in continuous production for over ten years. It was used all over the world not only by the military and several of the earliest airlines, but also by many private owners. **Admiral Byrd** used this aircraft in his expedition to the Arctic in 1925. Until his death in 1976, Loening remained active in aviation as designer, author, consultant, and lecturer in the true spirit of the aviation pioneer.

Fearless pioneer fliers learned that airplanes could do aerobatics. **Adolphe Pegoud,** a French pilot, proved

Figure 3.37 Harriet Quimby

in 1913 that it was possible to fly upside down in an airplane. The next year a Curtiss exhibition pilot, **Lincoln Beachey** (1887–1915), "looped the loop" more than a thousand times. Beachey demonstrated the tailspin, flew inside a building, and was the first of the great daredevil stunt pilots.

In 1915 Lieutenant **Max Immelmann** (1890–1916) of Germany invented the Immelmann turn, which was a combination short climb and half-roll.

In 1914, at the beginning of World War I, all of the countries involved in the war had aircraft but none were suitable for reconnaissance purposes. Observing enemy movements from the air required an aircraft that would allow an observer, in addition to the pilot, to look over the countryside. A camera was necessary but a machine-gun was considered useless. Opposing pilots and observers eventually began to throw things at each other. Bricks were the favorite missiles. Some pilots were known to throw a chain hoping to snare the enemy's propeller and cause the aircraft to crash. Pistols were inaccurate and rifles were little better. The observer had to be the gunner while the pilot would maneuver to put the airplane in firing position. Unfortunately many observer-gunners shot their own aircraft structures and propeller blades, thus causing more damage than the enemy.

The next step was to carry a machine gun aloft. A British pilot did this by 'borrowing' a gun from the Company's storeroom. It was a very heavy Lewis machine gun. It was so heavy that the aircraft could fly no higher than 3,500 feet, while the German aircraft could easily fly at 5,000 feet. Eventually more powerful airplanes were developed to lift heavier guns as well as fly faster, higher and be more maneuverable. There was the problem of where to locate the machine gun without hitting their own aircraft. Some guns were placed on the top wing above the propeller. The pilot had to stand up to fire and reloading was next to impossible.

The best innovator, **Roland Garros,** (See Figure 3.39) was the first real combat pilot. He was a music student who had gone to Paris to study the piano. While there he saw his first airplane and very quickly the airplane replaced the piano as his major interest. Garros met and convinced the famous pilot, Alberto Santos-Dumont, to teach him to fly. Garros was an excellent student and soon became one of the best pilots. He participated in air races and exhibition flights in Europe as well as the United States. In 1913 he was the first person to fly across the Mediterranean Sea from southern France to Tunisia. The 453 mile distance took less than eight hours.

When World War I was declared Garros was in Germany where he had been giving exhibition flights. As a French citizen he was an enemy alien. Although he was closely guarded he was able to take off and fly back to France. He accomplished this because it was not expected for anyone to fly at night. Upon returning to France, he joined the military and soon was flying above Germany as an observer. While flying, he thought about using a gun on the airplane and determined that a pilot should be able to fire in a forward direction and not to the side as the rear seat observers were doing. Garros heard about a French flyer, Eugene Gilbert, who had tried wrapping propeller blades with steel-wire tape to deflect any bullets that struck them. While Gilbert

Figure 3.39
Roland Garros.

Roland Garros was the first flying "Ace"

was trying out this idea, ricocheting bullets killed two men who were helping him.

Garros calculated that about seven percent of the bullets fired would actually strike the propeller. He designed triangular metal shields to place on the back of the propeller blades. They were angled so as to deflect any bullets away from the pilot and the propeller. Garros started his work in February 1915, and by April 1st was ready to try out his new invention. Shortly after takeoff he saw four German Albatross observation airplanes heading toward the French lines. He soon caught up with them and turned into the nearest aircraft and fired. The last thing the enemy pilot expected was a burst of bullets. The Albatross went down. Garros headed for the next airplane and with another burst of fire it blew up in midair. Seeing this, the two remaining enemy aircraft turned and headed home to report what had happened.

In the next two weeks, using his forward firing machine-gun, he shot down five more German aircraft and became the first allied ace. The word "ace" had been applied to anyone who had accomplished something outstanding, such as a long distance bicycle race, or a soldier for some special act of bravery. The local newspapers called him an ace among pilots and the word became legendary thereafter.

The German pilots, upon spotting Garros' aircraft, were very cautious and did not wish to be anywhere near him. However, his luck ran out when engine trouble forced Garros to make an emergency landing behind German lines. Upon landing he attempted to burn his aircraft but was not successful because the airplane was wet due to a local shower. He was taken prisoner and his airplane went to Berlin where the Germans asked Anthony Fokker, a Dutch airplane designer working for the Germans, to examine the aircraft. He was instructed to make something like that for German aircraft. Fokker, a brilliant engineer, decided this was not efficient because sooner or later the propeller would splinter, become out of balance and cause engine failure. Fokker determined that the two blades of the propeller passed the gun 2400 times a minute and the gun fired 600 times a minute. He reasoned that it would be possible to figure out a way to fire the gun only when the propeller blade would not be in the way. Fokker then designed a mechanism that would prevent the gun firing if the propeller was in the way of the bullet. Within forty-eight hours he had perfected an interrupter device which worked on ground tests. In less than a month,

FLIGHTS OF FANCY

Cal Rogers

Calbraith Perry Rogers (See Figure 3.40) was a descendant of the famed Perry and Rogers U.S. Naval dynasties. He was an experienced motorcycle racer when he decided to learn to fly in 1911. After only ninety minutes of instruction from the Wright brothers, he purchased an airplane to participate in the Chicago Air Meet to be held in August. At that event he gained national fame as an aviator by capturing several endurance records. A month later he announced that he intended to win the $50,000 prize offered by William Randolph Hearst for the first pilot who could fly coast-to-coast in 30 days or less. On September 17, 1911, he took off from Sheepshead Bay, New York, in his Wright biplane which he christened the *Vin Fiz* for a new soft drink made by his financial backer. The name was on the airplane. Less than 100 miles later he had crashed three times. Each time that he crashed the airplane was repaired and Rogers continued the flight. By the time he reached Chicago it was obvious that he had lost the prize. However his venture continued and Rogers paused at cities along his route to entertain the crowds who came to see him by performing his aerobatics.

On November 5th, 49 days later, he landed at Pasadena, California. He had covered 4,250 miles with 30 unscheduled stops and 39 crashes. His actual flying time was 3 days, 10 hours, and 4 minutes. During the trip he completed 68 take-offs. A special train was sent ahead of him with spare parts and repair facilities. His airplane was rebuilt so many times that of the original aircraft only a strut, rudder and an engine drip pan remained.

When he landed, one leg was encased in a cast as a result of a crash landing in Arizona. He was met by a crowd of more than 20,000 people who wrapped an American flag around him. Rogers lost the prize money but won wide acclaim for his efforts. His claim to fame was short-lived because four months later he crashed into the Pacific Ocean at Long Beach while performing an exhibition and was killed.

Cal Rogers had obtained the mechanical assistance of Charlie Taylor, who had made the Wright brothers first engine. He went along in the train and helped with the repairs when Rogers repeatedly crashed. Rogers said of him "he was the greatest airplane mechanic in the country." Taylor later lived in California and worked at North American Aviation in Los Angeles where he was discovered by Henry Ford in 1937. Ford asked Taylor to help him in the restoration of the exhibit of the Wright brothers cycle shop in Dearborn, Michigan. Taylor returned to California and died at the age of 87, in 1955, alone and destitute. In 1965 he was then honored when his name was placed in the Aviation Hall of Fame at Dayton, Ohio. It was an honor long overdue.

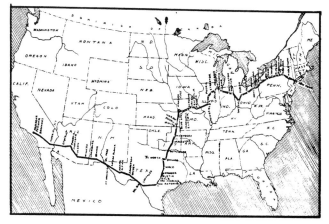

Route flown by Cal Rogers

Figure 3.40 The first transcontinental flight was made by Cal Rogers in 1911; it took him 49 days to accomplish 82 flying hours.

Figure 3.41   Arch Hoxsey.

German aircraft equipped with the new device were shooting down French and British aircraft. Aerial combat had arrived.

During World War I there was a tremendous improvement in airplanes, engines, and manufacturing. Glenn L. Martin, who had started building airplanes in 1909, produced bombers of advanced design in 1918, using two powerful new 400-horsepower Liberty engines. Donald Douglas was chief engineer for Martin during the war, and in 1920 organized his own airplane manufacturing company. In Seattle, Washington, William Boeing began building planes during the war. Anthony Fokker of the Netherlands built many outstanding military planes for Germany and came to the United States after the war to build civilian and military airplanes. Willi Messerschmitt, a German, built airplanes for Germany, not only in World War I but also in World War II. In Russia, Igor I. Sikorsky built the first multiengine airplane and later developed the first successful helicopter (See Figures 3.43 and 3.44). He came to the United States after the war. These manufacturers and others gained experience through the war and began making airplanes that were safer and more useful than had been previously possible.

After the war **Dornier,** in Germany, was the first to apply Duralumnin to aircraft. In 1922 **Fokker** offered his welded steel fuselage.

Between World Wars I and II many aviators, like the pioneer fliers of the earlier period, risked their lives to set new records. (See Table 3.1.) Nonstop transcon-

FLIGHTS OF FANCY

Lafayette Escadrille

Long before the United States entered World War I, American volunteer pilots joined the French Army. In March/April 1916, American pilots serving in the French army were gathered together and formed a separate squadron. It was first named the *Escadrille Americaine* but became the **Lafayette Escadrille** on December 6, 1916. This squadron was financed by William Vanderbilt who paid the bills for training, uniforms, and food. The bonus paid for shooting down a German airplane was $250 and three days leave in Paris. A total of 180 American pilots flew with the French.

Pilots of the Lafayette Escadrille with their lion cub mascot named "Whiskey."

FLIGHTS OF FANCY

Roosevelt's First Flight

In the United States races, competitions, and exhibitions were held in many cities to show off this new stunt called flying. The Wright Flying team, which was organized to demonstrate the Wright brothers' airplanes, established many altitude, endurance, and distance records. But in 1910 two of its star pilots, Ralph Johnstone and Arch Hoxsey, (See Figure 3.41) were killed in crashes within a month of each other. It was Hoxsey who gave Teddy Roosevelt his first flight in October 1910, at the St. Louis air meet (See Figure 3.42). While waving to the crowd below, Roosevelt almost fell out of the airplane.

Table 3.1 Aviation Records from 1906 to 1914

Altitude

Date	Place	Name	Airplane	Engine	Height Feet
1908 13 XI	Issy (F)	Henri Farman	Voisin	40 hp Vivinus	82
1908 13 XI	Auvours (F)	Wilbur Wright	Wright	24 hp Wright	82
1908 18 XII	Auvours (F)	Wilbur Wright	Wright	24 hp Wright	360
1909 18 VII	Douai (F)	Louis Paulhan	Voisin	50 hp Gnome	492
1909 29 VIII	Reims (F)	Hubert Latham	Antoinette	50 hp Antoinette	508
1909 20 IX	Brescia (I)	Rougier	Voisin	50 hp E.N.V.	633
1909 18 X	Juvisy (F)	De Lambert	Wright	24 hp Wright	984
1909 1 XII	Chalons (F)	Hubert Latham	Antoinette	50 hp Antoinette	1436
1910 7 I	Chalons (F)	Hubert Latham	Antoinette	50 hp Antoinette	3444
1910 12 I	Los Angeles (USA)	Louis Paulhan	H. Farman	50 hp Gnome	4110
1910 14 VI	Indianapolis (USA)	Walter Brookins	Wright	40 hp Wright	4379
1910 7 VII	Reims (F)	Hubert Latham	Antoinette	50 hp Antoinette	4539
1910 10 VII	Atlantic City (USA)	Walter Brookins	Wright	40 hp Wright	6237
1910 11 VIII	Lanark (USA)	Armstrong Drexel	Blériot	50 hp Gnome	6603
1910 29 VIII	Le Havre (F)	Léon Morane	Blériot	50 hp Gnome	7042
1910 3 IX	Deauville (F)	Léon Morane	Blériot	50 hp Gnome	8469
1910 8 IX	Issy (F)	Geo Chavez	Blériot	50 hp Gnome	8484
1910 1 X	Mourmelon (F)	Jan Wijnmalen	H. Farman	50 hp Gnome	9118
1910 31 X	Belmont Park (USA)	Ralph Johnstone	Wright	60 hp Wright	9600
1910 9 XII	Pau (F)	Geo Legagneux	Blériot	50 hp Gnome	10,168
1911 9 VII	Buc (F)	Loridan	H. Farman	70 hp Gnome	10,496
1911 5 VIII	Étampes (F)	Cap. Félix	Blériot	70 hp Gnome	10,988
	Chicago (USA)	Lincoln Beachey	Curtiss	60 hp Curtiss	11,578
1911 4 IX	St-Malo (F)	Roland Garros	Blériot	70 hp Gnome	12,824
1911 6 IX	Dinard (F)	Roland Garros	Blériot	70 hp Gnome	16,269
1912 17 IX	Issy, Villalonblay (F)	Geo Legagneux	Morane	80 hp Gnome	18,050
1912 11 XII	Tunisi (TN)	Roland Garros	Morane	80 hp Gnome	18,400
1913 11 III	Buc (F)	Édouard Perreyon	Blériot	80 hp Gnome	19,290
1913 29 XII	St-Raphaël (F)	Geo Legagneux	Nieuport	60 hp Le Rhône	20,060
1914 9 VII	Johannisthal (D)	Gino Linnekogel	Rumpler	100 hp Mercedes	21,653
1914 14 VII	Lipsia (D)	Harry Oelerich	D.F.W.	100 hp Mercedes	25,725

Speed

Date	Place	Name	Airplane	Engine	Speed per hour
1908 21 IX	Auvours (F)	Wilbur Wright	Wright	24 hp Wright	27.2 mi
1909 31 V	Juvisy (F)	Léon Delagrange	Voisin	45 hp Antoinette	27.9
1909 3 IX	Juvisy (F)	Cap. Ferber	Voisin	45 hp Antoinette	29.7
1909 28 VIII	Reims (F)	Blériot	Blériot	60 hp E.N.V.	47.7
1910 29 X	Belmont Park (USA)	Alfred Leblanc	Blériot	100 hp Gnome	67.5
1911 1 VIII	Eastchurch (GB)	C. Weymann	Nieuport	100 hp Gnome	70.5
1912 9 IX	Chicago (USA)	Jules Védrines	Deperdussin	100 hp Gnome	105
1913 29 IX	Reims (F)	Marcel Prévost	Deperdussin	160 hp Le Rhône	124.5

Table 3.1 Aviation Records from 1906 to 1914 (continued)

Duration

Date	Place	Name	Airplane	Engine	Time (h m s)
1906 12 XI	Bagatelle (F)	Santos-Dumont	Santos-Dumont	50 hp Antoinette	0 0 21
1907 26 X	Issy (F)	Henri Farman	Voisin	40 hp Vivinus	0 0 52
1908 13 I	Issy (F)	Henri Farman	Voisin	50 hp Antoinette	0 1 28
1908 21 III	Issy (F)	Henri Farman	Voisin	50 hp Antoinette	0 3 39
1908 11 IV	Issy (F)	Léon Delagrange	Voisin	40 hp Vivinus	0 6 39
1908 30 V	Roma (I)	Léon Delagrange	Voisin	50 hp E.N.V.	0 15 26
1908 6 VII	Issy (F)	Henri Farman	Voisin	50 hp Antoinette	0 20 19
1908 6 IX	Issy (F)	Léon Delagrange	Voisin	40 hp Vivinus	0 29 53
1908 21 IX	Auvours (F)	Wilbur Wright	Wright	24 hp Wright	1 31 25
1908 18 XII	Auvours (F)	Wilbur Wright	Wright	24 hp Wright	1 54 53
1908 31 XII	Auvours (F)	Wilbur Wright	Wright	24 hp Wright	2 20 23
1909 27 VIII	Béthény (F)	Louis Paulhan	Voisin	50 hp Gnome	2 43 24
1909 27 VIII	Béthény (F)	Henri Farman	H. Farman	50 hp Gnome	3 4 56
1909 3 XI	Mourmelon (F)	Henri Farman	H. Farman	50 hp Gnome	4 17 53
1910 9 VII	Reims (F)	Labouchère	Antoinette	50 hp Antoinette	4 19 0
1910 10 VII	Reims (F)	Jan Olieslaegers	Blériot	50 hp Gnome	5 3 5
1910 28 X	Étampes (F)	Maurice Tabuteau	M. Farman	70 hp Renault	6 0 0
1910 18 XII	Étampes (F)	Henri Farman	H. Farman	50 hp Gnome	8 12 23
1911 1 IX	Buc (F)	Fourny	M. Farman	70 hp Renault	11 1 20
1912 11 IX	Buc (F)	Fourny	M. Farman	70 hp Renault	13 17 57
1914 4 II	Johannisthal (D)	Langer	L.F.G. Roland	100 hp Mercedes	14 7 0
1914 24 IV	Étampes (F)	Poulet	Caudron	50 hp Gnome	16 28 56
1914 24 VI	Johannisthal (D)	Basser	Rumpler	100 hp Mercedes	18 10 0
1914 28 VI	Johannisthal (D)	Landmann	Albatros	100 hp Mercedes	21 50 0
1914 10 VII	Johannisthal (D)	Boehm	Albatros	100 hp Mercedes	24 12 0

Distance

Date	Place	Name	Airplane	Engine	Distance
1906 14 IX	Bagatelle (F)	Santos-Dumont	Santos-Dumont	50 hp Antoinette	8.6 yd
1906 12 XI	Bagatelle (F)	Santos-Dumont	Santos-Dumont	50 hp Antoinette	244.4 yd
1907 26 X	Issy (F)	Henri Farman	Voisin	40 hp Vivinus	855.5 yd
1908 13 I	Issy (F)	Henri Farman	Voisin	50 hp Antoinette	0.625 mi
1908 21 III	Issy (F)	Henri Farman	Voisin	50 hp Antoinette	1.25
1908 11 IV	Issy (F)	Léon Delagrange	Voisin	40 hp Vivinus	2.50
1908 30 V	Roma (I)	Léon Delagrange	Voisin	50 hp E.N.V.	7.7
1908 6 IX	Issy (F)	Léon Delagrange	Voisin	40 hp Vivinus	15.3
1908 17 IX	Issy (F)	Léon Delagrange	Voisin	40 hp Vivinus	41.5
1908 21 IX	Auvours (F)	Wilbur Wright	Voisin	24 hp Wright	60.9
1908 18 XII	Auvours (F)	Wilbur Wright	Wright	24 hp Wright	62
1908 31 XII	Auvours (F)	Wilbur Wright	Wright	24 hp Wright	77.5
1909 26 VIII	Reims (F)	Henri Farman	H. Farman	50 hp Gnome	112
1909 3 XI	Mourmelon (F)	Henri Farman	H. Farman	50 hp Gnome	150
1910 10 VII	Reims (F)	Jan Olieslaegers	Blériot	50 hp Gnome	139.5
	Reims (F)	Jan Olieslaegers	Blériot	50 hp Gnome	245
1910 28 X	Étampes (F)	Maurice Tabuteau	M. Farman	70 hp Renault	290
1910 30 XII	Étampes (F)	Maurice Tabuteau	M. Farman	70 hp Renault	362.7
1911 16 VII	Kiewitt (D)	Jan Olieslaegers	Blériot	50 hp Gnome	393.7
1911 1 IX	Buc (F)	Fourny	M. Farman	70 hp Renault	448.3
1911 24 XII	Pau (F)	Gobé	Nieuport	70 hp Gnome	460
1912 11 IX	Étampes (F)	Fourny	M. Farman	70 hp Renault	633
1914 28 VI	Johannisthal (D)	Landmann	Albatros	100 hp Mercedes	1178

Figure 3.42 Theodore Roosevelt became the first former president to fly. On October 10, 1910, at an air meet at Lambert Field, Mo., he took off in a Wright Type B pusher, piloted by flying instructor Arch Hoxsey. The former chief executive, an avid proponent of the strenuous life, termed the airplane "a practical and safe vehicle of transit."

Figure 3.44 Igor Sikorsky testing his VS-300, the world's first practical helicopter. His flight uniform consisted of a business suit and a derby hat.

Figure 3.43 This Igor Sikorsky aircraft was the world's first heavy bomber; capable of carrying 2,200 pounds of bombs. More than 75 were built.

Figure 3.45 Captain Eddie Rickenbacker, leading ace of World War I with 26 victories, commanded the famous 94th Aero Pursuit Squadron. Much later he established Eastern Air Lines.

Figure 3.46   U.S. Navy NC-4 during its world flight.

tinental flights, transoceanic flights, and polar flights kept aviation news on the front pages of newspapers. Speed, altitude, endurance, and distance records were made and broken time after time. Newspapers, aviation organizations, and individuals offered large prizes to aviators to perform certain designated flights.

The first great flight after World War I was the transatlantic crossing by the United States Navy seaplane NC-4 (See Figure 3.46). The plane started from Rockaway, Long Island, New York, on May 8, 1919, and arrived at Plymouth, England, on May 31. The route included stops at the Azores, Lisbon, Portugal, and Marengo, Spain. Three NC planes started the flight, but two were unable to complete the trip. Lieutenant Commander Albert C. Read was in command of the NC-4 and the crew of five other Navy and Coast Guard airmen.

The early transatlantic flights were made from west to east so that the fliers could take advantage of the prevailing west-to-east winds to increase their speed. **Sir John Alcock** (1892–1919) and **Sir Arthur Whitten-Brown** won a $50,000 prize offered by the *London Daily Mail* when they made the first nonstop airplane flight across the Atlantic. They flew from Newfoundland to Ireland on June 15, 1919, in a Vickers "Vimy" twin-engine biplane (See Figure 3.47).

The most noted flier of the 1920s was **Charles A. Lindberg** (See Figures 3.48 and 3.49) who on May 10, 1927, flew a record solo flight from San Diego to New York in 21 hours and 20 minutes. Ten days later, on

May 20, he took off from New York alone and headed across the Atlantic Ocean for Paris. His airplane was only slightly larger than the Wright brothers' first airplane. When he landed safely at LeBourget Field near Paris, he won over to aviation many persons who before his flight had regarded the airplane as impractical.

The most disastrous air race of the period was the Dole Race of 2,400 miles over the Pacific Ocean from San Francisco to Honolulu in 1927. Before and during the race ten fliers were killed. The $25,000 prize was won by Arthus C. Goebel. He flew the distance in 26 hours, 17 minutes and 33 seconds.

Many engineers, designers, and manufacturers were responsible for the improvements in the power, speed, and safety of airplanes. **William B. Stout** produced a successful all-metal airplane in 1924 which later led to the Ford Trimotor passenger transport.

Commercial airlines developed during this period and began carrying airmail and then passengers. This, however, is the story of the growth and development of air transportation. Throughout the early years of its development, until the end of World War I, the airplane had yet to be used commercially. The first commercial use of the airplane took place in 1918 when the United States Post Office began scheduled airmail flights. Throughout the history of airplane development human beings achieved their goal of flight and have now embarked on the next step—space flight and reaching for the stars.

Alcock and Brown take-off from Newfoundland heading for Ireland on their transatlantic flight in June 1919 in a Vickers Vimy.

Alcock and Brown made it to Ireland but crashed on landing.

Figure 3.47   Alcock and Brown.

Figure 3.48   Charles Lindbergh.

Figure 3.49   Lindbergh's "Spirit of St. Louis."

CLAUDE DORNIER

Claud Dornier was an industrialist who was born at Kempten, Germany, May 14, 1884. His early career as an engineer in metal construction and super structures provided him an excellent background for his later involvement in aircraft construction. After graduation from the Munich Institute of Technology in 1910, he served briefly with the Graf Zeppelin Company where he was introduced to aviation. Unable to persuade Zeppelin officials to diversify into airplanes, he formed his own

FLIGHTS OF FANCY

Female Aviators

Many women became famous as fliers. **Amelia Earhart** (1899–1937) was the first woman to fly across the Atlantic in 1928 and to solo across the Atlantic in 1932. She disappeared during an attempted round-the-world flight in 1937. **Ruth Nichols,** who learned to fly in 1922, was the first woman ever to hold three international records at one time for altitude, speed, and distance. In 1932, she became the first woman airline pilot. **Jacqueline Cochran** won the Bendix Transcontinental Race in 1938 in a competition with nine male fliers. She also set a number of national and international records. In 1953, Cochran became the first woman to fly faster than the speed of sound.

company with his brother and enjoyed immediate success with flying boats and some of the world's earliest, large, all metal aircraft. His DO-X was the largest passenger airplane in 1929. In the face of widespread skepticism concerning its practicality, the giant 12-engined craft flew from Germany to New York in 1931. In 1932, Dornier turned his talents to military aircraft, developing two distinctive thin-fuselaged, twin-engined bombers, the DO-17 and the DO-217, which became mainstays of the Luftwaffe's bomber and reconnaissance fleet in World War II. As a consequence of World War II, Dornier lost his business. In 1947, he moved to Zug, Switzerland where he consulted in aeronautical engineering until his death in 1969. Claude Dornier's vision coupled with his technological skills permitted him to lead the world in the advancement of metal aircraft. In 1987 he was installed into the International Aerospace Hall of Fame.

The Treaty of Versailles of 1919, which banned construction of engine-powered aircraft for fifteen years in Germany, forced Claude Dornier to look elsewhere in order to continue his aircraft business. Most of the Dornier flying boats included the two that were purchased by Roald Amundsen for his 1925 Arctic expedition. It is interesting to note that the huge Savigliano hangar that was used for major structural repairs on the DO-X, still exists in Marina di Pisa. Dornier moved to Spain and then to Switzerland due to the aircraft pro-

FLIGHTS OF FANCY

Aircraft Development

In the years between World War I and World War II aircraft development increased rapidly. Two notable efforts in constructing giant size flying boats were the DO-X and the Hercules HK-1 known as the "Spruce Goose."

duction prohibition. Dornier's company was banned from producing aircraft in Germany from 1945–1955 under a general government ban on aircraft production. The company continued to exist and was owned by Claude Dornier until his death in 1969. His sons managed it after his death. The company eventually became a part of the Fairchild Aircraft Company.

DO-X

Ten years before the building of the first Boeing Flying Boat Clippers, Dr. Claude Dornier in Germany created world interest with the DO-X. It was the largest, heaviest and most powerful aircraft in the world at the time. He anticipated using it for transatlantic passenger service. The German Transport Ministry financed it. It was a colossal flying boat powered by twelve engines. It had a wingspan of $157\frac{1}{2}$ feet, a length of 131 feet 5 inches and a height of 33 feet. Takeoff weight was 110,250 pounds. It had a metal hull and wings of

Figure 3.50

metal framework covered with the fabric. It had seating capacity for 66 to 100 passengers depending on the length of the flight. On October 21, 1929, with 169 persons aboard consisting of 150 passengers, 10 crew members and nine stowaways, it weighed 48 tons when it took off from Lake Constance, the water boundary between Germany and Switzerland. It took fifty seconds to lift off the water surface. It slowly ascended to a maximum of 650 feet; it flew forty minutes at a top speed of 105 mph before successfully landing on the lake. Never before had that many people been carried aloft at one time in a single aircraft. The famous Graf Zeppelin was limited to seventy passengers. The test was successful and a flight to the United States was planned.

The twelve engines were Siemens-Halske Jupiters placed on top of the wing in six tandem tiers, delivering 6000 horsepower. They could lift fifty-two tons of weight off the water in fifty seconds and attain a top speed of 134 mph. The aircraft could remain airborne on eight engines. The triple-decked duralumin hull was equal to that of a ship; its main passenger deck was 64 feet long. On board was a corridor with doors opening into sleeping compartments leading to a luxurious lounge with soft carpets, expensive chairs, deep plush cushions, and a phonograph. The cabin also contained a recreation room, bathroom, kitchen, and dinette.

The aircraft proved to be vastly under powered. To correct this, Dornier substituted Curtiss Conqueror engines for the European engines—thus increasing horsepower to 7200.

At last the planned flight started from Lake Constance on November 5, 1930 with a crew of nineteen under command of Captain Friedrich Christiansen. On board were 180,000 pieces of mail. The route was along the coast of Africa then across the Atlantic Ocean to South America. The DO-X reached New York on August 27, 1931, by following the route flown by Pan American Airways. The crew was given a ticker-tape parade and received medals from Jimmy Walker, the mayor. The DO-X created public interest wherever it went. However, the grand tour was less than triumphal because of a series of unpredictable events. It took ten months to reach New York, a distance of 12,000 miles. After visits to Holland and England, the leviathan was forced down at sea by fog and had to taxi sixty miles to a French harbor for repairs. Repairs took more than a month. A wing was damaged due to a fuel tank fire. After continuing the tour, the hull was badly damaged in Las Palmas, Canary Islands, by waves during takeoff. This repair took three months.

The twelve engines consumed 400 gallons of fuel an hour. To permit a maximum fuel load, the crew was reduced to twelve for the next long flight and the airplane was stripped of all expendable weight, including spare clothing. However, it still could not gain altitude and flew the 1400 miles to Fernando de Noronha at an altitude up to thirty feet.

At New York it was placed in dry-dock for the winter for overhaul. It left for Germany on May 19, 1932 with a woman added to the crew. She was a German actress and a pilot named Antonie Strassman. She became the second woman to cross the Atlantic in a heavier-than-air-craft.

Two more DO-X airplanes were constructed and designated the X2 and X3. They were sold to Italy where they were used primarily by the military for prestige flights. In 1933, Mussolini ordered them to be destroyed.

Little more was heard of the DO-X after that. It was eventually placed in the Berlin Air Museum in 1934 but was destroyed in 1943, during World War II, by allied aerial bombardment.

While the DO-X was not a commercial success, it was an important experiment. It was extraordinary because of its physical strength and size and earned a place in seaplane history.

HERCULES HK-1 SPRUCE GOOSE

This aircraft is probably the largest aircraft ever flown. There was critical need to fly over enemy submarines that were sinking Allied ships during World War II, especially in the Atlantic Ocean. It was originally conceived by Henry Kaiser, famous for the production of liberty ships during World War II. He contacted Howard Hughes who had acquired fame as a designer, builder and pilot of fast aircraft. Originally designated the HK-1 for Howard Hughes and Henry Kaiser, it later became the H-4 Hercules when Henry Kaiser withdrew from the project. This huge flying boat became known as the "Spruce Goose."

The project was a remarkable story of sacrifice, determination, and technological development. The HK-1 was far ahead of its time in the early 1940s. It revolutionized jumbo aircraft having large lift capability.

The aircraft was a cargo-type flying boat designed to transport men and materials over long distances. It had a single hull with fixed wing-tip floats as large as small yachts, cantilever wing and tail surfaces. The entire airframe and surface structures were composed of laminated wood, primarily birch not spruce. All primary control surfaces except the flaps were fabric covered.

The hull was divided into two areas: a flight deck for the operating crew and below it a large cargo deck. Access between the two decks was provided by a circular stairway. Below the cargo decks were fuel bays divided by watertight bulkheads. Each engine had 28 cylinders, with two spark plugs each, totaling 56 spark plugs per engine, or 448 spark plugs per aircraft. For in-flight inspection and repair, the engines were accessible through the spar of the 13-foot thick wing. A sight station located behind each engine allowed a mechanic/engineer to observe the engine.

While being developed it encountered and dealt with tremendous design and engineering problems. These included the testing of new concepts for large-scale hulls and flying control surfaces; the incorporation of complex power boost systems that gave the pilot the power of a hundred men in controlling the Hercules. Eight of the most powerful engines available were installed. A fuel storage and supply system was created to allow for the long, over-water flights. Hughes and his engineers built the aircraft with nonessential materials, which some industry persons considered impossible. All of this was accomplished under the constrictions of building materials during World War II.

The Hughes flying boat was to be the biggest airplane ever built and probably the most prodigious aviation project of all time. Only the courage and solitary dedication of Howard Hughes, and his small development group, caused this project to advance. He was subject to much criticism and doubt about the aircraft's ability to fly. During a senate investigation committee, a disgruntled United States Senator dubbed it the "flying lumberyard." This resulted in Hughes' announcement that he was going to begin taxi tests in Long Beach Harbor, near where it was constructed. On November 2, 1947, Howard Hughes and a small crew taxied the airplane for taxi tests and thrilled thousands of people assembled along the shore. This was as a result of criticism by the congressional committee as well as many other skeptics. The purpose was to show that it could operate on the water and not sink. After making a few long powered taxi runs, Howard Hughes, at the controls, lifted the flying boat seventy feet off the water. It flew one mile in less than a minute at a speed of eighty miles an hour before gently settling on the water for a perfect landing. The flight was ample proof that Hughes was correct. The event is recognized as a great moment in aviation history. Hughes, feeling vindicated, took the aircraft back to its dry dock. It never flew again. Many years later it was put on display in Long Beach Harbor next to the Queen Mary. After being there for many years, where it was seen by millions of visitors, it was disassembled and floated to Seattle, Oregon, where a museum is being built to house it.

The Spruce Goose is now regarded as a true American icon and deserves to be preserved so future generations can see this true marvel.

Because of its uniqueness, specifications for this flying boat are listed below for comparisons to other aircraft now known or planned in the future.

Wing Span	320 feet	Gross Weight	300,000 pounds
Wing Root Chord	51 feet 9³/₄ inches	Payload	130,000 pounds
Wing Tip Chord	19 feet 7³/₄ inches	Fuel Capacity	14,000 gallons
Maximum Wing Thickness	11 feet 6 inches	Power	24,000 horsepower
Wing Area	11,430 square feet	Maximum Speed	218 mph
Overall Length	218 feet 6¹/₄ inches	Cruise Speed	175 mph
Overall Height	79 feet 3³/₈ inches	Landing Speed	78 mph
Hull Width	25 feet	Range	3,500 miles
Hull Height	30 feet	Eight Engines	Pratt & Whitney
Tail Span	113 feet		28 cylinder
Horizontal Stabilizer Area	2,610 square feet		3,000 horsepower
Vertical Stabilizer Chord	53 feet	Propellers	17 feet 2 inches diameter
Vertical Stabilizer Area	1,699 square feet		

Figure 3.51. Howard Hughes' HK-1 Flying Boat has been airborne only once—on November 2, 1947. Photo courtesy of the Captain Michael King Smith, Evergreen Aviation Educational Institute, McMinnville, Oregon.

Air Force Bases Located in the United States Which Were Named for Noted Aviation, Pioneers, Heroes and Personalities

Andersen
In Guam two miles north of Yigo. Named in 1945 for General James Roy Andersen, lost at sea between Kwajalein and Hawaii in February 1945.

Andrews
Ten miles southeast of Washington, DC. Activated May 1943. Named for Lt. General Frank M. Andrews, air pioneer and WW II commander of the European theater, died in May 1943 in an aircraft accident in Iceland.

Arnold
Seven miles southeast of Manchester, TN. Dedicated June 25, 1951 for General H.H. (Hap) Arnold, the WW II chief of the Army Air Force.

Barksdale
In Bossier City, LA. Named on February 3, 1933 for Lt. Eugene H. Barksdale, a WW I airman who died in a crash near Wright Field, OH in August 1926.

Beale
Thirteen miles east of Marysville, CA. Named in April 1948 for General E.F. Beale, an Indian agent in California prior to the Civil War.

Bolling
Three miles south of Washington, DC. Activated in October 1917 for Col. Raynal C. Bolling, the first high ranking Air Service officer killed in WW I.

Brooks
In San Antonio, TX. Activated December 8, 1917 for Cadet Sydney J. Brooks, Jr., who died November 13, 1917 on his commissioning flight.

Cannon
Eight miles west of Clovis, NM. Named in August 1942 for General John K. Cannon, WW II commander of allied forces in the Mediterranean Theater.

Davis-Monthan
In Tucson, AZ. Named in 1927 for two local early aviators: Lt. Samuel H. Davis who died on December 28, 1921 and Lt. Oscar Monthan, who was killed March 27, 1924.

Dyess
Located near Abilene, TX. Named in December 1956 for Col. William E. Dyess, a WW II fighter pilot who escaped from a Japanese prison camp. He died in a P-38 crash at Burbank, CA, December 1943.

Edwards
Twenty miles east of Rosamond, CA. Originally called Muroc in September 1933. Renamed in 1949 for Captain Glen W. Edwards, who died June 5, 1948 in a crash of the YB-49 Flying Wing.

Eglin
Seven miles northeast of Fort Walton Beach, FL. Activated 1935 and named for Colonel Frederick I. Eglin, a WW I pilot killed in an aircraft accident on January 1, 1937.

Eielson
Twenty-six miles southeast of Fairbanks, AK. Activated 1944 and named for Carl Ben Eielson, an aviation pioneer who died in an arctic rescue mission in November, 1929.

Ellsworth
Ten miles east of Rapid City, SD. Activated January 1942 but renamed in 1953 for General Richard E. Ellsworth, who died in an RB-36 crash in Newfoundland, Canada, March 18, 1953.

Elmendorf
In Anchorage, AK. Activated and named in 1940 for Captain Hugh Elmendorf, who died on January 13, 1933 at Wright Field, OH, while testing a new pursuit airplane.

Fairchild

Twelve miles west-southwest of Spokane, WA. Opened and named in 1942 for General Muir S. Fairchild, USAF Vice Chief of Staff at his death in 1950.

Francis E. Warren

At Cheyenne, WY. Named in 1930 for Frances Emory Warren, a senator and first governor of the state.

Goodfellow

Southeast of San Angelo, TX. Named in 1941 for Lt. John J. Goodfellow, Jr., WW I observation pilot killed in combat on September 14, 1918.

Grand Forks (Exception to the Naming Rule)

Sixteen miles west of Grand Forks, ND. Activated in 1956. Named after the town of Grand Forks whose citizens bought the property for the Air Force.

Hanscom

Seventeen miles northwest of Boston, MA. Named for Laurence G. Hanscom, a pre-WW II advocate of general aviation who died in a light airplane crash in 1941.

Hickam

Nine miles west of Honolulu, HI. Named in September 1938 for Lt. Col. Horace M. Hickam, an aviation pioneer killed in a crash on November 5, 1934 in Texas.

Hill

Twenty-five miles north of Salt Lake City, UT. Activated and named in 1940 for Major Ployer P. Hill, who died on October 30, 1935 while testing the first B-17.

Holloman

Seven miles west of Alamogordo, NM. Named in 1942 for Col. George Holloman, a guided missile pioneer.

Hurlburt

Five miles west of Fort Walton Beach, FL. Named in 1943 for Lt. Donald W. Hurlburt, a WW II pilot who died in a crash near Eglin on October 1, 1943.

Keesler

In Biloxi, MS. Named on June 12, 1941 for Lt. Samuel R. Keesler, Jr., an aerial observer killed on October 9, 1918 near Verdun, France.

Kelly

Five miles southwest of San Antonio, Texas dating since November 21, 1916. Named in 1942 for Lt. George E. M. Kelly, the first Army pilot killed flying a military aircraft on May 10, 1911. This is the oldest continuously active air base in the United States.

Kirtland

In southeast Albuquerque, NM. Named in 1941 for Col. Roy C. Kirtland, an aviation pioneer and commandant of Langley Field in the 1930s. He died May 2, 1941.

Lackland

Eight miles southwest of San Antonio, TX. Named in 1941 for General Frank D. Lackland, an early commandant of Kelly Field flying school who died in 1943.

Langley

Three miles north of Hampton, VA. Activated December 30, 1916. One of the oldest continuously active air bases in the U.S. Named for Samuel Pierpont Langley, aviation scientist and pioneer.

Laughlin

Six miles east of Del Rio, TX. Named in July 1942 for Lt. Jack Thomas Laughlin, a Del Rio native and B-17 pilot killed over Java on January 29, 1942.

Luke

Twenty miles west-northwest of Phoenix, AZ. Named in 1941 for Lt. Frank Luke, Jr., an ace in WW I and the first American pilot to receive the Medal of Honor; he died in action on September 28, 1918 in France.

Malmstrom

One and a half miles east of Great Falls, MT. Activated December 15, 1942. Named for Col. Einar A. Malmstrom, a WW II fighter commander killed in an air accident August 21, 1954.

MacDill

Near Tampa, FL. Named on April 15, 1941 for Col. Leslie MacDill in 1941 who died in an airplane accident near Washington, DC on November 8, 1938.

Maxwell

Near Montgomery, AL. Named in 1918 for Lt. William C. Maxwell, who died in an airplane accident in the Philippines on August 12, 1920.

McChord

Ten miles south of Tacoma, WA. Named on May 5, 1938 for Col. William C. McChord, who died on August 18, 1937 making a forced landing at Maidens, VA.

McClellan

Nine miles northeast of Sacramento, CA. Named on May 25, 1939 for Major Hezekiah McClellan, who died in a crash in May 1936. He was a pioneer in Arctic aeronautical experiments.

McConnell

In southwest corner of Wichita, KS. Named on June 5, 1951 for three McConnell brothers from Wichita, Lt. Col. Edwin M. McConnell, Captain Fred J. McConnell and Lt. Thomas L. McConnell, B-24 pilots in WW II. Thomas was killed in an attack on Bougainville in the Solomon Islands, South Pacific, in 1943. Edwin died September 1, 1997. Fred died in a private aircraft crash on October 25, 1945.

McGuire

Eighteen miles southeast of Trenton, NJ. Named in 1949 for Major Thomas B. McGuire, Jr., a P-38 pilot and the second leading U.S. ace in WW II. He died in action on January 7, 1945 in the Philippine Islands.

Moody

Ten miles northeast of Valdosta, GA. Named in June 1941 for Major George P. Moody, killed testing a Beech AT-10 on May 5, 1941.

Nellis

Eight miles northeast of Las Vegas, NV. Named in 1949 for Lt. William H. Nellis, a WW II P-47 fighter pilot killed on December 27, 1944 in Europe.

Offutt

Eight miles south of Omaha, NE. Named for Lt. Jarvis J. Offutt, a WW I pilot who died of injuries in France, August 13, 1918.

Patrick

Two miles south of Cocoa Beach, FL. Named in 1940 for General Mason M. Patrick, chief of AEF Air Service in WW I.

Peterson

At Colorado Springs, CO. Named in 1942 for Lt. Edward J. Peterson, killed in a crash at the base on August 8, 1942.

Pope

Twelve miles north-northwest of Fayetteville, NC. Named in 1919 for Lt. Harley H. Pope, a WW I pilot who died on January 7, 1917 when his Curtiss Jenny crashed near Fayetteville, NC.

Randolph

Seventeen miles east-northeast of San Antonio, TX. Named in 1930 for Captain William M. Randolph, who died at Gorman, TX when his AT-4 crashed on take-off on February 17, 1928.

Robins

Fifteen miles south-southeast of Macon, GA. Named in March, 1942 for General Augustine Warner Robins, an early chief of the Materiel Division of the Air Corps who died on June 16, 1940.

Schriever

Ten miles east of Colorado Springs, CO. Originally Falcon Air Force Base. Renamed in June 1998 for General B.A. Schriever.

Scott

Six miles east-northeast of Belleville, IL. Named on June 14, 1917 for Cpl. Frank S. Scott, the first enlisted man to die in an airplane accident on September 28, 1912 in a Wright Flyer at College Park, MD.

Seymour Johnson

At Goldsboro, NC. Named June 12, 1942 for Navy Lt. Seymour A. Johnson, who died in an aircraft accident in Maryland on March 5, 1941.

Shaw

Ten miles west-northwest of Sumter, SC. Named on August 30, 1941 for Lt. Ervin D. Shaw. He was one of the first Americans to see action in WW I. He died when his fighter was shot down on July 9, 1918 in France.

Sheppard

Four miles north of Wichita Falls, TX. Named on June 14, 1941 for Morris E. Sheppard, a U.S. senator from Texas who died on April 9, 1941.

Tinker

Eight miles southeast of Oklahoma City, OK. Named in March 1942 for General Clarence L. Tinker whose early model B-24 went down at sea southwest of Midway Island on June 7, 1942.

Travis

Fifty miles northeast of San Francisco, CA. Named May 17, 1943 for General Robert F. Travis, who died in a B-29 accident on August 5, 1950.

Tyndall

Twelve miles east of Panama City, FL. Named on December 7, 1941 for Lt. Frank B. Tyndall, a WW I fighter pilot killed on July 15, 1930 in a P-1 crash.

Vance

Three miles south-southwest of Enid, OK. Activated November 1941 and named for Col. Leon R. Vance, Jr., an Enid native and a 1939 graduate of West Point, who died on July 26, 1944 when his airplane went down at sea in the Atlantic Ocean near Iceland.

Vandenberg

Eight miles north-northwest of Lompoc, CA. Originally Camp Cooke, renamed June 7, 1957 for General Hoyt S. Vandenberg, the second chief of staff of the USAF.

Whiteman

Two miles south of Knob Noster, MO. Named in 1942 for Lt. George A. Whiteman, the first pilot killed in aerial combat during the attack on Pearl Harbor in 1941.

Wright-Patterson

Ten miles east-northeast of Dayton, OH. Two bases were merged on January 13, 1948. Named for aviation pioneers Orville and Wilbur Wright and Lt. Frank S. Patterson, who died in a DH-4 crash on June 19, 1918. This is the site of Huffman Prairie where the Wright brothers did much of their early flying.

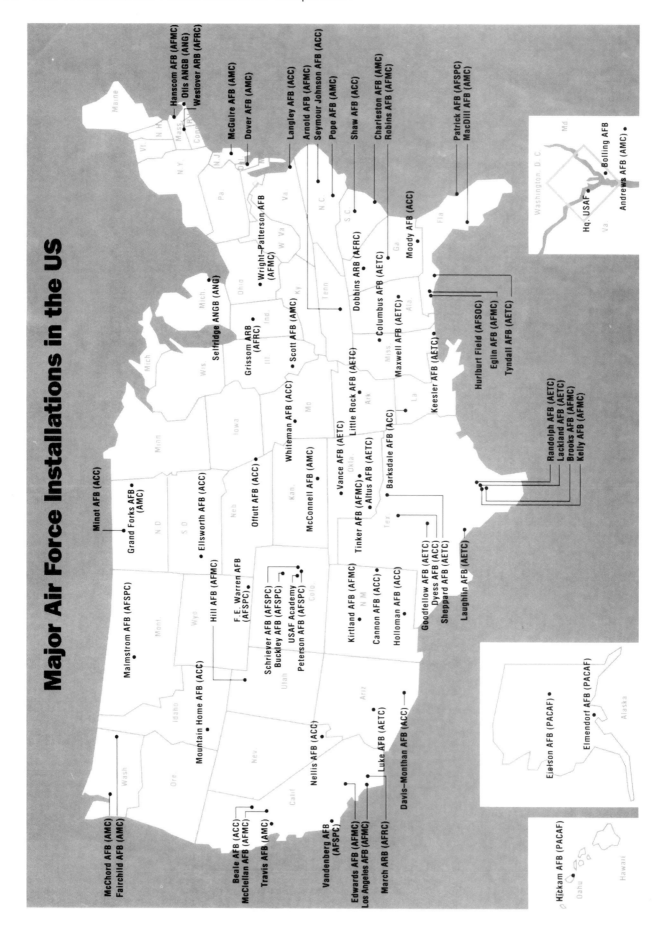

Major Air Force Installations in the US

CHAPTER 4

The Beginning of Commercial Air Transportation

Since the Wright Brothers' first successful flight on December 17, 1903, it took the airplane more than six decades to attain recognition and utility in the role of a commercial vehicle. Its first practical use in this respect was as a mail carrier. The airmail story has been one of healthy growth in which determination made possible the final acceptance of airmail into the U.S. transportation and economic system.

Airmail was born during the week of September 23 to 30, 1911 on Long Island (See Figure 4.1). There an airplane took off and delivered mail to the Mineola post office, about ten miles away. The pilot, **Earl Ovington,** (See Figure 4.2) flying a Bleriot monoplane, carried about 15 pounds of letters daily during the week-long air meet. He flew the short distance to the Mineola post office where he dropped the mail pouches to the ground. The postal employees picked them up, and the mail continued on its way in the usual surface manner. Although the mail did go by air, there was no practical value to it other than its being an attraction for the air show. These letters marked "Aeromail" have become valuable as a collector's item.

The following year, 31 additional such experimental airmail flights occurred. In every flight the Post Office Department cooperated by giving permission and supplying the mail, but did not assist with the expense.

The authorization for these experiments came from a law introduced by Morris Sheppard, a Representative from Texas, in June, 1910 "to definitely determine whether aerial navigation may be utilized for the safe and rapid transmission of the mails."

In 1912 the Post Office Department, encouraged by the success of these experimental airmail flights, urged Congress to appropriate money to launch an air-mail service. However, the Congress was far from convinced and preferred to keep the mail on the ground; they did not appropriate any money.

It was not until 1916 that Congress made available for airmail service the lavish sum of $50,000 out of its "steamboat or other powerboat service" appropriation. World War I interrupted development; but before the

Figure 4.1 The first airmail flight in the United States, September 23, 1911

Figure 4.2   Earl Ovington, Long Island, New York, September 1911.

war ended in 1918, Congress appropriated $100,000 for the establishment of an experimental airmail route as well as for the purchase, operation, and maintenance of airplanes. Sheppard again was responsible for this appropriation. **Captain Benjamin B. Lipsner,** an army engineer who helped perfect an improved aircraft engine oil during the war, was put in charge and made responsible for this operation. The War Department furnished the planes and the pilots from the Army Signal Corps. The pilots were to be engaged in cross-country flight training, and the transporting of the mail was secondary.

Lipsner had earlier convinced **Otto Praeger,** the Second Assistant Postmaster General, that the airmail service was feasible and that he could develop a system showing the cost of operation. After establishing the service, Lipsner was discharged from the army and became the first "Superintendent of the Aerial Mail Service," on July 15, 1918. He resigned some months later due to a disagreement over the expenditure of funds.

Much credit for the impetus in the inauguration for airmail service goes to Otto Praeger, often called "The Father of Airmail." As Second Assistant Postmaster General, from 1915 to 1921, he possessed a long-range vision that, during the early years of national air policy, contributed immensely to the establishment of commercial aviation. Praeger's goal was not only to foster air commerce so that private capital could be attracted to create a new industry, but also to make the airplane a mail carrier that could measure up to requirements of dependability and regularity, which would develop its potential. He could not have been more correct. The development of commercial aviation almost exactly paralleled his early thinking.

THE FIRST EXPERIMENTAL AIRMAIL ROUTE

The first experimental airmail route was between Washington, D.C., and New York City, with a stop at Philadelphia to change pilots and airplanes. The total distance of the first route was 218 miles. Four Curtiss Jenny (JN-4H) (See Figure 4.3) army training airplanes were used. They had 150-horsepower Hispano Suiza engines and a capacity of 150 pounds of mail. The Jenny had an average block speed of 50 to 60 miles per hour. The first Jenny, Aircraft number 38262, was delivered from Philadelphia to Washington, D.C., by **Major Rueben Fleet** and was turned over to Captain Lipsner on the morning of May 15, 1918. Fleet later left the army and eventually became head of the Consolidated Aircraft Corporation.

The inauguration of the first official airmail route took place the same morning that President Wilson autographed the first letter addressed to the Postmaster of New York City (See Figure 4.4). This letter and along with three pouches of mail was placed in the front cockpit of the Jenny. The load amounted to 140 pounds of about 6,600 letters, 300 to which were addressed to Philadelphia. The gross revenue for this mail was about $1,584.

The President's party included Mrs. Wilson, Postmaster General Burleson, Otto Praeger, Assistant Postmaster, and the Assistant Secretary of the Navy, Franklin D. Roosevelt (See Figure 4.5). The press and many spectators were also present to view the memorable occasion. The location chosen was the polo grounds in Potomac Park, Washington, D.C. Although it had not been built as a flying field, it had ample level ground.

Lt. George Boyle (See Figure 4.6) was selected to make the first flight. At 10:30 A.M. May 15, 1918, with the mail on board and everything ready, the order was

Figure 4.3   The Curtiss "Jenny."

Figure 4.4   At Philadelphia on May 15, 1918, mail is transferred to a waiting JN-4H to complete the first official flight from New York to Washington, D.C.

Figure 4.5   May 15, 1918, the beginning of the first official United States airmail route. Shown are Otto Praeger, Assistant Postmaster; Merit Chance, Washington Postmaster; Albert Burleson, Postmaster General; President Woodrow Wilson.

Figure 4.6   Postmaster General Albert S. Burleson gives a mail pouch to Lieutenant George L. Boyle for the beginning of the first airmail flight from Washington, D.C. to New York City. Unfortunately Boyle got lost and never arrived.

given to start the engine of the Jenny. The mechanic called "contact," the ignition switch was turned on, and five mechanics forming a chain pulled the propeller. The engine coughed once but failed to start. Four more times they tried with the same result. After much confusion and embarrassment it was discovered that someone had neglected to fill the gas tank. Only after three cans of gas had been siphoned from a nearby dismantled airplane and poured into the empty tank did Lt. Boyle get his engine started.

With order restored and the crowd cheering, the airplane took off. Lt. Boyle, a student pilot, for some unexplained reason turned south instead of north and became lost. It was not long before he had to make an emergency landing in an open field near Waldorf, Maryland, and damaged the airplane. The mail was sent back to Washington by truck and went on to Philadelphia and New York by train.

The day was not lost, however, because the plans for the first day called for **Lt. Torrey Webb** (who later became an executive of the Texas Oil Co.) to take-off from Belmont Park Race Track in New York at 11:30 A.M. with the first southbound airmail (See Figure 4.7). He arrived at Bustleton Field, Philadelphia, without incident and turned the mail over to **Lt. James Edgerton,** who flew it on to Washington, D.C. He delivered it there safely and made the inauguration of airmail a success.

> **The Post Office spent $138,000 in that first year, and the total revenue from airmail postage was $160,000.**

The airmail schedule soon settled down to a routine with Edgerton, Webb, and four other army pilots alternating between Washington, D.C., Philadelphia, and New York.

Two months later, 88 flights had been completed out of 100 which had been scheduled. During the first year 1,263 flights had been scheduled, but 55 had to be cancelled. Another 53 were forced down by bad weather, and 37 others were cancelled because of engine trouble. The record was nearly 90% and 128,000 miles were flown carrying 193,000 pounds of mail.

The Post Office spent $138,000 in that first year, and the total revenue from airmail postage was $160,000. The success of this effort made the United States the first country to have daily scheduled airmail service.

The experimental airmail service between New York-Philadelphia-Washington launched on May 15, 1918, continued until August 10, 1918.

Since it was the intention of the Post Office Department to operate the service with the Postal Service's own equipment, an order for six custom-built mail planes was placed with the Standard Aircraft Company of Elizabeth, New Jersey. These planes, advanced for their day, were powered with 150-horsepower Hisso engines and had special mail pits located underneath the center sections of the upper wings. The

Figure 4.7 One of the pioneer mail planes, a Jenny, taking off from Belmont Park on Long Island. (U.S. War Dept. General Staff Photo in the National Archives.)

FLIGHTS OF FANCY

The Jenny Stamp

A special stamp was quickly designed for airmail service. It had a rose-colored background with a picture of a Jenny in blue. The stamp sold for 24 cents. On May 14, 1918, the day before the first Post Office flight, it was discovered that the Jenny on the stamp had been printed in an inverted position. The upside down stamps had been sold at the Washington post office. Only one sheet had not been recovered; the rest had been found in time and destroyed. The one sheet had been sold to a stamp collector who did not notice the error immediately. The post office tried to buy back the 100 stamps for the purchase price of $24.00, but the buyer refused to sell, realizing their value. The sheet was eventually broken up and if one were

to be sold today, its value to collectors would be enormous. A center line block of four once sold for nearly $50,000. The entire sheet would be priceless if it were still intact.

Figure 4.8 The special stamp issued for the inauguration of the airmail service in which the "Jenny" was printed upside down.

---

acceptance of these airplanes marked the real beginning of commercial aviation. Six civilian pilots were hired at a salary of $3,600 to $5,000 a year to replace the army pilots.

PERMANENT CIVILIAN AIRMAIL

On Monday, August 12, 1918, the Post Office Department began the world's first regular permanent civilian airmail service. Pilot **Max Miller** was at the controls of the first airplane taking off that day with airmail from Washington, D.C. Miller was an experienced pilot for those days, since he had accumulated over 1,000 flying hours and had been an army flight instructor at San Diego, California. He was the first civilian pilot hired. He met and later married Otto Praeger's stenographer who was actually the first airmail employee. Max Miller burned to death over New Jersey two years later while carrying the mail. **Edward Radel** was hired as the chief mechanic. He was also a musician and later played the saxophone for many years with the Fred Waring orchestra. The base of operations was moved from the polo grounds to the flying field at College Park, Maryland.

The airplane left Washington, D.C., August 12 at 11:35 A.M. carrying 222 pounds of mail and arrived at Philadelphia at 1:00 P.M. There Maurice Newton took

> The dream of transcontinental airmail service became a reality.

over and landed at Belmont Park Race Track, New York, at 2:15 P.M. Two other pilots flew the southbound trip from New York to Washington in three and one-half hours starting at noon.

On May 15, 1919, service was established between Cleveland and Chicago, with a stop at Bryan, Ohio. This was the first step in what later became the first transcontinental route linking New York and San Francisco.

On July 1, 1919, operations were extended from Cleveland to New York with a stop at Bellefonte, Pennsylvania, thus opening the New York to Chicago route. The service performance during that period was remarkable, considering that there were no radio facilities, no marked airways, or other navigational aids. Airmail was flown on those routes in connection with the railroad service. The airplane would carry the mail during the day, and at night the mail would be turned over to a train to carry it, since aircraft did not fly in the night-time hours. During 1919, over the three routes in operation, eight planes flew 1,900 route miles daily with a performance record showing more than 95% of scheduled miles completed.

On May 15, 1920, service was extended westward from Chicago to Omaha, Nebraska, and on August 16, the St. Louis to Chicago route was opened. This is the route that Charles Lindbergh later flew as an airmail pilot. On September 8, 1920, the last leg of the transcontinental route was opened from Omaha, Nebraska to San Francisco. The dream of transcontinental airmail service became a reality. Even though airplanes flew only during the daylight hours, airmail bettered coast-to-coast train time by 22 hours.

On February 22, 1921, the first through-transcontinental airmail airplane took to the air. This was a truly great moment, for it meant flying the mails through long, black, beaconless nights. It took 33 hours and 21 minutes to complete the flight from the West Coast to Long Island.

The heroics of this flight are an epic in the annals of aviation history. The first airplane to leave New York westbound was forced down shortly after take-off. The second airplane made it to Chicago but could go no further due to bad weather. The first eastbound airplane to leave San Francisco crashed in Nevada, and the pilot was killed.

The second eastbound plane got to Reno, Nevada. There another pilot took it on to Cheyenne, Wyoming, where he arrived 12 hours after the mail had left San Francisco. Another pilot carried it on to North Platte, Nebraska. The hero of the flight, **Jack Knight** (See Figure 4.9) took off late in the evening in a DeHaviland, and while enroute, some people on the ground lighted

> **The next time you receive a letter by air, remember the airmail pioneers.**

fires for him to follow. He landed at Omaha at 1:00 A.M. only to find that the airplane that was planned to meet him had been grounded in Chicago. In cold, ice, and snow, and being unfamiliar with the route, Knight continued on with only an automobile road map to guide him. He could not land at Des Moines, Iowa, his intended stop, because of snow at the airport, so he went on to Iowa City. There the ground crew, which was supposed to light the guiding bonfires, had gone home thinking the flight had been cancelled. A night watchman at the airfield heard the engine of the airplane and lighted a flare. As Knight landed, he ran out of gas. The watchman helped refuel the airplane, and in snow and sleet Knight again took off and encountered fog. By some miracle he found Chicago and landed safely at 8:40 in the morning. The airmail was then uneventfully carried on to New York to complete the first thorough transcontinental delivery.

Jack Knight demonstrated that the old motto of mail carriers, "Neither rain, nor snow, nor heat, nor gloom of night can stay these couriers from the swift completion of their appointed rounds," could now be applied to airmail pilots.

In the first half of 1923 the Post Office built a lighted airway between Cheyenne and Chicago; and in August, for a four-day period, a regular schedule was flown from New York to San Francisco using this lighted airway during the night-time hours. Another test period of 30 days in July, 1924, demonstrated the feasibility of transcontinental airmail and it continued on as a regular operation.

From this beginning grew our present system of navigable airways. It was the Post Office that gave aviation not only this beginning, but also the first practical night flying. (See Figure 4.10.)

In 1927 the lighted airways and radio communication were transferred to the authority of the Department of Commerce.

By July, 1924 regular 24-hour transcontinental airmail service was in operation. A scheduled airmail flight took 34 hours westbound and 29 hours eastbound. Aircraft and crew changed at six points (Cleveland, Chicago, Omaha, Cheyenne, Salt Lake City, and Reno) along the route. The three postal zones created for determining rates were New York—Chicago, Chicago—Cheyenne, and Cheyenne—San Francisco. In those days it cost 24 cents to send a letter across the country. By July 1925 businesses in Chicago and New York were receiving overnight airmail service; this route developed the largest volume of airmail.

Figure 4.9 Jack Knight. Cross-country flight over unlighted airways by ten airmail pilots February 22, 1921 brought a $1,250,000 appropriation by Congress for continuation of airmail, with funds for lighting airways. Knight was the hero of the flight which secured the future of commercial aviation.

Figure 4.10 The early days; preparing to board.

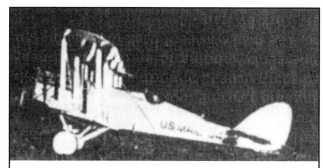

Figure 4.11 Night Flight. A DeHaviland-4 mail plane readying for a night take-off in the early 1920s. Routes were covered by means of beacons. (Smithsonian Institution, National Air Museum.)

Aircraft equipment was a problem for the fledgling airmail service. In November 1918, DeHaviland DH-4 military observation planes (See Figure 4.11) were placed in service flying the airmail. They had to be withdrawn because of weak spots in their design and modified by strengthening the landing gear and moving the gasoline tank to the center section immediately behind the engine. Before the modification the tank had been located behind the pilot's cockpit. Making a crash landing practically guaranteed a flaming death when the pilot found himself pinned between a ruptured fuel tank and a red-hot Liberty engine. For this reason the DH-4s were nicknamed "Flying Coffins." With modifications the DH-4B became the standard work-horse of the airmail service and held that place until 1926, although many other types were also used.

> **With no navigational aids, aerial sign posts, nor radios, the pilots still carried the mail in weather that stopped all surface traffic.**

It was the requirement of airmail which fostered the development of:

- night flying,
- instrument flying,
- meteorological service,
- federal airways,
- hard surface runways,
- radio communications,
- multi-engined airplanes.

When the airplane was forced to produce the exacting performance necessary to keep the system of American business flowing smoothly, it literally had to either show up or quit. It conformed, but it wasn't easy. Those persons working against great handicaps made it work; they were of the United States Airmail Service. Thus the commercial value of air transportation became a reality.

These pages and many more could not do justice to the historic achievements in the lives of all those pioneers who contributed so greatly to make air transportation the great and vital operation it is today.

The next time you receive a letter by air, remember the airmail pioneers—those whose tireless efforts and confidence in the future provided the foundation upon which commercial air transportation was built.

FLIGHTS OF FANCY

Early Piloting

The instrument panel on the DH-4 contained an ignition switch, an air speed indicator, a tachometer, a water temperature gauge, and an altimeter which registered 1,000 feet of altitude for each half inch around the periphery of its scale. Since the latter was more sensitive to changes in temperature than it was to altitude, the pilot almost had to be a mathematician, statistician, and magician to interpret what the altimeter readings meant.

There was a magnetic compass, which on an easterly or westerly heading, oscillated all the way from north to south when the air was rough.

With no navigational aids, aerial sign posts, nor radios, the pilots still carried the mail in weather that stopped all surface traffic. The pilots strapped a road map to their thigh; and if there were no clouds, fog, rain, sleet, or snow to obstruct the view, they could look over the side of the open cockpit and locate a river, railroad track, distinctive barn, or some other landmark and thus determine their course. Flying the "iron beam" literally meant following a railroad track. During bad weather and low ceilings, more than one pilot had to climb suddenly to avoid a head-on collision with a railroad locomotive.

PART 2

REGULATION
OF
AIR TRANSPORTATION

PART 2

BRIEF OVERVIEW OF CHAPTERS

5. THE AIR CARRIER INDUSTRY AND FEDERAL LEGISLATION

- Describes the early federal laws that provided incentive and stability to the air industry.

6. DEPARTMENT OF TRANSPORTATION

- Identifies the development, organization, functions and responsibilities of the DOT.

7. THE FEDERAL AVIATION ADMINISTRATION

- Discusses the organizational structure and responsibilities of this branch of government including air traffic control.

8. AVIATION SAFETY AND THE NATIONAL TRANSPORTATION SAFETY BOARD

- Examines FAA safety and air traffic control systems as well as the functions and responsibilities of the NTSB.

9. AVIATION ACCIDENT INVESTIGATION AND SAFETY PERFORMANCE

- Describes activities of National Transportation Safety Board's "Go-team" and gives examples of aircraft accident investigations.

10. AIR CARRIER ECONOMIC REGULATIONS

- Studies the depth of economic regulation of the Department of Transportation and how it affects air transportation, along with a review of the historical effects of deregulation.

11. AIR CARRIERS

- Explains growth and development of the air carrier industry from 1914 to present and describes classification of air carriers; also provides current industry data.

12. INTERNATIONAL AIR TRANSPORTATION LAW

- Explores influence of aviation meetings, conferences, and conventions and the concept of International deregulation.

13. INTERNATIONAL AIR TRANSPORTATION ORGANIZATIONS

- Focuses on major international air transportation organizations.

14. NON UNITED STATES AIR CARRIERS

- A brief review.

15. COMMERCIAL SPACE TRANSPORTATION

- Defines the use of space vehicles for commercial purposes.

CHAPTER 5

The Air Carrier Industry and Federal Legislation

The Post Office Department, through the development of airmail, was directly responsible for the beginning of commercial air transportation and of the airline industry. Therefore, the Post Office can be credited with being the father of United States commercial air transportation.

Benjamin Franklin, who established the Postal Service at the birth of the United States, recognized the importance of such a service. He said that a progressive nation requires a good communication system. His policy for the Post Office was that it should assist development of all new forms of transportation, which would, in turn, provide better mail delivery. Examples of this were the mail subsidies paid to the early stagecoach lines, which depended upon mail pay to stay in operation; only then were they able to provide passenger service. Their real income was from the transportation of mail. The famous Pony Express was established solely because of the lucrative mail payment offered to the contractors.

Government assistance in the early railroads is further evidence of the federal policy to encourage new forms of transportation. In this case, the government granted land to the railroads to lay their tracks, and then loaned or gave them money for equipment.

By 1925 the Post Office had conducted airmail service long enough to prove the practicability of such a commercial, nonmilitary use of the airplane. It was generally understood that the Post Office operation would only be temporary, and that as soon as it was feasible, carrying mail by air would be turned over to private industry.

> **A progressive nation requires a good communication system.**

In 1918, it was estimated that it would be at least five years before this transfer could take place. By the mid-1920s the Post Office was ready to ask private industry to take over the airmail operation.

The story of private companies beginning to carry airmail is also the story of the inception and growth of the commercial airline industry.

The last flight of the Post Office operation took place on September 9, 1927. Beginning in June 1927, the Post Office pilots were released as the newly formed airlines took over the airmail routes. There were 43 pilots at that time in the Postal Service, and an additional 600 employees in ground jobs. All of these had contributed to more than 12 million airmail miles having been flown.

The entire cost to the United States government for the airmail service, from its beginning in 1918 until the last flight in 1927 was $17.5 million. During these nine years about $5 million in airmail postage was sold to the public. The difference of $12.5 million cannot be counted as a loss, since it was a very small price to pay for the establishment of commercial air transportation and the United States airline industry. This industry has repaid the debt many times over, not only in taxes, but in valuable service to both the government and to the public.

AIRMAIL ACT OF 1925 (THE KELLY ACT)

Civil air transportation got its start in the United States when on February 2, Congress passed the Airmail Act of 1925. It is also known as the Kelly Act, because it was Representative Clyde Kelly of Pennsylvania who sponsored and led the congressional fight for its passage.

This Act made possible the awarding of contracts to private contractors for the transportation of airmail. Therefore, the purpose of the law was to provide for private airmail contractors, as clearly indicated in the title of the Kelly Act: "An Act to Encourage Commercial Aviation and to Authorize the Postmaster General to Contract for the Mail Service."

One important feature of the Kelly Act was that the amount of compensation paid to an air carrier could not be more than four-fifths, or 80%, of the revenue derived from the sale of airmail postage for such mail. This feature was a compromise with those in Congress who were opposed to the federal government paying for the development of the airline industry. The remaining 20% was for the ground handling expense of the airmail. In essence, the operation of the airmail under the Kelly Act would not cost the government—this feature proved to be the main weakness in the Kelly Act.

By the middle of 1925 Postmaster General Harry S. New advertised for bids on eight airmail routes. These routes were to be short feeder routes in order to allow the airlines time to gain experience; after the airlines had proved themselves, the transcontinental routes would be awarded. Only those companies with proper experience and equipment were eligible to bid.

On September 15, 1925, bids for the eight routes were filed with the Postmaster General, and they were opened on October 7. There were 10 companies which submitted 17 bids. Three were dispensed with due to the lack of proof of financial responsibility. As a result, only five routes were immediately awarded. By the beginning of 1926, 12 contract airmail (CAM) routes had been awarded. (Table 5.1.)

The first of these awards went to companies supported by men of various backgrounds and personalities. Colonial Airlines, the forerunner of American Airlines, was sponsored by individuals of civic, financial, and social prominence. Within these groups was Juan Trippe of Pan American fame. Another company, later to join American, was Robertson Aircraft Corporation, which was founded by two brothers, one of whom gained experience during World War I. One of their three employees was Charles A. Lindbergh. Wall Street

> **The story of private companies beginning to carry airmail is also the story of the inception and growth of the commercial airline industry.**

promoter Clement M. Keys was Chairman of the Board and President of Curtiss Aeroplane and Motor Company. Keys succeeded in getting CAM 3 for National Air Transport, later to join United Airlines. The Los Angeles-Salt Lake City award went to Western Air Express. Western was formed by journalist Harry Chandler, publisher of the *Los Angeles Times*. Awards to Henry Ford of routes 6 and 7 attracted the most publicity because of his influence on the business community.

Florida Airways Corporation received CAM 10 between Atlanta and Jacksonville, Florida. Its president was Reed Chambers who sought his former flying companion from the 94th Aero Squadron, Eddie Rickenbacher, to assist Florida Airways' growth.

CAM 11 had the most interesting award. It went to Clifford Ball who was the Hudson-Essex automobile dealer in McKeesport, Pennsylvania. As a result of a real estate transaction, Ball acquired land near Pittsburgh that pilots had been using as an airport. When they could not pay the rent, he seized their aircraft as payment. Since he had an airport and airplanes, Clifford Ball bid and won the Pittsburgh-Cleveland route.

These first contract airmail routes awarded under the Kelly Act were feeder lines branching off into the main transcontinental route. Because of economic conditions and a desire to reduce costs in the Department, it was then decided that bids would be given on main routes.

Although Colonial Air Lines received the first airmail contract, the honor for being the first in operation goes to Henry Ford, who owned Ford Air Transport. In the early days of commercial aviation the name Ford was known in aviation equally as well as in the automobile industry. As early as 1923 Ford became interested in an all metal, internally braced wing, monoplane designed by William B. Stout. Ford bought Stout's factory and put three engines on the aircraft instead of one. The result became known as the Ford TriMotor, or more affectionately, the *Tin Goose*. It was such a strong and dependable aircraft that it became the leading passenger aircraft for many years. This type of aircraft was later used to found air transportation in South America. In fact, some of them are still in operation today, a record unequaled by any other type of airplane.

In April 1925, Ford, using his single-engine airplanes, began flying a scheduled route from Detroit to Chicago to Cleveland for the exclusive use of the Ford

Table 5.1 The First Contract Airmail Routes

Route #	Company	Route	Began Operating
CAM 1	Colonial Air Lines	New York to Boston	June 18, 1926
CAM 2	Robertson Aircraft Corp.	Chicago to St. Louis	April 15, 1926
CAM 3	National Air Transport	Chicago to Dallas	May 12, 1926
CAM 4	Western Air Express	Los Angeles to Salt Lake City	April 17, 1926
CAM 5	Varney Speed Lines	Elko, Nevada to Pasco, Washington	April 6, 1926
CAM 6	Ford Air Transport	Detroit to Cleveland	February 16, 1926
CAM 7	Ford Air Transport	Detroit to Chicago	February 15, 1926
CAM 8	Pacific Air Transport	Los Angeles to Seattle	September 15, 1926
CAM 9	Charles Dickenson	Chicago to Minneapolis	June 7, 1926
CAM 10	Florida Airways Corp.	Atlanta to Jacksonville	September, 1926
CAM 11	Clifford Ball	Cleveland to Pittsburgh	April 21, 1927
CAM 12	Western Air Express	Pueblo, Colorado to Cheyenne, Wyoming	December, 1926

Company. Thus Ford not only operated the first airmail route by a private contractor, but also is credited with having one of, if not the first, air freight operations as well as with having one of the first airlines to carry passengers.

Under the Kelly Act a contract airmail carrier was paid up to 80% of the postal revenue of the airmail he carried. In trying to avoid subsidy Congress created a problem in computing payment to the carrier. Because the airmail was handled both by the Post Office and by the airline, each letter had to be counted before it was loaded aboard the airplane so that the postage could be apportioned between the Post Office and the air carrier. Under this system, an irrational distribution of airmail payments occurred.

The Postmaster solved these inequalities by the first amendment to the Kelly Act, approved June 3, 1926. New contracts were provided for at rates not to exceed $3.00 per pound for the first 1,000 miles and thirty cents a pound for each additional 100 miles. Again compensation was based upon nonsubsidy; this was still a weakness.

On January 25, 1927, the bid for the San Francisco to Chicago portion of the route was awarded to the Boeing Airplane Company and Edward Hubbard. Several months later the joint contract was turned over to Boeing Air Transport. Boeing Air Transport bid $2.89 per pound on the Chicago-San Francisco route; their nearest competitor bid $5.09 per pound. At that rate and with the aircraft available, Boeing critics predicted

substantial losses. When the contract was awarded, William Boeing went to Pratt & Whitney and requested that they build an air-cooled Wasp radial engine for his Boeing 40-A. By June 30, 1927, 25 Boeing 40-A's were ready. The airplane carried two passengers in addition to its airmail load. During its first two years Boeing Air Transport carried over 1,200 tons of airmail and approximately 6,000 passengers. The Post Office and Boeing urged lower rates to stimulate the use of airmail. At the time the western sector was awarded, no acceptable bid was received for the route east of Chicago. This was determined later by awarding a contract to National Air Transport on March 8, 1927.

In February 1927, an airmail postage rate of ten cents per half ounce between any two points in the United States became effective and provided a great impetus to the public in the use of airmail. In August 1928, rates were reduced to five cents for the first one-half ounce and ten cents for each additional ounce.

The first amendment to the Kelly Act did away with the difficult method of counting each letter carried, and the second amendment, passed in May 1928, did away with assuring the government against losses. Thus subsidy quietly came into the airline industry. The second amendment also reduced the airmail postage to five cents an ounce, and a 95% increase in airmail traffic resulted. The airlines could actually receive more money for carrying the airmail than the cost of the postage on the mail carried. To the young profit-starved airlines, this presented a golden opportunity. Now that they were being paid by the pound to carry the airmail, several of the airline companies began sending large quantities of airmail, as private citizens, destined to go over their own routes. They sent thousands of letters stuffed with paper, even telephone directories and spare parts. One airline contractor mailed two tons of lithograph material from New York to Los Angeles. It cost him over $6,000 in postage; but he was paid $25,000 by the Post Office to carry it, a neat profit in anyone's estimation.

Obviously, the opportunity for these inequalities had to be corrected; and so the third amendment to the Kelly Act so completely changed it that it was, in reality, the second major law passed by Congress having to do with airmail carried by the private contractors. This piece of legislation was called the Airmail Act of 1930.

AIR COMMERCE ACT OF 1926

When the Kelly Act provided that the airlines would carry the airmail, it was apparent that they were neither financially able, nor large enough, to provide for the maintenance and operation of the airway system organized for the Post Office operation.

Therefore, on the heels of the Kelly Act, Congress passed another major piece of legislation known as the Air Commerce Act of 1926, the purpose of which was to promote air commerce. This law charged the Federal Government with the operation and maintenance of the airway system as well as all aids to air navigation, and to provide safety in air commerce generally through a system of regulation.

It was unlike the other mail legislation acts. It left no doubt that the Federal Government was strongly in the picture of growth and development of aviation by way of aiding and encouraging air transportation.

The function of safety regulation was to be carried out by the Department of Commerce; therefore, the Bureau of Air Commerce was established.

Among the safety regulations provided were the requirements of registration and licensing of aircraft and the certification and medical examination of pilots. Civil penalties were allowed to enforce these requirements. This was the start of what later became the Civil Aeronautics Administration, and today the Federal Aviation Administration.

The Kelly Act and the Air Commerce Act provided the foundation of civil air transportation in the United States.

The late 1920s brought many new ventures in aviation. Four major groups developed:

- United Aircraft and Transport Corporation
- North American Aviation
- Aviation Corporation of Delaware
- Transcontinental Air Transport

AIRMAIL ACT OF 1930 (MCNARY-WATRES ACT)

The Airmail Act of 1930, also known as the McNary-Watres Act, was passed April 29, 1930, in an attempt to unify the industry. Up until this time, the newly organized airlines were not interested in carrying passengers. During the 1930s the airline airplanes were referred to as mail planes. (See Figure 5.1.) Today, when an airliner passes overhead, it is thought of as a passenger airplane, even though airmail is aboard.

An important event which vastly effected development of the airline industry, took place in November 1928, when Herbert Hoover was elected President and shortly thereafter appointed Walter Brown as the new Postmaster General. Brown initiated passage of the McNary-Watres Airmail Act of 1930. (See Figure 5.2.)

Brown served under Hoover as Assistant Secretary of Commerce in the Coolidge Administration and had served as Hoover's campaign manager. He was previously chairman of the Republican National Committee.

Figure 5.1 Mail plane of the 1930s.

Figure 5.2   Three-engined airplane of the 1930s meets the three-engined airplane of the 1960s.

When Brown assumed the office of Postmaster General there existed 44 small airline companies lacking capital and dependent upon government airmail contracts.

Brown felt that the responsibility to encourage commercial aviation was not being carried out by competitive bidding although airmail was being carried at the lowest cost. Brown defined the airline problems as:

1. Being unwilling to invest in new equipment,

2. Operating obsolete aircraft,

3. Demonstrating questionable safety performance resulting from cost cutting, and

4. Maintaining marginal operations with no growth.

Figure 5.3.
Postmaster Walter Folger Brown

To Brown the solution was to eliminate competitive bidding and use airmail pay to support those corporations strong enough to encourage commercial aviation. To accomplish his solution Brown needed legislation. This legislation was the Airmail Act of 1930. The law received difficult passage because Brown failed to consult Congressman Clyde Kelly. Kelly had gone on record supporting new legislation. Brown's oversight resulted in Kelly's vigorously opposing the law and succeeded in making critical amendments to it.

The new legislation authored by Brown himself contained three important provisions—

1. Operators would be paid for flying mail according to the space available for mail in their airplanes. As much as $1.25 per mile was paid for large aircraft like the Ford TriMotor.

2. The Postmaster could extend or consolidate routes at his discretion.

3. Routes would be awarded to the lowest responsible bidder who had owned an airline operating on a daily schedule for at least 250 miles over a six-month period.

Brown's goal was to build a viable and safe commercial airline system. Once put into place, the airmail contract system subsidized large operations at the expense of smaller air carriers. This gave substantial incentives to airlines to acquire large multiengine airplanes and to develop passenger routes. The new system actually did result in a strong commercial aviation system early in the 1930s. No other Postmaster, before or since, has held such power over the United States air carrier system as did Walter Brown. Brown alienated many airlines by his insistence on forced mergers.

It was under Brown's administration that the second phase of the airline industry's development took place. Brown became a most controversial figure and even today is both violently criticized and praised for the part he played in the development of civil air transportation and airline history.

Upon taking the office of Postmaster General, given to him for being partly responsible for Hoover's nomination, he began a thorough study of the problems of aviation. He felt the airlines should be able to develop profitably without the help of airmail payments. He also believed that competition was necessary in the airline industry to stimulate growth.

Brown was almost 50 years ahead of time in his thinking—The Airline Deregulation Act of 1978 was passed for the purpose of encouraging an air transportation system which relies on competitive market forces to determine quality and price. In a meeting with airline leaders, Brown encouraged them to develop a profitable passenger business to become independent of the subsidy of airmail contracts. Postmaster Brown's goal was a system of three self-supporting transcontinental airline systems, and so he urged the airlines to form three large transcontinental companies.

The Airmail Act of 1930 gave Brown dictatorial power over the airline industry; therefore, commercial air transportation took on the characteristics of a federally regulated industry. The law gave Brown extensive power—he could grant an airmail contract without competitive bidding. He stated at the time that if the airlines were ever to become self-supporting they had to carry passengers and compete with each other. He felt that the airline industry needed leadership and that he was the one to give it. Postmaster Brown arranged that his office extend or consolidate routes in the public interest. This resulted in several smaller companies joining together to qualify for an airmail contract.

> **The Airline Deregulation Act of 1978 was passed for the purpose of encouraging an air transportation system which relies on competitive market forces to determine quality and price.**

The new law brought about a change in the method of computing mail pay rates, paying the airlines for space instead of weight. This encouraged the airlines to purchase larger aircraft, which in turn gave rise to passenger traffic. In addition to computing the new airmail rates on space, the McNary-Watres Act also provided for variables such as bad terrain, bad weather, night flying, radio equipment, and multi-engine aircraft.

Brown met with the contracting airlines to discuss the new airmail contracts and plan for passenger service. It became clear that the airlines were not willing, as yet, to move in this direction. This further forced Brown into assuming the responsibility of leadership of the airline industry and using the far reaching powers granted to him under the McNary-Watres Airmail Act of 1930.

Meeting with the airlines, Brown outlined his philosophy and his plan for development of a national air transportation system. Brown disliked the reckless competition that was going on, but even more so he disliked a monopoly. Brown's solution was regulated competition. He made it apparent that he believed an airline should be a large, sufficiently financed company, and that the transcontinental airmail routes must be conducted by one company. Since there was no large single airline, mergers of several smaller companies resulted. This action contributed to the beginning of the corporate entities of airlines that we know today, such as United Air Lines, American Airlines, and Trans World Airlines. Many smaller companies were left out. To them it meant no mail contract, and no contract meant going out of business. Brown got the large transcontinental airline companies he wanted. The four years Brown was Postmaster General resulted in the emergence of a consolidated airline route pattern and the formation of the great air carrier companies of today.

Brown has been called both good and evil because he acted in this direct fashion. In retrospect, however, it becomes obvious that the airline industry development would have been much slower were it not for his accomplishments.

The complaints of the small airlines were heard in Washington. With a presidential election coming up, Brown's actions made a good basis for political discussion. Hoover lost to the Democratic candidate, Franklin D. Roosevelt, who upon taking office, named James A. Farley of New York Postmaster.

When Brown left office there were 34 established airmail routes. The per mile cost of airmail was 54 cents, down from $1.10 when he entered office. The result of his reign was good if no attention were paid to those who had been trampled upon.

Roosevelt's New Deal program created many investigations, one of which was to examine mail contracts subsidizing the Merchant Marine. This congressional investigation committee was chaired by a second-term Senator from Alabama, Hugo Black, who later became a Supreme Court Justice.

One small airline that lost its bid on an airmail route was the Ludington Line. Although Ludington was making a profit flying passengers between New York, Philadelphia, and Washington, the bid was won by Eastern Air Transport. But Ludington Line was innovative. In 1930 they introduced a concept not duplicated again until 1960; the operation consisted of flights leaving New York and Washington every hour on the hour.

In 1932, word was circulating through Congress for the cancellation of the airmail contracts awarded in 1930. In early 1933 a House committee expressed its

FLIGHTS OF FANCY

The Case Against Walter Brown

The investigating committee, with the cooperation of small carriers who lost contracts, found that apparent favoritism had been used by Walter Brown.

Senator Black found little interest in investigating the Merchant Marine, but airmail contracts added fuel to a growing political career. The committee hearings took on the form of a prosecution of Walter Brown. Cross-examination and witnesses developing full statements were not acceptable to Chairman Black. Black's line of attack focused on two points. First, small operations were forced out of business by Wall Street seeking a monopoly. Second, enormous profits were made through stock manipulations.

The main outcome was to crucify Walter Brown by saying he had favorites among the airlines and by charging him with collusion with the larger airlines. His methods drew the attention of the Black Committee. Brown's defense was that he acted in a manner according to his beliefs for the public interest.

The new Postmaster General, James Farley, maintained that the routes had been awarded at a series of secret meetings held in May and June of 1930, called the Spoils Conferences.

The main point was that all but two of 20 contracts went to United Aircraft and Transport Corporation, Aviation Corporation of Delaware, and the North American Aviation Group of General Motors.

Senator Black's committee overlooked the issue of how much growth and progress took place during Walter Brown's handling of airmail contracts. Little time was spent on how United Aircraft and Transport Corporation, Eastern Air Transport, and American Airways had improved passenger service, safety, and aircraft development.

The airlines were not entirely without fault. Expense account favors were utilized in entertaining government officials. Jobs and loans to postal officials were offered. Relatives of senators and congressmen were hired as consultants. However, as far as Walter Brown was concerned, no testimony or evidence was ever recorded that showed that he benefited financially or otherwise. Walter Brown acted as he felt was best for the United States. If a small carrier's contract was awarded to a large carrier, Brown made it a condition that the large carrier would buy the small carrier at a fair price.

Black went to the White House in January 1934 to present to the President the findings of his committee. Roosevelt said he would study the matter. Black then met with the United States Solicitor General, and both men went to Postmaster General Farley. Farley felt many of Black's statements were for publicity. He asked the Solicitor General to verbally sum up the volume of evidence, and he was eventually convinced.

The Postmaster General and Solicitor General met with the President and again discussed the findings. Farley wanted to advertise for new bids and then cancel the existing contracts. Roosevelt accepted Black's view for immediate cancellation. The Democrats accused Brown with nine charges of favoritism, collusion, and misconduct of office.

Brown subsequently retired to his home in Ohio and became the dean of Toledo politics and the head of the Republican Party there. He was vindicated in 1941. He died at the age of 91 in 1961.

feelings that certain interlocking relationships had prevented the development of aviation and resulted in wasteful expenditures of public funds. It was the committee's recommendation that the powers of the Postmaster be restrained.

On February 9, 1934, as a result of the Black Committee investigation, James Farley issued an order which canceled all domestic airmail contracts on charges of collusion. The Army, he said, carried the airmail originally in 1918 and they could do it again. General Benjamin Foulois, an aviation pioneer and Chief of the Air Corps, was called upon to do the job.

The airline pilots at the time of the cancellation were experienced even for a fledgling industry. Most of the pilots had over 4,000 hours of flying time and some had as much as 9,000 hours. They had day and night flying time and knew their routes well. They were used to the particular weather associated with the route and their aircraft were equipped with radio for air-to-ground communication.

In contrast, the Army assigned open-cockpit airplanes to carry the airmail and their pilots had been restricted to flying 170 hours a year. The Army aircraft were not equipped for weather or night flying, and only 500 men were assigned to the entire operation, which had been handled by several thousand airline employees.

In taking over the airmail on February 19, 1934, the route mileage was greatly reduced. The Army was given ten days to get the schedules in operation. The Air Corps itself was struggling for recognition and had not been given adequate funds to accomplish their growth.

The ill-prepared and poorly equipped Air Corps had tragic results in its effort to carry out Farley's order. Three days before they were to take over the airmail routes three pilots were killed on their way to begin their assignment, and another crashed but escaped serious injury.

The record for the first week's operations was equally tragic. Five Army pilots were killed and six more were seriously injured. Eight airplanes were ruined, and there was $300,000 worth of property damage. A few days later two more pilots were killed and one was critically injured.

The needless slaughter went on into March of 1934. Finally, after 66 crashes, 12 deaths, and governmental cost of nearly $4 million, President Roosevelt ordered the Army to cease flying the airmail on June 1, 1934, after nearly six months' operation.

At the time of the cancellation of airmail contracts, the airlines were receiving from 42.5 cents to 54 cents per mile. It cost the Army $2.21 during its operation. It was obvious that for economy, service, and safety, the airlines could do a much better job.

As a result, all the former airmail contractors were given three-month contracts to transport airmail. Before the time expired it was apparent that airmail legislation had to be completely revamped.

FLIGHTS OF FANCY

The Last Industry Airmail Flight

The day before the Army took over airmail, the airlines demonstrated their progress and ability to carry the mail, as well as to show the ridiculousness of the postmaster's order. A new Douglas airliner, the DC-2, with two famous pilots at the controls, Jack Frye of Trans World Airlines and Eddie Rickenbacker of Eastern, flew the last load of mail from Los Angeles, California to Newark, New Jersey and set a new transcontinental flying record of 13 hours.

Frye and Rickenbacker wanted everything perfect for their transcontinental flight. It was their desire to make the last trip carrying airmail in less than 15 hours. Scheduled to fly on board were several journalists to record the event. The flight was to land in Newark before midnight to prove that air transportation had progressed to a point of flying an accurate schedule.

The new DC-2 took off on schedule at 9:00 P.M. from Los Angeles; en route to Albuquerque the flight averaged 230 miles per hour. Donald Douglas had guaranteed 180 miles per hour for the new aircraft. The first stop was Kansas City for ten minutes to refuel, then on to Pittsburgh. Weather reports received en route indicated a storm over Pittsburgh; therefore, Columbus was chosen as the second refueling point. After take-off, they passed the storm and landed at Newark 13 hours and two minutes after leaving Los Angeles.

It was neither the President nor Black who received the criticism for the failure of the Army in carrying the airmail; it was James A. Farley who signed the cancellation order.

In March 1934 Roosevelt asked Congress to provide adequate legislation for returning airmail to private companies.

It was not until 1941 that Brown was vindicated when the United States Court said that the charges of collusion against him were untrue. Therefore, the cancellation of the airmail contracts, the deaths of the pilots, the property damage, and the high expense were all unnecessary—except as a period in the historical development of United States air transportation. This action of the court made it possible for the airlines, whose airmail contracts had been cancelled by Farley, to claim and receive about $2.5 million dollars in damages.

AIRMAIL ACT OF 1934 (BLACK-MCKELLAR ACT)

The remedial act meant to prevent the happenings of Brown's administration again was passed in June 1934 and is known as the Airmail Act of 1934, or the Black-McKellar Act.

Under the provisions of this act airmail contracts were to be granted upon competitive bidding, as was the case before 1930. However, no contract would be awarded to any company who had been involved in the supposed collusion. The three air carriers involved in the alleged collusion did show up at a meeting called by Farley on April 20, 1934, to issue new contracts. The three airlines had disguised themselves by changing their names slightly; American Airways became American Airlines, Eastern Air Transport became Eastern Airlines, and Transcontinental & Western Air just added the suffix "Inc." Furthermore, the control of the industry was placed in the hands of three agencies of the Federal government. This joint administration was divided between the Post Office, the Interstate Commerce Commission, and the Department of Commerce.

The Post Office awarded all airmail contracts and enforced the regulations governing airmail. The Interstate Commerce Commission set the rates of mail pay to the contracting airlines as well as reviewing all rates periodically. The Department of Commerce had established the Bureau of Air Commerce (the ancestor of the present Federal Aviation Administration) whose func-

tion was to provide safety in air transportation and to maintain, operate, and develop the airway system.

The old airmail contracting airlines were awarded most of their previous airmail routes. To ensure regaining these routes, some airlines submitted extremely low bids; several were only a fraction of a cent per mile.

By midsummer the airlines were financially weakened because their airmail income was less than one-half the former amounts. The depression and the publicity of the Black hearings also added to the difficulty. The situation reached a point where the airlines almost suspended operations.

Many of the smaller airlines were successful in obtaining routes; some lasted only a year or two. By World War II almost half of these companies had merged or suffered financial collapse and no longer existed. This seemed to confirm Walter Brown's philosophy.

The Act of 1934 also created a Federal Aviation Commission to study aviation policy headed by Clark Howell of Atlanta. The commission submitted its report on February 1, 1935, and recommended that a separate organization be created to control the airline industry. Senator Pat McCarran, during debate on the Black-McKellar Act, suggested this same course of action.

The Commission, in discussing the reorganization of regulatory agencies, came to two possible choices: control by the Interstate Commerce Commission, or control by a new independent agency. The White House was in favor of an independent agency.

At about this time the airlines were forming a trade association, known as the Air Transport Association, whose function it would be to speak in unity for the airline industry.

A minor provision of the Act of 1934, seemingly unimportant at the time, required the separation of airline companies and aircraft manufacturers. It was considered a matter of safety that airplane users not be controlled by those who controlled the airplane builders. Had this been allowed, an airline might be required to buy an airplane from a manufacturer owned by the same holding company. This action resulted in the final organization of the present day airline corporate names. This provision of the Airmail Act of 1934 required North American Aviation to divest itself of its airline companies. Through a loophole in the law, General Motors was allowed to keep Eastern. However, Eastern was in poor financial condition.

The responsibility for building Eastern was given to Eddie Rickenbacker. As a result, Eastern's condition

Airmail Stamps

FLIGHTS OF FANCY

First Stewardesses

The world's first airline stewardesses were hospital nurses. This group was on the Chicago to San Francisco route of United Air Lines in 1930. The woman at top left is Ellen Church who proposed the idea and recruited the women.

substantially improved so that John Hertz, of Hertz Rent-A-Car, offered General Motors $3 million for Eastern Airlines. Rickenbacker went to the chairman of General Motors, Alford Sloan, and asked for an opportunity to match the Hertz offer. After receiving that option he set about securing financing for the deal. Rickenbacker called upon friends on Wall Street, and financing was acquired. The completion of the sale took place in Eastern's hangar at Newark airport. Rickenbacker also had obtained a half million dollars for operating funds.

Both the air transport industry and the Federal government learned many valuable lessons during the early months of 1934. Among these was the conviction that a healthy air transport service was essential to the nation's social, economic, and political strength, and that the time was at hand to revise the existing air legislation. It took four years of discussion before satisfactory legislation was finally enacted.

To do a good job for both the airlines and the public, the Federal government decided it must have regulatory power over the airline industry and that it must regulate air commerce in the same way it regulated interstate and foreign commerce. The authority by which it conducted these functions stemmed from the United States Constitution.

By 1938, the airline industry was an established and recognized segment of the American way of life. The airlines had airmail contracts, and they were developing passenger service. The economic and business condition of the entire United States was improving after the disastrous years of the depression. Aircraft manufacturers had begun providing aircraft to the airlines for passenger service.

All seemed well with the industry—in fact, too well. Uneconomic passenger route duplication and rate cutting began to surface.

CIVIL AERONAUTICS ACT OF 1938 (MCCARRAN-LEA ACT)

The airlines approached the Federal government and suggested working out a basic set of guiding principles. The three agencies under the Airmail Act of 1934 were overlapping in authority, causing further hardship on the airlines.

After several months of study by the industry leaders and government officials, a completely new all-encompassing law was passed affecting civil aviation in the United States. The new law found its basis in Article I, Section 8, of the United States Constitution known as the Commerce Clause. The progression of authority was the Interstate Commerce Commission Act of 1887, and the essentials of the new law came from the then recently passed Motor Carrier Act of 1935.

The Civil Aeronautics Act, introduced by Senator Pat McCarran and Representative Clarence Lea, passed the Congress on June 23, 1938. The McCarran-Lea Act amended or repealed all major existing and previous legislation having to do with aviation.

The mechanics of the Civil Aeronautics Act were simple. All air transportation regulation, both economic and safety, was administered by three separate agencies.

These original three agencies were:

1. The Civil Aeronautics Authority, composed of five members who were to establish aviation policies by legislation of safety and economics of air transportation.

2. The Administrator of Aviation, appointed to carry out the safety policies of the Authority, while the Authority provided for the execution of the economic regulations concerning the air transport industry.

3. The Air Safety Board, formed as an independent group of three people responsible for the investigation of aircraft accidents.

For the first time the airline industry could look upon a firm regulatory system, making it possible to plan for future development.

After the functioning of the Authority, the Administrator, and the Air Safety Board began, it became obvious that some duplication of authority existed and that an adjustment was necessary. Therefore, President Roosevelt in April and June of 1940 proposed changes that became effective on June 30, 1940, and became known as the 1940 Amendment of the Civil Aeronautics Act.

The result of the organizational changes was the reshuffling of functions into two agencies instead of three. The first as the Civil Aeronautics Board, which was to be an independent group of five people reporting to the President. Its function was to exercise legislative and judicial authority over civil aviation, as well as executive control in the area of air carrier economic regulation. The investigation of aircraft accidents also became a responsibility of the Civil Aeronautics Board.

The second agency created by the 1940 Amendment was the Civil Aeronautics Administration, headed by an Administrator, whose function was solely to be the execution of safety regulations. This was to include enforcement and promotion of aviation safety as well

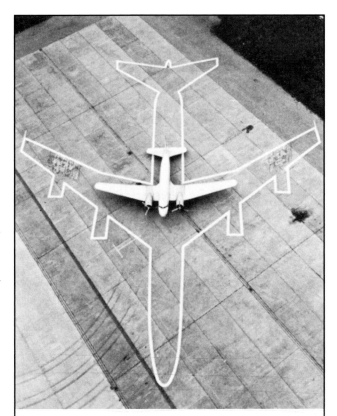

Figure 5.4   A DC-3 of the 1930s superimposed on the outline of a Boeing 747 of today.

as safety in the entire operation of the airway system. The Civil Aeronautics Administration was placed under the Department of Commerce.

THE GRANDFATHER CLAUSE

Included in Title IV of the economic regulation of the Civil Aeronautics Act of 1938 was section 401e, which stated that the carriers who had provided adequate and continuous airmail service from May 14 to August 22, 1938, the effective date of the Act, would receive a permanent Certificate of Convenience and Necessity for those routes. This clause was a grandfather clause, and the first airline to receive this award was Delta Air Corporation. (Table 5.2.) Only a violation of the Act can cause an airline to lose its grandfather rights.

Of these 16 carriers, six have faded away through mergers or reorganization. Chicago and Southern, and Northeast merged with Delta; Inland merged with Western; Mid-Continent merged with Braniff; Pennsylvania-Central became Capital, which later merged with

FLIGHTS OF FANCY

Passenger Service

An indirect, but most important result of the 1934 Airmail Act was the growth of passenger service. The airlines realized that their future lay not upon dependence on airmail contracts, but upon the development of passenger traffic. Therefore, the major airlines began forming traffic and sales departments for the purpose of promoting and selling passenger travel. By the end of 1936 income from passengers exceeded income from airmail transportation.

Table 5.2 Airlines That Received Permanent Certification by the Grandfather Clause

American Airlines	Eastern Airlines
Braniff Airways	Inland Airlines
Chicago and Southern Airlines	Mid-Continent Airlines
Continental Airlines	National Airlines
Delta Air Corporation	Northeast Airlines
Northwest Airlines	United Airlines
Pennsylvania-Central Airlines	Western Air Express
Transcontinental & Western Air	Wilmington-Catalina Airlines

United; Transcontinental and Western changed their corporate name to Trans World Airlines. Additional carriers were merged and others are no longer operating because of bankruptcies.

Civil air transportation continued under the Civil Aeronautics Act for a period of 20 years, and the Act provided the practical machinery for the development of civil air transportation. It formulated continuing public service objectives and provided the means whereby these objectives could be established. The purpose of the Act was not only to regulate civil air transportation, but also to develop and encourage its growth.

> **The writers of the Civil Aeronautics Act agreed that air transportation must be kept a strong and dynamic force.**

Because of the growing importance of the air transport industry to the economy and the national defense of the United States in the later 1930s, the writers of the Civil Aeronautics Act agreed that air transportation must be kept a strong and dynamic force.

Time alone proved the truth of their wisdom.

THE FEDERAL AVIATION ACT—1958*

The Civil Aeronautics Act of 1938 was basically a constitution of aviation upon which the aviation industry could expand and develop. It was general in character and left the interpretation of the specific nature to the Civil Aeronautics Board in the matter of economic regulation, and to the Civil Aeronautics Administration in the area of adherence to air safety.

Since 1938 and development of the air industry, particularly after World War II, it became apparent that changes had to be made. Amendments and revisions were passed to take care of minor current adjustments; however, the main points of contention became more severe. Many plans were forthcoming, ranging from overhauling and modernizing the Civil Aeronautics Act, to a completely new method of aviation regulation. Some people proposing changes had been responsible for the writing and enactment of the Civil Aeronautics Act in 1938; a few felt that aviation regulation had not been carried out according to their intended meaning. Some of their arguments, no doubt, were justified. It is sufficient to state that no major change came about and the Civil Aeronautics Act remained in effect until the passage of the Federal Aviation Act in 1958.

The Federal Aviation Act of 1958, however, is not entirely new; it is largely a reenactment, in amendment form, of the prior Civil Aeronautics Act. The economic regulatory provisions set forth therein are unchanged. Therefore, pre-1959 judicial and administrative decisions interpreting and applying predecessor provisions of the Civil Aeronautics Act are of precedential value with respect to the Federal Aviation Act. The Federal Aviation Act is the old Civil Aeronautics Act in practically every respect except one—the expanding of power in the area of air safety. The Civil Aeronautics Administration became the Federal Aviation Agency. Whereas, the Civil Aeronautics Administration was under the Department of Commerce, the Federal Aviation Agency was organized at an independent level answerable only to Congress and the President. With the enactment of the Department of Transportation in 1966, the Federal Aviation Agency became the Federal Aviation Administration and was placed under the Secretary of Transportation.

The Federal Aviation Agency was granted expanded authority in air safety. It would not be hampered organizationally or budgetwise as had been the case of the Civil Aeronautics Administration. The Federal Aviation Agency was able to make long-range plans and to implement these plans without interference.

The Federal Aviation Act of 1958 worked virtually no changes of substance into the economic regulatory provisions, but made several revisions in the safety

---

*As amended by the Airline Deregulation Act of 1978.

program. While the Board retained its duties in the fields of air carrier economic regulation and aircraft accident investigation, the Board's safety rule-making powers were transferred to the administrator of the Federal Aviation Agency, with the result that the latter official then promulgated the very regulations and standards which he administers and enforces. The Board's role in safety rule-making is presently limited to participation as an interested party in FAA proceedings.

A second important revision of prior law concerns procedure in certificate suspension and revocation cases (Section 609). Whereas under the former law, only the Board could suspend or revoke in the first instance; the new act contemplated initial action by the Administrator, subject to the certificate holder's privilege of appeal to the Board. Apart from these matters, the Federal Aviation Administrator has substantially all the powers and duties of his predecessor under the 1938 Act, plus a clearer authority to allocate the navigable airspace between military and civilian users.

Whereas the Civil Aeronautics Board had been responsible for the enactment of air safety legislation, and such regulations carried out by the Civil Aeronautics Administration in their executive capacity, the power of air safety legislation was transferred to the Federal Aviation Agency. The Civil Aeronautics Board retained the responsibility of aircraft accident investigation and economic regulation of the air carriers.

All ongoing air safety research and development was consolidated and placed in the care of the Federal Aviation Agency. Therefore, the work of such agencies as the Airways Modernization Board, the Air Coordinating Committee, and the National Advisory Committee for Aeronautics could be coordinated at one location and under one agency, the Federal Aviation Agency.

The area of economic regulation of the air transportation industry was not altered in any way. The Federal Aviation Act was passed hurriedly in the closing days of Congress in 1958. No attempt was made to change or modify any economic regulation of the air transport industry.

FLIGHTS OF FANCY

Mid-air Collisions

The circumstances which led to the Federal Aviation Act of 1958 were a series of mid-air collisions, some of which involved military aircraft. These highlighted the need for improved air traffic control.

• The first of these accidents occurred on June 30, 1956, over the Grand Canyon. The aircraft involved were a Trans World Airlines Constellation and a United Airlines DC-7. Both aircraft fell into the Canyon.

TWA Flight 2 left Los Angeles International Airport at 9:00 A.M. bound for Kansas City; and three minutes later, bound for Chicago, UAL Flight 718 took off from the same runway. At 10:31 A.M. Flight 2 and Flight 718 collided over the Grand Canyon.

The probable cause, according to the official Civil Aeronautics Board Accident Report, was that the pilots did not see each other in time to avoid the collision. It is not possible to determine why the pilots did not see each other, but the evidence suggests any one, or a combination of the following factors: intervening clouds, visual limitations, preoccupation with normal cockpit duties, attempting to provide passengers with a more scenic view, physiological limits to human vision, or insufficiency of en route air traffic advisory information due to inadequacy of facilities and lack of personnel in air traffic control.

• The second accident involved a DC-7B owned by Douglas Aircraft Company and a USAF F-89J near Sunland, California on January 31, 1957. The DC-7B crashed into a junior high school playground killing three students and injuring 70 others. The F-89J crashed in the Verdugo Mountains.

The probable cause was the high rate of near head-on closure at high altitude, which, together with physiological limitations, resulted in a minimum avoidance opportunity during which the pilots did not see the other's aircraft.

• The third accident involved a United Airlines DC-7 and a USAF F-100F near Las Vegas, Nevada, on April 21, 1958.

The probable cause of this mishap, according to Civil Aeronautics Board investigation, was a high rate of near head-on closure at high altitude; human and cockpit limitations; and the failure of the Nellis Air Force Base and the Civil Aeronautics Administration to take every measure to reduce a known collision exposure.

These accidents and other occurrences caused Congressional action.

In the study of present Federal regulation of air transportation, it must be remembered that such regulation is now much as it was in 1938 except in the area of air safety including air traffic control.

Although the Federal Aviation Act is the law of the land in aviation matters, it is very broad and in many cases loose in definition. This fact is not a weakness, for the Civil Aeronautics Board and the Federal Aviation Agency were to interpret and apply the law within the framework of the Act.

The Federal Aviation Act was passed by Congress on August 23, 1958. That part of the law dealing with the creation and organizational structure of the Federal Aviation Agency became effective on that date. The main body of the law was placed in effect on December 31, 1958.

The Airline Deregulation Act of 1978 substantially changed the Federal Aviation Act of 1958. (Refer to Chapter 13, *Deregulation*.)

> **Aeronautics is the science and art of flight.**

Officially the Federal Aviation Act is known as Public Law 85-726, 85th Congress, S.3880. The introductory paragraph very clearly states the purposes of the new law as:

1. Continuing the Civil Aeronautics Board (disbanded 1/1/85).
2. Creating a Federal Aviation Agency (Administration).
3. Providing for the regulation and promotion of Civil Aviation.
4. Providing for the safe and efficient use of the airspace.

Structurally, the Act is divided into 15 main divisions called "Titles." Each title is divided into various sections which have several sub-sections. Reference is made to any part of the Act by stating the title number and section combined; thus 411 means the eleventh part of the fourth title.

Title II deals with the organization, functions, and general powers of the Civil Aeronautics Board which ceased to exist on January 1, 1985. Title IV, Air Carrier Economic Regulation, was the direct responsibility of the Civil Aeronautics Board and indicated the majority of the work which they performed. Title VII, Aircraft Accident Investigation, was a function of the Civil Aeronautics Board, but it was transferred to the National Transportation Safety Board under the Department of Transportation.

The organization, powers, and duties of the Federal Aviation Administration, headed by Administrator, are outlined in Title III. The main responsibilities of the Administrator, and therefore the Federal Aviation Administration, are stated in Title V, Nationality and Ownership of Aircraft, as well as Title VI, Safety Regulations of Civil Aeronautics.

The remaining titles of the Act, although important, deal with miscellaneous aviation matters.

SECTION 101—DEFINITIONS

Except for the minor changing of words to a more modern connotation, the definitions had not been altered until the passage of the Airline Deregulation Act on October 24, 1978. In 1938 the writers of the Civil Aeronautics Acts wanted to be sure the terms and words were generally understood by all; therefore, the definitions represent an effort at standardization. There are now 41 definitions.

The statutory definitions are of great importance since application of the substantive regulatory provisions of the Act depend upon them to a large extent, and since the definitions also include certain substantive grants of power. Thus, the definition of "air commerce" largely fixes the scope of the Federal Aviation Administrator's jurisdiction in the safety field because the substantive provisions of Title VI, Safety Regulations of Civil Aeronautics, are couched in terms of "air commerce." It should be observed that the definition of "air commerce" is exceedingly broad. It includes not only what is traditionally regarded as interstate and foreign commerce (physical movement of aircraft across state and international boundaries and the transportation within a single state of persons or property moving to or from another state), but also includes all transportation of mail, operations, or navigation within the limits of any federal airway, and any operation or navigation, which may endanger safety in air commerce. This definition is generally regarded as conferring federal jurisdiction in safety matters with respect to all flights of aircraft, since all flights, whether commercial or private, and irrespective of whether they cross state lines or operate within a federal airway, represent a potential danger to interstate commerce. Moreover, counsel for the Board and the Administrator, and thus far some courts, have considered the definition to be so broad as to vest in the Federal government exclusive jurisdiction in safety matters, thus preempting the states from enacting air safety regulations under their general police powers.

On the other hand, the definition of "air transportation," which fixes the scope of the Board's regulation under Title IV, Air Carrier Economic Regulation, is considerably narrower than the definition of "air commerce." "Air transportation" includes only common carriage by aircraft "in commerce between" the states, etc., and the carriage of mail by aircraft. This definition is believed to confer jurisdiction over the common carriage of persons and property only in those areas traditionally regarded as constituting interstate and foreign commerce. Unlike in the safety field, the definition does not preempt the entire economic field to the exclusion of the states, and the courts have in certain context so held. Thus, while the Board's economic jurisdiction was believed to extend to all common carrier movements of aircraft across state lines and within the territories, and to movements of aircraft within a state but engaged in interstate transportation of more than a minimum amount, there was no direct economic jurisdiction over purely intrastate transportation. Air transportation of mail, whether interstate or purely intrastate, falls within the definition of air transportation, except for certain special transportation defined elsewhere.

Another important term is "air carrier" defined as any U.S. citizen "who undertakes, whether directly or indirectly or by a lease or any other arrangement, to engage in air transportation." This definition serves to fix the Board's jurisdiction over "indirect air carriers." The definition provides further that the Board "may by order relieve air carriers who are not directly engaged in the operation of aircraft" from the various regulatory provisions of the statute. This provision has been used to establish the classification of Air Freight Forwarder and to exempt both them and other indirect air carriers such as Railway Express (an "air carrier" as to air express) from the Certificate of Convenience and Necessity and other provisions of the Act.

Mention should also be made of the term "aeronautics," which is defined as "the science and art of flight." Since the control provisions of the statute (Sections 408 and 409) confer jurisdiction over relationships between air carriers and persons engaged in a "phase of aeronautics," this definition permits considerable breadth in the application of the statute. It has been held to include manufacturing companies, leasing companies, and a host of other persons engaging in activities closely related to air carrier operations.

The examples listed are for the purpose of illustration, and only those which bear special attention will be discussed.

Administrator—the Administrator of the Federal Aviation Administration.

Board—the Civil Aeronautics Board.

Aircraft—any contrivance now known or hereafter invented, used, or designed for navigation of or flight in the air.

Civil aircraft—any aircraft other than public aircraft.

Civil aircraft of the United States—any aircraft registered as provided in this Act.

Public aircraft—an aircraft used exclusively in the service of any government or of any political subdivision, but not including any government-owned aircraft engaged in carrying persons or property for commercial purposes.

Citizen—anyone, a partnership, or corporation, who is a citizen of the United States or its possessions.

Persons—any individual, firm, co-partnership, corporation, company, association, joint-stock association, or body politic; and includes any trustee, receiver, assignee, or other similar representative thereof.

Foreign air carrier—any person, not a citizen of the United States, who undertakes, whether directly or indirectly or by lease or any other arrangement, to engage in foreign air transportation.

Charter Air Carrier—an air carrier holding a certificate of public convenience and necessity authorizing it to engage in charter air transportation.

Charter Air Transportation—charter trips, including inclusive tour charter trips, in air transportation rendered pursuant to authority conferred under this Act under regulations prescribed by the Board.

Interstate air commerce, overseas air commerce, and *foreign air commerce,* respectively—the carriage by aircraft of persons or property for compensation or hire, or the carriage of mail by aircraft, or the operation of aircraft in the conduct of a business or vocation.

Interstate air transportation, overseas air transportation, and *foreign air transportation,* respectively—the carriage by aircraft of persons or property as a common carrier for compensation or hire or the carriage of mail by aircraft.

Airman—any individual who engages, as the person in command or as pilot, mechanic, or member of the crew in the navigation of aircraft while under way; and any individual who is directly in charge of the inspection, maintenance, overhauling, or repair of aircraft, engines, or propellers; and any individual who serves in the capacity of aircraft dispatcher or air traffic control tower operator.

Ticket agent—any person, not an air carrier and not a bona fide employee of an air carrier who, as principal or agent, sells or offers for sale any air transportation, or negotiates for, or holds him or herself out by solicitation, advertisement, or otherwise as one who sells such transportation.

Airport—a landing area used regularly by aircraft for receiving or discharging passengers or cargo.

Landing area—any locality, either land or water, including airports, which is used or intended to be used for the landing and take-off of aircraft, whether or not facilities are provided for the shelter, servicing, or repair of aircraft, or for receiving or discharging passengers and cargo.

Federal airway—a portion of the navigable airspace of the United States designated by the Administrator as a federal airway.

Appliances—instruments, equipment, parts, and accessories, which are used in the navigation, operation, or control of aircraft in flight, and which are not parts of the aircraft, aircraft engines, or propellers.

Spare parts—pans, appurtenances, and accessories of aircraft (other than aircraft engines and propellers), of aircraft engines (other than propellers), of propellers, and of appliances, maintained for installation or use in an aircraft, aircraft engine, propeller, or appliance, but which at the time are not installed or attached.

Propeller—all parts, appurtenances, and accessories thereof.

Mail—United States mail and foreign-transit mail.

Navigable airspace—airspace above the minimum altitudes of flight prescribed by regulations issued under this Act, and shall include airspace needed to insure safety in take-off and landing of aircraft.

Navigation of aircraft or *navigate aircraft*—the piloting of aircraft.

Operation of Aircraft or *operate aircraft*—the use of aircraft, for the purpose of air navigation. Any person who authorizes the operation of aircraft, whether with or without the right of legal control (in the capacity of owners, lessee, or otherwise) of the aircraft, shall be deemed to be engaged in the operation of aircraft within the meaning of this Act.

Possessions of the United States—(a) the Canal Zone, but nothing herein shall impair or affect the jurisdiction which has heretofore been, or may hereafter be, granted to the President in respect of air navigation in the Canal Zone; and (b) all other possessions of the United States. Where not otherwise distinctly expressed or manifestly incompatible with intent thereof, references in this Act to possessions of the United States shall be treated as also referring to the Commonwealth of Puerto Rico.

United States—the several States, the District of Columbia, and the several Territories and possessions of the United States, including the territorial waters and the overlying airspace thereof.

Predatory—any practice which would constitute a violation of the antitrust laws as set forth in the first section of the Clayton Act.

The Declaration of Policy, Sections 102 and 103 state the guiding principles which the Civil Aeronautics Board and the Federal Aviation Administration follow to accomplish their three basic objectives of:

1. Economic regulatory control of air carrier activity.
2. Promotion of maximum progress in aeronautics.
3. Promotion of air safety.

Since the Deregulation Act the Department of Transportation has assumed the responsibilities of the Civil Aeronautics Board, therefore, any reference to the Board in the following Sections of the Federal Aviation Act of 1958 are now meant for the Department of Transportation.

Sections 102 and 103 are a preface to every section of the Federal Aviation Act pertaining to either the Civil Aeronautics Board or the Administrator. Therefore, consideration must be given to the effects of these two sections for complete understanding.

SECTION 102—DECLARATION OF POLICY: THE BOARD FACTORS FOR INTERSTATE, OVERSEAS AND FOREIGN AIR TRANSPORTATION

This section, originally a part of the Civil Aeronautics Act of 1938, is analogous to the National Transportation Policy contained in the Interstate Commerce Act and provides that the Board shall consider, among other things, the specific factors there set forth "as being in the public interest, and in accordance with the public convenience and necessity." Since, throughout the substantive provisions of the Act, the Board is required as a prerequisite to various actions to find either "public interest" or "public convenience and necessity," Section 102 serves in part as a statutory definition of these terms. It speaks, however, only in terms of air carriers and air transportation. Counsel for the Board have contended that this section, among others, permits the Board to award operating authority to air carriers and to take other regulatory action with respect to air transportation without regard to the possible adverse competitive impact that such action might have upon surface carriers.

In performing its responsibilities under the Act with respect to interstate and overseas air transportation, the Board shall consider the following, among other things, as being in the public interest and in accordance with the public convenience and necessity:

1. Maintaining safety as the highest priority in air commerce.

2. Preventing any deterioration in established safety procedures.

3. Availability of economic, efficient, and low-price air carrier service without discrimination or deceptive practices.

4. Rely upon competition to provide needed air transportation and to encourage well-managed air carriers to earn adequate profits.

5. To develop and maintain regulation responsive to the public need of air transportation for the commerce, Postal Service, and national defense of the United States.

6. Encourage air service at major areas through secondary airports consistent with local authorities when endorsed by state entities encouraging air carriers whose responsibility is to provide service at secondary airports.

7. Prevent unfair, deceptive, predatory, or anti-competitive practices in air transportation and avoid:

   a. Unreasonable industry concentration, excessive market domination, and monopoly.

   b. Any other conditions that would allow an air carrier(s) to unreasonably increase prices, reduce services, or exclude competition.

8. Maintain a system of scheduled air carrier service for small communities with direct federal assistance where appropriate.

9. Encourage, develop, and maintain an air transport system relying on competition to provide efficiency and low prices.

10. Encourage entry into markets by new and existing air carriers, and the strengthening of small air carriers to assure a competitive air carrier industry.

11. Promote, encourage and develop civil aeronautics and a viable privately owned U.S. air transport industry.

12. Strengthen the competitive position of U.S. air carriers to at least assure equality with foreign air carriers.

Factors for All-Cargo Air Services. In addition to the declaration of policy above, the Board in performing its duties with respect to All-Cargo Air Service shall consider the following, among other things, as being in the public interest:

1. Encourage and develop All-Cargo Air Service by private enterprise responsive to the needs of shippers, the commerce of the United States, and national defense.

2. Encourage and develop an integrated transportation system relying upon competition to determine quality and price.

3. Provide service without discrimination, deceptive practices, or predatory prices.

SECTION 103—DECLARATION OF POLICY: THE SECRETARY OF TRANSPORTATION

In this exercise and performance of his powers and duties under this Act the Secretary of Transportation shall consider the following among other things, as being in the public interest:

a. To regulate air commerce to promote and develop safety.

b. To promote, encourage, and develop civil aeronautics.

c. To control use of the navigable airspace of the United States and to regulate both civil and military operations therein.

d. To consolidate research and development of air navigation facilities.

e. To develop and operate an air traffic control system for both civil and military aircraft.

This section was originally written in 1958 at the time the Federal Aviation Agency was created by the legislation of the Federal Aviation Act. It parallels the previous section concerning the Civil Aeronautics Board in that it specifies several factors which the Administrator shall consider as being in the public interest.

As previously stated, the Federal Aviation Act created the Federal Aviation Agency to replace the Civil Aeronautics Administration. The name of Agency was changed to Administration in 1966 when the Department of Transportation Act was passed. The Administrator is charged with encouraging civil aviation and air commerce in the United States. In exercising his authority, he must consider the needs of the national defense and of commercial and general aviation, as well as the public right to use the navigable airspace of the United States.

Specifically, the Administrator is authorized to prescribe rules governing the safe and efficient use of the navigable airspace; to provide for necessary air navigation facilities; to promulgate air traffic rules; to grant exemptions from his own regulations when the public interest requires it; to veto federal nonmilitary expenditures for airports and air navigation facilities if such are deemed by him as being not reasonably necessary for use in air commerce, or not in the interest of national defense; to make recommendations to the Secretary of Transportation concerning weather services for air commerce; to disseminate and exchange information relative to civil aviation; to engage in long-range planning, research, and development with respect to the utilization of the navigable airspace; and to provide for improved control of air traffic.

SECTION 104—PUBLIC RIGHT OF TRANSIT

This section of the Act recognizes the right enjoyed by free people; it is a precious right that is not abundant in many countries on earth. To a person born in the United States, Section 104 is taken for granted, because it recognizes the public right of freedom of the United States citizen to use the navigable air space of the United States.

The declaration of a public right of freedom of transit through the navigable airspace of the United States has been the subject of considerable controversy in lawsuits involving low-flying aircraft. "Navigable airspace" is defined as airspace above the minimum altitudes of flight prescribed by regulations issued under this Act, and it includes airspace needed to insure safety in take-off and landing of aircraft. The Administrator prescribes such altitudes in the exercise of his safety rule-making powers. Prior to the passage of the Federal Aviation Act, when the Board was the body which

promulgated the minimum altitude regulation, the Board's position in the courts was that the freedom of transit provision relieved aircraft operators from technical claims of trespass, but that it did not serve to extinguish a landowner's rights in the case of an actual "taking" of property occasioned by low-flying aircraft. In such latter circumstances, contended the Board, the landowner would have his state law remedies against the person causing the damage.

The Secretary shall consult with the Architectural and Transportation Barriers Compliance Board established under Section 502 of the Rehabilitation Act of 1973, prior to issuing or amending any order, rule, regulation, or procedure that will have a significant impact on the accessibility of commercial airports or commercial air transportation for handicapped persons.

SECTION 105—FEDERAL PREEMPTION

A. No state or interstate agency can enact or enforce any law or rule relating to rates, routes, or services of any air carrier having authority to provide interstate air transportation except for air transportation conducted within the State of Alaska.

B. Nothing here shall be construed to limit the authority of any State or interstate agency as the owner or operator of an airport served by certificated air carriers.

SECTION 106—REPORT ON SUBSIDY COST-SHARING

Not later than January 1, 1980, the Secretary of Transportation, shall submit a comprehensive report to the Congress on the feasibility and appropriateness of devising formulas by which States and their political subdivisions could share part of the costs being incurred by the United States under sections 406 and 419 of this Act. Such report shall include any recommendations of the Secretary for the implementation of such cost sharing formulas.

SECTION 107—SAFETY STUDY

Congress intends that the Airline Deregulation Act of 1978 will not result in any diminishing of safety attained.

Not later than January 31, 1980, and each April 1 thereafter, the Secretary of Transportation shall prepare and submit to the Congress and the Board a comprehensive annual report on the extent to which the implementation of the Airline Deregulation Act of 1978 has affected, during the preceding calendar year, or will affect, in the succeeding calendar year, the level of air safety. Each such report shall, at a minimum, contain an analysis of each of the following:

1. All relevant data on accidents and incidents occurring during the calendar year covered by such report in air transportation and on violations of safety regulations issued by the Secretary of Transportation occurring during such calendar year.

2. Current and anticipated personnel requirements of the Administrator with respect to enforcement of air safety regulations.

3. Effects on current levels of air safety of changes or proposals for changes in air carrier operating practices and procedures which occurred during the calendar year covered by such report.

4. The adequacy of air safety regulations taking into consideration changes in air carrier operating practices and procedures which occurred during the calendar year covered by such report.

Based on such report, the Secretary shall take steps necessary to ensure that the high standard of safety in air transportation is maintained in all aspects of air transportation in the United States.

SECTION 108—REPORT ON AIR CARRIER MARKETING OF TOURS

The Board shall prepare and submit a report to the Congress which sets forth the recommendations of the Board on whether this Act and regulations of the Board should be amended to permit air carriers to sell tours directly to the public and to acquire control of persons authorized to sell tours to the public. The report shall evaluate the effects on the following groups of allowing air carriers to sell tours:

1. The traveling public.

2. The independent tour operator industry.

3. The travel agent industry.

4. The different classes of air carriers.

CIVIL AERONAUTICS BOARD

A rare instance of a government agency being legislated out of existence took place on January 1, 1985, when the Civil Aeronautics Board ceased to exist.

The Airline Deregulation Act of 1978 provided for a slow phasing out of its authority. "Sunset Provisions" (Title XVI of the Act) provided for termination of the Civil Aeronautics Board and its legislative foundation provided by Title II of the Federal Aviation Act of 1958. This Act is a revision of the Civil Aeronautics Act of 1938 which established the powers of the Civil Aeronautics Board. These powers were economic in nature and dealt with the rates that the air carriers charged for their services and the routes over which these services were offered.

When the Civil Aeronautics Board was created, the United States air carrier system was a struggling, subsidized collection of private companies earning little or no profit. When the Deregulation Act was passed the air carrier industry had become one of the world's most efficient and carefully controlled competitive route networks that served high density markets as well as small cities.

> **January 1, 1985, the Civil Aeronautics Board ceased to exist.**

The legislative demise of the Civil Aeronautics Board left a competitive free-for-all air carrier industry marked by disruptions in air service (especially to small cities), lower fares in high density markets and an industry of leaner but more efficient air carriers. Occasional bankruptcies also occurred.

Because the efforts of the Civil Aeronautics Board will long remain and be remembered, a brief presentation of its organization and functions is presented below.

The Civil Aeronautics Board derived its authority from, and was organized in accordance with, the Federal Aviation Act of 1958 as amended by the Department of Transportation Act of 1966 and the Airline Deregulation Act of 1978. It was an independent federal agency comprised of five members appointed for six-year terms by the President with the advice and consent of the Senate, with no more than three members appointed from the same political party. Each year the President designated one member as Chairman and another as Vice Chairman.

Each member of the Board had to be a citizen of the United States, and no member could have any pecuniary interest or own any stock or bonds in any civil aeronautics enterprise. Also, no member of the Board could engage in any other business, vocation, or employment. Three members of the Board constituted a quorum.

The Board exercised its power independently. Its decisions were not subject to review by any executive department or agency, except for the approval of the President required in Board decisions granting or affecting certificates for overseas and foreign air transportation, and foreign air carrier permits.

In general, the Board performed two major functions:

1. Regulation of the economic aspects of domestic and international United States air carrier operations and of the operations of foreign air carriers to and from the United States.

2. Participation in the establishment and development of international air transportation.

Economic Regulations. The Board's responsibilities changed dramatically under the Airline Deregulation Act of 1978. Routes, rates, mergers, foreign air carrier permits, and all other economic matters were amended.

International Civil Aviation. The Board consulted with and assigned the Department of State in the negotiation of agreements with foreign governments for the establishment or development of air routes and services between the United States and foreign countries.

The Board's function dealing with aviation safety was transferred to the Department of Transportation several years before the Board went out of existence.

The Board's authority over Certificates of Convenience and Necessity (CCN), rates, and the transportation of mail ceased to be in effect on December 31, 1981. The Act of 1978 provided that the authority of the Board relating to the air carriers filing tariffs; filing of accounts, records, and reports; and complaints and investigations ceased on January 1, 1983. The finale occurred on January 1, 1985, when Title II ceased.

FUNCTIONS OF THE BOARD MEMBERS

The Board members were charged with carrying out the duties and responsibilities of the Board under the Act and the statutes. Action initiated pursuant to the Board's own initiative or by any document authorized or required to be filed with the Board originated in or was referred to the appropriate organizational unit for study and recommendation to the Board. The Board had the authority to delegate any of its functions to a division of the Board, an individual Board member, an Administrative Law Judge, or any employee or employees of the Board.

In addition to duties as a member of the Board, the Chairman served as presiding officer at meetings of the Board, determined the order in which day-to-day matters received attention of the Board, and acted as Spokesman for the Board before committees of Congress. The Chairman was responsible for the executive and administrative functions of the Board.

The Board's staff was composed of the following Offices and Bureaus:

Managing Director

Public Affairs

Management Systems

Community and Congressional Relations

Secretary

Civil Rights

Human Resources

Administrative Support Operations

General Counsel

Comptroller

Administrative Law Judges

Carrier Accounts and Statistics

International Aviation

Domestic Aviation

Economic Analysis

Compliance and Consumer Protection

FEDERAL AIRPORT ACT OF 1946

Orville Wright, in a statement before the House of Representatives, Committee on Interstate and Foreign Commerce, October 12, 1925, said:

The greatest present drawback to the use of aircraft for civil purposes, such as commerce, mail travel, and sport, is the lack of suitable airports.

Prior to 1946, the airports of this country were financed and operated by state, county, or municipal governments. The cost of building and maintaining these airports was very high, and because of this the development of airports was slow. It was the purpose of the Federal Airport Act to give the United States a comprehensive system of airports, administered by the Civil Aeronautics Administration. Small communities which needed airports to help develop their social and economic structure, theoretically were supposed to benefit from this program.

Congress appropriated $520 million over a seven-year period to aid in the development of this airport system; however, the money had to be spent on operational facilities (runways, etc.). This federal aid program was organized so that the Federal government would pay as much as 50% of the cost and that the airport (sponsor) would pay the balance, or at least 50% of the cost. As far as large cities were concerned, this was excellent, because they could issue and sell bonds to pay their share of the cost. However, for small cities even 50% of the cost of development was too much of a burden. The purpose of the legislation was failing, since small cities did not benefit.

In 1953, President Dwight D. Eisenhower suggested that the Act be amended to include a provision that the money could be spent on public buildings (terminals) as well as operational facilities.

In 1958, Congress passed a bill which would continue the Act until 1963 with an increase in appropriations. However, the Eisenhower administration disagreed, and the Undersecretary of Commerce for transportation said that the construction, maintenance, and operation of civil airports was primarily a matter of local responsibility. The President vetoed the bill by saying, "I am convinced that the time has come for the federal government to begin an orderly withdrawal from the airport grant program."

The Senate Committee on Interstate and Foreign Commerce then stated that, "The committee is convinced that the capital investment required to bring airport facilities up to the present and future needs of this Nation is far beyond the financial capacity and capabilities of local communities with continued effective assistance and encouragement from the federal government."

Congress later passed, and the President approved, a bill which extended the Act through 1961.

For an airport or governmental unit to be available for such money, it is necessary that the airport be in the National Airport Plan. Under the Federal Airport Act, the Administrator of the Federal Aviation Administration is directed to prepare such a plan. In formulating the plan the Administrator shall take into account the needs of both air commerce and private flying, technological developments, probable growth, and any other considerations he may find appropriate.

The money which is appropriated for use is divided into two areas: 75% is distributed for projects among the several states and 25% is placed in a discretionary fund for the Administrator to use as he sees fit for airport construction. One-half of the 75% is apportioned to the States, based on population, and the other half is based on land areas. The discretionary fund allows the Administrator to choose the projects regardless of their location.

As a condition to his approval of a project, the Administrator shall receive in writing a guarantee that the following provisions will be adhered to:

1. The airport will be available for public use without unjust discrimination.
2. The airport will be suitably operated and maintained.
3. The aerial approaches will be cleared and protected, and future hazards will be prevented.
4. Proper zoning will be provided to restrict the use of land adjacent to the airport.
5. All facilities developed from federal aid shall be made available to the military.
6. All project accounts will be kept in accordance with a standard system.
7. All airport records will be available for inspection by an agent of the Administrator upon reasonable request.

On May 17, 1966, the Senate Commerce Committee gave approval to a bill to continue for an additional three years a program authorizing $75 million annually in federal matching funds for airport construction. This extended the Federal Airport Act to June 30, 1970. This program was expanded in 1970 to include a separate Airport and Airway Trust Fund.

The airlines and the air industry can develop only as rapidly as the facilities they use; the Federal Airport Act has aided this development.

AIRPORT AND AIRWAY DEVELOPMENT ACT OF 1970 (AIRPORT DEVELOPMENT AID PROGRAM)

The Second Session of the 91st Congress passed an act to provide for the expansion and improvement of the airports and airway systems of the United States. In order to do this Congress also provided for the imposition of an airport and airway user charge. In declaring the policy of this law they stated that the nation's airport and airway system was inadequate to meet the current and projected growth in aviation; and in order to meet the demands of interstate commerce, the postal service, and the national defense, substantial expansion and improvement were necessary to meet the proper requirements of the future.

The Secretary of Transportation is directed by this Act to prepare and publish a national airport system plan for the development of public airports. The plan shall show the type and estimated costs of airport development necessary to provide a system of public airports adequate for the needs of civil aeronautics. In developing this plan the Secretary is directed to consider the relationship of each airport to the rest of the transportation system, including all modes of intercity transportation.

One section of this Act provides for the Secretary to make available grants of funds to planning agencies to develop airport master plans.

In order to develop a proper airway system and adequate airports, the Secretary may authorize grants for the purpose of acquiring, establishing, and improving air navigation facilities; and for existing airports served by air carriers certificated by the Civil Aeronautics Board. Included in this group of airports are those general aviation airports, which serve to relieve congestion at airports having high density traffic serving other segments of aviation. Thirty million dollars was made available for the fiscal years 1971 through 1975 for airports serving segments of aviation other than air carriers.

The Secretary is authorized to apportion funds in the following manner for air carrier airports:

a. One-third of the funds will be distributed to the various states, one-half of this amount distributed according to the geographic size of the state and the other half according to the size of the population.

b. One-third of the funds will be distributed to the sponsors of airports served by certificated air carriers in the same ratio as the number of passengers enplaned at each airport of the sponsor bears to the total number of passengers enplaned at all such airports.

c. One-third will be distributed at the discretion of the Secretary.

The Secretary is authorized to apportion the funds for general aviation airports in the following manner:

a. 73.5% to the states based on the distribution related for air carrier airports.

b. 1.5% for Hawaii, Puerto Rico, Guam, and the Virgin Islands.

c. 25% to be used at the discretion of the Secretary.

The most controversial section of this Act appears to be a section which amends the Federal Aviation Act of 1958 by adding Section 612. This section is titled "Airport Operating Certificates." The Administrator is empowered to issue airport operating certificates to airports serving air carriers certificated by the Civil

Aeronautics Board and to establish minimum safety standards for the operation of these airports.

Any person desiring to operate an airport serving certificated air carriers must file with the Administrator an application for an airport operating certificate. If, after an investigation, the Administrator finds the applicant properly equipped and able to conduct a safe operation, he shall issue an airport operating certificate. The details for this procedure of airport certification may be found in the Federal Aviation Regulation Part 139.

It shall be unlawful for any person to operate an airport serving certificated air carriers without an airport operating certificate, or in violation of the terms of that certificate.

Title II of the Airport and Airway Revenue Act of 1970 established new and increased taxes which are imposed on the users of the airport and airway system. These taxes include the following:

1. A 10% tax on airline tickets for domestic flights.

2. A $6.00 charge on airline tickets for most international flights beginning in the United States.

3. A 6.25% tax on air freight waybills.

4. A 7¢ tax on fuels used in noncommercial aviation.

5. A basic annual registration tax of $25.00, plus an added charge (2¢ per pound for piston aircraft, and 3–4¢ per pound for jets) applicable to aircraft over 2,500 pounds.

As a result of the Airport and Airway Development Act of 1970, the Federal Aviation Administration adopted a Federal Aviation Regulation, titled Airport Aid Program. The new regulation prescribes the policies and procedures for administering the Airport Development Aid Program and the Planning Grant Program. Both of these programs were established by the Airport and Airway Development Act of 1970. The new regulation, Part 152, incorporates the general requirements of Part 151 which governed the old Federal Aid Airport Program and remained in effect for that program until all of its projects were completed.

AIRPORT IMPROVEMENT PROGRAM

Currently, federal assistance for airports is provided by the Airport Improvement Program, which awards grants to airports proportionally based on formulas considering use (enplaned passengers or pounds of cargo) and location (land area and popu-

FLIGHTS OF FANCY

Criticism of The Act of 1970

The operation of the Act of 1970 has been severely criticized because the money collected for the aviation trust fund is placed in the general budget of the nation. Any expenditures are counted against the budget total which usually has a ceiling set by the President.

Critics state that about half of the money collected has not been used for aviation safety projects but rather to make the general budget deficit appear to be smaller than it is. At the end of fiscal year 1991 the surplus in the trust fund was over $15 billion.

Legislation has been proposed to remove the trust fund from the general budget, thus allowing expenditures from the aviation fund to be freed from the restrictions of the general budget.

The Government has proposed, and will probably approve, the elimination of several airports from the group of those that receive grants under the Airport Development Aid Program (ADAP). This action has been called "airport defederalization."

Airport interests are outspoken on the fact that surplus money is being used to off-set the federal deficit rather than to aid airports as the Act intended. At the same time, airports are to be removed from the list of recipients of the trust fund money.

---

lation of the State). A separate discretionary fund also exists, but disbursements are largely driven by congressional mandate.

The adequacy of the Nation's airports and airways continues to be a priority issue. Among the most prominent problems is the sufficiency of airport capacity, or the ability of airports to accommodate demand for takeoffs and landings at certain times. The Federal Government takes an interest in airport capacity in order to meet military, commercial, and safety needs. It accomplishes this by its management of air travel through the Air Traffic Control System and by meeting airport capital assistance needs through the Airport Improvement Program.

The Airport Improvement Program is the Federal Government's capital grant funding program that helps airports sustain or increase their capacity through facility expansion and improvement. Grant allocation is based on the type of project and airport involved and other funding goals outlined in authorizing legislation. Capital grants address, at least partially, the problem of airport capacity; other difficulties, however, arise from implementation of the Airport Improvement Program.

There are a number of economic and legislative issues that face airport managers, the Federal Aviation Administration, and Congress. Among them is the notion of appropriate allocation of funds to meet national airport goals. Some analysts have argued that Congress

> The Airline Deregulation Act of 1978 was signed into law by President Carter on October 24, 1978.

has, on occasion, attempted to take too much control of the funding decision-making process. Additionally, local, state, and national goals may not always be compatible, requiring resolution at the federal level.

Congress has continued to support the Airport Improvement Program largely to meet national needs; numerous issues, however, remain unresolved. Pressure to minimize the federal deficit, as well as questions about the effectiveness of capital spending in addressing airport capacity problems suggest that increased funding for the Airport Improvement Program is unwise. Other viewpoints, however, indicate that the need for a safe and effective aviation system, as well as the need to confront noise and other ongoing problems may be sufficient incentive to repel attacks on this program's budget. Legislation by Congress indicates that it is satisfied with the Airport Improvement Program and that curtailing its growth is not a likely outcome in the near future.

AIRLINE DEREGULATION ACT OF 1978

The Airmail Act of 1925 provided for the encouragement of the air carrier industry. The Civil Aeronautics Act in 1938 established economic and other regulations upon which the industry matured and developed.

Human nature is such that not everyone is satisfied when legislation is enacted. Laws passed by Congress for the benefits of the public are compromises at best. Many factions and individuals representing the aviation industry, government, and the general public continued to express dissatisfaction after the Civil Aeronautics Act was passed in 1938 and again after the Federal Aviation Act became law in 1958. Dissent and criticism with federal aviation regulation continued with increasing force until the 1970s. As early as 1975 a law was proposed known as the Federal Aviation Act of that year. It was not passed, but opposition grew regarding the economic regulation of the aviation industry. Almost every opinion was heard—from complete abolishment of economic regulation to total control. Some people were in favor of operation of the industry by the government. Somewhere in between these diverse ideas lies a compromise.

The idea of retaining economic regulation on the one hand, and allowing the air transportation industry greater freedom on the other persisted and merited further consideration.

In the early 1970s, many academic economists questioned the need for economic regulation of air carriers. As a result, President Ford began to press for deregulation. Then President Carter appointed Alfred Kahn as Chairman of the Civil Aeronautics Board. He moved the Civil Aeronautics Board quickly toward deregulation in areas of pricing, entry, and exit.

In 1975, Senator Edward Kennedy began an investigation of the regulatory practices of the Civil Aeronautics Board and the effects of these practices upon the air carrier industry. He was seeking answers to such fundamental questions as, why were rates so high and why was there so little route competition.

Kennedy was concerned that between November 1973 and January 1975 the standard coach fare rose 16% and the average yield rose 20%. The solution to these problems was rather simple, he said. By allowing new entry and pricing freedom, air carriers would be forced to operate more efficiently, and consumers would reap the benefit of competition in the form of lower fares.*

As early as 1975, the Civil Aeronautics Board began adjusting for deregulation. For the following four years until 1979 the Board engaged in five major domestic regulatory actions. These were:

1. Scheduled operating rights and new entry

2. Charter rules and entry

3. Pricing

4. Agreements, antitrust and control relationships

5. Air taxis, commuters, and air freight forwarders

The result of industry comment, congressional study, and rhetoric by almost every side involved during the years would require a volume many times larger than this text. The final result was the Act by Congress was signed into law by President Carter on October 24, 1978, known as the Airline Deregulation Act of 1978.

The new law consists of amendments to the Federal Aviation Act of 1958. Those Titles substantially changed were:

  I General Provisions

 IV Air Carrier Economic Regulation

VIII Other Administrative Agencies

  X Procedures

 XI Miscellaneous

XVI Sunset Provisions (This was a new part added to the Act.)

In addition to these changes the Airline Deregulation Act amended certain sections of the Airport and Airway Development Act of 1970.

The purpose of the Airline Deregulation Act of 1978 is given in its opening paragraph and states as its purpose to amend the Federal Aviation Act of 1958, "to encourage, develop, and attain an air transportation system which relies on competitive market forces to determine the quality, variety, and price of air services, and for other purposes."

The Deregulation Act of 1978 caused many changes, the most important of which are briefly summarized below.

1. Elimination of most of the economic regulations which were a barrier to competition.

2. Provided for the guarantee of future air service to small communities.

---

*Hearings on Oversight of Civil Aeronautics Board Practices and Procedures before the Subcommittee on Administrative Practice and Procedure of the Committee of the Judiciary, Senate, 94th Congress, 1st Session Vol. 1 at 1–3 (1975).

3. The ease of air carriers, both new and established, to enter new market areas.

4. The protection of air carrier employees if bankruptcy occurs within ten years or a 75% reduction in employment in one year due to the effects of deregulation.

5. The elimination of the Civil Aeronautics Board and its authority over domestic routes and fares which then became subject to U.S. anti-trust laws.

Much has been said about deregulation over the past several years and much more will be said about it in the future. Many people say that it is the best thing to ever happen to the United States air transportation industry, while others take the view that it is the most disastrous.

DEREGULATION

Deregulation—What is it? What does it mean? What brought it about? How does it affect the air carrier industry? What does it mean to the flying public? The dictionary defines "regulation" as the act of governing or directing according to rule, bringing under control and fixing the amount or rate by adjusting. This definition describes the United States air carrier industry from 1938 to 1978. The prefix "de" means separation, reversing or undoing an action or freeing from a rule. Placing the "de" in front of "regulation" reverses its meaning. Therefore, "deregulation" denotes the freeing from governing rules which control the amount or rate.

Specifically, deregulation of the air carrier industry provides for the removal of rules which control the routes the air carriers fly and the rates which they charge the public. Directly, deregulation allowed for the removal of Civil Aeronautics Board control thus permitting open competition, primarily in routes and rates. Deregulation in the United States is also prevalent in such industries as trucking, railroads, communications, and banking.

Since 1938 the Civil Aeronautics Board had held tight economic control over the air carriers. It was the Board that decided which cities would get service and when they would get it. The Board decided what air carriers would serve these cities and what prices they would charge. Also, it was the Board that decided which air carriers could merge and when and under what conditions they could do so. Some mergers may even have been forced by the Board. The Civil Aeronautics Board made so many decisions for the air carriers that about the only decisions they did not make were what types of aircraft were used, and how frequently service was provided.

Many reasons were given to support the Civil Aeronautics Board's tight control. The main reason, it was believed, that without regulatory control, the air carrier industry would become embroiled in cut-throat competition which would force some companies out of business and result in an industry structure of a few large companies with a considerable amount of power. A few small weak air carriers might remain, fighting for the leftover "crumbs."

FLIGHTS OF FANCY

Economic Regulation Needed?

During the mid-1970s, Kennedy and other Congressmen started to listen to the questions that economists had been raising for many years about the need for close regulation of the air transportation industry. They argued that there was no longer a need for detailed economic regulation, if, in fact, there ever had been a need. They theorized that air transportation was like any other business and that air carrier man-

agements should be allowed to make all, or almost all, of the decisions affecting them.

As examples they pointed to Intrastate Air Carriers, under no federal economic regulations, that were operating successfully in California, Florida, and Texas. These air carriers were making large profits charging low rates, while the regulated air carriers were earning little or no profit while charging higher rates. This seemed to prove the economic theories of competition—supply and demand and pricing.

These questions concerning the need for economic regulation could not bring forth any valid answers.

These reasons provided the basis for opposition to deregulation. Opponents of deregulation said that it would leave the air carrier industry in ruin and that even safety would be jeopardized. One valid point was that small communities might lose their air carrier service. It was decided that this point had merit and therefore the Airline Deregulation Act contains protection for small communities.

One reason Congress began listening to arguments for deregulation was the growing public mood that government was getting to be too large and too intrusive.

The decision to deregulate the air carrier industry was premised upon the fundamental economic principle that the air carrier industry is inherently competitive. Congress concluded that the industry sells a basically homogeneous product and that there are no serious barriers to entry at the firm level. This reflected a substantial change from prior government regulatory principles. For 40 years the air carrier industry existed in an environment that was virtually exempted from antitrust laws. Actually, the Civil Aeronautics Board, through its control over air carrier routes and rates, was acting as a cartel agent directed by Congress to promote and to protect the industry.

In a system of limited entry and rigidly controlled prices, no real competition could exist. Over the years the Board had established a policy of parallel growth for the various air carriers, and the aviation industry market shares remained relatively constant for 40 years.

No doubt, the Civil Aeronautics Board believed it was promoting competition in certain city-pair routes. However, the air carriers had no incentive to seriously compete in individual markets or at the national level. The system that had evolved was one of sharing. Each air carrier got its share of an ever increasing population.

During the debate over deregulation, Congress found that this system created few, if any, incentives for operating efficiently and that it led to high costs and higher rates. Congress concluded that deregulation would be in the public interest.

Deregulation has affected more than just the air carrier industry. It has also affected the travel agency industry, the operation of airports, the methods of selling and distributing aviation fuel, and even the development of aircraft technology.

The debate on air carrier industry deregulation which had begun in early 1975 ended with the passage of the Airline Deregulation Act in October 1978. The case for reduced government intervention in air carrier pricing and services decisions had won.

Three major interrelated arguments were advanced by the proponents of deregulation and accepted by Congress. They were:

1. That supply and demand would be in balance; that air carrier service would be provided at the level of demand in all markets that could be profitably served. Transitional problems and economic air service would be provided for by means of explicit subsidy.
2. That improvements, which would be reflected in lower costs and therefore lower prices, would come from improved efficiency.
3. That the air carrier industry would profit sufficiently to provide for the cost of capital replacement and expansion.

The air carrier industry today does not resemble the same industry of the 1970s; many areas have been affected. The ultimate restructuring of airline organizations and capitalization has been widespread through the industry.

COMMENTS

Deregulation has been criticized since its inception. There are many opposed to it as well as those who claim that it was the best thing that happened to the Air Transportation Industry. Many of the problems associated under the days of regulation are claimed under deregulation. Regulation was criticized for obstructing creativity and expansion in the air carrier industry. Now that deregulation has been in effect for more than a couple of decades, its critics claim that the industry is being obstructed and expansion stifled. The opponents to deregulation give three classic examples. The first is the telephone industry since the court ordered the breakup of the Bell Telephone system. Telephone users now must have a "provider" in addition to paying a server. This means that one company provides the telephone system while another transmits the messages. There is intense competition for your telephone business. Advertisements received by mail and TV commercials encourage the user to switch services. Each company promises better service at cheaper rates, however, upon close examination this is not always the case. Information assistance was once provided free but now information is provided at a nominal cost. When the information service is used the dialer is asked if they want to be connected. If the answer is yes then an additional charge will be levied to dial the number.

A second example of problems resulting from deregulation is to be found in the electrical generating industry. Deregulation is given as the blame for the outages and problems in the state of California; although in fairness this may or not be entirely true. A closer examination of each individual circumstance is necessary.

A third example presented by the opponents to deregulation is the trucking industry. Cutthroat competition brought on by deregulation has turned those knights of the road into road warriors.

Summarily, deregulation in any shape or form, wherever it is found does have its problems but so did regulation. Deregulation has not been found to be the panacea of regulatory problems. Inefficiencies, many of which existed during the regulations years, can be found in one way or another under deregulation. One critic was quoted as saying "somebody is profiting and the rest of us are paying for deregulation."

Thomas Jefferson once said that "the art of life is the art of avoiding pain." This could well be applied to the present problem of deregulation versus regulation.

LABOR RELATIONS

The changing pattern of air carrier service brought about by deregulation has made it difficult for labor unions representing air carrier personnel to negotiate contracts that will keep their members within the mainstream of the economic spiral.

Unions and air carrier management officials differ in their opinions about the impact of deregulation. Unions attribute layoffs of their members to deregulation; while management says they are necessitated by economic conditions. Negotiations between unions and airline management have become difficult and many strikes have resulted. Labor demands for higher compensation have not usually been met due to higher airline operation costs and decreased profits; in some cases bankruptcies have occurred.

ESSENTIAL AIR SERVICE

The Deregulation Act contains a provision for air service to small communities. It provided that a minimum level of essential air service to all certificated cities be guaranteed. The Board was directed to solicit applications from air carriers to perform the service and, when necessary, to pay a specific cost based subsidy for the service if it would not be provided without subsidy.

Not every community benefits to the same degree under deregulation. Some have different kinds of air service than they had before deregulation. Different air service does not mean less or bad service.

Several years before deregulation, the Civil Aeronautics Board had exempted commuters from some regulations so that they could develop air services to better meet the needs of small communities.

Under deregulation, an air carrier must give notice before eliminating service in a city. The Department of Transportation must then determine if the elimination will cause service to fall below what is considered essential for the community in order for it to have access to the national air transportation system. If it is determined that the city would be left without essential air service, the Department of Transportation may require the air carrier to continue service to that city until a replacement is found. In nearly every case so far, commuter air carriers have been eager to serve the city and to do so without the benefit of subsidy. In very few cases is subsidy being provided. For example, in Jamestown, North Dakota, Northwest Airlines was providing one flight each day using large jet aircraft. When Northwest gave notice of its intention to vacate Jamestown, the Board determined that essential air service to that town would be two flights a day westward to Bismark and two flights eastward to Minneapolis. Air Wisconsin replaced Northwest with three daily flights to Minneapolis and two to Bismark using a 19-seat aircraft on a non-subsidized basis. In the first month of the new service traffic doubled. This illustrates that the flexibility of frequent flights with small aircraft very often serves the need of the small town better than one flight a day using large aircraft.

In Providence, Rhode Island, American Airlines moved out; but TWA, Air New England, and Pilgrim moved in. Providence soon set a record for passenger boardings. This evidence indicates that if a market exists and the community responds, air service will be provided.

AIRPORTS

Deregulation has caused problems not only in the air carrier industry; it has also brought about massive difficulties with airport facilities. Due to the route freedom allowed by deregulation, air carriers found it difficult to obtain airport terminal facilities for loading and unloading passengers and cargo. It may be that airport space will come to dictate air carrier operations at all major cities and many other cities as well.

The established air carriers have made large investments to expand their terminal facilities and are now being challenged by new companies whose equal access is provided for by law under deregulation. The problem is complicated by the trend to reduce federal funds for building and expanding airport facilities. Airport authorities will have to devise standards for the utilization of airport terminals.

The Federal Government operates Washington National Airport through the Federal Aviation Administration, and it has taken the lead in devising new procedures for allocating airport "slots" after the air carriers serving the airport and others who wanted to do so were unable to negotiate a satisfactory solution.

Other airport problems brought about by deregulation are: increased noise from aircraft and highway traffic, increased road congestion, and airport parking limitations. Section 105 of the Federal Aviation Act of 1958 was amended by the Airline Deregulation Act of 1978. It prohibits any attempt by a local airport or government to control the markets served by the airport.

Some new airport leases may contain provisions allowing the airports to buy back underutilized areas and reassign them to other air carriers who have a greater demand. This would assure more efficient use of gates and other terminal facilities. New leases at Miami International Airport, for example, allow the air carriers a preferential, but not nonexclusive, right to the use of gate space.

POSTAL SERVICE

When the Civil Aeronautics Board ceased to exist on January 1, 1985, its authority over the mail rate also ceased. From that time on, it has been the responsibility of the U.S. Postal Service to determine the rates to be paid air carriers for transporting the mail. This has been accomplished by competitive bidding, and the Postal Service contracts for air transportation when and where it is needed.

This change has had the largest effect on the air carriers. Historically, the Civil Aeronautics Board has used airmail rates as a method of subsidizing some air carriers. The Postal Service has no interest in subsidizing air carriers.

INTERNATIONAL

The United States Government, together with other governments, has begun to question the conventional system of international and foreign air transportation

and to suggest that a competitive system would lead to a healthier industry.

Domestically, the competition encouraged by deregulation has led to a realignment of the industry. Internationally, the elimination of restrictions on competition should also lead to greater efficiency and traveler benefits. However, few countries appear willing to change as the U.S. has, opting for a competitive regime including multiple designations, dual disapproval pricing, and third country matching.

Pro-competition policies have been endorsed by the Congress and the President in the International Air Transportation Competition Act passed on February 15, 1980. This Act encourages pro-competitive arrangements. It dictates a resolute yet flexible approach to bilateral negotiation. The Act's Declaration of Policy states that the U.S. shall consider in the public interest the placement of maximum reliance on competitive market forces. The U.S. recognizes that there are substantial differences between countries and markets. For example, the grounds upon which the U.S. is willing to compromise with a small and/or isolated country may differ substantially from what might be considered liberalization by a large country even though the air route from each country to the U.S. is the same or very similar. Domestic flexibility in pricing and freedom of entry and exit have permeated the international scene which now appears to be more open minded toward a competitive system. The U.S. has negotiated more liberal agreements with a number of countries and has achieved liberalization with others. As a result, increased rate competition in international markets has been achieved and the public has benefited. The entire structure of international aviation fares has been made more complicated by the newly negotiated bilateral agreements.

Some important markets are still restricted. The U.S. will have to continue to negotiate for more liberal agreements to bring the benefits of competition to more international travelers. The bilateral agreements that were negotiated before deregulation exchanged route rights for route rights. The new agreements give foreign air carriers route rights in exchange for foreign market access by U.S. carriers. Market access is difficult to enforce because foreign countries may seek to deny the U.S. air carriers' rights indirectly through intimidation—making the other country's breach of the bilateral agreement more difficult to detect. Preserving the United States international aviation system requires that the U.S. take steps which are necessary to assure that its bilateral agreements do not become one way deals.

SUMMARY OF DEREGULATION CHANGES

1. During 1979 and 1980 new domestic route automatic entry was allowed, multiple permissive awards were made, simplified procedures for obtaining route certificates were provided, and reasonable domestic fares were implemented.

2. As of December 31, 1981, most regulation of domestic route authority expired, including Civil Aeronautics Board authority of air carrier and route selections.

3. On December 31, 1982, authority over domestic passenger fares was terminated. Board authority over domestic mergers and interlocking relationships were transferred to the Department of Justice.

4. On December 31, 1983, a report was sent to Congress on the success or failure of deregulation. This report consisted of before and after comparisons and recommendations for the future of the Civil Aeronautics Board and its remaining programs.

5. On December 31, 1984, authority over foreign air transportation was transferred to the Department of Transportation and authority over domestic mail rate determinations transferred to the Postal Service. Air transportation subsidy programs went to the Department of Transportation.

6. On the same date, authority over agreements and foreign matters transferred to the Department of Transportation. All other programs and the Civil Aeronautics Board ceased to exist.

7. Title II of the Federal Aviation Act of 1958 concerning the Civil Aeronautics Board ceased to be effective on January 1, 1985.

Congress must be sensitive to any losses of public service, the possible financial failure of any large air carrier, continued service suspensions, and any failure of the commuter air carriers to provide necessary service to small communities.

Few can doubt the economic principle embodying the view that the competition process inevitably leads to the most efficient and socially desirable utilization of resources. One fundamental conclusion to be drawn from the benefits of deregulation is a direct link between a competitive environment and the increases in industry productivity.

The impact of deregulation continues to alter the commercial aviation industry. October 1988 marked the tenth anniversary of the Airline Deregulation Act. During the decade a number of significant structural and operational changes in the commercial aviation industry have occurred. The industry went through three distinct phases:

1. Expansion (from 30 large air carriers in 1978 to 105 in 1985)

2. Consolidation (11 mergers and 16 buyouts of smaller regionals/commuters in 1986–1988) to 61 active carriers at the end of 1988

3. Concentration (4 largest carriers accounted for 60.4 percent of traffic in 1988—up from 52.5 percent in 1978)

The regional/commuter airlines experienced similar changes, with the number of carriers increasing from 210 in 1978 to 250 in 1981, then declining to 170 in 1988. In addition, the regional/commuter airlines became increasingly integrated with the large scheduled air carriers through code-sharing agreements and/or through acquisition in part or totally by their larger partners. Airlines changed the structure of the routing system from predominantly linear operations to a system of hub and spoke. The development of connecting hub airports led to high frequencies in peak hours at major air carrier airports and has significantly increased the demand for FAA services at these airports. The U.S. deregulation experience has become a model for the rest of the world. As the current movement toward worldwide deregulation progresses, it opens the possibility of the creation of multinational carriers throughout the world. The U.S. experience with code-sharing agreements between large air carriers and regionals/commuters suggests that smaller regionals/commuters benefit from working relationships with a larger airline. In future years, the same could hold true for competition in international markets.

In 1978 when Congress deregulated the commercial aviation industry, it argued that the U.S. commercial airline industry had matured and no longer needed the protection afforded them through economic regulation. With the passage of the Airline Deregulation Act of 1978 several expectations were widely held regarding the benefits of deregulation:

1. There would be improved service to the traveling public;

2. The public would be offered lower fares;

3. U.S. carriers would achieve higher profits; and

4. The resultant commercial airline industry would be more competitive.

The following review by the Federal Aviation Administration shows the results of the past in light of the expectations held earlier. In June 1978, U.S. certificated airlines (the designation prior to deregulation) served a total of 470 airports in 48 states (no service in Delaware and South Dakota) and the District of Columbia. By December 1988, however, the number of airports served by large U.S. air carriers totaled only 232, less than half the number served in 1978. Only two states (Florida and Washington) had service to more airports in 1988 than in 1978. Five states (Indiana, Maryland, New York, Ohio, and Rhode Island) and the District of Columbia received service to the same number of airports in both periods. All of the other states had service to a smaller number of airports in 1988.

Included in the total of the 232 airports served in 1988 are 16 airports which did not receive certificated air carrier service in 1978. This means that over the 10-year period since deregulation, a total of 254 airports have lost certificated air carrier service. At first glance it would appear that deregulation has resulted in some 254 cities receiving less service today than they had in 1978. However, the fact is that few, if any, of these cities actually lost all their air service. In fact, many of the cities are receiving air service that is superior, at least from a marketing standpoint, to the service they received in 1978. In 1978, service to many of these cities was subsidized and generally consisted of one or two flights daily. In addition, service generally was not at the most convenient travel times. Most of the service was provided by local service or regional carriers, operating smaller aircraft similar to the aircraft operated by the commuter/regional airlines of today.

Many communities are served by commuters/regional carriers that operate new technology turboprop aircraft with the comfort and amenities of larger air carrier jet aircraft. With the advent of commuter code-sharing agreements and schedule tie-ins with the larger air carriers, most communities receive more frequent service as well as an increase in the number of available destinations. This is because the commuter/regional flights are timed to connect at the larger hub airports with connecting flights to many different destinations. Despite a cutback in the number of cities served, air carrier activity has increased substantially (up 26.2 percent) during the 10-year period since deregulation. This is largely the result of a proliferation of hub airports supporting carriers' hub-and-spoke route systems. Prior to deregulation, some hub-and-spoke networks did exist, although they were not as numerous as the number in existence today. (See Figure 5.5.) This was due to the difficulty of obtaining new routes. Deregulation changed all this by making it easier for a carrier to enter more markets and to fly any routes it chooses.

Saturation of the larger hub airports, and the attendant congestion and delays, led to the establishment of secondary hub airports. One of the major disadvantages associated with the development and expansion of the hub-and-spoke route system is that it has resulted in a greater number of air carrier operations being scheduled into relatively few airports. The only possible result of such behavior is readily apparent and predictable. That is, increased airport congestion and an increase in the number and length of delays in the National Airspace System.

The proponents of deregulation may view these shifts as a restructuring of pricing policy to better reflect the actual costs of providing service. Critics of deregulation may say that short-haul travel is now subsidizing long-haul service. Whichever view is held, the fact remains that there has been a dramatic shift in pricing policies since the passage of the Act.

On average, "real" fares have fallen since 1978, but this phenomena has not been uniformly distributed among all city-pair markets. Some fares are significantly lower than they were prior to deregulation: e.g., Los Angeles to Phoenix—actual fare down 30%; "real" fare down 58% since 1979. On the other hand, some fares are significantly higher than they were prior to deregulation: e.g., Indianapolis to St. Louis—actual fare up 297% since 1979.

Whether the fare an individual traveler pays is higher or lower than would have been the case without deregulation ultimately depends on: where one lives; which cities one wishes to fly between; the number of competing carriers in those markets; whether one is able to plan his or her travel in advance; whether one is able to travel at non-peak hours or days of the week; and often, whether one is willing to accept substantial cancellation penalties. Discount fares are available in most, if not all, markets. The individual air traveler must seek them out.

Conceivably, the final phase of the deregulation process may have begun in December 1987 when United Airlines announced a marketing merger with British Airways, whereby the two carriers would begin code-sharing operations in the Seattle-Chicago-London and Denver-Chicago-London markets. In addition, the agreement called for the two carriers to share facilities at the Seattle/Tacoma, Chicago O'Hare, and New York Kennedy airports. Since that time, a number of agreements between U.S. and foreign flag carriers have been proposed and/or put into effect. Most notable among them is the agreement between the Texas Air Corporation and Scandinavian Airways.

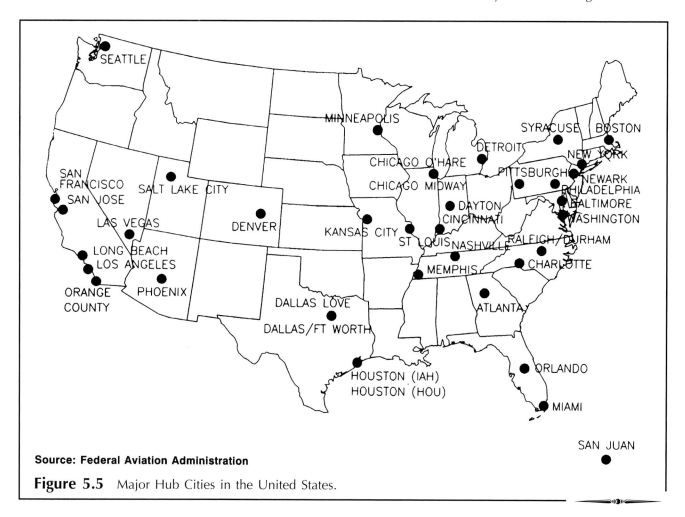

Source: Federal Aviation Administration

Figure 5.5 Major Hub Cities in the United States.

What makes these agreements particularly important is the movement toward deregulation and merger/consolidation among Europe's 21 national carriers. In December 1988, the European Community's transport ministers agreed to start freeing up European skies, a move which could possibly lead to the creation of transnational "megacarriers" inside Europe. The European Common Market became completely deregulated in December 1992. When these factors are considered along with the current U.S./foreign flag agreements, it opens the possibility of the creation of multinational "megacarriers" throughout the world. The U.S. experience with code-sharing agreements has shown that, while the smaller regionals/commuters have benefited from a working relationship with a larger airline, those without such a relationship find it difficult to compete. In future years, the same could hold true for competition in international markets.

The moves today toward regulatory reform around the world are limited essentially to commercial matters (fares, rates, capacity, market entry and frequency). There is no question that governments might relax their control over things like safety, airworthiness requirements, licensing of flying and maintenance staff, air traffic control, and similar matters.

Some countries view their airline as an arm of the state, designed to serve broad national interests. Generally, airlines seek, with varying degrees of success, both to provide essential public service and to support national goals, while at the same time at least breaking even if not achieving profit.

In a far-reaching domestic experiment, cargo deregulation within the U.S. was introduced in December 1977, followed by passenger deregulation in November 1978. In parallel, the U.S. began to seek liberalized bilateral agreements for international services on various routes. These new agreements place emphasis on more flexible fare structures, services to new destinations, direct or point-to-point service, and increased numbers of competing airlines.

In Britain, there is increasing emphasis on airline competition and in the European Economic Community a growing interest is being shown in how airlines organize their operations and the level of fares and rates. However, there is a recognition in Europe that, while greater competition is desirable, it should be an evolutionary process and should not prejudice the public service character of airline operations, avoiding any disruption which could have harmful effects for the consumer.

There is a considerable difference between applying deregulatory principles domestically within a single country and seeking, as the U.S. has done, to extend them throughout the global system. The latter cannot be done unilaterally, since it involves the susceptibilities of numerous countries in differing stages of development. Ironically, one effect of the U.S. international deregulatory thrust has not been to "get governments off the back of aviation"—for which there is considerable sympathy—but rather to increase government involvement in airline affairs.

This has come about because, where the multilateral airline tariff coordination process becomes hamstrung or inoperable, governments have found themselves getting into the details of fare and rate setting in bilateral negotiations. Thus deregulation can create a situation internationally which is the exact opposite of that of the U.S. domestic scene—more government involvement in airline commercial activities rather than less. Where there are differing regulatory philosophies this could mean clashes between governments over issues capable of solution between airlines multilaterally at the tariff coordination level.

One "spin-off" effect of deregulatory policies and the push for cheaper air travel is an emphasis on point-to-point fares. Internationally, this could lead to fragmentation of the unique interlining system painstakingly built up over the years to enable passengers and cargo to move easily and simply from one country to another. The flexibility of the interlining system also enables passengers to change their plans en route—a feature of particular importance to business travelers—and to arrange or rearrange their schedules on short notice.

The successful operation of this system requires standardization of airline paperwork, procedures and practices, and a pattern of agreed tariffs so that each airline involved in an itinerary knows what share to expect of the total fare. Point-to-point fares cannot be accommodated, it is claimed, because they are calculated with margins that prohibit any division of revenue. The challenge for the airline industry—and for governments—is to find the right balance between the demands for cheap point-to-point travel and for full-scale interlining facilities, because there are clearly markets for both.

REGIONAL/COMMUTER AIRLINE INDUSTRY

The regional/commuter airline industry is defined as those air carriers that provide regularly scheduled passenger service and whose fleets are composed predominantly of aircraft having 60 seats or less. During 1988, 176 regional/commuter airlines reported traffic data.

Since 1984, the regional/commuter airline industry has been in a period of transition. In 1985, there was a dramatic growth in the number of code-sharing agreements with the major air carriers. This was followed in 1986 by a wave of large jet air carrier acquisitions of, or equity interest in, their regional/commuter code-sharing partners. In 1988, this consolidation process continued.

In fiscal year 1988, the growth of the regional/commuter airline industry again outpaced the growth of the larger commercial air carriers. Total revenue passenger enplanements increased by 8.9% to $30.5 million, while revenue passenger miles increased by 9.0% to just over $4.4 billion. For the 48 states, enplanements increased 12.5%, and passenger miles increased by 11.7%. Traffic in Hawaii, Puerto Rico, and the U.S. Virgin Islands posted a significant decline due to the cessation of operations by Mid-Pacific Airlines. Passenger enplanements and revenue passenger miles dropped 29.2% and 38.4% respectively.

While dramatic, these impressive growth statistics belie the depth of the significance of the changes that have occurred within the industry. During the 10-year period following deregulation, the fundamental character of the industry changed from the relative size and sophistication of airline operations and aircraft fleets to the industry relationship with the large commercial air carriers in the national air transportation system.

The primary role of the industry, in the past and today, is to provide feeder service to the large hubs served by the large commercial air carriers. Over the course of time the scope of this role has increased.

From its formal recognition in 1969, the regional/commuter airline industry developed and grew in an unregulated environment. However, this is not to say that the industry has not been impacted by the Airline

Deregulation Act of 1978. Dramatic changes occurred within the industry in the 10 years following deregulation. To illustrate these changes one needs only to trace the major developments that shaped the industry, and compare with the industry as it existed in 1988.

In 1978, 210 regional/commuter operators enplaned just under 10.4 million passengers, an average of approximately 49,500 enplanements per carrier. Then, as in 1988, the industry was dominated by a relatively small group of carriers, generally defined as the top 50 operators. In 1978, the top 50 carriers enplaned over 8.7 million passengers, an average of approximately 174,500 per carrier, and accounted for 84.0 percent of the total industry enplanements.

By 1988, 176 regional/commuter operators enplaned just over 31.7 million passengers, an average of approximately 180,200 enplanements per carrier. This represents an increase of over 205% in total passenger enplanements, or an average annual growth rate of 11.8% for the 10-year period. The top 50 operators enplaned just under 29.1 million passengers, an average of 581,000 enplanements per carrier, and accounted for 91.7 percent of the industry total.

> It seems that the majority of the traveling public has benefited from better service since deregulation.

Industry growth prior to deregulation was spurred by the conversion to large turbojet aircraft by the large scheduled commercial air carriers. This led to the abandonment of low density short-haul markets in favor of concentration on the high density medium- and long-haul markets best suited for the large jet aircraft. The route rationalization programs of the large jet operators accelerated in the first few years following deregulation. The commuter operators moved into the abandoned markets in which they could provide greater schedule frequency more economically than large jet aircraft. Following deregulation, the regional/commuter industry posted dramatic growth rates both in the level of traffic and the number of new operators.

While the growth in industry traffic was sustained at relatively high levels throughout the 10-year period following deregulation, the same cannot be said for the number of operators. The number of operators peaked at about 250 in 1981 and then declined. Within a 2-year period after 1981 the number of operators dropped significantly, primarily due to bankruptcies resulting from a severe economic recession and the dramatic increase in fuel costs during this time. While most failures were among the smaller operators, a number of the larger industry operators also failed. However, there were a number of new entrants after 1978 which were among the industry leaders in passenger traffic in 1988.

The success of the large survivors and the large new entrants in the industry is attributable to their relationship with the major/national air carriers. The development and growth of the hub-and-spoke route systems of the majors, with its emphasis on traffic feed and control of passenger traffic from origin to destination, has changed the role of the regional/commuter airline industry. The hubbing operations of the majors and nationals gave rise to the development of code-sharing agreements between the major/national air carriers and regional/commuter airlines, becoming a widespread practice in 1985 and growing since then. The importance of the traffic feed to the major/national air carriers by the regional/commuter operators is further evidenced by the fact that selected regionals/commuters have been acquired totally or in part by their larger partners beginning in 1986 and continuing into 1988. This all constitutes a trend toward increasing integration of the regional/commuter airline industry into a total air transportation system with the major/national air carriers.

Significant changes occurred within the industry during the 10 years after deregulation, especially in the composition of the dominant industry carriers; many of which began operating during this time. Of the current top 50 regional/commuter airlines, 28 were in operation prior to 1978, while 22 began operating after 1978.

Two distinct but interrelated trends had shaped the industry by 1988. These were industry consolidation and growing integration of operations with the major and national air carriers.

Delays in the National Airspace System increased by 34.5% between 1979 and 1987, growing from an average of 5.8 minutes per operation in 1978 to 7.8 minutes per operation in 1987. Delays at many of the larger hub airports (Chicago O'Hare, New York Kennedy, Newark, Atlanta) exceed the average system delay. In addition, by 1988 delays had increased significantly at the new secondary hub airports (up 82.1% at Phoenix, up 86.8% at Raleigh/Durham) and were fast approaching the average delays associated with more congested larger hub airports. Clearly, there was a delay cost associated with the increased hubbing activity and improved service that occurred following deregulation. The question was to what extent the traveling public was willing to pay the delay cost that is associated with more frequent, lower cost flights to more destinations. Airline management found it necessary to increase published flight times in 1988, largely in response to the public outcry and media attention given to flight delays and airport congestion during much of 1987. This could mean that the industry believed that the average traveler was not willing to pay that cost.

The number of communities served by the larger commercial airlines has been halved since 1978, although few, if any, communities actually lost air service. An increase in the number of hub-and-spoke route systems and hub airports has greatly increased the number of travel destinations available to a large number of potential air travelers. Hubbing is also responsible for the increase in the number of air carrier operations that has occurred since 1978 and, consequently, is partially responsible for the increase in airport congestion and flight delays. Overall, it would appear that the majority of the traveling public has benefited from better service since deregulation.

In summary, it appears that the commercial airline industry has become more concentrated among fewer carriers than it was before deregulation. Only 17 of the 77 new carriers that began scheduled passenger service during the past decade have survived, and a number of these carriers are in financial trouble. Whether there is more or less competition in the U.S. commercial aviation industry today compared with 10 years ago, is openly debated. How an individual air traveler benefits from the changes that have occurred is often dependent on where one lives and where one wants to fly.

For years, one of the criticisms leveled at the airline industry has been that the fare structure is too complex. In an emerging deregulatory climate it tended to become even more diversified and complicated, and the passenger must be prepared to shop around in the open market to find the best offer to suit his travel needs. This can prove very time-consuming and confusing for the public as well as for airlines and travel agents. This could in turn lead to pressure for more simplicity, not inhibiting competition, but bringing it within a coherent and comprehensible framework.

Deregulation has not affected all sectors of the economy equally and has not affected all individuals equally. There have been numerous winners and losers in the deregulation process. Proponents and opponents

What Remains Regulated
• International Services
• Mergers
• Essential Air Services
• Safety

of deregulation have each advanced significant arguments to articulate their respective positions. (Table 5.3.)

It is not yet possible to make any definitive judgment about the future course of regulatory reform. Airlines, by the very nature of their business, are going to continue to be regulated across a wide area. The aim should be to encourage the emergence of a balanced pattern of airline competition sufficient to stimulate innovation but not so extreme as to prejudice service to the public.

It is still too early to form a clear assessment of the effects of regulatory reform. For the consumer, deregulation has meant increased variety and depth of discounts, new carriers entering the market, increased service on heavily-traveled routes, and increased commuter service. However, there are unmistakable signs that the initial rush of deep discount promotional fares may well have provided only a short-term benefit for certain consumers, that mergers between airlines—meaning greater concentration in the industry—are very much more likely than before, that some airlines may disappear from the scene completely, and that service to smaller communities on some of the less traveled routes has suffered.

WHAT REMAINS REGULATED*

International: Among the Civil Aeronautics Board functions shifted to other parts of the government was the responsibility for awarding landing rights and other privileges in foreign countries to U.S. carriers. All international air service is governed by bilateral agreements between nations. The agreements specify such things as the cities each nation's airlines may serve, the number of flights they may operate, and the range of fares they may offer. Bilateral negotiations involving the United States are led by the State Department with active Department of Transportation participation. When the United States secures new international rights, it is the task of the Department of Transportation to decide which U.S. airlines will get those rights. When more than one airline is interested in a new route, an administrative law judge will hold public hearings to allow each airline to make a case for why it is best suited to operate the new service. The judge then makes a recommendation to the Secretary of Transportation, who makes the final decision.

*Air Transportation Association "Airline Handbook"

Table 5.3 Aspects of Deregulation

Positive	Negative
1. Airline fares have increased at a rate far lower than that of inflation. Average fares (measured as yield/revenue earned per mile) have risen 59.8% in the period from 1977 through 1990. During the same period the consumer price index has risen an estimated 120.3%.	1. Fares may have gone down initially, but they have risen dramatically as industry concentration has increased. Fare increases were particularly apparent in 1990 according to some estimates. Fare increases have been much greater in certain markets for reasons that are not always apparent or rational to the traveler.
2. More discount fares are available than ever before; 91.4% of all airline traffic (measured on a revenue passenger mile basis) during 1990 was carried at a discount. This compares with a discount level of only 48% in 1978. The average discount in 1990 was 65.4% of the average full fare.	2. Hub-and-spoke systems have resulted in the creation of concentrated hubs where there is little competition between airlines. A recent study by the General Accounting Office indicates that air fares for trips originating at these hubs are higher on average than fares for trips originating at unconcentrated hubs.
3. According to a 1990 survey by the U.S. General Accounting Office, fares to small-city airports, long thought by many to be well above those to larger cities, were only 3% higher than those charged at major airports.	3. Non-stop flights between many destinations have disappeared as a result of the industry transition to a hub-and-spoke route system. The circuitous routes now required for travel between certain destinations are time consuming, inconvenient, and add significant time-related costs to air travel.
4. Airlines and airline passengers have saved large sums as a result of deregulation. One 1989 estimate is that deregulation has provided travelers and airlines with $14.9 billion of annual benefits.	4. Rural areas have been adversely affected by greatly reduced flight schedules and much higher fares. Some rural destinations feel that they have not only not received any benefit from deregulation, but have been effectively disenfranchised from the national air transportation system as well.
5. Changes in industry route structure resulting primarily from the adoption of extensive hub-and-spoke route structures by most carriers have led to a significant increase in flight frequencies between most destinations. As a result most travelers have significantly greater flexibility and opportunity to choose when and where they want to fly.	5. The airline industry has not paid adequate attention to consumer issues. Too many flights are delayed or canceled, flights are too crowded, too much baggage is misplaced and too many flights are overbooked. Inadequate enforcement by the Department of Transportation has allowed airlines to treat their passengers in a manner that would have been unthinkable prior to 1978.
6. Airlines have been very innovative in their transition to a deregulated environment. The airlines have shown an ability to develop new marketing tools, such as frequent flyer programs, that are very popular with travelers. In addition they have developed new and beneficial route structures. All of these activities would likely have been prevented by continued Civil Aeronautics Board regulation.	6. The fare system created over the last 10 years is confusing to most travelers. Only the most knowledgeable can decipher the system and even for these individuals there is no guarantee that they are not paying more for the same transportation as the person who will sit next to them. This situation raises numerous questions about equity as far as the traveler is concerned.
7. Average airline industry earnings, which have always been below those of other industries, showed improvement prior to the onset of a recession in 1990. In fact, the airlines collectively achieved record profit levels in 1988. This allowed the industry to place massive orders for new aircraft desired by the traveling public. The new aircraft will be more comfortable, quieter and more reliable. In addition, airline industry growth results in record levels of employment.	7. Deregulation is leading to ever greater industry concentration as major airlines fail and are not replaced. This development is detrimental to competition and creates skepticism that a competitive industry will survive over the long term. As weak remaining airlines fail in the 1990s, concentration is likely to increase even further with only a few carriers controlling the vast majority of traffic. Real competition amongst the few survivors is viewed as doubtful.

Mergers: Another Civil Aeronautics Board function assigned to the Department of Transportation was the review and approval of airline mergers. The Department of Transportation must decide if a merger will result in reduced service and less competition—in short, whether it is in the best interests of the traveling public. In addition, the Department of Transportation must consider the effect of the merger on employees of the two airlines. Department of Transportation has the power to impose "labor protective provisions" (LPPs) as a condition of the merger. LPPs are designed to guarantee adequate severance and relocation pay to employees. They also establish procedures for merging seniority lists, which is particularly important to flight crews, who bid on work assignments based on years of service with the airline. LPPs were last imposed by the Civil Aeronautics Board when it approved the merger of Mohawk Airlines into Allegheny Airlines (later renamed USAir). In all recent mergers, LPP issues have been resolved through collective bargaining. The Department of Transportation has never imposed them.

Essential Air Service: A third Civil Aeronautics Board function the Department of Transportation assumed following deregulation was the responsibility for maintaining air service to small communities. With carriers free to go wherever they want, Congress anticipated that some of the lightly traveled routes would lose service, and it did not want that to happen. So it established the Essential Air Service program, which provided subsidies to carriers willing to provide services that otherwise would be money-losers. The Department of Transportation administers the program determining subsidy levels and soliciting bids from carriers.

Safety: The government continues to regulate the airlines on all matters affecting safety. It has performed this regulatory role since 1926, and continues to do so through the Federal Aviation Administration, a part of the Department of Transportation since the department was founded in 1967. The Airline Deregulation Act ended government regulation of airline routes and rates, but not airline safety.

EFFECTS OF DEREGULATION

Airline deregulation has had a tremendous effect on the airline industry. Almost immediately following passage of the act, carriers began revamping their route structures for greater efficiency and moved into markets they had not served previously.

Hub and Spoke: A major development in the decade following deregulation was the widespread development of hub and spoke networks, which existed on a very limited basis prior to 1978. Hubs are strategically located airports used as transfer points for passengers traveling from one community to another in the region surrounding the hub. They also are collection points for passengers traveling to and from the immediate region and other parts of the country or points overseas. Airlines schedule "banks" of flights into and out of their hubs several times a day. Each bank typically entails dozens of planes arriving within minutes of each other so that, once on the ground, the passengers on those flights can transfer conveniently to the planes that will take them to their final destination. Total ground time for each bank usually is about 45 minutes.

Airlines developed hub and spoke systems because they enable them to serve far more markets than they could with the same size fleet if they offered only direct, point-to-point service. At a hub, travelers can connect to dozens, sometimes hundreds, of flights to different cities, and often can do so several times of the day. An airline with a hub and spoke system thus has a better chance of keeping its passengers all the way to their final destination rather than hand them off to other carriers, and travelers enjoy the convenience of staying with a single airline.

The carriers also found that with hub and spoke systems they could achieve higher load factors (percentage of seats filled) on flights to and from small cities, which in turn lowered unit operating costs and enabled them to offer lower fares. A city of 100,000 residents, for example, is unlikely to generate enough passengers to any single destination to fill more than a handful of seats aboard a commercial jet. However, it many very well generate enough passengers to a dozen different destinations to fill a high percentage of seats. Operating a jet into a hub where passengers can connect to dozens of different cities, therefore, makes economic sense for small-city markets.

Hub and spoke systems also have disadvantages, which by 1993 were leading some large carriers to reduce their hub operations and increase direct service. To work efficiently, hubs require a large number of ground service personnel to transfer baggage, assist passengers with connections, and perform other tasks. The additional ground personnel needed to handle each bank of flights are largely idle between banks—an inefficiency that can increase unit costs. In addition, when bad weather moves in on a hub, a carrier's whole system can be affected as planes are delayed and/or re-routed.

Most of the major airlines, nonetheless, continue to maintain hub and spoke systems, with hubs in several locations across the United States. Geographic location, of course, is a prime consideration in deciding where to put a hub. Another is the size of the local market. Airlines prefer to "hub" at cities where there already is significant "origin and destination" traffic to help support their flights.

New Carriers: Deregulation did more than prompt a major reshuffling of service by existing carriers. It opened the airline business to newcomers, and dozens of them stepped through the door, just as Congress intended. In 1978, there were 36 carriers certified under Section 401 of the Federal Aviation Act for scheduled service with large aircraft (defined as planes seating 60 or more passengers). By 1984, there were 123 such carriers.

The number declined in the late 1980s as weaker airlines went out of business or were taken over by stronger companies. By 1993, however, the number again was on the rise as new airlines offering direct, low cost, no-frills service began to emerge. The new airlines were a result of several factors, most notably low prices for used aircraft and the availability of pilots, mechanics, and other airline professionals from some of the bankrupt carriers.

Increased Competition: The appearance of new airlines, combined with the rapid expansion into new markets by many of the established airlines, resulted in unprecedented competition in the airline industry. A study by the Department of Transportation a decade after deregulation found that well over 90% of airline passengers had a choice of carriers compared with only two-thirds in 1978. There have been some well-publicized airline bankruptcies and mergers, but the big airlines still in business compete with one another in virtually all major markets, as well as with the numerous new airlines on the scene today.

Between 1990 and 1996 the Department of Transportation certified about fifty new air carriers, 39 of them by 1993. By the end of 1996 only 25 of the first 39 were still flying and only 13 of those were carrying passengers.

Small airlines can offer significantly lower fares to passengers because they have much lower costs than the big airlines. Usually they start with older used aircraft models that were leased or bought inexpensively. They are not burdened by the costly labor contracts that the large air carriers must maintain. High costs have forced the failure of many smaller air carriers because of their limited financial support. Their financial reserves soon dissipated during economic slowdown or fare wars with the larger air carriers that could match or undercut the low fare of the smaller start-up air carrier. Some of these small new air carriers failed because of poor management and bad decision making.

Several major air carriers began price wars to discourage the new entrants. In some markets the larger air carriers engaged in predatory practices and engaged in below cost pricing.

The future of small air carriers is in doubt for several reasons. In addition to those discussed above there is the problem of acquiring gates and slots at air terminals to board and deplane their passengers. The major air carriers are having difficulty competing for terminal gates at the present. The chance of a new small air carrier obtaining a gate is indeed very slim. Their alternative is to schedule at off-hours. There are many in the air carrier industry, and particularly those of the small air carrier group, who are petitioning Congress to provide government help. This is a difficult matter because the local airports are governed by the political organization in which they are located.

Discount Fares: Increased competition spawned discount fares, and from the traveler's perspective, the discounts are the most important result of airline deregulation. Fares have risen half as fast as the rate of inflation since 1978. They have become so low, in fact, that interstate bus and rail service has been hard pressed to compete with the airlines, which today provide the primary means of public transportation between cities in the United States.

The Brookings Institute in 1993 estimated that the traveling public was saving $17.7 billion a year as a result of deregulation, measured in 1993 dollars. Fifty-five percent of the savings resulted from lower fares and 45% from increased service frequency which helps reduce the number of nights travelers must spend on the road. More than 90% of air travel today involves a discount, with discounts averaging two-thirds off full fare.

Growth in Air Travel: With greater competition on the vast majority of routes, extensive discounting, and more available flights, air travel has grown rapidly since deregulation, recessionary periods excluded. In 1977, the last full year of government regulation of the airline industry, U.S. airlines carried 240 million passengers. By 1993 they were carrying nearly 490 million. A Gallup survey that same year revealed that 77% of the U.S.

adult population had flown at least once, more than 30% of them in the past 12 months.

Frequent Flyer Programs: Deregulation also sparked marketing innovations that equate to fare discounts, the most noteworthy being frequent flyer programs, which reward repeat customers with free tickets and other benefits. Most major airlines have such a program, and many small carriers have tie-ins to those programs. While the programs vary, the essential elements are the same. Once a customer enrolls, he or she is credited with points for every mile flown with the sponsoring carrier or with other airlines tied into the sponsor's program. The rewards (free tickets and upgrades that convert coach tickets to first class or business class tickets) are pegged to certain point totals.

A more recent development has been the marriage of frequent flyer programs with promotions in other industries, the credit card industry in particular. It is now possible to build up frequent flyer points by purchasing things other than airline tickets, and in some cases to exchange miles for other goods and services, like hotel rooms.

Computerized Reservations: Another important development following deregulation was the advent of computer reservation systems (CRSs). These systems help airlines and travel agents keep track of fare and service changes, which occur much more rapidly today than they did when the government controlled such things. The systems also enable airlines and travel agents to efficiently process the millions of passengers who fly each day.

Several major airlines developed their own systems and later sold partnerships in their systems to other airlines. The systems list not only the schedules and fares of their airline owners, but those of any other airline willing to pay a fee to have their flights listed. Travel agents using the systems to check schedules and fares for clients, as well as to print tickets, also pay various fees for those conveniences.

Code Sharing: Computer reservation systems spurred the development of code sharing agreements in the mid-1980s between the major airlines and smaller, regional airlines. The agreements allow the small carriers to share the two-letter code used to identify their larger partners in the CRSs. Their flights then are displayed as "through" flights rather than connecting flights, which appear lower in the computer listings.

The agreements also usually tie the regional carriers into their partners' marketing and frequent flyer programs, provide for schedule coordination for convenient connections between carriers, and in most cases permit the smaller airlines to paint their planes with markings similar to those used by their bigger partners.

All the major airlines have code sharing agreements with regional carriers, in most cases with several regionals. Some also own regional carriers outright, giving them greater control over these important services that feed traffic from outlying areas into the major hubs.

Code sharing also spread to international routes. Many U.S. and foreign airlines now have code sharing agreements that essentially enable those airlines to expand their global reach through the services operated by their partners.

Code sharing differs from "interlining," a much older industry practice where a carrier simply hands off a passenger to another carrier to get the passenger to a destination the first carrier does not serve directly. In such situations, the passenger buys a single ticket, and the airline issuing the ticket makes the arrangements for the traveler on the second carrier. However, schedules are not necessarily coordinated, there are no frequent flyer tie-ins, and there is no sharing of codes in computer reservation systems. The flights of each carrier appear independently in the CRS.

Express Package Delivery: There was one other important development following deregulation—the rapid expansion of overnight delivery of documents and small packages.

As mentioned above, air cargo was deregulated a year before the passenger airline business, with dramatic results for all aspects of the cargo business but particularly express package delivery. Overnight delivery of high value and time sensitive packages and documents began in the early 1970s. However, it was deregulation that really opened the door to success for such services. Deregulation gave express carriers the operating freedom such high-quality services demand, and the result was outstanding growth for that end of the aviation industry over the next decade. In 1994, Congress further deregulated this part of the airline industry by preempting state efforts to regulate intrastate air/truck freight and express package shipments.

DEPARTMENT OF TRANSPORTATION ACT—1966

See Chapter 6.

INTERNATIONAL AIR TRANSPORTATION COMPETITION ACT OF 1979

See Chapter 12.

Department of Transportation*

I n March 1966 President Lyndon B. Johnson sent a special message to Congress requesting that they create a twelfth cabinet department to cope with the country's transportation problems. One of the main reasons for creating such a department was to centralize, under one department, the many federal agencies regulating the transportation systems.

On October 15, 1966, President Johnson signed the act creating the U.S. Department of Transportation. He said:

The act which I sign today is the most important transportation legislation of our lifetime. It is a logical result of our nation's growth and development. It is one of the essential building blocks in our preparation for the future. Transportation has truly emerged as a significant part of our national life. As a basic force in our society, its progress must be accelerated so that the quality of life can be improved.

The old system was inadequate even though transportation is the nation's biggest industry which involves one dollar of every five dollars in the United States economy.

It is important to note that in passing the law Congress provided that it would not give up its control on transportation. The Secretary's recommendations must be approved by the President and by Congress before they can take effect. (Refer to the Department of Transportation Act 1966, Section 4(a).)

The Department of Transportation Act created a department consisting of parts of 31 agencies and employs approximately 100,000 persons. Its first budget exceeded $6.5 billion. The bill that created the DOT is known as Public Law 89-670, 89th Congress, H.R. 15963.

The purposes of the Act are stated in Section 2; that Congress established a Department of Transportation in the public interest to:

1. Assure the coordinated, effective administration of the transportation programs of the Federal Government.
2. Facilitate the development and improvement of transportation service.
3. Encourage government, carrier, labor, and others to cooperate in achieving transportation objectives.
4. Stimulate technological advances.
5. Provide general leadership.
6. Recommend policies and programs to the President and the Congress.

The goals of the U.S. Department of Transportation are:

1. To ensure the safety of all forms of transportation.
2. To protect the interest of consumers.
3. To conduct planning and research for the future.
4. To help cities and states meet their local transportation needs.

---

*For current information go to the Website at http.www.//dot.gov

The official seal of the Department of Transportation is described as a white abstract triskelion figure signifying motion appears within a circular blue field. The figure is symmetrical. The three branches of the figure curve outward in a counter-clockwise direction, each tapering almost to a point at the edge of the field. Surrounding the blue circle is a circular ring of letters. The upper half of the ring shows the words "Department of Transportation." The lower half of the ring shows the words "United States of America."

HISTORY

The Department of Transportation (DOT) was established by an act of Congress, signed into law by President Lyndon B. Johnson on October 15, 1966. Its first secretary, Alan S. Boyd, took office on January 16, 1967. The department's first official day of operation was April 1, 1967.

The mission of the DOT, a cabinet-level executive department of the United States government, is to develop and coordinate policies that will provide an efficient and economical national transportation system, with due regard for need, the environment, and the national defense. It is the primary agency in the federal government with the responsibility for shaping and administering policies and programs to protect and enhance the safety, adequacy, and efficiency of the transportation system and services.

The Department of Transportation contains the Office of the Secretary and twelve individual operating administrations: the United States Coast Guard, the Federal Aviation Administration, the Federal Highway Administration, the Federal Motor Carrier Safety Administration, the Federal Railroad Administration, the National Highway Traffic Safety Administration, the Federal Transit Administration, the Maritime Administration, the Saint Lawrence Seaway Development Corporation, the Research and Special Programs Administration, and the Bureau of Transportation Statistics, each headed by a presidential appointee, and the Transportation Administrative Services Center (TASC), and the Surface Transportation Board, an independent adjudicatory body administratively housed within the Department.

From its inception the United States government has wrestled with its role in developing transportation infrastructure and transportation policy. Often, the result has been confusion and needless complexity, leading to an overabundance of aid for some means of transportation and inadequate support for others. The law that established a cabinet-level Department of Transportation did not pass Congress until ninety-two years after one was first introduced. Lyndon Johnson called it "the most important transportation legislation of our lifetime . . . one of the essential building blocks in our preparation for the future. . . ."

Passage of the Department of Transportation enabling act in 1966 fulfilled a dream at least as old as that of Thomas Jefferson's Treasure secretary, Albert Gallatin. Even before that, the Coast Guard and the Army Corps of Engineers had helped to foster trade and transportation. To enhance the prosperity of struggling new states and to fulfill the need for rapid, simple, and accessible transportation, Gallatin recommended in 1808 that the federal government subsidize such internal improvements as the National Road.

Before he left office in June 1965, Najeeb Halaby, administrator of the independent Federal Aviation Agency (as it was then), proposed the idea of a cabinet-level Department of Transportation to Johnson administration planners. He argued that the department should assume the functions then under the authority of the under secretary of commerce for transportation. More-

Table 6.1   Secretaries of the Department of Transportation

Secretaries	(dates in office)
Alan S. Boyd	1967–1969
John A. Volpe	1969–1973
Claude S. Brinegar	1973–1975
William T. Coleman	1975–1977
Brockman Adams	1977–1979
Neil Goldschmidt	1979–1981
Andrew L. Lewis, Jr.	1981–1983
Elizabeth H. Dole	1983–1987
James H. Burnley	1987–1989
Samuel K. Skinner	1989–1991
Andrew H. Card	1992–1993
Federico F. Peña	1993–1997
Rodney E. Slater	1997–2001
Norman Y. Mineta	2001–

over, he recommended that the Federal Aviation Agency become part of that department. As he later wrote, "I guess I was a rarity—an independent agency head proposing to become less independent."

Frustrated because he thought the Defense Department had locked the Federal Aviation Agency out of the administration's supersonic transport decision-making, Halaby decided that a Department of Transportation was essential to secure decisive transportation policy development. After four and a half years as administrator, he concluded that the agency could do a better job as part of an executive department that incorporated other government transportation programs. "One looks in vain," he wrote Johnson, "for a point of responsibility below the President capable of taking an evenhanded, comprehensive, authoritarian approach to the development of transportation policies or even able to assure reasonable coordination and balance among the various transportation programs of the government."

Charles Schultze, director of the Bureau of the Budget, and Joseph A. Califano, Jr., special assistant to the president, pushed for the new department. They urged Boyd, then under secretary of commerce for transportation, to explore the prospects of having a transportation department initiative prepared as part of Johnson's 1966 legislative program. On October 22, 1965, the Boyd Task Force submitted recommendations that advocated establishing a Department of Transportation that would include the Federal Aviation Agency, the Bureau of Public Roads, the Coast Guard, the Saint Lawrence Seaway Development Corporation, the Great Lakes Pilotage Association, the Car Service Division of the Interstate Commerce Commission, the subsidy function of the Civil Aeronautics Board, and the Panama Canal.

With modifications, Johnson agreed, and on March 6, 1966 he sent Congress a bill to establish a Department. The new agency would coordinate and effectively manage transportation programs, provide leadership in the resolution of transportation problems, and develop national transportation policies and programs. The department would accomplish this mission under the leadership of a secretary, an under secretary, and four staff assistant secretaries whose functions, though unspecified, expedited the line authority between the secretary and under secretary and the heads of the operating administrations.

With the proposed legislation Johnson sent Congress a carefully worded message recommending that it enact the bill as part of his attempt to improve public safety and accessibility. Johnson recognized the dilemma the American transportation system faced. While it was the best-developed system in the world,

it wasted lives and resources and had proved incapable of meeting the needs of the time. "America today lacks a coordinated transportation system that permits travelers and goods to move conveniently and efficiently from one means of transportation to another, using the best characteristics of each." Johnson maintained that an up-to-date transportation system was essential to the national economic health and well-being, including employment, standard of living, accessibility, and the national defense.

After much compromise with a Congress that was jealous of its constitutional power of the purse and its relationship with the older bureaucracies, Johnson signed into law the Department of Transportation enabling act on October 15, 1966. Compromise made the final version of the bill less than what the White House wanted. Nevertheless, it was a significant move forward, producing the most sweeping reorganization of the federal government since the National Security Act of 1947.

On April 1, 1967 the Department opened for business, celebrating the "Pageant of Transportation" five and a half months after Johnson had signed the enabling legislation. Dignitaries from the department, the Smithsonian Institution, the transportation industry, and the public gathered for ceremonies on the Mall celebrating the start of the new department. Alan S. Boyd, named by Johnson as its first secretary, guaranteed that the new department would "make transportation more efficient, more economical, more expeditious and more socially responsible."

By April 1, this newest cabinet-level department was suddenly the fourth largest, with a blueprint of organization, an order providing for essential authorizations, and several leading officials on the job. It brought under one roof more than thirty transportation agencies and functions scattered throughout the government and about ninety-five thousand employees, most of whom had been with the Federal Aviation Agency, the Coast Guard, and the Bureau of Public Roads.

To Alan S. Boyd, the former Civil Aeronautics Board chairman and under secretary of commerce for transportation, fell the challenge of setting up the new department: structuring it around Congress's recommendations in the enabling act, organizing it, and setting it in motion. The new secretary faced a host of problems: creating his own immediate office, providing appropriate missions for his assistant secretaries, building the new Federal Highway Administration and the Federal Railroad Administration, helping to start the National Transportation Safety Board, and setting up an organization and management plan for the entire department.

Acknowledging the connection between transportation systems and the needs of urban areas, the White House drafted a plan to transfer urban mass transit functions to the Department that formerly resided in the Department of Housing and Urban Development (HUD). As mandated by the Department of Transportation Act, Johnson directed the secretaries of housing and urban development and transportation to inform Congress where the most "logical and efficient organization and location of urban mass transportation functions within the Executive Branch" would be. When this failed to resolve the issue, Johnson transferred most of HUD's mass transit capacity to the DOT, effective July 1, 1968. Responsibility for these programs resided in the newly established Urban Mass Transportation Administration (now the Federal Transit Administration).

By the conclusion of Boyd's administration, the department embraced the Coast Guard, the renamed Federal Aviation Administration, the Federal Highway Administration, the Federal Railroad Administration, the Saint Lawrence Seaway Development Corporation, the Urban Mass Transportation Administration, and, tangentially, the National Transportation Safety Board. Boyd's most significant achievement was to organize the department and to get it operating as a constructive governmental entity.

During his first administration, Richard M. Nixon presided over several transportation-related matters, including the bailout of the Penn Central Railroad, the launching of Amtrak, and the attempted extension of federal support for supersonic transport. He nominated as his secretary of transportation the moderate, thrice-elected governor of Massachusetts, John A. Volpe. A modern Horatio Alger, Volpe headed a construction firm that built hospitals, schools, shopping centers, public buildings, and military installations along the Eastern Seaboard and in other parts of the country. In 1968, the former federal highway administrator had been a rumored vice presidential nominee—until Maryland governor Spiro Agnew received the nod.

In 1970, the Highway Safety Act authorized the establishment of the National Highway Traffic Safety Administration. Although the law added somewhat to the department's safety mission, the Federal Highway Administration originally had handled most of the functions that the new agency assumed. Besides establishing another operating administration and adding to the secretary's span of control and coordination workload, the Highway Safety Act separated highway administration into two parts: design, construction, and maintenance on the one hand; and highway and automobile safety on the other. Such organization ran counter to

the original Departmental organizing concept for the various modes of transportation: unlike the Coast Guard and the Federal Aviation Administration, for example, the Federal Highway Administration no longer bore responsibility both for facilities and infrastructure and for safety programs.

Volpe gave highest priority to coordinating the missions of the diverse agencies placed under the department's umbrella and developing a "balanced" transportation policy. Symbolic of this effort was the establishment of the Transportation Systems Center in Cambridge, Massachusetts. He thought that he had effectively begun to coordinate separate agencies, each of which had its own constituencies on Capitol Hill, in industry, and among the public. For years, these agencies had acted autonomously and with little coordination or teamwork among themselves. Volpe believed he had begun to forge them into a united transportation agency.

During Volpe's tenure the Department assumed a higher profile in resolving national transportation problems. These included airline hijackings, the sick-out of the fledgling Professional Air Traffic Controllers Organization, the decision to end federal support for production of the supersonic transport and to handle applications for Concorde landing slots, the financial insolvency of the Penn Central Railroad and the creation of Amtrak, and the Coast Guard's handling of the case of the defection of the Lithuanian seaman Simas Kudirka.

On December 6, 1972, Nixon named Dr. Claude S. Brinegar to succeed Volpe. Brinegar, a senior vice president of the Los Angeles-based Union Oil Company, had a Ph.D. in economic research and was a self-styled "non-political" professional manager. Reserved in management style and pragmatic in political philosophy, Brinegar successfully steered the department through Watergate and the energy crisis of 1973–1974. Moreover, he charted the Administration's response to the "Northeast Rail Crisis," the Regional Rail Reorganization Act of 1973, and at the urging of Congress, drafted a written *National Transportation Policy* in March 1974.

When Gerald R. Ford, Nixon's successor, decided to run for president in his own right, Brinegar indicated that he had no wish to join the campaign. He returned to California, and Ford named William T. Coleman, Jr., to succeed him. Coleman had served on several airline and transit boards, including the Southeastern Pennsylvania Transportation Authority, Philadelphia's transit system. Coleman was a distinguished lawyer who, with Thurgood Marshall, had played a major role in landmark civil rights cases, including Brown v. the Board of Education of Topeka, which ended de jure school segregation in 1954. Later, Coleman met and impressed Ford, when the then-House Minority Leader served on the Warren Commission investigating the assassination of John F. Kennedy; Coleman was senior consultant and assistant counsel to the commission. During Coleman's tenure, on April 1, 1975, Congress granted the National Transportation Safety Board, which had been established within the Department, its independence from the department. On the other hand, Coleman delineated a *Statement on National Transportation Policy* in September 1975 and *National Transportation Trends and Choices* in January 1977, which, while set aside by his immediate successor, "used the knowledge of the past to look into the future" and "to creat[e] a planning and decisionmaking framework to guide that future."

Ford lost the election of 1976 to Jimmy Carter, the former governor of Georgia. For secretary of transportation, Carter chose Brock Adams, a six-term member of the House of Representatives from Washington. Adams, a leading authority on transportation matters in the House, had been Brinegar's nemesis and the primary author of the legislation that reorganized the bankrupt northeastern rail lines into the government-backed Conrail system.

Adams's establishment of the Research and Special Programs Administration (RSPA), on September 23, 1977, was a significant institutional development. When Adams created RSPA, he combined the Transportation Systems Center, the hazardous materials transportation and pipeline safety programs, and diverse program activities from the Office of the Secretary that did not readily fit in any of the existing operating administrations. The establishment of the RSPA set a precedent in that it was a creation of the secretary, not Congress. (Passage of the Pipeline Safety Act of 1992 gave RSPA equal statutory standing with the other operating administrations.) RSPA simultaneously moved crosscutting research and development pursuits from the Office of the Secretary to an autonomous operating administration.

During Adams's administration, the Inspectors General Act of 1978 established for the department, and most other executive agencies as well, an inspector general, appointed by the president and confirmed by the Senate. The mission of the inspector general was to help the secretary cope with waste, fraud, and abuse. Although housed in the department and given the rank of assistant secretary, the inspector general was generally autonomous.

Before leaving office, Adams recommended that the Federal Highway Administration and the Urban Mass Transportation Administration be reorganized into a Surface Transportation Administration, an idea to which James Burnley and Federico Peña would later return. Adams was succeeded by Neil E. Goldschmidt, mayor of Portland, Oregon, since 1972, and later president of the United States Conference of Mayors. Meanwhile, legislative triumphs in transportation deregulation included the Railroad Regulatory Act (better known as the Staggers Rail Act), the Truck Regulatory Reform Act, the International Airlines Reform Act, and the Household Goods Regulatory Reform Act.

Goldschmidt expressed an interest in government industrial policy, an early example of which was the Chrysler Corporation Assistance Program, worked out largely by the Treasury Department. When Congress drafted the Chrysler Loan Guarantee Act of 1979, he began a review of the automobile industry's problems. Goldschmidt also established the Office of Small and Disadvantaged Business Utilization in the Office of the Secretary. It was responsible for carrying out policies and procedures consistent with federal statutes to provide guidance for minority, women-owned, and disadvantaged businesses taking part in the department's procurement and federal financial assistance activities.

Ronald Reagan's first secretary of transportation, Andrew L. ("Drew") Lewis, Jr., a management consultant and political leader from Pennsylvania, successfully negotiated the transfer of the Maritime Administration from the Commerce Department to DOT and provided the department with the maritime connection it needed to formulate national transportation policy. The department assumed greater visibility during the air traffic controllers' strike in August 1981, during which Lewis spoke for the administration. After personally negotiating with the Professional Air Traffic Controllers Organization in the days leading up to the strike, Lewis forcefully explained the government's response to the strike-firings and no amnesty for strikers.

Lewis's successor, Elizabeth Hanford Dole, had been Reagan's assistant for public liaison. A consumer adviser in two administrations and a member of the Federal Trade Commission during the Nixon and Ford administrations, Dole brought to her new position experience in consumer and trade matters. At DOT, she focused on many safety-related issues, including drunk driving and the so-called "Dole brake light." Responding to a Supreme Court ruling, Dole authorized deadlines for the installation of air bags and other passive restraints in motor vehicles, which resulted in major increases in seat belt usage by the public, and incentives to manufacturers to equip new cars with air bags.

While Dole was secretary, the Commercial Space Launch Act of 1984 gave the department a multifaceted new mission to promote and to regulate commercial space launch vehicles. Because no operating administration had a comparable mission and because of its modest funding, Dole located the Office of Commercial Space Transportation in the Office of the Secretary.

The Airline Deregulation Act of 1978 and the Civil Aeronautics Board Sunset Act of 1984 had abolished the board and transferred to the department many of its functions relating to the economic regulation of the airline industry. Specifically, these included the aviation economic fitness program, functions related to consumer protection, antitrust oversight, airline data collection, and the review of international route negotiations and route awards to carriers. On January 1, 1985, the Office of the Secretary took over most of these functions, under the jurisdiction of the Office of the Assistant Secretary for Policy and International Affairs.

Continuing a trend begun when the department transferred the Alaska Railroad to the state of Alaska, the Department divested itself of entities that it thought should be in the private sector. Dole moved to end Federal Railroad Administration ownership of Conrail, finally realized in April 1987. She also encouraged the establishment of the Metropolitan Washington Airports Authority in June 1987, transferring administration of Washington National Airport and Dulles International Airport from the Federal Aviation Administration to that authority.

To succeed Dole, Reagan chose James H. Burnley IV, her deputy and former general counsel. While deputy secretary, Burnley had helped to negotiate the sale of Conrail, directed the privatization of Amtrak, enabled the transfer of the Washington airports to the regional authority, and helped to assemble an air traffic control work force in the wake of the 1981 strike. He also helped to produce the department's policies on aviation safety and security.

Disappointed with the Federal Aviation Administration's apparent foot-dragging on safety regulations, and seeking to increase the secretary's management oversight capacity within the department, Burnley proposed to curtail the autonomy of the operating administrations. A working paper recommended integration of the functions of the Maritime Administration, the Federal Aviation Administration, and the surface transportation administrations under three under secretaries, for water, air, and surface transportation, respectively. Burnley offered his reorganization proposal at the conclusion of Ronald Reagan's second term in the hope that it would provide Congress, his successor, and the public an al-

ternative to proposals according to which one agency or another would leave the department.

His successor, Samuel K. Skinner, a George Bush appointee, chose instead to emphasize the establishment of a National Transportation Policy. Skinner also welcomed expansion of the department's role in crisis management response. His handling of a succession of disasters, both natural and manufactured, earned Skinner the Washington moniker "the Master of Disaster." For Skinner, it began with additional evidence that a terrorist bomb had destroyed Pan American Airways flight 103. (The explosion over Lockerbie, Scotland, on December 21, 1988, had killed 270, including eleven on the ground.) In rapid sequence followed the machinists' strike at Eastern Airlines (March 1989) and the company's subsequent bankruptcy, the Exxon Valdez oil spill (March 1989), the Loma Prieta earthquake (October 1989), and Hurricane Hugo (September 1990), all high-profile incidents that took place during Skinner's first twenty-one months in office.

For Skinner, establishment of a national transportation policy became the department's highest priority. In Moving America, national transportation policymakers outlined six objectives: to maintain and expand America's national transportation system; to nurture a sturdy financial footing for transportation; to keep the nation's transportation industry vigorous and competitive; to guarantee that the transportation system enhances public safety and the national security; to maintain the environment and the quality of life; and to ready American transportation technology and expertise for the next century. By March 1990, conditions had persuaded Skinner that to realize these goals, diverse departmental offices would have to work together. As a result, the secretary launched the National Transportation Policy—Phase 2 under the leadership of Thomas Larson, administrator of the Federal Highway Administration. NTP—Phase 2 activities combined to help the department inventory its strengths and weaknesses and identify room for improvement.

On December 18, 1991, Bush signed into law the Intermodal Surface Transportation Efficiency Act (ISTEA), derived in part from the NTP, which provided a six-year reauthorization to restructure the department's highway, highway safety, and transit programs. One effect of this legislation was that the Urban Mass Transportation Administration became the Federal Transit Administration. The ISTEA legislation also required the department to establish two new organizational entities: the Bureau of Transportation Statistics, which was to provide timely transportation-related information through the compilation, analysis, and publishing of comprehensive transportation statistics, and the Office of Intermodalism, in the Office of the Assistant Deputy Secretary, which was charged with coordinating and initiating federal policy on intermodal transportation.

Skinner, meanwhile, had become White House chief of staff. A month and a half later, Bush named Andrew H. Card, Jr., his deputy White House chief of staff, to be secretary of transportation. Disaster response to Hurricane Andrew, which hit southern Florida in August 1992, highlighted Card's term at the department.

Bush lost the election of 1992 to Arkansas governor Bill Clinton. In a move to enhance diversity in his cabinet, Clinton selected Federico Peña, an Hispanic American and the former mayor of Denver, Colorado, initially to the "cluster group" that dealt with transportation issues during the transition, and ultimately to manage the Department of Transportation.

In March 1993, Clinton announced an initiative that the Democratic Leadership Council embraced, a plan for a six-month National Performance Review of the federal government. Following a highly successful program analysis by Texas governor Ann Richards, Clinton asked Vice President Al Gore to head his administration's effort to improve the quality of the government and to reduce the cost of delivering services to the American taxpayer. The National Performance Review challenged federal agencies to identify what worked and what did not, to propose new ways of doing the job that would eliminate red tape and improve both operations and customer service, and to think about doing their work in smarter, more cost-effective ways.

While the National Performance Review laid the groundwork for "reinventing government," the department had been responding to several congressional initiatives, including the Chief Financial Officers Act of 1990, the Federal Managers' Financial Integrity Act, and the Government Performance and Results Act of 1993. The outcome was the DOT strategic Plan, which Peña announced in January 1994.

The plan delineated the department's mission and enumerated seven broad strategic goals to carry out: "tying America together" through an effective intermodal transportation system; investing strategically in transportation infrastructure; creating a new alliance between the nation's transportation and technology industries in order to make them more efficient and economically competitive; promoting safe and secure transportation; actively enhancing the environment; "putting people first" in the transportation system; and transforming the Department. Meanwhile, the department continued to be at the center of the federal government's crisis management response team, as exemplified by its response to flooding in the Mississippi River Basin in the summer of 1993 and the Northridge earthquake of January 1994.

The National Performance Review had promised a government that not only did its job better, but cost less as well. Consequently, the Clinton administration was able, by December 19, 1994, to propose a "middle-class" tax cut, one that would be funded in part by restructuring several federal departments and agencies, including the Department of Transportation. That same day, Peña outlined a plan to restructure the department by the end of the decade. After a month and a half of workshops and discussions with Congress, the public, and department employees throughout the country, Peña announced a restructuring plan for the department. Pending congressional approval, three operating administrations, a Federal Aviation Administration, a new Intermodal Transportation Administration, and the Coast Guard, would replace the current ten. Where Congressional approval was not necessary, Peña moved ahead, transferring the Office of Commercial Space Transportation from the Office of the Secretary to the Federal Aviation Administration, and launching the Transportation Administrative Services Center to provide fee-based administrative services previously financed by the Working Capital Fund, both within Department of Transportation and to other government agencies.

Following his reelection in 1996, Clinton selected Federal Highway Administrator Rodney E. Slater to succeed Peña at Department of Transportation. The second former federal highway administrator (after Volpe) and the second African-American (after Coleman) to become Secretary, Slater was instrumental in getting ISTEA reauthorized, with the passage of the Transportation Equity Act for the 21st Century, the largest public works legislation in history. During his first year and a half at Department of Transportation, airline and railroad mergers again became fashionable. Department negotiators helped to avert a strike against Amtrak—and Congress mandated that Corporations overhaul; the National Highway Traffic Safety Administration issued regulations allowing consumers to turn off their airbag switches where necessary; and the United States finalized a long-sought, liberalized aviation agreement with Japan.

Also, in keeping with his conviction that transportation was about "more than concrete, asphalt, and steel," Slater announced the Garrett A. Morgan Technology and Transportation Futures program to encourage students to choose careers in transportation; a "Safe Skies for Africa" Initiative to promote sustainable improvements in aviation safety and airport security in Africa;

and on October 8, 1998, proposed the idea of creating a unified Department, ONE DOT, able to act as an integrated, purposeful leader increasing transportation efficiency and effectiveness.

ORGANIZATIONS OF THE DEPARTMENT OF TRANSPORTATION

The Department of Transportation (DOT) is headed by the Secretary of Transportation, who is appointed by the President with the advice and consent of the Senate. The Office of the Secretary provides staff and advisory support for the Secretary and supports and coordinates the activities of the various administrations within the Department. In addition, the Office of the Secretary has primary or sole responsibility for carrying out certain programs. (See Figure 6.1.)

The Secretary is responsible for exercising leadership, under the direction of the President, in transportation matters including those involving national defense. The Secretary is also directed to provide leadership in the development of national transportation policies and programs, and to make recommendations to the President and the Congress. The Secretary is to promote and undertake development, collection, and dissemination of technological, statistical, economic, and other information pertaining to domestic and international transportation. The Secretary consults with the Secretary of Labor involving labor management relations, contracts, problems, and in promoting stable employment conditions.

The Secretary of Transportation is directed to undertake research and development relating to transportation with particular attention to aircraft noise. Also, the Secretary is directed to consult with other federal departments and agencies on the transportation requirements of the government, including the procurement of transportation or the operation of their own transport services. The Secretary must also consult with state and local governments. Any orders and actions of the Secretary or the National Transportation Safety Board in the exercise of their functions, powers, and duties shall be subject to judicial review.

The President, with the advice and consent of the Senate appoints the Under Secretary of Transportation. The Under Secretary is to perform such powers, functions, and duties as the Secretary shall prescribe, and

during the absence or disability of the Secretary he shall exercise the duties of the Secretary.

The Secretary of Transportation is assisted by Deputy and Assistant Secretaries who are appointed by the President with the advice and consent of the Senate. Their duties will be prescribed by the Secretary. The Secretary and Deputy Secretary are assisted by the Executive Secretariat, the Office of Civil Rights, the Board of Contract Appeals, the Office of Small and Disadvantaged Business Utilization, the Office of Intelligence and Security, Public Affairs and Office of Chief Information Officer all of which report to the Secretary. The Assistant Secretaries, the General Counsel, the Inspector General, and the Regional Representatives of the Secretary also report directly to the Secretary. There is in the Department an Assistant Secretary for Administration who is appointed by the Secretary under civil service classification with the approval of the President.

The Department of Transportation consists of intra-agency operating departments. The staff assignments are carried out by the Assistant Secretaries and the General Counsel. The Department of Transportation was established to assure the coordinated, effective administration of the transportation programs of the Federal Government and to develop national transportation policies and programs conducive to the provision of fast, safe, efficient, and convenient transportation at the lower cost consistent therewith. It became operational in April 1967 and was comprised of elements transferred from eight other major departments and agencies.

The central management concept of the Department is that operating programs are carried out by the operating administrations, which are organized generally by mode (e.g., air, rail, etc.). The Secretary and Deputy Secretary are responsible for the overall planning, direction, and control of all departmental activities and the Office of the Secretary focuses its attention largely on policy formulation, resource allocation, interagency and intradepartment coordination, evaluation of programs, and on matters of an intermodal nature, which require integration and balancing of modal interests. The Assistant Secretaries and the General Counsel are essentially staff officers, having one or more functional areas in which they assist the Secretary in matters of Department-wide scope. These officials do not exercise line control over the operating administrations.

Effective management of the Department is dependent for its efficient operation on a high degree of teamwork between the Assistant Secretaries and the heads

Figure 6.1 U.S. Department of Transportation.

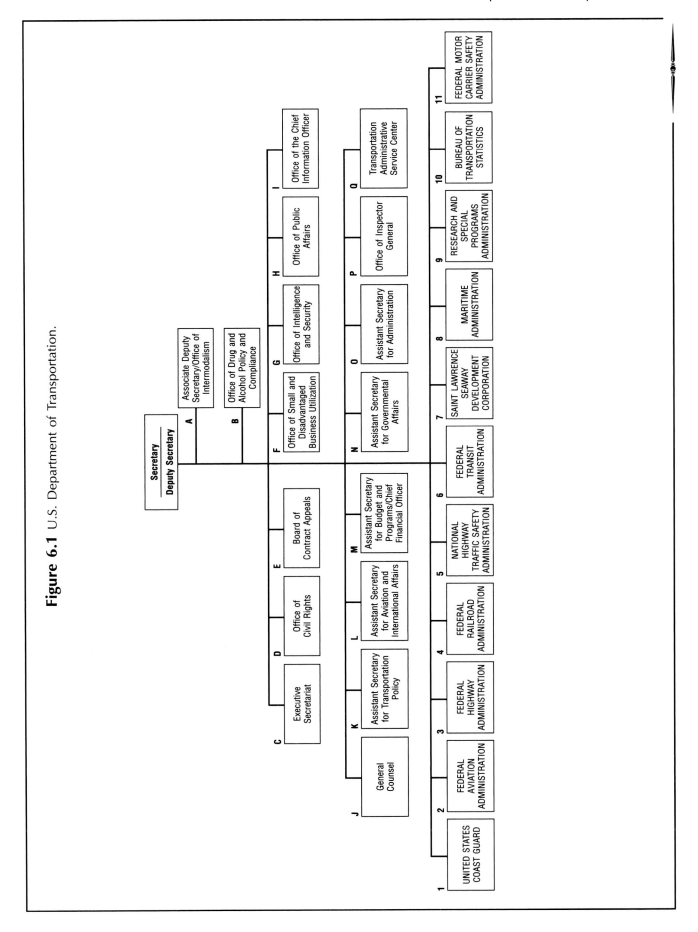

of the operating administrations. Although operating generally within the standard regional boundaries, the field organizations of the various operating administrations differ widely in character primarily due to the nature of their work—some essentially providing funds to state and/or local governments for transportation undertakings such as road building, airport development, etc., others providing a vital nationwide public service such as air traffic control. The Department relies on Regional Representatives of the Secretary to coordinate the diverse programs of the Department in the field. (Figure 6.1.)

The Department of Transportation is administered by the Secretary of Transportation, who is the principal adviser to the President in all matters relating to Federal transportation programs. He is the principal representative of the President's Administration in relations with Congress, other elements of Government, the transportation community and the public, with respect to transportation needs, policies, programs, resources, and actions. He provides executive direction and leadership to the Department of Transportation.

U.S. Department of Transportation*

Secretary
Deputy Secretary

A. Associate Deputy Secretary/Office of Intermodalism
B. Office of Drug and Alcohol Policy and Compliance
C. Executive Secretariat
D. Office of Civil Rights
E. Board of Contract Appeals
F. Office of Small and Disadvantaged Business Utilization
G. Office of Intelligence and Security
H. Office of Public Affairs
I. Office of the Chief Information Officer
J. General Counsel
K. Assistant Secretary for Transportation Policy
L. Assistant Secretary for Aviation and International Affairs
M. Assistant Secretary for Budget and Programs/ Chief Financial Officer
N. Assistant Secretary for Governmental Affairs
O. Assistant Secretary for Administration

P. Office of Inspector General
Q. Transportation Administrative Service Center

Agencies

1. United States Coast Guard
2. Federal Aviation Administration
3. Federal Highway Administration
4. Federal Railroad Administration
5. National Highway Traffic Safety Administration
6. Federal Transit Administration
7. Saint Lawrence Seaway Development Corporation
8. Maritime Administration
9. Research and Special Programs Administration
10. Bureau of Transportation Statistics
11. Federal Motor Carrier Safety Administration

Additional

Surface Transportation Board

The Secretary is assisted in the administration by a Deputy Secretary of Transportation who assists the Secretary of Transportation in the discharge of the Secretary's responsibilities, with authority to act for the Secretary in all matters not reserved to the Secretary by law, order, or instructions of the Secretary.

A. OFFICE OF INTERMODALISM

In - ter - mo - dal - ism is defined as *the use of more than one form of transportation*

The Office of Intermodalism was established in 1992 within the Office of the Secretary of Transportation and is responsible for coordinating Department of Transportation projects, programs and policies involving more than one mode of transportation.

The concepts of "intermodalism" have been applied by the freight industry for many years to provide the shipper with the most efficient movement of goods for the best value. The same concepts that work for freight have broad applications to all types of transportation.

In its simplest terms, "intermodalism" covers all of the issues and activities which may affect or involve more than one mode of transportation. It has several aspects:

Connections: the convenient, rapid, efficient, and safe transfer of people or goods from one mode to another (including end-point pick-up and delivery) during a

---

The letters and numbers on this outline are the same on the organizational chart and relate to the text in this chapter. Select an item on the organization chart, look for it on the outline then find it in the text.

single journey to provide the highest quality and most comprehensive transportation service for its cost.

Choices: the provision of transportation options through the fair and healthy competition for transportation business between different modes, independently or in combination.

Coordination and Cooperation: collaboration among transportation organizations for the purpose of improving transportation services, quality, safety, and economy for all modes or combinations of modes in an environmentally sound manner.

Intermodal Hazardous Materials Programs Office

The purpose of this office is to improve Intermodal Hazardous Materials transportation safety by facilitating improved strategic planning, program coordination, and effective program delivery.

Responsibilities of this Office include: implementation of the recommendations contained in the Department-wide Hazardous Materials Program Evaluation (HMPE), published in March 2000, (*http://hazmat.dot.gov/hmpe.htm*); providing coordination of intermodal and cross-modal hazardous materials activities; and coordination of Department of Transportation-wide outreach and data activities. The IHMP team has initially identified several short and long term initiatives to improve the Department's program, including outreach, training, and exploring methods of improving Department of Transportation-wide sharing of shipper data to better identify problem shippers and potential trends.

In recent years, people in transportation have been stressing a concept called "intermodalism." Intermodalism means the way different kinds of transportation like trucks and trains and ships and airplanes are needed to complete a single trip or journey. The radio one buys in a store may have been shipped from the factory in a truck, then aboard a ship or an airplane, and finally another truck. To get to work in the morning, many people must drive to the station, and then take a commuter train.

We often think that we use airplanes to travel great distances. In all cases, though, we must first get to the airport. That means that a flight to Europe is, really, an intermodal journey.

Many people get to the airport by driving. In a number of American cities, though, it is now possible to take a train to the plane. (Table 6.2.)

B. OFFICE OF DRUG AND ALCOHOL POLICY AND COMPLIANCE

The Secretary of Transportation established the Office of Drug and Alcohol Policy and Compliance to develop policy, provide guidance and offer consultation on drug and alcohol issues within the transportation industry to the Secretary, Department of Transportation Operating Administrations, the transportation industry, and other Federal Executive Agencies.

The purpose of this office will ensure that the drug and alcohol testing policies and goals of the Secretary of Transportation are developed and carried out in a consistent, efficient, and effective manner within the transportation industries for the ultimate safety and protection of the traveling public. This is accomplished through program review, compliance evaluation, and the issuance of consistent guidance material for Department of Transportation Operating Administrations and for their regulated industries.

The functions of this office are:

a. Provides expert advice and recommendations on policy matters to the Secretary of Transportation on drug and alcohol testing issues at the national and international level.

b. Provides guidance to the Operating Administrations in developing compliance and enforcement plans to foster consistency and ensure effectiveness across the transportation industries.

c. Conducts program reviews of Operating Administrator drug and alcohol industry oversight procedures.

d. In partnership with the Operating Administrations, develops drug and alcohol rules and procedures, and makes appropriate regulatory modifications for regulated transportation workplace testing.

e. Provides Department of Transportation regulatory interpretations, technical assistance, and information to the Operating Administrations, the Operating Administrations regulated industries, the public, and other federal agencies on drug and alcohol testing and related issues.

f. In conjunction with Operating Administrations and other appropriate federal agencies monitors and reviews compliance of drug and alcohol service providers where deemed necessary.

g. Provides consultation, guidance, and technical assistance to foreign governments and/or foreign industries regarding implementation of Department of Transportation drug and alcohol testing rules.

Table 6.2   The Cities Where Rail Transit Serves the Local Airport

City	Airport	Directions by Mass Transit
Atlanta	Hartsfield International (ATL)	Take MARTA North-South Line rapid transit from downtown Atlanta to Airport Station
Baltimore	Baltimore-Washington International (BWI)	Take MARC commuter rail service operating over the Penn Line between Washington and Baltimore to BWI Station; free shuttle bus to various terminals. Note: some Amtrak Metroliner and Northeast Direct service also stops at BWI Station. MTA Central Light Rail Line will also soon be serving BWI directly from downtown Baltimore
Boston	Logan International (BOS)	Take the MBTA Blue Line rapid transit from downtown Boston to Airport Station; free shuttle bus from the station to various terminals
Chicago	Midway (MDW)	Take southbound CTA Orange Line rapid transit from the Loop Elevated in downtown Chicago to terminal station on the airport grounds
Chicago	O'Hare International (ORD)	Take northbound CTA Blue Line rapid transit in the Dearborn Street subway in downtown Chicago to terminal station on the airport grounds
Chicago/South Bend	Michiana Regional (SBN)	Take Chicago, South Shore & South Bend commuter rail service from Chicago to South Bend. South Bend terminal is on the airport grounds
Cleveland	Hopkins International (CLE)	Take westbound GCRTA Red Line rapid transit to Airport Station
Los Angeles	Los Angeles International (LAX)	Take LACMTA Green Line light rail transit to Aviation Station; shuttle bus to various terminals
Miami	Miami International (MIA)	Take Tri-Rail commuter rail service from any station between Miami and West Palm Beach to the southern end of the line; shuttle bus to the various terminals
New York	John F. Kennedy International (JFK)	Take NYCT's A Train subway, the 8th Avenue-Washington Heights Express, to Howard Beach Station, shuttle bus from station to the various terminals
New York/Newark	Newark International (EWR)	transit connection under construction
Philadelphia	Philadelphia International (PHL)	Take SEPTA commuter rail service R-1 train from Suburban Station in downtown Philadelphia, or Amtrak's 30th Street Station, direct to the airport
St. Louis	Lambert International (STL)	Take westbound Metrolink light rail transit from East St. Louis, Illinois or downtown St. Louis, to Airport/Main Terminal station on the airport grounds
San Francisco	San Francisco International (SFO)	BART extension under construction
San Francisco/Oakland	Oakland International (OAK)	Take BART rapid transit from downtown San Francisco or Oakland headed for either Dublin/Pleasanton or Fremont to Coliseum/Oakland Airport Station
Washington	Washington National (DCA)	Take WMATA Metrorail Yellow Line or Blue Line rapid transit from downtown Washington to National Airport Station

h. Develops and maintains working relationships with industry association groups and other takeholders relative to drug and alcohol policies and programs.

i. Serves as the Department of Transportation liaison with the Office of National Drug Control Policy, Department of Health and Human Services, and other executive branch agencies concerning demand reduction activities and workplace substance abuse programs.

j. Analyzes and evaluates information and data related to transportation.

Drug and Alcohol Regulations— Testing Procedures

The Department of Transportation's rule, **49 CFR Part 40**, describes required procedures for conducting workplace drug and alcohol testing for the Federally regulated transportation industry.

Operating Administration's Regulations

The Federal Aviation Administration's rules, **14 CFR Parts 61, et al.**, provides drug and alcohol testing requirements for employers and employees working in the aviation industry.

The Federal Motor Carrier Safety Administration's rule, **49 CFR 382**, provides drug and alcohol testing requirements for carriers and commercial driver's license holders.

The Federal Railroad Administration's rule, **49 CFR Part 219**, provides drug and alcohol testing requirements for employers and employees working in the railroad industry.

The Federal Transit Administration's rule, **49 CFR Parts 653 & 654**, provides drug and alcohol testing requirements for employers and employees working in the mass transit industry.

The Research and Special Programs Administration's rule, **49 CFR Part 199**, provides drug testing requirements for operators and employees working the pipeline industry.

The United States Coast Guard's rule, **33 CFR Part 95**, provides drug and testing requirements for employers and employees operating commercial vessels.

C. EXECUTIVE SECRETARIAT

The Office of the Executive Secretariat is located in the Immediate Office of the Secretary of Transportation and is under the direction of the Director, Executive Secretariat. It is composed of: the Immediate Office of the Executive Secretariat, the Information Analysis Staff, and the Document Review and Control Staff.

The Secretariat provides an organized staff service for the Secretary and the Deputy Secretary to assist them in carrying out their management functions and facilitate their responsibilities for formulating, coordinating, and communicating major policy decisions. The functions include assisting the principal officers of the Immediate Office of the Secretary in carrying out their responsibilities and in assuring the responsiveness of all elements of the Department.

D. OFFICE OF CIVIL RIGHTS

The Director of the Office of Civil Rights is the principal adviser to the Secretary on civil rights and equal opportunity matters. The Director acts for and represents the Secretary to assure full and affirmative implementation of civil rights and equal opportunity precepts within the Department in all its official actions, including departmental employment practices; services rendered to the public, employment practices of contractors and subcontractors under direct or federally assisted contracts; operation of federally assisted activities, and other programs and efforts involving departmental assistance, participation, or endorsement. This Office is also responsible for the implementation of Executive Order 12320 of September 15, 1981, on aid to historically black colleges and universities.

F. BOARD OF CONTRACT APPEALS

The Board of Contract Appeals, established pursuant to the Contract Disputes Act of 1978 (92 Stat.2383; 41 U.S.C. 601), is responsible for hearings and decisions on appeals from decisions of departmental contracting officers. When sitting as the Contract Adjustment Board, it acts on petitions for extraordinary contractual relief under the Act of August 28, 1958 (72 Stat. 972; 50 U.S.C. 1431).

F. OFFICE OF SMALL AND DISADVANTAGED BUSINESS UTILIZATION

The Office of Small and Disadvantaged Business Utilization, established in July 1980 pursuant to Pub. Law 95-507 (92 Stat. 1757), is responsible for the Department's implementation and execution of the functions and duties under sections 8 and 15 of the Small

Business Act (15 U.S.C. 637, 644) for developing policies and procedures consistent with Federal statutes to provide policy direction for minority, women-owned, and small and disadvantaged business participation in the Department's procurement and Federal financial assistance activities. The Office is also responsible for setting the Department's goals for minority, women-owned, and small disadvantaged businesses, which includes monitoring and evaluating the accomplishments of these goals.

Also contained within the Office is the responsibility of the Minority Business Resource Center, under the direction of the Director of the Office of Small and Disadvantaged Business Utilization, established under section 906 of the Railroad Revitalization and Regulatory Reform Act (90 Stat. 149; 49 U.S.C. 1657a), which establishes, maintains, and disseminates information to minorities on opportunities available in departmental procurement and Federal financial assistance activities.

OFFICE OF COMMERCIAL SPACE TRANSPORTATION

This Office has been moved to the Federal Aviation Administration.
See Chapter 7.

G. OFFICE OF INTELLIGENCE AND SECURITY

This office advises the Secretary on domestic and international intelligence and security matters; to coordinate the development and implementation of long-term strategic plans, information management systems and integrated research and development programs affecting the security of the traveling public and of cargo; to be the focal point in the Department for transportation intelligence and security policy; and to provide

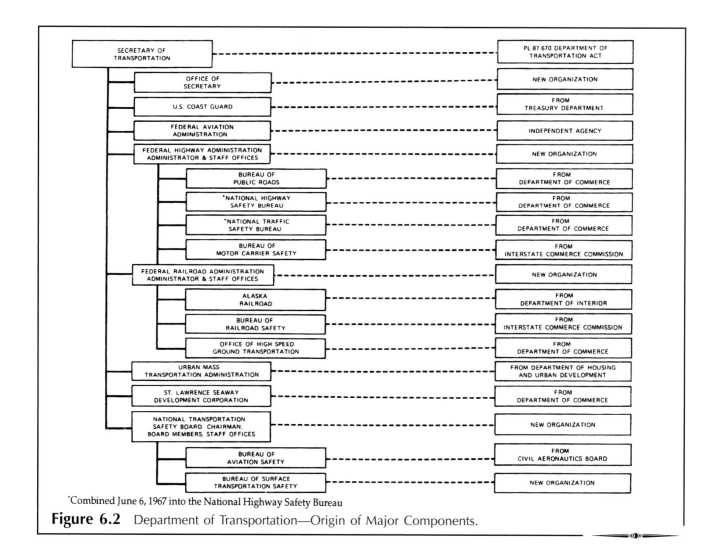

*Combined June 6, 1967 into the National Highway Safety Bureau

Figure 6.2   Department of Transportation—Origin of Major Components.

oversight of transportation security and intelligence programs.

H. OFFICE OF PUBLIC AFFAIRS

The Assistant Secretary for Public Affairs is the principal adviser to the Secretary on the dissemination of information to the public and news media concerning the Department's policies and programs. The Assistant Secretary is responsible for the overall public information program and supervises the information activities of the operating elements of the Department. This Office is composed of the Offices of Public Information; Speechwriting and Research; Special Projects; and Media Relations.

The staff functions of the Department of Transportation are listed and explained in the following paragraphs.

I. OFFICE OF THE CHIEF INFORMATION OFFICER

The Department invests more than $2.5 billion each year on information technology to help in carrying out their mission and programs. Investment in information technology is growing to create a transportation system that is safe and sustainable.

In addition to the Immediate Office of the CIO, the organization consists of five divisions:

1. Strategic Planning and Policy
2. Operations and Architecture
3. IT Security
4. Capital Planning
5. E-Government

Strategic Planning & Policy

The Department of Transportation invests more than $2.5 billion annually in information technology to improve safety and increase the mobility of American citizens. The Strategic Planning and Policy Division of the Office of the CIO ensures that this large information technology program supports the strategic goals and objectives of the Department as outlined in the Department of Transportation Strategic Plan 2000–2005 Performance Plan. There are opportunities to streamline and improve how citizens interact with the Department as required by law. This division provides leadership and establishes policy to address these many regulatory requirements including accessibility to information and systems by individuals with disabilities, reducing paperwork burden on the public and protect-

ing their privacy when citizens do business electronically with the Department.

Operations & Technology

The Operations staff provides complete information technology support for over 500 persons in the Office of the Secretary.

A central Help Desk staff and engineering support team provide full service, multilevel support for all end-user desktop computing needs. Services include:

- Hardware maintenance
- Configuration control
- Standard software loads
- Technology planning services
- Technical services
- Technology refreshment for PC systems
- Systems integration
- System security monitoring Network monitoring
- Remote user access
- Asset management
- Software distribution
- Remote desktop control
- Server management.

The staff uses a variety of servers to provide electronic mail, file and print services, internet access, connection encryption, and database hosting.

Information Technology (IT) Security

The Department of Transportation relies heavily on the use of Information Technology (IT) to conduct business. Maintaining the security of these IT systems is vital to their mission. The Office of the Chief Information Officer (OCIO) is responsible for the overall management and guidance of the Department's IT Security Program. OCIO promulgates IT Security policy and guidance for DOT. The DOT Operating Administrations are responsible for the implementation of this policy in the management of their IT system.

Capital Planning and Investment Control

An initiative is currently underway within the Office of the CIO to establish an effective Capital Planning and Investment Control (CPIC) policy and process as envisioned in the Clinger-Cohen Act of 1996, OMB Circular A-130 (Management of Federal Information Resources) and other related guidance and regulations. The overall goal is to establish and maintain a Department wide CPIC process that will use long-range strategic planning and a disciplined budget process as the basis for efficient management of a portfolio of capital assets. This will enhance the ability of DOT to achieve agency missions, and performance goals with the lowest life-cycle costs and least risk. In 1999, the Office of the CIO, in partnership with all DOT operating administrations, spearheaded an intensive effort to develop and coordinate a new CPIC policy. The DOT Council, Subcommittee For Capital Planning, is now leading this undertaking, and in cooperation with OMB, plans to have a final DOT CPIC policy and process in place in 2001.

E-Government

At the Department of Transportation, E-Government means transforming the way they do business by using technology and the internet to conduct all business processes with the public and the Department of Transportation staff. The goal is to provide better, more efficient services; make it easy to do business with the Department; and increase productivity.

This is a big goal; but they are already making progress! Here are a few examples:

- *Do-it-Yourself* web site makes it easy to make on-line payments using your card.

- *Docket Management System* lets the public review and comment on items on the docket.

- Federal Motor Carriers Safety Administration web site provides real-time up-to-date information contained in their *Licensing & Insurance* database; and the

- National Highway Traffic Safety Administration has put *recall* information at your fingertips!

The Office of the CIO E-Government Division is responsible for providing leadership throughout the Department of Transportation for the transition to digital government, including managing the departmental internet and intranet web sites. The goal is to create the synergy to bring E-Government ideas to life. The role is to foster, encourage, promote and facilitate the transformation to becoming a truly electronic department.

The private sector has already made substantial progress in utilizing web technology in streamlining internal and external business processes. They hope to inspire similar efficiencies within the DOT through the

Intranet. Similarly, they envision the DOT Internet becoming a leading on-line platform for the conduct of DOT business with the public any time and any place. They also manage the Departmental internet site at www.dot.gov and the departmental intranet. They are currently active with both the Federal CIO and DOT CIO Councils' E-Government Committees.

J. GENERAL COUNSEL

The General Counsel is the chief legal officer of the Department and the final authority within the Department on questions of law; represents the Department in proceedings before regulatory agencies; supervises legal aspects of the Department's legislative program; and promotes and coordinates the efficient use of departmental legal resources. This Office is composed of the Offices of Legislation, Litigation; Regulation and Enforcement; Environmental, Civil Rights, and General law; International Law; Board for Correction of Military Records; and Aviation Enforcement and Proceedings.

The General Counsel provides legal services as the chief legal officer of the Department, legal advisor to the Secretary and the Office of the Secretary; final authority within the Department on questions of law; professional supervision, including coordination and review, over the legal work of the legal offices of the Department; drafting of legislation and review of legal aspects of the legislative matters; point of coordination for the Office of the Secretary and Department Regulations Council; advice on questions of international law; exercise of functions, powers, and duties as Judge Advocate General under the Uniform Code of Military Justice (Chapter 47 of Title 10, U.S.C.) with respect to the United States Coast Guard; advice and assistance with respect to uniform time matters; review and final action on applications for reconsideration of initial decisions not to disclose unclassified records of the Office of the Secretary requested under 5 U.S.C. 552(a)(3); promotion and coordination of efficient use of Departmental legal resources; recommendation, in conjunction with the Assistant Secretary for Administration, of legal career development programs within the Department; review and final action on applications for correction of military records of the United States Coast Guard.

K. TRANSPORTATION POLICY

The Assistant Secretary for Transportation Policy is delegated authority to establish policy and maintain oversight of implementation of the National Environmental Policy Act of 1969, as amended, within the DOT.

The Secretary oversees the implementation of section 4(f) of the Transportation Act; he represents the Secretary of Transportation on various interagency boards, committees and commissions to include the Architectural and Transportation Barriers Compliance Board and the Advisory Council of Historic Preservation. He carries out the functions vested in the Secretary by section 656 of the Department of Energy Organization Act which pertains to planning and implementing energy conservation matters with the Department of Energy and service as the Department's principal conservation officer.

L. AVIATION AND INTERNATIONAL AFFAIRS

The Assistant Secretary for Aviation and International Affairs is delegated authority to represent the Secretary of Transportation on various inter-agency boards, committees and commissions to include the Trade Policy Review Group and the Trade Policy Staff Committee; carries out the functions of the Secretary pertaining to aircraft with respect to Transportation Orders under the Act of September 8, 1950. He serves as Department of Transportation member of the Interagency Group on International Aviation and serves as chairman. He serves as second alternate representing the Secretary of Transportation to the Trade Policy Committee. He carries out the functions vested in the Secretary by the appropriate sections of the Federal Aviation Act, which relates to the security of foreign airports.

The Secretary carries out various statutory provisions relating to consumers protection by taking such actions and issuing regulations as may be necessary to complete the responsibilities relating to enforcing the duty of carriers to provide safe and adequate service. He investigates any air carrier or ticket agent that is engaged in unfair or deceptive practices or unfair methods of competition appropriate to consumers protection functions.

The Designated Senior Career Official in the Office of the Assistant Secretary for Aviation and International Affairs is delegated exclusive authority to make decisions in all hearing cases to select a carrier for limited designation, international route authority, and in any other case that the Secretary designates under the authority transferred to the DOT from the Civil Aeronautics Board; this includes the authority to adopt, reject or modify recommended decisions of administrative law judges.

M. BUDGET AND PROGRAMS AND CHIEF FINANCIAL OFFICER

In order for the Department of Transportation to be successful in achieving its Presidential and congressionally mandated goals, it must possess and exercise a continuing capability to evaluate and improve the allocation of its resources and the effectiveness of its programs in meeting the Nation's transportation priorities. The Assistant Secretary for Budget and Programs is the principal staff advisor to the Secretary on the development, review, and presentation of the Department's budget resource requirements and on the evaluation and oversight of the Department's programs. The Assistant Secretary is responsible for reviewing the impact and programs in achieving their objectives, advising the Secretary on major problem areas that impede attainment of departmental program plans and objectives, and advising the Secretary on program and legislative changes necessary to resolve them. Important, too, is this Office's responsibility for coordinating the impact on departmental resources of legislative and other proposals, establishing procedures for development of long-range budgetary resource planning, and making recommendations on the budget and program aspects of proposals for acquisition of major new technical systems.

This Office is composed of the Offices of Programs and Evaluation; and Budget.

N. GOVERNMENTAL AFFAIRS

The Office of Governmental Affairs is responsible for maintaining liaison with the Congress, State and local governments, and public and private interest groups; coordinating matters of congressional concern within the Department; coordinating the presentation to the Congress of the Department's legislative program; ensuring effective communication and coordination with other Federal agencies and State and local governments with respect to DOT programs; working with State and local governments in identifying their specific transportation needs and problems and assuring that information on new transportation technologies and assistance on possible solutions or improvements are made available in a timely and useful manner; and, as the Department's point of contact for public and private organizations and groups, maintaining consumer awareness.

This Office is composed of the Offices of Congressional Affairs; Intergovernmental and Consumer Affairs; and Technology and Planning Assistance.

O. ADMINISTRATION

The Department's management program includes formulating, prescribing, assuring compliance with, and evaluating the effectiveness of policies in the areas of personnel and training, manpower utilization, financial and information management systems (including telecommunications and automated data processing management), procurement and contracting, installations and logistics, and security. The program also includes the provision of comprehensive administrative services and computer support services to the Office of Secretary and certain other components of the Department. These programs are under the direction and control of the Assistant Secretary for Administration, who also serves as the principal advisor to the Secretary and Deputy Secretary in matters involving the internal management of the Department.

This Office is composed of the Offices of Personnel; Management Planning; Information Resource Management; Administrative Services and Property Management; Hearings; Acquisition and Grant Management; Security; Financial Management; and Departmental Accounting and Financial Information System (DAFIS) Development and Implementation.

P. INSPECTOR GENERAL

The Department's Inspector General performs all audit functions, evaluates the effectiveness of programs to ensure uniform adherence to policy and procedures, promotes economy and efficiency in the administration of programs, and maintains a system of program review and follow-up on audit findings. The Inspector General performs all of the Department's investigative functions relating to waste, fraud, and abuse in Department programs and operations, including coordinating such matters with the Justice Department and other law enforcement agencies in accordance with the Inspector General Act of 1978 (92 Stat. 1101; 5 U.S.C. App.). The Inspector General also operates the Department's Hotline Complaint Center.

The Inspector General will conduct, supervise, and coordinate audits and investigations, review existing and proposed legislation and make recommendations to the Secretary and Congress (Semi-annual reports) concerning their impact on the economy and efficiency of program administration, or the prevention and detection of fraud and abuse; recommend policies for and conduct, supervise, or coordinate other activities of the Department for the purpose of promoting economy and efficiency in program administration, or preventing and detecting fraud and abuse.

The Inspector General shall report to and be under the general supervision of the Secretary and Deputy Secretary. In accordance with the statutory intent of the Inspector General Act to create an independent and objective unit, the Inspector General is authorized to make such investigations and reports relating to the administration of the programs and operations of the Department as are, in the judgement of the Inspector General, necessary and desirable. Neither the Secretary nor the Deputy Secretary shall prevent or prohibit the Inspector General from initiating, carrying out, or completing any audit or investigation, or from issuing any subpoena during the course of any audit or investigation. The duties and responsibilities of the Office of Inspector General are carried out by the Assistant Inspector General for Auditing; the Assistant Inspector General for Investigations; and the Assistant Inspector General for Policy, Planning, and Resources.

Q. TRANSPORTATION ADMINISTRATIVE SERVICE CENTER

The Transportation Administrative Service Center (TASC) provides technical and administrative services for the Department of Transportation's (DOT) operating administrations and other Government entities, ranging from the latest in information technology support services to printing and personnel management services. TASC is an entrepreneurial organization that offers competitive quality services that are responsive to its customers' needs. TASC services are not financed through Congressional appropriations but instead, are billed according to actual customer usage on a fee-for-service basis.

REGIONAL REPRESENTATIVES

A Secretarial Representative is located in the headquarters' city in each of the six standard regions. This representative provides a single focal point for representation of departmental or Secretarial interests in the field to assure effective administration of Federal transportation programs. The Regional Representative works with State and local agencies, public interest and user groups, and with other Federal agencies on matters involving two or more elements of the Department.

REGIONAL REPRESENTATIVES OF THE SECRETARY—DEPARTMENT OF TRANSPORTATION

REGIONS I, II, III (Suite 1000, 434 Walnut St., Philadelphia, Pa. 19106)

REGION IV (Suite 515, 1720 Peachtree Rd. NW., Atlanta, Ga. 30309)

REGION V (Room 700, 300 S. Wacker Dr., Chicago, Ill. 60606)

REGION VI (Room 7A29, 819 Taylor St., Fort Worth, Tex. 76102)

REGIONS VII, VIII (Room 634, 601 E. 12th St., Kansas City, Mo. 64106)

REGIONS IX, X (Suite 1005, 211 Main St., San Francisco, Calif. 94105)

Included in the Department of Transportation are eleven operating agencies:

1. U.S. Coast Guard.
2. Federal Aviation Administration.
3. Federal Highway Administration.
4. Federal Railroad Administration.
5. National Highway Traffic Safety Administration.
6. Federal Transit Administration.
7. St. Lawrence Seaway Development Corporation.
8. Maritime Administration.
9. Research and Special Programs Administration.
10. Bureau of Transportation Statistics.
11. Federal Motor Carrier Safety Administration.

The Department of Transportation Act of 1966 transferred to the Secretary all the functions, powers, and duties of the Civil Aeronautics Board and of the chairman, members, and offices under Title VI (Safety Regulation of Civil Aeronautics) and Title VII (Aircraft Accident Investigation) of the Federal Aviation Act of 1958; provided, however, that these functions shall be exercised by the National Transportation Safety Board (NTSB). Decisions of the NTSB shall be administratively final. Appeals as authorized by law shall be taken directly to the courts.

UNITED STATES COAST GUARD

Since 1790, when Alexander Hamilton created the Coast Guard to combat smugglers, it has lived up to its motto, "Semper Paratus" (Always Ready). Coast Guard personnel go out on 71,000 search and rescue missions each year—and save about 800 lives—and have become famous around the world for their lifesaving skills.

The Coast Guard, established by the Act of January 28, 1915 (14 U.S.C. 1), became a component of the DOT on April 1, 1967, pursuant to the Department of Transportation Act of October 15, 1966 (80 Stat. 931). The Coast Guard is a branch of the Armed Forces at all times and is a service within the DOT except when operating as part of the Navy in time of war or when the President directs. (Table 6.3.)

The predecessor of the Coast Guard, "The Revenue Marine," was established in 1790 as a Federal maritime law enforcement agency. Many other major responsibilities have since been added.

Historically the United States Coast Guard development was based upon the integration of the following Services:

1. The Revenue Cutter Service—established August 4, 1790.
2. The Lifesaving Service—established June 20, 1874.
3. The Lighthouse Service—established August 7, 1789.
4. The Bureau of Marine Inspection and Navigation was derived from several Bureaus which were established between 1838 and 1936.

FUNCTIONS AND ACTIVITIES

Search and Rescue: The Coast Guard maintains a system of rescue vessels, aircraft and communications facilities to carry out its function of saving life and property in and over the high seas and the navigable waters of the United States. This function includes flood relief and removing hazards to navigation.

Maritime Law Enforcement: The Coast Guard is the primary maritime law enforcement agency for the United States. It enforces or assists in the enforcement of applicable Federal laws and treaties and other international agreements to which the United States is party, on and under the high seas and waters subject to the jurisdiction of the United States, and may conduct investigations into suspected violations of such laws and international agreements. The Coast Guard works with other Federal agencies in the enforcement of such laws as they pertain to the protection of living and nonliving resources and in the suppression of smuggling and illicit drug trafficking.

Commercial Vessel Safety: The Coast Guard is charged with administering and enforcing various safety standards for the design, construction, equipment, and maintenance of commercial vessels of the United States

Table 6.3   District and Field Organizations—United States Coast Guard

ATLANTIC AREA	**Governors Island,** **New York, N.Y. 10004,** **212-668-7196**
1st District: Maine, Massachusetts, New Hampshire, Rhode Island, Vermont	150 Causeway St., Boston, Mass. 02114, 617-223-3601
2nd District: Arkansas, Colorado, Illinois, Indiana, Iowa, Kansas, Kentucky, Minnesota, Missouri, Nebraska, North Dakota, Ohio, Oklahoma, western Pennsylvania, South Dakota, Tennessee, West Virginia, Wisconsin, Wyoming	1430 Olive St., St. Louis, Mo. 63103, 314-425-4601
3rd District: Connecticut, Delaware, New Jersey, eastern New York, eastern Pennsylvania	Governors Island, New York, N.Y. 10004, 212-668-7196
5th District: District of Columbia, Maryland, North Carolina, Virginia	431 Crawford St., Portsmouth, Va. 23705, 804-398-6000 (switchboard only)
7th District: Florida, Georgia, Puerto Rico, South Carolina, Virgin Islands	51 SW., 1st Ave., Miami, Fla. 33130 305-350-5654
8th District: Alabama, Louisiana, Mississippi, New Mexico, Texas	500 Camp St., New Orleans, La. 70130, 504-589-6298
9th District: Great Lakes area	1240 E. 9th St., Cleveland, Ohio 44199, 216-522-3910
PACIFIC AREA	**2 Government Island,** **Alameda, Calif. 94501,** **415-536-6150**
11th District: Arizona, southern California	400 Oceangate Blvd., Long Beach, Calif. 90822, 213-590-2211
12th District: northern California, Nevada, Utah	2 Government Island, Alameda, Calif. 94501, 415-536-6150
13th District: Oregon, Idaho, Montana, Washington	915 2d Ave., Seattle, Wash. 98174, 206-442-5078
14th District: American Samoa, Guam, Hawaii, Pacific Islands	9th Floor, 300 Ala Moana Blvd., Honolulu, Hawaii 96850
17th District: Alaska	P.O. Box 3-5000, Juneau, Alaska 99802, 907-586-7347
U.S. COAST GUARD ACADEMY, SUPERINTENDENT	New London, Conn. 06320, 203-444-8286

and offshore structures on the Outer Continental Shelf. The program includes enforcement of safety standards on foreign vessels subject to U.S. jurisdiction and administration and enforcement of vessel personnel manning and crew qualification standards.

Investigations are conducted of reported marine accidents, casualties, violations of law and regulations, misconduct, negligence, and incompetence occurring on commercial vessels subject to U.S. jurisdiction. Surveillance operations and boardings are conducted to detect violations of law and regulations. The program also functions to facilitate marine transportation by admeasuring vessels, supervising the employment and records of employment of merchant marine personnel, and administering the vessel documentation laws.

Great Lakes Pilotage: The Coast Guard administers the Great Lakes Pilotage Act of 1960 which regulates pilotage services on the Great Lakes.

Marine Environmental Response: The Coast Guard has major responsibilities in implementing the Nation's policies for protection of the marine environment. The program objectives are to maintain or improve the quality of the marine environment and to minimize the damage caused by pollutants discharged into the marine environment.

> **The Coast Guard is, as its motto suggests, *Semper Paratus,* Always Ready.**

The functions conducted include boarding tank vessels, monitoring transfer operations, and inspecting liquid bulk facilities to ensure compliance with the laws, executive orders, and agreements that constitute the legal mandate for the marine environmental protection program. A National Strike Force also has been established to provide response capability in the event of a major pollution incident.

Port and Environmental Safety: This program is administered by the Coast Guard Captains of the Port (COTPs). Title 14 of the U.S. Code authorizes the Coast Guard to enforce rules and regulations governing the safety and security of ports and the anchorage and movements of vessels in U.S. waters. Port safety and security functions include supervising cargo transfer operations, both storage and stowage, boarding of Special Interest Vessels, conducting harbor patrols and waterfront facility inspections, establishing security zones as required, and the control of vessel movement, including the operation of Vessel Traffic Services, in selected ports.

Aids to Navigation: The Coast Guard establishes and maintains U.S. aids to the navigation system, which include lighthouses, lightships, buoys, beacons, fog signals, marine radiobeacons, racons, and long-range radionavigation aids (including Loran). With the exception of Loran, which extends to the Western Pacific, Arctic, Europe, and Middle East, aids are established in or adjacent to waters subject to the jurisdiction of the United States. These aids to navigation are intended to assist a navigator to determine his or her position or safe course, or to warn of dangers or obstructions to navigation. Other aids to navigation-related functions include origin of marine information radio broadcasts and publication of Local Notices to Mariners and Coast Guard Light Lists.

Bridge Administration: The Coast Guard administers the several statutes regulating the construction, maintenance, and operation of bridges across U.S. navigable waters to provide for safe navigation through and under bridges.

Ice Operations: The Coast Guard operates the Nation's icebreaking vessels (icebreakers and ice-capable cutters), supported by aircraft, for ice reconnaissance, to facilitate maritime transportation and aid in prevention of flooding in domestic waters, and support logistics to U.S. polar installations. Icebreakers also support scientific research in Arctic and Antarctic waters.

Deepwater Ports: Under the provisions of the Deepwater Port Act of 1974, the Coast Guard administers a licensing and regulatory program governing the construction, ownership (international aspects), and operation of deepwater ports on the high seas to transfer oil from tankers to shore.

Boating Safety: The Coast Guard develops and directs a national boating safety program aimed at making the operation of small craft in U.S. waters both pleasurable and safe. This is accomplished by establishing uniform safety standards for recreational boats and associated equipment; encouraging State efforts through a grant-in-aid and liaison program; coordinating public education and information programs; administering the Coat Guard Auxiliary; and enforcing compliance with Federal laws and regulations relative to safe use and safety equipment requirements for small boats.

Coast Guard Auxiliary: The Auxiliary is a non-military volunteer organization of private citizens who own small boats, aircraft, or radio stations. Auxiliary members assist the Coast Guard by conducting boating education programs, patrolling marine regattas, participating in search and rescue operations, and conducting courtesy marine examinations.

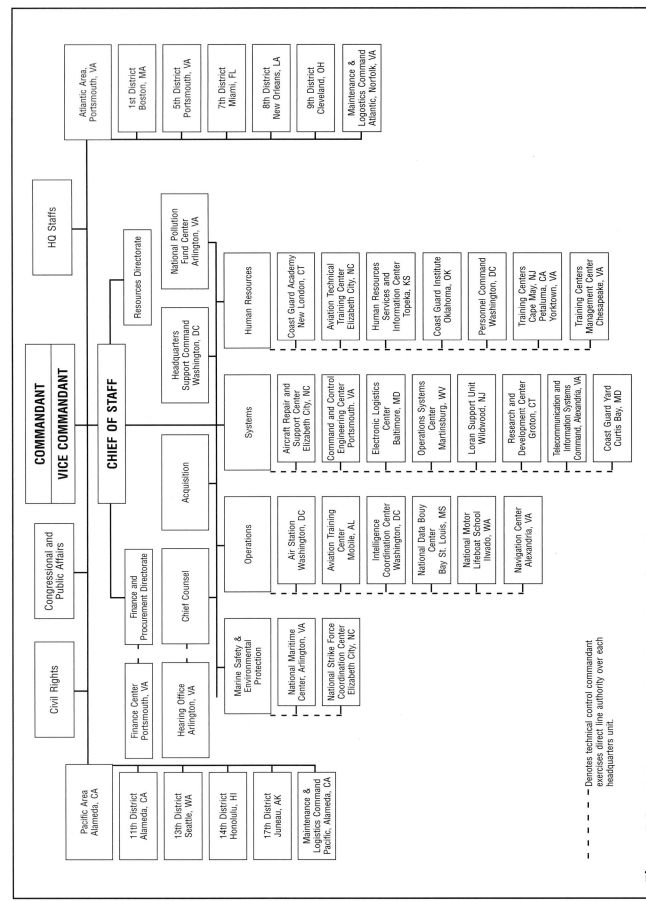

Figure 6.3 United States Coast Guard Districts and Headquarters Units.

Military Readiness: As required by law, the Coast Guard maintains a state of readiness to function as a specialized service in the Navy in time of war.

Reserve Training: The Coast Guard Reserve provides qualified individuals and trained units for active duty in time of war or national emergency and at such other times as national security requires. In addition to its role in national defense, the Reserve augments the active service in the performance of peacetime missions during domestic emergencies and during routine and peak operations.

Marine Safety Council: The Marine Safety Council acts as a deliberative body to consider proposed Coast Guard regulations and to provide a forum for the consideration of related problems. (See Figure 6.3.)

FEDERAL AVIATION ADMINISTRATION

The Federal Aviation Administration (FAA), originally the Federal Aviation Agency, was established by the Federal Aviation Act of 1958 (72 Stat. 744) and became a component of the Department of Transportation in 1967 pursuant to the Department of Transportation Act (80 Stat. 931; 49 U.S.C. 1652).

FAA is charged with regulating air commerce in a manner that promotes its development and safety and fulfills the requirements of national defense; controlling the use of navigable airspace of the United States and regulating both civil and military operations in such airspace in the interest of safety and efficiency; promoting, encouraging, and developing civil aeronautics; consolidating research and development with respect to air navigation facilities; installing and operating air navigation facilities; developing and operating a common system of air traffic control and navigation for both civil and military aircraft; and developing and implementing, in coordination with other departmental elements and other Federal agencies, a program to achieve a system solution to the aircraft noise and sonic boom problems.

The Federal Aviation Administration (FAA) oversees the safety of civil aviation. The safety mission of the FAA is first and foremost and includes the issuance and enforcement of regulations and standards related to the manufacture, operation, certification and maintenance of aircraft. The agency is responsible for the rating and certification of airmen and for certification of airports serving air carriers. It also regulates a program to protect the security of civil aviation, and

enforces regulations under the Hazardous Materials Transportation Act for shipments by air. The FAA, which operates a network of airport towers, air route traffic control centers, and flight service stations, develops air traffic rules, allocates the use of airspace, and provides for the security control of air traffic to meet national defense requirements. Other responsibilities include the construction or installation of visual and electronic aids to air navigation and promotion of aviation safety internationally. The FAA, which regulates and encourages the U.S. commercial space transportation industry, also licenses commercial space launch facilities and private sector launches. **(See Chapter 7 for an organization chart and a more complete description of the FAA).** (Table 6.4.)

FUNCTIONS AND ACTIVITIES

Safety Regulation: The FAA Administrator issues and enforces rules, regulations, and minimum standards relating to the manufacture, operation, and maintenance of aircraft as well as the rating and certification (including medical) of airmen and the certification of airports serving air carriers. FAA performs flight inspection of air navigation facilities in the United States and, as required, abroad.

Airspace and Air Traffic Management: To meet its primary objective of safe and efficient use of navigable airspace, FAA operates a network of airport traffic control towers, air route traffic control centers, and flight service stations; develops air traffic rules and regulations and allocates the use of airspace; and provides for the security control of air traffic to meet national defense requirements.

Air Navigation Facilities: FAA is responsible for the location, construction or installation, maintenance, and operation of Federal visual and electronic aids to air navigation. It operates and maintains communications equipment, radio teletype circuits, and equipment at flight service stations, airport traffic control towers, and air route traffic control centers.

Research and Development: The research and development activities of FAA are directed toward providing the systems, procedures, facilities, and devices needed for a safe and efficient system of air navigation and air traffic control to meet the needs of civil aviation and the air defense system. FAA also is involved in developing and testing improved aircraft, engines, propellers, and appliances.

Airport Planning and Development Programs: FAA administers programs to identify the type and the cost of development of public airports required for a national airport system and to provide grants of funds to assist public agencies in airport system planning, airport master planning, and public airport development.

Registration and Recordation: FAA provides a system for the registration of an aircraft's nationality, its engines, propellers, and appliances, as well as a system for recording aircraft ownership.

Other Programs: FAA administers the aviation insurance and aircraft loan guarantee programs. It is an allotting agency under the Defense Materials System with respect to priorities and allocation for civil aircraft and civil aviation operations and develops specifications for the preparation of aeronautical charts. It publishes current information on airways and airport service and issues technical publication for the improvement of safety in flight, airport planning and design, and other aeronautical activities.

Wartime Service: The wartime mission of the Federal Aviation Administration is to support the Department of Defense and appropriate military commanders through air traffic control, aeronautical communications, aids to navigation, and other essential services, to support essential civil aviation operations, including preservation and restoration of the capability of the civil air transport system; to support civil government; civil survival and recovery operations; and to provide for the protection of FAA personnel and the continuity of executive direction and for safety and survival of FAA personnel.

Executive Order 11161, Relating to Certain Relationships Between the Department of Defense and the Federal Aviation Administration, contemplates that the FAA will be transferred to Department of Defense in event of war and will function as an adjunct of the Department of Defense. It is further contemplated that while functioning as an adjunct of Department of Defense, FAA will remain organizationally intact, and the Administrator will retain responsibility for administration of statutory functions.

FEDERAL HIGHWAY ADMINISTRATION

The Federal Highway Administration (FHWA) carries out the highway transportation programs of the Department of Transportation under pertinent legislation or provisions of law.

The Federal Highway Administration was established on April 1, 1967, as one of the operating admin-

istrations of the Department of Transportation. Representing the Federal interest in the Nation's highway transportation system, its components included organizational entities transferred with their functions and facilities from the Department of Commerce and the Interstate Commerce Commission. The primary programs and responsibilities of the Administration were carried out by three bureaus, the Bureau of Public Roads, the Bureau of Motor Carrier Safety, and the National Highway Safety Bureau. (See Figure 6.4.)

FHWA encompasses highway transportation in its broadest scope, seeking to coordinate highways with other modes of transportation to achieve the most effective balance of transportation systems and facilities under cohesive Federal transportation policies.

FHWA is concerned with the total operation and environment of highway systems, including highway safety. In administering its highway transportation programs, FHWA gives full consideration to the impacts of highway development and travel, transportation needs, engineering and safety aspects, and project costs. FHWA ensures balanced treatment of these factors by utilizing a systematic, interdisciplinary approach in providing for safe and efficient highway transportation.

The Federal Highway Administration (FHWA) coordinates highway transportation programs in cooperation with states and other partners to enhance the country's safety, economic vitality, quality of life, and environment. Major program areas include the Federal-Aid Highway Program, which provides federal financial assistance to the States to construct and improve the National Highway System, urban and rural roads, and bridges. This program provides funds for general improvements and development of safe highways and roads. The Federal Lands Highway Program provides access to and within national forests, national parks, Indian reservations and other public lands by preparing plans and contracts, supervising construction facilities, and conducting bridge inspections and surveys. The FHWA also manages a comprehensive research, development, and technology program.

FUNCTIONS AND ACTIVITIES

Federal-Aid Highway Program: FHWA administers the Federal-aid highway program of financial assistance to the States for highway construction and improvement of efficiency in highway and traffic operations. This program provides for construction and preservation of the approximately 42,500-miles National System of Interstate and Defense Highways, financed

Table 6.4 Major Field Organizations—Federal Aviation Administration

ALASKAN—Alaska	P.O. Box 14, 701 C St., Anchorage, AK 99513
EASTERN—New York, New Jersey, Pennsylvania, Delaware, Maryland, West Virginia, Virginia	Federal Bldg., JFK International Airport, Jamaica, NY 11430
CENTRAL—Iowa, Kansas, Missouri, Nebraska	601 E. 12th St., Kansas City, MO 64106
GREAT LAKES—Illinois, Indiana, Michigan, Minnesota, North Dakota, Ohio, South Dakota, Wisconsin	2300 E. Devon Ave., Des Plaines, IL 60018
NEW ENGLAND—Maine, Vermont, New Hampshire, Massachusetts, Connecticut, Rhode Island	12 New England Executive Parkway, Burlington, MA 01803
NORTHWEST MOUNTAIN—Colorado, Idaho, Montana, Oregon, Utah, Washington, Wyoming	17900 Pacific Highway S., Seattle, WA 98168
SOUTHERN—Alabama, Georgia, Florida, Kentucky, Mississippi, North Carolina, Puerto Rico, South Carolina, Tennessee	P.O. Box 20636, Atlanta, GA 30320
SOUTHWEST—Arkansas, Louisiana, New Mexico, Oklahoma, Texas	P.O. Box 1689, Fort Worth, TX 76101
WESTERN-PACIFIC—Arizona, California, Hawaii, Nevada	P.O. Box 92007, Los Angeles, CA 90009
MIKE MONRONEY AERONAUTICAL CENTER	P.O. Box 25082, Oklahoma City, OK 73125
FAA TECHNICAL CENTER	Atlantic City, NJ 08405

on a 90% Federal, 10% State basis, and the improvement of approximately 800,000 miles of other Federal-aid primary, secondary, and urban roads and streets, with financing generally on a 75–25% basis. In addition, FHWA administers an emergency program to assist in the repair or reconstruction of Federal-aid highways and certain Federal roads, which have suffered serious damage by natural disasters over a wide area and catastrophic failures. Revenues derived from special taxes on highway users are deposited into the general funds of the Treasury and credited to the Highway Trust Fund to meet the Federal share of highway program costs.

Special emphasis is directed toward making highway improvements that are the highest priority needs in each State, improving the safety design of new highways, correcting highway hazards on existing roads, replacing or rehabilitating deficient bridges, reducing

traffic congestion, and facilitating the flow of traffic. Other activities include improving access for the handicapped, encouraging the joint use and development of highway corridors, providing relocation assistance to those displaced by highway construction, encouraging minority business enterprises to participate in highway construction, and preserving along highways the natural beauty of the countryside, public parks and recreation lands, wildlife and water-fowl refuges, and historic sites. FHWA also administers a technology transfer program aimed at promoting the use and adoption of innovative highway engineering practices.

Highway Safety Programs: FHWA is responsible for several of the highway safety programs undertaken by the Federal Government. Under the authority of the Federal-aid highway acts, highway construction programs to increase safety are administered through matching grants to the States. These safety construction pro-

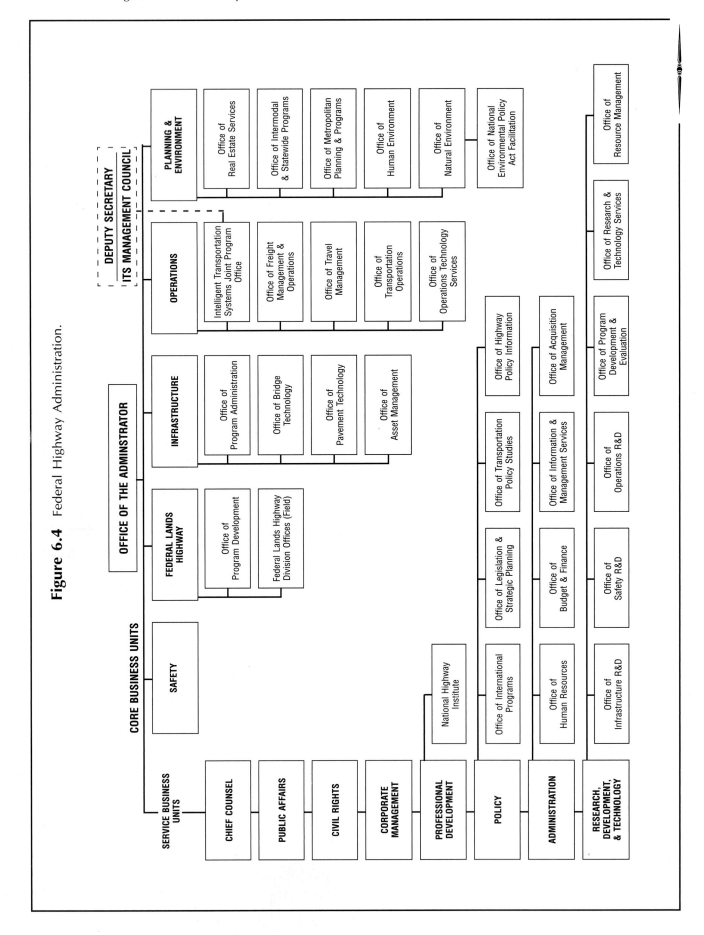

Figure 6.4 Federal Highway Administration.

grams fund activities which eliminate roadside obstacles, identify and correct hazardous locations, eliminate hazards at railroad crossings, and improve signing, pavement markings, and signalization.

Under the Highway Safety Act of 1966, the Federal Government is authorized to provide funding assistance in the form of matching grants to States, which establish specific highway safety programs in accordance with national standards promulgated by the Secretary of Transportation. FHWA administers highway-related safety standards, which provide for the identification and surveillance of accident locations; highway design, construction, and maintenance; traffic engineering services; and highway-related aspects of pedestrian safety. These standards form the foundation for the State and local programs dealing with street and highway safety.

Motor Carrier Safety: Under the authority of the motor carrier safety provisions, title 49, chapter 31, of the United States Code (96 Stat. 2437; 49 U.S.C. 3101 et seq.) and the Hazardous Materials Transportation Act (88 Stat. 2156; 49 U.S.C. 1801), FHWA exercises Federal regulatory jurisdiction over the safety performance of all commercial motor carriers engaged in interstate or foreign commerce. FHWA deals with some 200,000 carriers, who collectively operate over 4 million commercial vehicles on public highways, employing approximately 4.5 million full- or part-time professional drivers and approximately 22,000 shippers of hazardous materials. Federal safety regulations enunciating safe operating practices are published in accordance with the Administrative Procedure Act (5 U.S.C. 551 et seq.). Implementing work activities are conducted by FHWA to promote observance by carriers of these safe practices. Safety management audits are conducted at the carrier's facilities to determine the safety performance of the carrier's over-the-road operations. Checks of vehicles and drivers are conducted at roadside. Compliance investigations are conducted with a view toward enforcement action, which may involve criminal prosecution or civil forfeiture proceedings against violators of the Federal motor carrier safety regulations or the hazardous materials transportation regulations.

FHWA also has jurisdiction over the safe movement of the Nation's highways of dangerous cargoes such as hazardous wastes, explosives, flammables, and other volatile materials; the safety and comfort of migrant workers; motor carrier employees' health; as well as programs in noise abatement in motor carrier operations and encouraging State adoption and enforcement of Federal regulations. In addition, FHWA has responsibility for administering the motor carrier safety assis-

tance program under the provisions of sections 401-404 of the Surface Transportation Assistance Act of 1982 (96 Stat. 2154–2156; 49 U.S.C. 2301–2304). The act provides for grants to qualified States for the development or implementation of programs for the enforcement of Federal or compatible State regulations applicable to commercial vehicle safety and hazardous materials transportation by highway.

Federal Lands Highway Program: FHWA, through cooperative agreements with Federal land managing agencies, administers a coordinated Federal lands program consisting of forest highways, defense access roads, public lands highways, park roads, parkways, and Indian Reservation roads. This program provides for the funding of more than 75,000 miles of federally owned roads or public roads—which serve Federal lands. FHWA's direct Federal program provides for the program, coordination and administration and directs transportation planning, engineering studies, designs and construction engineering assistance.

Research and Development: FHWA coordinates a wide-ranging research and development program directed toward the problems of traffic congestion; street and highway safety; effective design and reduced construction and maintenance costs, energy conservation, and the social, economic, and environmental impact of highway transportation. A major effort of FHWA is the transfer of the technology developed through research and other means to the State, county, city, and other local highway jurisdictions.

Training: Through its National Highway Institute, FHWA develops and administers, in cooperation with State highway agencies, training programs of instruction designed primarily for State and local highway agency employees engaged or about to be engaged in Federal-aid highway work. It also administers fellowship programs in highway safety and transportation education, as well as a highway technician scholarship program.

Additional Programs: FHWA administers a highway planning program, the highway beautification program, the highway construction phase of the Appalachian regional development program, and the territorial highway program; administers on-the-job training programs for unskilled highway construction workers; and provides assistance and advice to foreign governments in various phases of highway engineering and administration. FHWA administers a civil rights program affecting the internal practices of the agency together with the equal employment and equal opportunity practices by recipients of Federal assistance. Some of the issues

Table 6.5

Region	Location of Regional Office	State
I	Cambridge, Massachusetts	Connecticut, Maine, Massachusetts, New Hampshire, Rhode Island, and Vermont
II	White Plains, New York	New York, New Jersey, Puerto Rico, and the Virgin Islands
III	Hanover, Maryland	Delaware, District of Columbia, Maryland, Pennsylvania, Virginia, and West Virginia
IV	Atlanta, Georgia	Alabama, Florida, Georgia, Kentucky, Mississippi, North Carolina, South Carolina, and Tennessee
V	Homewood, Illinois	Illinois, Indiana, Minnesota, Michigan, Ohio, and Wisconsin
VI	Fort Worth, Texas	Arkansas, Louisiana, New Mexico, Oklahoma, and Texas
VII	Kansas City, Missouri	Iowa, Kansas, Missouri, and Nebraska
VIII	Denver, Colorado	Colorado, Montana, North Dakota, South Dakota, Utah, and Wyoming
IX	San Francisco, California	Arizona, California, Hawaii, Nevada, Guam, and American Samoa
X	Seattle, Washington	Alaska, Idaho, Oregon, and Washington

addressed include: disadvantaged business enterprise and women's business enterprise programs, title VI of the Civil Rights Act of 1964; and contract compliance as affected by Executive Order 11246 of September 24, 1965, and title 23 of the United States Code.

Major Field Organizations—Federal Highway Administration: Each region is under the supervision and direction of a Regional Administrator. The Associate Administrator for Regional Operations provides executive direction and supervision over the Regional Administrators. Technical direction and guidance will be provided to the Regional Administrators by appropriate headquarters program and staff elements. The field structure consists of ten regions. The Regions, location of the regional offices, and the states included are shown in Table 6.5.

FEDERAL RAILROAD ADMINISTRATION

The purpose of the Federal Railroad Administration (FRA) is to promulgate and enforce rail safety regulations, administer railroad financial assistance programs, conduct research and development in support of improved railroad safety and national rail trans-

portation policy, provide for the rehabilitation of Northeast Corridor rail passenger service, operate the Alaska Railroad, and consolidate government support of rail transportation activities. (Table 6.6.)

The Federal Railroad Administration was created pursuant to section 3(e)(1) of the Department of Transportation Act of 1966 (80 Stat. 932). Other sections of the Act provided for the transfer to the new Department of The Alaska Railroad from the Department of the Interior; the railroad safety activities of the Bureau of Railroad Safety and Service of the Interstate Commerce Commission; and the Office of High Speed Ground Transportation of the Office of the Under Secretary for Transportation, Department of Commerce. These organizational elements were assigned to the Federal Railroad Administration by the Secretary of Transportation under authority granted by the Act. (See Figure 6.5.)

FUNCTIONS AND ACTIVITIES

Railroad Safety: FRA administers and enforces the Federal laws and related regulations designed to promote safety on railroads; and exercises jurisdiction over all areas of rail safety under the Rail Safety Act of 1970, such as track maintenance, inspection standards, and equipment standards. It also administers and enforces

Table 6.6 Major Field Organizations—Federal Railroad Administration

1. NORTHEASTERN—Connecticut, Maine, Massachusetts, New Hampshire, New Jersey, New York, Rhode Island, Vermont	10th Floor, 55 Broadway, Cambridge, MA 02142
2. EASTERN—Delaware, District of Columbia, Maryland, Pennsylvania, Virginia, West Virginia	Room 1020, 434 Walnut St., Philadelphia, PA 19106
3. SOUTHERN—Alabama, Florida, Georgia, Kentucky, Mississippi, North Carolina, South Carolina, Tennessee	Suite 440, 1720 Peachtree Rd. NW., North Tower, Atlanta, GA 30309
4. CENTRAL—Illinois, Indiana, Michigan, Minnesota, Ohio, Wisconsin	14th Floor, 165 N. Canal St., Chicago, IL 60606
5. SOUTHWESTERN—Arkansas, Louisiana, New Mexico, Oklahoma, Texas	Room 7A35, 819 Taylor St., Fort Worth, TX 76102
6. MIDWESTERN—Iowa, Kansas, Missouri, Nebraska	Room 1807, 911 Walnut St., Kansas City, MO 64106
7. WESTERN—Arizona, California, Colorado, Nevada, Utah	Room 1018, 211 Main St., San Francisco, CA 94105
8. NORTHWESTERN—Idaho, Montana, North Dakota, Oregon, South Dakota, Washington, Wyoming	Room 450, 900 SW. 5th St., Portland, OR 97204

regulations resulting from railroad safety legislation for locomotives, signals, safety appliances, power brakes, hours of service, transportation of explosives and other dangerous articles, reporting and investigation of railroad accidents. Railroad and related industry equipment, facilities, and records are inspected and required reports reviewed.

Research and Development: A ground transportation research and development program is administered to advance all aspects of intercity ground transportation and railroad safety pertaining to the physical sciences and engineering, in order to provide leadership to national railroad and advanced ground system technology.

Transportation Test Center: This 50-square mile facility, located near Pueblo, Colo., provides testing for advanced and conventional systems and techniques designed to improve ground transportation. The facility has been managed and staffed for FRA by the Association of American Railroads since October 1, 1982. The United States and Canadian Governments and private industry use this facility to explore, under controlled conditions, the operation of both conventional and advanced systems. It is used by the Urban Mass Transportation Administration for testing of urban rapid transit vehicles.

Policy and Program Development: Program management for new and revised policies, plans, and projects related to railroad transportation economics, finance, system planning and operations is provided; appropriate studies and analyses are performed; and relevant tests, demonstrations, and evaluations are conducted. Analyses of issues before regulatory agencies are carried out and recommendations are made to the Secretary as to the positions to be taken by DOT.

Federal Assistance to Railroads: FRA administers a program of Federal assistance for national, regional, and local rail services. Programs include rail freight service assistance programs; Conrail monitoring; rail service continuation programs and State rail planning; labor/management programs; and for rail passenger service on a national, regional, and local basis.

Northeast Corridor Improvement Project: FRA administers programs to develop, implement, and administer rail system policies, plans, and programs for the Northeast Corridor in support of applicable provisions of the Railroad Revitalization and Regulatory Reform Act of 1976 (90 Stat. 31; 45 U.S.C. 801), the Rail Passenger Service Act (84 Stat. 1327; 45 U.S.C. 501), and related legislation.

Figure 6.5 Federal Railroad Administration.

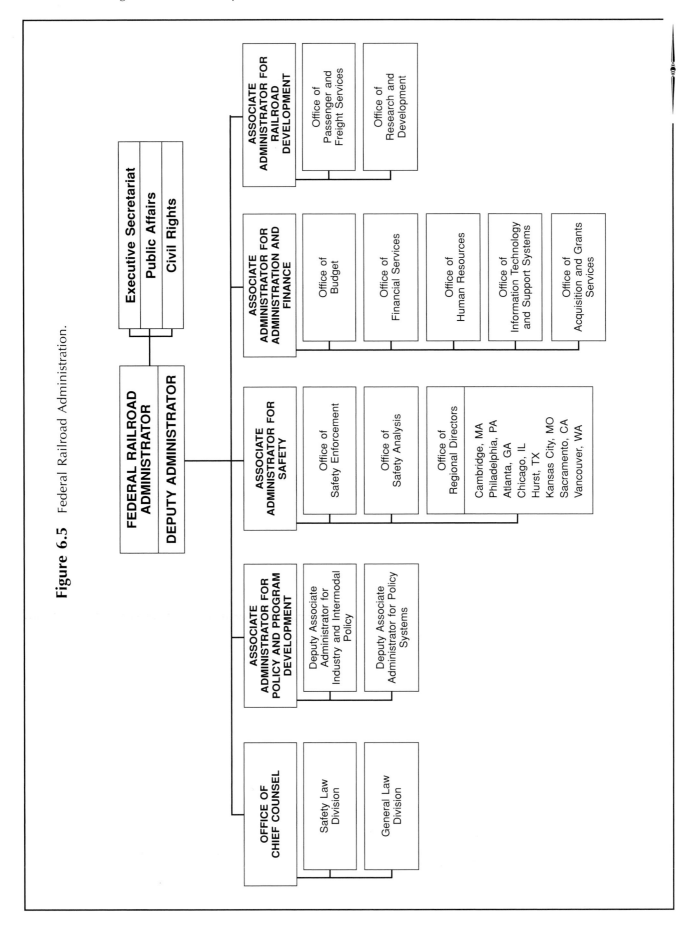

Alaska Railroad: The Alaska Railroad provides transportation to stimulate settlement and the industrial and agricultural development of the State of Alaska and serve the national defense. A 482-mile main line extending from Seward and Whittier through Anchorage to Fairbanks, including branch lines to Eielson Air Force Base and to the Matanuska and Suntrana coal fields is operated to provide transportation for persons and property.

NATIONAL HIGHWAY TRAFFIC SAFETY ADMINISTRATION

The National Highway Traffic Safety Administration is a composite of two separate agencies established in the Department of Commerce pursuant to the National Highway Safety Act of 1966 and the National Traffic and Motor Vehicle Safety Act of 1966. Pursuant to section 6(a) of the DOT Act, these two agencies were transferred to the DOT on April 1, 1967, and were merged into a single National Highway Safety Bureau to carry out the provisions of both acts by Executive Order 11357 of June 6, 1967. By administrative action of the Secretary of Transportation, the Bureau was placed within the Federal Highway Administration. Effective March 20, 1970, the Secretary separated the Bureau from the Federal Highway Administration and established the Bureau as one of the operating administrations of the Department reporting directly to him. This reorganization was affirmed with the establishment of the National Highway Traffic Safety Administration as an operating administration in the Department of Transportation by the Highway Safety Act 1970 (P.L. 91-605).

The Administration carries out programs relating to the safety performance of motor vehicles and related equipment, motor vehicle drivers and pedestrians, and a uniform nationwide speed limit under the National Traffic and Motor Vehicle Safety Act of 1966 (80 Stat. 718), as amended, and the Highway Safety Act of 1966 (80 Stat. 731), as amended. Under the authority of the Motor Vehicle Information and Cost Saving Act (86 Stat. 947), as amended, the Administration carries out programs and studies aimed at reducing economic losses in motor vehicle crashes and repairs, through general motor vehicle programs; administers the Federal odometer law; and promulgates average fuel economy standards for passenger and nonpassenger motor vehicles.

Under the authority of the Clean Air Amendments of 1970 (84 Stat. 1700), the Administration certifies as to the consistency of Environmental Protection Agency State grants with any highway safety program developed pursuant to section 402 of title 23 of the United States Code.

The National Highway Traffic Safety Administration was established to carry out a congressional mandate to reduce the mounting number of deaths, injuries, and economic losses resulting from traffic accidents on the Nation's highways and to provide motor vehicle damage susceptibility and ease of repair information, motor vehicle inspection demonstrations, and protection of purchasers of motor vehicles having altered odometers, and to provide average standards for greater vehicle mileage per gallon of fuel for vehicles under 10,000 pounds (gross vehicle weight). (See Figure 6.6.)

The National Highway Traffic Safety Administration is responsible for reducing deaths, injuries and economic losses resulting from motor vehicle crashes. NHTSA sets and enforces safety performance standards for motor vehicles and equipment, and through grants to state and local governments enables them to conduct effective local highway safety programs. NHTSA investigates safety defects in motor vehicles, sets and enforces fuel economy standards, helps states and local communities reduce the threat of drunk drivers, promotes the use of safety belts, child safety seats and air bags, investigates odometer fraud, establishes and enforces vehicle anti-theft regulations and provides consumer information on motor vehicle safety topics. Research on driver behavior and traffic safety is conducted by NHTSA to develop the most efficient and effective means of bringing about safety improvements. A toll-free Auto Safety Hotline, 1-888-DASH-2-DOT, furnishes consumers with a wide range of auto safety information. Callers also can help identify safety problems in motor vehicles, tires and automotive equipment such as child safety seats.

FUNCTIONS AND ACTIVITIES

Rulemaking and Enforcement Programs: The Administration is implementing motor vehicle safety programs to:

- Reduce the occurrence of highway crashes;

- Reduce the severity of injuries in such crashes as do occur;

- Improve survivability and injury recovery by better postcrash measures;

- Reduce the economic losses in crashes;

Figure 6.6 National Highway Traffic Safety Administration.

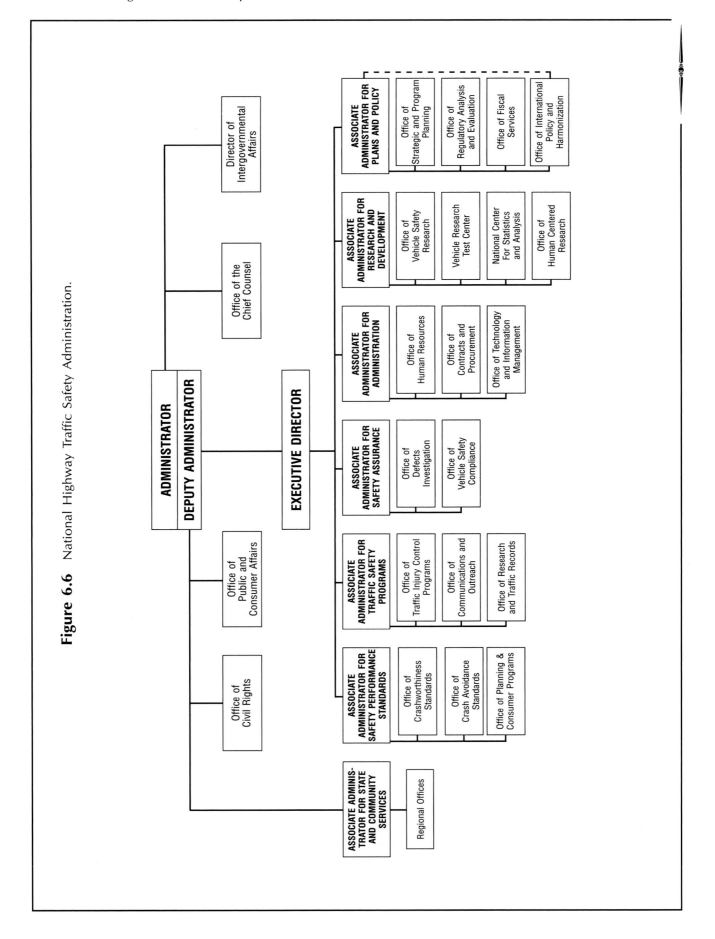

- Conduct a consumer information study to determine motor vehicle damage susceptibility, degree of crashworthiness, and ease of diagnosis and repair; and

- Establish safeguards for the protection of purchasers of motor vehicles having altered or reset odometers.

Under the Administration's program, Federal Motor Vehicle Safety Standards are issued which prescribe safety features and levels of safety related performance for vehicles and motor vehicle equipment. Damage susceptibility, crashworthiness and ease of repair are to be studied and reported to the Congress and public. The Administration establishes safeguards to protect purchasers of motor vehicles from vehicles with altered or reset odometers. The Administration conducts an intensive testing program to determine whether vehicles and equipment comply with applicable standards. It also investigates reports of safety-related defects. The Administration can require a manufacturer of motor vehicles or motor vehicle equipment to take corrective action.

The Energy Policy and Conservation Act, as amended (89 Stat. 871; 42 U.S.C. 6201 note), sets automotive fuel economy standards for passenger cars for model years 1985 and thereafter. The Administration has the option of altering the standards for the post-1985 period.

The Administration develops and promulgates mandatory fuel economy standards for light trucks for each model year and administers the fuel economy regulatory program. The Administration establishes rules for the collection and reporting of information required concerning manufacturer's technological alternatives and corporate economic capabilities in meeting fuel economy standards.

Traffic Safety Programs: The law provides for Federal matching funds to assist States with their driver, pedestrian, and motor vehicle safety programs. The Administration has issued standards as guidelines and provides technical assistance to State and local community safety programs. Areas of primary emphasis are the implementation of countermeasures to reduce accidents and resultant deaths and injuries attributable to the use of alcohol and drugs, to increase occupant restraint usage, to improve emergency medical systems, and to control the aberrant driver. The Administration maintains a register of persons who have had their operator's license withdrawn or revoked for more than 6 months. The National Highway Safety Advisory Committee of the Department of Transportation provides valuable advice and counsel on standards and other highway safety matters.

Research and Development: To provide a foundation for the development of motor vehicle fuel economy and highway safety program standards, the Administration administers a broadscale program of research, development, testing, demonstration, and evaluation of motor vehicles, motor vehicle equipment, operator and pedestrian safety, and accident data collection and analysis.

The research program covers numerous areas that affect safety problems and includes provision for appropriate laboratory testing facilities to obtain necessary basic data. In this connection, research in both light and heavy vehicle crashworthiness and crash avoidance is being pursued. The objectives are to encourage industry to adopt advanced motor vehicle safety designs, stimulate public awareness of safety potentials, and provide a base for vehicle safety information.

The Administration maintains a collection of scientific and technical information related to motor vehicle safety, and operates the National Center for Statistics and Analysis, whose activities include the development and maintenance of highway accident data collection systems and related analysis efforts. These comprehensive motor vehicle safety information resources serve as documentary reference points for Federal, State, and local agencies; industry, universities, and the public. (Table 6.7.)

Table 6.7 Regional Offices—National Highway Traffic Safety Administration

I.	Kendall Sq., Code 903, Cambridge, MA 02142
II.	222 Mamaroneck Ave., White Plains, NY 10605
III.	793 Elkridge Landing Rd., Linthicum, MD 21090
IV.	1720 Peachtree Rd. NW., Atlanta, GA 30309
V.	18209 Dixie Hwy., Homewood Heights, IL 60430
VI.	819 Taylor St., Fort Worth, TX 76102
VII.	P.O. Box 19515, Kansas City, MO 64141
VIII.	1st Floor, 555 Zang St., Denver, CO 80228
IX.	Suite 1000, 211 Main St., San Francisco, CA 94105
X.	915 2d Ave., Seattle, WA 98174

FEDERAL TRANSIT ADMINISTRATION

The Urban Mass Transportation Administration is operated under the authority of the Urban Mass Transportation Act of 1964. The Administration was established as a component of the Department of Transportation by section 3 of the President's Reorganization Plan No. 2 of 1968, effective July 1, 1968. The Intermodal Surface Transportation Efficiency Act of 1991 renamed the Urban Mass Transportation Administration to the Federal Transit Administration.

The missions of the Administration are: to assist in the development of improved mass transportation facilities, equipment, techniques, and methods; to encourage the planning and establishment of areawide urban mass transportation systems where they are cost-effective; to provide assistance to State and local governments in financing such systems; and to encourage private sector involvement in local mass transportation systems. (See Figure 6.7.)

The Federal Transit Administration assists in developing improved mass transportation systems for cities and communities nationwide. Through its grant programs, FTA helps plan, build, and operate transit systems with convenience, cost and accessibility in mind. While buses and rail vehicles are the most common type of public transportation, other kinds include commuter ferryboats, trolleys, inclined railways, subways, and people movers. In providing financial, technical and planning assistance, the agency provides leadership and resources for safe and technologically advanced local transit systems while assisting in the development of local and regional traffic reduction. The FTA maintains the National Transit images (NTL), a repository of reports, documents, and data generated by professionals and others from around the country. The NTL is designed to facilitate document sharing among people interested in transit and transit related topics.

Functions and Activities: The Federal Public Transportation Act of 1982 (96 Stat. 2140), also known as title III of the Surface Transportation Assistance Act of 1982, extended through fiscal year 1986 authorizations for several programs of the Urban Mass Transportation Act of 1964. Under the act, UMTA's financial assistance programs, provided under the Discretionary Capital Grant Program (section 3) and the Capital and Operating Formula Assistance Program (section 5), were continued during fiscal year 1983. Under Title III, in fiscal year 1983 only, a Mass Transit Account Distribution Program (section 9A), a formula-apportioned re-

source, was made available for planning and for any eligible capital purpose. In fiscal year 1984, section 9A was replaced by another new program, a Formula Grant Program (section 9) which may be used for capital, planning, and operating assistance.

Discretionary Capital Assistance Grants and Loans, Advance Land Acquisition Loans: Grants or loans are authorized to assist communities in acquiring or improving capital equipment and facilities needed for urban mass transit systems, both public and private. Only State, regional, or local governmental bodies and public agencies are eligible as applicants. Private transit operators may be assisted under the program through arrangements with an eligible public body.

The grant is 75% (reduced from 80% by Title III) of new project cost if the urban area has completed a program for a unified or officially coordinated urban transportation system as a part of the comprehensive planned development of the area. Capital loans may be made to qualified public agencies at a moderate rate of interest, if financing cannot otherwise be obtained at reasonable terms.

Advance land acquisition loans may be made at a moderate rate of interest to finance the purchase of land or interests in land for future use on urban mass transportation systems. Loans are secured by the land or interests in land financed by the loans. Only State, regional, and local government agencies are eligible as applicants. Land and interests in land are eligible providing that they are reasonably expected to be required in connection with an urban mass transportation system and will be used for the purpose within 10 years of the date of the loan agreement.

Formula Operating and Capital Assistance: Section 5 of the Urban Mass Transportation Act of 1964, as amended, contains formula based programs for capital and operating assistance. Funds are apportioned to urbanized areas by a formula based one-half on population and one-half on population density. These funds can be used either for construction, operating, or capital assistance. The Federal matching share for funds used for capital purposes is up to 80%, and the matching share for operating purposes is up to 50%. Funds are apportioned among urbanized areas on the basis of fixed guideway and commuter rail mileages and commuter rail train mileages. These funds can be used for capital and operating expenses related to both fixed guideway and commuter rail purposes.

Technical Assistance: The Administration provides funds for research, development, and demonstration projects in all phases of urban mass transportation for the purpose of increasing productivity and efficiency in

Figure 6.7 Federal Transit Administration.

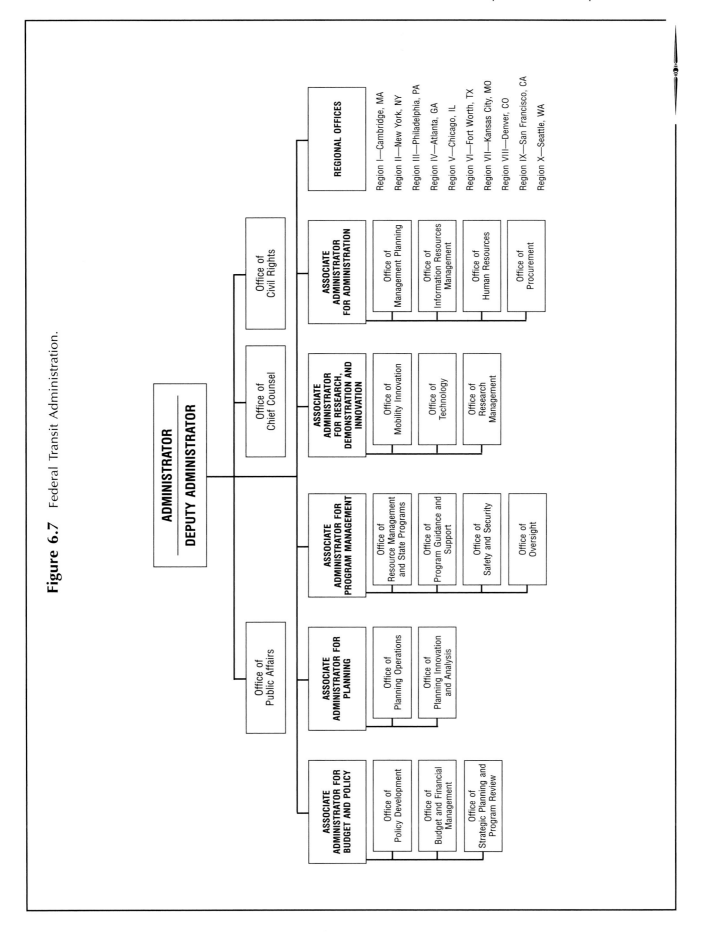

urban mass transportation systems, improving mass transportation service and equipment, and assisting State and local governments in providing total urban transportation services in a cost-effective manner. A comprehensive program of research, development, and demonstration is conducted, addressing the following principal areas of concern: bus, paratransit and rail technology, new systems and automation, safety and product qualification, socioeconomic factors, service and methods demonstrations, planning methodology, policy development, program evaluation, and management techniques and methods.

Major projects in these areas are:

- Development, testing, and evaluation of energy saving components and subsystems for transit buses and rail cars;

- Demonstrations of innovative techniques for reducing the costs of constructing tunnels and elevated track structures, and quieting the noise generated by rail transit vehicles, and economical means of rehabilitating and extending the useful life of existing transit facilities;

- Demonstration of new techniques of traffic management, such as priority for high occupancy vehicles;

- Innovative pricing policies;

- New computerized techniques for planning urban transportation systems and;

- Special features enabling elderly and handicapped individuals to use transit vehicles.

Most projects are conducted under contracts with private organizations, both profit and nonprofit, public bodies, including State and local governments, and expert individuals.

University Research and Training Grants: Grants may be awarded to public and private nonprofit institutions of higher learning to assist in carrying out research on problems of urban mass transportation and in providing training for students and working professionals in the field of urban transportation analysis, planning, engineering, and operations. The objective is to encourage and support university research and training that addresses and is responsive to Federal, State, and local transportation concerns, and advances the understanding and resolution of critical transportation problems facing the Nation's cities.

Managerial Training Grants: Grants to governmental bodies and agencies and operators of public transportation services provide fellowship for training

in public or private training institutions for personnel employed in managerial, technical, and professional positions in the public transportation field. The assistance provided under this section toward each fellowship shall not exceed the lesser of $5,000 or 75% of the sum of: (1) tuition and other charges to the fellowship recipient, (2) any additional costs incurred by the training institution in connection with the fellowship and billed to the grantee, and (3) the regular salary of the fellowship recipient for the period of the fellowship (to the extent that salary is actually paid or reimbursed by the grantee).

Technical Studies Grants: Grants to governmental bodies and agencies are authorized for up to 100% but, by policy, are awarded up to 80% of the cost of planning, programming, engineering, and designing urban mass transportation projects. Grants also are made for other types of transit studies to enhance the design and operation of transit systems.

Capital and Operating Formula Assistance for Nonurbanized Areas: The Capital and Operating Formula Assistance Program (section 18) of the Urban Mass Transportation Act of 1964, as amended, contains a program of capital and operating assistance for exclusive use in nonurbanized areas (under 50,000 population). Funds under this program are available for planning and program development activities, demonstration programs, vehicle acquisition, and other capital investments in support of general or special transit services, including services provided for the elderly, handicapped, and other transit-dependent persons. Like most other UMTA programs, the matching ratio of Federal to non-Federal shares for the section 18 program is 80/20 for capital assistance and 50/50 for operating assistance. (Table 6.8.)

SAINT LAWRENCE SEAWAY DEVELOPMENT CORPORATION

The Saint Lawrence Seaway Development Corporation was established by an act of Congress approved May 13, 1954 (33 U.S.C. 981–990). The Corporation, one of the operating administrations of the Department of Transportation, is self-sustaining, being financed from revenues received from tolls charged for the use of its facilities.

The Corporation, a wholly Government-owned enterprise, is responsible for the development, operation, and maintenance of the part of the Seaway be-

Table 6.8 Regional Offices—Urban Mass Transportation Administration

I.	c/o Transportation System Center, 55 Broadway, Cambridge, MA 02142
II.	26 Federal Plaza, New York, NY 10278
III.	434 Walnut St., Philadelphia, PA 19106
IV.	1720 Peachtree Rd. NW., Atlanta, GA 30309
V.	300 S. Wacker Dr., Chicago, IL 60606
VI.	819 Taylor St., Fort Worth, TX 76102
VII.	6301 Rockhill Rd., Kansas City, MO 64131
VIII.	1050 17th St., Denver, CO 80265
IX.	211 Main St., San Francisco, CA 94105
X.	915 2d Ave., Seattle, WA 98174

tween Montreal and Lake Erie, within the territorial limits of the United States.

The Saint Lawrence Seaway Development Corporation (SLOC) operates and maintains a safe, reliable and efficient waterway for commercial and noncommercial vessels between the Great Lakes and the Atlantic Ocean. The SLSDC, in tandem with the Saint Lawrence Seaway Authority of Canada, oversees operations safety, vessel inspections, traffic control, and navigation aids on the Great Lakes and the Saint Lawrence Seaway. Important to the economic development of the Great Lakes region, SLSDC works to develop trade opportunities to benefit port communities, shippers and receivers and related industries in the area.

It is the function of the Seaway Corporation to provide a safe, efficient, and effective water artery for maritime commerce, both in peacetime and in time of national emergency. The Seaway Corporation charges tolls in accordance with established rates for users of the Seaway, which it negotiates with the St. Lawrence Seaway Authority of Canada. The Corporation coordinates its activities with its Canadian counterpart particularly with respect to overall operations, traffic control, navigation aids, safety, season extension, and related programs designed to fully develop the fourth seacoast. As a self-sustaining entity, it encourages the development of traffic through the Great Lakes Seaway system so as to contribute significantly to the comprehensive economic and environmental development of the entire region. (See Figure 6.8.)

MARITIME ADMINISTRATION

The Maritime Administration is the successor of several Government agencies dating back to the establishment of the independent U.S. Shipping Board in 1916. Executive Order 6166 made the Shipping Board part of the Department of Commerce in 1933. However, in 1936, following passage of the Merchant Marine Act, the maritime function was again made independent with the establishment of the United States Maritime Commission. (See Figure 6.9.)

The Maritime Administration was established by Reorganization Plan 21 of 1950, effective May 24, 1950. The Maritime Act of 1981 (95 Stat. 151; 46 U.S.C. 1601) transferred the Maritime Administration from the Commerce Department to the Transportation Department. The transfer was effective August 6, 1981.

The Maritime Administration administers programs to aid in the development, promotion, and operation of the U.S. merchant marine. It is also charged with organizing and directing emergency merchant ship operations.

The Maritime Administration administers subsidy programs, through the Maritime Subsidy Board, under which the Federal Government, subject to statutory limitations, pays the difference between certain costs of operating ships under the U.S. flag and foreign competitive flags on essential services, and the difference between the costs of constructing ships in U.S. and foreign shipyards. It provides financing guarantees for the construction, reconstruction, and reconditioning of ships; acquires old ships for credit on the construction of new ships; and enters into capital construction fund agreements which grant tax deferrals on moneys to be used for the acquisition, construction, or reconstruction of ships.

The Maritime Administration (MARAD) promotes development and maintenance of an adequate, well-balanced, United States merchant marine, sufficient to carry the Nation's domestic waterborne commerce and a substantial portion of its waterborne foreign commerce, and capable of serving as a naval and military auxiliary in time of war or national emergency. MARAD also seeks to ensure that the United States enjoys adequate shipbuilding and repair service, efficient ports, effective intermodal water and land transportation systems, and reserve shipping capacity in the time of national emergency.

The Administration constructs or supervises the construction of merchant type ships for the Federal Government. It helps industry generate increased business for U.S. ships and conducts programs to develop

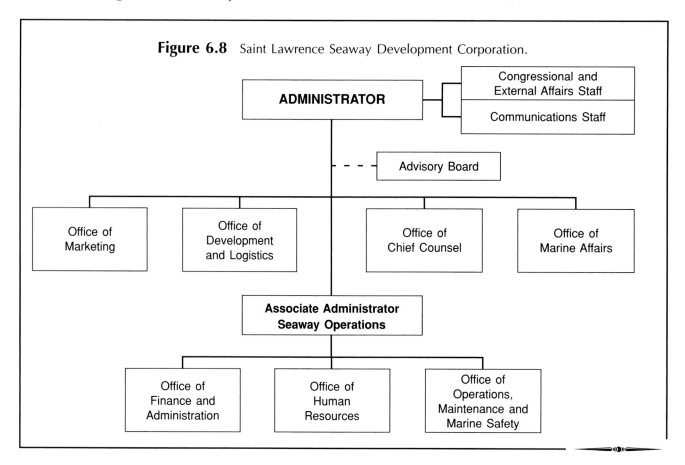

Figure 6.8 Saint Lawrence Seaway Development Corporation.

ports, facilities, and intermodal transport, and to promote domestic shipping. Also, it administers a War Risk Insurance program which ensures operators and seamen against losses caused by hostile action if domestic commercial insurance is not available.

The Administration conducts research and development activities to improve the efficiency and economy of the merchant marine. Under emergency conditions it charters Government-owned ships to U.S. operators, requisitions or procures ships owned by U.S. citizens, and allocates them to meet defense needs. It maintains a National Defense Reserve Fleet of Government-owned ships which it operates through general agents when required in national defense interests. It regulates sales to aliens and transfers to foreign registry of ships which are fully or partially owned by U.S. citizens. It also disposes of Government-owned ships found nonessential for national defense.

The Administration operates the U.S. Merchant Marine Academy, Kings Point, NY, where young people are trained to become merchant marine officers, and conducts training in shipboard firefighting at Earle, NJ; San Francisco, Calif.; Toledo, Ohio; and New Orleans, La. It also administers a Federal assis-

tance program for the maritime academies operated by California, Maine, Massachusetts, Michigan, New York, and Texas. (Table 6.9.)

Table 6.9 Field Organization—Maritime Administration

EASTERN REGION	26 Federal Plaza, New York, NY 10278 Phone, 212-264-1300
CENTRAL REGION	2 Canal St., New Orleans, LA 70130 Phone, 504-589-6556
GREAT LAKES REGION	Rm. 260, 1301 Superior Ave., Cleveland, OH 44114 Phone, 226-522-7617
WESTERN REGION	450 Golden Gate Ave., San Francisco, CA 94102 Phone, 415-556-3816
U.S. MERCHANT MARINE ACADEMY	Kings Point, NY 11024 Phone, 516-442-5347

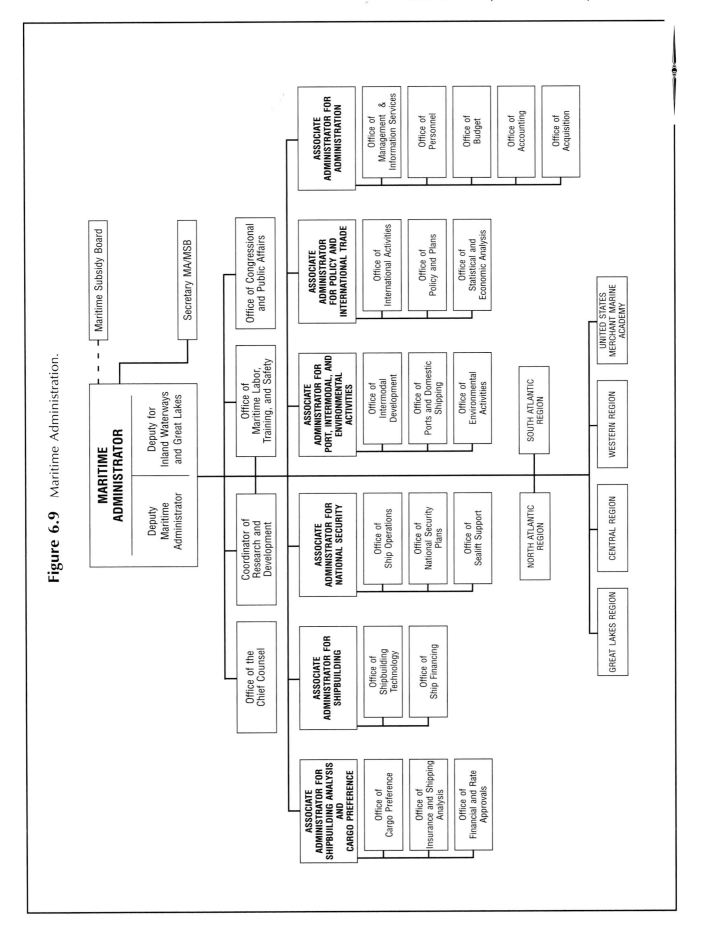

Figure 6.9 Maritime Administration.

RESEARCH AND SPECIAL PROGRAMS ADMINISTRATION

The Research and Special Programs Administration (RSPA) oversees rules governing the safe transportation and packaging of hazardous materials by all modes of transportation, excluding bulk transportation by water. RSPA also assists local and state authorities with training for hazardous materials emergencies. Pipeline safety standards are established and maintained by RSPA, ensuring public safety and environmental protection from gas and hazardous liquids transported by pipeline. Research and development plays a major role in RSPA's mission. With responsibility for research policy and technology sharing, the agency partners with national and international organizations and universities. In addition, RSPA operates the Volpe National Transportation Systems Center in Cambridge, Mass., which is dedicated to enhancing the effectiveness, efficiency, and responsiveness of other Federal organizations with critical transportation-related functions. (See Figure 6.10.)

BUREAU OF TRANSPORTATION STATISTICS

The 1991 Intermodal Surface Transportation Efficiency Act (ISTEA) established the Bureau of Transportation Statistics for data collection, analysis, and reporting and to ensure the most cost-effective use of transportation-monitoring resources. It strives to increase public awareness of the nation's transportation system and its implications and improve the transportation knowledge base of decisionmakers. (See Figure 6.11.)

This Bureau supplements the data collection programs of other agencies and serves as the lead agency in developing and coordinating intermodal transportation statistics. It is unique in that it is the only federal agency to combine statistical analysis, mapping, and transportation analysis under one roof.

It is committed to quality, accessibility, usability, and objectivity in transportation statistics and respect for privacy. These goals are accomplished in the following manner:

The Bureau strives to make high-quality data and information available for the transportation community and other individuals or groups interested in transportation. Strong leadership, planning, educational out-

reach, and the pursuit of a superior working team are maintained.

The Director guides data collection, analysis, and reporting to ensure the most cost-effective use of transportation resources.

A strategic plan outlines goals for 2000–2005 and beyond and plans to achieve them. Strategic goals focus on commitment to relevance, quality, timeliness, comparability, completeness, and utility.

This Bureau is an integral part of the strategic plan for the entire Department of Transportation and the larger scope of the American transportation system. The Strategic Plan discusses values and vision, relationships between goals, and the strategies that will enable the Department to achieve them.

To ensure the quality and effectiveness of transportation statistics, BTS tracks advances in data acquisition and information technology, promotes the use of successful technologies to reduce costs and respondent burden, and works to increase data accuracy and timeliness.

Because transportation is intimately linked to geography, they bridge many DOT statistical and mapping programs to provide a complete, accurate picture of transportation using a broad array of geographic data and geographic information systems technology.

The Bureau works to assure quality by evaluating transportation data needs and recommending improvements. Transportation information needs is a list of assessments and the studies and conferences upon which these assessments are based.

The most important responsibility is to make transportation statistics data accessible and understandable. To promote access to data, it publishes a wide variety of statistical and other information in printed and electronic form. It also compiles and disseminates inventories of all transportation data resources, making them available to government agencies, private industry, and the public at minimal or no cost.

To improve the usability of transportation statistics, the Bureau develops straightforward ways to measure transportation and present data visually.

In close cooperation with the DOT Safety Council, other operating administrations within DOT, and federal, state, local, and international agencies, this Bureau strives for common definitions, sampling procedures, and other guidelines to improve statistical quality and inter-comparability.

Figure 6.10 Research and Special Programs Administration.

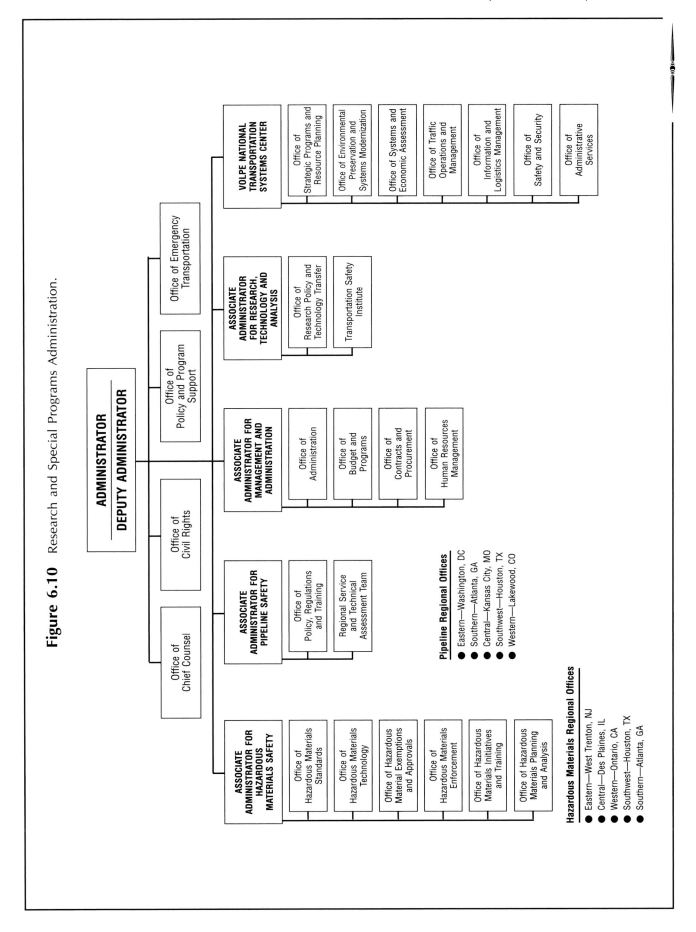

Pipeline Regional Offices
- Eastern—Washington, DC
- Southern—Atlanta, GA
- Central—Kansas City, MO
- Southwest—Houston, TX
- Western—Lakewood, CO

Hazardous Materials Regional Offices
- Eastern—West Trenton, NJ
- Central—Des Plaines, IL
- Western—Ontario, CA
- Southwest—Houston, TX
- Southern—Atlanta, GA

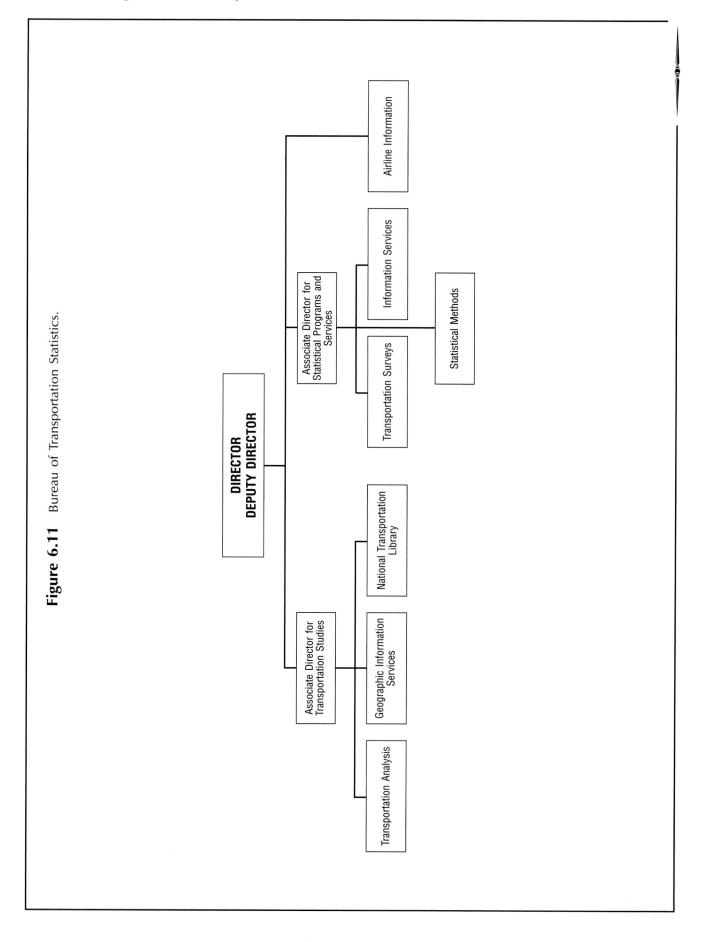

Figure 6.11   Bureau of Transportation Statistics.

FEDERAL MOTOR CARRIER SAFETY ADMINISTRATION

The Federal Motor Carrier Safety Administration was established within the Department of Transportation on January 1, 2000, pursuant to the Motor Carrier Safety Improvement Act of 1999 [Public Law No. 106-159, 113 Stat. 1748 (December 9, 1999)]. Formerly a part of the Federal Highway Administration, the Federal Motor Carrier Safety Administration's primary mission is to prevent commercial motor vehicle-related fatalities and injuries. Administration activities contribute to ensuring safety in motor carrier operations through strong enforcement of safety regulations, targeting high-risk carriers and commercial motor vehicle drivers; improving safety information systems and commercial motor vehicle technologies; strengthening commercial motor vehicle equipment and operating standards; and increasing safety awareness. To accomplish these activities, the Administration works with Federal, state, and local enforcement agencies, the motor carrier industry, labor safety interest groups, and others. (See Figure 6.12.)

PROGRAMS

Motor Carrier Safety Assistance Program

The Motor Carrier Safety Assistance Program is a Federal grant program that provides states with financial assistance for roadside inspections and other commercial motor vehicle safety programs. It promotes detection and correction of commercial motor vehicle safety defects, commercial motor vehicle driver deficiencies, and unsafe motor carrier practices before they become contributing factors to crashes and hazardous materials incidents. The program also promotes the adoption and uniform enforcement by the states of safety rules, regulations, and standards compatible with the Federal Motor Carrier Safety Regulations and Federal Hazardous Materials Regulations.

Regulatory Compliance and Enforcement

The Administration's compliance reviews and enforcement activities and the states' roadside inspection activities are the principal means of ensuring that the Federal Motor Carrier Safety Regulations and the Federal Hazardous Materials Regulations are enforced. Compliance and enforcement efforts are enhanced through the Performance and Registration Information Systems Management (PRISM) program, a Federal and state partnership to improve safety performance or remove high-risk carriers from the nation's highways. Through PRISM, compliance reviews are conducted on unsafe motor carriers and their safety performance is monitored and tracked. Continued poor safety performance may result in a Federal Operations Out-of-Service Order/unfit determination in conjunction with the suspension and/or revocation of vehicle registration privileges.

Licensing and Insurance

With the closing of the Interstate Commerce Commission (ICC) the licensing and insurance responsibility was transferred to the Office of Motor Carrier and now to the Federal Motor Carrier Safety Administration.

Commercial Driver's License Program

The Administration develops, issues, and evaluates standards for testing and licensing commercial motor vehicle drivers. These standards require states to issue a Commercial Driver's License only after drivers pass knowledge and skill tests that pertain to the type of vehicle operated. States are audited every three years to monitor compliance with Federal standards; noncompliance could result in loss of Federal funding.

Data and Analysis

The Administration collects and disseminates safety data concerning motor carriers. Data collected by Federal safety investigators and state partners from roadside inspections, crashes, compliance reviews, and enforcement activities are indexed by carrier. This information provides a national perspective on carrier performance and assists in determining Administration and state enforcement activities and priorities. Combined with data from other sources (including the National Highway Traffic Safety Administration), extensive analysis is performed to determine trends in performance by carrier and other factors such as cargo, driver demographics, location, time, and type of incident. Based on identified trends, the Administration directs resources in the most efficient and effective manner to improve motor carrier safety.

Research and Technology Program

The Administration identifies, coordinates, and administers research and development to enhance the safety of motor carrier operations, commercial motor

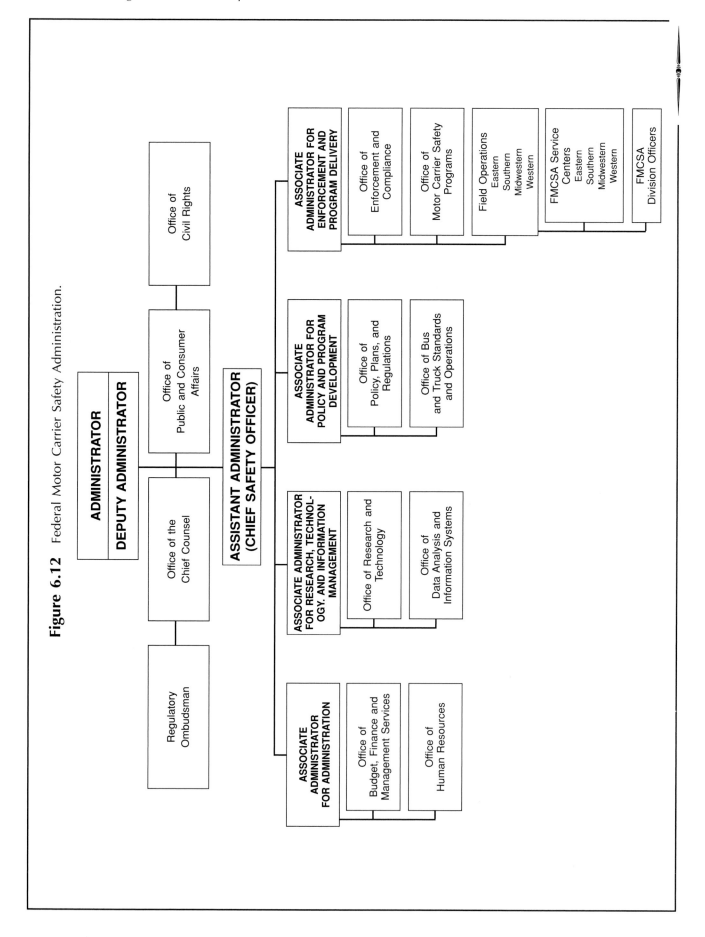

Figure 6.12 Federal Motor Carrier Safety Administration.

vehicles, and commercial motor vehicle drivers. The Administration promotes the use of information systems and advanced technologies to improve commercial vehicle safety, simplify government administrative systems, and provide savings to states and the motor carrier industry.

Border and International

The Administration supports the development of compatible motor carrier safety requirements and procedures throughout North America in the context of the North America Free Trade Agreement (NAFTA). It supports programs to improve the safety performance of motor carriers operating in border areas with other Federal agencies, and supports the development of state safety inspection facilities. The Administration participates in international technical organizations and committees to share best practices in motor carrier safety.

Other

Hazardous Materials. The Administration enforces regulations for the safe transportation of hazardous materials by highway and rules governing the manufacture and maintenance of cargo tank motor vehicles, as set forth in Chapter 51 of Title 49 of the United States Code.

Household Goods. The Administration has established a task force to identify and investigate those household good carriers which have exhibited a substantial pattern of consumer abuse. Consumer awareness/self-help packages are available.

Hotline. The Federal Motor Carrier Safety Administration provides a toll-free hotline for reporting dangerous safety violations involving a commercial truck or bus: 1-888-DOT-SAFT (1-888-368-7238).

FIELD OFFICES

The field organizations deliver program services to the Federal Motor Carrier Safety Administration's (FMCSA) partners and customers. This organization consists of Field Operations, Service center and State-level motor carrier division offices.

These offices are here to answer questions and to provide guidance concerning the Federal Motor Carrier Safety Regulations.

SURFACE TRANSPORTATION BOARD

The Surface Transportation Board is an independent, bipartisan, adjudicatory body organizationally housed within the Department of Transportation. It is responsible for the economic regulation of interstate surface transportation, primarily railroads, within the United States. Its mission is to ensure that competitive, efficient, and safe transportation services are provided to meet the needs of shippers, receivers, and consumers. The Board is charged with promoting, where appropriate, substantive and procedural regulatory reform in the economic regulation of surface transportation, and with providing an efficient and effective forum for the resolution of disputes. The Board continues to strive to develop, through rulemakings and case disposition, new and better ways to analyze unique and complex problems, to reach fully justified decisions more quickly, to reduce the costs associated with regulatory oversight, and to encourage private-sector negotiations and resolutions to problems where appropriate.

NATIONAL TRANSPORTATION POLICY

STATEMENT OF THE SECRETARY OF TRANSPORTATION

An investment in transportation is an investment in America's future. No industry in the Nation is more important to U.S. economic growth and international competitiveness than transportation. Every household and every business, our mines and farms, manufacturers and utilities, export trade and national security, all depend on transportation. Americans spend nearly $800 billion for transportation products and services every year (See Figure 6.13).

As we begin a new decade and prepare for the 21st century, the United States must renew its commitment to maintaining our transportation system as the finest in the world. We are entering an era in which our ability to compete internationally is critical to our economic vitality and quality of life. To meet the changing demands of the international marketplace, we must have safe, efficient transportation to carry people where they want to go and to move the vast quantities of goods we produce and consume. Projected transportation needs

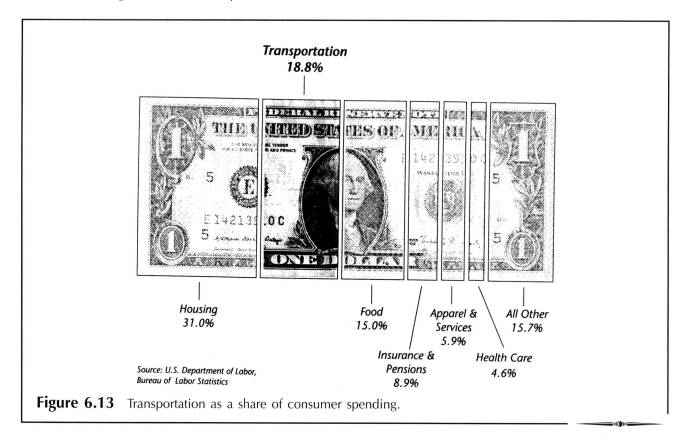

Figure 6.13   Transportation as a share of consumer spending.

for the 21st century eclipse our present public and private sector programs. We must broaden the base of support for transportation, reinvigorate investment, and tap new sources of ideas and capital to meet growing demands.

As we face the challenges of a changing society, an evolving world economy, and new technologies, we must restructure the transportation partnership to give other levels of government and the private sector the tools they need to address critical requirements in transportation. All of those who have a stake in efficient transportation must participate—Federal, State, and local governments, private businesses, academic institutions, transportation interest groups, communities, and individuals. The measure of our Federal policies will lie in their success at unleashing private resources and at using public resources most efficiently to meet the Nation's transportation needs.

The mission of the Department of Transportation, as set forth in the legislation establishing the Department, is to "provide general leadership in identifying and solving transportation problems," to "develop and recommend . . . transportation policies and programs" to the President and Congress, and to "achieve transportation objectives considering the needs of the public, users, carriers, industry, labor, and national defense."

The Federal Government's direct role in achieving transportation objectives is anchored in Constitutional responsibilities to promote and facilitate interstate commerce, conduct the Nation's foreign affairs, and provide for the general welfare and national defense. Beyond these responsibilities, the Federal Government must be involved in transportation decisions where other compelling national interests are involved. In all cases, Federal programs and policies should be designed to contribute to attaining national goals; based on cost-effective use of resources in relation to public benefits; responsive to market needs and based on market principles; directed to factors such as safety or the environment that are not adequately reflected in market prices; equitable in dealing with the various modes and forms of transportation; and flexible enough to address varying circumstances and needs.

THE NATIONAL POLICY AGENDA

To respond to views expressed around the country during the public outreach effort and to prepare for future challenges and opportunities, the Department has developed an ambitious agenda to fulfill both short- and long-term needs. This agenda revolves around six key themes.

1. Maintain and expand the Nation's transportation system.

2. Foster a sound financial base for transportation.

3. Keep the transportation industry strong and competitive.

4. Ensure that the transportation system supports public safety and national security.

5. Protect the environment and the quality of life.

6. Advance U.S. transportation technology and expertise for the 21st century.

1. Maintain and Expand the Nation's Transportation System.

The transportation infrastructure is vital to the Nation's economy, and it must serve the needs of all Americans, including the young and old, minorities, disadvantaged and disabled individuals, and people living in urban and rural communities. There are increasing signs, however, that the system is beginning to break down. We cannot afford inadequate, inefficient transportation.

The Federal Government is committed to maintaining transportation infrastructure and providing the tools, incentives, and flexibility for State and local governments and the private sector to renew the capacity and performance of the transportation system. The Department is particularly committed to reducing congestion in the aviation and highway systems by fostering improved management and use of key transportation facilities, new technology, and capacity enhancements.

To achieve the transportation system the Nation needs for the future, we must recognize the changing Federal, State, and local roles. The Federal Government must concentrate more of its transportation resources on facilities and projects that advance the performance of transportation systems of national significance. Within Federal-aid programs for transportation, grant recipients must be provided the flexibility to achieve diverse transportation goals through broad, multi-purpose programs. Rigid project requirements can be replaced with performance criteria.

The most immediate task for the transportation sector is to maintain the assets we have. If facilities are not kept in sound condition, they cannot support the level of operations they were designed to handle. The Federal Government will help to address this issue by emphasizing capital maintenance in Federal-aid programs. Federal-aid recipients, in turn, will have to make a commitment to preserving critical elements of the infrastructure by, for example, instituting comprehensive plans for managing capital assets and maintaining facilities.

To use the Nation's resources most effectively, we must improve management of existing and new transportation facilities. The Department is particularly committed to implementing the National Airspace System Plan and installing a new generation of air traffic control. In urban and intercity travel, Department programs will encourage system management improvements, peak-period pricing, and other initiatives to reduce congestion.

Federal transportation assistance must be structured so that it does not encourage unnecessary or unwise investment. Programs must allow for a broad range of options, permitting investment in cost-effective projects that enhance capacity or make better use of existing resources, such as high-occupancy vehicle lanes for carpools and buses. However, to meet long-term transportation needs, the Nation must anticipate and plan for expansion of our current transportation system. In partnership with State, local, and private interests, the Department will support construction of new facilities and new capacity on existing facilities to address priority national needs in the transportation network.

Smooth, efficient travel depends on good connections between different parts of the transportation system. For example, many freight movements rely on connections between railroads and ports, while intercity passenger travel often requires links between airports and ground transportation. Improved connections, particularly among intercity, urban, and rural systems, will contribute to sounder, more efficient transportation.

2. Foster a Sound Financial Base for Transportation.

We must ensure that the necessary funds will be available to support our transportation system. There will be increasing demands for investment in transportation to keep up with rising costs and emerging national transportation system needs, and the necessary funding will have to come from a variety of sources. The Federal Government is prepared to provide the leadership, in partnership with State and local governments and the private sector, to assure an adequate financial base for transportation.

The Federal Government will emphasize reliance on user charges as the key element in financing the Federal share of transportation expenditures. The user charges paid into transportation trust funds must be dedicated to transportation to preserve the integrity of the trust funds and the user fee concept and to serve critical transportation needs.

The Department is proposing to institute user fees to recover the costs of Federal railroad safety and Coast Guard inspection activities and to increase the Federal aviation program and improve cost recovery for Federal aviation activities. The Federal Government must also continue to review the structure and level of Federal transportation user charges to ensure that they provide adequate and equitable cost recovery. In addition, where groups of users who benefit from facilities or services supported by Federal funds do not pay fees, the Federal Government should determine whether there is an efficient method to recover Federal costs from them.

We must stimulate increased investment in transportation by State and local governments and the private sector by expanding the range of available tools and choices. Federal policies should provide greater incentives and increased flexibility in financing for other levels of government and the private sector. For example, local passenger facility charges at airports and tolls on highways offer significant potential as financing mechanisms where there is heavy travel demand. Federal policy should relax restrictions on the use of such mechanisms. In addition, State and local governments and the private sector need greater flexibility to employ innovative financing techniques, such as benefit assessments, joint development rights, and other means of capturing the value of transportation investments in fees assessed on the private firms that benefit from transportation service or facilities.

Continuing and substantial infusions of private capital will be required to sustain the performance of the transportation system and accommodate increasing traffic. While government bodies at all levels must encourage and welcome private investment in transportation, many laws and policies deter such participation. Future policy must minimize barriers to private participation in the ownership, planning, financing, construction, maintenance, and management of transportation facilities and services, while encouraging State and local governments to do the same.

3. Keep the Transportation Industry Strong and Competitive.

The efficiency and competitiveness of transportation providers are essential to economic growth and productivity and the ability of the United States to compete in the world market. Providers of transportation service can meet transportation needs most effi-

ciently if they have the latitude to respond to demand and if they are competing on an equitable basis. Federal programs and policies must treat modes and carriers fairly, and avoid unnecessary restrictions that hinder efficient transportation operations. We must remove the barriers that impede efficiency and restrict the free flow of interstate and international commerce, and work to ensure that policies do not unfairly provide competitive advantages to one mode over another.

Transportation deregulation has been a notable success. We must build on that success by eliminating remaining economic regulation of trucking and other transportation industries where regulation is unnecessary and outmoded. We need greater uniformity in the State motor carrier registration and taxation procedures. Federal requirements that place unique and burdensome costs on carriers should be repealed, including a variety of archaic labor requirements that prevent the railroads from operating efficiently and competing on an equal basis with other modes. We must develop a balanced approach for aviation that reduces aircraft noise and takes into account both the needs of interstate commerce and the desire of local areas to limit aircraft noise.

The principles of market competition must be brought to bear in transit programs to improve performance and reduce costs. The Federal Government must also achieve greater consistency and flexibility in rural transportation programs. In intercity rail passenger service, Amtrak has made considerable progress toward improving efficiency and reducing its subsidy requirement. Under current budget constraints, no Federal funding is proposed for Amtrak in FY 1991, but the Administration is eager to work with the Congress, Amtrak, and other interested public and private parties to determine how best to obtain needed investment from the private sector and to make Amtrak services more cost-effective.

The U.S. merchant marine must be more competitive if it is to survive and support national security needs. That effort must begin with a reexamination of Federal maritime programs, including reform of the Operating Differential Subsidy program. The Federal Government must also actively pursue agreements to improve access to international markets for U.S. carriers in all modes and redouble our efforts to eliminate practices that discriminate against U.S. maritime, air, and motor carriers, inhibiting operations and sapping our carriers' competitive strength. In the newest element of the transportation system, commercial space transportation, the Nation should work to foster the development of a vigorous industry.

A well-qualified workforce is critical to building, managing, maintaining, and operating the transportation system. Federal, State, and local governments must work with private industry to assure effective recruitment and training for the transportation work force, especially minorities and women, disabled citizens, and economically disadvantaged individuals.

4. Ensure That the Transportation System Supports Public Safety and National Security.

Safety remains the top priority of the Department. Across all modes, the Department will expand efforts to improve public safety and security, through better driver and operator training in all modes, increased public awareness of transportation safety matters, more effective anti-drug and alcohol programs, improved vehicle designs, and effective regulation of hazardous materials movements.

By far the greatest number of transportation-related accidents each year occurs on the Nation's streets and highways. More than 47,000 people died on our highways in 1988. We cannot tolerate such senseless loss. The Federal Government is committed to a broad, cooperative, and multifaceted campaign to reduce the highway death toll and to meet the President's safety improvement goals.

The aviation system faces major challenges to its consistently high safety record: revolutionary changes to aircraft and other aviation technology, the pressure increasing travel demand has placed on aviation system capacity, substance abuse within the work force, and terrorist acts against aviation operations. The Department will take a number of actions, including modernization of the air traffic control system, to ensure that rising demand does not compromise the safety of the system. The Department will also provide leadership in addressing human factors issues that affect aviation safety.

The Department has many other safety responsibilities. Safety on the waters is the major mission of the U.S. Coast Guard. The Department will assure that shipments of hazardous materials by water, highway, railroad, and pipeline do not pose a safety hazard to nearby communities, and that the transportation system is prepared to withstand natural disasters, such as hurricanes and earthquakes. In addition, the Department working with other agencies and industry, must maintain vigilance to detect and interdict movements of illicit drugs, and prevent acts of terrorism against transportation at home and abroad.

During peacetime and wartime, the Nation's civilian transportation system and the U.S. Coast Guard are vital to supporting national defense. The Department is committed to working with the Department of Defense to identify national defense transportation needs and assure that they are met. In particular, a viable and competitive merchant marine is essential to meeting the Nation's military sealift requirements, and the Departments of Transportation and Defense must work together to implement the President's National Sealift Policy.

5. Protect the Environment and the Quality of Life.

Federal transportation policy must support national efforts for environmental protection. We must continue to protect our air, water, and land resources and the long-term health and well-being of citizens. For example, the Nation must take stronger steps to reduce vehicle emissions, as proposed in the amendments to the Clean Air Act advanced by the President.

Many parties will have to work together to achieve more effective application of vehicle emissions control technology, reduce the release of toxic chemicals into the environment during transportation, comprehensively address issues related to global climate change and environmental degradation, and implement a "no net loss" goal for wetlands.

Catastrophic oil spills like the *Exxon Valdez* disaster must be prevented, and quick and effective response must be assured for those spills that do occur. The Federal Government must ensure that the necessary rules are in place to achieve safe, effective transport of crude oil and petroleum products. The Department is committed to working with State, local, and regional officials to develop improved and more consistent contingency planning procedures to respond to oil spills.

An improved quality of life requires increased mobility and access; this is especially true for the transportation of the disadvantaged and those who are elderly and disabled. All Americans have the right to enjoy the benefits of transportation, and we must assure that transportation services and facilities accommodate their needs. This includes working with private carriers and public transportation agencies in preparing plans or standards for assuring that their vehicles are accessible to disabled passengers in a timely and cost-effective manner.

6. Advance U.S. Transportation Technology Expertise.

The United States has a long and proud history of breakthroughs in transportation technology and innovations in transportation management and operations. We must renew and strengthen our focus on technology and innovation if we are to meet the expectations and needs of the Nation and maintain U.S. technological leadership in the world. Although many of the resources, the imagination, and creativity necessary to support transportation advances will come from the private sector, the Federal Government can play a key role in increasing the awareness of technological needs, and can serve as a leader and a catalyst for research, innovation, and expertise.

The opportunities to improve transportation through research and innovation are many. An intensive national program of research into human factors in transportation will lead to major breakthroughs in efficiency as well as safety. Improved data, communications, and information technology, innovative management and financing techniques can make a significant contribution to the efficiency and performance of the transportation system. Research on methods of reducing vehicle noise and air pollution must also be a significant focus of attention.

Although technological advances alone cannot solve our transportation problems, new forms of freight and passenger transportation offer exciting potential for the future. In cooperation with State, local, and private groups, the Department will foster research, evaluation, and demonstration of promising new technologies to carry travelers in high-density intercity corridors, including such options as high-speed rail, magnetically levitated trains, and tiltrotor aircraft. The Administration will also work with State and local governments and private industry to develop "intelligent vehicle/highway systems" that integrate the latest computer and communication technology to improve the safety and efficiency of our highways.

Many other Federal initiatives are under way that will affect motor vehicles. DOT will work actively with other Federal agencies involved in research on automobiles and other motor vehicles to improve fuel efficiency, reduce vehicle emissions, promote alternative fuels, and increase design safety, occupant protection, and crashworthiness of vehicles.

Transportation innovation relies upon effective dissemination of information and research results. The Department is committed to enhancing and making more widely available transportation data and research results, and reinforcing the program of transportation research in the Nation's academic and business communities. Greater awareness of the opportunities and challenges in transportation and improved transportation education are both vital to the effort to build transportation expertise in the 21st century.

The Department is in a unique position to learn of and share information about innovative transportation technologies and operations being developed around the world. Through its cooperative programs with other countries, the Department will step up its efforts to make certain that the U.S. transportation community is aware of and has access to emerging technological advances.

WHERE DO WE GO FROM HERE?

It is critically important to begin immediately the national effort to implement this transportation policy. Major reauthorizing legislation will be enacted in the near future to ensure that the Federal Government can carry out its obligations to provide safe and adequate airport and airspace operations, to sustain a safe and adequate national network of highways, and to support vital urban mass transportation systems. Other legislation will be proposed by the Department to address key concerns involving railroad, merchant marine, Coast Guard, and safety functions. During this year, the Department will also begin pursuing a number of important regulatory policy changes, many of which will require new legislative authority.

Much can be done to achieve national transportation policy objectives by redirecting the resources and endeavors of the Department of Transportation. The Department will work to ensure that this policy is fully implemented. As years pass, the results of these initial efforts will be available to support future decision-making.

For the longer term, the Federal Government must maintain the mechanisms for integrating ideas from all parts of the transportation community that have worked so well to support development of this policy. The Department of Transportation will establish a continuing strategic planning capability to carry on the forward-looking, multidisciplinary, multimodal approach to transportation that this process has fostered.

We must make wise use of existing resources and launch longer term efforts to put new systems and facilities in place. The Department will ensure that programs and individuals actions fit within a sound overall national policy framework and that those programs and actions remain sensitive to the changing conditions and needs the transportation system is facing. The Nation must invest today to meet tomorrow's transportation needs.

INTERMODAL SURFACE TRANSPORTATION EFFICIENCY ACT OF 1991

The National Transportation Policy was the forerunner to the Intermodal Surface Transportation Efficiency Act of 1991. This landmark legislation restructured the Federal aid to highway and transit programs to meet the Interstate needs of the nation. It is the current authorizing legislation for these programs.

On December 28, 1991, the President signed the Intermodal Surface Transportation Efficiency Act of 1991 providing authorizations for highways, highway safety, and mass transportation for the next 6 years. Total funding of about $155 billion was available in fiscal years (FY) 1992–1997.

The purpose of the Act is clearly enunciated in its statement of policy:

To develop a National Intermodal Transportation System that is economically efficient, environmentally sound, provides the foundation for the Nation to compete in the global economy and will move people and goods in an energy efficient manner.

The provisions of the Act reflect these important policy goals. Some of the major features include:

1. A National Highway System, consisting primarily of existing Interstate routes and a portion of the Primary System, is established to focus Federal resources on roads that are the most important to interstate travel and national defense, roads that connect with other modes of transportation, and are essential for international commerce.

2. State and local governments are given more flexibility in determining transportation solutions, whether transit or highways, and the tools of enhanced planning and management systems to guide them in making the best choices.

3. New technologies, such as intelligent vehicle-highway systems and prototype magnetic levitation systems, are funded to push the Nation forward into thinking of new approaches in providing 21st Century transportation.

4. The private sector is tapped as a source for funding transportation improvements. Restrictions on the use of Federal funds for toll roads have been relaxed and private entities may even own such facilities.

5. The Act continues discretionary and formula funds for mass transit.

6. Highway funds are available for activities that enhance the environment, such as wetland banking, mitigation of damage to wildlife habitat, historic sites, activities that contribute to meeting air quality standards, a wide range of bicycle and pedestrian projects, and highway beautification.

This report, A Statement of National Transportation Policy, is the second of two reports entitled, *Moving America: New Directions, New Opportunities.*

Volume 1, Building the National Transportation Policy, provides an overview of the current situation, a snapshot of the U.S. transportation "landscape." It describes trends and external factors affecting transportation, sets out the key issues, and generally outlines the policy development process.

A related report to Congress, *National Transportation Strategic Planning Study,* was required by Section 317(b) of the FY 1988 DOT Appropriations Act. It provides information on the factors affecting transportation (including demographics, the economy, and energy) and the transportation setting (including regulations, safety, and technology), and reviews the conditions and issues facing each transportation mode. The report also contains current estimates of long-term costs to develop and maintain facilities and services for moving people and goods, and summarizes urban transportation case studies.

7. Highway safety is further enhanced by a new program to encourage the use of safety belts and motorcycle helmets.

8. State uniformity in vehicle registration and fuel tax reporting is required. This will ease the recordkeeping and reporting burden on businesses and contribute substantially to increased productivity of the truck and bus industry.

The bill's comprehensive coverage is reflected in its eight titles:

TITLE I—Surface Transportation (related to highways)

TITLE II—Highway Safety

TITLE III—Federal Transit Act Amendments of 1991

TITLE IV—Motor Carrier Act of 1991

TITLE V—Intermodal Transportation

TITLE VI—Research

TITLE VII—Air Transportation

TITLE VIII—Extension of Highway-Related Taxes and Highway Trust Fund

CHAPTER 7

The Federal Aviation Administration*

A BRIEF HISTORY OF THE FEDERAL AVIATION ADMINISTRATION AND ITS PREDECESSOR AGENCIES

The Air Commerce Act of May 20, 1926, was the cornerstone of the Federal government's regulation of civil aviation. This landmark legislation was passed at the urging of the aviation industry, whose leaders believed the airplane could not reach its full commercial potential without Federal action to improve and maintain safety standards. The Act charged the Secretary of Commerce with fostering air commerce, issuing and enforcing air traffic rules, licensing pilots, certificating aircraft, establishing airways, and operating and maintaining aids to air navigation. A new Aeronautics Branch of the Department of Commerce assumed primary responsibility for aviation oversight. The first head of the Branch was William P. MacCracken, Jr., who had played a key part in convincing Congress of the need for this new governmental role.

In fulfilling its civil aviation responsibilities, the Department of Commerce initially concentrated on such functions as safety rulemaking and the certification of pilots and aircraft. It took over the building and operation of the nation's system of lighted airways, a task that had been begun by the Post Office Department. The Department of Commerce improved aeronautical radio communications, and introduced radio beacons as an effective aid to air navigation.

In 1934, the Aeronautics Branch was renamed the Bureau of Air Commerce to reflect its enhanced status within the Department. As commercial flying increased, the Bureau encouraged a group of airlines to establish the first three centers for providing air traffic control (ATC) along the airways. In 1936, the Bureau itself took over the centers and began to expand the ATC system. The pioneer air traffic controllers used maps, blackboards, and mental calculations to ensure the safe separation of aircraft traveling along designated routes between cities.

In 1938, the Civil Aeronautics Act transferred the Federal civil aviation responsibilities from the Commerce Department to a new independent agency, the Civil Aeronautics Authority. The legislation also expanded the government's role by giving the Authority the power to regulate airline fares and to determine the routes that air carriers would serve.

In 1940, President Franklin Roosevelt split the Authority into two agencies, the Civil Aeronautics Administration (CAA) and the Civil Aeronautics Board (CAB). CAA was responsible for ATC, airman and aircraft certification, safety enforcement, and airway development. CAB was entrusted with safety rulemaking, accident investigation, and economic regulation of the airlines. Both organizations were part of the Department of Commerce. Unlike CAA, however, CAB functioned independently of the Secretary.

---

*For current information go to the Website at http://www.faa.gov/orgs.htm

On the eve of America's entry into World War II, CAA began to extend its ATC responsibilities to take-off and landing operations at airports. This expanded role eventually became permanent after the war. The application of radar to ATC helped controllers in their drive to keep abreast of the postwar boom in commercial air transportation. In 1946, meanwhile, Congress gave CAA the added task of administering the Federal-aid airport program, the first peacetime program of financial assistance aimed exclusively at promoting development of the nation's civil airports.

The approaching introduction of jet airliners, and a series of midair collisions, spurred passage of the Federal Aviation Act of 1958. This legislation transferred CAA's functions to a new independent body, the Federal Aviation Agency, which had broader authority to combat aviation hazards. The act took safety rulemaking from CAB and entrusted it to the new FAA. It also gave FAA sole responsibility for developing and maintaining a common civil-military system of air navigation and air traffic control, a responsibility CAA had shared with others.

The scope of the Federal Aviation Act owed much to the leadership of Elwood "Pete" Quesada, an Air Force general who had served as President Eisenhower's principle advisor on civil aeronautics. After becoming the first Administrator of the agency he had helped to create, Quesada mounted a vigorous campaign for improved airline safety.

In 1966, Congress authorized the creation of a cabinet department that would combine major Federal transportation responsibilities. This new Department of Transportation (DOT) began full operations on April 1, 1967. On that day, FAA became one of several modal organizations within DOT and received a new name, Federal Aviation Administration. At the same time, CAB's accident investigation function was transferred to the new National Transportation Safety Board.

Even before becoming part of DOT, FAA gradually assumed responsibilities not originally contemplated by the Federal Aviation Act. The hijacking epidemic of the 1960s involved the agency in the field of aviation security. In 1968, Congress vested in FAA's Administrator the power to prescribe aircraft noise standards. The Airport and Airway Development Act of 1970 placed the agency in charge of a new airport aid program funded by a special aviation trust fund. The same Act made FAA responsible for safety certification of airports served by air carriers.

Air Traffic Control Automation. By the mid-1970s, FAA had achieved a semi-automated air traffic control system based on a marriage of radar and computer technology. By automating certain routine tasks, the system allowed controllers to concentrate more efficiently on the vital task of providing separation. Data appearing directly on the controllers' scopes provided the identity, altitude, and groundspeed of aircraft carrying radar beacons. Despite its effectiveness, this system required enhancement to keep pace with the increased air traffic of the late 1970s. The increase was due in part to the competitive environment created by the Airline Deregulation Act of 1978. This law phased out CAB's economic regulation of the airlines, and CAB ceased to exist at the end of 1984.

To meet the challenge of traffic growth, FAA unveiled the National Airspace System (NAS) Plan in January 1982. The new plan called for more advanced systems for en route and terminal ATC, modernized flight service stations, and improvements in ground-to-air surveillance and communication.

While preparing the NAS Plan, FAA faced a strike by key members of its workforce. An earlier period of disharmony between management and the Professional Air Traffic Controllers Organization (PATCO) had culminated in a 1970 "sickout" by 3,000 controllers. Although controllers subsequently gained additional wage and retirement benefits, another period of tension led to an illegal strike in August 1981. The government dismissed over 11,000 strike participants and decertified PATCO. By the spring of 1984, FAA had ended the last of the special restrictions imposed to keep the airspace system operating safely during the strike.

FAA's organizational structure has continued to evolve since its creation. The agency's first Administrator favored a management system under which officials in Washington exercised direct control over programs in the field. In 1961, however, his successor began a decentralization process that transferred much authority to regional organizations. This pattern generally endured until a 1988 change again charged managers at national headquarters with more direction of field activities. Another notable change occurred in 1987, when Washington National and Dulles International Airports passed from FAA's management to that of an authority representing multiple jurisdictions. (National had been opened by CAA in 1941, Dulles by FAA in 1962.)

In November 1994, a reorganization structured FAA along its six key lines of business in order to make better use of resources. A seventh line of business was added one year later when the Office of Commercial Space Transportation was transferred to FAA from the Office of the Secretary of Transportation. The addition of this office gave the agency regulatory responsibilities concerning the launching of space payloads by the private sector. During 1996, reform legislation gave FAA increased flexibility regarding acquisition and personnel policies. Further legislation in 2000 prompted action to establish within the agency a new performance-based organization with responsibility for air traffic services.

FAA addressed a wide variety of technical issues as the rapid evolution of aeronautics continued. The Aviation Safety Research Act of 1988 mandated greater emphasis on long-range research planning and on study of such issues as aging aircraft structures and human factors affecting safety. In February 1991, FAA replaced the National Airspace System Plan with the more comprehensive Capital Investment Plan (CIP). The new plan included higher levels of automation as well as new radar, communications, and weather forecasting systems.

As the modernization program evolved, problems in developing ambitious automation systems prompted a change in strategy. FAA shifted its emphasis toward enhancing the air traffic control system through more manageable, step-by-step improvements. At the same time, the agency worked to speed the application of the Global Positioning System satellite technology to civil aeronautics. Other notable programs included Free Flight, an innovative concept aimed at providing greater flexibility to fly direct routes. At the opening of the 21st Century, Free Flight's initial phase was beginning to deliver benefits that added to the efficiency of air transportation.

Periodically a movement is presented to separate the FAA from the DOT and make it an independent agency as it was before 1966.

Directed by an Administrator, the FAA has as its primary function the fostering of the development and safety of American aviation. More specifically, the FAA is responsible for developing the major policies necessary to guide the long-range growth of civil aviation; modernizing the air traffic control system; establishing in a single authority the essential management functions necessary to support the common needs of civil and military operations; providing for the most effective and efficient use of the airspace over the United States; and for the rulemaking responsibilities relative to these functions.

The FAA constructs, operates, and maintains the National Airspace System and the facilities which are a part of the system; it allocates and regulates the use of the airspace; it ensures adequate separation between aircraft operating in controlled airspace; and, through

research and development programs, it provides new systems and equipment for improving utilization of the nation's airspace.

The Federal Aid to Airports Program (FAAP) authorized the FAA to make grants of federal funds to sponsors for airport development and for advanced planning and engineering. Under FAAP, approximately $1.2 billion was granted by FAA to airport sponsors for airport development purposes from 1947 through 1970. FAAP was superseded by the Airport Development Act of 1970 and the Airport and Airways Improvement Act of 1982. The FAA maintains and operates Washington National and Dulles International airports. Dulles International is the first airport in the world specifically designed for the use of commercial jet transports.

The FAA prescribes and administers rules and regulations concerning airmen competency, aircraft airworthiness, and air traffic control. It promotes safety through certification of airmen, aircraft, and flight and aircraft maintenance schools. It reviews the design, structure, and performance of new aircraft to insure the safety of the flying public.

Services provided by FAA toward the development of aviation and air commerce include:

1. Dissemination of news and information on civil aviation generally.

2. Publication of flight information data for pilots.

3. Technical aviation assistance to other governments, operation of overseas civil aviation missions, and the aviation training of foreign nationals.

4. Development of medical standards for airmen through aviation medical research.

5. Research and development in the field of aeronautics and electronics.

6. Other activities required to encourage and foster the worldwide development of civil aviation and air commerce.

Policies governing these programs are developed in the Washington headquarters of FAA, and are executed by field employees under the supervision of regional offices strategically located throughout the United States as well as the FAA Technical Center at Atlantic City, New Jersey, and the Mike Monroney Aeronautical Center at Oklahoma City, Oklahoma. Title 49, United States Code, contains air commerce and safety provisions of the Federal Aviation Administration. The missions of FAA are:

1. Assigning, maintaining, and enhancing safety and security as the highest priorities in air commerce.

2. Regulating air commerce in a way that best promotes safety and fulfills national defense requirements.

3. Encouraging and developing civil aeronautics, including new aviation technology.

4. Controlling the use of navigable airspace and regulating civil and military operations in that airspace in the interest of safety and efficiency of both of those operations.

5. Consolidating research and development for air navigation facilities and the installation and operation of those facilities.

6. Developing and operating a common system of air traffic control and navigation for civil and military aircraft.

7. Providing assistance to law enforcement agencies in the enforcement of laws related to regulation of controlled substances, to the extent consistent with aviation safety.

8. Developing and implementing, in coordination with other Departmental elements and other Federal agencies, of a program to achieve a system solution to the aircraft noise and sonic boom problem.

9. Regulating United States commercial space transportation.

The wartime mission of the Federal Aviation Administration is to support the Department of Defense and appropriate military commanders through air traffic control, aeronautical communications, aids to navigation, and other essential services; to support essential civil aviation operations, including preservation and restoration of the capability of the civil air transport system; support of civil government; civil survival and recovery operations; and to provide for the protection of FAA personnel and the continuity of executive direction and for safety and survival of FAA personnel.

Executive Order 11161 contemplates that the Federal Aviation Administration will be transferred to the Department of Defense in event of war and will function as an adjunct of the Department of Defense. It is further contemplated that while functioning as an adjunct of DOD, FAA will remain organizationally intact and the Administrator will retain responsibility for administration of statutory functions.

In very recent years the nature of governmental organizations has been drastically changing and will probably continue to do so. This has been caused by the attitude of the general public that those in the central government, who make the laws, need to be more cost conscious and reduce wastefulness. Pressures are on lowering the federal debt and producing a balanced budget. This has caused practically every United States government agency to improve its efficiency and lower its operating cost. The federal agencies involved with air transportation are not without exception.

The Federal Aviation Administration has been affected and is in a continuous process of reorganization. For this reason an accurate current organization chart depicting its department structure is difficult to present. Changes are constantly being made.

The overall structure of the Federal Aviation Administration probably changed while this text was being published. The reader is encouraged to obtain a current organization chart from the FAA and to compare it with the one shown in Figure 7.1.

Regardless of the technical organizational changes, the basic purposes of the FAA remain the same.

The Federal Aviation Administration consists of two basic administrative levels of organization: Headquarters and Regions.

The *Washington headquarters* in Washington, D.C., is responsible for agency-wide program planning, direction, control, and evaluation and for managing program activities, including aircraft certification, flight standards, aviation medical, airway facilities, air traffic, airports, civil aviation security, and legal.

Regions are responsible for logistics, accounting (where appropriate), management systems, public affairs, communications control, civil rights, human resource management, planning, and appraisal. Each region participates in general policy, planning, and budget information and execution and is responsible for the budgets of those areas over which executive direction is exercised.

The Aeronautical Center in Oklahoma City, and the FAA Technical Center near Atlantic City, where certain centralized activities are conducted; a Europe, Africa, and Middle East Office headquartered in Brussels, Belgium, with responsibility for FAA programs and policy in its assigned area; and an Aviation Standards National Field Office, located at the Aeronautical Center in Oklahoma City, which performs certain fleet maintenance, flight inspection, and regulatory support functions.

In the general plan of organization the FAA headquarters consists of the Office of the Administrator which is responsible for overall planning, direction, and control of FAA activities and the executive relationships with the Secretary and Deputy Secretary of Transportation, the Assistant Secretaries, the heads of other operating administrations, the Congress, other agencies, the aviation community, and the public.

Figure 7.1   Federal Aviation Administration

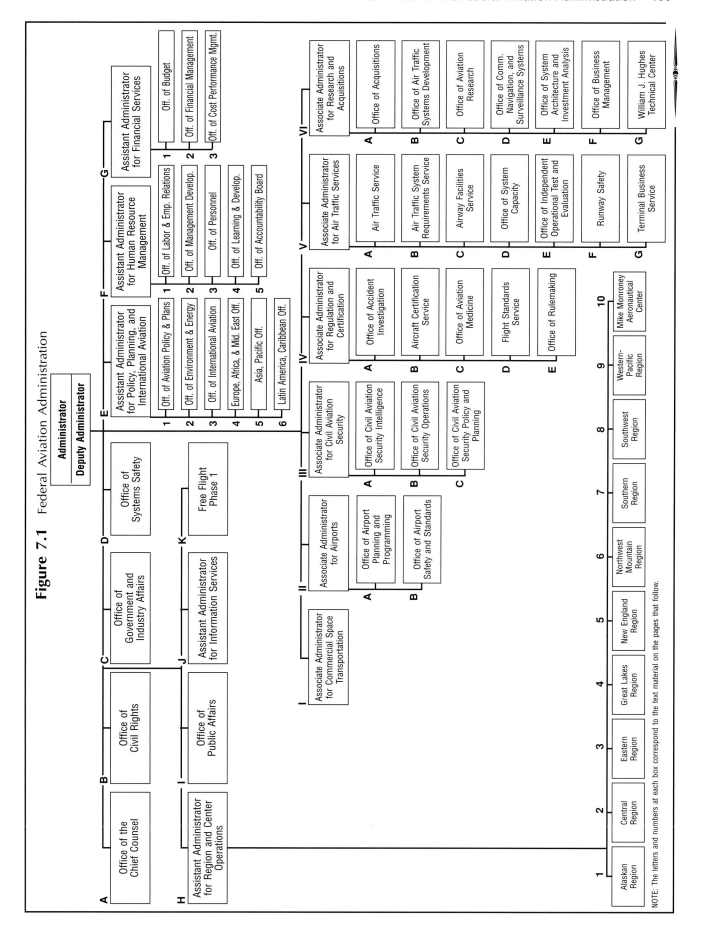

NOTE: The letters and numbers at each box correspond to the text material on the pages that follow.

The Associate Administrators direct, coordinate, control, and ensure the adequacy of FAA plans and programs within their spheres of responsibility and exercise executive direction over offices assigned to them.

Staff offices attached to the Administrator and Associate Administrators are responsible for:

1. Formulation of overall objectives, plans, policies, programs, standards, and procedures, for issuance by or on behalf of the Administrator.

2. Development of FAA rules and regulations to be promulgated by or on behalf of the Administrator for observance by FAA and members of the public.

3. Technical guidance, coordination, and review and evaluation of regional program performance.

4. Conduct of Seat-of-Government functions relating to such matters as legislation, request for appropriation, and interagency coordination at the national level.

5. Conduct of activities, which in the interest of effectiveness, efficiency, and economy must be performed centrally.

The structure of the Federal Aviation Administration is based upon a clear-cut concept of sound management and its organization is continually being changed for improvement as conditions necessitate. (Table 7.1.)

Regardless of what form the current FAA organization chart may appear, the functions are to be carried out by divisions and departments including a representation on the following pages.

Table 7.1 Federal Aviation Administration and Predecessor Agencies Administrators

Department of Commerce, Aeronautics Branch

Asst. Secretary of Commerce for Aeronautics:	
William MacCracken, Jr.	Aug. 1926 to Oct. 1929
Clarence Young	Oct. 1929 to June 1933
Director of Aeronautics:	
Eugene Vidal	Sept. 1933 to June 1934

Department of Commerce, Bureau of Air Commerce

Director of Air Commerce:	
Eugene Vidal	July 1934 to Mar. 1937
Fred Flagg, Jr.	Mar 1937 to Apr. 1938
Dennis Mulligan	Apr. 1938 to Aug. 1938

Civil Aeronautics Authority

Chairman:	
Edward Noble	Aug. 1938 to Apr. 1939
Robert Hinckley	Apr. 1939 to June 1940
Administrator:	
Clinton Hester	Aug. 1938 to June 1940

Department of Commerce, Civil Aeronautics Administration

Donald Connell	July 1940 to Jan. 1942
Charles Stanton	July 1942 to Sept. 1944
Theodore Wright	Sept. 1944 to Mar. 1948
Delos Rentzel	June 1948 to Oct. 1950
Donald Nyrop	Oct. 1950 to May 1951
Charles Horne	May 1951 to Mar. 1953
Frederick Lee	Apr. 1953 to Dec. 1955
Charles Lowen	Dec. 1955 to Sept. 1956
James Pyle	Dec. 1956 to Dec. 1958

Federal Aviation Agency

Administrator:	
Elwood "Pete" Quesada	Nov. 1958 to Jan. 1961
Najeeb Halaby	May 1961 to July 1965
William McKee	July 1965 to Mar. 1967

Department of Transportation, Federal Aviation Administration

Administrator:	
William McKee	Apr. 1967 to July 1968
John Shaffer	Mar. 1969 to Mar. 1973
Alexander Butterfield	Mar. 1973 to Mar. 1975
John McLucas	Nov. 1975 to Apr. 1977
Langhorne Bond	May 1977 to Jan. 1981
J. Lynn Helms	Apr. 1981 to Jan. 1984
Donald D. Engen	Apr. 1984 to June 1987
T. Allen McArtor	July 1987 to Feb. 1989
James B. Busey	June 1989 to Dec. 1991
Thomas C. Richards	June 1992 to Jan. 1993
David R. Hinson	Aug. 1993 to Nov. 1996
Jane F. Garvey	Aug. 1997 to —

FEDERAL AVIATION ADMINISTRATION*

ADMINISTRATOR

Deputy Administrator

Staff Departments

A. Office of the Chief Counsel

B. Office of Civil Rights

C. Office of Government and Industry Affairs

D. Office of System Safety

E. Assistant Administrator for Policy, Planning and International Aviation

   1. Office of Aviation Policy and Plans

   2. Office of Environment and Energy

   3. Office of International Aviation

   4. Europe, Africa and Middle-East Office

   5. Asia-Pacific Office

   6. Latin American-Caribbean Office

F. Assistant Administrator for Human Resource Management

   1. Office of Labor and Employee Relations

   2. Office of Management Development

   3. Office of Personnel

   4. Office of Learning and Development

   5. Office of the Accountability Board

G. Assistant Administrator for Financial Services

   1. Office of Budget

   2. Office of Financial Management

   3. Office of Cost Performance Management

H. Assistant Administrator for Region and Center Operations

   1. Alaskan

   2. Central

   3. Eastern

   4. Great Lakes

   5. New England

   6. Northwest Mountain

   7. Southern

   8. Southwest

   9. Western-Pacific

   10. Mike Monroney Aeronautical Center

I. Office of Public Affairs

J. Assistant Administrator for Information Services

K. Free Flight Phase 1

Associate Administrators

I. Associate Administrator for Commercial Space Transportation

   A. Space Systems Development

   B. Licensing and Safety

   C. Systems Engineering and Training Division

II. Associate Administrator for Airports

   A. Office of Airport Planning and Programming

   B. Office of Airport Safety and Standards

III. Associate Administrator for Civil Aviation Security

   A. Office of Civil Aviation Security Intelligence

   B. Office of Civil Aviation Security Operations

   C. Office of Civil Aviation Security Policy and Planning

IV. Associate Administrator for Regulation and Certification

   A. Office of Accident Investigation

   B. Aircraft Certification Service

   C. Office of Aviation Medicine

   D. Flight Standards Service

   E. Office of Rule Making

V. Associate Administrator for Air Traffic Services

   A. Air Traffic Service

   B. Air Traffic System Requirements Service

   C. Airway Facilities Service

   D. Office of System Capacity

   E. Office of Independent Operational Test and Evaluation

   F. Runway Safety

   G. Terminal Business Service

VI. Associate Administrator for Research and Acquisitions

   A. Office of Acquisitions

Note: The letters and numbers on this outline are the same on the organizational chart and relate to the text in this chapter. Select an item on the organization chart, look for it on the outline then find it in the text.

B. Office of Air Traffic Systems Development
C. Office of Aviation Research
D. Office of Communication, Navigation and Surveillance Systems
E. Office of System Architecture and Investment Analysis
F. Office of Business Management
G. William J. Hughes Technical Center

THE ADMINISTRATOR

The Administrator directs and controls the operations of the Federal Aviation Administration and acts as principal to the Secretary and Deputy Secretary of Transportation on civil aviation matters and air transportation.

The Administrator of the Federal Aviation Administration is appointed by the President and confirmed by the Senate. She also serves as principal aviation advisor to the Secretary of Transportation. Beginning in 1997, for the first time, the administrator serves for a period of five years and no longer serves at the pleasure of the President.

The Administrator is responsible for the exercise of all powers and the discharge of all duties of the Administration. In so doing, she does not have to submit her decisions for the approval of any individual or group.

The Administrator must be a United States citizen and a civilian and have experience in aviation. The individual cannot have any pecuniary interest in, or own any stock or bonds in any aeronautical enterprise, nor be engaged in any other business, vocation, or employment.

The responsibilities of the Administrator as outlined in the Federal Aviation Act of 1958 are:

1. The regulation of air commerce in such manner as to best promote its development and safety and fulfill the requirements of national defense.

2. The promotion, encouragement, and development of civil aeronautics.

3. The control of the use of the navigable airspace of the United States and the regulation of both civil and military operations in such airspace in the interest of the safety and efficiency of both.

4. The consolidation of research and development with respect to air navigation facilities as well as the installation and operation thereof.

5. The development and operation of a common system of air traffic control and navigation for both military and civil aircraft.

The functions of the Administrator are to:

1. Determine and establish FAA objectives and priorities.

2. Guide the development of and approve long-range plans for achieving FAA objectives.

3. Establish the policies and broad technological, operational, and managerial concepts to govern the development and accomplishment of FAA programs based on approved plans.

4. Issue FAA rules and regulations, or authorize their issuance pursuant to delegations of authority.

5. Approve broad legislative, budgetary, and fiscal proposals.

6. Represent FAA in its relations with the Secretary of Transportation and as an entity of the Department of Transportation in its relations with the President, the Congress, other agencies, the aviation community, and the general public.

7. Take individual actions of major significance, such as changes in the basic pattern of FAA organization, the selection and appointment of key personnel, the broad allocation of FAA resources, and individual matters of particular political or public sensitivity.

8. Exercise control over, evaluate, and take steps to ensure the adequacy and continued improvement of overall FAA performance.

9. Ensures the adequacy and continued improvement of overall FAA performance.

10. Oversees FAA's personnel management system.

11. Establishes procurement policies and procedures.

EMERGENCY OPERATIONS

The Administrator directs the operation of FAA during emergencies and continues to perform, as appropriate, those functions prescribed in the Federal Aviation Act of 1958 (as amended by Public Law 89-670), delegated to the Administrator by the Secretary of Transportation, various applicable executive orders, directives issued pursuant to other statutes, and various joint agreements and plans between FAA and other organizational elements of the Federal Government.

The Administrator, the Secretary of Defense, the Administrator of the National Aeronautics and Space Administration, and the Secretary of Transportation are directed to exchange information pertaining to their own programs and policies. The Federal Aviation Administrator with the Department of Defense, furthermore, develop plans in the event of war; this being, of course, for emergency conditions.

Related duties of the Administrator are the selection, employing, and appointing employees subject to civil service laws necessary to carry out her responsibilities, as well as the conducting of studies of personnel problems inherent to the provisions of the Act. She is directed to use the facilities of other civil or military agencies.

The President may transfer to the Administrator any functions for safe and efficient air traffic control. The Administration is authorized by the Federal Aviation Act to acquire, establish, and improve air navigation facilities wherever necessary, and to operate and maintain these facilities; to publish aviation maps and charts necessary for the safe flight of aircraft; and to provide facilities and personnel for the regulation and protection of air traffic. As such, the Federal Aviation Administration issues air traffic rules. The Administrator may grant exemptions from the requirements of any rule or regulation if she finds it necessary in the public interest.

When it is essential to the defense of the United States, prior notice will be given to the Administrator as soon as practicable, and every effort is so made to consult with her.

In order to conform to policies, no airport construction can be undertaken unless notice is given to the Administrator so that she may advise aviation activities as to the effects upon the use of the airspace.

With regard to developmental planning, the Administrator makes plans and formulates policies with respect to the orderly development and use of the navigable airspace; she supervises developmental work on aircraft as well as testing and evaluating systems, facilities, and devices to meet the needs for safe and efficient air traffic control.

The Administrator publishes written reports on all proceedings and investigations in which formal hearings were held, and states her conclusions and decisions. The compilation of these reports constitutes in part the annual report submitted to the President and the Congress. In the exercise of her duties the Administrator may delegate to any properly qualified person the functions of the examining, inspecting, and testing necessary to the issuing of airmen, aircraft, and other certificates.

In describing the mission of the Administrator, the Federal Aviation Act states that the Administrator determines and establishes the Administration objectives and priorities and guides the development of, and approves long-range plans for achieving Administration objectives. She establishes policy and issues Administration rules and regulations. She approves broad legislative, budgetary, and fiscal proposals. She represents the Administration with the President, the Congress, other agencies, the aviation community, and the general public, in addition to taking individual action of major significance. The Administrator exercises control over, evaluates, and takes steps to ensure the adequacy and continued improvement of overall Administration performance.

THE DEPUTY ADMINISTRATOR

The Deputy Administrator assists the Administrator in the discharge of the Administrator's responsibility with authority to act for the Administrator in all matters not reserved to the Administrator by law, order, or instruction of the Administrator.

The Deputy Administrator is also appointed by the President and confirmed by the Senate. The Deputy Administrator is responsible for the direction and execution of Administration operations and for coordinating the activities of the regions and various technical staff services and offices, as well as the operations of the Bureau of National Capital Airports. During the absence of the Administrator, the Deputy serves as Acting Administrator.

The Deputy Administrator must also be a citizen of the United States and is appointed with due regard for fitness to carry out the vested duties. As stated for the Administrator, the Deputy shall be experienced in aviation, have no financial interest in any aeronautical enterprise, nor engage in any other business or employment. The Deputy Administrator participates with and assists the Administrator in the overall planning, direction, coordination, and control of Administration programs.

Subject to policies, standards, and instructions issued by the Administrator, the Deputy Administrator is authorized to represent the Administrator and exercise the Administrator's full authority. All authority delegated by the Administrator to any element in the agency is also delegated to the Deputy Administrator, unless otherwise specifically provided.

STAFF FUNCTIONS

A. OFFICE OF CHIEF COUNSEL

The Chief Counsel has overall responsibility for the legal activities of the Administration and provides legal counsel to all offices and services. The office also conducts the Administration litigation, ruledrafting and interpretation, tort claims, enforcement, legislative, codification, and contract appeals programs.

In cooperation with legal staffs in the Regions, the Chief Counsel's Office oversees all legal activities of the Administration. These include providing necessary legal advice and services in support of all Federal Aviation Administration functions. The Chief Counsel is also responsible for the legislative program, protection of Administration legal interests in litigation and accident investigations, the legal aspects of rulemaking, and the interpretation and enforcement of rules and regulations. This office also deals with other departments and agencies in the formal negotiation of international aviation agreements.

This office is the principal staff element of the FAA with respect to:

1. Rules codification program.

2. Drafting, approval as to form and legality, and interpretation of FAA rules, regulations, orders, and obstruction evaluation determinations.

3. FAA legislative program.

4. Legal aspects of FAA's procurement programs, and its contracts and agreements, and the contract appeals function.

5. Tort claims by and against FAA.

6. Legal proceedings before courts, legislative committees, Government agencies, and other administrative hearings.

7. International law.

8. Legal aspects of the FAA's enforcement program.

9. Airports and environmental law.

10. Representation of the FAA headquarters in all condemnation matters.

11. Coordination and clearance of all FAA headquarters correspondence on matters with legal implications.

12. Investigations by the Office of the Special Counsel of the Merit Systems Protection Board.

13. Provides legal counsel and advice to the Office of the Administrator and other offices and services.

14. Coordinates and ensures the adequacy of legal aspects of defense readiness plans, programs, and functions.

15. Exercises executive direction over the legal functions in the regions and centers.

Special Delegations: Service of Process. The Chief Counsel, Deputy Chief Counsel, and Assistant Chief Counsel, Litigation Division, are authorized to exercise the authority of the General Counsel (C-1). Office of the Secretary of Transportation (OST), under Part 9 of the Regulations of the Office of the Secretary of Transportation with respect to the acceptance of service of legal process or pleadings on behalf of the Secretary of Transportation or the Administrator in any legal proceedings concerning FAA (49 CFR 9 17).

Issuance of Subpoenas and Compel Testimony. The Chief Counsel, Deputy Chief Counsel, and all assistant chief counsel are authorized to take evidence, issue subpoenas, take depositions, and compel testimony in conducting hearings and investigations authorized by 49 U.S.C. § 4101 et. seq., the Federal Aviation Act, the Airport and Airway Improvement Act of 1982, successor legislation: The Aviation, Safety, Capacity, and Expansion Act of 1990, and the Airport Noise and Capacity Act of 1990, and to exercise the authority vested in the Administrator by sections 313 (c) and 1004 of 49 U.S.C. § 4101 et. seq. the Federal Aviation Act. They may redelegate this authority to any attorney under their supervision, provided that such redelegation is limited to the specified hearing or investigation for which the authority is required.

Testimony of Employees and Production of Records. The Chief Counsel, Deputy Chief Counsel, and Assistant Chief Counsel for Litigation, are authorized under Part 9 of the Regulations of the Office of the Secretary of Transportation, to exercise the authority of the General Counsel (C-1), as to testimony by agency employees and the production of agency records (49 CFR Part 9).

B. OFFICE OF CIVIL RIGHTS

The Office of Civil Rights advises, represents, and assists the Administrator on civil rights and equal opportunity matters that ensures the elimination of unlawful discrimination on the basis of race, color, national origin, sex, age, religion, or creed and individuals with disabilities in federally operated and federally assisted transportation programs. The office ensures that all beneficiaries and potential beneficiaries of these programs, including employees and potential employees, are offered equal opportunities to participate in them, and that ensures a positive working environment in the Federal Aviation Administration by valuing, using, and managing the differences that individuals bring to the workplace.

The Office of Civil Rights:

1. Advises the Administrator on national and field civil rights programs, equal employment opportunity, diversity, procedures, regulations, reports, and related matters.

2. Evaluates the effectiveness of the agency's program for civil rights, equal employment opportunity, diversity and reporting to the head of the agency with recommendations for improvement or correction and follow-up.

3. Makes changes, as authorized by the Administrator, in programs and procedures designed to eliminate discriminatory practices and improve the agency's program for civil rights, equal employment opportunity and diversity.

4. Provides for counseling and mediation when requested by employees and applicants and members of class complaints in matters of discrimination.

5. Ensures that affirmative actions are taken to support the total Federal equal opportunity and diversity programs.

6. Ensures that small business concerns owned and/or controlled by socially and economically disadvantaged individuals are afforded the opportunity to participate in contracting and concession opportunities.

7. Ensures equal opportunity, nondiscrimination, and compliance regarding the Americans with Disabilities Act and Section 504 of the Rehabilitation Act.

8. Advises, represents, and assists the Administrator in the elimination of discrimination based on political affiliation, marital status, sexual orientation, or any other characteristic not bearing on job performance as part of the model work environment effort.

With respect to all matters within the Assistant Administrator's sphere of responsibility, the Assistant Administrator for Civil Rights is authorized to:

1. Take action and issue orders in the name of the Administrator, except for those matters for which the Administrator has specifically reserved authority or otherwise provided.

2. Represent the Administrator.

3. Act on any matter for which specific delegation of authority has been made to the Assistant Administrator or to any element under that position's executive direction.

C. OFFICE OF GOVERNMENT AND INDUSTRY AFFAIRS

Government and Industry Affairs serves as the Administrator's principal advisor and representative on matters concerning relations with the Congress, aviation industry groups, and other governmental organizations. In concert with other agency organizations, the office develops and reviews various plans and strategies involving these groups to enhance the promotion of aviation. To ensure consistent policy direction with the Department in carrying out the functions outlined below, these activities are conducted in close coordination and consultation with the Assistant Secretary for Governmental Affairs.

Government and Industry Affairs:

1. Provides advice and information to the Administrator, Deputy Administrator, Executive Directors, and other agency officials on the policies, actions, and positions of the Congress, State and local government officials, and industry representatives.

2. Develops programs to inform external groups about agency policies and actions and responds to requests for information.

3. Serves as FAA's focal point to coordinate agency actions relating to Congressional oversight of FAA programs.

4. Develop special programs to increase the agency's involvement with industry groups on matters which have significant impact on the aviation community.

5. Monitors aviation activities and issues of interest to State and local governments to ensure that agency policies are adequately represented.

6. Coordinates with Departmental officials to ensure consistency in furthering policies relating to Congressional and intergovernmental issues.

7. Serves as the FAA clearinghouse for authoritative data concerning the Congress, State and local governments, and aviation industry organizations.

8. Manages the Reports to Congress program within FAA. Serves as the FAA Reports Control Officer and is responsible for providing the DOT Congressional Reports Officer all information to disseminate to Congress and interested parties.

The Administrator is the official spokesperson for the Federal Aviation Administration. All statements, announcements, or presentations to the Congress will be made by the Administrator or on behalf of the Administrator, by another official, when designated by the Administrator to do so.

The Office of Government and Industry Affairs is responsible for the implementation of policies with respect to relations with the Congress. The office will:

1. Keep the Assistant Secretary for Government Affairs informed on all matters of significant interest.

2. Serve as the FAA focal point in monitoring and coordinating requests received by FAA from Congressional Members and Committees.

3. Assist the Office of the Chief Counsel on matters pertaining to Congressional hearings.

4. Keep the associate administrators and the offices and services informed of public and Congressional concerns which may influence their operational responsibility and will ensure proper coordination of material with offices having substantive responsibility prior to its being communicated to Congress.

The Office of the Chief Counsel is responsible for providing advice and assistance to the Administrator on the legislative aspects of agency policies and for conducting the agency's legislative program. The Office of the Chief Counsel will keep the Office of Government and Industry Affairs informed of legislative activities.

D. OFFICE OF SYSTEM SAFETY

The Office of System Safety fosters aviation safety by providing international leadership in the identification of safety issues through the collection, analysis, and distribution of safety data; and facilitating the application of system safety methods in FAA decision-making processes.

The Office of System Safety:

Advises the Administrator and is the principal focal point for identifying existing or incipient system safety issues.

Exercises executive direction and line authority over teams of safety experts with operational knowledge of all aspects of aviation.

Develops policy, standards, and procedures for the development, analysis and monitoring of data utilized in the identification of system safety concerns in the National Airspace System (NAS).

Promotes and maintains liaison on system safety issues, system safety analysis concepts, tools, and methodologies with other government agencies and the military, State and local governments, national and international aviation interest groups, and the aviation industry.

Initiates and implements innovative system safety outreach through products, publications, and actively participates in public, government, and non-government organizations-sponsored forums.

Provides expert advice and assistance and develops standard procedures in the application of system safety concepts, and proactive strategies for identifying and addressing safety issues.

E. ASSISTANT ADMINISTRATOR FOR POLICY, PLANNING, AND INTERNATIONAL AVIATION

The Assistant Administrator for Policy, Planning, and International Aviation advises and assists the Administrator in directing, coordinating, controlling, and ensuring the adequacy of environmental and energy programs; national and international aviation system policies, goals, and priorities.

The functions of the Associate Administrator are:

1. Develops and recommends national aviation policy relating to environmental energy programs and hazardous materials regulatory matters.

2. Develops and recommends long-range systemwide master plans and aviation system concepts.

3. Coordinates and integrates the FAA strategic planning efforts.

4. Develops, coordinates, recommends, and promulgates statements of FAA policy, goals, and priorities (both short- and long-range) and related achievement indicators.

5. Ensures the continuous coordination of such policies, goals, and overall plans with the Office of the Secretary of Transportation.

6. Provides the focal point for aviation, public, and Government participation in policy development and planning processes.

7. Identifies future demands for aviation services, forecasting aviation technology, and future operational environments.

8. Reviews and analyzes proposed FAA actions which significantly impact upon the national aviation system to identify the social, economic, or other consequences which are associated with FAA regulatory actions and other actions and to ensure consideration of all feasible alternative FAA policies and plans.

9. Ensures continuous and effective liaison with foreign governments and the adequacy of programs and operating policies of the Europe, Africa, and Middle East Office within its assigned geographic jurisdiction.

10. Administers the Aircraft Loan Guarantee and Aviation Insurance Programs.

11. Provides critical values and advisory assistance to other agency elements in the conduct of economic studies and performs independent cost and benefit-

cost analyses or reviews of selected FAA programs, functions, facilities, and equipment.

12. Serves as the designated safety and health official to assist the Administrator in ensuring a comprehensive occupational safety and health program for FAA employees.

13. Undertakes studies of FAA financing requirements, conducts cost allocation analyses, and performs evaluations of and develops proposals and/or recommendations for user taxes and fees.

The Assistant Administrator for Policy, Planning and International Aviation exercises executive direction over the:

1. Office of Aviation Policy and Plans.
2. Office of Environment and Energy.
3. Office of International Aviation.
4. Europe, Africa, and Middle East Office.
5. Asia-Pacific Office.
6. Latin America-Caribbean Office.

With respect to all matters within the assistant administrator's sphere of responsibility, the Assistant Administrator for Policy, Planning, and International Aviation is authorized to:

1. Take action and issue orders in the name of the Administrator except for those matters for which the Administrator has specifically reserved authority or otherwise provided.
2. Represent the Administrator.
3. Act on any matter for which specific delegation of authority has been made to the assistant administrator or to any element under the assistant administrator's executive direction.
4. Approve employee claims for foreign allowance.

Special Relations: The Assistant Administrator for Policy, Planning, and International Aviation is responsible for coordinating, but not dictating, agency policy and planning development so that operations and development activities are directed toward common goals and in accordance with approved priorities. All operational and development programs and activities are to be consistent with approved FAA policies, goals, and priorities.

1. Office of Aviation Policy and Plans

The Office of Aviation Policy and Plans formulates, coordinates, and documents aviation policy, system plans, goals, and priorities; develops and provides planning standards and facility establishment criteria; develops the strategic planning and management process; performs economic and regulatory analysis and independent cost analysis; and provides aviation statistical services.

2. Office of Environment and Energy

The Office of Environment and Energy develops, recommends and coordinates national aviation policy relating to environmental and energy matters. The office provides instructions, guidance, oversight, and technical assistance for FAA compliance with applicable environmental, occupational safety and health and energy statutes and regulations prescribing Federal environmental protection, worker protection, and energy conservation policies. The office formulates and implements technical programs leading to reduced aircraft noise and exhaust emissions and to improved environmental conditions around airports. The office develops, recommends, and promulgates regulations and standards, as appropriate to meet statutory requirements or Department agency policy. The office conducts analyses and studies of aircraft and airport operations and development programs which could lead to the reduction of any adverse impact on the environment while maintaining the efficiency and capacity of the National Airspace System; coordinates with other Federal agencies in developing aviation-related environmental and energy policies, goals, and priorities; and provides the agency focal point for coordinating and fostering community, State, local, and general public participation in the resolution of aviation-related environmental and energy matters.

3. Office of International Aviation

The Office of International Aviation achieves U.S. and agency objectives in international aviation through the:

a. Formulation and coordination of policy, plans, programs, and related matters affecting the international activities of the agency.

b. Provision of guidance and support to all agency elements having international responsibilities.

c. Management and coordination of agency international programs conducted by FAA domestic organizations outside the Washington headquarters.

d. Overall evaluation of agency international programs and activities.

e. Administration of aviation assistance programs conducted by the agency.

f. Formulation and coordination of cooperative efforts with other U.S. Government departments and agencies and the U.S. aviation industry on international aviation efforts.

4. Europe, Africa, and Middle East Office

The Europe, Africa, and Middle East Office discharges the responsibilities of FAA within the assigned areas of Europe, Africa, and the Middle East, including the Azores, Iceland, the countries of the former Soviet Union, and all countries on the continent west of Pakistan. The office works with elements of U.S. diplomatic missions with a view to encourage and foster the development of civil aeronautics and air commerce; and to provide for safety and efficiency of U.S. aviation.

5. Asia-Pacific Office

The Asia-Pacific Office discharges the responsibilities of FAA within the assigned areas of Asia and the Pacific, including all countries on the continent east of Pakistan. The office works with elements of U.S. diplomatic missions with a view to encourage and foster the development of civil aeronautics and air commerce; and to provide for safety and efficiency of U.S. aviation.

6. Latin America-Caribbean Office

The Latin America-Caribbean Office discharges the responsibilities of FAA within the assigned areas of Latin America and the Caribbean. The office works with elements of U.S. diplomatic missions with a view to encourage and foster the development of civil aeronautics and air commerce; and to provide for safety and efficiency of U.S. aviation.

F. ASSISTANT ADMINISTRATOR FOR HUMAN RESOURCES MANAGEMENT

The Federal Aviation Administration is committed to making the United States airspace increasingly safe, secure and efficient. To succeed in an environment of increased air and space travel, budget constraints, technological advances and regulatory change, it must have exceptional people in the right places at the right time and with the proper skills. The FAA needs human resource professionals who are strategic partners in accomplishing the purpose of the Federal Aviation Administration through a skilled, committed and diverse workforce.

1. Office of Labor and Employee Relations
2. Office of Management Development
3. Office of Personnel
4. Office of Learning and Development
5. Office of the Accountability Board

People are the foundation for accomplishment. The FAA's strategic plan stresses the importance of providing a model work environment where people with diverse skills, interests, and backgrounds can work together to assure safety, security, and system efficiency.

The FAA is faced with the challenge of accomplishing its mission in an environment that includes budget constraints, growth in air travel, regulatory changes, technological advances, privatization, and increased emphasis on customer satisfaction. Managers and supervisors in all lines of business rely on the support of human resource professionals to build the intellectual capital and work environment that truly support individual, team, and organization success.

Reforming the personnel system is part of the challenge—and part of the solution. Successful personnel reform will give FAA managers, employees, and Human Resource professionals the support and flexibility they need to accomplish the agency mission.

The strategic plan is a high level executive summary. The projects are strategic, multi-year, and cross organization boundaries. They are being accomplished through dozens of shorter term tactical projects and daily operations. These projects and shorter term actions will be listed, tracked, managed and communicated. The strategic plan and the new project management system will help leadership link resources, employee development, awards, recognition, and individual performance agreements more effectively. Each year, Human Resources leadership will select priority projects and focus their attention and resources on those projects. As customer needs and FAA goals change, priorities will shift. Updates of HR's strategic plan and priority projects are on the web site.

Human Resources is committed to accomplishing the strategic goals and business outcomes outlined in a plan. It will establish and examine performance measures every year. Also, conduct systematic program evaluations of key human resource management practices and innovative personnel reform initiatives. It will measure the organization's success in terms of completion and accomplishment of objectives, the quality of products, timeliness, and customers' satisfaction. Performance measurement will focus on attaining organization goals. Program evaluation will examine a broader range of information on program performance, including processes, operations, program impacts, and cost-effectiveness.

Human Resources is committed to conducting effective measurement and evaluation because these processes are the foundation for building better management and business practices and will provide valuable information for continuously improving products and customer service. To insure the commitment to measurement and evaluation is fully realized, it will educate human resource professionals about the value of measuring performance at all levels of organization and create learning opportunities to participate in ongoing human resource management evaluations.

Maintaining a focus on measurement and evaluation of human resource management will develop a more compelling business case for the value human resources adds to the agency and help to align human resource management with the FAA business strategy.

G. ASSISTANT ADMINISTRATOR FOR FINANCIAL SERVICES

The Assistant Administrator for Financial Services advises the agency of FAA plans and programs for budget, financial management, and performance management.

The Assistant Administrator for Financial Services:

- Provides accounting, financial, and audit liaison services.

- Develops and evaluates FAA accounting systems.

- Maintains accounting operations for the Washington headquarters.

- Ensures that agency budgetary needs are identified.

- Ensures that agency funds and resources are utilized effectively.

- Develops policies, programs, standards, systems, and procedures for budget, financial, and performance management.

- Develops and administers the implementation of the organizational structure and issues administrative standards and procedures.

- Administers the cost accounting, and user fees.

- Administers OMB Circular A-76, Performance of Commercial Activities.

- Serves as the Chief Financial Officer.

Financial Services consists of the following:

1. Office of Budget
2. Office of Financial Management
3. Office of Cost Performance Management

The Management Staff is the principal advisor to the CFO, Deputy, and management team for all administrative requirements areas, including managerial, budgeting, personnel resource, training, and space administration. The staff also provides the focal point for internal policy, procedure, and coordination; and represents the CFO in matters relating to planning and utilization of program resources.

Office of Budget

Develops overall agency budgetary policies, standards, systems, and procedures pertaining to agency multiyear programming, budget estimates and justifications, allowances, allotments and apportionments, employment ceilings, staffing authorizations and any special budget controls. The Office of Budget ensures that agency budgetary needs are accurately identified and defined. The office ensures that agency funds and other resources are utilized effectively.

Office of Financial Management

To improve the operation of the FAA by providing financial information necessary to evaluate the use of agency resources, developing policy, systems, and programs which provide for a more effective use of resources, distributing funds, and ensuring resources are used properly and in accordance with governing laws and policy.

The Financial Management functions include:

- Establish FAA accounting, travel and financial management policy.

- Provide headquarters accounting and reporting for FAA allotments and general ledger.

- Prepare agency financial statements and reports.

- Provide accounting policy to regional and headquarters lines of businesses.

- Serve as the accounting systems requirements office for local and national systems and represent FAA on interdepartmental systems.

- Provide local accounting services or accounting operations for Washington headquarters offices, including major centralized F&E contract payments.

Office of Cost Performance Management

The Office of Cost Performance Management is responsible for designing and implementing cost and performance management initiatives, including the cost accounting system, labor distribution reporting and the overall cost and performance management program; and for providing executive-level management information, organizational analysis, management and productivity improvement, and paperwork management programs of the agency.

The Office of Cost Performance Management:

- Oversees implementation of the Government Performance and Results Act.

- Manages agency programs that measure performance and monitor cost and labor use (e.g., Cost and Performance Management, Cost Accounting System, and Labor Distribution Reporting programs); collects and issues performance information.

- Manages the agency overflight user fee program.

- Manages the agency programs for correspondence, printing, distribution, mail, records, forms, reports, and Advisory Circulars.

- Manages the process for documenting agency policy, procedures, and standards.

- Manages the Privacy Act program.

- Manages the organizational structure process, including the review and approval of cost center codes.

- Administers the committee management program.

- Serves as focal point for Department of Transportation-wide initiatives such as organizational assessments/ evaluations and employee and customer surveys.

- Produces agency-wide management information products such as the Monthly Performance Report, Administrator's Fact Book, and FAA Organizational Directory.

Policies

Directives are the primary means of issuing policy, instructions, and work information within the FAA. Directives include:

- Guidance or instructions that describe, establish, or explain agency policies, organization, methods, or procedures.

- Documents that require action or impose workload.

- Written information that is essential to the administration or operation of the agency or any of its programs.

Information Systems and Technology Services

This staff office provides technology services to all the employees in the CFO's office and automates financial business processes. Information technology services include installation/maintenance of personal computers, providing local area network and electronic mail services, and running a help desk. Information systems services include the development, implementation, and maintenance of automated systems ranging from the Cost Accounting System to identify the cost of agency services to the Automated Correspondence Express system for generating FAA letterheads.

Overflight Fees

On June 5, 2000 the Federal Aviation Administration announced aircraft operators will be required to pay fees for air traffic control services provided to aircraft that operate in U.S. airspace, but do not take off or land in the United States. Unlike other aircraft operations, these "overflights" have not been paying for the FAA air traffic control services they receive.

This rule assesses fees directly related to services provided by one of the safest air traffic control systems in the world. The charging of overflight fees is consistent with the practices of almost every other nation and will recover most of the costs of the services provided.

The authority to charge fees to aircraft conducting U.S. overflights was contained in the Federal Aviation Reauthorization Act of 1996. The agency issued an interim final rule in 1997 but a U.S. Court of Appeals decision in January 1998 determined that FAA's calculation of fees was inconsistent with the statute. In today's interim final rule, FAA has based its new overflight fees on the agency's costs as calculated by the FAA's recently developed cost accounting system.

Under the new rule, fees will be based on the distance flown through U.S.-controlled airspace. Overflights will be charged at the rate of $37.43 per 100 nautical miles in the enroute environment, and $20.16 per 100 nautical miles in the oceanic environment. These fees will apply to operators of aircraft that fly over U.S.-controlled airspace. There are some exceptions. No charges will be assessed on military and civilian aircraft operated by the U.S. government or by a foreign government. In addition, users who accrue $250 or less in fees per month will not be charged for these operations.

The FAA will bill users by sending a monthly invoice. Affected users are requested to designate and submit to the FAA the name and address of a U.S. agent for billing. Users not providing a billing address will be billed at the address of record of the aircraft owner as maintained in the country where the aircraft is registered.

The fees are directly related to the FAA's costs of providing the service rendered. The Act further states that services for which costs may be recovered include the costs of ATC, navigation, weather services, training and emergency services that are available to facilitate safe transportation over the United States, and other services provided by the Administrator or by programs financed by the Administrator to flights that neither take off from, nor land in, the United States.

H. ASSISTANT ADMINISTRATOR FOR REGION AND CENTER OPERATIONS

The Assistant Administrator for Region and Center Operations assists the Administrator with integrated field perspective of mission needs and performance; provides senior agency leadership in the regions to ensure customer responsiveness and program integration for mission accomplishment; and provides critical operational support to enable FAA to meet safety mission of the agency.

Assistant Administrator for Region and Center Operations:

1. Advises and assists the Administrator and the Management Board with a field perspective of mission needs and performance.

2. Provides leadership for improving agency systems and processes.

3. Administers the Freedom of Information Act program.

4. Oversees activities of the regional administrators to:

   —Provide senior agency leadership and cross-functional oversight in the regions.

   —Provide integrated agency interface with industry, the public, and various governmental organizations.

   —Provide services in the regions for acquisition, budget, civil rights, financial management, human resource management, information technology management, logistics, and other administrative programs.

   —Provide an operational communications control center and leadership for regional emergency preparedness and crisis management.

5. Oversees the activities of the Mike Monroney Aeronautical Center.

   —Provide technical training, National Airspace System Logistics support and business services (e.g., payroll, software application development, and special examinations) to FAA, other elements of the Department of Transportation, other Federal agencies, and foreign governments.

   —Manage the Aeronautical Center programs for civil rights, human resources, and other administrative programs.

   —Perform functions such as acquisition, information technology management, and logistics for direct report and straightlined organizations representing FAA and other elements of the Department of Transportation.

REGIONAL BOUNDARIES

The FAA regional boundaries are shown in Figure 7.2.

A summary of the geographic areas of responsibility of FAA's regions are as follows:

- ALASKAN REGION—Anchorage, Alaska.

  Geographical Areas of Responsibility:

  State of Alaska and the oceanic area within the Anchorage Flight Information Region, including the Arctic offshore area (control 1485) and the Arctic Control Area/Flight Information Region and flight inspection of assigned facilities in Canada.

- CENTRAL REGION—Kansas City, Missouri.

  Geographical Areas of Responsibility:

  States of Iowa, Kansas, Missouri, and Nebraska.

- EASTERN REGION—Jamaica, New York.

  Geographic Areas of Responsibility:

  States of Delaware, New York, New Jersey, Pennsylvania, Maryland, Virginia, and West Virginia; the District of Columbia; Canada, east of 100 west longitude; all of Canada for purpose of certification of foreign-made aircraft and components; and Greenland and Bermuda, excluding flight inspection; and that portion of the Atlantic Ocean in which domestic offshore control is exercised by air traffic control facilities of the Eastern Region.

Figure 7.2   Federal Aviation Administration Regional Boundaries Including Locations of Regional Headquarters and Centers.

- GREAT LAKES REGION—Des Plaines, Illinois.

  Geographical Areas of Responsibility:

  States of Illinois, Indiana, Michigan, Minnesota, North Dakota, South Dakota, Ohio, and Wisconsin.

- NEW ENGLAND REGION—Burlington, Massachusetts.

  Geographical Areas of Responsibility:

  States of Connecticut, Maine, Massachusetts, New Hampshire, Rhode Island, and Vermont, and that portion of the Atlantic Ocean in which domestic offshore control is exercised by air traffic control facilities of the New England Region.

- NORTHWEST MOUNTAIN REGION—Seattle, Washington.

  Geographical Areas of Responsibility:

  States of Colorado, Idaho, Montana, Oregon, Utah, Washington, and Wyoming; the designated oceanic area within the Oakland Flight Information Region that is north of a line drawn from the intersection of the southern boundary of Oregon and the coastline to

the northeast corner of the Honolulu Flight Information Region; Canada west of 100 west longitude, excluding certification of foreign-made aircraft and components within this geographic area.

- SOUTHERN REGION—Atlanta, Georgia.

  Geographical Areas of Responsibility:

  States of Kentucky, Tennessee, North Carolina, South Carolina, Georgia, Florida, Alabama, and Mississippi, the Caribbean area, South America, Central America (excluding Mexico), Panama, and that portion of the Gulf of Mexico and Atlantic Ocean in which domestic offshore control is exercised by air traffic control facilities of the Southern Region.

- SOUTHWEST REGION—Fort Worth, Texas.

  Geographical Areas of Responsibility:

  States of Arkansas, Louisiana, Texas, Oklahoma, and New Mexico; Mexico and that portion of the Gulf of Mexico covering the Oceanic Control Area and the domestic offshore control area under control of air traffic facilities located in the Southwest Region.

- WESTERN-PACIFIC REGION—Los Angeles, California.

Geographical Areas of Responsibility:

States of Arizona, California, Hawaii, and Nevada; the Pacific Ocean area west of the continental United States, including the designated area within the Oakland Flight Information Region, except for the area north of a line drawn from the intersection of the southern boundary of Oregon and the coastline to the northeast corner of the Honolulu Flight Information Region.

Mike Monroney Aeronautical Center

The Mike Monroney Aeronautical Center is a major organizational complex in Oklahoma City, Oklahoma, headed by a Director who reports to the Executive Director for Policy, Plans, and Resource Management. The Aeronautical Center has operating and support functions which are national in scope, which are not required to be performed in the Washington headquarters, and which are not susceptible of assignment to, or division among, the regions as regional operating programs. The term "Aeronautical Center" includes only those organizations that report to the Director, Aeronautical Center. Tenant organizations located on the Aeronautical Center property are not integral parts of the Aeronautical Center. The Aeronautical Center conducts centralized training and central warehousing and supply and provides certain automatic data processing (ADP) services for national and local programs.

The Aeronautical Center operates the FAA Academy which provides training for FAA employees and other governmental and nongovernmental employees. It provides for the management and distribution of FAA material and for the operation and maintenance of the centralized material system, also provides central data processing operations, systems, and programming services for assigned national and local ADP programs.

I. OFFICE OF PUBLIC AFFAIRS

The Office of Public Affairs maintains an FAA image that instills public trust and confidence in aviation safety by communicating the FAA message in ways that are consistent, seamless, and supportive of FAA offices. The office serves as the principal public spokesperson for FAA; initiates and participates in the execution of coordinated information plans and programs; and ensures that programs, policies, objectives, and all relevant information concerning FAA are consistently presented to the public, the aviation community, and

FAA employees in a factual, dignified, and timely manner. The Office:

- Serves as the source and point of primary coordination for supplying the employees, the public, the aviation community, State and local governments, and the news media with current, authoritative information about programs and objectives of FAA.

- Provides guidance to Regional Administrators and center directors on national public affairs policy.

- Provides public affairs counsel and staff assistance to the Administrator, Deputy Administrator, and other high-level officials in the exercise and performance of their statutory responsibilities in the promotion, encouragement, and development of aviation.

- Establishes public affairs standards and procedures, including releases to the media, press conferences, speeches, and radio and television presentations. Provides liaison with the aviation community regarding public affairs.

- Maintains liaison with representatives of communications media to provide news and background material about the growth, progress, and accomplishments of aviation.

- Serves as FAA's central office for the coordination of all agency audiovisual productions and procurements.

- Provides FAA employees, communities, organizations, and individuals with information about FAA through publications, audiovisuals, presentations, and by participation in public and organizationally sponsored meetings.

- Administers the FAA history program.

- Administers the FAA Freedom of Information Act program making information and records available.

- Administers the FAA external recognition and awards programs.

Within the office's sphere of responsibility, the Assistant Administrator for Public Affairs is authorized to:

- Take action in the name of the Administrator, except for those matters for which the Administrator has specifically reserved authority or otherwise provided.

- Represent the Administrator.

- Act on any matter for which specific delegation of authority has been made to the Assistant Administrator or to any element under the Assistant Administrator's executive direction.

The Assistant Administrator for Public Affairs is delegated authority to issue an administratively final decision to either sustain or overrule initial determinations to withhold records from the public after coordination with the Chief Counsel, FAA, and the Office of the General Counsel, Office of the Secretary of Transportation.

The Assistant Administrator of Public Affairs:

- Serves as principal advisor to the Administrator, Deputy Administrator, and key officials with respect to public affairs aspects of FAA activities.

- Represents FAA with respect to the formulation or implementation of Government-wide plans, policies, and programs concerning public affairs activities.

- Serves as the principal spokesperson of FAA to external sources on public affairs matters.

- Collaborates with the Office of International Aviation concerning public affairs aspects of international activities and objectives of FAA.

J. ASSISTANT ADMINISTRATOR FOR INFORMATION SERVICES

The Assistant Administrator for Information Services and Chief Information Officer serves as the principal advisor to the Administrator, Deputy Administrator, and FAA offices on information management and technology across the agency. As the agency's senior management official, serves as the spokesperson on information technology matters before Congress, other agencies, and the public.

This Administrator's mission is to provide agency policy and direction in the following areas:

- Strategic Planning
- Investment Analysis
- Process Engineering
- Information Management
- Information Security

These objectives are achieved by working with key constituents and understanding the information technology needs of the agency and teaming with other organizations.

K. FREE FLIGHT PHASE 1

The Federal Aviation Administrator established Free Flight Phase 1 in October 1998 as the agency's single accountable voice and point of contact. The Free Flight program provides benefits to the National Airspace System users as quickly as possible by taking an incremental building block approach to the fielding of new systems and promising new capabilities.

Free Flight enhances the aviation community's ability to collaboratively share data and to view and optimize all phases of flight—from planning and surface operations to en route flight paths. In collaboration with the aviation community, Free Flight is introducing new technologies and procedures. Free Flight is the industry-endorsed strategy that calls for the limited deployment of selected core capabilities that are already providing early benefits to users of the National Airspace System. Deployed systems are integrated into the traffic management system with operational procedures and training to minimize risk and achieve greater user satisfaction. Collaboration and sharing of information is becoming a new way of doing business.

The FAA Administrator is taking a building block approach to fielding new systems to provide benefits to users as soon as possible. Among the measurable benefits are the lifting of restrictions, fuel savings, reduction in delays, increased airport acceptance rates during rush periods, and more efficient use of available runways and ramp operations.

Free Flight Phase 1 was established in 1998 to deliver five "core capabilities" through a consensus process that drew upon the airline industry, labor organizations, the National Airspace System Modernization Task Force, and other Federal Aviation Administration offices. Free Flight Phase 1 tools are to be in place by the close of 2002. Free Flight Phase 1 has delivered on its charter, providing significant early benefits on time and within budget. Free Flight Phase 1 is a success.

Free Flight Phase 2 is chartered to geographically expand upon the successes of Free Flight Phase 1 as well as to conduct research to alleviate congestion and provide greater access to the National Airspace System. The Free Flight Phase 2 timeline is from October 2000 through December 2005. Free Flight Phase 2 activities will not conflict with the operation or commitments of the Free Flight Phase 1 program.

The Free Flight Phase 1 Program Office is focused on achieving the industry-recommended goals to:

- Achieve early benefits by deploying low-risk technology while maintaining or exceeding current levels of safety;

- Provide operational availability and evaluate performance of the core capabilities;

- Extend early benefits to National Airspace System users and to service providers;

- Employ an evolutionary development paradigm;

- Make leveraged use of proven technologies.

ASSOCIATE ADMINISTRATORS

The Associate Administrators assist the Administrator and Deputy Administrator in the discharge of agency management responsibilities and executive direction. Each Associate Administrator has a specific area of assigned responsibility. These responsibilities and the organizations under their direction are listed below.

I. ASSOCIATE ADMINISTRATOR FOR COMMERCIAL SPACE TRANSPORTATION

The Office of the Associate Administrator for Commercial Space Transportation (AST) is the newest, and only space-related Line of Business within the Federal Aviation Administration. Established in 1984 as the Office of Commercial Space Transportation in the Department of Transportation, AST was transferred to the FAA in November 1995.

Under Title 49, U.S. Code, Subtitle IX, Sections 70101–70119 (formerly the Commercial Space Launch Act), AST is given the responsibility to:

1. Regulate the commercial space transportation industry, only to the extent necessary to ensure compliance with international obligations of the United States and to protect the public health and safety, safety of property, and national security and foreign policy interest of the United States.

2. Encourage, facilitate, and promote commercial space launches by the private sector.

3. Recommend appropriate changes in Federal statutes, treaties, regulations, policies, plans, and procedures.

4. Facilitate the strengthening and expansion of the United States space transportation infrastructure.

In fulfilling its responsibilities under Title 49, AST issues Launch Operator's Licenses for commercial launches of orbital rockets such as the Atlas, Delta, Taurus, and Athena launch vehicles, and the air-launched Pegasus rocket. AST has also issued licenses for commercial launches of suborbital sounding rockets such as the Black Brant and Starfire. The first licensed was a suborbital launch of a Starfire on March 29, 1989. The 100th licensed launch was that of a Delta II from Vandenberg Air Force Base in California on September 8, 1998.

While the vast majority of licensed launch activities occur from U.S. Federal Ranges—such as the Cape Canaveral Air Station, Florida, Vandenberg Air Force Base, California, White Sands Missile Range, New Mexico, and Wallops Flight Facility, Wallops Island, Virginia—many future launch activities are expected to occur from private or State-operated launch sites. AST has licensed the operation of several non-Federal launch sites including the California Spaceport at Vandenberg Air Force Base, Spaceport Florida at Cape Canaveral Air Station, the Virginia Space Flight Center at Wallops Island, and Spaceport Alaska at Kodiak Island, Alaska. The first launch from a non-Federal range licensed by AST was that of NASA's Lunar Prospector aboard a Lockheed Martin Athena-2 rocket on January 6, 1998 from Spaceport Florida. AST is also evaluating a license application for a commercial launch which will take place from a mobile platform in the Pacific Ocean.

Commercial Space Transportation is divided into three functional components:

A. Space Systems Development Division

B. Licensing and Safety Division

C. Systems Engineering and Training Division

A. Space Systems Development

The Space Systems Development Division provides the space systems engineering, space policy, and economic and launch forecast capabilities for the Associate Administrator. AST-100's systems engineering expertise supports AST's regulatory mission through the development of requirements and criteria for the regulation of advanced launch concepts and launch site technologies. In particular, SSDD is developing regulations to ensure the safety of the many proposed reusable launch vehicles. Systems engineering support also includes the evaluation of environmental impacts of new launch vehicles and launch sites and the integration of space launch activities into a Space and Air Traffic Management System (SATMS) as part of the FAA's National Airspace (NAS) modernization.

The Space Systems Development Division also develops long-range commercial launch forecasts based on the markets for established and new satellite services, and identifies both domestic and international future space markets and industry trends. As part of its policy role, AST works with the interagency community to develop space transportation policies and works closely with other Federal agencies on issues relating to the use of U.S. commercial launch services. AST-100 also works with other government agencies to monitor trading practices in the worldwide launch market and to develop policy guidelines for free and fair trade in commercial launch services for international launch services providers.

B. Licensing and Safety

The Licensing and Safety Division's primary objective is to carry out AST's responsibility to ensure public health and safety through:

1. The licensing of commercial space launches and launch site operations.
2. Licensing the operation of non-Federal space launch sites.
3. Determining insurance or other financial responsibility requirements for commercial launch activities.

The Licensing and Safety Division seeks to ensure protection of public health and safety and the safety of property through its licensing and compliance monitoring processes. The components of the licensing process include a pre-licensing consultation period, policy review, payload review, safety evaluation, financial responsibility determination, and an environmental review.

About the Licensing Process

The primary objective of AST's licensing program, carried out by the Licensing and Safety Division, is to ensure public health and safety through the licensing of commercial space launches and reentries, and the operation of launch sites. For launches, the components of the licensing process include pre-application consultation, policy review and approval, safety review and approval, payload review and determination, financial responsibility determination, and an environmental review. For the operation of a launch site and for the reentry of a reentry vehicle, the FAA/AST evaluates an applicant's proposal on an individual basis. The FAA/AST issues a license when it determines that an applicant's launch or reentry proposal or proposal to operate a launch site will not jeopardize public health and safety, safety of property, U.S. national security or foreign policy interests, or international obligations of the United States. Statutes, regulations, and advisory circulars can be found at Statutes, Regulations, and Policies.

Applicants proposing to launch unguided suborbital launch vehicles, such as competitors for the Cheap Access To Space (CATS) prize, require a license unless the launch is exempt. To be exempt under the regulations (14 C.F.R. § 400.2), a launch must take place from a private site and involve a rocket that meets all three of the following conditions:

- has a motor or combination of motors with a total impulse of 200,000 pound-seconds or less; and

- whose motor or combination of motors have a total burning time or operating time of less than 15 seconds; and

- the rocket has a ballistic coefficient—i.e., gross weight in pounds divided by frontal area of rocket vehicle—less than 12 pounds per square inch.

AST issues two general types of launch licenses. A **launch-specific license** authorizes a license to conduct one or more launches, having the same launch parameters, of one type of launch vehicle from one launch site. The license identifies, by name or mission, each launch authorized under the license. A licensee's authorization to launch terminates upon completion of all launches authorized by the license or the expiration date stated in the license, whichever occurs first. A **launch operator license** authorizes a licensee to conduct launches from one launch site, within a range of launch parameters, of launch vehicles from the same family of vehicles transporting specified classes of payloads. A launch operator license remains in effect for five years from the date of issuance.

There are several key components to the launch licensing process:

- Pre-application consultation;

- Application evaluation, comprised of

  —Policy review and approval;

  —Safety review and approval;

  —Payload review and determination;

  —Financial responsibility determination; and

  —Environmental review.

- Compliance Monitoring.

Pre-application consultation is accomplished prior to the formal submittal of a license application. The policy review, safety review, payload review, financial responsibility determination, and environmental review are part of the launch license application evaluation. Compliance monitoring is performed after the license has been issued.

An applicant may submit data related to the policy review, safety review, and payload review together as a single package or separately. An applicant may also request a maximum probability of loss determination separately to determine its financial responsibility requirements early on in its launch program. Environmental information is required for evaluation if the proposed activity is not adequately addressed in AST programmatic documents.

The following is a brief description of each component of the launch licensing process:

Pre-Application Consultation: An applicant must consult with the FAA before submitting an application. Pre-application consultation consists of any and all meetings, communications, or draft application submittals that a potential applicant may undertake with the FAA prior to submitting a formal application. Pre-application consultation allows a prospective applicant to familiarize the FAA with its proposal and the FAA to familiarize the prospective applicant with the licensing process. It also provides a potential applicant with an opportunity to identify any unique aspects of its proposal, and develop a schedule for submitting an application.

Policy Review and Approval: The FAA reviews a license application to determine whether it presents any issues affecting U.S. national security or foreign policy interests, or international obligations of the United States. A major element of the policy review is the interagency review of the launch proposal. An interagency review allows government agencies to examine the proposed mission from their unique perspectives. The FAA consults with the Department of Defense, the Department of State, and other federal agencies such as the National Aeronautics and Space Administration that are authorized to address national security, foreign policy, or international obligation issues.

Safety Review and Approval: The purpose of the safety review is to determine whether an applicant can safely conduct the launch of the proposed launch vehicle(s) and any payload. Because the licensee is responsible for public safety, it is important that the applicant demonstrate an understanding of the hazards involved and discuss how the operations will be per-

formed safely. There are a number of technical analyses, some quantitative and some qualitative, that the applicant may perform in order to demonstrate that their commercial launch operations will pose no unacceptable threat to the public. The quantitative analyses tend to focus on the reliability and functions of critical safety systems, and the hazards associated with the hardware, and the risk those hazards pose to public property and individuals near the launch site and along the flight path, to satellites and other on-orbit spacecraft. The qualitative analyses focus on the organizational attributes of the applicant such as launch safety policies and procedures, communications, qualifications of key individuals, and critical internal and external interfaces.

For applicants proposing to launch from a federal launch range who have contracted with the federal launch range for the provision of safety-related launch services and property, the FAA issues a safety approval if the applicant satisfies the requirements of the regulations and if those launch services and the proposed use of launch property are within the federal launch range's experience. AST's **Launch Site Safety Assessments** document general information and range capabilities of a federal launch range, and provide a safety assessment of the federal launch range to support AST's licensing determination.

Payload Review and Determination: The FAA reviews a payload proposed for launch to determine whether a license applicant or payload owner or operator has obtained all required licenses, authorization, and permits, unless the payload is exempt from review. The FAA does not review payloads that are subject to regulation by the Federal Communications Commission (FCC) or the Department of Commerce, National Oceanic and Atmospheric Administration (NOAA); or owned or operated by the U.S. Government.

If not otherwise exempt, the FAA reviews a payload proposed for launch to determine whether its launch would jeopardize public health and safety, safety of property, U.S. national security or foreign policy interests, or international obligations of the United States. The FAA may review and issue findings regarding a proposed class of payload, e.g., communications, remote sensing or navigation. However, each payload is subject to compliance monitoring by the FAA before launch.

Financial Responsibility Determination: *Section 70112* of the Commercial Space Launch Act* requires

---

*The Commercial Space Launch Act of 1984, as codified at 49 U.S.C. Subtitle IX—Commercial Space Transportation, ch. 701, Commercial Space Launch Activities, 49 U.S.C. §§ 70101–70119 (1994).

that all commercial licensees demonstrate financial responsibility to compensate for the maximum probable loss (MPL) from claims by a third party for death, bodily injury, or property damage or loss resulting from an activity carried out under the license; and the U.S. Government against a person for damage or loss to government property resulting from an activity carried out under the license. Section 70112 also requires that the Department of Transportation set the amounts of financial responsibility required of the licensee. The licensee can then elect to meet this requirement by proving they have financial reserves equal to or exceeding the amount specified, or placing the required amount in escrow, or purchasing liability insurance equal to the amount specified. The most common and preferred method is via the purchase of liability insurance.

The MPL determination is based on an analysis and assessment of the maximum monetary losses likely to be incurred by government and third party personnel and property in the event of a mishap. It is calculated by assessing the dollar value of government and third party properties at risk by launch accidents likely to occur as the result of the conduct of launch activities.

Environmental Review: The environmental evaluation ensures that proposed launch activities pose no unacceptable danger to the natural environment. FAA/AST is required to consider the environmental effects of commercial space launches authorized under a license because the issuance of a license is considered to be a major federal action under the National Environment Policy Act, 42 U.S.C. 4321 et seq. (NEPA). An applicant must provide information sufficient to enable the FAA/AST to comply with the requirements of NEPA, the Council on Environmental Quality Regulations for Implementing the Procedural Provisions of NEPA, 40 CFR Parts 1500–1508, and the FAA's Procedures for Considering Environmental Impacts, FAA Order 1050. 1D.

Compliance Monitoring: The purpose of compliance monitoring is to ensure that a licensee complies with the Act, the regulations, and the terms and conditions set forth in its license. A launch licensee shall allow access by, and cooperate with, federal officers or employees or other individuals authorized by the FAA to observe any activities of the licensee, or of the licensee's contractors or subcontractors, associated with the conduct of a licensed launch.

C. Systems Engineering and Training

The **System Engineering and Training Division** defines safety standards for existing and emerging space launch systems, launch sites, re-entry systems, and re-entry sites. Additionally, defines methods to assure and verify that those standards are met. The System Engineering and Training Division develops and delivers training in unique aspects of space transportation to the Office personnel. The Division supports the other Divisions of AST with expert consultative support.

COMSTAC

COMSTAC is the Commercial Space Transportation Advisory Committee. (Figure 7.3.) Established in 1985, COMSTAC provides information, advice, and recommendations to the Administrator of the Federal Aviation Administration within the Department of Transportation on matters relating to the U.S. commercial space transportation industry.

Table 7.2   Commercial Space Launch Schedule

Recent Commercial Space Launches

#	Launch Date	Payload	Vehicle	Results	Company	Site
136	19 Jun 2001	ICO2	Atlas IIAS	Success	LMC	CCAFS
135	8 May 2001	XM-1	Zenit-3SL	Success	SLC	Pacific
134	18 Mar 2001	XM-2	Zenit-3SL	Success	SLC	Pacific
133	21 Oct 2000	THURAYA-1	Zenit-3SL	Success	SLC	Pacific
132	9 Oct 2000	HETE II	Pegasus	Success	OSC	KMR
131	23 Aug 2000	DEMOSAT	Delta III	Success	TBC	CCAFS
130	28 Jul 2000	PAS 9	Zenit-3SL	Success	SLC	Pacific
129	14 Jul 2000	ECHOSTAR VI	Atlas IIAS	Success	LMC	CCAFS
128	7 Jun 2000	TSX-5	Pegasus XL	Success	OSM	VAFB
127	24 May 2000	EUTELSAT W4	Atlas IIIA	Success	LMC	CCAFS

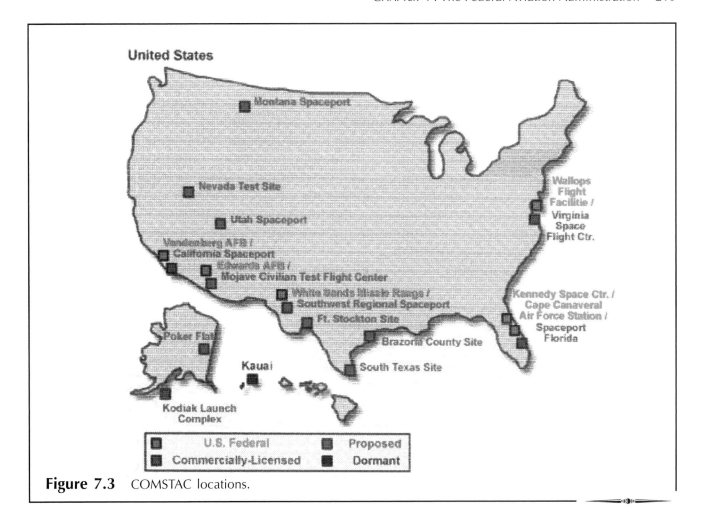

Figure 7.3   COMSTAC locations.

The primary goals of COMSTAC are to:

1. Evaluate economic, technological and institutional developments relating to the U.S. commercial space transportation industry.

2. Provide a forum for the discussion of problems involving the relationship between industry activities and government requirements.

3. Make recommendations to the Administrator on issues and approaches for Federal policies and programs regarding the industry.

COMSTAC membership is made up of senior executives from the U.S. commercial space transportation industry, including entrepreneurial firms as well as large aerospace companies; the satellite industry; space-related state government officials; and representatives from space advocacy organizations.

Industry issues are primarily addressed through **working groups** which provide information, reports and recommendations to the full Committee for adoption.

If a report or recommendation is adopted by the full Committee, it is then submitted to the FAA Administrator as an official industry recommendation. COMSTAC currently has four active working groups:

- Technology and Innovation
- Launch Operations and Support
- Risk Management
- Reusable Launch Vehicle Development

II. ASSOCIATE ADMINISTRATOR FOR AIRPORTS

The Associate Administrator for Airports advises and assists the Administrator in directing, coordinating, controlling, and ensuring the adequacy of the substantive aspects of FAA rulemaking actions relating to the certification and capacity of airports and the administration of airport grant programs; the adequacy of the technical standards, plans, and programs for the development of a national integrated system of airports and for the improvement of safety in airport operations.

The functions of the Associate Administrator are:

1. Develops standards for airport design, development, construction, maintenance, operation, safety, and data.

2. Manages the Airport Certification Program.

3. Administers airport program matters pertaining to national airport planning, environment and social requirements, airport grants, and passenger facility charges.

4. Serves as the FAA advocate for airport capacity programs to improve and enhance airport capacity programs in the National Airport System.

The Associate Administrator for Airports exercises executive direction over the:

A. Office of Airport Planning and Programming.

B. Office of Airport Safety and Standards.

With respect to all matters within the Associate Administrator's sphere of responsibility, the Associate Administrator for Airports is authorized to:

1. Take action and issue orders in the name of the Administrator, except for those matters for which the Administrator has specifically reserved authority or otherwise provided.

2. Represent the Administrator.

3. Act on any matter for which specific delegation of authority has been made to the associate administrator or to any element under the associate's executive direction.

Special Delegations: The Associate Administrator for Airports is delegated authority to:

1. Approve or modify Airport Improvement Program projects.

2. Approve final environmental impact statements or supplements to final environmental impact statements for actions subject to section 102(2)(C) of the National Environmental Policy Act of 1969 that involve:

(a) Any new airport serving a metropolitan area.

(b) Any new runway extension for an airport, any part of which is located in a metropolitan area and is either certified under section 612 of the Federal Aviation Act of 1958, as amended, or used by large aircraft (except helicopters) of commercial operators.

(c) Any project to which a Federal, State, or local government agency has expressed opposition on environmental grounds.

(d) Any project for which a notice of intended referral to the Council on Environmental Quality has been received from another Federal agency and the objections of that agency have not been met.

3. Approve or disapprove airport noise compatibility programs submitted by airport operators under Federal Aviation Regulations, Part 150, Airport Noise Compatibility Planning.

4. Approve or disapprove, in whole or in part, any application, request, or plan from a public agency that controls a commercial service airport; terminate the authority to impose Passenger Facility Charges previously granted; and offset Federal airport grant program apportioned funds, as required, under Federal Aviation Regulations, Part 158, Passenger Facility Charges (PFC's). This authority may be redelegated.

5. Approve or disapprove, in whole or in part, as required, under Federal Aviation Regulations, Part 161. This authority may be redelegated.

A. Office of Airport Planning and Programming

The Office of Airport Planning and Programming serves the principal organization of FAA responsible for all Airports program matters pertaining to national airport planning, environmental and social requirements, airport grants, property, transfers, passenger facility charges, and ensuring adequacy of the substantive aspects of FAA rulemaking actions relating to these programs.

The Office of Airport Planning and Programming serves as the principal staff element of FAA for airport planning and programming. It:

• Administers Airports grant programs, passenger facility charges, and conveyance or lease of Federal land and surplus property for airport purposes.

• Develops eligibility criteria governing airport grants, passenger facility charge program, and entry criteria for the National Plan of Integrated Airport Systems (NPIAS).

• Provides guidance and central control over national planning of integrated airport systems, including development and issuance of the NPIAS.

- Develops guidelines for coordination and implementation of intermodal and multimodal transportation planning relating to the Airports program.

- Provides for airport planning and planning support, including development of guidance for master and system planning.

- Analyzes and formulates the Airports program legislation on subject matters within the purview of the office.

- Administers the program for environmental review and approval of airport development, airport noise compatibility planning under Federal Aviation Regulations Part 150, airport noise and access restrictions under Federal Aviation Regulations Part 161, and other Airports Program activities relating to environmental issues. Administers the program for environmental review and documentation of airport projects, the airport noise compatibility planning.

- Provides representation at meetings of organizations concerned with matters within the purview of this office.

- Administers the application of the Uniform Relocation Assistance and Real Property Acquisition Policies Act of 1970 to airport improvement projects receiving Federal financial assistance.

B. Office of Airport Safety Standards

The Office of Airport Safety and Standards serves as the principal organization of FAA responsible for all airport program matters pertaining to standards for airport design, construction, maintenance, operations, safety, and data, including ensuring adequacy of the substantive aspects of FAA rulemaking actions relating to the certification of airports.

The Office of Airport Safety and Standards:

- Develops FAA standards and criteria for:

  —Airport design, construction, maintenance, safety, snow and ice control, aircraft rescue and firefighting, and data.

  —FAA-wide programs for continuous safe operation of airports and for airport safety certification.

  —Compliance with Federal airport assistance agreements, conveyance or lease of Federal land and surplus property for airport purposes, and airport certification requirements.

- Administers the Airport Safety and Certification Program.

- Manages the program for collecting and maintaining airport facilities data on the Nation's airports.

- Provides representation at meetings of organizations concerned with matters within the purview of this office.

- Cooperates with the Office of International Aviation in establishing international standards for airport design and representing the FAA interests and international activities relating to airport safety and standards.

- Provides guidance to regions for promoting emergency operations, vulnerability reduction, and damage control at civil airports; develops plans for emergency management and restoration of civil airports after attack or natural disaster, including determining the need for equipment, materials, and supplies.

- Identifies sponsors, and monitors airport design and safety-related research and development.

- Establishes and maintains liaison with other Federal agencies and other organizations to ensure effective coordination of airport design, construction, maintenance, operational, and safety matters within the purview of this office.

- Analyzes and formulates the Airport program legislation on subject matters within the purview of the office.

III. ASSOCIATE ADMINISTRATOR FOR CIVIL AVIATION SECURITY

The Associate Administrator for Civil Aviation Security advises and assists the Administrator in directing, coordinating, and ensuring the effective protection of the U.S. traveling public in air transportation throughout the world and providing for the integrity of the civil aviation security system. The associate administrator develops and implements regulatory policies, programs, and procedures to prevent criminal and other disruptive acts against civil aviation; assists in interaction of dangerous drugs and narcotics into the United States; protects FAA employees, facilities, and equipment; and supports the national security.

The Associate Administrator for Civil Aviation Security:

- Provides leadership in the promotion and management of initiatives to foster aviation security, managerial accountability, recognition, and organizational development and modernization.

- Establishes strategic goals and objectives for the physical security and safeguarding of FAA personnel, assets, facilities, and operations.

- Assures the integration and coordination of policy and planning within and across agency functional areas.

- Evaluates the effectiveness of organizational elements and programs.

- Promotes and practices positive human relations, open communications, and affirmative equal employment opportunity policies.

The Associate Administrator for Civil Aviation Security exercises executive direction and authority over the:

a. Office of Civil Aviation Security Intelligence.

b. Office of Civil Aviation Security Operations.

c. Office of Civil Aviation Security Policy and Planning.

With respect to all matters within the Associate Administrator for Civil Aviation Security's sphere of responsibility, the associate administrator is authorized to:

- Take action and issue orders in the name of the Administrator, except for those matters for which the Administrator has specifically reserved authority or otherwise provided.

- Represent the Administrator.

- Issue, amend, or withdraw orders, standards, and procedures pertaining to the physical security safeguarding of FAA personnel, assets, facilities, and operations. Prohibit disclosure of a record and information which contains provisions of Federal Aviation Regulations (FAR) 191 which ensure the safety of persons traveling in air transportation. Exercise the other authorities contained within FAR 191 concerning the release of information gathered within the FAA's civil aviation security role.

- Issue, amend, or cancel orders, standards, and procedures required to implement within FAA executive orders, national policy directives, and DOT policy and procedures pertaining to security of personnel, communications, technical surveillance countermeasures, national security, sensitive unclassified information, and FAA operations.

- Pursuant to the International Security and Development Cooperation Act of 1985, authorize Federal Air Marshals (FAM), in connection with the performance of their air transportation security duties, to carry firearms and to make arrests without warrant for any of-

fense against the United States committed in their presence, or for any felony recognizable under the laws of the United States if they have reasonable grounds to believe that the person to be arrested has committed a felony. This authority may not be redelegated.

- Pursuant to the Aviation Security Improvement Act of 1990, authorize the establishment of the Federal Security Manager (FSM) position at all airports within the United States necessary to meet the needs of air transportation security. This authority may not be redelegated.

A. Office of Civil Aviation Security Intelligence

The Office of Civil Aviation Security Intelligence manages the information collection effort; collates, researches, evaluates, analyzes, and disseminates aviation security information and intelligence; coordinates domestic and international aviation security intelligence activities with other Government agencies; provides indication and warning intelligence of potential criminal actions to the civil aviation community; assesses the threat of criminal actions against domestic and international aviation and FAA facilities; integrates specialized FAA-unique analysis with threat analysis efforts of the intelligence community and law enforcement agencies to provide estimates of the future threat to civil aviation and directs FAA's participation in the El Paso Intelligence Center.

B. Office of Civil Aviation Security Operations

The Office of Civil Aviation Security Operations ensures effective implementation of policies, regulations, programs, and procedures: to promote the security of civil aviation, including the prevention of acts of air piracy, aviation sabotage, and related criminal acts; to assist law enforcement in the program for interdiction of dangerous drugs and narcotics into the United States; to promote the security of agency operations, personnel, facilities, property, and communications; and to conduct investigations supporting the FAA mission.

C. Office of Civil Aviation Security Policy and Planning

The Office of Civil Aviation Security Policy and Planning ensures effective development of policies, regulations, and standards to: promote the security of civil aviation, including the prevention of acts of air piracy, aviation sabotage, and related criminal acts;

support law enforcement in its programs for interdiction of dangerous drugs and narcotics transported into the U.S. and promote the security of agency operations, personnel, facilities, property, and communication.

IV. ASSOCIATE ADMINISTRATOR FOR REGULATION AND CERTIFICATION

The Associate Administrator for Regulation and Certification advises and assists the Administrator in directing, coordinating, controlling, and ensuring the adequacy of the substantive aspects of FAA rulemaking actions related to aircraft certification and manufacturing; certification of airmen, and air agencies and maintenance aspects of air carrier, air operators and aircraft; plans and programs covering competence of airmen, air agencies, and air carriers, aviation medicine, accident investigation, civil aviation registry, foreign air carrier assessments; substantive aspects of FAA rulemaking related to the safety of flight; and safety analysis on related subjects.

The Associate Administrator for Regulation and Certification:

- Prescribes standards governing the design, production quality assurance, and airworthiness certification (or approval) of aeronautical products.

- Administers an aircraft certification program.

- Establishes certification standards for air carriers, commercial operators, air agencies, and airmen (except airport traffic control tower operators).

- Directs the certification, inspection, and surveillance activities to ensure the adequacy of flight procedures, operating methods, airmen qualifications and proficiency, aircraft maintenance, and the maintenance aspects of continued airworthiness programs.

- Manages and directs the FAA rulemaking program that is under the jurisdiction of the Associate Administrator for Regulation and Certification and other associated Administrators with rulemaking authority.

- Administers, manages and oversees the activities of the Aviation Rulemaking Advisory Committee (ARAC) sponsored by the Administrator.

- Oversees the management of the civil aviation registry.

- Investigates aircraft accidents and incidents, supports National Transportation Safety Board (NTSB) accident and incident investigation, and develops and manages a reporting program for accidents and incidents.

- Oversees the policy execution and administrative management aspects of the airman medical certification, medical research, aeromedical education, medical accident investigation, aviation industry and anti-drug, and airman medical standards.

- Prescribes policy for flight procedures development.

- Administers the aircraft Flight Proficiency Program for Aviation Safety Inspectors and Flight Test Pilots.

- Oversees the Aircraft Certification Service and the Flight Standards Service flight programs to ensure safe and efficient operations conform with the applicable Federal Aviation Regulations and with FAA policies and procedures governing these programs.

The Associate Administrator for Regulation and Certification exercises executive direction over the:

A. Office of Accident Investigation.

B. Aircraft Certification Service.

C. Office of Aviation Medicine.

D. Flight Standards Service.

E. Office of Rulemaking.

A. Office of Accident Investigation

The Office of Accident Investigation promotes safety and safety consciousness in air commerce while conducting investigations of accidents and incidents, evaluates the efficacy of selected programs on safety matters, analyzes trends, and conducts special analyses on accident/incident related and other safety issues, identifies relevant safety issues, and recommends corrective issues.

The Office of Accident Investigation:

- Conducts accident and incident investigations.

- Conducts special accident/incident investigations and analyses.

- Provides analyses of accident/incident trends and safety data.

- Manages National Transportation Safety Board and FAA safety recommendations programs.

- Establishes FAA accident and incident investigation policy.

- Accomplishes the responsibilities in paragraphs 2a through 2f by:

    —Identifying accident/incident investigation related safety issues that require further analysis and recommending correction actions.

—Developing, coordinating, and recommending national accident/incident investigation policies.

—Developing and implementing specific program goals and areas of emphasis to guide field program planning and performance.

—Evaluating the adequacy of existing regulations, policies, procedures, practices, and field program performance in meeting FAA safety goals.

—Developing and implementing programs and practices to ensure the professional competency and development of employees engaged in accident investigation and reporting.

—Conducting accident/incident investigation and analysis and identifying and recommending research and development programs.

—Conducting studies and analyses of safety data and issues within the purview of the Associate Administrator for Regulation and Certification.

B. Aircraft Certification Service

The Aircraft Certification Service administers the Aircraft Certification Regulatory Program. This program includes the development and administration of safety standards governing the type, production, and airworthiness certification of aircraft, engines, propellers, parts, and appliances. Noise and emission level determinations are also made during certification. This aircraft certification regulatory responsibility begins with the development of safety standards and continues through making findings of compliance, issuing certificates, monitoring safety performance of the system, and taking corrective action as required for safety and to ensure compliance.

The major activities of the Aircraft Certification Regulatory Program include:

• Regulatory Policy Development. The development of regulations, standards, policies, directives, and guidance material.

• Certifications and Approvals and the Granting of Appointments to "Representatives of the Administrator." The examination of civil aeronautical products, their design, the production quality assurance systems under which they are produced, and of private persons authorized to represent the Administrator in aircraft certification functions to determine compliance with applicable safety and qualification requirements.

• Continued Operational Safety. The monitoring of the safety performance of certified or approved civil aeronautical products, production quality assurance systems, and authorized Representatives of the Administrator, and taking corrective action or recommending legal enforcement action, as appropriate, to ensure the continued integrity of issued certificates, approvals, authorizations, and appointments.

• Flight Program. The administration of the Aircraft Certification Service Flight Program to ensure safe and efficient flight operations conform with the applicable Federal Aviation Regulations and with FAA policies and procedures governing the program.

C. The Office of Aviation Medicine

Serves as the principal office with respect to:

• Medical certification/qualification of airmen and other persons associated with safety in flight.

• Airman medical regulations, standards, policies, and procedures.

• Designated aviation medical examiner system.

• FAA employee medical standards, policies, and procedures.

• Occupational health programs of the agency.

• Aviation medical research.

• Aeromedical and human factors in civil aviation accident investigations.

• Biometric and biostatistical data for use in human factors evaluations.

• Aeromedical education.

• Agency health awareness activities.

• Implementation and oversight of industry antidrug and alcohol misuse prevention programs.

• FAA employee substance abuse testing.

• Medical review of all positive drug tests involving Department of Transportation employees and applicants for employment with DOT.

With respect to the functions in paragraph 2a, the office:

• Develops, recommends, and coordinates national policies for issuance by the Administrator.

• Develops and prescribes technical standards, systems, and procedures consistent with national policies.

- Prescribes national medical program goals and priorities for field guidance and execution.

- Maintains liaison with other governmental agencies and private, professional, and technical organizations to ensure maximum support of the national civil aviation medical effort.

- Evaluates the adequacy of policies, rules, regulations, procedures, and medical program execution in meeting agency goals and priorities.

- Coordinates with the National Transportation Safety Board and the Office of Accident Investigation in providing professional medical services for the investigation of civil aviation accidents.

- Ensures that medical certification activities conform with international medical standards and policies.

- Serves as the agency medical expert, providing professional and technical advice and assistance to the Administrator and other officials; and participates in all intra-agency deliberations which concern medical determinations.

- Determines the medical qualifications of FAA employees in positions with medical qualification standards, as well as applicants for these positions; and grants or denies medical clearances for employment or continued employment.

- Develops, implements, and conducts compliance and enforcement inspections for the agency's aviation industry drug and alcohol misuse prevention programs.

- Exercises line authority over regional Aviation Medical Divisions.

D. Flight Standards Service

The Flight Standards Service promotes safety of flight of civil aircraft in air commerce by:

- Setting certification standards for air carriers, commercial operators, air agencies, and airmen (except air traffic control tower operators).

- Directing, managing, and executing certification, inspection, and surveillance activities to ensure the adequacy of flight procedures, operating methods, airmen qualification and proficiency, aircraft maintenance, and the maintenance aspects of continued airworthiness programs.

- Managing the systems for registry of civil aircraft and all official airmen records, and supporting law enforcement agencies responsible for drug interdiction.

The Flight Standards Service is responsible for:

- Certification, operating methods, flight operations, and maintenance activities of U.S. air carriers and foreign air carriers operating in and over the U.S.

- Maintenance standards for U.S.-registered aircraft, including continued airworthiness.

- Certification and conduct of commercial, industrial, private, and general aviation operations including rotorcraft.

- Examination and certification (except medical) of airmen (except air traffic control tower operators) and air agencies.

- Examination and appointment of persons designated and authorized to act as representatives of the Administrator pursuant to Title 49 of the United States Code (49 U.S.C.) with respect to certification of flight airmen and the maintenance of civil aircraft and products.

- Use of air navigation facilities, appliances, and systems by civil aircraft; the minimum equipment capability of civil aircraft for operating in an established environment; and the operational aspects of flight procedures including en route and instrument approach procedures (except air traffic control procedures).

- Approval of and surveillance over the aircraft maintenance programs of operators and pilot schools.

- Assuring that appropriate operational considerations are accommodated with regard to aircraft maintenance policies, procedures, and practices.

- Operating requirements and criteria for use of aircraft systems; e.g., determining whether a navigation device can be used as a sole source of navigation or how many are required; and determining the type of airborne equipment required for low visibility approaches and landings.

- Ensuring that operational considerations are accounted for in the "Operating Limitations and Information" (including operational requirements and pilot procedures) requirements, policies, and practices for the development of airplane and rotorcraft flight manuals.

- Promoting safety through monitoring compliance with the Federal Aviation Regulations, including the gathering of evidence to support administrative or legal enforcement action and the preparation of Enforcement Investigative Reports to support the initiation of administrative and legal enforcement action, when appropriate.

- Administering and monitoring the FAA Safety Program through direction and oversight of the FAA's Senior Flight Safety Officer.

    With respect to the foregoing:

- Develops and recommends, or issues within the delegated authority of the Director, regulations and minimum standards.

- Develops and recommends national policies for issuance by the Administrator.

- Develops and issues guidance, procedures, practices, and program plans consistent with national policies.

- Develops and recommends specific program goals and areas of emphasis to guide field program planning and performance.

- Evaluates the adequacy of existing regulations, policies, procedures, practices, and program performance in meeting broad FAA goals, as well as specific program goals.

- Develops plans and technical guidance for the protection and use of civil aviation resources, except airports, in time of national emergency.

- Recommends budget levels for formulation of decision packages on national programs, and recommends allocations of appropriated resources based on review of Washington headquarters and regional requirements and quarterly review information.

- Develops and recommends programs and practices to ensure the professional competency and development of employees.

- Determines the need for and recommends research and development projects establishing the relative priority of those projects recommended.

- Administers the Flight Standards Service Flight Program to ensure safe and efficient operations conform with the applicable Federal Aviation Regulations and with FAA policies and procedures governing the program.

- Exercises line authority over the regional Flight Standards Division.

E. Office of Rulemaking

The Office of Rulemaking assists the Associate Administrator for Regulation and Certification in managing and directing all aspects of FAA rulemaking actions.

The Office of Rulemaking:

- Co-manages (administrative, nontechnical aspects), with the office of primary responsibility, rulemaking project activities (including flight standards, aircraft certification and manufacturing, security, medical, air traffic, airports, airspace, and energy and environmental rules.)

- Develops and recommends national policies on rulemaking procedures and priorities for issuance by the Administrator and develops procedures and program plans consistent with these policies.

- Represents the associate administrator in matters relating to rulemaking.

- Conducts regulatory review of rules and appraises the quality and effectiveness of rulemaking activities.

- Establishes and maintains a system of priorities for rulemaking activities and schedules regulatory projects.

- Assists in the development of rulemaking documents and develops rulemaking documents for which the Office of Rulemaking is the office of primary responsibility.

- Provides advice on rulemaking and recommends the initiation of rulemaking actions.

- Reviews and ensures the administrative adequacy of all safety and security regulatory material developed within FAA.

- Ensures that existing rules, regulations, standards, policies, procedures, and program performance are consistent with FAA goals and objectives.

- Arranges and chairs hearings and formal or informal meetings on rulemaking actions.

- Serves as the liaison between the Office of the Chief Counsel and other FAA offices on rulemaking and legislation.

- Serves as the operational and approval focal point for regulatory contact.

- Manages the Aviation Rulemaking Advisory Committee.

V. ASSOCIATE ADMINISTRATOR FOR AIR TRAFFIC SERVICES

The Associate Administrator for Air Traffic Services provides leadership, direction, and guidance relating to the safe and efficient utilization of the national airspace system. This includes the operation and maintenance of the national air traffic control and navigation system and the installation of air traffic and navigation facilities and equipment; the flight inspection of navigational aids; the formulation of system capacity programs; the conduct of training, warehousing and supply, and automatic data processing services; and the management of regional air traffic and airway facilities programs.

The Associate Administrator for Air Traffic Services:

- Provides leadership in the promotion and management of initiatives to foster aviation safety, managerial accountability, recognition, and organizational development and modernization.

- Establishes objectives and priorities that reflect FAA strategic goals and Administrator's policy initiatives.

- Ensures the integration and coordination of policy and planning within and across agency functional areas.

- Evaluates effectiveness of organizational elements and programs.

- Promotes positive human relations, open communications, and affirmative equal employment opportunity policies.

- Oversees the flight inspection flight program to ensure safe and efficient flight operations to conform with applicable Federal Aviation Regulations and FAA policies and procedures governing the program.

The Associate Administrator for Air Traffic Services exercises executive direction over the:

A. Air Traffic Service.

B. Air Traffic System Requirements Service.

C. Airway Facilities Service.

D. Office of System Capacity.

E. Office of Independent Operational Test and Evaluation.

F. Runway Safety.

G. Terminal Business Services.

A. Air Traffic Service

The Air Traffic Service provides for the management of civil and military air traffic in the navigable airspace by developing and recommending national policies and establishing national programs, regulations, standards, and procedures for management of the airspace; operation of air navigation and communications systems and facilities, separation and control of, and flight assistance to, air traffic; provides for the security control of air traffic to meet national defense requirements; operates the FAA national and international flight information and cartographic programs; develops and coordinates U.S. policies, standards, and procedures

related to international air traffic and telecommunications services and provides for the management of regional air traffic programs.

B. Air Traffic System Requirements Service

The Air Traffic System Requirements Service develops comprehensive National Airspace System (NAS) requirements and manages a disciplined process to fulfill the operational needs of the air traffic system. The service collects, validates, advocates, and implements system requirements to ensure operational effectiveness. The service establishes operational and support requirements for facilities and equipment programs; aviation weather services; national airspace programs; automation, communications, navigations and landing lights, environmental (including tower), and surveillance systems; infrastructure and power systems; and software and hardware for use in the National Airspace System.

C. Airway Facilities Service

The Airway Facilities Service promotes a safe and efficient use of the national airspace through transition, integration, sustaining, and maintenance engineering and field support of current systems that comprise the National Airspace System.

D. Office of System Capacity

The Office of System Capacity is responsible for development of user-driver performance measurements for the air traffic system. The strategy will encompass short-, medium- and long-term objectives that drive FAA to achieve its capacity goals. The office provides direction and management support required to increase the capacity of the National Airspace System (NAS).

E. Office of Independent Operational Test and Evaluation

The Office of Independent Operational Test and Evaluation is responsible for the objective, independent assessment of operational readiness for all acquisition programs designed by the Department of Transportation or the FAA Acquisition Executive for Independent Operational Test and Evaluation. Operational readiness is a combination of operational effectiveness and operational suitability.

ATS employees are Air Traffic controllers, engineers and technicians, pilots and flight inspection personnel, business managers, and support staff. Approximately 36,500 ATS employees:

- control 200,000 aircraft takeoffs and landings per day

- provide 24 hours of Air Traffic control daily

- manage the NAS infrastructure by operating and maintaining 32,500 facilities and systems

- maintain 8,200 terminal instrument flight procedures and 9,000 airway segments

- conduct over 11,000 flight inspections nationally and internationally each year to preserve the safety, quality, and reliability of the airspace system

- assign and protect more than 40,000 aeronautical radio frequencies used in Air Traffic control; and direct the modernization of the NAS infrastructure (Free Flight).

The Program Control aspect is responsible for monitoring and assessing the overall technical, schedule, and financial performance of the business unit.

Terminal Automation is responsible for terminal air traffic control capabilities provided by automation systems: the Standard Terminal Automation Replacement System (STARS), the Automated Radar Terminal System (ARTS), and Common ARTS.

Resource Management is responsible for workforce planning, facility management, labor/management relations, training, awards, and related personnel and work environment issues for the people who support the provision of terminal air traffic control capabilities.

F. Runway Safety

The FAA has recently developed and published the National Blueprint for Runway Safety, which provides a structured plan to improve runway safety across the nation. The Blueprint outlines several initiatives aimed at increasing runway safety. As part of implementing the Blueprint, the FAA has analyzed the severity of runway incursions for the first time. This analysis of runway incursion severity trends at towered airports in the United States will help guide implementation of these safety-related initiatives. The Runway Safety Program is pleased to present the National Blueprint for Runway Safety, a guide to achieve a measurably safer runway environment.

G. Terminal Business Service

To meet the continuing challenges in modernizing the FAA's terminal capabilities, the Terminal Business Service (ATB) was established on January 10, 2001. The new organization will consolidate and integrate all skills required to provide integrated terminal ATC capabilities.

Its purpose is to align capital investment, people, and processes with the most critical needs of the flying public. To accomplish this, the Terminal Business Service will combine acquisition and operational staffs and will consolidate funding, personnel, and planning in a single organization.

Initially, the Terminal Business Service will consolidate responsibility and accountability for terminal facilities, automation, and surveillance capabilities.

In its final form, ATB will add responsibility, authority, and accountability for terminal communications, weather, and surface.

The Standard Terminal Automation Replacement System (STARS) is a joint Federal Aviation Administration and Department of Defense program to replace Automated Radar Terminal Systems and other capacity-constrained, older technology systems at 172 FAA and up to 199 terminal radar approach control facilities and associated towers.

STARS is used by controllers to provide air traffic control service to aircraft in terminal areas. Typical terminal area ATC services include: the separation and sequencing of air traffic, the provision of traffic alerts and weather advisories, and radar vectoring for departing and arriving traffic. The system will reduce the life-cycle cost of ownership, accommodate air traffic growth, and provide for the introduction of new automation functions which improve the safety and efficiency of the National Airspace System.

The STARS program is being managed under the FAA's Terminal Business Service (ATB). The STARS effort is led by a product team with members integrated from acquisition and operations organizations of the FAA and DoD. The team works collaboratively to ensure that STARS development benefits from the insights and experience of each member. The controller and technician unions are also contributing to STARS efforts. Union representatives and working members participated in requirements development and the evaluation of the system before it was fielded and continue to support each increment in STARS capability.

The Planning, Control, and Integration staff ensures the provision of integrated terminal air traffic control capabilities by developing strategies and plans that reduce risk to service and improve performance across the domain, and by providing advice and insight about the probable effects of alternative courses of action.

VI. ASSOCIATE ADMINISTRATOR FOR RESEARCH AND ACQUISITIONS

The Associate Administrator for Research and Acquisitions provides leadership, direction, and guidance relating to FAA acquisition policy, research, system prototyping, and agency information resource management. As the FAA's Acquisition Executive, the Associate Administrator for Research and Acquisitions leads the agency's programs in the areas of:

- Definition and validation of requirements and planning for current and future systems supporting the National Airspace System, including air traffic management, airport technology, safety, capacity, and security.

- Complex initiatives for new management approaches, administrative techniques, and information technology solutions to improve resource allocation, cost efficiency, and productivity.

- Integration of operational requirements with system development, including system planning for design and material control, advanced technologies and concepts, and operations research.

- Development and management of centralized acquisition policy and programs.

The Associate Administrator for Research and Acquisitions exercises executive direction over the:

A. Office of Acquisitions.
B. Office of Air Traffic Systems Development.
C. Office of Aviation Research.
D. Office of Communications, Navigation, and Surveillance Systems.
E. Office of System Architecture and Investment Analysis.
F. Office of Business Management.
G. William J. Hughes FAA Technical Center.

The Associate Administrator for Research and Acquisitions:

1. Provides leadership over the definition and validation of needs/requirements and planning for current and future systems supporting the National Airspace System, including air traffic management services, airport technology, safety, capacity and security of the air transportation system.

2. Manages complex planning initiatives and makes recommendations to the Administrator on new management approaches, administrative techniques, and information technology solutions which would improve resource allocation, cost efficiency, and productivity.

3. Provides leadership over the integration of operational requirements with system development, including system planning for design and material control; advanced concepts, and operations research.

4. Provides leadership in the development and management of a centralized acquisition policy and program. Develops, implements, and evaluates agency acquisition policy and processes in compliance with all laws and directives.

5. Promotes positive human relations, open communications, and affirmative equal employment opportunity policies.

With respect to all matters within the Associate Administrator's sphere of responsibility, the Associate Administrator is authorized to:

1. Take action and issue orders in the name of the Administrator, except for those matters for which the Administrator has specifically reserved authority or otherwise provided.

2. Represent the Administrator.

3. Act as the agency's acquisition executive.

4. Act on any matter for which specific delegation of authority has been made to the Associate Administrator.

A. Office of Acquisitions

The Office of Acquisitions provides leadership, direction, and guidance related to acquisition policy and is responsible for planning, monitoring, controlling, scheduling, and implementing the acquisition of material, equipment, and services for the National Airspace System and for interagency and international programs. The office provides acquisition, quality assurance, and procurement support and management of real property for agency programs.

B. Office of Air Traffic Systems Development

The Office of Air Traffic Systems Development provides the leadership, management, direction, and coordination within FAA required to research, develop, acquire, test, integrate, implement, and support FAA air traffic systems.

C. Office of Aviation Research

The Office of Aviation Research advises and assists the Associate Administrator for Research and

Acquisitions and the Administrator in the management, direction, and coordination of the agency's research and development program including strategic planning and policy formulation, program assessment and development, collaborative activities with domestic and international partners, technology assessment, future system.

D. Office of Communications, Navigation, and Surveillance Systems

The Office of Communications, Navigation, and Surveillance Systems provides the leadership, management, direction, coordination within FAA required to research, develop, acquire, test, implement, and support communications, navigation, and surveillance system requirements for the National Airspace System through an Integrated Product Development Process.

E. Office of System Architecture and Investment Analysis

The Office of System Architecture and Investment Analysis advises and assists the Associate Administrator for Research and Acquisitions (ARA) and the Administrator in developing programs for applying new scientific and advanced technologies to meet National Airspace System (NAS) requirements. The office provides assistance and advice on: designing and planning the implementation of system improvements and interfaces of the NAS; managing and controlling the baseline configuration and architecture of the NAS; assessing systemwide performance; managing and controlling FAA financial baseline for research, engineering, and development and facilities and equipment appropriations; developing plans for modernization of the NAS; directing, coordinating, controlling, and ensuring the adequacy of FAA plans and programs for all research, advanced development, and applied development to support new systems and procedures for the NAS; managing the Federally Funded Research and Development Center as a program and technical administration of contracts impacting the NAS; establishing baseline procedures and productively metrics for organizational elements under ARA; and serving as the agency's safety advocate.

F. Office of Business Management

The Office of Business Management provides leadership and support to the Associate Administrator for Research and Acquisitions (ARA) and its corporate management in defining efficient and effective business plans and practices, human capital management (including development of human resource management guidance and processes), and partnership management (including the Integrated Product Development System for current and future reform and change management activities). The office is designed specifically to manage the task of converting ARA's strategic business goals into measurable outcomes and results.

G. William J. Hughes Technical Center

The William J. Hughes Technical Center (referred to as the Technical Center) conducts engineering, research and development, and test and evaluation activities in support of FAA-approved programs. The Technical Center operates and administers a national center providing laboratories, facilities, skills, and services responsive to the research, development, test implementation, field support, and maintenance programs of FAA; develops, tests, and evaluates new or substantially improved NAS equipment, systems, materials, processes, techniques, and procedures; and performs or participates in research, engineering, and development to provide new or improved techniques or methodologies related to the NAS. This includes advanced concepts exploration, human in-the-loop simulations, and real-time simulations. The Technical Center is a major organizational complex located near Atlantic City, New Jersey.

The missions of the FAA Technical Center are:

- Operates and administers a national test center providing laboratories, facilities, skills, and services responsive to the research, development, testing, implementation, field support, and maintenance programs of FAA.

- Develops, tests, and evaluates new or substantially improved NAS equipment, systems, materials, processes, techniques, and procedures.

- Performs or participates in research, engineering, and development to provide new or improved techniques or methodologies related to airport designs, layouts, construction, and operations; aviation security systems; improved or new aircraft safety systems and devices, improved crashworthiness designs and techniques, and improved or new aircraft control systems.

The functions within the assigned missions are:

- Manages and conducts test and evaluations of specified items (available systems, subsystems, equipment, devices, materials, concepts, or procedures) at any phase in the cycle of their development, from conception to acceptance and implementation.

- Plans long-range airport/aircraft safety and aviation security development programs and devises appropriate research and development programs for approved requirements.

- Manages and executes assigned aircraft safety and aviation security programs and executes assigned airport technology programs. Provides technical data required as a partial basis for improved procedures, criteria, minimum standards, and safety rules pertaining to the design, materials, construction, operation, and performance of civil aircraft, aircraft engines, equipment, airports, and aviation security systems.

- Conducts applied research, as appropriate and/or requested by a developmental office or service.

- Provides laboratory facilities and conducts hands-on research and development test and evaluation for the FAA advanced concepts program.

- Manages, operates, and maintains the various technical, aviation, laboratory, simulation, and plant facilities of the Center and plans, develops, and executes the acquisition and technical improvements required to ensure responsiveness to FAA requirements. Provides technical facility support consistent with assigned mission and program activity.

- Provides required support for the FAA research and development, flight inspection aircraft based at the FAA Technical Center, and services for visiting aircraft, as required.

- Provides for aircraft and avionics engineering and modification in support of the research and development projects.

- Manages and operates the FAA Technical Center, Atlantic City International Airport, ensuring conformance with airport safety regulations and criteria.

- Provides administrative, logistics, and space support to the other FAA, other Government, military, and contractor activities collocated at the FAA Technical Center.

- Develops and presents the annual FAA Technical Center budget with appropriate assistance from other organizations.

- Provides facilities for Federal law enforcement and military agencies in support of anti-hijacking and anti-terrorist exercises and training programs.

The operation of the Technical Center has expanded by a $25.8 million building for an air traffic control laboratory known as the Advanced Automation System Facility. Work there focused on the modernization of the air traffic control system through the end of the 1990s and also into the new century.

With the quantity of air passengers expected to increase to over a billion by 2012, it is imperative that work be done now to produce an air traffic control system that can accommodate this expanded activity.

The IBM Corporation, under contract to the Federal Aviation Administration, is working to overhaul the system to enhance safety and reduce airport congestion. The $3.8 billion project is part of the largest contract ever awarded by the FAA and the Department of Transportation. Most of IBM's work is the development of a new generation of air traffic control computers.

CHAPTER 8

Aviation Safety and the National Transportation Safety Board

AVIATION REGULATION

The regulation of aviation safety rests primarily in the hands of the Federal Aviation Administration. It is complete and encompasses all aspects of aviation safety including the proper registration of aircraft, the regulatory functions of air traffic control, the certification of aircraft and airmen, and the investigation of aircraft accidents. The basis of these rules is found in Titles V, VI, and VII of the Federal Aviation Act.

REGISTRATION OF AIRCRAFT

The registration of all aircraft nationally is required, and it is unlawful for any person to operate, in air navigation, any aircraft that is not properly registered by its owner; or to even operate any aircraft within the United States which is not eligible for registration. The registration requirements of aircraft are similar to the registration requirements for automobiles. However, automobiles are registered in various individual states, and aircraft are registered nationally with the Federal Government by the FAA. This makes for greater standardization and easier control. An aircraft in the United States may be eligible for registration if it is owned by a citizen of the United States and if it is not registered under the laws of any other country. Certain public aircraft of the local, state, and Federal Government are also registered, but military aircraft are not included.

It is the responsibility of the aircraft owner to see that the aircraft is legally registered. After making the necessary application to the FAA the aircraft owner is issued a certificate of registration. Therefore, any registration certificate may be suspended or revoked by the FAA for any cause which may render the aircraft ineligible for registration.

The issued certificate is conclusive evidence of nationality for international purposes, but not in any proceeding under the laws of the United States. Registration shall not be evidence of ownership of an aircraft in any proceedings in which the ownership is an issue.

It is the responsibility of the Federal Aviation Administration to establish reasonable rules and regulations for the registration and identification, of not only aircraft, but also aircraft engines, propellers, and appliances in the interest of safety. These items must not be used in violation of any rule or regulation of the FAA. The FAA maintains a system for recording any conveyance which affects title to any civil aircraft in the United States as well as any lease, mortgage, equipment trust, or contract of conditional sale. All conveyances or instruments of ownership must be valid and properly recorded in the office of the FAA.

> **Certain public aircraft of the local, state, and federal government are registered, but military aircraft are not included.**

The regulations state clearly the limitation of security owner's liability, in that no person having an interest in, or title to, any civil aircraft shall be liable by reason of his interest or ownership for any injury or death of persons or for damage or loss of property on the surface of the earth caused by such aircraft, unless the aircraft was in the actual control of the owner at the time of the injury, damage, or death that was caused.

In the public interest the Federal Aviation Administration provides for the issuance of dealers' aircraft registration certificates and for their use in the connection with aircraft eligible for registration by persons engaged in the business of manufacturing, distributing, or selling of aircraft. This system of recording aircraft ownership is very much like that of the system of recording deeds.

SAFETY REGULATION

The major change in the safety regulation of aviation was brought about with the passage of the Federal Aviation Act of 1958 in which the Federal Aviation Administration was created to supersede the Civil Aeronautics Administration. Unlike the Civil Aeronautics Administration which was in the Department of Commerce, the Federal Aviation Agency was organized with independent status responsible only to the President. With the passage of the Department of Transportation Act in 1966, the organization was transferred to that Department. Title VI of the Federal Aviation Act contains the principle substantive provisions relating to safety regulation in effect presently. Prior to the passage of the Federal Aviation Act of 1958, the Civil Aeronautics Act divided the authority for aviation safety between the Civil Aeronautics Board and the Civil Aeronautics Administration. The Board legislated safety rules, and the executive responsibilities rested upon the Civil Aeronautics Administration. The Federal Aviation Act divested the Civil Aeronautics Board of its former safety rule-making powers and transferred these to the Federal Aviation Administration where all aviation safety is administered by the Federal Aviation Administration. The National Transportation Safety Board possesses jurisdiction to review certain actions taken by the Federal Aviation Administration. The Administrator of the FAA has the power, as well as the duty, to promote safety of flight of civil aircraft in air commerce by prescribing and constantly revising, to keep up-to-date, the various safety regulations governing the standard for aviation safety.

These regulations of the Federal Aviation Administration include the following:

A. The minimum standards governing the design, materials, workmanship, construction, performance, inspection, servicing, and overhaul of aircraft, engines, propellers, and appliances, as well as the equipment and facilities for such inspection and production of aircraft to determine safety and the periods of time for inspection and overhaul.

B. The rules and regulations affecting the reserve supply of fuel to be carried in flight.

C. The rules in the interest of aviation safety which cover the maximum numbers of hours or periods of service which airmen may perform in a given period of time, such as daily, weekly, and monthly.

The regulation of safety includes all other practices and procedures connected with the national security and safety of aircraft that the Federal Aviation Administration may find to be necessary. Exemptions may be granted from the requirements of any safety regulation if the Federal Aviation Administration finds it to be in the public interest to do so.

In prescribing the many rules and regulations, the Federal Aviation Administration must give full consideration to the duty resting upon the air carriers to perform their services with the highest possible degree of safety in the interest of the flying public. This, in a manner of speaking, has placed the burden of responsibility upon the air carriers, in that as a public service industry it is their obligation to maintain the highest degree of aviation safety in airline operation.

SAFETY CERTIFICATES

The regulation of aviation safety is controlled through the issuance of various safety certificates by the Federal Aviation Administration. There are six major types of these certificates:

1. Airman
2. Aircraft
3. Air Carrier Operating
4. Air Navigation Facility
5. Air Agency
6. Airport Operating

1. Airman Certificates

The Federal Aviation Administration requires the certification of all persons engaged as airmen in con-

Flights of Fancy

Court Cases

The general safety powers and duties, as well as other sections of the Act relating to safety, have been tested in court. In Halaby v. Jones and Scott, 1962, the courts found that although the regulations provide for only one pilot-in-command, this does not alter the fact that the responsibility for the proper operation of the aircraft falls to the co-pilot who is in actual operation of the aircraft. The regulations which provide that no one will operate an aircraft against the instructions of air traffic control in areas where ATC is exercised are applicable to visual flight rule conditions, as well as instrument flight rule con-

ditions. This was determined in Halaby v. Lindsay, 1964. One general regulation that caused problems in the industry was mandatory retirement of pilots at 60 years of age by FAA rule. This rule was upheld in 1961 in Airline Pilots Assoc., Int'l v. Quesada. The courts held in 1946 that a government inspector must be admitted to the cockpit at any time in the performance of his duties. The federal regulations take precedence over company regulations (U.S. v. Northwest). In Southeastern v. Hurd, 1962, the decision was made that although the Federal Government has preempted the field of aviation, it does not supplant the common law principles of tort law. Therefore, state courts are not deprived of jurisdiction in trials of wrongful death arising out of an airplane accident. In Eastern Airlines v. U.S., 1953, the court ruled that a deviation from prescribed regulations is not negligence when the deviation is in the interest of safety.

---

nection with aircraft. Airmen are pilots, mechanics, traffic controllers, and the like. The Federal Aviation Administration establishes requirements, both mental and physical, in the testing of airmen to determine their qualifications before the necessary Airman Certification is issued. Any person is eligible to hold an Airman Certificate if he properly qualifies, however, the Federal Aviation Administration may prohibit or restrict the issuance of an Airman Certificate to an alien, or may make such issuance dependent upon the terms of the reciprocal agreements entered into with the foreign home government of the person involved. For a more detailed description of the Airman Certificate, the reader is directed to the current Federal Aviation Regulations governing Airman Certificates.

The courts have been asked to clarify the law regarding airman certificates. Court cases have been held challenging the Administrator's authority in regard to medical certificates. One such case upheld the FAA requiring blood pressure readings at stated intervals in the interest of air safety. A pilot may not disregard the fact that the FAA requires a license to operate a multi-engine aircraft, even though he considers himself qualified as was ruled in Somlo v. C.A.B., 1966.

Good moral character is not defined, but is required of an airline transport pilot. In McKee v. Roe, 1966, it was found that a pilot's pattern of conduct which departs from ordinary patterns of morality, and which shows that he is capable of acting without inhibitions in an unstable manner without regard for other's rights, establishes that he does not possess good moral character.

The courts have held that it is valid for a regulation to place the burden on the airman to prove that he has no history of clinical diagnosis of myocardial infarction (Day v. N.T.S.B., 1969). A petitioner proved that his excellence in aeronautical experience and skill offset his physical defect caused by the amputation of a leg nine inches above the knee.

2. Aircraft Certificates

Include those for Type, Production, and Airworthiness. Any interested person may file with the Federal Aviation Administration an application and subsequently be granted a Type certificate for an aircraft, aircraft engine, propeller, or appliance after the proper investigation and inspection has been made.

The Federal Aviation Administration may, and usually does, require the application to conduct tests in the interest of aviation safety, including flight tests and tests of materials. If the FAA finds that the aircraft, or other part, meets the minimum standards for safety, then the Type Certificate will be issued. In the process of obtaining this certificate, the applicant must submit all technical drawings and any other data, as well as a workable model to demonstrate the safety of the design. This inspection on the part of the Federal Aviation Administration is very costly and time consuming and is as complete technically as is humanly possible. The expense for this is borne by the designer or applicant for the Type Certificate. This process usually takes a long period of time. In the case of the first commercial jet transport it was a matter of several years.

No aircraft, aircraft engine, propeller, or aircraft appliance can be produced and sold to the public if there has not been a Type Certificate issued. This certificate is granted to the separate and exacting design and, as much, may be transferred or sold by an individual or corporation to another.

If at any time during production the design is altered or improved in any way, the Federal Aviation Administration must approve and either amend the original Type Certificate or, in the case of a major change, issue a new type certificate. This is what occurs when a new model aircraft of the same basic design is produced.

An aircraft or aircraft part cannot simply be produced. In order to do so the manufacturers must hold a valid Production Certificate issued by the Federal Aviation Administration. The FAA will inspect the facilities and other equipment to determine if the producer can satisfactorily produce exact duplicates of the aircraft or part of which a Type Certificate is in effect. The FAA makes various inspections and tests of the manufacturer holding a Production Certificate to assure that the products being made continue to conform with the Type Certificate. This is being continually done in the interest of aviation safety to protect the public. It is a complex system in the case of a large complicated structure such as a jet transport aircraft or its major component parts.

The certification of the type design and of the producer would appear sufficient to insure safety. It is complete, that is, until the aircraft is sold to the public. From then on it becomes the responsibility of the registered owner of the aircraft to see that it is maintained in an airworthy condition. Therefore, all aircraft being flown for any reason must have been issued, and currently hold, a valid Airworthiness Certificate issued by the Federal Aviation Administration. If the aircraft is found to be in a safe condition, the Airworthiness Certificate will be granted.

The Airworthiness Certificate is valid for a period of twelve months. Before the expiration of this time it is the responsibility of the owner to have the aircraft properly inspected and the certificate renewed. This is generally known as "relicensing" of aircraft and insures that the necessary maintenance and repair, as are necessary, will be performed before the Airworthiness Certificate is reissued. In some respects, although to a much greater detail, the Airworthiness Certificate of civil aircraft is similar to the automobile inspection sticker required by most municipalities and states in the country. No fee is charged for the issuance of the Airworthiness Certificate, however, it costs the owner to have the aircraft serviced,

prepared, and made ready for the inspection.

Many non-Federal Aviation Administration persons, who have the adequate experience and qualifications, are designated by the FAA to conduct this inspection. They are persons who own, operate, or are employed by an aircraft service company that is itself approved by the FAA. The persons designated will also be certificated airmen holding an Airframe and Powerplant Mechanic Certificate.

American Airlines did not test-fly an aircraft prior to a passenger flight after a defective component part was replaced on the automatic pilot. The court ruled in Nelson v. American Airlines that there was no negligence when the replacement of the part was not a repair or alteration within the meaning of the regulation that would require a test flight. Salem Air Service v. Devancy in 1947 determined that aircraft registered by the Federal Government need not be registered in a state over which the aircraft is operated. 1967 brought a court ruling that the Board was negligent in issuing a Type Certificate for the Lockheed Electra stating its airworthiness. The Board was aware that the engines were capable of ingesting birds on take-off causing loss of power and resulting in a serious hazard to the aircraft. Negligence was found in the failure of the Board to provide further tests to determine the effects of bird ingestion on take-off, and in failing to issue a Type Certificate that the aircraft could not be used in areas where birds are known to flock.

3. Air Carrier Operating Certificates

Air carrier operating certificates are issued to all carriers transporting the public for hire. This includes the noncertificated and supplemental air carriers as well as the certificated air carriers.

Federal aviation regulations require certification of all airline companies, as well as the equipment they use. The certificate, or license, to operate aircraft with 30 or more seats is called a Part 121 certificate in reference to the section of the Federal Aviation Regulations which spell out the requirements for engaging in large-plane service. These are operating requirements as opposed to the kind of financial, insurance, and citizenship requirements contained in Section 401 of the Federal Aviation Act (which applies to carriers operating aircraft with 60 or more seats).

Among other things, a Part 121 operator must have FAA-approved training and maintenance programs, as well as airworthiness certificates for each aircraft. The maintenance program must specify the intervals at which certain aircraft and engine parts will be inspected and, in some cases, replaced. In addition, the maintenance shops the airline intends to use (both its own shops and those of subcontractors) must be certified by FAA and open to inspection on demand. Records of all maintenance work must be kept and also must be open to FAA inspection. Other Part 121 requirements address such things as:

1. the equipment a carrier must have aboard each aircraft,

2. flammability standards for cabin materials,

3. floor lighting for emergency evacuation,

4. onboard smoking rules,

5. the number of flight attendants that must be on board,

6. the content of pre-flight announcements,

7. rules for carry-on baggage,

8. security procedures, and

9. aircraft de-icing procedures.

A certificated air carrier may possess a valid Certificate of Convenience and Necessity, but it cannot operate its aircraft until it has a current valid Air Carrier Operating Certificate. Each such certificate will prescribe the terms, conditions, and limitations as are reasonably necessary to assure safety in air transportation. Furthermore, it will specify the points to and from which, as well as the airways over which, the air carrier is permitted to operate. At any time the air carrier enlarges its route system and serves new airport cities or introduces a new type of aircraft, its Air Carrier Operating Certificate must be amended after proper inspection and approved by the Federal Aviation Administration.

Safety regulation concerning air carriers recognizes the duty and responsibility of the individual air carriers and charges them with conducting their aviation activities in the highest degree consistent with safety in the public interest. It is a function of the Federal Aviation Administration to make inspections of airline aircraft not only for the purpose of determining that a proper level of safety is being maintained but also for the purpose of advising and cooperating with the air carriers in the inspection and maintenance of their equipment.

The failure of the air carrier (Halaby v. Far West Airlines) to keep proper records for flight operations and airmen affects air safety, because these records are a means of achieving safety. In the same case in 1962, numerous irregularities that occurred in the conduct of a carrier's operations found that the carrier failed to meet the standards of fitness. The carrier's operations were conducted in a shell without funds, personnel, or equipment. An early case in aviation in 1939 involved Pan American and a court ruling on fit, willing, and able. This ruling set five standards to be met: (1) Proof that the applicant has had sufficient experience in the type of operation proposed, has made adequate surveys and test flights, is aware of particular weather problems, and has adequate training and maintenance facilities; (2) landing rights have been obtained; (3) proposed aircraft is satisfactory and available; (4) proof that the applicant has obtained or will obtain an air carrier operating certificate; and (5) the airline has the financial capacity to carry out the proposed service.

4. Air Navigation Facility Certificates

FAA has the power to inspect, classify, and rate any facility of air navigation available for the use of civil aircraft as to its suitability for such use. If found to be adequate for the needs of safety, a certificate is issued as an Air Navigation Facility. Landing areas, lights, radio-directional apparatus, and like equipment used in the navigation of aircraft are air navigation facilities.

5. Air Agency Rating Certificate

Representative of air agencies are flight and ground training schools, as well as aircraft maintenance and repair facilities.

Before a flight school, for example, can be awarded an Air Agency Certificate it must possess the necessary flight equipment, in good safe condition, the proper maintenance facilities and personnel, and certificated instructors. Not only must they have adequate facilities including classrooms and teaching equipment, but also the curriculum for flight and ground courses must be approved by the FAA.

A certificated aircraft repair agency must demonstrate that it has the proper tools, shops, equipment, and personnel to adequately repair an aircraft or engine commensurate with the best practices of safety.

6. Airport Operating Certificates

Airport operating certificates provide for the issuing of a certificate to land airports serving scheduled air carriers that hold Certificates of Public Convenience and Necessity and who operate large aircraft into and out of those airports.

Section 51 of the Airport and Airway Development Act of 1970 added, to the Federal Aviation Act of 1958, Section 612 that authorizes the Federal Aviation Administrator to issue Airport Operating Certificates to airports serving certificated air carriers. The administrator is to establish minimum safety standards for the operation of those airports. Section 612 originally provided that such terms, conditions and limitations as are reasonably necessary to assure safety in air transportation must be prescribed. This included those terms, conditions and limitations relating to the installation, operation and maintenance of adequate air navigation facilities and to the operation and maintenance of adequate safety equipment.

Currently, Federal Air Regulation (FAR) Part 139 provides for the certification and operation of airports. It prescribes rules governing the certification and operation of land airports that serve any scheduled or unscheduled passenger operations of an air carrier that is conducted with an aircraft having a seating capacity of more than thirty passengers.

AIRPORT REGULATION

The Federal Aviation Administration also regulates airports, to a lessor extent than airmen, airlines, and aircraft. It was empowered to do so by the Airport and Airway Development Act of 1970, whose primary purpose was to promote the development of new aviation infrastructure. The act states that all airports with commercial service must be certified by the FAA and that certification will be granted only if the airport complies with certain safety criteria set by the FAA. Among those criteria are ones dealing with the number and type of fire-fighting vehicles at the airport, runway lighting, and storage facilities for hazardous substances such as fuel.

The FAA also issues advisory circulars to airport operators on such topics as runway paving, drainage, and apron design, and it provides grants for airport projects that enhance safety and increase the capacity and efficiency of the airport.

The FAA, upon receiving an application, will investigate and inspect the airport to determine that it is adequately equipped to conduct a safe operation. If satisfied, the certificate will be issued. The certificate will state the terms, conditions, and limitations which are necessary to assure safety.

The FAA may exempt an air carrier airport, enplanning annually less than one-quarter of one percent of the total number of passengers enplaned at all air carrier airports, from the requirements relating to firefighting and rescue equipment. This special exemption may be granted if the FAA finds that the requirements are too costly and impractical. This situation would apply to small airports where small air carriers may serve occasionally. The detail procedure for acquiring an Airport Operating

Certificate is to be found in Part 139 of the Federal Aviation Regulations. Airports also may have to comply with state and local regulations, although these usually deal with environmental or administrative matters rather than strictly with safety.

REINSPECTION

Regardless of the type of certificate issued, the FAA has the power to reinspect any aircraft, airman, or any holder of a safety certificate at any time. If upon reinspection the FAA determines that safety is not being adhered to in the utmost standard, the FAA may order the amending, modifying, suspending, or revoking, in whole or in part, any certificate that has been issued. This can only take place after notification to the offender and a hearing held in which he may defend himself.

Any person whose certificate is so affected may appeal the Federal Aviation Administration order to the National Transportation Safety Board who may, after due notice and hearing, uphold, amend, modify, or even reverse the Federal Aviation Administrator's order. The filing of such an appeal with the National Transportation Safety Board can stay the effectiveness of the Administrator's order pending the final disposition of the case, unless the Administrator advises the National Transportation Safety Board that an emergency exists and aviation safety requires the order to become effective immediately. If this occurs, the National Transportation Safety Board must dispense with the appeal within sixty days.

The review proceeding by the National Transportation Safety Board actually takes the form of a new hearing in which the National Transportation Safety Board is not bound by the findings which led the Administrator to decide adversely to the defending applicant. After the hearing the National Transportation Safety Board issues its own decision, and the Administrator is bound by it. Anyone who is then unsuccessful in appealing to the National Transportation Safety Board has the privilege of going to the courts for review. In any court action the Administrator shall be made a party to the proceedings and is joined with the National Transportation Safety Board as party-respondent.

The Administrator also has the authority to amend, suspend, or revoke any of its certificates. An Airman's Airline Transport Pilot Certificate cannot be suspended for his failure to exercise care and responsibility in the absence of any regulation imposing such a standard (McKee v. Buchanan, 1966). An Air Agency Certificate was revoked when it was found that there was carelessness in approving as airworthy an aircraft that was not airworthy. In Shaffer v. Florida Atlantic Airlines, 1969, an air taxi disregarded the emergency suspensions of its operating authority and continued its unauthorized service to the Bahamas when it had the right to seek judicial relief. A prima facie case for careless and reckless operation was established when it was shown that a pilot landed short of the runway, that the blast pad where he landed was marked with chevrons, and that there were no mechanical or weather problems, (Halaby v. Lindstrom).

In McKee v. Rappattoni and Swanson, 1968, the courts found that the cockpit voice recorder may not be used in a safety enforcement proceeding, since it would be inhibiting the purpose of aiding in accident investigation. A respondent's certificate was suspended for his failure to follow a prescribed missed approach procedure in attempting to land, and for failing to maintain contact with the control tower. Courts have ruled that the Board may impose both remedial and punitive suspensions to attain safety.

A pilot's failure to successfully complete a required phase B pilot-in-command proficiency check in DC-8 aircraft relates to DC-8s and does not impair his qualifications on other aircraft (Shaffer v. Harrington, 1971).

The various regulations concerning aviation safety are most complete, definite, and positive. It is contrary to the laws to operate any civil aircraft that does not have current effective registration and Airworthiness Certificates, to perform in the capacity of an airman without having been issued the necessary Airman Certificate, or to employ such a person. No air carrier may conduct public air transportation without holding Air Carrier Operating Certificate, and no one possessing an Air Agency or Production Certificate may violate any term, condition, or limitation of the certificate.

Any violators of safety regulations are subject to civil penalties. Moreover, in appropriate cases the courts may enjoin such violators or direct compliances with the safety regulations. Criminal penalties do not exist for safety violations, however.

Foreign aircraft and airmen may be exempted from any safety regulatory provision if the Federal Aviation Administrator finds it to be in the public interest.

Together with the Federal Aviation Administrator's powers and duties as stated in Title III of the Federal Aviation Act, and aviation safety rule-making under Title VI, there exists a well-rounded, comprehensive system of safety regulation extending in its coverage from the designer's drawing board to all aspects of aviation functions.

AIR TRAFFIC CONTROL (ATC)

The government developed the Air Traffic Control system primarily to maintain safe separation of aircraft flying over the United States and in and out of U.S. airports. It is ATC's job to keep aircraft traffic moving as efficiently as possible throughout the system. ATC is aviation's traffic cop, working to ensure that aircraft do not run into each other and that traffic moves in an orderly fashion with a minimum of delay. The prime responsibility of the FAA is air safety. The Air Traffic Control system is a major part of this function and is composed of four components.

1. Air Route Traffic Control Centers
2. Airport Traffic Control Towers
3. Terminal Radar Approach Control facilities
4. Flight Service Stations

The air traffic control system in the United States is a vast network of facilities located in all 50 states and in Guam, American Samoa, Panama, and Puerto Rico. Included are 22 air route traffic control centers, more than 400 airport control towers, 123 flight service stations, more than 1,000 radio navigation aids, hundreds of instrument landing systems, and some 250 long-range and terminal radar systems. Moreover, nearly half of the agency's total complement of 55,000 plus people are engaged in some phase of air traffic control. An additional 10,000 technicians and engineers are involved in the installation and maintenance of this system.

In order to keep pace with the rapid growth of aviation, the FAA has implemented a computer-based semi-automated air traffic control system at all of the en route centers serving the contiguous 48 states and at all major terminal facilities. The system tracks controlled flights automatically and tags each target with a small block of information written electronically on the radar scopes used by controllers. The data block includes both aircraft identity and altitude. Automated radar systems, tailored to the varied traffic demands of terminal locations, already have been installed and are operational at more than 60 large and medium hub airports. Many more systems are being installed at airports in the small hub category.

The en route and terminal systems are tied together nationwide in a common network for the exchange of data between facilities. The capabilities of the automated system also include additional air traffic management functions such as warning systems that alert controllers when aircraft under their control are predicted to get too close to the ground or too close together. Another feature provides flow control in congested terminal situations. Satellites are now being used to enhance aircraft communications and surveillance on over-ocean routes, development of a new microwave landing system for more precise airport approaches in all weather conditions, and development of data link systems for automatic air-ground communications.

> **The prime responsibility of the FAA is air safety.**

1. AIR ROUTE TRAFFIC CONTROL CENTERS

Air route traffic control centers provide air traffic service to aircraft by using air and ground communications and radar. They primarily provide for en route separation of aircraft and safe, expeditious movement of air traffic operating under Instrument Flight Rules (IFR) within their particular controlled airspaces.

Air route traffic control centers handle en route aircraft operating under Instrument Flight Rules (IFR) between airport terminal areas. Together the 22 centers log more than 39 million flights a year with 17 centers recording in excess of one million operations each. The total exceeded 44 million by the end of the 1990s.

The typical center has responsibility for more than 100,000 square miles of airspace generally extending over a number of states. To keep track of aircraft in its area, a center may use as many as six or seven long-range radars and 10 to 20 remote air-ground communications sites. Each radar covers an area 200 miles in radius.

The controller staff can range from 300 to 700, with more than 150 on duty during peak periods at the busier facilities. In addition, each facility has its own airways facilities sector which may include as many as 125 engineers and technicians.

Each aircraft in the sector is represented by a blip or target symbol with a printed data block alongside showing flight information. Electronic devices in the aircraft continuously sent out coded signals on altitude and flight number. These signals are picked up and relayed by one of the seven radar antennas in the center's territory. A computer converts these signals into data blocks and projects them on the screen next to the moving blip for the appropriate aircraft. It also displays an upward pointing arrow if the plane is climbing and a downward pointing one if it is descending.

At the same time it automatically prints out paper strips giving the same information plus the destination and other pertinent information on the flight. The second controller tears off the strips and arranges them in sequence for the convenience of the controller monitoring the screen.

As the controllers monitor the radar, they check to see that no aircraft is getting too close to another or is on a course that would take it too close. If such a situation appears likely to develop, the controller tells one or both to change course. Or he might tell one or both to go to different altitudes.

The twenty-one ATC centers keep track of aircraft while they are "en route," or during the high-altitude, cruise phase of their flights. They are located in Albuquerque, Anchorage, Atlanta, Boston, Chicago (the busiest center), Cleveland, Denver, Fort Worth, Houston, Indianapolis, Jacksonville, Kansas City, Los Angeles, Memphis, Miami, Minneapolis, New York, Oakland, Salt Lake City, Seattle, and Washington, D.C. (Table 8.1.)

Air Route Traffic Control Centers (ARTCC)

Cleveland, Ohio

Denver, Colorado

Minneapolis, Minnesota

Fort Worth, Texas

2. AIRPORT TRAFFIC CONTROL TOWERS

A central operations facility in the terminal air traffic control system consists of a tower cab structure, including an associated IFR room if radar equipped, using air/ground communications and/or radar, visual signaling and other devices, to provide safe and expeditious movement of terminal air traffic.

Airport traffic control towers direct the movement of aircraft on and in the vicinity of an airport. (See Figure 8.1.) In addition to directing actual takeoffs and landings, approximately 180 of the more than 400 FAA-run towers also provide radar services to aircraft using the primary airport as well as many secondary airports in the terminal approach control area. These services include approach and departure control for IFR aircraft as well as other services to Visual Flight Rules (VFR) aircraft.

Table 8.1. IFR Aircraft Handled at FAA Air Route Traffic Control Centers
(In thousands)

| Fiscal Year | IRF Aircraft Handles | | | | |
	Air Carrier	Air Taxi/ Commuter	General Aviation	Military	Total
Historical*					
1995	20,993.1	6,946.3	7,824.3	4,385.4	40,149.1
1996	21,944.5	6,656.1	7,857.3	3,961.6	40,419.3
1997	22,514.7	6,826.7	8,175.0	3,895.4	41,411.8
1998	23,227.0	7,137.1	8,641.1	4,190.7	43,195.9
1999	24,044.8	7,732.1	8,808.1	4,069.7	44,654.7
2000	24,987.1	8,100.9	8,744.4	4,192.4	46,024.8
Forecast					
2001	25,636.8	8,279.1	8,919.3	4,192.4	47,027.6
2002	26,405.9	8,436.4	9,097.7	4,192.4	48,132.4
2003	27,224.4	8,579.8	9,288.7	4,192.4	49,285.4
2004	28,041.2	8,717.1	9,493.1	4,192.4	50,443.8
2005	28,994.6	8,926.3	9,682.9	4,192.4	51,796.3
2006	29,951.4	9,131.6	9,876.6	4,192.4	53,152.0
2007	30,849.9	9,359.9	10,074.1	4,192.4	54,476.4
2008	31,775.4	9,612.6	10,265.5	4,192.4	55,846.0
2009	32,728.7	9,853.0	10,460.6	4,192.4	57,234.7
2010	33,743.3	10,099.3	10,648.9	4,192.4	58,683.9
2011	34,789.3	10,341.7	10,829.9	4,192.4	60,153.3
2012	35,867.8	10,589.9	11,024.8	4,192.4	61,674.9

*Source: FAA Air Traffic Activity.
Note: Detail may not add to total because of rounding.

Airport Traffic Control Towers (ATCT)

Atlanta, Georgia
Bakersfield, California
Columbus, Georgia
Dayton, Ohio
District of Columbia, Washington National
Fairbanks, Alaska
Fayetteville, North Carolina
Houston, Texas Intercontinental
New Orleans, Louisiana
Orlando, Florida International
Pittsburgh, Pennsylvania
Prescott, Arizona
Raleigh, North Carolina
San Jose, California
Santa Barbara, California
Sarasota, Florida
St. Thomas, US Virgin Islands
Moline, Illinois

Figure 8.1 Airport Traffic Control Towers (ATCT)

Tower facilities can range from the familiar glass-walled cupola on top an airport terminal building to freestanding structures soaring more than 200 feet into the air. Similarly, staffing can range from a three- or four-person operation which keeps the tower open 10–12 hours a day to a controller workforce of more than 150 working shifts around the clock. Together the FAA staffed control towers direct nearly 60 million operations annually, and is forecast to be about 69 million by the year 2012. (Table 8.2.)

3. TERMINAL RADAR APPROACH CONTROL (TRACON) FACILITIES

TRACONs control the aircraft immediately prior to, and after, landings and takeoffs, or during the climb and descent phases of flight. There are 184 TRACONs, less than the number of towers because some TRACONs handle more than one airport. For example, a single TRACON handles the traffic approaching and departing from all three New York-area airports.

Table 8.2 Total Aircraft Operations at Airports with FAA Traffic Control Service
(In thousands)

Fiscal Year	Air Carrier	Air taxi/ Commuter	General Aviation	Military	Total
Historical*					
1995	13,589.7	9,823.8	32,265.6	2,294.8	57,973.9
1996	13,768.1	9,314.9	29,249.1	2,077.7	54,409.8
1997	14,112.0	8,968.8	28,232.5	1,942.9	53,256.2
1998	14,101.7	8,928.1	27,929.0	2,028.8	52,987.6
1999	14,423.8	9,318.1	29,144.7	2.181.9	55,068.5
2000	14,920.6	9,218.0	26,973.4	2,059.6	53,171.6
Forecast					
2001	15,313.7	9,420.8	27,449.7	2,059.6	54,243.8
2002	15,768.5	9,599.8	27,934.1	2,059.6	55,362.0
2003	16,258.9	9,763.0	28,453.9	2,059.6	56,535.4
2004	16,745.0	9,919.2	28,994.5	2,059.6	57,718.4
2005	17,306.0	10,157.3	29,539.1	2,059.6	59,061.9
2006	17,880.5	10,390.9	30,093.9	2,059.6	60,424.9
2007	18,415.2	10,650.6	30,647.4	2,059.6	61,772.8
2008	18,971.3	10,938.2	31,192.5	2,059.6	63,161.6
2009	19,546.1	11,211.7	31,735.0	2,059.6	64,552.4
2010	20,144.2	11,492.0	32,255.2	2,059.6	65,951.0
2011	20,758.6	11,767.8	32,783.9	2,059.6	67,370.0
2012	21,398.0	12,050.2	33,308.5	2,059.6	68,816.3

*Source: FAA Air Traffic Activity.

Terminal Radar Approach Control (TRACON) Facilities

Grant County, Washington

Houston, Texas Intercontinental

Orlando, Florida International

Pittsburgh, Pennsylvania

Potomac

San Francisco/Oakland Bay

4. FLIGHT SERVICE STATIONS

Flight Service Stations (FSS) are the Air Traffic Service facilities within the National Airspace System which have the prime responsibility for preflight pilot briefing, en route communications with VFR flights, assisting lost VFR aircraft, originating NOTAMS, broadcasting aviation weather information, accepting and closing flight plans, monitoring radio NAVAIDS, participating with search and rescue units locating missing VFR aircraft, and operating the national weather teletypewriter systems. In addition, at selected locations, FSSs take weather observations, issue airport advisories, administer airman written examinations, and ad-

vise Customs and Immigration of transborder flight. Flight service stations are the direct descendants of the airways communications stations established in the 1920s to provide weather data and other assistance to the early airmail pilots.

Like air traffic control towers, the size, staffing, and hours of operation for flight service stations vary from location to location. Busier facilities operate around the clock and may have a total complement of 50 specialists who brief pilots on weather, airport conditions, winds aloft, preferred routes, and other flight planning data. Many flight service stations also are equipped with direction-finding equipment that enables them to guide lost pilots to safety.

The FAA, in February 1990, modernized the national network of flight service stations by automating many of these facilities and locating them at airports with the heaviest general aviation activity. Eventually, these automated hubs will provide coverage for the entire country, allowing FAA to phase out the other flight service stations. Besides having the most advanced communications and weather reporting equipment, the automated facilities will give pilots direct access to services by means of computer terminals and telephones.

The Flight Service Station is a type of air traffic facility that the Federal Aviation Administration's air traffic control/air navigation system provides to ensure the safe and efficient use of the nation's airspace by both civil and military aircraft. There are 123 of these stations whose main concern is for safe flight. They provide pilots with assistance in their preflight planning and with continued assistance during flight. (Table 8.3.)

Flight service specialists undergo intensive training in weather briefing, procedures and techniques for providing pilot services, and the use of radio direction-finding equipment and weather radar. Upon completion of weather training, flight service specialists are certified as pilot weather briefers by the National Weather Service.

Federal Aviation Regulations require the pilot-in-command to familiarize himself with all available pertinent information prior to a flight, including weather and weather forecasts. Through the briefer's services, pilots and dispatcher receive weather intelligence that originates with observers, forecasters, and pilots. Briefers also provide current Notices to Airmen concerning the operational status of navigational aids, airport conditions, and any other special conditions which appear to be pertinent to a proposed flight except those that are the Airman's Information Manual (AIM).

To help pilots form their initial weather "picture," many flight service stations have Pilot Automatic Telephone Weather Answering Service (PATWAS). These tape-recorded briefings cover an area of about 200 miles around the station and describe the present and forecasted weather. PATWAS telephone numbers are listed in the Airman's Information Manual. (See Figure 8.2.)

TRANSCRIBED WEATHER BROADCAST (TWEB)

Another aid to assist pilots with their initial weather check, which many flight service stations have, is the Transcribed Weather Broadcast known as "TWEB." The TWEB broadcasts continuously on a low frequency navigational aid in the 200–415 KHz band. Like the PATWAS, the TWEB gives a synoptic picture of the present weather and forecasted weather. But the TWEB, in addition to the synopsis, broadcasts Notices to Airmen, pilot weather reports, weather radar reports, winds aloft forecasts, and hourly weather observations. Some TWEB locations also have telephone access to the TWEB broadcast. These numbers are listed in the Airman's Information Manual.

Automated Flight Service Stations (AFSS)

Albuquerque, New Mexico
Altoona, Pennsylvania
Anniston, Alabama
Buffalo, New York
Dayton, Ohio
Elkins, West Virginia
Fairbanks, Alaska
Fort Dodge, Iowa
Fort Worth, Texas
Grand Forks, North Dakota
Hawthorne, California
Jackson, Tennessee
Lansing, Michigan
Leesburg, Virginia
Macon, Georgia
McMinnville, Oregon
Raleigh-Durham, North Carolina
St. Petersburg, Florida
Gainesville, Florida
Williamsport, Pennsylvania
Kankakee, Illinois

Automated International Flight Service Stations (AIFSS)

Oakland, California
Miami, Florida
Kenai, Alaska

Figure 8.2   Automated Flight Service Stations

A more complete weather briefing, tailor-made to meet individual needs, can be obtained by telephoning and talking directly with the pilot weather briefer. The briefer will need to know the type of aircraft, whether the trip will be made strictly by Visual Flight Rules or if the trip can be flown on instruments. The briefer also will need to know the departure airport, intended route, stopover points and destination, expected time of departure (ETD), and estimated time en route (ETC), including stopover times. With this information, the pilot weather briefer can more accurately select the information pertaining to the trip.

A pilot can better visualize weather systems in relation to his proposed flight by looking at weather charts. And if the pilot then encounters unfavorable weather during the flight, he can better visualize an alternate course of action. The final decision, to make the flight or not, always rests with the pilot. Therefore, the most desirable briefing occurs when the pilot visits the flight

Table 8.3   Total Flight Services at FAA Flight Service Stations
(In thousands)

Fiscal Year	Flight Plans Originated	Pilot Briefs	Aircraft Contacted	Total Flight Services	Flight Services Including Duats
Historical*					
1995	6,328	9,162	4,240	35,220	46,740
1996	6,629	8,692	3,904	34,546	46,606
1997	6,725	8,724	3,704	34,602	48,010
1998	6,493	8,727	3,476	33,916	46,774
1999	6,252	8,293	3,325	32,415	45,785
2000	5,936	7,699	3,224	30,494	45,496
Forecast					
2001	5,986	7,630	3,176	30,408	46,590
2002	6,025	7,565	3,128	30,308	47,446
2003	6,056	7,504	3,035	30,155	47,961
2004	6,087	7,448	3,018	30,088	48,268
2005	6,114	7,396	2,989	30,009	48,485
2006	6,139	7,348	2,945	29,919	48,701
2007	6,164	7,303	2,899	29,833	48,929
2008	6,185	7,260	2,857	29,747	49,159
2009	6,207	7,224	2,814	29,676	49,412
2010	6,227	7,188	2,772	29,602	49,666
2011	6,248	7,152	2,730	29,530	49,930
2012	6,270	7,116	2,689	29,461	50,201

*Source: FAA Air Traffic Activity.
Notes: Total flight services is equal to the sum of flight plans originated and pilot briefs, multiplied by two, plus the number of aircraft contacted.

service station for an in-person briefing. The pilot weather briefer can show the pilot the latest surface weather chart depicting frontal activities and areas of potentially hazardous weather. He can also show the pilot forecasted surface systems depicted on a prognostic chart and a map showing pilot weather reports. In addition, selected flight service stations are equipped with a weather radar scope which gives the pilot a first-hand view of weather echoes.

In addition to a preflight weather briefing, pilots can obtain assistance in flight planning by requesting it. This assistance includes determining mileages, headings, time computations, navigational aids and frequencies, and landmarks. He can obtain information concerning preferential routings, customs and immigration service, air traffic control procedures, air traffic rules, orientation procedures, flight plan procedures, airport services available, and search and rescue procedures.

Pilots are urged to use Visual Flight Rules (VFR) flight plans. The use of a VFR flight plan for flying cross-country is not required but is highly recommended for the pilot's own peace of mind in knowing that search and rescue is assured in the event the flight is not ter-

minated as planned. Yet, the pilot may change his estimated time en route, course, or even his destination airport by merely advising a flight service station of his intentions and requesting a change in the flight plan. The pilot can also cancel the flight plan at any time, but he must cancel the flight plan at the termination of his flight. This closure prevents search and rescue operations from being initiated unnecessarily. The FAA, Air Force, Coast Guard, Civil Air Patrol, law enforcement agencies, and other organizations have pooled their resources to provide the flying public with an efficient emergency service. This service provides search for overdue or missing aircraft, survival aid, and rescue of personnel.

During flight, pilots can receive pilot weather services by radio. Because of radio frequency congestion, however, a radio preflight briefing is not recommended, but pilots are encouraged to make position reports and keep updated on en route weather. Pilots can request and receive the latest weather observations, forecasts, weather advisors, Notices to Airmen, and pilot weather reports along their route of flight as the information becomes available.

Aviation weather observations are normally received every hour, terminal forecasts are received three times every 24 hours, but revised forecasts and weather advisories are issued at any time conditions warrant. Notices to Airmen are issued as conditions occur.

A pilot who is unsure of his position can receive navigational assistance from the flight service specialist. To be able to provide this service, each specialist has acquired a detailed knowledge of the terrain and prominent landmarks with a hundred miles of the flight service station and has received training in locating lost aircraft through the use of VHF omnidirectional radio range stations (VORS). He also is trained in locating lost aircraft and providing navigational guidance with radio direction finder (DF) equipment where available. At present, more than one hundred flight service stations have VHF Doppler DF equipment. Each year, 3,000 to 4,000 pilots receive assistance under emergency conditions. About 85 percent of these "Assists" are due to pilots encountering bad weather or becoming lost. All pilots should remember that it is better to ask for assistance before a situation develops into an emergency.

EN ROUTE FLIGHT ADVISORY* SERVICE (EFAS)

The objective of Enroute Flight Advisory Service (EFAS) is to provide enroute aircraft with timely and meaningful weather advisories. These advisories consist of current complete, and accurate information pertinent to a specific flight, provided at a time that prevents unnecessary changes to a flight plan, but when necessary, permits the pilot to make a decision to terminate the flight or alter course before adverse conditions are encountered. A total of 44 flight service stations provide service throughout the conterminous U.S. along heavily-traveled flyways to the extent that any pilot at or above 5,000 feet above ground level will be able to obtain it. The system is manned by specially trained flight service station personnel who have received additional intensive training in meteorology.

All EFAS radio communications are conducted on 122.0 MHz simplex. The pilot need only call "Flight Watch" on 122.0 MHz for immediate assistance. Through its function as a "clearing house" for pilot reports (PIREPs) and its use of live and facsimile weather radar systems, it can provide timely severe weather avoidance information and other flight weather

data. Pilots are urged to cooperate and volunteer reports of cloud tops, upper cloud layers, thunderstorms, ice, turbulence, strong winds, and other significant flight conditions. Such in-flight observations between weather reporting stations are vitally needed. These reports are extremely helpful to other pilots and valuable to the National Weather Service in its efforts to provide more detailed and accurate forecasts.

EFAS is available between 6 A.M. and 10 P.M. local time, 7 days a week. Since EFAS is intended to provide real-time weather information, random sequence reports, position reports, filing or closing plans, or other routine requests should not be directed to EFAS but to the nearest FSS on the appropriate frequency.

Any flight service station located at an airport where a traffic control tower is not in operation provides Airport Advisory Service to arriving and departing aircraft. This service is offered for safety purposes and provides the following information: wind direction and velocity, favored runway, altimeter setting, pertinent known traffic, Notices to Airmen, airport taxi routes, airport traffic patterns, and instrument approach procedures.

Flight service stations monitor radio navigational aids to detect malfunctioning, operate a national teletypewriter communication system, and a national weather teletypewriter system. In addition, at selected locations, they take weather observations, administer airman written examinations, and advise Customs and Immigration of transborder flights.

The flight service specialist's main duty is to serve the flying public. Pilots and aviation enthusiasts are encouraged to visit the flight service stations to become better acquainted with the services offered. Service is their middle name; safety is their business.

THE NATIONAL TRANSPORTATION SAFETY BOARD (NTSB)*

The National Transportation Safety Board is an independent agency that determines the "probable cause" of transportation accidents and promotes transportation safety through the recommendation process. The Safety Board also conducts safety studies, evaluates the effectiveness of other government agencies' transportation safety programs, and reviews appeals of adverse actions by the U.S. Department of Transportation (DOT) involving pilot and mariner certificates and licenses.

To help prevent accidents, the Safety Board develops and issues safety recommendations to other government agencies, industry and other organizations that are in a position to improve transportation safety. These recommendations are always based on the Board's investigations and studies, and are the focal point of its efforts to improve safety in America's transportation systems.

The Safety Board's origins can be found in the Air Commerce Act of 1926, in which Congress charged the Department of Commerce with investigating the causes of aircraft accidents. Later that responsibility was given to the Civil Aeronautics Board's Bureau of Aviation Safety. In 1966, Congress consolidated all transportation agencies into a new Department of Transportation, and established the National Transportation Safety Board as an independent agency within the Department.

In creating the Safety Board, Congress envisioned that a single agency could develop a higher level of safety than the individual modal agencies working separately. Since 1967 the Board has investigated accidents in the aviation, highway, marine, pipeline and railroad modes.

In 1974, Congress made the Safety Board completely independent outside the DOT because "no Federal agency can properly perform such functions unless it is totally separate and independent from any other . . . agency of the United States." Because the DOT is charged with both the regulation and promotion of transportation in the U.S., and accidents may suggest deficiencies in the system, the Board's independence is necessary for objective oversight.

AUTHORITY

The Safety Board has no authority to regulate, fund or be directly involved in the operation of any mode of transportation. Therefore, it has the ability to oversee the transportation system, conduct investigations and make recommendations from a totally objective viewpoint, and to make recommendations for needed safety improvements. Its effectiveness depends on an ability to make timely and accurate determinations of the cause of accidents, along with comprehensive and well-considered safety recommendations.

The most visible portion of the Safety Board involves major accident investigations. Under its accident selection criteria, the Board's investigative response will depend primarily on:

1. the need for independent investigative oversight to ensure public confidence in the transportation system;

2. the need to concentrate on the most significant and life-threatening safety issues; and

3. the need to maintain a data base so that trends can be identified and projected.

Safety Board investigations include the participation of modal agencies and other parties (such as manufacturers, operators and employee unions). Within the transportation network, each governmental organization has been established to fulfill a unique role. Each modal agency investigates accidents to varying degrees of depth and with different objectives. The Board—as the only federal agency whose sole purpose is promoting transportation safety—conducts detailed, open, and thorough accident investigations that often uncover significant system-wide problems that need to be corrected to prevent future similar accidents.

> At an annual cost of less than 23 cents a citizen, the NTSB is one of the best bargains in the government.

Many safety features currently incorporated into airplanes, automobiles, trains, pipelines and marine vessels had their genesis in NTSB recommendations. At an annual cost of less than 23 cents a citizen, the NTSB is one of the best bargains in the government.

STAFF/RESOURCES

The National Transportation Safety Board is a small agency, with approximately 350 employees, whose primary responsibility is the investigation of transportation accidents and other safety problems, in all five modes of transportation. These investigations result in the development of safety recommendations to correct any safety problems uncovered.

The Safety Board accomplishes this large transportation role with a very small dedicated staff that has never exceeded 400 employees. During the early 1980s the staff was reduced to approximately 300 employees. This level disrupted the Safety Board's ability to accomplish its transportation safety responsibilities and it has been working diligently since 1982 with the Office of Management and Budget (OMB) and the Congress to rebuild its transportation safety programs to meet its statutory mandate.

The Safety Board reached its approximate target staffing level for FY 1994 in accordance with Executive Order 12839. In its core area of responsibility, accident investigation, the Board has minimized its need for resources by developing procedures to accomplish its responsibilities using the resources of others.

The Safety Board investigative staff manages other experts from industry and government in the collection of facts, conditions and circumstances surrounding the accidents it investigates. The participation of these other "parties" greatly multiples the Board's resources and without the donated assistance provided by these parties the Board could not accomplish its large volume of work with its current resources.

There is an additional safety benefit from this participation in that it ensures general agreement over the factual findings of the investigation, and allows first-hand access to information so that appropriate corrective actions may be taken immediately by the parties. The leveraging of Federal resources accomplished by this Safety Board policy is precisely the type of innovative management of Federal programs called for in the National Performance Review.

Another means by which the Safety Board multiplies the use of its limited accident investigation resources is by delegating the accidents with lesser accident prevention potential to other government agencies. For example, the Board currently delegates the investigation of some aviation accidents involving agricultural, experimental, and homebuilt aircraft to the Federal Aviation Administration while retaining the determination of the probable cause of these accidents. By selecting only those accidents with the most accident prevention potential, while delegating the investigation of other accidents, the Board achieves the maximum safety benefit from its limited resources.

By utilizing the resources of others, the Safety Board has maintained a relatively constant employment level in the face of continually increasing complexity in the accidents they are required to investigate. Technological advances in the aviation industry, for example, have resulted in glass cockpits, fly-by-wire and use of composite materials; advances in the railroad industry have resulted in satellite and ground based advanced train control systems, sophisticated electronic altering devices, digitized electronic event recorders, and end-of-train telemetry devices; and marine industry technological advances have included satellite electronic navigation and small water plane area twin hulls. These and other advances in technology have contributed to the necessary specialization of staff and the lack of staffing depth in most specialty areas.

IMPROVEMENTS

The Safety Board has used technology and other management improvements to obtain great productivity from its limited staff. The Board has invested heavily in automation. Almost every employee at the Board has a desktop computer and many employees use laptops when traveling or on accident investigations. The Board installed a new technology local area network to connect all of its computers and enable the transfer of information between all employees, including the regional office staffs. The most recent technological improvement has been the installation of a paperless office concept using optical imaging equipment to allow the investigative staffs to develop their reports, which include pictures and graphics, without the transfer of paper. Additionally, the Board shares technology with the DOT agencies which it primarily interfaces.

The Safety Board has also implemented a significant number of management improvements to increase the efficiency and effectiveness of the staff. These initiatives are directly in line with the management practices described in the National Performance Review.

The first step the Board took was to streamline its organization so that managers are accountable for their functions and have all the resources under their control to complete their end products.

A second step was to decentralize the decision making responsibility, including budget authority, from top management to the divisions and regional offices. This change has allowed conversion of some support positions to additional investigative positions.

A third step was to have each Office develop a mission statement and goals and objectives for their organization. The objectives include specific measures of quality, quantity, and timeliness of all Board products, such as safety recommendations, accident investigation reports and safety studies. Periodic meetings are held to assess progress in meeting these goals and objectives. In addition, the goals and objectives are updated annually to assure improvements in effectiveness and efficiency.

Despite this significant long-term attention to improved efficiency, the Board welcomes the Report of the National Performance Review and the additional incentive of the President's plan to Streamline the Bureaucracy and plans to further improve its organization and programs in accordance with those guidelines.

Since its inception, the NTSB has investigated more than 100,000 aviation accidents, and over 10,000 surface transportation accidents. On call 24 hours a day, 365 days a year, NTSB investigators travel throughout the country and to every corner of the world to investigate significant accidents, developing a factual record and safety recommendations with one aim—to ensure that such accidents never happen again.

To date, the NTSB has issued almost 10,000 safety recommendations pertaining to the various transportation modes to more than 1,250 recipients. As the board has no authority to regulate the transportation industry, its effectiveness depends on its reputation for conducting thorough and accurate investigations, and for producing timely, well considered recommendations to enhance transportation safety. The NTSB's role in fostering advances in transportation safety has been significant—more than 82 percent of its recommendations have been adopted by the regulatory authorities and the transportation industry.

ORGANIZATION OF NTSB

Policy at the National Transportation Safety Board is established by the Chairman, Vice Chairman, and Members of the Board, and carried out by the various line and staff departments. (See Figure 8.3.)

To carry out the responsibilities of the Safety Board as prescribed in the Independent Safety Board Act of 1974, Board Members establish policy on transportation safety issues and problems and on Board goals, objectives, and operations. Board Members review and approve major accident reports as well as safety recommendations, and decide appeals of FAA and Coast Guard certificate actions. Individual Members preside over hearings and testify before Congressional committees. Some of the offices and divisions relating to aviation are listed below.

Office of Administrative Law Judges

Under 49 U.S.C. Section 1133, the NTSB's administrative law judges conduct formal hearings and issue initial decisions on appeals from all FAA certificate actions and civil penalty actions involving pilots, engineers, mechanics, and repairmen. Also covered are petitions for certification that have been denied by the FAA.

The *Office of the Managing Director* implements the Safety Board's programs by coordinating the day-to-day operations of the staff. The office schedules and manages the Board's review of major reports, and provides executive secretarial services to the Board. The office's financial management division manages Safety Board funds so that they are properly controlled and spent. To accomplish this, the financial management staff prepares annual budget requests to the Office of

Management and Budget and Congress. It also evaluates program operations and conducts reviews to ensure that appropriated funds are expended in accordance with approved programs.

This division maintains an accounting system that provides accountability for expenditures and furnishes timely external and internal financial management reports. It audits and certifies bills and vouchers for payment, and conducts audits of Board functions. This procurement and contracting for needed goods and services also is handled by this division.

The *Office of Government, Public and Family Affairs* answers questions from the public, the news media, and the transportation industry to keep the public informed about the work of the Safety Board and its efforts to improve transportation safety. Public Affairs staff members also work with the media at accident sites, Board meetings and hearings and disseminate safety information to increase public awareness of the NTSB's activities in transportation safety. At major accidents, members of the Board conduct regular media briefings with assistance from Public Affairs staff.

This office keeps Congress and federal, state, and local government agencies informed on the Safety Board's efforts to improve transportation safety. This office responds to oral and written inquiries, and addresses problems and concerns raised by the Congress and other government entities. It prepares testimony for Board participation in Congressional hearings, and provides information legislation at the federal, state and local government levels.

The Safety Board's state liaison program serves as an advocate for Board recommendations to state and local governments, and provides information and insights to the Board on state policies and activities.

The *Office of Safety Recommendations and Accomplishments* helps to ensure that the Safety Board issues appropriate and effective recommendations for enhancing safety in all transportation modes. The office develops other programs to increase the acceptance of Board recommendations and also coordinates the "Most Wanted" safety recommendations program, alcohol and drug policy, and international accident prevention activities. In the latter regard, the office has assisted in the establishment of an International Transportation Safety Association a new global organization. Safety Recommendations are issued by the NTSB as a result of the investigation of transportation accidents and other safety problems. Recommendations usually identify a specific problem uncovered during an investigation or study and specify how to correct the situation. Letters

Figure 8.3 National Transportation Safety Board.

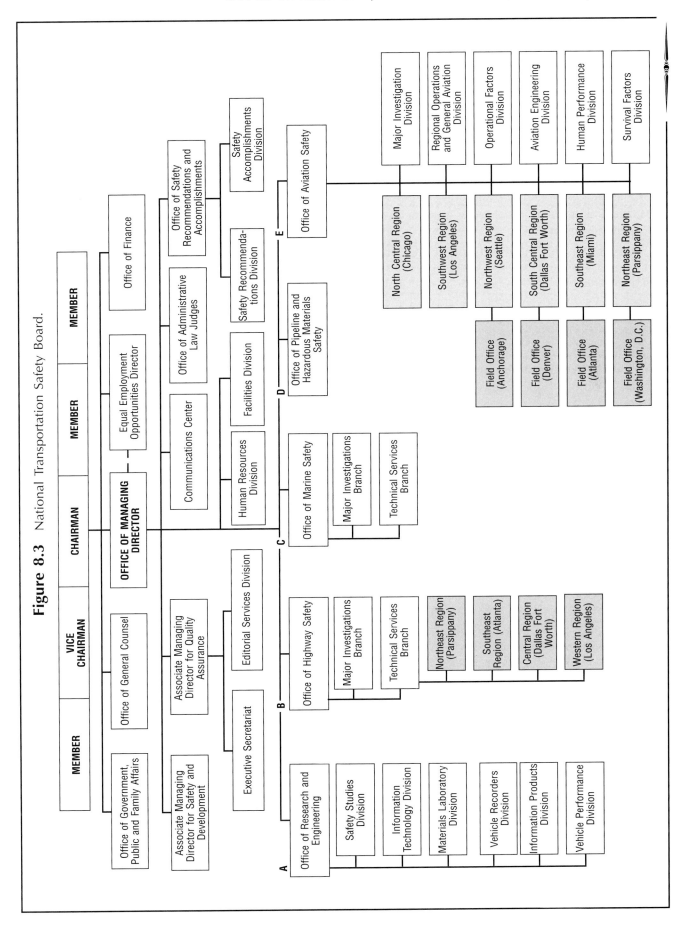

containing the recommendations are directed to the organization best able to act on the problem, whether it be public or private.

The *Office of the General Counsel* provides legal advice on policy, legislation, Safety Board rules, and other legal matters. The office helps to ensure that the Board's review of airman and seaman certificate and license appeals is timely and objective, and assists the Department of Justice in representing the Board in court proceedings. The general counsel's office also provides legal assistance and guidance to the Board's other offices regarding hearings, appearances as witnesses, and the taking of depositions.

Since 1967, the National Transportation Safety Board has served as the "court of appeals" for any airman, mechanic or mariner whenever certificate action is taken by the Federal Aviation Administration or the U.S. Coast Guard Commandant.

Under 49 U.S.C. section 1133 and 49 C.F.R. Part 821, the Board's *Administrative Law Judges* hear, consider and issue initial decisions on appeals of FAA certificate actions taken under 49 U.S.C. sections 44106, 44709 and 44710. Also covered are petitions for certification that have been denied by the FAA pursuant to 49 U.S.C. Section 44703. The judges' decisions in these cases may be appealed to the five-member Board by either the airman or the Federal Aviation Administration.

The Federal Aviation Administration Civil Penalty Administrative Assessment Act of 1992 transferred all civil penalty appeals for enforcement cases involving pilots, engineers, mechanics and repairmen from the Federal Aviation Administration to the National Transportation Safety Board (The civil penalty act is now codified at 49 U.S.C. Sections 46301, *et. seq.* That law also gave the Federal Aviation Administration the right to appeal certain decisions of the five-member Board (in both certificate action and civil penalty cases) to the U.S. Court of Appeals. Airmen and mechanics have always had the right to appeal adverse Board decisions to the federal appeals courts.

Under the Equal Access to Justice Act of 1980, as amended ("EAJA"), the judges also review and decide applications for attorneys' fees and expenses from airmen against the Federal Aviation Administration in cases brought pursuant to 49 U.S.C. Sections 44709. Equal Access to Justice Act applications filed in connection with actions brought by the Federal Aviation Administration under 49 U.S.C. Section 46301(d) (civil penalty

cases) are also decided by the Board's judges and, on appeal from the judges' decision, by the full Board.

The Board's review on appeal of its administrative law judges' decisions is based on the record of the proceeding, which includes hearing testimony (transcript), exhibits and the judge's decision, as well as appeal briefs submitted by the parties.

Upon review of the Board's decision, the U.S. Courts of Appeals have the power to affirm, modify or set aside that decision in whole or in part—or, if need is found, to order further proceedings by the Board. The judgment and decree of the Court of Appeals is subject to review by the U.S. Supreme Court on a writ of *certiorari*.

Marine certificate actions are heard first by Coast Guard's administrative law judges, and may be appealed to the Commandant of the Coast Guard. The ruling of the Commandant may be appealed to the National Transportation Safety Board where the Board follows the same appellate process as it does in considering the initial decisions of its law judges in aviation cases.

The Federal Aviation Act of 1958 and the Independent Safety Board Act of 1974 placed the responsibility for investigating and determining the probable causes of all civil aviation accidents with the Safety Board. Although it may delegate the actual investigation of the accident, the National Transportation Safety Board is the only entity that may determine the official probable cause. The Board is also charged with carrying out studies, special investigations, evaluations, and assessments on issues that are aviation-related.

Because of the international nature of the industry and America's leading role in aviation technologies, the Safety Board's investigation of domestic accidents and participation in international aviation investigations is essential to the enhancement of worldwide airline safety. The Board fulfills the U.S. obligations for international aviation accident investigations established by an International Civil Aviation Organization treaty by sending an accredited representative to the investigation of major accidents where American interests exist.

Foreign governments often request special assistance and expertise from the Safety Board. The Board's major aviation accident reports, safety recommendations, and accident statistics are disseminated worldwide and have a direct influence on the safety policy of foreign airlines.

Another important aspect of the Board's mandate is to investigate the more than 2,000 general aviation

> **The National Transportation Safety Board is the only entity that may determine the official probable cause.**

accidents that occur annually. On a selective basis, the NTSB will investigate accidents involving only property damage in which data is collected in a relatively limited but highly focused investigation. In addition, certain incidents not meeting the definition of an accident may be investigated as they often provide information that may be helpful in preventing accidents.

The NTSB serves as the nation's primary repository of aviation accident statistics and other related data, but its approach goes beyond the collection of data and a narrow determination of probable cause. Typically, NTSB investigators examine all factors, surrounding an accident or series of accidents, thereby ensuring that the regulatory agencies are provided with a thorough and objective analysis of actual as well as potential deficiencies in the transportation system. Only then can solutions be proposed to correct deficiencies that may have caused the accident.

When the Board is notified of a major accident, it launches a "Go Team," which varies in size depending upon the severity of the accident and the complexity of the issues involved. The team consists of experts in as many as 14 different specialties. Each expert manages other specialists from industry and government in the collection of the facts, conditions, and circumstances surrounding the accident.

The participation of these parties multiplies the Board's resources and fosters a greater likelihood of general agreement over the findings of the investigation, allowing firsthand access to information so that corrective actions may be taken by the appropriate parties.

A hearing may be convened, or depositions taken, to collect additional factual information. After the investigation is complete, a detailed narrative report is prepared that analyzes the investigative record and identifies the probable cause of the accident.

A board member usually accompanies the Go-Team to the scene of an accident. Also a public affairs officer is assigned to the team to coordinate media activities.

Assisting the Safety Board are agencies of the U.S. Department of Transportation that have day-to-day oversight of the transportation industry: the Federal Aviation Administration, the Federal Railroad Administration, the Research and Special Programs Administration, the Coast Guard, the National Highway Traffic Safety Administration, and the Federal Highway Administration. These agencies, and other State agencies and/or law enforcement organizations, often conduct their own parallel investigations. However, determining the probable cause of NTSB-investigated transportation accidents is the job of the Safety Board.

It is important to note that the NTSB was established as an independent agency because, during the course of its investigations, it often must investigate the role that the appropriate Department of Transportation agency may have played in the accident scenario.

Additionally, the NTSB enlists the support and oversees participation in its accident investigation of technically knowledgeable industry representatives and local police and emergency/rescue units that have special information and/or capabilities. This relationship is known as the "party system." It is through the party system, under the direction of the NTSB, that much of the background technical information is gathered for use in NTSB factual reports. It is important to remember that all investigatory activities are supervised by the NTSB experts, and that the determination of probable cause and the issuance of any safety recommendations resulting from the investigation are made solely by the five presidentially appointed Board Members.

The length of time a Go-Team remains on the accident site varies with need, but generally a team completes its on-scene work in 7 to 10 days. The NTSB takes very seriously its responsibility to keep the public informed. It follows a policy at a major accident site of providing factual information on the progress of the investigation at press briefings. Often, when a major accident occurs and the probable cause is not readily apparent, there is considerable speculation by the press and public about what happened. To minimize this, the NTSB issues periodic press statements, and a Board Member often meets directly with the press to brief the media and to answer questions in the days following an accident. These briefings convey the known facts of the investigation. They do not speculate about possible causes of the accident.

Within 3 to 6 months after an accident, factual reports written by NTSB investigators are made available in a public docket at NTSB headquarters in Washington, D.C. If additional, relevant factual material is developed later, it also is added to the public docket of the accident. All of this information may be obtained, at the cost of reproduction of the documents, from the NTSB's Public Inquiries Branch in Washington, D.C.

The Public Hearing—Following an accident, the Board may decide to hold a public hearing to clarify accident information and to air in a public forum significant new safety issues. A Board Member presides over the hearing, and witnesses provide technical testimony under oath. Every effort is made to hold the hearing promptly and close to the accident site.

The Final Report—With the completion of the fact-finding phase, the accident investigation process enters its final stage—analysis of the factual findings. The analysis of major investigations is conducted at the Board's Washington, D.C. headquarters, and results in what the Board terms "the probable cause of the accident."

A draft accident report for major investigations is then presented to the full five-Member Board for discussion and approval at a public meeting in Washington. The entire process—from accident investigation to final report—normally takes nine to twelve months. Accidents investigated by the Board's field investigators generally are reported in "brief" format.

The Laboratory—The Board operates its own technical laboratories to support investigations in the field with unbiased analysis. For example, the engineering services laboratory has the capability to "read out" aircraft cockpit voice recorders (CVR) and decipher flight data recorders (FDR). These so-called "black boxes" provides investigators with a profile of an aircraft during the often crucial last minutes of flight. The Board's readout capability is not confined to aviation. Similar techniques are applied to marine course recorders taken from ships involved in accidents and railroad event recorders from locomotives.

Metallurgy is another of the laboratory skills. Materials laboratory engineers and metallurgists perform post-accident analysis of components involved in all modes of transportation, ranging from components of jet aircraft engines of railroad tankcars. The laboratory uses state-of-the-art investigative equipment, such as scanning electron microscopes and x-ray analyzers, to document anomalies found during accident investigations and to determine causes of failures.

The Safety Recommendation—The safety recommendation is the Board's most important product. The recommendation is vital to the Board's basic role of accident prevention since it is the lever used to bring changes and improvements in safety to the nation's transportation system. With human lives at stake, timeliness is an essential part of the recommendation process. As a result, the Board issues safety recommendations as soon as a problem is identified, without necessarily waiting until an investigation is completed and the probable cause of an accident is determined.

The "Most Wanted" safety recommendations program is intended to spotlight safety recommendations issued by the Safety Board that would have the greatest impact on transportation safety at the national level. Follow-up efforts for safety recommendations on the "Most Wanted" list are more aggressive than for others.

In its mandate to the Board, Congress clearly emphasized the importance of the safety recommendation, saying the Board shall "advocate meaningful responses to reduce the likelihood of recurrence of transportation accidents." In each recommendation, the Board designates the person, or the party, expected to take action, describes the action the Board recommends, and clearly states the safety need to be satisfied. Although the Board's recommendations are not mandatory, to emphasize their importance, Congress has required that the Department of Transportation respond to each Board recommendation within 90 days.

> **The entire process—from accident investigation to final report—normally takes nine to twelve months.**

Operational factors division in three disciplines (air traffic control, operations, and weather) support major investigations with intensive work in their specialties. *Air traffic control (ATC) specialists* examine ATC facilities, procedures, and flight handling, including ground-to-air voice transmissions, and develop flight histories from Air Route Traffic Control Center and terminal facility radar records. Other specialists examine factors involved in the flight operations of the carrier and the airport, and in the flight training and experience of the flightcrew. *Weather specialists* examine meteorological and environmental conditions that may have caused or contributed to an accident.

Human Performance Division examine the background and performance of persons associated with the circumstances surrounding an accident—including the person's knowledge, experience, training, and physical abilities, decisions, actions and work habit patterns. Also examined are company policies and procedures, management relationships, equipment design and ergonomics, and work environment.

Aviation Engineering Division in four areas provide strong technical investigative skills. *Powerplant specialists* examine the airworthiness of aircraft engines, while *structures experts* examine the integrity of aircraft structures and flight controls as well as the adequacy of design and certification. *Systems specialists* examine the airworthiness of aircraft flight controls, and electrical, hydraulic, and avionic systems. And *maintenance specialists* examine the service history and maintenance of aircraft systems, structures, and powerplants.

Survival Factors Division investigates factors that affect the survival of persons involved in accidents, including the causes of injuries and fatalities. These investigators also examine cabin safety and emergency procedures, crashworthiness, equipment design, emergency responsiveness, and airport certification.

REGIONAL OPERATIONS AND GENERAL AVIATION

The Safety Board's Regional Operations and General Aviation consist of aviation investigators located in the Washington, D.C. headquarters and 10 regional and field offices across the United States. The offices provide support to major investigations and manage the investigation of smaller accidents that usually are investigated by one person or a partial team from the Board. They investigate about two hundred accidents and incidents monthly.

Field accident and incident investigations are conducted in a manner similar to a major investigation, but because the investigation is usually much smaller in scope, it is often conducted by a single investigator who, working with representatives from other parties, gathers all of the detailed information pertinent to the accident. During each investigation, investigators must always consider ways to prevent similar types of accidents from recurring through an informal on-scene recommended solution, or through the Board's formal safety recommendation process. In addition, field investigators provide support to major aviation accidents.

Limited investigations generally are conducted for non-fatal aviation accidents in which the aircraft is substantially damaged or destroyed.

"PUBLIC USE" AIRCRAFT

Under a 1994 law, which took effect in April 1995, the NTSB was granted new authority to investigate accidents and incidents involving "public use" aircraft, i.e., those that are owned, operated or leased by government entities (excluding military and intelligence agency aircraft). Previously, the Board did investigate some "public use" aircraft accidents under agreements with several government agencies. In investigating "public use" aircraft accidents, the NTSB's role will be the same as in civil aircraft cases—determining the facts and probable cause, and making recommendations for safety improvements.

FOREIGN INVESTIGATIONS

Around the world, the Safety Board is considered the leader in aviation accident investigations. Because it is the United States' sole accredited representative to the International Civil Aviation Organization (ICAO), Board staff frequently participates in foreign investigations. U.S. manufacturers and operators, in addition to foreign governments, seek the Board's assistance to determine the causes of accidents and incidents.

A. OFFICE OF RESEARCH AND ENGINEERING

The National Transportation Safety Board's Office of Research and Engineering provides technical support to accident investigations, conducts investigations of hazardous materials accidents and incidents (including explosions in transportation), and conducts safety studies that examine safety issues in all modes of transportation. The office is also responsible for maintaining the Safety Board's aviation accident data base, providing periodic statistical reviews of aviation accidents, and responding to public inquiries regarding Board investigations and studies.

An important unit of this office is the Safety Studies Division. This division, in collaboration with the Aviation and Surface Transportation offices, conducts field studies of safety issues in all transportation modes and performs analyses of accident statistics to detect trends and patterns. The division also evaluates the effectiveness of federal, state and local government and industry transportation safety programs by examining policy issues and performance. Comprehensive reports containing recommendations for corrective action are prepared for public release.

Safety studies are performed to stimulate improvements in the policies, programs, or statutory authority of government agencies, or to advance technological improvements in a transportation system or component.

In selecting subjects for safety studies, the Board identifies ongoing or potential safety problems or issues of national significance. Close consideration is given to matters that have the potential for reducing accident losses, improving the safety effectiveness of other government agencies and to attaining implementation of previous Board recommendations. The adequacy of program resources committed by other government agencies, the timeliness of studies with regard to transportation agency program planning and implementation, and the potential impact on regulatory or other safety programs are also considered.

B. OFFICE OF HIGHWAY SAFETY

Selecting a manageable number of highway accidents for investigation requires careful screening of millions of traffic accidents every year. The Board generally investigates highway accidents involving issues with wide-ranging safety significance. Specifically, accidents that involve the collapse of a highway bridge structure, a fatality on a public transportation vehicle (such as an intercity bus), and grade crossing accidents that involve collisions between trains and public transportation vehicles or hazardous materials vehicles are investigated. The investigative team is usually composed of an automotive engineer, a civil engineer, a hazardous materials expert, a metallurgist, and a human factors expert.

The Board's recommendations in the highway mode are directed to the U.S. Department of Transportation as well as State and local agencies, operators, manufacturers, and trade associations. As part of the Board's responsibilities, it also examines the safety programs of such agencies as the Federal Highway Administration and the National Highway Traffic Safety Administration.

C. OFFICE OF MARINE SAFETY

The Safety Board investigates all major marine accidents on navigable waters of the United States. In addition, it investigates major marine accidents that involve U.S. merchant vessels in international waters and collisions involving U.S. public and nonpublic vessels. Under the Board's criteria, a major marine accident is one that involves the loss of six or more lives, the loss of a self-propelled vessel of 100 or more gross tons, property damage estimated at more than $500,000, or an accident involving a serious threat from hazardous materials.

Under joint regulations promulgated by the Safety Board and the U.S. Coast Guard, the Coast Guard conducts the preliminary investigations of all marine accidents and notifies the Board if an accident is within its jurisdiction. The Safety Board then responds in one of three ways: (1) by conducting its own investigation, (2) by participating in a joint Safety Board/Coast Guard investigation, or (3) by asking the Coast Guard to conduct an investigation for the Board. As a result of its investigations, the Safety Board directs safety recommendations to agencies such as the Coast Guard, U.S. Army Corps of Engineers, shipping firms, and maritime trade organizations.

D. OFFICE OF RAIL, PIPELINE AND HAZARDOUS MATERIALS

Rail

Although the Safety Board investigates many kinds of railroad accidents, including freight train collisions and derailments, the Board places special emphasis on train accidents that involve the traveling public, such as passenger train and rail rapid transit accidents. The Board's criteria for a railroad accident investigation include any accident involving a passenger or employee fatality, or any accident resulting in substantial damage.

As a result of railroad accident investigations, the Board has directed safety recommendations to such agencies as the Federal Railroad Administration, the Federal Transit Administration (formerly the Urban Mass Transportation Administration), the National Railroad Passenger Corporation (Amtrak), State regulatory agencies, rapid transit agencies, trade associations, and common carriers. Safety studies in the rail mode have involved such areas as the transportation of hazardous materials and rapid transit systems.

Pipeline

Under its Congressional mandate, the Safety Board investigates all pipeline accidents involving a fatality or substantial property damage. Additionally, the Board may investigate accidents of a recurring nature. Once notification of an accident is received, the Board dispatches an investigator to the site who takes charge of a team composed of investigatory personnel from agencies such as the State public utility commission, local fire and police units, pipeline companies, and the U.S. Department of Transportation. In recent years, the Board has conducted investigations of accidents on pipelines that transport natural gas, highly volatile liquids, and other petroleum products, some of which pass through highly populated urban areas.

Hazardous Materials

The Safety Board investigates selected accidents involving the release of hazardous materials, including fatal accidents or those causing major disruptions to a community. Safety Board investigations are especially concerned with the effects of any materials released upon the public or emergency responders, the handling of the emergency by local authorities, and the adequacy of Federal standards for the transportation of hazardous materials.

When the accident is primarily the result of the transportation of the hazardous material, the investigation is focused on the performance of containers, the preparation for and handling of the materials during their transport, the health and safety hazards of the materials, the marking and hazard communication for the shipments, and the effectiveness of responses to emergencies resulting from the release of hazardous materials. In recent years, the Safety Board has investigated accidents in all modes of transportation of hazardous materials ranging from the release of gasoline to the explosion of military bombs.

E. Office of Aviation Safety

The Office of Aviation Safety is responsible for fulfilling a number of functions. It has the primary responsibility for investigating aviation accidents and incidents, and proposing probable causes for Board approval. Working with other Board offices, the office also formulates aviation safety recommendations.

The staff is located in 10 regional and field offices in major metropolitan areas throughout the United States. The office is composed of six divisions: major investigations, field operations and general aviation, operational factors, human performance, aviation engineering, and survival factors.

The Board investigates thousands of accidents annually, including all air carrier, commuter and air taxi accidents, in-flight collisions, and fatal general aviation accidents. The Board also participates in the investigation of major airline crashes overseas involving American carriers or U.S.-manufactured airlines as part of the U.S. obligation to The International Civil Aviation Organization.

The majority of the Board's air safety recommendations are directed to the Federal Aviation Administration. The recommendations have resulted in a wide range of safety improvements in areas such as pilot training, aircraft maintenance and design, air traffic control procedures, and post-accidental survival. The Board also is authorized to conduct safety studies of transportation problems. A safety study allows the Board to go beyond the single accident investigation to examine a safety problem from a broader perspective. In the past, for example, the Board has conducted safety studies in the areas of air traffic control, weather, crashworthiness, in-flight collisions, and commuter airlines.

Airline Accident Classification

The National Transportation Safety Board has developed a system for classifying airline accidents based upon the severity of their consequences. An improved classification system is required by the *FAA Reauthorization Act* of 1966. The Board believes that its proposal is fully responsive to the law, and in fact exceeds its requirements toward the goal of providing more meaningful measures of the level of safety of airline transportation. There is no intention to change the definition of an accident—*an occurrence associated with the operation of an aircraft which takes place between the time any person boards the aircraft with the intention of flight and all such persons have disembarked, and in which any person suffers death or serious injury, or in which the aircraft receives substantial damage.*

The statistics that the Board publishes relating to airline safety are: the number of accidents and fatal accidents; overall and fatal accident rates using flight hours, departures, and miles as normalizing factors; and the numbers of fatalities aboard and total. These statistics have been presented for each year of a seven-year series. None of the statistics, taken alone, necessarily can be considered an accurate measure of airline safety. Some fatal accidents involving ground crew fatalities pose no threat to the aircraft or its occupants. Yet the statistics have counted such an accident as one fatal accident, just as they counted the total destruction of an aircraft with no survivors. While the Board has found no single index that perfectly indicates the state of airline safety, the new classification system, it believes, is an improvement over current statistics.

Provided here is a description of the proposed classification system as well as several additional accident parameters that the Board intends to publish regularly.

In the proposed classification system below, each accident involving a Part 121 aircraft is placed into one of four mutually exclusive and collectively exhaustive categories. If an accident involves more than one Part 121 aircraft, the accident is placed into the category appropriate to the most severe consequences to any of those aircraft. Such an accident counts only once (rather than counting once for each of the Part 121 aircraft involved.) The four accident categories, defined in terms of the injuries and aircraft damage that resulted from the accident are:

A. Major Accident—an accident in which any of three conditions is met:

- a Part 121 aircraft was destroyed, or

- there were multiple fatalities, or

- there was one fatality and a Part 121 aircraft was substantially damaged.

B. Severe Accident—an accident in which at least one of two conditions is met:

- there was one fatality without substantial damage to a Part 121 aircraft, or

- there was at least one serious injury and a Part 121 aircraft was substantially damaged.

C. Injury Accident—a nonfatal accident with at least one serious injury and without substantial damage to a Part 121 aircraft. *(These often involve abrupt maneuvers, turbulence, evacuation, or scalding.)*

D. Damage Accident—an accident in which no person was killed or seriously injured, but in which any aircraft was substantially damaged.

The NTSB reports the numbers of accidents in each category and corresponding accident rates per flight hour and/or departure. These statistics are reported for the industry as a whole and not by airline or aircraft type. The Board believes that accident statistics reported in this form will be useful to the aviation safety community, the press, and the public in assessing the state of aviation safety.

The National Transportation Board reports several measures of airline safety in addition to the accident classification statistics above.

The NTSB reports the number of destroyed aircraft and the corresponding rate by hours and/or departures. These statistics are reported for U.S. airline operations as a whole and are not reported by airline or aircraft type. Accident statistics reported in this form are expected to be of particular interest to the aviation safety community, and will help the press and the public understand the state of aviation safety as well.

The NTSB reports numbers of fatally- and seriously-injured passengers and their corresponding passenger injury rates by passenger miles and/or passenger enplanements. Rates will be reported inversely to the way they are customarily presented—for example, passenger miles per fatality rather than fatalities per million passenger miles. This gives greater meaning to the typical consumer of the information. These statistics are reported for U.S. airline passenger operations as a whole and are not reported by airline or aircraft type. Passenger injury statistics reported in this form are expected to be particularly useful to the press and the public in assessing aviation safety, and will be another safety indicator of interest to the aviation community.

The NTSB publishes a list of accidents that caused passenger fatalities aboard U.S. airlines. The list includes the airline, the aircraft model, and the number of passenger fatalities and survivors.

The NTSB publishes a graphical portrayal of passenger fatalities aboard U.S. airlines. This graphic shows at a glance the number of passenger fatalities and the time between the accidents that caused them.

CHAPTER 9

Aviation Accident Investigation and Safety Performance

The National Transportation Safety Board is charged to carry out studies, special investigations, evaluations, and assessments of matters pertaining to aviation safety, including human injury avoidance, other agencies' aviation safety consciousness and efficacy in preventing aviation accidents, and the adequacy of safeguards and procedures for transporting hazardous materials by air.

Because of the international nature of the world's aviation industry and the leading role of the U.S. in the technological progress of aviation, the Safety Board's role in the investigation of domestic and international aviation accidents is essential to the enhancement of worldwide airline safety for all persons who travel by air. The worldwide public reaction of any major air disaster has an adverse effect on U.S. airlines and the confidence of U.S. citizens in the safety of airlines in general.

The Board is charged with fulfilling the U.S. obligations for international aviation accident investigations established by the International Civil Aviation Organization treaty. As such, the Safety Board appoints a leader (U.S. Accredited Representative) of the U.S. team who participates in the investigation of major accidents overseas. These accidents include U.S. airline accidents in foreign territory and accidents involving U.S. manufactured aircraft operated by foreign airlines overseas. Because the United States maintains a reputation as the world leader in aviation safety, many governments and aircraft industry representatives look to the Safety Board for the results of its investigations and safety recommendations. In addition, because of its advanced laboratory equipment and analysis capabilities, the Safety Board often is called upon by foreign governments to provide expertise in examining data from their aircraft accident investigations. The Safety Board is pleased to provide such services to the extent that it can, and still provide technical support to domestic accident investigations. The Board's major aviation accident reports, safety recommendations, and accident statistics are disseminated worldwide and have a direct influence on the safety of foreign airlines.

> **On 24-hour alert, a Go-team is a group of Safety Board technicians who possess a wide range of accident investigation skills.**

A less visible portion of the Safety Board's aviation accident investigation role involves the investigation of non-catastrophic and general aviation accidents. These accidents involve specific issues of special concern to the Board:

- air carrier and other large aircraft accidents;
- fatal and serious injury commuter and air taxi accidents;
- midair collisions;
- in-flight breakup;
- in-flight fire accidents;
- accidents involving newly certified aircraft;
- accidents involving high performance turbine-powered airplanes; and
- accidents implicating air traffic control services, facilities, or procedures.

FLIGHTS OF FANCY

NTSB Laboratory

The technical heart of the Board's investigative process is its laboratory. The lab is renowned as a center for analysis of accident information and wreckage. For example, the laboratory's expertise includes the ability to "readout," or decipher, the cockpit voice recorders (CVR) and the flight data recorders (FDR) which are required aboard large commercial aircraft. These two so-called "black-boxes," (which normally are painted orange or yellow to make them more visible amid accident wreckage) are crucial investigative tools. The CVR produces a magnetic tape recording of the last 30 minutes of cockpit crew conversa-

tions, and the crew's radio transmissions. But the CVR also provides a wealth of other information. For example, the cockpit is equipped with many audible warning signals, including altitude alert warnings, fire bells, stallwarning devices, and overspeed warnings. The equally important Flight Data Recorder records the flight parameters from the aircraft itself. In most aircraft, these are the aircraft's heading, airspeed, altitude, and vertical acceleration versus elapsed time. However, wide-bodied aircraft—including Boeing 747s, DC-10s, A-300s, and the Lockheed 1011—are equipped with even more sophisticated Digital Flight Data Recorders which can measure more than 100 points of information over a 25-hour flight period, including the monitoring of engine parameters, cockpit control positions, and flight control surface positions—i.e., flaps, aileron, rudder.

The Safety Board also investigates accidents involving property damage only, in which a relatively limited, but highly focused, investigation suffices for data collection purposes. Further, the investigation of selected incidents not meeting the definition of an accident often provides valuable prevention measures to prevent a serious accident from occurring.

As the result of an agreement with the U.S. Department of Transportation, the NTSB investigates commercial space launch accidents.

Immediately following a serious aircraft accident causing loss of life and/or considerable property damage, the Safety Board undertakes an exhaustive investigation to determine the probable cause of the accident and the circumstances which may have contributed to its cause. One of the more publicly visible aspects of a Board accident investigation is the Go-team concept. On 24-hour alert, a Go-team is a group of Safety Board technicians who possess a wide range of accident investigation skills. A Go-team roster could include one of the five Members of the Safety Board, air traffic control specialists, meteorologists, aircraft engine and structures technicians, as well as experts trained in witness interrogation, aircraft operations, and aircraft maintenance records.

> **"Black-boxes" are usually painted orange or yellow for higher visibility.**

REVIEWS

Under the Independent Safety Board Act, the Board has been given the role of a court of appeal for airmen and seamen. Specifically, the Act states that the Board shall . . . "review on appeal the suspension, amendment, modification, revocation, or denial of any operating certificate or license issued by the Secretary of Transportation." Air traffic controllers are included in this category as well as air carriers and air agencies authorized by the FAA to perform aircraft maintenance and to certify aircraft as airworthy. To carry out this mandate is the role of the Board's Office of Administrative Law Judges. The proceedings range from an appeal by a commercial airline pilot whose license had been revoked after his aircraft exhaused its fuel and crashed, killing 10 persons, to a proceeding involving a commuter airline whose operating certificate was revoked for violating FAA regulations. The hearings held by the judges are in the nature of an administrative proceeding and the judges have the option to either issue an initial decision from the bench or to write a decision after a review of the hearing transcript. The judges' decisions can be appealed to the five-member Safety Board. The right to appeal to the full Board is for either party—the FAA or the airman. The Board's review of

FLIGHTS OF FANCY

Accident Investigation

The crash of a four-engine British-owned Bristol Britannia air cargo flight in a wooded area near Billerica, Massachusetts resulted in the Board centering attention again on a long-standing problem in aviation—the rapid dissemination of severe weather forecasts. In its report on the accident, the Safety Board said the aircraft took off from Boston's Logan International Airport with an accumulation of ice and snow on the airframe and then encountered severe icing conditions. With the increased drag, and its lift capability degraded, the aircraft crashed eight minutes later.

Developing the probable cause of this accident required a particularly detailed investigation sequence. To begin with, the Board sent a nine-member Go-Team to the accident site, and it was joined by a representative of the British govern-ment. Additional "parties" to the investigation included rep-resentatives from British Aerospace Industries, Rolls-Royce, and Redcoat Air Cargo, the operator of the aircraft. The team completed the field phase investigation in 14 days, while the Cockpit Voice Recorder (CVR) and Flight Data Recorder (FDR) groups worked in Washington, D.C., to analyze the aircraft's reaction to the existing meteorological conditions.

A performance group was formed which, because of the lack of complete FDR data from the accident aircraft, also ana-lyzed FDR's from several aircraft operating in the vicinity of Boston at the time of the accident. This information and air traffic control data from the same aircraft were analyzed to evaluate meteorological phenomena which may have influ-enced the accident aircraft. The information derived from these analyses was then evaluated using a National Aeronau-tics and Space Administration computer program in conjunc-tion with the air traffic data from the accident aircraft to determine the accident aircraft's reaction to the weather events it encountered. These investigative techniques were then combined with an interview with the surviving flight engineer to determine the probable cause of the accident.

---

the appeal is based on a review of the transcripts of the proceeding, the Judge's decision, and appeal briefs submitted by the parties.

The Board considers only these issues:

- The findings of each fact are supported by a pre-ponderance of reliable, probative, and substantial evidence.

- Conclusions are made in accordance with precedent and policy.

- Are the questions on appeal substantial?

- Have any prejudicial errors occurred?

AIRCRAFT ACCIDENT INVESTIGATION

The following cases are examples of the NTSB accident investigation procedure. The detailed report on any accident investigation can be obtained from the National Technical Information Service (NTIS), 5285 Port Royal Road, Springfield, VA 22161. The telephone number is (800) 553-6847.

Case Study 1 ▰▰▰▰▰▰▰▰▰▰▰▰▰▰

The National Transportation Safety Board reported that an American Airlines McDonnell Douglas DC-10 stalled, rolled and crashed after takeoff in Chicago because of partial left wing slat retraction and the loss of two cockpit warning systems—all the end result of maintenance damage which caused separation of the left engine and pylon. The separation, at a critical point in takeoff, "resulted from damage by improper maintenance procedures which led to failure of the pylon structure," the Board ruled. In determining probable cause of the May 25, 1979, crash, the Safety Board emphasized that the flightcrew had "inadequate information and opportunity" to recognize and avoid the impending aerodynamic stall.

Factors cited by the Board as contributing to the accident were:

- The "vulnerability of the design of the pylon attach points to maintenance damage."

- The "vulnerability of the design of the leading edge slat system to the damage which produced asymmetry."

- "Deficiencies in the FAA surveillance and reporting systems which failed to detect and prevent the use of improper maintenance procedures."

- "Deficiencies in the practices and communications" among operators, McDonnell Douglas and FAA which failed to detect and make known previous maintenance damage incidents.

- The "intolerance of prescribed operational procedures" for takeoff to "this unique emergency."

The wide-body jetliner was taking off from Chicago-O'Hare International Airport's Runway 32 Right. It was "rotating"—its nose rising for liftoff—when the left pylon and engine tore loose from the wing, passed over it, and fell to the runway.

The aircraft lifted off the runway and maintained a steady climb and heading for 20 seconds. It then began a left turn and continued rolling to the left until its wings passed the vertical. Out of control, the DC-10 nosed down, crashed and exploded on impact in an open field.

All 258 passengers, the crew of 13, and two persons on the ground were killed—the highest death toll in any airline crash in the United States.

Safety Board investigation showed that separation of the pylon from the wing had damaged hydraulic and flight control components located there. This caused uncommanded retraction of the left wing's six outboard leading edge slats—aerodynamic lift enhancement surfaces, eight of which extend from each wing.

Two cockpit warning systems were disabled by the loss of that portion of the electrical system powered by the left engine. One was a slat disagreement system which alerts the crew when the slats are not in the selected position. The second, a stall warning device, literally shakes the control wheel when airspeed is dropping too close to an aerodynamic stall.

The Safety Board concluded that the uncommanded slat retraction, which induced an asymmetric stall, and the loss of the two systems which could have warned of it, caused the flightcrew to lose control. "Each by itself would not have caused a qualified flightcrew to lose control of its aircraft, but together during a critical portion of flight," they left the crew with "an inadequate opportunity to recognize and prevent the ensuing stall."

☀ Investigation

The investigation showed that the American flightcrew had followed prescribed engine-out procedure during the climbout. Post-accident flight simulation showed that the crew might have been able to overcome the partial slat retraction without stalling and losing control had they maintained higher than prescribed airspeed. Since many other carriers still use the same airspeed schedules as American then had in effect, the Board said these schedules "should be examined to insure that they afford the maximum possible protection."

Examination of the separated pylon showed there had been a pre-existing 10-inch crack in the forward flange of the pylon aft bulkhead—rearmost of three DC-10 pylon-to-wing attach points. A crescent-shaped deformation on the fracture surface was determined to have been produced when the pylon was installed or removed from the wing, not by the crash.

During maintenance about eight weeks before the accident, American Airlines had used a forklift hoisting device to remove the left engine and pylon as a single unit, rather than separately as recommended by McDonnell Douglas. Post-accident inspections and investigations revealed eight other cracked bulkhead flanges on DC-10s of American Airlines and Continental Airlines, which also was using the single-unit, fork-lift hoister technique.

The Safety Board held that the pylon had separated in Chicago "by a complete failure of the forward flange of the aft bulkhead after its residual strength had been critically reduced by a maintenance-induced crack which was lengthened by service loads."

Although the pylon met strength requirements prescribed by regulation, the Board said, "neither the designers nor the FAA certification review team adequately considered the vulnerability of the structure to damage during maintenance. In several places, clearances were unnecessarily small and made maintenance difficult to perform."

Two of the four Continental DC-10 flange failures were detected immediately and repaired. The Board expressed concern that FAA and key engineering and maintenance personnel at American Airlines were not aware of the incidents, both of which preceded the Chicago crash.

Determination

The Safety Board said it believes the regulatory reporting structure which permitted this "had and still has a serious deficiency." It also voiced concern that "this accident may be indicative of a climate of complacency."

"Although the accident in Chicago on May 25 involved only one manufacturer and one carrier, the Safety Board is concerned that the nature of the identified deficiencies in design manufacturing, quality control, maintenance and operations may reflect an environment which could involve the safe operation of other aircraft by other carriers."

Case Study 2

A mid-air collision that claimed 17 lives was caused by the failure of the pilots of both airplanes to follow the recommended communications and traffic advisory practices for uncontrolled airports, the National Transportation Safety Board reported.

The collision—which occurred August 24, 1984—involved a Wings West Airlines Beech C-99 and a Rockwell Commander, a single engine general aviation airplane. Wings West Flight 628 had departed San Luis Obispo County Airport enroute to San Francisco International Airport. The Rockwell Commander was on a training flight and descending toward San Luis Obispo County Airport which operates as an "uncontrolled airport"—an airport that does not have a control tower. The planes collided head-on at an altitude of about 3,400 feet, killing all aboard.

Investigation

Since the weather was clear each flightcrew had the regulatory responsibility to see-and-avoid the other. But the Board's investigation indicated that neither flightcrew detected the other airplane in sufficient time to either begin—or execute—an evasive maneuver.

The accident might have been avoided if the pilots of both airplanes had followed recommended procedures cited in the Airman's Information Manual. But two key recommendations were not followed: The pilot of the Rockwell Commander failed to advise the Air Route Traffic Control Center that he was approaching the runway at San Luis Obispo, foreclosing the opportunity for the air traffic controller to issue a traffic advisory to the Wings West flight, and the Wings West flight itself failed to monitor the airport communication facility for the recommended distance from the airport. As a result, the Wings West flight did not hear a communication from the Rockwell Commander flight on the local frequency that the aircraft was on an inbound course to the runway.

Determination

In determining the probable cause of the accident, the Board said the pilots of both planes failed to follow "the recommended communications and traffic advisory practices for uncontrolled airports contained in the Airman's Information Manual to alert each other to their presence, and to enhance the controller's ability to provide timely traffic advisories. Underlying the accident were the physiological limitations of human vision and reaction time. Also underlying the accident was the short time available to the controller to detect and appraise radar data and to issue a safety advisory. Contributing to the accident was the Wings West Airline policy which required their pilots to tune one radio to the company frequency at all times."

The Board long has recognized the deficiencies of the see-and-avoid concept and since 1968, repeatedly has recommended the development and installation of a collision avoidance system to supplement the see-and-avoid concept and to support other air traffic services.

The Board said also it was concerned the Wings West flightcrew elected to depart the San Luis Obispo Airport under Visual Flight Rules (VFR) and then request an air traffic control clearance after becoming airborne. This decision, though legally permissible, severely limited the time available to the controller—about 28 seconds—to make a radar identification of the flight before the collision occurred.

In summary, the Board said it recognized the inherent need for the see-and-avoid concept of visual flight. However, it said "the facts of this accident demonstrate that there may be occasion in which the physical factors of a traffic conflict can approach or may even exceed the physiological capabilities of the pilots to see-and-avoid an oncoming airplane. But compliance with recommended communications procedures can provide additional safeguards since they may—when used—provide the VFR pilots with advance warning of existing traffic, and may, in some cases, require the Air Traffic Control system to provide advisory and traffic separation services. Consequently, the Board believes that, if accidents of this type are to be prevented, action must be taken, where feasible, to encourage pilots more strongly to use these recommended procedures."

Case Study 3

On April 4, 1979, a Trans World Airlines B-727 entered a high-speed spiral dive while cruising at 39,000 feet (FL390) near Saginaw, Michigan. The aircraft did not recover from the dive until the aircraft reached an altitude between 5,000 and 6,000 feet msl despite flightcrew actions to counteract the maneuver. The aircraft was then landed under emergency conditions at an alternate airport. The aircraft was damaged extensively, and the No. 7 leading edge slat on the right wing, the No. 10 spoiler panel, and several other components were missing.

Investigation

During its investigation, the Safety Board examined the effects of full extension of the No. 7 slat on aircraft performance and control during level flight and descent. Using a Boeing engineering simulator, it was determined that the extended slat will generate a right roll which will be countered by the autopilot until its roll authority is exceeded. At the onset, the roll is readily recognizable and controllable as long as lateral controls are used with minimal delay and only to the extent needed to return the aircraft to a wings-level attitude. If the application of corrective controls is delayed and then used to full travel, an uncontrollable, steep descending spiral will develop. This occurs at certain Mach number and angle of attack relationships where the extended slat generates rolling moments that exceed the control authority available to the pilot. The spiral will continue until Mach number and angle of attack values are reduced or until the slat separates from the aircraft. The simulation results confirm the flightcrew's description of the spiral dive and the loss of roll control until the slat separated from the aircraft. Under certain conditions, recovery would not be possible.

Determination

The Safety Board believes that an extended No. 7 slat precipitated control problems that culminated in a loss of control. The Safety Board is also aware of TWA Safety Bulletin 79-3 and Boeing Operations Manual Bulletin 75-7 that, to a degree, inform flightcrews of the recognition and control aspects of an asymmetric slat configuration. The Safety Board believes that flightcrews must be able to recognize and react to such a condition and that there is a need to more widely disseminate comprehensive guidance to flightcrews.

Case Study 4

On February 26, 1980, a Cessna Model 172K (XP) crashed during normal takeoff from the Eagle Creek airport near Indianapolis, Indiana. The pilot, a commercial flight instructor and the only occupant of the aircraft, was killed. According to witnesses, the aircraft pitched up to a steep nose high attitude, about 60° or 70°, and the sound of engine power reduced abruptly from takeoff power to idle. The aircraft then pitched down and rotated about 160° to the left before crashing on the edge of the asphalt runway.

 Investigation

The investigation revealed that the pilot's seat was not locked and had slid rearward on the seat rails during liftoff. The pilot weighed 105 pounds and was 5 feet 2 inches tall. Acquaintances stated that she flew all types of aircraft with her seat in a full-forward position and required an extra seat cushion to enable her to see over the glareshield of the instrument panel. Because of her relatively short stature, she could not reach the throttle or rudder pedals or fully manipulate the control wheel of the above aircraft with her seat in its rearmost position. Consequently, once the seat slid aft, she was not able to maintain control or regain control when the pitch angle increased abruptly. The pitch up of the aircraft to a steep nose high attitude and the reduction in power would be the expected consequences of the pilot's holding onto the control yoke and the throttle as her seat slid aft.

 Determination

If the pilot had attempted to position and lock her seat in the full-forward position, the left front corner of the seat would have contacted and wedged against the door jamb. This interference, which is typical in this aircraft model, can prevent the seat locking pins from reaching the forwardmost locking holes. More importantly, however, the wedging of the seat can lead the pilot to believe that the seat is locked when, in fact, the locking pins are actually positioned between locking holes. Any subsequent forces on the seat, such as those occurring during takeoff, liftoff, or landing, can cause the seat to release abruptly and slide aft.

The pilot's operating handbook for the Cessna model 172K (XP) aircraft includes the pilot's check of the adjustment and locking of the seats, belts, and shoulder harnesses on the "before starting engine" checklist. However, because some pilots may find it necessary to readjust the seat before takeoff, the Safety Board believes that a check to ensure that front seats, belts, and harnesses are adjusted and locked also should be included on the "before takeoff" checklist.

Between 1970 and 1979, various Cessna aircraft were involved in 20 accidents in which slippage of the pilot's seat during takeoff or landing was determined to have been a causal element.

Case Study 5

A decision by the flightcrew to initiate and continue a landing approach through a thunderstorm, lack of specific procedures for wind shear avoidance, and lack of wind shear information led to the fatal crash of Delta Flight 191 at Dallas-Fort Worth airport August 2, 1985, the National Transportation Safety Board has concluded. The crash killed 135 people.

 Investigation

The Board said the airplane, a Lockheed L-1011 with 163 people aboard, penetrated a microburst wind shear below the thunderstorm, successfully flew through the first part of the microburst, then, attempting to transit the second part, touched the ground over a mile north of the approach end of the runway.

According to the Board, initial ground contact was soft. In fact, the plane got airborne again before crossing State Highway 114 at the north end of the airport. There, the plane struck a car and a light pole and began to break up. It subsequently collided with two water tanks on airport property 1,700 feet beyond the highway.

Determination

In determining the flightcrew's role in the accident, the Board evaluated the information about the thunderstorm available to the crew, including a sighting by the first officer of lightning in front of the airplane about 90 seconds before the crash. The Board concluded the flightcrew had enough information to decide that they should avoid the thunderstorm.

The failure of that flightcrew to recognize the severity of the weather, the Board explained, may have been due to the fact that the wind shear detection equipment at Dallas-Fort Worth airport did not give an alarm until after the accident—because the weather at the airport was clear within two minutes of landing—or because several flightcrews of airplanes landing before Delta 191 (some of which had seen lightning north of the airport) had not reported any difficulties or unusual conditions either on the approach or after landing.

The Board said the radar at Fort Worth's Air Route Traffic Control Center Weather Service Unit probably detected the cell as it intensified, but because no one was monitoring the radar display at the time, no alert was transmitted to the air traffic control tower.

The Board also noted that guidance to the crew on thunderstorm avoidance in the Delta Flight operations procedures manual was not specific enough. The manual states only that below 10,000 feet, thunderstorms are to be avoided by five miles.

According to the Board, "Although . . . the accident could have been avoided had the procedures contained in the Delta thunderstorm avoidance policy been followed, the absence of more specific operational guidelines for avoiding thunderstorms in the terminal areas provided less than optimum guidance to the captain and flightcrew. The circumstances of this accident indicate that there is an apparent lack of appreciation on the part of some, and perhaps many, flightcrews of the need to avoid thunderstorms and to appraise the position and severity of the storms pessimistically and cautiously. The captain of flight 191 apparently was no exception. Consequently, the Safety Board believes that thunderstorm avoidance procedures should address each phase of an air carrier's operation and in particular, the carriers should provide specific avoidance procedures for terminal area operations."

The Board said the probable causes of the accident were: "the flightcrew's decision to initiate and continue the approach into a cumulonimbus cloud which they observed to contain visible lightning, the lack of specific guidelines, procedures, and training for avoiding and escape from low-altitude wind shear, and the lack of definitive, real-time wind shear hazard information. This resulted in the aircraft's encounter at low altitude with a microburst-induced, severe wind shear from a rapidly developing thunderstorm located on the final approach course."

As a result of its crash investigation of Delta Flight 191, the Safety Board issued recommendations to the Federal Aviation Administration (FAA), the National Weather Service, the National Oceanic and Atmospheric Administration, the Dallas-Fort Worth airport, the American Association of Airport Executives, the Airport Operations Council International, and the National Fire Protection Association. The recommendations related to thunderstorm avoidance, detection and dissemination of weather information, disaster notification and emergency response, and flight attendant restraint systems.

Case Study 6

A DC-8 cargo plane crashed near Toledo, Ohio because the crew failed to recover in time from an unusual aircraft attitude, the National Transportation Safety Board has found. While the reason for that unusual attitude could not be positively determined, the Board said it probably resulted from the captain's apparent spatial disorientation brought about either by physiological factors or by the failure of cockpit instrumentation, or a combination of the two.

Air Transport International flight 805, operating under a contract for Burlington Express, was executing its second missed approach at Toledo Express Airport when it crashed into a field at 3:26 A.M. There was light rain and fog in the area and visibility was limited to two miles. The three crew members and an observer aboard the aircraft died in the accident, and the aircraft was destroyed.

 ## Investigation

Air traffic control radio communications and a transcript of the cockpit voice recording indicate that the first officer, who was at the controls until the second missed approach, was having difficulty aligning the aircraft with the instrument landing system (ILS) flight path. The ILS is used by pilots to navigate to a runway during instrument flying conditions. Shortly after the captain assumed control for the second missed approach, the transcript shows him asking twice " . . . what's the matter here?" The captain relinquished control back to the first officer, but the aircraft crashed within seconds.

 ## Determination

The Board determined that the captain apparently became spatially disoriented while executing the second missed approach, either because of physiological factors or because his attitude direction indicator—a type of artificial horizon gauge used to determine the aircraft's attitude—malfunctioned, or both. After the captain became disoriented, the first officer was righting the aircraft after he reassumed control, but he could not complete the recovery before it impacted trees and then hit the ground at more than 300 knots. The accident was not survivable.

Case Study 7

After exhaustive investigative efforts, the National Transportation Safety Board did not find conclusive evidence to explain the 1991 crash of United Airlines B-737 at Colorado Springs until 2001 when it was determined that for an unknown reason the rudder moved full right.

The accident occurred as United flight 585 was completing a turn onto the final approach course to runway 35 at Colorado Springs Municipal Airport. In clear skies and at an altitude of approximately 1,000 feet above ground, the aircraft suddenly rolled to the right, pitched nose down until it reached a nearly vertical attitude, and impacted the ground at Widefield Park. All 25 persons aboard the flight were killed. The flight had originated in Peoria, Illinois with intermediate stops in Moline, Illinois and Denver.

The Safety Board did report that the two most likely events that could have resulted in the accident were a malfunction of the aircraft's lateral or directional control system, or an encounter with an unusually severe atmospheric disturbance.

 ## Investigation

More than 170 witnesses were interviewed in the course of the 20-month long investigation. The majority of them observed the aircraft operating normally until it suddenly rolled to the right and descended into the ground in less than 10 seconds.

Evidence from the flight data and cockpit voice recorders indicated that 16 seconds prior to the crash, the engines' thrust was increased from 3,000 pounds per engine to 6,000 pounds per engine. As the thrust was increasing, the first officer made the 1,000 foot (above ground) call-out. Within the next four seconds—nine seconds before the crash—the rate of change of the aircraft's heading increased to about five degrees per second, nearly twice that of a standard rate turn. The first officer said "oh God," and the captain—in the last eight seconds—called for flaps to be set at 15 degrees. The aircraft's altitude decreased rapidly while the indicated airspeed increased to more than 200 knots. The plane impacted the ground 3.47 nautical miles from the end of the airport's runway 35, leaving a 15 foot deep crater that measured approximately 39 feet by 24 feet.

The Safety Board said the most likely atmospheric disturbance to cause an uncontrollable roll would be a horizontal axis vortex, commonly known as a rotor. Some witness observations support the existence of a rotor at or near the time and location of the accident, and conditions have been identified that were conducive to the formation of a rotor.

Determination

The Safety Board concluded that the flight encountered a number of topographically-induced atmospheric phenomena including updrafts and downdrafts, gusts, and vertical and horizontal axis vortices. The flight data recorder, however, does not conclusively support an encounter with a rotor strong enough to cause a jetliner to roll. The Board said that too little is known about rotors to decisively conclude whether such an event was a factor in the accident.

The Safety Board also concluded that the airplane was properly maintained, and actions to correct previous discrepancies related to uncommanded rudder inputs were proper. The Safety Board could not find evidence of any pre-impact failure or malfunction of the aircraft structure or in any electrical, instrument or navigation system.

There were anomalies found in the aircraft's hydraulic and flight control systems, but none that would explain an uncommanded rolling motion or initial loss of control of the airplane. Neither member of the crew reported any malfunctions or difficulties.

The captain and first officer were qualified, according to the Safety Board, with no evidence that the flightcrew was affected by illness, incapacitation, fatigue or other factors associated with their personal or professional lives.

In an effort to determine what caused the crash, the Safety Board conducted an intensive examination—and in some cases functional testing—of 46 components from the aircraft. The components included engine indicating instruments, yaw damper electronics, rudder, ailerons, elevator, secondary flight controls, spoilers, leading edge devices, flap control module and trailing edge flap control valve.

In addition, sophisticated atmospheric numeric computer modeling of air movements in the Rocky Mountains near Colorado Springs helped the Safety Board define potential flow fields that might have been present, and a specialized computer simulation was used to define possible roll angle and sideslip angle time histories that would be consistent with the crash scenario. Finally, the investigation employed simulation exercises to examine the effects of various atmospheric disturbances and/or flight control malfunctions on a B-737-200 aircraft. Approximately 250 such runs were completed.

No new recommendations were issued with the final report. On August 20, 1991 the Safety Board recommended that the Federal Aviation Administration (FAA) require airlines to inspect B-737 and B-727 rudder standby actuator units, with the replacement of input shafts in which rotation of the bearing occurs or where excessive force is needed to move the input lever. To date, the FAA has not taken any final action on that recommendation.

On July 20, 1992 the Safety Board urged the FAA to develop and implement a program to document and analyze potential meteorological threats to aircraft operating in the Colorado Springs area and, as a result, develop a meteorological aircraft hazard program for airports in or near mountainous terrain.

Case Study 8 ▮▬▬▬▬▬▬▬▬▬

The National Transportation Safety Board has cited a faulty stall warning design, inadequate airline maintenance, and poor crew coordination for the crash on takeoff of Trans World Airlines flight 843 from New York's JFK International Airport.

Calling again for better training of pilots to deal with abnormal situations during takeoffs, the Safety Board said the plane would have flown if the flight had not been suddenly aborted.

Two hundred ninety-two people aboard the aircraft escaped safely when the San Francisco-bound L-1011 burst into flames after the aborted takeoff. The flightcrew believed the aircraft would not fly because of a warning indicating an aerodynamic stall. The emergency evacuation of the plane was exemplary with only one serious injury and several minor ones, the Safety Board said. The aircraft was destroyed by fire.

 Investigation

The Safety Board found that a malfunction in the stall warning system caused a false indication. The malfunction was not detectable by the pilots because of the system's design deficiency. Previous such malfunctions went undetected by TWA's quality assurance program because the airline used a calendar day, rather than a flight-hour basis for detecting repetitive problems, the Safety Board said.

The Safety Board urged the Federal Aviation Administration to require air carriers to improve rejected takeoff training through crew coordination briefings as well as by simulator training. The training should include actions to take under abnormal conditions during takeoff and climb, including the transfer of the aircraft's control to the captain when an emergency or abnormal situation occurs while the first officer is flying the aircraft.

Flight 843's takeoff roll was proper until the first officer, who was the flying pilot, incorrectly perceived that the airplane was in an aerodynamic stall, according to the Board. He suddenly turned over the controls to the captain, who aborted the flight. The plane was about 15 feet off the ground at the time. It touched down very hard, some 9,500 ft down the 14,572-foot runway, 13R/31L, and the captain guided it into the left shoulder to avoid a jet blast fence at the end of the runway.

 Determination

The Safety Board determined that the probable causes of this accident were design deficiencies of the stall warning system that permitted a defect to go undetected, the failure of TWA's maintenance program to correct a repetitive malfunction of the stall warning system, and inadequate crew coordination between the captain and the first officer that resulted in their inappropriate response to a false stall warning.

The Safety Board said the first officer reacted to the stall warning by immediately deciding to let the captain take over and he transferred control of the airplane without proper warning or coordination. This action is not consistent with nearly universal practice in the aviation community regarding transfer of control in a two-pilot aircraft.

It concluded that the first officer pushed the control column forward or allowed it to move ahead in reaction to the false stall warning. Then, the captain made a split second decision to reject the takeoff by reducing engine thrust, a decision very likely based, in part, on his perception of available runway to stop the plane, the NTSB added.

Although the Safety Board believes that the flightcrew's reactions to the false stall warning were inappropriate, it believes that the malfunction in the angle of attack sensor that caused the warning should have been detected and repaired by TWA's maintenance and quality assurance program, thereby eliminating the precipitating event in this accident.

It found that the airplane's right wing spar broke when the airplane landed hard and that this fracture was not fatigue induced. The damaged wing spar resulted in a release of fuel, which then caught fire. The Board also found that the airport rescue and fire fighting services responded to the accident in a timely and efficient manner.

Also as a result of the accident, the Board issued recommendations involving cabin interior furnishings, L-1011 windows and seat belts.

Case Study 9

The inherent limitations of the concept known as "see-and-avoid" used by all general aviation pilots resulted in the 1992 mid-air collision of two aircraft southeast of Indianapolis, according to the National Transportation Safety Board. Six persons were killed and two others seriously injured in the accident.

The collision occurred when a Mitsubishi MU-2B departed Greenwood Municipal Airport and was struck by a Piper PA-32 Saratoga as the MU-2B was climbing through an altitude of 2,100 feet two miles northeast of the airport. The Saratoga was en route to the airport, which is an uncontrolled facility, and was descending from 2,500 feet when it struck the MU-2B, which was en route to Columbus, Ohio. Weather at the time of the accident was reported to be high scattered clouds and 15 miles visibility.

In addition to citing the limitations to see-and-avoid, the Safety Board determined that a contributing factor in the accident was the failure of the MU-2B pilot to activate his instrument flight rules flight plan prior to takeoff.

Before the collision, the Saratoga had departed Terry Airport 14 miles northwest of Indianapolis and had been receiving air traffic control radar services from the Indianapolis airport until it was three miles north of the Greenwood airport. Forty-four seconds after radar services for the Saratoga were terminated, the MU-2B pilot reported that he was "off Greenwood" and sought the instrument flight rules clearance. The controller at Indianapolis issued a discrete beacon code, but the flight had not yet been identified on the controller's radar screen when the collision occurred.

 ## Investigation

During its investigation of the accident, the Safety Board found that the Saratoga would have appeared briefly in the lower left corner of the MU-2B windshield at least 20 seconds before impact. Similarly, the Board found that the MU-2B would have appeared in the right front windshield of the Saratoga 25 seconds before the accident. The sun, according to the Safety Board, would not have been in the normal field of vision of either pilot.

When weather conditions permit, federal aviation regulations require that vigilance shall be maintained by each person operating an aircraft so as to see and avoid other aircraft. The Safety Board said many constraints have been shown to reduce a person's ability to exercise the required degree of vigilance to make the regulation effective. According to the Board, these limitations are affected by the age and workload of the individual who is supposed to be doing the seeing, the size and color of the object to be seen, and weather conditions such as glare and clouds. Research gleaned from military studies indicate that it takes an individual 12.5 seconds to see an object and take evasive action in response to a perceived collision threat.

Determination

The Safety Board said the see-and-avoid limitations would have been compounded for the pilot of the MU-2B by a heavy workload immediately upon takeoff. In addition to watching for other aircraft, the MU-2B would normally perform an after-takeoff checklist, make radio calls to UNICOM and departure control, raise the landing gear and flaps, adjust the transponder, and adjust the engine and propeller controls. Even though the MU-2B was flying through a relatively high traffic density environment, the pilot had less time available to scan for other aircraft that might have posed a threat to his own airplane as a result of the workload. Had the MU-2B pilot received his instrument flight rules clearance before takeoff, controllers could have provided traffic advisories and thereby reduced his workload.

As a result of its investigation, the Safety Board has recommended that the Federal Aviation Administration develop departure and arrival procedures for uncontrolled airports near high density areas while requiring pilot compliance with local departure and arrival procedures at all uncontrolled airports. The Board also wants the FAA to establish entry and departure corridors at uncontrolled airports for high performance airplanes such as the MU-2B that are separate from low performance airplanes such as the Saratoga.

The Safety Board has also recommended that the FAA require pilots who intend to use an instrument flight rules flight plan to obtain an air traffic clearance prior to take-off when two-way communications with controllers are available on the ground. It has also reiterated a five year old recommendation urging the development and production of low-cost proximity warning and conflict detection systems for use on general aviation aircraft.

Finally, the Safety Board recommended that the FAA revise the Airman's Information Manual to include information on see-and-avoid scanning techniques and inform instructor pilots about the necessity for emphasizing scanning techniques during biennial flight reviews.

Case Study 10

The National Transportation Safety Board cited the design of a cockpit handle that operates the wing flap/slat system as the cause of a fatal high-altitude upset of a China Eastern Airlines MD-11 over the Pacific.

Investigation

The Safety Board discovered during its investigation the need to replace deficient fire retardant seat material in that wide-body jet and possibly in other airliners worldwide.

The NTSB determined that flight 583 pitched violently after an inadvertent deployment of leading edge wing slats. It was cruising at 33,000 and lost 5,000 feet of altitude. Lack of the use of restraints led to the death of two passengers and injured 160 others.

The plane, on a scheduled flight from Beijing, China to Los Angeles, with a stop-over in Shanghai, made an emergency landing at Shemya Air Force Base, Alaska. It suffered severe damage to the interior passenger cabin.

Although it was not a factor in the accident, the Safety Board was concerned when its examination of the plane's cabin revealed that premature deterioration of fire-retardant material used on passenger seats resulted from severe wear from normal use, and no longer provided fire protection to the cushions. The Board said the deficiency could potentially jeopardize the safety of passengers in accidents that result in interior cabin fires, and recommended corrective action by the Federal Aviation Administration.

Determination

The NTSB said the probable cause of the accident was the inadequate design of the flap/slat handle by Douglas Aircraft Co. that allowed the handle to be easily and inadvertently moved. The captain's attempt to recover from the slat extension, given the reduced longitudinal stability and the associated light control force characteristics of the MD-11 in cruise flight, led to several violent pitch oscillations, according to the Board.

It added that the violence of the pitch oscillations was due to the lack of specific pilot training in recovery from high altitude upsets in MD-11 aircraft, and the influence of the stall warning system on the captain's control responses.

The Board said this was the worst of 12 incidents of inadvertent or uncommanded in-flight slat extensions involving the MD-11. Normally, slats are never used in cruise flight. They are deployed for take-off and landings, and extend from the front of a wing to provide greater aerodynamic lift.

According to the Safety Board, the majority of those passengers aboard didn't have their seat belts fastened tightly or at all, nor were they required to. The Board said, however, that contributing to the severity of the injuries was the lack of seat restraint usage by the occupants. Most of the injuries occurred in the mid and rear of the passenger cabin.

The China Eastern accident resulted in Safety Board recommendations that prompted McDonnell Douglas to make an interim modification in the flap/slat system to prevent inadvertent deployment. The Board also recommended at that time that a new system be developed to replace the mechanical one in use.

In its new recommendations, the Safety Board urged that the FAA review the MD-11's high altitude longitudinal stability and control characteristics, and require better pilot training to recover from upsets in this part of flight. It also called for replacement of deficient fire-blocking materials, establishment of a requirement to have the effectiveness of seat fire-blocking material tested periodically while in use, and dissemination of information to foreign aviation authorities about the problem.

Case Study 11

A failure by the captain of an American Airlines DC-10 to use proper aircraft directional control techniques resulted in the plane's departure from the runway after a landing at Dallas-Fort Worth International Airport, according to the National Transportation Safety Board. Although there were no serious injuries as a result of the accident, two persons were seriously injured while evacuating the airplane, which was declared a total loss.

The accident occurred as the DC-10, American Airlines' flight 102 from Honolulu, landed on runway 17L at Dallas/Fort Worth. About 15 seconds after the main landing gear touched the runway, the airplane departed the right side of the runway and came to a stop in grass and mud.

Investigation

The Safety Board's investigation of the accident revealed that a line of moderate to heavy showers and thunderstorms was crossing runway 17L as the plane touched down, although no microbursts or windshears were recorded in the vicinity of the airport at the actual time of the landing. Flight 102 was subjected to crosswinds of 15 to perhaps 20 knots.

Once on the runway, the captain failed to compensate for moderate crosswinds from the right, allowing the airplane to weathervane and drift off the right side of the runway with minimal rudder commands, inappropriate tiller nosewheel steering commands, and lack of forward pressure on the control column. There was no evidence of hydroplaning of the airplane on the runway, nor was any reverted rubber found on the airplane's tires.

Determination

Although air traffic control was not a factor in the accident, because of procedural shortcomings, windshear advisory information was not provided to the flightcrew in a timely fashion. The practice of displaying only the centerfield wind on the low level windshear alert system limited the amount of information the controller had available to issue to the flightcrew.

The evacuation of the passengers was handled in an expeditious and professional manner, the Board said. Emergency lighting did not operate properly, however, because the emergency lighting battery packs were found to be out of sequence. The manufacturer's instructions did not describe the importance of properly sequencing the batteries in each pack.

Case Study 12

On July 19, 1989, United Airlines flight 232, a DC-10-10, was on a scheduled flight from Denver to Philadelphia, with an intermediate stop in Chicago, when it experienced a catastrophic failure of the number 2 (tail) engine while cruising at 37,000 feet. The flightcrew immediately noticed a complete loss of the aircraft's hydraulic pressure and severe flight control difficulties. While attempting an emergency landing at Sioux City, the aircraft crashed. Of the 296 passengers and crew aboard, 111 received fatal injuries. A 112th victim died 31 days later.

Investigation

Investigation revealed that the first stage fan disk had separated in flight, releasing metal fragments that disabled two of the plane's three hydraulic systems powering the airplane's flight controls; portions of the remaining system adjacent to the engine separated during the engine failure, leaving the aircraft without hydraulic power to manipulate vital flight controls. The disk, which wasn't recovered for almost three months, underwent extensive metallurgical examination.

Determination

The Board determined that the failure originated in a metallurgical flaw that had existed since the disk's manufacture. A fatigue crack propagated from this flaw and grew until the disk failed. Discoloration of the crack found after the accident and metallurgical analysis convinced the Safety Board that the crack was present when the disk was last inspected by the airline 760 flights before the accident. The crack could have been detected if a proper inspection had been conducted, the Board said.

The Board said that personnel generally work independently and receive very little supervision. The Board stated, "There is minimum redundancy built into the [inspection] process to prevent human error or other task or workplace factors that can adversely affect inspector performance." The Board said it is concerned that inspections in general, and fluorescent penetrant inspections in particular, may not be given the detailed attention that such a critical process warrants. United used FPI during what turned out to be its final inspection of the disk.

The disk was manufactured by GEAE in 1971. The flaw in the titanium ingot from which the disk was forged was present following its original melting. The Board concluded that the defect was probably not detectable when GEAE ultrasonically inspected the still-unfinished piece upon its arrival at GE's Evandale, Ohio plant. The Board believed, however, that had the final shape been macro-etch inspected by GEAE, the flaw would have been apparent since it was on the surface of the final shape. During a macro-etch inspection, the metal surface is treated with an etchant that highlights different metallurgical structures, allowing flaws to be detected.

The Board considered the DC-10's certification process and said that, in retrospect, "The potential for hydraulic system damage as a result of random debris could have been given more consideration in the original design and certification requirements of the DC-10. As a result of lessons learned from this accident, the hydraulic system enhancement mandated by the FAA should serve to preclude loss of flight control as a result of a number 2 engine failure." The Board urged the FAA to give all possible consideration to the redundancy of, and protection for, power sources for aircraft flight and engine controls.

During the 44 minutes between the engine failure and the attempted landing, the crew discussed many possible procedures and also attempted to get assistance from United maintenance and operations personnel on the ground. The Board viewed the interaction of the pilots, including a DC-10 captain who came up to the cockpit from his seat in the cabin, as indicative of the value of cockpit resource management training. As to the crew's performance, the Board concluded that the aircraft, while flyable even though it had lost its hydraulic flight controls, "could not have been successfully landed on a runway. Under the circumstances, the UAL flightcrew performance was highly commendable and greatly exceeded reasonable expectations."

Case Study 13

A poor decision, an overweight aircraft, and an overly ambitious trip itinerary led to the crash of a private general aviation aircraft that killed a young girl, her father and a flight instructor. The accident killed seven year old Jessica Dubroff in a crash that occurred on April 11, 1996, shortly after a Cessna 177-B took off from a Cheyenne, Wyoming airport as part of a highly publicized cross country trip.

Investigation and Determination

The National Transportation Safety Board determined the probable cause of the accident was the improper decision by the flight instructor, who was the pilot in command, to take off into deteriorating weather conditions. Weather included air turbulence, gusty winds, an advancing thunderstorm and associated precipitation. The four seat airplane was overweight and the density altitude was higher than the flight instructor was accustomed to. This resulted in a stall caused by failure to maintain airspeed. Contributing to the decision by the pilot in command to take off was a desire to adhere to an overly ambitious itinerary, in part because of media commitments, the NTSB stated.

The Safety Board also urged the Federal Aviation Administration to incorporate the lessons of this accident into educational materials on aeronautical decision-making and expand information and dissemination of materials on the hazards of fatigue to general aviation pilots.

The board reached numerous other conclusions about the accident including:

- The pilot in command was at least assisting Jessica Dubroff, the pilot trainee, if he was not the sole manipulator of the controls during the takeoff and climb-out sequence. At the time of impact the pilot in command was the sole manipulator of the airplane's controls.

- There was no evidence that airplane maintenance was a factor in the accident and there was no evidence of airframe, engine or control malfunction during the takeoff and subsequent crash. Airframe icing was not likely a factor and there were no air traffic control factors that contributed to the cause of the accident.

- The airplane was 96 pounds over maximum gross takeoff weight at takeoff, and 84 pounds over the maximum gross takeoff weight at the time of the impact.

- The airplane experienced strong crosswinds, moderate turbulence and gusty winds during its takeoff and attempted climb. The pilot in command was aware of these adverse wind conditions prior to takeoff.

- The accident sequence took place near the edge of a thunderstorm and the pilot in command decided to turn right immediately after takeoff to avoid the thunderstorm and heavy rain that would have been encountered on a straight-out departure.

- The right turn into a tailwind may have caused the pilot in command to misjudge the margin of safety above the airplane's stall speed. In addition the pilot may have increased the airplane's pitch angle to compensate for the perceived decreased climb rate, especially if the pilot misperceived the apparent ground speed for airspeed or if the pilot became disoriented.

- The high density altitude and possibly the pilot in command's limited experience with this type of takeoff contributed to the loss of airspeed that led to the stall.

- The pilot in command suffered from fatigue during the day before the accident and information on fatigue and its effects and methods to counteract it, might have assisted the pilot to recognize his own fatigue on the first day of the flight and possibly enhance the safety of the flight.

Case Study 14

On February 19, 1996, at 0902 central standard time, Continental Airlines (COA) flight 1943, a Douglas DC-9-32, N10556, landed wheels up on runway 27 at the Houston Intercontinental Airport, Houston, Texas. The airplane slid 6,850 feet before coming to rest in the grass about 140 feet left of the runway centerline. The cabin began to fill with smoke, and the captain ordered the evacuation of the airplane. There were 82 passengers, 2 flightcrew members, and 3 flight attendants aboard the airplane. No fatalities or serious injuries occurred; 12 minor injuries to passengers were reported. The airplane sustained damage to its lower fuselage. The regularly scheduled passenger flight was operating under Title 14 Code of Federal Regulations (CFR) Part 121 and had originated from Washington National Airport about 3 hours before the accident. An instrument flight rules (IFR) flight plan had been filed; however, visual meteorological conditions prevailed for the landing in Houston.

Investigation

The first officer began the descent, and at 0841:32, the cockpit voice recorder (CVR) recorded the captain reading the descent checklist. At 0841:40, the first officer asked the captain to verify that the calculation of 132 knots as the target airspeed for the approach was correct, to which the captain replied in the affirmative. The descent checklist was called complete by the captain at 0842:03.

At 0845:31, the first officer called for the in-range checklist. The data from the digital flight data recorder (FDR) indicated that the airplane was descending through 19,000 feet at this time. Between 0845:37 and 0846:10, the captain referred to each of the seven items on the in-range checklist, in the correct order, *except for the fourth item, "Hydraulics,"* to which the captain did not refer. The first officer responded "checked set" to the third item, "Flight Instruments, Altimeters," and "on" to the fifth item, "Shoulder Harness."

At 0854:49, the first officer called for the approach checklist. Between 0854:49 and 0855:18, the captain referred to the first four of the nine items on the checklist. At 0855:27, the checklist was interrupted by the first officer informing the captain that he intended to use manual spoilers at 40° of flaps for the landing. The captain resumed completing the checklist at 0855:56, and accomplished the next three items before he was interrupted again at 0856:06, when the controller transmitted "Continental nineteen-forty-three, thirteen miles from the marker, maintain two thousand till established on the localizer, cleared ILS two seven approach." At 0857:02, the controller instructed flight 1943 to maintain a speed of 190 knots or faster to the outer marker and to contact the tower.

After making the landing public address announcement, the captain contacted the Houston Intercontinental Air Traffic Control Tower Local East controller, and at 0857:58, the flight was cleared to land. At 0858:08, the captain said, "Now, where was I," referred to the last two items on the approach checklist and stated, "Approach check complete."

During postaccident interviews, neither pilot recalled seeing "any" landing gear indicator lights; both pilots recall the gear handle being moved to the down position.

According to FDR data, at 0900:58, the airplane was traveling at 216 knots indicated airspeed, approximately 504 feet above field elevation, and 34 seconds from touchdown. At 0901:02, the first officer stated, "want to take it around?" and the captain replied, "No, that's alright keep your speed up." Regarding his decision to continue the approach, the captain later stated, "It was a VFR day, we had a 10,000 foot runway, we had gear and flaps, I felt there was not a problem." The first officer later stated that there was no time for discussion with the captain because the approach was so fast.

At 0901:07, the landing gear warning horn stopped sounding. At 0901:08, the first officer stated, "I can't slow it down here now," and the captain replied, "You're alright." At 0901:10, the first officer said, "We're just smokin' in here." At 0901:13, the ground proximity warning system (GPWS) alerted, "Whoop whoop pull up" three times, and silenced at 0901:18. During the second GPWS alert, at 0901:15, the landing gear warning horn resumed sounding and continued to do so until after touchdown. According to the first officer, the captain reached up to the overhead panel as the GPWS was alerting. The captain did not recall doing this and stated that he had interpreted the GPWS alerts as a high sink rate warning.

At 0901:18, the first officer said, "Want to land it?" At 0901:20, the captain replied, "Yeah," and, according to the first officer, took control of the airplane. According to the captain, the first officer was "uncomfortable with the situation and relinquished the controls." The captain stated that at the time he took over, the airspeed was high, but he felt comfortable. The transfer of control from the first officer to the captain occurred as the airplane was traveling at 204 knots indicated airspeed, approximately 161 feet AFE, and 12 seconds from touchdown. At 0901:24, the first officer asked the captain, "You want it?" and the captain said, "Yeah."

At 0901:32, the airplane touched down hard with the wheels up at 193 knots indicated airspeed. As the airplane slid down the runway, two controllers on duty in the tower and two airport groundskeepers observed smoke and fire coming from beneath the airplane. The captain said that as the airplane slid down the runway, he was able to maintain directional control with the rudder. The airplane came to a stop in the grass off to the left side of the runway.

The first officer stated that after the airplane came to rest, he made the PA announcement, "Remain seated, remain seated, remain seated." According to the captain, he called for the evacuation checklist and pulled both engine fire handles.

Physical evidence indicated that the airplane touched down about 3,300 feet from the approach end (beginning) of runway 27, almost directly on the runway centerline. A continuous scrape mark started at this point and led down the runway to the location of the airplane. The scrape mark remained close to the runway centerline for approximately 5,000 feet and then diverged to the left, departing from the pavement about 6,730 feet after it began. About 10 feet further than that, both inboard main landing gear doors and the left forward nosegear door were located. Small fragments of skin from the belly of the airplane were scattered along the runway.

Examination of the cockpit revealed that the landing gear handle was in the down position and the flap handle was set to 50°. The left and right engine-driven hydraulic pump switches were in the *"LOW"* position, and the LAT and AUX hydraulic pump switches were in the *"OFF"* position. The left hydraulic system gauge indicated 1,600 psi, and the right gauge indicated 0 psi.

The evidence indicates that the airplane's hydraulic system was not configured for landing. Because the hydraulic system remained in the low pressure mode, hydraulic pressure was not available to lower the landing gear and deploy the flaps. The flightcrew failed to detect this configuration error and continued its approach into Houston. Comments on the CVR and post-accident statements by the flightcrew indicate that both pilots recognized that the flaps did not deploy after the flaps were selected to 15°, but the flightcrew did not determine the cause of this problem or execute a go-around.

The landing checklist was not performed, and the flightcrew did not confirm that the gear was down and locked. The gear warning horn sounded during the approach, indicating that the landing gear was not extended, but it was ignored. When the airplane descended through 500 feet, it was traveling 84 knots faster than the target airspeed of 132 knots. Although, under standard operating procedures, this excessive airspeed mandated that the approach be discontinued, the captain rejected a go-around request from the first officer, who was the flying pilot. The GPWS sounded an alert 19 seconds before impact and was ignored. Unaware that the gear was not down, the captain assumed control of the airplane and made a wheels-up landing.

 ## Determination

Performance deficiencies exhibited by the flightcrew during this flight include:

1. Failure to configure the hydraulic system for landing during the performance of the in-range checklist,

2. Failure to detect initially that the flaps did not extend,

3. Failure to determine the reason the flaps did not extend after detection,

4. Failure to perform the landing checklist and to confirm the landing gear status, and

5. Failure to discontinue the approach.

Had the landing checklist been properly performed, the flightcrew would have detected the failure of the landing gear to extend.

The National Transportation Safety Board determined that the probable cause of this accident was the captain's decision to continue the approach contrary to Continental Airlines standard operating procedures that mandate a go-around when an approach is unstabilized below 500 feet or a ground proximity warning system alert continues below 200 feet above field elevation. The following factors contributed to the accident:

1. The flightcrew's failure to properly complete the in-range checklist, which resulted in a lack of hydraulic pressure to lower the landing gear and deploy the flaps,

2. The flightcrew's failure to perform the landing checklist and confirm that the landing gear was extended,

3. The inadequate remedial actions to ensure adherence to standard operating procedures, and

4. The Federal Aviation Administration's inadequate oversight to ensure adherence to standard operating procedures.

Case Study 15 ▰▰▰▰▰▰

On November 19, 1996, at 1701 central standard time, United Express flight 5925, a Beechcraft 1900C, N87GL, collided with a Beechcraft King Air A90, N1127D, at Quincy Municipal Airport, near Quincy, Illinois. Flight 5925 was completing its landing roll on runway 13, and the King Air was in its takeoff roll on runway 04. The collision occurred at the intersection of the two runways. All 10 passengers and two crewmembers aboard flight 5925 and the two occupants aboard the King Air were killed. Flight 5925 was a scheduled passenger flight operating under the provisions of Title 14 Code of Federal Regulations (CFR) Part 135. The flight was operated by Great Lakes Aviation, Ltd., doing business as United Express. The King Air was operating under 14 CFR Part 91.

🔍 Investigation

According to a Cherokee pilot and his passenger, as well as a pilot who saw the approach and landing of flight 5925 as he was driving to the airport, flight 5925 had its landing lights on. The passenger in the Cherokee said the airplane made a normal landing on runway 13.

A pilot employed by the airport's fixed-base operator (FBO) and two Beech 1900C-qualified United Express pilots, who had been waiting for flight 5925 to arrive, were the first people to reach the accident scene. One of the United Express pilots remained some distance from the airplanes while the other United Express pilot and the FBO pilot approached the airplanes. They saw that the King Air and the right side of the Beech 1900C were engulfed in fire. The United Express pilot said that he opened the left aft cargo door of the Beech 1900C and black smoke poured out. The FBO pilot said that he could not see the interior of the cabin through the passenger windows because the cabin appeared to be filled with dark smoke. They then ran to the forward left side of the Beech 1900C fuselage where the FBO pilot said he saw the captain's head and arm protruding from her window on the left. She asked them to "get the door open."

The FBO pilot stated that he found the forward air stair door handle in the 6 o'clock (unlocked) position. He said that he attempted unsuccessfully to open the door by moving the handle in all directions and pulling on the door. He said that he did not see any instructions for opening the door, but he was able to rotate the handle upward to the 5 o'clock position but no further. The United Express pilot stated that he then intervened because he believed that the FBO pilot probably did not know how to open the door. The United Express pilot stated that he depressed the button above the handle while rotating the handle from the 3 o'clock position downward to the unlocked position. He stated that the handle felt "normal" as he rotated it. However, he was unable to open the door. The FBO pilot then tried again to open the door by rotating the handle upward, but he was again unsuccessful.

The Beech 1900C was visible to other airport traffic during its approach. Witnesses, including the occupants of the Cherokee taxiing behind the King Air, said that they could see the airplane and that it had its landing lights on. Further, the Beech 1900C flightcrew discussed the fact that two airplanes were planning to take off on runway 04, and they had an alternate plan to use runway 04 if necessary. The captain's request at 10 miles out for other traffic to "please advise" gave them sufficient time to revert to this alternate plan if needed. The pilots observed when the King Air entered runway 04, and later attempted to ensure that runway 13 would remain clear for their landing by asking whether the airplane on the runway (i.e., the King Air) intended to hold or take off.

The Safety Board concludes that given the Beech 1900C flightcrew's frequent radio broadcasts of the airplane's position during the approach, and the lack of any prohibition on straight-in approaches to uncontrolled airports, the flightcrew's decision to fly a straight-in approach to runway 13 was not inappropriate.

The flightcrew made radio transmissions about 30 miles out, at 1652:07, ("Any traffic in the area please advise"); 10 miles out, at 1656:56, ("We'll be inbound to enter on a left base for runway one three at Quincy any other traffic please advise"); 5 miles out, at 1659:29, ("Just about to turn, about a six mile final for runway . . . one three, more like a five mile final for runway one three at Quincy;"); and on short final, at 1700:16, ("Aircraft gonna hold in position on runway four or you guys gonna take off?"). Although these callouts did not exactly match those recommended in the AIM and AC 90-42F, they were appropriate for the straight-in approach being flown. Even though under 14 CFR Part 91.113, flight 5925, as a landing aircraft, had the right of way over aircraft on the surface, the captain took the precaution of asking whether the airplane on the runway was going to hold or take off. It would have been prudent for the captain to refer specifically to the "King Air," to leave no doubt about which airplane she was addressing; however, her transmission was sufficiently specific that she could reasonably expect to be understood.

The Cherokee pilot's transmission, at 1700:28, ("seven six four six Juliet uh, holding uh, for departure on runway four . . . on the uh, King Air") immediately followed the captain's inquiry, and appeared to be in response to her question. The transmission was interrupted by the GPWS alarm in the Beech 1900C. Although it would have been prudent for the captain to ask that the transmission be repeated, her reply, at 1700:37, ("OK, we'll get through your intersection in just a second, sir—we appreciate that") made it clear that she believed she was communicating with the airplane that was to take off next on the runway, and it would have been reasonable for her to expect a clarification if that was not the case.

Subtle cues indicated that the transmission did not come from the King Air. Specifically, the speaker gave a different "N" number, and the voice and gender of the speaker were different than heard in previous transmissions from the King Air. However, because the pilots were most likely preoccupied with landing the airplane, and because the speaker said "King Air" but did not say "Cherokee" and the pilots had no reason to expect a response from any aircraft other than the King Air, they probably did not notice or focus on those cues. Having received what they believed was an assurance from the airplane on the runway that it was going to hold, the pilots may have become less concerned about continuing to watch the King Air during their landing.

The airplane touched down at 1700:59. The captain was recorded as calling for "Max reverse" at 1701:01; expletives from the flightcrew were also recorded.

The King Air pilot's flying history suggests that he may not have placed sufficient importance on the basics of safe flying. His previous gear-up incident during an instructional flight suggests carelessness, and his subsequent comments to the FAA indicate that he did not consider the incident significant. The fact that he sat on an active runway for an extended time and comments from students indicating that he seemed to be rushing them are consistent with a careless attitude. Further, during his last year as a TWA pilot, the pilot had been downgraded from captain to flight engineer because of poor performance during recurrent training.

The accident occurred at 1701, a time often associated with fatigue. According to the pilot's wife, he slept normally in the days before the accident but awoke earlier than his usual time of 0800 on the day of the accident. The detection of lorazepam in the pilot's urine indicates that he ingested the medication in the previous days or weeks. However, the absence of the medication in his blood indicates that he was not impaired by the medication at the time of the accident. Nevertheless, his potentially recent use of the medication suggests that he may have had some difficulty sleeping. Based on his early wake-up time, the time of day that the accident occurred, and the possibility that he had difficulty sleeping recently, he was most likely not at his peak alertness at the time of the accident. However, the Safety Board could not determine the extent to which this may have affected his performance.

The King Air pilot might have been in a hurry to get home after a long day of flying potential purchasers of the King Air on a demonstration flight to Tulsa. After the King Air pilot returned to Quincy, two of the passengers said that he seemed to be "in a hurry" or "anxious to get home."

Determination

A combination of these factors (preoccupation with providing instruction to the pilot/passenger, careless habits, possible fatigue, and rushing) could explain why the King Air pilot did not properly scan for traffic.

The National Transportation Safety Board determines that the probable cause of this accident was the failure of the pilots in the King Air A90 to effectively monitor the common traffic advisory frequency or to properly scan for traffic, resulting in their commencing a takeoff roll when the Beech 1900C (United Express flight 5925) was landing on an intersecting runway.

Contributing to the cause of the accident was the Cherokee pilot's interrupted radio transmission, which led to the Beech 1900C pilot's misunderstanding of the transmission as an indication from the King Air that it would not take off until after flight 5925 had cleared the runway.

Contributing to the severity of the accident and the loss of life were the lack of adequate aircraft rescue and fire fighting services, and the failure of the air stair door on the Beech 1900C to open.

Case Study 16 ▮▮▮▮▮▮

On May 11, 1996, at 2:13 P.M. eastern daylight time, a Douglas DC-9-32 crashed into the Everglades about ten minutes after takeoff from Miami International Airport, Miami, Florida. The airplane, N904VJ, was being operated by ValuJet Airlines as flight 592. Both pilots, three flight attendants and all 105 passengers were killed. Visual meteorological conditions existed in the Miami area at the time of the takeoff. Flight 592 was destined for the Hartsfield International Airport, Atlanta, Georgia.

🔍 Investigation

ValueJet flight 591, the flight preceding the accident flight on the same aircraft, was operated by the accident crew. Flight 591 was scheduled to depart Atlanta at 10:50 A.M. and arrive in Miami at 12:35 P.M. ValuJet's dispatch records indicated that it actually departed the gate at 11:25 and arrived in Miami at 1:10 P.M. The delay resulted from unexpected maintenance involving the right auxiliary hydraulic pump circuit breaker.

Flight 592 had been scheduled to depart Miami for Atlanta at 1:00 P.M. The cruising altitude was to be flight level 35,000 feet with an estimated time en route of one hour 32 minutes. The ValueJet DC-9 weight and balance and performance form completed by the flightcrew for the flight to Atlanta indicated that the airplane was loaded with 4,109 pounds of cargo (baggage, mail and company-owned material—COMAT. According to the shipping ticket the COMAT consisted of two main tires and wheels, a nose tire and wheel and five boxes that were described as "Oxy Canisters Empty." According to the ValuJet lead ramp agent on duty at the time, he asked the first officer of flight 592 for approval to load the COMAT in the forward cargo compartment. He showed the first officer the shipping ticket. According to the lead ramp agent he and the first officer did not discuss the notation "Oxy Canisters Empty" on the shipping ticket. According to him the estimated total weight of the tires and the boxes was 750 pounds and the weight was adjusted to 1,500 pounds for the weight and balance form to account for any late arriving luggage. Within five minutes of loading the COMAT the forward cargo door was closed. He could not remember how much time elapsed between his closing the cargo compartment door and the airplane being pushed back from the gate. Flight 592 began its taxi to runway 9L(left) about 1:44 P.M. At 2:03 Air Traffic Control cleared the flight for takeoff and the flight crew acknowledged the clearance.

At 2:07:22, the departure controller instructed flight 592 to "turn left heading three zero and maintain one six thousand." The first officer acknowledged the transmission.

At 2:10:03 an unidentified sound was recorded on the cockpit voice recorder (CVR) after which the captain remarked. "What was that?" According to the flight data recorder (FDR), just before the sound, the airplane was at 10,634 feet mean sea level (m.s.l.), 260 knots indicated airspeed (KIAS) and both engine pressure ratios were 1.84.

At 2:10:15, the captain stated, "We got some electrical problem," followed five seconds later with, "We're losing everything." At 2:10:22, the captain stated, "We need to go back to Miami," followed three seconds later by shouts in the background of "fire, fire, fire, fire." At 2:10:27, the CVR recorded a male voice saying, "We're on fire. We're on fire." At 2:10:31, the first officer radioed that the flight needed an immediate return to Miami.

According to the CVR, at 2:10:36 the sounds of shouting subsided. Four seconds later the captain stated, "Fire" and the first officer replied, "Uh smoke in the cockp . . . smoke in the cabin." At 2:11:12 a flight attendant shouted, "Completely on fire." The FDR and radar data indicated that flight 592 began to change heading to a southerly direction about 2:11:20. At 2:11:26, the north departure controller advised the controller at Miami Center that flight 592 was returning to Miami with an emergency. At 2:11:37 the first officer transmitted that they needed the closest available airport. No other transmission was received from flight 592.

The accident occurred at 2:13:42. Ground scars and wreckage scatter indicated that the airplane crashed into the Everglades in a right wing down, nose down attitude. The location was 17 miles northwest of Miami.

Two witnesses, fishing from a boat in the Everglades when flight 592 crashed, stated that they saw a low flying airplane in a steep bank. The bank increased and the nose of the airplane dropped. The airplane struck the ground in a nearly vertical attitude. The witnesses described a great explosion, vibration and a huge cloud of water and smoke. One observed that the landing gear was up and all the airplanes parts appeared to be intact and there was no sign of fire.

Other witnesses who were sightseeing in a private airplane in the area at the time provided similar accounts of the accident. These witnesses, and those in the boat who approached the accident site, described seeing only part of an engine and other debris scattered around the impact area. One witness remarked that the airplane seemed to have disappeared upon crashing into the Everglades.

Analysis

The passenger oxygen system is composed of oxygen generators that upon activation provide emergency oxygen to the occupants if the cabin pressure is lost. The flightcrew was properly certified and had received the appropriate training prescribed by federal regulations. Evidence indicated that the airplane was equipped and maintained according to approved procedures. There was no evidence of pre-existing mechanical malfunction in the airplane. Both engines were developing power at ground impact. The CVR revealed that about six minutes after takeoff from Miami the crew became aware of a fire in the passenger cabin. Approximately four minutes later the airplane crashed into the Florida Everglades. The accident was not survivable. The recovered wreckage provided evidence of fire damage in the forward cargo compartment and areas above it. Other areas of the airplane did not show significant fire damage, including the cockpit and the electronics compartment located beneath the cockpit. Examination of the heat damaged wires and cables revealed no physical evidence of short circuits or of burning that could have initiated the fire. The heat and fire damage to the interior of the cargo compartment was more severe than the damage to the exterior.

Investigation revealed that shortly before departure from Miami, five boxes of unexpended oxygen generators were loaded into the forward cargo compartment in the area where the fire damage was the most severe. Further investigation found that safety caps were not installed over the percussion caps that start a chemical reaction in the oxygen generators. The generators were not packed adequately to prevent generators from striking the actuation mechanism on adjacent generators.

Determination

The NTSB determined that the probable cause of the accident was activation of one or more oxygen generators, which initiated the fire, being improperly carried as cargo in the forward cargo compartment of the airplane. They were not properly packed or identified as unexpended.

Case Study 17

On July 17, 1996 about 8:31 P.M. EDT, Trans World Airlines (TWA) flight 800, a Boeing 747-131, N93119, crashed in the Atlantic Ocean near East Moriches, New York. The flight was operating as a scheduled international passenger flight from John F. Kennedy International Airport, New York, to Charles DeGaulle International Airport, Paris, France. The flight departed JFK about 8:19 P.M. with 18 crew members and 212 passengers. All 230 people were killed and the airplane was destroyed.

On the day of the accident the aircraft departed Athens, Greece as TWA flight 881 at 5:37 A.M. It landed at JFK about 4:31 P.M. The flight crew did not observe any operational problems during the flight. A flight crew change was made and the aircraft was refueled. It remained at the gate with its auxiliary power and two of its three air conditioning units running for two and a half hours until it departed as Flight 800. The flight was delayed shortly because of a problem with a passenger's luggage. The pilot was informed that the bags had been placed aboard. The cockpit door closed at 8:00 P.M. and the flight crew continued to prepare for departure. During the subsequent departure the pilot received a series of altitude assignments and heading changes from New York Terminal Radar Approach Control and Boston controllers. The airplane reached its assigned altitude.

 **Investigation**

At 8:29 P.M. the cockpit police recorder recorded the captain saying, "Look at that crazy fuel flow indicator there on number four . . . see that?" The next thirty seconds the cockpit recorder contained the following: a sound similar to a mechanical movement in the cockpit; an unintelligible word; and sounds similar to recording tape damage noise. At 8:31 P.M. the recording ended with a very loud sound then lost power.

According to the Boston Air Route Traffic Control Center transcript at 8:31 P.M., the captain of an Eastwind Airlines Boeing 737 reported that "We just saw an explosion out here." About ten seconds later he said "We just saw an explosion up ahead of us about 16,000 feet or something like that; it just went down into the water." Many ATC facilities received reports of an explosion from other pilots operating in the area.

Many witnesses in the vicinity of the accident stated that they saw or heard explosions accompanied by a large fireball falling over the ocean, and observed debris, some of which was burning, falling into the water. About one-third of these witnesses reported that they observed a streak of light, resembling a flare, moving upward in the sky to the point where a large fireball appeared. Several witnesses reported seeing this fireball split into two fireballs as it descended toward the water. Pieces of the airplane wreckage were discovered floating on and beneath the surface of the Atlantic Ocean about eight miles south of East Moriches, New York. The main wreckage was found on the ocean floor. The accident occurred in dusk lighting conditions. The airplane was destroyed by the explosion, fire, break up and impact forces. According to insurance company records the airplane was valued at $11 million. No structures on the ground were damaged. The Safety Board reviewed the flight crew's duty and rest time and found that they were within the limits established by Federal regulations.

On the basis of the initial information, investigators considered several possible causes for the in-flight breakup. These included a structural failure and decompression; detonation of a high-energy explosive device such as a bomb exploding inside the airplane or a missile warhead exploding upon contact with the aircraft; and finally a fuel/air explosion in the center wing fuel tank.

Close examination of the wreckage revealed no evidence of preexisting aircraft structural faults that could have contributed to the in-flight breakup. It was suggested that the breakup could have been initiated by the separation of the forward cargo door from the aircraft. However, all of the latching cams remained attached to the pins and there were no indications of pre-impact failure of the hinges. Therefore, evidence indicates that the door was closed and locked at time of impact. Despite being unable to determine traces of explosive residue found in the wreckage, evidence indicated that the explosion did not result from the detonation of a high-energy explosive device. Accordingly the safety board concluded that the in-flight break up of TWA flight 800 was not initiated by a bomb or a missile strike. It was clear from the wreckage recovery locations that the first pieces to depart from the airplane were from the area in and around the wing and center section of the aircraft.

Several factors led to speculation that the accident might have been caused by a bomb or missile strike. These factors included heightened safety and security concerns because of the 1996 Olympics then being held in the United States, the fact that TWA flight 800 was an international flight, and the sudden and catastrophic nature of the in-flight breakup. In addition, numerous witnesses to the accident reported seeing a streak of light and then a fireball, which some people believed represented a missile destroying the airplane. Further, some anomalous primary radar targets were recorded by the Islip, New York, radar site in the general vicinity of TWA flight 800 at the time of the accident that apparently could not be explained. Accordingly, the Safety Board considered the possibility that a bomb exploded inside the airplane or that a missile warhead from a shoulder-launched missile exploded upon impact with the airplane.

Pieces of the forward portion of the wing and the fuselage directly forward of the wing were recovered, and among the first pieces to separate from the airplane. Most of the remainder of the airplane, including the wings, fuselage, and the empennage, was found in a relatively small area indicating that this portion of the airplane remained intact for some time after the separation of the forward fuselage section.

According to the study, the combined load of normal cabin pressurization and vented overpressure generated a downward force on the fuselage belly structure and resulted in additional downward loading on the keel beam. Stress analysis showed that these loads were sufficient to cause separation of the forward portion of the keel beam from the lower skin panel and then to cause the keel beam to fracture about 22 inches aft of the mid spar. The report indicated that when the large piece of fuselage belly structure separated, a large opening in the bottom of the fuselage resulted.

As the belly structure separated, adjacent pieces of the remaining fuselage skin and structure continued to crack and tear. Nearly symmetric pieces of fuselage skin above the right side and left side of the large hole in the belly separated from the rest of the airplane in an outward, upward, and aft direction. A curl of metal was created on both of these two pieces at the final point of separation. After these pieces of fuselage skin separated, the hole in the fuselage extended across the entire bottom of the airplane between the main cabin window belts.

As the airplane continued to depressurize through the large hole in its underside, the nose of the airplane began to bend down, creating compression stresses, in the window belts above the hole. The window belts collapsed from these compression stresses and compression buckling spread upward toward the crown of the airplane, where evidence of tension failure was found. Subsequently, pieces of fuselage skin began to separate from right to left across the top of the airplane; some of these pieces had curls similar to the two symmetric curls below the window belt. This loss of fuselage structure around the airplane's circumference resulted in the separation of the airplane's forward fuselage from the remainder of the airplane, which included most of the wings, the aft fuselage, and the empennage. A study stated that upward crushing damage found on the lower portion of the aft fuselage indicated that most of this portion of the fuselage struck the water as a large single piece.

Determination

The National Transportation Safety Board determined that the probable cause of the TWA flight 800 accident was an explosion of the center wing fuel tank. This resulted from ignition of the flammable fuel-air mixture in the tank. The source of ignition for the explosion could not be determined with certainty. Of the sources evaluated by the investigation, the most likely was a short circuit outside of the fuel tank that allowed excessive voltage to enter it through electrical wiring associated with the fuel quantity indication system.

Contributing factors to the accident were the design concept that fuel tank explosions could be prevented solely by precluding all ignition sources. Also, the design and certification of the Boeing 747 with heat sources located beneath the center wing fuel tank with no means to reduce the heat transferred into the tank or to render the fuel vapor in the tank nonflammable.

Terrorism Attack

On the morning of September 11, 2001, the United States suffered the greatest catastrophe in its history. Nineteen Islamic hijackers took over four aircraft shortly after takeoff from Boston, Newark and Washington, D.C. Two were flown into each of the World Trade Center buildings in downtown New York City. The third was flown into the Pentagon Building in Washington, D.C. There is evidence that the fourth hijacked aircraft was headed for the Capitol building but somehow the male passengers fought with the hijackers and the aircraft crashed south of Pittsburgh, Pennsylvania.

At 8:00 A.M. American Airlines flight 11, a Boeing 767, took off from Boston airport enroute to Los Angeles, California, with sixty-five passengers and eleven crewmembers aboard. At 8:45 A.M. it was deliberately crashed into the north tower of the World Trade Center in New York City. Eighteen minutes later at 9:03 A.M., United Airlines flight 175, a Boeing 767 with fifty-six passengers and nine crewmembers on board was flown into the South Tower. It had departed Boston airport at 7:58 A.M. heading for Los Angeles, California.

At 9:43 A.M. American Airlines flight 77, a Boeing 757, was crashed into the Pentagon Building. It had taken off from Washington, D.C. Dulles International Airport at 8:10 A.M. bound for Los Angeles, California. This was shortly followed by United Airlines flight 93, also a Boeing 757, crashing in a field near Somerset, south of Pittsburgh, at 10:10 A.M. It had left Newark Airport at 8:01 A.M. with a destination of San Francisco, California.

The 110 story buildings were made of vertical steel columns encircled by steel beams that girded each tower. The intense heat of the fires of the burning jet fuel, which reached over a thousand degrees Fahrenheit, affected the steel. At 9:50 A.M. the South Tower collapsed, followed at 10:29 A.M. by the North Tower.

The debris of the two towers was estimated to be 1.2 million tons and was as high as an eight-story building. Normally 40,000 to 50,000 people worked in the twin towers. After the first crash some were able to go down the staircases and escape. More than 3,000 people were killed in these traumatic events. About 300 firemen and police, called when the first airplane struck the North Tower building, were caught under the collapse of the buildings.

It was determined that the hijackers had learned to fly in Florida and California, among other places in the United States. They also did simulator training in the Boeing 757 and 767 aircraft, not to take off or land but only to control it in flight. It was a well planned and executed terroristic attack.

Within minutes all flights throughout the country were grounded and those aircraft in the air were told to land immediately at the nearest airport. It was believed that other possible hijackers were planning to take over aircraft and crash into more government buildings. It was several days before aircraft were permitted to resume flying.

This horrific event caused untold losses of revenue to the air transportation industry. The air carriers had been suffering financial losses due to the effects of a recession throughout the country. It was feared that they could now be forced into bankruptcy. Thousands of their employees were laid-off from their jobs. Since the air transport industry is of vital concern to the economy and operation of the country, the United States government came to its aid with billions of dollars in subsidy.

The federal government imposed stronger surveillance and passenger screening at all airports, and sky marshals began flying on scheduled passenger flights.

ACCIDENT CATEGORY CHANGES

In an effort to provide more meaningful measures of airline safety, the National Transportation Safety Board developed classifications of accidents based on the severity of the accident. Development of the new categories was mandated by Congress in the Fiscal 1997 Federal Aviation Administration Reauthorization Act.

The new categories did not change the existing definition of an aircraft accident. The purpose of the change was to make it easier for the public to understand the accident status of U.S. airlines. The NTSB defines an aircraft accident as occurring when a person is seriously injured or dies, and/or an aircraft is substantially damaged.

The four categories of accidents are as follows:

1. Major accident—Defined as one that results in the destruction of an aircraft operated under FAR Part 121, or in which there were multiple fatalities, or that an aircraft operated under Part 121 is substantially damaged and at least one fatality occurs. Any one condition must occur. The old definition of an accident did not consider what section of the Federal Aviation Regulations an aircraft was operating under at the time an accident occurs.

2. Severe accident—When only one fatality occurs and an aircraft operated under Part 121 is not substantially damaged, or there was at least one serious injury and the aircraft was substantially damaged.

3. Injury accident—A non-fatal accident having at least one serious injury but without substantial damage to an aircraft. The Safety Board said this type of accident often involves abrupt aircraft maneuvers, turbulence, evacuation injury or scalding.

4. Damage accident—An accident in which there are no fatalities or serious injuries but an aircraft is substantially damaged.

Another analysis would report the number of passengers who receive fatal or serious injuries and provide their corresponding injury rates by passenger miles flown and/or enplanements instead of fatalities or injuries per million passenger miles flown. The Safety Board also is proposing to report a list of accidents that resulted in fatalities on board U.S. airlines that would include the name of the airline, aircraft type, the number of passenger fatalities and survivors.

SOURCES OF ACCIDENT INFORMATION

The Safety Board conducts an accident investigation in a public environment. For a major accident press briefings are held on the scene in the days immediately following the accident. A public docket containing factual information about the accident is available within a few months. Usually within a year, the Board Members will review a draft of the accident report in a public meeting at Safety Board headquarters in Washington,

D.C. Soon after the meeting the Board's Public Affairs Office issues an abstract containing the Board's conclusions, probable cause statement and safety recommendations from the accident report. The final report of a major accident is subsequently printed for public distribution. For non-major accidents the investigator-in-charge is available to answer media inquiries; a public docket containing factual information is also available. Non-major accident reports generally are available in a computerized format (brief of accident) and are issued about a year after the accident. Almost all factual information about an accident and all final documents issued by the Board are available to the public in some form.

The following is a listing of sources of information from the NTSB. An asterisk (*) indicates that the information can be found on the Internet; (ntsb.gov).

- **Public Affairs Office:** (202) 314-6100. Press releases*, speeches*, annual reports to Congress, post-meeting abstracts, news media liaison.

- **Public Inquiries Branch:** (800) 877-6799 or (202) 314-6551. All docketed material such as factual reports on pending accidents and final accident reports. Accidents must be cited by date and location of occurrence.

- **Office of Safety Recommendations:** (202) 314-6170. List of Most Wanted Safety Recommendations*, recommendation letters (cited by recommendation number), printouts of status of pending recommendations (by number).

- **Freedom of Information Act Officer:** (202) 314-6540 or (800) 877-6799.

- **Administrative Law Judges:** (202) 314-6150. Inquiries about pending appeals of airmen, mechanics or manners to certificate actions taken by the Department of Transportation. See below for copies of Opinions and Orders. Law Judge hearings are open to the public.

- **Analysis and Data Division:** (202) 314-6550. Data base research of aviation accidents and incidents. Produces monthly* and annual* aviation accident statistics.

- **National Technical Information Service:** (800) 553-6847. An agency of the Department of Commerce, NTIS sells Safety Board publications such as final accident reports, safety studies, statistical compilations and Opinions and Orders. NTIS publication numbers* may be obtained from the NTSB Public Inquiries Branch.

AVIATION ACCIDENTS AND SAFETY PERFORMANCE

The four leading causes of aviation accidents in the United States, in order of occurrence, are human error (flightcrew members, air traffic controller), weather (fog, ice, windshear), airframe or engine failure, and maintenance. A fifth cause that shows up in worldwide accident statistics (currently third just behind weather) is sabotage/military action. Attempts to rank causal factors more precisely can be misleading due to low accident rate among U.S. carriers and difficulties inherent in determining accident causes.

Leading Causes of Aviation Accidents
- **human error**
- **weather**
- **airplane failure**
- **maintenance**
- **sabotage/military action**

Most accidents involve multiple factors. Finding the primary cause can be difficult and may require subjective judgments. The National Transportation Safety Board must at times decide which is the primary cause by consensus, leaving room for disagreement. Some potentially important factors, such as an airline's management philosophy, are difficult to assess in terms of causal factors. Accidents can also be analyzed in a variety of ways including primary cause, initial cause, sequence of events, phase of operation, type of operation, etc., and over different time frames, which can lead to confusing results.

Despite problems with the fault-finding process, most analyses point to human error, usually on the part of the flightcrew, as the leading cause of aviation accidents. The Office of Technology Assessment analyzed 22 fatal air carrier accidents in the United States. It found that human error was the initiating factor in approximately 60% of the accidents, and a causal factor in over 70%. In response to recommendations made by the Office of Technology Assessment, Congress passed the Aviation Safety Research Act of 1988 (P.L. 100-591), directing the Federal Aviation Administration to establish a Human Factors Research Program. A program has been established and is currently under the direction of a Human Factors Coordinating Committee.

Studies carried out by the National Aeronautics and Space Administration (NASA) over 10 years indicate that most pilot-error accidents are the result of a breakdown in communications among crew members, not a lack of skills. These studies point to a deficiency in pilot training procedures in areas related to human factors.

A Flight Safety study prepared by its Approach and Landing Accident Reduction Task Force found that a frequent cause of an aircraft accident on landing is the failure to establish an early, stabilized approach. According to the study, 30 percent of pilots involved in approach and landing accidents were too fast or too high on the approach and 83 percent of pilots did not execute a go-around or missed approach when conditions dictated such action was necessary.

The task force also identified high workload situations caused by a need to maintain the company's schedules and the pilot's acceptance of demanding air traffic control clearances. It also determined that although the percentage of time spent making an approach and landing accounts for only 16 percent of a typical flight, 56 percent of accidents occur in this phase.

The following is extracted from a report of a study conducted by the Boeing Commercial Airplane Group.

The safety record of the world's airlines will decline in the next 20 years unless the industry focuses more on preventing accidents than determining what caused them, according to a study conducted by the Boeing Commercial Airplane Group. The studies indicate that airline safety will decline further as more new aircraft are added to the global airline fleet. The global airline jet fleet currently stands at 11,507 active aircraft. The fleet will grow to 18,200 aircraft by the year 2010 and could reach 19,700 by 2014. Based on projected fleet growth one jet transport hull loss every week will occur by 2010 unless strong, preventive measures are taken by the industry to reduce accidents. We have to change from concentrating on the cause of an accident to how it could have been prevented.

Boeing's studies are based on transport category, commercial jet-engine aircraft with takeoff gross weights in excess of 60,000 lbs. The company has based its conclusions upon accident data from around the world, except for information from China and the former Soviet Union, which is generally not reliable.

Traditionally, accident investigation analysis has centered on a single, primary cause when most accidents involve a chain of events. As a result, such procedures tend to limit the scope of future accident prevention actions. Boeing advocates creation and implementation of prevention strategies designed to interrupt and thwart the accident process before it progresses too far.

More than 80% of the accidents were caused by the flightcrew. In another series of accidents, about 58% were caused by practices or procedures used by the airline; nearly 38% were the fault of air traffic control or an airport facility, 25% were caused by the aircraft and 18% by maintenance actions. Weather caused less than 10% of the accidents.

In its study of hull loss accidents Boeing found that on scheduled flights of 1.6 hr. duration, nearly 70% of the accidents occurred during takeoff and landing operations. Specifically, 24.8% of the accidents occurred during the crucial takeoff and initial climb phases, which represents a mere 2% of total flight time. Analysis of airline hull losses since 1968 shows a clear correlation between *controlled flight into terrain* (CFIT) and the use of *ground proximity warning system* equipment. GPWS warns pilots that the aircraft is too low and in close proximity to terrain. Since 1974–1975, when GPWS was implemented by airlines, 44 accidents have occurred involving aircraft that did not have the system installed, according to Boeing. Only about 5% of the world's airline aircraft lack such equipment.

Another 43.4% of the accidents occurred during the final approach and landing phases, which account for only 4% of the flight time. The U.S. airline system of hub-and-spoke airports tends to increase the possibility of such accidents by virtue of the number of takeoff and landing operations at such facilities.

Although takeoff and landing operations accounted for nearly 70% of all accidents since 1959, CFIT remains the leading cause of airline deaths worldwide. During the past decade, an average of 550 people have died each year in CFIT-related accidents, according to Boeing's studies.

About five or six CFIT accidents occur each year worldwide, and estimates indicate that 75% of these accidents happen during non-precision instrument approach procedures that lack vertical, or glideslope, guidance. In such cases, a GPWS probably would have provided warning of the impending crash. Boeing's analysis indicates that slow, incorrect or no pilot response to GPWS alerts was responsible for at least 19 accidents since 1975.

Boeing's study of 63 accidents in the U.S. and Canada from 1982–1991, for example, showed that prevention strategies applicable to the flying pilot's adherence to procedures may have been a factor in as much as 41% of the crashes. This compares with 43% of 38 accidents in Europe during the same period, 48% of 47 accidents in Latin America, 32% of 37 accidents in Africa and 52% of 37 accidents in Asia. They found that strategies linked to improvements in aircraft design, maintenance, air traffic control and basic piloting skills would have played important roles in preventing the accidents. Basic piloting skills, for example, were a factor in 16% of the U.S.-Canada accidents, 34% of those occurring in Latin America, 29% in Africa and 32% in Asia.

AVIATION SAFETY ECONOMICS

Aviation safety is a matter of economics. The viability of the entire $75 billion plus commercial aviation industry depends on having an almost zero accident rate. The best ever performance of the industry in safety occurred during the years 1980–1984. The period from 1985–1989 was an abrupt reversal of the trend. If the system cannot be made more efficient safely, then the economic foundation of the entire commercial aviation industry could be threatened with collapse. The airlines must make their aircraft more crashworthy. The industry competes for consumer dollars based on its safety efforts as well as price and convenience. There is growing evidence that the cost-cutting, overscheduling, and crowded conditions at airports are eroding the safety margins and posing a growing threat to the flying public.

> **The airlines must make their aircraft more crashworthy.**

Many people involved in the airline industry agree that the most pressing challenge facing safety is the aging of the commercial jet transport fleet. The airlines—pressed for dollars—will skimp on maintenance in order to cut costs. Fraud and falsification of maintenance records is also a concern. The FAA is understaffed and underfunded and is forced to rely on the good faith of the airlines to comply with safety. Unfortunately the FAA does not have the resources or the inspection force to adequately police the airlines.

Cockpit Resource Management (CRM) training is designed to rid the flightcrew of authoritarian attitudes. The idea is to open communications among flightcrew so that they will act as a team.

> **The U.S. air carrier industry is one of the safest in the world.**

These are troubled times for the industry. Airlines are losing billions of dollars a year, the FAA is overwhelmed with work and underwhelmed with resources, the aircraft fleet is aging, the sky is growing increasingly crowded, terrorism is a growing threat, and the aviation system, when taken as a whole, appears to be suffering a slow motion slide toward less safe conditions.

The U.S. air carrier industry is one of the safest in the world. One observing spokesman jokingly said that the only country with a better safety record is the Republic of Zykrestand. They have only one small airplane and do not know how to fly it.

TRANSPORTATION ACCIDENT STATISTICS—2000

Transportation fatalities in the United States rose 0.2 percent in the year 2000 over those in 1999, according to preliminary figures contained in a report released by the National Transportation Safety Board.

Preliminary figures show that in 2000, 44,186 persons died in highway, rail, marine, aviation and pipeline accidents, up from 44,093 in 1999. Increases in fatalities were registered in highway, aviation, and pipeline while rail and marine fatalities declined.

Highway fatalities, which account for more than 94 percent of all transportation deaths, rose from 41,717 in 1999 to 41,800 in 2000. Fatalities at roadway/railway grade crossings increased from 402 to 425.

Rail fatalities declined from 783 to 770, despite an increase in pedestrian fatalities associated with intercity rail operations. Deaths among passengers on trains declined from 14 to 4. Fatalities occurring on light rail, heavy rail and commuter rail dropped from 196 to 194.

Marine fatalities dropped from 874 to 801, with most fatalities occurring in recreational boating. Cargo transport, commercial fishing, and commercial passenger deaths all decreased from the previous year.

Aviation deaths rose from 693 to 777. The vast majority of deaths in aviation occur in general aviation (592 deaths). Airline fatalities increased from 12 to 92, of which 88 were aboard Alaska Airlines flight 261, which crashed off the coast of California. Air taxi fatalities increased from 38 to 71. Detailed aviation statistics are found on the NTSB web site, www.ntsb.gov.

Pipeline fatalities increased from 26 to 38. Deaths related to gas pipelines increased from 22 to 37, while liquid pipeline fatalities decreased from 4 to 1.

Aviation statistics are compiled by the NTSB. Numbers for all other modes are from the respective Department of Transportation modal agencies. All numbers for 2000 are preliminary. (Table 9.1 and see Figure 9.1.)

Table 9.1. National Transportation Safety Board 1999–2000 U.S. Transportation Fatalities

		1999	2001[1]
Highway	Passenger cars	20,862	20,455
	Light trucks and vans	11,265	11,439
	Pedestrians	4,939	4,727
	Motorcycles	2,483	2,680
	Pedalcycles	754	738
	Medium and heavy trucks	759	746
	Buses	59	31
	Other	596	984
	Total	**41,717**	**41,800**
Grade Crossings[2]		(402)	(425)
Rail	Intercity[3]		
	Trespassers and nontrespassers[4]	530	544
	Employees and contractors	43	28
	Passengers on trains	14	4
	Transit[5]		
	Light, heavy, and commuter rail	196	194
	Total	**783**	**770**
Marine	Recreational boating	734	701
	Cargo transport	47	36
	Commercial fishing[6]	57	41
	Commercial passengers	36	23
	Total	**874**	**801**
Aviation	General aviation	630	592
	Airlines	12	92
	Air taxi	38	71
	Commuter	12	5
	Foreign/unregistered[7]	1	17
	Total	**693**	**777**
Pipeline	Gas	22	37
	Liquids	4	1
	Total	**26**	**38**
	Total	44,093	44,186

[1]Numbers for 2000 are preliminary estimates. Aviation data come from the NTSB; all other data are from the U.S. Department of Transportation (DOT).

[2]Grade crossing fatalities are not counted as a separate category for determining the grand totals because they are included in the highway and rail categories, as appropriate.

[3]Data reported to Federal Rail Administration (FRA).

[4]Does not include motor vehicle occupants killed at grade crossings.

[5]Data reported to Federal Transit Administration (FTA). Fatalities for commuter rail operations may also be reported to the FRA and may be included in the intercity railroad fatalities.

[6]Refers to operational fatalities.

[7]Includes non-U.S. registered aircraft involved in accidents in the United States.

FLIGHTS OF FANCY

The Chicken Gun Story

It has been reported that apparently the Federal Aviation Administration has a gun that fires a chicken (a store-bought dead one of course) at airplane windshields to test the strength of the windshield. Midair collisions with birds are a serious problem for aircraft, particularly during takeoff and landing. An unidentified railroad company (alleged to be British Rail), supposedly borrowed this gun when they were testing a new high-speed locomotive. They wanted to see if their locomotive's windshield would be able to withstand the impact of a bird that might not get out of the way of the train in time.

They carefully set up the gun according the FAA specifications, loaded a chicken into it, and fired. They were amazed to find that not only did the windshield not stop the chicken, it did not even slow it down. The bird shattered the windshield, penetrated right through the back of the operator's seat, and embedded itself about eight inches deep in the rear wall of the cab.

The flabbergasted railroad officials sent the results of the experiment to the FAA and wanted to know what had gone wrong to cause such destruction. After several months' investigation into the ill-fated experiment, the FAA returned their findings. The terse reply was "Use a thawed chicken."

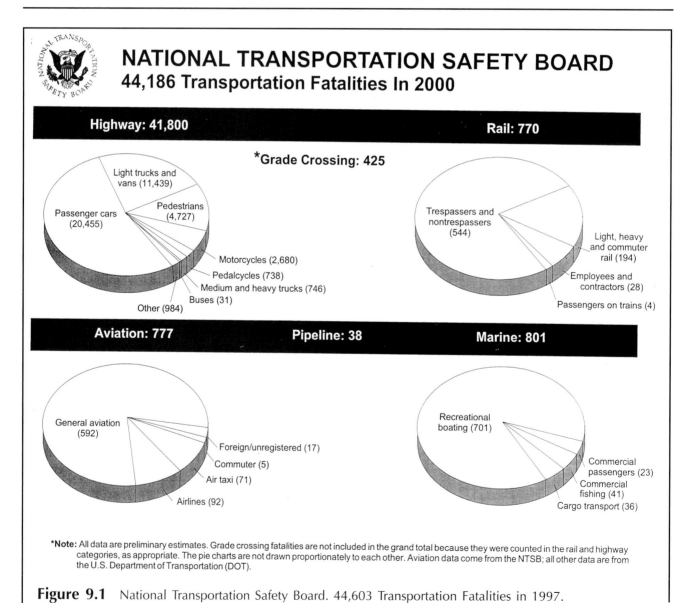

Figure 9.1   National Transportation Safety Board. 44,603 Transportation Fatalities in 1997.

TRANSPORTATION SAFETY WORLD WIDE WEB LINKS

www.aashto.org/main/home_page.html American Association of State Highway Transportation Officials
www.air-transport.org/ Air Transportation Association
http://bst-tsb.gc.ca/ Transportation Safety Board of Canada
www.ntsb.gov National Transportation Safety Board
www.taic.org.nz New Zealand Transport Accident Investigation Commission
www.dot.gov U.S. Department of Transportation
www.dot.gov/useful.html Dot Links
www.cam.org/~icao/ International Civil Aviation Organization
www.camc.ca The Canadian Aviation Maintenance Council
www.imo.org International Maritime Organization
http://www.maiif.net Marine Accident Investigators' International Forum
www.amtrak.com National Railroad Passenger Corporation
www.aar.com Association of American Railroads
www.trucking.org American Trucking Association
http://raru.adelaide.edu.au/icadts/ ICADTS
http://nasdac.faa.gov/safety_data Federal Aviation Administration safety data base
www.ite.org Institute of Transportation Engineers
www.nas.edu/trb/indexf2.html Transportation Research Board of the National Academy of Sciences
www.nas.edu/trb/link/govf2.html Transportation Research Board global transportation links page
www.apta.com American Public Transit Association
www.saferoads.org Advocates for Highway & Auto Safety
www.hwysafety.org Insurance Institute for Highway Safety
www.startext.net/homes/mikem Air Safety Investigation Resource
www.db.erau.edu/www_virtual_lib/aviation/research.html Aviation Research
www.albany.edu/sph/injr_012.htm The Electronic Highway Safety Library
http://dragon.princeton.edu/~dhb/index.html The Directory of Transportation Resources
www.nga.org The National Governors' Association
www.avweb.com AVweb—an aviation magazine and news service
www.flightsafety.org Flight Safety Foundation
http://www.alpa.org Air Line Pilots Association
http://awgnet.com/safety/isasi.htm International Society of Air Safety Investigators
www.cami.jccbi.gov FAA Office of Aviation Medicine/Civil Aeromedical Institution
www.casa.gov.au Civil Aviation Authority—Australia
www.aicc.org Aviation Industry Computer Committee
http://www.dot.gov/dotinfo/uscg/hq/g-m/gmhome.htm U.S. Coast Guard Marine Safety Site
www.wdi.co.uk/msnet/home.html Marine Safety Network
www.oli.org Operation Lifesaver—Rail/Highway grade crossing safety
www.rotor.com Helicopter Association International
www.swisspropilot.ch Swiss Professional Pilots Association
http://www.irlgov.ie/tec/aaiu Irish Air Accident Investigation Unit
www.aviation.org Aviation Safety Connection
www.generalaviation.org/safety.htm General Aviation Manufacturers Association
www.usroads.com/index.html Road Safety Information
www.engr.usask.ca/tc/index.html University of Saskatchewan Transportation Centre
www.iht.org Institute of Highways and Transportation
www.pacts.org.uk United Kingdom—Parliamentary Advisory Council for Transport Safety

AVIATION TRANSPORTATION FATALITIES

The National Transportation Safety Board released statistics showing that U.S. civil aviation accidents in the year 2000 decreased to 1,975 from 2,053 the previous year, while the number of fatalities increased from 697 to 748.

The Safety Board reported that 92 persons were killed in accidents involving U.S. air carriers operating under 14 CFR 121 (generally aircraft with 10 or more seats or large cargo airplanes). These included: 88 persons who died in the crash of Alaska Airlines flight 261 off the coast of California on January 31; three crewmembers of an Emery Worldwide Airlines' DC-8 that crashed February 16, near Sacramento, CA; and an American Airlines flight attendant who was fatally injured during an emergency evacuation on November 20, in Miami, FL.

There were 49 accidents involving Part 121 scheduled carriers, up one from the previous year, although the accident rate for this category per 100,000 departures decreased from 0.449 to 0.440.

No fatalities were reported for charter airlines operating under 14 CFR 121. The number of accidents increased from four in 1999 to five in 2000; the accident rate per 100,000 departures went from 0.979 to 1.131.

There were five fatalities in Part 135 scheduled airline service in 2000, down from 12 in 1999. The accident rate per 100,000 departures dropped to 1.231 from 1.546.

Air taxis reported an increase to 80 accidents in 2000 from 73 the year before, with the number of fatalities at 71—almost double the total for 1999. The accident rate per 100,000 hours increased to 3.29 from 3.23.

Accidents involving U.S. general aviation aircraft (virtually all except Part 121, Part 135 and military aircraft) fell to 1,835 from 1,913 in 1999. Fatal accidents decreased by one in 2000 to 341, with the number of fatalities also falling to 592 from 630. The general aviation rate per 100,000 flight hours in 2000 decreased to 5.96 from 6.49 the previous year.

Foreign registered aircraft accounted for 11 accidents in the U.S. in 2000, with eight fatalities. The previous year's report showed a total of six accidents with no fatalities.

Current aviation accident data can be found on the NTSB web site http://www.ntsb.gov/aviation/Stats.htm.

Aviation accident statistics released on March 27, 2002 by The National Transportation Safety Board show a decline in the scheduled U.S. airline accident rate in 2001.

In 2001 there were 36 accidents on U.S. scheduled airlines, including the four crashes of September 11. Because the crashes of September 11, 2001 were the results of criminal activity, those crashes are included in the totals for scheduled U.S. airline accidents and fatalities, but are not used for the purpose of accident rate computation. The remaining 32 accidents in 2001 resulted in an accident rate of .317 per 100,000 departures. These numbers represent a decrease from 2000, when 51 accidents were reported for a rate of .463 accidents per 100,000 departures.

The 531 fatalities associated with crashes involving U.S. scheduled airliners last year is the highest total since 1977, when two jumbo jets collided in the Canary Islands. Half of last year's fatalities—265—occurred aboard the four hijacked airliners on September 11. Other than a ground worker who was struck by a propeller at an airport in August, the remaining fatalities (265) occurred when American Airlines flight 587 crashed in New York on November 12.

Accident rates for both scheduled and non-scheduled 14 CFR part 135 service decreased in 2001. The scheduled service rate decreased from 1.965 accidents per 100,000 departures in 2000 to 1.407 in 2001. For unscheduled, on-demand air taxis, the rate decreased from 2.28 to 2.12 per 100,000 flight hours.

Despite reporting fewer accidents in 2001, the accident rate for general aviation aircraft increased slightly from 6.33 accidents per 100,000 flight hours in 2000 to 6.56 accidents in 2001. General aviation was the only category of air transportation to report an increase in its accident rate, which is attributable to the fact that less hours were flown by general aviation aircraft in 2001 than in 2000.

Table 9.2 Accidents Involving Passenger Fatalities U.S. Airlines (Part 121)

The NTSB wishes to make clear to all users of the following list of accidents that the information it contains cannot, by itself, be used to compare the safety either of operators or of aircraft types. Airlines that have operated the greatest number of flights and flight hours could be expected to have suffered the greatest number of fatal-to-passenger accidents (assuming that such accidents are random events, and not the result of some systemic deficiency). Similarly, the most used aircraft types would tend to be involved in such accidents more than lesser used types. The NTSB also cautions the user to bear in mind when attempting to compare today's airline system to prior years that airline activity (and hence exposure to risk) has risen by almost 100% from the first year depicted to the last.

Date	Location	Operator	Aircraft Type	Fatal	Surv
01/13/82	Washington, DC	Air Florida	Boeing 737-222	70	4
01/23/82	Boston, MA	World Airways	McDonnell Douglas DC-10-30	2	198
07/09/82	New Orleans, LA	Pan American World Airways	Boeing 727-235	137	0
11/08/82	Honolulu, HI	Pan American World Airways	Boeing 747-100	1	274
01/09/83	Brainerd, MN	Republic Airlines	Convair 580-11-A	1	29
10/11/83	Pinckneyville, IL	Air Illinois	Hawker Siddeley HS-748-2A	7	0
01/01/85	La Paz, Bolivia	Eastern Air Lines	Boeing 727-225	21	0
01/21/85	Reno, NV	Galaxy Airlines	Lockheed 188C	64	1
08/02/85	Dallas/Ft Worth, TX	Delta Airlines	Lockheed L-1011-385-1	126	26
09/06/85	Milwaukee, WI	Midwest Express Airlines	Douglas DC-9-14	27	0
12/12/85	Gander, Newfoundland	Arrow Airways	Douglas DC-8-63	248	0
02/04/86	Near Athens, Greece	Trans World Airlines	Boeing 727-231	4	110
02/14/87	Durango, Mexico	Ports of Call	Boeing 707-323B	1	125
08/16/87	Romulus, MI	Northwest Airlines	McDonnell Douglas DC-9-82	148	1
11/15/87	Denver, CO	Continental Airlines	McDonnell Douglas DC-9-14	25	52
12/07/87	San Luis Obispo, CA	Pacific Southwest Airlines	British Aerospace BAE-146-200	38	0
08/31/88	Dallas/Ft Worth, TX	Delta Airlines	Boeing 727-232	12	89
12/21/88	Lockerbie, Scotland	Pan American World Airways	Boeing 747-121	243	0
02/08/89	Santamaria, Azores	Independent Air	Boeing 707	137	0
02/24/89	Honolulu, HI	United Airlines	Boeing 747-122	9	328
07/19/89	Sioux City, IA	United Airlines	McDonnell Douglas DC-10-10	110	175
09/20/89	Flushing, NY	USAir	Boeing 737-400	2	55
12/27/89	Miami, FL	Eastern Air Lines	Boeing 727-225B	1	46
10/03/90	Cape Canaveral, FL	Eastern Air Lines	McDonnell Douglas DC-9-31	1	90
12/03/90	Romulus, MI	Northwest Airlines	McDonnell Douglas DC-9-14	7	33
02/01/91	Los Angeles, CA	USAir	Boeing 737-300	20	63
03/03/91	Colorado Spgs, CO	United Airlines	Boeing 737-291	20	0
03/22/92	Flushing, NY	USAir	Fokker 28-4000	25	22
07/02/94	Charlotte, NC	USAir	Douglas DC-9-30	37	20
09/08/94	Aliquippa, PA	USAir	Boeing B-737-300	127	0
10/31/94	Roselawn, IN	American Eagle	ATR-72-212	64	0
12/20/95	Cali, Colombia	American Airlines	Boeing B-757	152	4
05/11/96	Miami, FL	ValuJet Airlines	McDonnell Douglas DC-9	105	0
07/07/96	Pensacola, FL	Delta Airlines	McDonnell Douglas MD-88	2	140
07/17/96	Moriches, NY	Trans World Airlines	Boeing 747	212	0
08/02/97	Lima, Peru	Continental Airlines	Boeing 757-200	1	141
12/28/97	Pacific Ocean	United Airlines	Boeing 747	1	373
06/01/99	Little Rock, AR	American Airlines	McDonnell Douglas MD-80	10	129
01/31/00	Point Mugu, CA	Alaska Airlines	McDonnell Douglas MD-83	83	0

Source: National Transportation Safety Board

Table 9.3   Accidents Involving Passenger Fatalities U.S. Commuters (Part 135)

The NTSB wishes to make clear to all users of the following list of accidents that the information it contains cannot, by itself, be used to compare the safety either of operators or of aircraft types. Airlines that have operated the greatest number of flights and flight hours could be expected to have suffered the greatest number of fatal-to-passenger accidents (assuming that such accidents are random events, and not the result of some systemic deficiency). Similarly, the most used aircraft types would tend to be involved in such accidents more than lesser used types. The NTSB also cautions the user to bear in mind when attempting to compare today's airline system to prior years that airline activity (and hence exposure to risk) has risen by more than 35% from the first year depicted to the last.

Accident Date	Location	Operator (DBA)	Aircraft Type	Passengers Fatal	Passengers Surv
08/17/1983	Peach Springs, AZ	Las Vegas Airlines	Piper PA-31-350	9	0
03/05/1984	Cumberland, MD	Cumberland Airlines	Piper PA-31	2	0
07/21/1984	Tau, Manua	ISL South Pacific Island	DeHavilland DHC-6-300	1	10
08/02/1984	Vieques, PR	Vieques Air Link, Inc.	Britten-Norman BN-2A Islander	8	0
08/24/1984	San Luis Obispo, CA	Wings West Airlines, Inc.	Beech C-99	13	0
09/07/1984	Naples, FL	ProvincetownBoston Airlines	Cessna 402C	1	4
12/06/1984	Jacksonville, FL	ProvincetownBoston Airlines	Embraer Bandeirante EMB-110P1	11	0
12/17/1984	Bainbridge, NY	Susquehanna Airlines, Inc.	Piper PA-23-250	2	0
02/04/1985	Soldotna, AK	North Pacific Airlines	Beech 65-A80	7	0
02/06/1985	Altus, OK	Altus Airline, Inc.	Cessna 402B	1	0
04/26/1985	New York, NY	New York Helicopters	Aerospatiale SA360C Dauphin	1	5
08/25/1985	Auburn, ME	Bar Harbor Airlines	Beech 99	6	0
09/23/1985	Grottoes, VA	Henson Airlines	Beech B99	12	0
11/01/1985	Bethel, AK	Hermens Air, Inc.	Cessna 208	1	2
03/13/1986	Alpena, MI	Simmons Airlines	Embraer EMB-110P1	2	5
10/28/1986	St. Croix, VI	Virgin Island Seaplane Shuttle	Grumman G-73	1	12
01/15/1987	Kearns, UT	Sky West Airlines Inc. (Sky West Airlines/Western Expr)	Swearingen SA-226TC	6	0
03/04/1987	Romulus, MI	Fisher Brothers Aviation Inc. (Northwest Airlink)	CASA C-212-CC	7	9
04/01/1987	Anchorage, AK	Wilbur's Flight Operations (Wilbur's Inc.)	Cessna 402	1	0
11/23/1987	Homer, AK	Ryan Air Service, Inc.	Beech 1900C	16	3
12/23/1987	Kenai, AK	South Central Air, Inc.	Piper PA-31-350	5	2
12/23/1987	Maunaloa, HI	Panorama Air Tours (Panorama Air Tours)	Piper PA-31-350	7	0
01/19/1988	Bayfield, CO	Trans Colorado Airliness (Trans Colorado)	Fairchild SA-227-AC	7	8
02/19/1988	Cary, NC	Avair, Inc. (American Eagle)	Fairchild SA-227-AC	10	0
04/19/1989	Pelican, AK	Channel Flying Service	DeHavilland DHC-2	1	0
07/30/1989	Haines, AK	Skagway Air Service	Piper PA-32-301	2	2
10/28/1989	Halawa, Molokai, HI	Aloha Islandair	DeHavilland DHC-6-300	18	0
12/26/1989	Pasco, WA	NPA/United Express (United Express)	British Aerospace BAE-3101	4	0
09/03/1990	Kaltag, AK	Frontier Flying Service	Piper PA-31-325	3	6
02/01/1991	Los Angeles, CA	Skywest Airlines, Inc.	Fairchild SA-227-AC	10	0
04/05/1991	Brunswick, GA	Atlantic Southeast Airlines	Embraer EMB-120RT	20	0
07/10/1991	Birmingham, AL	L'Express Airlines, Inc.	Beech C99	12	1
08/20/1991	Ketchikan, AK	Temsco Helicopters, Inc. (Temsco Airlines)	Pilatus Britten-Norman BN-2A-26 Islander	3	0

Accident Date	Location	Operator (DBA)	Aircraft Type	Passengers Fatal	Passengers Surv
09/11/1991	Eagle Lake, TX	Continental Express	Embraer 120	11	0
12/10/1991	Temple Bar, AZ	Las Vegas Airlines, Inc.	Piper PA-31-350	4	0
01/03/1992	Gabriels, NY	Commutair (USAir Express)	Beech 1900C	1	1
01/23/1992	Clewiston, FL	Air Sunshine Inc.	Cessna 402C	1	0
06/07/1992	Mayaguez, PR	Executive Air Charter, Inc. (American Eagle)	CASA 212	3	0
06/08/1992	Anniston, AL	GP Express Airlines, Inc.	Beech C99	2	2
10/27/1992	Saipan, MP	Pacific Island Aviation, Inc	Cessna 310R	2	0
10/31/1992	Grand Junction, CO	Alpine Aviation (Alpine Air)	Piper PA-42	2	0
11/08/1992	Kiana, AK	Baker Aviation Inc.	Cessna 402C	2	0
04/03/1993	Nome, AK	Ryan Air Service, Inc	Cessna 207	1	0
07/12/1993	Las Vegas, NV	Air Nevada Airlines	Cessna 402C	2	0
12/01/1993	Hibbing, MN	Express Airlines II, Inc. (Northwest Airlink)	Jetstream BA-3100	16	0
01/07/1994	Columbus, OH	Atlantic Coast Airlines (United Express)	Jetstream 4101	2	3
12/13/1994	Morrisville, NC	Flagship Airlines (American Eagle)	BAE Jetstream 3201	15	5
08/21/1995	Carrollton, GA	Atlantic Southeast Airlines (Delta Connector)	Embraer EMB-120RT	7	19
11/19/1996	Quincy, IL	Great Lakes Aviation (United Express)	Beech 1900	10	0
01/09/1997	Ida, MI	Comair	Embraer 120	26	0
02/08/1997	St. Thomas, VI	Air Sunshine	Cessna 402C	2	2
04/10/1997	Wainwright, AK	Hageland Aviation	Cessna 208B	4	0
06/27/1997	Nome, AK	Olson Air Service	Cessna 207	1	0
11/08/1997	Barrow, AK	Hageland Aviation Services	Cessna 208B	7	0
09/05/1999	Westerly, RI	New England Airlines	Piper PA-32-260	2	2
12/07/1999	Bethel, AK	Grant Aviation	Cessna 207	5	0
09/18/2000	Nuiqsut, AK	Cape Smythe Air Service	Piper PA-31T3	4	5

Source: National Transportation Safety Board

Table 9.4 Accidents, Fatalities, and Rates—2000 Preliminary Statistics, U.S. Aviation

	Accidents		Fatalities		Flight Hours	Departures	Accidents per 100,000 Flight Hours		Accidents per 100,000 Departures	
	All	Fatal	Total	Aboard			All	Fatal	All	Fatal
U.S. air carriers operating under 14 CFR 121										
Scheduled	49	3	92	92	17,170,000	11,145,000	0.285	0.017	0.440	0.027
Nonscheduled	5	—	—	—	870,000	442,000	0.575	—	1.131	—
U.S. air carriers operating under 14 CFR 135										
Scheduled	12	1	5	5	550,000	975,000	2.182	0.182	1.231	0.103
Nonscheduled	80	22	71	68	2,430,000	n/a	3.29	0.91	n/a	n/a
U.S. general aviation	1,835	341	592	582	30,800,000	n/a	5.96	1.11	n/a	n/a
U.S. civil aviation	1,975	365	748	747						
Other accidents in the U.S.										
Foreign registered aircraft	11	4	8	8						
Unregistered aircraft	17	7	9	9						
Military aircraft that collided with civil aircraft	1	1	1	—						
U.S. registered aircraft operated abroad by foreign air carriers	7	3	35	31						

Notes: All data are preliminary.

Flight hours and departures are compiled and estimated by the Federal Aviation Administration.

n/a—not available.

Accidents and fatalities in the categories do not necessarily sum to the figures in U.S. civil aviation because of collisions involving aircraft in different categories.

Source: National Transportation Safety Board

Table 9.5 Accidents, Fatalities, and Rates—1982 through 2000, for U.S. Air Carriers Operating Under 14 CFR 121, Scheduled Service (Airlines)

(since March 20, 1997 includes aircraft with 10 or more seats formerly operated under 14 CFR 135)

Year	Accidents All	Accidents Fatal	Fatalities Total	Fatalities Aboard	Flight Hours	Miles Flown	Departures	Accidents per 100,000 Flight Hours All	Accidents per 100,000 Flight Hours Fatal	Accidents per 1,000,000 Miles Flown All	Accidents per 1,000,000 Miles Flown Fatal	Accidents per 100,000 Departures All	Accidents per 100,000 Departures Fatal
1982	16	4	234	222	6,697,770	2,806,885,000	5,162,346	0.224	0.045	0.0053	0.0011	0.291	0.058
1983	22	4	15	14	6,914,969	2,920,909,000	5,235,262	0.318	0.058	0.0075	0.0014	0.420	0.076
1984	13	1	4	4	7,736,037	3,258,910,000	5,666,076	0.168	0.013	0.0040	0.0003	0.229	0.018
1985	17	4	197	196	8,265,332	3,452,753,000	6,068,893	0.206	0.048	0.0049	0.0012	0.280	0.066
1986	21	2	5	4	9,495,158	3,829,129,000	6,928,103	0.211	0.011	0.0052	0.0003	0.289	0.014
1987	32	4	231	229	10,115,407	4,125,874,000	7,293,025	0.306	0.030	0.0075	0.0007	0.425	0.041
1988	29	3	285	274	10,521,052	4,260,785,000	7,347,575	0.266	0.019	0.0066	0.0005	0.381	0.027
1989	24	8	131	130	10,597,922	4,337,234,000	7,267,341	0.226	0.075	0.0055	0.0018	0.330	0.110
1990	22	6	39	12	11,524,726	4,689,287,000	7,795,761	0.191	0.052	0.0047	0.0013	0.282	0.077
1991	25	4	62	49	11,139,166	4,558,537,000	7,503,873	0.224	0.036	0.0055	0.0009	0.333	0.053
1992	16	4	33	31	11,732,026	4,767,344,000	7,515,373	0.136	0.034	0.0034	0.0008	0.213	0.053
1993	22	1	1	0	11,981,347	4,936,067,000	7,721,870	0.184	0.008	0.0045	0.0002	0.285	0.013
1994	19	4	239	237	12,292,356	5,112,633,000	7,824,802	0.146	0.033	0.0035	0.0008	0.230	0.051
1995	34	2	166	160	12,776,679	5,328,969,000	8,105,570	0.266	0.016	0.0064	0.0004	0.419	0.025
1996	32	3	342	342	12,971,676	5,449,997,000	7,851,298	0.247	0.023	0.0059	0.0006	0.408	0.038
See notes below													
1997	44	3	3	2	15,061,662	6,334,559,000	9,920,569	0.292	0.020	0.0069	0.0005	0.444	0.030
1998	43	1	1	0	15,929,308	6,348,484,000	10,540,481	0.270	0.006	0.0068	0.0002	0.408	0.009
1999	48	2	12	11	16,550,145	6,646,805,000	10,684,222	0.290	0.012	0.0072	0.0003	0.449	0.019
2000	49	3	91	92	17,170,000	6,755,500,000	11,145,000	0.285	0.017	0.0073	0.0004	0.440	0.027

Notes   Flight hours, miles, and departures are compiled by the Federal Aviation Administration.

Effective March 20, 1997, aircraft with 10 or more seats must conduct scheduled passenger operations under 14 CFR 121.

The 62 total fatalities in 1991 include the 12 persons killed aboard a Skywest commuter aircraft and the 22 persons killed aboard the USAir airliner when the two aircraft collided.

The following suicide/sabotage cases are included in "Accidents" and "Fatalities" but are excluded from accident rates in this table.

Year	Location	Operator	Fatalities Total	Aboard
1982	Honolulu, HI	Pan American	1	1
1986	Near Athens, Greece	Trans World	4	4
1987	San Luis Obispo, CA	Pacific Southwest	43	43
1988	Lockerbie, Scotland	Pan American	270	259
1994	Memphis, TN	Federal Express	0	0

Source: National Transportation Safety Board

Table 9.6 Accidents, Fatalities, and Rates—1982 through 2000, for U.S. Air Carriers Operating Under 14 CFR 121, Scheduled and Nonscheduled Service Airlines

since March 20, 1997 includes aircraft with 10 or more seats formerly operated under 14 CFR 135

Year	Accidents All	Accidents Fatal	Fatalities Total	Fatalities Aboard	Flight Hours	Miles Flown	Departures	Accidents per 100,000 Flight Hours All	Fatal	Accidents per 1,000,000 Miles Flown All	Fatal	Accidents per 100,000 Departures All	Fatal
1982	18	5	235	223	7,040,325	2,938,513,000	5,351,133	0.241	0.057	0.0058	0.0014	0.318	0.075
1983	23	4	15	14	7,298,799	3,069,318,000	5,444,374	0.315	0.055	0.0075	0.0013	0.422	0.073
1984	16	1	4	4	8,165,124	3,428,063,000	5,898,852	0.196	0.012	0.0047	0.0003	0.271	0.017
1985	21	7	526	525	8,709,894	3,631,017,000	6,306,759	0.241	0.080	0.0058	0.0019	0.333	0.111
1986	24	3	8	7	9,976,104	4,017,626,000	7,202,027	0.231	0.020	0.0057	0.0005	0.319	0.028
1987	34	5	232	230	10,645,192	4,360,521,000	7,601,373	0.310	0.038	0.0076	0.0009	0.434	0.053
1988	30	3	285	274	11,140,548	4,503,426,000	7,716,061	0.260	0.018	0.0064	0.0004	0.376	0.026
1989	28	11	278	276	11,274,543	4,605,083,000	7,645,494	0.248	0.098	0.0061	0.0024	0.366	0.144
1990	24	6	39	12	12,150,116	4,947,832,000	8,092,306	0.198	0.049	0.0049	0.0012	0.297	0.074
1991	26	4	62	49	11,780,610	4,824,824,000	7,814,875	0.221	0.034	0.0054	0.0008	0.333	0.051
1992	18	4	33	31	12,359,715	5,039,435,000	7,880,707	0.146	0.032	0.0036	0.0008	0.228	0.051
1993	23	1	1	0	12,706,206	5,249,469,000	8,073,173	0.181	0.008	0.0044	0.0002	0.285	0.012
1994	23	4	239	237	13,124,315	5,478,118,000	8,238,306	0.168	0.030	0.0040	0.0007	0.267	0.049
1995	36	3	168	162	13,505,257	5,654,069,000	8,457,465	0.267	0.022	0.0064	0.0005	0.426	0.035
1996	37	5	380	350	13,746,112	5,873,108,000	8,228,810	0.269	0.036	0.0063	0.0009	0.450	0.061
See notes below													
1997	49	4	8	6	15,838,109	6,691,693,000	10,313,826	0.309	0.025	0.0073	0.0006	0.475	0.039
1998	50	1	1	0	16,821,641	6,741,691,000	10,985,345	0.297	0.006	0.0074	0.0001	0.455	0.009
1999	52	2	12	11	17,381,999	7,032,971,000	11,092,839	0.299	0.012	0.0074	0.0003	0.469	0.018
2000	54	3	92	92	18,040,000	7,134,600,000	11,587,000	0.299	0.017	0.0076	0.0004	0.466	0.026

Notes 2000 data are preliminary.

Flight hours, miles, and departures are compiled by the Federal Aviation Administration.

Effective March 20, 1997, aircraft with 10 or more seats must conduct scheduled passenger operations under 14 CFR 121.

The 62 total fatalities in 1991 include the 12 persons killed aboard a Skywest commuter aircraft and the 22 persons killed aboard the USAir airliner when the two aircraft collided.

The following suicide/sabotage cases are included in "Accidents" and "Fatalities" but are excluded from accident rates in this table.

Year	Location	Operator	Fatalities Total	Aboard
1982	Honolulu, HI	Pan American	1	1
1986	Near Athens, Greece	Trans World	4	4
1987	San Luis Obispo, CA	Pacific Southwest	43	43
1988	Lockerbie, Scotland	Pan American	270	259
1994	Memphis, TN	Federal Express	0	0

Source: National Transportation Safety Board

Table 9.7 Passenger Injuries and Injury Rates—1982 through 2000,
for U.S. Air Carriers Operating Under 14 CFR 121

since March 20, 1997 includes aircraft with 10 or more seats formerly operated under 14 CFR 135

Year	Passenger Fatalities	Passenger Serious Injuries	Total Passenger Enplanements (millions)	Million Passenger Enplanements per Passenger Fatality
1982	210	17	299	1.4
1983	8	8	325	40.6
1984	1	6	352	352.0
1985	486	20	390	0.8
1986	4	23	427	106.8
1987	213	39	458	2.2
1988	255	44	466	1.8
1989	259	55	468	1.8
1990	8	23	483	60.4
1991	40	19	468	11.7
1992	25	14	494	19.8
1993	0	7	505	No Fatalities
1994	228	15	545	2.4
1995	152	15	561	3.7
1996	319	19	592	1.9
See notes below				
1997	2	18	641	320.5
1998	0	11	631	No Fatalities
1999	10	37	646	64.6
2000	83	9	665	8.0

Notes   Injuries exclude flight crew and cabin crew.

Effective March 20, 1997, aircraft with 10 or more seats must conduct scheduled passenger operations under 14 CFR 121.

Source: National Transportation Safety Board

Table 9.8 Number and Rate of Destroyed Aircraft—1982 through 2000,
for U.S. Air Carriers Operating Under 14 CFR 121

since March 20, 1997 includes aircraft with 10 or more seats formerly operated under 14 CFR 135

Year	Hull Losses	Aircraft Hours Flown (millions)	Hull Losses per Million Aircraft Hours Flown
1982	3	7.040	0.426
1983	2	7.299	0.274
1984	2	8.165	0.245
1985	8	8.710	0.918
1986	2	9.976	0.200
1987	5	10.645	0.470
1988	3	11.141	0.269
1989	7	11.275	0.621
1990	3	12.150	0.247
1991	5	11.781	0.424
1992	3	12.360	0.243
1993	1	12.706	0.079
1994	3	13.124	0.229
1995	3	13.505	0.222
1996	5	13.746	0.364
See note below			
1997	2	15.838	0.126
1998	0	16.822	0.000
1999	2	17.382	0.115
2000	3	18.040	0.166

Note Effective March 20, 1997, aircraft with 10 or more seats must conduct scheduled passenger operations under 14 CFR 121.

Source: National Transportation Safety Board

Table 9.9 Accidents, Fatalities, and Rates—1982 through 2000, for U.S. Air Carriers Operating Under 14 CFR 135, Scheduled Service

since March 20, 1997 only aircraft with fewer than 10 seats

Year	Accidents All	Accidents Fatal	Fatalities Total	Fatalities Aboard	Flight Hours	Miles Flown	Departures	Accidents per 100,000 Flight Hours All	Fatal	Accidents per 1,000,000 Miles Flown All	Fatal	Accidents per 100,000 Departures All	Fatal
1982	26	5	14	14	1,299,748	222,355,000	2,026,691	2.000	0.385	0.1169	0.0225	1.283	0.247
1983	16	2	11	10	1,510,908	253,572,000	2,328,430	1.059	0.132	0.0631	0.0079	0.687	0.086
1984	22	7	48	46	1,745,762	291,460,000	2,676,590	1.260	0.401	0.0755	0.0240	0.822	0.262
1985	18	7	37	36	1,737,106	300,817,000	2,561,463	1.036	0.403	0.0598	0.0233	0.703	0.273
1986	14	2	4	4	1,724,586	307,393,000	2,798,811	0.812	0.116	0.0455	0.0065	0.500	0.071
1987	33	10	59	57	1,946,349	350,879,000	2,809,918	1.695	0.514	0.0940	0.0285	1.174	0.356
1988	18	2	21	21	2,092,689	380,237,000	2,909,005	0.860	0.096	0.0473	0.0053	0.619	0.069
1989	19	5	31	31	2,240,555	393,619,000	2,818,520	0.848	0.223	0.0483	0.0127	0.674	0.177
1990	15	4	7	5	2,341,760	450,133,000	3,160,089	0.641	0.171	0.0333	0.0089	0.475	0.127
1991	23	8	99	77	2,291,581	433,900,000	2,820,440	1.004	0.349	0.0530	0.0184	0.815	0.284
1992	23	7	21	21	2,335,349	507,985,000	3,114,932	0.942	0.300	0.0433	0.0138	0.706	0.225
1993	16	4	24	23	2,638,347	554,549,000	3,601,902	0.606	0.152	0.0289	0.0072	0.444	0.111
1994	10	3	25	25	2,784,129	594,134,000	3,581,189	0.359	0.108	0.0168	0.0050	0.279	0.084
1995	12	2	9	9	2,627,866	550,377,000	3,220,262	0.457	0.076	0.0218	0.0036	0.373	0.062
1996	11	1	14	12	2,756,755	590,727,000	3,515,040	0.399	0.036	0.0186	0.0017	0.313	0.028
See notes below													
1997	16	5	46	46	982,764	251,650,000	1,394,096	1.628	0.509	0.0636	0.0199	1.148	0.359
1998	8	0	0	0	353,735	50,773,000	707,071	2.262	—	0.1576	—	1.131	—
1999	13	5	12	12	452,031	81,429,000	841,040	2.876	1.106	0.1596	0.0614	1.546	0.595
2000	12	1	5	5	550,000	112,000,000	975,000	2.182	0.182	0.1071	0.0089	1.231	0.103

Notes   Flight hours, miles, and departures are compiled by the Federal Aviation Administration.

Effective March 20, 1997, aircraft with 10 or more seats must conduct scheduled passenger operations under 14 CFR 121.

The 99 total fatalities in 1991 include the 12 persons killed aboard a Skywest commuter aircraft and the 22 persons killed aboard the USAir airliner when the two aircraft collided.

The following attempted suicide case is included in "Accidents" and "Fatalities" but is excluded from accident rates in this table.

			Fatalities	
Year	Location	Operator	Total	Aboard
1992	Lexington, KY	Mesaba Airlines	0	0

Source: National Transportation Safety Board

Table 9.10   Accidents, Fatalities, and Rates—1982 through 2000, for U.S. Air Carriers
Operating Under 14 CFR 135, Nonscheduled Service

(On-demand Air Taxis)

Year	Accidents		Fatalities		Flight Hours	Accidents per 100,000 Flight Hours	
	All	Fatal	Total	Aboard		All	Fatal
1982	132	31	72	72	3,008,000	4.39	1.03
1983	142	27	62	57	2,378,000	5.97	1.14
1984	146	23	52	52	2,843,000	5.14	0.81
1985	157	35	76	75	2,570,000	6.11	1.36
1986	118	31	65	61	2,690,000	4.39	1.15
1987	96	30	65	63	2,657,000	3.61	1.13
1988	102	28	59	55	2,632,000	3.88	1.06
1989	110	25	83	81	3,020,000	3.64	0.83
1990	107	29	51	49	2,249,000	4.76	1.29
1991	88	28	78	74	2,241,000	3.93	1.25
1992	76	24	68	65	1,967,000	3.86	1.22
1993	69	19	42	42	1,659,000	4.16	1.15
1994	85	26	63	62	1,854,000	4.58	1.40
1995	75	24	52	52	1,707,000	4.39	1.41
1996	90	29	63	63	2,029,000	4.44	1.43
1997	82	15	39	39	2,250,000	3.64	0.67
1998	77	17	45	41	2,751,000	2.80	0.62
1999	73	12	38	38	2,260,000	3.23	0.53
2000	80	22	71	68	2,430,000	3.29	0.91

Notes   2000 data are preliminary.

Flight hours are estimated by the Federal Aviation Administration (FAA).

Source: National Transportation Safety Board

Table 9.11   Accidents and Accident Rates by NTSB Classification—1982 through 2000, for U.S. Air Carriers Operating Under 14 CFR 121

(since March 20, 1997, includes aircraft with 10 or more seats formerly operated under 14 CFR 135)

Year	Accidents				Aircraft Hours Flown (millions)	Accidents per Million Hours Flown			
	Major	Serious	Injury	Damage		Major	Serious	Injury	Damage
1982	3	4	6	5	7.040	0.426	0.568	0.852	0.710
1983	4	2	9	8	7.299	0.548	0.274	1.233	1.096
1984	2	2	7	5	8.165	0.245	0.245	0.857	0.612
1985	8	2	5	6	8.710	0.918	0.230	0.574	0.689
1986	4	0	14	6	9.976	0.401	0.000	1.403	0.601
1987	5	1	12	16	10.645	0.470	0.094	1.127	1.503
1988	4	2	13	11	11.141	0.359	0.180	1.167	0.987
1989	8	4	6	10	11.275	0.710	0.355	0.532	0.887
1990	4	3	10	7	12.150	0.329	0.247	0.823	0.576
1991	5	2	10	9	11.781	0.424	0.170	0.849	0.764
1992	3	3	10	2	12.360	0.243	0.243	0.809	0.162
1993	1	2	12	8	12.706	0.079	0.157	0.944	0.630
1994	4	0	12	7	13.124	0.305	0.000	0.914	0.533
1995	3	2	14	17	13.505	0.222	0.148	1.037	1.259
1996	6	0	18	13	13.746	0.436	0.000	1.309	0.946
See note below									
1997	2	4	24	19	15.838	0.126	0.253	1.515	1.200
1998	0	3	21	26	16.822	0.000	0.178	1.248	1.546
1999	2	1	20	29	17.382	0.115	0.058	1.151	1.668
2000	3	3	20	28	18.040	0.166	0.166	1.109	1.552

Note   Effective March 20, 1997, aircraft with 10 or more seats must conduct scheduled passenger operations under 14 CFR 121.

Definitions of NTSB Classifications

Major—an accident in which any of three conditions is met:
- a Part 121 aircraft was destroyed, or
- there were multiple fatalities, or
- there was one fatality and a Part 121 aircraft was substantially damaged.

Serious—an accident in which at least one of two conditions is met:
- there was one fatality without substantial damage to a Part 121 aircraft, or
- there was at least one serious injury and a Part 121 aircraft was substantially damaged.

Injury—a nonfatal accident with at least one serious injury and without substantial damage to a Part 121 aircraft.

Damage—an accident in which no person was killed or seriously injured, but in which any aircraft was substantially damaged.

Source: National Transportation Safety Board

Table 9.12   Accidents, Fatalities, and Rates—1982 through 2000, U.S. General Aviation

Year	Accidents		Fatalities		Flight Hours	Accidents per 100,000 Flight Hours	
	All	Fatal	Total	Aboard		All	Fatal
1982	3,233	591	1,187	1,170	29,640,000	10.90	1.99
1983	3,077	556	1,069	1,062	28,673,000	10.73	1.94
1984	3,017	545	1,042	1,021	29,099,000	10.36	1.87
1985	2,739	498	956	945	28,322,000	9.66	1.75
1986	2,582	474	967	879	27,073,000	9.54	1.75
1987	2,495	447	838	823	26,972,000	9.25	1.65
1988	2,385	460	800	792	27,446,000	8.69	1.68
1989	2,232	431	768	765	27,920,000	7.98	1.53
1990	2,215	443	767	762	28,510,000	7.77	1.55
1991	2,175	433	786	772	27,678,000	7.85	1.56
1992	2,073	446	857	855	24,780,000	8.36	1.80
1993	2,039	398	736	732	22,796,000	8.94	1.74
1994	1,994	403	725	718	22,235,000	8.96	1.80
1995	2,053	412	734	727	24,906,000	8.23	1.64
1996	1,909	360	632	615	24,881,000	7.67	1.45
1997	1,851	352	641	635	25,464,000	7.27	1.38
1998	1,090	368	631	625	25,349,000	7.53	1.45
1999	1,913	342	630	622	29,496,000	6.49	1.16
2000	1,835	341	592	582	30,800,000	5.96	1.11

Notes   2000 data are preliminary. 1999 flight hours are preliminary.

Flight hours are estimated by the Federal Aviation Administration.

Suicide/sabotage cases included in "Accidents" and "Fatalities" but excluded from accident rates in this table are: 1982 (3 acc., 0 fatal acc.); 1983 (1, 0); 1984 (3, 2); 1985 (3, 2); 1987 (1, 1); 1988 (1, 0); 1989 (5, 4); 1990 (1, 0); 1991 (3, 2); 1992 (1, 1); 1993 (1, 1); 1994 (2, 2); 1995 (4, 3); 1997 (1, 1)

Since April, 1995 the NTSB is required by law to investigate all public use accidents. The effect upon the number of general aviation accidents has been an increase of approximately $1\frac{3}{4}$ percent.

Source: National Transportation Safety Board

Table 9.13   Accidents, Fatalities, and Rates—1982 through 2000, for U.S. Air Carriers Operating Under 14 CFR 121, Nonscheduled Service (Airlines)

Year	Accidents All	Accidents Fatal	Fatalities Total	Fatalities Aboard	Flight Hours	Miles Flown	Departures	Accidents per 100,000 Flight Hours All	Accidents per 100,000 Flight Hours Fatal	Accidents per 1,000,000 Miles Flown All	Accidents per 1,000,000 Miles Flown Fatal	Accidents per 100,000 Departures All	Accidents per 100,000 Departures Fatal
1982	2	1	1	1	342,555	131,628,000	188,787	0.584	0.292	0.0152	0.0076	1.059	0.530
1983	1	0	0	0	383,830	148,409,000	209,112	0.261	—	0.0067	—	0.478	—
1984	3	0	0	0	429,087	169,153,000	232,776	0.699	—	0.0177	—	1.289	—
1985	4	3	329	329	444,562	178,264,000	237,866	0.900	0.675	0.0224	0.0168	1.682	1.261
1986	3	1	3	3	480,946	188,497,000	273,924	0.624	0.208	0.0159	0.0053	1.095	0.365
1987	2	1	1	1	529,785	234,647,000	308,348	0.378	0.189	0.0085	0.0043	0.649	0.324
1988	1	0	0	0	619,496	242,641,000	368,486	0.161	—	0.0041	—	0.271	—
1989	4	3	147	146	676,621	267,849,000	378,153	0.591	0.443	0.0149	0.0112	1.058	0.793
1990	2	0	0	0	625,390	258,545,000	296,545	0.320	—	0.0077	—	0.674	—
1991	1	0	0	0	641,444	266,287,000	311,002	0.156	—	0.0038	—	0.322	—
1992	2	0	0	0	627,689	272,091,000	365,334	0.319	—	0.0074	—	0.547	—
1993	1	0	0	0	724,859	313,402,000	351,303	0.138	—	0.0032	—	0.285	—
1994	4	0	0	0	831,959	365,485,000	413,504	0.481	—	0.0109	—	0.967	—
1995	2	1	2	2	728,578	325,100,000	351,895	0.275	0.137	0.0062	0.0031	0.568	0.284
1996	5	2	38	8	774,436	423,111,000	377,512	0.646	0.258	0.0118	0.0047	1.324	0.530
1997	5	1	5	4	776,447	357,134,000	393,257	0.644	0.129	0.0140	0.0028	1.271	0.254
1998	7	0	0	0	892,333	393,207,000	444,864	0.784	—	0.0178	—	1.574	—
1999	4	0	0	0	831,854	386,166,000	408,617	0.481	—	0.0104	—	0.979	—
2000	5	0	0	0	870,000	379,100,000	442,000	0.575	—	0.0132	—	1.131	—

Notes   2000 data are preliminary.

Flight hours, miles, and departures are compiled by the Federal Aviation Administration.

Source: National Transportation Safety Board

Table 9.14 Fatal Accidents, 2000 Preliminary Data for All Operations Under 14 CFR 121 and for Scheduled Operations Under 14 CFR 135

Date	Location	Operator	Service	Aircraft	Fatalities			Total	No. Aboard	Circumstances
					Psgr	Crew	Other			
Scheduled 14 CFR 121										
1/31/2000	Point Mugu, CA	Alaska Airlines	Psgr	MD-83	83	5	—	88	88	Structural failure resulting in crash into ocean
2/16/2000	Rancho Cordova, CA	Emery Worldwide Airlines	Cargo	DC-8-71F	—	3	—	3	3	Crashed into auto salvage yard after takeoff
11/20/2000	Miami, FL	American Airlines	Psgr	A300B4	—	1	—	1	130	Flight attendant fatally injured during emergency evacuation
Nonscheduled 14 CFR 121										
None in 2000										
Scheduled 14 CFR 135										
9/18/2000	Nuiqsut, AK	Cape Smyth Air Service	Psgr	Piper PA-31T3	4	1	—	5	10	Crashed during go around following a gear-up landing

Source: National Transportation Safety Board

CHAPTER 10

Air Carrier Economic Regulations

T he air transportation industry of the United States has been federally regulated to a far greater extent than many other industries. In fact, since 1938, when the Civil Aeronautics Act was passed, federal regulatory control has increased. Unlike any other segment of American business enterprise, the air carriers found themselves, wholly or in part, under government control since their inception in the 1920s. It was the action of the Federal Government, through the Post Office promotion of airmail, that led to the creation of the commercial air transport industry. Since governmental control was so positive, hardly any action could be taken without Federal knowledge or approval. This was true in the area of air carrier economics as well as safety.

In 1977 and 1978 there was much discussion and controversy about deregulation or regulatory reform. The result was the amending of the Federal Aviation Act of 1958 by the Airline Deregulation Act of 1978.

> **Economist Alfred Kahn oversaw airline industry deregulation.**

DEREGULATION

Although Title IV of the Federal Aviation Act was the foundation of air carrier economic regulation, the Civil Aeronautics Board, which was the agency responsible for carrying out economic regulatory activities, issued economic regulations which governed the daily economic business affairs of the air carriers.

The basis of the Airline Deregulation Act of 1978 was a report by the U.S. General Accounting Office that said air fares might have been 22 to 25% cheaper, and air travelers might have saved as much as $1.8 billion between 1969 and 1974 if the airlines had to compete on the basis of price.

Discussion of deregulation of the airline industry started during the Ford Administration and developed into legislation during the Carter Administration. President Carter selected economist Alfred Kahn to lead the Civil Aeronautics Board through the deregulation of the airline industry. The legislative hearings took a substantial amount of time, and it was Chairman Kahn's belief that much deregulation could be accomplished through the Board's administrative processes and a liberal interpretation of the Act. This opinion resulted in a new Board philosophy toward fare deregulation, entry and exit of routes, and cargo deregulation.

Chairman Kahn believed that there was no reason to fear that competition would be destructive. He stated that most city-pair markets will support only one carrier, and most of the traffic is concentrated in markets that will support only a few carriers, so oligopolistic restraint is far more likely than cutthroat price rivalry.

One lesson learned from the history of the airlines is that, in the absence of price competition, rivalry among carriers tends to take the form of costly improvements in service, particularly additional schedules. A statistical analysis showed that air carriers with almost identical route systems had differing unit costs. This suggested that differences in management have at least as important an impact on the relative abilities of different air carriers to compete on particular routes as the quality of their overall route structures.

The feeling in Washington was that free entry would reduce fares. However, Chairman Kahn, seeing the slow pace of the legislative process, urged that the air carriers seek fare reductions through the Board. Following was the new, developing philosophy of the Civil Aeronautics Board.

Historically, the CAB had established market prices and an industry-wide rate of return on the basis of industry-wide average costs at a prescribed load factor. Under this regime individual companies could do well or badly depending upon how their efficiency compared with industry average, or varied relative to it; cost reductions produced by good management were reflected in increased profits. There is some indication, however, that even this relatively liberal form of regulation led to lower efficiency than would have occurred under open competition. This leaves open the possibility that even the most efficient air carriers perform poorly relative to what is absolutely achievable. Indeed, this is likely to be the case, because industries which are protected from the pressures of competition in their product or service markets are likely to differ in the ways in which they bargain with employees over wages and in the results that they achieve.

Unregulated intrastate carriers have achieved costs far lower because of the higher productivity they get. The head of the pilot's union of North Central testified in the Chicago Midway Case that they accepted a 15% reduction in pay and a substantial liberalization of their work rules to enable their company to compete with carriers in Chicago markets at the very low fares that were proposed.

FARES

It was clearly in response to the charter liberalization that American Airlines first introduced its Super Saver fare in April of 1977 between New York and Los Angeles and San Francisco. The response to the great expansion of charters and of Laker's Skytrain brought about the new budget fares, standby fares, and all the variations of the Super theme.

Standbys are an obvious example of low fares offered for a service lower in value. They carry no assurance of getting on a flight of one's choice, and are lower in cost because they make available only seats that would otherwise fly empty. The passengers who pay the full coach fare are paying for the assurance of a seat, for being able to make reservations in advance on a flight of their choice, and for the privilege of not showing up at flight time without having to pay a penalty.

The restricted advance purchase discount fares on scheduled service, like the Super Apex and Super Saver, have many of the characteristics of standbys, even though they provide advance reservations of guaranteed seats. That is because, in principle, they are made available only in limited numbers, varying from flight to flight, providing approximately the number of seats that would otherwise fly empty. They cost less to provide, because, in contrast with regular coach service, many of them carry a cancellation fee. Like charters, therefore, the advance purchase and cancellation fee transfer part of the risk of less than 100% load factors from the air carrier to the passengers.

Discount fares represent obvious efforts to reach for the elastic demand discretionary travelers, while continuing to charge full fares to travelers who must plan trips on short notice and stay for only brief periods of time. The ability to segregate inelastic demand markets and charge them considerably higher prices than the elastic demand is a clear sign of continuing monopoly power.

> **Freedom of entry is the heart of competition.**

Other consequences of the spread of these discount fares have been confusion among travelers and resentment on the part of travel agents. The discount fares have caused an enormous upsurge of traffic which, in turn, has contributed to congestion at airports and in reservation systems, and a general deterioration in the quality of service. Many air carriers have concluded that the marginal costs of these discount fares are markedly higher than they had expected, especially taking into account their effect on the quality of service to regular fare-paying passengers.

An additional reason for the wide diffusion of the new fare offerings is that a large proportion of the elastic demand customers to whom they appeal are vacationers. Travelers thinking about going someplace on a vacation may not have made up their minds about where to go, and the air fare may make a difference. That means the airlines that compete for traffic to Miami also have to worry about competition from airlines that fly to California and Hawaii. A reduction in fares to one of these locations exerts strong pressure on the airlines serving the other vacation spots to reduce fares as well.

Some carriers responded to these competitive pressures by introducing inherently lower average cost service at low fares uniformly available to all comers. TWA, losing money on its Chicago-Los Angeles runs, reduced its daily flights from five to two, reconfigured its aircraft for closer seating, cut down on the quality of meals it served, introduced its Spartan Super Coach at fares 37% below Domestic Passenger Fare Investigation level, and transformed a losing operation into a moneymaking one.

Less obvious is how discount fare availability is limited to the number sold on each flight, on a totally nonrestricted and nondiscriminatory basis; no advance purchase and no minimum stay requirements. The pioneer was Texas International's Peanuts Fare which was offered only on selected off-peak flights.

The ultimate demonstration of success will be the imitation of competition in regular coach fares. The question is, in markets with several air carriers already operating, will one of them break ranks and reduce its standard coach fare in hope of filling its aircraft with regular fare-paying passengers diverted from its rivals; or whether, knowing that such cuts would surely be matched by rivals, all will prefer to retain the present multi-tiered, discriminatory structures. After the formal decision in August 1978 to give carriers a wide margin of discretion in reducing basic fares, TWA attempted to set off the next of the customary six-month rounds of price changes by announcing increases and was followed by most of its competitors. Delta, however, held the line.

We already have evidence that an immediate threat of competitive entry can produce large reductions. The pioneering example was Western's "No-Strings" between Miami and Los Angeles.

Several carriers have taken dramatic steps toward simplifying their fare structures, as well as providing separate accommodations to the several classes of customers.

Similarly, the CAB decision to permit free entry between Chicago's Midway Airport and a number of Midwestern cities led directly to Northwest's offer of substantially reduced fares in these markets. The entrants that are certified in that case promised uniform reductions up to 50% for a commuter-type turn-around service. The decision in the Transcontinental Low Fares case represents the culmination of the effort, extending over more than a decade, of World Airways to introduce regularly scheduled transcontinental service at a basic one-way fare of $99. This compares with regular coach round-trip level of $202. The four carriers the CAB decided to admit into the U.S. market promised fares on regularly scheduled service comparable to the ones Laker charged between London and New York.

Price competition increases the break-even load factor, and there is strong evidence that the higher the break-even load factor the higher the achieved load factor. The response to the introduction of the Super Saver between New York and California brought a more than offsetting increase in load factors. In the Los Angeles/San Francisco-New York market, for example, the third quarter yield in 1976 was about 6.4 cents per passenger mile, and the average load factor about 62%. In the same quarter a year later, the yield declined to six cents, but the average load factor increased to 76%.

ROUTES

Another important part of the Board's philosophy prior to the enactment of the Airline Deregulation Act of 1978 was the entry of air carriers into new routes.

Freedom of entry is the heart of competition. The extreme exemplification of this policy was the route moratorium of the early 1970s, during which the Board refused to entertain the hundreds of applications that applied for new route authority. Less obvious, but equally effective, was the indescribably intricate maze of restrictions on the operating rights of each of the existing carriers.

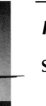

FLIGHTS OF FANCY

Secret Meetings

Mr. Kahn had been told by people from the Civil Aeronautics Board that in the past the Board would often secretly choose among competing applicants for the right to operate a particular route. Somehow out of that process emerged a name of an air carrier attached to the route in question. The Chairman would then pick up the telephone, call the general counsel, and tell him who the lucky winner was and nothing more. Then a lawyer on the General Counsel's staff, amply supplied with blank legal tablets and a generous selection of tried and true clichés—some like "beyond area benefits," "route strengthening," or "subsidy need reduction," and others the desperate product of a feverish imagination—would construct a work of fiction that would then be published as the Board's opinion. Any resemblance between it and the Board's actual reasons for the decision would be purely coincidental.

Another component was the CAB's sympathetic consideration of applications by supplemental air carriers to engage in scheduled service; by combination air carriers and all-cargo carriers to compete with one another; and by air carriers traditionally restricted to international routes to enter domestic markets. The Board had been permitting domestic air carriers to move in the opposite direction, of foreign carriers to have access to additional U.S. gateways in exchange for reciprocal relaxations by foreign governments, particularly in their willingness to receive our charters and low fare scheduled flights.

The CAB grasped the opportunity to make the first major grant of universal authority to all applicants. It was the belief that this would ensure the fullest and most rapid possible exploitation of the market, and that the competitive market would do a better job than the Board of deciding what service, and how much, would be economically feasible, and which carriers would be best equipped to provide it.

The basic problem is that airports, for the most part, are separately owned. Each airport charges landing fees based on its own costs. The choices by air carriers and passengers of flying times and airports are uninfluenced by what must be vast differences in marginal opportunity costs.

The Board was unwilling to settle for a very poor second best. They certificated Colonial and advised Newark to put pressure on the New York Port Authority to introduce marginal cost pricing, which would mean reducing Newark landing fees and increasing fees at the other two.

The Carter Administration had strong feelings toward deregulation of awarding new routes to the air carriers. The Board, under Alfred Kahn, used the Board's administrative power to award permissive authority to the air carriers prior to the enactment of the Airlines Deregulation Act of 1978.

AIR FREIGHT

Fares and routes are not the only areas touched by deregulation. Air freight has been affected. Deregulation came to air freight in 1977 and was firmed up in 1978. One year after the signing of the cargo deregulation legislation, air carriers and freight forwarders were permitted to file for 418 certificates to fly air cargo anywhere in the United States, including Puerto Rico and the Virgin Islands. Seventy-five air carriers and cargo shippers have qualified as cargo air carriers under a grandfather clause of the 1977 law that granted

that designation to entities already in the business. Some freight forwarders are seriously considering the purchase of aircraft to supplement their service. Airline observers expect few changes as a result of total deregulation. However, some concern had been expressed that cargo prices would go wild now that the CAB no longer required filing of tariffs. The CAB prepared to monitor the marketplace to evaluate whether there were wild fluctuations of prices. Shippers had to negotiate for the best rate and live by the adage "let the buyer beware."

All air carriers naturally seek only the most profitable routes. They are not interested in operating marginal flights or in feeding the competition. Thus, the result is reductions and abandonments of service, instability and unreliability resulting from air carrier management business decisions being based on the vagaries of the marketplace at any given time. If medium-sized or smaller markets are to receive adequate service, and they will demand it, most of them could require direct public subsidy.

An inconsistency in the Deregulator's arguments is their concern that there be more price competition but less service competition. Yet the free marketplace is filled with examples of service competition, even where free price competition is available. The automobile, fast-food, motion picture theatre, service station, and computer industries—virtually all industries compete on many bases, including service or other nonprice features.

To describe the air carriers' fare system as nonprice competitive shows a lack of understanding of that system. Throughout the years the air carriers have offered, individually and collectively, a multiplicity of fares for the traveling public, ranging from full first class, coach, and economy fares, to numerous discounts.

What is commonly overlooked by observers of the scheduled air carriers' system is that 30% of domestic traffic is produced by 70 larger city-pair markets; 40% in 840 markets; and the final 30% in some 57,000 smaller markets. The smaller and middle-sized markets are an integral part of the system, and it is the lower load factor flights on those markets which feed the higher load factor flights beyond or connecting to them. Maintenance of regular scheduled service on a continuing basis, despite seasonal, weekly, and time of the day peaks and valleys, requires some degree of peaking and lessening of load factors.

The comprehensive Domestic Passenger Fare Investigation established strict efficiency standards on air carriers for rate-making purposes. These precedent-setting Board efficiency standards resulted in higher-

FLIGHTS OF FANCY

Sunset

The sunset of the Civil Aeronautics Board on December 31, 1984 was a milestone event. For the airline industry Sunset marked the end of the agency that for almost 50 years regulated nearly every economic aspect of commercial air transportation. It established an important precedent for deregulation of other transportation industries. The phasing out of government regulation of domestic airline operations has provided convincing evidence that not only can a regulated industry make the successful transition to independent economic decisionmaking, but also the transportation consumer can benefit through a wider choice of services and prices.

density seating and more efficient air carriers' operations, and help to guarantee that management errors will not be passed on to consumers.

Due to many problems, deregulation of the air carrier industry has not brought about the results that were expected. However, the industry has become more efficient while becoming more competitive but not necessarily more profitable. The airline industry has become more concentrated with three air carriers capturing more than 60% of the domestic market.

For a further presentation of the Airline Deregulation Act, see Chapter 5.

ECONOMIC REGULATIONS ADMINISTERED BY THE DEPARTMENT OF TRANSPORTATION

On January 1, 1985, most of the functions of the Civil Aeronautics Board transferred, together with the associated staff, to the Department of Transportation. The Department of Transportation chose not to consolidate these functions in a new and separate operating administration because that would have perpetuated the notion that the airline industry requires a special agency. The Board's residual functions have been integrated into the existing organizational structure of the Department of Transportation.

Seven major sections of the Department of Transportation carry out the remaining airline economic regulatory functions as follows:

1. The Assistant Secretary for Governmental Affairs is responsible for airline consumer protection matters, including consumer assistance and consumer protection regulations.

2. The Research and Special Programs Administration oversees airline data collection and dissemination.

3. A newly established Office of Essential Air Service administers the Essential Air Service Program.

4. The Assistant Secretary for Aviation and International Affairs is responsible for airline economic licensing, international aviation matters, antitrust functions, and the employee protection program.

5. The Office of the General Counsel provides legal support for the transferred airline functions, including enforcement, litigation, rulemaking, documentary services, and advice to decisionmakers.

6. The Assistant Secretary for Administration includes a new Office of Hearings, which is staffed by administrative law judges who conduct oral evidentiary hearings.

7. The Office of the Inspector General provides auditing services for the Essential Air Service Program and other airline economic program functions.

DESCRIPTION OF REGULATORY FUNCTIONS

The following description of airline economic regulatory functions is a simplified guide to the administration of these functions at the Department of Transportation. It summarizes various statutory and regulatory requirements, but it is not legally authoritative. In all cases, the statutes and regulations contain the final and binding legal requirements.

LICENSING AND CERTIFICATION

Certification of air carriers is the responsibility of the Assistant Secretary for Aviation and International Affairs. Ordinarily, the Assistant Secretary or delegate will perform these functions for the Department, but the Secretary may exercise this authority in lieu of the Assistant Secretary. Staff actions are subject to review by the Assistant Secretary and ordinarily are effective 10 days after the action is served.

CERTIFICATES UNDER SECTION 401 OF THE FEDERAL AVIATION ACT

Each applicant for a certificate for scheduled or charter air transportation should file an application with the Documentary Services Division in the Office of the General Counsel. Separate applications for interstate/overseas and foreign authorities must be filed, with the required filing fees. There are basically three types of 401 certificate cases:

1. those requiring primarily a determination of fitness;
2. those requiring primarily a determination of public convenience and necessity (which includes international carrier selection cases); and
3. continuing fitness reviews.

Fitness Determinations

To receive a section 401 certificate, a carrier must be found fit for the type of service it will provide. Applicants that have not been found fit previously or that are proposing substantial changes in operations (such as going from cargo to passenger service or charter to scheduled operations, or proposing the start up of service after a two-year dormant period) are required to establish their fitness to operate. After receiving a fitness application, the Documentary Services Division will assign it a docket number, date it, and forward it to the Special Authorities Division of the Office of Aviation Operations for review and action. Within 21 days they will determine whether the application is complete. If it is not complete, the application will be rejected or the applicant will be notified and asked to provide further information. After the application is complete one of the following actions will take place:

1. Issue a show cause order tentatively finding the carrier fit and proposing to issue the requested certificate. The order will allow for objections to be filed. A final decision on the fitness application will be made within 180 days after the application is complete.
2. Institute formal proceedings before an administrative law judge in order to determine fitness. This course will be followed in cases where there is controversy concerning the applicant and where the case involves novel issues or where the facts are in dispute. In this event, a decision will be made according to the process applicable to formal proceedings.

Public Convenience and Necessity Determinations

For carriers desiring to provide foreign air service, a determination of public convenience and necessity is required, in addition to the fitness finding described above. Applicants previously found fit, and which hold certificates for operations comparable to those sought may file applications for additional authority, amendments, alterations, modifications, and renewals of their 401 certificates. The Documentary Services Division will give each application a docket number, date it, and forward it to the Public Proceedings Division of the Office of Aviation Operations for review and action. Within 21 days, this Division will determine if the application is complete. If the application is not complete, the applicant will be notified and asked to provide the required information. Within 90 days after the application is complete, a decision will be made to process the application in one of the following ways: dismiss the application; handle it under simplified procedures without an oral evidentiary hearing; or institute a formal hearing case where, for example, a choice must be made between competing applications for limited-designation international route authority.

Continuing Fitness Reviews under Section 401(r)

U.S. certificated and commuter air carriers which do not institute service within two years of being found fit, or which cease operations for at least two years, must undergo a new fitness determination before commencing operations. Certificated carriers applying for a "two-year fitness review" should file an application with the Office of the General Counsel. The application will be given a docket number, dated, and forwarded to Special Authorities Division of the Office of Aviation Operations for review. Commuters seeking a two-year review should file an original application directly with the Special Authorities Division. This Division will determine if the application is complete. If it is not complete, the applicant will be notified and asked to provide further information. After the application is complete, DOT will either issue a show cause order tentatively finding that the carrier continues to be fit and allowing 15 days for objections to be filed, or institute formal proceedings before an administrative law judge in order to determine fitness.

AIR CARRIER ALL-CARGO CERTIFICATES UNDER SECTION 418

An applicant for a domestic all-cargo certificate under section 418 of the Federal Aviation Act should file an application with the Documentary Services Division in the Office of the General Counsel. The application will be given a docket number, dated, and forwarded to the Special Authorities Division of the Office of Aviation Operations for review and action. Within 14 working days they will determine if the application is complete. If not complete the applicant will be notified and asked to provide further information. Once complete, a notice of the application will be published in the *Federal Register* and 21 days will be allowed for objections to a favorable fitness finding and issuance of the certificate.

FOREIGN AIR CARRIER PERMITS UNDER SECTION 402

Applicants for section 402 permits, including renewal, amendment, and/or transfer of a permit, should file an application with the Documentary Services Division in the Office of the General Counsel. The application will be given a docket number, dated, and forwarded to the Licensing Division of the Office of Aviation Operations for review and action. Within 21 days, the Licensing Division will determine if the application is complete. If it is not complete, the applicant will be notified and asked to provide further information. If the additional information is not supplied within a specified, reasonable period, the application may be rejected. After the application is complete and as soon as possible after the date answers are due, DOT will do one of the following:

1. issue a final order;

2. issue a show cause order setting forth tentative findings and conclusions on the case and allowing a specified number of days for objections to be filed; or

3. institute oral evidentiary proceedings before an administrative law judge.

For (1) and (2) above, except when there are unusual or controversial circumstances, a decision will be made within the Office of the Assistant Secretary for Policy and International Affairs. For (3) above, a decision will be made according to the process applicable to all formal proceedings.

COMMUTER AIR CARRIER FITNESS DETERMINATIONS UNDER SECTION 419

Under section 419 of the Federal Aviation Act, commuter air carriers must be found fit to provide scheduled passenger service. Those wishing to establish a commuter air carrier service should file an application with the Documentary Services Division of the Office of the General Counsel. They will refer the application to the Special Authorities Division of the Office of Aviation Operations. This office will review the application to determine whether it is complete and contact the applicant for additional information when necessary. When all required information is received, DOT will issue a show cause order stating tentative findings and allowing 15 days for objections to be filed.

Prior to commencing operations, commuter air carriers must also have a registration form and an insurance certificate on file. (See the section on "Registrations and Insurance Monitoring" for more information on this requirement.)

Commuter air carriers are also subject to the continuing fitness requirement of section 401(r) of the Federal Aviation Act. (See the preceding section on "Continuing Fitness Reviews under Section 401(r)" for further information which applies to commuters which do not institute service within two years of being found fit or which cease operations for at least two years.)

EXEMPTIONS FROM SECTIONS 401, 402, AND 1108(B), INCLUDING EMERGENCY CABOTAGE

Applicants for exemptions from sections 401, 402 (and 403 when accompanying either a 401 or 402 exemption application), or 1108(b) should file an application with the Documentary Services Division in the Office of the General Counsel. The application will be given a docket number, dated, and forwarded to the Licensing Division of the Office of Aviation Operations. The Licensing Division will recommend an appropriate action on the application. Except in unusual or controversial cases, a decision on the application will be made by the Director of the Office of Aviation Operations.

NAME CHANGE OR USE OF TRADE NAME

U.S. certificated and foreign air carriers proposing to change the name in which their certificate or permit is issued, or proposing to use a trade name should file an application with the Documentary Services Division in the Office of the General Counsel. The application will be given a docket number, dated, and forwarded to the Office of Aviation Operations. Answers to the application will be due within 30 days, unless the Department specifies a different period. After the answer period has ended the Division will issue an order granting permission for the change of name or use of the trade name, if the use of such name would not be contrary to the public interest because of the potential for public confusion between the proposed name and one of an existing carrier. A decision on whether to allow the use of the name will normally be made by the Director of the Office of Aviation Operations.

REGISTRATIONS AND INSURANCE MONITORING

U.S. Air Taxis and Commuters

Prior to commencing operations, air taxi operations and commuter air carriers must have on file a registration form and an insurance certificate covering their proposed operations. These forms, as well as subsequent amendments and insurance filings, are to be filed directly with the Licensing Division of the Office of Aviation Operations. If the registration form is properly filled out and the insurance certificate provides coverage for the service proposed, the Licensing Division will return an approved copy of the registration to the applicant. In the case of new commuter applicants, the registration to provide scheduled passenger service will be approved when the carrier's fitness has been determined.

Canadian Charter Air Taxis

Canadian charter air taxi operators desiring to conduct small aircraft transborder services into the United States must file with the Licensing Division a registration form, a certificate of insurance form and a Waiver of the Warsaw Convention. If the above forms are properly filled out and the insurance certificate demonstrates required coverage for the service proposed, DOT will publish notice of the registration by posting it in the public reference room of the Licensing Division and by including it in the Weekly Summary of Applications Filed, which is issued by the Documentary Services Division of the Office of the General Counsel. Interested parties are allowed 28 days to answer. If no objections are received, the Licensing Division will return an approved copy of the registration to the applicant as evidence of operating authority.

Foreign Air Freight Forwarders

Foreign air freight forwarders desiring to conduct operations in interstate or overseas air transportation of property outbound from the United States must be registered before commencing operations. Applicants must file two copies of a completed registration form with the Licensing Division not later than 60 days before start-up. The application will be posted in the Licensing Division and noted in the Weekly Summary of Applications Filed. Upon expiration of the 28-day period for filing answers, the registration will be approved or rejected. Except in unusual or controversial cases, the decision will be made by the Director of the Office of Aviation Operations.

Foreign Charter Operators

Foreign charter operators desiring to conduct public charters in interstate or overseas air transportation, and/or in foreign air transportation carrying U.S. originating traffic, must be registered before filing charter prospectuses and commencing operations. Applicants must file, with the Licensing Division, two copies of completed Form OST F 4530. Applications are posted and noted in Weekly Summary of Applications Filed. Upon expiration of the 28-day answer period, the registration will be approved or rejected. Except in unusual or controversial cases, the decision will be made by the Director of the Office of Aviation Operations.

U.S. and Foreign Air Carrier Liability Insurance

Insurance documents, including certificates evidencing current liability insurance coverage, amendments, and cancellation notices, for U.S. and foreign air carriers should be filed in the Licensing Division. If the certificate does not provide the required coverage, or if it is subsequently canceled, the air carrier will be notified by the Licensing Division to provide the necessary coverage.

CHARTERS

Public Charter Prospectuses

Public charter prospectuses should be filed with the Licensing Division of the Office of Aviation Operations. These prospectuses must include certifications from the charter operator, air carrier, depository bank, and securer that required charter contracts, escrow accounts and security agreements have been established for the proposed program. The Licensing Division will review these filings and advise the charter operator within 10 days whether the program may be advertised or whether additional information is required.

Charter Waivers

Requests for waivers of the charter regulations should be filed with the Licensing Division. Waivers are to be filed at least 30 days in advance of the proposed flights. The Licensing Division will review the request and the applicant will be notified of its disposition.

Overseas Military Personnel Charter Operating Authorizations

Persons proposing to operate charter flights for military are required to obtain an operating authorization as an Overseas Military Personnel Charter operator. Applicants should file an original and one copy of an application, directly with the Licensing Division. The Division will review the application to determine whether it is complete, and, where necessary, contact the applicant for additional information. When the required information is received an order will be issued through the Documentary Services Division, finding the applicant capable of performing the proposed transportation and issuing it an operating authorization.

Air Carrier Financial Security Agreements

U.S. and foreign air carriers operating U.S. originating passenger charter flights are required to obtain a surety bond or establish an escrow account for the protection of customer charter deposits. Copies of these security agreements should be filed with the Licensing Division. The Division will review the agreement and advise the carrier whether it is acceptable or requires modification.

U.S. Charter Operations in Certain Foreign Markets

U.S. carriers desiring to conduct charter operations in a foreign market, where a bilateral agreement or other intergovernmental arrangement requires the U.S. Government to formally advise the other government of the consistency of U.S. carrier charters with that undertaking, should follow procedures administered by the Licensing Division. Such procedures usually involve providing the Licensing Division with advance notice of the carrier's proposed charter operations in those markets.

Japan Charter Authorizations

U.S. carriers desiring to conduct charter operations to and from Japan should contact the Licensing Division for information on availability of Japan charter slots, and the procedures to be followed to obtain and exercise these authorizations.

Statements of Authorization for Foreign Air Carrier Charters

Foreign air carriers, which are required to obtain statements of authorization for various charter operations, should request this authority by filing three copies of completed Form OST F 4540 with the Licensing Division. Applications may also be made by letter. Applications are posted in the Licensing Division and noted in Weekly Summary of Applications Filed. The advance filing requirement varies with the type of authority sought:

- 5 business days for Fifth Freedom charters,
- 30 days for Third or Fourth Freedom charters subject to prior approval,
- 45 days for long-term wet leases, and
- 14 days for carriers requiring prior approval for national security reasons.

Late applications will be accepted upon a showing of good cause.

MISCELLANEOUS FOREIGN AUTHORITIES

Wet Leases

A U.S. carrier desiring to wet lease aircraft to a foreign carrier, or a foreign carrier desiring to wet lease aircraft either to a U.S. or to another foreign carrier for long-term operations of more than 60 days' duration, should file an application for a statement of authorization. They should follow the procedures outlined above under "Statements of Authorization for Foreign Air Carrier Charters." If the applicant lacks the underlying authority to conduct charter operations, it should request this authority by certificate, permit, or exemption.

Operations by Foreign Civil Aircraft Not in "Air Transportation"

Operators of foreign civil aircraft desiring to conduct commercial operations, including agricultural, industrial, and commercial air operations requiring a foreign aircraft permit or special authorization, should file a request with the Licensing Division. The Division posts applications and they also appear in Weekly Summary of Applications Filed. The application must include a complete description of the proposed operation, a statement as to whether the applicant's homeland extends similar privileges to U.S. operators, and the reasons the applicant believes its request to be in the public interest. Applications should be filed at least 15 days before the proposed commencement of operations; however, late applications will be accepted upon a showing of good cause. A foreign aircraft permit or special authorization will be issued, if and as appropriate. Except in unusual or controversial cases, a decision on the application will be made by the Director of the Office of Aviation Operations.

Blind Sector Authorizations

Applications by foreign carriers for authority to conduct blind sector operations (mingling on the same aircraft traffic moving in foreign air transportation with traffic not moving in foreign air transportation) should be filed by letter with the Licensing Division 60 days before commencement if the operations will extend for a period of three months or longer, or 20 days in advance if the operational period is less than three months. The application must include a complete description of the proposed operation, a statement as to whether the applicant's homeland extends similar privileges to U.S. carriers, and the reasons the applicant believes its request to be in the public interest. Except in unusual or controversial cases, a decision on the application will be made by the Director of the Office of Aviation Operations.

Schedule Filing

Filings of U.S. carriers' schedules provided for by intergovernmental arrangements or agreements are to be submitted to the Director, Office of International Aviation Relations, 15 days before the schedules are required to be filed with the foreign government. Filing of foreign air carrier schedules pursuant to regulations, intergovernmental arrangements or agreements should also be submitted to the Director, Office of International Aviation Relations.

Intermodal Cargo Services

Foreign carriers desiring to conduct intermodal cargo services should file one of the following two types of applications. (1) If intermodal authority is provided for in a bilateral agreement, memorandum of consultations, or diplomatic note or letter, between the United States and the applicant's homeland, the applicant may request a statement of authorization for intermodal cargo services by filing two completed copies of DOT Form OST F 4500 with the Licensing Division. (2) If there is no formal agreement between the United States and the applicant's homeland covering intermodal services, the applicant may request an exemption, following the procedures discussed under the section on "Exemptions from Sections 401, 402, and 1108(b)."

Waiver or Modification of Filing Fees

A foreign carrier desiring a waiver of all filing fees should file a letter requesting such waiver with the Licensing Division. The request should include evidence of whether the applicant's homeland charges U.S. carriers any fees analogous to those assessed by DOT.

TARIFFS, FARES, AND RATES

Tariff, fare, and rate matters are the responsibility of the Office of the Assistant Secretary for Policy and International Affairs. Ordinarily, the Assistant Secretary or delegate will perform these functions for the Department, but the Secretary may exercise this authority in lieu of the Assistant Secretary. Staff actions are subject to review by the Assistant Secretary and ordinarily are effective 10 days after the action is served.

TARIFF ADMINISTRATION

Tariff Filing Procedures

Each air carrier or foreign air carrier is required to file its tariffs, including revisions thereof, in the Tariffs Division, Office of Aviation Operations. Tariffs must be accompanied by a letter of tariff transmittal in duplicate.

Special Tariff Permissions

Carriers may request permission to implement tariff changes on less than lawful notice. The requests should be made to the Tariffs Division in duplicate. The request must be accompanied by the applicable filing fee. Action will normally be taken on such requests within seven working days, except those requests which require further analysis.

Tariff Exemption and Rules (Other Than Exemptions under Section 416)

Carriers may request waiver or modification of any of the requirements of the tariff regulations or for modifications of section 403 with respect to the filing and posting of tariffs. Requests should be made to the Tariffs Division in duplicate. The request must be accompanied by the applicable filing fee. Action will normally be taken within seven working days.

Tariff Certifications

Individuals who desire certificated copies of tariff pages may submit requests by letter or telephone to the Tariffs Division. The requester must provide his/her name and address, origin and destination of the transportation involved, name of carrier, and date to be certified (date of commencement of transportation). The Tariffs Division will photocopy the appropriate pages, prepare necessary documentation, obtain required signatures and forward the certified documents to the requestor.

Automated Tariff System

The Tariffs Division is responsible for long range planning of operating standards and policies to permit carriers or their agents to file tariffs electronically. The Division is also responsible for the planning, development and maintenance of automated fare and rate monitoring systems to assure that there is compliance with fare policies. Department of Transportation will continue in effect the arrangements for the exchange of fare data that existed between tariff agents and the Civil

Aeronautics Board. Copies of reports produced by the automated systems will be placed in the public reference room adjacent to the Tariffs Division.

FARES AND RATES

Exemptions from Sections 403(a) and (b)

Carriers seeking exemption from section 403(a) to carry traffic that otherwise could not fly under the terms of their effective tariffs should file a request with the Documentary Services Division in the Office of the General Counsel. The Division will date the request, assign it a docket number, and turn it over to the Fares and Rates Division of the Office of Aviation Operations for action. The Division will review the request and prepare a response. Carriers seeking permission to carry free and reduced rate traffic not otherwise authorized by section 403(b) must file a request with the Fares and Rates Division, which will review and respond to the request.

Complaints/Suspensions

Complainants seeking suspension of tariffs under section 1002(j) of the Federal Aviation Act should file a complaint with the Documentary Services Division in the Office of the General Counsel. The complaint will be given a docket number, dated, and forwarded to the Fares and Rates Division of the Office of Aviation Operations for action. This Division will review and analyze the complaint and formulate a recommended order to be issued. This order will either dismiss the complaint, grant partial relief or suspend the tariffs for a period of 365 days and institute formal proceedings before an administrative law judge. The Assistant Secretary for Policy and International Affairs will ordinarily make the final decision, subject to Presidential review under section 801 of the Federal Aviation Act.

Intercarrier Agreements Regarding International Fares and Rates

An applicant for section 412 approval and section 414 antitrust immunity of intercarrier agreements establishing international fares and rates should file its request with the Documentary Services Division. The Division will date the application, give it a docket number, and refer it to the Fares and Rates Division. This Division will review and analyze the agreement, formulate a recommendation, and draft an order to issue. If the agreement involves major changes in foreign air transportation, the Assistant Secretary for Policy and International Affairs will ordinarily make the final decision. If it involves routine matters, the Director of the Office of Aviation Operations will issue a tentative decision which will become final ten days after the order is served, unless within such period a petition for review is filed or the Assistant Secretary gives notice that he will review the order on his motion.

Standard Foreign Fare and Rate Indices/Formulas

The Fares and Rates Division is responsible for establishment of benchmarks used to measure the non-suspend zones for international and transborder (U.S.-Canada) passenger fares and cargo rates. The Division will receive carrier cost data. An order updating the indices will be issued every two months.

Airmail Rates (International and Alaska)

Proceedings for the determination of rates of compensation for the transportation of mail by aircraft may be commenced by the filing of a petition by an air carrier whose rate is to be fixed by the U.S. Postal Service, or upon the issuance of an order by the Department of Transportation. A petition must set forth the rate or rates to be established and a detailed economic justification sufficient to establish rate reasonableness. The petition should be filed with the Documentary Services Division and also served upon the Postal Service. The petition will be given a docket number, dated, and forwarded to the Fares and Rates Division. This Division will either recommend that a formal hearing process be instituted or will prepare a show-cause order with provisional findings. In the first instance, a decision will be made according to the process described in the section on "Formal Proceedings Requiring Oral Evidentiary Hearings." In the second instance, persons having objections should file their objections within 10 days after the order's service date. Written answers and any supporting documents must be filed within 30 days after the service of the show cause order. If an answer raises a material issue of fact, the Assistant Secretary for Policy and International Affairs will issue a final order dealing with the issue and fixing the fair and reasonable rate or rates. If no notice of objection is filed, the Director of the Office of Aviation Operations will issue a final order fixing the fair and reasonable rate or rates as specified in the show cause order. Once mail rates are established, they are automatically updated by the Fares and Rates

Division (usually semiannually) to reflect changes in unit operating costs reported by carriers.

Airmail Contracts

Any certificated air carrier, which is a party to certain contractual arrangements with the Postal Service for the transportation of mail in foreign air service or within the State of Alaska, entered into under section 5402(a) of the Postal Service Reorganization Act, must file each contract with the Documentary Services Division not later than 90 days before the effective date of the contract. The Division will refer the filing to the Fares and Rates Division for further action. Unless DOT disapproves the contract not later than 10 days prior to its effective date, the contract automatically becomes effective.

INTERNATIONAL AVIATION RELATIONS

International aviation relations are the responsibility of the Office of the Assistant Secretary for Policy and International Affairs. The Assistant Secretary or delegate, under the supervision of the Secretary, will perform the functions associated with the conduct of international aviation relations in cooperation with the Department of State.

NEGOTIATIONS WITH FOREIGN GOVERNMENTS—FORMAL AND INFORMAL

Comments and recommendations on formal and informal negotiations with foreign governments and on bilateral aviation issues are to be submitted in duplicate to the Director of the Office of International Aviation Relations in the Office of the Assistant Secretary for Aviation and International Affairs. This Office will forward a copy of the submission to the General Counsel for International Law.

DESIGNATIONS OF U.S. CARRIERS UNDER BILATERAL AGREEMENTS

Designations of U.S. carriers to serve international routes under bilateral air transport agreements will be made only in response to requests by the U.S. carrier concerned. Requests for designations are to be submitted to the Director, Office of International Aviation Relations. Only if the carrier possesses the requisite operating authority will the Office recommend the carrier's designation to the Department of State.

U.S.-CANADA NONSCHEDULED AIR SERVICES AGREEMENT

U.S. carriers (certificated carriers and Part 298 operators) which desire to be designated under the U.S.-Canada Nonscheduled Air Services Agreement should contact the Office of International Aviation Relations and indicate whether the carrier desires a large or small aircraft designation. As appropriate, the Office will send the carrier pertinent forms and information regarding its designation request. Once the carrier holds the requisite U.S. operating authority and the appropriate forms have been properly filed, the Office will recommend the carrier's designation to the Department of State for transmission through diplomatic channels to the appropriate Canadian authorities.

IATCA COMPLAINTS

A U.S. carrier desiring to file a formal complaint under the International Air Transportation Competition Act, alleging restrictions or discriminatory or unfair competitive practices by a foreign government or carrier, should file its complaint with the Documentary Services Division in the Office of the General Counsel. The complaint will be given a docket number and forwarded to the Director, Office of Aviation Operations and the Assistant General Counsel for International Law for review and recommendations. Action on the complaint will normally be taken by the Assistant Secretary for Aviation and International Affairs. However, in the event that a formal hearing is instituted, a decision will be made according to the process described later in the section on "Formal Proceedings Requiring Oral Evidentiary Hearings."

ESSENTIAL AIR SERVICE PROGRAM

The Essential Air Service Program is administered by the Office of Essential Air Service in the Office of the Secretary of Transportation. Decisions and recommendations of the Director of the Office of Essential Air Service are subject to review and action by the Assistant Secretary for Policy and International Affairs. The Secretary may exercise this authority in lieu of the Assistant Secretary.

EAS DETERMINATIONS, REVIEWS, AND HEARINGS ON APPEAL

All points named on the certificate of at least one air carrier on October 24, 1978, or later designated under section 419(b) of the Federal Aviation Act, are eligible for essential air service with Federal subsidy support if necessary. A determination of the level of service necessary to meet a community's essential air service needs is required for those points that have been served by no more than one carrier. Such determinations will be issued by the Office of Essential Air Service, subject to review by the Assistant Secretary for Policy and International Affairs. Prior to the issuance of such an order, the Office will seek the views of the community and any relevant State agencies on the level of service required by sending a questionnaire for them to complete. Once the determination is issued, the affected community or State agency may appeal the determination within 60 days of the issuance of the order. Appeals should be filed with the Documentary Services Division and should state how the determination departs from the guidelines for essential air service and what level of service should be required. To process the appeal, the Assistant Secretary for Policy and International Affairs will appoint an appeal panel consisting of three senior employees (to be drawn from the Office of EAS, the Office of the General Counsel, and the Office of the Assistant Secretary for Governmental Affairs). The panel may or may not hold an informal conference, and after considering all relevant information, will make a recommendation to the Assistant Secretary, who will issue a final order resolving the appeal. *Ad hoc* petitions for modification or review of determinations may be filed whenever circumstances warrant. Absent such petitions, determinations will be reviewed by the Office of EAS at least once every three years or periodically as circumstances warrant. In such cases, the procedures described above for initial determinations will be followed.

CARRIER SELECTION AND RATE DETERMINATION

Carrier proposals to provide essential air service, with subsidy if necessary, are generally requested by an order which is served on all carriers that have expressed an interest in providing essential air service in the region. A service list is maintained by the Office of EAS. These orders identify the docket number of the case, specify the essential air service to be provided and generally contain complete instructions on selection procedures and data to be submitted with a proposal. A carrier's proposal should be filed with one of the two Service Analysis Divisions of the Office of Essential Air Service as specified in the order. Proposals are normally due within 30 days of the service date of the requesting order. When the deadline for filing proposals has passed, all those from whom proposals are received will be contacted by the Service Analysis Division handling the case to serve copies of their proposals on all parties to the selection case. After a brief (10–14 days) comment period (all comments are to be filed with the appropriate Service Analysis Division), a rate conference is held with each applicant. Rate conferences are scheduled and conducted by the Subsidy Division of the Office of EAS. After conferences are completed a summary of the results for all applicants is sent by the Service Analysis Division to all parties for final comments, which are generally due in 21 days. If a carrier applicant has not provided essential air service previously, staff from one of the Divisions of the Office of EAS and/or the Office of Community and Consumer Affairs may visit the carrier's headquarters to review its operating procedures. These operational reviews generally take place after the rate conference stage is completed and are arranged by the appropriate Service Analysis Division. Occasionally, an on-site financial audit may be performed by the Office of Inspector General to assess the applicant's financial stability. Based on the public record, a recommended selection will be forwarded from the Office of EAS to the Assistant Secretary for Policy and International Affairs for a decision.

RATE RENEWALS

At the end of a normal one or two-year carrier selection/subsidy rate period, subsidy rates and selections of incumbent carriers will be renewed in a significant number of cases. Those generally are cases where the incumbent has performed satisfactorily. In these cases the Office of EAS will initiate contact with incumbent carriers several months before rates are due to expire in order to determine if there is interest in submitting proposals to continue service. Such proposals will be analyzed and rates will be negotiated with the carriers by the subsidy and essential air service staffs. When analyses and rate negotiations are complete, renewal deci-

sions will be reflected in a show cause order to afford other carriers an opportunity to submit competing bids.

RESPONSES TO SUSPENSIONS AND REDUCTIONS OF SERVICE (HOLD-IN PROCEEDINGS, COMPENSATION, AND FINDING REPLACEMENTS)

Carriers are required to file notices if they intend to terminate or suspend service in a manner that will result in less than the defined essential air service level for an eligible point, or that will result in certain types of service losses (more than 33% of all service, the last certificated service or service by the next-to-last certificated carrier). Notices should be filed with the Documentary Services Division either 90, 60 or 30 days in advance of the proposed suspension or reduction, depending upon the type of service reduction and the type of carrier (certificated or commuter). Affected parties may file responses to these notices. The Office of EAS will review the notices and an order acting on the proposed service reduction or suspension will be issued. In cases where essential air service will not be maintained, an order will be issued prohibiting the carrier from terminating service required to meet the essential air service requirements and seek proposals from carriers interested in providing replacement service. Procedural deadlines for processing such proposals will be established by the Office of EAS. While attempting to secure replacement service, the Service Analysis Division of the Office of EAS will issue orders requiring the incumbent to maintain essential air service for consecutive 30-day periods. Applications for compensation for losses for service provided on a hold-in basis should be filed with Division. The Office of EAS will establish by final order or show-cause order interim rates of compensation for the incumbent carrier's hold-in service. A carrier's final hold-in subsidy normally will be established only after an audit of its claim by the Office of the Inspector General.

INDEPENDENT REPRESENTATION OF STATE AND COMMUNITY VIEWS IN ESSENTIAL AIR SERVICE DECISIONS

In order to provide independent representation of State and community views in essential air service decisions, the Office of Community and Consumer Affairs in the Office of the Assistant Secretary for

Governmental Affairs administers a community assistance program. The focus of this program is to keep communities apprised of their rights to air service under the EAS program and to help them develop and meet their own air service needs. The Office monitors cases to ensure State and local views are considered.

ANTITRUST MATTERS AND UNFAIR METHODS OF COMPETITION

Antitrust matters and unfair methods of competition are the responsibility of the Office of the Assistant Secretary for Aviation and International Affairs, acting in cooperation with the Office of the General Counsel. Ordinarily, the Assistant Secretary or delegate will perform this function for the Department, but the Secretary may exercise this authority in lieu of the Assistant Secretary. Staff actions are subject to review by the Assistant Secretary and ordinarily are effective 10 days after the action is served.

MERGERS AND INTERLOCKS UNDER SECTIONS 408 AND 409

Applicants for approval of airline mergers, reorganizations, and interlocks should file an application with the Documentary Services Division in the Office of the General Counsel. A true copy of the application should also be sent to the Assistant Attorney General of the Antitrust Division of the Justice Department. The Division will give the application a docket number, date it and send it to the Office of the Assistant General Counsel for Litigation and to the Industry Economics and Finance Division of the Office of Economics for review. These offices will determine within 10 days whether the application is complete. If it is not complete, the applicant will be asked to provide the missing information. If the application is complete the DOT will, within 30 days, either issue a show cause order tentatively approving or disapproving the application, or issue an order instituting a formal hearing proceeding before an administrative law judge. In the first case, the decision will be made by the Assistant Secretary for Policy and International Affairs. In the second case, a decision will be made according to the procedures applicable to all formal proceedings.

In emergency situations, the DOT can exempt parties to a contemplated merger or acquisition from the procedural requirements of section 408 of the Federal Aviation Act, provided that the applicant clearly shows that the public interest and competition will suffer no harm from immediate approval. The Office of the Assistant General Counsel for Litigation or the Industry Economics and Finance Division may be contacted for further information.

INTERCARRIER AGREEMENTS UNDER SECTION 412

If a carrier wishes to have the DOT approve or grant antitrust immunity for an agreement (other than one related to International Air Transport Association conferences), or a meeting to discuss possible cooperative working arrangements, or any modification or cancellation of such agreements, it should file the agreement or request with the Documentary Services Division. They will assign a docket number, date it, and forward it for review to the Industry Economics and Finance Division of the Office of Economics and to the Office of the Assistant General Counsel for Litigation or, in the case of agreements relating to foreign air transportation, to the Industry Economics and Finance Division and the Office of the Assistant General Counsel for International Law. These offices will determine within 10 days whether the application is complete. If it is not complete, the applicant will be asked to provide the missing information. If the application is complete, DOT will, within 30 days, either issue a show cause order tentatively approving or disapproving the application, or issue an order instituting a formal hearing proceeding before an administrative law judge. In the second case, a decision will be made according to the procedures applicable to all formal proceedings. In emergency situations the DOT can provide relief from procedural requirements.

GRANTS OF ANTITRUST IMMUNITY

If a carrier wishes the DOT to grant antitrust immunity for an airline merger or intercarrier agreement, the request for immunity should be included with the carrier's request for approval of the merger or agreement. The immunity request will be processed together with the merger or agreement approval request. Section 414 of the Federal Aviation Act will govern decisions on whether to grant immunity.

UNFAIR METHODS OF COMPETITION

Any person who wants the DOT to investigate charges that a particular carrier is engaged in an unfair method of competition in violation of Section 411 of the Federal Aviation Act or the DOT regulations should file a complaint with the Documentary Services Division in the Office of the General Counsel. They will give the complaint a docket number, date it and forward it to the Office of the Assistant General Counsel for Aviation Enforcement and Proceedings which will handle it in the same manner as other third-party complaints.

Industry practices that are potentially unfair methods of competition, that may require other action under section 411 of the Federal Aviation Act, will be reviewed (in the case of domestic air transportation) by the Industry Economics and Finance Division of the Office of Economics and the Office of the Assistant General Counsel for Litigation or, in the case of foreign air transportation, the Industry Economics and Finance Division and the Office of the Assistant General Counsel for International Law. These offices will recommend appropriate action.

CONSUMER PROTECTION

Consumer protection matters are primarily the responsibility of the Office of the Assistant Secretary for Governmental Affairs. Ordinarily the Assistant Secretary for Governmental Affairs or delegate will perform this function for the Department, but the Secretary may exercise this authority in lieu of the Assistant Secretary for Governmental Affairs.

CONSUMER ASSISTANCE REGARDING AIRLINE SERVICES

Beginning January 1, 1985, the Office of Community and Consumer Affairs began handling both written and telephone complaints from consumers regarding such problems as lost baggage, passenger bumping, smoking, unfair or deceptive practices, and refunds. The Office works with State and local consumer offices and organizations across the country.

Consumers should remember that they should **first contact the air carrier with their complaints.** The vast majority of complaints can be quickly resolved by the air carrier. However, if a consumer is unable to obtain assistance or believes the assistance offered by the carrier is less than required by law, they should contact the Office of Community and Consumer Affairs. A consumer representative will then assist the consumer with his or her complaint. This person will contact the air

carrier if the carrier has not provided a satisfactory response. The representative will also advise individuals of the current consumer regulations relating to air travel.

The Office of Community and Consumer Affairs will continue to issue monthly reports listing the number of consumer complaints received by the Office that involve air carriers, as well as the number of passengers denied confirmed seats (bumped).

CONSUMER ASSISTANCE REGARDING AVIATION SAFETY

Airline passengers who have complaints or inquiries regarding aviation **safety** should contact the FAA's Community and Consumer Liaison Division.

INVESTIGATIONS OF ALLEGED RULE VIOLATIONS AFFECTING CONSUMERS

Possible violations of consumer regulations by an air carrier can lead to an investigation. These investigations will be conducted by the Investigations Division of the Department of Transportation Office of Community and Consumer Affairs.

INFORMAL AND FORMAL ENFORCEMENT OF CONSUMER REGULATIONS

The DOT may take either informal or formal enforcement action against an airline that violates consumer regulations. In the case of informal enforcement, the Office of Community and Consumer Affairs will be responsible for recommending civil penalties against a carrier. The Deputy General Counsel will be responsible for actually assessing civil penalties. Persons wishing formal enforcement action to be taken against a carrier should refer to the section on "Enforcement" under the heading "Rulemaking, Litigation, and Enforcement," for further information.

CONSUMER PROTECTION RULEMAKING AND EXEMPTIONS

Consumer protection regulations and exemptions related to baggage liability, denied boarding compensation, ticketing notices, and smoking restrictions will be the primary responsibility of the Assistant Secretary for Governmental Affairs. For certain other regulations which are both consumer matters and licensing matters, such as those related to liability insurance and airline charter operations, the Office of the Assistant Secretary for Governmental Affairs and the Office of the Assistant Secretary for Policy and International Affairs share responsibility.

DATA COLLECTION AND DISSEMINATION

Data collection and dissemination are the responsibility of the Research and Special Programs Administration, acting in cooperation with the Office of the Assistant Secretary for Aviation and International Affairs.

AIR CARRIER ACCOUNTING AND GUIDANCE

Air Carriers receiving section 401 certificates are required to comply with the "Uniform System of Accounts and Reports for Large Certificated Air Carriers." The Research and Special Programs Administration's Office of Aviation Information Management is responsible for accounting and related systems design and modification, as well as interpretation of the regulations. Inquiries regarding waivers from accounting regulations, proposed rulemakings or suggestions on new or revised rules should be directed to the Director.

The Office of Aviation Information Management provides technical accounting expertise and guidance to air carriers and other Government agencies, including the Securities and Exchange Commission. The Data Requirements and Public Reports Division of the Office of Aviation Information Management also assists small air carriers participating in the Essential Air Service program, such as air taxi operators, who may elect to implement the "Voluntary Accounting System for Small Air Carriers" and new or growing certified carriers who may need assistance to familiarize themselves with the required accounting systems and related rules in the "Uniform System of Accounts and Reports for Large Certificated Air Carriers."

The Office of Aviation Information Management continuously evaluates the airline industry accounting systems and related rules and coordinates with the Office of Inspector General on the need for audit assistance. Questions on accounting or reporting issues concerning the aviation information data banks may be addressed to the Data Requirements and Public Reports Division of the Office of Aviation Information Management.

FINANCIAL AND STATISTICAL REPORTING

Air carrier reporting requirements established by the Civil Aeronautics Board continue in effect until changed. Authority to maintain these rules and manage the aviation information program is delegated to the Administrator of the Research and Special Programs Administration. Program operation is accomplished by the Office of Aviation Information Management.

Petitions for rulemaking on reporting matters should be filed with the Documentary Services Division in the Office of General Counsel. The petition will be given a docket number, dated, and referred to the Office of Aviation Information Management for processing. Rules proposed and issued by them will be docketed.

New reporting instructions, changes to existing instructions, interpretations of reporting instructions, or special reporting requirements for air carriers will be promulgated by the Office of Aviation Information Management. These instructions, as well as written requests for waivers, interpretations, extensions of filing dates, substitution of forms or formats, or confidential treatment of reports will be handled by the Director of the Office of Aviation Information Management.

Air carrier submissions will be reviewed for acceptability by the Data Administration Division of the Office of Aviation Information Management. This Division may contact air carriers concerning the form and/or substance of their reports.

PUBLIC ACCESS TO AIR CARRIER REPORTS

Copies of air carrier reports as well as recurrent publications, unpublished studies, listings and microfilm end products may be viewed by the public in the Data Requirements and Public Reports Division of the Office of Aviation Information Management. Telephone inquiries by the public about the different kinds of reports and data available, and the air carriers who have filed, are recorded by a 24-hour message recorder. Inquiries are answered in turn as staff time is available.

The U.S. Government Printing Office services requests for financial and statistical publications. Copies of magnetic tape data banks are available from the National Archives and Records Services' Machine Readable Archives Division. Copies of Passenger Origin and Destination Survey books and microfilm are sold by the Air Transport Association. Copies of recurrent financial and cost analyses are available for inspection in the Office of Aviation Information Management public reports area.

Certified copies of air carrier reports are provided upon written application. Access to confidential and/or restricted air carrier data may be discussed with the Data Requirements and Public Reports Division staff, but written requests must be sent to the Director.

DATA PROCESSING SERVICES FOR AVIATION INFORMATION

The Data Processing Division is responsible for providing systems analysis, programming and technical support covering all existing automated systems that were formally in use at the Civil Aeronautics Board. This includes maintenance of the systems which process the various air carrier submissions for editing and validating purposes.

EMPLOYEE PROTECTION PROGRAM

Section 43 of the Airline Deregulation Act of 1978 contains two employee protection provisions; a federal assistance payment provision and a first-right-of-hire provision, both of which are described below. (Note, however, that on May 18, 1984, the U.S. District Court for the District of Columbia declared all of section 43 unconstitutional because it contained a legislative veto.)

FEDERAL ASSISTANCE PAYMENT PROVISION

Airline employees who lose their jobs or suffer loss in pay as a result of the change in regulatory structure provided by the Airline Deregulation Act of 1978 can become eligible for federal assistance payments if both the DOT and the Department of Labor make certain determinations. The DOT must first determine whether a carrier has experienced a major contraction in employment, which is defined as a 7.5% reduction in its total number of full-time employees within a 12-month period. Ten airlines were found to have suffered major contractions: Airlift International, Air New England, American, Braniff, Continental, Mackey International,

Pan American, TWA, United and Western as well as Republic. The DOT must then commence a proceeding to determine whether any of the major contractions amounted to a qualifying dislocation, that is, a bankruptcy or major contraction, the major cause of which was deregulation. Prior to Civil Aeronautics Board sunset, the Board set the 10 cases listed above for hearing, and scheduled five of them (Air New England, Mackey International, Braniff, Pan American, and United) for the initial round of hearings before administrative law judges. Following the court decision on the constitutionality of Section 43, the Civil Aeronautics Board stayed all further actions in the dislocation proceedings. For those cases pending before administrative law judges and any other cases set for formal hearings, the DOT procedures applicable to all formal hearings would apply.

If the DOT finds that any carrier has suffered a qualifying dislocation, it will be up to the Department of Labor to determine which protected employees are eligible for benefits and the amounts of assistance to which they are entitled, subject to availability of appropriations. An employee of such carrier would be protected if, as of October 24, 1978, he or she had been employed by that carrier for four years. Information concerning payment of benefits and funding for the program may be obtained by writing to the Director, Office of Program Management, Employment and Training Administration, U.S. Department of Labor.

If an employee of a carrier not among the eleven listed above wants to apply for a determination of qualifying dislocation, he or she should contact the Office of the Assistant General Counsel for Environmental, Civil Rights, and General Law for information. In order for the employee to be protected under the statute, the carrier must have received a section 401 certificate from the Civil Aeronautics Board no later than October 24, 1978.

Employees of the eleven carriers listed need not resubmit their applications for assistance, since their cases transferred automatically from the Civil Aeronautics Board. An employee may be kept apprised of developments in a case by requesting to have his or her name placed on the service list for that case. To do so, an employee should contact the Documentary Services Division in the Office of the General Counsel.

FIRST-RIGHT-OF-HIRE PROVISION

Section 43(d) of the Airline Deregulation Act provides first-right-of-hire rights within the airline industry for protected employees who have been terminated or furloughed. Unlike the assistance payment provision, no DOT determination is required for an employee to be eligible for this program; it is administered solely by the Department of Labor.

RULEMAKING, LITIGATION, ENFORCEMENT, AND LEGAL COUNSEL

All legal functions of the Civil Aeronautics Board transferred to the Department of Transportation Office of the General Counsel. This includes the preparation and coordination of rulemakings to be conducted by the Department, presentation of the views of the Department on legislation, conduct of litigation, representation of the Department's position as enforcement or public counsel in all hearing cases, and advice and counsel on all final actions of the Department under authority transferring from the Civil Aeronautics Board. To ensure a separation of functions, a new Office of the Assistant General Counsel for Aviation Enforcement and Proceedings was established to perform the enforcement and public counsel roles in hearing cases. That Office will report only to the Deputy General Counsel. The Deputy General Counsel and the Office of the Assistant General Counsel for Aviation Enforcement and Proceedings will be segregated from staff participating in the decision-making process in all hearing cases.

RULEMAKING

Any interested person may petition the DOT for the issuance, amendment, or repeal of any rule. A petition for rulemaking should be filed in the Documentary Services Division. In addition, petitioners are encouraged to file 10 additional copies of the petition to help expedite the government's review. Each petition will be given a docket number and placed in a separate file. The petition and related public documents will be placed in that docket and become a matter of public record. The docket may be examined and copies made.

Any interested person may file an answer to a petition. Filing an answer is purely permissive and failure to do so does not prejudice any interested person in any rulemaking proceeding that may be instituted. Petitions are either denied by order, or a rulemaking proceeding is initiated.

A rulemaking proceeding may also be begun directly by the Department. This may be done by issuance of an advance notice of proposed rulemaking or a notice of proposed rulemaking. Most of DOT initiated rulemakings are listed in the United Agenda of

Federal Regulations. Anyone who would like to be placed on a mailing list for the Department's Regulatory Agenda (and specific rulemaking documents of the Office of the Secretary of Transportation) may do so by making a request. If the Department decides to clarify an ambiguity in a rule, it may issue an interpretative amendment or an editorial correction. Likewise, it may issue final rules without a prior notice because of an emergency.

For most notices the DOT provides 45 or 60 days to file comments. In some cases, the public will be invited to file reply comments. As a matter of practice, the Department considers all comments filed. Late filed comments are considered so far as possible without incurring additional expense or delay. All comments should be sent to the specified docket number at the Documentary Services Division, Office of the General Counsel, Department of Transportation. All comments are available for public inspection and duplication. Final rules are generally effective not less than 30 days after publication in the *Federal Register.*

LITIGATION

Any person who wishes to obtain judicial review of a final DOT decision taken under the Federal Aviation Act or Section 43 of the Airline Deregulation Act, must file a petition for review in an appropriate court of appeals. Copies of the petition should also be sent to the General Counsel of the Department of Transportation and, for most matters affecting the airline industry, to the Appellate Section of the Antitrust Division of the Department of Justice. The Assistant General Counsel for Litigation will represent the DOT in all such cases.

ENFORCEMENT

Informal Complaints

Informal complaints should be made in writing to the Office of the Assistant General Counsel for Aviation Enforcement and Proceedings or to the Investigation Division of the Office of the Assistant Secretary for Governmental Affairs. In coordination with the Office of the Assistant General Counsel for Aviation Enforcement and Proceedings, the Investigation Division will conduct any necessary investigation to determine if violations of the regulations have occurred and to obtain any other information necessary to enable resolution of the complaint on an informal basis. Should the investigation indicate a need for formal enforcement action, an enforcement proceeding may be instituted by the Office of the Assistant General Counsel for Aviation Enforcement and Proceedings or the Deputy General Counsel. The filing of an informal complaint does not bar the complainant from subsequently filing a formal enforcement complaint.

Formal Complaints

A person filing a formal enforcement complaint should file the complaint with the Documentary Services Division in the Office of the General Counsel. The complaint will be given a docket number, dated, and forwarded to the Office of the Assistant General Counsel for Aviation Enforcement and Proceedings. A 15-day period is allowed for answers to the complaint. Where necessary, the Office of the Assistant General Counsel for Aviation Enforcement and Proceedings will request an investigation from the Investigation Division of the Office of the Assistant Secretary for Governmental Affairs to determine if violations of the regulations have occurred and to obtain documentary evidence in support of the charges made in the formal complaint. Based on the results of such investigation, the Office of the Assistant General Counsel for Aviation Enforcement and Proceedings or the Deputy General Counsel will either institute a formal enforcement proceeding as to all or part of the complaint or dismiss it. If the Office does not act on the complaint within 60 days from the date it is filed (subject to approved extensions of time), the complainant or respondent may ask the Deputy General Counsel that the complaint be docketed or dismissed. A notice dismissing the complaint shall become effective, as a final order, 30 days after its service. Whenever a formal enforcement proceeding is initiated, a decision will be made according to the process applicable to all formal proceedings.

LEGAL COUNSEL

Legal advice and counsel on decisions of the Assistant Secretary for Policy and International Affairs and the Assistant Secretary for Governmental Affairs, and their delegates, will be the responsibility of the Office of the General Counsel. The Assistant General Counsel for Environmental, Civil Rights and General Law, will be responsible for legal advice and counsel on EAS matters, employee protection cases, consumer protection decisions, and air carrier fitness determinations. The Assistant General Counsel for Litigation will be responsible for legal advice and counsel on mergers, interlocking relationships, intercarrier agreements, and unfair methods of competition in domestic air transportation. The Assistant General Counsel for International Law will be responsible for legal advice and counsel on decisions relating to foreign air transportation, including intercarrier agreements and unfair methods of competition.

FORMAL PROCEEDINGS REQUIRING ORAL EVIDENTIARY HEARINGS

GENERAL

This section describes how the Department of Transportation will process cases and make decisions on matters warranting oral evidentiary hearings before administrative law judges. Cases which may be set down by the Department for an oral evidentiary hearing include international carrier selection cases, fitness investigations, antitrust matters, employee protection determinations, and formal enforcement actions.

THE OFFICE OF HEARINGS

The Department of Transportation Office of Hearings is responsible for conducting all formal proceedings requiring an oral evidentiary hearing involving the regulatory powers transferred to the DOT under Titles IV and X of the Federal Aviation Act and Section 43 of the Airline Deregulation Act. Upon institution of a hearing case and its assignment by the Chief Administrative Law Judge, the presiding administrative law judge will proceed to the scheduling and holding of prehearing conferences, hearings, and arguments as may be required, to issue the necessary notices and procedural orders, to receive evidence and briefs, and to issue initial or recommended decisions. The Department of Transportation Rules of Practice and Rules of Conduct apply to all hearings, which will be conducted in the Hearing Room of the Department of Transportation Headquarters or other room as specified.

THE PUBLIC COUNSEL

The Office of the Assistant General Counsel for Aviation Enforcement and Proceedings will act as public counsel in all formal hearings. Exhibits, analyses, and written and oral testimony will normally be prepared by the DOT staff office that has substantive functional responsibility for the subject of the hearing. (For example, the Special Authorities Division of the Office of Aviation Operations will prepare analyses, exhibits, and testimony for fitness cases; the Public Proceedings Division of the Office of Aviation Operations will perform the same function for international carrier selection cases.)

To ensure separation of functions, the Office of the Assistant General Counsel for Aviation Enforcement and Proceedings will report only to the Deputy General Counsel, who will be independent for the purposes of the public counsel role. DOT staff who prepare analyses, exhibits, and testimony for formal hearings will also be subject to the separation of functions requirement of the Administrative Procedure Act.

FINAL DECISIONS

At the completion of the hearing process, the presiding administrative law judge will issue a recommended decision on the case. For international carrier selection cases and other cases as deemed appropriate by the Secretary, a recommended decision will be referred to the senior career official in the Office of the Assistant Secretary for Policy and International Affairs for a final decision. This decision is reviewable at the discretion of the Assistant Secretary for Policy and International Affairs or the Secretary of Transportation. However, these officials may only affirm the decision or remand it to the senior career official for reconsideration, with a full explanation of the basis for the remand.

For cases other than those described in the preceding paragraph, the recommended decision of the administrative law judge will be referred to the Assistant Secretary for Policy and International Affairs for a decision. The Secretary may exercise this authority in lieu of the Assistant Secretary.

DOCUMENTARY SERVICES

RECEIPT AND DISTRIBUTION OF FORMAL PLEADINGS AND PETITIONS, INCLUDING MAINTENANCE OF A SERVICE LIST AND PUBLIC REFERENCE ROOM

Documents required to be filed with the Department of Transportation (other than those related to certain undocketed applications to the Office of Aviation Operations) shall be filed with the: Docket Section, Documentary Services Division, Office of the General Counsel.

Such documents shall be deemed filed on the date on which they are actually received by the Docket Section. The hours for the filing of documents are from 9:00 A.M. to 5:00 P.M., eastern standard or daylight saving time, whichever is in effect in the District of Columbia at the time, Monday through Friday, inclusive, except for legal holidays for the Department. The Docket Section receives all formal pleadings (applications, complaints, motions, petitions, answers, comments, replies) filed in connection with docketed matters. All applications must be accompanied by the appropriate number of copies and an appropriate filing fee, as specified in applicable DOT regulations. All applications must include a service list with the names and addresses of the parties served as well as a certificate of service verifying service on parties. All applications must include proper identification on the cover of the pleading as to docket number (if previously assigned), the type of pleading (i.e., answer, motion, etc.) and the name, address, and telephone number of the carrier and/or counsel who prepared the pleading. If the document is proper in every respect, it is then date-stamped, assigned a docket number (if one is not previously assigned) and distributed to the appropriate offices for further processing. A copy of each pleading filed is posted on a bulletin board in the Docket Section for public inspection.

MAINTENANCE OF OFFICIAL RECORDS OF ALL FORMAL ACTIONS AND CERTIFICATION OF OFFICIAL DOCUMENTS FOR COURTS

The Documentary Services Division obtains and keeps records of all formal actions and certifies official documents for courts. Requests for certification of Certificates of Public Convenience and Necessity, Foreign Air Carrier Permits currently in effect, orders, and regulations should be made directly to the Coordination Section. Requests for documents in a specific docket should be made directly to the Docket Section. Requests for certification of other official documents should be made to the appropriate offices that are responsible for the documents requested.

DISTRIBUTION OF NOTICES OF ACTIONS AND DECISIONS

The Documentary Services Division makes official service on all parties to proceedings of orders, notices, and decisions issued by DOT. All official documents are served by regular mail and contain a certificate of service to substantiate validity of service.

WEEKLY CALENDAR OF FORMAL HEARINGS AND SUMMARY OF ACTIONS

A weekly calendar of formal hearings entitled "Calendar of Prehearing Conferences, Hearings, and Oral Arguments" as well as a weekly summary of applications, orders, opinions and regulations are prepared by the Docket Section. Copies are sold on a subscription basis and may be obtained from the Superintendent of Documents of the U.S. Government Printing Office.

REQUESTS FOR ORAL ARGUMENT

If any party desires to argue a case orally, that party, in its exceptions or brief, may request leave to make oral argument. If DOT rules that oral argument is to be allowed, all parties to the proceeding will be advised of the date and hour set for argument; each party wishing to participate in the oral argument must notify the Chief of the Documentary Services Division in writing on or before the date established, together with the name of the person who will represent it at the argument. Each participant will be notified by the Documentary Services Division of the amount of time allowed for argument. Requests for oral argument on petitions for discretionary review will not be entertained. Pamphlets, charts, maps, and other written data may be presented at the oral argument only in accordance with the following rules: All such material shall be limited to facts in the record of the case being argued. All such material shall be served on all parties to the proceeding and transmitted to the Docket Section of the Documentary Services Division at least five calendar days in advance of the argument.

EXTENSIONS OF TIME

Whenever a party has the right or is required to take action within a period prescribed by the Rules of Practice, by a notice given thereunder, or by an order or regulation, request for extension of the time set may be made by letter, before expiration of the prescribed period, to the Chief of the Documentary Services Division. After the expiration of the specified time, where the failure to act is clearly shown to have been the result of excusable neglect, request for extension of the prescribed period may be made by motion filed with the Docket Section, Documentary Services Division. Where an administrative law judge has been assigned to a proceeding, requests for continuance or extensions of time shall be directed to the Chief Administrative Law Judge.

CHAPTER 11

Air Carriers

Although it was not until after 1925 that the airline industry began to emerge and develop, there were two notable early attempts at purely commercial passenger operation in the United States.

ST. PETERSBURG-TAMPA AIRBOAT LINE

The first scheduled commercial airline in the world was the St. Petersburg-Tampa Airboat Line. It was formed in the Tampa Bay area during 1913 by Percival E. Fansler, Tom Benoist, and Tony Jannus. (See Figure 11.1.) The inaugural scheduled airline flight originated in St. Petersburg in a Benoist airboat, powered by a six cylinder aluminum engine, flown by Jannus on January 1, 1914, at 10 A.M. The flight ended 21 miles and 23 minutes later across the bay in Tampa. The seaplane could carry two passengers in an open cockpit at a price of five dollars each. Anyone weighing over two hundred pounds had to pay overweight charges. This new service competed with existing transportation. The time to travel between the two cities was nine hours by train, six hours by automobile and two hours by steamboat. The airline was organized by Percival Fansler, a visionary engineer sales representative for a marine engine company in Jacksonville, Florida. He arranged financing by thirteen prominent business leaders in St. Petersburg and acted as business manager for the company. (See Figure 11.2.)

Figure 11.1 Tony Jannus.

The company flew seasonally for only a three-month period and established the remarkable record of 1,274 passengers with no injuries or fatalities. A surprisingly accurate schedule was maintained with but a few days of foul weather preventing some flights. By the end of March 1914 the company closed down after not having made sufficient money to warrant continuing; but the future success of the airplane as a commercial transport had been heralded.

Benoist, of St. Louis, was an experienced designer and builder, specializing in flying boats. He enthusiastically joined Fansler in forming the airline by providing three airboats, considerable personal expertise, and his highly qualified aviator-engineering staff headed by Tony Jannus. Based upon this significant first step in scheduled commercial aviation, the St. Petersburg *Times* newspaper predicted:

"Airlines in the very near future will be used generally for transit purposes and the line from this city across the bay to Tampa is only the pioneer of them all."

That first small step has evolved to a giant step whereby scheduled commercial aviation now touches the lives of everyone in some manner.

Following that historic flight, Tony Jannus and his brother Roger worked together to establish the St. Petersburg-Tampa Airboat Line. Later they opened a flying school and did exhibition work. Tony eventually went to work for a Canadian airplane manufacturing firm as a test pilot during World War I. On October 16, 1916, Tony, at age 27, died while testing a Curtiss H-7 airplane he was piloting for the Russians.

In 1964, on the 50th anniversary of the Tony Jannus inaugural flight, the chambers of commerce of St. Petersburg and Tampa sponsored a commemorative project by establishing the Tony Jannus Award. The award is given each year to an individual who has contributed to

Figure 11.2   Pilot Tony Jannus and passenger A.C. Pheil fly the first commercial passenger airline service on the St. Petersburg-Tampa Airboat Line, January 1, 1914.

the growth and improvement of the scheduled airline industry.

A second commemorative project was to build and fly a reproduction of the 1913 Benoist Airboat, model 14, number 43 flown by Jannus. The Florida Aviation Historical Society, assisted by interested supporters, completed the authentically detailed reproduction of the famous Benoist Airboat. It was flown on January 1, 1984, at 10 A.M. from St. Petersburg to Tampa following the route Jannus pioneered 70 years earlier. This historic replica is displayed in the St. Petersburg Historical and Flight One Museum within a few hundred yards of the site where the Jannus flight originated in 1914.

AEROMARINE AIRWAYS

The next notable early venture in passenger air transportation took place in November 1919. Aeromarine Airways flew passengers, airmail, and freight between Key West and Havana. Three seaplanes were used by the airline which was organized by the manufacturer of the airplanes. The fare was $50.00. One year later Aeromarine received an airmail contract. In May 1921

the airplanes were flown North and service began between New York and Atlantic City, New Jersey; and later that summer between Detroit and Cleveland. (See Figure 11.3.) The following winter season service was expanded from Miami to Bimini and Nassau for $85.00 a passenger. Service ceased in 1924, when airmail payments ended. Records indicate that during the period 1920 to 1924, 6,814 passengers were carried using eleven flying boats. The company ceased operating because of the lack of sufficient profit.

CIVIL AERONAUTICS ACT—1938

By the time of the passage of the Civil Aeronautics Act in 1938, the air carrier industry had begun to mature. A section of this Act stated that the Civil Aeronautics Authority (later to become the Civil Aeronautics Board) could classify airlines for the purpose of regulatory control. Later new classes were added and several changes were made. It is necessary to review the various ways air carriers have been classified through the years, because the classifications have functioned in the development of the U.S. commercial air transport industry. An understanding of the historical classi-

Figure 11.3 Aeromarine Airways, Inc., 1921–24.

fications is needed to fully appreciate the changes brought about by the Airline Deregulation Act of 1978.

At the outset it must be recognized that an air carrier is a *common carrier*. A common carrier transports the public for hire and operates on a fixed schedule. There are two other types of carriers: contract and private. A *contract carrier* is one who transports the public for hire but not on a fixed schedule. A *private carrier* is a privately owned and operated vehicle such as an automobile.

In addition to air carriers, there are four other types of common carrier transportation systems. They are road, rail, water, and pipe. All forms of public transportation fall within these five types or modes of common carriers.

Almost all air carriers in the U.S. today, transporting the majority of the air traveling public, are certificated air carriers. To be certificated, in the past, an air carrier had to have been granted, by the Civil Aeronautics Board, a Certificate of Convenience and Necessity. This has changed under deregulation.

The Civil Aeronautics Act required the possession of a Certificate of Convenience and Necessity by a certificated air carrier and made the Civil Aeronautics Board the responsible authority for granting the certificate in the public interest. Public interest, or being in the public need, means for the *commerce, postal service, and/or national defense* of the United States.

The Civil Aeronautics Act further provided for the automatic granting of a Certificate of Convenience and Necessity, in 1938, to those air carriers who had been in continuous operation, and in possession of an airmail contract, for a period of ninety days prior to the passage of the Act. This was known as the grandfather clause and was Section 401e of the Civil Aeronautics Act of 1938.

DOMESTIC TRUNKS

As a result of the grandfather clause, sixteen major domestic airlines were granted Certificates of Convenience and Necessity. Thus, the first classification of air carriers became known as **Domestic Trunks** and formed the nucleus of the air carrier industry. They can trace their beginning from the early days of the airmail private contractors after the passage of the Airmail Act in 1925.

The main characteristics of a Domestic Trunk were the operation of medium and long stage length routes serving large metropolitan areas and medium-size cities. These routes had relatively high density traffic volume, and in order to perform this type of operation, large equipment (aircraft) were needed. The Trunks took on a new look, however. They dropped many of the medium stage routes to medium-size cities and now concentrated on the long stage routes to metropolitan areas. Domestic service originally was limited to the continental limits of the United States; now most of them go outside of the country as well.

The Trunks were granted permanent Certificates of Convenience and Necessity. In fact, at the time this class was established as a result of the Civil Aeronautics Act in 1938, there was no thought of a temporary Certificate of Convenience and Necessity.

Of the original sixteen air carriers granted permanent Certificates of Convenience and Necessity under the Grandfather Clause, six remain, although in different classifications.

American Airlines	Dallas, Texas
Continental Air Lines	Houston, Texas
Delta Air Lines	Atlanta, Georgia
Northwest Airlines	St. Paul, Minnesota
Trans World Airlines	New York, New York
United Air Lines	Chicago, Illinois

The second classification established in 1938 was **International Air Carriers** which were United States-flag airlines that operated between the United States and foreign countries. Later, the class was expanded to International and Overseas which included routes defined as being between the continental United States and one of its territories or possessions.

Another classification established in 1938 was **Territorial Air Carriers,** which was for those air carriers conducting certificated flight operations within particular territories of the United States. However, with the expansion of the air carrier industry, the original classes had to be realigned and new classes were formed.

This classification then became known as **International and Territorial Air Carriers** and included those U.S. air carriers operating between the United States and foreign countries as well as those operating over international waters to territories and possessions of the United States. Examples of the latter are flights to the Caribbean.

In the International and Territorial class were those air carriers that were strictly international; they did not operate within the United States but entirely outside of the country.

Another group within this class was the Domestic Trunk Air Carriers that had been granted international routes by the extension of their domestic routes into Mexico, South and Central America, and the Caribbean, as well as to other foreign countries.

The characteristics of an International and Territorial Air Carrier were the flying of routes outside the continental limits of the United States. This included

from the United States to foreign countries, between foreign countries, and over international waters. This required the use of large equipment over long stage length routes. Permanent Certificates of Convenience and Necessity were possessed by air carriers in this group.

The third classification was the **Intra-Hawaiian Air Carriers** that flew between the many islands of the State of Hawaii. Their unique characteristic was inter-island flying which dictated the use of medium-size aircraft, usually twin-engine, and short stage length routes.

The fourth classification of air carriers became the **Intra-Alaskan Air Carriers,** who operated solely within the State of Alaska. For the most part they were characterized by seasonal operation due to the trends of business and weather. They used small and medium equipment on short to medium stage length routes. Passenger service in Alaska was started in 1924 by Noel Wien, of Fairbanks. By 1929 the company incorporated under the name of Northern Air Transport. Today, it operates as Wien Air Alaska. Weather made road travel difficult if not impossible. Railroad travel existed only between Fairbanks and Anchorage. Therefore, it was the airplane that Alaskans relied upon for transportation.

Another early pioneer in Alaskan aviation was Robert Reeve, a bush pilot, who specialized in flying the Aleutian Islands. One route in the system of Reeve Aleutian Airways covered almost 2,500 miles from Anchorage to Attu Island. During the early 1930s these carriers made their first move forward by outbidding dog teams for airmail contracts. In 1942, 21 air carriers were issued certificates by the Civil Aeronautics Board.

DOMESTIC LOCAL SERVICE AIR CARRIERS

The fifth major air carrier classification, **Domestic Local Service Air Carriers,** (also unofficially called Feeders), did not come about until 1945, when the establishment of their particular type of air service was permitted by the Civil Aeronautics Board. They had a difficult development.

During World War II about fifty percent of the airlines' aircraft were engaged in military contracts, leaving a severe shortage for civilian use, particularly at a time when the demand for air travel increased. One notable lack of air service was between small communities and the major trunk airline cities. As early as August 1943 the Civil Aeronautics Board began investigating the feasibility of such local air service. The investigation showed there was no immediate prospect of profitable passenger traffic. Since route distances would be so short, there was no indication that airmail service could be improved upon over the existing surface facilities. As far as air cargo was concerned, there simply was not any demand.

In spite of the bleak picture with regard to local service profitability, the Civil Aeronautics Board allowed the certification, in 1945, of twenty companies in 45 states on the basis of the Board's power to experiment in air transportation. Since it was to be an experiment, the Certificates of Convenience and Necessity were granted for a three-year period. This was the first time temporary certificates were issued.

The Trunk airlines opposed the certification of the Local Service Air Carriers, no doubt because they were afraid they would grow larger in time and create competition. In issuing the order for certification, the Civil Aeronautics Board made it quite clear that this was not to be the case. It was the Civil Aeronautics Board's intention to restrict the Feeders to small cities of approximately 25,000 population and less. They were also to confine their route operation within their small geographic areas and were not allowed to give nonstop through service between any one small city and the terminus Trunk airline stop. Once this policy was established the Trunks were satisfied and favored the Local Service air carriers, because it meant they would bring added traffic to them from the smaller cities and communities.

The Local Service Air Carriers' costs were high due to short routes, low traffic density, and the use of small aircraft. This condition improved with the expansion of their routes and the purchase of jet aircraft. Due to the obvious lack of sufficient profit, the Local Service airlines required a large subsidy payment in the form of mail pay. Several of these new airlines never started flying, while others did not have their Certificates of Convenience and Necessity renewed at the expiration of their three-year certificate.

In 1948, while still receiving the major portion of their income from mail pay, the remaining Local Service Airlines had their Certificates of Convenience and Necessity renewed for a five-year period. About the time these certificates expired in 1953, the Local Service Air Carriers were requesting that their certificates be made permanent. Their valid argument was that since they only had a temporary life they could not attract investment capital, make long-range bank loans, or enter

into funded debt. Without new money they could not hope to acquire better facilities and more economical aircraft to lower unit cost, and thus lessen their dependence on subsidy.

The Civil Aeronautics Board denied their pleas on the grounds that the experimental period was to continue, and in 1953 the Certificates of Convenience and Necessity were again renewed for another five-year period. Before they expired an investigation was started resulting in a Civil Aeronautics Board case. By 1958 the outcome of this case was that the Civil Aeronautics Board reluctantly granted permanent certification but in a unique manner. A review of all the routes was made. Those that proved profitable were permanently certificated. The cities that were not supporting enough traffic, for at least a break even condition, were continued on the temporary basis. This policy is known by the CAB as "Use It or Lose It." A minimum standard was set of five passengers boarded daily to be reached after a year and a half. If this did not occur, the route was to be ordered abandoned or continued for a longer temporary period. The responsibility for supporting and continuing air service to these unprofitable cities was placed upon the cities themselves, hence the term "Use It or Lose It."

The turning point for the Local Service Air Carriers occurred when the Civil Aeronautics Board adopted the Class Mail Rate. This is the formula which determines the subsidy to the Local Service Air Carriers for providing service to cities which do not produce sufficient revenue to cover the cost. This action gave these carriers a future to look forward to and an impact on the financial community.

As a result of permanent certification the Local Service Air Carriers could and did acquire much needed capital to purchase new F-27 and F-227 turbo-prop aircraft and twin-engine jet aircraft. Their plight was also aided by Congress providing a guaranteed loan for the purchase of new aircraft. Therefore, their condition improved greatly. The Local Service Air Carriers gave better service and became less dependent on subsidy (public service revenue).

As in the case of the Trunks, increasing costs darkened the profit picture for the Local Service Air Carriers, and they looked for merger partners. As the Trunks (Majors) reduced their medium stage routes, the Locals picked them up; and the classification, Local Service Air Carrier, became a misleading name. The Local Service Air Carrier concept of "Feeder" is now gone. They are now classified as Nationals and Regionals with two companies having been elevated to the Major group.

ALL-CARGO AIR CARRIERS

The next classification of air carriers to appear were the **All-Cargo Air Carriers.** Shortly after the close of World War II several individuals and small, independent companies entered into charter, nonscheduled activities. This was a result of available surplus military cargo aircraft and discharged servicemen who had gained experience during the war in the various services, such as the Air Transport Command and the Naval Air Transport Service.

They conducted their civilian post war flights under the exemption of certain economic regulations of the Civil Aeronautics Acts which permitted charter flights by noncertificated air carriers. Predominantly they were one or two airplane operations that carried air freight wherever the business opportunity appeared, and for whatever rates the traffic and competition would allow. When the competition became too great, as a result of the appearance of literally hundreds of them, many began carrying passengers in the same manner. This created chaos in the air industry, not only within their own ranks, but also with the certificated air carriers.

Eventually the Civil Aeronautics Board legislated economic regulatory control. The laws were mainly directed toward these passenger-carrying noncertificated air carriers. This caused a hardship upon the truly air cargo companies since they were not carrying passengers but transporting air freight only. The Civil Aeronautics Board recognized their situation, and after an investigation and a case, concluded that they should have a valued position in air transportation. This was the Air Freight Case of July 1949 which allowed for the awarding of Certificates of Convenience and Necessity to all-cargo air carriers. For the second time since the requirement of Certificates of Convenience and Necessity in 1938, the certificates were granted for a temporary period which was to be five years.

The four original All-Cargo air carriers were Slick Airways, United States Airlines, The Flying Tiger Line, and Air News.

Of the original group certificated in 1949, Air News was not successful and never really got underway. United States Airlines, after a somewhat successful time but a difficult financial and organizational period, also ceased operations. Both companies' certificates were not renewed after a time of inactivity.

Slick Airways lasted for a number of years but then faded away. Seaboard World Airlines became certifi-

cated as an all-cargo air carrier and operated successfully; they have since merged with the Flying Tiger Line.

The certificated All-Cargo carriers enjoyed the same rights and privileges as did other certificated airlines. However, certain limitations were placed upon them at first, due to the nature of their business activities. Such limitations were that they could not transport passengers and would not be permitted to engage in conducting air mail services, simply because they did not have definite routes. The Civil Aeronautics Board then allowed All-Cargo air carriers to enter into contracts with the Post Office and also to transport passengers on a charter-only basis.

Due to the growth of their air cargo activities, the All-Cargo air carriers now conduct scheduled service between designated areas in the United States which serve major cities along the route. It is even now possible, due to necessity, to reserve space on board a given flight for an amount of air freight.

The potential of the all-cargo industry is still immense when it is understood that less than one-tenth of one percent of the intercity freight in the United States today travels by air, and most of this upon the passenger-carrying air carriers.

> **In November 1977 Congress passed a law permitting free entry into the industry.**

The All-Cargo air carriers had to sustain themselves with military contracts. The lack of economically operating air cargo aircraft has been one of the major problems. Only now, since the introduction of the widebody aircraft such as the Boeing 747, is there a glimmer of optimism for the future.

The first major change in air cargo since its beginning took place in November 1977 when Congress passed a law permitting free entry into the industry. The law deregulated the air cargo industry from Civil Aeronautics Board regulation.

Open entry into the domestic all-cargo industry was allowed by the change. It took effect in two stages. In the first stage the grandfather clause was applied so that those carriers who had held certificates to give all-cargo services received a certificate under the new law. They had to have applied within 45 days of the law, and the Civil Aeronautics Board had to approve within 60 days. By December 31, 1977, 83 applications had been filed with the Board and 73 were certificated by mid-1978. The effect of the new air cargo ruling increased competition. Theoretically, competition should result in lower rates. The immediate result during 1978 was a wide fluctuation in rates and an overall increase in the amount of air freight transported.

The second stage became effective January 1, 1979. Any citizen of the United States could apply for an all-cargo certificate and the Civil Aeronautics Board would grant it if they found the applicant fit, willing, and able to conduct all-cargo services. This meant that any citizen of the United States could go into the all-cargo business. Any air carrier so doing was able to serve any city it desired without Civil Aeronautics Board permission. Companies could set their own rates without Civil Aeronautics Board approval and operate any size aircraft.

HELICOPTER AIR CARRIERS

Although Leonardo da Vinci first presented the idea of the rotary wing, it was over two hundred years until the idea was developed into what we know today as the helicopter. "Spiral wing" is the literal meaning of the word helicopter. The first successful helicopter in the United States was built by Igor Sikorsky in 1939, after he started experimenting in Russia as early as 1908.

Helicopters were produced for the military by the end of World War II but were of no real practical use until 1946. It was then that the first helicopter was certificated for commercial purposes. Using the helicopter for local air mail service was experimented with by the Post Office shortly thereafter and received enthusiastic support of the Postmaster General in his 1947 fiscal report.

The vertical take-off and landing ability and lack of necessity for conventional runway made the helicopter ideal for intra-city service. Due to the size of the metropolitan areas and traffic congestion delaying air mail delivery, the helicopter was tried as a mail carrier in Los Angeles. The service so speeded up delivery of mail from the airport, central post office, and outlying districts, that the first air carrier company to use helicopters was formed and started flying in October 1947. Los Angeles Airways, using helicopters exclusively, became the first air carrier of its kind to be granted a temporary Certificate of Convenience and Necessity. In so doing, the Civil Aeronautics Board recognized the unusual serviceable advantages of the helicopter and created the classification Helicopter Airmail Lines. Originally they were restricted to a fifty-mile radius of the main post office and could carry only mail. However, with the advent of larger and better models of helicopters, they became certificated by the Civil Aeronautics Board to carry not only airmail, but also passengers and air cargo. The classification became known as **Helicopter Air Carriers.**

> "Spiral wing" is the literal meaning of the word helicopter.

Two other air carriers utilizing helicopters in the same manner were certificated to operate in Chicago and New York. Later, another Helicopter Air Carrier started service in the San Francisco-Oakland area.

The Helicopter Air Carrier was characterized by extremely short stage length, intra-city, or metropolitan area. The expenses of operating helicopters are extremely high in comparison to conventional aircraft. As a result of this and the extremely short stage length, the Helicopter Air Carriers had to rely heavily upon government subsidy in the form of air mail payments. Although the major portion of their gross revenues was form mail pay, the helicopter companies proved the value of this type of service. In 1965 the policy of the government was changed to eliminate subsidy to Helicopter Air Carriers.

Unfortunately, due to the high cost of operation and little or no profits, none of the Helicopter Air Carriers remain in operation today.

SUPPLEMENTAL AIR CARRIERS

For an understanding of the **Supplemental Air Carrier** classification of air carriers, it is necessary to recall the events already discussed in the history of the establishment of the all-cargo air carriers which pertain to the passenger-carrying activities of the non-certificated airlines, many of which were only interested in passenger traffic and not air cargo. They equipped their aircraft to carry passengers and did so in charter flights.

Their facilities were inadequate, and their maintenance generally poor. This led to a relatively high accident rate and subsequent enforcement by the Civil Aeronautics Administration, of safety regulations.

Economic regulations were also soon forthcoming; and in some cases the companies or individuals acted in flagrant and direct violation of such controls. Only after years of litigation was a place in air transportation recognized for the honest, well meaning and equipped, non-certificated air carrier. This became the classification of Supplemental Air Carriers. The reason for their existence was to relieve pressure on high-density Domestic Truck routes, when this occurred seasonally. On such routes as New York-Miami, during the height of the winter season, if the Trunk Air Carriers did not have sufficient seats available, it was the intention of the Civil Aeronautics Board that this overload of traffic could be carried by a Supplemental Air Carrier. Therefore, their flight operations each month were limited between any two domestic cities. They could conduct unlimited charter flights.

Since the advent of the jet transport, which brought about a sufficient number of available passenger seats, the purpose of the Supplemental Air Carrier became less necessary. In Civil Aeronautics Board cases they were denied operations because the existing Trunk Air Carriers have the capacity to serve even an abnormally high seasonal demand. This situation did not bother them too greatly, because practically all the Supplemental Air Carriers were under contract with the military to transport troops and supplies—a lucrative and dependable source of income.

The Supplementals found another extremely lucrative, but less dependable, source of income in charter work throughout the United States and foreign countries. This type of service came to be strongly opposed by the Trunks, Internationals, "Regionals," and Foreign Air Carriers.

Although the Supplemental Air Carriers were certificated, it was only to the extent of the meaning and scope of their services as defined by the Civil Aeronautics Board. Their Certificate of Convenience and Necessity did not contain the same requirements and authorizations granted to the other classes of air carriers previously discussed. Their operations were conducted by exempting them from requirements for scheduled passenger and airmail service.

In some states there was a classification of air carrier that developed in recent years known as **Intra-State Air Carriers.** Their operations were limited to the area within the borders of one state, and their right to operate was granted by an agency of that state. They were not subject to the economic regulations of the Civil Aeronautics Board since their operations did not cross state lines. Characteristically they resemble the Local Service Air Carriers when they began operation in 1945. They serve small and medium-size communities whose traffic density is low. Their routes are designed to originate and terminate at the larger airport cities.

The **Noncertificated Air Carriers** were miscellaneous air transportation operators. It was not their intention or function to offer scheduled flight activities. In lieu of a Certificate of Convenience and Necessity they were required to possess a Letter of Registration issued by the Civil Aeronautics Board. This class was composed of two divisions—Air Taxis and Air Freight Forwarders.

Air Taxis, as the name implies, offer air transportation when and to wherever the passenger desires. The rates for this special service were much higher than for a certificated air carrier. Air Taxi operations were allowed by Federal Aviation Regulations Parts 135 and 298. They could operate aircraft with a maximum of 60 passenger seats and a maximum payload capacity of 7,500 pounds. Many helicopters were found in the Air Taxi group. Those carrying cargo only could operate aircraft up to 18,000 pounds payload capacity. Air Taxi companies operate throughout the United States at airports of all sizes.

Air Freight Forwarders also conduct business freely under deregulation. Surface freight forwarding has been in existence as long as there has been business. With the advent of the airplane it was natural that freight forwarding should take to the air.

An Air Freight Forwarder is a consolidator or middleman between the shipper and the airline company. His business is to collect individual shipments, consolidate them into a large load destined for a given city, and have the airline carry them. He is actually a customer of the airline and earns a profit only by the spread between what he receives from the individual shipper and the price he pays to the airline company for quantity shipments. Further income is derived by providing extra services, such as packing and special handling, to the shipper. The Air Freight Forwarder does not own or operate aircraft, but since he receives public property for transportation by air, he is engaged indirectly in air transportation.

In late January 1979, the Civil Aeronautics Board deregulated Air Freight Forwarders. This followed the passage of the Airline Deregulation Act which became effective on October 24, 1978. The purpose of deregulation is to allow competition to adjust rates and services.

The deregulation of Air Freight Forwarders and cooperative shippers associations eliminated the requirement of filing tariffs. Under deregulation, Forwarders are allowed to negotiate individually with direct carriers (airlines) and will not be required to hold public liability or cargo liability insurance. Reporting requirements are simplified and the former fitness applications are reduced to a registration procedure.

Airline companies registered in foreign countries, but nonetheless conducting air transport services to and from the United States, are termed Foreign Air Carriers. In order to conduct such scheduled flights they needed to be granted a Foreign Air Carrier Permit by the Civil Aeronautics Board.

Foreign Air Carriers are allowed to discharge and enplane traffic at gateway or international airports of entry, but they are not allowed to carry traffic between two points within the United States.

A more detailed discussion concerning this subject will be found in the chapter dealing with International and Foreign Air Transportation, Chapter 12.

COMMUTER AIR CARRIERS

As the Local Service Air Carriers started to expand by seeking longer stage routes, larger metropolitan areas, and larger aircraft, a new group of airlines started to appear. The Local Service Air Carriers were plagued with outdated equipment and low-density routes. The new aircraft being developed at this time were capable of carrying 90 to 120 passengers while the Local's outdated equipment handled 44 to 50 passengers. In order to fill these new aircraft, higher-density routes were sought and approved by the Civil Aeronautics Board. The result was that many communities on low-density routes felt a reduction in air service.

Out of this came a new breed of air carrier; the **Commuter Air Carriers.** Many Commuters developed from Air Taxis, while others were totally new corporations. Commuter Air Carriers differed from Air Taxis in that they flew a published schedule on specific routes, whereas the Air Taxi flew only on demand. The Commuters had two basic controls placed upon them in addition to safety requirements. These were (1) meeting prescribed liability insurance, and (2) operating aircraft with a gross take-off weight of less than 12,500 pounds. The 15-passenger Beech-99 and 19-passenger DeHavilland Twin Otter were the most popular commuter aircraft of this type. The CAB stated that Commuter Air Carriers were to be encouraged to continue, but that they "shouldn't be allowed to enter long-haul, high-density markets except possibly to provide specialized service with noncompetitive equipment."

Commuter Air Carriers were not issued Certificates of Convenience and Necessity by the Civil Aeronautics Board, and therefore were not controlled as far as the routes they served or the fares they charged. However, the Federal Aviation Administration did regulate their safety programs. Some of these carriers provided service into cities where Trunks and Locals had suspended service, however the Major carrier was responsible for serving these cities if a Commuter failed to provide adequate service. Commuter Air Carriers now serve as designated air mail carriers in many markets.

For a Commuter Air Carrier to be successful, it must start with the proper financial backing and have a management team that controls the flow of cash adhering to sound principles. Careful selection of equipment and routes tied to a service that is highly passen-ger-oriented are other features necessary for a viable carrier.

Commuter air service differed from certificated service in that it generally was performed in smaller aircraft in short-haul, low-density markets where surface transportation can be an attractive alternative. Commuters providing such service must have flexibility to enter and exit markets quickly.

Deregulation created a major impetus for the Commuter segment of the air transportation industry. While deregulation for the traditional certificated air carriers brought freedom from rate and route regulations, it brought more regulation to the Commuter air carriers. However it did not alter the Commuters' basic route and rate freedoms. The reason is that the Civil Aeronautics Board never had any economic regulations for this smallest segment of the air carrier industry. Since 1952, the Commuters and their predecessors had been free to fly whatever routes they chose and charge the rates which they determined. The reasons for the absence of regulatory control were that these very small air carriers were predominately intrastate at their beginning and that they constituted a very small part of the industry, so small, in fact, as to be negligible in comparison to the total revenue passenger miles flown by the entire air carrier industry.

From the middle 1960s, the Commuters grew rapidly with the advent of the new, more cost-efficient aircraft such as the Beech-99 and the DeHavilland Twin Otter. Immediately following this rapid growth there was a general collapse in the Commuter industry and then a slow growth.

The only requirements of the Civil Aeronautics Board were for the filing of a registration statement showing proof of a valid Federal Aviation Administration Operating Certificate and liability insurance coverage. Later the Board asked for traffic data on a route basis as well.

After deregulation became effective in 1978, the Board allowed the Commuters greater liberty regarding aircraft size by permitting the use of larger aircraft if route market conditions warranted it. The Board allowed for an increase in aircraft size to 60 seats immediately prior to passage of the Deregulation Act.

Commuter traffic grew during the 1970s at an average rate of 11%. Since deregulation, passenger traffic has continued to grow. Twenty-five Commuters had become certificated passenger air carriers and twenty-two as air cargo air carriers by the end of 1980. (See Figure 11.4.)

As the major air carriers have taken advantage of the entry-exit provisions of the Deregulation Act by

Figure 11.4
Current Air Carriers

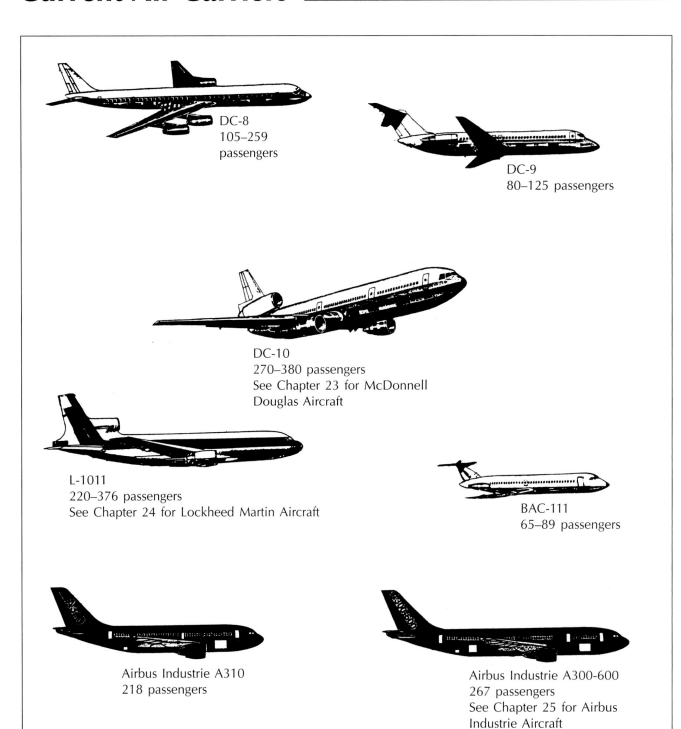

DC-8
105–259
passengers

DC-9
80–125 passengers

DC-10
270–380 passengers
See Chapter 23 for McDonnell
Douglas Aircraft

L-1011
220–376 passengers
See Chapter 24 for Lockheed Martin Aircraft

BAC-111
65–89 passengers

Airbus Industrie A310
218 passengers

Airbus Industrie A300-600
267 passengers
See Chapter 25 for Airbus
Industrie Aircraft

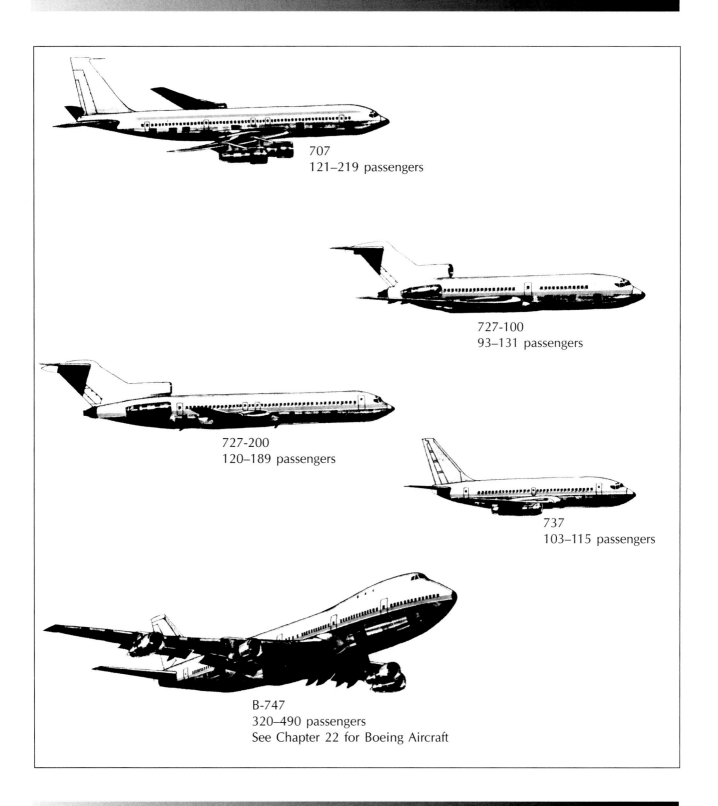

707
121–219 passengers

727-100
93–131 passengers

727-200
120–189 passengers

737
103–115 passengers

B-747
320–490 passengers
See Chapter 22 for Boeing Aircraft

suspending service to small communities, Commuters have expanded their operations by taking their place. The Deregulation Act provided fewer economic regulations for the old certificated air carriers; however, it meant a change from no economic regulation to some regulation for the Commuters. Since deregulation, the Commuter air carriers have committed to the purchase of more than one billion dollars' worth of new aircraft. This amount is double the value of the entire existing Commuter aircraft fleet in operation before deregulation. The Federal Aviation Administration forecasts that the Commuter Air Carriers will experience the highest growth rate of all domestic air transportation over the next several years.

RECLASSIFICATION OF AIR CARRIER GROUPS

Passage of the Airline Deregulation Act on October 24, 1978, represented the culmination of much study and discussion. It was a major legislative action which completely changed government, industry and labor relationships. The passage was the dawn of a new era for the U.S. air transportation industry. The principal objective of deregulation was to reduce government economic regulation of the U.S. domestic air carrier industry. The air carriers were to begin operating freely in a competitive environment, subject only to the antitrust and other laws applicable to all other industries in the nation. The full impact of deregulation is yet to be determined.

Since the Act was passed there has been considerable change in the aviation industry. The once clear-cut distinctions among Trunk, Local Service, Commuter, and other classes of air carriers are becoming increasingly blurred. Route structures, services, and aircraft used have changed in response to the conditions of the marketplace for air transportation services.

The history of aviation has been one of change— change in legislative framework, technology, operations, procedures, and economic conditions. In spite of these changes, the general trend of the U.S. air carrier industry has been that of continued growth. Examined in this light, the current changes resulting from deregulation are not that different from the changes and challenges presented in the past.

In a major move toward deregulation the Civil Aeronautics Board, on October 3, 1981, adopted a plan that greatly reduced the number and frequency of reports air carriers are required to file with the Board. For the smallest non-subsidized certificated air carriers, this meant a 62% reduction in reporting.

The new system not only reduced costs for the air carriers and the government but also removed an obstacle for entry into the air transport industry. The burden of Federal Government paperwork for the air industry was lessened. This demonstrates that a regulatory agency can continue to carry out its function with a smaller work staff and with less information from the industry it regulates.

In addition to reducing the filing burden on certificated carriers, the plan eliminated the use of the pre-deregulation categories for the air carrier industry such as Trunk, Local Service, etc. Since the Airline Deregulation Act was passed in October 1978, the old categories no longer have significance. Beginning in January 1981, the Board began a gradual change to tabulating financial and statistical information on the basis of annual revenues.

Certificated air carriers need to file only about one-half as many reports under the new plan. Because Commuter air carriers providing essential air service are to file more data than before, the total reduction in paperwork required by the Board was approximately 40%.

A three-fold increase in the number of certificated air carriers occurred within two years after passage of the Airline Deregulation Act of 1978. However, the Civil Aeronautics Board information-gathering staff was reduced 44% in anticipation of reduced reporting requirements.

The changing nature of air carrier operations under deregulation necessitated a reevaluation and restructuring of air carrier groupings for statistical and financial data aggregation and analysis. The historical groupings, such as Trunks, Local Service, etc., lost significance as new air carriers entered certificated service and as some pre-deregulation certificated carriers either restructured their operations or merged with other air carriers. The Board eliminated the prederegulation, or historical, air carrier groupings and adopted newly defined groupings based on size of annual total operating revenues.

TYPES OF AIRLINE CERTIFICATION

U.S. scheduled airlines are classified by the government on the basis of the amount of revenue generated from operations. These classifications are major, national and regional. All airlines hold two certificates from the federal government: a fitness certificate and an operating certificate. The Department of Transportation issues fitness certificates—called certificates of public convenience and necessity—under its statutory authority. The certificate establishes that the carrier has the financing and the management in place to provide scheduled service. The certificate typically authorizes both passenger and cargo service. Some airlines, however, obtain only cargo-service authority. Commuter airlines that use aircraft with a seating capacity of 60 or fewer seats or a maximum payload capacity of no more than 18,000 pounds can operate under the alternative authority of Part 298 of Department of Transportation's economic regulations.

Operating certificates, on the other hand, are issued by the Federal Aviation Administration under Part 121 of the Federal Aviation Regulations, which spell out numerous requirements for operating aircraft with 10 or more seats. The requirements cover such things as the training of flight crews and aircraft maintenance programs. All majors, nationals and regionals operate with a Part 121 certificate. (Table 11.1.)

MAJORS

Major airlines generate operating revenues of more than $1 billion annually. Previously called trunk carriers, they generally provide nationwide, and in some cases, worldwide service. There were 15 major U.S. passenger airlines in 2000: Alaska, America West, American, American Eagle, American Trans Air, Continental, Delta, Northwest, Southwest, Trans World, United and US Airways. In addition, three all-cargo airlines were classified as majors: DHL Airways, FedEx and United Parcel Service.

All of the majors hold two certificates from the Federal Government, a fitness certificate and an operating certificate. The Department of Transportation issues fitness certificates under Section 401 of the Federal Aviation Act. Basically, the certificate establishes that the carrier has the financing and management in place to provide scheduled service with large aircraft (defined as aircraft with 60 or more seats and a payload of more than 18,000 pounds.)

Operating certificates, on the other hand, are issued by the Federal Aviation Administration under Section 121 of the Federal Air Regulations, which spell out numerous requirements for operating aircraft with 30 or more seats and more than 9,000 pounds payload capacity. The requirements cover such things as the training of flight crews and aircraft maintenance programs.

Table 11.1 Active U.S. Large Certificated Air Carriers

Majors (15) (Annual revenues over $1 billion)	Nationals (37) (Annual revenues of $100 million to $1 billion)		Regionals (44) (Annual revenues under $100 million)		
Alaska	Air Transport Int'l	Kitty Hawk	Accessair	Miami Air	Trans Air Link
America West	Air Wisconsin	Kitty Hawk Int'l	Allegiant	Nations Air	Transmeridian
American	AirTran	Legend	Amerijet	North American	UFS
American Eagle	**Aloha**	Mesaba	Ameristar	Northern Air	Zantop
American Trans Air	Atlantic Southeast	Midway	Arrow	Omni	
Continental	**Atlas Air**	**Midwest Express**	Asia Pacific Int'l	Pace Aviation	
Delta	Challenge	National	Capital Cargo	Pan American	
DHL Airways	Comair	**Polar Air Cargo**	Casino Express	Panagra	
FedEx	Continental Express	Ryan Int'l	Champion Air	Planet	
Northwest	Continental Micronesia	Spirit Air	Custom Air	Pro Air	
Southwest	**Emery Worldwide**	Sun Country	Discovery	**Reeve Aleutian**	
Trans World	**Evergreen Int'l**	Tower	Eastwind	Reliant	
United	Executive	Trans States	Express.Net	Renown	
United Parcel Service	Express One	USA Jet	Falcon Air	Sierra Pacific	
US Airways	Fine	US Airways Shuttle	Florida West	Southeast	
	Fontier	Vanguard	Gulf and Caribbean	Southern	
	Gemini	World	Kiwi	Sun Pacific	
	Hawaiian		Laker	Sunworld	
	Horizon Air		Lorair	Tatonduk	
	JetBlue		Lynden	Trade Winds	

Source: Air Transport Association

NATIONALS

National carriers are scheduled airlines with annual operating revenues between $100 million and $1 billion. Many of the airlines in this category serve particular regions of the country, although some provide long-haul and even international service. Among the nationals are some of the former local service lines that, prior to deregulation, were licensed by the Civil Aeronautics Board to operate between major cities and smaller communities surrounding them. Also in this category are some of the former supplemental carriers, previously licensed by the Civil Aeronautics Board to operate unscheduled charter service, which supplemented the capacity of the trunk carriers.

Like the majors, nationals operate mostly medium- and large-sized jets. They are subject to Department of Transportation fitness requirements, as well as the FAA Part 121 operating requirements. Among today's nationals are Aloha, Atlas Air, Emery Worldwide, Evergreen, Hawaiian, Midwest Express and Polar Air Cargo.

REGIONALS

As their name implies, regional carriers are airlines whose service, for the most part, is limited to a single region of the country, transporting travelers between the major cities of their region and smaller, surrounding communities. This has been one of the fastest growing and most profitable segments of the industry since deregulation.

Regional carriers are divided into three sub-groups: large, medium and small.

Large regionals are scheduled carriers with operating revenues of $20 million to $100 million. Most of their aircraft seat more than 60 passengers, so they hold Department of Transportation fitness certificates and must comply with FAA Part 121 operating requirements.

Medium regionals follow the same market-niche strategy as the large regionals and operate many of the same type of aircraft. Their distinction is simply that they operate on a smaller scale, with operating revenues under $20 million.

Small regionals, sometimes called commuters, represent the largest segment of the regional airline business. There is no official revenue definition of a small regional. What distinguishes them as a group, more than anything else, is the size of the aircraft they operate. All have less than 61 seats, which means they do not require a fitness certificate from Department of Transportation; Department of Transportation only requires that

they register their service and make certain annual reports to the department under Section 298 of the Department of Transportation economic regulations.

CARGO CARRIERS

Within the categories of major, national and regional airlines are not only passenger carriers, but cargo carriers as well. While much of the cargo that moves by air is carried in the bellies of passenger jets or in combination aircraft where the main deck is divided into two sections, one for cargo and one for passengers; other aircraft in use by principally all cargo carriers, called freighters, carry nothing but freight.

Freighters are, most often, passenger jets that have been stripped of their seats to maximize cargo-carrying capacity. In addition, their decks are reinforced to accommodate heavier loads, and they typically have other cargo-handling features, such as rollers, built into the floors, extra-large doors, and hinged nose and tail sections. Department of Transportation has a special fitness review procedure for all-cargo carriers, but most of the large ones hold a certificate of public convenience and necessity. Among the largest cargo carriers are companies that began in the small package and overnight document-delivery business. These are the integrated carriers, so called because they offer door-to-door service, combining the services of the traditional airline and the freight forwarder. (Table 11.2.)

THE AIR CARRIER INDUSTRY

In the year 2000 there were 87 U.S. commercial air carriers including both scheduled and nonscheduled. There were 62 passenger airlines (operating aircraft with over 60 seats) and 24 all-cargo carriers.

Forty-three of the airlines provided scheduled passenger service. Forty-two of the carriers provided scheduled domestic service within the 50 States, the District of Columbia, Puerto Rico, and the U.S. Virgin Islands, while 17 of the carriers provided scheduled international service. Of the carriers providing scheduled international service, eight served Atlantic routes, ten served Latin American routes, and seven served Pacific routes. (Table 11.3.)

FINANCIAL RESULTS

In 2000 operating revenues for the U.S. commercial airline industry exceeded operating expenses. This was the eighth consecutive year that operating revenues

Table 11.2   Top 50 Regional/Commuter Airlines Ranked by Total Passenger Enplanements
Fiscal Year 2000

Carrier	Enplanements	Carrier	Enplanements
1. American Eagle	12,085,877	26. Astral	391,876
2. Comair	7,818,419	27. Aloha Island Air	390,912
3. Continental Express	7,621,394	28. Shuttle America	265,507
4. Mesaba	6,008,305	29. Chicago Express	232,576
5. Atlantic Southeast	5,986,069	30. Colgan Air	186,831
6. SkyWest	5,727,490	31. Peninsula	180,486
7. Horizon	5,056,439	32. United Feeder Service	144,335
8. Atlantic Coast	3,550,440	33. Big Sky	140,654
9. Piedmont	3,132,583	34. Corporate Express	116,614
10. Mesa	2,738,582	35. Freedom Air	90,111
11. Allegheny	2,446,967	36. Hagland Aviation	84,313
12. Trans States	2,044,987	37. Pacific Island Aviation	82,351
13. Executive Airlines	1,919,102	38. Samoa Air	72,835
14. PSA	1,135,508	39. Seaborne Aviation	65,496
15. Great Lakes	1,082,758	40. Grant Aviation	61,926
16. Express Airline I	1,076,630	41. Harbor Airlines	58,832
17. Chautauqua	1,069,487	32. Kenmore Air Harbor	55,614
18. Business Express	1,067,291	43. Bering Air	51,495
19. Gulfstream International	925,894	44. Vieques Air Link	50,998
20. Air Midwest	915,565	45. Cape Smythe	45,506
21. CCAir	758,815	46. Frontier Flying Service	44,338
22. Cape Air	590,544	47. Promech	39,060
23. Commutair	563,113	48. Chalks Flying Boat	38,180
24. Eagle Canyon	544,480	49. Taquan Air Service	35,121
25. ERA	432,549	50. Wings of Alaska	34,234

Source DOT Form 298-C and Form 41

were higher than operating expenses. Since 1993, cumulative operating profits have exceeded $47.2 billion. The financial success of the industry in 2000 was based on strong growth in traffic and yields offsetting higher fuel and labor costs. Capacity growth in 2000 was well below that of traffic, resulting in an increase in system load factor of 1.4 points to a record 72.2 percent. Labor turmoil at United was one of the major contributors to slower capacity growth in 2000.

The industry operating profit was $7.6 billion in 2000. Although operating profit was down $1.1 billion in 2000, it was the fourth highest year for operating profit since deregulation.

The industry had an operating profit in all four quarters. For the year, operating revenues increased 8.3 percent, while operating expenses increased 10.0 percent. By comparison, operating expenses were up 4.8 percent in 1999, 3.8 percent in 1998, and 5.7 percent in 1997.

The large increase in operating expenses in 2000 was largely due to a sharp increase in fuel costs. After declining 18.6 and 9.3 percent in the past 2 years, fuel prices rose an estimated 48 percent in 2000, escalating industry operating expenses by more than $4.8 billion.

Industry domestic nominal yields increased 3.2 percent, while yields, adjusted for inflation, increased 0.1 percent. Throughout much of the year, carriers have raised fares to offset rising fuel prices. However deep discounting by carriers in order to stay competitive and boost demand has offset much of the increase in posted fares. Competition in the industry is intense, and is expected to continue in both the domestic and international markets throughout the forecast period. (Table 11.4.)

Nominal international yields also increased during the year. In the Atlantic real yields declined 1.9 percent while in Latin American and Pacific markets real yields increased 0.4 and 7.6 percent, respectively. The falling

Table 11.3 Top 25 Airlines in 2000
Scheduled Service

Carriers certificated under Section 401, Federal Aviation Act

	Passengers (thousands)		Revenue Passenger Miles (millions)		Freight Ton Miles (millions)		Total Operating Revenues (millions)
1 Delta	105,591	1 United	126,880	1 Federal Express	7,401.9	1 United	$19,331
2 American	86,240	2 American	116,515	2 UPS**	4,339.1	2 American	18,117
3 United	83,854	3 Delta	107,782	3 United	2,529.9	3 FedEx	15,597
4 Southwest	72,568	4 Northwest	79,101	4 Northwest	2,205.1	4 Delta	15,321
5 US Airways	59,772	5 Continental	62,314	5 American	1,916.7	5 Northwest	10,957
6 Northwest	56,835	6 US Airways	46,827	6 Delta	1,435.0	6 US Airways	9,181
7 Continental	45,139	7 Southwest	42,230	7 Emery Worldwide**	1,048.3	7 Continental	9,129
8 Trans World	26,365	8 Trans World	27,215	8 Polar Air Cargo	1,047.2	8 Southwest	5,650
9 America West	19,942	9 America West	19,102	9 Atlas Air**	995.1	9 Trans World	3,585
10 Alaska	13,512	10 Alaska	11,979	10 Continental	887.0	10 United Parcel Service	2,530
11 American Eagle	12,176	11 American Trans Air	7,488	11 Evergreen Int'l**	792.0	11 America West	2,309
12 Continental Express	7,770	12 Hawaiian	4,196	12 Airborne Express	648.2	12 Alaska	1,760
13 AirTran	7,547	13 AirTran	4,111	13 DHL Airways	452.4	13 American Eagle	1,246
14 Atlantic Southeast	6,096	14 American Eagle	3,145	14 US Airways	277.7	14 DHL Airways	1,231
15 Mesaba	6,068	15 Continental Micronesia	3,050	15 Gemini	223.5	15 American Trans Air	1,182
16 American Trans Air	5,940	16 Continental Express	2,947	16 Arrow	154.1	16 Airborne Express	1,126
17 Hawaiian	5,887	17 Spirit Air	2,741	17 Challenge	153.4	17 Emery Worldwide	1,013
18 Comair	5,655	18 Sun Country	2,697	18 Trans World	129.6	18 Continental Express	845
19 Aloha	5,177	19 Frontier	2,596	19 Kitty Hawk Int'l	74.6	19 Atlas Air	790
20 Horizon Air	5,044	20 National	2,571	20 Southwest	69.1	20 AirTran	624
21 Air Wisconsin	3,857	21 Comair	2,148	21 Alaska	57.4	21 Atlantic Southeast	622
22 Midway	2,937	22 Atlantic Southeast	2,116	22 Hawaiian	53.7	22 Hawaiian	607
23 Fronteir	2,893	23 Midwest Express	1,969	23 Kitty Hawk	47.1	23 Continental Micronesia	512
24 Spirit Air	2,836	24 Mesaba	1,692	24 Air Transport Int'l	45.8	24 Frontier	451
25 Sun Country	2,203	25 Horizon Air	1,429	25 Continental Micronesia	44.3	25 Horizon Air	443

* Includes carriers certificated under Chapter 411 of Title 49 of the U.S. Code (formerly Section 401 of the Federal Aviation Act).
** Includes non-scheduled service.
Source: Air Transportation Association

yields in the Atlantic markets can be attributed to supply side effects of increased competition and growth in capacity. The Latin region increase reflected a shift in the mix of traffic to higher yielding Caribbean destinations while the Pacific yield increase was due to an increase in the yen/dollar exchange rate and an increase in demand. During 2000, six major passenger carriers reduced their real unit costs (estimated without fuel and oil expenses). U.S. Airways had the largest decline—down 6.4 percent, followed by Southwest with unit costs declining 6.1 percent. Alaska showed the largest increase, with unit costs up 5.8 percent.

System average real operating cost per available seat mile (excluding fuel and oil) for the major passenger carriers was 8.64 cents in 2000, down 0.6 percent from 1999. System real unit costs (including fuel and oil) increased 3.3 percent. In 2000, American Trans Air had the lowest operating cost (excluding fuel and oil) per available seat mile (5.80 cents). The highest unit cost among the major network carriers was U.S. Airways with 12.38 cents.

In 2000, U.S. airlines posted a net profit of $3.6 billion, $1.7 billion below that of 1999. Net profit between the 1994 and 1998 period totaled $14.7 billion. Total net profit for the seven-year period was $23.6 billion. The following two graphs show operating and net loss for the 12 major passenger air carriers. Of the 12 carriers, 10 had operating profits in 2000 while TWA and US Airways recorded operating losses of $364.1 million and $15.0 million, respectively. American and Delta recorded the highest operating and net profits of the major passenger carriers.

During the next several years, competition, capacity expansion, and productivity gains in the industry are expected to push real yields downward. Falling yields plus economic growth will continue to expand aviation activity and increase passenger revenues. Cost control will be key to the industry's ability to sustain profits at a relatively high level throughout the forecast period.

Table 11.4 U.S. Scheduled Airlines, 1990–2000 Summary

in millions, except when noted

	1990	1991	1992	1993	1994	1995	1996	1997	1998	1999	2000
TRAFFIC—SCHEDULED SERVICE											
Revenue Passengers Enplaned	465.6	452.3	475.1	488.5	528.8	547.8	581.2	599.1	612.9	636.0	665.5
Revenue Passenger Miles	457,926	447,955	478,554	489,684	519,382	540,656	578,663	605,574	618,086	652,047	692,505
Available Seat Miles	733,375	715,199	752,772	771,641	784,331	807,078	835,071	860,803	874,090	918,419	956,502
Passenger Load Factor (%)	62.4	62.6	63.6	63.5	66.2	67.0	69.3	70.3	70.7	71.0	72.4
Average Passenger Trip Length (miles)	984	990	1.007	1,002	982	987	996	1,011	1,008	1,025	1,041
Freight & Express Revenue Ton Miles	10,546	10,225	11,130	11,944	13,792	14,578	15,301	17,959	18,131	19,317	21,143
Aircraft Departures (thousands)	6,924	6,783	7,051	7,245	7,531	8,062	8,230	8,192	8,292	8,627	8,992
FINANCIAL DATA											
Passenger Revenues	$58,453	$57,092	$59,828	$63,945	$65,422	$69,594	$75,286	$79,471	$80,986	$84,318	$93,572
Freight & Express Revenues	5,432	5,509	5,916	6,662	7,284	8,616	9,679	10,477	10,697	11,415	11,993
Mail Revenues	970	957	1,184	1,212	1,183	1,266	1,279	1,362	1,708	1,739	1,975
Charter Revenues	2,877	3,717	2,801	3,082	3,548	3,485	3,447	3,575	3,821	4,030	4,365
Total Operating Revenues	76,142	75,158	78,140	84,559	88,313	94,578	101,938	109,568	113,465	119,038	129,463
Total Operating Expenses	78,054	76,943	80,585	83,121	85,600	88,718	95,729	100,982	104,138	110,638	122,390
Operating Profit (Loss)	(1,912)	(1,785)	(2,444)	1,438	2,713	5,860	6,209	8,586	9,327	8,400	7,073
Interest Expense	1,978	1,777	1,743	2,027	2,347	2,424	1,981	1,733	1,742	1,821	2,165
Net Profit (Loss)*	($3,921)	($1,940)	($4,791)	($2,136)	($344)	$2,314	$2,804	$5,170	$4,903	$5,360	$2,638
Revenue per Passenger Mile (cents)	12.76	12.74	12.50	13.06	12.60	12.87	13.01	13.12	13.10	12.93	13.51
Rate of Return on Investment (%)	(6.0)	(0.5)	(9.3)	(0.4)	5.2	11.9	11.5	14.7	12.0	11.1	6.6
Operating Profit Margin (%)	(2.5)	(2.4)	(3.1)	1.7	3.1	6.2	6.1	7.8	8.2	7.1	5.5
Net Profit Margin (%)	(5.1)	(2.6)	(6.1)	(2.5)	(0.4)	2.4	2.8	4.7	4.3	4.5	2.0
EMPLOYEES (average full-time equivalent)	545,809	533,565	540,413	537,111	539,759	546,987	564,425	586,509	621,058	646,410	679,967

*Excludes fresh-start accounting extraordinary gains of Continental and Trans World in 1993.

Source: Air Transport Association

In 2000, total scheduled U.S. commercial air carrier activity (domestic plus international) continued to grow at rates above those of the U.S. and world economies. In 2000, system revenue passenger miles (RPMs) increased 6.4 percent, while enplanements increased 4.7 percent. (Table 11.5.) Since 1991, system RPMs have increased 4.8 percent a year—roughly 27 percent higher than the rate of growth of U.S. Gross Domestic Product (GDP) and 64 percent higher than world GDP growth, adjusted for inflation. System available seat miles (ASMs) increased 4.4 percent in 2000, resulting in a load factor increase of 1.4 percentage points to 72.2 percent—the highest figure ever. Since 1991, the system load factor has increased 9.9 percentage points.

ECONOMICS OF AIR CARRIER ROUTES

The basic air carrier route structure in the United States today has progressed through many evolutionary stages and is continually changing. The air carrier route system presently in effect has been, and is currently, influenced by many factors, the most important of which are the general economic-business conditions of the nation and the air industry, air carrier management policies, technological progress, and government action.

The earliest air routes were determined by the requirements of the airmail. Early airmail routes were established between the large cities and areas of population which were separated by many miles. Not long after, transcontinental routes were developed. The rate of expansion of air routes in the decade of 1925 to 1935 was determined by the Post Office. It was not until after World War II that local routes and long international routes were developed. Today a large portion of the population in the United States has direct access to certificated air carrier routes. Many people in the country indirectly benefit by the service of air transportation.

Economics is a broad subject of study. It is a social science, with science meaning an organized body of

Table 11.5   U.S. Commercial Air Carriers
Scheduled Passenger Traffic

FISCAL YEAR	REVENUE PASSENGER ENPLANEMENTS (Millions)			REVENUE PASSENGER MILES (Billions)		
	DOMESTIC	INTERNATIONAL	TOTAL	DOMESTIC	INTERNATIONAL	TOTAL
*Historical**						
1995	496.3	48.6	544.9	392.6	144.3	536.9
1996	524.5	50.0	574.5	418.9	150.9	569.8
1997	543.0	52.3	595.3	440.9	158.8	599.7
1998	555.0	53.1	608.1	451.5	163.3	614.8
1999	576.1	53.3	629.4	473.1	169.7	642.8
2000	604.1	54.6	658.7	502.8	181.3	684.0
Forecast						
2001	624.3	58.1	682.4	522.4	194.0	716.4
2002	643.3	62.1	705.4	541.2	207.9	748.1
2003	665.5	66.4	731.9	562.8	222.9	785.7
2004	690.0	70.8	760.8	587.0	238.5	825.5
2005	717.0	75.2	792.2	612.9	253.8	866.7
2006	745.3	79.6	824.9	640.4	269.1	909.5
2007	773.6	84.1	857.7	668.6	284.5	953.1
2008	802.2	89.1	891.3	697.4	301.3	998.7
2009	831.6	94.3	925.9	726.6	318.9	1,045.5
2010	862.1	99.8	961.9	757.2	337.7	1,094.9
2011	893.8	105.4	999.2	789.0	356.6	1,145.6
2012	926.6	111.0	1,037.6	822.1	376.0	1,198.1

*Source: Form 41, U.S. Department of Transportation

knowledge or facts. The body of facts in a social science cannot be as exact as in the physical sciences which have more predictable results. Economics as a social science is the study of the social aspects of business. It is a science that investigates the conditions affecting the production and use of labor, materials, and equipment for the public interest.

With respect to air carrier routes, economics means management and control with regard to their productivity. Special attention is given to the costs and revenues of producing the air route service for the commercial, postal, and national defense needs of the United States. (Table 11.6.)

AIR CARRIER ROUTE DETERMINANTS

In general, the factors which determine air carrier routes fall within three areas, namely:

1. Economic
2. Political
3. Geographic

1. Economic determinants include all the activities of producing an air transportation service, activities which create and satisfy a demand. The demand in this case includes that of air passengers for reasons of both business and pleasure; all forms of air cargo; and the transportation of mail by air, including priority airmail and non-priority first class mail transported on a space availability basis.

2. For want of a better term the word "political" is used to describe this air carrier route determinant. This includes all legislative and regulatory actions of governments from local, State, and Federal to the relations of nations internationally. An air carrier may find it inexpedient to refuel its aircraft in one state rather than another because of the fuel tax levied. Taxes of all kinds tend to influence management when they consider a location for the building of overhaul facilities. The treaties between nations in negotiating and granting reciprocal agreements also will affect air carrier route structure.

3. The final route determinant, geography, though less important than formerly due to the expanded capa-

Table 11.6 U.S. Commercial Air Carriers
Scheduled Passenger Capacity, Traffic, and Load Factors

FISCAL YEAR	DOMESTIC			INTERNATIONAL		
	ASMs (BIL)	RPMs (BIL)	% LOAD FACTOR	ASMs (BIL)	ROMs (BIL)	% LOAD FACTOR
*Historical**						
1995	602.1	392.6	65.2	202.3	144.3	71.4
1996	621.1	418.9	67.4	206.9	150.9	73.0
1997	639.9	440.9	68.9	213.8	158.8	74.3
1998	644.3	451.5	70.1	223.3	163.3	73.1
1999	677.9	473.1	69.8	229.6	169.7	73.9
2000	709.1	502.8	70.9	238.6	181.3	76.0
Forecast						
2001	741.0	522.4	70.5	257.5	194.0	75.3
2002	770.4	541.2	70.2	275.2	207.9	75.5
2003	804.0	562.8	70.0	293.9	222.9	75.8
2004	835.6	587.0	70.3	313.2	238.5	76.1
2005	870.5	612.9	70.4	331.9	253.8	76.5
2006	908.4	640.4	70.5	351.7	269.1	76.5
2007	948.4	668.6	70.5	372.0	284.5	76.5
2008	989.2	697.4	70.5	394.2	301.3	76.4
2009	1030.7	726.6	70.5	417.5	318.9	76.4
2010	1074.0	757.2	70.5	442.2	337.7	76.4
2011	1119.1	789.0	70.5	467.3	356.6	76.3
2012	1166.1	822.1	70.5	492.9	376.0	76.3

*Source: Form 41, U.S. Department of Transportation

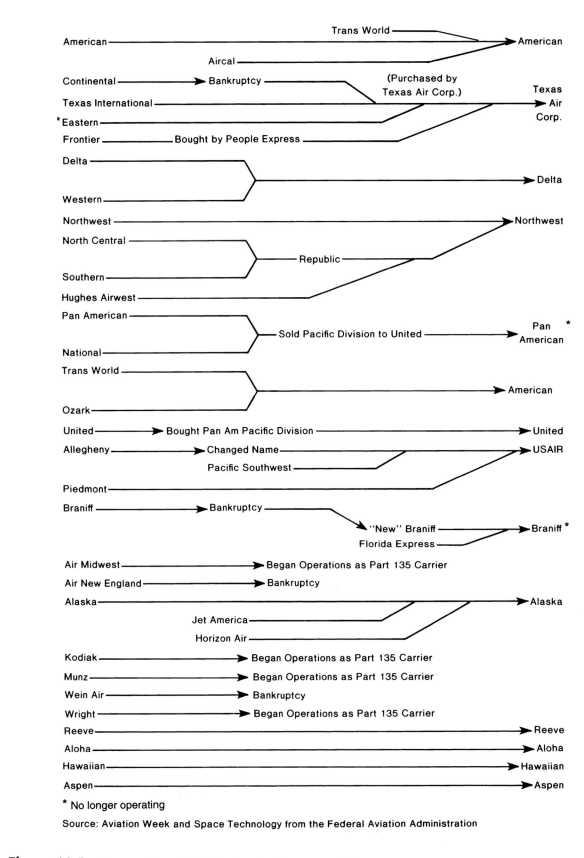

Figure 11.5   Restructuring of Air Carriers by Mergers and Acquisitions.

bilities of modern commercial aircraft, still bears important consideration. Our concepts of world geography have had to change. No longer can we think that the shortest route between the Pacific coast of the United States and Tokyo, Japan, is a south-southwest direction; in reality it is northwest by way of Alaska. This is because of the globular shape of the earth which makes it practical to follow the natural curve. This type of route which takes advantage of the earth's curve is known as a great circle. It is the shortest distance between any two points on the surface of the earth. Air carriers are not carrying passengers in scheduled service on routes that cross over the top of the world. Many flights from the United States non-stop to Europe and Asia follow this direct, much shorter route. (See Figure 11.6.)

Meteorology and the study of weather is a part of the natural science of geography. Pressure-pattern flying, high altitude flights, and within recent years the discovery and use of the jet streams, fast-moving rivers of air criss-crossing the earth at extremely high altitudes and speeds, have caused a change in the geographical concepts of air carrier routes.

The interaction of these three route determinants have played and will continue to play a decisive role in formulating air carrier route structure.

ECONOMIC ROUTE CHARACTERISTICS

There are several factors which determine the economic characteristics of an air carrier route. They are most all included when considering profitable, unprofitable, and competition factors.

First must be considered those factors which tend to make a particular route economically successful. These profitable route factors are:

1. Stage length of the route.

2. Degree of density of traffic carried on that route.

3. Average length of haul.

1. Stage length is the overall physical length of the route in miles. The greater number of miles produced on a certain route by an aircraft will tend to decrease the per-mile cost of operating the aircraft. A fixed cost for a given flight will remain fixed regardless of the

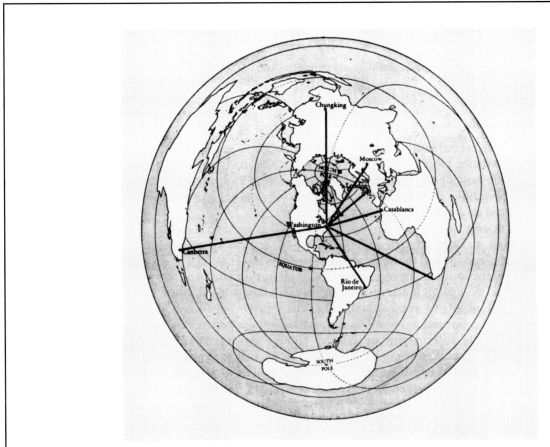

Figure 11.6 Great Circle Routes.

total miles flown. This fixed cost, spread over more miles will result in a lower fixed cost per mile. It is a basic economic fact that greater production will lower unit costs.

2. Density of traffic refers to the quantity of passengers or other traffic carried on a route. A route may be sufficiently long in miles, but if the average density of traffic carried is low it will offset the advantages of the lowered cost per mile. In fact, long routes and low densities are disastrous to profit.

3. The distance the average passenger flies along an air carrier route is known as the average length of haul. A route may be a thousand miles long, but if the average passenger disembarks after two or three hundred miles his vacated seat may well remain empty for the remainder of the flight. This, of course, can be prevented by non-stop flights. The air carriers are most desirous of non-stop flights, since the average length of haul would be equal to the stage length of the route. Non-stop routes are not always possible, because air carriers must also serve immediate points along the route as provided in their Certificate of Convenience and Necessity. The average length of haul has increased from 775 miles in 1970 to 990 miles in 1991.

All these factors—stage length, density of traffic carried, and the average length of haul—must be present for an air carrier route to be economically profitable. Usually any two of these must be favorable if the company is to break even. The degree to which any one of these factors is weak or lacking will be the cause of relatively unprofitable operations. A route may be relatively short, but this disadvantage could be off-set if the density of traffic and the average length of haul is high. An example of this condition is the Boston-New York-Washington route.

A lesser degree of profitability will exist if the size of the route is sufficient and the average length of haul is good but the density of traffic is low.

Likewise, poor financial operation will result if the size of the route is good and the density of traffic is high but the average length of haul is low. The weakening of any one of these three factors will tend to decrease the success or profitable nature of the air carrier route.

Air transportation is basically short-haul oriented. Fifty percent of all U.S. passenger trip lengths are 500 miles or less, and 75% of all trips are 1,000 miles or less. It would seem obvious that short-haul transportation is destined for an increasingly important role in the total U.S. air transportation system.

A recent study to determine the effect of stage length on local service operations found that there is no way to avoid heavy losses on the short stage length trips that serve smaller cities. The study stated that, "As flight distance decreased, operating losses increased acutely. When the stage length fell below 100 miles the traffic, service, and expense elements all combined to create an operating loss situation that no normal increase in traffic or fares, or decrease in expenses, could overcome."

While it is true that the reverse of the factors which lead to an economically successful route will cause an uneconomic condition, specifically, unprofitable air carrier route factors are a result of one or more of the following:

1. Low load factors.

2. Cities too small in population or otherwise unable to generate sufficient air traffic to support air service.

3. Unhealthy or excessive competition on the route from other air carriers or even surface carriers.

1. Load factor is expressed as a percentage showing the relation between production of an air carrier, usually available seat miles, and sales, or the revenue passenger miles actually sold. A break-even load factor is computed for any model or type of aircraft over any given route; this is equal to the percentage of the aircraft which must be filled by passengers or other traffic in order for the air carrier to cover its costs for the flight. This point must obviously be reached before a profit can be attained. It is detrimental if a scheduled flight does not achieve a sufficient load factor to cover costs for a route, then an uneconomic condition results.

2. This condition may be due to the second uneconomic route factor. If the cities along the route that the air carrier serves are too small in population or for some other reason do not have the ability to generate enough traffic, this would result in an unprofitable situation. This is particularly true in the case of local service air carriers.

3. The third uneconomic route factor is excess competition. It was the policy of the Civil Aeronautics Board, since its inception, to increase competition in order to produce better air service in the public interest. Since the U.S. air carrier route system was not planned on an overall pattern, several instances of unhealthy competition have resulted. Unprofitableness results when there is not enough air traffic to support the air carriers serving a route. This situation has been further aggravated since the introduction of the widebody jet

transport aircraft. This type aircraft, because of its greater capacity of seats, is able to produce a greater number of available seat miles; this, therefore, further aggravates the competition situation.

Because competition is perhaps the most direct cause of an uneconomic route, it bears further examining. There are four general factors which cause competition on air carrier routes:

- The creation of new air carriers.

- New routes of existing air carriers into areas being served by other air carriers.

- Mergers of companies or any type of route consolidations including interchanges.

- Competitive rate structure brought about by the Airline Deregulation Act of 1978.

There had been relatively few new air carriers permitted before deregulation. No new Domestic Trunk air carriers had been certificated since 1938. In fact, the number of major air carriers decreased due to mergers. As general economic inflation in the Untied States continues, costs will continue to rise. In order to lower costs through eliminating duplication, more mergers will no doubt take place.

Early in its history, the Civil Aeronautics Board established the policy of balanced competition within each classification of air carriers. In determining the extent of competition necessary for adequate public service, consideration was given to the total traffic potential which the route may be expected to produce. The result will indicate whether the route is able to support one or more air carriers. Duplication of air carriers on a route is justified only when all of them can be expected to at least break even with their load factors, and furthermore, to increase their volume of traffic in due course, thus allowing profits for all air carriers concerned.

The present economic condition of the United States air carrier industry is due to a multiplicity of causes, and much attention is being given by the Federal Government in the area of economic activity.

Since the establishment of the air carrier industry, particularly with the passage of the Civil Aeronautics Act in 1938, air carrier routes have increased until they now crisscross the United States in a web-like pattern. A large percentage of these routes have a high degree of competition in that two or more air carriers serve them. This competition coupled with increased costs and declining profits resulted in losses to the U.S. air

carrier industry. The air carriers consistently requested an increase in rates to offset the rising cost, but the policy of the Civil Aeronautics Board pertaining to rates had been to not allow any substantial increases to offset these losses. Some air carriers increased their route miles through the acquisition of new routes in order to alleviate declining profits. These actions have resulted in creating more competition and further aggravating an already intense uneconomic condition. Deregulation has played a dominant role in this process. To acquire a new route is not necessarily the solution to the problem

On domestic routes the airlines decide what service they want to offer. There is no Federal restriction on what destinations a certificated U.S. air carrier is allowed to provide. Prior to deregulation the Civil Aeronautics Board selected carriers on a route-by-route basis and limited the number of competitors on a route. Even in a period of airline industry consolidation, with a concomitant smaller number of airlines, there is general agreement that most communities are served by a larger number of airlines.

Deciding which markets to serve has become primarily a business decision, although non-business factors play a role in this process. An airline, in very oversimplified terms, looks at the revenue potential of a market—population, airport access, local economy, etc., then looks at the costs associated with providing service—aircraft, needed airport infrastructure, labor, etc., and looks for a situation where it will make a profit. In some instances the airline's profit might not occur on that specific route, but may instead come from carrying passengers to some destination beyond the original route.

PUBLIC UTILITY ASPECTS OF AIR CARRIERS

The air transport industry has many characteristics like those of public utilities. Although they are responsible for air service in the public interest, they are not true public utilities according to the strict definition of the term.

A public utility is one which is:

A. Privately owned by the public (stockholders)

B. Subject to governmental regulatory control

This regulation covers three areas:

1. Geographic areas of operational services, (routes in the case of air carriers before deregulation)

2. Rates or fares charged to the public

3. Percentage of return on investment allowed

Being a public utility usually implies a monopoly in that it is granted a franchise to conduct its business. This is true of electric, telephone, and water companies, and intracity bus companies. Most franchises are granted by the state Public Utilities Commission or equivalent state authority. Higher costs and rates would result if there were more than one public utility serving a city or area. The duplication of equipment would not be warranted.

The air transport industry operated in much the same way. The Civil Aeronautics Board granted air carriers franchises to serve certain routes. No air carrier could do so without the Civil Aeronautics Board approval. In this sense the air carriers were protected monopolies. The difference between air carriers and public utilities stops at that point. Within the air industry there is much competition, especially since the Airline Deregulation Act became law in October 1978. The Civil Aeronautics Board encouraged competition on routes. Those air carriers serving a route are monopolies as an industry, yet at the same time they compete with each other. This fact was the basis of the complaint against the Civil Aeronautics Board. The Civil Aeronautics Board's rationale was that they encouraged competition to develop a better air service and lower fares in the public interest. As contradictory as it may sound, nonetheless, the air carriers did conduct their business in a framework of monopolistic competition. It was one of the very few industries to do so.

The advantage of a pure public utility operating as a monopoly is offset by the disadvantage of having the rates it charges the public controlled by government authority. This was true of air carriers before deregulation. The Civil Aeronautics Board disapproved a fare submitted to it if it believed the rate was too high or too low. The low rate, which may or may not be below cost, would be unfair competition. The Civil Aeronautics Board saw to it that the same type of air service on the same route by competing air carriers was about identical. Competition tends to equalize fares under regulation or deregulation.

Another offsetting disadvantage to being a public utility monopoly is that the amount of profit earned is controlled, limited, or set by government authority. In the air transport industry this was true. The Civil Aeronautics Board established a percentage as a fair return on investment depending upon the class of air carrier. Different routes of the same air carrier even had different allowable percentages of profit or return on investment. The Board's opinion dealing with rate of return

Air carriers are like public utilities with certain unique differences.

on investment stated in the Domestic Passenger-Fare Investigation (Civil Aeronautics Board, Docket 21866 8, April 9, 1971) was that the fair and reasonable rate of return on investment for domestic passenger fare services of the trunk air carriers was 12%. This was based upon a 6.2% cost of debt, a 16.75% cost of equity, and an optimum capital structure consisting of 45% debt and 55% equity. A load factor of 55% was used as the basis for rates. The rate of return on investment for local service air carriers was 12.35%, however.

If the air carrier's percentage of profit return exceeded its limit set by the Civil Aeronautics Board, then fare reductions resulted. An alert management saw to it in advance that any would-be excess profits were plowed back into the company by expanding or improving its equipment. This results in a larger capital investment and, therefore, a higher dollar return for the same allowable percentage. The next result of expanded equipment is an expanded service, and the cycle is complete and back to where it started but the circle is now larger.

The public obviously is the beneficiary of this chain of events.

Strict public utilities that operate at a fixed return on investment can normally adjust upward or downward to maintain consistency in that return, because they are pure monopolies. The Civil Aeronautics Board set a rate of return standard for airlines, but few have been able to attain it. Since airlines are not pure monopolies and do not have consistent demand, as does the local electric, gas, or telephone company, pricing is a competitive tool. It cannot be used freely to make up rate of return deficiencies.

This is the way it is supposed to happen and usually does. However, some economists and air industry managements raised questions which helped bring about the Deregulation Act in 1978. In summary it can be said that air carriers are like public utilities with certain unique differences.

ESTABLISHMENT OF RATES ON AIR CARRIER ROUTES

The economic theory of rate-making generally applies when considering how air carrier rates for service are determined. Generally the rate on an air carrier route is supposed to be sufficient to allow the company to earn a fair rate of return on its investment. Only with such a return can they pay dividends to their stockholders, show capital gains, and attract invested capital.

As in the establishment of any rate or product price, there are two considerations. The first is the cost of producing the service or product, and the second is the demand, or the value, for that service or product. This is expressed in the formula P = C + D. "P" is the price or rate established, "C" is the cost, and "D" is demand. The average total cost per unit of producing air service will decrease to a point and then increase as the "law of diminishing returns" takes effect.

The demand or value of the service to the air transport public is not a fixed quantity but rather several quantities of the service which the public will buy at various rate levels. A demand curve is simply a schedule of rates. Generally, as air carrier rates are decreased, the quantity of purchases will increase. Air carriers have a high elasticity of demand, which means that normally they will experience a change in quantity or volume as rates are changed. The air industry is said to have a high demand sensitivity.

The graph (See Figure 11.7) illustrates the typical condition in the air carrier industry for any given route on a per unit basis. The lower break-even point is at A. The upper break-even point is at B.

The quantity of miles that will yield the maximum profit is determined by the intersection of marginal costs and marginal revenue. This is XY on the graph. Any increase of quantity beyond that point will result in an increase in cost and a decrease in profit. When the upper break-even point is passed a loss occurs. The reason for this is that the marginal cost (the amount added to total cost for one more unit) increases, while the marginal revenue (the amount added to total revenue for one more unit) remains constant.

For example:

If the horizontal axis were a flight from Miami to Boston, with the take-off from Miami at point "O," the lower break-even point for the flight might be reached at Atlanta, point "A." The flight's termination at New York could be point "XY," thereby yielding the maximum profit. If the flight were to continue to Boston at point "B" the profit would be eliminated. If for some reason the flight continued beyond Boston a loss would occur.

The same example above can be expressed in hours of flight time and cost per hour. If the flight, when reaching its destination (point XY), is unable to land and must hold due to a back-up of air traffic for weather conditions or other reasons, the profit earned will be eliminated and loss will continue to mount as the holding time increases. This is the reason why "on time" arrivals are so important in an economic sense as well as to good service.

THE AIR TRANSPORT ASSOCIATION OF AMERICA (ATA)*

Founded by a group of 14 airlines meeting in Chicago in 1936, the Air Transport Association of America (ATA) was the first, and today still remains, the only trade organization for the principal U.S. airlines. In that capacity it has played a major role in all the major government decisions regarding aviation since its founding, including the creation of the Civil Aeronautics Board, the creation of the air traffic control system, and airline deregulation.

The purpose of the ATA is to support and assist its members by promoting the air transport industry and the safety, cost effectiveness, and technological advancement of its operations; advocating common industry positions before state and local governments; conducting designated industry-wide programs; and assuring governmental and public understanding of all aspects of air transport.

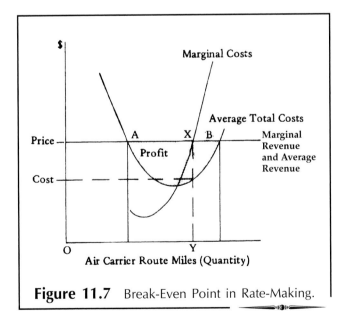

Figure 11.7 Break-Even Point in Rate-Making.

---

* For current information go to the Website at: http://www.air-transport.org

The ATA has represented the needs and promoted the interests of the commercial airline industry for almost 60 years. During its history, ATA has seen the airline industry and its members evolve from the small, pioneering companies of the 1930s into key players in the global transportation market. The industry continues to evolve with the addition of new carriers, which are playing a major role in shaping the future of air transportation.

As airlines continue to look for ways to reduce costs and maximize efficiencies while maintaining the safest transportation system in the world, ATA offers carriers that very opportunity. ATA is respected by Congress, state legislatures, the Department of Transportation, the Federal Aviation Administration, the press and the public for its professional and accomplished representation of the industry. As its members chart their futures in a changing market, ATA provides invaluable expertise, guidance and assistance.

ATA's structure is similar to most airlines and provides an interface between the carriers and various government and private sector organizations. Key departments within the association deal with operations and safety, engineering, maintenance and material, airport operations, air traffic management, cargo, electronic data interchange, facilitation, federal and state government affairs, international affairs, legal affairs, passenger service, public relations and security. Working with these established functions are a variety of ATA councils, committees, subcommittees and task forces, composed of experts from member airlines, formed to address industry issues. (See Figure 11.8.)

Today, the ATA continues to represent the industry on major aviation issues before Congress, federal agencies, state legislatures, and other governmental bodies. It continues to promote safety by coordinating industry and government safety programs, and it serves as a focal point for industry efforts to standardize practices and enhance the efficiency of the air transport system.

The Air Transport Association serves its member airlines and their customers by:

1. Assisting the airline industry in continuing to provide the world's safest system of transportation.

2. Transmitting technical expertise and operational knowledge among the member airlines to improve safety, service and efficiency.

3. Advocating fair airline taxation and regulation worldwide, ensuring a profitable and competitive industry.

The Air Transport Association is the nation's oldest trade association. Its membership of twenty-three United States and five associate non-United States airlines, carries over 600 million passengers and more than 25 billion tons of cargo each year. The United States members account for more than 95% of the passenger and cargo traffic carried by the scheduled U.S. airlines. In an extraordinary dynamic industry, the Air Transport Association enables air carriers to pool their unparalleled experience, technical expertise and operational knowledge so that the industry as a whole can better serve the public and improve airline safety, service and efficiency.

The Air Transport Association also represents its members on major airline issues in the technical, legal and political arenas. Its activities are designed to advocate and support measures which enhance aviation safety, ensure efficiency, foster growth and protect the ability of the airline industry to invest in the future, in order to meet the emerging demands of consumers.

While the Air Transport Association agenda of issues continuously changes, its major priorities remain constant. These include:

1. Assisting the airline industry in providing the world's safest system of transportation.

2. Advocating the modernization of the Federal Aviation Administration air traffic control system to provide service for airline customers and to benefit the environment.

3. Improving and refining the protection and security of airline passengers and cargo against threats directed at the United States.

4. Encouraging appropriate government action while seeking to prevent legislative and regulatory intervention that would penalize airlines and their customers by imposing rate, route, service and schedule controls on the industry.

5. Endeavoring to reduce the disproportionate share of taxes and fees paid by airlines and their customers at the federal, state and local levels.

6. Improving the industry's ability to attract capital necessary to meet future demand.

7. Helping to shape international aviation policy and to ensure that the United States and foreign carriers can compete on equal terms.

During its long history, the Air Transport Association has seen the airline industry grow from the small pioneering companies of the 1930's into key players in the global transportation market. The ATA and its members continually play a vital role in shaping the future of Air Transportation. (Table 11.7.)

Table 11.7 Air Transport Association (ATA) Member Airlines—2001

Airborne Express
145 Hunter Drive
Wilmington, OH 45177
937-382-5591

Alaska Airlines
P.O. Box 68900
Seattle-Tacoma Int'l Airport
Seattle, WA 98168
206-433-3200

Aloha Airlines
P.O. Box 30038
Honolulu, HI 96820
808-836-4101

America West Airlines
4000 E. Sky Harbor Blvd.
Phoenix, AZ 85034
480-693-0800

American Airlines
P.O. Box 619616
DFW Airport, TX 75261
817-963-1234

American Trans Air
P.O. Box 51609
Indianapolis Int'l Airport
Indianapolis, IN 46251-0609
317-247-4000

Atlas Air, Inc.
2000 Westchester Avenue
Purchase, NY 10577
914-701-8476

Continental Airlines
1600 Smith Street
Houston, TX 77002-4607
713-324-5000

Delta Air Lines, Inc.
P.O. Box 20706
Atlanta, GA 30320-9998
404-715-2600

DHL Airways
P.O. Box 75122
Cincinnati, OH 45275
859-283-2232

Emery Worldwide
One Lagoon Drive, Suite 400
Redwood City, CA 94065
415-596-9600

**Evergreen International
Airlines, Inc.**
3850 Three Mile Lane
McMinnville, OR 97128
503-472-0011

FedEx Corporation
942 South Shady Grove Road
Memphis, TN 38120
901-369-3600

Hawaiian Airlines
P.O. Box 30008
Honolulu Int'l Airport
Honolulu, HI 96820
808-535-3700

Midwest Express Airlines
6744 South Howell Avenue
Oak Creek, WI 53154
414-570-4000

Northwest Airlines
5101 Northwest Drive
St. Paul, MN 55111
612-726-2111

Polar Air Cargo
100 Oceangate, 15th Floor
Long Beach, CA 90802
562-528-7200

Southwest Airlines Co.
P.O. Box 36611, Love Field
Dallas, TX 75235
214-792-4000

United Airlines
P.O. Box 66100
Chicago, IL 60666
847-700-4000

United Parcel Service Airlines
1400 N. Hurstbourne Parkway
Louisville, KY 40223
502-329-3000

US Airways
2345 Crystal Drive
Arlington, VA 22227
703-872-7000

ASSOCIATE MEMBERS

Aeromexico
Paseo de la Reforma 445
12th Floor
Mexico City, D.F. 06500
Mexico
525-133-4004

Air Canada
Air Canada Centre, 1271
P.O. Box 14000
Dorval, Quebec H4Y 1H4
Canada
514-422-5000

KLM Royal Dutch Airlines
Amsterdamseweg 55
1182 GP Amstelveen
The Netherlands
31-20-649-9123

Mexicana
Xola 535, 30th Floor
Mexico City, D.F. 03100
Mexico
525-448-3000

I. OPERATIONS AND SAFETY DEPARTMENT

Since ATA's formation, the speed with which passengers and cargo can be transported great distances has increased dramatically. Along with advanced aircraft capability came a heightened awareness of ways in which technology can make flying a safer and more pleasant experience.

Operations and Safety works to improve safety, efficiency, and reliability in the national airspace system and to solve technical problems encountered in operating aircraft. ATA's annual Safety Agenda and Capacity and Efficiency Agenda outline the airlines' goals and

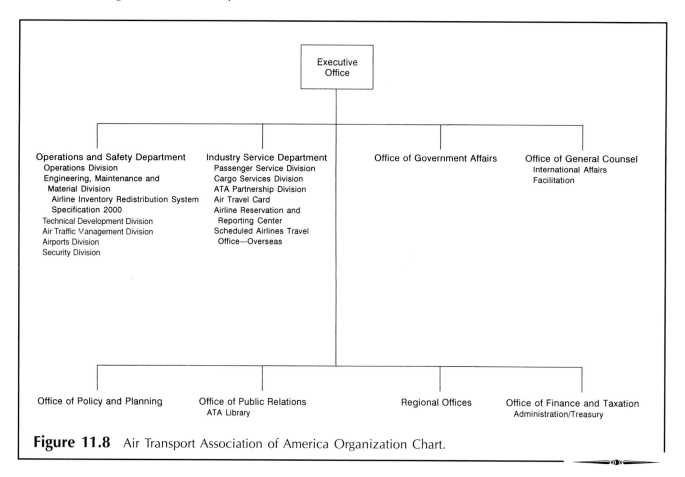

Figure 11.8 Air Transport Association of America Organization Chart.

areas of emphasis in operations and safety for the coming year.

ATA often approaches problem solving in these issues as the catalyst, combining the resources of many organizations. For example, in its efforts to eliminate wind shear as a major cause of accidents, ATA involves industry experts from the Federal Aviation Administration (FAA), the National Center for Atmospheric Research, aircraft and wind shear sensor manufacturers as well as academic institutions. Six divisions within the department address operations and safety issues:

Operations Division

Has responsibility for regulations, standards and procedures affecting aircraft operations, including flight operation rules, standards and requirements for certification, training and proficiency checking of crew members. In addition, the division oversees medical certification rules; navigation requirements; avionics and systems integration and related standards development. The group works closely with the FAA, the National Transportation Safety Board (NTSB), National Aero-

nautics and Space Administration (NASA) and other technical agencies.

The division also created a Human Factors Task Force, which addresses aspects of aviation safety which are affected by human performance, including workload, resource management, and the human/machine interface.

Engineering, Maintenance and Material Division

Advances industry positions on all aspects of airworthiness, integration of new safety technology, and operational engineering. Engineering and maintenance plays a significant role in material support, maintenance management, digital data communication standards, industrial safety and health, aircraft noise reduction, and other environmental matters such as handling and disposal of hazardous substances, recycling and fuel conservation. The department played a key role in the development of an industry-wide maintenance and inspection program for the safe operation and special needs of the industry's older aircraft.

The division also administers two programs that provide for supply and cost-efficient procurement of aircraft parts. Through standardized, computerized procurement methods, this unit provides member airlines with ready access to multiple sources of supply, helping to reduce inventory levels and costs. Two programs instrumental in this effort are AIRS and SPEC 2000.

1. **Airline Inventory Redistribution System (AIRS)** is an international automated program for sale and purchase of aircraft and engine parts. A central data base tracks global availability of millions of parts offered by airlines for resale to other carriers.

2. **Specification 2000 (SPEC 2000)** is an order forwarding system developed by air carriers to provide instant worldwide transmittal of purchasing data and order status. A central data base, under strict security, displays current price and lead time for aircraft replacement parts from over 70 major suppliers.

Technical Development Division

Focuses on technical matters of interest to the airlines, Congress and the FAA with the objective of enhancing air safety through technological advancements. The group typically deals with special technical matters that cross several disciplines and require coordination with various industry and government groups. For example, airport design and development issues and reduction of noise and other environmental concerns associated with airline operations at airports are handled by the department, as well as exploration of future technology, such as the use of space-based navigation systems.

Air Traffic Management Division

The air traffic control (ATC) system has become a critical, sophisticated element of the nation's air transportation system. ATA's air traffic management staff evaluates ATC standards, procedures and efficiency, airspace modernization and planning, local and regional operational requirements, and communications support. In addition, they are responsible for all aspects of day-to-day ATC system operation, including rules, standards and procedures, as well as communications and meteorological requirements to support airline operations. The division works closely with FAA, the National Weather Service, National Aeronautics and Space Administration and the Federal Communications Commission to minimize the impact of ATC-related delays. Today's agenda for air traffic control includes modern-

ization of ATC system elements to improve safety, capacity and efficiency and integration of new technology, such as collision avoidance systems, and technology to predict and detect complex weather phenomena such as wind shear and microbursts.

Airports Division

Together with the Air Traffic Management division, the Airports Division plays a critical role in the development of adequate capacity for air transportation. The division is involved in the review and assessment of federal funding requirements for airports, airport planning, use and access, development and design, and long-range planning. The team works cooperatively with airports and related associations to provide the airline industry perspective in dealing with airport and other infrastructure issues.

Security Division

This division leads industry efforts to assure that airline programs maximize passenger and cargo security. Activity is designed to prevent or deter acts of sabotage, hijacking and related crimes against civil aviation. The group's working relationship with many government branches and state, local, and federal law enforcement agencies ensures maximum security for passengers and shippers.

II. INDUSTRY SERVICES DEPARTMENT

Industry Services is charged with developing and administering programs, standards, and practices where an industry-wide approach improves customer service and achieves economies and efficiencies for ATA members and their customers. ATA was instrumental in creating industry standards and automation to handle movement of passengers, baggage and cargo between various airlines.

Industry Services advises ATA members of regulatory developments affecting the airlines. Its five divisions focus on operations as well as commercial aspects of the air travel industry.

Passenger Services Division

Works closely with airline counterparts to develop internationally acceptable standards and procedures for handling passengers and their baggage, enabling airlines to function more smoothly in the world travel market. Passenger Services is responsible for creating constant technological improvements to the system that allows customers to buy one ticket, with flights on multiple airlines traveling through different airports, and arrive at a final destination with their baggage.

Cargo Services Division

This group addresses the concerns of the various types of airlines that handle cargo and mail—passenger/freight, all cargo and express package carriers. Cargo Services maintains interline cargo traffic agreements to facilitate the smooth transfer between air carriers; serves as industry liaison between agencies, such as the U.S. Postal Service, Department of Transportation and U.S. Customs Service; coordinates safety programs for shipping hazardous materials; and develops industry programs to prevent freight loss, reduce claims and improve packaging.

ATA Partnership Program

The Industry Providers Partnership Program has been developed in response to increasing demand for reliable, cost-effective and up-to-date information on the activities of North American airlines and governmental entities from their suppliers and other aviation-related businesses. For an annual fee, the Partnership gives participating companies access to specialized data, information, publications and educational activities through a single source. Participants receive material that is specifically relevant to their business interests and needs by selecting one or more of a series of specialized options, such as engineering and maintenance, passenger services or government affairs.

Air Travel Card

The ATA, through the Universal Air Travel Plan (UATP), administers the Air Travel Card for the international airline industry. Established in 1936, the card is issued by 32 airlines for charging airfare on over 200 international airlines. The Air Travel Card staff works closely with corporations and travel agents to meet business traveler needs, provide insurance, and offer other enhancements through the card.

Airline Reservation and Reporting Center

Landing and take-off rights at four major airports, or slots, are traded, bought and sold among carriers. Established in 1986 as a central clearinghouse for slow transfer and related activities involving the four high-density airports, the Center serves the industry by ex-

pediting slot transfers among domestic and foreign airlines and securing FAA approval of the transfers.

Scheduled Airlines Travel Office-Overseas (SATO-OS)

Created in 1972, this program exists under an agreement between a group of ATA airlines and the U.S. military services to provide airline tickets and related travel services to American military personnel located overseas. Through ATA, member airlines provide on-site representation in foreign countries to offer full transportation services for both official and recreational travel by military personnel.

Commercial airlines play a key role in national defense as part of the Civil Reserve Air Fleet program. During Operations Desert Shield and Desert Storm the airlines carried two-thirds of the troops and 25% of the cargo airlifted to the Middle East. Thousands of airline personnel, including pilots, also served the nation during these efforts as part of the reserve forces.

III. OFFICE OF GOVERNMENT AFFAIRS

In addition to the work of the technical and industry service staffs are several ATA offices which provide specialized expertise to member airlines. These specialties address legal, political, communications and financial aspects of the industry, and also complement counterpart functions of member airlines.

As the commercial aviation industry's voice in Washington, state capitals, and city halls, Government Affairs identifies, tracks and interprets for ATA members the impact of federal, state and local issues and legislation. Working with other ATA departments, government organizations and member airlines, this office articulates airline positions in a unified voice before Congress, the executive branch and state and local governments. It presents industry views before Congress and state legislatures, gathers information, presents testimony and responds to legislators' requests for information about the industry. At the state and local level, the staff coordinates goals and activities of a cadre of airline representatives throughout the 50 states.

IV. OFFICE OF GENERAL COUNSEL

The legal staff counsel for all ATA departments, councils and committees, generates and advocates industry positions in hearings, proceedings and investigations at both the federal and state governmental levels, and manages litigation on behalf of the industry.

International Affairs

International Affairs represents industry interests on U.S. delegations for bilateral negotiations and treaties between the U.S. and dozens of other nations on international air rights, and works with the Departments of Transportation and State in establishing and maintaining the international agreements which govern overseas air transportation. The group also studies and evaluates issues in the evolving international marketplace to assist members in their decisions to seek new rights and expand services and to determine the competitive impact of these actions on the airlines and their passengers.

FACILITATION

Facilitation represents member carriers' interests to U.S. government agencies whose policies and regulations affect the efficiency and cost-effectiveness of international air transport of passengers and cargo. It also advocates government/industry employment of new technology and alternative inspection systems to accommodate the fast-growing volumes of international travel and trade.

V. OFFICE OF POLICY AND PLANNING

This office focuses on positioning ATA to serve long-term interests of the airline community, based on in-depth knowledge of both current issues and impact of legislation on industry performance. Whereas much of ATA's day-to-day work is directed at improving the present airline operating climate, the Office of Policy and Planning projects industry trends into the long-term future.

VI. OFFICE OF PUBLIC RELATIONS

Public Relations fosters understanding of the airline industry, its challenges, objectives and the vital role of the airlines in the economy. As spokesman for the industry, this office is a principal source of industry information, producing regular statistical and other reports for ATA members, the media and the public.

ATA Library

ATA maintains an extensive aviation library. The library's collection contains over 14,000 volumes covering a vast range of topics related to the airline industry, and includes general reference material, aviation history, industry statistics, legal and legislative works and other current information. It also offers ready reference, bibliography and online data base services. The library is available to ATA members and the public.

VII. ATA REGIONAL OFFICES

Six regional Offices are located in Atlanta, Denver, Chicago, Los Angeles, New York and Ft. Worth. Their primary function is to support air traffic control, airport and governmental concerns at the regional and local level.

VIII. OFFICE OF FINANCE AND TAXATION

Working with tax experts and chief financial officers at member airlines, this office interprets and seeks to minimize the impact on the industry of government tax measures. Its financial activities involve credit, insurance, corporate accounting, industry auditing and overseeing settlement of more than $9 billion in annual inter-airline payments through the Airline Clearing House.

Administration/Treasury

Responsible for the ATA budget and personnel support services, including physical facilities, conference management, and management information services.

AIR TRANSPORT ASSOCIATION COUNCILS AND COMMITTEES

The Air Transport Association committees and councils are composed of senior executives from member airlines. Committee members bring a broad range of experience and specialized skill to the table to set the industry's agenda in their respective areas, help resolve issues and employ technological advances in developing standards for improved service. Each of the six councils has a variety of committees, panels, task forces and working groups under its purview which concentrate on specific sets of issues.

I. Law Council

Deals with a variety of legal matters affecting industry, including government rules and procedures, development of international trade, tourism and international aviation policy, equal employment opportunity, affirmative action and personnel matters.

Litigation Committee
International Affairs Committee
Facilitation Committee
Human Resources Committee

II. Government and Public Affairs Council

Focuses on legislation-related and other governmental issues at the federal, state and local levels. Develops and recommends industry policy and political approach on key issues.

Federal Affairs Committee
Public Affairs Committee
Public Relations Committee

III. Operations Council

The focal point for ATA efforts to improve safety and efficiency of airline operations. Activity includes development of action programs and recommended policy on safety regulations governing operations, crew training and certification, control, navigation, and guidance of aircraft, requirements for air traffic services, meteorological support services, and airport matters.

Air Traffic Control Committee
Airports Committee
Airspace Systems Implementation Committee
Aviation Safety Committee
Flight Systems Integration Committee
Meteorological Committee
Security Committee
Training Committee
Cabin Operations Panel
Communications Panel
Medical Panel

IV. Engineering, Maintenance and Material Council

Responsible for developing industry-wide standards, procedures and positions relative to airworthiness, engineering and maintenance, aircraft performance, environment and industrial health, and digital data standards. The Council advances these positions with regulatory

authorities, domestic and international airlines, suppliers, and manufacturers. The Council's objective is to improve employee and passenger safety, increase transportation reliability, expand passenger and cargo capacity, and minimize costs.

Airworthiness and Engineering Committee
Maintenance Engineering Committee
Material Management Committee
Environmental Committee
Technical Information and Communications Committee

V. Air Cargo Council

Handles cargo-related concerns such as mail transportation, air freight services and automation systems, the shipment and handling of certain dangerous goods.

Dangerous Goods Board
Cargo Services Development Committee
Airlines Postal Advisory Committee

VI. Passenger Council

Considers industry passenger service resolutions, procedures, programs, and objectives which will facilitate effective air transportation at the lowest cost. Includes interline services such as reservations, ticketing, baggage, and other passenger services.

Baggage Committee
Reservations Committee
Passenger Processing Committee
ATA/IATA Reservations Interline Message Procedures Board
Passenger Data Interchange Standards Board
Industry Fares and Rules Exchange Standards Board

ATA INITIATIVES

ATA represents the interests of its membership in technical, legal, and political arenas. Its activities are designed to advocate and support measures which will further aviation safety, assure industry efficiency and growth, and promote financial health. The association's work includes seven major initiatives: (See Figure 11.9.)

1. Advocates the modernization of the Federal Aviation Administration's (FAA) air traffic control (ATC) system to improve the movement of aircraft. An upgraded ATC system will enhance safety and result in fewer delays for airline passengers and shippers. ATA seeks a comprehensive government approach that considers the integration of airport and air traffic control

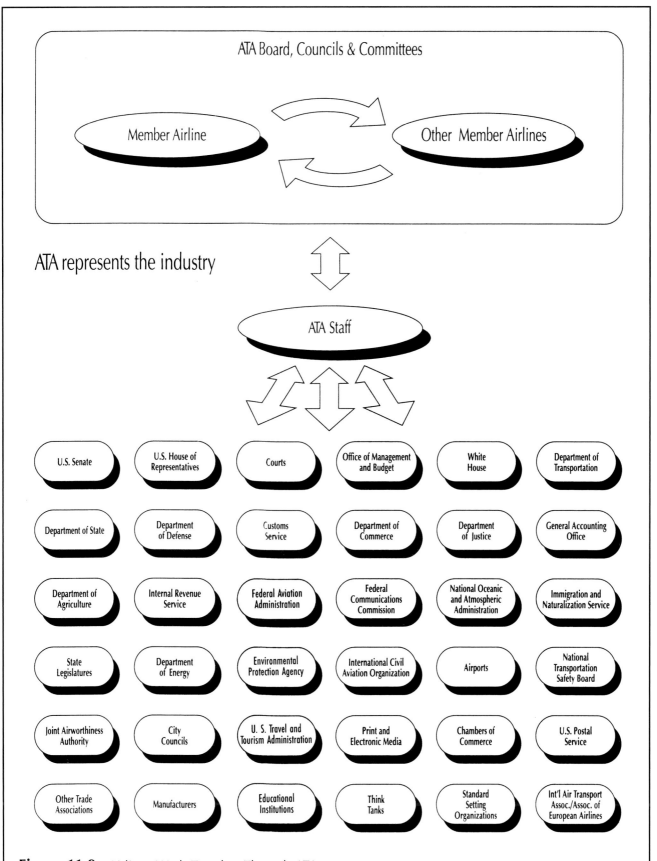

Figure 11.9   Airlines Work Together Through ATA.

system operations resulting in greater capacity and efficiency in the ATC system.

2. Seeks to improve the industry's ability to attract capital. Air carriers need to raise billions to fund the acquisition of new, quiet, fuel-efficient aircraft to meet federal noise standards and to make needed capital improvements in airports and related facilities. The airlines are seeking support in Washington for a variety of proposals, including an investment tax credit and changes in the alternative minimum tax that would create jobs and make aircraft and the airlines a good investment.

3. Works to build broad understanding of the industry's public service performance in a deregulated environment and seeks to prevent legislative and regulatory actions which would impose rate, route, service or schedule controls on the airlines—many of which would penalize passengers and shippers.

4. Focuses industry efforts to improve the airlines' strong safety record and minimize the impact of airline operations on the environment. The annual safety agenda identifies opportunities for improvement and ATA staff and member airlines prepare an action plan to achieve the objectives. Examples include measures that ensure continued airworthiness of older aircraft and reduce the risk of airborne or ground collision.

5. Participates in shaping international aviation policy to assure that U.S. carriers can compete on equal terms with foreign carriers. ATA continues to urge ratification of the Montreal Protocols which provide additional compensation for families in the event of an international accident.

6. Seeks to increase the protection and security of passengers and cargo, ensuring that security measures used by both U.S. and foreign carriers meet the same high standards.

7. Endeavors to reduce the disproportionate share of taxes and user fees placed on airlines and their passengers and opposes legislation and other initiatives which attempt to impose burdensome costs or taxes on the air travel industry and the traveling and shipping public at the federal, state or local level.

CHAPTER 12

International Air Transportation Law

The growth and development of international and foreign air transportation has not paralleled that of domestic air transportation in the United States. It is necessary to understand exactly what is included in the terms international and foreign as used in air transportation. As generally used, international air transportation[1] is the conducting of air transportation by an air carrier of the United States outside the nation to another country. The class of U.S. air carrier known as International and Territorial represents this definition and was discussed in the previous chapter. Foreign air transportation,[2] on the other hand, is the operation of air carriers of nations other than the United States. In some cases foreign air carriers perform air service to and from the United States.

"Overseas" refers to a type of air route and is geographic in nature; it is not a classification of air carrier. It is a type of operation conducted by U.S. air carriers flying from the continental United States to a point outside the continental limits that is a state, territory, or possession of the United States. This type of operation can be performed by an International and Territorial Air Carrier. An example would be a flight from Miami, Florida, to San Juan, Puerto Rico, or from San Francisco, California to Honolulu, Hawaii.

One point to be noted in the study of international and foreign air transportation is that while the U.S. international air carriers are privately owned corporations, foreign air carriers for the most part are either wholly or partially owned by their governments.

CONFERENCES AND CONVENTIONS

The progression of international conferences and conventions which resulted in the evolution of the present legal framework under which international and foreign aviation operates is reviewed briefly below.[3]

PARIS CONFERENCE—1910

International law presented aviation pioneers with many challenges. In 1910 it was seen that aviation was going to link different languages, cultures and legal systems to a far greater degree than sea or rail. It was

---

[1] The Warsaw Convention and the Chicago Convention have two slightly different definitions of what constitutes International Transportation.

[2] The term "foreign air transportation" is unique only to the United States and can be offensive to some non-United States air carriers and aeronautical authorities.

[3] Much of the text subject on conferences and conventions has been supplemented by Aero-Accords, Inc. of Seattle, Washington, Earl R. Scott, President. For a complete study of the International Conferences and Conventions reviewed in this chapter, the book recommended is "Compendium of International Civil Aviation" by Adrianus D. Groenewedge, published by the International Aviation Development Corporation, 3460 Peel Street, Suite 1803, Montreal, Quebec, Canada H3A 2M1.

also recognized that if maritime law were to be applied to aviation it would have to be expanded or, at the very least, adjusted to deal with the unique risks and demands of air travel.

A conference held in Paris in 1910 was attended by representatives from 19 European countries. It was the first attempt to reach international agreement on matters dealing with civil aviation. Those attending could not come to any basic agreements. They were divided between the concept of a freedom of the air, paralleling that of the sea; and the concept of a national sovereignty that extended into international air space. However, not all of the work of 1910 was lost. Many of the convention's less controversial draft articles were later reused in the conventions of 1919, 1926, 1928, and 1944. Their contemplated efforts were left to the Aeronautical Commission of the Paris Peace Conference, which was established in March of 1919.

In the world today, communication and transportation are the two factors that support the global society. Before World War II, efforts were made to establish an international legal framework to ensure the development of international civil aviation. After World War II the potential of the airplane was recognized for international commercial purposes as well as for its future role as an instrument of better understanding among the people of the world.

PARIS CONVENTION—1919

A meeting known as the Convention Relating to the Regulation of Aerial Navigation was held on March 6, 1919. The delegation met to accomplish what was not agreed upon in 1910. The countries represented were: Belgium, Brazil, the British Empire, Cuba, France, Greece, Italy, Japan, Portugal, Romania, the Kingdom of the Serbs, Croats and Slovenes, and the United States. At their first meeting the commission agreed to produce a set of basic principles in preparing the Convention and its Annexes.

Having established the guidelines for the drafting of the Convention, the Commission established three Sub-Commissions which were legal, technical, and military. These three were aided by draft conventions submitted by France, Great Britain, and the United States. Italy submitted a draft proposal for aerial navigation laws. In actuality, the influence of the International Commission Air Navigation was limited, as well as its implementation of the convention, because during the 1920s and 1930s the airplane was not capable of world wide trans-

port. It was not until after World War II that international air services expanded because of the improvements in the airplane to fly long distances.

This international convention for air navigation recognized that each nation had complete and exclusive control of the air space above its territory, thus preventing the air carriers of a country from flying over another country without permission. This convention:

1. Established basic principles of air sovereignty.
2. Prescribed for national registration of aircraft.
3. Placed restrictions on movement of military aircraft.
4. Established basic rules of airworthiness of aircraft.
5. Regulated pilots and others in charge of aircraft.
6. Provided for police measures.

For the purpose of the convention, the territory of a country was understood to include its national territory, that of the mother country, of the colonies, and the international waters adjacent therein.

A permanent commission was created by the Paris Convention to provide for the continued study of international aviation legal problems. This commission was known as the C.I.N.A. (Commission Internationale de Navigation Aerienne.)

The Convention was ratified by 26 countries and served as the legal document for international air transportation outside the Western Hemisphere. The United States signed the convention papers, however, it was not ratified by the United States because the convention was associated with the League of Nations to which the United States did not belong. Russia also did not ratify it, thus the two largest countries of leading importance in post World War I civil aviation never ratified the Paris Convention. The main accomplishment of this convention was the establishment of sovereignty of air space theory.

MADRID CONVENTION—1926

The Ibero-American Convention Relating To Air Navigation was formulated at a 1926 conference by Spain, Portugal and 19 Latin American countries. The 1926 Convention largely mirrored the text and appendices of the Paris Convention of 1919. It was developed as a reaction to the unequal voting procedures and certain other features in the Paris Convention at that time. The Madrid Convention was never registered with any international body and was totally ignored in the Chicago Convention of 1944. Its lack of success was due to three factors. First, aircraft of the period were not sufficiently developed to tie together Iberia and Latin America. Second, Spain's political environment during the period was very unsettled, deteriorating into Civil War. And third, two years later the Havana Convention focused Latin American energies on North America and away from Iberia.

PAN AMERICAN CONVENTION ON COMMERCIAL AVIATION—1928

At Santiago, Chile, in 1923, a Pan American Conference was held to establish basic rules for operating international commercial air services. The intent was to formulate a legal document for the needs of the countries of the Western Hemisphere. It was to be related to the Monroe Doctrine of the United States. This convention reviewed the provisions proposed at the Santiago conference. It was modeled after the Paris Convention and recognized that every country had complete and exclusive sovereignty over the air space above its country and adjacent territorial waters.

Although the Paris Convention of 1919 solved most of the problems for European countries, it was not satisfactory for the countries of the Western Hemisphere. The Sixth International Conference of American States was convened in Havana in 1928.

From this conference came the Commercial Aviation Convention, properly known as the Havana Convention of 1928. The Havana Convention contains most of the basic principles established by the Paris Convention and some new ones. It differed in that it also contained some provisions relating to private international aviation law and did not provide for any continuing commission such as the C.I.N.A. This agreement was signed on February 20, 1928, by 21 countries including the United States.

The differences between the Paris Convention of 1919 and the Havana Convention of 1928 were:

1. The Havana Convention had no Annexes; all rules were contained in the treaty itself.

2. The Havana Convention was applicable only to private aircraft; government aircraft were not included.

3. Aircraft regulation was to be done according to the laws of each country. No uniformity was provided.

4. Pilots were required to demonstrate a knowledge of the regulations of each country in which they flew. This meant they were to know the rules of the twenty other countries in addition to their own.

There were no provisions for a permanent way of effecting civil aviation progress and development. Each country was expected to take the initiative in civil aviation.

The Paris Convention and the Havana Convention caused some degree of confusion in actual practice since they were two separate sets of rules. It was soon realized that there would have to be only one international organization to bring together international civil aviation developments. This did not occur until 1944.

WARSAW CONVENTION—1929

The Warsaw Convention was the result of two international conferences held in Paris in 1925 and Warsaw in 1929. The purpose of the conferences was twofold. The first was to establish some degree of uniformity in travel/shipping documentation, i.e. tickets and waybills, etc. The second was to limit the potential liability of the air carrier in the case of accidents.

This was the first international convention pertaining to liability and has been ratified by more than sixty countries, including the United States.

The Warsaw Convention was signed in October 1929 and went into effect on February 13, 1933. It was recognized almost immediately as the most important document in international and foreign commercial air transportation. In 1934 the United States Senate gave its consent to the Convention.

The Warsaw Convention provides the rules of air carrier accident liability in international air transportation. It prescribes that the airline is liable for damages for death or injury to passengers; destruction, loss, or damage to baggage and goods; and loss resulting from delay in transporting passengers, baggage, and merchandise. It also sets standards for passenger tickets, cargo waybills, and other air travel documents.

After World War II ended many people, especially in Great Britain, suggested a revision of the Warsaw Convention. Those in the United States who urged for a revision wanted an increase in the liability limits which at that time were only $8,300 per person. These discussions continued until September 1955, when the Convention was amended. The diplomatic conference called for this event met at The Hague, Netherlands. The United States was represented, and the so-called Hague Protocol to the Warsaw Convention was signed. This Protocol made two major changes in the Convention. First it doubled the monetary limit to $16,600 as the maximum recovery for death; and second, it extended to agents of the carrier the limitation of liability now provided to the carrier. The Protocol has been signed and ratified by some 45 countries. The United States signed the Protocol on December 1, 1964. The subject of ratification of this document by the United States has been most controversial. Willful misconduct and the location of the crash can abrogate the limitation of liability.

During the early 1960s many countries expressed concern regarding the limits of liability which were doubled by the Hague Protocol of 1955. Some countries believed that limits were too low and did not relate to their economic conditions. Other countries feared that the limits were too high and imposed a financial burden on their national air carriers. In 1965, the United States denounced the original Warsaw Convention. The International Civil Aviation Organization held a special meeting in Montreal, in February 1966, in an attempt to find a solution, but no compromise was achieved.

This meeting became known as the Montreal Agreement of 1966. It was not an international agreement or a formal revision of the Warsaw Convention of 1929. It was an interim arrangement among air carriers operating passenger transportation to and from the United States. The Malta Agreement was a name given to an informal meeting of civil aviation authorities from the European governments who agreed upon the general increase in air carrier limits of passenger liability equal to that of the Montreal Agreement.

By virtue of the Montreal Agreement, the air carriers agreed to include in their tariffs a special contract permitted under the Warsaw Convention, which provided for a limit of liability for each passenger in case of death or bodily injury to the amount of $75,000. This amended the application of the Warsaw Convention as amended by the Hague Protocol of 1955. The air carriers who agreed to this arrangement must not avail themselves to any defense under the Convention, which provides that a carrier is not liable if they prove that they or their agents have taken all necessary measures to avoid the damage, or that it was impossible for them to take such measures. Thus the principle of strict liability regardless of fault had been contractually introduced by this action.

Current air carrier liability limits for international passengers range from $10,000 according to the Warsaw Convention of 1929 to a maximum of $150,000 depending upon the circumstances where the ticked was purchased.

CONVENTION ON DAMAGE CAUSED BY FOREIGN AIRCRAFT TO THIRD PARTIES ON THE SURFACE—1933

This Convention dealt with damage caused by foreign aircraft to people and property on the ground, and was signed in Rome on May 29, 1933. It imposed a strict liability on aircraft operators for sums limited by reference to the maximum permitted weight of the aircraft. Liability was secured by compulsory insurance, cash deposits, or bank guarantees. The Convention was formally adopted by very few countries, but the principles have been copied by other countries. An amended Convention in 1952 was intended to replace the original Convention of 1933. The new amendments included an increase in the liability limits and the matter of security was no longer compulsory but at the option of the individual contracting countries. The 1952 convention was revised by the Montreal Protocol of 1978. As of June 30, 1995, 38 countries have ratified the Convention of 1952.

CHICAGO CONVENTION ON INTERNATIONAL CIVIL AVIATION—1944 (CHICAGO CONFERENCE)

With the end of World War II near, many countries foresaw the peaceful applications of international air transportation. It was obvious that action would have to take place to provide for any international agreements in aviation. The U.S. Government invited the allied and neutral powers to attend an international conference in Chicago in November and December 1944. This conference came about after discussions between the United States and Great Britain in 1943. Fifty-two nations attended; only Saudi Arabia and the Soviet Union did not attend.

The purpose was to establish a basic legal framework for operating international civil air transportation services. An opening message by President Franklin D. Roosevelt said that the purpose of the conference was "to establish a fundamental law that would give full recognition of the sovereignty and judicial equality of all nations so that airways would serve humanity. The future development of International Civil Aviation can greatly help to create and preserve friendship and understanding among the nations and peoples of the world." This quote is from the preamble to the Convention on International Civil Aviation signed at Chicago on December 7, 1944.

The conference had three major objectives:

- The establishment of an International Air Interim Council.

- The establishment of provisional world air routes and arrangements.

- An agreement on principles for a permanent aeronautical body and a multilateral aviation convention.

Four different proposals for the organization of civil aviation were presented by the United States, Great Britain, Canada, and Australia-New Zealand. Secret talks between the United States, Great Britain and Canada finally resolved the issue. After 37 days of continuous meetings the Chicago Conference established not one but four treaties or conventions. They were:

1. The Interim Agreement on International Civil Aviation, (U.N. Treaty Series 501, Vol. 171, page 345). Its purpose was to provide for a temporary mechanism to allow for operation until the Convention would be formally ratified. It became effective on June 6, 1945 when twenty-six countries accepted it and established the Provisional International Civil Aviation Organization. Its first meeting was held on August 15, 1945. The PICAO functioned well until it was replaced by the permanent ICAO on April 4, 1947.

2. The main Chicago Convention on International Civil Aviation (U.N. Treaty Series 102, Vol. 15, page 295), setting up the International Civil Aviation Organization (ICAO) as a permanent organization.

3. The International Air Services Transit Agreement, (U.N. Treaty Series 252, Vol. 84, page 389) whereby contracting nations mutually exchange the privileges of overflight and noncommercial landing by scheduled flights, commonly referred to as the Two Freedoms Agreement. It should be noted that the Chicago Convention provides these privileges for non-scheduled flights. This agreement became effective on June 30, 1945.

4. The International Air Transport Agreement, commonly known as the Five Freedoms Agreement (U.N. Treaty Series 502, Vol. 171, page 387), whereby parties mutually exchange the additional commercial privileges of carrying passengers, mail and freight to and from the other contracting parties, as well as beyond to other countries. This multilateral agreement is by far the least successful of the group because it ignores the capacity to be provided and the amounts to be charged for the service, the two most important issues.

It was understood that many countries would not accept this agreement. It was eventually signed by 19 countries, which reciprocally applied its provisions. Many countries denounced the agreement and only a handful remain a party to it.

The International Civil Aviation Organization as a permanent organization began on April 4, 1947.

The Five Freedoms presented in the International Air Transport Agreement entered into by members of the treaty are summarized below.

Freedom One. *The right to fly over territory of a foreign country without landing.*

Freedom Two. *The right to make a landing in a foreign country for technical reasons but not to pick up or discharge traffic.*

Freedom Three. *The right to carry traffic from the home country of an air carrier into a foreign country.*

Freedom Four. *The right to carry traffic from a foreign country back to the home country of an air carrier.*

Freedom Five. *The right to carry traffic between two or more foreign countries on flights coming from, or going to, the home country of an aircarrier.*

In addition to these recognized Five Freedoms other conditions have been expressed as freedoms and are presented below:

Freedom Six. *The right to carry traffic between two foreign countries through the home country. This a combination of Freedoms Three and Four which has resulted from a bilateral agreement for exchanging air traffic rights.*

Freedom Seven. *The right to carry traffic between two foreign countries by an air carrier operating entirely outside of its own country. This is a combination of the Fifth Freedom rights.*

Freedoms Six and **Seven** are essentially supplementary freedoms and have no official recognition.

Cabotage is an air carrier carrying traffic between two points in a foreign country and is usually prohibited. The term Grand Cagbotage is used if these points are located in separate parts of the same foreign country.

Freedom Eight. *The right to carry traffic between two points within a foreign country, therefore acting as a domestic carrier in a foreign country.*

OUTCOMES OF CHICAGO CONFERENCE—1944

BILATERAL AGREEMENTS

One of the three major objectives of the Conference concerned air routes. At first it was the desire of the leaders of the conference to develop a multilateral air transport agreement, by which many countries would enter into an agreement regarding air routes. However, the Multilateral Transport Agreement was rejected by a majority of the States, and all that was left to work out commercial freedoms were bilateral negotiations.

As a result of this rejection the Final Act of the Chicago Convention includes a "Form of Standard Agreement for Provisional Air Routes." One of the first of these bilateral agreements, and by far the most significant, was the Bermuda Agreement, which will be discussed later in this chapter.

The current system of bilateral agreements, which started back in the 1940s, severely restricts competition in international markets. History has amply demonstrated that competition improves efficiency, productivity, and worldwide economic growth. At the present time, DOT is attempting to create a more competitive international aviation environment for the U.S. airlines through the continuing expansion of open-skies agreements. DOT is also assessing the pros and cons of modifying cabotage constraints, modifying seventh freedom rights,[4] and increasing foreign investment in U.S. air carriers from the current 25 percent.

During the last eight years, the Administration has achieved 89 new and expanded bilateral agreements, 50 of which are open-skies. An analysis conducted by DOT showed that from 1996 to 1999, on routes connecting interior cities in both the United States and European countries, the average decline in fares was 20 percent where open-skies was in effect. In markets where there were no open-skies agreements, the average decline in fares was only 10.3 percent.

In 2000, new bilateral agreements were reached with Colombia and open-skies agreements were signed with four countries from Asia, one each from South America and Europe, and four countries from Africa. Included in the open-skies agreements was the first multilateral "Open-Skies" agreement. The agreement included Brunei, Chile, New Zealand, and Singapore and permits unrestricted international air service for all flights among the five countries for these countries' carriers.

Discussions concerning the liberalization of markets are also proceeding with other countries throughout the world. The expansion of these agreements over the next several years could significantly increase the level of activity of the more efficient U.S. carriers vis-a-vis foreign flag carriers.

The industry is expected to continue toward globalization, through the use of code-sharing agreements and alliances. Four large alliances have formed and are continuing to add members and network connections. The four are SkyTeam (Delta-Air France), Star Alliance (United-Lufthansa), Oneworld (American-British Airways), and Northwest-KLM. The alliances have been able to reduce costs through economics of scale. They have also increased revenues and passenger traffic by expanding the reach of the networks and providing seamless travel for their passengers.

PROVISIONAL INTERNATIONAL CIVIL AVIATION ORGANIZATION

An interim organization was established by an agreement on June 6, 1945. Most of its structure patterned along the lines of what the permanent organization was to be: provisional Assembly, provisional Council, and a provisional Secretariat. It was to have advisory powers only and to operate until the permanent organization (ICAO) was created. The PICAO functioned for twenty months. This provisional organization was replaced by the permanent organization when the Chicago Conference was ratified by the necessary 26 States on April 4, 1947.

In the short life of the PICAO the foundation for an international organization devoted to the needs of civil aviation was laid and fifty contracting states took concerted action to provide and maintain the facilities and services necessary for the operation of air services across national borders.

PERMANENT INTERNATIONAL CIVIL AVIATION ORGANIZATION (ICAO)

At the invitation of the government of Canada, the city of Montreal was chosen as the site for the headquarters of the organization.

---

[4] Seventh Freedom rights allow a carrier to pick up passengers from a country other than its own and deliver them in a third country, also not its own, on flights that do not connect to its homeland. (Source: ALPA)

Membership in the ICAO comes under three classes of States: (1) signatory States which include all those States who were first to ratify the Conference; (2) members of the United Nations other than original members; and (3) other States which were those who were at war with the Allies (Italy, Austria, Finland, Japan, and Germany). The ICAO has obtained the status of a United Nations specialized agency.

The organization of ICAO is divided into three main bodies which are the Assembly, the Council and the Secretariat.

The Assembly of the Organization is much like the General Assembly of the United Nations. Each of the States has one vote, and decisions in most cases are taken by a simple majority vote. (Refer to Chapter 13 "International Air Transportation Organizations" for the complete organizational structure of the International Civil Aviation Organization.)

INTERNATIONAL AIR SERVICES TRANSIT AGREEMENT

This is the Two Freedoms agreement which is referred to as the technical freedoms. The first of these freedoms is the right of an aircraft to fly over the territory of another country who has agreed to it. This would allow an airline to fly from New York to Rome, passing over such other countries as Great Britain, France, and Switzerland. The second of these freedoms conveys the right of an airplane to land for technical reasons, such as refueling or repairs, but not for commercial purposes, such as picking up or discharging passengers. For example, the flight to Rome from New York could land at London to refuel.

This Agreement is one of the most important agreements in world aviation. If this Agreement had been the only result of the Chicago Conference the effort would have been worthwhile. The United States surrounded by two oceans and two friendly neighbors does not truly appreciate the significance of the Transit Agreement.

INTERNATIONAL AIR TRANSPORT AGREEMENT (FIVE FREEDOMS AGREEMENT)

This agreement was signed by 16 States and consisted of the two technical freedoms plus three more commercial freedoms.

The first of these commercial freedoms is the right to carry traffic from the plane's country of origin to another country, for example, an airline carrying pas-

sengers from New York to Paris. The second commercial freedom refers to the right to pick up traffic in other countries and return to the home country of the airline, such as a flight originating in Rome and carrying passengers to New York. The third commercial freedom is the right for an airline to carry traffic between countries outside its own country.

By the end of 1994, 191 nations had deposited instruments of either ratification or adherence to the Chicago Convention and joined ICAO. Of these, 100 nations had accepted the International Air Services Transit Agreement, but only 11 accepted the International Air Transport Agreement.

The two technical freedoms and the three commercial freedoms are referred to as the "Five Freedoms of the Air." Today few countries are willing to exchange these "Freedoms" on a multilateral basis, but all accept the concept of exchanging them bilaterally. By the terms of Article 80 of the Convention on International Civil Aviation, popularly known as the Chicago Convention of 1944, all contracting States agreed to give notice of denunciation of the Paris Convention of 1919 and the Havana Convention of 1928 upon the coming into force of the Chicago Convention of 1944. Since the Convention on International Civil Aviation came into force on April 4, 1947, the Paris Convention of 1919 and the Havana Convention of 1928 are rendered ineffective except for historical purposes.

BERMUDA AGREEMENT—1946 (U.N. TREATY SERIES 36, VOL. 3, PAGE 253)

The Bermuda Agreement was not the first bilateral agreement involving civil aviation entered into by two countries. The Agreement between the U.S. and Spain was signed on December 2, 1944; Denmark and Sweden was signed on December 16, 1944; Iceland was signed on January 27, 1945; Canada was signed on February 7, 1945; Switzerland was signed on July 13, 1945; and Norway was signed on July 13, 1945. Additionally, many bilateral agreements existed under both the Paris and Havana Conventions.

Although not the most complicated bilateral air agreement in existence it was the "father" of modern bilateral air service agreements. One observer stated that these agreements could no longer be regarded as merely temporary arrangements without any general significance but together with the Chicago Convention and the Air Transit Agreement they formed a well delineated law of international air transport.

If the Chicago Convention of 1944 represents the farthest advance toward multilateral accord, then the Bermuda Agreement of 1946 represents a triumph of bilateral achievement in influencing multilateral behavior.

The two great protagonists at Chicago were the United States and the United Kingdom. At that time the United States had the world's only fleet of long-range transports, and a history of separation of business and government. At Chicago the United States had campaigned for "Open Skies," i.e., unregulated air services.

On the other hand, the United Kingdom had only a few transports—each with limited range. The United Kingdom also had a long history of government participation in commercial aviation. At Chicago the United Kingdom had campaigned for "Order in the Air" or regulated air services. The United States had economic strength, but the United Kingdom had position. London was the hub of the English speaking world, and also in those days a necessary refueling stop on the way to Europe.

In 1946, diplomats from the two nations met in Bermuda to iron out their bilateral differences. The standard format in the Final Act of the Chicago Convention was a starting point but it ignored the main issues. In the end the United States accepted the United Kingdom concept that the airlines could mutually set the tariffs to be charged (fares and rates), subject to prior review and acceptance by the two governments. For its part the United Kingdom accepted the United States concept that the individual airlines could unilaterally select capacity, i.e., its own aircraft size and service frequency, with only an "ex-post-facto" review to guard against unfair practices.

In addition to the issues of capacity and tariffs, the Bermuda Agreement also reinforced the concepts that (1) Routes were to be mutually allocated by common consent on the basis of a fair and equitable exchange, and (2) the Fifth Freedom shall likewise be allocated by common consent on a fair and equitable basis. And most importantly, the governments also agreed that this new agreement would form the model for all the future bilateral agreements each would negotiate. As a result, the Bermuda Agreement replaced the Chicago Form as the world's standard Air Service Agreement.

Though it might seem that multilateral conventions provide all that could be desired in international aviation agreements, there are limitations. There are practical, international, political, and economic relations which prevent, or deter, some nations from entering into general multilateral agreements. At the same time, various combinations of nations can work out agreements on a bilateral basis. Therefore, existing concurrently with, and in some instances complementary to multilateral agreements, the United States has entered into bilateral agreements concerning Air Navigation; Air Transport; Airworthiness of Export Aircraft; and Reciprocal Recognition of Pilot Licenses. Of particular note among these agreements are those following the pattern suggested by Resolution No. VIII—Standard Form of Agreement for Provisional Air Routes resolved at the Chicago Conference of 1944, and those following the provisions of the Bermuda Agreement. These agreements are sometimes referred to as the Chicago-Type Agreement and the Bermuda-Type Agreement.

In addition to the general multilateral and bilateral aviation agreements referred to above, there are numerous multilateral and bilateral agreements concerning Double Taxation, Radio Communications, Sanitary Regulations, and Postal Arrangements.

RIGHTS IN AIRCRAFT CONVENTION

The Convention on the International Recognition of Rights in Aircraft was signed in Geneva in June of 1948 and entered into force on September 17, 1953. Through this Convention the recovery of seized aircraft is assured. In ratifying this Convention the Mexican Government reserved "the rights belonging to it to recognize the priorities granted by Mexican Laws to fiscal claims and claims arising out of work contracts over other claims."

Both the United States and Mexico became Contracting Parties to this Convention but the United States does not recognize Mexico's reservation. As a result, over the next two decades it was nearly impossible for United States owners to recover aircraft stolen for the drug trade and confiscated in Mexico.

As of the end of 1994, 61 nations have deposited their instruments of ratification or adherence to this Convention. Of these only the Netherlands and Sweden have adopted the United States position regarding Mexico.

GROUND DAMAGE CONVENTION

The Convention on Damage Caused by Foreign Aircraft to Third Parties on the Surface was signed in Rome in October of 1952 and entered into force on February 4, 1958.

As of the end of 1994, 38 nations have deposited their instruments of either ratification or adherence to this Convention. The United States was not as yet a Contracting Party.

AIR OFFENSES CONVENTION

The Convention on Offenses and Certain Other Acts Committed on Board Aircraft was signed in Tokyo in September of 1963 and entered into force on December 4, 1969. This Convention insures that offenses committed on board aircraft will be placed under the jurisdiction of at least one State, i.e., the one of aircraft registration. The Convention also contains provisions relating to the duties of States, the extradition of an accused offender and the powers of the aircraft commander.

As of the end of 1994, 149 nations deposited their instruments of either ratification or adherence to this Convention. The United States became a Contracting Party on December 4, 1969.

HIJACKING CONVENTION

Due to the increased incidents of seizure of aircraft for various purposes in recent years, many nations of the world met at The Hague in 1970.

As a result, the Convention for the Suppression of Unlawful Seizure of Aircraft was completed on December 16, 1970. The terms of the Convention were to become effective thirty days after the ratification by the tenth country. With the acceptance by the United States Senate and the President, ratification by the Senate was completed on September 14, 1971 and proclaimed by the President on October 18, 1971. The Convention entered into force on October 14, 1971; as of the end of 1994, 149 nations had become Contracting Parties.

SABOTAGE CONVENTION

The Convention for the Suppression of Unlawful Acts Against the Safety of Civil Aviation entered into force on January 26, 1973. The law gives effect to the Hijacking Convention by providing the President of the United States with authority to suspend air service to any country which he determines is encouraging hijacking in opposition to the Hijacking Convention.

The law orders the Federal Aviation Administration to provide regulations requiring that all air carrier passengers and their carry-on baggage be screened by detection devices. Also, it requires a federal air transportation security force to be stationed at major airports under the auspices of the Federal Aviation Administration.

As of the end of 1994, 151 nations have deposited their instruments of either ratification or adherence to this Convention. The Untied States became a Contracting Party on November 1, 1972.

INTERNATIONAL AIR TRANSPORTATION COMPETITION ACT OF 1979

A new law was enacted by Congress on February 15, 1980, which directs the future of the United States in international aviation affairs. This Act amended the Federal Aviation Act of 1958 in areas of international aviation matters.

The United States government extended its attitude concerning competition in the air carrier industry, formulated by the Airline Deregulation Act of 1978, into international air transportation.

The purpose of the Act is to amend the Federal Aviation Act of 1958 in order to:

- Promote competition in international air transportation.

- Provide greater opportunities for United States air carriers.

- Establish goals for developing United States international aviation negotiating policy.

The Act contains a Declaration of Policy directed to the Civil Aeronautics Board containing factors for interstate, overseas, and foreign air transportation. The Board is directed to consider the following in accordance with the public convenience and necessity:

1. Maintenance of safety as the highest priority.

2. Prevention of any deterioration of safety.

3. Availability of a variety of adequate, economic, efficient, and low-priced services by U.S. and foreign air carriers.

4. Maximum reliance on competitive market forces.

5. Development and maintenance of a sound regulatory environment which is responsive to the need of the public.

6. Encouragement of air service in major urban areas of the United States through secondary airports.

7. Prevention of unfair, deceptive, and anticompetitive practices in air transportation, and avoidance of unreasonable industry concentration.

8. Maintenance of a system of continuous scheduled interstate and overseas airline service for small communities.

9. Encouragement of an air transportation system relying on competition to provide low prices.

10. Encouragement of new carriers and existing air carriers into new markets, and strengthening of

small air carriers to assure a competitive air carrier industry.

11. Promotion of civil aeronautics and a privately owned U.S. air transport industry.

12. Strengthening of the position of U.S. air carriers to assure competitive equality with foreign air carriers.

The above policy declarations are reflected in the addition to Section 1102, International Agreements, of the Federal Aviation Act by establishing "Goals for International Aviation Policy." These goals state that in formulating United States international air transportation policy Congress intends that there shall develop a negotiating policy which emphasizes the greatest degree of competition. This includes, among other things:

1. Strengthening of the competitive position of U.S. air carriers to at least assure quality with foreign air carriers including opportunities to increase their profitability in foreign air transportation.

2. Freedom of all air carriers (U.S. and foreign) to offer rates which correspond with consumer demand.

3. Minimizing restrictions on charter air transportation.

4. Maximizing the degree of multiple and permissive international authority for U.S. air carriers so that they will be able to respond quickly to shifts in market demand.

5. Elimination of operational and marketing restrictions to the greatest extent possible.

6. Integration of domestic and international air transportation.

7. Increasing the number of nonstop United States gateway cities.

8. Increasing access opportunities for foreign air carriers to United States cities on a reciprocal basis for U.S. air carriers.

9. Elimination of discrimination and unfair competition faced by U.S. air carriers in foreign air transportation.

10. Promotion of civil aeronautics and a privately owned United States air transport industry.

INTERNATIONAL DEREGULATION

Deregulation began with air cargo in 1977 as an experiment in the United States. The following year passenger deregulation came about with the passage of the Airline Deregulation Act. The purpose of deregulation was to provide for open competition in the market-place and to influence the future economic and business decisions of the air carriers. This reform was limited to fares, rates, and charges. Aviation safety and air traffic control were not affected; they remained the responsibility of the government.

The application of deregulation in international civil aviation is a much different concept than domestic deregulation in the United States. This is obvious because international deregulation means the involvement of many different governments and has brought about a condition whereby more government involvement in airline activities has taken place.

In Europe it was recognized that a competitive condition was desirable, but that it would come about at a slower rate than it occurred in the United States because of the public service aspect of air carrier operations. Many countries of the world view their air carriers as an important instrument of their country designed to operate for the public good. This is especially true in the smaller developing nations.

Due to many problems, deregulation of the air carrier industry in the United States has not brought about the results that were expected. The industry has become more efficient while becoming more competitive, but not necessarily more profitable. The U.S. airline industry has become more concentrated with three air carriers capturing more than 60% of the domestic market.

As a result of deregulation in the United States, other countries have undertaken efforts to create a more competitive environment. The results in Canada were similar to the effect of deregulation in the United States. Since 1984 the Canadian air carrier industry had become highly concentrated before the National Transportation Act became effective in 1987. International deregulation evolves slowly, particularly where the major air carriers are owned wholly or in part by their governments.

In April 1986, a decision by the European Court of Justice said that air transportation agreements are subject to the competition rules of the Treaty of Rome, signed by six European countries in 1957. This meant that the air carriers could be prosecuted for violations unless permission had been extended to them by the Council of Ministers. In 1987, this Council of Ministers legislated rules and took the first step toward liberalizing the air transportation industry in Europe.

The European Civil Aviation Conference was formed consisting of 33 European countries. They developed two International Agreements concerning intra-European fares and capacity sharing. Soon other regulatory changes took place providing for more free market access. The European trend toward concentration of airline activities and their market share will no doubt continue in the future as a result of these and more measures to be put into effect.

International air carriers continue to find new ways to increase their strength in the market place by mergers, buying other air carriers, and several types of marketing agreements and cooperative ventures. An important tool is the worldwide computer reservation system which has been created by groups of airlines in different parts of the world. This is playing an increasing role in marketing and selling air transportation and is among the most important forces influencing international civil aviation developments in the future. As time passes more will be heard concerning international air carrier deregulation.

The worldwide computer reservation system plays an important role in influencing future international civil aviation developments.

THE UNITED STATES POLICY ON INTERNATIONAL AND FOREIGN AIR TRANSPORTATION

Prior to World War II, the United States had no policy on international and foreign air transportation except to develop flag carriers through airmail payments. Almost all these operations were conducted by Pan American World Airways. Pan American's position as the only carrier in international competition resulted in its achieving a dominant position and always seeming to be in the position of the best qualified carrier to receive air mail contracts. Congress encouraged the concentration of one airline effort, since our laws made no such provision. Pan American's monopoly policy was a result of its own initiative. Since the close of World War II the Board has taken the position that it is in the public interest to have more than one carrier, whenever possible, of the United States operating on international routes. As a result, many Trunk Air Carriers were awarded international routes as extensions of their domestic routes.

After World War II, the United States adopted a policy which was that there should be adequate incentives to stimulate efficiency in operations; also, that by reducing costs and rates, the full economic potential of the industry would be realized. Our policy was that the United States should continue to develop and use the newest equipment and best procedures; also, to ensure that the U.S.-flag carriers would carry passengers pro-

portional with the importance of the United States as a transportation market, and that healthy financial conditions would ensure an influx of adequate capital. The importance of international air transportation parallels the social, economic, and political factors discussed in Chapter 1.

During the 1950s U.S.-flag carriers carried the largest percentage of passengers in international flights. Today, the percentage is dwindling steadily, and it appears the trend will continue. U.S. maritime shipping has declined until only a fraction of the world's shipping is done by U.S. shipping interests. This must not be allowed to happen to U.S. international air carriers.

Many international problems have come from smaller countries who feel their air carriers cannot compete directly with U.S. air carriers. All too often these countries have attempted to restrict U.S. air carriers by influencing their schedules and service. Our government has usually been unwilling to protest or request arbitration. These smaller countries, also, are reluctant to furnish statistical data regarding fifth-freedom traffic. The United States, if it is going to regain some of its losses, must engage in more realistic negotiations for route exchanges.

After World War II, the policy changed to one of maximum development of international air transportation. It became policy that no foreign-flag airline seeking part of the industry would be excluded.

The United States' policy was described in the "International Air Transport Policy" of the 79th Congress (1945–1946). This policy was fivefold:

1. United States aviation would continue to be progressive in the development of new equipment and operating procedures.

2. Adequate incentives would compel efficiency in operation.

3. Full economic potentialities of air transport would be realized by widening the market.

4. Healthy financial condition would assure the inflow of adequate capital.

5. United States airlines would carry a volume of world traffic proportional with the importance of the United States as a market for air transport services.

The International Air Transportation Policy of the United States has undergone several changes since 1946. Richard Nixon, while President, presented his policy which superseded President John F. Kennedy's policy adopted on April 24, 1963. In September 1976, President Gerald Ford changed the policy once again.

UNITED STATES POLICY FOR THE CONDUCT OF INTERNATIONAL AIR TRANSPORTATION NEGOTIATIONS (AUGUST 21, 1978)

INTRODUCTION

United States international air transportation policy is designed to provide the greatest possible benefit to travelers and shippers. Our primary aim is furthering the maintenance and continued development of affordable, safe, convenient, efficient and environmentally acceptable air services. Our policy for negotiating civil air transport agreements reflects our national goals in international transportation. This policy provides a set of general objectives, designed particularly for major international air markets, on the basis of which United States negotiators can develop specific negotiating strategies.

Maximum consumer benefits can be best achieved through the preservation and extension of competition between airlines in a fair marketplace. Reliance on competitive market forces to the greatest extent possible in our international air transportation agreements will allow the public to receive improved service at low costs that reflect economically efficient operations. Competition and low prices are also fully compatible with a prosperous U.S. air transport industry and our national defense, foreign policy, international commerce, and energy efficiency objectives.

Bilateral aviation agreements, like other international agreements, should serve the interest of both parties. Other countries have an interest in the economic prosperity of their airline industries, as we do in the prosperity of ours. The United States believes this interest is best served by a policy of expansion, of competitive opportunity rather than restriction. By offering more services to the public, in a healthy and fair competitive environment, the international air transport industry can stimulate the growth in traffic which contributes to both profitable industry operations and maximum public benefits.

GOALS OF U.S. INTERNATIONAL AIR TRANSPORTATION POLICY

The U.S. will work to achieve a system of international air transportation that places its principal reliance on actual and potential competition to determine the variety, quality, and price of air service. An essential means for carrying out our international air transportation policy will be to allow greater competitive opportunities for U.S. and foreign airlines and to promote new low-cost transportation options for travelers and shippers.

Especially in major international air transport markets, there can be substantial benefits for travelers, shippers, airlines, and labor from increasing competitive opportunities and reducing protectionist restrictions. Increasing opportunities for U.S. flag transportation to and from the United States will contribute to the development of our foreign commerce, assure that more airlift resources are available for our defense needs, and promote and expand productivity and job opportunities in our international air transport industry.

TRANSLATING GOALS INTO NEGOTIATING OBJECTIVES

U.S. International Air Transportation Policy cannot be implemented unilaterally. Our objectives have to be achieved in the system of international agreements that form the basic framework for the international air transportation system.

Routes, prices, capacity, scheduled and charter rules, and competition in the marketplace are interrelated, not isolated problems to be resolved independently. Thus, the following objectives will be presented in negotiations as an integrated U.S. position:

1. Creation of new and greater opportunities for innovative and competitive pricing that will encourage and permit the use of new price and service options to meet the needs of different travelers and shippers.

2. Liberalization of charter rules and elimination of restrictions on charter operations.

3. Expansion of scheduled service through elimination of restrictions on capacity, frequency, and route and operating rights.

4. Elimination of discrimination and unfair competitive practices faced by U.S. airlines in international transportation.

5. Flexibility to designate multiple U.S. airlines in international air markets.

6. Encouragement of maximum traveler and shipper access to international markets by authorizing more cities for non-stop or direct service, and by improving the integration of domestic and international airline services.

7. Flexibility to permit the development and facilitation of competitive air cargo service.

EXPLANATION OF OBJECTIVES

1. *Pricing.* The U.S. will develop new bilateral procedures to encourage a more competitive system for establishing scheduled air fares and rates. Charter pricing must continue to be competitive. Fares, rates, and prices should be determined by individual airlines based primarily on competitive considerations in the marketplace. Governmental regulation should not be more than the minimum necessary to prevent predatory or discriminatory practices to protect consumers from the abuse of monopoly position, or to protect competitors from prices that are artificially low because of direct or indirect governmental subsidy or support. Reliance on competition and encouragement of pricing based on commercial considerations in the marketplace provides the best means of assuring that the needs of consumers will be met and that prices will be as low as possible given the costs providing efficient air service.

2. *Charters.* The introduction of charters acted as a major catalyst to the expansion of international air transportation in the 1960s. Charters are a competitive spur and exert downward pressure on the pricing of scheduled services. Charters generate new traffic and help stimulate expansion in all sectors of the industry. Restrictions which have been imposed on the volume, frequency, and regularity of charter services as well as requirements for approval of individual charter flights have restrained the growth of traffic and tourism and do not serve the interests of either party to an aviation agreement. Strong efforts will be made to obtain liberal charter provisions in bilateral agreements.

3. *Scheduled Services.* We will seek to increase the freedom of airlines from capacity and frequency restrictions. We will also work to maintain or increase the route and operating rights of our airlines where such actions improve international route systems and offer the consumer more convenient and efficient air transportation.

4. *Discrimination and Unfair Competitive Practices.* U.S. airlines must have the flexibility to conduct operations and market their services in a manner consistent with a fair and equal opportunity to compete with the airlines of other nations. We will insist that U.S. airlines have the business, commercial, and operational opportunities to compete fairly. The United States will seek to eliminate unfair or destructive competitive practices that prevent U.S. airlines from competing on an equal basis with the airlines of other nations. Charges for providing airway and airport properties and facilities should be related to the costs due to airline operations and should not discriminate against U.S. airlines. These objectives were recognized by the Congress in legislation enacted in 1975, and their attainment is required if consumers, airlines, and employees are to obtain the benefits of an otherwise competitive international aviation system.

5. *Multiple Airline Designations.* The designation of new U.S. airlines in international markets that will support additional service is a way to create a more competitive environment and thus encourage improved service and competitive pricing. Privately owned airlines have traditionally been the source of innovation and competition in international aviation, and it is, therefore, particularly important to preserve for the U.S. the right of multiple designation.

6. *Maximum Access to International Markets.* Increasing the number of gateway cities for non-stop or direct air service offers the potential for increasing the convenience of air transportation for passengers and shippers and improving routing and market opportunities for international airlines. In addition, enhancing the integration of U.S. airlines' domestic and international air services benefits both consumers and airlines.

7. *Cargo Services.* We will seek the opportunity for the full development of cargo services. Frequently demand for such services requires special equipment and routes. Cargo services should be permitted to develop freely as trade expands. Also important in the development of cargo services are improved facilitation, including customs clearance, integration of surface and air movements, and flexibility in ground support services.

NEGOTIATING PRINCIPLES

The guiding principle of United States aviation negotiating policy will be to trade competitive opportunities, rather than restrictions, with out negotiating partners. We will aggressively pursue our interests in expanded air transportation and reduced prices rather than accept the self-defeating accommodation of protectionism. Our concessions in negotiations will be given in return for progress towards competitive objectives, and these concessions themselves will be of a liberalizing character.

Proposed bilateral agreements which do not meet our minimum competitive objectives will not be signed without prior Presidential approval.

INTERAGENCY COMMITTEE ON INTERNATIONAL AIR TRANSPORTATION POLICY

Chaired by: Department of Transportation

Member Agencies: Department of State
Department of Justice
Department of Defense
Department of Commerce
Council of Economic Advisors
Council on Wage and Price
Stability
Domestic Policy Staff—
The White House
National Security Council
Office of Management and
Budget

The principle of liberal competition for the United States domestic air carriers brought about by Deregulation has permeated into the United States government's attitude with respect to its international air carrier operation and the negotiating of agreements with other countries. Parallel to domestic Deregulation, international agreements having to do with competitive actions by air carriers have become more important.

The most competitive bilateral agreement includes multiple designations, dual disapproving pricing, equal access to marketing outlets, the right to self handle, and an open charter regime. From air carrier management's perspective, such an agreement is an invitation to exercise marketing judgments to meet the public demand for service. Management has responded to this new freedom, and the effect on the industry and the public has been beneficial.

The benefits of a more world-wide competitive environment are that competition

1. Provides substantial new benefits to customers,

2. Forces the airlines to operate more efficiently, whether they are privately or publicly owned, and

3. Does not hinder the ability of airlines to earn a normal return on investment.

On August 21, 1978, President Carter announced a pro-competitive policy on international aviation. The principles contained in it were subsequently adopted by Congress in the International Air Transport Competition Act of 1979. The President stated:

"Our policy for negotiating civil air transport agreements reflects our national goals in international air transportation. This policy provides a set of general objectives designed particularly for major international air markets on the basis of which United States negotiations can develop specific negotiating strategies."

The United States' international policy has caused much controversy. Many foreign government-owned air carriers and some foreign governments have been critical of it. The criticisms may not stand up under close examination because they may be intended to protect their special interests. They fall into six areas:

1. That the United States is attempting to foist its approach on other nations which may have different national goals and is ignoring the basic principles of sovereignty.

2. That Deregulation will quickly lead to the loss of the regular high-frequency service that is required by the world business community.

3. That open competition is inconsistent with sound energy policy which may require severe restrictions in leisure travel to assure maintenance of service for business travelers.

4. That although competition may look good during the boom of a business cycle, history has shown that excessive discount pricing during growth periods has led to overcapacity and financial disaster during downturns.

5. That careful regulation and capacity control can achieve lower fares than can open entry and competition.

6. That it is foolish to talk about open skies when the industry is so dependent upon external constraints such as limited airport capacities, air traffic control, tourists' organizations, and so forth.

The foreign criticism of the United States' policy of international competition is that the United States violated the spirit of international cooperation and equality which was established at the Chicago Conference in 1944. This Conference was a milestone in the history of international aviation; it resulted in cooperation on many aspects of international civil aircraft operation.

The one area where no multilateral agreement could be reached, however, was the subject of how commercial air carriers would be permitted to compete. Presently, as it did in 1944, the United States advocates a system of essentially free entry and price flexibility. Some countries favor more regulation as a solution. No multilateral agreement has ever been reached, so the establishment of these relationships is dependent upon bilateral negotiations between participating countries.

The United States' International Air Transport Policy is a policy of commitment to creating an efficient system that can provide greater service and price options to travelers and shippers. Basically it is a return to the principles of equal competitive opportunities which the United States proposed at the Chicago Conference in 1944. The policy also provides that bilateral agreements should be designed to create a market environment where competition can flourish.

What the United States challenges is the presumption that the international system can function only if air carriers are allowed to agree on rates and if seat capacity is strictly controlled.

Between 1968 and 1977 the average load factor for U.S. air carriers on the North Atlantic route never exceeded 57%. In 1979 it rose to 69%; by 1991 it had increased slightly to 69.5%. The North Atlantic route has always been a highly seasonal market. Load factors have varied 15% to 20% between winter and summer.

Under Deregulation the domestic U.S. air carriers have adjusted their operations to accommodate for seasonal highs and lows. This flexibility is obviously beneficial and can be utilized by the international and foreign air carriers.

The public benefits of competition are not limited to greater access for leisure travelers. Business travelers also gain by the expansion of nonstop gateways to many destinations and increased frequency of service to many cities.

The result of the liberal competition policy was seen immediately as indicated by the traffic statistics for the year ended June 30, 1980.

- Traffic to Europe increased 12%
- Traffic to France increased 19%
- Traffic to Italy increased 3%
- Traffic to the Far East increased 20%
- Traffic to Korea increased 166%
- Traffic to Singapore increased 76%

Competition benefits air carriers in several ways. The potential for growth in international air transportation is directly connected to the development of non-business travel. The competitive process is better suited to developing low fares than the old system of regulation-controlled discriminate fares. Competition forces all air carriers in the international and foreign market to operate at their greatest efficiency. There is little doubt that all future bilateral negotiations will reflect the policy of competition.

A recent Gallup survey indicated that 68% of the United States population would travel abroad if they had the time and the money. In the United Kingdom the figure was 74%, and for the population of France it was 84%. This survey showed that the large majority of people want to travel. A competitive air transportation system will provide economic incentives to the air carrier industry to find methods to serve this relatively untapped market.

In April 1980 the Civil Aeronautics Board issued a tentative opinion in the International Air Transportation Association Show-Cause Proceeding approving IATA traffic conferences. Highlights of the opinion were:

1. The IATA traffic conference system was approved and granted anti-trust immunity for two years.
2. U.S. air carriers may not participate in rate conferences for travel over the North Atlantic between the United States and Europe.
3. Approval of the conferences will be effective only as long as the Civil Aeronautics Board receives assurance from IATA that in markets touching the United States, innovative fare proposals will not be subject to approval or delay by other IATA members.

The Civil Aeronautics Board affirmed its commitment to achieving a competitive international environment with individual air carrier initiative as the primary rate-setting mechanism.

Individual Civil Aeronautics Board members supporting the opinion indicated that it did not go far enough. They felt the participation of U.S. air carriers in traffic conferences should have been prohibited.

The foundation for the Civil Aeronautics Board's analysis of the International Air Transport Association traffic conference procedures is the Sherman Anti-trust Act which provides that any contract that restrains trade or commerce among the States or with foreign countries is illegal in the United States. The Board has concluded that the traffic conference procedures substantially reduce competition because they are designed primarily to establish the rates to be charged by competing air carriers.

The International Civil Aviation Organization at its Assembly meeting in September–October 1980, stated that the industry grew appreciably faster than the general economy during the 1970s and that the growth is expected to continue. World scheduled international air traffic grew at a 10% annual rate compared to the world's gross product growth rate of 3.8%. An average yearly decline in rate levels of 3.4% would appear to have contributed to this growth. Future growth will be affected by world economic growth which was predicted to be 4% a year. In light of this, yearly passenger increases were forecast to be 9%.

The effect of deregulation in the United States has spread to other countries. England has passed a law that makes it mandatory for their Civil Aviation Authority to consider the beneficial effects of competition when awarding routes. The British Civil Aviation Act became law in November 1980. It legally enabled the British government to sell all or part of British Airways to private investors.

The new law strengthens the powers of the British CAA in granting new air carrier routes by eliminating the power formerly held by the trade minister to give guidance to the CAA in determining what routes to award to which air carrier.

The entire world is watching the United States' system of air carrier deregulation. If successful, deregulation may spread to areas where the economic regulation is still being practiced.

> **The United States will offer to negotiate 'open skies' agreements with all European countries willing to permit U.S. carriers essentially free access to their markets.**

The United States will offer to negotiate 'open skies' agreements with all European countries willing to permit U.S. carriers essentially free access to their markets. Discussions will be limited to European countries since Europe is moving toward the free flow of passengers and goods. After reexamining its policy, the U.S. has decided it should be willing to offer open skies agreements to countries who agree with our free market principles.

The U.S. has already taken an important step in this direction with its underserved cities program, opening U.S. gateway cities to service by foreign airlines without insisting on prior negotiations for such rights. Foreign airlines have authority to provide service to selected American cities under the program.

During the 1980s, the U.S. developed more market-oriented agreements with its aviation partners than ever before. The more liberal environment is being challenged now by a number of countries. He noted there have been attempts by the U.S.'s trading partners to limit the rights of U.S. airlines under existing agreements. The United States places a very high value on its bilateral agreements; respect those agreements, and honor them. The same is expected from their trading partners. In the past, the U.S. has offered such agreements only to a few of its largest aviation partners.

FREE TRADE

The standard nation-to-nation bilateral is the present manner for international agreements. However, a new concept is being discussed and promoted by many air carriers and countries who desire the abandonment of the bilateral system and replace it with the method of international "free trade."

Free Trade advocates open market access and competitive pricing, rules to safeguard competition, no nationality limitations on airline ownership and transitional measures to ease acceptance of the new system.

Small nations and their air carriers are concerned that globalization of airlines will be further supported by a liberal, multilateral system and lead to domination by a few airlines. Those favoring Free Trade countered that the bilateral system restricts competition and stifles the growth of the air carrier industry, which is critically needed for economic development.

If the industry is to respond to consumer needs it must be free of the constraints on competition and market access that bilaterals have imposed in the past. The only point of agreement is that a hybrid system of bilaterals and new styled multinational agreements will coexist for awhile. In the meantime the free trade advocates seem to have their method for change. Many have endorsed the concept of nations joining together in a bilateral agreement and then allowing other nations to accept the liberal trading rules when they are willing and able. Thus the multilateral agreement could come into being and expanded to other nations until Free Trade becomes accepted. This process will speed up as regions join in economic groupings in order to grow. A useful product of open skies negotiations would be a model agreement that could put Free Trade on its way.

The change, if and when it comes, will require several years and much negotiation.

BIBLIOGRAPHIC NOTE

One of the problems in the study of international civil aviation has been the lack of total concentrated research material. Several independent sources and their materials would have to be gathered together and then carefully searched for the particular subject matter required. This is very time consuming. Fortunately, since 1996, this is no longer the case. A very worthwhile text has been prepared by Adrianus Groenewege entitled the *Compendium of International Civil Aviation*. This book is published by the International Aviation Development Corporation, 3460 Peel Street, Suite 1803, Montreal, Quebec, Canada H3A 2M1. The book costs under $200. Any up-to-date well-stocked library will have a copy available. It is highly recommended for further study of any subject matter presented in this chapter.

The text covers the major milestones in international civil aviation from 1990 through 1996 and is a general review of historical events.

A detailed analysis of the structure of international civil aviation covers the basic legal foundations of the several conferences, conventions and agreements that formulate the present legal aspect of international civil aviation.

An alphabetical listing of worldwide organizations and a description of each is included. A section presents the definition of the aviation terms commonly used throughout the industry and is a very good resource for the meaning of various technical as well as non-technical terms.

A larger section of the book is devoted to abbreviations, acronyms, world airport codes and other important research information including countries, capitals and their population, and distances between major world airports. Available are conversion tables for area, distance, pressure, speed, temperature and volume. A wealth of statistics is accessible for anyone desiring data.

This book is a valuable reference for any serious-minded aviation enthusiast or student.

CHAPTER 13

International Air Transportation Organizations

The conferences, conventions, regulations, and laws under which International Aviation exists today began in 1919 with the Paris Conference. Since then, international organizations have been created pertaining to the economics of air carriers, airports, technical operations of aircraft, safety, and air traffic control.

The structure of these organizations varies as widely as their purposes. The organizations and their functions, as well as membership list and statistical data are presented in this chapter. Included are:

- International Civil Aviation Organization
- International Air Transport Association
- International Transportation Safety Association
- Airports Council International
- Aviation Authorities (See Appendix D)

INTERNATIONAL CIVIL AVIATION ORGANIZATION*

In the years before World War I people with foresight realized that the advent of the airplane added a new dimension to transport which could no longer be contained within strictly national confines. It was for this reason that, on the invitation of France, the first important conference on an international air law code was convened in Paris in 1910. This conference was attended by 18 European States, and a number of basic principles governing aviation were laid down. (See Figure 13.1.)

The technical developments in aviation arising out of World War I created a completely new situation at the end of the hostilities, especially with regard to the safe and rapid transport of goods and persons over prolonged distances. However, the war had also shown the ugly potential of aviation and it had therefore become much more evident than this new, and now greatly advanced, means of transport required international attention.

The treatment of aviation matters was a subject at the Paris Peace Conference of 1919 and was entrusted to a special Aeronautical Commission, which had its origin in the Inter-Allied Aviation Committee created in 1917. At the same time, civil air transport enterprises were created in many European States and in North America, some of which were already engaged in international operations (Paris-London, Paris-Brussels). Also in 1919, two British airmen, Alcock and Brown, made the first West-East crossing of the North Atlantic from Newfoundland to Ireland and the "R-34," a British dirigible, made a round trip flight from Scotland to New York and back.

Events like these prompted a number of young aviators to propose that the international collaboration in aviation matters which had been born out of military necessity during and immediately after World War I should not stop with the end of hostilities. They felt that this collaboration should be directed toward peaceful endeavors such as the development of post-war civil

---

*For current information go to the Website at http://www.icao.org

aviation because they believed that aviation had to be international or not at all. This proposal was formally taken up by France and submitted to the other principal Allied powers who received it favorably. This action resulted in the drawing up of the International Air Convention, which was signed by 26 of the 32 Allied and Associated powers represented at the Paris Peace Conference, and it was ultimately ratified by 38 States. The Convention consisted of 43 articles that dealt with all technical, operational and organizational aspects of civil aviation. It also foresaw the creation of an International Commission for Air Navigation to monitor developments in civil aviation and to propose measures to States to keep abreast of developments. It should be noted that this Convention took over all the principles that had already been formulated by the Conference held in 1910 in Paris.

To assist the Commission, it was agreed to establish a small permanent Secretariat under the direction of a General Secretary. In December 1922 this Secretariat assumed its duties with Mr. Albert Roper from France as General Secretary. The Secretariat was located in Paris, where it remained throughout its existence. In fact, it should be noted that Mr. Roper also became the first Secretary General of International Civil Aviation Organization and the European Office of ICAO in Paris, on its foundation, took over the offices of the ICAN Secretariat and remained there for its first 19 years until August 1965 (60 bis avenue d'Iéna). This seems to demonstrate certain continuity, at least as far as organizational measures in international civil aviation are concerned.

The years between the two World Wars were marked by a continuous growth of civil aviation in both the technical and the commercial fields, even though flying was not yet opened to the masses but remained a rather exclusive means of personal transport. In fact, it was around 1930 when, after an ICAN Meeting, three prominent General Directors of Civil Aviation, met at the Paris Gare du Nord, and that the famous phrase was coined: "The layman flies, the expert takes the train," a phrase which perfectly reflected the uncertainties which surrounded flying at that time, especially during the bad weather periods in Europe. However, the search for higher speed, greater reliability and the covering of greater distances continued throughout this period in all industrialized States and each step forward in these fields brought the great potential inherent to air transport closer to reality.

The aviation made during World War II not only resulted in horror and human tragedies, but its utiliza-

tion also significantly advanced the technical and operational possibilities of air transport in a peaceful world. For the first time large numbers of people and goods were transported over long distances and ground facilities were developed to permit this in an orderly and expeditious manner. It was for this reason that, in 1943, the U.S. initiated studies of post-war civil aviation problems. These studies confirmed the belief that they needed to be tackled on an international scale or it would not be possible to use aviation as one of the principal elements in the economic development of the world and the first available means to start "healing the wounds of war" as President Roosevelt put it.

The consequence of the studies initiated by the U.S. and subsequent consultations between the Major Allies was that the U.S. government extended an invitation to 55 States or authorities to attend, in November 1944, an International Civil Aviation Conference in Chicago. Fifty-four States attended this Conference. At the end of the Conference a Convention on International Civil Aviation was signed by 32 States to set up the permanent International Aviation Organization (ICAO) as a means to secure international co-operation for the highest possible degree of uniformity in regulations and standards, procedures and organization regarding civil aviation matters. At the same time, the International Services Transit Agreement and the International Air Transport Agreement were signed.

The most important work accomplished by the Chicago Conference was in the technical field because the Conference laid the foundation for a set of rules and regulations regarding air navigation as a whole—bringing safety in flying a great step forward and paved the way for the application of a common air navigation system throughout the world.

Because of the inevitable delays in the ratification of the Convention, the Conference had signed an Interim Agreement, which foresaw the creation of a Provisional International Organization of a technical and advisory nature with the purpose of collaboration in the field of international civil aviation (PICAO). This Organization was in operation from August 1945 to April 1947 when the permanent ICAO came into being. Its seat was in Montreal, Canada and in 1947 the change from PICAO to ICAO was little more than a formality. However, it also brought about the end of ICAN because, now that ICAO was firmly established, the ICAN member States agreed to dissolve ICAN by naming ICAO specifically as its successor Organization.

From the very assumption of activities of PICAO/ ICAO, it was realized that the work of the Secretariat, especially in the technical field, would have to cover two major activities:

a. those which covered generally applicable rules and regulations concerning training and licensing of aeronautical personnel both in the air and on the ground, communication systems and procedures, rules for the air and air traffic control systems and practices, airworthiness requirements for aircraft engaged in international air navigation as well as their registration and identification, aeronautical meteorology and maps and charts. For obvious reasons, these aspects required uniformity on a world-wide scale if truly international air navigation was to become a possibility. Activities in these fields had therefore to be handled by a central agency, i.e. ICAO headquarters, if local deviations or separate developments were to be avoided;

b. those concerning the practical application of air navigation services and facilities by States and their co-ordinated implementation in specific areas where operating conditions and other relevant parameters were comparable.

To meet the latter objective it was agreed to subdivide the surface of the earth into a number of regions within which distinct and specific air navigation problems of a similar nature existed. A typical example of this process is illustrated by a comparison of the North Atlantic Region (NAT), where the primary problems concern long-range overseas navigation, with the European-Mediterranean Region (EUR) where the coordination of trans-European operations with domestic and short-range international traffic constitutes the major problem. Once the regions were created, bodies were needed to assist States in the resolution of their specific regional problems. It was agreed that this could best be achieved by the creation of a number of Regional Offices which were to be located either in the Region they served or, if more than one Region was to be served by such an Office, as close as possible to the Region concerned.

As a consequence, the ICAO adopted the concept of Regions and Regional Offices, on the understanding that any regional activities could only be undertaken provided they did not conflict with the world-wide activities of the Organization. However, it was also recognized that such activities could vary from Region to Region taking into account the general economic, technical or social environment of the Region concerned.

Convention on International Civil Aviation (also known as *Chicago Convention*), was signed on December 7, 1944 by 52 States. Pending ratification of the Convention by 26 States, the Provisional International Civil Aviation Organization (PICAO) was established. It functioned from June 6, 1945 until April 4, 1947. By March 5, 1947 the 26th ratification was received. ICAO came into being on April 4, 1947. In October of the same year, ICAO became a specialized agency of the United Nations linked to Economic and Social Council (ECOSOC).

The Convention on International Civil Aviation *set forth the purpose of ICAO:*

"WHEREAS the future development of international civil aviation can greatly help to create and preserve friendship and understanding among the nations and peoples of the world, yet its abuse can become a threat to the general security; and

WHEREAS it is desirable to avoid friction and to promote that co-operation between nations and peoples upon which the peace of the world depends;

THEREFORE, the undersigned governments having agreed on certain principles and arrangements in order that international civil aviation may be developed in a safe and orderly manner and that international air transport services may be established on the basis of equality of opportunity and operated soundly and economically;

Have accordingly concluded this Convention to that end."

STANDARDIZATION

One of the chief activities of the ICAO is standardization—the establishment of International Standards, Recommended Practices and Procedures covering the technical fields of aviation: licensing of personnel, rules of the air, aeronautical meteorology, aeronautical charts, units of measurement, operation of aircraft, nationality and registration marks, airworthiness, aeronautical telecommunications, air traffic services, search and rescue, aircraft accident investigation, aerodromes, aeronautical information services, aircraft noise and engine missions, security and the safe transport of dangerous goods. After a Standard is adopted it is put into effect by each ICAO Contracting State in its own territories. As aviation technology continues to develop, the Standards are kept under constant review and amended as necessary.

In keeping pace with the rapid development of international civil aviation, ICAO is conscious of the need to adopt in its specifications modern systems and techniques. In recent years, extensive work has been undertaken by ICAO in the areas of reporting aircraft accident and incident data, all-weather operations, automation of air traffic services, the application of computers in meteorological services, aircraft noise, engine emissions and the carriage of dangerous goods by air. ICAO has dealt with the subject of unlawful interference with civil aviation and with questions regarding aviation and the human environment.

CNS/ATM

Among ICAO's more recent significant achievements has been the development of a satellite-based system concept to meet the future Communications, Navigation, Surveillance/Air Traffic Management (CNS/ATM) needs of civil aviation.

CNS/ATM, formerly known as the Future Air Navigation Systems (FANS) concept, is essentially the application of today's high technologies in satellites and computers, data links and advanced flight deck avionics, to cope with tomorrow's growing operational needs. It will make obsolete much of today's expensive ground-based equipment, which uses line-of-sight technology and has inherent limitations. It will also produce economies, efficiencies and greater safety. But it is not these characteristics that make it a new frontier for aviation. It will be its impact as an integrated global system with consequential changes to the way air traffic services are organized and operated.

The CNS/ATM systems concept, which has received the endorsement of ICAO Member States, is now in its implementation phase. This major task includes the development of standards, recommended practices and guidance material which will be applied well into the 21st century.

REGIONAL PLANNING

Not all aviation problems can be dealt with on a world-wide scale and many subjects are considered on a regional basis. ICAO, therefore, recognizes nine geographical regions which must be treated individually for planning the provision of air navigation facilities and services required on the ground by aircraft flying in these regions.

In each of the regions, keeping in mind the objective of producing a seamless global air traffic management system, careful planning is necessary to produce the network of air navigation facilities and services upon which the aeroplanes depend—the aerodromes, the meteorological and communications stations, the navigation aids, the air traffic control units, the search and rescue bases, the thousands of facilities to be established and operated, and the services to be rendered. This planning is done at ICAO regional air navigation meetings, held from time to time for each of the regions, where the need for facilities and services is carefully considered and decided upon. The plan which emerges from a regional meeting is so designed that, when the States concerned implement it, it will lead to an integrated, efficient system for the entire region and will contribute to the global system.

When States require assistance in this regard, help is available through ICAO's seven regional offices—each one accredited to a group of Contracting States. These offices have, as their main function, the duty of encouraging, assisting, expediting and following up on the implementation of the Air Navigation Plans and maintaining them. In addition, regional planning and implementation groups have been established in ICAO regions to assist the regional offices in keeping the regional plans up-to-date and in fostering their implementation.

As financial and technical resources vary widely between nations, and as air transport's demands involve complex and costly equipment and well-qualified personnel for staffing and maintaining the facilities, there may be uneven implementation of parts of the Air Navigation Plans. ICAO can assist States through its technical assistance activities (described in the following pages). It has succeeded, also, in a few cases, in arranging for joint financing. Certain facilities in the North Atlantic are financed by the States whose airlines make use of them: communication systems for transmitting messages of interest to aviation, and air navigation aids and meteorological and air traffic control facilities in Greenland and Iceland.

FACILITATION

The obstacles placed by customs, immigration, public health and other formalities on the free and unimpeded passage of passengers and cargo across international boundaries have been a serious impediment to air travel. The problem is inherent in the speed of air travel itself; if, for example, formalities at each end of a trans-oceanic flight of six hours take up one hour, this means that the passenger's trip time has been increased by one-third, while the same formalities add only about two percent to a five-day sea voyage across the same ocean. For the past two decades ICAO has tried to persuade its Contracting States to reduce red tape, and International Standards on facilitation have been adopted to place an upper limit on what States may demand. In addition to reducing procedural formalities, ICAO's efforts are also aimed at providing adequate airport terminal buildings for passengers and their baggage as well as for air cargo, with all related facilities and services.

ECONOMICS

The Convention on International Civil Aviation requires that international air transport services be established on the basis of equality of opportunity and operated soundly and economically. In fact, ICAO's basic objective is the development of safe, regular, efficient and economical air transport. To assist States in planning their air transport services, ICAO collects and publishes comprehensive world aviation statistical data, and undertakes extensive economic studies in line with Resolutions of the ICAO Assembly and Recommendations of world-wide conferences. ICAO also produces manuals for the guidance of States in such areas as statistics, air traffic forecasting, airport and air navigation facility tariffs, the economic regulation of air transport and the establishment of air fares and rates. Workshop meetings are conducted in various regions to provide States with information and advice on ICAO activities and to exchange pertinent information and views.

TECHNICAL CO-OPERATION FOR DEVELOPMENT

Communities, since the beginning of time, have been connected to or separated from one another by surface conditions. Jungles, swamps, mountains, rivers and deserts presented almost insurmountable obstacles to movement—a condition which is characteristic even today in many developing countries where road and railway networks are insufficient or non-existent. The airplane's advantage here is obvious: it moves along a boundless highway in the sky and the only actual roadway needed is for take-off and landing. By the creation of an airstrip, remote towns and villages can be linked quickly to the modern world, whereas surface connections could take years or even generations to build. ICAO, therefore, pays special attention to promoting civil aviation in developing countries. An important instrument in this work has been the United Nations Development Programme. So far most of the Organization's work in this area has been directed toward the development of the ground services required for civil aviation and, in particular, toward aerodromes, air traffic control, communications and meteorological services; in the past few years, and with the advent of larger and more complex aircraft, requests for assistance in the more sophisticated fields of aviation, including airport operations, have been increasing in number. In response to the alarming incidents in recent years of acts of unlawful interference against aircraft and airports, ICAO also provides assistance to States to improve their aviation security facilities and procedures.

Assistance in general has consisted of advising on the organization of government civil aviation departments and on the location and operation of facilities and services, and particularly in the recruitment and administration of experts, fellowships training and procurement of equipment. Many large civil aviation training centers have been created or assisted by ICAO in, for example, Egypt, India, Indonesia, Jordan, Kenya, Morocco, Nigeria, Pakistan, Thailand and Tunisia; in most cases these are regional training centers which take students of many nationalities and for which the local governments pay a large share of the costs and take over complete operation of the projects after a set time. Smaller national training centers have also been established by ICAO technical cooperation missions, and nationals of many countries have received ICAO fellowships for study abroad.

ICAO technical cooperation missions consisting of one or more technical experts have gone to nearly one hundred States all over the world. Over 100,000 students have attended training schools registered with ICAO.

LAW

Within the more than one hundred and eighty Contracting States of ICAO there are many legal philosophies and many different systems of jurisprudence. There is need, therefore, for a unifying influence, in certain areas, for the development of a code of international air law. It is a function of ICAO to facilitate the adoption of international air law instruments and to promote their general acceptance. So far international air law instruments have been adopted under the Organization's auspices involving such varied subjects as the international recognition of property rights in aircraft, damage done by aircraft to third parties on the surface, the liability of the air carrier to its passengers, crimes committed on board aircraft, the marking of plastic explosives for detection and unlawful interference with civil aviation.

Table 13.1   ICAO Contracting States (187)

Afghanistan	Djibouti	Latvia	Russian Federation
Albania	Dominican Republic	Lebanon	Rwanda
Algeria		Lesotho	
Andorra	Ecuador	Liberia	Saint Lucia
Angola	Egypt	Libyan Arab Jamahiriya	Saint Vincent and the Grenadines
Antigua and Barbuda	El Salvador	Lithuania	Samoa
Argentina	Equatorial Guinea	Luxembourg	San Marino
Armenia	Eritrea		Sao Tome and Principe
Australia	Estonia	Macedonia, The former	Saudi Arabia
Austria	Ethiopia	Yugoslav Republic of	Senegal
Azerbaijan		Madagascar	Seychelles
	Federated States of	Malawi	Sierra Leone
Bahamas	Micronesia	Malaysia	Singapore
Bahrain		Maldives	Slovakia
Bangladesh	Fiji	Mali	Slovenia
Barbados	Finland	Malta	Solomon Islanda
Belarus	France	Marshall Islands	Somalia
Belgium		Mauritania	South Africa
Belize	Gabon	Mauritius	Spain
Benin	Gambia	Mexico	Sri Lanka
Bhutan	Georgia	Moldova	Sudan
Bolivia	Germany	Monaco	Suriname
Bosnia and Herzegovina	Ghana	Mongolia	Swaziland
Botswana	Greece	Morocco	Sweden
Brazil	Grenada	Mozambique	Switzerland
Brunei Darussalam	Guatemala	Myanmar	Syrian Arab Republic
Bulgaria	Guinea		
Burkina Faso	Guinea-Bissau	Namibia	Tajikistan
Burundi	Guyana	Nauru	Thailand
		Nepal	The former Yugoslav Republic
Cambodia	Haiti	Netherlands, Kingdom of	Togo
Cameroon	Honduras	the	Tonga
Canada	Hungary	New Zealand	Trinidad and Tobago
Cape Verde		Nicaragua	Tunisia
Central African Republic	Iceland	Niger	Turkey
Chad	India	Nigeria	Turkmenistan
Chile	Indonesia	Norway	
China	Iran, Islamic Republic of		Uganda
Colombia	Iraq	Oman	Ufraine
Comoros	Ireland		United Arab Emirates
Congo	Israel	Pakistan	United Kingdom
Cook Islands	Italy	Palau	United Republic of Tanzania
Costa Rica		Panama	United States
Côte d'Ivoire	Jamaica	Papua New Guinea	Uruguay
Croatia	Japan	Paraguay	Uzbekistan
Cuba	Jordan	Peru	
Cyprus		Philippines	Vanuatu
Czech Republic	Kazakhstan	Poland	Venezuela
	Kenya	Portugal	Viet Nam
Democratic People's	Kiribati		
Republic of Korea	Kuwait	Qatar	Yemen
Democratic Republic of the	Kyrgyzstan		
Congo		Republic of Korea	Zambia
Denmark	Lao People's Democratic	Romania	Zimbabwe
	Republic		

ICAO STRUCTURE

The constitution of ICAO is the Convention on International Civil Aviation, drawn up by a conference in Chicago in November and December 1944, and to which each ICAO Contracting State is a party. According to the terms of the Convention, the Organization is made up of an Assembly, a Council of limited membership with various subordinate bodies and a Secretariat. The chief officers are the President of the Council and the Secretary General.

The Assembly, composed of representatives from all Contracting States, is the sovereign body of ICAO. It meets every three years, reviewing in detail the work of the Organization and setting policy for the coming years. It also votes a triennial budget.

The Council, the governing body which is elected by the Assembly for a three-year term, is composed of 33 States. The Assembly chooses the Council Member States under three headings:

1. States of chief importance in air transport.
2. States which make the largest contribution to the provision of facilities for air navigation.
3. States whose designation will ensure that all major areas of the world are represented.

As the governing body, the Council gives continuing direction to the work of ICAO. It is in the Council that Standards and Recommended Practices are adopted and incorporated as Annexes to the Convention on International Civil Aviation. The Council is assisted by the Air Navigation Commission (technical matters), the Air Transport Committee (economic matters), the Committee on Joint Support of Air Navigation Services and the Finance Committee.

Regional Offices—Location

Asia and Pacific Office—Bangkok (Thailand)

Eastern and Southern African Office—Nairobi (Kenya)

European and North Atlantic Office—Seine Cedex (France)

Middle East Office—Cairo (Egypt)

North American, Central American and Caribbean Office—Mexico City (Mexico)

South American Office—Lima (Peru)

Western and Central African Office—Dakar (Senegal)

THE SECRETARIAT

The Secretariat, headed by a Secretary General, is divided into five main divisions:

1. Air Navigation Bureau
2. Air Transport Bureau
3. Technical Cooperation Bureau
4. Legal Bureau
5. Bureau of Administration and Services.

ICAO works in close cooperation with other members of the United Nations family such as the World Meteorological Organization, the International Telecommunication Union, the Universal Postal Union, the World Health Organization and the International Maritime Organization. Non-governmental organizations which also participate in ICAO work include the International Air Transport Association, the Airports Council International, the International Federation of Air Line Pilots' Associations, and the International Council of Aircraft Owner and Pilot Associations. (Figure 13.1.)

AIR NAVIGATION BUREAU

This Bureau is responsible for: provision of expert secretariat assistance required by the Assembly, the Council, the Air Navigation Commission and its divisions, panels, and working groups and Regional Air Navigation meetings and other air navigation meetings that may be convened; the maintenance and amendment of the air navigation work program and the preparation of studies and documentation and the making of recommendations on this program for consideration by the Air Navigation Commission; preparation of commentaries on recommendation of air navigation meetings for International Standards, Practices and Procedures for submission to the Air Navigation Commission; preparation for publication of material covering approved amendments; compilation and promulgation of lists of differences notified by Contracting States between their national regulations and practices and the International Standards, Practices and Procedures; the planning of air navigation meetings and the preparation of agenda and supporting documentation. The Director of the Air Navigation Bureau serves as the Secretary of the Air Navigation Commissions. The Deputy Director assists with work coordination and staff direction of the Bureau.

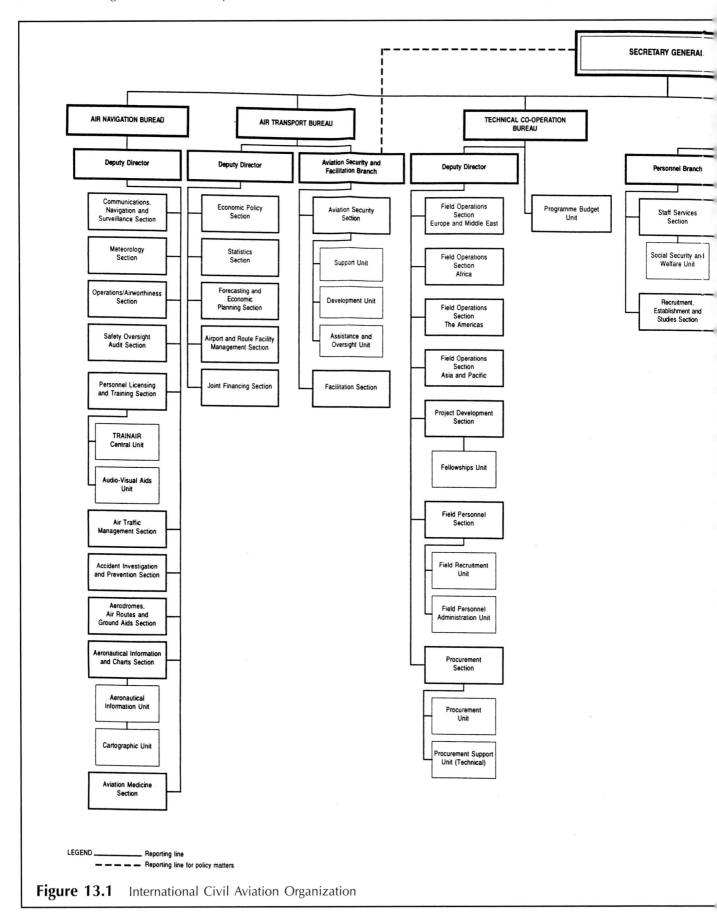

Figure 13.1   International Civil Aviation Organization

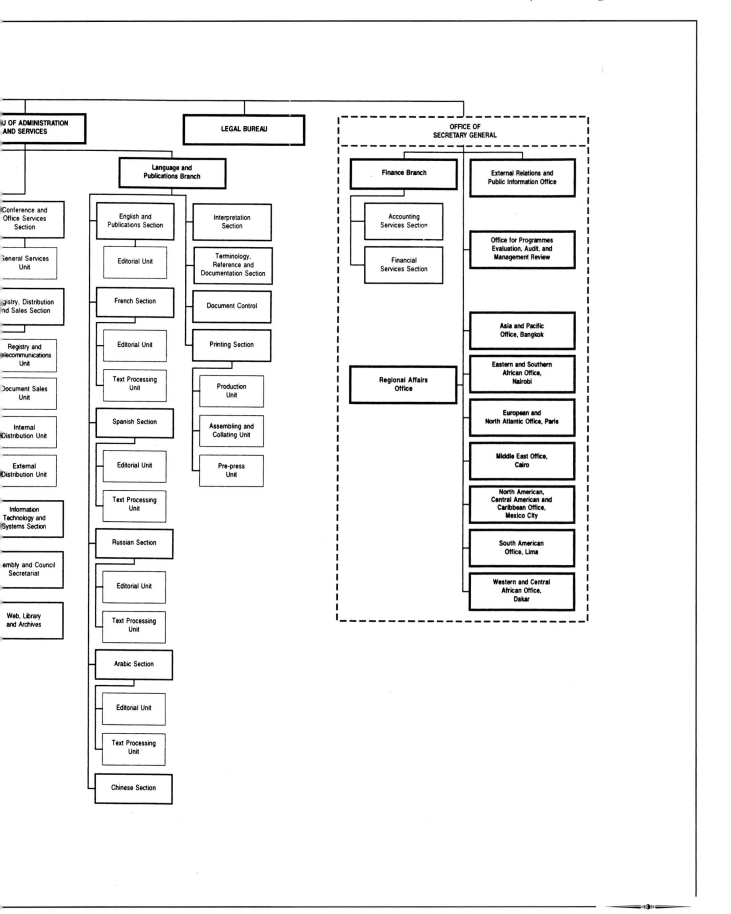

Table 13.2 ICAO Contact Information

ICAO Headquarters, Montreal, Canada

For general information on ICAO contact:

ICAO, External Relations and Public Information Office

999 University Street, Montreal, Quebec H3C 5H7, Canada

Tel.: + 1 514 954 8219; Fax: + 1 514 954 6077;

Telex: 05-24513; SITATEX: YULCAYA

Internet e-mail: icaohq@icao.int

Internet home page:http://www.icao.int

For information on ICAO publications and audio-visual training aides contact:

ICAO, Document Sales Unit

999 University Street, Montreal, Quebec H3C 5H7, Canada

Tel.: + 1 514 954 8022; Fax: + 1 514 954 6769

E-mail: sales_unit@icao.int

The Regional Offices

Asia and Pacific Office

ICAO, Asia and Pacific Office

252/1 Vipavadee Rangsit Road, Ladyao, Chatuchak, Bangkok 10900, Thailand

Mail: P.O. Box 11, Samyaek Ladprao, Bangkok 10901, Thailand

Tel.: + 662 537 8189; Fax: + 662 537 8199; Telex: TH87969 ICAOBKK TH

Cable: ICAOREP, Bangkok; SITATEX: BKKCAYA

Internet e-mail: icao_apac@bangkok.icao.int

Internet home page: http://www.icao.int/apac

Eastern and Southern African Office

ICAO, Eastern and Southern African Office

United Nations Accommodation, Limuru Rd., Gigiri, Nairobi, Kenya

Mail: P.O. Box 46294, Nairobi, Kenya

Tel.: + 254 2 622 395; Fax: + 254 2 226 706; Telex: KE25295 ICAOREP

Cable: ICAOREP, Nairobi; SITATEX: NBOCAYA

Internet e-mail: icao@icao.unon.org

Internet home page: http://www.icao.int/esaf

European and North Atlantic Office

ICAO, European and North Atlantic Office

3 bis villa Émile-Bergerat, 92522 Neuilly-sur-Seine Cedex, France

Tel.: + 33 1 46 41 85 85; Fax: + 33 1 46 41 85 00

Cable: ICAOREP, Paris; SITATEX: PAREUYA; AFTN: LFPSYAYU

E-mail: icaoeurnat@paris.icao.int

Documentation and Sales Unit e-mail: docsales_unit@paris.icao.int

Middle East Office

ICAO, Middle East Office

Egyptian Civil Aviation Complex, Cairo Airport Road, Cairo, Egypt

Mail: P.O. Box 85, Cairo Airport Post Office Terminal One, Cairo 11776, Arab Republic of Egypt

Tel.: + 202 267 4840; Fax: + 202 267 4843

Cable: ICAOREP, Cairo: SITATEX: CAICAYA

Internet e-mail: icao@idsc.net.eg

Internet home page: http://www.icao.int/mid

North American, Central American and Caribbean Office

ICAO, North American, Central American and Caribbean Office

Av. Presidente Masaryk No. 29—3rd floor

Col. Chapultepec Morales, C.P. 11570 México, D.F.

Mail: Apartado postal 5-377, C.P. 06500, México, D.F.

Mail: 1605-B Pacific Rim Court, PMB MX34-300/ 439015, San Diego, CA 92143-9015, U.S.A.

Tel.: + 525 250 3211; Fax: + 525 203 2757; Cable: ICAOREP, México

SITATEX: MEXCAYA

Internet e-mail: icao_nacc@un.org.mx

Internet home page: http://www.icao.int/nacc

South American Office

ICAO, South American Office

Edificio CORPAC, Zona Comercial, Aeropuerto Internacional Jorge Chávez

Lima (Callao), Perú

Mail: Apartado 4127, Lima 100, Perú

Tel.: + 51 1 575 1646; Fax: + 51 1 575 0974; SITATEX: LIMCAYA

Internet e-mail: mail@lima.icao.int

Internet home page: http://www.lima.icao.int

Western and Central African Office

ICAO, Western and Central African Office

15, boulevard de la République, Dakar Sénégal

Mail: Boîte postale 2356, Dakar, Sénégal

Tel.: + 221 839 9393; Fax: + 221 823 6926; Telex: SG61348 ICAOREP SG

Cable: ICAOREP, Dakar; SITATEX: DKRCAYA

Internet e-mail: icaodkr@icao.sn

Internet home page: http://www.icao.int/wacaf

AIR TRANSPORT BUREAU

This Bureau is responsible for: provision of expert assistance required by the Assembly, Council, Air Transport Committee, Joint Support Committee and the specialized divisional, conference, panel, and working group meetings that may be convened in the air transport field; maintenance and amendment of the air transport and joint support work program and preparation of studies and documentation and making of recommendations on these programs for consideration, as appropriate, by the Air Transport Committee or Joint Support Committee; preparation of statistical digests and other statistical publications; preparation and revision of manuals on airport and air navigation facility tariffs, route air navigation facility economics, airport economics, the ICAO statistical program, the establishment of international air carrier tariffs and air traffic forecasting; preparation of documentation and meeting reports in the economic regulatory, statistical, facilitation and joint financing fields, and preparation of Chapter I of the Council's *Annual Report* which provides a worldwide survey of international civil aviation; planning of periodic air transport meetings and preparation of agenda and supporting documentation; preparation for publication of material covering approved amendments to Annex 9 on Facilitation and the compilation and promulgation of lists of differences to this Annex which are notified by Contracting States; coordination of the work of the regional civil aviation organizations with ICAO air transport programs; and liaison and cooperation with international and regional organizations on air transport matters. The Director of the Air Transport Bureau serves as the Secretary to the Air Transport Committee.

TECHNICAL COOPERATION BUREAU

This Bureau is responsible for: the execution of ICAO's Technical Assistance Program, advising and assisting States, UNDP Headquarters and UNDP Resident Representatives in all matters relating to the formulation of country and intercountry programs and of project requests and for the over-all planning, preparation and management of civil aviation assisted projects financed by the United Nations Development Program (UNDP), by Trust Funds (TF) agreements and similar activities. In particular, this involves all aspects of project formulation; arrangements for funding from appropriate sources; project implementation which includes recruitment and administration of field staff; procurement and control of equipment required for field projects and the awarding of fellowships or scholarships; policy direction to field staff and the establishment of methods and procedures for systematic evaluation in order that inspections and evaluations of approved country programs and inter-country projects may be undertaken and reported upon. The Bureau's responsibilities also include the administration and execution of technical assistance funded from Voluntary Contributions; the budgetary control of assistance funds; the preparation of reports and field technical and training directives; the representation of ICAO at UNDP and other meetings involving technical assistance, and the maintenance of appropriate liaison with Government authorities responsible for civil aviation, UNDP Headquarters and Resident Representatives, other UN Specialized Agencies, ICAO Regional Representatives and other International Organizations. The Bureau is also responsible for the provision of telecommunications, travel and procurement services for the entire Organization as well as automation activities within the Bureau. The Bureau makes and maintains contacts with sources of funding with a view of expanding the resource basis of the ICAO Technical Assistance program. The Bureau is responsible for coordination of personnel actions of Headquarters and Regional Offices Technical Assistance staff.

LEGAL BUREAU

The First Session of the ICAO Assembly in 1947 established a permanent Legal Committee to advise on matters referred to it by the Council concerning the interpretation and amendment of the Chicago Convention, to study and make recommendations on such other questions relating to public international air law as may be referred to it by the Assembly or the Council and to study problems of private law affecting international civil aviation. With respect to the last mentioned function, the Legal Committee replaced the Comité International Technique d'Experts Juridiques Aériens (CITEJA) which had been responsible for the development of a code of private international air law since 1926. During the years in which the Legal Committee has been operating it has prepared drafts of 13 international instruments, the first of which was adopted by the ICAO Assembly and the last 12 by diplomatic conferences.

- *The Geneva Convention of 1948*
- *The Rome Convention of 1952*
- *The 1955 Protocol of Amendment to the Warsaw Convention of 1929*

- *The 1971 Protocol of Amendment to the Warsaw Convention of 1929*
- *The 1975 Protocol of Amendment of the Warsaw System*
- *Convention for the Suppression of Unlawful Acts Against the Safety of Civil Aviation*

For detailed information on these conferences see Chapter 12—International Air Transportation Law.

BUREAU OF ADMINISTRATION AND SERVICES

This Bureau is responsible for: the provision, coordination and administration of the financial allotments of services covering:

1. Personnel services involving the development and implementation of personnel policies, the recruitment, placement and promotion of staff, except field project staff, and the administration of salaries and conditions of service applicable to Secretariat staff.
2. Language services involving the use of four full working languages (English, French, Russian, Spanish), one gradually increasing working language (Arabic) and one limited working language (Chinese) to meet interpretation needs at meetings; the translation, typing, proofreading, the editorial preparation and the printing of documentation and publications, the development and revision of a lexicon.
3. Administration services involving the arrangements for meetings, the distribution and sale of publications, the provision of office services, supplies, equipment and furniture and the custody of the official records and archives.
4. Office automation services involving the feasibility, planning and implementation of fully operational computerized systems at Headquarters and at Regional Offices.
5. Library services, documents control and administrative direction of the Internal Audit Service.

ANNEXES TO THE ICAO CONVENTION ON INTERNATIONAL CIVIL AVIATION

A major responsibility of the Council is to adopt international standards and recommended practices. These are incorporated as Annexes to the Convention on International Civil Aviation. The following Annexes have been provided.

Annex 1—Personnel Licensing. Licensing of flight crews, air traffic controllers and aircraft maintenance personnel.

Annex 2—Rules of the Air. Rules relating to the conduct of visual and instrument flights.

Annex 3—Meteorological Service for International Air Navigation. Provision of meteorological services for international air navigation and reporting of meteorological observations from aircraft.

Annex 4—Aeronautical Charts. Specifications for aeronautical charts for use in international aviation.

Annex 5—Units of Measurement to Be Used in Air and Ground Operations. Dimensional systems to be used in air and ground operations.

Annex 6—Operation of Aircraft. Specifications which will ensure in similar operations throughout the world a level of safety above a prescribed minimum.

Part I—International Commercial Air Transport—Airplanes

Part II—International General Aviation— Airplanes

Part III—International Operations—Helicopters

Annex 7—Aircraft Nationality and Registration Marks. Requirements for registration and identification of aircraft.

Annex 8—Airworthiness of Aircraft. Certification and inspection of aircraft according to uniform procedures.

Annex 9—Facilitation. Specifications for expediting the entry and departure of aircraft, people, cargo, and other articles at international airports.

Annex 10—Aeronautical Telecommunications. Standardization of communications equipment and systems (Volume I) and of communications procedures (Volume II).

Annex 11—Air Traffic Services. Establishment and operation of air traffic control, flight information, and alerting services.

Annex 12—Search and Rescue. Organization and operation of facilities and services necessary for search and rescue.

Annex 13—Aircraft Accident Investigation. Uniformity in the notification, investigation of and reporting on aircraft accidents.

Annex 14—Aerodromes. Specifications for the design and operations of aerodromes (Volume I) and heliports (Volume II).

Annex 15—Aeronautical Information Services. Methods for the collection and dissemination of aeronautical information required for flight operations.

Annex 16—Environmental Protection. Specifications for aircraft noise certification, noise monitoring, and noise exposure units for land-use planning (Volume I) and aircraft engine emissions (Volume II).

Annex 17—Security—Safeguarding International Civil Aviation against Acts of Unlawful Interference. Specifications for safeguarding international civil aviation against acts of unlawful interference.

Annex 18—The Safe Transport of Dangerous Goods by Air. Specifications for the labeling, packing and shipping of dangerous cargo.

INTERNATIONAL AIR TRANSPORT ASSOCIATION (IATA)*

As a result of an effort by England in August 1919, representatives of six air transport companies met at The Hague. Two of these companies had recently begun operations, three were recently organized, and one was in the process of being formed. After four days of discussion they decided that the organization representing the airline industry of the various countries should be a free and voluntary association. On August 28, 1919, the agreement was signed. It stated that the representatives of the companies agreed to form the International Air Traffic Association with a view to cooperate to mutual advantage in preparing and organizing international air traffic. This is commonly known as the old IATA. The chairman of the meeting was Sir W. Sefton Brancker. The Association continued until 1945 when it became the International Air Transport Association.

The International Air Transport Association (IATA) is the world trade organization of scheduled airlines. Its members carry more than 95% of the world's scheduled international air traffic under the flags of over 120 independent nations. IATA is therefore able to speak with the greatest authority on the opportunities and problems presented by today's air transport operating environment.

While that environment has changed since the modern IATA was founded in Havana, Cuba, in 1945, with 57 members from 31 countries, the major purpose of the Association has not changed. It is to ensure that worldwide airline traffic moves with the greatest possible speed, safety, security, convenience, and efficiency for passengers and cargo shippers and with the utmost economy for the airlines.

The modern IATA is part of the structure of post-second world war aviation which grew out of the Chicago Conference of 1944. The Association, a non-governmental organization, draws its legal existence from a special Act of the Canadian Parliament, given Royal Assent in December 1945. However, IATA is as old as international air transport itself. The first international scheduled air service flew in 1919—the year that the International Air Traffic Association was founded in The Hague.

That earlier IATA was concerned with all the cooperative effort necessary for maintaining a worldwide air transport system that is seen in the modern IATA. But the earlier IATA was not concerned with tariffs which, in the pioneering days of a few simple routes, were negotiated by governments on a bilateral basis.

In 1919 the IATA members carried 3,500 passengers and performed 700,000 passenger kilometres—so the average international passenger flight was of 200 kilometers, or much less than the distance from Paris to London. The IATA Members now carry more than 200 million scheduled international passengers and perform about 700,000 million passenger-kilometers in doing so. The average international flight distance is more than 3,000 kilometers. The industry is therefore carrying some 60,000 times as many people as in the year of its birth. It is carrying each of those people an average of about 15 times as far as in that pioneering year of 1919.

This growth has happened through the technical development of aircraft, increased disposable incomes, greater leisure time, and changed social attitudes. It has also happened through the application of standard principles developed by the airlines through IATA.

---

* Refer to Appendix B for list of IATA members. For current information go to the Website at http://www.iata.org

In both its organization and its activity, the modern IATA has been closely associated with the International Civil Aviation Organization (ICAO)—established in 1944. ICAO is the UN agency which creates standards and recommendations at the international governmental level for the world's civil aviation.

The Association has two main offices, one in Montreal, Canada and the other in Geneva, Switzerland. Regional offices are maintained in Amman, Bangkok, Buenos Aires, Dakar, London, Nairobi, Rio de Janeiro, Singapore and Washington, D.C.

The IATA is a voluntary, non-exclusive, non-political and democratic organization. Membership is automatically open to any operating company which has been licensed to provide scheduled air service by a government eligible for membership in ICAO. Airlines engaged directly in international operations are Active Members, while domestic airlines are Associate Members.

IATA's declared purposes are:

- To promote safe, regular, and economical air transport for the benefit of the peoples of the world, to foster air commerce and to study and solve the problems connected therewith.

- To provide a forum for discussion and consultation on the industry's problems among Member air carriers or with other market participants, authorities and institutions. To provide comprehensive information analyses about the industry's activities and to perform such centralized services and research as Member carriers may decide and ask for.

- To cooperate with the International Civil Aviation Organization (ICAO), other international organizations and regional airline associations.

- To represent an association of air carriers which is committed to the principle of competition and free trade in air transportation.

IATA services four groups interested in the smooth operation of the world air transport system: airlines, governments, third parties such as travel and cargo agents or equipment suppliers, and the general public.

- For the airlines, joint solutions to the exploitation of opportunities or solving problems, beyond the resources of any single company, can be found within IATA. Airlines knit their individual networks into a worldwide system through IATA, despite differences in languages, currencies, laws, and national customs. Its secretariat is a pool of experience and information, and the administrator of many common services and enterprises. The Association represents the collective personality of over 200 companies. It functions as the international air transport industry's link with governments, with many third parties involved in the industry, and with the public.

- For governments, industry working standards are developed within IATA. It is thus the most effective source of airline experience and expertise upon which governments can draw. In fostering safe and efficient air transport, IATA serves the stated policy of most of the governments of the world. The IATA saves much effort and expense that would otherwise have to be expended in bilateral negotiations, for example, on tariffs.

- For third parties, IATA is a collective link between themselves and the airlines. Passenger and cargo agents are able to make representations to the industry through IATA and derive the benefit of neutrally applied agency service standards and levels of professional skill. Equipment manufacturers and others are able to join in the very meetings which define the way air transport goes about its business.

- For the general public IATA simplifies the travel and shipping process. By helping to control airline costs, IATA contributes to cheaper tickets and shipping costs. Thanks to airline cooperation through IATA, individual passenger can make one telephone call to reserve a ticket, pay in one currency and then use the ticket on several airlines in several countries or even return it for a cash refund.

International air transportation is one of the most dynamic industries in the world. The mission of IATA is to represent and to serve the airline industry in the smooth operation of the world air transport system. The specific goals which IATA has established for itself are:

1. **Safety and Security.** To promote safe, reliable and secure air services.

2. **Industry Recognition.** To achieve recognition of the importance of a healthy air transport industry to worldwide social and economic development.

3. **Financial Viability.** To assist the industry to achieve adequate levels of profitability.

4. **Products and the Services.** To provide high quality, value for money, industry-required products and services that meet the needs of the customer.

5. **Standards and Procedures.** To develop cost-effective and environmentally friendly standards and pro-

cedures to facilitate the operation of the international air transport.

6. **Industry Support.** To identify and articulate common industry positions and support the resolution of the key industry issues.

7. **Good Employer.** To provide a working environment which attracts, retains and develops committed employees.

SPECIFIC TASKS OF IATA

IATA's commercial objective is to ensure that people, freight, and mail can move on the vast global network as easily as if they were on a single airline within a single country.

IATA's operational task is to ensure that the aircraft used to carry the world's passengers and goods are able to operate with maximum safety and efficiency under clearly defined and universally understood regulations. Safe and secure airline operations contribute to a continuing positive perception of the industry, on the part of the general public. Efficient operations are in general the most economical—thereby helping to keep passenger fares and cargo rates as low as possible. As early as the 1930s, the airlines within the original IATA recognized that one more ingredient was necessary in order to achieve both safety and economy: "Safety in flight . . . and economy in operating costs . . . are two goals towards which the airlines must constantly strive. Safety and economy are unfortunately very often opposed. But standardization irreproachably conceived and widely carried out—offers a straight way to both of these essential aims, at the same time."

THE SERVICES OF IATA

Internally, the Association is organized to serve three distinct types of activity:

- **Core Functions** such as industry spokesmanship and maintaining close contacts with governments and other authorities, on behalf of all Members. These activities are financed entirely from Membership dues, however, when products are developed in order to carry on these functions more effectively (for example, non-confidential data bases) the products are sold to both Members and third parties. This helps to keep the Membership dues as low as possible.

- **Industry Coordination Activities** such as tariffs, scheduling, traffic services, and agency administration. These activities are financed partly from Membership dues and partly from revenues generated by the secretariat.

- **Self-Financing Services** such as publications, financial services, agents' accreditation and training, and symposia. As the name implies, these activities are financed entirely by revenue generated from their sale.

The basic source of authority in IATA is the Annual General Meeting (AGM) in which all the Active Members have an equal vote. Year-round policy direction is provided by an elected Executive Committee (of airline Chief Executives). Three standing committees report to the Executive Committee—Technical, Financial, and Traffic. These committees decide priorities and exercise oversight for the ongoing work of the Association. (See Figure 13.2.)

CORE FUNCTIONS OF IATA

Government and Industry Affairs

IATA monitors worldwide aeropolitical and regulatory developments, lobbies governments and government departments; analyzes what governments purpose and what they are doing; has liaison with ICAO and other international/regional organizations about information on IATA services and activities.

Strategic Plan—IATA's future work program and the annual review.

Membership Liaison—contact between the secretariat and individual members and potential Members.

IATA Consumer Dialogue—maintaining a constant dialogue with international consumer groups on questions of mutual airline/consumer concern, such as safety, security, taxation, denied boarding and air transport congestion.

IATA Environmental Coordination—acting as a "clearinghouse" for information on environmental issues, monitoring international debate and promoting, where feasible, common industry positions on environmental problems e.g., noise-compatible land use planning.

Regional Offices—liaison with airlines and governments on a regional basis.

Industry Human Resources Development—administering the Programme for Developing Nations' Airlines and airline training (over 120 courses in 65 subjects offered each year), consultancy, scholarships and administering the International Airline Training Fund.

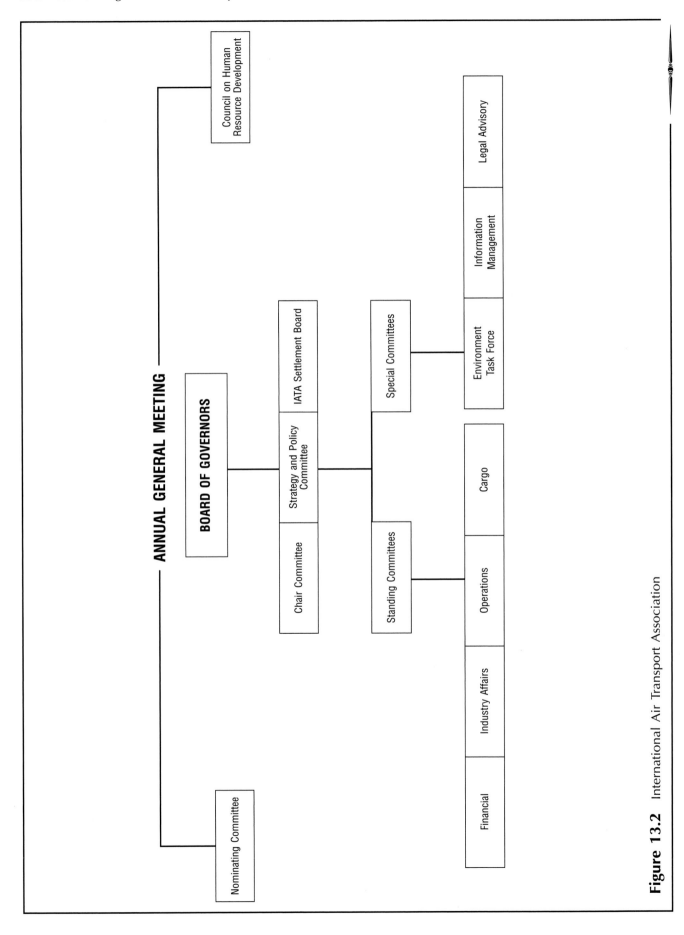

Figure 13.2   International Air Transport Association

Industry Automation and Finance

IATA Management Information includes statistical data collection and dissemination; cost/revenue and other financial analysis; industry and economic forecasts.

Industry Monetary Affairs

User Charges—monitoring ATC and airport fees and lobbying for reduction. This activity regularly saves the world's airlines up to $100 million dollars a year.

Currency—lobbying with authorities to speed repatriation of airlines' overseas revenues.

Fuel Trade—monitoring jet fuel prices worldwide and lobbying for reduction—particularly in cases where prices are inflated by local supply or handling monopolies, or by government taxation. This activity regularly saves the world's airlines (particularly those operating in or to the less developed countries) up to $50 million dollars a year.

Taxation—advice to Members on taxation matters and lobbying to reduce the impact of specific taxes. More than 600 different taxes, fees and charges are imposed on airlines by governments, mainly at airports around the world. Many of these are contrary to ICAO principles and the situation worsens monthly.

Automation

Automation activities within IATA have two principal goals: firstly, to support industry-wide initiatives on evolving standards—such as Electronic Data Interchange and Open Systems Interconnection; secondly, to implement and support IATA's internal automation requirements.

The United Nations have sponsored an EDI known as EDIFACT—Electronic Data Interchange For Administration, Commerce and Transport. IATA is now developing message formats to this standard for the exchange of passenger, cargo, fuel invoice and fuel delivery ticket information among airlines and their business partners. EDIFACT is already being implemented in the reservations field and in departure control.

IATA is working, through the airlines' information management committee, for the adoption of open telecommunications standards—away from the industry's "closed" networks, to universal EDI standards.

Technical

Airports—representing airlines in contacts with airport authorities. Since airlines are the prime users of airports and airport costs are reflected in the price of an airline ticket—the airlines need to be sure that investments in facilities and real estate are adequate to meet demand, while not exceeding that required for functional efficiency.

Avionics—fostering developments in avionics which pay back to the airlines in increased safety and reduced costs. The rapidly advancing technology embraces communications, surveillance, air traffic services, anti-collision systems and landing aids.

Engineering and Environment—covering the safe and economic operation and maintenance of aircraft and airborne systems, monitoring of fuel standards and development of IATA policies for minimizing the environmental impact from aircraft engine noise and emissions.

Flight Operations—is concerned with the selection, training and performance of flight deck crew. By collective analysis of individual airline operating experience the lessons can be shared by the whole industry. Safety issues predominate particularly with the introduction of new systems such as on board collision avoidance and precision landing aids and long-range twin engine operations.

Security—is essentially a cooperative matter since passengers, baggage and cargo pass between carriers. IATA Security staff represent the industry view in the formulation of national and international standards and work cooperatively with members to advise on their implementation. Close coordination is maintained with airports to which IATA offers security surveys.

Safety—maintaining and improving the safety standards of civil aviation has been the main pre-occupation of both airlines and administrators since the very beginning of industry. Working closely with the IATA Flight Operations Advisory Sub-Committee, the Safety Advisory Sub-Committee monitors safety trends to identify specific areas for corrective action.

Regional Technical Offices—six offices cover the world to work with ICAO and State Authorities in the provision of efficient air traffic infrastructure and optimum routings.

Infrastructure Capacity—for several years IATA has been working with the providers of Air Traffic Control and airport capacity to match the rapidly increasing demand to supply. Supported by the Air Transport Action Group representing wider interests in the continued expansion of the industry, IATA acts as a focus for industry initiatives.

Legal Services

Consultation processes for group litigation; updating and maintenance of international conventions and protocols (e.g., carrier liability, terrorism) in consultation with ICAO and national governments.

Public Relations

The air transport industry is becoming more competitive and more complex. As the industry is changing, IATA changes in terms of what it does and of the services it offers. As a result, there is a need for a more pro-active Public Relations function. Public Relations is the interface between collective industry information, decisions and views, the airlines, members of the traveling public and the media. IATA provides regular information to the Press and also holds press briefings and special presentations.

INDUSTRY COORDINATION ACTIVITIES

Tariff Coordination

IATA provides a forum for airlines to develop fares and rates proposals for submission to governments. This process arises from the special nature of air transport. Any country in the world is accessible by air. Airlines fly between most major cities over a maze of interrelated routes. Most governments reserve control over their own airspace, who may fly between their own country and other countries, how much capacity is offered, and what prices are charged.

Because of the time-consuming complexity of negotiating fares and rates in a series of bilateral discussions with other countries, most nations instruct their carriers to take part in the multilateral IATA sessions. Proposals coming from the sessions are studied by the governments and then approved, modified, or even refused. Governments decide fares; IATA is the fares negotiating forum.

There is an increasing tendency for some governments to abrogate their powers of oversight of air tariffs provided the tariffs fall within a certain pre-set range. This is currently true of the European Community countries. With completion of the internal market, a system of "double disapproval" is scheduled to operate. Under this system any tariff published by any carrier on a route (by whatever method that tariff may have been developed) will automatically remain in force unless both the governments at either end of the route disapprove it.

Most governments and carriers see tariff coordination as a necessary part of the worldwide interlining system. If a passenger or a shipper of goods wishes to use the services of any carrier on the world system, having purchased the transport on the paper of only one, then all the potential carriers have to be certain of the revenue benefit of undertaking parts of the carriage (and, in the case of most carriers, receiving credit for that carriage through the IATA Clearing House). This predictability is to some extent guaranteed by tariff coordination.

At the same time, the tariff coordination framework is intended to provide considerable flexibility. Since members need to respond quickly to market changes, provisions exist for them to introduce innovative passenger fares or cargo rates without necessarily affecting other tariffs in their area of operation.

Tariff coordination thus recognizes the fact that IATA members simultaneously compete and cooperate. The framework allows for the flexibility inherent in competition while maintaining sufficient predictability to enable the world interlining system to work. This is what is meant whenever IATA refers to "workable competition."

Third parties (e.g., consumer organizations) are able to make representations to tariff coordination meetings. Observers from ICAO, national governments, and regional organizations regularly attend.

Scheduling Services

Demand for air transport has grown rapidly over the past four decades. During this time the necessary infrastructure capacity—mainly Air Traffic Control (ATC) services and airports—has not grown sufficiently in all areas of the world to service that demand safely. Safety is never compromised—aircraft are kept on the ground until they can be handled safely. As a result there are now more than 100 international airports which are severely congested during certain hours of the day.

IATA and its members are taking strong action to remedy that situation. But in the meantime the available capacity has to be allocated among the users. There are four ways of doing this: government action, random selection, a lottery, market mechanisms, and consensus among the airlines affected. None of these methods are completely satisfactory. Current economic thinking might suggest that market mechanisms are the best choice. However, there is great merit in voluntary allocation.

Over the years, the airlines have developed a voluntary mechanism to deal with scheduling problems through negotiation and mutual adjustment of timetables.

Meetings are held on a worldwide basis because changes to schedules in one area or by one airline can have global repercussions. About 600 people from 200 airlines attend today's scheduling sessions.

Agency Accreditation

This is the process of overseeing the airline industry's passenger and cargo sales agency programs. No airline can afford to set up sales offices in every city of the world, yet most airlines wish to have the opportunity to carry people and goods originating from every city of the world. Travel and cargo agents are the marketplace intermediaries who make this possible.

The programs are designed to assure airlines and other agents in the agent community of high professional standards at individual agencies. The standards are concerned with financial soundness, proficiency of staff and suitability and security of agency premises.

Over the years IATA has built up a working relationship with the Universal Federation of Travel Agents' Associations and the International Federation of Freight Forwarders' Associations.

In the United States, the classic agency rules dealing with accreditation on the basis of the standards mentioned above have been replaced by a system whereby agents are registered on a central record for member airlines to use or not, depending on their commercial policy and judgement. A European program along similar lines has recently been accepted by the European Commission.

Traffic Services Coordination

More than 1.25 billion passenger journeys (domestic plus international) are made by air, worldwide, every year. Twenty million tons of high-value freight are carried by air. Commercial air activity on this scale would not have been possible without passenger, cargo and airport handling standards developed over the years through airline participation in IATA Traffic Services work.

Traffic Services' most significant success has been the creation of the Multilateral Interline Traffic Agreements (MITA). These have integrated the routes of individual airlines into a coordinated world air network—over which passengers, baggage, and cargo can be carried on very complex itineraries with a minimum of documentation. IATA worked closely with the U.S.-based Air Transport Association in developing MITA. More than 200 airlines belong to the agreements. They accept each other's passenger and cargo traffic, tickets and air waybills on a routine basis.

Today it normally takes only one telephone call to an airline or agent to obtain confirmed space aboard any flight. This is followed by the issue of a standard interline passenger ticket, permitting travel anywhere in the world, regardless of how many airlines participate in the carriage. Extensive airline-owned communications networks make this possible. The networks are run both by individual carriers and special companies such as Société Internationale de Télécommunications Aéronautiques and Aeronautical Radio, Inc.

Passenger services aim to speed travellers through airport terminals and on to flights in the least time at the lowest cost—within the limitations set by security requirements and local border formality requirements. Automation plays a big part in this. Reservations, ticketing and the associated accounting procedures will all benefit from increased use of automation in coming years. Message formats (e.g., the UN-sponsored EDIFACT) are developed and suggested for worldwide adoption. In addition, a standard now exists for the new-generation Automated Ticket and Boarding Pass (ATB2). Innovative features include a ticket and boarding pass on one piece of paper and a magnetic stripe on the reverse.

Precise industry standards for carrying disabled passengers have been developed over the years through Traffic Services. These standards benefit handicapped people, physicians, and the airlines themselves.

With more than one billion pieces of checked baggage handled worldwide every year, the potential for loss or misdirection could be high. In fact, through careful application of automated handling systems the loss rate is very low. Items that are lost or misdirected are in most instances recovered through standard procedures, including the IATA/SITA baggage tracing system. Standards and educational programs are also developed and regularly updated for the carriage of live animals and the prevention of carriage of dangerous goods.

Facilitation

This is the name given to attempts to eliminate "red tape" in the movement of people and goods, both inbound and outbound, through airports. As the pressure on airport handling capacity grows, this effort becomes increasingly important. In some cases it is clear that what is first identified as a terminal capacity problem is, in fact, a problem of government (immigration, passport control, health checks, exchange control, customs) procedures.

Fraud Prevention

Stolen and fraudulently used tickets cost the industry millions of dollars a year. The IATA Fraud Prevention Training Program equips people who process tickets to recognize invalid travel documents. TICKETS is the name of a joint Aeronautical Radio, Inc. (ARINC)/IATA automated service which provides real-time listing and inquiry to/from an industrywide data base of black-listed tickets.

SELF-FINANCING SERVICES

Of these services, the long-established Clearing House is preeminent. The Clearing House enables members to settle credits and debits among themselves at one location while minimizing the need to make actual transfers of money. Three hundred sixty members now clear each month; the annual throughout exceeds $22 billion dollars. Next in longevity is the Agency Program. Nearly 64,000 agents are accredited. Bank Settlement Program now cover nearly 29,000 locations with more than 200 participating airlines and a net sales volume in excess of $36 billion dollars. Cargo Account Settlement Systems cover more than 1,800 locations with nearly 120 participating airlines and a net sales volume of nearly $5 billion dollars.

BSP and CASS

Bank Settlement Plans (BSP) for airlines and their passenger agents and Cargo Account Settlement Systems (CASS) for airlines and their cargo agents are devices for the computerized processing of accounts between agents and airlines on a country-by-country basis. Agents deal with all airlines through one central control office rather than having to deal, themselves, with each airline.

Agency Training

IATA/UFTAA passenger agent training courses—originally intended purely for home study but now augmented by classroom and Computer Based Training options—have now been successfully completed by more than 20,500 students worldwide. On the cargo side, more than 9,600 students have passed the IATA/FIATA examinations.

Program for Human Resources Development

This represents an important contribution to skill enhancement for people working in airlines in less developed countries. It is financed through course fees, through the United Nations Development Program, ICAO and the International Airline Training Fund (IATF)—which receives financial contributions from a wide range of sources, corporate and governmental, and awards scholarships for people to attend IATA-approved courses. The IATF has foundations both in Geneva and Washington, D.C.

IATA provides more than 5,000 hours of classroom training for over 1,500 managers and specialists from around the world. At the same time, following the guidelines of the Committee on Human Resources Development, more than half of the 150 training weeks were regional, including those at the Regional Training Center in Singapore.

Revenue Accounting Training

Courses in this subject are offered in the IATA training centers in Geneva and Singapore. In 1990 the first in a series of self-study manuals was introduced entitled "Currency Conversion for Passenger Billings." These provide a top quality alternative to classroom training.

Automated Interline Revenue Data Exchange (EAIRDES)

This enables ticket images to be transferred electronically within 24 hours by a ticket issuing airline to any other AIRDES airline named on a sector. The result is better and faster data capture, pro-rating, and billing.

Proration Service

Proration is the allocating of revenue to the individual carriers who provide part of the transport service on a multi-leg journey—when that journey has been purchased on the ticket of only one carrier. Proration is a routine clearing house procedure according to agreed rules. A more cost-effective automated system is to be introduced, once the potential users have defined their needs.

Computer Based Training

Originally developed to provide training in the standards developed by Traffic Services, CBT modules—on diskette—have sold well. New subjects/modules are being developed.

Insurance Services

Airline Mutual Insurance, Ltd. was created by the industry for the exclusive use and benefit of airlines to cover part of their hull insurance. Other programs cover both airlines and their staff and third parties. One example of the latter is Travel Agents Protector Plus. This provides insurance coverage and bonds for owners of travel agencies in the U.S., who are listed by the local Agency program.

Yield Management Program

The growth of automation in reservations and ticketing has enabled the airlines to apply increasingly sophisticated control techniques to the business of matching supply and demand on a per-flight basis in ways that maximize the revenue per flight. IATA sells a system which does that. It is ideal for small and medium sized airlines.

IATA Currency Clearance Service

Every month the airline industry moves funds worth billions of dollars around the world. The ICCS provides a neutral, central platform which airlines can use to offset their equal but opposite currency flows. This leads to lower costs, rapid transfers and more beneficial exchange rates through consolidation of like currencies into larger amounts.

Automation Consultancy

Services are offered both to individual airlines and to air-transport related industries. One current example is development of core software for individual country's Bank Settlement Plans.

Aircraft Availability Service

A data base of aircraft for sale or lease is matched with potential purchases or leases.

Market and Economic Analysis, Traffic and Airport Forecasting, Data Collection Development

Typical of these activities are post-flight surveys of transatlantic passengers (service expectations and experience), attitude and awareness surveys, surveys of airline economic results and prospects and long-term traffic forecasts for leading world airports.

Registered Suppliers Program

Third parties—such as equipment builders and software suppliers—are able to take part in the Services Conference and thus participate in the standards setting process.

Seminars and Symposia

IATA convenes and organizes about 10 such events every year. Subjects include aircraft finance, air trans-port and tourism forecasting and economics, liberalization and interlining.

Publications

IATA sells many publications. These cover Traffic Services standards, airline operating statistics and airport and en route navigation charges, amongst others.

General Consultancy Services

IATA has a pool of airline industry expertise from two sources—inhouse staff and a vetted list of recent airline retirees. It is thus able to offer tailor-made consultancy services across a wide spectrum of subjects.

IATA EDUCATION PROGRAMS

In cooperation with Concordia University, IATA is conducting a Master of Business Administration program. IATA has recognized the need for a specialized aviation post-graduate university program to educate aviation managers to meet the challenges of the future.

The program is entirely self-financing without government grants although Canada and the cities of Quebec and Montreal assisted with the initial feasibility study. The Société du Centre de Conférences Internationales in Montreal supported IATA and Concordia University in launching the program.

Another on-going aviation education program is IATA's prestigious Diploma in Airline Management. Student candidates are selected for their potential in assuming leadership positions in their airline companies.

The program combines high level management courses with on-the-job assignments and specific airline training to help participants expand their business knowledge and to develop the sound commercial attitude needed to operate effectively in a leadership role.

These programs fill a need in the airline industry by providing students with a broad understanding of strategic issues affecting airline management and acquiring the ability to make efficient decisions.

INTERNATIONAL TRANSPORTATION SAFETY ASSOCIATION

The purpose of this organization is to improve transport safety in each member country by learning from experiences of others. The objectives of the International Transportation Safety Association are:

Table 13.3 U.S. Commercial Air Carriers Scheduled International Passenger Traffic

Fiscal Year	Revenue Passenger Enplanements (Mil)				Revenue Passenger Miles (Bil)			
	Atlantic	Latin America	Pacific	Total	Atlantic	Latin America	Pacific	Total
1995	16.2	18.0	14.3	48.6	64.4	24.4	55.5	144.3
1996	15.8	19.2	15.3	50.0	64.9	26.3	59.7	150.9
1997	16.5	20.2	15.8	52.3	68.2	29.5	61.1	158.8
1998	18.0	21.0	14.1	53.1	74.6	32.0	56.7	163.3
1999	19.1	21.9	12.3	53.3	79.6	34.1	56.1	169.7
2000	20.9	22.5	11.2	54.6	87.1	35.8	58.4	181.3
Forecast								
2001	22.2	24.1	11.8	58.1	92.9	38.7	62.4	194.0
2002	23.6	25.9	12.5	62.1	99.2	42.0	66.7	207.9
2003	25.1	27.9	13.3	66.4	106.1	45.5	71.3	222.9
2004	26.6	29.9	14.3	70.8	112.9	49.2	76.4	238.5
2005	28.0	32.0	15.2	75.2	119.2	52.9	81.7	253.8
2006	29.5	34.0	16.1	79.6	125.6	56.6	86.9	269.1
2007	30.8	36.2	17.1	84.1	131.6	60.5	92.4	284.5
2008	32.2	38.7	18.2	89.1	138.0	64.9	98.4	301.3
2009	33.7	41.3	19.3	94.3	144.6	69.6	104.7	318.9
2010	35.2	44.0	20.5	99.8	151.7	74.6	111.4	337.7
2011	36.8	46.8	21.7	105.4	158.8	79.7	118.1	356.6
2012	38.4	49.7	23.0	111.0	165.9	85.0	125.1	376.0

Source: Form 41, U.S. Department of Transportation.

Note: Detail may not add to total because of rounding.

1. To improve transportation safety in each member's country by learning from experience of other investigation boards.

2. To promote the practice of independent investigation into the causes and safety deficiencies of transportation accidents.

3. To exchange information on transportation safety on such matters as safety deficiencies, safety studies, safety recommendations, accident data and accident investigation techniques.

4. To share information on the implementation of important safety recommendations.

5. To identify common concerns, problems, methods and solutions and to share these both nationally and internationally.

The advantages of being a member in this organization are:

1. It brings together similar national investigation organizations.

2. Members receive structured information about the independent investigation of transportation accidents and incidents in other countries.

3. Sharing national experience on the findings and safety recommendations derived from in-depth investigation of accidents.

4. Establishing personal contacts with professional colleagues worldwide.

5. Extending intermodal experience to similar problems in other modes of transportation.

6. Contributing to a safer transportation system worldwide.

The International Transportation Safety Association is made up of national independent accident investigation boards whose objective is to improve transportation safety in each member country by learning from the experiences of others. The objective is accomplished by exchanging information on the causes of accidents, safety studies, recommendations, accident data and investigation methodology.

The members of the International Transportation Safety Association are:

Canada—*Transportation Safety Board of Canada*

The Commonwealth of Independent States—*Air Transport Accident Investigation Commission*

Finland—*The Accident Investigation Board*

India—*The Commission of Railway Safety*

Netherlands—*Dutch Transport Safety Board*

New Zealand—*Transport Accident Investigation Commission*

Sweden—*Board of Accident Investigation*

United Kingdom—*Marine Accident Investigation Branch*

United States of America—*National Transportation Safety Board*

AIRPORTS COUNCIL INTERNATIONAL*

On October 2, 1991, the Airports Council International (ACI) was formed, achieving a long desired goal by airport operators to establish a single, integrated and comprehensive worldwide organization. ACI's structure gives the global aviation scene an association that will facilitate cooperation and representation of airport interests at international, regional and national levels; thus bringing together, under one international organization, hundreds of public authorities responsible for operating the world's airport system.

For years, airport operators had searched for the formula that would unify airports under one organization. During that time, the Airport Associations Coordinating Council served as an umbrella organization for other airport operator groups: the Airport Operators Council International, the International Civil Airports Association and, for a time, the Western European Airports Association. Much effort began to develop a structure and process that would rationalize and enhance the integration efforts of airports. ACI is the culmination of that work.

Increasing worldwide economic integration also called for the integration of airports into a single world-wide organization. The regional focus of much of this economic integration argue for a regional orientation for the airports association. In Europe, in North America, in Latin America, in many other parts of the globe, markets are being broadened, trade is expanding, challenges are more complex. Air transportation will be a great catalyst and facilitator, and the airport role will be crucial. The organizational structure of ACI enable airports to fulfill that role more effectively.

The structure of ACI reflects the need to focus efforts on international issues that affect all airports, while enhancing services and programs to the member government bodies through regional organizations. ACI spearheads airport involvement in the affairs of other important international organizations. The Geneva office coordinates worldwide programs and conferences, as well as the administration of the ACI Governing Board and Standing Committees.

The Airports Council International is the "voice of the world's airports." Its membership consists of international airports and airport authorities, running close to 1,000 airports, in over 140 countries. ACI integrates AOCI and ICAA, the former airport associations, and succeeds their coordinating council—AACC. ACI is a non-profit organization whose primary purpose is to foster cooperation among its member airports and with other partners in world aviation. Through such cooperation, ACI aims to contribute significantly towards achieving an air transport system that is safe, secure, efficient and compatible with the environment. ACI represents the world's airports in interacting with the International Civil Aviation Organization (ICAO), with which it has observer status, and other world bodies. ACI has consultative status with the United Nations. ACI has its World Headquarters in Geneva and is made up of six geographical regions: Africa, Asia, Europe, Latin America/Caribbean, North America, and the Pacific. (See Figure 13.3.)

The six regions of AACI will govern their own affairs, thereby assuring a responsiveness to the needs and concerns of airport operators in the region. Each region will have its own Board of Directors, Committees, budget and headquarters staff.

ACI has the depth and breadth of membership to give airports their rightful place in the world aviation community. From the giant intercontinental passenger and cargo hubs that are more complex and dynamic

> The Airports Council International is the "voice of the world's airports."

---

* Refer to Appendix C for the ACI membership list. For current information go to the Website at http://www.airports.org

ACI - ONE ORGANIZATION, SIX REGIONS

REGIONAL OFFICES

AFRICA
PO Box 6019
Terminal 2
Cairo International Airport
CAIRO
EGYPT
Tel: (+20.2) 304 6955 / Fax: (+20.2) 304 6954
E-mail: aci2000afr10@hotmail.com

ASIA
c/o Institute of Aviation Management
Airports Authority of India
Gurgaon Road
110037 NEW DELHI
INDIA
Tel: (+91.11) 565 2307 / Fax: (+91.11) 565 2674/2830

EUROPE
6 Square de Meeus
1000 BRUXELLES
BELGIUM
Tel: (+32.2) 552 0978 / Fax: (+32.2) 513 2606
E-mail: info@aci-europe.org
www.aci-europe.org

LATIN AMERICA/CARIBBEAN
c/o IAAIM
Edificio Sede - Piso 8
Aeropuerto de Maiquetía
CARACAS
VENEZUELA
Tel: (+58.2) 3551 232 / Fax: (+58.2) 3551 654
E-mail: acilac@telcel.net.ve
www.acilac.com.ve

NORTH AMERICA
1775 K Street, N.W., Suite 500
WASHINGTON, DC 20006
USA
Tel: (+1.202) 293 8500 / Fax: (+1.202) 334 1362
E-mail: postmaster@aci-na.org
www.aci-na.org

PACIFIC
c/o Vancouver International Airport Authority
PO Box 23750
Airport Postal Outlet
RICHMOND BC V7B 1Y7
CANADA
Tel: (+1.604) 276 6773 / Fax: (+1.604) 276 6070
E-mail: ldaley@aci-pacific.org
www.aci-pacific.org

ACI WORLD HEADQUARTERS
PO Box 16
1215 GENEVA 15 - Airport
SWITZERLAND
Tel: (+41.22) 717 8585
Fax: (+41.22) 717 8888
E-mail: aci@airports.org
www.airports.org

ACI LIAISON OFFICE WITH ICAO
c/o Aéroports de Montréal
1100 Blvd René-Lévesque West - Suite 2100
MONTREAL, QUEBEC
CANADA H3B 4X8
Tel: (+1.514) 394 7321
Fax: (+1.514) 394 7356
E-mail: Rodheitm@aol.com

ACI FUND FOR DEVELOPING NATIONS' AIRPORTS
PO Box 16
1215 GENEVA 15 - Airport
SWITZERLAND
Tel: (+41.22) 717 8585
Fax: (+41.22) 717 8888
E-mail: aci@airports.org
www.airports.org

Figure 13.3

than many large cities, to the airfields that serve as a small community's link to the air transportation system and its world markets. The diversity and inclusiveness of ACI's membership brings with it the capability and authority to speak on behalf of the airports of the world.

The goals of the Airports Council International are to:

- Promote legislation, regulations and international agreements that support member airports' interests.

- Contribute to increased cooperation, mutual assistance, information exchange and learning opportunities for member airports.

- Provide member airports with timely information and analysis of domestic and international developments.

- Develop and promote programs that stimulate public awareness of the economic and social importance of airports.

- Generate programs and services which meet members' needs and contribute to membership retention and growth.

In the not too distant future, airports in all regions may have to handle aircraft capable of carrying 600 passengers. The major manufacturers have developed plans for these giants. ACI is ensuring that all the factors arising out of the operation of these aircraft are taken into consideration, including increased wingspan and wheelbase, gross weight, the effect of wake vortices and the design implications for terminal facilities. Wingspan will not be the only problem when operating new large aircraft at current facilities. Fuselage length, wheelbase and undercarriage configuration may also be limiting factors.

Present indications suggest that the phase-out of Chapter 2 aircraft by 2002 will not alleviate the noise problem as effectively as was once thought. As air traffic increases, overall aircraft noise levels around airports are expected to rise some time after 2002.

ACI's goal is to ensure that traffic growth can be maintained within the environmental capacity limitations imposed upon airports by governments. These limits may be set lower than the current capacity of airports. Future traffic growth will only be possible if noise and emissions are reduced at the source. More stringent noise and emissions certification standards have to be achieved in order to encourage manufacturers and airlines to produce and operate quieter and cleaner aircraft. It is the aim of the ACI to encourage the adoption of such standards.

The changing business environment of the aviation industry will affect the management and operation of airports. Airports need to make money. They provide an important service, which must be commercially viable like all the other services which make up air travel. Airlines have a tendency to blame airport charges for their financial problems. However, airport charges worldwide have been a very stable component of the operating costs of airlines.

ACI champions the widespread implementation of the key principles of ICAO Council Statements on Airport Charges. It provides assistance and advice to its members in dealing with users on matters relating to airport charges and other economic issues.

ACI

STRUCTURE OF AIRPORTS COUNCIL INTERNATIONAL (ACI)

The General Assembly is ACI's supreme authority. At least twice annually, the Governing Board's 29 members meet to decide ACI policy and review anything not referred to the Assembly. The Executive Committee's eight members supervise the work of ACI between board meetings. The Chairman of ACI heads the two bodies.

Headquartered in Geneva, ACI is made up of six geographical areas: Africa, Asia, Europe, Latin America/Caribbean, North America and the Pacific. Regional offices are located in Cairo, New Delhi, Brussels, Caracas, Washington, D.C. and Vancouver. In 1994, a liaison office with ICAO was established in Montreal. (See Figure 13.4.)

The regional offices represent the regional governmental and non-governmental organizations. They are supported by specialized committees and task forces. ACI's main officer and spokesperson is the Director General and is charged with implementing the policies of the General Assembly and the Governing Board. The day-to-day operations of the ACI are the responsibility of the Secretary General. Directors covering aeropolitical, economic, environmental, facilitation, security, technical and regional affairs report to the Secretary General.

Five World Standing Committees create airport policies in their specific areas of expertise:

Economics Standing Committee responsibilities: airport charging systems; security, noise and passenger-service charges; consultation with users; development of revenues from concessions; peak pricing; hard/soft currencies; financial statistics; airport financing and ownership; state taxation; the economic

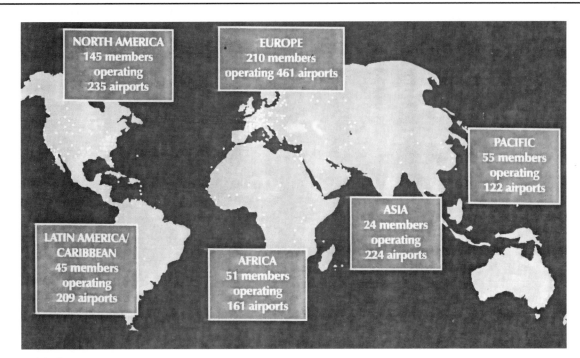

Figure 13.4 ACI membership—530 members operating over 1,400 airports in 162 countries

implications for airports with regard to issues such as airline deregulation and consolidation, competition between air transport and other modes of high-speed transport; route development; and non-aeronautical revenues.

Environmental Standing Committee responsibilities: noise management, including certification, abatement techniques and operational restrictions; air and water quality management, fuel storage and site remediation; land use compatibility; environmental capacity; natural resource management, energy conservation, wildlife and natural sites management; and environmental management systems including monitoring, training, certification and community relations.

Facilitation & Services Standing Committee responsibilities: the facilitation of passengers and their baggage; freight and mail; quality of service; surface access to airports and intermodal issues; automated services for passengers, baggage, freight and mail; hazardous goods; measures to stop drug trafficking; slot allocation and schedule coordination; and the inter-relationship between facilitation and security.

Security Standing Committee responsibilities: security in airport design; passenger and baggage screening; access control; security technology; the impact of security on airport operations; cargo security; planning for natural disasters; and measures to combat biological and chemical threats to aviation.

Technical/Safety Standing Committee responsibilities: airport planning, design and development; airspace and airport capacity; aviation and airspace technologies; physical characteristics of runways, taxiways and aprons; aircraft/airport compatibility; visual aids for navigation; airport equipment and installations; operational safety; aerodrome emergency planning; rescue and fire fighting; and removal of disabled aircraft.

COOPERATION WITH INTERNAL ORGANIZATIONS

ACI works closely with the International Air Transport Association (IATA) and also with the International Civil Aviation Organization (ICAO) and other United Nations agencies. ACI also keeps in contact with the International Federation of Air Line Pilots' Associations (IFALPA), the International Federation of Air Traffic Controllers' Associations (IFATCA), the International Coordinating Council of Aerospace Industries Associations (ICCAIA), and other worldwide organizations.

The International Industry Working Group (IIWG), of which ACI is a member, brings together the main areas of the civil aviation industry, which consist of airports, airlines and manufacturers. The entire group (ACI, IATA and ICCAIA) has the task of working on common problems regarding design, development and compatibility of aircraft and airports.

ACI AND THE PUBLIC

ACI must continuously monitor the interests of all airport customers in addition to the communities in the vicinity of all airports. ACI adopts, presents, and promotes positions on issues which are designed to eliminate or lessen current problems. It also strives to encourage optimum air travel growth while taking into account the environmental concerns. Current areas of interest include:

Aviation Security—ACI urges governments to enhance aviation security and ensure the highest level of safety in keeping with the threat. Its experts work with local airport security to create committees and programs. ACI works in conjunction with IATA and other groups to create guidelines on airside and landside security as well as aviation security technology, which it promotes in discussions with governments and in the context of ICAO. ACI maintains that States have the final responsibility to fight terrorism and ensure the implementation of ICAO security provisions. If the States do not meet the basic mandates, there is little confidence in the integrity of the global aviation security system.

Facilitation—ACI works to lessen red tape and bureaucratic holdups by government inspection services at many international airports. These cause slow and inefficient processing of passengers, baggage, freight and mail. Because of rigorous requirements to handle problems of security and drug trafficking, extra delays occur. Governments, airlines and airports need to make efforts to allow facilitation, yet meet security requirements. Increasing numbers of elderly and disabled passengers shows that easier access is needed to airports and through airports. ACI also reviews surface access to airports and intermodal facilities.

Environmental Protection—ACI asks for government restrictions with regard to the operation of noisy aircraft so that areas near airports are protected from the effects of aircraft noise and airports can increase traffic without restrictions. ACI encourages land use planning around airports so that construction of homes or other noise-sensitive buildings is avoided in certain areas. ACI also calls for a reduction in engine emissions to further decrease its share of air pollution, which is currently very small.

Congestion—Airspace and airport congestion hinder air transport, and ACI looks for ways to diminish the problem. Possible solutions include upgrading current terminal facilities; a safe reduction of minimum separation distances between parallel runways; reducing performance gaps between ATC and aircraft systems; and the creation of new airports and runways where feasible. It also encourages airlines to use large aircraft as a way to gain the highest productivity out of limited runway slots, as well as using quieter aircraft so as to increase traffic without disturbing communities near airports.

Airport Information Technology and Automation—The increased use of automation is important to simplify and speed up the handling of passengers, their baggage, freight and mail at airports. ACI and IATA have set a basic technical standard for automated baggage sorting in an effort to reduce the risk of mishandling, allow automated sorting and handling in airports, simplify passenger/baggage reconciliation and increase baggage security. ACI and IATA have also put in place a standard for EDI messages between airports and airlines and produced guidelines for interconnected and shared systems. ACI is working with other groups to further the Simplifying Passenger Travel concept in order to speed up passenger transit. This is based on a "one-stop" control process when the passenger checks in. This would meet the requirements of all Control Authorities for advance data, to allow pre-clearance for most passengers who would be determined to be low-risk. This would involve machine readable travel documents and the use of biometric data to identify the passenger. ACI also advocates the use of Information Technology to clear, handle and track freight and encourages the development of new procedures that will make work easier for shippers.

Total passenger traffic between the United States and the rest of the world is expected to grow from 139.2 million in 2000 to 267.0 million in 2012, an average annual growth rate of 5.6 percent. Passenger traffic is expected to be strongest in Latin American and Pacific markets, growing at annual rates of 6.7 and 6.2 percent, respectively, over the forecast period. Passenger traffic is projected to grow 4.9 percent annually in Atlantic markets and 4.0 percent a year in Canadian markets.

Table 13.4   Top 100 ACI Airports—January–December 2000

PASSENGER TRAFFIC		CARGO VOLUME		AIRCRAFT MOVEMENTS	
AIRPORT	PASSENGERS	AIRPORT	CARGO	AIRPORT	MOVEMENTS
1 Atlanta, GA (ATL)	80 171 036	1 Memphis, TN (MEM)	2 489 070	1 Atlanta, GA (ATL)	915 657
2 Chicago, IL (ORD)	72 135 887	2 Hong Kong, CN (HKG)	2 267 175	2 Chicago, IL (ORD)	908 989
3 Los Angeles, CA (LAX)	68 477 689	3 Los Angeles, CA (LAX)	2 054 212	3 Dallas/Ft Worth Airport, TX (DFW)	837 779
4 London, GB (LHR)	64 607 185	4 Tokyo, JP (NRT)	1 932 694	4 Phoenix, AZ (PHX)	636 848
5 Dallas/Ft Worth Airp., TX (DFW)	60 687 122	5 Anchorage, AK** (ANC)	1 883 825	5 Los Angeles, CA (LAX)	560 878
6 Tokyo, JP (HND)	56 402 206	6 Seoul, KR (SEL)	1 874 228	6 Detroit, MI (DTW)	555 375
7 Frankfurt, DE (FRA)	49 360 620	7 New York, NY (JFK)	1 825 906	7 Minneapolis/St Paul, MN (MSP)	523 014
8 Paris, FR (CDG)	48 240 137	8 Frankfurt, DE (FRA)	1 710 144	8 Paris, FR (CDG)	517 657
9 San Francisco, CA (SFO)	41 173 983	9 Singapore, SG (SIN)	1 705 410	9 Miami, FL (MIA)	517 440
10 Amsterdam, NL (AMS)	39 604 589	10 Miami, FL (MIA)	1 642 484	10 Las Vegas, NV (LAS)	515 293
11 Denver, CO (DEN)	38 748 781	11 Louisville, KY (SDF)	1 519 558	11 Denver, CO (DEN)	509 092
12 Las Vegas, NV (LAS)	36 856 186	12 Chicago, IL (ORD)	1 463 941	12 Cincinnati, OH (CVG)	486 671
13 Seoul, KR (SEL)	36 727 124	13 London, GB (LHR)	1 402 088	13 Philadelphia, PA (PHL)	484 308
14 Minneapolis/St Paul, MN (MSP)	36 688 159	14 Paris, FR (CDG)	1 380 068	14 Houston, TX (IAH)	483 570
15 Phoenix, AZ (PHX)	35 889 933	15 Amsterdam, NL (AMS)	1 267 386	15 St Louis, MO (STL)	481 025
16 Detroit, MI (DTW)	35 535 080	16 Taipei, TW (TPE)	1 208 838	16 Boston, MA (BOS)	478 323
17 Houston, TX (IAH)	35 246 176	17 Indianapolis, IN (IND)	1 173 967	17 London, GB (LHR)	466 815
18 Newark, NJ (EWR)	34 194 788	18 Newark, NJ (EWR)	1 082 668	18 Frankfurt, DE (FRA)	458 731
19 Miami, FL (MIA)	33 569 625	19 Osaka, JP (KIX)	1 000 693	19 Washington, DC (IAD)	457 482
20 New York, NY (JFK)	32 779 428	20 Dallas/Ft Worth Airport, TX (DFW)	904 994	20 Seattle/Tacoma, WA (SEA)	455 025
21 Madrid, ES (MAD)	32 765 820	21 Atlanta, GA (ATL)	871 602	21 Charlotte, NC (CLT)	452 009
22 Hong Kong, CN (HKG)	32 746 737	22 Bangkok, TH (BKK)	871 000	22 Newark, NJ (EWR)	449 498
23 London, GB (LGW)	32 056 942	23 San Francisco, CA (SFO)	870 113	23 Oakland, CA (OAK)	449 050
24 Orlando, FL (MCO)	30 822 580	24 Dayton, OH (DAY)	832 205	24 Pittsburgh, PA (PIT)	448 785
25 St Louis, MO (STL)	30 546 698	25 Tokyo, JP (HND)	769 733	25 Amsterdam, NL (AMS)	432 479
26 Bangkok, TH (BKK)	29 621 898	26 Oakland, CA (OAK)	703 043	26 San Francisco, CA (SFO)	429 222
27 Toronto, OT, CA (YYZ)	28 820 326	27 Brussels, BE (BRU)	634 342	27 Toronto, OT, CA (YYZ)	426 178
28 Singapore, SG (SIN)	28 618 200	28 Dubai, AE (DXB)	581 997	28 Memphis, TN (MEM)	388 412
29 Seattle/Tacoma, WA (SEA)	28 404 312	29 Sydney, AU (SYD)	564 616	29 Santa Ana, CA (SNA)	387 862
30 Boston, MA (BOS)	27 412 926	30 Philadelphia, PA (PHL)	562 752	30 New York, NY (LGA)	382 284
31 Tokyo, JP (NRT)	27 389 915	31 Beijing, CN (PEK)	554 833	31 Long Beach, CA (LGB)	373 624
32 Rome, IT (FCO)	25 921 886	32 Kuala Lumpur, MY (KUL)	524 442	32 Sanford, FL (SFB)	371 787
33 Paris, FR (ORY)	25 399 111	33 Shanghai, CN (SHA)	492 092	33 Phoenix, AZ (DVT)	370 779
34 New York, NY (LGA)	25 233 889	34 Honolulu, HI (HNL)	482 274	34 Daytona, FL (DAB)	368 538
35 Philadelphia, PA (PHL)	24 900 621	35 Sharjah, AE (SHJ)	475 122	35 Orlando, FL (MCO)	368 172
36 Sydney, AU (SYD)	23 553 878	36 Denver, CO (DEN)	469 737	36 Salt Lake City, UT (SLC)	366 933
37 Munich, DE (MUC)	23 125 872	37 Boston, MA (BOS)	465 796	37 Madrid, ES (MAD)	358 478
38 Charlotte, NC (CLT)	23 073 894	38 Ontario, CA (ONT)	464 165	38 Honolulu, HI (HNL)	345 771
39 Honolulu, HI (HNL)	22 660 349	39 Cologne, DE (CGN)	442 191	39 New York, NY (JFK)	344 623
40 Zurich, CH (ZRH)	22 649 539	40 Seattle/Tacoma, WA (SEA)	440 977	40 Vancouver, BC, CA (YVR)	337 397
41 Cincinnati, OH (CVG)	22 537 525	41 Toledo, OH (TOL)	426 733	41 Cleveland, OH (CLE)	331 899
42 Beijing, CN (PEK)	21 659 077	42 Sao Paulo, BR (GRU)	421 713	42 Brussels, BE (BRU)	325 979
43 Brussels, BE (BRU)	21 604 478	43 Copenhagen, DK (CPH)	419 342	43 Zurich, CH (ZRH)	325 622
44 Mexico City, MX (MEX)	21 042 610	44 Zurich, CH (ZRH)	417 111	44 Baltimore, MD (BWI)	321 627
45 Milan, IT (MXP)	20 716 815	45 Manila, PH (MNL)	390 154	45 Munich, DE (MUC)	319 009
46 Osaka, JP (KIX)	20 472 060	46 Washington, DC (IAD)	384 283	46 Anchorage, AK** (ANC)	314 922
47 Washington, DC (IAD)	19 971 449	47 Cincinnati, OH (CVG)	381 253	47 Sydney, AU (SYD)	307 058
48 Salt Lake City, UT (SLC)	19 900 810	48 Minneapolis/St Paul, MN (MSP)	369 888	48 Copenhagen, DK (CPH)	303 713
49 Pittsburgh, PA (PIT)	19 813 174	49 Houston, TX (IAH)	368 496	49 Portland, OR (PDX)	299 911
50 Barcelona, ES (BCN)	19 797 135	50 Tel-Aviv, IL (TLV)	344 054	50 Chicago, IL (MDW)	298 115
51 Baltimore, MD (BWI)	19 602 856	51 Phoenix, AZ (PHX)	339 356	51 Washington, DC (DCA)	297 879
52 Palma De Mallorca, ES (PMI)	19 401 807	52 London, GB (LGW)	338 240	52 Raleigh-Durham, NC (RDU)	296 679
53 Manchester, GB (MAN)	18 804 322	53 Madrid, ES (MAD)	331 285	53 Mexico City, MX (MEX)	296 408
54 Taipei, TW (TPE)	18 681 418	54 Bombay, IN (BOM)	304 520	54 Fort Lauderdale, FL (FLL)	292 675
55 Stockholm, SE (ARN)	18 446 309	55 Jakarta, ID (CGK)	301 170	55 San Jose, CA (SJC)	286 888
56 Copenhagen, DK (CPH)	18 294 387	56 Milan, IT (MXP)	300 108	56 Rome, IT (FCO)	280 811
57 Melbourne, AU (MEL)	16 442 312	57 Detroit, MI (DTW)	298 146	57 Stockholm, SE (ARN)	279 383
58 Vancouver, BC, CA (YVR)	16 245 209	58 Cheju, KR (CJU)	282 565	58 Tampa, FL (TPA)	278 863

Table 13.4 Top 100 ACI Airports—January–December 2000 (continued)

PASSENGER TRAFFIC		CARGO VOLUME		AIRCRAFT MOVEMENTS	
AIRPORT	PASSENGERS	AIRPORT	CARGO	AIRPORT	MOVEMENTS
59 Tampa, FL (TPA)	16 041 486	59 Portland, OR (PDX)	281 990	59 Indianapolis, IN (IND)	261 816
60 Dusseldorf, DE (DUS)	16 028 038	60 Orlando, FL (MCO)	271 046	60 London, GB (LGW)	260 858
61 Fort Lauderdale, FL (FLL)	15 856 663	61 Liege, BE (LGG)	270 307	61 Barcelona, ES (BCN)	256 799
62 Istanbul, TR (IST)	15 830 526	62 Salt Lake City, UT (SLC)	258 124	62 Dallas, TX (DAL)	256 790
63 San Diego, CA (SAN)	15 826 221	63 Vancouver, BC, CA (YVR)	251 771	63 Tokyo, JP (HND)	256 394
64 Washington, DC (DCA)	15 724 613	64 Delhi, IN (DEL)	246 133	64 Houston, TX (HOU)	254 435
65 Kuala Lumpur, MY (KUL)	15 648 029	65 Fort Lauderdale, FL (FLL)	236 669	65 Fresno, CA (FAT)	251 907
66 Chicago, IL (MDW)	15 591 487	66 Istanbul, TR (IST)	233 689	66 Tucson, AZ (TUS)	250 943
67 Sao Paulo, BR (GRU)	14 218 788	67 Baltimore, MD (BWI)	231 962	67 Milan, IT (MXP)	248 985
68 Oslo, NO (OSL)	14 214 554	68 Campinas, BR (CPQ)	229 937	68 Nashville, TN (BNA)	247 576
69 Dublin, IE (DUB)	13 843 528	69 Shanghai, CN (PUG)	227 480	69 San Antonio, TX (SAT)	245 737
70 Portland, OR (PDX)	13 790 115	70 Rome, IT (FCO)	210 086	70 Paris, FR (ORY)	243 586
71 Cleveland, OH (CLE)	13 288 353	71 Jeddah, SA (JED)	209 103	71 Columbus, OH (CMH)	238 011
72 San Jose, CA (SJC)	13 096 355	72 Charlotte, NC (CLT)	199 948	72 Seoul, KR (SEL)	236 272
73 Manila, PH (MNL)	12 764 916	73 East Midlands, GB (EMA)	193 519	73 St. Petersburg, FL (PIE)	235 740
74 Shanghai, CN (SHA)	12 354 676	74 Hahn, DE (HHN)	191 508	74 Albuquerque, NM (ABQ)	233 491
75 Dubai, AE (DXB)	12 320 660	75 Auckland, NZ (AKL)	187 665	75 Las Vegas, NV (VGT)	225 505
76 Bombay, IN (BOM)	12 043 204	76 Pusan, KR (PUS)	183 872	76 Colorado Springs, CO (COS)	221 995
77 Vienna, AT (VIE)	11 939 571	77 London, GB (STN)	182 583	77 Milwaukee, WI (MKE)	221 855
78 Kansas City, MO (MCI)	11 910 654	78 Penang, MY (PEN)	171 856	78 Kansas City, MO (MCI)	219 508
79 London, GB (STN)	11 874 894	79 Riyadh, SA (RUH)	170 676	79 Nice, FR (NCE)	217 369
80 Brisbane, AU (BNE)	11 774 135	80 Sacramento, CA (MHR)	167 091	80 Austin, TX (AUS)	212 620
81 Memphis, TN (MEM)	11 769 213	81 Hartford/Springfield, CT (BDL)	160 926	81 Montreal, QU, CA (YUL)	209 689
82 Johannesburg, ZA (JNB)	11 680 598	82 Austin, TX (AUS)	160 383	82 Vienna, AT (VIE)	206 968
83 Moscow, RU (SVO)	10 828 178	83 Fort Wayne, IN (FWA)	155 338	83 San Diego, CA (SAN)	206 889
84 Oakland, CA (OAK)	10 620 798	84 Stockholm, SE (ARN)	155 108	84 Oslo, NO (OSL)	204 492
85 Jeddah, SA (JED)	10 603 060	85 Kansas City, MO (MCI)	150 433	85 Tulsa, OK (TUL)	198 970
86 Jakarta, ID (CGK)	10 442 993	86 Bahrain, BH (BAH)	148 533	86 Wichita, KS (ICT)	198 210
87 Raleigh-Durham, NC (RDU)	10 440 561	87 Munich, DE (MUC)	148 017	87 Bangkok, TH (BKK)	195 037
88 Berlin, DE (TXL)	10 343 630	88 San Jose, CA (SJC)	146 909	88 Dusseldorf, DE (DUS)	194 019
89 Helsinki, FI (HEL)	10 014 873	89 Pittsburgh, PA (PIT)	146 634	89 Hong Kong, CN (HKG)	193 916
90 Hamburg, DE (HAM)	9 949 269	90 Rio de Janeiro, BR (GIG)	144 552	90 Manchester, GB (MAN)	193 400
91 New Orleans, LA (MSY)	9 874 257	91 Nairobi, KE (NBO)	140 643	91 West Palm Beach, FL (PBI)	192 515
92 Pusan, KR (PUS)	9 440 244	92 San Diego, CA (SAN)	139 261	92 Melbourne, FL (MLB)	192 153
93 Malaga, ES (AGP)	9 438 373	93 Columbia, SC (CAE)	138 008	93 Beijing, CN (PEK)	187 190
94 Lisbon, PT (LIS)	9 395 761	94 Vienna, AT (VIE)	134 994	94 Sao Paulo, BR (GRU)	186 109
95 Nice, FR (NCE)	9 392 408	95 St. Louis, MO (STL)	130 487	95 Singapore, SG (SIN)	184 533
96 Gran Canaria, ES (LPA)	9 374 399	96 Colombo, LR (CMB)	128 385	96 Louisville, KY (SDF)	181 548
97 Tel-Aviv, IL (TLV)	9 301 604	97 San Antonio, TX (SAT)	124 348	97 Dublin, IE (DUB)	180 245
98 Kaohsiung, TW (KHH)	9 138 417	98 Manaus, BR (MAO)	123 098	98 Sarasota, FL (SRQ)	179 844
99 Cheju, KR (CJU)	9 125 892	99 Manchester, GB (MAN)	121 881	99 Palma De Mallorca, ES (PMI)	176 847
100 Houston, TX (HOU)	9 105 778	100 Cleveland, OH (CLE)	119 424	100 Kahului, HI (OGG)	174 855

**includes transit freight.

Total Passengers   Total passengers enplaned and deplaned, passengers in transit counted once.

Cargo   Loaded and unloaded freight and mail (in metric tons).

Aircraft Movements   Landing and take-off of an aircraft.

Source: Airports Council International

CHAPTER 14

Non-U.S. Air Carriers

Throughout the world, there are approximately 300 air carriers in operation at any given time. These range from the very largest global companies to the smallest with only a few aircraft and sometimes only one aircraft.

The following is a listing of selected air carriers that are not of the United States. Log onto the web site by Sarah Ward: *http://airlines.afriqonline.com/* to learn their history, aircraft used, and the routes they fly. Over the years many companies evolved from mergers or simply inherited the activities of a predecessor. Most air carriers were either the operation of their country or were significantly subsidized by their government. Individual web sites for air carriers are also listed if available.

ABA-Swedish Air Lines

Adelaide Airways

Aer Lingus *www.aerlingus.ie/*

Aeroflot Russian Airlines *www.aeroflot.org/*

Aerolineas Argentinas

Aeromexico

Aeropostale

Air Afrique

Air Botswana

Air France *www.airfrance.fr/*

Air India

Air Jamaica *www.airjamaica.com/*

Air Namibia

Air New Zealand *www.airnz.com*

Air Tanzania

Air Zimbabwe

Alitalia *www.alitalia.it/*

All Nippon *www.ana.co.jp/*

Atlantis Airways

Australia
Ansset Airways
Kendell Airlines
Guinea Airways
Qantas
Trans Australia Airlines

Austrian Airlines *www.aua.com/*

Avensa

Aviateca

British European Airways

British Midland *www.iflybritishmidland.com*

BOAC

British Airways *www.british-airways.com/*

BWIA International *www.bwee.com*

Cathay Pacific Airways

Cubana *www.cubana.cu/*

Deta Mocambique

Egyptair

El Al Israel *www.elal.co.il*

Finnair

Ghana Airways

Hamburg Airlines

Iberia *www.iberia.com/*

Icelandair *www.icelandair.com*

Indian Airlines Corporation

Iran Air

Japan Airlines *www.jal.co.jp/*

Kenya Airways

KLM *http://www.klm.nl/*

Korean Air

LAN Chile *www.lanchile.com/*

Lauda Air

Libyan Arab Airlines

Lufthansa *www.lufthansa.de/*

Malayasia

Malert-Hungarian A.T.

Mexicana *www.mexicana.com/*

National Airways Corporation

Nigera Airways

Nordair

Olympic Airways

Pakistan International

Philippine Air Lines

REAL Transportes Aereos

Royal Brunei

Sabena World Airlines

Saudia

Scanair

Singapore Airlines *www.singaporeair.com/*

TABA Amazonica

TACA International

Tasman Empire Airways

Thai Airways International *www.metrotel.co.uk/ travlog/thaiair.html*

Trans Canada Air Lines-Air Canada *www.aircanada.ca/*

Transport Flug

Ukraine

Varig *www.varig.com.br/*

Wideroe *www.wideroe.no*

Xiamen Airlines

Yemenia Airways *www.home.earthlink.net/~yemenair*

Zambia Airways

CHAPTER 15

Commercial Space Transportation

The Federal Aviation Administration's Associate Administrator for Commercial Space Transportation (AST) licenses and regulates U.S. commercial space launch activity as authorized by Executive Order 12465, *Commercial Expendable Launch Vehicle Activities,* and the *Commercial Space Launch Act of 1984,* as amended. AST's mission is to license and regulate commercial launch and reentry operations to protect public health and safety, the safety of property, and the national security and foreign policy interests of the United States. The *Commercial Space Launch Act of 1984* and the *1996 National Space Policy* also direct the FAA to encourage, facilitate, and promote commercial launches.

INTRODUCTION TO COMMERCIAL SPACE TRANSPORTATION

The term "commercial space transportation" refers to the launch (or reentry) of an object into (or from) space by a private sector, nongovernmental entity. Within the United States commercial space launches are conducted by corporations such as Boeing, Lockheed Martin, and Orbital Sciences using expendable launch vehicles (ELVs)[1] to place spacecraft into orbit. Worldwide, commercial launch services are currently offered by companies from six countries—the United States, Europe, Russia, China, Japan, and Ukraine.

A "commercial launch" may carry a commercial, civil, or military payload into space, but is considered commercial because the launch service is commercially procured by the payload owner. For example, some U.S. Government payloads are commercially procured by the Government while others are launched by the U.S. Air Force or the National Aeronautics and Space Administration (NASA) using the same rockets. The FAA licenses those launches within the United States that are commercially procured, including those for U.S. and foreign governments.

The FAA also regulates and licenses noncommercial launches conducted by private citizens within the United States, providing an exception for amateur rocket launch activities.

COMMERCIAL USE OF SPACE

Since the launch of Sputnik in 1957, the use of space and the launching of objects into space has largely been a government endeavor. Governments launched vehicles to deploy satellites for both civil and military purposes, and the business of launching space vehicles has been dominated by governments until only recently. Satellites serving commercial or quasi-commercial purposes, however, were first launched in the early 1960's, even though the business of launching them was strictly a government affair. Many of the early commercial satellites launched were telecommunications spacecraft located in geostationary orbit[2] (GEO) for video broadcasting and international telephony under the auspices

---

For current information go to the Website at: http://www.ast.faa.gov

[1] Expendable launch vehicles are used only once, with stages falling back to Earth or remaining in orbit after use.

[2] A spacecraft in geostationary orbit remains over the same spot on Earth, orbiting once every 24 hours, as does the Earth itself. GEO is a circular orbit at an altitude of 22,300 miles with a low inclination (i.e., over the equator).

of international governmental treaty organizations, such as Intelsat, the International Telecommunications Satellite Organization (formed in 1971).

Launches of satellites that serve commercial purposes have steadily increased since the early 1980's, and now represent about 40 to 45 percent of launches conducted worldwide annually. Until the last couple of years, commercial spacecraft were almost exclusively telecommunications satellites located in geostationary orbit. Now commercial spacecraft serve more diverse applications. In 1997, full-scale deployment began of the first low Earth orbit (LEO)[3] constellations for mobile communications. Commercial satellites also now include spacecraft for remote sensing. Commercial launch service providers have conducted test launches of their new vehicles, and while these launches did not deploy a satellite for a paying customer, they do represent non-government launch activity. Even flights to the Russian Mir space station have received financing from a private entity.

U.S. COMMERCIAL LAUNCH SERVICES

Up until the early 1980s, commercial spacecraft were launched on rockets owned and operated by the U.S. Government, including the Space Shuttle, and no other nation launched satellites for commercial entities. When Europe's Ariane began offering launch services for commercial satellites in 1983, an international launch market was created, and has since grown to over 15 vehicle families worldwide. Following the passage of the *Commercial Space Launch Act of 1984*, the U.S. Government and industry began to transition from government to commercial operations for expendable launch vehicles. The *Commercial Space Launch Act* authorized the Department of Transportation to regulate and license commercial launch activities.

Commercial launches licensed by the Department of Transportation (now by the FAA) actually began in 1989 after the U.S. Government decided to stop launching commercial payloads on the Space Shuttle following the *Challenger* explosion in 1986. A commercial launch licensed by the FAA, as distinct from a commercial satellite, can orbit satellites from commercial, non-profit, or government entities, as long as the launch was procured as a service through one of the U.S. commercial launch service providers. The U.S. government, through the Department of Defense and NASA, still launch some spacecraft through vehicle procurement contracts, as opposed to launch service contracts. Such launches are not licensed by the FAA. U.S. expendable launch vehicles vary in size and the companies licensed by the FAA to conduct launches are:

1. Lockheed Martin
   - Atlas 2 and 3 (intermediate class)
   - Athena 1 and 2 (small class)
2. Boeing
   - Delta 2 (medium class)
   - Delta 3 (intermediate class)
3. Sea Launch
   - Zenit 3SL (intermediate class)
4. Orbital Sciences
   - Pegasus and Taurus (small class)

U.S. commercial launches to GEO are launched from the Cape Canaveral Air Force Station (CCAFS) in Florida. Launches to LEO take place from the Cape, Vandenberg Air Force Base (VAFB) in California, or the Wallops Flight Facility in Virginia depending on the inclination of their intended orbit. (See Figure 15.1.)

The FAA has issued four launch site operator licenses to state-run organizations to operate commercial launch sites, or spaceports. They are:

1. Spaceport Florida, at Cape Canaveral Air Force Station, Florida
2. California Spaceport, at Vandenberg Air Force Base, California
3. Virginia Space Flight Center, at Wallop's Island, Virginia
4. Kodiak Launch Complex, Kodiak Island, Alaska, the first spaceport not located on a federal range (See Figure 15.2.)

REVIEW OF 2000

Commercial launch activity worldwide remained relatively steady in 2000 compared to recent years, despite the fallout over the Iridium and Orbcomm bankruptcies, and skepticism surrounding LEO constellations in general. This drop-off was averted due to launches

---

[3] Satellites in LEO do not remain above a fixed point on Earth; rather they orbit every 90 minutes to 12 hours, depending on their altitude. Non-geostationary orbits (NGSO) include medium Earth orbit (MEO) and elliptical orbits.

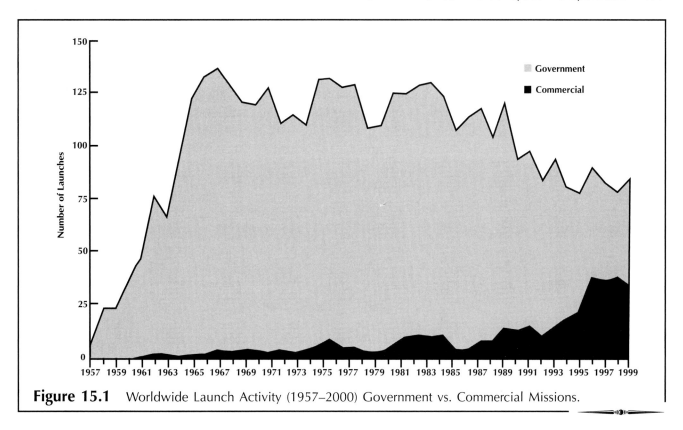

Figure 15.1   Worldwide Launch Activity (1957–2000) Government vs. Commercial Missions.

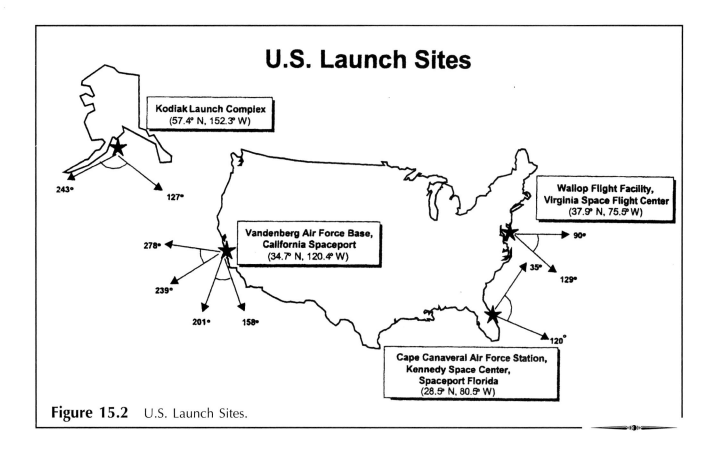

Figure 15.2   U.S. Launch Sites.

dedicated to new services such as direct radio broadcasting, commercial remote sensing, and even privately financed flights to Mir.

There were 35 commercial launches out of a total of 85 orbital flights in 2000, including two FAA-licensed launches for U.S. government customers. The figure represents just over 42 percent of total launches. Despite the continued robustness of the overall market, the number of FAA-licensed commercial launches fell in 2000, from 17 in 1999 to 10 in 2000. Seven of these launches were conducted for commercial customers, two for U.S. government payloads, and one was a test flight for Boeing's Delta 3.

Of the seven for commercial customers, three were conducted by the multinational Sea Launch partnership led by Boeing. Lockheed Martin's International Launch Services (ILS) successfully flew its first Atlas 3A launch vehicle, which featured an entirely new first stage using a Russian-built engine. ILS also deployed two GEO communications satellites on Atlas 2AS vehicles, Boeing successfully tested its Delta 3 vehicle to deploy a dummy payload, and deployed four Globalstar satellites to LEO using a Delta 2. Orbital Sciences Corporation deployed two small U.S. government satellites on two Pegasus vehicles. In addition to the seven licensed commercial launches conducted from U.S. ranges, there were 21 U.S. civil and military launches including the Space Shuttle.

Russian launch ranges deployed 13 vehicles for commercial missions, and Europe's Ariane vehicles flew 12 times. China did not launch any commercial payloads in 2000. Therefore, including the seven launches from U.S. ranges and the three flights for Sea Launch, a total of 35 commercial launches were conducted this year. (See Figure 15.3.)

COMMERCIAL SPACE TRANSPORTATION FORECASTS

In May 2000, the FAA and the Commercial Space Transportation Advisory Committee (COMSTAC) published their annual forecast for commercial launch demand. The forecast combined the *COMSTAC 2000 Commercial Geostationary Launch Demand Model* for satellites that operate in geosynchronous orbit with the FAA's 2000 Commercial Space Transportation Projections for Non-Geosynchronous Orbits (NGSO) *2000 Commercial Space Transportation Forecasts*.

The forecasts project an average of just over 41 commercial space launches annually worldwide through 2010. The business failures of NGSO systems accounted

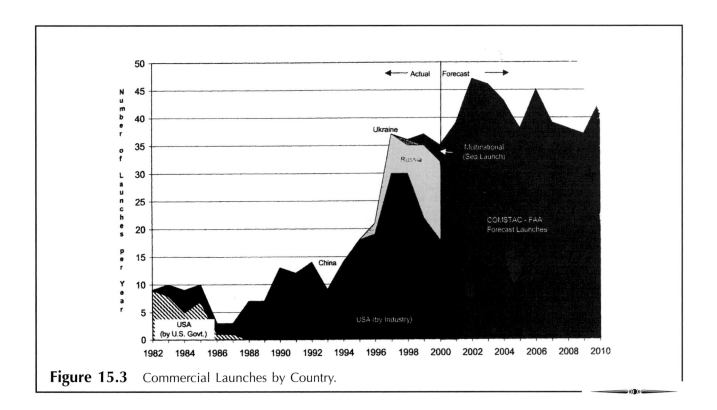

Figure 15.3 Commercial Launches by Country.

for the reduction from 51 annual launches projected in the 1999 forecast.

The forecasts projects an annual average of:

A. 23.5 launches of medium-to-heavy vehicles to deploy GEO communications satellites

B. 7.5 launches of medium-to-heavy vehicles to LEO or other NGSO orbits

C. 10.4 launches to LEO by small vehicles

These estimates account for dual-manifesting payloads, an important factor especially for NGSO launches.

The forecast is based on inputs from across the satellite and launch service industry and represents the demand for launch services for actual or projected satellite programs in a given year. This would be the peak load on the launch service providers if all projected satellite launches were conducted and is not a prediction of what will actually be launched in a given year.

Several factors can affect the execution of a scheduled launch including launch failures, launch vehicle components problems, or manifesting issues. Regulatory issues such as satellite export compliance or FCC licensing can come into play. Also, changes in business environment can cause satellite companies to reassess their priorities and alter their plans for deploying space assets. (See Figure 15.4.)

GENERAL TRENDS

The commercial space transportation market is driven largely by the demand for launches of telecommunications satellites, and therefore, developments in the industry over the next five years will parallel developments in satellite systems, including:

1. Continued strong demand for launch of GEO communications satellite systems and an increasing demand for remote sensing systems.

2. Lower than anticipated demand for LEO deployments due to business difficulties faced by first constellations.

3. An introduction of new larger launch vehicles to meet the demand for launches of heavier GEO spacecraft, including introduction of new U.S. vehicles, Delta 4 and Atlas 5.

4. Continued international competition for launch services by Europe, Russia, and China. Possible new entrants in the launch market from India, Israel, and Brazil.

5. Continued development of technologies and demonstrators for Reusable Launch Vehicles (RLVs). (See Figure 15.5.)

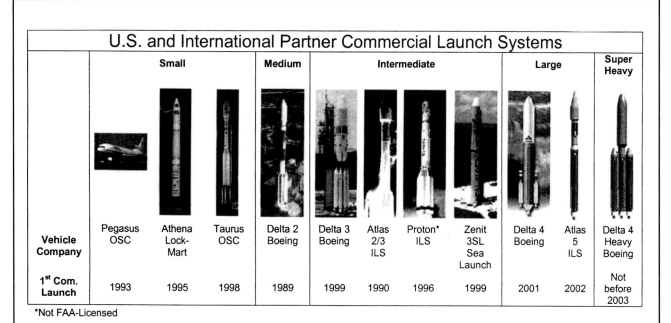

	U.S. and International Partner Commercial Launch Systems									Super Heavy
	Small			**Medium**	**Intermediate**				**Large**	
Vehicle Company	Pegasus OSC	Athena Lock-Mart	Taurus OSC	Delta 2 Boeing	Delta 3 Boeing	Atlas 2/3 ILS	Proton* ILS	Zenit 3SL Sea Launch	Delta 4 Boeing	Atlas 5 ILS	Delta 4 Heavy Boeing
1ˢᵗ Com. Launch	1993	1995	1998	1989	1999	1990	1996	1999	2001	2002	Not before 2003

*Not FAA-Licensed

Figure 15.4   U.S. and International Partner Commercial Launch Systems.

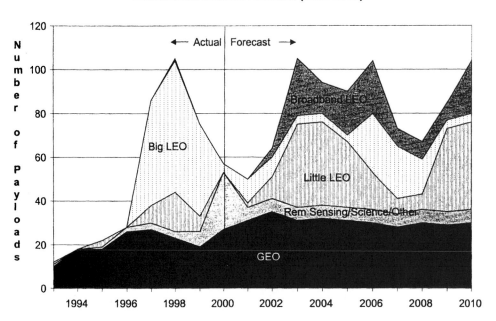

Commercial Satellite Forecast (1993-2010)

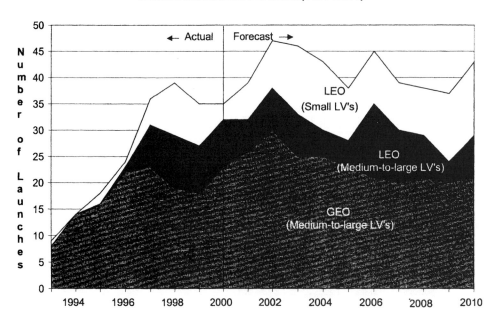

Commercial Launch Forecast (1993-2010)

Figure 15.5

PART 3

ADMINISTRATION
OF
AIR TRANSPORTATION

PART 3

BRIEF OVERVIEW OF CHAPTERS

16. AIR CARRIER MANAGEMENT AND ORGANIZATION

- Reviews application of management strategies and organization of air carrier functions.

17. AIR CARRIER MARKETING

- Explains "Marketing Mix" and its application to the air carrier industry and discusses the concept of supply and demand.

18. AIR CARRIER ACCOUNTING AND FINANCIAL STATUS

- Demonstrates accounting and reporting procedures required by the Federal Government and analysis of reports.

19. LEGAL ASPECTS OF AIR TRANSPORTATION

- Illustrates legalities of air transportation industry, particularly liability limits.
- Reviews the general Aviation Revitalization Act.

20. AVIATION INDUSTRY PERFORMANCE AND FORECASTS

- Analyzes performance activities of the aviation industry and presents forecasts for future aviation activities.
- Discusses air carrier traffic, route structure, and load factor.

CHAPTER 16

Air Carrier Management and Organization

Although charged with the responsibility of functioning in the public interest, and to a great extent having had its business activities regulated by the Federal Government, a certificated air carrier is, nonetheless, organized to be a profit-making enterprise.

Notwithstanding past government action, the success of an air carrier directly depends on the success of management. Most air carrier businesses will have good profits when the economic cycle is up and passenger loads are high. When the economy is good, managers can show profits in spite of less-than-acceptable management policies and control. The true test of good management comes when the economic cycle drops, when competition becomes intensified (either normally or induced), or when the general level of costs increase without a proportionate income increase by way of increased fares or traffic.

According to a major air carrier president:

There does not have to be an air carrier in the country that isn't making a profit; some have simply lost sight of the goals of free enterprise. The air industry's problem is in management. The companies that control costs can earn a profit and conversely, managements that do not concentrate on cost control effectively are the money losers.

An air carrier produces a product similar to a company manufacturing consumer goods for household use. The difference, of course, is that the manufacturing company produces a tangible product that the purchaser can see and touch and keep for future use. An air carrier produces an intangible product which is a service.

This service, like the services of a doctor, lawyer, or teacher, is not a physical object. The product of service of an air carrier is air transportation. Once the passenger has used the service purchased, it is gone, and all that is left to show for it is a receipted ticket and the fact that the individual is in a different place than before receipt of the product. This change of location was the reason for the purchase. This fact has to do with the economic theory of time and place utility.

Specifically, the production of an air carrier is an Available Seat Mile (or Ton Mile). This is one seat, flown one mile, in scheduled air transportation service. The sole purpose of all the air carrier equipment, facilities, and personnel is directed toward that end.

The sales or income of the air carrier occurs when this seat is filled with a fare-paying passenger. It then becomes a Revenue Passenger Mile. The relationship of what the air carrier sells, Revenue Passenger Miles (RPM), to what it produces, Available Seat Miles (ASM) is expressed in a percentage known as Load Factor.

$$LF = \frac{RPM}{ASM}$$

A measure of air carrier success can be taken by its load factors, including planned, actual, and break-even. Load factor is a most important guide for air carrier management. Unless it can keep its production (ASM) in balance with its sales (RPM), earnings will suffer.

Since efficient management is an absolute necessity to air carrier achievement, it is necessary to understand what is meant by management and what it does or is supposed to do. Philosophically, management is defined as the art and science of planning, organizing and controlling financial, human, and physical resources to attain a desired objective. Management is not only the collective group of those who conduct the affairs of an organization, but also the activities performed by that group. An air carrier, by definition in the Federal Aviation Act, Title I, Section 101-3, means any citizen of the U.S. who undertakes, whether directly or indirectly or by a lease or any other arrangement, to engage in air transportation. By combining the definition of management with that of an air carrier, the definition of Air Carrier Management is then [that group involved in] the art of science of planning, organizing, and controlling a company engaged in transporting the public by air for profit.

The traditional functions of management are to plan, organize, and control. The fundamental element in management is decision-making. Decisions are made by gathering the facts relating to the subject at hand, then studying those facts, and finally using this knowledge gained to reach a logical conclusion—the decision.

In the process of managing, established rules, laws, truths, and facts are used as guides, or tools of the trade. These are reliable and irrefutable and have been discovered throughout humankind's experience in business activity. They are known as Principles of Management. These principles are used in much the same way the scientists uses reliable principles, laws of physics, and mathematics.

Many principles of management have been established since the industrial revolution and the rise of big business. One of the earliest modern day contributors was Frederick W. Taylor, known as the "father of scientific management."

Not all principles of management are equally applicable to all commercial enterprises. Their use and degree of importance depend upon the nature of the particular product of the company.

PRINCIPLES OF AIR CARRIER MANAGEMENT

There are certain basic principles of management that are of particular importance to air carriers because of their producing an air transportation service. Some of these are discussed below:

- Fixed Responsibility
- Lines of Authority
- Lines of Communication
- Span of Control
- Organizational Structure
- Functionalization
- Flexibility

FIXED RESPONSIBILITY

Responsibility is the obligation to do a job; this principle fact includes being held accountable for the day-to-day successful operation of the company. Adequate maintenance and safety is not only a moral obligation to the flying public, but also an economic fact. Preventive maintenance is the air carrier policy rather than "replace when worn out."

All levels of management personnel, whether at the line or staff level, must possess a high degree of reliability. For example late departures play havoc with the entire scheduled operation of an air carrier. Flight delays sometimes are beyond the control of management. With proper planning and assumption of responsibility, delays may well be reduced.

Fixed responsibility means that each person must perform his job properly and at the necessary time. When a job is not completed adequately, the cause should be readily determined and steps taken to correct that cause and prevent it from reoccurring. Air carriers have traditionally had a high level of fixed responsibility due to the very nature of their operation. All pilots will attest to this; their lives and those of their crew and passengers depend not only upon their ability to accept an obligation to do their job properly, but also upon the entire work force who back them up.

LINES OF AUTHORITY

If responsibility is the obligation to do a job, then the right to get that job done is known as authority, which implies the right to command. Responsibility must always be coupled with corresponding authority. Fixed responsibility and authority must be assigned for each activity and job if a successful operation of the air carrier is to be achieved.

The exact extent of responsibility and authority must be clearly defined and understood by all personnel. Confusion results when this principle is violated. Certainly no one can be held accountable if he does not know exactly what is expected of him. A company handbook or organizational manual should be prepared showing an organization chart and explaining in detail the lines of responsibility and authority at all levels. Job descriptions should also be included.

Authority and responsibility fall into two general categories, formal and informal. Formal is depicted on the organization chart and refers to the positions in the plan of the company. Informal refers to the individuals assigned to the positions as a result of their experience, knowledge of the tasks involved, and ability to lead.

LINES OF COMMUNICATION

This principle is extremely important to air carriers because of the nature of their business activities. A manufacturing plant with all its activities and personnel under one roof, or in one location, will have less difficulty with this principle. The degree of complexity comes into focus when the extent of the air carrier's activities is considered. The air carrier's business is spread over its entire route structure which may extend worldwide. The movement of aircraft requires an efficient communication system. To keep pace with the increased demand for information, most major air carriers use electronic data processing systems to aid in scheduling maintenance on aircraft. Also, electronic reservation systems are used to speed and control the multitude of reservations that take place system-wide. This allows a passenger to be given immediate confirmation for a seat on a flight. Many years ago when reservations were practically hand processed it could take up to 24 hours for seat confirmations.

A successful air carrier must build and maintain a communication network that will supply information to all levels of authority. When decisions and policies are made, all personnel affected must be notified. Likewise, all levels must receive communication from those levels responsible to them. In this way they are receiving information to provide for better control and coordination. Communication works two ways: from the top of the company down through all levels to the work force, and upward in reverse order. Only in this manner can all levels be properly informed. The flow of communication must be kept simple and direct to be effective.

Economic losses can occur as a result of communication system breakdowns—for example, an error in the reservations for a flight reporting in full when in reality it is not. Much embarrassment, to say nothing of loss of revenue, takes place when the flight is ready for boarding and few passengers show up. It has been known to happen. Or perhaps when an aircraft has not been prepared for a flight due to a breakdown in communi-

cations, resulting in passengers waiting and no aircraft available to carry them.

Management control is closely dependent upon communication procedures and information systems.

SPAN OF CONTROL

This principle refers to limiting the number of subordinates that any one individual in the organization is required to supervise. There is a limit to the number of people an individual can supervise effectively. Although there is no fixed rule, five to seven subordinates reporting to a major supervisor is sufficient. Circumstances and the individual executive's abilities vary extensively.

> **Responsibility must always be coupled with corresponding authority.**

Supervision of too many persons will lead to trouble, if not confusion, since the supervisor will not have time or capacity, or both, to supervise any one subordinate adequately. The supervisor can become distracted by the large number of contacts required, and therefore may neglect more important matters. As the number of subordinates increases arithmetically, the number of relationships increases geometrically until a point is reached which is beyond the control of the supervisor. When this happens some subordinates tend to make their own decisions, sometimes out of necessity, and a total breakdown in the structure may soon result.

As the organization level descends from the president of the company to the supervisor level, the number of persons to be supervised can increase to ten to fourteen.

The senior executives control the activities of personnel having charge of more complicated and diverse functions. The supervisor or crew chief can handle more subordinates, because they are all usually in his immediate area within his sight. For example, a maintenance crew chief in charge of a turn-around inspection of an aircraft between flights, or the reservation supervisor whose telephone reservationists are located in one room. In both examples all workers are doing essentially the same job.

ORGANIZATIONAL STRUCTURE

Organization is the structural framework, depending upon the work to be done, of grouping the activities of the company according to their purposes for administration and control. It is a process of combining the work that groups and individuals have to perform to achieve maximum results. Organization is the formation of an efficient machine to operate effectively and attain the required objectives of the enterprise.

The traditional and oldest type of organizational structure is the Line organization. This is characterized by chain of command, direct lines of responsibility, authority, and communication. It best exists in very small firms.

The Staff organization is an extension to the Line. It provides specialized, advisory personnel whose job it is to advise the Line on matters of decision but not to command. The Line may or may not use the Staff advice accordingly as they see fit to. The Staff advises and the Line commands. The responsibility of the air carrier management is to keep the Line and Staff departments and functions in proper balance. All large enterprises are of the Line and Staff type of organization.

FUNCTIONALIZATION

Air carriers, due to their complex nature of business activity, have developed into the highest, or functional, type of organization structure. The functional type of organization provides for the staff to have authority over lower line personnel. However, this authority is only in the staff's area of speciality of function. Examples of air carrier functionalization follow.

Maintenance, inspection, and repair of aircraft is a detailed function. Before an air carrier can place a new type of aircraft into service it must submit, and have approved by the FAA, a complete maintenance manual. All maintenance on every part of the aircraft must be performed according to this manual of standard operating procedures. It is the responsibility of the engineering and maintenance staff members to prescribe, in detail, the exact manner that any aircraft component will be inspected and maintained as well as the criteria for its period of use and replacement. No matter where or when throughout the air carrier geographic system the job takes place, it will be done according to the procedure outlined by the staff. If difficulties arise or unusual questions are to be answered, it is the staff who are to be contacted for direction. Who does the job, and at what physical time, is the responsibility of the immediate Line organization. What and how the worker does his job is established by the Staff. When and where he does it is the responsibility of the Line.

Another example of air carrier functionalization appears in the accounting and reporting of financial and traffic statistical data. The Civil Aeronautics Board had established a detailed uniform system of accounting and reporting. The financial and traffic recording throughout the entire air carrier system is the responsibility of the finance department staff. Seeing to it that the job is done and information transmitted to the management is a line responsibility.

FLEXIBILITY

The ability to change is the broad definition of flexibility. As applied to management it provides for adjustment to varying levels of production.

The air carrier industry, in part due to its ever changing dynamic nature, must operate with a great degree of flexibility to provide for the ever occurring uncertainties. It is said that the only sure fact one can depend on, while employed by an air carrier, is that conditions will change constantly. This constant change makes the industry attractive to many people.

Technological flexibility is the change to new types of aircraft to produce a better service to the air traveling public.

> **The flow of communication must be kept simple and direct to be effective.**

Marketing flexibility exists when management policies of air carriers are able to vary the services offered to the public, such as new types of promotional flights, vacation plans, tours, and delayed and round trips. Air carrier management proves its worth when it can adjust to seasonal changes and business cycle changes without serious losses to its economy or efficiency.

Although flexibility means change, it does not mean change simply for the sake of changing. A balance between liberalism and conservatism is essential. There are those who, once they have found a good workable method, will not depart from it. Changing methods, policies, etc., are always occurring. The key to good management is knowing when to change in order to keep up with or exceed the competing air carriers.

Examples exist where an air carrier converted its entire fleet to a new untried type of aircraft. The aircraft, although sound in the safety sense, proved too costly to operate on the company's route structure; serious losses resulted. Another air carrier used the same type aircraft to its advantage, because it had a route structure to which the aircraft proved to be well adapted.

Some air carrier managements have taken the "wait and see" attitude by letting their competition break in a new type of aircraft, a new electronic reservation system, or a new approach to management-labor relations. If the "new" proves successful then they adopt it. The cost for this delay is relinquishing the advantage.

Some managements rush to the new equipment, techniques, or policies without adequate fact-gathering to substantiate their decision. This borders on speculation and, although profits may result, the odds are against this type of management success. However, the pressure of competition may force management to rapid decisions. Air carrier management is continuously faced with the question "to change or not to change"; and, if so, when?

CHARACTERISTICS OF AIR CARRIERS

All things have certain physical characteristics. Human beings, in addition, have certain mental characteristics which make for individual behavior patterns. Industries, like people, and different companies within an industry, have their own individual characteristics. To truly appreciate the service this industry performs is to understand the characteristics which influence its development, performance, and success.

In many respects, the airline business is no different from other businesses. The objective is to provide a service at a price that people are willing to pay and to keep costs below that price so that a profit can be made. However, recognizing certain characteristics of the airline business is essential to understanding the industry. Some of the more important characteristics of air transportation follow.

GOVERNMENT REGULATION

Perhaps no other industry in the United States has been more closely regulated than air transportation. Although the air carriers are privately owned financial corporations with public stockholders, they were not free to manage as they pleased.

The air transportation industry, very much like a public utility, exists in the public interest, to serve the public. In order for them to do so effectively the Federal Aviation Act, the aviation law of the land, provides for controls. The Civil Aeronautics Board was, and the F.A.A. remains, the federal agencies that exercised these controls.

The FAA controls all aspects of the safety of aircraft, their operation, maintenance, and flight crews. Before deregulation the CAB controlled all aspects of economics pertaining to the routes air carriers flew and the rates charged the public for being carried on those routes. To a lesser degree, other federal agencies and state and local governments regulate less obvious aspects of air carrier operations. The President of the United States has direct power over international routes.

It is interesting to note that while air carrier rates were regulated, air carrier costs were not, nor could they be. This usually resulted in costs rising faster than rates, resulting in a profit squeeze.

A SERVICE INDUSTRY

Air transportation is a service industry. The product of the air carrier is intangible, it is a service providing time and place utility. After receiving the service the passengers have no evidence of it other than being in a different location than where they started.

The air carrier produces for sale an available seat mile (one seat flown one mile). When the seat is occupied by a fare-paying passenger it becomes a revenue passenger mile (one passenger flown one mile). The airline product of an "available seat mile" is highly perishable, because once the flight has ended and the seat was not occupied by a paying passenger, it is lost forever. It cannot be put on a shelf or placed back in inventory to be used at a later time.

Because of all the equipment and facilities involved in air transportation, it is easy to lose sight of the fact that this is a service industry, not a manufacturing industry. Airlines perform a service for their customers, transporting them or their products, in the case of cargo, from one given point to another for an agreed price. In that sense, the airline business is similar to other service businesses like banks and insurance companies. There is no product given in return for the money paid by the customer, nor inventory created and stored for sale at some later date.

Capital Intensive

Unlike many service businesses, airlines need an enormous range of expensive equipment and facilities, from airplanes to flight simulators to maintenance hangars. It is a capital intensive business, meaning that large sums of money are required continually since all of an airline's equipment at some point needs to be replaced. Most equipment is financed through loans or the issuance of stock, rather than purchased outright. Increasingly, airlines are leasing equipment, including equipment they owned previously but sold to someone else and leased back. Whatever arrangements an airline chooses to pursue, its capital needs require consistent profitability over the long term.

High Cash Flow

Because large airlines own large fleets of expensive aircraft which depreciate in value over time, they typically generate a substantial positive cash flow (profits plus depreciation). Most airlines use their cash flow to repay debt or acquire new aircraft. When profits and cash flow decline, an airline's ability to repay debt and acquire new aircraft is jeopardized.

Labor Intensive

Airlines are labor intensive. Each major airline employs a virtual army of pilots, flight attendants, mechanics, baggage handlers, reservation agents, gate agents, security guards, cooks, cleaners, managers, accountants, lawyers, etc. Computers have enabled airlines to automate many tasks, but in a service business customers require, and often demand, a lot of personal attention. More than one-third of the revenue generated each day by the airlines goes to pay its workforce.

Highly Unionized

In part because of its long history as a regulated industry, the airlines are highly unionized and labor costs are among the highest of any industry. Prior to deregulation, air fares and freight rates were set on a cost plus basis, so unions were able to negotiate high rates of pay. Now, with unbridled competition and the appearance of low-cost competitors, many airlines are under pressure to lower their labor costs. Accomplishing that goal, however, is complicated by the ease with which competitors can move in on an airline's customers and markets when employees go on strike.

Thin Profit Margins

The bottom line result of all these characteristics is razor thin profits, even in the best of times. Airlines through the years have earned a net profit between 1 and 2.0% of revenue compared to an average of 5.0% for U.S. industry as a whole. To travelers, the cost of tickets sometimes looks high compared with the amount of money they spend on other goods and services. However, the cost of providing the transportation service they are getting is almost as high as the price they are paying. For the airlines, earning enough profit to satisfy stockholders and invest in the equipment and facilities needed for the future is a real challenge.

Seasonal

The airline business is very seasonal. The summer months are extremely busy as many people take vacations at that time of the year. Winter, on the other hand, is slow, with the exception of the Christmas holidays. The result of such peaks and valleys in travel patterns is that airline revenue also rises and falls significantly through the course of the year.

HIGHLY SENSITIVE DEMAND

Until recently business reasons accounted for the greatest demand for air travel. A recent survey indicated that business travelers continue to make the most repeat trips. However, among all air passengers, 61% now travel for pleasure or other personal reasons, while 26% travel for business, and 13% travel for both pleasure and business.

Like many industries, air transportation has high and low seasons of demand for services. Some months of the year have higher passenger demand than others; for instance, summer vacation months and the East Coast route to Florida following the Christmas/New Year season. One major air carrier does one-third of its yearly passenger volume business during the three summer months. An uneven demand exists certain weeks of the month as well as days of the week, with the weekend being the peak travel days. Hours throughout the day are also uneven in demand. The highest daily demand for air travel is in the early morning before 10:00 A.M. and in the late afternoon after 4:00 P.M.

Uneven demand creates cost problems. It is too costly to equip for high demand periods, then have personnel and aircraft idle during slack times.

Air transportation is a highly elastic demand. The volume of passengers is greatly affected by any moderate change in price or any service where price is involved. Lower fares will generate more traffic, while higher fares will discourage air travel. For this reason changes in fares are usually very slight. The advantages of air travel are greater than any small increase in price to the average air traveler.

HIGHLY COMPETITIVE INDUSTRY

The policy of the CAB was to provide competition between air carriers to produce improved air service to the public. An unprofitable condition will result if there are not enough passengers to support the air carriers serving a route. Competition will result with new routes, mergers of companies, interchange agreements, and the creation of new companies and new classes of air carriers.

Of the top leading domestic passenger markets, most now have competition by at least two air carriers.

When air fares were regulated, any change would affect all air carriers on the same route. Competition therefore was mainly in service to the passengers.

When an air carrier starts serving a route already being served by another air carrier, it must offer competitive schedules. An excessive capacity of available seats results, that is, more seats than passengers to fill them.

Alliances

Due to the intense competition in the air carrier industry, many executives are proposing marketing alliances in such areas as reservations, ticketing, and other areas. This, hopefully, will reduce costs and therefore satisfy customer demand for lower fares. Deregulation has proved that lower fares will fill seats. Since the air transport industry has a high fixed cost and a lower marginal cost structure, return on investment is low. Alliances are creative solutions in such situations.

A GROWTH INDUSTRY

Because of the population and industrial expansion of the United States, the annual increase in the Gross National Product, the yearly total of all goods and services produced, averages about 3.5% normally. The yearly growth rate for the air transport industry averages about 12%. The growth of air transportation has been phenomenal in the years since the industry had its beginning in 1925 with Ford TriMotor aircraft. Since 1925, especially since World War II, the assets of the industry have repeatedly doubled. A share of air carrier common stock, although not a noted yearly dividend earner, grows considerably in value. The air transport industry is a growth industry, in that its total investment has rapidly increased and will no doubt continue to do so.

SENSITIVE TO FLUCTUATION IN NATIONAL ECONOMY

Air transportation is not a vital consumer commodity such as food and shelter. The majority of air travelers today fly for pleasure reasons. Therefore, the air transportation industry is very susceptible to the ups and downs of the national economy. Both business and pleasure travel are reduced during periods of sustained downward trends in the general economy of the United States. In an economic recession people tend not to travel for pleasure and for business only when necessary.

During periods of national prosperity the airlines experience a high rate of traffic growth, in some cases as much as 18% or more a year.

The time between ordering a new aircraft and delivery ranges from three to five years. Air carriers place their orders for aircraft based upon their future planned capacity to handle the normal increase. If an economic recession should occur and these aircraft are delivered, then the companies find themselves with a substantial excess seating capacity. The delivery of new aircraft requires much lead time to allow the air carrier time to hire and train additional pilots, mechanics, flight attendants, ramp personnel, and other specialists required in their operation. The overall expansion of the economy of the nation will no doubt increase at an average rate notwithstanding the highs and lows experienced. The total result will be a continued average growth in airline expansion. A problem arises when average growth is not constant each year. In a period of a sluggish economy the growth rate of the air industry is decidedly cut back. A problem can also result in a period of unusually high national economy, when the growth rate is too great and the airline capacity cannot keep up with it. Either condition will cause a higher than normal cost of operation resulting in lower profits, or in some cases no profits or even losses.

> **Deregulation has proved that lower fares will fill seats.**

Forecasting the future economic condition of the country is a very difficult task; it approaches the impossible in air transportation. The Civil Aeronautics Board forecasted traffic growth and its estimates differed from those made by the FAA. These in turn differ from the forecasts of the Department of Transportation, the Air Transport Association, and the individual air carriers. It is the hope of the industry that the highs and the lows can be evened out more.

INTERDEPENDENCE OF FUNCTIONS

One unique characteristic of an air carrier is that all departments and every function are interrelated and dependent upon each other in much the same way that each link in a chain depends upon all the others. Each department, like each link, must carry its own responsibility and contribute its strength for the success of the entire operation. Every activity of an air carrier, from reservations to aircraft maintenance, is so interrelated that when one event occurs it has an effect on all other activities. This is one reason for the necessity of the high degree of coordination and control required and the functionalized organization structure. In few large industries is teamwork and "esprit de corps" so essential or evident.

GEOGRAPHIC DISTRIBUTION

This characteristic is associated with the subject of "centralization-decentralization." Centralization is practical when activities are located in one location or under one executive having responsibility for all activities of a specific type. Therefore all decisions, plans, policies, and orders emit from a central point. Centralization is used to advantage in purchasing materials and supplies. It results in savings and better prices by buying in quantities. Reservations is an example of centralized control. All stations selling seats on a given flight must coordinate through one central point. Flight operations is another activity that must be centralized for successful results. Certain air carrier activities must be centralized for planning, control, and general administration purposes. The system established may be generated centrally, but the accomplishment of the system is done wherever necessary.

Decentralization is somewhat a division of labor whereby decisions and functions are the responsibility of all levels where they occur. This reduces the amount of communication necessary with the headquarters. Decentralization prevents costly delays and stimulates initiative. It permits freedom for those in the field to concentrate on things where their greater "on the spot" knowledge can achieve faster action, better service, and lower costs. Decentralization aids in eliminating frustration of those in the field from having to go through headquarters for decisions they can best make locally. Good management will delegate responsibility to the field levels where significant contributions can be made.

OBSOLESCENCE AND TECHNOLOGICAL CHANGE

Because of the dynamic nature of air carriers resulting from their rapid growth, equipment and policies are in a constant state of going out of use. This applies to methods and techniques as well as to systems. A new model aircraft is just placed into operation when its successor is in the final stages of development. Too rapid a change is costly. Some turboprop aircraft were hardly introduced when jet aircraft were being delivered. Aircraft, from an operational standpoint, never wear out, because their parts are constantly being replaced. What does wear out is their usefulness in an economic sense.

The introduction of the jet age was a technologically revolutionary change. The methods of flying, servicing, and maintaining were radically new. So too were the new management systems the air carriers had to adopt. Those companies with less flexible managements were slower in adjusting to the changes and suffered higher costs and diminishing profits as a result. Many air carrier managements were replaced, and many reorganizations occurred during the introduction of, and adjustment to, the jet age.

The rate of technological progress has been extremely high in air transportation. This is typical of a rapidly expanding industry. The air traveling public benefits as air service continually improves. The improvement results in more, safer, faster, larger, and more comfortable aircraft. To make these technological advances the carriers have had to use a large amount of capital. For the past twenty years the air industry has led all other United States industries, including public utilities, manufacturing, and communications, in the rate of increase in capital spending.

Technological advancements have created a re-equipment cycle about every eight to ten years. In addition to the capital spending required for these cycles, high costs are incurred in the hiring, training, and re-training of personnel as well as for buildings and other facilities to accommodate and maintain the new aircraft. Generally, one year is the introductory period for a new model aircraft, and it is two to three years before the air carrier can realize the full cost benefits of the new equipment. The large air carriers are once again in a major re-equipment cycle with the wide-bodied jets, including the Boeing 757 and 767, McDonnell Douglas DC-10, MD-80, MD-11, and the Airbus 300 series.

NATURE OF COSTS

Costs fall into two general groups: fixed and variable. Fixed costs do not change for a given volume of production, such as the quantity of revenue passengers carried. Fixed costs are usually attributed to the rental and maintenance of land, buildings, hangars, and terminal space. Utilities, insurance and taxes are examples of fixed costs. Interest expense on loans and payments to bondholders are also included in fixed costs.

Variable costs vary directly with production; examples are labor and materials. Total costs are the sum of fixed and variable costs.

The best test of whether a cost is fixed or variable is to determine if it exists if the company is not in operation, as occurs when the company is closed because of a strike. If the cost continues it is fixed; if it does not exist then the cost is a variable.

Because of the large amount of investment in capital items, manufacturing industries tend to have a high fixed cost. Also, railroads, for the same reason, have a high fixed cost. This means that the major part of their total costs are of the fixed type. Since the major costs continue whether the train runs or not, the decision is made to run. The only added expense is the small amount of variable costs. The decision to operate the train is made if the expected income will cover the added variable cost. Any additional income above this can then be applied to the fixed cost. The result may be a total loss by running the train, but the loss would have been greater had the train not been run.

The economics of air carriers, in comparison with other types of transport industries and manufacturing, tend to have a relatively lower level of fixed costs because of lower capital investment. Conversely this means substantially higher variable costs. The decision to schedule a flight is predicated on its anticipated income. On scheduled flights all seats are available, but only about one-half are filled on a yearly average. Those seats not filled are wasted production. The costs of operating the flights are about the same regardless of how many seats are sold.

Part of the reason for the advantage of lower fixed costs is that airways' control, navigation aids, and airport facilities are generally provided at government expense or borne by the public through taxation.

The high speed of aircraft lessens the amount of capital equipment required than would otherwise be needed.

Constant costs are variable costs that do not change with the volume of passengers carried. In this sense it satisfies the definition of a fixed cost although it is not. Constant costs are variable costs and sometimes called fixed-variable.

An example of a constant cost is air crew salaries; they are not paid according to the number of passengers carried on their flight. Fuel costs and even depreciation costs are of the constant type. The cost of ticketing a passenger and placing him aboard a flight is the same regardless of the income generated by the price of the ticket he purchased. These are examples of variable costs which do not exist if there is no flight. However, they are practically unaffected once the flight departs. They are, in effect, a fixed type of variable costs which are constant costs.

Air carrier costs also can be looked upon from another standpoint. Common and separable costs are categories necessary for management control. Common costs are those that are common to the different types of air carrier income: passenger, mail and air cargo. The cost of a flight carrying these various sources of income cannot be applied separately to the income source. For example, the pilot's ability and salary for flying the aircraft cannot be proportionately applied to the income from passengers, mail, and air cargo.

Separable costs are those which can be applied to each type of income source. For example, the flight attendants' salaries as well as food service cost is attributed to passenger income only. The same is true in cargo handling costs attributed directly to air cargo income.

The economic future of the air transportation industry depends on its achieving financial and economic stability. This does not necessarily mean a constant rate of return on investment, or the same rate for each individual company. It does, however, mean an adequate rate of return over a period of years.

Due to its high technological change and sensitivity to general economic conditions, the air transportation industry has erratic economic business cycles. These swings to highs and lows will even out as the industry further matures. The industry will have to make adequate profits in good years in order to offset years of poor earnings.

MANAGERIAL ECONOMICS

The subject of **economics** is a social science concerned chiefly with the description and analysis of the production, distribution and consumption of goods and services. Basically it deals with the flow of money. **Econometrics** is the application of statistical methods to the study of economic data and problem solving. Within the subject of economics there are two major areas involved. The first is that of **macroeconomics**, which has to do with the entire industry. **Microeconomics** has to do with a study of one individual company in that industry. The application of statistical analyses can be extremely helpful in formulating decisions and problem solving.

The administration of an air carrier may use microeconomics as a management tool in making decisions concerning such things as the price to charge passengers for a given flight and the quantity of available seat miles. The application is also known as **managerial economics**.

Presented below is a precise distillation of this vast subject into practical use. The basic cost data is obtained from the accounting department and entered on a table. Upon completion of the table certain columns of numbers are used to construct curves on a grid or graph paper. The places where the curves intersect will show important facts.

TABLE PREPARATION

Observe Table 16.1, while relating to the following: There are a total of 13 columns on the table.

Column 1, *Quantity*—represents the amount of production. Numbers 1 to 14 are used for simplicity. They represent the amount of seat miles or numbers of passengers. They represent hundreds, thousands, millions or billions.

Column 2, *Total Fixed Costs*—obtained from accounting records.

Column 3, *Average Fixed Costs*—obtained by dividing total fixed costs by the quantity. (Column 2 divided by column 1)

Column 4, *Total Variable Costs*—obtained from accounting records.

Column 5, *Average Variable Costs*—obtained by dividing total variable costs by the quantity. (Column 4 divided by column 1)

Column 6, *Total costs*—obtained by adding total fixed costs and total variable costs. (Column 2 plus column 4)

Column 7, *Average Total Costs*—obtained by dividing total costs by the quantity. (Column 6 divided by column 1)

Column 8, *Marginal Costs*—are the incremental changes from one total cost to the next total cost below it. For example: 2, 4, 7, 11 are total costs. The difference between 2 and 4 is 2; between 4 and 7 is 3; between 7 and 11 is 4. Therefore marginal costs are 2, 3 and 4.

Column 9, *Price* (demand), also *Average Revenue*—The suggested price is established by management. It may well be changed after the curves are drawn.

Column 10, *Total Revenue*—Price multiplied by the quantity. (Column 9 multiplied by column 1)

Column 11, *Marginal Revenue*—the incremental change from one total revenue to the next total revenue below it. When the price column is constant for every quantity then marginal revenue will be the same as the price column.

Column 12, *Marginal Profit or Loss*—subtract marginal costs from marginal revenue. (Column 11 minus column 8)

Column 13, *Total Profit or Loss*—subtract total costs from total revenue. (Column 10 minus column 6)

Table 16.1   Sample Table

1	2	3	4	5	6	7	8	9	10	11	12	13
Quantity	Total Fixed Costs	Average Fixed Costs	Total Variable Costs	Average Variable Costs	Total Costs	Average Total Costs	Marginal Costs	Price-Average Revenue	Total Revenue	Marginal Revenue	Marginal Profit or Loss	Total Profit or Loss
1	$100.00	$100.00	$50.00	$50.00	$150.00	$150.00		$40.00	$40.00	$40.00		–$110.00
2	100.00	50.00	80.00	40.00	180.00	90.00	$30.00	40.00	80.00	40.00	$10.00	–100.00
3	100.00	33.33	105.00	35.00	205.00	68.33	25.00	40.00	120.00	40.00	15.00	–85.00
4	100.00	25.00	127.00	31.75	227.00	56.75	22.00	40.00	160.00	40.00	18.00	–67.00
5	100.00	20.00	148.00	29.60	248.00	49.60	21.00	40.00	200.00	40.00	19.00	–48.00
6	100.00	16.67	168.00	28.00	268.00	44.67	20.00	40.00	240.00	40.00	20.00	–28.00
7	100.00	14.29	188.00	26.86	288.00	41.14	20.00	40.00	280.00	40.00	20.00	–8.00
8	100.00	12.50	210.00	26.25	310.00	38.75	22.00	40.00	320.00	40.00	18.00	10.00
9	100.00	11.11	240.00	26.67	340.00	37.78	30.00	40.00	360.00	40.00	10.00	20.00
10	100.00	10.00	285.00	28.50	385.00	38.50	45.00	40.00	400.00	40.00	–5.00	15.00
11	100.00	9.09	350.00	31.82	450.00	40.91	65.00	40.00	440.00	40.00	–25.00	–10.00
12	100.00	8.33	440.00	36.67	540.00	45.00	90.00	40.00	480.00	40.00	–50.00	–60.00
13	100.00	7.69	559.00	43.00	659.00	50.69	119.00	40.00	520.00	40.00	–79.00	–139.00
14	100.00	7.14	700.00	50.00	800.00	57.14	141.00	40.00	560.00	40.00	–101.00	–240.00

GRAPH CONSTRUCTION

The next step after completing the table is to use selected columns on it to construct the various curves on the graph paper. The proper columns to use for this purpose are as follows:

Average Fixed Costs
Average Variable Costs
Average Total Costs
Marginal Costs
Price (Average Revenue)
Marginal Revenue—(same as Price)

Completing the table and the graph sheet may be difficult at first but with care and patience they can be done quite easily.

The left side of the graph is the 'X' axis and represents dollars. The bottom of the graph is the 'Y' axis and represents the quantity of production. See Figure 16.1.

After the necessary curves are completed, their resulting locations and intersections are the subject of interest for analysis.

There are two places where the average total cost curve intersects with marginal revenue (price). These are the lower and upper break-even points. To the left of the lower intersection the company was operating at a loss. Profit will continue until the place where they intersect for the second time at the upper break-even point. The distance between the two is the profit range. In this area profit increases to a maximum and then decreases.

The intersection of marginal costs and the marginal revenue (price) is the quantity of maximum efficiency. This is the quantity that will result in the most profit. Although total profit will continue beyond this point, average total costs are increasing at a greater amount than marginal revenue (price). This continues until the upper break-even point is reached where losses will again occur. At all intersecting places the quantity of production can be indicated by extending a line from the intersection to the 'Y' axis at the bottom of the graph to determine the quantity number.

As quantity of production increases it becomes obvious that marginal costs increase at a skyrocketing rate while marginal revenue (price) increases at a constant amount.

ANALYSIS

Various price lines (marginal revenue) can be inserted on the completed graph for a 'what if' situation. Each new price (marginal revenue) will present different break-even locations.

On the graph, Figure 16.1, a second price line of $45.00 is indicated by the line marked P2. The change in price will create changes on the table of columns 9 through 13. With the new price change to $45.00 the lower break-even quantity is now 5.8 while the lower break-even point at the $40.00 price was quantity 7.5. The same conditions of change will exist for the upper break-even locations. From a quantity of 10.3 at the $40.00 price to a quantity of 12 at the $45.00 price.

The average fixed costs, the average variable costs and the average total cost for any given quantity can be determined from the graph by drawing a line from the cost to the quantity 'y' axis on the bottom of the graph.

The air transport industry, in comparison to other transport and manufacturing industries, tends to have a relatively lower level of fixed costs. Therefore, it has substantially higher variable costs. This means that if the company does not even fly its aircraft, fixed costs are still being incurred. If it does fly, variable costs are generated. Obviously, to be profitable, the income must be more than the total cost consisting of the fixed costs added to the variable costs. In a highly competitive market, such as the air transport industry, price is important but knowledge of costs is critical.

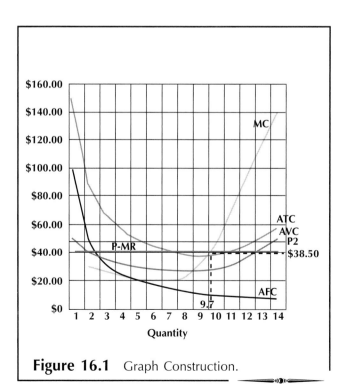

Figure 16.1 Graph Construction.

If competition on a given route forces a lower price, management must decide how low the price can go before they must cease flying the route. This can be determined by using the graph. Fixed costs exist if the flight does not take place. When the decision is made to fly, variable costs are added. The decision to fly or not can be determined if the income will at least cover the variable cost even if a total loss will result. But—and this is most important to understand—if the income is enough to cover the variable costs, any added income will contribute to the fixed costs. Less money will be lost if the decision is made to fly than if the flight did not take place. There is a play on words that says "when is it profitable to operate at a loss?" The answer is—when income is sufficient to cover the variable costs and any additional income can be applied to the fixed costs. In plain words—income must at least be enough to pay the variable costs when the decision is made to make the flight. Any more income will help pay towards the fixed costs. A total loss will result but—(important again)—if the flight was not made then a greater loss would exist. Therefore it becomes "profitable to operate at a loss." (Again, a play on words.) Of course, this situation cannot go on for too long a time. If a good air carrier management has control of its costs, it will be able to stay in operation when its competitor has a higher cost condition. The first company can operate until its competitor is forced to stop. Then, after a short time, the company can raise its price to a point where it will cover all costs and result in a total profit.

This scenario is constant throughout the air carrier industry. It is not a matter of the strongest who survives, but the smartest who knows the application of econometrics. The use of the above exercise of using the graph will result in profitable decisions. Those managements that do not, unfortunately, will cease to exist.

So, back to our basic example. At the $40.00 price, what is the lowest price that can be allowed before it becomes necessary to cease operations? The answer is simple. Look at the graph and locate the lowest point on the average variable cost curve. Read the quantity on the 'Y' axis and the price on the dollar axis. It will be seen that a quantity of 8 at a price of $26.25 is the lowest price that the air carrier can afford to fly. This price can also be seen on the table at quantity 8. If even one dollar more income occurs, then it can be applied to the fixed costs.

Table 16.2 can be completed from information on the graph. It summarizes all that has been discussed. The two prices of $40.00 and $45.00 are used. In the third column enter a different price between $30.00 and

Table 16.2   Data Obtained from the Graph

1	Price (average revenue per unit)	$40.00	$45.00
2	Quantity (most profit or least profit)	9.7	10
3	Cost per unit	$38.50	$40.00
4	Profit (or loss) per unit (1 − 3)	$1.50	$5.00
5	Total revenue (1 × 2)	$388.00	$450.00
6	Total cost (2 × 3)	$373.45	$400.00
7	Total profit (or loss) (2 × 4)	$14.55	$50.00
8	Profit margin (7 ÷ 5)	3.75	11.1
9	Lower breakeven quantity	7.5	5.8
10	Upper breakeven quantity	10.3	12
11	Profit range	2.8	6.2
12	Lowest competitive price	$26.25	$26.25
13	Lowest competitive quantity	8	8

$50.00. Then complete the blank column by determining the numbers from the graph.

This exercise is only one example of the use of the graph. For further interest it is suggested you refer to books on the subject that delve into it at greater length than is available here.

For practice, use the table and redo it by using different prices. On the graph try entering the different price lines and see their effect on quantity. Try constructing a new table using different cost data. Evaluate the circumstances and how they would affect decisions concerning the quantity to operate.

AIR CARRIER ORGANIZATION

The manner in which an air carrier produces its air transport service is by its organization. Organization can be defined as a structure. Buildings are physical structures in which activities take place. Likewise the human skeleton is a basic structure by means of which the human body can move about. Organization is the structure by which management can achieve its objectives. Industries and companies within an industry have different structures, just as people are physically different from each other.

Air carriers, due to their producing an air transport service, have certain common organizational structures. Air carrier organizations, though basically the same, will vary from one company to another. This is due to several reasons, namely: historical growth, the influence of strong administrators, the classification of air carriers (see Chapter 11), their route structures (domestic as opposed to international or local service, for example), as well as the size of the company.

The formal organization of a company is depicted by its organization chart. This chart shows the line of authority, chain of command, and relationship of functions, among other things.

Regardless of their differences they all bear a family resemblance. Since they are producing an air transport service they would, of necessity, have a commonality. This commonality appears in both their line and staff department structure. The staff advisory and specialized department functions are indirectly related to the production and sale of air transport services. Beyond the staff departments are the line departments whose activities are directed toward the sale and delivery of air transportation.

That group of air carrier line departments having the responsibility of attracting, selling, and placing the air passenger in the aircraft is known as Marketing.

Those line departments responsible for delivering the product to the passenger, or seeing to it that he gets what he purchased, are known as the Operations.

The purpose of the chart in Figure 16.2 is to describe the general functions of the various departments that constitute an air carrier. It would be of little value and very confusing to describe any particular, or all air carrier organizations as they now exist. For this reason the organization chart presented is a composite of a typical, average air carrier. The titles used for the department names reflect the functions they perform. Actual company department names are not standardized and will be somewhat different from one air carrier to another. Actual department names are constantly changing due to the continuing reorganization that takes place. If the functions performed by the departments are understood, then any actual air carrier organization chart will appear familiar and their activities recognizable.

Air carriers are private, profit-making organizations. They are owned by the stockholders those ownership represents equity. As in all large corporations,

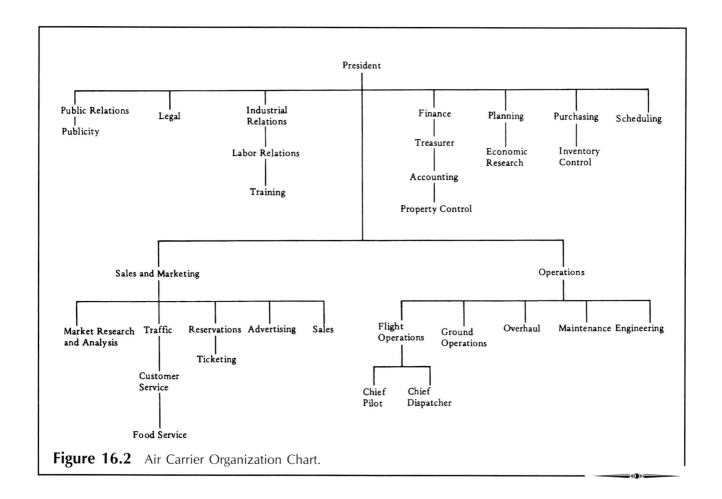

Figure 16.2 Air Carrier Organization Chart.

the stockholders elect a Board of Directors who designate one of their members as chairman. The Board's main policy is to establish major objectives and goals for the company.

The Board employs the top administrative officer who is the president. It is his function to set major policies, make final decisions, and to be ultimately responsible for the success of the company. The president must answer to the Board for his actions and that of all levels of the organization.

The president is aided in carrying out his responsibility by several vice presidents who are in charge of major areas. Some areas are more complex and larger in size than others and carry the higher rank of executive or senior vice president.

The typical air carrier is a functionalized line and staff organization. It has several staff departments separated according to the function the department performs.

The line section of the air carriers is usually divided into two main divisions, although others of lesser importance may be established according to circumstances and individual company requirement. The lower levels of the line are spread throughout the air carrier's entire geographic route structure. Each line and staff department will have many subdepartments and branches.

STAFF DEPARTMENTS

Staff departments are not only responsible for their particular areas of specialization but they also act in an advisory capacity to the policy-making administrative executives. These include specialists in such fields as law, accounting, finance, employee relations, and public relations. Their function is to support the work of line personnel so that the airline runs efficiently and earns a profit. For the most part, staff personnel work out of corporate headquarters and fall into seven broad job categories typical of major corporations.

PUBLIC RELATIONS DEPARTMENT

This department endeavors to interpret company policies to the general public, to government agencies, and to the air carrier employees. Also, it is this department's job to present to the public the good image of the company. It is not paid advertising. This department is in continuous contact with the news media and supplies newspapers and television with photographs and news items. Whenever a very important person (VIP) is an airline passenger, photos are taken which

are submitted to the press. These photos will show the air carrier's name very inconspicuously somewhere in the background.

Some large air carriers have developed their public relations department to the extent of providing community services of many kinds. A few companies have developed large information centers which publish guide books and other sources of educational materials including extensive audiovisual aids. This department welcomes public groups to tour their facilities to learn about the workings of an air carrier. Public speakers are supplied to address civic groups on many subjects, usually relating to air transportation in some way.

LEGAL DEPARTMENT

All companies in the business today need advice and help in legal matters. The air carrier industry, unlike many other large industries, has a multiplicity of Federal, State, and local statutes, laws and regulations in addition to the economic and safety regulations to which they must unfalteringly adhere. Contracts of all types need the benefit of expert legal assistance.

Much of the responsibility for dealing with the public and other government agencies rests with the general counsel who heads this department. The legal department represents the company regarding legal actions, claims, and suits both for and against the company. The department processed economic cases before the Civil Aeronautics Board for the company when such actions were required.

INDUSTRIAL RELATIONS DEPARTMENT

This function is the company's internal dealings with its employees. Included are recruiting, interviewing, hiring, training, and placing new employees; wage and salary administration; and employee services. Complete records and files are kept on all employees showing their history of performance with the company. Raises, advancements, and promotions are compiled from these historical records.

Dealing with unions in labor relations is a very important part of this department, from hearing grievances to negotiating labor union contracts and complying with government labor laws. In these matters the legal department works in close relationship with this department.

Athletic teams and interdepartment sports competition are often established by this department to generate employee morale.

FINANCE DEPARTMENT

The control of the company's money is the basic responsibility of this department. Included are budget formulation and control, the accounting and record keeping function, insurance, taxes, and property control.

PLANNING DEPARTMENT

To research and develop plans for the future operation of the company is the entire description of this department's function. This department assists the legal department in preparing exhibits for presentation to the Civil Aeronautics Board in economic proceedings. Formulation of statistical data for management needs in decision making is a part of this department's work.

PURCHASING DEPARTMENT

The procuring of materials and supplies necessary to keep the company in operation is an important function resting in this department. Some specific responsibilities include:

- Processing purchase requisitions
- Maintaining a file of vendors or suppliers
- Material specification formulation
- Shipping and receiving
- Inventory control
- Issuance of purchase orders

SCHEDULING DEPARTMENT

This department is found in almost any position in the company organization. In a larger air carrier it should be a separate staff function if only to allow it independence, thus freedom pressures of line departments. Scheduling flights is not a simple matter when consideration must be given to traffic needs, competition from other air carriers, flight crews, and maintenance and overhaul of aircraft.

Scheduling is always a matter of compromise; never can there be an ideal, perfect schedule which satisfies all demands, yet this must be the objective of this department.

LINE DEPARTMENTS

These include everyone directly involved in producing or selling an airline's services—the mechanics who maintain the planes, the pilots who fly them, the flight attendants who serve passengers and perform various in-flight safety functions, the reservation clerks, airport check-in and gate personnel who book and process the passengers, baggage handlers, security guards, etc. Line personnel fall into three broad categories: engineering and maintenance, flight operations, and sales and marketing. These three divisions form the heart of an airline and generally account for 85% of an airline's employees.

SALES AND MARKETING

This division encompasses such activities as pricing, scheduling, advertising, ticket and cargo sales, reservations, and customer service, including food service. While all of them are important, pricing and scheduling in particular can make or break an airline, and both have become more complicated since deregulation. Airline prices change daily in response to supply and demand and to changes in the prices of competitors. Schedules change less often, but far more often than they used to when the government regulated the industry. Airlines use sophisticated computer reservation systems to advertise their own fares and schedules to travel agents and to keep track of the fares and schedules of competitors. Travel agents, who sell the majority of all airline tickets, use the same systems to book reservations and print tickets for travelers.

MARKET RESEARCH AND ANALYSIS DEPARTMENT

This department's responsibility includes determining what the customers want and what they will buy by seeking out methods of expanding current markets of users of air service and of expanding into new markets for air service. This department should have a complete description of the company's customers available for management use, accumulated by an analysis of those who purchased the air carrier's product.

A major source of information is a short questionnaire to determine such facts as the frequency of flights made by passengers, the reason for the flight, and information concerning service and rates. Surveys are made for the following objectives:

- To measure the characteristics of the passenger
- To ascertain the group structure of air travelers
- To learn the preferences of air travelers
- To gain a basis for estimating the response to changes in rates

TRAFFIC DEPARTMENT

This department's responsibility is servicing the passengers and seeing to their needs. Food service and baggage handling are a large part of this department's function.

RESERVATIONS DEPARTMENT

This department's responsibility is that of maintaining the complicated system necessary to see to it that all space on the aircraft scheduled for flight is properly controlled. The ticketing function is the act of consummating the sale to the customer.

ADVERTISING DEPARTMENT

Large air carriers maintain their own advertising departments, while smaller companies find it economically feasible to contract this function to independent advertising agencies. The large air carriers sometimes conduct their own commercial art, drawing, and print shops.

Advertising is the function of deliberately presenting the company's product before the public. This is done by the purchase of newspaper, magazine, radio, and television services.

SALES DEPARTMENT

This department's principal responsibility is to obtain customers to purchase the company's product— air service. Large air carriers divide this department into several levels of subdepartments specializing in contacting and selling in the areas of passengers, conventions, charter, cargo, military, mail, interline, etc.

OPERATIONS

The Operation function is carried out by several departments, some of which are presented here.

FLIGHT OPERATIONS DEPARTMENT

Flight operation is responsible for operating the airline's fleet of aircraft safely and efficiently. It schedules the aircraft and flight crews to meet the scheduling needs of the marketing division, and it develops and administers all policies and procedures necessary to maintain safety and meet all FAA operating requirements. It is in charge of all flight crew training, both initial and recurrent training for pilots and flight attendants, and it establishes the procedures crews are to follow before, during, and after each flight to ensure safety.

Dispatchers are part of flight operations. Their job is to clear flights for take-off following a review of all factors affecting a flight. These include the weather, routes the flight may follow, fuel requirements, and both the amount and distribution of weight on board the aircraft. Weight must be distributed evenly aboard an aircraft for it to fly safely.

This department is responsible for all matters affecting the piloting and controlling of all the air carrier's flights. It is usually divided into two subdepartments having equal responsibility. They are the offices of chief pilot and chief dispatcher. An illustration of equal responsibility is that usually before a scheduled flight takes off, the pilot in command of the flight and the dispatcher on duty must equally agree upon the disposition and plan for the flight. They are held equally responsible for the safe conduct and conclusion of the flight.

While the plane is in the air, the dispatcher is in constant radio contact with the pilot from the dispatch center on the ground. The dispatcher's job is to notify and assist the pilot on matters pertaining to the flight. The information includes fuel load and rate of consumption, weather conditions, reporting over check points, flight time, and other important matters.

GROUND OPERATIONS DEPARTMENT

This department is responsible for all activities that take place on the airport location assigned to the company. Included are the administration of stations, maintenance of aircraft other than at the home airport, servicing aircraft for flight, and operation of ground communication systems.

OVERHAUL DEPARTMENT

This department is responsible for the major replacement of parts and components which compose the aircraft structure.

No longer is the aircraft taken out of service for an extended period of time during which its expense continues while it is producing no income. A system known as "block overhaul" is now used. In this system the aircraft is under continuous overhaul. During the hours between flights certain planned replacements of parts takes place.

It is surprising how efficient overhaul mechanics are in completely stripping an aircraft to the point where one would believe it could not be put back together, and have it accomplished and ready for flight in an unbelievably short period of time.

MAINTENANCE DEPARTMENT

Much credit must be given to the air carrier rank and file personnel who quite literally "keep them flying."

Maintenance is the hourly and daily care of the aircraft, its equipment, and all its parts. No sooner have the aircraft wheels stopped and the engines wound down than the line maintenance crew are at work servicing and inspecting the aircraft in preparation for its next flight. Safety is not accidental; accidents are caused, they do not just happen. An interruption of a scheduled air carrier flight today is almost nonexistent, attesting to the high technological state of the art of aircraft construction and maintenance.

Maintenance accounts for approximately 10% of an airline's employees and 10–15% of its operating expenses. Its mission is to keep aircraft in safe, working order, ensure passenger comfort, preserve the airline's most valuable physical assets (its aircraft), and ensure maximum utilization of those assets by keeping planes in the condition they need to be in to keep flying. An airplane costs its owner money every minute of every day, but makes money only when it is flying with freight or passengers aboard. It therefore is vital to an airline's financial success that aircraft are properly maintained to avoid extensive downtime for repairs stemming from neglect.

Airlines typically have one facility for major maintenance work and aircraft modifications. It is called the "maintenance base." Smaller, slightly less sophisticated facilities are maintained at an airline's hubs or primary airports where aircraft are likely to be parked overnight. Usually called "major maintenance stations," these facilities perform the lion's share of routine maintenance and stock a large supply of spare parts.

A third level of inspection and repair capability is maintained at airports where a carrier has extensive operations, although less so that at its hubs. These maintenance facilities simply are called "maintenance stations."

ENGINEERING DEPARTMENT

This department is concerned with the improvement of the use of aircraft. They continually study records, methods, and parts to find a "better way." Some of the several areas involved in engineering include electrical, hydraulic, pneumatic, fuel, control, and communication. Standard operating procedures for flight, maintenance, and overhaul are determined by the engineering department.

SUBCONTRACTORS

While major airlines typically do most of their own work, it is common for them to farm out certain tasks to other companies. These tasks would include aircraft cleaning, fueling, airport security, food service, and some maintenance work. Airlines might contract out for all of this work or just some of it, keeping the jobs in house at their hubs and other key stations. However, whether an airline does the work itself or relies on outside vendors, the carrier remains responsible for meeting all federal safety standards where they apply.

SUMMARY

The Airline Deregulation Act of 1978 has caused restructuring and reorganization of most of the air carriers. Since air transportation is such a dynamic industry, this has happened many times in the past and will, no doubt, continue to occur in the future.

CHAPTER 17

Air Carrier Marketing

To satisfy the public need for air transportation services, while doing so at a profit, is the reason for the existence of the air carrier industry. This can be accomplished by acceptable marketing practices.

In the study of the application of marketing principles to the air carrier industry there are three questions that need to be answered to create an understanding of the subject.

- What is air carrier marketing?

- Exactly what does it do?

- How does it do it?

DEFINITION OF AIR CARRIER MARKETING

Perhaps the most simplified definition is that marketing is the process of getting the product of the air carrier, a transportation service, to the consumer of such service—passenger or shipper. Marketing directs the flow of air transport services from the producer, the air carrier, to satisfy the needs of the air transportation consumer. The further objectives of the company must be met; the most important of which is profit.

Air carrier marketing is an organized system of activities by which the air carrier services are matched with the markets of users. The marketing concept is that air carriers exist to satisfy market requirements and to do so at a profit. The market is the potential demand for services, that is, markets are people with purchasing power. The term 'market' refers to a place, actual or hypothetical, where buyers and sellers exchange goods and services.

Air carriers provide four basic economic utilities to satisfy the public need.

- Form—producing an air transportation service which is an available seat (or cargo space).

- Time—having the service of an available seat when the passenger wants it.

- Place—having the seats to take the passengers where they want to go.

- Possession—a system of selling the seat to the passenger and delivering the desired transportation.

Successful air carrier marketing is getting the service (form utility) of air transportation to passengers or cargo user, when (time utility) they need it to carry them or their cargo, where (place utility) they want to go at a price of which they can avail themselves (possession utility).

Air carrier marketing can be defined as activities performed as well as a social process. More specifically, airline marketing is micro-marketing those activities which anticipate passenger needs and provide services to satisfy those needs. This is an integral part of the total air carrier economic system.

FUNCTIONS OF AIR CARRIER MARKETING

The purpose of the functions of air carrier marketing is to give the passenger or shipper the:

- right product or service
- at the right place where it is needed
- at the right price
- at the right time that it is wanted

The successful air carrier must design a total marketing system which satisfies consumer needs and is market oriented according to modern marketing concepts.

ACTIVITIES OF AIR CARRIER MARKETING

The 'market strategy' includes the selection of a product or service and a target group to whom the service is offered; then development of a mixture of marketing factors to accomplish the objective.

Strategy is a planned action to achieve a predetermined objective. Strategy is the skill in planning, organizing and controlling facilities to obtain the best results and/or to gain the most advantageous position. Market strategy is the process of using the Marketing Mix, which is a mixture of several factors.

Marketing strategy is developed by selecting a target group; a group of consumers that the air carrier wants to buy its service, and then creating a Marketing Mix. The Marketing Mix determines how marketing accomplishes its task.

THE MARKETING MIX

The Marketing Mix refers to the use of certain variables referred to as the four P's which are controlled by the management of the air carrier.

- Product—To satisfy the target group.
- Place—Getting the product to the target group.
- Promotion—Telling the target group about the product.
- Price—Establishing a fair and reasonable price.

The Marketing Mix combines the elements of those factors that the management must use in order to satisfy the needs or wants of the target group. The four P's must create the needed or wanted right product, where and when needed at the right time and place and be able to do so at the right price. (See Figure 17.1.)

There are certain uncontrollable factors that are beyond the control of the air carrier management because they occur outside of the company's environment. These factors are variables which affect marketing strategy:

- Cultural and social environment
- Political and legal environment
- Economic environment
- Current business conditions
- Resources and objectives of the company

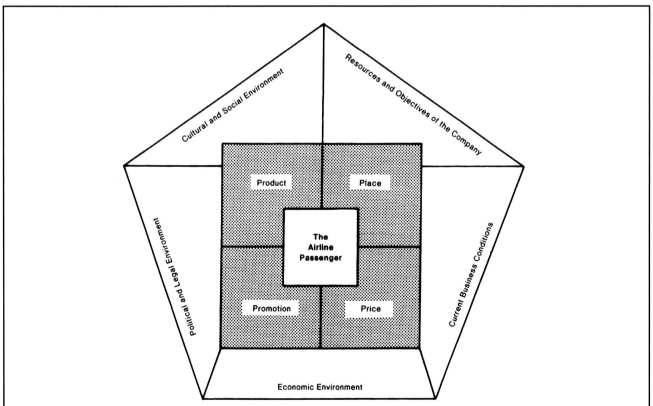

Figure 17.1 The controllable factors of the marketing mix are shown in the four sections of the square above the noncontrollable environmental factors surrounding them. All activity is directed toward the airline passenger consumer shown in the center.

MARKETING RESEARCH

Market strategy requires information about the target groups and marketing mixes including controllable and non-controllable factors. The function of gathering information for decisions regarding sales activities is that of marketing research.

Marketing research provides information about what the customer wants or needs. It shows the value of the air carrier service to the passenger and obtains the facts to base decisions affecting service to the public. It is a continuous process providing feedback to management.

The American Marketing Association defined marketing research as "The systematic gathering, recording and analyzing of data about problems relating to the marketing of goods and services."

PRODUCT

The purpose of the product is to satisfy the demand of the target group; it is the first "P" of the Marketing Mix. The product must be viewed as the passenger sees it.

Air carriers offer two general kinds of products that are of value to the traveling consumer; they are air transportation for business and pleasure. Business travel is usually not sensitive to price (inelastic demand). Included in this group are industry and government. Pleasure travel is very sensitive to price (elastic demand). Included in this group are those passengers traveling for vacations and holidays. The needs and wants of the pleasure traveler are much different from those of the business traveler.

Offering lower fares during the low period of passenger demand or sales activity will increase sales by offering inducements to the flying public to buy at other than peak traffic demand periods. Since most air passengers prefer to fly during the daylight hours, air carrier fares are lower at night. The purpose is to draw those price-conscious passengers from day flights to night flights. This method is also true regarding days of the week and seasons of the year.

The production unit of service of an air carrier is an "available seat mile" (one available passenger seat flown one mile in scheduled flight). The schedule for the product is a tariff and describes the service by listing prices (fares), frequency of services, departure and arrival times, type of service (non-stop, local or connecting), in-flight service such as food, drinks, and entertainment.

Marketing of air transportation is unique because it is a service and marketing a service is different from marketing a tangible product such as a television set. Marketing air transportation services is also different from marketing other types of services because of industry competition. The air carrier product is produced in groups (flights) not individually.

The demand for air transportation is elastic when total revenue increases. This happens when the quantity of seats sold increases as price changes (either up or down). (See Figure 17.2.)

The Civil Aeronautics Board at one time had control over prices in the domestic market, however, now prices are set by competition. In air carrier marketing, price cannot usually be used for competition purposes. Once a new price is set, all carriers will offer the same price to be competitive.

PLACE

When the air carrier product or service has been determined the questions which then must be answered are:

● Where is the product and how does the passenger get it?

The answers have to do with the location of the product, the distribution channels to reach the target group and getting the product to the air passenger. Distribution is the identification of the path followed by a product or service in moving from the producer (air carrier) to the customer (passenger), and is a complex process.

The function of place, the second "P" of the Marketing Mix, is to have the product readily available to the passengers so that they can get the service when they need it. Place is concerned with the location of the product and its utilitarian value. Place must be examined in terms of supply and demand. The job of the air carrier management is to match up supply capabilities to the demands of the target group by having the product where it will satisfy the passenger needs and wants. An excellent product or service has no value to the passenger if it is not where it is wanted, when it is wanted. Place is generally concerned with the location of marketing facilities.

"P" of the Marketing Mix, Product, has to do with developing a satisfactory product that provides utility. The utility of a product has no value unless it is combined with "Time" and "Place" utility to permit posses-

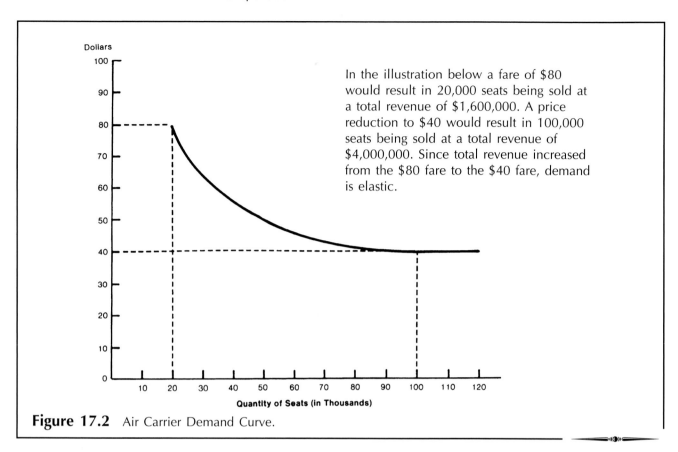

In the illustration below a fare of $80 would result in 20,000 seats being sold at a total revenue of $1,600,000. A price reduction to $40 would result in 100,000 seats being sold at a total revenue of $4,000,000. Since total revenue increased from the $80 fare to the $40 fare, demand is elastic.

Figure 17.2 Air Carrier Demand Curve.

sion. Time utility refers to the product being available when the consumer needs it—at the right time. Place utility refers to the product being available where the consumer needs it—in the right place.

An air carrier schedule to a businessman may not be a life and death situation but when he must make an emergency trip the service available to him is high in utility value.

Telephone reservations, air carrier ticket offices and travel agencies are the principal channels of distribution for air carrier service. The service of air transportation is even more important than a physical product because of its perishability. Scheduled available seats in a jet cannot be stored; once the flight takes off the unsold seats are lost. Passengers want flights available to them not only when they want or need them but also available conveniently. They want flights available to the place or location they want or need to go. (Table 17.1.)

Place is therefore the channels of distribution, the manner in which the passenger can purchase the service made available by the air carriers. The objective of "Place" is to deliver the air carrier service desired by the passenger.

AIR CARRIER DISTRIBUTION CHANNELS

Place refers to the different places passengers can buy tickets and the system that provides for them to do so conveniently.

The airline distribution system has two elements:

1. Sales Outlet—where passengers can purchase the services.
2. Reservation System—the purpose of which is to provide the company with information on the sales for future flights.

In the air carrier industry there are three basic types of sales outlets: they are the company's sales offices (direct sales), interline sales (other air carriers) and travel agencies.

Direct airline sales account for about 25% of domestic air carrier business.

Interline sales account for about 20% of domestic air carrier business and consists of sales made by other air carriers. The air carriers are competitors as well as good customers to each other. In fact, other air carriers

Table 17.1 Top 30 Domestic Airline Markets*
Passengers—Outbound plus Inbound (Twelve months ended September 2000, in thousands)

1	New York	Los Angeles	3,637	16	Honolulu	Lihue, Kauai	1,733
2	New York	Chicago	3,067	17	New York	Las Vegas	1,602
3	New York	Orlando	2,978	18	Los Angeles	Oakland	1,590
4	New York	Boston	2,966	19	New York	Dallas/Ft. Worth	1,583
5	New York	San Francisco	2,807	20	New York	West Palm Beach	1,563
6	New York	Atlanta	2,771	21	Chicago	Detroit	1,524
7	New York	Ft. Lauderdale	2,671	22	Chicago	Atlanta	1,513
8	Honolulu	Kahului, Maui	2,607	23	Chicago	Dallas/Ft. Worth	1,478
9	New York	Miami	2,542	24	Honolulu	Kona, Hawaii	1,466
10	New York	Washington, D.C.	2,534	25	Chicago	Minneapolis/St. Paul	1,447
11	Los Angeles	Las Vegas	2,405	26	Atlanta	Washington, D.C.	1,428
12	Dallas/Ft. Worth	Houston	2,289	27	Chicago	Las Vegas	1,410
13	New York	San Juan	1,986	28	New York	Houston	1,382
14	Los Angeles	San Francisco	1,959	29	Boston	Washington, D.C.	1,381
15	Chicago	Los Angeles	1,817	30	Los Angeles	Phoenix	1,376

*Includes all commercial airports in a metropolitan area. Does not include connecting passengers.
Source: DOT Passenger Origin-Destination Survey.

are the second largest group of customers. Many reservations for small air carriers are handled by large air carrier computer systems.

Travel agencies are the air carrier's single largest group of customers and are the largest channel of distribution, amounting to about 55% of the domestic air carrier business. Through travel agencies the air carriers get quantity distribution at virtually no cost. They are their representative or agent and do most of the selling at their own cost. The advantages of travel agencies in air transportation are many. There are more than 15,000 travel agencies throughout the United States and Canada serving the air carriers. About two-thirds of the travel agency business is air travel. Travel agency commissions range from 7 to 11%. Use of home computers and the Internet has introduced a new sales outlet for purchase of tickets.

The passage of the Airline Deregulation Act caused rapid changes and confusion in the air carrier industry that extended into the travel agency industry. The Civil Aeronautics Board controlled routes and approval of rates. They never had control over travel agencies nor the power to regulate directly the appointment of travel agencies by the air carriers.

The Civil Aeronautics Board reviewed the Air Carrier-Travel Agency relationship in its "Competitive Marketing Investigation." After the Civil Aeronautics Board went out of operation on January 1, 1985, travel agents are no longer the exclusive sales agents for the air carriers. This means that anyone may sell airline tickets, even department stores, chains, and supermarkets. However, the air carriers still have the authority to say who does and who does not sell tickets for their product. The Airline Deregulation Act gave the air carriers the freedom to fly where they wanted and to charge what they wanted as well as the flexibility to market their product in the manner in which they wanted.

Travel agencies are aware of their increased competition. No doubt the air carriers will continue the same arrangement with the travel agencies.

WEBSITES

Since the advent of the Internet the number of reservations made by air travelers has been increasing at a very rapid rate. The two most popular online travel websites currently have a larger quantity of visitors each month than the six leading airline websites, but their dominance is being challenged. The air carriers are offering incentives on the Internet to further attract customers. A ticket purchased on the air carrier's website costs the company from one to three dollars. The fees airlines pay to third party vendors and traditional travel agencies can be as high as twenty-five dollars.

Airline websites are being called the sleeping giants of the online air travel industry. A research firm recently released data showing that visitors to airline websites increased twenty-six percent in early 2001 compared with seven percent growth for online travel agencies.

Combined, the number of monthly inquiries to air carrier websites and online travel agencies grew to more than 30 million in February 2001 compared with 24.5 million in the year 2000.

One leading air carrier had 58 percent more Internet visitors in February 2001 than the year before. They also reported an increase in ticket sales on their website by 25 percent.

Another major air carrier said that it would no longer pay commissions to travel agency websites. This will probably be adopted by other companies indicating more intense competition in the future between the air carriers and those who sell tickets online.

Most of the major air carriers offer special deals on their web sites. Apparently the air carriers and the online travel websites are going to have increased competition. This means good news for the air travelling public.

PROMOTION

The third "P" of the Marketing Mix is promotion, the purpose of which is to tell the target group about the product. The importance of promotion in the air carrier industry, as a marketing activity, is due in part to the proliferation of the rate structure and the various kinds of flights offered to the flying public brought about by increased competition. About 9 to 13% of the major air carriers' gross operating revenue is spent on promotion, including sales and advertising. Advertising is an important part of promotion and therefore it plays an essential part in the Marketing Mix. It is the air carrier's major form of promotion.

The function of promotion is to tell the target group that the right product is available at the right place, time and price. Promotion is the action of communication between the air carrier producing the service and the passengers to whom they want to buy their service. Promotion includes advertising, public relations and publicity.

Advertising is paid for by the air carriers seeking to promote their product. The amount spent is approximately 1 to 2% of their gross operating revenue. This amounts to about $100 to $300 million yearly for all major air carriers. Studies show that an air carrier's share of the market is dependent upon its schedules. Surveys indicate that most passengers' selection of an air carrier is based upon its schedule. Until recently

few companies have reflected this in their advertising. Of the total advertising budget for major air carriers, one-half is spent on newspapers, one-fourth on television and one-fourth on magazines, radio and billboards.

Many advertisements are ineffective and fail to convince potential passengers to fly their air carrier. The advertisements of glamorous flight attendants is exploited when in reality their function is one of safety for the passengers, as required by the FAA. A uniform is for the purpose of passengers being able to identify the flight attendants in case of emergency and not for glamor. The purpose of advertising is to induce potential passengers to select a certain air carrier. It should stress service features that are important to the passengers and feature a service that competing air carriers do not have.

Public relations has the function of communicating information that will help in achieving marketing goals. Public relations is broadly defined as a planned program of non-advertising communication to influence understanding, acceptance and cooperation by people outside of the management group. Public relations is non-advertising communication paid for by the air carrier. In the air carrier industry, public relations is involved in practically all of the air carriers communications. Its approach is entirely different from advertising. The company's publics are those groups with whom they deal. A partial list would include not only passengers but also travel agencies, employees, suppliers, stockholders, creditors, the community and the government. Proper use of public relations techniques makes a substantial contribution to the flow of information necessary for attaining the objectives of marketing, namely, satisfying the customer so as to meet the company's profit goal.

Publicity is public relations most valuable, flexible and most frequently used tool. It is defined as information designed to advance the interest of the air carrier and used by mass media without charge because it is of interest to the public. Unlike paid advertising, publicity items are submitted to a newspaper, radio station or television channel with the understanding that they will be edited to conform to the general interest of the readers, listeners or viewers and not to conform to the wishes of the air carriers. The only characteristic that publicity and advertising have in common is the use of mass media.

The objectives of promotion can be summed up in three short words which are: inform, persuade and remind. The three methods of promotion are personal selling, mass selling, and sales promotion.

Personal selling is a method of promotion involving face to face contact between the seller and the potential buyer. It is the most effective method because it allows the salesman to adapt to the individual personality and characteristics of the buyer. Maximum flexibility is permitted for the current circumstances and allows for the particular behavior patterns of the buyer. The disadvantage of this method is the high cost ratio of sales. It is simply impractical for air carrier sales people to personally contact every potential passenger. Air carriers sales personnel are utilized to contact civic organizations and associations. When a national group is going to hold a convention, the airline sales personnel call upon the organization leaders as well as some of the leading individual participants. There are airline sales people who specialize in selling to business, military, the government and the Post Office, to mention a few.

Mass selling is a method of promotion designed to reach large numbers of people. It is less effective than personal selling because no immediate feedback is available. Mass selling can reach the general public, or target group, over large areas immediately whereby personal selling cannot. The advantage of mass selling is low cost ratio to sales. Advertising is therefore the main form of mass selling. Publicity is a form of free advertising and can be more effective than paid advertising.

Sales promotion is a method of promotion used to supplement both personal and mass selling. It makes them more effective. The term sales promotion is widely used with much confusion. To some it means the entire marketing function while to others it means only a minor activity related to sales. Manufacturers use the term differently than air carriers. Sales promotion is properly defined as those activities supplementing personal and mass selling and coordinates them to make them more effective. It includes the relationship between the air carrier and its travel agencies for the purpose of aiding them to increase sales. Sales promotion may also include the relationship between a producer and the consumers of his product. Sales promotion educates and arouses the enthusiasm of sales people and customers through a variety of devices, which the company controls, including signs, window displays, trade show exhibits, special promotion events, direct mail, contests, etc. These and many more have the purpose of influencing the passenger to buy the product.

Competition causes promotion to be a very important part of the air carrier marketing activity. Most of the promotion costs are found in advertising and sales budgets. As much as 50% of the entire cost of marketing for an air carrier is spent on promotion.

Any method of promotion must be plausible and creditable, honest and believable. Promotion must get the message across quickly, easily, simply, and understandably.

AIR CARRIER SALES

Sales is perhaps the most important function of promotion, therefore, it requires special attention. The action of making the sale completes the purpose of the Marketing Strategy and objectives of a company. Buying and selling have to do with human behavior. People and their situations differ greatly and a theory based upon standardized prospects is not likely to be widely effective. This idea minimizes the uniqueness of prospects and oversimplifies consumer motivation and buying behavior particularly when dealing with the users of air carrier services. The need satisfaction theory is based upon the fact that people buy to increase their sense of satisfaction. When individuals become conscious of something they want, they are expected to take the initiative in buying.

PRICE

The fourth and final "P" of the Marketing Mix is price. Price is often considered to be the most important of all the "Ps" in the Marketing Mix. The proper determination of price, or fare offered to the flying public, can mean economic success or failure regardless of how skillful the other three "Ps" of the Marketing Mix were developed.

There are several methods of determining price. The method used is based upon several conditions in the air carrier industry. Since the price charged is about the same for all air carriers who offer the same service, because of competition an air carrier can increase its sales only by offering a different service.

Price theory establishes a framework in which price decisions are made. The price of a product or service is the result of the interaction of two economic forces known as supply and demand. Their interaction is like a pair of scissors; neither blade by itself can do the job of cutting. Only when both blades are functioning in their proper relationship to each other can action take place at the point of contact or intersection. An understanding of price requires an understanding of these two forces which together result in price determination.

Since deregulation, airlines have had the same pricing freedom as companies in most other industries. They have set fares and freight rates in response to both customer demand and the prices of competitors. As a result, fares change much more rapidly than they used to, and passengers sitting in the same section on the same flight often are paying different prices for their seats.

Although this price discrepancy may seem nonsensical to some travelers, it makes perfect sense considering that a seat on a particular flight is of different value to different people. It is far more valuable, for instance, to a salesman who suddenly has an opportunity to visit an important client than it is to someone contemplating a visit to a friend. The latter customer likely will make the trip only if the fare is relatively low. The salesman, on the other hand, likely will pay a premium in order to make his appointment.

For the airlines, the chief objective in setting fares is to maximize the revenue from each flight by offering the right mix of full fare tickets and various discounted tickets. Too little discounting in the face of weak demand for the flight, and the plane will leave the ground with a lot of empty seats, and revenue-generating opportunities will be lost forever. On the other hand, too much discounting early on can sell out a flight far in advance and preclude the airline from booking last-minute passengers that might be willing to pay higher fares (another lost-revenue opportunity).

The process of finding the right mix of fares for each flight is called yield, or revenue, management. It is a complex process, requiring sophisticated computer software that helps an airline estimate the demand for seats on a particular flight so it can price the seats accordingly. And it is an on-going process, requiring continual adjustments as market conditions change. Unexpected discounting in a particular market by a competitor, for instance, can leave an airline with too many unsold seats if it does not match the discounts.

DEMAND

Demand is defined as a want or need and the ability to pay for it. As prices rise, the desire for airline seats decreases and the amount of money paid also decreases. This means that fewer tickets will be purchased at higher prices and more at lower prices. If there is a substantial change in sales, due to a small change in price, and total revenue increases, the demand is considered to be Elastic. If there is little or no change in sales with a large change in price and total revenue decreases, the demand is considered to be Inelastic. (See Figure 17.3.)

An increase in demand (sales) can take place in three ways:

- Price can increase or decrease so that more or less will be purchased, causing a change in demand.

- A company may increase its portion in the market by aggressive promotion.

- Consumers (passengers) may buy (demand) more of the product or service at the same price. This causes a shift in demand which creates a new demand curve. (See Figure 17.4.)

There are two pricing concepts in airline marketing. The first is "not sensitive to price." Under some conditions, the quantity sold will change very little or not at all as price changes. The increasing or decreasing of price will not increase or decrease the amount of seats sold appreciably. In this pricing concept the quantity of seats sold is not a direct result of price. This is an inelastic demand market. It is represented by first class passengers who are simply not price sensitive. Some business executives, whose fare is paid by their company, fall into this group. There are also those in the "snob" class who would not fly any other way simply because of their so-called prestigious position.

The second pricing concept is price "capable of being levelled." A big problem in airline marketing is that demand is not consistent with capacity. If sufficient seat capacity is provided to meet peak demand it

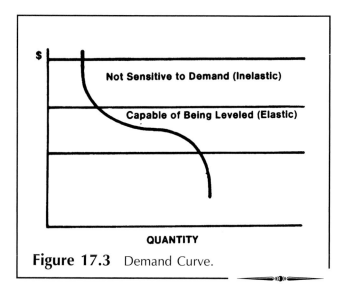

Figure 17.3 Demand Curve.

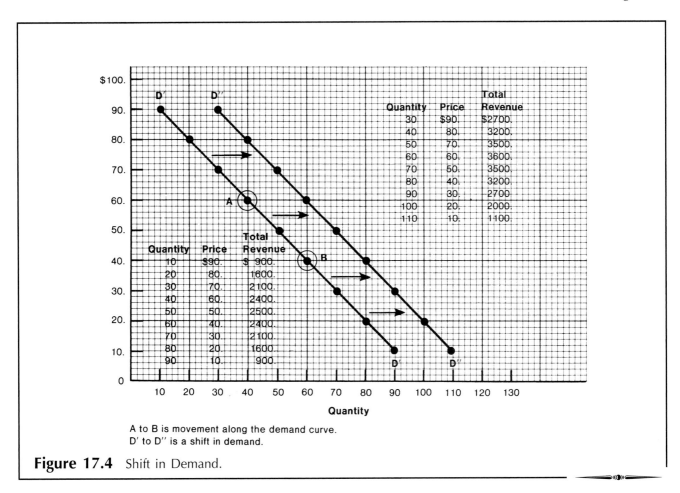

A to B is movement along the demand curve.
D' to D'' is a shift in demand.

Figure 17.4 Shift in Demand.

means that during low demand periods capacity is wasted and aircraft sit idle or are mostly empty if flown. Passenger demand is not time complementary. This means that peaks do not occur at the same time. Airlines do not always have other markets or routes that they can assign excess capacity. No airline is large enough so that they have sufficient alternate markets that they can change their capacity to utilize all of their excess capacity that is unused during low periods but necessary during peak periods.

An effort to overcome this problem is to formulate a price strategy. Price strategy is changing (reducing) the price to increase quantity of seats sold and gain additional passengers and total revenue. A good example of this was the "no frills" fare that was intended to even-out the high and low capacity ranges, or level the market, so that more passengers are carried at low periods but still carry as many passengers as possible at the high periods.

Not only are there seasonal highs and lows but also there are weekly, daily and hourly peaks. To the market segment that is capable of being levelled, prices are established to direct passengers to the low demand period by offering price reductions to travel at the low traffic periods.

Pleasure travel is a segment of the airline market that is highly price sensitive. It includes vacation and holiday travel. The pleasure market does not care about flexibility, choice of destination, time, day, date, speed, comfort, etc., but is very interested in price. This market can be served at a lower cost and will bring a lower price. Pleasure travel is capable of being levelled.

Consumer demand is a term used loosely to describe people's ability to pay and willingness to buy. Consumer demand represents the quantity of a product or service that the consumer will buy at various prices, assuming all other conditions are constant. These other conditions include consumer income, substitute products and services and consumer preferences.

A demand curve or schedule can be estimated by an airline. This will show the quantity of seats purchased at different prices. Demand must be expressed in terms of numbers of passengers.

ELASTIC-INELASTIC

The laws of demand in economic theory state that when the price increases, a decrease in the quantity sold or demanded will result; conversely, if the price decreases, an increase in the quantity sold or demanded will result.

Each product has its own demand schedule and demand curve in a potential market. Figures 17.5 and 17.6 show a basic demand schedule and a demand curve. In Figure 17.5 the increased demand will stretch enough to increase total revenue as price is decreased. This is an elastic demand.

In Figure 17.6 although demand increased as price decreased it did not do so enough to offset the price decrease. This caused total revenue to decrease, therefore, demand is Inelastic. The total revenue decreased as price decreased; this is an undesirable situation.

Although the quantity demanded increased as price decreased, the quantity demanded did not stretch enough, that is, it is not elastic enough to increase total revenue.

It is important to know that elasticity is defined in terms of changes in total revenue. If total revenue decreases as price decreases, demand is Inelastic. If total revenue increases as price decreases, demand is Elastic. The reverse situations will occur. For instance, read columns on Figures 17.5 and 17.6 from the bottom up. This will make movements on the curve from right to left. In an inelastic demand, total revenue is increased as price is increased although the quantity decreases. In an elastic demand, total revenue is decreased as price is increased although the quantity decreases.

In Figure 17.7, as price decreased from $300 to $150 demand continued to increase and total revenue increased but at a decreasing amount. Demand is elastic. Price below

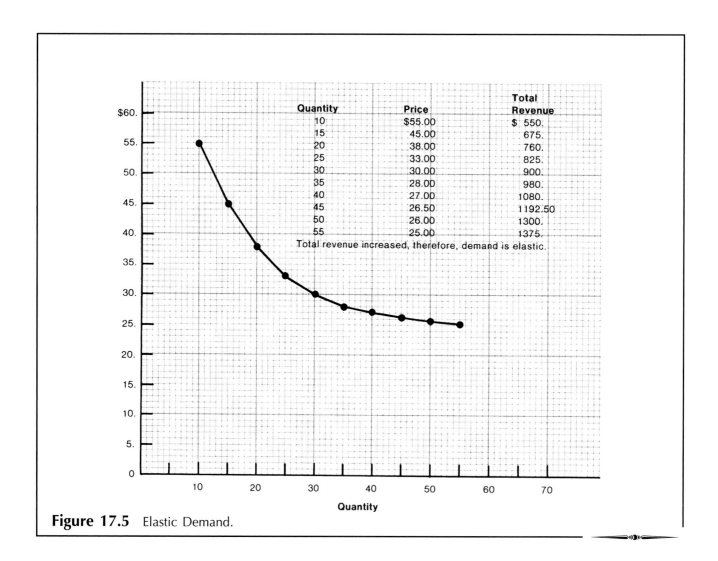

Figure 17.5   Elastic Demand.

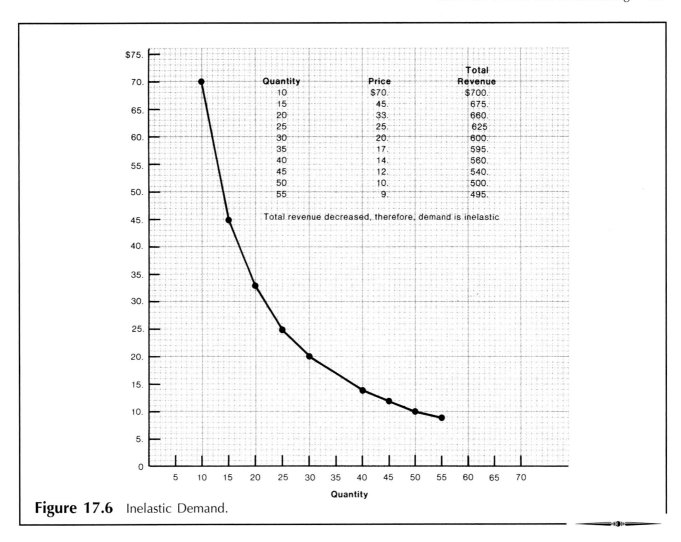

Quantity	Price	Total Revenue
10	$70.	$700.
15	45.	675.
20	33.	660.
25	25.	625
30	20.	600.
35	17.	595.
40	14.	560.
45	12.	540.
50	10.	500.
55	9.	495.

Total revenue decreased, therefore, demand is inelastic

Figure 17.6 Inelastic Demand.

$150 still increased demand but total revenue decreased. Therefore, demand became inelastic.

An entire demand curve for a product or service is not totally elastic or inelastic. Elasticity for a particular product curve refers to the change in total revenue between two points (prices and quantities) on the curve and not the entire curve. If demand for a product is totally elastic, the demand curve is completely flat and parallel to the quantity axis. In this case the company has no control over price because consumers do not see any difference in the product than that offered by competing air carriers. Therefore, the use of the other three "Ps" is considerably more difficult. This is a situation of pure competition.

If the air carrier's demand curve is inelastic, the company has much use in varying the other three "Ps." Although all of the companies in the air carrier industry together serving the same route have a down sloping demand curve, each individual air carrier has a demand curve that is perfectly flat at the market price. (See Figure 17.8.)

All companies, including air carriers, want to avoid pure competitive situations. They want a market in which they have some control. To avoid a purely competitive situation they try to develop a different product or service of special interest directed to certain target groups. Thus the demand curve for their product, a different kind of air service that their competitors do

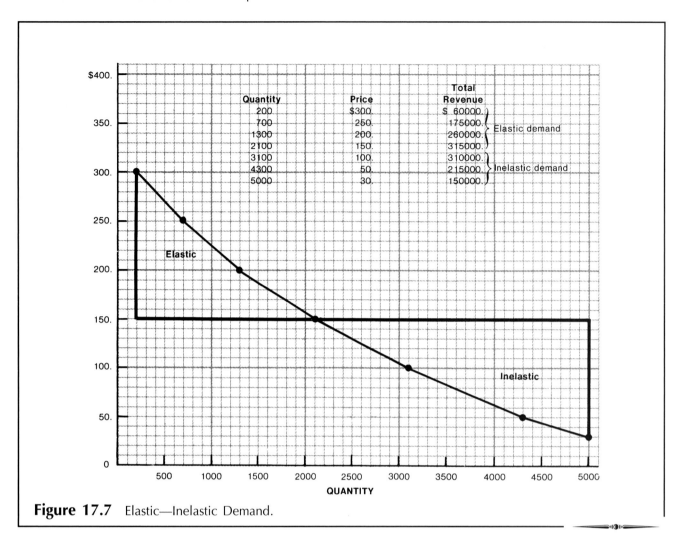

Quantity	Price	Total Revenue	
200	$300	$ 60000.	Elastic demand
700	250	175000.	
1300	200	260000.	
2100	150	315000.	
3100	100	310000.	
4300	50	215000.	Inelastic demand
5000	30	150000.	

Figure 17.7   Elastic—Inelastic Demand.

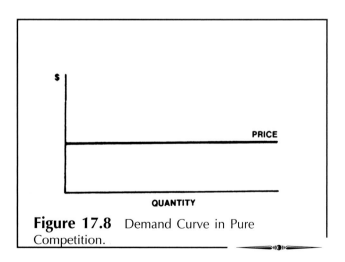

Figure 17.8   Demand Curve in Pure Competition.

not have, ceases to be flat but takes on the shape of a demand curve for the industry. Such a market is then called "monopolistic competition" which simply means offering something different for sale in a highly competitive situation.

In air transportation all air carriers operate within the "industry" whose rates and routes are competitive. All air carriers with approximately the same schedule and type of aircraft sell their product at the same price. Yet each individual air carrier tries to offer a uniquely different kind of service. Their advertisements reflect this competition, which is not in price, but in a different type of service or product which they hope will attract the passenger to their company.

SUPPLY

Supply depends on the quantity the company will produce. Cost affects their supply curves. A demand curve shows the quantity customers will buy at various prices while a supply curve shows the quantity the company will produce at various prices. As prices (demand) increase, suppliers (air carriers) will tend to produce a greater quantity. (See Figure 17.9.)

The demand and supply curves summarize the action of buyers and sellers for a certain product in a given market and their effect upon price. (Table 17.2.)

The point at which demand and supply intersect determines the price of the product and the quantity produced. At this point the market is said to be in equilibrium or balance. Since costs reflect supply, cost and demand determine the price. A supply curve can be considered a cost curve for the air carriers. Thus the equation of $P = C + D$. "P" is price, "C" is cost and "D" is demand. This equation is extremely important to understand because it reflects the theory of pricing. (See Figure 17.10.)

Price determined by supply and demand occurs when the supply and demand curves, moving in opposite directions, meet at the point of equilibrium. Price

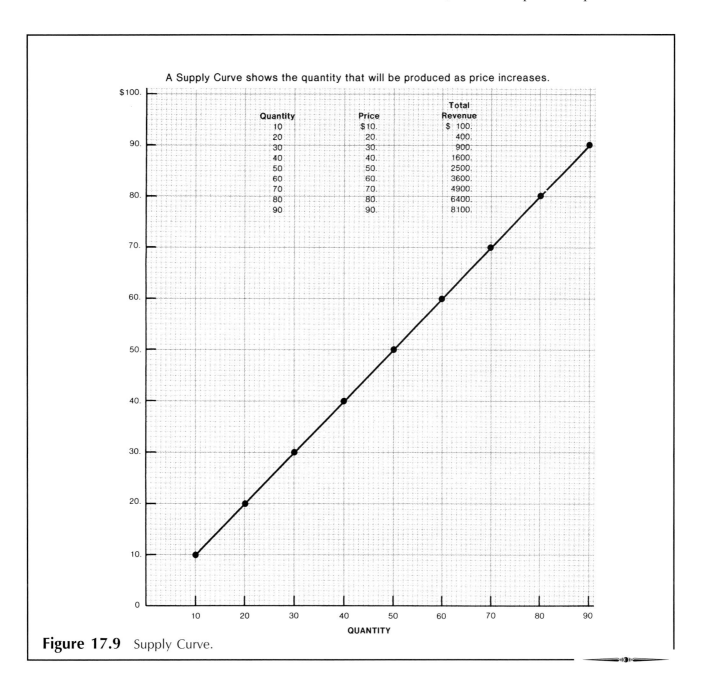

A Supply Curve shows the quantity that will be produced as price increases.

Quantity	Price	Total Revenue
10	$10.	$ 100.
20	20.	400.
30	30.	900.
40	40.	1600.
50	50.	2500.
60	60.	3600.
70	70.	4900.
80	80.	6400.
90	90.	8100.

Figure 17.9 Supply Curve.

Table 17.2 Price Determined by Supply and Demand

Quantity	Price	Total Revenue	Average Total Cost	Total Cost	Profit or Loss
10	$10.00	$100.	$1.80	$ 18.	$ 82.
20	7.00	140.	2.00	40.	100.
30	6.00	180.	2.20	66.	114.
40	5.00	200.	2.50	100.	100.
50	4.20	210.	3.00	150.	60.
60	3.50	210.	3.50	210.	0.
70	2.80	196.	4.00	280.	−84.
80	2.40	192.	4.70	367.	−184.
90	2.10	189.	5.30	477.	−288.
100	1.80	180.	6.00	600.	−420.
110	1.60	176.	7.00	770.	−594.

Demand Curve—Quantity and Price are used.
Supply Curve—Quantity and Average Total Costs are used.

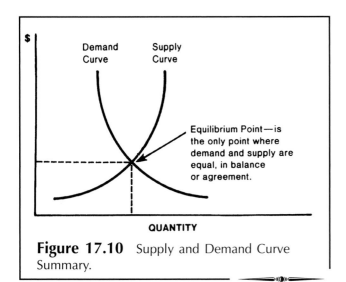

Figure 17.10 Supply and Demand Curve Summary.

is determined by the interaction of these forces of supply and demand. The quantity produced is equal to the quantity demanded. (See Figure 17.11.) If a higher price is asked, the quantity demanded will be less and the quantity produced will be more. Producers will offer more than buyers will take. Price will then decrease. Some producers will withdraw and some buyers will come in and reestablish the equilibrium price.

Pricing under pure competition is a situation in which individual buyers and sellers are unable to influence the market. Pure competition assumes an infinite number of buyers and sellers and identical products so that no one seller can influence demand.

The supply and demand curves, in a purely competitive market, would look as follows: (See Figure 17.12.)

OBJECTIVES OF PRICE

The three major objectives of price are:

1. Profit—to gain a certain percentage on sales for a fixed amount of profit for either a short or long period of time.
2. Sales—to achieve a given amount of sales or total revenue but not necessarily a profit.
3. Maintain status quo—to meet competition, avoid it, or to stabilize prices.

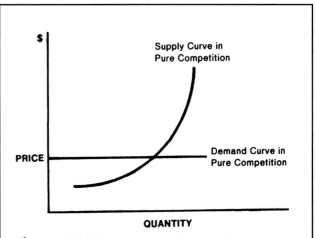

Figure 17.12 Supply and Demand Curve in Pure Competitive Market.

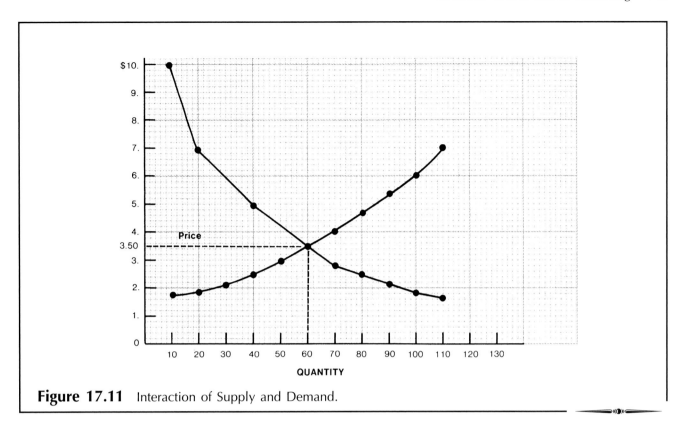

Figure 17.11 Interaction of Supply and Demand.

CHAPTER 18

Air Carrier Accounting and Financial Analysis

Accounting is the language of business; it is a primary means of reporting, measuring, and communicating business data and information. All business enterprises practice various types of accounting procedures to keep records of their business transactions. The United States government requires that records be accurately kept for tax reporting purposes. The air carrier industry is no exception. Accounting records are required for the needs of adequate managerial control.

Financial statements reflect the information recorded in the accounting system or the records of transactions. The principal financial statements include the Balance Sheet and the Income Statement, traditionally known as Profit and Loss.

The *Balance Sheet* is a statement of financial condition of a business at one particular moment of time. It shows assets, liabilities, and owners' equity. Assets represent what the company owns. Liabilities represent obligations of a company, or what it owes. Owners' equity represents the stockholders' interest in the company; the excess of assets over liabilities.

The *Income Statement* shows activities of the company during the period of time covered by the statement including revenue, expense, and profit or loss. Revenue is income from the sale of goods or services. Expense is cost incurred in the process of earning revenue. Profit or loss is the resulting difference between revenue and expense. The income statement is considered to be far more important than the balance sheet because of the greater emphasis upon earnings.

Since the air carrier industry functions in the public interest, they, like all other public utilities, are required to record and submit to the government, financial and statistical data.

The Federal Aviation Act charged the Civil Aeronautics Board with the responsibility for the economic regulation of the air carrier industry. Accordingly the Civil Aeronautics Board established Economic Regulation 241, known as the "Uniform System of Accounts and Reports for Certificated Air Carriers." This system is a standardized method so that all air carriers will keep financial data in the same manner. The purpose of the system was to provide the Civil Aeronautics Board with information on air carriers' economic activity so that it may have the necessary financial information for its economic regulation of the air carrier industry.

All financial reporting responsibilities of the Civil Aeronautics Board were transferred to the Department of Transportation on January 1, 1985, as a result of the "Airline Deregulation Act of 1978" and the "Civil Aeronautics Board Sunset Act of 1984." The system of accounts and reports was designed to permit limited contraction or expansion to reflect the varying needs and capacities of different air carriers without impairing basic accounting comparability between air carriers.

Balance Sheet and Profit and Loss account groupings are designed, in general, to embrace all activities, both air transport and other than air transport, in which the air carrier engages.

In order to afford air carriers as much flexibility and freedom as possible in establishing ledger and subsidiary accounts to meet their individual needs, a minimum number of account subdivisions had been prescribed in the system of accounts. It is intended that each air carrier, in maintaining its accounting records, would provide subaccount and subsidiary account segregations of accounting elements which differ in nature of accounting characteristics, in a manner which will render individual elements readily discernible and traceable throughout the accounting system. This provided for relating profit and loss elements to applicable balance sheet counterparts.

The general books of account, and all books and records which support in any way the entries therein, are kept in a manner to provide full information at any time relating to any account. The entries in each account must be supported by detailed information to render certainty to the identification of all facts. The books and records referred to include not only accounting records, but also all other records which develop the history of facts regarding any accounting or financial transaction.

The Uniform System of Accounts and Reports for Certificated Air Carriers was issued, prescribed, and administered under provisions of the following sections of the Federal Aviation Act.

SECTION 204(A)

The Department of Transportation is empowered to perform acts, to conduct investigations, to issue and amend orders, and to make rules, regulations and procedures, pursuant to and consistent with the Federal Aviation Act as it shall deem necessary to carry out and perform its powers and duties under the Act.

SECTION 407(A)

The Department of Transportation is empowered to require annual, monthly, periodic, and special reports from any air carrier; to prescribe the manner and form in which such reports shall be made; and to require from any air carrier specific answers to all questions upon which the Board may deem information to be necessary.

SECTION 407(D)

The Department of Transportation shall prescribe the form of any and all accounts, records, and memoranda to be kept by air carriers, including the accounts, records and memoranda of the movement of traffic, as well as the receipts and expenditures of money. It shall be unlawful for air carriers to keep any accounts or records other than those prescribed or approved. Any air carrier may keep additional accounts or records if they do not impair the integrity of the accounts and records prescribed or approved and do not constitute an undue financial burden on such air carrier.

SECTION 407(E)

The Department of Transportation shall at all times have access to all land, buildings, equipment, accounts, and records required to be kept by air carriers; it may employ auditors to inspect and examine these at any time.

As a result of deregulation the Civil Aeronautics Board reduced the paperwork it had required of air carriers, especially of small companies. Under deregulation the Board reduced excessive reporting requirements and took steps to remove the government from information collection and dissemination activities that could be performed by the private sector. This was consistent with the Paperwork Reduction Act of 1980. There are a number of private sector firms in the business of disseminating air carrier data collected by the Civil Aeronautics Board. Secondary users of Board data may secure the information they need from these sources. At least three automated data processing firms make most of the Board's data available throughout the United States by way of computer terminals; and one firm offers worldwide access.

The information reported by the air carriers has been essential to the conduct of many of the government regulatory responsibilities. The data provided a broad spectrum for the Civil Aeronautics Board in its decision making process. This produced a situation in which the Board maintained basic financial and traffic data for the air transportation industry as well as for secondary users of the data. The financial and statistical data is used by various Offices and Bureaus of the Government to carry out their program responsibilities.

BALANCE SHEET

The Balance Sheet of the Uniform System of Accounts is designed to show the financial condition of the air carrier at a given date, reflecting the asset and liability balances carried forward subsequent to the closing of the air carrier's books of account.

The Balance Sheet items and their explanation follow:

CURRENT ASSETS

Included in current assets are all resources which may reasonably be expected to be realized in cash or sold or consumed within one year, such as: unrestricted cash, assets that are readily convertible into cash or are held for current use in operations, and current claims against others that settlement is reasonably assured.

INVESTMENT AND SPECIAL FUNDS

Included are long term investments in securities of others exclusive of United States Government securities, securities which are not readily marketable, funds set aside for special purposes, contract performance deposits, and other securities, receivables, or funds not available for current operations.

PROPERTY AND EQUIPMENT

Included are all investments in land, tangible property, and equipment. Property and Equipment is subclassified into:

1. Operating Property and Equipment
   This encompasses items used in air transportation services.
2. Non-operating Property and Equipment
   This encompasses investments in property and equipment not separately accounted for within a non-transport division but assigned to other than air transportation and its incidental services, and property and equipment held for future use.

CURRENT LIABILITIES

Included are all debts the payment of which is reasonably expected to be within one year. Current liabilities include payables incurred in the acquisition of materials.

NONCURRENT LIABILITIES

Included are all debts the payment of which is not reasonably expected to require the use within one year of resources of a type which are classifiable as current assets or the creation of current liabilities.

DEFERRED CREDITS

Included are all credit balances in general clearing accounts, including credits held in suspense pending receipt of information necessary for final disposition and premiums on long-term debt securities of the air carrier.

STOCKHOLDERS' EQUITY

Included are all items which record the aggregate interests of stockholders in assets owned by the air carrier. Subdivisions are:

1. Paid-in capital—direct contributions of the stockholders.
2. Retained earnings—income retained from the operation of the air carrier.
3. Treasury stock—the cost of the air carrier of capital stock issued which has been reacquired and is held for disposition.

PROFIT AND LOSS

The Profit and Loss accounts are designed to reflect the elements of income and expense, resulting in profit or loss accruing to the proprietary interests during each accounting period.

The system provides that profit and loss elements be grouped in accordance with their inherent characteristics within the following primary classifications:

OPERATING REVENUES

This classification includes revenues ordinarily derived from the performance of air transportation, and net revenues from services performed incidental to it.

Operating Revenues and their explanation follow:

1. Transport Revenues
   Included are all revenues from the air transportation of traffic. Revenues are derived from direct aviation activity of:

   Passenger
      first class
      coach
   Mail
      priority
      nonpriority
      foreign
   Property
      freight
      excess passenger luggage
   Charter
      passenger
      property
   Air Transport—Other
      reservation cancellation fees
      miscellaneous operating revenues
   Public Service Revenues (subsidy)

2. Transport Related Revenues
Included are all revenues for providing air transportation facilities, but not as direct payment for the carriage of traffic, and all revenues (less expenses) directly associated with the performance of services that are incidental to air transportation services performed by the air carrier. Included is revenue from the operation of hotels, restaurants, food services, surface transportation, and services to other air carriers.

OPERATING EXPENSES

This classification includes expenses ordinarily incurred in performing air transportation services.

Operating Expenses and their explanation follow:

1. Flying Operations
Included are expenses for salaries of flight personnel, aircraft fuels and oils, fuel taxes, rental of flight equipment, and insurance.

2. Maintenance
Included are expenses identified with the repair and upkeep of equipment, expense of labor, and materials.

3. General Services and Administration
This is a general inclusive classification of expenses for Passenger Service, Aircraft and Traffic Servicing, Promotion and Sales, and Administration.

4. Depreciation and Amortization
Included are expenses brought about by exhaustion of the serviceability of property and equipment due to use, wear, and the passage of time. Separate accounts are maintained for the depreciation of airframe, engines, and their respective parts.

5. Transport Related Expenses
Included are all expenses applicable to generating transport related revenues such as revenues from the United States Government as direct grants or aids for providing air transportation facilities and revenues from various services incidental to air transportation services performed.

NONOPERATING INCOME AND EXPENSE

This classification represents the net income or loss from ventures not directly related to the performance of air transportation service.

INCOME TAXES

This classification includes provisions for taxes for the current period, provisions for deferred federal income taxes, and investment tax credits deferred and amortized.

AIRLINE REVENUE

About 90% of the U.S. airline industry's revenue comes from passengers and 10% from cargo shippers, the biggest of which is the U.S. Postal Service. For the all-cargo carriers, cargo is the sole source of revenue. For the major passenger airlines which also carry cargo, less than 10% of revenue comes from cargo.

Most of the passenger revenue (about 75%) comes from domestic travel, while 25% comes from travel to and from destinations in other countries. More than 90% of the tickets sold by U.S. airlines are discounted to some extent, with discounts averaging two-thirds off full fare. Fewer than 10% ever pay full fare, most of them last minute business travelers. The majority of business travelers receive some discount when they travel. A relatively small group of travelers (the frequent flyers who take more than 10 trips a year) account for a significant portion of air travel. While these flyers represent only 8% of the total number of passengers flying in a given year, they make about 45% of the trips. They are the prize customers.

Travel agencies play an important role in airline ticket sales. More than 85% of the industry's tickets are sold by agents, most of whom use airline-owned computer reservation systems to keep track of schedules and fares, to book reservations, and to print tickets for customers. Airlines pay travel agents a commission for each ticket sold. There are more than 30,000 travel agents in the United States, providing a vast network of retail outlets for air transportation that would be enormously expensive for the airlines to duplicate on their own.

Similarly, freight forwarders book the majority of air cargo space. Like travel agents, freight forwarders are an independent sales force for airline services, in their case working for shippers.

AIRLINE COSTS— WHERE THE MONEY GOES

According to reports filed with the Department of Transportation, airline costs usually are approximately as follows:

31.0%	*Flying Operations*—essentially any cost associated with the operation of aircraft, such as fuel and pilot salaries
15.7%	*Aircraft and Traffic Service*—basically the cost of handling passengers and aircraft on the ground and including such things as the salaries of baggage handlers, dispatchers, and airline gate agents
10.9%	*Promotion/Sales*—including advertising, reservations, and travel agent commissions
12.3%	*Maintenance*—both parts and labor
10.3%	*Transport Related*
8.6%	*Passenger Service*—mostly in-flight service and including such things as food and flight attendant salaries
5.6%	*Administrative*
5.6%	*Depreciation/Amortization of equipment and plants*

Labor costs are common to nearly all of those categories. When looked at as a whole, labor accounts for 35% of the airlines' operating expenses and 75% of its controllable costs. Fuel is another major cost item (about 15% of total expenses). So are travel agent commissions (about 10%). Commissions have been one of the fastest rising airline costs since deregulation, when they accounted for less than 5% of total costs. Another rapidly rising cost has been airport landing fees and rents, which have been rising at four times the rate of inflation in recent years.

BREAK-EVEN LOAD FACTORS

Every airline has what is called a break-even load factor. It is the percentage of the seats the airline has in service that it must sell at a given yield, or price level, to cover its costs.

Since revenue and costs vary from one airline to another, so does the break-even load factor. Escalating costs push up the break-even load factor, while increasing prices have just the opposite effect, pushing it lower. Overall, the break-even load factor for the industry in recent years has been a little over 65%.

Airlines typically operate very close to their break-even load factor. The sale of just one or two more seats on each flight can spell the difference between profit and loss for an airline.

REPORTING SYSTEM

The Uniform System of Accounts and Reports for Certificated Air Carriers contains two major divisions. The first pertains to accounting procedures. The second, pertaining to the procedures of reporting financial and operating statistical data, is presented below.

Every certificated air carrier must submit monthly, quarterly, semiannual, and annual reports of financial and operating activity. The method used is known as Form 41 Reports.

The system prescribed provides for the submission by each air carrier of five classes of financial and operating statistics, on individual schedules of Form 41 report, grouped as follows:

A. Certification

B. Balance Sheet Elements

P. Profit and Loss Elements

T. Traffic and Capacity Elements

The prescribed system of reports provides that the frequency of reporting shall be monthly for some schedules, quarterly for some, an annually for others. It also provides for the classification of air carriers into Group I, Group II, and Group III, with the form and content differentiated as between groups and by types of certification.

Each schedule of the prescribed Form 41 report has been assigned a specific code. The prefix alphabetical codes A, B, P, and T, respectively, have been employed to denote certification, balance sheet, profit and loss, traffic and capacity, and general corporate elements. The digits immediately following the alphabetical prefix designate the particular schedule.

Upon approval, the carrier may supply its own computer prepared forms provided each schedule conforms with the size and format of the forms prescribed herein.

Four separate air carrier entities shall be established for route air carriers for the purpose of submitting the reports hereinafter prescribed. They are as follows:

1. Domestic operations;

2. Operations via the Atlantic Ocean;

3. Operations via the Pacific Ocean; and

4. Operations within the Latin American areas.

With respect to the first classification, the domestic entity shall embrace all operations within the 50 States of the United States and the District of Columbia, and shall also include Canadian transborder operations.

The Airline Deregulation Act passed in October 1978 brought about a vast decrease in economic regulations. This reduced the government's need for statistical data.

The Deregulation Act specifies its concern for air service to small communities. Points within the continental United States are to be monitored as essential air service points in order to ensure their continued service.

Information on international operations is still necessary. The government will continue to need information for monitoring the condition of the air transportation industry.

Although the Deregulation Act does not provide for data collection, it does imply the need for data through its continuation of programs that require it.

The Board's financial information system used to provide basic data for other federal organizations, the aviation industry, aircraft manufacturers, and other users of economic data. That activity is now carried out by private business.

When the Board "faded into the sunset" on January 1, 1985, the Department of Transportation took over responsibility for regulatory programs including foreign air transportation and subsidy for essential air service to the small communities.

It is not the intention of this text to delve into the contents of the schedules required in the reporting system. For a further study the reader is referred to the actual system available from the Department of Transportation.

The Form 41 Balance Sheet and Income Statement follow for general information. (See Figures 18.1 and 18.2.)

Uniform System of Accounts and Reports for Certificated Air Carriers

ASSETS

Current Assets:
Cash
Short-term investments
Notes receivable
Accounts receivable
Net investment in direct financing
    and sales-type leases—current
Less: Allowance for uncollectible
    accounts
    Notes and accounts receivable—
    net
Prepaid items
Other current assets

    Total current assets

Investments and Special Funds:
Investments in associated
    companies
Other investments and receivables
Special funds
    Total investments and special
    funds

Operating Property and Equipment:
Flight equipment
Ground property and equipment
Less: Allowances for depreciation
    Property and equipment—net
Land

Equipment purchase deposits and
    advance payments
Construction work in progress
Leased property under capital
    leases
Leased property under capital
    leases—accumulated
    amortization

    Total operating property and
    equipment

Non-operating Property and Equipment:
Less: Allowance for depreciation
Nonoperating property and
    equipment

Other Assets:
Long-term prepayments
Unamortized developmental and
    preoperating costs
Other assets
    Total other assets

Total Assets

Figure 18.1   Form 41—Balance Sheet.

LIABILITIES AND STOCKHOLDERS' EQUITY

Current Liabilities:
Current maturities of long-term debt
Notes Payable—Banks
Notes Payable—Others
Trade accounts payable
Accounts payable—Others
Current obligations under capital leases
Accrued salaries, wages
Accrued vacation liability
Accrued interest
Accrued taxes
Dividends declared
Air traffic liability
Other current liabilities

   Total current liabilities

Noncurrent Liabilities:
Long-term debt
Advances from associated companies
Pension liability
Noncurrent obligations under capital leases
Other noncurrent liabilities

   Total noncurrent liabilities

Deferred Credits:
Deferred income taxes
Deferred investment tax credits
Other deferred credits

   Total deferred credits

Stockholders' Equity:
Capital stock:
   Preferred shares issued
   Common shares issued
   Subscribed and unissued
Total capital stock
Additional capital invested
Total paid-in capital
Retained earnings
Total stockholders' equity
Less: Treasury stock shares
   Net stockholders' equity

Total Liabilities and Stockholders' Equity

Figure 18.1   continued.

Before deregulation the Board prescribed an extensive accounting and reporting system for both financial and statistical information. The Board used to receive approximately 32,000 reports from air carriers annually. These included periodic and annual reports from 45 certificated air carriers in addition to operational reports from 220 commuter air carriers and 350 Air Freight Forwarder reports.

In November 1979, 81 certificated air carriers were making 17,581 reports each year. The average air carrier was formerly required to submit 205 reports annually.

Deregulation brought about a new era of information requirements. Shortly after passage of the Deregulation Act the number of certificated air carriers increased by 71%, many of which were small new companies interested in serving small communities. The number of Air Freight Forwarders increased by 20%. As a result, the annual report to the Board increased more than 6% to 34,000.

The Board suggested a greater reliance upon nongovernment, private sources for providing basic air transportation data and information in the future.

A new air carrier classification system was instituted by which the air carriers are classified by total

FORM 41—STATEMENT OF OPERATIONS

Uniform System of Accounts and Reports for Certificated Air Carriers

OPERATING REVENUES

Passenger
Mail
Property
Charter
Air transport—other
Public Service Revenues (Subsidy).
Transport Related Revenues
    Total Operating Revenues

OPERATING EXPENSES

Flying operations
Maintenance
Passenger Service
Aircraft and Traffic Servicing
Promotion and Sales
General and administrative
Depreciation and amortization
Transport Related Expenses
    Total operating expenses
    Operating profit or loss

NONOPERATING INCOME AND EXPENSE

Interest on long-term debt and
    capital leases
Other interest expense
Capital gains and losses

Foreign exchange gains and losses
Other income and expense—net
    Nonoperating income and expense
    Income before income taxes

INCOME TAXES FOR CURRENT PERIOD

Income before discontinued
    operations, extraordinary items and
    accounting changes

DISCONTINUED OPERATIONS

EXTRAORDINARY ITEMS

Income taxes applicable to
    extraordinary items

ACCOUNTING CHANGES

Net income

Figure 18.2 Form 41—Statement of Operations.

revenues rather than the old method of classification as Trunks, Local Service, and so forth. Data collecting and reporting will be on the basis of this new system.

An immediate benefit of the change in reporting was to reduce the reporting burden for small air carriers and new companies. This helped assure that reporting would not be a barrier to, or an unnecessarily high cost of, entry into the air transport industry.

The Board contacted 25 "outside" users of the data. The largest number were air carriers, 27%. They were followed by aircraft manufacturers, 10%; consultants, 13%; state and local governments, 8%; and other federal government users, 22%; and various other users, 20%.

The Board reviewed the grouping of classification of air carriers. During the regulatory years before the

Table 18.1   Income Statement—U.S. Scheduled Airlines

thousands of dollars

| | 2000 | | |
	Domestic	International	Total
Operating Revenues			
Passenger	$74,041	$19,531	$93,572
Freight & Express	6,021	5,972	11,993
Mail	1,693	282	1,975
Charter	3,273	1,092	4,365
Public Service	5	—	5
Other	13,657	3,896	17,553
Total Operating Revenues	98,690	30,773	129,463
Operating Expenses			
Flying Operations	28,450	9,439	37,889
Maintenance	11,981	3,060	15,041
Aircraft & Traffic Servicing	14,658	4,528	19,186
Passenger Services	7,355	3,211	10,566
Promotion & Sales	10,079	3,263	13,342
Administrative	5,258	1,622	6,880
Transport Related	10,245	2,422	12,667
Depreciation & Amortization	5,087	1,732	6,819
Total Operating Expenses	93,113	29,277	122,390
Operating Profit or (Loss)	**5,577**	**1,496**	**7,073**
Other Income or (Expense)			
Interest Expense	(1,557)	(608)	(2,165)
Income Taxes	(2,045)	(408)	(2,453)
Other	136	47	183
Net Profit or (Loss)	**$2,111**	**$527**	**$2,638**
Operating Profit Margin (%)	**5.7**	**4.9**	**5.5**
Net Profit Margin (%)	**2.1**	**1.7**	**2.0**

Source: Air Transport Association

Deregulation Act of 1978, the scope of an air carrier's operations rarely changed. Terms such as Trunk and Local Service could be used as standard. The new reduced reporting procedures group air carriers on the basis of their annual operating revenues. Annual revenues are better for classification purposes than other factors such as fleet size or annual revenue passenger miles because of simplicity and easier administration. The new classification/grouping of Majors, Nationals, and Regionals (large and medium) reflects the kinds of direct air carriers in the deregulated air carrier industry.

Due to the importance of air transportation industry data being made available to government, industry, and other users, provision was made to ensure continuation of the necessary basic data system after the Board ceased to exist. The responsibility rests upon the Department of Transportation.

The future of air carrier financial reporting has become doubtful. In January 1985, the Department of Transportation stated that it regards Form 41 as overly burdensome and unwarranted since the Airline Deregulation Act of 1978 is now in full effect after the elimination of the Civil Aeronautics Board.

FINANCIAL ANALYSIS

Recording and reporting financial and operational activities is a subject in itself. However, in order to manage and control an air carrier, it is necessary to analyze and to interpret the data shown in the financial statements when the financial condition or the progress of a company is to be determined. In doing so, three important factors are to be considered:

- Solvency is a company having sufficient funds to meet its liabilities.

- Financial Stability is the financial strength of a company and is a factor in appraising profitability.

- Profitableness is success in realizing an appropriate amount of income in relation to the capital employed.

The most important interest in financial statements is evidenced by management who must plan, organize, and control the activities of the company to attain the desired objective, normally profit. Financial statements provide management with a tool, or a blueprint, by which they may determine the financial strengths and weaknesses of their operation. Financial statements and

their interpretation are essential to the successful management of an air carrier. (Table 18.2.)

Interpretation and analysis of financial statements is used by management to:

- Measure the costs of producing various incomes.

- Determine efficiency of operations.

- Measure profitability.

- Measure performance.

- Evaluate operations and effect changes or improvements.

- Make sound decisions.

- Account to stockholders.

- Establish future plans.

When interpreting financial statements, comparisons should be made between related items. The data of one

Table 18.2   Balance Sheet U.S. Scheduled Airlines
thousands of dollars

Assets	1999	2000
Current Assets	$26,847	$28,161
Investments and Special Funds	16,187	14,667
Flight Equipment Owned	86,269	97,899
Ground Equipment and Property	21,826	21,702
Reserve for Depreciation (Owned)	(39,060)	(41,440)
Leased Equipment and Property Capitalized	9,657	9,230
Reserve for Depreciation (Leased)	(3,504)	(3,473)
Other Property	11,285	14,241
Deferred Charges	4,204	4,488
Total Assets	$133,711	$145,475
Liabilities		
Current Liabilities	$33,909	$38,326
Long-Term Debt	24,115	29,805
Other Non-Current Liabilities	23,342	22,695
Deferred Credit	14,369	16,837
Stockholders' Equity—Net of Treasury Stock	37,976	37,812
Preferred Stock	1	235
Common Stock	813	821
Other Paid-In Capital	17,939	18,303
Retained Earnings	22,067	21,963
Less: Treasury Stock	2,844	3,510
Total Liabilities and Stockholders' Equity	$133,711	$145,475

Source: Air Transport Association

FLIGHTS OF FANCY

Annual Reports

Most annual reports can be presented in three sections:

- The **Executive Letter** to stockholders which presents a broad overview of the company's business and financial performance.

- The **Business Review** summarizes the recent developments, trends and objectives of the company.

- The **Financial Review** shows performance of the company in money. This usually is the most important and of greatest interest.

The Financial Review has two major parts: *discussion and analysis* and *financial statements*. In discussion and analysis the management explains changes in operating results from year to year. This is presented in a narrative form with charts and graphs depicting comparisons. The operating results are numerically presented in the financial statements. The principal components in the financial statements are the balance sheet, income statement, statement of changes in shareholders' equity and cash flow. The balance sheet portrays the financial strength of the company by showing what the company owns and what it owes on a certain date. The balance sheet can be thought of as a snapshot photograph since it reports the financial position as of the end of the year. The income statement is like a moving picture because it reports on how the economy performed during the year and shows if results were a profit or loss. The statement of changes in stockholders' equity reconciles the activity in the equity section of the balance sheet from year to year. Changes in equity result from company profits or losses, dividends or stock issues.

Annual reports, including financial statements, are used by investors and other interested persons to analyze the financial condition of the company.

Table 18.3 Traffic and Operations Data—U.S. Scheduled Airlines

(In millions, except where noted)

	1999			2000		
	Domestic	International	Total	Domestic	International	Total
PASSENGER TRAFFIC—SCHEDULED SERVICE						
Revenue Passengers Enplaned	582.9	53.1	636.0	610.0	55.5	665.5
Revenue Passenger Miles	480,134	171,913	652,047	508,151	184,354	692,505
Available Seat Miles	687,502	230,917	918,419	714,006	242,496	956,502
Passenger Load Factor (%)	69.8	74.4	71.0	71.2	76.0	72.4
Average Passenger Trip Length (miles)	824	3,238	1,025	833	3,322	1,041
CARGO TRAFFIC—SCHEDULED SERVICE						
Total Revenue Ton Miles	9,087	12,526	21,613	9,884	13,727	23,611
Freight & Express Revenue Ton Miles	7,289	12,028	19,317	7,943	13,200	21,143
Mail Revenue Ton Miles	1,798	498	2,296	1,941	527	2,468
OVERALL TRAFFIC AND OPERATIONS DATA						
Total Revenue Ton Miles—Charter Service	5,932	3,093	9,025	5,598	2,561	8,159
Total Revenue Ton Miles—All Services	63,032	32,811	95,843	66,297	34,724	101,021
Total Available Ton Miles—All Services	110,137	55,650	165,787	114,915	57,659	172,574
Weight Load Factor—All Services (%)	57.2	59.0	57.8	57.7	60.2	58.,5
Revenue Aircraft Departures—Scheduled Service (thousands)	8,126	501	8,627	8,453	539	8,992
Revenue Aircraft Miles—Scheduled Service	5,057	1,110	6,167	5,388	1,172	6,560
Revenue Aircraft Hours—Scheduled Service (thousands)	12,470	2,228	14,698	13,256	2,367	15,623

Source: Air Transport Association

company should be compared with similar companies or with the standard of the industry.

Statistics prepared are standards, ratios, trends, and percentages. They represent the financial and operating accomplishments of the company or the industry.

The analysis of financial statements consists of a study of relationships and trends to determine if the financial position, financial progress, and the rules of operations of a company are satisfactory.

The objective of analysis is to simplify or reduce the statistical data to understandable terms. The analyst must first compute and organize the data and then analyze and interpret it in order for it to be meaningful. Methods and techniques used in analyzing financial statements include:

Comparing:

- Dollar amounts
- Percentages
- Increases and decreases in dollar amounts
- Increases and decreases in percentages
- Ratios
- Percentages of total

Computing:

- Trend ratios of selected items

Data selected from financial statements may be compared and shown graphically. By studying charts the analyst may obtain an idea of the changes that have taken place. In comparison with a table of figures, a chart is more meaningful since variations are more noticeable.

ANALYSIS OF AIR CARRIER FINANCIAL STATEMENTS

The financial strength of an air carrier and the efficiency of its management may be measured and evaluated by comparisons with the company's data from year to year, and also by comparison with other air carriers of its class and with the total industry. In order to make comparisons practical, the data obtained from accounting records and reports must be summarized into statistics that are comprehensive, comparable, readable, and understandable.

The key to analysis of financial statements is the calculation of certain critical ratios. The analyzer must know the meaning of the data used in the ratios as well as their use.

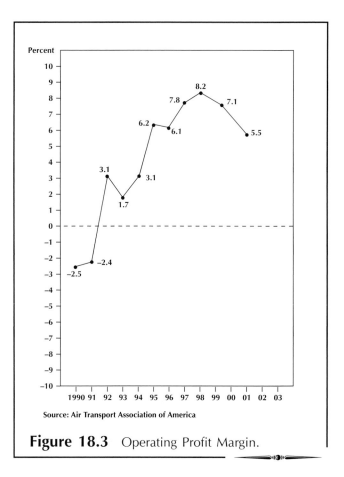

Source: Air Transport Association of America

Figure 18.3 Operating Profit Margin.

TREND RATIOS

The use of trend percentages (index numbers) is a valuable aid in analyzing financial and operating data. (See Table 18.4.)

OPERATING RATIO

Operating Ratio is determined by dividing the operating expenses by the operating revenues. The resulting operating ratio is regarded as an index of operating efficiency. (See graph in Figure 18.3.)

$$\left(\frac{\text{Operating Expenses}}{\text{Operating Revenues}} \right)$$

COMPARISONS OF OPERATING REVENUE AND OPERATING EXPENSE

Revenue and expense can be compared from year to year for one company to show the percentage of change. Revenue and expense of one air carrier can

Table 18.4 Trend Ratios of Financial Statement Items

index numbers total U.S. scheduled air carriers in thousands of dollars

	1991	1992	1993	1994	1995	1996	1997	1998	1999	2000
Total Assets	70,375,984	75,426,091	82,399,203	83,062,951	89,827,486	95,022,326	105,822,000	118,308,000	132,928,000	145,475,000
Index Number	100	107	117	118	128	135	150	168	189	207
Liabilities	57,144,706	65,455,186	69,159,151	70,169,495	72,737,928	73,545,825	78,007,000	85,915,000	95,114,000	107,661,000
Index Number	100	114	121	123	127	129	137	150	166	188
Stockholder's Equity	13,231,278	13,240,052	13,240,052	12,893,456	17,089,558	21,476,501	27,815,000	32,393,000	37,814,000	37,812,000
Index Number	100	100	100	97	129	162	210	245	286	286
Total Operating Revenue	75,113,859	78,140,243	84,559,130	87,567,451	94,577,657	101,918,628	109,535,000	113,465,000	119,038,000	129,463,000
Index Number	100	104	113	116	125	136	146	151	158	172
Total Operating Expense	76,837,293	80,584,703	83,121,041	84,801,434	88,718,139	95,693,889	100,925,000	104,138,000	110,638,000	122,390,000
Index Number	100	105	109	110	115	125	131	136	145	159
Operating Income or Loss	−1,723,434	−2,444,460	1,438,172	2,766,017	5,859,518	6,224,739	8,611,000	9,327,000	8,400,000	7,073,000
Net Profit or Loss	−1,869,974	−4,791,284	−2,135,626	−279,407	2,313,591	2,824,328	5,195,000	4,903,000	5,360,000	2,638,000
Net Profit Margin %	−2.5	−6.1	−2.5	−0.3	2.4	2.8	3.9	4.3	4.5	2.0

Source: Air Transport Association

also be compared to that of other air carriers of like class and also to the total of the industry.

The operating expense and revenue can be compared for the following items:

- The dollar amounts
- Cents per mile
- Percentage of operating revenue and expense
- Cents per mile flown (revenue and expense)

CURRENT RATIO

The current ratio is a useful indication of the financial strength of the air carrier and is obtained by dividing current assets by current liabilities.

$$\left(\frac{\text{Current Assets}}{\text{Current Liabilities}} \right)$$

RETURN ON INVESTMENT

Expressed as a percentage, return on investment is obtained by dividing the profit by the total assets of the company.

$$\left(\frac{\text{Profit}}{\text{Total Assets}} \right)$$

PROFIT MARGIN

A more exacting test of a company's operating success, for a period of time, is the profit margin. This is expressed as a percentage and is determined by dividing the profit by the revenue or income from sales. The higher the resulting percentage, the more successful the company has been. This ratio shows operating efficiency in a competitive situation and is considered a true test of management's ability.

$$\left(\frac{\text{Profit}}{\text{Revenue}} \right)$$

OPERATING COST

The operating cost percentage is the complement of the profit margin. If a company experienced a profit margin of 10%, then the operating cost figure is 90%. The lower this percentage the higher the profit margin.

TRAFFIC AND SERVICE

$$\text{Load Factor} = \frac{\text{Revenue Passenger Miles}}{\text{Available Seat Miles}}$$

$$\text{Utilization} = \frac{\dfrac{\text{Hours Flown}}{\text{Number of Aircraft}}}{\text{Number of Days}}$$

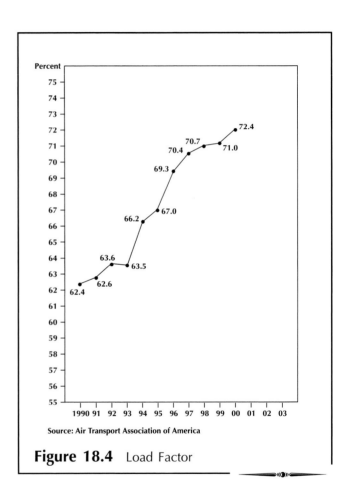

Figure 18.4 Load Factor

Source: Air Transport Association of America

UNIT COSTS

Expressed in operating expenses per seat mile.

YIELD

The amount that passengers pay, expressed in cents per mile flown.

FACTORS AFFECTING AIR CARRIER FINANCIAL SUCCESS

When making a complete and detailed analysis of an individual air carrier, consideration must be given to various external factors which are beyond control of the management. The most important of these are:

- Various Government regulations.

- Excessive competition.

- Business cycle. In analyzing air carrier trends, it is necessary to recognize the general business activity and economic condition of the country.

On the following pages are examples of tables and graphs using the ratios stated above. Several pages of statistical data follow which can be used to prepare additional tables and graphs for analysis of several aspects of air carrier operation.

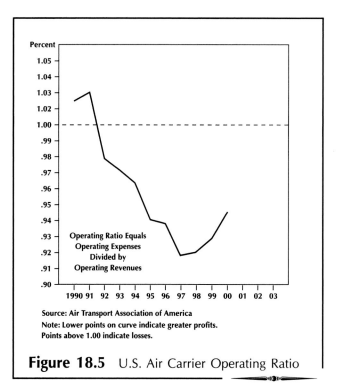

Source: Air Transport Association of America
Note: Lower points on curve indicate greater profits.
Points above 1.00 indicate losses.

Figure 18.5 U.S. Air Carrier Operating Ratio

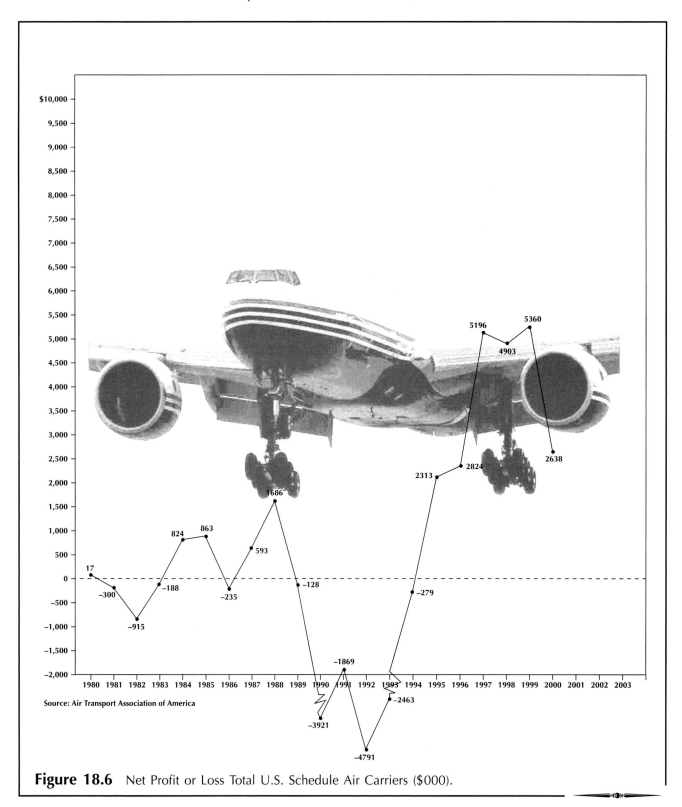

Figure 18.6   Net Profit or Loss Total U.S. Schedule Air Carriers ($000).

Source: Air Transport Association of America

Table 18.5   Total U.S. Scheduled Air Carriers
thousands of dollars

Year	Total Operating Revenue	Net Profit or Loss	Operating Profit Margin
1991	73,133,859	−1,869,974	−2.5
1992	78,140,243	−4,791,284	−6.1
1993	84,559,213	−2,135,626	−2.5
1994	87,567,451	−279,407	−0.3
1995	94,577,657	2,313,591	2.4
1996	101,938,000	2,804,328	6.1
1997	109,535,000	5,195,000	7.9
1998	113,465,000	4,903,000	8.2
1999	119,038,000	5,360,000	7.1
2000	129,463,000	2,638,000	5.5

Table 18.6   Total U.S. Scheduled Air Carriers

Year	Available Seat Miles (000)	Revenue Passenger Miles (000)	Load Factor
1991	714,974,175	447,795,703	62.6
1992	752,772,435	478,553,708	63.6
1993	771,640,648	489,684,421	63.5
1994	783,839,740	519,161,222	66.2
1995	807,077,839	540,656,211	67.0
1996	835,078,294	578,663,509	69.3
1997	860,564,000	605,434,000	70.4
1998	874,090,000	618,086,000	70.7
1999	918,419,000	652,047,000	71.0
2000	956,502,000	692,505,000	72.4

CHAPTER 19

Legal Aspects
of Air Transportation*

The comparatively young field of aviation law has developed its own distinctive body of statutes, treaties, regulations, and case law. Nevertheless, the cases in the field of aviation have borrowed from, and are related to, other branches of the law that deal with transportation, railroads, admiralty, automobiles, civil, and military.

Public international aviation law is defined as the body of law concerning agreements between nations pertaining to landing rights, transit agreements, transport agreements, sanitary agreements, radio agreements, etc., involving international operations of civil aircraft with no direct concern for the particular rights of individual persons of the contracting nations. The rights and liabilities of private individuals constitute the subject matter of a body of law known as private international law.

Public international aviation law started with the close of World War II which awakened the world to the possibilities of aviation as a civilian industry and a military weapon. Jurists of all nations realized that an understanding between nations was necessary to prevent this new mode of travel and fighting from upsetting the age-old concepts of sovereignty and international trade.

NATIONAL SUPREMACY IN AIR SPACE

The authority of the Federal Government is derived from the authority delegated by the States. The specific authority delegated to the Federal Government is set forth in the United States Constitution.

With the advent of air travel it became apparent that, in the matter of air travel and air regulation, there would be a conflict between the authority delegated to the Federal Government and the authority of the States.

Some of the legal questions that arise in this area are:

- Who has sovereignty over the airspace—the States or the Federal Government?

- It is acknowledged that the United States has sovereignty over the three nautical-mile belt beyond the low water mark. How does this precedent in land and water rights affect the newer law of air rights?

- Is there a difference between "sovereignty" of air rights and "ownership" of air rights?

- What are the spheres of authority to tax aircraft which are constantly moving from one state to another? Can all states tax the property equally? Are the states preempted of their taxing authority by the Federal Government?

---

*This chapter consists of excerpts from the text "Aviation Law—Fundamental Cases," by Dr. Gerard Pucci, Kendall/Hunt Publishing Company.

- Which branch of government has jurisdiction over crimes on board aircraft? Are the state criminal laws violated? Are federal criminal laws violated? Where is the crime committed when a plane is traveling at 600 miles per hour? Is the crime committed in one State, in a second State, or in both States?

This section sets forth the steps taken to delineate the responsibility and authority of these two branches of government.

RELATIONSHIP OF FEDERAL AND STATE GOVERNMENTS

The national responsibility for regulating air commerce has been acknowledged by the Congress of the United States and by the United States Supreme Court. Precedence for recognizing the federal supremacy was developed from such cases as the Tidelands Oil Case (U.S. v. Texas); and U.S. v. Causby.

TAXATION

Taxation of aircraft that were continually flying, landing, and being repaired in many different States was an important question that had to be resolved. The authority of States in preference to the Federal Government was decided. Then the question of which State could tax these aircrafts arose—was it the State in which the airline was domiciled or was it every State into which the aircraft flew? This question was resolved by many cases, two of which were Northwest Airlines v. Minnesota, and Braniff Airways v. Nebraska. The States then further clarified the matter by agreeing to a Council of States Allocation Formula that allocated the percentage of taxes permitted to the different states based on the percentage of the number of stops, the tonnage, and the revenue originating in each state.

CRIMES ON AIRCRAFT

Another conflict of responsibility between the two levels of government was the commission of a crime on board an aircraft. There was little precedence for this area of aviation law. It was difficult to determine over exactly what location of land the crime was committed in a moving aircraft. There were few parallels in the common law jurisprudence of criminal law.

The Federal Government had to enact a body of laws that would cover these new crimes against society.

AIRPORTS AND LIABILITY

The question of liability of airports due to the noise which results by their use is considered. The question raised is whether the noise created is a "taking" of the property of adjacent landowners, or whether the airport and airplane noise constitute a "tort" against the neighboring landowners.

A sovereign government can be sued only if it consents to be sued. The United States, by enactment of the Tucker Act in 1887, consented to be sued only in five situations, and expressly forbade lawsuits against the United States based on torts.

In 1946 the Federal Tort Claims Act was passed, which, in general, permitted a citizen to sue the United States Government for torts committed by a federal employee while acting within the scope of his employment.

Similarly, a sovereign State of the United States, cannot be sued unless it consents to be sued. There are provisions in State constitutions which permit the State to be sued.

A State constitution may contain a provision for compensation for "taking," in which case if a court declares the State's airport noise as a commission of a tort, then the adjacent landowner could not recover. If, however, the State constitution mentioned "damages," the landowner could recover on the grounds that lawsuits against the State were permitted for "torts" in which "damages" are the result. In cases involving a "taking" the landowner is considered entitled to compensations for the taking of an easement over his property by operation of the airport. In this situation, the "taking" by the airport constitutes depriving the landowner of one or more useful functions of the land, due to the noise resulting from the airport operation.

A distinction should be made between a "Tort" and a "Taking":

- A "Tort" is any wrongful act (not involving contract) to which a civil action can be brought for damages.

- A "Taking" exists where the owner of land is either prevented from his rightful use of his land, or his land is actually taken from him for public use. In either situation the owner must be compensated for the loss of his land or for the loss of the use of his land.

DAMAGES AND INJURIES ON GROUND

This section examines the extent of liability of persons operating aircraft above land and causing injury to persons and property on the land, by descent or ascent of the aircraft, or by dropping any object from the aircraft.

In the area of aerial agriculture there are several cases that can be summarized here. The task of pinpointing liability is impeded by the difficulty of establishing the source of the harmful spray, and in proving the negligence of the defendant.

The following are brief descriptions of cases where it was held that the aircraft operation was liable for injury to plant life or animal stock on the ground.

- The case of Hammond Ranch Corporation v. Dodson, 136 SW 2d 484 (Ark. 1940), involved the unauthorized spraying, with herbicides or pesticides, of the plaintiff's property adjacent to the property intended to be sprayed, which resulted in the death of the plaintiff's cattle.

- The case of Burke v. Thomas, 313 P 2d 1082 (Okla. 1957), involved the destruction of shade trees as a result of the unauthorized spraying with pesticides or herbicides.

LIABILITY TO PASSENGERS AND OTHERS

The purpose of this section is to emphasize the legal considerations involved when a pilot, passenger, or employee is injured as a result of an aircraft crash or collision.

The legal questions that arise are:

- Whether the passenger has the burden of proving that the carrier was negligent; or whether the carrier has the burden of proving that it was not negligent.

- Whether the lawsuit should be tried under the laws of the State in which the accident occurred; or whether the lawsuit should be tried under the Laws of Admiralty, or the Death on the High Seas Act; or whether it should be tried under the laws of the foreign country in which the plane is registered; or whether the case is covered by Workmen's Compensation laws in the case of an employee. This question is important because in some cases State laws make it easier for a plaintiff to recover damages; or the laws of the foreign country make it difficult for a plaintiff to recover damages; or the Workmen's Compensation cases limit the amount of damages that a plaintiff may recover for injuries.

- Whether the Federal Government is an employer, and whether it is liable for the acts of its employees under the Federal Tort Claims Act. The United States Government is not liable under the Federal Tort Claims Act if the facts in the case considered come within one of the exceptions set forth in the act.

ADMIRALTY LAWS AND DEATH ON THE HIGH SEAS ACT

In 1920 Congress passed the Death on the High Seas Act (41 Stat. 537), and thereby created a remedy, or right of action, for death caused by wrongful act, neglect, or default, on the high seas.

The First National Bank of Greenwich v. National Airlines, demonstrates how the courts resolved the question of whether to apply the State law or the Death on the High Seas Act. In this case the court applied the Death on the High Seas Act, because the crash occurred in the Gulf of Mexico beyond the three-mile limit from the Alabama shore.

When the Death on the High Seas Act created the right of action to sue for death occurring on the high seas, several other aspects arose.

The first task was to determine whether to apply the law of the United States or the laws of the foreign country in which the aircraft was registered.

The second task was to determine whether to afford the injured employee the relief of unlimited liability of employer, as provided by the Death on the High Seas Act; or whether to give the injured employee the limited liability of his employer as provided by the Workmen's Compensation laws.

The laws and rules of admiralty are old and settled. Some of these laws and rules have been made applicable to the laws of aviation, and others have not.

UNITED STATES AND THE FEDERAL TORT CLAIMS ACT

A previous section discussed application of the Federal Tort Claims Act (1946) to airports and the liability of airports to their neighbors.

In this section the application of the Federal Tort Claims Act on the liability of the United States Government in military activities is examined.

The next several cases illustrate special applications of provisions of the Federal Tort Claims Act (FTCA).

1. FTCA Section 2680(k) states that FTCA shall not apply to a claim arising in a foreign country. In U.S. v. Spelar, 338 U.S. 217 (1949), the court ruled that a military base in Newfoundland, leased to U.S. for a long term, was considered a foreign country for purposes of 2680(k), and therefore the U.S. was not liable.

2. In the case of Eastern Airlines v. Union Trust Co., 221 F. 2d 62 (1954), the executors of the deceased brought action for death arising out of a mid-air collision between a commercial airliner and a privately owned surplus fighter aircraft. The airport was owned by the U.S. Government. It was determined that the negligence of the tower operator controlling aircraft movement was the proximate cause of the accident and of the death. The court held that the U.S. was liable, because the tower operator was a federal employee within the meaning of 1346(b).

   In order to escape liability the defendant U.S. Government advanced two arguments:

   a. The airport was a discretionary function, and therefore the U.S. Government was not liable under FTCA Section 2680(a).

   b. A private individual could not perform this function, and therefore the U.S. Government was not liable within the meaning of FTCA Section 2674. The court rejected both of the government's arguments and ruled that the government was liable, because the airport function was not discretionary; and that anyone can operate an airport, hire tower operators, and get them certified by the Federal government.

3. Another case in which the court held that the discretionary function provision of Section 2680(a) did not preclude a suit under FTCA is Bullock v. U.S., 133 F. Supp 885 (Utah 1955), in which the court ruled that

the fallout damage to a flock of sheep, as a result of nuclear tests conducted by the Atomic Energy Commission, did not prevent a suit under FTCA.

TARIFFS— LIMITATION OF LIABILITY

A tariff is a list or schedule of charges for services and for transportation of goods and people, and the conditions therefor.

The study of tariffs in aviation cuts across many fields of study, including the Warsaw Convention and the Interstate Commerce Commission.

In the aviation industry tariffs for air carriage must be filed with the Civil Aeronautics Board. Properly filed, tariffs become a part of the contract of the carriage between the carriers and the shipper, and therefore, are binding on both parties. Tariff rates and schedules have been held to be binding on all parties whether or not the shipper has knowledge of the tariff rates and schedules.

The United States Supreme Court has applied its Interstate Commerce Act tariff rulings to cases under the FAA and under the CAB. Following are several cases decided by the Supreme Court under the Interstate Commerce Commission, as applicable to cases that might be brought under the Civil Aeronautics Board:

- In the case of Texas & Pacific R.R. Company v. Mugg & Dryden, 202 U.S. 242, the shipper was quoted a lower rate than that filed with the Interstate Commerce Commission. The Supreme Court held that the shipper must pay the full rate recited in the tariff.

- In Chicago & Atlantic R.R. Company v. Kirby, 255 U.S. 155 (1912), a carrier agreed to expedite a shipment of horses over its own lines in order to make connections with a fast freight train of a second carrier. The first carrier was not able to make the connection, and the shipper sued for recovery of damages for breach of an agreement. The Supreme Court held that the shipper could not recover damages for breach of an agreement, because the agreement constituted an unreasonable preference, forbidden by the Interstate Commerce Act. The shipper was charged only regular through rates with no provision for such service.

- In Jones v. Northwest Airlines, 157 P. 2d 728 (1945), the court applied the rulings under the ICC to aviation cases and tariffs filed under CAB. The tariff in question permitted the carrier to cancel a flight at any time it deemed necessary, and further stated that the carrier was not responsible for failure of the aircraft to depart or arrive at the scheduled time. The court held that, even though the passenger claimed he had a special contract with carrier which recognized the limited time he had for the trip, the alleged contract was void because it was inconsistent with the terms of the tariff schedules. The court stated that the ticket was sold subject to tariff regulations, which were in conflict with the alleged contract.

The general reasoning of many courts in cases similar to the above is based not on the fiction of constructive notice or of lack of contracts, but rather on the requirement for equality and uniformity of rates, and the application thereof.

WORKMEN'S COMPENSATION—LIMITATION OF LIABILITY

Workmen's Compensation acts are within the province of the states and, therefore, are covered by state laws and statutes. Workmen's Compensation acts provide benefits and care to employees who suffer injury or death in connection with their employment. The cost of these benefits is borne by the employer.

The primary task in Workmen's Compensation cases is to determine whether the injury or death of an employee occurred during the course of his employment. These are fact situations that are peculiar in themselves and cannot be readily applied to other cases.

The following are summaries of cases in which it was held that the injury or death of the employee occurred during the course of his employment and, therefore, the employee was covered by the Workmen's Compensation Act of his state.

- In Markoholz v. General Electric Co., 243 N.Y.S. 2d 853 (1963), an employee was on a one-week personal visit to Italy after attending a business conference in France. The court held that his death occurred while he was in the course of business and, therefore was covered by Workmen's Compensation Act.

- In Dunham Co. v. Industrial Commission, 156 NE 2d 560 (Ill. 1959), an engineer was traveling as a passenger from Chicago to Seattle in a commercial airliner which was destroyed in mid-air by an act of sabotage. The court held that his death occurred during the course of his employment and, therefore, was covered by the Workmen's Compensation Act of his state.

- In Indiana Steel Products Company v. Leonard, 131 N.E. 2d 162 (Ind. 1956), a salesman piloting a rented aircraft to make a call on a customer crashed the aircraft; and the court held he was covered by Workmen's Compensation Act.

The following are summaries of cases in which the courts held that the employee's injury or death did not occur within his duties of employment.

- In Ruffi v. American Fly Away Service Inc., 104 N.W. 2d 37 (Ohio 1950), a pilot ferrying an aircraft departed from flight altitude, buzzed a fishing boat, and as a consequence, crashed the aircraft. The court held that he was not acting within the scope of his employment and, therefore, was not covered by Workmen's Compensation Law of his state.

- In Lange v. Memphis, St. Paul Metropolitan Airport Commissions, 99 N.W. 2d 915 (Minn. 1959), an airport supervisor was instructed by his employer that flying aircraft was not a part of his duties and that flying was not permitted during working hours. The supervisor, while flying in violation of these instructions, crashed the aircraft. The court held he was not covered by Workmen's Compensation Act of his state.

- In Whitely v. King Radio Corporation, 375 Pac. 2d 593 (Kansas 1962), an engineer was taking flying lessons at the expense of his employer. The flying, however, had no relationship to the duties of his employment. The court held he was not covered by Workmen's Compensation.

WARSAW CONVENTION—LIMITATION OF LIABILITY

In the 1920s, the insurance industry provided protection to the airlines at high cost. Aircraft were mechanically unreliable and relatively frail. The first in-depth discussions about insurance took place in 1925. For those airlines which did get coverage, premiums were high—20% or more of the aircraft's value. If a State-owned airline did not have formal insurance coverage, claims were paid out of the Treasury. It was unusual for an aircraft to be fully insured, meaning that operators were exposed to considerable financial risk.

The airlines' insurance problems were largely solved by the Warsaw Convention whose purpose was to limit their liability. This Convention—the direct result of one of IATA's first major lobbying campaigns in the 1920s—defines a transporter's liability in case of death or injury to passengers or loss of or damage to cargo and baggage on international flights.

The Warsaw Convention has been modified since its first implementation in 1929 to meet changing economic conditions.

There is legal opinion that the limited liability provision, Article 22, and the venue provision, Article 28, of the Warsaw Convention deny equal rights of U.S. citizens under the Constitution. On November 7, 1968, Judge Nicholas J. Bua of the Circuit Court of Cook County, Illinois, handed down a lengthy Memorandum Opinion on this question (Burdell v. Canadian Pacific Airlines, No. 66L—10799, Cook County Circuit Court, Nov. 7, 1968). This case did not go to a higher court for appeal, because it was settled for $215,000 in favor of the plaintiff. The air carrier requested the court to withdraw that part of the ruling which related to constitutionality. The court granted the motion, but stated that, as concerns this case, the venue and damage limitation provisions of the Warsaw Convention were unconstitutional. This opinion, therefore, remains an important precedent on the constitutionality of Warsaw Articles 22 and 28. (Also refer to Illinois Bar Journal, February 1970, John J. Kennelly.)

The following summarized cases utilize and refer to several articles of the Warsaw Convention.

- In Mertens v. Flying Tiger Lines, 8 CCH Av. Cases 18023 (Dec. 5, 1963), an aircraft, with crew, was chartered to the U.S. Government, and the tickets were not delivered to passengers until after the aircraft was airborne. The plaintiff passenger, in this case, asserted that there was not sufficient delivery of tickets under Warsaw Convention Article 3, and therefore the limited liability provisions of the Warsaw Convention did not apply to the air carrier. The court held that there was sufficient delivery and, therefore, the limited liability provisions of Warsaw Convention Article 22 were applicable.

- In Kraus v. K.L.M., 92 N.Y.S. 2d (Oct. 17, 1949), an air freight "airwaybill" did not give a list of agreed stopping places as required by Warsaw Convention Article 8. However, the air freight "airwaybill" did make reference to a timetable list of scheduled stopping places. The plaintiff shipper asserted that, since the "airwaybill" did not set forth the stopping places, Warsaw Convention Article 9 would apply, and the carrier would not be able to use the limited liability provision of the Convention. The court held that the reference to the timetable was sufficient compliance with Warsaw Convention Article 8, and, therefore, the

limited liability provided by Article 20 would be applied in favor of the carrier defendant.

AIRLINE MUTUAL INSURANCE (AMI)

When insurance premiums rose in the mid-1980s IATA supported the foundation of Airline Mutual Insurance Ltd (AMI) for the exclusive use and benefit of the airlines. Located for tax reasons in Bermuda, AMI is termed a "mutual" because members mutually share their risk. Any profits are put back into the operation, so that the company can gain capital strength.

Since its launch in 1986, AMI has grown to provide coverage for more than 100 airlines. AMI functions as a classic aviation insurance company, insuring 5% of an operator's coverage.

AMI proved immediately beneficial to the airlines. It was more than mere coincidence that rates declined at the time of AMI's launch. Rates have not risen markedly although there are signs that rates will increase considerably in coming years for reasons related to the insurance market's structure.

AMI provides coverage for:

1. Hull all risks and liabilities
2. Hull war risks
3. Hull deductible risks
4. Aero-engine breakdown

In addition to its involvement with AMI, the IATA has successfully launched a range of competitively priced insurance schemes specially designed to meet airline industry needs. These include protection for an airline against loss of income following a disaster and against loss of license of a crew member due to unsatisfactory medical checks.

LIABILITY OF MANUFACTURERS AND REPAIRS

The liability of manufacturers and repairs to the buyers or passengers of their products is a dynamic aspect of aviation law. The two landmark cases are MacPherson v. Buick and Goldberg v. Kollsman.

The first question that must be resolved in manufacturer liability cases is whether there is privity of contract between the buyer and the manufacturer; and whether that privity of contract is necessary to hold the manufacturer liable to the buyer for injury inflicted on the buyer by the manufacturer's products. The courts have held that privity of contract is not necessary to hold the manufacturer liable.

The second question that must be resolved is whether the manufacturer is liable to the buyer on the legal theory that there is a tort, or on the theory that there is a breach of contract liability. This is an important question to be resolved.

If the manufacturer is liable on the basis of torts, then the plaintiff buyer has the burden of proving that the defendant manufacturer is negligent, because the manufacturer is presumed innocent until proved negligent. In addition, the defendant manufacturer has the following defenses by which he can wholly or partially escape liability:

1. The defendant can allege contributory negligence by the plaintiff buyer.

2. The defendant can allege that the plaintiff buyer assumed an unjustifiable risk.

3. The defendant can allege that the plaintiff violated a statute or ordinance.

If the manufacturer is liable on the contractual basis, whether it is actually written or implied, then the same manufacturer can be sued by the buyer on the basis that the manufacturer breached a warrant of contract. The warranty can be written or implied. Of course, in this contractual situation the plaintiff is in a stronger position than in that of tort liability. If the plaintiff buyer can sue the defendant manufacturer on the basis that the manufacturer breached a warranty of contract, then the advantage to the plaintiff is threefold:

1. The plaintiff buyer does not have the burden of proving that the defendant manufacturer is negligent.

2. The defendant manufacturer is presumed negligent and, therefore, has the burden of proving he was not negligent.

3. The defendant does not have the three defenses set forth above in the theory of tort liability.

The case of MacPherson v. Buick covers the general analysis of the liability theories. The case of Goldberg v. Kollsman applies the theory to the aircraft.

PRODUCT LIABILITY AND GENERAL AVIATION

A serious situation developed concerning product liability throughout the manufacturing industries of the United States after 1979. Builders of products are be-

ing sued and large court awards of money have been granted—even though sometimes the product was not to blame. For instance, if a person misuses a kitchen paring knife and cuts himself, it is not the fault of the person who made the knife. Yet courts have found the knife maker liable and have granted large financial awards. This example is hypothetical but it serves to illustrate the problem. Of course if the product were defective and caused the accident or injury then the liability grant is justified.

A survey showed that 47% of U.S. manufacturers withdrew their products from markets for liability reasons. Thirty-nine percent decided against introducing a new product and 25% discontinued new product research.

Some cities have had to close their playgrounds because they no longer found it practical to pay the high cost of liability insurance. Diving boards have been removed from public swimming pools and some pools have closed.

The liability problem has seriously affected general aviation in the production of small, light aircraft of the training and pleasure type. All small aircraft producers have either drastically reduced or completely ceased production.

Unfair and exorbitant product liability costs have devastated the United States general aviation manufacturers, consumers and service organizations. Claims paid by the industry along with product liability costs have increased even though the general aviation safety record has steadily improved. These higher costs result in higher prices and put the purchase of a general aviation aircraft beyond the means of many potential consumers. The costs have been driven up by an expansion of insurance liability costs and an increase in the size of court awards. Settlements and rapidly increasing costs fall directly upon the manufacturers—and ultimately upon the customer.

The increase in the number and the size of verdicts and settlements have driven some general aviation manufacturers out of business. Piper Aircraft Corporation's legal fees were in excess of $250,000 a month and used solely for legal defense. This is in addition to their liability insurance premium costs. One small aircraft component manufacturer said that his company had been sued even though his company's product, a magneto, was not a part of the aircraft that crashed. After $5,000 in legal fees and months of investigation it was proved that his product was not a part of the aircraft. The suing party and their attorney did not even bother to read the label on the magneto—which did not contribute to the crash when pilot error was the cause.

The suing attorney then would not dismiss the suit until the company signed an agreement not to sue because of the mistake. One company scrapped a year's research on a completely new electronic ignition system. The reason was not economic or technical; it was the potential product liability risk of being the pioneer of an innovative product.

The main cause of the liability problem is not the quality of the product manufactured or the insurance industry but the manner in which the laws have been abused. General aviation has suffered as a result. The general aviation manufacturers sold 964 light aircraft in 1993; in 1978 they sold 17,811 aircraft. Employment has decreased accordingly; by 65% since 1980. Foreign aircraft manufacturers are moving to fill the void caused by the product liability crisis. This further increases the United States' unfavorable balance of trade.

The cause of the liability problem is found in the courts which have expanded liability to unexpected situations. The most common judicial justification is that expanded liability provides a form of compensation insurance to victims who may not have insurance coverage for themselves. The corporate defendants passed along part of the compensation cost to consumers in the product price. This form of insurance is very expensive; perhaps five to ten times as costly as standard first-party insurance. That is because going to court entails greater legal expenses and often the payment of enormous amounts to cover pain and suffering, which no consumer is compensated for in first-party insurance coverage.

Our legal system cannot survive as a compensation insurance system. If courts insist on using the legal system as a compensation system, they must reduce tort damages and approve other tort reform measures to make the compensation system more coherent. The New York State Court of Appeals moved in this direction by restricting recovery for "loss of enjoyment of life," which again is uninsurable in a first-party policy. Much of modern tort reform also seeks this end by such steps

FLIGHTS OF FANCY

Piper Aircraft v. Cleveland

At dawn on July 7, 1983, a pilot by the name of Edward Cleveland crashed his 13 year old Piper Super Cub aircraft into a van parked at an airfield near Albuquerque, New Mexico. The van had been placed there by its owner to keep the pilot from taking off. Cleveland and the company for whom he was employed had been known for unsafe flying practices. The van owner did not want him using the runway. A local company hired Cleveland's firm to film an advertisement. Cleveland removed the front seat of his two-seater aircraft and installed a camera facing toward the rear. The cameraman was squeezed in behind the camera with his back covering the instrument panel and front window while the pilot was in the rear seat.

To prevent the take-off the airport owner parked his van a thousand feet down the runway with its lights on. The pilot started his take off and either did not see the van or thought he could clear it. He did not make it; he hit the van and smashed his face into the camera mount in front of him suffering severe brain damage.

His family sued the owner of the van and was awarded $300,000. Upon winning, their lawyer then sued Piper Aircraft. According to him the design of the Super Cub was defective. On the ground it is impossible to see out the front from the rear seat. He also contended that the airplane should have been equipped with a rear shoulder harness. Nothing was said about the cameraman blocking the view of the pilot. The jury was convinced and awarded $1,042,000 in damages. That award gave liability lawyers a great opportunity.

Piper became a target thereafter. Operators of corporate jets usually carry adequate insurance and can be sued when an accident occurs. The operators of Piper's small airplanes usually do not have such insurance, therefore lawyers went after the aircraft manufacturer. The Piper Company paid $10 million a year from 1987 through 1991 to settle lawsuits. Piper stopped buying insurance in 1987 because by then insurance became pointless. The last policy the company owned carried a $100,000,000 deductible. In July 1991, Piper entered bankruptcy under Chapter 11.

The design of the Super Cub, one of the most popular and safest aircraft in history, had long since been approved by the Federal Aviation Administration. This included a 1977 ruling that only a front seat shoulder harness was required.

FLIGHTS OF FANCY

Who's to Blame?

Airplane manufacturers blamed greedy lawyers for the distress of their industry. For example, Beech Aircraft noted that in four years during the 1980s, their company was sued 203 times for accidents involving their aircraft. In none of these cases did the National Transportation Safety Board find Beech equipment to be defective. The company said that it spent an average of $530,000 to defend itself in each case.

as limiting awards for pain and suffering. Those states that have capped awards left the amounts so high that continued problems are inevitable.

Industry in the U.S. remains liable in most states for over 200,000 domestic airplanes in service which is a risk exposure not shared by foreign competitors. This is an unreasonable burden especially considering that these airplanes average over 25 years of service and have been subject to modifications, maintenance and operation beyond the control of the manufacturer. This policy gives foreign air carriers a competitive advantage.

General aviation is totally regulated by the federal government from the design and manufacture of aircraft and component parts, and federal licensing of pilots and mechanics to the control of air traffic and accident investigation. However, liability is decided after an accident based upon laws which differ significantly from State to State. The inherent conflicts between Federal regulatory standards and widely divergent State liability laws can only be resolved through the establishment of Federal standards of liability by Congress.

Federal law had been proposed to set uniform Federal standards for product liability in general aviation. There tort reform measures have the support of the aviation industry and consumers including the Experimental Aircraft Association, the General Aviation Manufacturers Association, the Helicopter Association International, the National Agricultural Aviation Association, the National Aeronautic Association, the National Air Transportation Association and the National Business Aircraft Association.

GENERAL AVIATION REVITALIZATION ACT

Legal reformers and manufacturers pressed Congress for over eight years to pass a bill limiting lawsuits against manufacturers of small airplanes. Their claim was that such suits were unfair and could be brought about after the plane had been rebuilt or major parts replaced.

The legal profession represented by the American Trial Lawyers Association fought against any change and argued that some defects require many years to emerge.

On August 17, 1994, President Clinton signed a new law known as the General Aviation Revitalization Act which prevents lawsuits against an airplane or parts manufacturer more than 18 years after manufacture. This is known as the "statute of repose." Before then manufacturers could be held liable for defects for the life of their products. This exemption from lawsuits applies to about half of the 180,000 private aircraft in the United States, many of which are more than 25 years old. This new law immediately prompted renewed interest in private flying. Small aircraft manufacturers have re-opened production lines. The Cessna Aircraft Company is building piston engine powered aircraft including models 172, 182, and 206 which they had ceased building in 1986 because of the product liability costs. Independence, Kansas is the site for the single-engine assembly facility. One thousand employees at that location conduct final assembly, paint and flight operations, engineering, finance, marketing, and human resource functions.

The General Aviation Manufacturers Association which represents Beech, Cessna, Learjet, and about 50 other makers of private airplanes, predict that the new Act will create 25,000 more jobs within five years after the passage of the law.

The passage of the Revitalization Act represents a broader victory because for the first time Congress limited the ability of lawyers to sue manufacturers for product liability. Such limits have long been opposed by the trial lawyers of the nation who have one of the toughest lobbies in Washington. The Association of Trial Lawyers of America opposed the general aviation legislation for the same reason that it opposes all such legislation.

They stated that when consumers' rights are taken away, it is an important issue for their organization. Further they stated that the small aviation industry was in the shape it was in not because of lawsuits but because of many factors including mismanagement of companies and their decisions to build the wrong type of aircraft.

GENERAL AVIATION REVITALIZATION ACT OF 1994

Following is a reprint of Public Law 103-298.

Public Law 103-298
One Hundred Third Congress of the United States of America
At the Second Session

Begun and held at the City of Washington on Tuesday, the twenty-fifth day of January, one thousand nine hundred and ninety-four

AN ACT

To amend the Federal Aviation Act of 1958 to establish time limitations on certain civil actions against aircraft manufacturers, and for other purposes.

Be it enacted by the Senate and House of Representatives of the United States of America in Congress assembled,

SECTION 1. SHORT TITLE

This Act may be cited as the "General Aviation Revitalization Act of 1994."

SEC. 2. TIME LIMITATIONS ON CIVIL ACTIONS AGAINST AIRCRAFT MANUFACTURERS

(a) In General—Except as provided in subsection (b), no civil action for damages for death or injury to persons or damage to property arising out of an accident involving a general aviation aircraft may be brought against the manufacturer of the aircraft or the manufacturer of any new component, system, subassembly, or other part of the aircraft, in its capacity as a manufacturer if the accident occurred—

(1) after the applicable limitation period beginning on—

(A) the date of delivery of the aircraft to its first purchaser or lessee, if delivered directly from the manufacturer; or

(B) the date of first delivery of the aircraft to a person engaged in the business of selling or leasing such aircraft; or

(2) with respect to any new component, system, subassembly, or other part which replaced another component, system, subassembly, or other part originally in, or which was added to, the aircraft, and which is alleged to have caused such death, injury, or damage, after the applicable limitation period beginning on the date of completion of the replacement or addition.

(b) Exceptions—Subsection (a) does not apply—

(1) if the claimant pleads with specificity the facts necessary to prove, and proves, that the manufacturer with respect to a type certificate or airworthiness certificate for, or obligations with respect to continuing airworthiness of, an aircraft or a component, system, subassembly, or other part of an aircraft knowingly misrepresented to the Federal Aviation Administration, or concealed or withheld from the Federal Aviation Administration, required information that is material and relevant to the performance or the maintenance or operation of such aircraft, or the component, system, subassembly, or other part, that is causally related to the harm which the claimant allegedly suffered;

(2) if the person for whose injury or death the claim is being made is a passenger for purposes of receiving treatment for a medical or other emergency;

(3) if the person for whose injury or death the claim is being made was not aboard the aircraft at the time of the accident; or

(4) to an action brought under a written warranty enforceable under law but for the operation of this Act.

(c) General Aviation Aircraft Defined—For the purposes of this Act, the term "general aviation aircraft" means any aircraft for which a type certificate or an airworthiness certificate has been issued by the Administrator of the Federal Aviation Administration, which at the time such certificate was originally issued, had a maximum seating capacity of fewer than 20 passengers, and which was not, at the time of the accident, engaged in scheduled passenger-carrying operations as defined under regulations in effect under the Federal Aviation Act of 1958 (49 U.S.C. App. 1301 et seq.) at the time of the accident.

(d) Relationship to Other Laws—This section supersedes any State law to the extent that such law permits a civil action described in subsection (a) to be brought after the applicable limitation period for such civil action established by subsection (a).

SEC. 3. OTHER DEFINITIONS

For purposes of this Act—

(1) the term "aircraft" has the meaning given such term in section 101(5) of the Federal Aviation Act of 1958 (49 U.S.C. 1301(5));

(2) the term "airworthiness certificate" means an airworthiness certificate issued under section 603(c) of the Federal Aviation Act of 1958 (49 U.S.C. 1423(c)) or under any predecessor Federal statute;

(3) the term "limitation period" means 18 years with respect to general aviation aircraft and the components, systems, subassemblies, and other parts of such aircraft; and

(4) the term "type certificate" means a type certificate issued under section 603(a) of the Federal Aviation Act of 1958 (49 U.S.C. 1423(a)) or under any predecessor Federal statute.

SEC. 4. EFFECTIVE DATE; APPLICATION OF ACT

(a) Effective Date.—Except as provided in subsection (b), this Act shall take effect on the date of the enactment of this Act.

(b) Application of Act.—This Act shall not apply with respect to civil actions commenced before the date of the enactment of this Act.

TAXPAYER RELIEF ACT OF 1997*

The Taxpayer Relief Act was signed into law August 5, 1997. It is known as Public Law 105-35, and provides for the future of aviation funding for the Federal Aviation Administration and its capital improvement programs. New laws present questions for the taxpayer and/or the collector on how these provisions will be administered. The Secretary of the Treasury has the authority to develop regulations regarding the administration of this law. The Act includes six basic areas which include the following:

1. Aviation Gasoline
2. Jet Fuel
3. Transportation Taxes
4. Special Provisions For Rural Airports
5. International Flights
6. Other Tax Provisions

Aviation Gasoline

The act extends the federal excise taxes imposed on aviation gasoline and jet fuel to September 30, 2007. All federal excise taxes imposed on aviation gas are assessed as the product is lifted from the terminal rack or refinery. The first of these taxes is the 15 cents a gallon producer's tax. Revenue collected from the deficit reduction tax break (4.3 cents a gallon) that was previously deposited into the U.S. Treasury's General Fund is now deposited in the Airport and Airway Trust Fund. The previously expired Leaking Underground Storage Tank tax is reinstated as the listed rate and is also collected by the producer.

*Excerpts from The National Air Transportation Association publication "The Aviation Industry Guide to the Taxpayer Relief Act of 1997."

Those operators that qualify for aviation gas fuel credits are allowed to continue claiming 15 cents a gallon tax credit on commercial flights. Even though the 4.3 cents a gallon deficit reduction tax is now deposited into the Aviation Trust Fund, this tax is paid by all users, both commercial and noncommercial, and is not refundable.

Jet Fuel

All federal excise taxes imposed on jet fuel are assessed as the product is sold by the wholesale distributor. The major component of the taxes is a 17.5 cents a gallon wholesale distributor's tax. Revenue collected from the deficit reduction tax (4.3 cents a gallon) that was previously deposited into the U.S. Treasury's General Fund is now deposited in the Airport and Airway Trust Fund. The previously expired Leaking Underground Storage Tank tax is reinstated at the listed rate and is also collected by the wholesaler. Those operators that qualify for jet fuel tax credits are allowed to continue claiming 17.5 cents a gallon tax credit on commercial flights. Even though the 4.3 cents a gallon deficit reduction tax is now deposited into the Aviation Trust Fund, this tax is paid by all users, both commercial and non-commercial, and is not refundable.

Transportation Taxes

The Taxpayer Relief Act of 1997 dramatically revised aviation excise taxes on domestic and international transportation of persons. However, the tax rate and application on transportation of cargo remains unchanged.

The federal excise tax of 6.25% for cargo shipped within the United States before October 1, 1997, remains unchanged and is extended through September 30, 2007. Cargo that arrives from or departs to international locations is exempt from the domestic transportation of cargo tax.

After September 30, 1997, the rate of tax for transportation of persons will decrease incrementally over the next three years to a final level of 7.5%. However, this tax is now coupled with a second tax on domestic segments. The incremental decrease in the transportation of persons tax is: 8% after September 30, 1998; 7.5% between September 30, 1999 and September 30, 2007.

In addition to decreasing the transportation of persons tax, the Act also imposes a *domestic segment fee*. The term "domestic segment" is defined as any segment consisting of one takeoff and one landing by a flight that is defined as taxable transportation by the Internal Revenue Service. The domestic segment fee applies to each segment of paid transportation.

Those operators that charge one person or company for the use of an entire aircraft will see this fee applied once per flight segment, regardless of the number of passengers on the aircraft. Operators that sell seats on flights (tickets) must assess this tax on each paid passenger seat per flight segment.

The Internal Revenue Service Chief Counsel's office has not ruled on how the domestic segment fee will apply. However, the bill language states that this tax is imposed on amounts paid for each segment of domestic transportation rather than on transportation of persons by air (a head tax) as seen with the international facilities tax. Air carriers should determine how to address the collection of domestic segment fees until the Internal Revenue Service releases further guidance.

Note that the domestic segment fee is not subject to the transportation of persons tax. This fee is added after the total flight cost and tax are calculated for a particular flight. (Table 19.1.)

Occasionally situations may result in a change of the original route planned for a flight between two points that requires diverting to an alternate location. Such situations occur for weather delays, in-flight medical emergencies and aircraft malfunctions. These diversions that do not require an additional charge are exempt from additional domestic segment charges.

Special Provisions for Rural Airports

Recognizing the special needs of small, rural airports, Congress adopted a provision that provides an incentive for service to small community airports. Beginning on October 1, 1997, flights that begin or end at rural airports are charged the transportation of persons tax at a rate of 7.5%. Additionally, the per-flight segment fee does not apply to any segment that begins or ends at a rural airport. A rural airport is defined as an airport with less than 100,000 commercial passengers

Table 19.1 Incremental Increase in Domestic Segment Fee

Transportation after	Domestic Segment Fee
9/30/98	$2.00
9/30/99	$2.25
12/31/99	$2.50
12/31/2000	$2.75
12/31/01	$3.00
12/31/02	Indexed to the Consumer Price Index.

departing (passenger enplanements) during the second preceding calendar year. Additionally, the airport must not be located within 75 miles of another airport that has 100,000 or more commercial passenger departures. Also, airports that receive federally-subsidized essential air service as of August 5, 1997, are considered rural if that airport has less than 100,000 enplanements.

While on the surface this provision appears to necessitate an additional burden on air carriers, customers traveling to rural airports will pay less federal excise tax compared to non-rural airport flights for a period of two years. After September 30, 1999, rural airports continue to qualify for the domestic segment fee exemption.

The Internal Revenue Service in conjunction with the Department of Transportation and the Federal Aviation Administration, is developing a listing of rural airports that qualify for the special provision. Until guidance is issued from the IRS regarding rural airports, operators are required to determine if each flight qualifies for the exemption. A list of rural airports will be released when it is developed and approved.

Inevitably, additional charges such as pilot waiting fees, overnight expenses, crew travel and expenses, airport landing fees, and FBO handling fees must be charged to the customer. These additional expenses are subject to the transportation of persons tax. However, flights involving multiple legs may travel to rural airports and therefore are assessed a different tax rate. Any charge associated with a flight that departs from or arrives at a rural airport is taxed at the rural airport rate of 7.5%. In-flight catering remains exempt from any federal excise tax.

International Flights

Operators that perform international flights have many changes in the international tax rates and the application of these taxes. Passengers on flights arriving from or departing to international locations are subject to a $12 international facilities charge each way.

Flights that began in the United States or in the 255 mile zone and end in the United States or in the 225 mile zone are subject to the domestic transportation of persons tax. The "225 mile zone" means of those portions of Canada and Mexico that are not more than 225 miles from the nearest point in the continental United States. The act extends this prohibition for ten years.

The Taxpayer Relief Act of 1997 applies special provisions to international flights arriving and departing from Alaska and Hawaii. Flights from the continental United States to Hawaii and Alaska travel significant distances over international territory. The Internal Revenue Service can only assess fees on flights that travel over United States land. As a result, Congress has adopted a special provision for those domestic flights traveling to or from Alaska or Hawaii. All domestic flights to and from Alaska and Hawaii are subject to the domestic transportation of a persons tax for the distance traveled over United States territory. Additionally each person is charged a $6 international facilities fee.

Other Tax Provisions

Congress has provided an exemption for flights involved in skydiving from the transportation of persons tax. Flights that are exclusively dedicated to skydiving are taxed as non-commercial aviation flights and pay the fuel tax.

The Act permits a refund of the tax previously paid on aviation jet fuel when a registered producer purchases the fuel, tax included. Fuel sold at most airports is sold by the retail dealers that do not qualify as wholesale distributors. This fuel is purchased by the retailers with the tax included in the price-per-gallon. In certain instances, fuel that has been purchased tax-paid by a retailer is resold to a registered producer. This is to enable the producer to serve one of its other customers at the airport. When this fuel is resold by the producer, a second tax is imposed. Previously the Internal Revenue Code contained no provision that allows for a refund of the first tax in such cases. The Act now allows registered producers to receive a refund for the previously paid tax on jet fuel.

Tax law places sole liability for payment of any excise taxes on the person or company paying for transportation by air. After September 30, 1997, the initial air carriers providing transportation will be held secondarily liable for payment of any excise taxes that are paid by the customer at the time transportation is provided for international flights. For air carriers, this means that the excise tax for all legs of air transportation must be collected and remitted by the air carrier providing the initial domestic leg, even if multiple carriers are used.

In 1996, Congress authorized an exemption from the domestic transportation of persons tax for operators that use aircraft equipped for, and exclusively dedicated to, acute air medical transportation. Congressional report language did not clarify how the exemption applied to specific flights. The Act clarifies the exemption to apply on a flight-by-flight basis rather than on a dedicated aircraft basis. Emergency Medical Service flights also qualify for a fuel tax credit.

The transportation of persons tax rate incrementally decreases over the next 3 years. As pre-payments for air transportation are received, the tax must be computed based on the date the transportation occurs, not the date the payment is received.

CODE OF FEDERAL REGULATIONS

The Code of Federal Regulations is a codification of general and permanent rules that were first published in the Federal Register by agencies and departments that belong to the Executive Branch of the Federal Government. The Code is divided into fifty Titles, which represent broad areas subject to federal regulations. The various Titles list regulations that set the standards affecting most segments of aviation and transportation as well as other public activity.

TITLES

1. General Provisions
2. Reserved
3. The President
4. Accounts
5. Administrative Personnel
6. Reserved
7. Agriculture
8. Aliens and Nationality
9. Animals and Animal Products
10. Energy
11. Federal Elections
12. Banks and Banking
13. Business Credit and Assistance
14. Aeronautics and Space
15. Commerce and Foreign Trade
16. Commercial Practices
17. Commodity and Securities Exchanges
18. Conservation of Power and Water Resources
19. Custom Duties
20. Employees' Benefits
21. Food and Drugs
22. Foreign Relations
23. Highways
24. Housing and Urban Development
25. Indians
26. Internal Revenue
27. Alcohol, Tobacco Products and Firearms
28. Judicial Administration
29. Labor
30. Mineral Resources
31. Money and Finance: Treasury
32. National Defense
33. Navigation and Navigable Waters
34. Education
35. Panama Canal
36. Parks, Forests and Public Property
37. Patents, Trademarks and Copyrights
38. Pensions, Bonuses and Veterans' Relief
39. Postal Service
40. Protection of Environment
41. Public Contracts and Property Management
42. Public Health
43. Public Lands: Interior
44. Emergency Management and Assistance
45. Public Welfare
46. Shipping
47. Telecommunication
48. Federal Acquisition Regulations System
49. Transportation
50. Wildlife and Fisheries

Each of the fifty Titles is divided into Chapters, which usually bear the name of the issuing agency. For instance, Title 14, Aeronautics and Space, is of interest to those in the Air Transportation/Aviation Industry. There are four Chapters in Title 14; Chapter 1 is the only one that deals with Federal Aviation Regulations (FAR'S). The remaining chapters deal with the Department of Transportation rules, National Aeronautics and Space Administration regulations and so forth. Each chapter is further subdivided into Subchapters. For example, Title 14 Subchapter A, contains only Part 1, Definitions. Subchapter B, Procedural Rules, contains five Parts. Subchapters C, Aircraft, has eleven Parts in the Subchapter. The entire 199 Parts that comprise the Federal Aviation Regulations are divided in this manner. To emphasize, in Chapter 1, there are 199 Parts assigned to Federal Aviation Regulations.

Parts contain regulations dealing with a subject, such as Part 39, Airworthiness Directives or Part 145, Repair

Stations. Parts are further divided into Subparts and Subsections. Subparts make up a specific group within the Part. For example, Subpart 21 deals with Aircraft Type Certificates. Sections are individual rules. For example,

Federal Aviation Regulations (FAR) 43.13, Performance Rules, is a section of a subpart, which is part of a part, which is found in a chapter, which is a subdivision of a Title. Thus there are Titles, Chapters, Subchapters, Parts, Subparts and Sections. The government has a system or code on how each Part, Subpart and Section is identified. For example: Title 14, Chapter 1, Part 39, Subpart A, Section 39.1.

The code starting with Parts is numerical, then Subpart A is alphabetical, and then Section 43.13 is numerical. The Federal Aviation Administration uses odd numbers first such as Part 1, 11, 21, 43, 91, 121, 145 and so forth. With few exceptions, only slightly more than half, 106, of the 199 Parts assigned to the Federal Aviation Regulations is being used.

The same identification system is used to identify the Federal Aviation Regulation Parts from each other is also used within each Part. Each original individual section or rule is identified with an odd number, for example 21.95 or 43.1. A new Part or Section can be recognized because it has an even number.

Title 14
AERONAUTICS AND SPACE
CHAPTER 1
FEDERAL AVIATION ADMINISTRATION
DEPARTMENT OF TRANSPORTATION

Part
1   Definitions and Abbreviations
11   General rulemaking procedures
13   Investigation and enforcement procedures
14   Rules implementing the Equal Access to Justice Act of 1980
15   Administrative claims under Federal Tort Claims Act
16   Rules of practice for Federally-assisted airport enforcement proceedings
17   Procedures for protests and contracts disputes
21   Certification procedures for products and parts
23   Airworthiness standards: Normal, utility, acrobatic, and commuter category airplanes
25   Airworthiness standards: Transport category airplanes
27   Airworthiness standards: Normal category rotorcraft
29   Airworthiness standards: Transport category rotorcraft
31   Airworthiness standards: Manned free balloons
33   Airworthiness standards: Aircraft engines
34   Fuel venting and exhaust emission requirements for turbine engine powered airplanes
35   Airworthiness standards: Propellers
36   Noise standards: Aircraft type and airworthiness certification
39   Airworthiness directives
43   Maintenance, preventive maintenance, rebuilding and alteration
45   Identification and registration marking
47   Aircraft registration
49   Recording of aircraft titles and security documents
50–59 Reserved

PART 1:
DEFINITIONS AND ABBREVIATIONS

The aviation dictionary can be found in Part 1. It gives the proper legal definition of the words used in Federal Aviation Regulations. Words and terms used are subject to explicit definition so that their meaning cannot be misinterpreted. Some words in general usage may have a totally different meaning as used in aviation. An example of this is *airframe, appliance* and *airworthiness,* among others.

Section 1.3, Rules of Construction, defines the way words are used in Federal Aviation Regulations. For example: words referring to the singular include the plural and vice-versa. Words importing a masculine gender also include the feminine. The word *shall* is used in an imperative sense. The word *may* is used in a permissive sense; such as a person may or may not be authorized or permitted to do the act prescribed. The word *includes* means "includes, but is not limited to."

PART 11:
GENERAL RULEMAKING PROCEDURES

Subpart C of this Part is where the average person has regulatory authority to change the way the Federal Aviation Administration does business by requesting a rulemaking action. The average citizen has the power as written in Title 14, Chapter 1, Part 11, to petition the Federal Aviation Administration to make a rule, change an existing one, or delete a rule altogether. Especially important is Section 11.25, which explains not only the rulemaking process but also how to obtain an exemption from one or more rules.

PART 13:
INVESTIGATIVE AND ENFORCEMENT PROCEDURES

This Part is where aviation people should go first when they get a letter of investigation from the Federal Aviation Administration. Lawyers involved in cases must be fully aware of this Part when representing their clients in an investigation or procedures case.

PART 21:
CERTIFICATION PROCEDURES FOR PRODUCTS AND PARTS

A rule in this part is worth noting in Section 21.181. It refers to the duration of Airworthiness Certificates. It states that the Airworthiness Certificate is effective as long as the maintenance, preventative maintenance and alterations are performed in accordance with Parts 43 and 91 of this Chapter and the aircraft is registered in the United States. This statement can be found on the standard white Airworthiness Certificate found on board the aircraft in seat pockets or on cockpit doors. This indicates that the Registration Certificate, not the Airworthiness Certificate, is the most important document in the aircraft because the Airworthiness Certificate is worthless without it.

Look at an Airworthiness Certificate, Block 1, because it identifies the "N" number of the aircraft, which is found on the Registration Certificate.

Section 21.197, Special Flight Permits, is another rule worth knowing. This rule allows an aircraft that does not meet all the applicable airworthiness requirements, but is flyable, to make a flight. There are five reasons for a special flight permit to be used:

1. Flying the aircraft to a base where repairs, alterations or maintenance are to be performed or to a point of storage.
2. Delivering or exporting the aircraft.
3. Flight testing new production aircraft.
4. Evacuating aircraft from areas of impending danger.

5. Conducting customer demonstration flights in new production aircraft that have satisfactorily completed production flight test.

If any of the above special permits are required, the Federal Aviation Administration Airworthiness Inspector must be contacted to help in processing the necessary forms in accordance with Section 21.199.

Another important rule in Part 21 can be found in Section 21.303, Replacement and Modification of Parts. This rule states that no person may produce a modification or a replacement part for sale for installation on a type certificate product unless it has a Parts Manufacturer Approval (PMA). However, there are four exceptions to this:

1. Parts produced under a type or production certificate.
2. Parts produced by an owner or operator for their own product.
3. Parts produced under a Technical Standard Order (TSO).
4. Standard parts conforming to an established United States or industry standard.

Another regulation not usually understood is Export Airworthiness Approvals found in Part 21, Subpart 1. Exports are divided into three classes. A Class I product is a complete type certificated aircraft, engine or propeller. A Class II product is a major component of a Class I product including a wing or control surfaces. A Class III product is anything not included in the above two classes.

The document required for a Class I product is an Export Certificate of Airworthiness, FAA Form 8130-4. This document does not authorize the operation of aircraft. It merely states that the aircraft meets its type design and is in airworthy condition. Used aircraft being exported must have an annual type inspection completed no less than thirty days before the date of application is made for the Export Certificate of Airworthiness.

PART 39:
AIRWORTHINESS DIRECTIVES

This Part has a very specific purpose. It corrects unsafe conditions discovered in either the manufacturing of the product or corrects a defect that occurred during the life service of the product. Each Airworthiness Directive (AD) is an individual rule or section with its own amendment number. There are currently more than 11,000 amendment numbers making Part 39 the largest Part in the Federal Regulations.

Airworthiness Directives are divided into three Books. Book 1 has all of the Airworthiness Directives issued from the beginning through 1979. Book 2 covers all of the AD's issued from 1980 through 1989. Book 3 covers the AD's from 1990 to the present date. Each Book is divided into five sections: large aircraft, small aircraft, appliances, powerplants and propellers.

There are three types of Airworthiness Directives:

1. The emergency or priority letter

2. The immediate adopted rule

3. The notice of proposed rulemaking

Because safety is most important, the emergency or priority letter and the immediate adopted rule are exempt from the long rulemaking process. The notice of proposed rulemaking moves along the same route that other proposed rules must travel. It is not unusual for a proposed Airworthiness Directive to be canceled by the rulemaking process. This usually happens when there is a large amount of unfavorable comments to the notice of proposed rulemaking by the public.

The quickest way to determine the difference between the emergency or priority letter is that the emergency AD starts with the words "prior to flight." Most emergency AD's will ground the aircraft until the correction is made. An immediate adopted rule does not ground the aircraft; it allows a little time to have it corrected. Immediate adopted rules usually begin with the words "within the next ten hours/cycles/days perform the following." The language used in the AD issued by the normal rule-making process usually gives the owner a certain number of hours or months to make the correction.

The Airworthiness numbering system is clear and concise. The first two numbers are in the year; the second group of two numbers describe the bi-weekly issue that the AD was assigned. The last two numbers identify its position within that year and a bi-weekly issue.

PART 43:
MAINTENANCE, PREVENTIVE MAINTENANCE, REBUILDING AND ALTERATIONS

Part 43 is of extreme importance to aircraft mechanics. There are twelve regulations, which they must know. Eleven apply to United States certificated mechanics. The twelfth regulation applies to work done on United States aircraft by certain Canadian persons. In addition there are six appendices. Appendix C is "reserved" and contains nothing.

The eleven rules or sections of Part 43 can be stated as containing five elements:

1. Applicability (for what has Part 43 been used?)

2. Who can do the work on the aircraft

3. Who can sign off on the work

4. Record-keeping

5. Performance standards

Applicability

Section 43.1: Applicability, limits its authority to only aircraft having a United States Airworthiness Certificate and foreign registered aircraft used in a Part 121, 127 or 135 air carrier operation. This rule allows a United States certificated mechanic to work on a German 'N' number A320 Airbus operated by United Airlines. Paragraph (b) of this section states that Part 43 does not apply to any aircraft which has only been issued an experimental Airworthiness Certificate, such as an amateur built aircraft. The Federal Aviation Administration does not impose maintenance standards on an unknown aircraft and hold a mechanic responsible to that standard.

Who can work on an aircraft?

Section 43.3 gives a long list of individuals who can perform maintenance; such as manufacturers, repair stations, air carriers, mechanics, and people working under the supervision of mechanics. It even allows pilots to work on aircraft. Almost anyone can work on an aircraft either by holding the proper certification or working under the supervision of a mechanic who possesses it.

Section 43.5 and 43.7 allows only a privileged few to approve an aircraft to return to service. Although mechanics, repair stations, manufacturers, air carriers and pilots can perform preventive maintenance and approve an aircraft for return to service, the real power and responsibility is the authority given by the government to approve an aircraft for return to service.

Record-keeping

Aircraft mechanics need to sign only three documents. The airplane and powerplant mechanic has the authority to approve the aircraft or component for return to service in only two of the three documents. The first two are maintenance and inspection logbook entries. Section 43.9 refers to maintenance entries and Section 43.11 relates to inspection entries. The third document is Form 337. While a certificated mechanic can perform a major repair or major alteration, it is the responsibility of the repair station or air carrier to return the aircraft or component to service. Appendix B in Part 43 is the appendix that refers to maintenance entries on Form 337 and maintenance releases for major repairs and major alterations. Examples of these follow:

Section 43.9, Maintenance entries, requires all log entries to have the following:

1. A description or reference to acceptable data used.
2. The date the work was completed.
3. The name of the person performing the work.
4. Signature and kind of certificate held.

There is no requirement to approve the work for return to service in Section 43.9. This has been provided for in paragraph (a) (4) and states very plainly that the signature constitutes approval for return to service for only the work performed. Also, the person who signs off on the work does not necessarily have to be the one who performs the work. If an individualis working under supervision of another, even if he is not certified, his name must be included as well as the one signing the document.

Period of Responsibility

For maintenance work, such as minor repairs and alterations, the mechanic is held responsible only for work that he or she performed until that work is rein-spected, altered, replaced, damaged or reached its life limit. Part 91 states that the maximum amount of time to be held responsible is approximately one year or until the next annual inspection.

Section 43.11, Inspections entries, requires all log-book entries to have the following:

1. The type of inspection and a brief description of the extent of the inspection.
2. The date and total time in service. Time in service is defined as time accumulated from takeoff to landing. (Hobbs meter and Tach time are acceptable—except the two cannot be mixed.)
3. The signature and certificate number of the person approving or disapproving the aircraft or component part for return to service.

It is important to know that inspections, either large or small, conducted on Part 91 aircraft cannot be delegated to another individual. The one who signed the logbook entry must be the one who performed the inspection.

Time Held Responsible for an Inspection

The mechanic is held responsible for the inspection only until he or she signs the logbook. This may not sound correct but the truth is that the mechanic has no control over the airworthiness condition of the aircraft once it leaves his or her care. The Federal Aviation Administration would be unreasonable to hold the mechanic responsible for the future airworthiness of the entire aircraft for an undetermined period of time, especially when the aircraft becomes the responsibility of every pilot that flies it.

Section 43.11 states that the inspection logbook entry declares that every major and minor repair and alteration is airworthy at that moment of time when completed. An inspection approves only the past and not for the future. While Part 43 acquires a Form 337 to be completed for a major repair or alteration, it is Section 91.417, Record-keeping, that states the length of time the owner or operator is required to keep Form 337. For a major repair, Section 91.417(a)(1) requires only one year. The thinking behind this rule is based on the fact that the major repair returns the aircraft or component part back to its original type design, so nothing has been changed. In most cases, within a year repair would be accomplished again by a new inspector so the form can be discarded because a copy of the major repair is kept in the file of the aircraft in the Federal Aviation Administration Office at Oklahoma City. However, it is wise to retain a copy of Form 337 in the maintenance records in order to recall who, what, when, where, and how the aircraft was repaired. It is in the best interest of the owner to save all major repair Forms 337.

Section 43.2 is relatively new. This rule defines the term "overhauled" and "rebuilt." This section defines the major difference between an overhauled unit and one that has been rebuilt by stating the overhauled unit must meet manufacturing service limits and a rebuilt unit must meet new part limits.

Mechanics have it much easier because the Federal Aviation Administration set the standard for overall quality of work, or how the work is done. Section 43.13, Performance Rules, is a three paragraph rule. Paragraph (a) sets the standard for data and tools that must be used. The rule requires that each mechanic performing maintenance shall use the methods, techniques, and practices in the current manufacturer's manuals or instructions for continuing Airworthiness or other methods, techniques and practices acceptable to the Federal Aviation Administration. The mechanic must also use the tools, equipment and test apparatus to assure completion of the work in accordance with acceptable industry practices. Paragraph (b) sets the standard for acceptable quality of work. The rule requires that each mechanic performing maintenance shall do the work in such manner and use materials of such quality, that the condition of the aircraft is at least equal to its original or properly altered condition. The reference in the rule "equal to" is very important. If a mechanic made a repair better than the original then that mechanic made either a major or minor alteration to the type design of the aircraft. Paragraph (c) provides special provisions for air carriers. This paragraph basically states that an air carrier's manual and operating specifications constitute an acceptable means of compliance with Section 43.13.

PART 91: GENERAL OPERATING AND FLIGHT RULES

The rules in Part 91 that concern airplane mechanics are the General Operating Rules. These rules are divided into two broad Subparts. Subpart C refers to additional equipment that must be maintained and Subpart E is about maintenance, preventive maintenance, and alterations.

Subpart C refers to equipment that was never part of the original aircraft Type Design. This additional equipment was added to the aircraft because it either enhances the environment of the operating aircraft or because it was required by regulation. An example of the equipment that enhances the aircraft operating environment are transponders, oxygen and even lights. An example of equipment required by mandatory law passed by Congress is the Emergency Locator Transmitter (ELT).

Section 91.213 refers to inoperative instruments and equipment. It states that "no person may take off in an aircraft with inoperative instruments or equipment installed————." This could mean a logbook entry describing inoperative equipment that does not constitute a hazard to the aircraft. It is not part of the aircraft equipment for the kind of flight to be conducted.

Part 91, Subpart E, contains requirements for inspections including annuals, 100 hour, progressive and inspections for large and turbine aircraft under Section 91.409 (e)(f). This is the Subpart where the mechanics favorite rule can be found. Section 91.403(a) is the rule that the Federal Aviation Administration puts the primary responsibility for maintaining the aircraft in an airworthy condition on the owner or operator of the aircraft.

CHAPTER **20**

Aviation Industry Performance and Forecasts*

Performance data and forecasts are developed annually for use by the Federal Aviation Administration in future planning and are widely used not only by government organizations but also by the aviation community and other interested groups. These forecasts cover the years through 2009.

Generally, the forecast predicts expansion of the U.S. economy and therefore a positive growth in the air transportation industry. The U.S. economy is expected to grow at an average rate of 3% to the year 2012.

It must be recognized that forecasting is not an exact science; it has its limits. Accuracy is dependent on economic and political assumptions. Forecasts will require revisions and adjustments as time advances in the forecast period. The FAA's accuracy in its forecasting of two to three years has been very high in the short term and reasonably accurate in the long term of ten to twelve years.

COMMERCIAL AVIATION PERFORMANCE

In 2000, the large U.S. air carriers' system capacity (ASMs or available seat miles) increased by 4.4 percent, only slightly less than the 4.6 percent increase recorded in 1999. Passenger demand (RPMs and enplanements) grew by 6.4 and 4.7 percent, respectively. As a result of faster traffic growth relative to growth in capacity, the system-wide load factor (including domestic and international services) increased to 72.2 per-

cent, an all-time record high. The previous highest system load factor was the 70.9 percent recorded in 1998.

Domestic capacity (50 states, Puerto Rico, and the U.S. Virgin Islands) increased by 4.6 percent in 2000. Domestic capacity is up 10.1 percent over the past 2 years, the highest consecutive year increase recorded since 1986–1987 (up 19.5 percent). RPMs and passenger enplanements grew by 6.3 and 4.9 percent, respectively, the result being a 1.1 point increase in load factor to 70.9 percent. This is also an all-time record high, surpassing the previous high of 70.1 percent recorded in 1998.

Traffic growth would have been higher in 2000 except for the "Y2K effect" on traffic. It appears that a relatively large number of travelers avoided travel by air around the first of the year for fear of the Y2K impact on airline safety. In December 1999 and January 2000, domestic passengers were up only 1.5 and 1.7 percent, respectively. International passengers were down 7.0 and 7.1 percent during the same time period. Although some of the lost travel may have been rescheduled for later in the year, it is possible that passenger traffic could have been between 0.5 and 1.0 percent higher.

Regional/commuter airline traffic continued to grow at rates significantly higher than that of larger air carriers, with RPMs and enplanements up 18.2 and 7.1 percent, respectively. Regionals/commuters capacity increased by 15.3 percent in 2000, the result being a 1.5 point increase in load factor to 59.0 percent—a new all-time high.

---

*Federal Aviation Administration Aviation Forecasts

489

In 2000, it is estimated that U.S. and foreign flag carriers combined transported a total of 139.2 million passengers between the United States and the rest of the world, an increase of 6.0 percent over 1999. This traffic volume is distributed among the four world travel markets as follows: 52.7 million (up 8.2 percent) in Atlantic markets; 39.4 million (up 1.7 percent) in Latin American markets; 26.5 million (up 9.5 percent) in Asia/Pacific markets; and 20.6 million (up 4.0 percent) between the United States and Canada.

On the other hand, international enplanements on U.S. flag carriers alone grew by only 2.4 percent in 2000, less than half the estimated growth in total international traffic to and from the United States. U.S. carrier passenger enplanements were up 9.3 percent in Atlantic markets and 2.8 percent in Latin American markets. However, the number of passenger enplanements in Asia/Pacific markets declined by 8.9 percent in 2000, the third consecutive year of declining passenger traffic. During this three-year period, U.S. air carriers Asia/Pacific enplanements have declined by 29.1 percent while total passengers in the market are up 8.2 percent. While these declines may reflect some loss of market share by U.S. flag carriers, the large decline in U.S. carrier passenger counts is a bit misleading. A large part of the decline is the result of the restructuring and/or elimination of intra-Asia routes by Northwest and United, the two largest U.S. carriers operating in the region. The elimination of the shorter-haul intra-Asia markets also helps to explain the large increase in the average Asia/Pacific passenger trip length (up 1,342 miles) between 1997 and 2000.

U.S. air carriers' air cargo traffic was up 6.7 percent in 2000, with domestic RTMs up 4.9 percent and international RTMs up 8.4 percent. This represents a significant turnaround from 1999 when cargo traffic declined 0.9 percent, the first recorded decline since 1985. The decline in 1999 was largely due to a 2.7 percent decline in international cargo traffic, in particular freight movements between the U.S. and Latin American and Asian markets. It appears that these markets have turned around in 2000.

Domestic freight/express RTMs (12.1 billion) were up 5.3 percent while domestic mail RTMs (2.5 billion) were up 3.2 percent over 1999 levels. International freight/express (14.8 billion) and mail (531.9 million) RTMs were up 8.6 and 4.4 percent, respectively, in 2000.

Industry operating and net profits totaled $7.6 and $3.6 billion, respectively in 2000. This represents declines of $1.1 billion in operating profits and $1.7 billion in net profits from 1999. Operating revenues were up 8.3 percent in 2000, due to a combination of strong traffic growth and a 3.5 percent increase in passenger yield. Operating expenses were up 10.0 percent, due, in large part, to a 48.0 percent increase in the price of jet fuel—from 49.69 to 73.83 cents per gallon. The run-up in oil prices is estimated to have increased industry operating expenses by over $4.8 billion in 2000.

The impact of higher fuel prices on individual carrier' profits varied considerably, largely depending on the percentage of fuel requirements that each carrier was able to hedge at lower-than-market costs. Generally, the larger air carriers were more favorably impacted by use of these fuel-hedging strategies. For example, in September 2000 domestic jet fuel prices averaged 89.98 cents per gallon. However, the average price paid for jet fuel ranged from a low of 67.51 cents by American Airlines to a high of $1.91 per gallon by Tatonduk, a cargo carrier in Alaska.

In general, hedging appears to have further heightened the disparity that exists among the individual U.S. carriers with regard to financial profitability and/or viability. In 2000, all but two of the 15 majors[1] reported positive earnings, with operating and net profits for the group totaling $7.3 and $3.7 billion, respectively. Operating results for the majors ranged from a high of $1.4 billion (American) to a loss of $364.1 million (Trans World). Three carriers (American, Delta, and United) accounted for over half (54.1 percent) of the group's total earnings. Not surprisingly, these three carriers were among the leaders in the percentage of fuel hedged in 2000.

The financial results of many of the smaller nationals[2] and regionals[3] worsened in 2000, with 22 of the 53 reporting carriers incurring operating losses. The combined operating profits of the nationals and regionals totaled just under $500 million in 2000, with earnings ranging from an operating profit of $220 million (Atlas Airlines) to an operating loss of nearly $51 million (Vanguard Airlines).

---

[1] Defined by the U.S. DOT as carriers with annual operating revenues greater than $1 billion.

[2] Defined by the U.S. DOT as carriers with annual operating revenues between $100 million and $1 billion.

[3] Defined by the U.S. DOT as carriers with annual operating revenues less than $100 million.

A number of the smaller carriers cited the burden of escalating fuel prices and the lack of hedging protection as major factors for their poor financial performance in 2000. The record for the low cost, low-fare, new entrant carriers was mixed in 2000, with several of the carriers posting large operating losses. Since December 1999, a total of 10 carriers have filed Chapter 11 bankruptcy, including several startup carriers.

The regional/commuter airline industry posted an operating profit of $546.2 million in 2000, $162.4 million less than the $708.6 million profit recorded in 1999. The nine Form 41 carriers (operating at least one aircraft with more than 60 seats) reported operating profits of $341.4 million while 81 Form 298-C carriers (operating only aircraft with 60 seats or less) posted profits of $204.8 million. The lower profits reflect the significantly higher fuel prices in 2000.

Orders for commercial jet aircraft totaled 1,450 during the first 3 quarters of 2000, a 54.7 percent increase over the same period in 1999. The smaller regional jets (37 to 70 seats) accounted for 45.6 percent of the orders (661 aircraft) during 2000, a 51.6 percent increase over the 436 aircraft ordered during the first 9 months of 1999. While the total number of jets in the U.S. regional/commuter fleet totaled only 569 in 2000 (547 defined as regional jets), the 1,582 orders over the past eleven quarters show that this will continue to be the fastest growing segment of the industry over the next several years.

A total of 788 commercial jet aircraft were delivered during the first 3 quarters of 2000, a slight decline from the same 1999 period. A total of 206 regional jets were delivered during the first 9 months of 2000, a 53.7 percent increase over deliveries during the same 1999 period.

DOMESTIC AIR CARRIER PASSENGER TRAFFIC

Domestic air carrier RPMs and passenger enplanements are forecast to increase at annual rates of 4.2 and 3.6 percent, respectively, over the 12-year forecast period. The forecast assumes that domestic RPMs and enplanements will grow by 3.9 and 3.3 percent, respectively, in 2001, then slow marginally in 2002, growing by 3.6 and 3.0 percent, respectively. U.S. carriers are expected to achieve somewhat higher growth beginning in 2003, with RPMs and enplanements averaging 4.3 and 3.7 percent over the remainder of the forecast period.

Higher passenger yields are expected to impact domestic traffic demand in the short-term. Domestic passenger yields are expected to increase by 2.9 and 2.4 percent during the first 2 years of the forecast period (basically flat in real terms), due in part to higher fuel costs in 2001 and expected higher labor costs in both years. Yield increases moderate thereafter, averaging 0.9 percent over the remaining ten years of the forecast period. Real yields decline by an average 1.7 percent during the same ten-year period.

The relatively large decline in real yields over the latter years of the forecast is based on the assumption that increased competitive pressures (both domestically and internationally) will force carriers to hold the line on fare increases. Competition in domestic markets will come from established low-fare carriers such as Southwest; as well as from low cost carriers, such as Frontier and JetBlue. Internationally, increased competition will come from expanded open sky agreements and new and existing global alliances. Additionally, the expanded use of electronic ticketing should continue to reduce the costs associated with this marketing/distribution function. There should also be considerably less pressure exerted on operating costs from rising oil prices throughout the forecast period.

Air carrier aircraft operations are forecast to increase at an annual rate of 3.1 percent during the 12-year forecast period. The slower growth in activity at FAA air traffic facilities relative to expected traffic increases (3.6 percent growth in domestic enplanements) reflects the efficiencies which result from the assumed increases in both domestic average aircraft size (up 0.7 seats annually) and the passenger trip length (up 4.6 miles annually). However, very little gain is expected to result from increased domestic passenger load factors. The current forecast assumes that load factors will decline gradually from 70.9 percent in 2000 to 70.0 percent in 2003, then resume its upward trend and average 70.5 percent for most of the remaining years of the forecast period.

In fiscal year 2000 there were 87 U.S. commercial airlines (both scheduled and nonscheduled) reporting traffic and financial data to the Bureau of Transportation Statistics (BTS), U.S. Department of Transportation (DOT), on Form 41. There were 62 passenger airlines (operating aircraft with over 60 seats) and 24 all-cargo carriers.

Forty-three of the airlines provided scheduled passenger service and constitute the focus of the air carrier forecasts (both domestic and international) discussed in this chapter. Forty-two of the carriers provided scheduled domestic service (within the 50 States, the District of Columbia, Puerto Rico, and the U.S. Virgin Islands), while 17 of the carriers provided scheduled international service. Of the carriers providing scheduled international service, eight served Atlantic routes, ten served Latin American routes, and seven served Pacific routes.

REVIEW OF 2000

FINANCIAL RESULTS

In 2000 operating revenues for the U.S. commercial airline industry exceeded operating expenses. This was the eighth consecutive year that operating revenues were higher than operating expenses. Since 1993, cumulative operating profits have exceeded $47.2 billion. The financial success of the industry in 2000 was based on strong growth in traffic and yields offsetting higher fuel and labor costs. Capacity growth in 2000 was well below that of traffic, resulting in an increase in system load factor of 1.4 points to a record 72.2 percent. Labor turmoil at United was one of the major contributors to slower capacity growth in 2000.

The industry operating profit was $7.6 billion in 2000. Although operating profit was down $1.1 billion in 2000, it was the fourth highest year for operating profit since deregulation.

The industry had an operating profit in all four quarters. For the year, operating revenues increased 8.3 percent, while operating expenses increased 10.0 percent. By comparison, operating expenses were up 4.8 percent in 1999, 3.8 percent in 1998, and 5.7 percent in 1997.

The large increase in operating expenses in 2000 was largely due to a sharp increase in fuel costs. After declining 18.6 and 9.3 percent in the past 2 years, fuel prices rose an estimated 48 percent in 2000, escalating industry operating expenses by more than $4.8 billion.

Industry domestic nominal yields increased 3.2 percent, while yields, adjusted for inflation, increased 0.1 percent. Throughout much of the year, carriers have raised fares to offset rising fuel prices. However deep discounting by carriers in order to stay competitive and boost demand has offset much of the increase in posted fares. Competition in the industry is intense, and is expected to continue in both the domestic and international markets throughout the forecast period.

Nominal international yields also increased during the year. In the Atlantic real yields declined 1.9 percent while in Latin American and Pacific markets real yields increased 0.4 and 7.6 percent, respectively. The falling yields in the Atlantic markets can be attributed to supply side effects of increased competition and growth in capacity. The Latin region increase reflected a shift in the mix of traffic to higher yielding Caribbean destinations while the Pacific yield increase was due to an increase in the yen/dollar exchange rate and an increase in demand.

During 2000, six major passenger carriers reduced their real unit costs (estimated without fuel and oil expenses). US Airways had the largest decline—down 6.4 percent, followed by Southwest with unit costs declining 6.1 percent. Alaska showed the largest increase, with unit costs up 5.8 percent.

System average real operating cost per available seat mile (excluding fuel and oil) for the major passenger carriers was 8.64 cents in 2000, down 0.6 percent from 1999. System real unit costs (including fuel and oil) increased 3.3 percent. In 2000, American Trans Air had the lowest operating cost (excluding fuel and oil) per available seat mile (5.80 cents). The highest unit among the major network carriers was US Airways with 12.38 cents.[4]

In 2000, U.S. airlines posted a net profit of $3.6 billion—$1.7 billion below that of 1999. Net profit between 1994 and 1998 period totaled $14.7 billion. Total net profit for the seven-year period was $23.6 billion.

Data indicates that of 12 carriers, 10 had operating profits in 2000 while TWA and US Airways, recorded operating losses of $364.1 million and $15.0 million, respectively. American and Delta recorded the highest operating and net profits of the major passenger carriers.

During the next several years, competition capacity expansion, and productivity gains in the industry are expected to push real yields downward. Falling yields plus economic growth will continue to expand aviation activity and increase passenger revenues. Cost control will be key to the industry's ability to sustain profits at a relatively high level throughout the forecast period.

---

[4] Although American Eagle by definition is a major carrier, they have been excluded from this discussion, as their costs more closely resemble those of a commuter carrier rather than a network carrier.

SCHEDULED PASSENGER TRAFFIC AND CAPACITY

In 2000, total scheduled U.S. commercial air carrier activity (domestic plus international) continued to grow at rates above those of the U.S. and world economics. In 2000, system revenue passenger miles (RPMs) increased 6.4 percent, while enplanements increased 4.7 percent. Since 1991, system RPMs have increased 4.8 percent a year—roughly 27 percent higher than the rate of growth of U.S. Gross Domestic Product (GDP) and 64 percent higher than world GDP growth, adjusted for inflation.

System available seat miles (ASMs) increased 4.4 percent in 2000, resulting in a load factor increase of 1.4 percentage points to 72.2 percent—the highest figure ever. Since 1991, the system load factor has increased 9.9 percentage points.

DOMESTIC PASSENGER TRAFFIC AND CAPACITY

In 2000, a strong economy and flat real yields pushed RPMs and enplanements up 6.3 and 4.9 percent, respectively. Growth was consistently strong throughout the year, except in December and January reflecting the impact of the Y2K effect. Although capacity grew at a relatively rapid pace, 4.6 percent, the load factor increased by 1.1 percentage points to an all-time high of 70.9 percent. Since 1991 the domestic load factor has increased 10.1 percentage points.

U.S. AIR CARRIERS' INTERNATIONAL PASSENGER TRAFFIC AND CAPACITY

Strong world and U.S. economic growth in 2000, along with declining real fares in the Atlantic markets, drove total U.S. air carrier international traffic to record levels.

In 2000, total international RPMs increased 6.8 percent in the ninth consecutive year of growth and the highest growth rate since 1992. Enplanements also increased, up 2.4 percent, as strong growth in Atlantic markets more than offset continued declines in the Asia/Pacific markets. The growth in both RPMs and enplanements occurred despite the negative impact of Y2K on traffic during the December/January time frame.

Since the U.S. economic expansion began in 1991, international RPMs have increased 59.7 percent, while enplanements increased 37.3 percent. During the same period, domestic RPMs and enplanements increased 50.7 and 46.3 percent, respectively.

Total international ASMs grew 3.9 percent in 2000 as carriers continued to increase capacity rapidly in the robust Atlantic region. Capacity in the Asia/Pacific market increased slowly following two years of declines while capacity was flat in the Latin American market. Capacity growth in the Atlantic, Asia/Pacific, and Latin American markets was 7.1, 1.9, and 0.5 percent respectively.

NONSCHEDULED TRAFFIC AND CAPACITY

The number of nonscheduled (charter) passengers flying on U.S. commercial air carriers fell 12.1 percent in 2000 to 9.7 million—5.2 million in domestic markets (down 22.3 percent) and 4.5 million in international markets (up 3.8 percent). Nonscheduled ASMs and RPMs declined 15.3 and 13.9 percent, respectively, in 2000, the result being a 1.2 point increase in load factor to 69.5 percent.

AIR CARGO TRAFFIC

Air cargo revenue ton miles (RTMs) flown by U.S. air carriers totaled 30.0 billion in 2000, up 6.7 percent from 1999. Domestic cargo RTMs (14.7 billion) were up 4.9 percent, while international RTMs (15.3 billion) increased 8.4 percent.

Freight/express RTMs (26.9 billion) increased 7.1 percent in 2000. This included 12.1 billion domestic RTMs (up 5.3 percent) and 14.8 billion international RTMs (up 8.6 percent). Mail RTMs (3.1 billion) increased 3.5 percent in 2000. This included 2.5 billion domestic RTMs (up 3.3 percent) and 531.9 million international RTMs (up 4.4 percent).

Air cargo RTMs flown by all-cargo carriers were 59.3 percent of total RTMs in 2000; passenger carriers flew the remainder, or 40.7 percent of the total. Total RTMs flown by all-cargo carriers increased 4.1 percent in 2000, from 17.1 billion to 17.8 billion. Total RTMs flown by passenger carriers were 12.2 billion in 2000 (up 10.8 percent).

GLOBAL INDUSTRY AND MARKET ASSUMPTIONS

The background against which the present forecasts for the next 12-year period (2001 to 2012) are developed are based upon a set of assumptions concerning changes in the economy, structural changes in the air carrier industry, and changes in the market for air transportation. Clearly, the probability of achieving the forecasts is largely dependent upon the probability of realizing the economic projections and industry assumptions.

INDUSTRY STRUCTURE

Significant changes in the structure of the industry, both domestically and internationally, are intensifying competition, moving carriers to increase efficiency and productivity, reduce operating costs, and lower fares.

New, low-cost carriers are entering the domestic market, encouraged by the financial success of Southwest Airlines and large profit margins on many routes. Since CY 1989, 88 new entrant scheduled passenger carriers have applied for certification. Currently, 17 are still operating and four have been authorized but have not yet started operations.

Two carriers that began operations in 2000 are JetBlue Airways and Legend Airlines. Some of the new carriers who are authorized but have yet to start operations include Cardinal Airlines and Puerto Rico Airlines. New entrants are needed to ensure that competitive forces remain strong in the industry. The benefits to the American consumer brought about by low-cost, low-fare airlines have been substantial. A recent report by DOT estimated that consumer savings, due to low-cost service, are now $6.3 billion annually.

Higher cost carriers are continuing to restructure to reduce their unit costs to the levels achieved by the more efficient airlines. The restructuring includes elimination of unprofitable routes or transfer of those routes to an aligned commuter carrier, seeking work rule changes, acquiring more efficient aircraft, and increasing employee productivity. In addition, with the recent spike fuel prices, carriers have increased their hedging activity in order to minimize the impact of further oil price increases.

While higher cost carriers seek ways to reduce their unit costs, a resurgent airline labor movement is making the task more difficult. After a period of labor peace with givebacks and small increases in wages despite record profitability, labor has re-established itself as a force to be reckoned with in the industry. Beginning with the pilots strike at Northwest in 1998, the near strike by flight attendants at US Airways in late March 2000, and the just recently concluded pilots agreement at United Airlines, labor has shown that it will not tolerate its demands being subservient to the idea of cost competitiveness. There are currently contracts in negotiation at United (flight attendants, mechanics), Delta (pilots), American (pilots), Continental (pilots), and Northwest (mechanics). It remains to be seen if the United pilots contract serves as a catalyst for higher wage demands and/or renewed labor unrest following a period of labor peace. If so, the industry could see a reduction or reversal of the decline in unit costs that it has experienced during the past decade.

The airline industry could also be entering a new era of consolidation with United's proposed acquisition of US Airways. Immediately there was speculation that other major carriers would get together and, in fact, American and Northwest held merger discussions. The ensuing months since the United announcement has seen a number of lawmakers and various consumer groups voice opposition to the merger, fearing that competition would be reduced. As of this writing no recommendation to allow or deny the merger has been issued by the Department of Justice. If the merger is allowed to proceed, it is likely to significantly alter the structure of the industry and could have a far-reaching effect on the forecasts presented in this document.

To summarize, the industry is dynamic, with new entrants, but faces the possibility of a period of labor unrest and a number of mergers and international agreements that could fundamentally alter the industry structure. Although some of these changes could result in decreased demand in the short term, in the long run the net effect of these changes will be increased demand for air travel, increased air carrier efficiency, and reduced unit costs and fares.

MARKET CHANGES

There are a number of important trends occurring in the industry. Among these are:

1. the ability of air carriers to more closely adjust the number of discounted seats to maximize revenues and profits

2. the growth of competition by low-cost carriers during most of the 1990s

3. increased numbers of open-skies agreements

4. increased efficiency and productivity

5. expanding global alliances

6. declining real fares.

Offsetting some of the positive benefits of the above is the increased willingness of labor to use its strike power to counter large carriers' attempts to reduce unit costs. On the demand side, we see increasing sensitivity of business travelers to the cost of air trips, a shift in consumer preference for pleasure travel by air, and a long-term expansion of the economy.

Business demand for air travel will become more price elastic for two reasons. First is the increase in the availability of substitutes. Not only is innovative new technology, such as videoconferencing, expanding rapidly but also the development of more productive and efficient corporate aircraft has given business travelers more choices than previously. Second, as the relative price of business travel increases vis-a-vis discounted travel, business travelers will become more tolerant of the conditions of discounted travel (advance purchase, Saturday night stays, etc.) in order to qualify for the discounts.

The demand for leisure travel during the 1990s has also experienced major shifts because of increasing consumer preference for air travel, increasing disposable income, expanding personal wealth, and lower relative fares. The 1998 Air Travel Survey conducted by the Air Transport Association of America shows that the percent of individuals who have ever flown increased from 74 percent in 1990 to 81 percent in 1997.

Atlantic Routes

In 2000, transatlantic RPMs were up for the ninth consecutive year, increasing 9.5 percent from 79.6 million to 87.1 million. Enplanements were up 9.3 percent. Continued strong growth can be attributed to the strong economies in the U.S. and Europe, intense competition, and continued fare discounting.

Following a decline in capacity between 1994 and 1997 of about 1.0 percent a year, ASMs have increased at an annual rate of 9.2 percent over the past three years. RPM growth since 1997 has averaged a healthy 8.5 percent driving the load factor up 0.5 points, from 78.7 percent in 1997 to 79.2 percent in 2000. Since 1991, the Atlantic load factor has increased 9.7 percentage points.

Immigration and Naturalization Service (INS) data, which is compiled by the U.S. Department of Commerce, showed that in 1999 U.S. flag carriers' market share in the region continued its steady decline, dropping 1.0 percentage point to 38.5 percent. U.S. flag carriers' market share peaked in 1988 at 48.5 percent.

In 2000 the U.S. passenger carriers serving the market had an operating profit of $634.3 million, making the Atlantic market the most profitable of the international regions. In 1999 the Atlantic market had an operating profit of $658.8 million.

Latin American Routes

Traffic demand to Latin America (destinations in South America, Central America, Mexico, and the Caribbean) continued to grow, albeit at rates slower than in the recent past. In 2000, RPMs and passenger enplanements were up 4.9 and 2.8 percent, respectively. For the period 1991 through 2000, RPMs increased at an annual rate of 7.7 percent, while enplanements increased 4.8 percent a year.

Expansion in traffic in 2000 was the result of a strong U.S. economy and mixed growth in Latin America. Slow capacity growth (up 0.5 percent) resulted in a load factor increase of 2.9 percentage points to 68.8 percent—a record high for the region.

The continued expansion of U.S. carriers into deep South America—Argentina, Brazil and Chile—plus the expansion of service to the Caribbean from Northeast destinations increased the average trip length 2.1 percent (32.6 miles) in 2000. Since 1990, the average trip length has expanded 29.7 percent, or 364.4 miles, increasing from 1,227.3 miles to 1,591.7 miles.

The U.S. passenger carriers serving the Latin American market had an operating profit of $240.8 million, down 28.1 percent versus 1999.

The embracing of free markets in Latin America has resulted in the privatization and restructuring of Latin American carriers. Clearly, these industry changes along with the move towards open-skies agreements will pose additional challenges for the U.S. carriers over the next several years.

Pacific Routes

Following two years of declines, traffic in Asia/Pacific markets increased modestly in 2000, with RPMs up 4.2 percent over 1999. The region's continued recovery from the financial and economic crisis of 1997/98 plus the strong U.S. economy were the principle drivers of the growth. Enplanements continued to fall however, down 8.9 and 12.8 percent in 2000 and 1999, respectively. These large declines are the result of a significant restructuring of the regional route networks in April 1999.

After two years of declines U.S. flag carrier ASMs increased by 1.9 percent as carriers began to slowly add capacity back to the region. The slow growth in ASMs, coupled with the increase in RPMs, resulted in the load factor for the region increasing to 76.2 percent, 1.6 points higher than in 1999.

The recovery in traffic, coupled with a strong Japanese yen for most of the year, resulted in a turnaround in regional profitability for U.S. passenger carriers. Following operating losses of $180.6 million in 1999 and $369.8 million in 1998, U.S. passenger carriers recorded an operating profit of $198.1 million in 2000.

The recent open-skies agreements reached with Malaysia, New Zealand, Taiwan, Singapore, Brunei, and Korea, as well as new liberal bilateral agreements with Japan and China, will continue to stimulate aviation growth. Over the long-term, these agreements will provide travelers with service to more cities and lower fares.

It is an inescapable conclusion that increasing productivity, growth in capacity, and competitive markets must be achieved to keep relative fares declining. These market conditions will assure growth in demand and provide the industry with acceptable rates of return on capital.

GLOBAL RISKS AND UNCERTAINTIES

The forecasts of scheduled commercial air carrier demand are based on a specific set of assumptions concerning economic growth in the United States and abroad, the political environment in which they will take place, Government tax policy, and changes in industry structure. There are many uncertainties in all these areas that could alter the short- and long-term environment, and cause the outcomes to be different from those forecasts. Developments that could alter the forecasts include:

1. the strength and duration of the current United States economic expansion and economic growth in the rest of the world;
2. the impact of regional jets;
3. the number of business cycles that occur over the forecast period;
4. the movement of future oil prices;
5. structural changes in the international markets that affect U.S. carrier shares;
6. the degree of competition in both the domestic and international markets;
7. how far carriers can reduce unit costs, especially in light of a resurgent labor movement;
8. how fast yields decline due to increased competition and cost reductions;
9. when and if the industry reaches equilibrium;
10. the impact of industry consolidation; and
11. the impact of continued air traffic delays.

In addition, the network of bilateral pacts that the United States currently has in place in Europe, the Far East, and South America could significantly inhibit the expansion plans of air carriers operating in these international regions and restrain traffic growth. On the other hand, the move towards deregulation, privatization of national carriers, and expansion of open-skies agreements could result in significantly greater traffic growth.

Passenger Yields

During the period 1970 through 1977 domestic real yields declined at a rate of 1.3 percent a year. Since deregulation, the decline in real yields has accelerated, so that by 2000 real yield fell to 14.42 cents, an average yearly decline of 1.9 percent—1.5 times higher than the rate achieved during the 1970s.

In the 1970s the dominant reason for the decrease was the introduction of large numbers of more efficient jet aircraft into the fleets operated by air carriers. In the 1980s the airlines started to adjust to a deregulated industry by rationalizing their route structures, and increasing labor productivity.

Financial weakness of the industry in the early 1990s along with excess capacity, the growth of new-entrant, low-cost carriers, and the expansion of Southwest into new markets has brought about intense fare competition. Competition has pushed high-cost carriers into restructuring, increasing productivity, and lowering unit costs.

Since deregulation, unit costs (real operating costs adjusted for ASMs) have been declining along with yields. In fact, our analysis has shown that there is a high positive correlation between domestic real yields and unit costs, and that a 1.0 percent decline in unit costs will, *on average,* reduce real yields by about 0.9 percent. Also, productivity in the industry, as measured by ASMs per dollar of real operating costs less fuel and oil expenses, has increased by approximately 1.2 percent a year since 1978.

In 1999 nominal yields declined every quarter, real yields were down 3.3 percent for the year, and capacity increased 5.2 percent, the largest increase since 1990. Nominal yields were up in every quarter in 2000, driven in part by fuel related fare increases. However, real yields increased only 0.1 percent for the year. Capacity growth was 4.6 percent but would have been higher were it not for operational difficulties at United during the summer of 2000. (Table 20.1.)

Nominal yields are forecast to go up to 2.9 percent in 2001, 2.4 percent in 2002, and 1.7 percent in 2003. Real yields decrease at an average annual rate of 0.3 percent during the same period. The relatively large increases experienced in the short-term are for the most part due to the rising unit costs driven by relatively high fuel prices and rising labor costs. In 2002 and 2003, oil prices are forecast to decline 25 percent and then

Table 20.1   Domestic Passenger Yields Fiscal Year 1999/2000

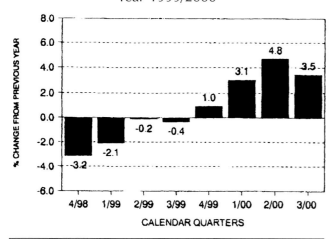

grow slower than general inflation for the balance of the forecast, resulting in unit costs returning to their long run decline. It is also assumed that the air carriers will optimally adjust their capacity to meet future demand. For the period 2005 through 2012, continued competition and expanding capacity results in nominal yields increasing 0.8 percent a year, while real yields fall 1.9 percent. Over the 12-year forecast period, nominal yields increase from 14.42 cents in 2000 to 16.68 cents in 2012, while real yields decline 1.4 percent a year.

Passenger Trip Length

In 2000 the average domestic passenger trip length increased 11.1 miles. This was due largely to the continued turning over of short-haul routes to code-sharing regional partners and the expansion of Southwest, Continental, TWA, and US Airways into longer-haul markets.

The rapid integration of new state-of-the-art aircraft into the regional/commuter fleet—especially regional jets and large, high-speed turboprops with ranges of up to 1,000 miles—could significantly alter the route system of the industry. These new aircraft are enabling regional/commuters to greatly expand the number of markets they serve.

The continued turnover of short-haul markets by the majors to their code-sharing regional partners, expansion of low-cost carriers into longer-haul markets, restructuring of the regional/commuter fleets, and expansion of point-to-point service are expected to increase the domestic trip length modestly during the forecast period. For the entire forecast period, the av-

erage trip length increases 4.6 miles per year, increasing from 832.3 miles in 2000 to 887.3 miles in 2012.

Passenger Load Factor

Domestic load factors were relatively stable over the period 1978 through 1993, ranging from a low of 57.7 percent to 63.0 percent. From 1993 through 2000, the load factor increased 9.6 percentage points, expanding from 61.3 percent to 70.9 percent. During this period, the carriers developed the capability to rapidly adjust capacity to changing conditions in both the domestic and international markets to meet demand while pushing up load factors.

Despite capacity increases of almost 10 percent over the past two years, traffic growth in excess of 11 percent has resulted in the load factor increasing to 70.9 percent—the highest average yearly level ever achieved on domestic routes.

Relatively large increases in capacity as new aircraft enter the fleet, along with the impact of slowing of U.S. economic growth and higher fares, will put downward pressure on load factors through 2003. ASMs are forecast to increase 4.6 percent in 2001, 4.0 percent in 2002 and 4.4 percent in 2003. Load factor is forecast to decline in 70.5 percent in 2001, 70.3 percent in 2002, and 70.0 percent in 2003. As carriers adjust capacity by 2004, the load factor begins to increase, reaching 70.5 percent in 2006. For the remainder of the forecast period it is assumed that ASMs will be adjusted at the same rate in response to changes in demand so that demand and supply will be in equilibrium. For the period 2007 through 2012, capacity and RPMs are expected to grow 4.2 percent a year, resulting in an average load factor of 70.5 percent.

FORECASTS

Revenue Passenger Miles

Since the most recent economic expansion began in 1991, domestic RPMs have been continuously increasing, averaging 4.7 percent growth per year over the 9-year period. Scheduled domestic RPMs totaled 502.8 billion in 2000, up 6.3 percent compared to 4.8 percent in 1999. The strong traffic growth in 2000 was driven by strong growth in the U.S. economy, lower real fares, and heightened consumer confidence.

The expected slowing of the U.S. economy in 2001 through 2004 will slow the growth of traffic. Domestic traffic increases 3.9 percent in 2001, 3.6 percent in 2002, and 4.0 percent in 2003. As the economy returns to its long-term growth rate in 2004, traffic increases, on average, 4.3 percent a year for the remainder of the forecast period. The average annual increase in domestic RPMs over the 12-year planning horizon is forecast to be 4.2 percent, with domestic RPMs reaching 822.1 billion in 2012.

Passenger Enplanements

U.S. scheduled domestic air carriers enplaned a total of 604.1 million passengers in 2000, up 4.9 percent compared to 3.8 percent increase in 1999. Domestic passenger enplanements are forecast to increase 3.3 percent in 2001, 3.0 percent in 2002, and 3.5 percent in 2003. For the remainder of the forecast period, enplanements increase 3.7 percent a year. The growth in enplanements is projected to average 3.6 percent annually during the 12-year forecast period, with the number of domestic enplanements reaching 926.6 million in 2012.

ATLANTIC MARKET

U.S. Air Carriers' Yields and Operational Variables

Passenger Yields

In 2000 current dollar yield (9.72 cents) increased 1.1 percent, while real yields in the market fell 1.9 percent. This followed a drop in real yield in 1999 of 6.9 percent. Yields fell in the first half of 2000 and then increased in the latter half of the year. The decline in yields in 2000 can be attributed to the significant increase in capacity (ASMs up 7.1 percent) and competition in the market.

Passenger Trip Length

In 2000 the average passenger trip length in the Atlantic market increased 6.4 miles down from the 26.5 miles increase in 1999. The small increase in trip length was primarily due to a shift in the carrier mix from relatively longer haul carriers (United, TWA, and American) to shorter haul carriers (Continental and US Airways). Since 1990, average trip length has increased from 3,341.4 miles to 4,168.3 miles—up 826.9 miles. The increase in average passenger trip length over the period was primarily due to more direct flights and expanded service into Central and Eastern Europe. This trend is expected to continue over the 12-year forecast period.

The average trip length is forecast to increase 19.5 miles in both 2001 and 2002. For the remainder of the planning period—2003 through 2012—trip length increases average 11.5 miles annually. For the period 2000 through 2012, the Atlantic market trip length increases from 4,168.3 miles to 4,322.3 miles—up 154 miles.

Average Aircraft Size

The average aircraft size in the Atlantic market continuously increased during the 1970s and early 1980s as the widebody DC-10s/L-1011s and B-747s dominated the market, peaking at 332.0 seats in 1985. Since the mid 1980s the advent of the B-767 and other aircraft flying extended-range twin-engine operations (ETOPS), has resulted in the average seat size steadily declining. In 2000 the average aircraft size was 233.7 seats—a decline of 98.3 seats from 1985.

Over the 12-year forecast period, the average aircraft size in the Atlantic market gradually increases as the major carriers expand the number of non-stop city-pair services and use of larger two-engine widebody aircraft. Average aircraft size increases to 250.7 seats by 2012—an increase of approximately 1.4 seats per year.

Passenger Load Factor

With the exception of 1986*, Atlantic market load factors were relatively stable over the period 1980 through 1989, ranging from a low of 63.8 to 65.7 percent. From 1989 through 2000, the load factor increased 13.5 percentage points, from 65.7 percent to 79.2 percent.

Although capacity expanded 7.1 percent in 2000, RPM growth of 9.5 percent increased the load factor to 79.2 percent—the highest average yearly level ever achieved in the Atlantic market.

Relatively smaller increases in capacity are expected through 2004 as U.S. carriers move capacity back into an expanding Asia/Pacific market. ASMs are forecast to increase 7.3 percent in 2001, then 6.1 percent in 2002, and 6.6 percent in 2003. RPMs will grow slightly less than capacity in 2001 resulting in a load factor decline in 78.8 percent. Load factor then increases steadily up to 80 percent by 2005 as traffic increases, driven by economic growth and falling real yields, outpace capacity increases. For the balance of the forecast period, load factor remains at 80 percent as the market achieves equilibrium.

---

* The load factor in 1986 was 56.0 percent, the result of increased terrorism on these routes.

Total Passengers: U.S. and Foreign Flag Carriers

Based on Immigration and Naturalization Service (INS) data, which is compiled by the Department of Commerce, total passengers in the Atlantic market grew 4.4 percent in 1999 (the latest full year for which data is available). Preliminary data shows total passengers increasing about 8.2 percent in 2000.

U.S. air carrier's market share for the Atlantic region has been steadily declining since 1988, when it peaked at 48.5 percent. In 1999 U.S. market share declined to 38.5 percent. However, preliminary data indicate that U.S. carrier market share increased to 39.0 percent in 2000. Additionally, the percent of total passengers that are U.S. citizens traveling in the Atlantic market has been falling. From a peak of 67.7 percent in 1985, the ratio has fallen to 51.0 percent in 1999.

Using the latest forecasts of GDP for the U.S. and Atlantic regions, total passengers traveling in the Atlantic market are expected to increase 5.1 percent in 2001 and 5.6 percent in 2002. Over the entire forecast period, total passengers increase an average of 4.9 percent per year, from 52.7 million in 2000 to 93.2 million in 2012.

The International Civil Aviation Organization (ICAO) North Atlantic Traffic Forecasting Group (Canada, U.S., U.K., and Portugal) was formed with the primary objective of developing forecasts of air traffic over the North Atlantic and between North America and the Caribbean. Annual forecasts are provided for both total passengers and aircraft movements to support air navigation systems planning activity for ICAO and its member states.

The Group develops baseline, optimistic, and pessimistic forecasts based upon changing assumptions of available capacity, yields and economic growth. The Group's baseline forecast shows passengers increasing 7.0 percent a year for the period 1999 through 2005. For the optimistic scenario, passengers increase 7.8 percent per year, while the pessimistic scenario shows an annual growth rate of 5.5 percent. Aircraft movements for the baseline scenario expand 5.6 percent a year. The optimistic and pessimistic scenarios show growth rates of 7.2 and 4.0 percent, respectively.

Copies of the report entitled, *"North Atlantic Air Traffic Forecasts for the Years 2000–2005, 2010 and 2015,"* can be obtained from the FAA's Statistics and Forecast Branch, Office of Aviation Policy and Plans, phone (202) 267-3355.

U.S. Flag Carriers' Passenger Enplanements

U.S. scheduled air carriers in the Atlantic market enplaned a total of 20.9 million passengers in 2000, up 9.3 percent. Atlantic market passenger enplanements are forecast to increase 6.1 percent in 2001 and increase on average 5.2 percent annually during the 12-year forecast period. The number of Atlantic market enplanements reaches 38.4 million in 2012—83.7 percent higher than in 2000.

U.S. Flag Carriers' Revenue Passenger Miles

Since 1991, Atlantic market RPMs have been continuously increasing due to strong, steady economic growth in the U.S. and Europe and declining real yields. For the period 1991 through 2000, RPMs increased 7.1 percent a year. Atlantic market RPMs totaled 87.1 billion in 2000, up 9.5 percent from 1999. In 2001, Atlantic market RPMs are forecast to increase 6.6 percent. The average annual increase in RPMs over the 12-year forecast horizon is 5.5 percent, reaching 165.9 billion in 2012.

LATIN AMERICAN MARKET

U.S. Air Carriers' Yields and Operational Variables

Passenger Yields

In 2000 Latin American yield (13.21 cents) increased 3.5 percent and real yield increased 0.4 percent. In 1999 nominal and real yield declined 7.0 and 8.7 percent, respectively. Since 1994, real yield in the market has declined 19.1 percent.

In 2000, regional capacity increased 0.5 percent, following increases of 1.6 percent in 1999 and 13.6 percent in 1998. Since 1994 capacity in the market is up 43.7 percent. Capacity growth is expected to be rapid in the next few years (up 9.3 percent annually) as U.S. carriers continue to expand service into both the Caribbean and South America. The softening of the U.S. economy over the next several years, intense competition, and increased productivity should continue to push real yields down in both the short- and long-term. (Table 20.2.)

Real yields are expected to decline 2.0 percent a year through 2003, and continue to fall throughout the remainder of the forecast period but at a slower rate of 0.5 percent a year. Over the forecast period, real yields are declining at a rate of 0.9 percent a year, while nominal yields increase at an annual rate of 1.8 percent, reaching 16.35 cents in 2012.

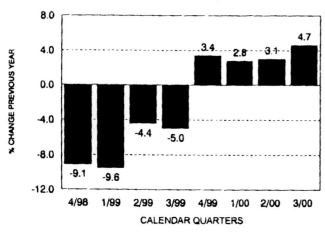

Table 20.2   Latin American Route Passenger
Yields Fiscal Year 1999/2000

Passenger Trip Length

The continued expansion of U.S. carriers into South America—Argentina, Brazil and Chile—and the expansion of routes from the Northeast to the Caribbean resulted in the average trip length increasing 32.6 miles in 2000. Since 1990 average trip length increased 364.4 miles, from 1,227.3 miles to 1,591.7 miles. This trend is expected to continue over the 12-year forecast period.

The average trip length is forecast to increase 15.0 miles in 2001, 13.5 miles in 2002, and 12.0 miles in 2003. For the balance of the forecast period—2004 through 2012—trip length increases average 8.7 miles a year. During this time, Latin American market trip length expands from 1,591.7 miles to 1,710.7 miles.

Average Aircraft Size

The average aircraft size in the Latin American market increased during the 1970s and early 1980s as widebody aircraft dominated the market, peaking at 220.2 seats in 1986. With the advent of the B-757 and other flying ETOPS since the mid-1980s, the average seat size has steadily declined. In 2000 the average aircraft size was 173.5 seats—a decline of 46.7 seats from 1986.

Over the 12-year forecast period, the average aircraft size in the Latin American market is expected to gradually increase as the major carriers expand the number of non-stop city-pair services into deep South America, and begin using larger two-engine widebody aircraft. The average aircraft size is forecast to increase

to 185.0 seats by 2012—an increase of just under one seat per year.

Passenger Load Factor

Load factors in the Latin American market showed little variability from 1987 through 1994, ranging from a low of 57.9 percent to 62.5 percent. From 1994 through 2000, the load factor increased almost 8.0 percentage points, expanding from 60.9 percent to 68.8 percent.

In 2000, RPM growth of 4.9 percent combined with capacity growth of only 0.5 percent pushed the load factor up to 68.8 percent—the highest average yearly level ever achieved in the Latin American market. In 1999, capacity increased 1.6 percent, while RPMs increased 6.5 percent, which resulted in the load factor increasing 3.0 percentage points to 65.9 percent.

Through 2002, large increases in capacity are forecast to occur which leads to a decrease in load factor over this period. ASMs are forecast to increase 9.4 percent in 2001, and 9.3 percent in 2002. Slower growth in RPMs in 2001 and 2002 will result in the load factor falling to 67.5 percent. After 2002, the load factor gradually increases during the next four years and levels off at 68.5 percent in 2006 and remains at this level for the balance of the forecast period as the market reaches equilibrium.

Total Passengers: U.S. and Foreign Flag Carriers

Based on INS data, total passengers in Latin American market (South America, Central America/Mexico, and the Caribbean) grew 3.1 percent in 1999. Preliminary data indicate that total passengers grew 1.5 percent in 2000. The largest increase in 1999 occurred in the Central America/Mexico region, which was up 6.6 percent. The Caribbean region increased 4.6 percent, while the South American region decreased 4.5 percent. Despite the decrease in 1999, the South American region has been the fastest growing since 1990, with passengers increasing 8.4 percent annually. During this time, the Central America/Mexico market increased 5.4 percent per annum, while the Caribbean market increased only 1.4 percent a year.

U.S. air carriers' market share of the Latin American region has been increasing steadily since 1991. Between 1991 and 1996, U.S. air carriers' market share increased from 58.8 to 64.3 percent. Following a decline in share in 1997, U.S. carriers' market share has increased from 61.7 percent to 63.2 percent in 1999. The market shares for the Caribbean, Central America/ Mexico, and South America in 1999 were 70.9, 59.2, and 59.7 percent, respectively.

Between 1990 and 1998 the percent of total passengers that were U.S. citizens traveling in the Latin American market decreased steadily from 67.3 percent to 63.4 percent. In 1999 the ratio increased to 64.8 percent.

Using the latest forecasts of GDP for the U.S. and Latin American regions, total passengers traveling in the Latin American market are expected to increase 6.6 percent in 2001 and 7.1 percent in 2002. Over the entire forecast period, total passengers increase 6.7 percent per year, from 39.4 million in 2000 to 86.2 million in 2012.

U.S. Flag Carriers' Passenger Enplanements

U.S. scheduled air carriers in the Latin American market enplaned a total of 22.5 million passengers in 2000, up 2.8 percent following 1999's increase of 4.2 percent. Latin American market passenger enplanements are forecast to increase 7.2 percent in 2001. The growth in enplanements is expected to average 6.8 percent annually during the 12-year forecast period, with the number of Latin American market enplanements reaching 49.7 million in 2012—more than double the level achieved in 2000.

U.S. Flag Carriers' Revenue Passenger Miles

Since 1993, Latin American market RPMs have been increasing due primarily to strong economic growth in the U.S. and Latin America and declining real yields. From 1993 through 2000, RPMs increased 8.1 percent a year. Latin American market RPMs totaled 35.8 billion in 2000, up 4.9 percent from 1999. In 1999, RPMs grew 6.5 percent. Latin American RPMs are forecast to increase 8.1 percent in 2001. The average annual increase in RPMs over the 12-year forecast horizon is 7.5 percent, reaching 85.0 billion in 2012.

PACIFIC MARKET

U.S. Air Carriers' Yields and Operational Variables

Passenger Yields

A stronger Japanese yen and firming demand helped propel nominal yield in the Pacific market (9.99 cents) up 11.0 percent in 2000. Real yield in 2000 increased 7.6 percent. The gain in real yield followed declines of 4.5 and 11.9 percent in 1999 and 1998, respectively. The rise in yields is another indication that the market is recovering from the financial and economic problems that began in 1997. (Table 20.3.)

Table 20.3 Pacific Route Passenger Yields Fiscal Year 1999/2000

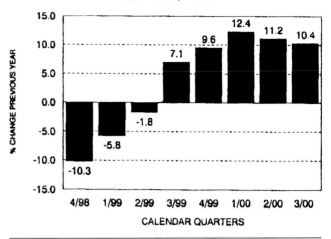

Real yield is expected to decline 0.7 percent in 2001 and 0.5 percent in both 2002 and 2003. Over the balance of the forecast real yield decreases an average of 1.0 percent per year. Nominal yield during the forecast period increases from 9.99 cents in 2000 to 12.36 cents in 2012—an increase of 1.8 percent a year.

Passenger Trip Length

In 2000 the average passenger trip length in the Pacific market increased 656.5 miles following an increase of 539.9 miles in 1999. These large increases are the result of the restructuring of the route networks of the two dominant carriers in the region (United and Northwest) in April 1999, which eliminated a number of shorter intra regional routes. Since 1990 the average trip length increased from 3,718.0 miles to 5,219.9 miles—up 1,501.9 miles. However the increase in trip length between 1990 and 1998 was only 305.6 miles. The increase in average passenger trip length between 1990 and 1998 was primarily due to more direct flights and expanded service into the Asia/Pacific region. A return to more moderate increases in trip length similar to the 1990–1998 experience is expected to continue over the 12-year forecast period.

The average trip length is forecast to increase 60.0 miles in 2001 and 40 miles in 2002. For the remainder of the planning period—2003 through 2012—the average trip length increases 13 miles a year. For the 12-year forecast period, the Pacific market trip length increases 230 miles from 5,219.9 to 5,449.9 miles.

Average Aircraft Size

The average aircraft size in the Pacific market increased from 318.6 eats in 1990 to 329.1 seats in 1997. As traffic rapidly increased during this period, a large percentage of the additional capacity provided by the U.S. carriers came from adding larger B-747s to the routes.

When activity in the region began to shrink in 1998 due to the economic problems of the region, U.S. carriers began shifting capacity to other markets. ASMs declined 5.4 percent in 1998 and 3.4 percent in 1999. The average number of seats per aircraft in the Pacific market declined 10.9 in 1998 and 14.4 in 1999.

Average seat size in 2000 increased by 4.2 seats and is expected to continue to grow through the remainder of the 12-year forecast period, as the carriers expand their fleets with larger widebody aircraft. The average aircraft size is forecast to increase from 308.0 seats in 2000 to 331.0 seats by 2012.

Passenger Load Factor

Between 1991 and 1997 the Pacific market load factor increased from 66.7 to 74.3 percent. In 1998 load factor fell 1.5 points as capacity declined 5.4 percent and RPMs fell 7.3 percent. Load factor increased 1.7 points in 1999, as capacity declined 3.4 percent, while RPMs fell only 1.1 percent. In 2000 load factor increased 1.6 points to a record 76.2 percent as traffic grew 4.2 percent—the first increase since 1998—while capacity increased 1.9 percent.

Load factor is forecast to decline to 75.5 percent in 2001 as capacity expands at a faster rate than RPMs. As traffic returns to its long-term growth path from 2002 to 2005, the load factor increases steadily from 76.0 percent in 2002 to 77.5 percent by 2005. The load factor is projected to remain at 77.5 percent for the period 2006 through 2012 as ASMs and RPMs expand at the same rate.

TOTAL PASSENGERS: U.S. AND FOREIGN FLAG CARRIERS

Based on INS data total passengers in the Pacific market increased 5.8 percent in 1999 following a decline of 6.4 percent in 1998. Preliminary 2000 data indicates that total passengers will increase about 9.5 percent to 26.5 million. After peaking in 1990, U.S. air carrier's market share has declined 15.1 percentage points to 40.0 percent in 1999.

Using the latest forecasts of GDP for the U.S. and Pacific regions, total passengers traveling in the Pacific market are projected to increase 7.2 percent in 2001, 6.7 percent in 2002, and 6.3 percent in 2003. Over the entire forecast period total passengers increase at an average rate of 6.2 percent per year from 26.5 million in 2000 to 54.7 million in 2012.

U.S. Flag Carriers' Passenger Enplanements

U.S. scheduled air carriers in the Pacific market enplaned a total of 11.2 million passengers in 2000, down 8.9 percent. This follows declines of 12.8 and 10.6 percent in 1999 and 1998, respectively. Enplanements decreased primarily due to a change in the route structures of the two dominant carriers in the region. Enplanement growth is forecast to return in 2001 with enplanements increasing 5.7 percent, then rising 6.1 percent in 2002, and 6.4 percent in 2003. Enplanement growth is projected to average 6.2 percent annually during the 12-year forecast period, with Pacific market enplanements reaching 23.0 million in 2012—more than double the number in 2000.

U.S. Flag Carriers' Revenue Passenger Miles

Before the economic and financial problems developed in the Asia/Pacific region in 1997, U.S. air carrier traffic in the Pacific market was growing significantly faster than all other markets—both domestic and international. Between 1980 and 1997, RPMs were expanding at 8.4 percent a year—about double the rate of growth experienced in the domestic market. After declining in 1998 and 1999, RPMs increased 4.2 percent in 2000. Traffic in the Pacific market is forecast to increase 6.9 percent per year from 2001 to 2003, and 7.2 percent in 2004 as the economies of the region return to their long-term historical growth. The average annual increase in RPMs over the 12-year forecast is 6.6 percent, with RPMs totaling 125.1 billion in 2012.

U.S./CANADA TRANSBORDER TRAFFIC

In 1995, the U.S. and Canada signed an open-skies agreement. Between 1995 and 1998, transborder traffic grew 8.8 percent a year. Transborder traffic growth is estimated to have moderated somewhat in 1999 and 2000, increasing at rates of 3.1 and 4.8 percent, respectively. For the 12-year forecast period transborder traffic increases from 20.6 million in 2000 to 32.9 million in 2012—an average of 4.0 percent a year.

AIR CARGO

Air cargo traffic is comprised of domestic and international revenue freight/express and mail. The demand for air cargo transportation is a derived demand resulting from economic activity. Cargo is moved in the bellies of passenger aircraft and in dedicated all-cargo aircraft, on both scheduled and nonscheduled service. In addition, a portion of the cargo activity, as reported on DOT Form 41, is handled exclusively by truck.

In 2000, the total number of domestic and international air cargo RTMs flown by U.S. commercial air carriers was 30.0 billion. The top five carriers accounted for approximately two-thirds of this total. The top five carriers in terms of RTMs and their percentage shares were: Federal Express (25.9 percent), United Parcel Service (14.2 percent), United Airlines (10.6 percent), Northwest Airlines (8.3 percent), and American Airlines (7.6 percent).

The total number of enplaned domestic and international air cargo tons at U.S. airports by U.S. commercial air carriers in 2000* was 16.6 million. The top five airports accounted for more than a quarter of the nation's enplaned cargo tonnage. The top five airports in terms of enplaned tons and their percentage shares were: Memphis International (8.2 percent), Louisville International (5.1 percent), Willow Run Detroit (4.9 percent), Los Angeles International (3.9 percent), and Indianapolis International (3.7 percent). Memphis and Louisville serve as hubs for Federal Express and United Parcel Service, respectively. Willow Run handles a large quantity of shipments related to the transportation industry. Los Angeles is a major international gateway. Indianapolis serves as a hub for Federal Express and as an express mail hub for the U.S. Postal Service.

HISTORIC FREIGHT/EXPRESS TONNAGE

Historic data were derived for domestic and international freight/express tonnage. The domestic figures represent enplaned domestic freight/express tons at U.S. airports on U.S. commercial air carriers. These data were compiled on a calendar year basis using the DOT Onboard T3 and T100 databases. (The domestic estimates include some transborder tonnage to Canada that is not reported separately.) Enplaned domestic freight/express tonnage grew from 6.4 million tons in 1990 to 10.8 million tons in 1999, an average annual increase of 5.9 percent. The 1999 level represents a 0.4 percent increase from the 10.7 million tons enplaned in 1998.

The international figures are enplaned and deplaned international freight/express tonnage at U.S. airports on U.S. and foreign flag carriers. These data were compiled on a calendar year basis using the DOT International T100 database. International freight/express tonnage on U.S. and foreign flag carriers grew from 3.9 million tons in 1990 to 7.1 million tons in 1999, an average annual increase of 2.3 percent from 7.0 million tons in 1998. The U.S. flag carrier portion of the total international tonnage has increased from 40.3 percent in 1990 to 42.2 percent in 1999. The distribution of total tonnage for U.S. and foreign flag carriers by world region in 1999 was: Atlantic (41.0 percent), Pacific (36.5 percent), Latin American (21.3 percent), and Canada (1.2 percent).

REVENUE TON MILES

Historic data and forecasts are presented for domestic and international freight/express and domestic and international mail RTMs. In addition, within each of these four components, trends and forecasts are presented for all-cargo carriers and passenger carriers. Passenger carriers transport cargo predominantly in the bellies of their aircraft.

Historically, air cargo activity has been highly correlated with GDP. Additional factors that have affected the growth in air cargo traffic include declining real yields, improved productivity, and globalization. In the future, other factors that could potentially stimulate demand for air cargo include increased market opportunities from open-skies agreements, decreased costs from global airline alliances, and increased business volumes attributable to e-commerce. Factors that could potentially limit growth include increased use of e-mail, decreased costs of sending documents via facsimile, and the increased cost to airlines in meeting environmental restrictions.

Forecasts of domestic freight/express and mail RTMs were developed from regression equations using real U.S. GDP as the independent variable. Projections of international freight/express and mail RTMs were derived from equations that related these variables to

---

* 12 months ending June 2000.

world GDP, adjusted for inflation. This methodology implicitly assumes that adequate capacity will be available and that other influences will impact cargo in a manner similar to that in the past. The distribution of RTMs between passenger carriers and all-cargo carriers was forecast based on an analysis of historic trends in shares and discussions with industry representatives.

From 1990 to 2000, total cargo flown on U.S. commercial air carriers increased from 16.3 billion to 30.0 billion RTMs. This growth, which averaged 6.3 percent per year, was faster than the rate of growth in passengers. The fastest growing component of air cargo activity has been international freight/express, which increased an average of 8.1 percent annually from 1990 to 2000.

Growth in domestic freight/express RTMs, which averaged 4.9 percent annually between 1990 and 2000, has been dominated by all-cargo carriers. These carriers have significantly increased their market share, accounting for more than three-quarters of domestic freight/express RTMs in 2000. Federal Express and United Parcel Service are the two largest domestic all-cargo carriers. Both of these carriers are integrated carriers who provide door-to-door service using intermodal systems.

Revenue Ton Miles Forecast

The total number of air cargo RTMs flown by U.S. commercial air carriers was 30.0 billion in 2000, an increase of 6.7 percent over 1999. Total RTMs are forecast to increase to 59.1 billion in 2012. This represents a 5.8 percent average annual increase from 2000 to 2012.

Freight/Express Revenue Ton Miles

Total freight/express RTMs flown by U.S. commercial air carriers was 26.9 billion in 2000, a 7.1 percent increase from 1999. Domestic freight/express RTMs, which increased by 5.3 percent in 2000 to 12.1 billion, is forecast to increase to 22.2 billion in 2012. This represents an average annual growth rate of 5.2 percent over the 12-year forecast period. Historically all-cargo carriers have increased their share of domestic freight/express RTMs flown, from 61.3 percent in 1990 to 78.5 percent in 2000. This has resulted from the significant growth of express service by Federal Express and United Parcel Service and the lack of growth of domestic freight/express business for passenger carriers. These carriers have increased passenger load factors almost 10 percentage points since 1990 and thus are increasingly using belly capacity for passenger luggage. The trend in market shares is expected to continue through-

out the forecast period, resulting in a forecast market share for the all-cargo carriers of 87.7 percent in 2012.

International freight/express RTMs increased to 14.8 billion in 2000, an increase of 8.6 percent from 1999. International freight/express RTMs are forecast to increase by an average of 6.7 percent over the entire forecast period to 32.0 billion. This forecast is based on the projected strong economic growth in the world GDP, especially in the Latin America and Asia/Pacific regions. The all-cargo carriers increased their share of international freight/express RTMs flown from 48.6 percent in 1990 to 57.1 percent in 1998. This share declined to 50.7 percent by 2000, due in part to a shortage of all-cargo capacity. All-cargo carriers share of international freight/express RTMs is forecast to increase to 60.3 percent by 2012.

Mail Revenue Ton Miles

Total mail RTMs flown by U.S. commercial air carriers was 3.1 billion in 2000, an increase of 3.5 percent from 1999. Domestic mail increased by 3.3 percent in 2000 to 2.5 billion RTMs. Domestic mail is forecast to grow an average of 4.1 percent per year over the forecast period. The forecasted total for domestic mail RTMs in 2012 is 4.1 billion. Historically passenger carriers have accounted for the majority of domestic mail RTMs. The all-cargo carriers have increased their share though from 3.8 percent in 1990 to 28.5 percent in 2000. This trend has resulted from the increased use of all-cargo carriers such as Emery Worldwide by the U.S. Postal Service as a means to improve control over delivery. Factors cited by the U.S. Postal Service in determining the use of all-cargo versus passenger carriers includes capacity, availability, and on-time performance. The all-cargo share of domestic mail is forecast to increase to 35.7 percent by 2012.

THE REGIONAL/COMMUTER JET AGE

The introduction of the regional jet into the dynamics of the demand for air transportation services has significantly expanded the role and market presence of the regional/commuter industry. The phenomenal customer acceptance of the regional jet, coupled with the success operating carriers have experienced in markets where the aircraft is deployed, positions its operators to move beyond the current boundaries of traditional regional/commuter markets. The regional jets' range and speed opens up new opportunities for regional/commuter carriers to serve longer-haul markets and also by-pass congested hub airports by providing point-to-point service.

While jet aircraft have been operated by regional/commuter airlines for quite some time, the first true regional jet was introduced into service in 1993—four carriers operated jet aircraft in that year. Since 1993, four new regional jet aircraft models have been introduced into the market, ranging in size from 30 to 70 seats. Today, 15 regional/commuter airlines operate a total of 569 regional jet aircraft.

To assess the impact of the introduction and growing importance of the regional jet on the industry, regional/commuter schedules from the Official Airline Guide were analyzed for the 10-year period between 1991 and 2000. This analysis included fleet composition, activity and industry operational measures, airports and markets served, and the impact on the industry as a whole.

FLEET COMPOSITION

In 1991, three regional/commuter air carriers operated a total of 20 jets, consisting largely of the British Aerospace 146 and the Fokker F28. These aircraft accounted for only one percent of the total fleet, and just over 4.0 percent of seats offered for sale. By 1993, the year the regional jet was first introduced, four carriers operated a total of 29 jet aircraft. This relatively slow growth in the numbers of jet aircraft continued through 1996, totaling 90 in that year.

It was not until 1997 that the introduction of the regional jets started to accelerate, increasing by over 100 aircraft per year during the next four years. Between 1996 and 2000 the number of jet aircraft increased more than six-fold, from 90 aircraft in 1996 to 569 in 2000. The jet aircraft's share of the total regional/commuter fleet increased from 4.2 percent in 1996 to 24.6 percent in 2000. Additionally, jets accounted for just over one-third of regional carrier seats in 2000, up from only 6.7 percent in 1996.

MARKETS/ROUTES SERVED

The new regional jets are providing the flying public with significantly more travel options to choose from in making their travel plans. With the addition of the Bombardier, Embraer, and Fairchild-Dornier regional jets, more small- and medium-sized hubs are being served by regional jets. Consequently, the number of airports and city-pairs benefiting from jet service are at an all-time high.

The number of U.S. airports receiving regional/commuter jet service increased from a total of only six in 1991 to 184 in 2000. During 2000, the number of U.S. airports receiving regional jet service increased by 14 airports. The percentage of airports receiving regional jet service is also on the rise. In 1991, only 1.1 percent of the airports served by regional/commuter aircraft had jet service. In 2000, 38.7 percent of all airports served by regional/commuter carriers received jet service. At present, Hawaii and Alaska do not have airports offering regional jet service.

Travelers between points in the United States and Canada and Mexico are also witnessing an increase in the numbers of airports served by jet aircraft. In 2000, regional/commuter jet aircraft flew to nine Canadian airports from the United States, up from just two airports in 1992. In Mexico, 13 of the 15 airports with regional/commuter service are served by jet aircraft; up from only one airport in 1998.

Correlating to the increase in airports with commuter jet service is the increase in the number of city-pairs served by jet aircraft. Regional/commuter city-pairs with jet service grew from 10 in 1991 to 1,270 in 2000. In the year 2000 alone, an additional 369 city-pairs received regional/commuter jet service, raising the percentage of total regional/commuter city-pairs with jet service to over 37 percent.

Out of the 1,270 city-pairs served by regional jets in the year 2000, 62 were flown in international transborder service. Between the United States and Canada, 46 of 97 regional/commuter city-pairs were served by jets. Between the U.S. and Mexico, 16 of the 26 regional/commuter city-pairs received jet service.

TOP 10 REGIONAL/COMMUTER AIRPORTS

The top ranked airport in 2000, as measured by regional jet departures, was Cincinnati/Northern Kentucky International (CVG), the main hub for Comair. Scheduled jet departures at CVG totaled 112,548 in 2000, 90.4 percent of all regional/commuter departures and 55.4 percent of all commercial departures at the airport.

Chicago O'Hare ranked a distant second to CVG in 2000, with a total of 69,404 jet departures in 2000. Cleveland Hopkins (38,802), Atlanta Hartsfield (38,382), and Washington Dulles (32,504) round out the list of top five airports with scheduled jet service from regional/commuter carriers. (Table 20.4.)

Table 20.4 Top 10 Airports Ranked by Commuter Jet Departures Calendar Year 2000

Airport	Departures Commuter* Jet Only	Departures Commuter* Total	Commercial**	Commuter Jet Departures As % of Total Commuter Departures	Commuter Jet Departures As % of Total Commercial Departures
Cincinnati/N. Kentucky International	112,548	124,501	203,197	90.4	55.4
Chicago O'Hare International	69,404	103,183	433,515	67.3	16.0
Cleveland-Hopkins International	38,802	85,558	143,564	45.4	27.0
William B. Hartsfield International	38,382	91,791	424,566	41.8	9.0
Washington Dulles International	32,504	121,303	193,123	26.8	16.8
Houston International	31,605	68,845	215,630	45.9	14.7
New York La Guardia	31,757	66,283	199,565	47.9	15.9
Raleigh-Durham International	31,212	51,505	101,058	60.6	30.9
Dallas/Fort Worth International	23,494	123,689	395,792	19.0	5.9
Newark International	21,189	48,598	192,550	43.3	11.0
Departures—Top 10	430,897	885,616	2,502,560	48.7	17.2
Total Departures—48 U.S.	1,004,606	4,208,797	10,553,544	23.9	9.5

Source: Official Airline Guide

* Scheduled Commercial Passenger Aircraft with seat size >=3 and <69.

** Scheduled Commercial Passenger Aircraft with seat size >=3.

Regional jet departures at the top 10 ranked regional/commuter airports accounted for 48.7 percent of total regional/commuter departures and 17.2 percent of total commercial departures at these 10 airports. In the 48 contiguous states, commuter jet departures accounted for 23.9 percent of all regional/commuter departures, and 9.5 percent of all commercial departures.

INDUSTRY IMPACT

The regional/commuter segment of air transportation has distinguished itself as a "high-flying" member of the commercial aviation industry. The past several years have seen rapid development of routes utilizing regional jets, much to the increasing satisfaction of the traveling public. However, even with the high traffic growth being experienced by the industry, there are some down sides as the regional/commuter carriers move toward a fleet composed of greater numbers of jet aircraft.

In 1991, a total of 3,475 city-pairs received regional/commuter service. By the end of 2000, regional/commuter carriers still served a total of 3,424 city-pairs, only 51 less than served 10 years earlier. However, of the 3,475 city-pairs served in 1991, only 1,811 (52.1 percent) received regional/commuter in 2000. While another 156 of the city-pairs received replacement service from large air carriers, the fact remains that 1,508 city-pairs no longer receive air carrier service of any kind.

Passenger Yield

The nominal passenger yield for the nine Form 41 regional/commuter air carriers was 33.75 cents in 2000, down 6.9 percent from 1999 and 18.6 percent lower than in 1998. This decline can be attributed largely to the increased utilization of regional jets operating at higher load factors and flying longer passenger trip lengths. Even with these declines, the Form 41 regional/commuter carriers' yield is still almost two and one-half times higher than that of the larger air carriers (14.35 cents in 2000).

The nominal yield is expected to increase throughout the forecast period (up 1.2 percent annually), from 33.75 cents in 2000 to 39.05 cents in 2012. The real yield is projected to remain steady during the first years of the forecast period, then decline thereafter and reach 28.35 cents in 2012. This represents an average annual decline of 1.4 percent over the 12-year forecast period.

Average Aircraft Size

The most significant change in fleet composition will result from the integration of large numbers of regional jet aircraft into the fleet, most of which occur in the "41 to 60 seat" category. These aircraft will contribute to increase public acceptance of regional airline service, and will offer the greatest potential for replacement service on selected jet routes.

The regional/commuter aircraft fleet will continue to grow rapidly during the forecast period. As such, the average seats per aircraft (calculated by dividing available seat miles by miles flown) is expected to increase by 0.7 seats annually over the 12-year forecast period, from 37.5 seats in 2000 to 46.0 seats in 2012.

Most of the growth in seat size is expected to come from those carriers operating the larger turboprop and regional jets. The average aircraft size of the Form 41 carriers is projected to increase from 44.9 seats in 2000 to 53.0 seats in 2012. The average aircraft size for the Form 298-C carriers is expected to grow from 30.9 seats in 2000 to 36.5 seats in 2012.

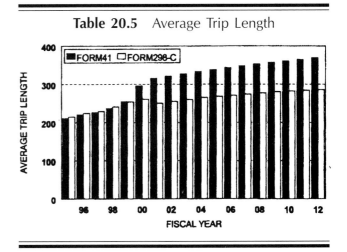

Table 20.5   Average Trip Length

Passenger Trip Length

The growth in the average passenger trip length, and the resultant higher growth in RPMs relative to enplanements, will be driven, in large part, by the increased numbers of larger regional jets and high-speed turboprops entering the regional/commuter carrier fleet during the forecast period. With increased speed and capacity, these aircraft will serve expanded market areas on a timely and efficient basis. The average trip length is projected to increase from 280.4 miles in 2000 to 338.8 miles in 2012, an increase of just under 4.9 miles annually.

The trip length for the Form 41 carriers is forecast to increase from 295.6 miles in 2000 to 369.0 miles in 2012. For Form 298-C carriers, the trip length is expected to increase from 260.9 miles in 2000 to 286.0 miles in 2012. (Table 20.5.)

Passenger Load Factor

With the introduction of larger jet aircraft into the regional fleet, the industry load factor is expected to rise slowly over the 12-year forecast period. The average regional/commuter industry load factor is expected to increase from 59.0 percent in 2000 to 62.8 percent in 2012. It is also assumed the regional/commuter industry will continue to emphasize frequency of service and this should keep the regional/commuter load factors from reaching the level of the major airlines.

The load factor for Form 41 carriers is projected to increase from 62.0 percent in 2000 to 65.7 percent in 2012. The load factor for the Form 298-C carriers increases from 55.2 percent to 57.0 percent over the same time period.

Revenue Passenger Miles

Regional/commuter RPMs are expected to total 24.8 million (up 11.2 percent) in 2001, then slow to an average growth of 8.0 percent over the next 5 years. RPMs are forecast to increase an average annual rate of 7.3 percent over the 12-year forecast period, and total 52.1 billion in 2012.

Passenger miles for the Form 41 carriers are forecast to increase 25.8 percent (to 16.6 billion) in 2001 and 9.0 percent in 2002 (to 18.1 billion). During the 12-year forecast period, RPMs are expected to increase at an annual rate of 8.7 percent, totaling 36.1 billion in 2012. During the final 10 years of the forecast period, these carriers' RPMs are expected to grow at an average annual rate of 6.1 percent and total 16.0 billion in 2012.

REGIONAL/COMMUTERS PASSENGER FLEET

The current composition of the regional/commuter fleet underscores the growth of the industry and quality of service provided. From a fleet once composed predominantly of general aviation aircraft, today's fleet is increasingly composed of new state-of-the-art turboprops and regional jets offering amenities similar to those found on larger jet aircraft. Today's regional/commuter airlines have a large variety of aircraft from which to choose. As such, regional/commuter carriers are able to tailor their fleet to the specific markets they serve.

The regional/commuter aircraft seat categories were changed last year to more accurately reflect the changing nature of this fast growing industry. More specifi-

Table 20.6 Top 50 Regional/Commuter Airlines Ranked by Total Passenger Enplanements
Fiscal Year 2000

Carrier	Enplanements	Carrier	Enplanements
1. American Eagle	12,085,877	26. Astral	391,876
2. Comair	7,818,419	27. Aloha Island Air	390,912
3. Continental Express	7,621,394	28. Shuttle America	265,507
4. Mesaba	6,008,305	29. Chicago Express	232,576
5. Atlantic Southeast	5,986,069	30. Colgan Air	186,831
6. SkyWest	5,727,490	31. Peninsula	180,486
7. Horizon	5,056,439	32. United Feeder Service	144,335
8. Atlantic Coast	3,550,440	33. Big Sky	140,654
9. Piedmont	3,132,583	34. Corporate Express	116,614
10. Mesa	2,738,582	35. Freedom Air	90,111
11. Allegheny	2,446,967	36. Hagland Aviation	84,313
12. Trans States	2,044,987	37. Pacific Island Aviation	82,351
13. Executive Airlines	1,919,102	38. Samoa Air	72,835
14. PSA	1,135,508	39. Seaborne Aviation	65,496
15. Great Lakes	1,082,758	40. Grant Aviation	61,926
16. Express Airline I	1,076,630	41. Harbor Airlines	58,832
17. Chautauqua	1,069,487	42. Kenmore Air Harbor	55,614
18. Business Express	1,067,291	43. Bering Air	51,495
19. Gulfstream International	925,894	44. Vieques Air Link	50,998
20. Air Midwest	915,565	45. Cape Smythe	45,506
21. CCAir	758,815	46. Frontier Flying Service	44,338
22. Cape Air	590,544	47. Promech	39,060
23. Commutair	563,113	48. Chalks Flying Boat	38,180
24. Eagle Canyon	544,480	49. Taquan Air Service	35,121
25. ERA	432,549	50. Wings of Alaska	34,234

Source: DOT Form 298-C and Form 41

cally, the changes made were intended to include categories which cover the three seating configurations of regional jets that are projected to enter the regional fleet over the forecast period—32, 50, and 70 seats—as well as eliminate categories for which relevant aircraft no longer exist.

The regional/commuter passenger fleet is projected to grow at an average annual rate of 3.9 percent, increasing from 2,312 aircraft in 2000 to 3,673 aircraft in 2012. The growth in the regional/commuter fleet is considerably less than that forecast for passenger demand (5.6 percent annually), and reflects the increased efficiencies which result from the use of larger aircraft and the achievement of higher load factors. The average seat size of the regional/commuter fleet is expected to increase from 37.5 seats in 2000 to 46.0 seats in 2012. The average load factor is projected to increase from 59.0 percent in 2000 to 62.8 percent in 2012.

Changes in the regional/commuter airline industry

are being defined by the changes taking place in the composition of the regional/commuter aircraft fleet. The introduction of regional jet aircraft will accelerate greatly during the forecast period. By the year 2012, it is projected that more than 1,600 new regional jet aircraft, ranging in size from 32 to 70 seats, will be added to the fleet. While the overall average annual growth in the regional fleet is expected to be 3.9 percent, the number of regional jets will grow at an average annual rate of 11.9 percent. Regional jets account for 24.6 percent of the fleet today. By 2012, it is forecast that they will account for almost 60 percent of the fleet.

Most of the aircraft in the "less than 10 seats" category are operated by Alaskan regional carriers. Regional aircraft in this category once made up the bulk of the fleet—60.9 percent in 1980. In 2000, this category totaled 400 aircraft and accounted for only about one-fifth of the total regional fleet. Between 2000 and 2012, the number of aircraft in this category is expected to decline to 314 aircraft, and account for only 8.5 percent of the total fleet in 2012. It is assumed that the decline in this category will occur almost entirely among regional airlines operating within the 48 contiguous states.

In 2000, the "10 to 20 seats" category, which made up the largest portion of the fleet during the early to mid 1990s, continued to decline. In 2000, aircraft in this category totaled 452 (down 3.6 percent from 1999) and accounted for only 19.6 percent of the total fleet. The recent decline in this group is expected to continue throughout the current forecast period. It is projected that the "10 to 20 seats" aircraft category will decline to 328 in 2012, and account for only 8.9 percent of the fleet in that year.

The greatest growth in the regional/commuter fleet is expected to occur from aircraft having between 21 and 70 seats. This is due to the continued substitution of service and new route opportunities created through the use of larger, longer-range regional aircraft. It is projected that almost 2,200 regional jets (with up to 70 seats) will be in operation by the end of the forecast period, compared to an estimated 569 aircraft in 2000. By 2012, it is estimated that 12.4 percent of the regional jets will be in the "21 to 40 seats" category, 71.1 percent in the "41 to 60 seats" group, and 16.5 percent in the "61 to 70 seats" category.

In 2000, aircraft in the "21 to 40 seats" category accounted for 34.0 percent of the regional fleet, the "41 to 60 seats" category made up 24.2 percent, and aircraft with "61 to 70 seats" accounted for only 5.0 percent. However, it is the growth in the "41 to 60 seats" category that will be most dramatic over the forecast period. The bulk of the regional jets that will be introduced into the fleet will fall in this category.

By the year 2012, these three aircraft categories are expected to account for a combined 82.5 percent of the total fleet—26.5 percent in the "21 to 40 seats" category, 44.6 percent in the "41 to 60 seats" group and 11.4 percent in the "61 to 70 seats" category. During the 12-year forecast period, aircraft having 21 to 40 seats are forecast to increase from 785 to 972, an average annual increase of 1.8 percent. The number of aircraft in the "41 to 60 seats" category is projected to increase from 559 to 1,639, up 9.4 percent on an annual basis. During the same time frame aircraft in "61 to 70 seats" category are expected to increase from 116 in 2000 to 420 in 2012, an average annual growth of 11.3 percent.

FLIGHT HOURS

Regional/commuter flight hours, as reported on DOT Form 298-C and on Form 41, totaled 3.8 million hours in 2000, up 2.3 percent compared to 1999. During the forecast period industry flight hours are expected to increase to 4.0 million (up 4.7 percent) in 2001 and to just under 4.2 million (up 4.4 percent) in 2002. During the 12-year forecast period, flight hours are forecast to increase at an average annual rate of 4.6 percent, totaling just over 6.5 million hours in 2012.

PART 4

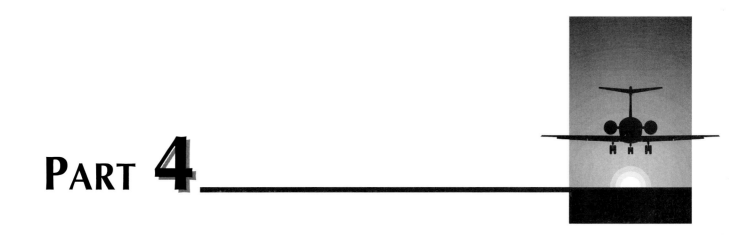

AIRCRAFT

PART 4

BRIEF OVERVIEW OF CHAPTERS

21. AIRCRAFT PERFORMANCE

- Discusses the performance of aircraft in terms of fleet size.

22. THE BOEING COMPANY

- Presents the history and development of The Boeing Company and gives descriptions of several Boeing aircraft.

23. THE McDONNELL DOUGLAS CORPORATION

- Presents the history and development of The McDonnell Douglas Corporation and gives descriptions of several of their aircraft.

24. THE LOCKHEED MARTIN CORPORATION

- Presents the history and development of The Lockheed Martin Corporation and gives descriptions of several of their aircraft.

25. AIRBUS INDUSTRIE

- Presents the history and development of the Airbus Industrie and gives descriptions of their aircraft.

26. FUTURE AIRCRAFT

- The feasibility of future aircraft and spacecraft under development.

CHAPTER 21

Aircraft Performance

In earlier days of air transportation, passengers left the air terminal at ground level, walked several yards across the loading ramp, and climbed a steep flight of steps in order to board an aircraft. They were often exposed to inclement weather conditions during their walk. Sometimes air carrier personnel provided umbrellas for partial protection from the weather, but feet often splashed through puddles.

The design of major airport terminals now enables passengers to check their baggage at the curb and proceed through the main terminal area, through one of the long hallways (concourses) to one of several numbered boarding lounges ("gates"). There they are issued boarding passes and assigned seats on the aircraft. When their flight is called for boarding, they leave the lounge area and walk through an enclosed, carpeted hallway to the door of the aircraft. There the flight personnel welcome them and direct them to their seats. After entering the airport terminal passengers are not exposed to outside weather conditions. At the end of the flight the reverse procedure takes place. Passengers make their way to the outside of the airport terminal for surface transportation. In fact, if they did not know better, they would not realize they had been in an aircraft because they did not at any time see the aircraft except from the inside, possibly in the middle seat of ten seats across the width of the aircraft. Many passengers do not even see the outside of their aircraft.

Of course, many small cities and many small air carriers still use the old "walk out to the aircraft" system. Airport terminals have had to change because of the changes in the air carrier aircraft which they service. Jet passenger aircraft have grown greatly in size, speed, and service. Today's wide-bodied aircraft carry

> **Many small cities and many small air carriers still use the old "walk out to the aircraft" system.**

more cabin attendants than previous aircraft carried in total passengers. As one air carrier captain put it when asked what it is like to pilot one of these aircraft, he said, "It's like sitting on the front porch of a hotel containing three hundred or more people and flying it!"

Modern aircraft have improved in response to the demand for more efficiency. Since the inception of the commercial air transportation industry in the late 1920s, the technological advancement of passenger-carrying aircraft has made possible a decrease of one-third every 10 years in real cost to the air traveling public. Even greater benefits have resulted from increases in aircraft speed, causing a greater value of time, convenience, reliability, and safety to produce economic benefits. Technological advancements partly explain the rapid growth of air travel.

From almost the beginning of the manufacture of passenger aircraft, research and development has been derived from the building of military aircraft. This was true from the early Boeing and Douglas aircraft to the first jet transport, the Boeing 707, which was based upon the United States Air Force B-47 bomber.

The first jet transport commercial airplane built in the U.S. was the Boeing Stratoliner Model 707, first tested July 15, 1954 by "Tex" Johnston at Renton, Washington. It had four Pratt & Whitney J-57 engines with more than 10,000 pounds of thrust, weighed 190,000 pounds and cost $20 million. Designed to carry 150 passengers at 550 mph, the first one was delivered to Pan Am on August 16, 1958.

Since the early 1970s, the military has been moving toward defense systems other than fixed-wing aircraft. This means that the burden of research and development of air carrier aircraft has substantially increased for manufacturers and, therefore, sale prices have increased as well. The effect is a decrease in the rate of technological advancement. The real price decreases in passenger rates cannot continue. This will slow down the air carrier industry market expansion of about 15% a year.

Technological improvements of passenger aircraft producing greater efficiency have been in three areas—speed, range, and size. Speed and range have probably reached their practical limits; therefore, aircraft size is the only area where efficiency can be improved. The wide-bodied aircraft are designed for large-scale operations. The Boeing 747, in its most "stretched" design, for example, could accommodate nearly 1,000 seats. Substantial cost reductions on a seat mile basis are still possible for wide-body aircraft. Larger versions may not be economically practical in domestic U.S. service for some time to come.

The present thrust on technological improvements is for fuel-efficient aircraft. This includes not only the engines but also aerodynamic improvements. The new aircraft have greater efficiency improvements over their smaller versions. On a seat mile basis these aircraft can be up to 40% more fuel-efficient.

Many aircraft have reached the point where they require replacement. The problem is not so much age, but the need for quieter and more fuel-efficient operation. The capital needs of the major airlines for the years 1975 to 1990 were estimated at $20 to $40 billion. Furthermore, it is estimated that the capital needs more than doubled during the 1980–1995 time frame. These estimates determined that starting in the mid-1990s, the air carrier industry would enter a major equipment replacement cycle comparable to the replacement of piston engine aircraft with jet transports.

FLEET PLANNING

Selecting the right aircraft for the markets an airline wants to serve is vitally important to its financial success. As a result, the selection and purchase of new aircraft usually is directed by an airline's top officials, although it involves personnel from many other divisions such as maintenance and engineering, finance, marketing, and flight operations.

There are many factors to consider when planning new aircraft purchases, beginning with the composition of an airline's existing fleet—how old are the planes, how much fuel do they burn per mile, how much are maintenance costs, and how many people are needed to fly them.

In general, newer aircraft are more efficient and cost less to run than older aircraft. A 727, for example, is less fuel efficient than the 757 that Boeing designed to replace it. The 727 also is smaller than the 757, so there are fewer seats to sell, and it requires a flight crew of three, versus two for the 757. As planes get older, maintenance costs can also rise significantly.

Productivity gains must be weighed against the cost of acquiring a new aircraft. Can the airline afford to take on more debt? What does that do to profits? What is the company's credit rating, and what must it pay to borrow money? What are investors willing to pay for stock in the company if additional shares are floated? A company's finances, like those of an individual considering the purchase of a house or new car, play a key role in the aircraft acquisition process.

Marketing strategies are important, too. An airline considering expansion into international markets, for example, cannot pursue that goal without long-range, widebody aircraft. If it has been largely a domestic carrier, it may not have that type of aircraft in its fleet. What's more, changes in markets already served may require an airline to reconfigure its fleet. Having the right size aircraft for the market is vitally important. Too large an aircraft can mean that lots of unsold seats will be moved back and forth within a market each day. Too small an aircraft can mean lost revenue opportunities.

Since aircraft purchases take time (often two or three years, if there is a production backlog), airlines must do economic forecasting before plunging ahead with new aircraft orders. This is difficult because no one knows for certain what economic conditions will be like many months or years into the future. An economic downturn coinciding with the delivery of a large number of expensive new aircraft can cause major financial losses for a carrier. Conversely, an unanticipated boom in the travel market can mean lost market share for an airline that held back on aircraft purchases while competitors were making them.

Sometimes, airline planners determine their company needs an aircraft that does not exist. In such cases they may approach the aircraft manufacturers about developing a new model or the manufacturers may have anticipated their needs and approached the airline first. In any event, new aircraft usually reflect the needs of several major airlines. Because start-up costs for the production of new aircraft are enormous, manufacturers must sell hundreds just to break even. They usually will not proceed with a new aircraft unless they have a "launch customer," meaning an airline willing to step forward with a large order for the plane, plus smaller purchase commitments from several other airlines.

AIR CARRIER FLEET

U.S. air carriers placed orders for an estimated 831 jet aircraft during 1999 continuing the boom in aircraft orders that began in 1996. The 831 orders are the second highest total ever made by the industry, surpassed only by the 1998 total of 911. The number of orders placed during the past three years (2,507) is greater than the number placed during the prior 8-year period, 1989 through 1996. During the past 40 years, the average number of orders per year was 260.

A majority of the orders, 489 aircraft (58.8 percent) were for narrowbody two-engine aircraft (A-318/319/320/321 and B-717/737/757). Regional jet orders (CRJs, EMBs, and Fairchild/Dornier) accounted for 34.1 percent of the total (283 aircraft). Orders for two-engine (A-300/330 and B-767/777) widebody aircraft totaled 52 (6.2 percent) in 1999.

Aircraft manufacturers delivered 519 jet aircraft to U.S. customers in 1999—the largest number of deliveries ever. Of this total, 290 (55.9 percent) were two-engine narrowbody aircraft, 60 (11.6 percent) were for two-engine widebody aircraft, and 140 were for regional jets (27.0 percent). (Table 21.1.)

Passenger Jet Aircraft

In 2000, the fleet of passenger jet aircraft for U.S. air carriers expanded by an estimated 309 aircraft, the largest yearly increase during the past 10 years. As expected, there was a large increase in two-engine

Table 21.1 Jet Aircraft Deliveries U.S. Customers

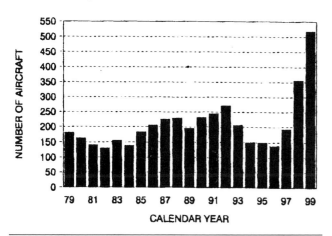

narrowbody aircraft (up 160 aircraft or 5.1 percent), two-engine widebody aircraft (up 71 or 19.7 percent), and regional jets (up 182 aircraft or 49.9 percent).

Based on the backlog of aircraft orders and the projections of air carrier traffic, seat capacity, load factors, fleet requirements, and aircraft productivity, the U.S. commercial air carrier passenger fleet is projected to increase from an inventory of 4,964 aircraft in 2000 to 8,503 aircraft by 2012. This involves a net addition to the fleet (after retirements of obsolete aircraft) of approximately 295 aircraft annually. (Table 21.2.)

The two-engine narrowbody fleet is projected to grow by an average of 153 aircraft annually. By 2012, two-engine narrowbody aircraft are expected to account for 60.3 percent of the fleet, down from 66.5 percent in 1990. The number of three-engine narrowbody (B-727) aircraft declines from 378 aircraft (7.6 percent of fleet) in 2000 to 127 (1.5 percent of fleet) by 2012. The number of four-engine narrowbody aircraft remains constant through the forecast period at 19 aircraft.

The two-engine widebody fleet (A-300/310/330 and B-767/777) is the fastest growing of the widebody group. This group is expected to increase by an average of 34 aircraft per year (5.7 percent), expanding from 432 aircraft in 2000 to 840 aircraft in 2012. The three-engine widebody fleet (MD-11, DC-10, and L-1011) is projected to shrink at an average annual rate of 8.6 percent, from 171 aircraft in 2000 to 58 aircraft in 2012.

Four-engine widebody (B-747 and A-340) aircraft are forecast to increase from 118 aircraft in 2000 to 140 aircraft in 2012, an annual average increase of 1.4 percent. There are currently no U.S. customers for the proposed large A-380 aircraft (formerly referred to as the A-3XX), and our current forecast does not project any of these aircraft entering the U.S. fleet during the forecast period. However if the program is launched, it would not be surprising if U.S. customers did order a handful of these very large aircraft.

The regional jet fleet consisting of aircraft ranging in size from 35 to 70 seats, is forecast to expand from 547 aircraft in 2000 to 2,190 aircraft in 2012, an increase of 12.3 percent a year. By 2012 the regional fleet will account for 25.8 percent of the total passenger jet fleet. In 2000, the regional jet fleet accounted for only 11.0 percent of the fleet.

Average Aircraft Size

Between 1978 and 1983, the average seating capacity of aircraft used by U.S. commercial air carriers in domestic markets increased by over 17 seats (136.4

Table 21.2   Aircraft on Order—Air Transport Association U.S. Members

	Number		Firm Order Delivery Date			
Aircraft Type	Firm	Options	2001	2002	2003	2004
Airbus						
A300	83	80	15	9	10	49
A318	15	8			5	10
A319	111	31	39	45	27	
A320	136	273	48	37	30	21
A330	28	28	3		6	19
Ayres						
LM-200	75			1	32	42
Boeing						
B-717	48	57	27	13	8	
B-737	399	702	125	117	37	120
B-747	17	23	4	7	1	5
B-757	76	138	31	24	19	2
B-767	54	112	25	17	8	4
B-777	41	129	21	13	3	4
Total	**1,083**	**1,581**	**338**	**283**	**186**	**276**

Note: The value of firm aircraft orders was $59.2 billion.

Source: Air Transport Association

seats to 153.6 seats). Between 1983 and 1993, however, the average number of seats remained relatively stable at 152.1, with a standard deviation of only 1.3 seats. From 1993 through 2000, the average number of seats fell precipitously from 149.7 to 139.9 seats—the largest decline during the past 20 years.

The large increase in domestic short-haul traffic by the low-cost, low-fare carriers (Southwest, AirTran, etc.) had been only partly responsible for this occurrence. The most probable cause of the big decline in the average number of seats was the increased number and activity of regionals/commuters reporting on DOT Form 41.

To test this premise, the number of seats for the domestic fleet was calculated for the period of 1986 through 1999 without the regional carriers reporting on Form 41. These carriers generally operate in short-haul markets with turboprop or the new regional jet aircraft. Their average seating capacity for the 1986–1999 period was 35.5 seats. For the period, excluding the regional carriers, average yearly seating capacity for the large air carriers was 4.3 seats higher and almost static since 1995.

In 2000 the average number of seats for all domestic Form 41 carriers declined 2.0 seats. The average number of seats for the large air carriers decreased by 0.6 seats, while the average number of seats for regional carriers reporting on DOT Form 41 increased 2.2 seats.

Current fleet plans by both the large air carriers and regionals/commuters show that the average seat size is increasing. Most new aircraft entering the fleet—either for replacement or expansion of capacity—will be larger. The result will be an increase in the average seat size throughout the forecast period.

The seating capacity for domestic large air carriers is forecast to increase, on average, one seat per year, while the regionals reporting on DOT Form 41 are forecast to increase 0.6 seats per year. For all DOT Form 41 domestic carriers, average seating capacity increases 0.7 seats per year. (Table 21.3.)

CARGO JET AIRCRAFT

In 2000, the jet fleet of U.S. air carrier cargo aircraft increased by 4.3 percent to 1,073 aircraft. Based on the backlog of aircraft orders and the projections of air cargo demand, the U.S. commercial cargo fleet is projected to increase to 1,760 aircraft by 2012. This involves an average net addition to the fleet (after retirements of obsolete aircraft) of 57 aircraft annually or 4.2 percent per year.

Narrowbody aircraft, which accounted for 63.7 percent of the cargo fleet in 2000, are projected to account for 46.1 percent in 2012. The fleet of two-engine narrowbody aircraft is expected to increase from

Table 21.3   Aircraft Operating Statistics—2000

(Figures are averages for most commonly used models)

	Seats	Cargo Payload (*in tons*)	Airborne Speed (*in miles per hour*)	Flight Length (*in statute miles*)	Fuel (*in gallons per hour*)	Operating Cost (*per hour*)
B747-400	379	8.74*	546	4,375	3,257	$6,964
B747-200/300	369	7.72*	521	2,951	3,664	8,615
B747-F		72.25	508	2,277	3,530	7,740
L-1011	322	5.71	503	1,576	2,524	6,565
DC-10-10	309	3.13	509	2,012	2,395	4,372
DC-10-10-F		46.44	473	1,062	2,212	7,239
DC-10-40	285	5.12	495	1,631	2,580	6,313
B-777	273	10.51	524	3,435	2,201	4,497
MD-11	264	9.94*	515	3,910	2,485	7,204
DC-10-30	252	9.24*	517	2,724	2,708	6,879
A300-600	238	4.48*	475	1,271	1,698	6,033
B767-300ER	211	8.99	446	2,076	1,486	3,696
B767-200ER	180	4.31	487	2,191	1,450	4,103
B-757	174	1.82	464	1,195	1,070	2,931
B-737-800	150	0.58	459	1,155	770	2,459
MD-90	148	0.40	431	711	815	4,392
B727-200	147	0.47*	434	707	1,317	2,868
B727-F		15.16	431	609	1,386	4,583
A320-100/200	146	0.53	454	1,107	811	2,324
B737-400	141	0.34	411	675	803	2,446
MD-80	137	0.33	428	782	950	2,539
B737-300	131	0.34	414	620	782	2,150
DC-9-50	127	0.27	359	282	912	2,130
A319	121	0.39	451	1,058	755	2,029
B737-100/200	116	0.17	389	515	829	2,275
B717-200	114	0.11	322	492	582	1,690
DC-9-40	112	0.23	393	519	855	1,771
B737-500	109	0.29	408	584	755	2,271
DC-9-30	98	0.29	372	512	814	2,188
F-100	92	0.13	380	482	664	2,304
DC-9-10	69	0.39	390	468	742	2,000
CRJ-100	50		436	502	464	1,585
CRJ-145	50		375	466	419	987
ERJ-145	50		335	437	337	869
ERJ-135	37		339	402	280	791

*Passenger aircraft models only.

Source: Air Transport Association

167 aircraft in 2000 to 286 aircraft in 2012, an average annual increase of 4.6 percent.

The number of three-engine narrowbody aircraft is expected to grow from 339 aircraft in 2000 to 348 aircraft in 2012. The number of four-engine narrowbody aircraft is expected to remain relatively constant over the forecast period, totaling 178 aircraft in 2012.

Widebody aircraft accounted for 36.3 percent of the cargo fleet in 2000. The fleet of widebody aircraft is forecast to increase to 53.9 percent of the cargo fleet in 2012. The largest increase in the number of widebody aircraft is projected to occur in the two-engine widebody category. This category is expected to grow by an average of 32 aircraft per year (10.8 percent annually), expanding from 160 aircraft in 2000 to 548 aircraft in 2012.

Table 21.4 Operating Fleet of Air Transport Association Members
As of December 31, 2000

Air Carrier	B-747	A-340	L-1011	B-777	A-330	DC-10	MD-11	A300	B-767	B-757	MD-90	B-727	A-320
Airborne Express									17				
Alaska													
Aloha													
America West										13			45
American				27			7	35	79	102	5	60	
American Trans Air			19							15		24	
Atlas Air	37												
Continental				16		17			7	41			
Delta			15	7			15		112	118	16	87	
DHL Airways								6				19	
Emery Worldwide						8							
Evergreen International	13												
Federal Express						59	30	36				152	
Hawaiian						15							
Midwest Express													
Northwest	45					44				48		25	70
Polar Air Cargo	14												
Reeve Aleutian												2	
Southwest													
Trans World									16	27			
United	44			48		3			54	98		75	68
United Parcel Service	18							7	30	75		61	
US Airways					6				11	34			24
Aeromexico									5	8			
Air Canada	3	12			4				42				34
Canadian	4	13							22				
KLM Royal Dutch	33						10		12				
Mexicana										7		22	16
Totals	211	25	34	98	10	146	62	84	407	586	21	527	257

Source: Air Transport Association

319	B-717	B-737	MD-80	DC-9	A310	DC-8	F-100	L-188	CRJ	F-27	SD-360	Cessna 208	Totals
				73		31							121
		61	34										95
		21											21
9		61											138
		51	276				75						717
													58
													37
		225	65										371
		120	120										610
							7						32
							30						38
				7									20
					41					32	11	261	622
			13										28
			10	24									34
20			172										424
													14
								3					5
		344											344
	15		103	27									188
2		182											604
					49								240
6		182	31	23			40						417
			40	16									69
5				17					25				172
		43											82
		29					5						89
							12						57
72	15	1319	679	372	41	117	132	3	25	32	11	261	5,647

The three-engine widebody fleet is projected to increase from 166 aircraft in 2000 to 308 aircraft in 2012. This represents an average annual increase of 12 aircraft or 5.3 percent per year. Conversions of DC-10 passenger aircraft to MD-10's and new MD-11F orders drive the growth in this category. The number of four-engine widebody aircraft is forecast to increase from 63 aircraft in 2000 to 92 aircraft in 2012, an average annual increase of 3.2 percent. (Table 21.4.)

AIRBORNE HOURS

U.S. large commercial air carriers (passenger and cargo but excluding regional jets) flew an estimated total of 14.4 million hours in 2000, up from 13.7 million hours in 1999. Two aircraft categories accounted for more than 80 percent of total airborne hours: two-engine narrowbody (68.7 percent), and two-engine widebody (12.2 percent).

In 2012, the total number of hours is forecast to expand to 22.7 million, an average annual increase of 3.9 percent. Airborne hours are projected to increase 2.3 percent in 2001 to 14.7 million, and 3.9 percent in 2002, to 15.3 million.

Two-engine aircraft (both narrowbody and widebody) are expected to account for 89.2 percent of all airborne hours flown in 2012. Narrowbody two-engine aircraft hours, which make up 71.8 percent of total hours in 2012, increase, on average, 4.3 percent per year. Widebody two-engine aircraft hours, which account for 17.4 percent of total hours in 2012, increase 7.0 percent per year. Four-engine widebody aircraft hours flown are forecast to increase at an average annual rate of 1.8 percent.

The number of hours flown by three-engine aircraft is projected to decline through 2012. Three-engine widebody hours flown are expected to remain essentially flat, increasing just 0.1 percent a year. Although the fleet of three-engine widebody aircraft is forecast to increase over the forecast period, the growth in this aircraft category occurs among cargo operators. Cargo utilization rates for hours are typically lower than utilization rates for passenger applications. Three-engine narrowbody aircraft hours are forecast to fall 3.8 percent annually, reflecting the retirement of large numbers of B-727 aircraft. The share of total hours flown by three-engine aircraft will decrease from 14.3 percent in 2000 to 7.1 percent in 2012. Hours for the four-engine narrowbody fleet, made up primarily of DC-8 cargo aircraft, increase slowly at a rate of 0.3 percent a year. (Tables 21.5 and 21.6.)

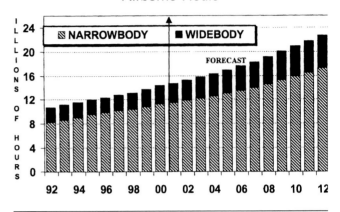

Table 21.5 U.S. Commercial Air Carriers: Airborne Hours

Source: Federal Aviation Administration

AEROSPACE INDUSTRIES ASSOCIATION

The Aerospace Industries Association (AIA) of America, Inc., based in Washington, DC, is the premier trade association representing the nation's manufacturers of commercial, military, and business aircraft, helicopters, aircraft engines, missiles, spacecraft, materials, and related components and equipment.

Founded in 1919, AIA actively conveys industry goals and accomplishments and voices common concerns to Congress, relevant federal agencies, international organizations, news media, and the American public. The association provides an excellent forum for industry and government to exchange views and resolve issues on matters that relate to aerospace industries.

A Board of Governors, consisting of chief executive officers and other senior executives of member companies, guides AIA's activities. A hallmark of AIA is that it receives its leadership from the highest levels of the country's major aerospace companies.

Serving as the voice of our nation's aerospace manufacturers since 1919, AIA represents the vital interests of this industry, not only to the nation, but also to the world at large.

AIA is committed to addressing a wide range of critical issues affecting the entire aerospace community. These range from near-term legislative and regulatory issues to more structural concerns.

The United States aerospace industry generated $144 billion in sales during the year 2000, down 4.9%, or $7.4 billion, from a record of $151 billion. Civil

Table 21.6 U.S. Commercial Air Carriers Passenger Jet Aircraft

Calendar Year	Large Narrowbody			Large Widebody			Regional Jets	Total
	2 Engine	3 Engine	4 Engine	2 Engine	3 Engine	4 Engine		
Historical								
1995	2,715	522	44	248	256	112	35	3,932
1996	2,810	537	47	262	258	143	62	4,119
1997	2,824	532	37	288	243	139	10	4,073
1998	2,949	508	32	309	226	122	221	4,367
1999	3,139	436	21	361	204	129	365	4,655
2000E	3,299	378	19	432	171	118	547	4,964
Forecast								
2001	3,413	293	19	478	149	116	702	5,170
2002	3,554	230	19	510	136	113	848	5,410
2003	3,680	176	19	543	124	115	997	5,654
2004	3,816	118	19	571	118	119	1,110	5,871
2005	3,935	115	19	609	105	123	1,225	6,131
2006	4,069	116	19	637	98	125	1,346	6,410
2007	4,199	118	19	667	91	126	1,499	6,719
2008	4,376	120	19	697	84	127	1,657	7,080
2009	4,569	122	19	729	78	129	1,800	7,446
2010	4,743	124	19	767	71	131	1,941	7,796
2011	4,924	125	19	808	58	134	2,071	8,139
2012	5,129	127	19	840	58	140	2,090	8,503

Source: Federal Aviation Administration

aircraft sales, commercial transport deliveries in particular, accounted for the majority of the sales decline. The industry also attained an estimated $9.4 billion in profits during the year 2000, down from $10.2 billion from the year before. This is the second highest year on record. This is the fifth consecutive year that the aerospace industry has earned profits in excess of $7 billion. Industry sales were projected to be $145 billion as commercial transport production increases after the year 2000 record $155 billion in total orders.

Fewer shipments of commercial jetliners reduced civil aircraft sales to $5.9 billion in 2000. Sales of large civil transport aircraft declined approximately $7.2 billion to an estimated $31 billion. General aviation experienced rising sales during the year. General aviation billings are projected to surpass the year 2000 record of $6.9 billion by approximately $1.3 billion. Civil helicopter sales also increased $49 million to $236 million. Together, civil aircraft shipments declined $5.8 billion to $39 billion in 2000. Sales in the civil aircraft sector, which also includes engines and parts, declined 11.4% to $46 billion.

Sales of military aircraft, engines and parts increased $2.7 billion to $33 billion in 2000. Reduced exports were largely responsible for the military aircraft sales

decline during the year. Fewer foreign deliveries of fighter aircraft and military transports reduced military aircraft exports by $1.2 billion to $3 billion. The military aircraft sector is fundamentally funding by the Defense Department for aircraft procurement, which Congress reduced in fiscal year 2000.

Foreign sales fell $3.5 billion from the previous year of $62.4 billion. Military aerospace exports, which peaked in 1998 at $12 billion, declined for the second straight year to $9.6 billion. Civil aerospace exports fell $1.2 billion to $49 billion after reaching a high in 1998. (Table 21.7.)

The largest component of civil aircraft exports, commercial transports, comprised $23.6 billion of the total; down $2.1 billion from the previous year of $25.7 billion. General aviation exports also declined in 2000, down 21% or $0.3 billion to $1 billion.

Imports rose in 2000 from a record level. Total imports of aerospace products increased $0.6 billion on the $26 billion. Imports of complete civil aircraft rose by $1.7 billion to $10.4 billion. Aircraft engine imports decreased $0.8 billion to $3.7 billion. Aircraft and engine parts imports decreased $0.1 billion dollars to $10.8 billion reflecting reduced domestic production of commercial airline aircraft.

Table 21.7   U.S. Civil Jet Transport Aircraft
Shipments—2000
(In Thousands)

Total Number	**485**
U.S. Customers	276
Foreign	209
B-737, Total	**278**
U.S. Customers	161
Foreign	117
B-747, Total	**24**
U.S. Customers	5
Foreign	19
B-757, Total	**45**
U.S. Customers	25
Foreign	20
B-767, Total	**44**
U.S. Customers	35
Foreign	9
B-777, Total	**55**
U.S. Customers	27
Foreign	28
MD-11, Total	**4**
U.S. Customers	0
Foreign	4
MD-80, Total	**0**
U.S. Customers	0
Foreign	0
MD-90, Total	**3**
U.S. Customers	0
Foreign	3
MD-95 (B-717), Total	**32**
U.S. Customers	23
Foreign	9
Total Value (000s)	**$30,872**

Source: Aerospace Industries Association

Total orders increased 21% to a projected $155 billion in 2000. With shipments totaling $136 billion, the unfilled order backlog grew $19 billion to $210 billion. Similarly, the unfilled order backlog for commercial jetliners grew $9.8 billion through the first nine months of 2000 to $83 billion. As of September 30th, 2000, a total of 1620 commercial transport aircraft remained in the unfilled order backlog. Foreign customers held orders for 487 aircraft.

Although there are early indications that total employment may soon begin rising, aerospace industry employment steadily declined through the year 2000. (Tables 21.8, 21.9, 21.10, 21.11.)

The United States aerospace industry sales are forecast to rise $1.6 billion to $145 billion. Sales to the Department of Defense are expected to rise $2.2 billion to $48 billion as aircraft spending increases, while NASA and other non-defense federal agencies space related spending will fall $1.5 billion to $11.4 billion. Sales to customers other than the United States government are expected to rise slightly to $62 billion. Other customers, such as air carriers and private corporations, account for $0.6 billion of the year's sales growth. Shipments of complete civil aircraft will soon total 3,827 aircraft worth approximately $41 billion. AIA estimates that 530 airliners will be shipped in 2001 and will comprise 80%, or $33 billion, of the total value of civil aircraft shipments. Shipments of civil helicopters are projected to remain strong.

The aerospace industry manufacturers and producers have been experiencing a series of acquisitions, consolidations and mergers for the past several years. This has been caused by the usual corporate reasons resulting from competition and increasing costs. The overall effort has been to operate at a more efficient level.

The following charts are descriptive of what has happened. No doubt more will occur in the future. (See Figures 21.1 and 21.2.)

Table 21.8 Total Employment in the Aerospace Industry—1990–2000
(In Thousands)

Year/Month	Total Aerospace Related Employment	Aircraft and Parts				Guided Missiles, Space Vehicles and Parts		All Other Aerospace Related Employment
		Total	Aircraft	Aircraft Engines & Engine Parts	Aircraft Parts & Auxiliary Equipment	Total	Guided Missiles & Space Vehicles	
1990	1,302	712.3	381.0	151.7	179.5	185.1	132.6	405
1991	1,214	669.2	355.6	143.2	170.3	167.6	120.4	378
1992	1,100	611.7	332.1	126.6	153.0	146.4	105.9	342
1993	966	542.0	301.4	109.2	131.4	123.7	88.9	300
1994	855	481.5	271.3	95.1	115.1	107.5	75.9	266
1995	796	450.5	243.6	93.0	113.9	98.2	69.0	248
1996	796	458.1	243.1	94.7	120.4	90.4	62.7	248
1997	859	500.6	262.4	99.8	138.4	91.4	62.9	267
1998	896	525.1	271.6	103.3	150.2	92.0	63.3	279
1999	846	494.9	254.3	100.0	140.7	88.1	60.9	263
2000	794	459.1	231.7	95.4	132.1	87.8	61.8	247
2001*	787	455.9	229.2	93.4	133.3	86.7	61.2	245

*Estimated
Source: Aerospace Industries Association

Table 21.9 Employment of Women in the Aerospace Industry—1990–2000
(In Thousands)

Year/Month	Aerospace Industry Total	Aircraft and Parts				Guided Missiles, Space Vehicles and Parts	
		Total	Aircraft	Aircraft Engines & Engine Parts	Aircraft Parts & Auxiliary Equipment	Total	Guided Missiles & Space Vehicles
1990	209.3	161.1	92.2	28.5	40.5	48.2	36.4
1991	193.0	150.0	84.7	26.5	38.8	43.0	32.7
1992	171.8	135.1	77.8	23.0	34.3	36.7	28.7
1993	147.6	116.0	67.9	19.6	28.5	31.6	24.4
1994	128.1	100.9	59.7	16.7	24.5	27.2	20.7
1995	117.8	93.3	53.1	16.0	24.3	24.5	18.5
1996	117.4	95.7	53.0	16.5	26.1	21.7	15.9
1997	129.1	107.4	59.3	17.3	30.8	21.7	15.6
1998	137.4	115.3	63.2	18.3	33.8	22.1	15.8
1999	130.5	109.0	58.5	18.3	32.2	21.5	15.1
2000	123.1	101.5	54.3	17.8	29.5	21.6	15.5
2001*	121.6	100.1	52.8	17.2	30.0	21.5	15.8

*Estimated
Source: Aerospace Industries Association

U.S. Industry Consolidation: A Work in Progress

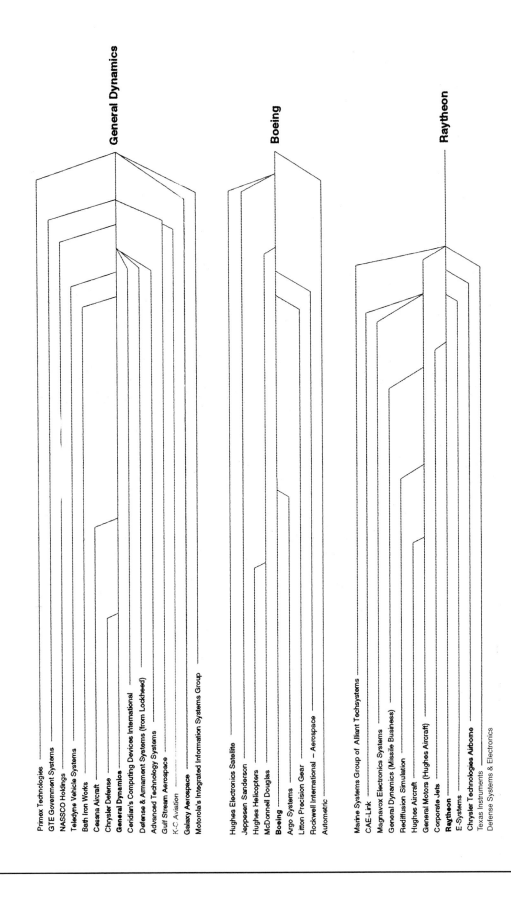

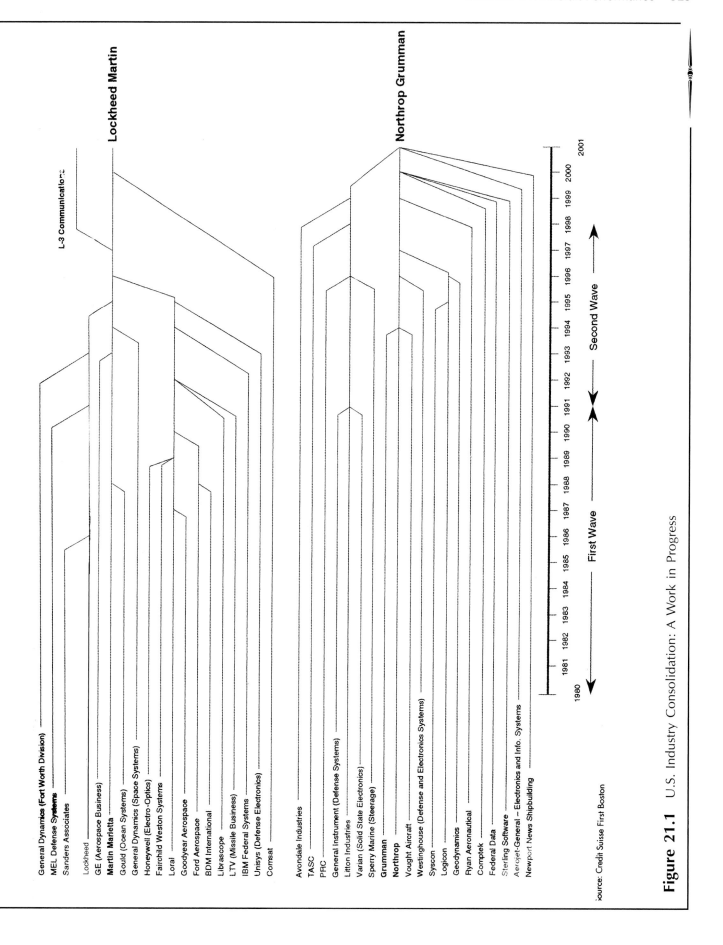

Figure 21.1 U.S. Industry Consolidation: A Work in Progress

Table 21.10   Average Hourly Earnings in the Aerospace Industry—1990–2000
(Production Workers Only)

Year/ Month	Aerospace Industry Total	Aircraft and Parts				Guided Missiles, Space Vehicles and Parts	
		Total	Aircraft	Aircraft Engines & Engine Parts	Aircraft Parts & Auxiliary Equipment	Total	Guided Missiles & Space Vehicles
1990	14.73	14.79	15.66	14.84	13.37	14.39	14.82
1991	15.51	15.60	16.72	15.38	14.05	14.90	15.21
1992	16.46	16.53	17.70	16.28	14.89	15.99	16.45
1993	17.18	17.23	18.43	16.70	15.72	16.80	17.43
1994	17.89	17.95	19.50	17.31	16.01	17.48	18.29
1995	17.99	18.02	19.97	17.34	15.93	17.74	18.58
1996	18.56	18.57	20.49	18.22	16.42	18.51	19.34
1997	18.94	18.88	20.76	18.58	16.76	19.53	20.75
1998	19.24	19.17	21.08	18.93	17.02	19.96	21.38
1999	19.79	19.75	21.78	19.67	17.38	20.24	21.76
2000	20.71	20.75	23.04	20.73r	18.22	20.34	21.63
2001*	21.20	21.24	23.82	21.35	18.47	20.73	21.79

*Estimated
Source: Aerospace Industries Association

Table 21.11   Average Weekly Earnings in the Aerospace Industry—1990–2000
(Production Workers Only)

Year/ Month	Aerospace Industry Total	Aircraft and Parts				Guided Missiles, Space Vehicles and Parts	
		Total	Aircraft	Aircraft Engines & Engine Parts	Aircraft Parts & Auxiliary Equipment	Total	Guided Missiles & Space Vehicles
1990	624	626	656	637	570	612	634
1991	648	651	694	654	583	632	649
1992	685	689	736	689	615	652	666
1993	714	717	756	715	657	696	727
1994	754	756	800	753	688	738	779
1995	758	757	809	770	677	765	812
1996	801	802	859	813	721	790	837
1997	844	844	918	838	756	842	896
1998	847	847	932	840	751	840	892
1999	844	845	928	871	735	836	881
2000	895	901	995	937r	774	842	887
2001*	928	933	1027	986	799	877	916

*Estimated
Source: Aerospace Industries Association

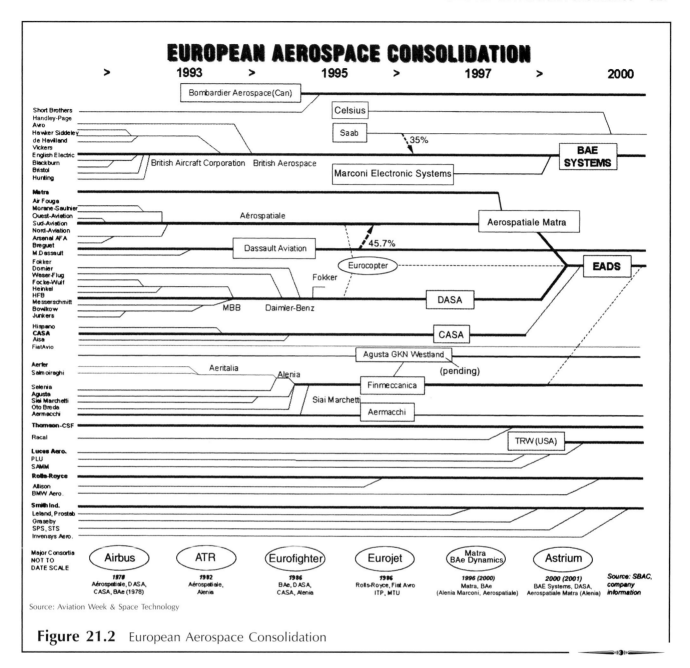

Figure 21.2 European Aerospace Consolidation

CHAPTER 22

The Boeing Company*

The Boeing Company, founded on July 15, 1916 in Seattle, Washington, has produced more commercial jetliners than any other company. It has also become a leader in the missile, rocket, helicopter, and space fields.

The company was founded by William E. Boeing after the building of two biplanes at a shop on Seattle's Lake Union. Only 21 men made up the company's first work force.

By December 1915 a plane Boeing and G. Conrad Westervelt had designed, called "The B & W seaplane," was under construction.

The first of two "B & Ws" was finished early in 1916, and it was apparent that the United States might enter World War I. Boeing knew what that would mean, and he felt he could build superior airplanes—types that might serve the armed forces. On July 15, 1916, he founded the Pacific Aero Products Company, incorporating it for $100,000 under laws of the State of Washington. The name was changed to Boeing Airplane Company on April 18, 1917, and the present name was adopted on May 3, 1961.

> **Boeing summed up the new joint operation by applying their well known term "Working Together."**

Boeing and his associates held a conference. Was there any future in the aircraft business? They decided there was, but that aircraft manufacture alone was not enough to keep the company going. Hence, for a while, the Boeing plant manufactured Hickman sea sleds and, when the boat market was slack, bedroom furniture.

Meanwhile, Boeing was buying materials—a few rolls of piano wire, some spruce lumber, some linen fabric—and hiring carpenters and other workmen.

When the United States entered into World War I, the Boeing plant became a busy place with the building of 50 Model C trainers. The government placed orders for a number of flying patrol boats, but only a few were built before the armistice was signed and production stopped.

Boeing's two years of study at Yale Sheffield School of Science had taught him the importance of research and experimentation. Idea men, he decided, were essential if the company were to grow. Among the first men Boeing hired were two promising engineering students from the University of Washington. One was Philip G. Johnson, who died in 1944, and whose genius for production geared the Boeing company for its unmatched World War II output. The second was Claire L. Egtvedt, chairman of Boeing who retired in 1966, and died in 1975. Egtvedt was an idea man above all else. Johnson and Egtvedt took part in the earliest developments, beginning with the Model C trainer.

Expansion of civil aviation in the United States in the 1920s was concerned mainly with carrying mail, and in 1919 Eddie Hubbard, an Army pilot, discussed with Boeing the possibilities of a commercial airmail contract. They made their first survey flight on March 3, 1919, and carried a pouch of 60 letters on the return trip from Vancouver, B.C., Canada, to Seattle in a Boeing C-700 seaplane. The first contract international airmail route, linking Seattle and Victoria, B.C., was awarded to Hubbard on October 15, 1920, with the Boeing B-I flying boat used for the service.

---

* For current information go to the Website at: http://www.boeing.com/commercial

FLIGHTS OF FANCY

Boeing's Interest in Flying

William Edward Boeing, son of a wealthy timberman, took up flying at the age of 34 for his own amusement. After a couple of rides in a hydroplane being flown in 1914 by Terah Maroney from Seattle's Lake Washington, Boeing became convinced he could build a better airplane. He and G. Conrad Westervelt, a Navy officer assigned to engineering work at a Seattle shipyard, decided to build a pair of seaplanes.

In preparation, Boeing learned to fly in 1915 at a flying school operated by Glenn L. Martin in Santa Ana, California. Late that year he bought a Martin seaplane and had it shipped to Seattle where it was assembled. It soon was flying over the city with Boeing at the controls.

William Edward Boeing

One year later the company won its first major postwar airplane order, 111 observation airplanes, followed the next year by the largest postwar contract awarded any airplane manufacturer—200 MB-3A pursuits.

From 1921 until 1927, the company devoted its airplane production primarily to military types, producing 268 trainers, pursuits, observation craft, torpedo planes and patrol bombers for the Army, Navy, Marines and the governments of Peru and Cuba. Two exceptions to this military production were one mail plane in 1924 (a modification of an Army observation type) and another in 1925—the Boeing Model 40.

The Navy's order in early 1927 for 27 fighter planes is illustrative of the production speed of those days. The first FB-5 flew on October 7, 1926, and all 27 airplanes were delivered to the Navy by January 1, 1927.

When the United States government, under President Coolidge's economy program, stopped flying the mail in 1926, Boeing bid for and received the contract for carrying transcontinental airmail. Boeing Air Transport, Inc., was organized in 1926 and in five months 24 Boeing 40-As were designed and built to fly the route from Chicago to San Francisco.

The Model 40-A was designed to carry two passengers and 1,200 pounds (544 kg) of mail. It signaled the beginning of regular commercial passenger service over long distances, and in 1930 served as the vehicle for the first regular passenger and mail night flights. A 40-B mail plane also pioneered commercial use of voice radio communication with the ground. The 40-A had a top speed of 135 miles an hour (217 km/h) and a maximum range of 550 miles (885 km). Its 420-horsepower "Wasp" engine enabled it to climb to an absolute ceiling of 18,000 feet (5486 m).

By 1928 the Boeing factory, with 800 employees, had become one of the largest aircraft plants in the country. Boeing could see that his own financial resources would not be enough for future activities. On November 1, 1928, Boeing Airplane & Transport Corporation stock went on the market and sold quickly.

This was a time of expansion and combination for business in general, and the aircraft industry was no exception. Soon after the sale of Boeing stock, the United Aircraft & Transport Corporation was founded, with William Boeing as the firm's chairman. The corporation included Boeing Airplane Co., Pratt & Whitney, Chance Vought, Sikorsky, Hamilton Propeller Co., Pacific Air Transport, and Boeing Air Transport.

In 1931, Boeing Air Transport, National Air Transport, Pacific Air Transport and Varney Air Lines were combined under the name United Air Lines.

Following a lengthy government hearing in 1933–34 and the subsequent passage of a law prohibiting air mail contractors from being associated with any aviation manufacturing companies, United Aircraft and Transport Corporation was forced to split up. On September 26, 1934, the corporation was split into three new companies: United Air Lines, which took over air transport; United Aircraft Corporation, which took all the eastern manufacturing firms; and Boeing Airplane Company, which retained the western manufacturing portion. Stearman Aircraft of Wichita, acquired by United Aircraft and Transport in 1929, became part of Boeing.

The Boeing Monomail, completed in the spring of 1930, marked the beginning of the era of low-wing all-metal transport construction. The Monomail had many other special features including retractable landing gear, a sleek aerodynamically clean exterior, oleo shock absorbers, and revolutionary internal structure. Its design was so advanced that its full utilization was compelled to await the variable pitch propeller, a development which came a few years later.

The Monomail was powered by one 575-horsepower P & W "Hornet" engine. Originally designed as an all-cargo plane, it later was refined to carry from six to eight passengers as well as freight and mail. A development of this airplane type was the B-9 bomber, which outdistanced all pursuit aircraft of its day.

The Boeing 247, delivered in 1933, was an outgrowth of the Monomail and B-9. It was the first all-metal, twin-engine transport. Its basic design is still dominant in transport aircraft. Among the innovations were control-surface trim tabs, an automatic pilot, de-icing equipment, and supercharged engines of the type formerly used only on military airplanes. It was one of the first twin-engine airplanes capable of climbing to altitude on one engine with a full load. With accommodations for ten passengers and a crew of two plus a stewardess, the 247 revolutionized air traffic by making possible 20-hour coast-to-coast flights with only seven intermediate stops. Seventy-five were built, and some were still flying in the late 1960s.

In 1934, the prototype of the Boeing Kaydet was first flown at the Wichita plant. In all, Boeing built 10,346 of these standardized primary training planes used by both the Army and the Navy—nearly as many as the total primary trainers from all other United States manufacturers. It was a two-place, open cockpit biplane of welded steel tube fuselage frame construction, with built-up fabric-covered wings.

In the middle and late 1930s aircraft designs pioneered by The Boeing Company appeared throughout the country, not only in the Boeing 247s flying the airways, but in the aircraft of competing companies. Competitors followed the Boeing trend, added some flourishes of their own, and quickly sold their products.

In 1934 the Army announced competitive tests for a "multi-engined" bomber. Other aircraft companies interpreted "multi-engined" to mean "two-engined." Boeing engineers concentrated on four, and the resources of the company were devoted to the task.

The Boeing Model 299 was the result. It was built in 1935 and flew in record time from Seattle to Wright Field, Ohio. Later it crashed and burned there when an Army pilot inadvertently took off with the flight controls locked. But the Army had seen enough—it ordered more of the same type, tried them, and ordered more. They were called B-17s.

This early model Flying Fortress was the first airplane to combine long range—more than 3,010 miles

(4844 km), a carrying capacity of eight men, 4800-pound (2177 kg) bomb load, five guns, and the speed of a pursuit plane—236 miles an hour (380 km/h).

The new Boeing bomber was so advanced that its acceptance was slow. The company had been solely responsible for its development, even to the financing. While the Air Corps officers connected with it were enthusiastic, the War Department was not prepared to accept such an advanced airplane.

But World War II was brewing, and urgency eventually brought about the triumph of the Flying Fortress—a major weapon in itself. Even then, however, Boeing engineers realized that although the Flying Fortress was good, it was not enough. They knew that in the thin, high air a plane could fly faster on less fuel. If it were a bomber, it could evade much of the enemy's fire and cope more effectively with fighters.

The early Flying Fortress was not a high-altitude aircraft, but, fitted with turbo-superchargers, it soon became one. The chief difficulty was that its crew had to wear cumbersome oxygen masks. The problem was to build an airplane that carried normal atmospheric pressure with it. Boeing engineers had achieved this in the Stratoliner, the first successful pressurized passenger transport. A limited number of these had been built, along with the huge, 72-passenger Boeing 314 Flying Boat, when war turned the entire Boeing plant to bomber production.

By war's end, 12,731 B-17s had been built—6,981 by Boeing and the others by Douglas and Lockheed. They had dropped 640,036 tons of bombs, and had shot down 6,659 enemy fighters—nearly as many as all other American airplanes combined, including fighters.

Early in the war, American military planners realized that neither the Flying Fortress, nor any other airplane of its size, would be able to carry the war over the vast distances of the Pacific. They needed an airplane which would combine even greater range and striking power with the ruggedness of the B-17.

Such a plane was the B-29 Superfortress, the first of which was completed by Boeing in September 1942. It became the first pressurized heavy bomber produced in quantity and the first with a complete remote-controlled gun-firing system. It, too, set the pattern for bombers which followed.

By the end of the war, 3,970 of the 60-ton bombers had been built—2,766 of them by Boeing. The Superfortress had four 2,200-horsepower Wright engines, cruised at 250 miles an hour (402 km/h) with a top speed of 368 miles an hour (592 km/h), had a range of over 4,500 miles (7,242 km), and could carry a 20,000-pound (9,071 kg) bomb load.

A postwar development of the B-29 was the B-50 Superfortress. Though outwardly very similar to the B-29, the B-50 was actually 75% a new airplane, with 69% more power and a wing 16% stronger although 650 pounds (294 kg) lighter.

The 400-mile-an-hour (643 km/h) B-50's range was 6,000 miles (9,656 km). With inflight refueling, its range was virtually unlimited. In the spring of 1949 the B-50 Superfortress "Lucky Lady II" proved this by making the first round-the-world nonstop flight, covering the 23,452 miles (37,742 km) with the aid of four aerial refuelings. Time for the trip was 94 hours and 1 minute.

The company's first postwar commercial airliner was the 72-ton double-deck Stratocruiser. This 300- to 340-mile-an-hour (482 to 547 km/h) luxury transport was completely air-conditioned and cruised at altitudes of 15,000 to 25,000 feet (4571 to 7620 m) with a maximum range of 4,600 miles (7403 km). It normally carried 75 passengers, and included a lower deck and lounge.

To the Strategic Air Command, Boeing delivered the B-47 six-engined Stratojet and the eight-jet B-52 bombers. Various models of the B-52 still form the principal striking force for SAC.

The B-47, first of the swept-wing bombers, was described by the United States Air Force as a medium bomber in the 600-mile-an-hour (965 km/h) class, capable of carrying nuclear devices. First flight of the original XB-47 was on December 17, 1947, and the last of 1,390 Boeing-built B-47s was delivered by the company's Wichita facility on October 24, 1956. Total deliveries to the Air Force, including B-47s built by Douglas and Lockheed, came to 2,041 units.

B-47s set spectacular records for their day, among them a 1949 flight in which the XB-47 covered 2,289 miles (3683 km) from Larson Air Force Base in central Washington State to Andrews AFB, Md., in 3 hours, 46 minutes, at an average speed of 607.8 miles an hour (978 km/h).

The XB-52 and YB-52, prototypes for the eight-jet Stratofortress, first flew in 1952; and the first production model, the B-52A, made its initial flight August 5, 1954. Prototype planes featured tandem seating for pilot and co-pilot, but the production models, with designations of A through H, have a side-by-side cockpit arrangement. In all, 744 were built, including 277 at Seattle, with the last B-52 rolling out of the factory at Wichita in June 1962.

Performance of the B-52 has been outstanding from the outset. Three of the big planes landed at March AFB, Calif., in January 1957, after a nonstop flight around the world, covering the 24,325 miles (39,147 km) from Castle AFB, Calif., in 45 hours and 19 minutes at an average speed of 530 miles an hour (852 km/h). This was less than half the time of the previous around-the-world record of the B-50 "Lucky Lady II." In January 1962, a B-52H flew nonstop 12,519 miles (20,147 km) from Okinawa to Spain without refueling, breaking eleven distance and speed records.

All A through F models of the B-52 have similar external appearance, with a wing span of 185 feet (56.39 m) and sweepback of 35 degrees. Features of the G and H models include extended unrefueled range, more refined electronics, low altitude capabilities, and the ability to launch supersonic Hound Dog and SRAM missiles. Development of the B-52 as a cruise missile carrier is in progress. The vertical fin was shortened on the G and H models, and the tail gunner's position was moved to the forward fuselage section. A 20 mm cannon replaced the four 50-caliber gun on the H models, and 17,000-pound thrust turbofan engines were installed. The G and H models were expected to remain in service through the 20th century.

Flying teammates of the B-47 and B-52 included the KC-97 Flying Boom Tanker and the KC-135 jet Stratotanker. The C-97 Stratofreighter, a 74-ton (67.131 kg), double-deck carrier, was capable of carrying 68,500 pounds (31.071 kg) of cargo. The last of 888 Stratofreighters was rolled from the Renton production facility on July 18, 1956.

A military jet plane was derived from Boeing's 70 prototype—the KC-135 tanker transport built for the Air Force. Altogether, 732 jet tankers were delivered with the final delivery in January 1965 at the Renton plant. In February 1961, the Military Air Transport (now the Military Airlift Command) ordered a sister ship, the C-135A jet cargo transport. A later model, the C-135B, had turbofan engines. Forty-five of the cargo transports were built by Boeing in 1961 and 1962.

In mid-1964, Boeing delivered the first of a fleet of 17 new EC-135C airborne command posts to the Strategic Air Command. Designed and built specifically for the command-post mission, the EC-135C can serve as a tanker or can receive fuel in flight from other tankers. These aircraft are used around the clock as backup control from the air for America's strategic forces, with mission duration limited only by flight crew endurance. Twenty-six other C-135s were built for various missions—a grand total of 820 in the KC/C-135 series.

In August 1952, Boeing announced it was investing $16 million of its own money in the development of a prototype jet transport. That was a substantial part of the company's net worth, so it was a high-risk investment. From the company's background in sweptwing B-47 and B-52 production came extensive experience with high-performance jet aircraft. But the forerunner of all Boeing planes to follow—designated the 367-80 and more frequently called "the Dash Eighty"—was a departure from the military bombers.

The Model 707 prototype, the Dash Eighty, was rolled from the Renton factory in May 1954, and made its first flight on July 15, the 38th anniversary of Boeing's founding. In October 1955, the first order for a commercial jet was received from Pan American World Airways, which put the first Boeing jet airliner in service on its transatlantic route on October 26, 1958.

William E. Boeing, as an honored guest at the 1954 rollout, watched his wife christen the aircraft which ushered in the jet for America. Although no longer associated with the company, he was able to view the fruits of his pioneering efforts which had begun four decades earlier. Boeing died September 28, 1956, at the age of 74. In 1972, the Dash Eighty was presented to the Smithsonian Institution.

In early 1960 the 707-120B and 720B airlines made their appearance. These models were equipped with Pratt & Whitney JT3D turbofan engines giving improved performance and efficiency. Announcement of the 707-320B Intercontinental with advanced JT3D-3 turbofan engines was made in early 1961.

Wingspan of the basic 707-120 and the medium-range 720 is 130 feet 10 inches (39,87m). The Intercontinental has a wing span of 145 feet 9 inches (44,42 m). Length of the 720 is 136 feet 9 inches (41,50 m); of the 707-120 airplanes, 145 feet 1 inch (44,04 m), and of the Intercontinental, 152 feet 11 inches (46,60 m). The maximum gross weight is 235,000 pounds (106,819 kg) for the 720B and up to 336,000 pounds (152,720 kg) for the Intercontinental.

The Air Force versions of the 707-120B and the 707-320B Intercontinental are the VC-137B and VC-137C, respectively. The military models are used for the rapid transportation of government officials and high-priority cargo.

The 727 differs in appearance, power, and capabilities from other members of Boeing's jetliner family. Designed initially for short- to medium-range routes and a passenger capacity of about 130, the popular tri-jet has gone through successive stages of improvement and now boasts a variety of optional equipment that makes it one of the most versatile aircraft ever designed. Gross weight has risen from 142,000 pounds to a maximum of 208,000 pounds (96,350 kg), with a passenger capacity of 189 and a range of more than 2,800 nautical miles. Currently offered in a choice of many gross weights, depending on airline requirements, the Advanced 727-200 features a new superjet-look interior as standard equipment. The contemporary cabin treatment patterned after the 747 has proved popular with both passengers and crew.

Boeing announced the 727 in December 1960. The initial flight took place February 9, 1963, and on December 26 of that year the Federal Aviation Administration certificated the type for commercial service. In one of the final phases of the FAA tests, a 727 flew more than 94,000 miles (151,246 km) on a world tour of 26 nations.

The first 727 delivery was to United Air Lines in October 1963. Both United and Eastern Air Lines put the new Boeing jet with its distinctive T-tail into service in February 1964. Cargo models (all -100 versions) have a forward cargo door the same size as that on the 707-320C and can take the same size cargo pallets. It is convertible from passenger to cargo configuration or vice versa in as little as 30 minutes.

The smallest member of the Boeing jetliner family is the twinjet 737. Four versions of the short-to-medium-range airliner are in production at Boeing's Renton, Washington, facility with major body construction at the Wichita, Kansas, factory. Depending on interior configuration, the 737 can carry up to 169 passengers.

The first production model made its first flight on April 9, 1967, with FAA certification and delivery to airlines late that same year. All 737s being built are equipped with "Quiet Nacelle" engine treatment to meet noise regulations. The first 737 equipped with quiet nacelles was delivered to Canada's Eastern Provincial airlines in October 1973.

The 737 also has been outfitted as an airborne navigator-trainer for the Air Force. The first of a fleet of 19 of these "flying classrooms," called T-43s by the Air Force, was delivered in 1973, and the final plane in the 19-airplane order was delivered in 1974.

The spacious 747 entered airline service in early 1970, and within six months more than one million passengers had flown on the superjets.

The 747 was conceived in the early 1960s, when Boeing market research indicated an airplane of its size would be required to meet the growth in airline passenger and cargo traffic predicted for the 1970s.

In April 1966, Pan American World Airways announced its purchase of 25 747s, and in the next few months a total of $1.8 billion in airline orders for the superjets was received—one of the largest pre-production orders in commercial airplane history. A 200 million-dollar manufacturing plant was begun at Everett, Washington, about 30 miles north of Seattle, and the huge assembly building was occupied and activated just a year after the program go-ahead.

On February 8, 1969, the first 747 took to the air and began the flight phase of the most extensive test program ever undertaken in commercial aviation history. In addition to laboratory tests of parts and components, the program included assignment of five of the giant airplanes for a multi-million-dollar, year-long Boeing and FAA flight test program. The five superjets involved logged more than 1,400 flight hours by the program's conclusion. Further flight-testing resulted in the certification of a higher-gross-weight standard 747, as well as the advanced 747B, the 747F Freighter, the 747C convertible passenger/cargo jetliner, and the 747SR short-range version for high-density routes.

In August 1973, Boeing announced plans to produce a smaller member of the 747 family—the 747SP special performance aircraft. The 747SP has the same wing platform but is 47 feet shorter than the basic 747s. It offers greater range and better economics and performance than any comparable aircraft of its size. Deliveries began in early 1976.

Except for the 747SP, all members of the 747 family have the same basic configuration: length—231 feet 10 inches; wing span—195 feet 8 inches; tail height—63 feet 5 inches; fuselage width—21 feet 4 inches. The 747SP is not only shorter, but it has a larger tail with a height of 65 feet and 5 inches. The 747s are powered by four Pratt & Whitney JT9D engines, each producing up to 47,670 pounds of thrust. Other engine options are available, including a 52,000-pound thrust P&W version, the Rolls-Royce RB211-524 with 50,000 pounds of thrust, and the General Electric CF6-50E fanjet with 52,500 pounds of thrust. (See Figure 22.1.)

The 747—The standard 71,000-pound version, operating at a maximum gross weight, carries an average load of 374 passengers and baggage a distance of 5,900 miles. A growth version of the standard 747 was developed to take advantage of the superjet's structural capability as determined in static structural tests. With minor changes, the takeoff gross weight was increased 25,000 pounds, making possible longer range, greater payload, or a combination of the two. Standard 747s can be retrofitted to the higher gross-weight configuration.

The 747B—This advanced 775,000-pound to 820,000-pound gross weight passenger plane can carry a standard 374-passenger load more than 6,600 miles nonstop. Another version, the new "Combination" 747 with a cargo door located on the left fuselage behind the wing, can operate as an all-passenger jetliner or can carry combination passenger/freight loads during less busy travel seasons.

The first of these versatile workhorses of the air went into service with Sabena Belgian World Airlines in early 1974. It was a standard passenger airplane which was modified by installing the side cargo door. The first Combi 747B off the production line featured a larger door and was delivered to Air Canada in February 1975.

The 747F (Freighter)—The freighter carries a maximum payload of about 260,000 pounds about 2,900 miles, or 200,000 pounds (100 tons) nearly 4,000 miles, well beyond transatlantic range. Its operating costs per ton-mile are expected to be about 35% lower than those of the 707. It features a swing-up nose and mechanical cargo handling equipment to permit fast, easy, straight-in loading of cargo, and also is offered with a main-deck side cargo to increase its versatility.

The 747C (Convertible)—The 747C is a convertible passenger/cargo airplane capable of carrying air travelers in the spacious surroundings and luxurious decor to which superjet passengers have become accustomed, yet upon conversion becomes a modern air freighter. A typical all-passenger flight can carry 380 persons and their baggage in a mixed-class configuration 5,800 statute miles. A typical North Atlantic nonstop cargo load will be 180,000 pounds. A full cargo payload of 250,000 pounds will be carried 2,850 miles. The 747C can also carry main-deck combination passenger/cargo loads. The 747C incorporates the same type of swing-up nose and mechanical cargo-handling equipment as the 747F freighter, and a main-deck side cargo door also can be installed in the 747C. First delivery was in April 1973.

The 747SR—Designed specifically to fill the need for high-capacity transports on routes as short as 200 miles, the 747SR is structurally strengthened to permit it to make twice as many landings in 20 years of short-range flights, yet retain its long-range capability. Gross weight can vary from 520,000 pounds at takeoff on short-range flights to 735,000 pounds for long-range flights.

The 747SP—This high-performance version of the 747 offers a typical mixed-class passenger capacity of 288 in its 185-foot fuselage. Takeoff field-length requirements are reduced and cruising altitude is 4,000 to 6,000 feet higher than that of any other wide-body jetliner. Gross weight is 650,000 pounds with a range up

Figure 22.1
Noted Boeing Aircraft

Boeing B&W

The B&W was the name of the first airplane model Boeing produced. Only two were built; both were sold to New Zealand.

Boeing Model 200

The Boeing Model 200 was a revolutionary all-metal airplane. It had an aerodynamic single-wing design that eliminated support wires. Flying at 158 mph this airplane carried a single pilot plus six passengers and cargo. The first flight was May 6, 1930.

Boeing 707

In 1958, the Boeing 707 became America's first jet airliner. Nearly twice as fast as most propeller-driven airliners, the 707 helped introduce the jet age to the world.

Boeing 314 Clipper

The Boeing Model 314 Clipper, a long distance flying boat, was the biggest and most luxurious airplane of its time. On overseas flights, passengers slept in full length berths and ate in a special dining room. The clipper carried 72 passengers at a cruising speed of 184 mph. The first flight was June 7, 1938.

Boeing Model 40-A

The Boeing Model 40-A was the company's first airliner. It had an all-steel fuselage and an air-cooled engine. It could carry two passengers and 1,000 pounds of mail at a cruising speed of 145 mph. The first flight was on May 20, 1927.

Boeing Model 247

The Boeing Model 247 was a twin-engine, ten passenger airplane that could cruise at 189 mph. Called the "three mile a minute" airliner, the 247 broke coast-to-coast records on its first scheduled flight. The first flight was on February 8, 1933.

Boeing B-17

From the beginning, Boeing has used its technologies to support America's armed services. Almost 13,000 of these B-17 bombers were built for World War II.

A 1917 photo of the "Red Barn" where Boeing built its first airplanes. The building has been restored and can be seen at the Museum of Flight, in Seattle, located next to Boeing Field.

to nearly 6,900 statute miles—or the capability of non-stop trips from New York to Tokyo, Casablanca to Los Angeles, or Tokyo to Amsterdam. Fuel consumption will be about 20% less than the basic 747.

747SUD—This version has a Stretched Upper Deck to provide for 60 passengers in the upper deck. Passenger capacity is increased by 44 seats.

By the mid-1970s it became apparent that fuel used per passenger had become an overriding design point for commercial airliners, second only to safety in importance. Boeing realized that rather than more speed or larger aircraft, fuel efficiency and jet operation would be the guiding criteria for the next generation of jet airliners.

Years of research and development work culminated in an announcement by United Airlines, on July 14, 1978, that it had ordered 30 Boeing 767 airliners. With two advanced design engines, the 767 carries up to 375 passengers in wide-body comfort. About four feet wider than present medium-range aircraft, the 767 is configured with five to eight seats across, divided by two aisles down the passenger cabin. Boeing Commercial Airplane Company engineers estimate that the 767, on a typical flight of 400 miles, will burn 40% less fuel per seat than earlier jets it will replace. First delivery to United Airlines was in 1982.

In size, the 767-300 is midway between the present 727 and wide-body trijets. Fuselage length is 180 feet. Engines can be any of three different manufacturers' designs, in the 40,000-pound thrust class.

The 777 resulted when market demand sized, shaped and launched the newest member of the Boeing family of aircraft. Designed to be the most preferred airliner in the medium size aircraft category, the 777 was the largest twinjet in the world when it entered service in 1995. The new airplane's design offers features, innovations and approaches to aircraft development that will set the standard well into the next century. The second member of the new-generation Boeing family is the 757-200, a 220 passenger airliner based on the 727 fuselage with a newly designed wing.

The 757, with engines in the 40,000-pound thrust class, has a gross weight of 200,000 pounds. It will have the lowest fuel consumption of any airplane its size—about 10 percent lower on a medium-range flight than the 727-200, even though the 757 will carry more passengers. With many electronic systems matching those of the 767, the smaller 757 offered exceptional economy when it went into service in early 1983.

THE 727

Boeing's 727-200 was the latest development in a continuing program of growth an improvement for the popular trijet. From an initial gross weight of 140,000 pounds, the 727 has grown to 210,000 pounds and a passenger capacity of up to 189 for the Advanced version.

More and more airlines have decided that the "long-bodied" 727 is the best available answer to high-capacity, medium-range "airbus" operations. It has proved to be a versatile aircraft equally suited for high-frequency scheduled routes between major cities, for medium range charter operations, and for multi-stop transcontinental service.

Structural improvements, more powerful engines, improved reliability, and greater fuel capacity led to Boeing's introduction of the 191,000-pound Advanced trijet in May 1971, and the 208,000-pound version one year later. Minor changes added 2,000 pounds gross weight capability since then. Structural changes include thicker wing skins, a stronger main landing gear, and a heavier nose gear. Up to 2,400 gallons more fuel can be carried in integral tanks in the center wing section and fuel cells in the lower body hold, as options, increasing range by more than 1,000 miles with a typical payload.

As part of Boeing's efforts to reduce noise levels of all its aircraft, the nacelle of the higher thrust JT8D-17 (16,000 pounds) engine has optional sound absorption treatment that makes the Advanced 727 one of the quietest jets flying. The FAA has certified that the Advanced airplane, with Quiet Nacelle modifications, meets U.S. Government noise standards for new aircraft. The 727, in fact, was the first airplane of its size to meet those stringent rules. It also meets ICAO noise requirements.

The "superjet look" interior cabin treatment is standard on all Advanced 727s. Fuselage width is the same as that of the 707 and 737 jetliners, 12 feet 4 inches, providing the same cross-sectional space and the same degree of luxury on short and medium-range routes. The generous cabin width allows six-abreast seating and greater airline earnings in high-density charter configurations than is possible with narrower cabins. The fuselage depth is 14 feet, leaving room for two large cargo compartments, one forward and one aft of the wing, with a combined capacity of 1,664 cubic feet. (See Figure 22.2.)

An aviation milestone was reached January 4, 1974, when the 1,000th 727 was delivered. No other commercial airliner has proved so successful. The historic

Figure 22.2
Boeing Transports

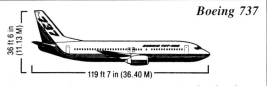

Boeing 737

36 ft 6 in (11.13 M)
119 ft 7 in (36.40 M)

The short- to medium-range Boeing 737 is a family of airplanes all by itself with three different models ranging in capacity from 108 passengers to 170. Airlines have made the 737 the most popular jetliner in history with orders for more than 2,900.

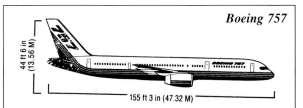

Boeing 757

44 ft 6 in (13.56 M)
155 ft 3 in (47.32 M)

The fuel-efficient Boeing 757 is a versatile airplane that airlines use on both domestic and international routes. It can carry as many as 230 passengers.

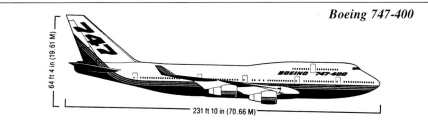

Boeing 747-400

64 ft 4 in (19.61 M)
231 ft 10 in (70.66 M)

The Boeing 747-400 is the largest airliner in commercial service, and has the greatest range. It can carry more than 450 passengers a third of the way around the world, nonstop.

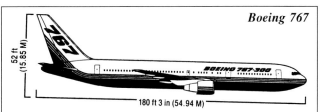

Boeing 767

52 ft (15.85 M)
180 ft 3 in (54.94 M)

The Boeing 767-200 can accommodate 216 passengers in a two-class cabin layout; the larger 767-300 has room for 261.

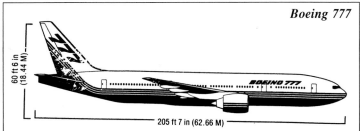

Boeing 777

60 ft 6 in (18.44 M)
205 ft 7 in (62.66 M)

The Boeing 777 is the newest airplane. The decision to build this new-generation jetliner was made in late 1990; the first model was delivered in 1995. The twin-engine 777 will carry from 360 to 390 passengers in multi-class cabin layouts; up to 440 in a single-class commuter configuration.

1,000th airplane went to Delta Air Lines, a major U.S. trunk carrier. Less than six years later—on July 2, 1979—the 1,500th 727 was turned over to United Airlines. The 727 is no longer being produced.

BOEING MODEL 737 SHORT- TO MEDIUM-RANGE JETLINER

The Boeing 737 was designed to bring to short- and medium-range routes the same popular features provided by 707s and 727s: dependability, wide-body comfort, and cargo width. The Advanced 737 offers operational capabilities and versatility found in no other twinjet airliner.

The first 737 flew April 9, 1967. After an intensive Boeing and Federal Aviation Administration flight testing program, during which a test fleet of six 737s flew more than 1,300 hours, the airplane was certificated for airline service in December 1967. Certification included approval for two-man crew operation and automatic approaches with a 100-foot ceiling and 1,200-foot forward visibility.

The 737 entered commercial service in Europe February 10, 1968—less than one year after its first flight. On April 28, 1968, the 737 began airline service in the United States. By December 31, 1979, more than 760 had been ordered by 90 airlines and the U.S. Air Force. Nearly 600 million passengers have been carried by 737s in commercial service.

One of the reasons for this airplane's continuing sales success has been the improvements which Boeing introduced into the Advanced 737 in May 1971. The Advanced version of the twinjet incorporates aerodynamic refinements, a stopping package with improved anti-skid and automatic brakes, and more powerful engines that greatly improved payload/range capability and short-field performance. Standard equipment now includes noise-reducing engine nacelle treatment that allows the 737 to be certified to U.S. and ICAO noise rules.

The newest Boeing 737s are fitted with a Performance Data Computer System (PDCS) as basic equipment. The Lear Siegler system gives flight crews advisory information on engine pressure ratios, temperatures, and airspeed. This data, together with target indicators on cockpit instruments, makes it easier for pilots to operate the airplane for maximum fuel efficiency. Now a full flight regime auto-throttle which couples with the performance data system will automatically set thrust levels throughout the flight to maintain desired airspeed or predetermined thrust limits.

Items recently incorporated as basic or standard options in the 737 also include a Performance Navigation Computer System that builds on the PDCS to add a lateral (horizontal) navigation function. There is a digital three-color weather radar, a heads-up visual approach and takeoff monitor, several choices of modern navigation aids (including Omega and Inertial Navigation System), and five-inch dials on the altitude director and horizontal situation indicators. The new dials replace older style four-inch instruments to allow better presentation and improve readability for the pilots. These and other improvements to the versatile 115 to 169-passenger 737 will ensure that the Boeing twinjets will meet airline requirements for years to come.

Four versions are available: all-passenger and convertible passenger/cargo. All have, as standard equipment, a contemporary new interior with large enclosed stowage bins to increase headroom and provide space for briefcases, garment bags, and other large items that previously had to be carried on the floor. Brighter lighting and a flatter ceiling add to the feeling of spaciousness and enhance passenger comfort even beyond that of earlier Boeing jetliners.

The more powerful engines, aerodynamic improvements, and better brakes allow the Advanced twinjet to operate profitably from air fields as short as 4,000 feet. Options such as low-pressure tires and gravel runway capability make it possible for the 737 to operate from unpaved fields anywhere.

The under-wing location of the engines results in savings in structure weight, a longer passenger section for a specific fuselage length, better in-flight balance characteristics, and easier maintenance (the engines can be easily serviced by a mechanic standing on the ground). Sealing of the wings provides two integral fuel tanks outboard of the body; installation of additional fuel tanks in the center wing section is optional for a maximum fuel capacity of 5,970 U.S. gallons.

The 737 owes its low-speed performance characteristics to high-lift devices similar to those of the 727. Lateral control is through single outboard ailerons operating in conjunction with two flight spoiler panels on each wing. Two additional ground spoiler panels on each wing are used only on landing. All flight controls are hydraulically operated by two independent systems. A third system is installed for the rudder, and manual backup is provided as a third control system for elevators and rudder.

A gas turbine engine located in the tail is the power source for cabin air conditioning, electricity, and en-

ADVANCED 727-200 SPECIFICATIONS

Wing Span	108 feet
Length	153 feet 2 inches overall
	Fuselage only: 136 ft. 2 in.
Height	34 feet
Gross Weight (Advanced)	191,000 pounds maximum taxi weight
(High GW Advanced)	208,000 pounds maximum taxi weight
	210,000 pounds maximum taxi weight
Landing Weight	160,000 pounds both models
Maximum speed	615 mph
Range:	2,464 miles with 27,500 pound payload

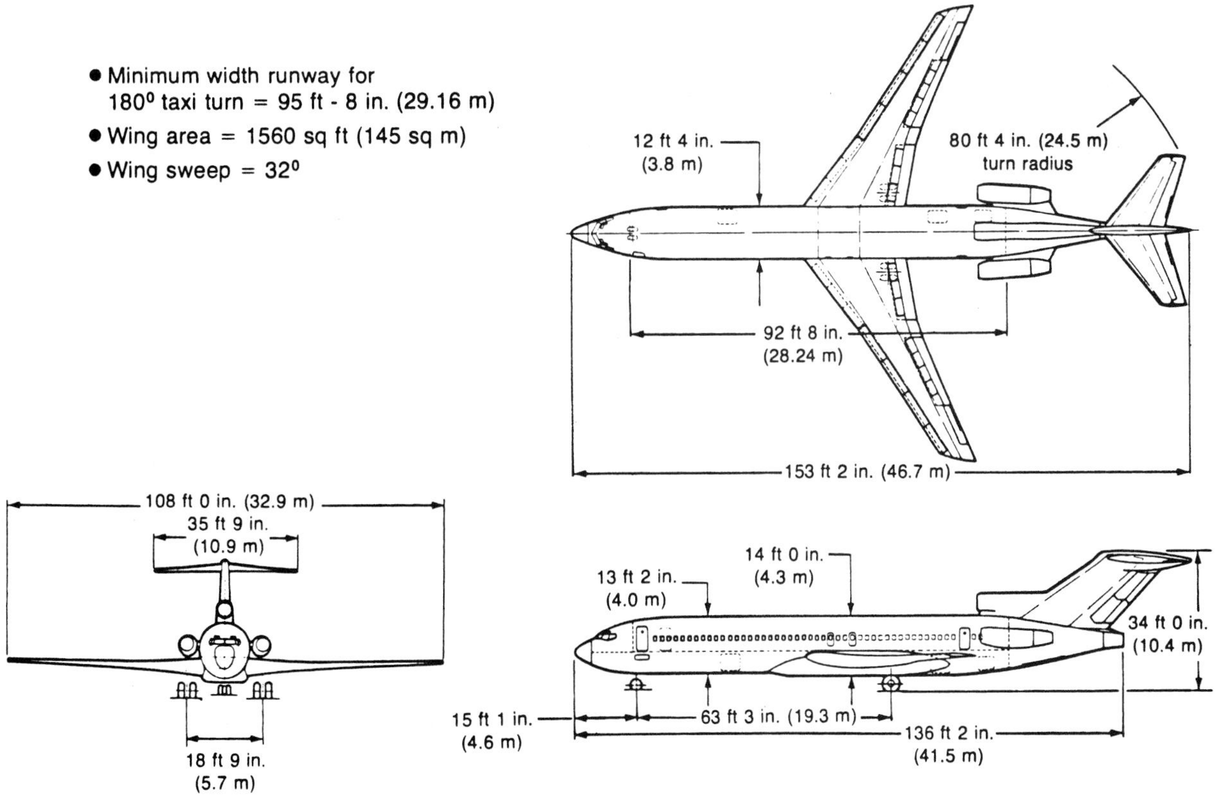

- Minimum width runway for
  180° taxi turn = 95 ft - 8 in. (29.16 m)
- Wing area = 1560 sq ft (145 sq m)
- Wing sweep = 32°

Figure 22.3 727-200 General Arrangement.

gine starting on the ground. It can be operated in flight for electrical power and air conditioning if required.

Passengers board through front and rear entry doors on the left side of the airplane. An electrically operated boarding stair is carried within the fuselage beneath the forward door as standard equipment on passenger ver-

sions. An integral boarding stair at the rear door is optional.

The standard Boeing cabin width—12 feet 4 inches—makes the 737 the only short-range jetliner offering six-abreast tourist seating, thus extending airline earning potential. (See Figure 22.6.)

ADVANCED 727-200 SPECIFICATIONS—CONTINUED

Power   3 Pratt & Whitney JT8D turbofans:
                           -9 rated at 14,500 pounds thrust
                           -15 rated at 15,500 pounds thrust
                           -17 rated at 16,000 pounds thrust
                           -17R rated at 17,400 pounds thrust
Cruising Speed   570 to 605 mph
Cruising Altitude   30,000 to 40,000 feet
Range   1,500 to 2,500 miles
Passenger Capacity   148 to 189
Fuel   8,186 gallons standard at lower gross wts.
                           9,806 gallons standard for 208,000 lbs.
                           10,606 gallons optional for 208,000 lbs.

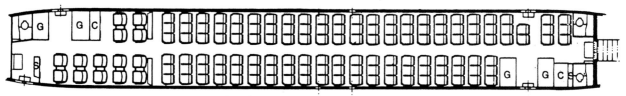

145 passengers (14 at 38″ pitch and 131 at 32″/33″ pitch)
U.S. mixed class

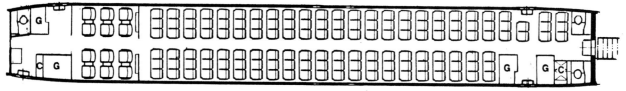

149 passengers (12 at 36″ pitch and 137 at 32″ pitch)
European mixed class

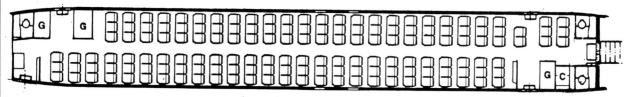

155 passengers at 34″ pitch
All tourist

Figure 22.4   Interior 727-200.

737-400 SPECIFICATIONS

Dimensions:

Wingspan	94.9 feet
Overall length	119.7 feet
Height	36.6 feet
Fuselage width (inside)	11.7 ft.
Wing sweepback	25 degrees
Passenger capacity	138–169 passengers 6 abreast
Landing gear:	Tricycle—dual wheel units
Crew:	Two: pilot and copilot
Maximum speed	565 mph at 26,000 feet
Cruising speed:	495 mph at 35,000 feet
Cruising altitude:	30,000 feet
Maximum altitude:	35,000 feet
Maximum taxi weight:	139,000–150,000 lbs.
Maximum landing weight:	124,000 lbs.
Range capability: (115 pas)	1,850 n. mi.
Fuel Capacity: (standard) (optional max)	5,701 U.S. gal.
Powerplant:	CFM56-382

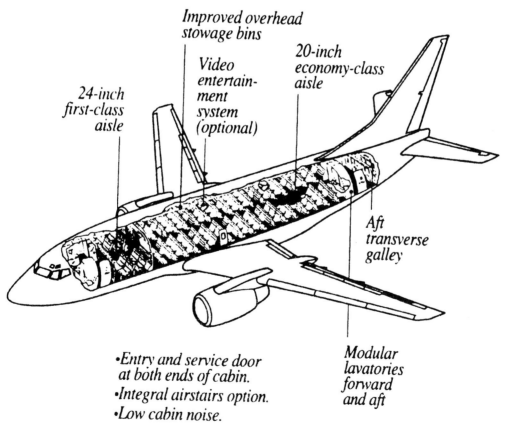

Figure 22.5 Boeing 737-400 Specifications.

737-400 SPECIFICATIONS

	737-500		737-300		737-400	
Passenger capacity	108 to 132		128 to 149*		146 to 168	
Maximum gross weight, lb	Standard	Options	Standard	Options	Standard	Options
Taxi	116,000	134,000	125,000	139,000	139,000	150,500
Takeoff	115,500	133,500	124,500	138,500	138,500	150,000
Landing	110,000	110,000	114,000	116,600	121,000	124,000
Zero fuel	102,500	103,000	105,000	109,600	113,000	117,000
Typical operating empty weight, lb	69,800	71,040	72,100	73,340	75,800	77,520
Engines, CFM56	-3C-1	-3C-1	-3C-1	-3C-1	-3C-1	-3C-1
SLST**, lb	18,500	20,000	20,000	22,000	22,000	23,500
Fuel capacity, U.S. gal	5,311	6,295†	5,311	6,295†	5,311	6,295†
Lower-hold cargo volume, ft³	822	546	1,068	792	1,373	1,097

*Exit limit
**Sea-level static thrust
†Assumes after-market auxiliary fuel tanks (STC)

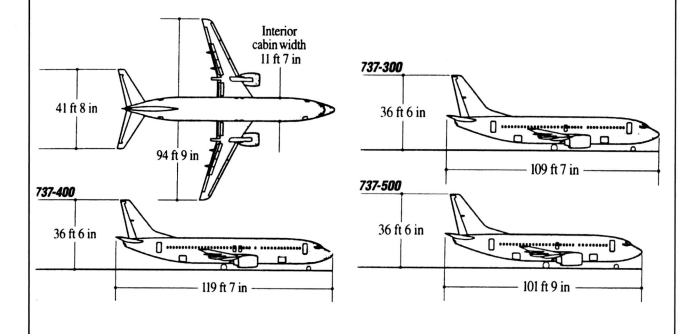

Figure 22.5 Continued.

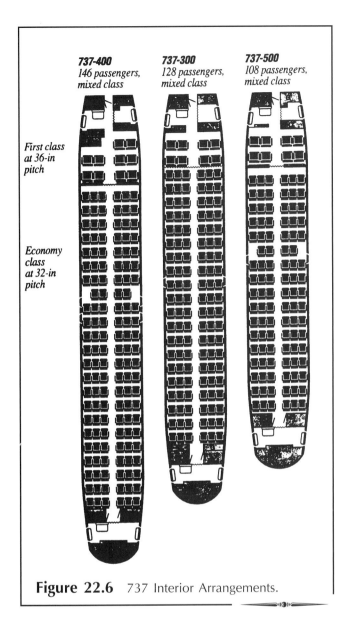

737-400
*146 passengers,
mixed class*

737-300
*128 passengers,
mixed class*

737-500
*108 passengers,
mixed class*

*First class
at 36-in
pitch*

*Economy
class
at 32-in
pitch*

Figure 22.6   737 Interior Arrangements.

The convertible cargo/passenger 737 incorporates an 86 by 134-inch forward cargo door and is available with either a cargo or quick-change pallet loading system. Because of its wide body, the aircraft can accept the same pallets used as conventional convertible jets permitting easy transfer of cargo loads. It can be converted in less than an hour to carry all passengers, all cargo, or a combination of cargo and passengers.

An electronically controlled cabin pressurization system—first of its kind—permits an essentially hands-off operation by the two-pilot crew and provides unparalleled passenger comfort at all altitudes.

Another contribution to cost control is crew size on the 737. The airplane was designed for two-pilot operation and certificated by the FAA for such crew size.

One operator says that there have been more cartoons and nicknames attributed to the Boeing 737 than to any other aircraft, which goes to prove public and airline acceptance. The chief pilot of one African airline put it this way: "You don't fly a 737—you have an affair with it."

THE BOEING 747

The first of the giant jetliners, the Boeing 747 is the largest airplane ever built for commercial service. Its beginnings can be traced to the early 1960s, when Boeing market research showed that an airplane of this size would be needed to meet the growth in airline passenger and cargo traffic predicted for the 1970s and 1980s.

The 747 reached formal project status in March 1966. One month later, Pan American World Airways announced it would purchase 25 of the new Boeing 747s. Within just five months, Boeing had received $1.8 billion in orders for the superjets—one of the largest backlogs of pre-production orders in commercial aviation history.

In June 1966, three months after the 747 program go-ahead, Boeing acquired 780 acres adjacent to Paine Field, in Everett, Washington, 30 miles north of Seattle, for the 747 manufacturing complex. The complex includes the world's largest-volume building.

In preparing to produce the 747, Boeing expended 14,000 hours of wind-tunnel testing and 10 million engineering man-hours. Four years of continuous testing ranging from metals selection to systems operation preceded the first superjet.

The 747 Division of Boeing Commercial Airplane Company was established and made directly responsible for designing, developing, and manufacturing the new jetliner. First production operations at the new Everett plant began in January 1967. The buildings were occupied in stages throughout the year as each was completed. Activation of the huge assembly building began on May 1, 1967, just over a year after the initial announcement of the program. Actual assembly of the first airplane began in September of the same year, and late in the year components for the first 747 nose section arrived at Everett from Boeing's Wichita, Kansas, Division. They went into assembly jigs also built at Wichita and shipped earlier. Concurrently, first components manufactured by Boeing's major contractors began arriving at Everett.

The first 747 wing was removed from the assembly jig in March 1968. The wing weighed 28,000 pounds, or 10 times the gross weight of the first airplane built by Boeing, the 1916 B&W.

In mid-June 1968, a JT9D high-bypass turbofan engine was test flown for the first time, on a B-52 leased from the U.S. Air Force by Pratt & Whitney, the engine manufacturer.

On September 30, the first 747 superjet made its world debut in a roll-out ceremony at the Everett plant. Following roll-out it was prepared for flight while production of the next units continued.

By January 1969, the first superjet's major systems had been activated and its major components, such as landing gear and flight controls, had been operationally tested. Compass calibration, fueling, and engine testing followed. The first flight was made February 9, 1969. Test Pilot Jack Waddell said afterward, "The plane is a pilot's dream."

The 747 test program was the most extensive ever undertaken in commercial aviation history. In addition to laboratory tests of parts and components, the program included assignment of five of the giant airplanes to a 28 million-dollar, year-long Boeing and Federal Aviation Administration flight-test program. The five superjets had logged more than 1,400 flight hours by the program conclusion. The 747 was certificated for commercial passenger service December 30, 1969.

The Boeing 747 structure verification test program made use of two structurally complete superjet airframes which would never fly. The program was aimed at proving the 747's structural soundness.

Static testing, using one of the non-flying airframes, verified the strength of the entire airframe. In one climactic test, the wing tips were deflected upwards 26 feet (7.9 m) before structural failure occurred—at 116% of the design ultimate load of the airplane.

Fatigue-testing made use of the second non-flying airframe and duplicated the stresses experienced in day-to-day airline flying to make certain that no undetected structural problems will be encountered in the service life of the airliner. The fatigue-test program took the airframe through the equivalent of 20,000 airline flights, or 60,000 hours. Following the normal testing, fail-safe testing with the structure cracked or sawed through in 28 critical places put the equivalent of 12,000 additional hours in airline flights on the structure. This was done to test its ability to continue to operate safely after damage.

Production of the Boeing 747 quickly built up to a peak of seven airplanes a month, then dropped substantially when demand declined in the recession of the early 1970s. By mid-1979, following a steady increase in orders, production resumed the seven-per-month rate.

747-400 PERFORMANCE SUMMARY

Passengers	412 (34 first, 76 business, 302 tourist class)
Cargo	5 pallets, 14 LD-1 containers
Engines	PW4056, CF6-80C2, RB211-524G, P&W JT9D-7A
Thrust (Lbs.)	56,000 nominal
Fuel Capacity (Gal.)	53,985 to 57,285
Maximum Takeoff Wt.	800,000 lbs.
(Options)	850,000 lbs.
	870,000 lbs.
Design Range	8,470 statute (7,365 nautical)
Wing Span	211 feet
Overall Length	231 feet 10.25 inches
Tail Height	63 feet 5 inches
Body Width	20 feet 1 inch
Crew	Two: pilot co-pilot
Avionics	Digital
Displays	Six cathode ray ray tubes (CRTs)
Controls, indicators	365 lights, gauges, switches
Cruising speed	560 mph at 35,000 feet
Maximum speed	615 mph at 27,500 feet

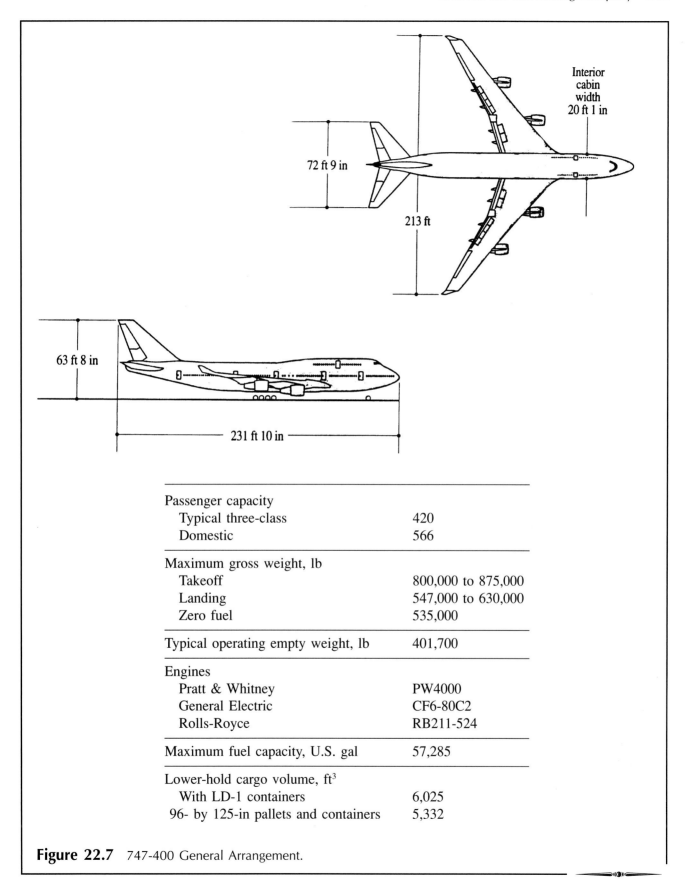

Passenger capacity		
Typical three-class	420	
Domestic	566	
Maximum gross weight, lb		
Takeoff	800,000 to 875,000	
Landing	547,000 to 630,000	
Zero fuel	535,000	
Typical operating empty weight, lb	401,700	
Engines		
Pratt & Whitney	PW4000	
General Electric	CF6-80C2	
Rolls-Royce	RB211-524	
Maximum fuel capacity, U.S. gal	57,285	
Lower-hold cargo volume, ft³		
With LD-1 containers	6,025	
96- by 125-in pallets and containers	5,332	

Figure 22.7 747-400 General Arrangement.

It remained at seven through 1980, leveling off at about five a month for 1981.

Supporting the production program from the beginning was one of the largest subcontracting efforts in the history of commercial aircraft manufacturing. About 65% of the weight (50% by dollar volume) of each 747 is subcontracted to firms other than Boeing. Approximately 1,500 prime suppliers and an additional 15,000 secondary suppliers, located in 47 states and 6 foreign countries, provide parts and equipment for the 747.

Much of the airplane's structure is built at locations other than Everett. Most major wing components are fabricated at Boeing's central fabrication facility in Auburn, Washington, and sent to Everett for assembly. Boeing's Wichita Division manufactures the forward fuselage section, with subcontracting firms building the remaining sections and supplying components and systems. All are shipped to Everett.

THE 747 FAMILY

As the first widebody, high-capacity commercial jet, the 747 more than doubled the passenger and cargo capacity of predecessor jetliners.

It offered passengers spaciousness unmatched by any other airplane. The main-deck cabin is 20 feet wide, permitting two 20-inch aisles to extend the 185-foot length of the cabin. Sidewalls of the cabin are nearly vertical, and the 8-foot-4-inch high ceiling is flat. Center-line galley and washroom installations divide the cabin into five separate compartments. The superjet has 10 double-width doors, five on each side of the cabin. Several are used for passenger boarding, others for airplane servicing, and all for emergency evacuation if required.

The flight deck, on a level above the main deck, permits straight-in loading through a hinged nose door in the freighter and convertible models. Behind the cockpit in the passenger-carrying 747s is the upper-deck compartment reached by a stairway from the main deck. The upper deck serves as a luxurious lounge or can seat up to 32 passengers; an optional lengthened version more than doubles upper-deck seating capacity.

The big airplane has a 16-wheel main landing gear (four units of four wheels each) and a two-wheel nose gear for even distribution of loads on airport ramps and runways. The airplane can be landed with only one main gear unit on each side extended.

The 747-200F (Freighter)—Using cargo containers on the lower deck and pallets and nets to carry cargo on the main deck, the Freighter can carry a maximum payload of about 250,000 pounds more than 3,000 miles. It will carry more than 200,000 pounds over 4,000 miles or well beyond transatlantic range. Maximum takeoff gross weight is 833,000 pounds.

The Freighter and Convertible 747s have a mechanized cargo handling system on the main deck. The nose swings up so that pallets or 8 x 8-foot containers in lengths up to 40 feet can be loaded straight in on the power-driven cargo system. Two individuals, one at the nose and one in the interior of the airplane, can complete the unload and load cycle in 60 minutes.

The 747SP (Special Performance)—A lower passenger-capacity version of the 747, the 747SP is shorter by 47 feet overall than current models of the Boeing superjet. It is designed to fly higher, faster, and farther than any other wide-body airliner. The 747SP broadens the 747 family, serving with excellent economy on the world's long-distance air routes where passenger traffic does not require airplanes the size of other 747 models. This derivative 747 design is capable of carrying 331 passengers nearly 5,900 statute miles. By varying the payload, it serves nonstop such long-range markets as New York-Tokyo and New York-Dhahran, Saudi Arabia. In addition to the shorter fuselage, the 747SP differs from other 747s in having lighter weight structure in parts of the wing, fuselage, and landing gear; a taller tail with double-hinge rudder for control equal to that of the 747s; and new trailing-edge wing flaps. The SP can also be used for high-payload lift from limited runway lengths, even on shorter stage lengths. Depending on options, maximum gross takeoff weights range from 630,000 pounds to 700,000 pounds.

Extended Upper Deck—(Option on all versions except Convertible, Freighter, and SP)—Provides seating for up to 69 passengers in the upper deck. The extension is about 23 feet (7.1 m) to the rear, but does not affect the fuselage length. Aircraft built with the extension can be equipped with current engine options. Besides a new profile for the 747, changes stemming from the extension include a new exit door, additional windows and placement of the interior stairway in the aft rather than forward area of the upper deck.

The lower holds of all versions of the 747 have a mechanized loading system using containers for both cargo and baggage. A main-deck cargo door is offered to make it possible for airlines to carry more cargo in periods of light passenger traffic, or to use 747s as side-cargo-door freighters. The cargo door is aft of the wing on the main deck between the fourth and fifth passenger doors on the left side. A ball-transfer floor panel at the door, and cargo roller tracks and tiedowns, as well

Figure 22.8   Boeing 747-400.

as a cabin divider for passenger/cargo combination loads, complete the interior requirements. Installed on freighter or convertible 747s, the side cargo door makes possible carrying of taller loads than can be put aboard through the nose loading door.

In addition to its primary use as a commercial jet-liner, the 747 has been specially adapted to military and space programs. Several modified 747-200Bs, equipped with extensive electronic systems, are in service with the U.S. Air Force as E-4 Airborne Command Posts. They would serve as the critical communication link between national command authorities and the nation's strategic retaliatory forces in the event of nuclear attack.

Boeing has also modified a 747-100 to serve as a carrier for ferrying the NASA Space Shuttle Orbiter from landing sites back to its launch area. Modifications included the addition of shuttle carrier struts, structural reinforcements, and vertical stabilizers.

The 747-400 is the latest model and hopes to be the world's most modern and fuel efficient airliner in commercial operation.

With the same fuselage dimensions as the 747-300, the new 747-400 delivers more range, better fuel economy and lower operating costs. Its range capability of 8,470 statute miles is an 1,100–1,300 statute mile increase over the 747-300. It will consume 9 to 12% less fuel than the 747-300 model, and improved performance of up to 25% per seat is expected over older 747s currently in service.

The first 747-400 was delivered in January 1989 to Northwest Airlines, which ordered ten.

The 747-400 design embodies technological advances in aerodynamics, structural materials, avionics, and interior design. The most noticeable aerodynamic improvements, designed to reduce fuel burn and extend the 747-400's range, are the six-foot longer wing with six-foot-high winglets, angled upward and slightly outward. The winglets provide even greater wingspan without causing airport space problems, and offer a fuel burn improvement of about 3%. The wing-to-body fairing has been recontoured for drag improvement. Additional efficiency is incorporated in newly designed nacelles and struts for the advanced engines: the Rolls

Boeing 747 Facts ■

- There are 6 million parts in the 747. Three million parts are fasteners, and about half of those are rivets.
- The wing area of the 747-400 is 5,600 square feet, an area large enough to hold 45 medium-sized automobiles.
- The diameter of the 747 engine nose cowl is 8 feet 6 inches.
- Four World War I vintage JN4-D "Jenny" aircraft could be lined up on each of the Boeing 747 wings.
- One wing of the 747 weighs 28,000 pounds, 10 times the weight of Boeing's first air-plane, the 1916 B&W.
- More than 15,000 hours of wind-tunnel testing were completed on the first 747.
- The 747 flight test program leading to certification for commercial service in December 1969 employed five airplanes, lasted 10 months and required more than 1,500 hours of flying.
- Seventy-five thousand engineering drawings were used to produce the first 747.
- There are 15 models of the 747. These include all-passenger versions, passenger and cargo configurations and all-cargo models. The newest model, the 747-400 Freighter, rolled out in February 1993 and delivered later that year.
- The 747-400 contains the greatest passenger interior volume of any commercial airliner at 31,285 cubic feet, the equivalent of more than three 1,500 square foot houses.
- The 747 has sixteen 49-inch main landing gear tires and two nose landing gear tires.
- The 747 has been in service since Jan. 21, 1970.
- The tail height of a 747, at 63 feet 8 inches, is equivalent to that of a six-story building.
- The Wright Brothers' first flight at Kitty Hawk could have been performed within the 150-foot economy section of a 747-400.
- Engine thrust on the 747-400 has grown from 43,500 to approximately 60,600 pounds per new generation engine. By comparison, total takeoff thrust of the four-engine 707-120 was 54,000 pounds.
- The first 747 had a design range of 5,290 miles. The 747-400 has a design range of 8,290 miles.
- The 747-400 consumes 8% to 13% less fuel than the 747-300, depending on engine selection. This is an improvement of up to 17% over the first 747s.
- There are 365 lights, gauges and switches in the 747-400 flight deck.
- The 747-400 can carry more than 57,000 gallons of fuel. This makes it possible for the airplane to fly extremely long routes, such as between San Francisco and Sydney, Australia.
- How much weight does an additional 6-foot wingtip extension and winglet add to the 747-400 wing? NONE! A weight savings of approximately 5,000 pounds was achieved in the wing by using new aluminum alloys, which offset the weight increase of the wing tip extension and winglet.
- According to one 747 operator, no less than five and a half tons of food supplies and more than 50,000 inflight service items are needed on a typical international flight.
- Engine noise from today's 747-400 is half what it was on the original airplanes delivered in 1970.

Royce RB211-524G, Pratt & Whitney PW4000 or General Electric CF6-80C2, which provide a minimum 56,000 pounds of thrust.

The 747-400's 8,000-mile range will make possible nonstop service with typical full passenger, three-class payloads on such routes as London-Tokyo, Los Angeles to Hong Kong, Singapore-London and Los Angeles-Sydney. An optional 3,300 U.S. gallon fuel tank in the horizontal tail will boost the 747-400's range an additional 400 statute miles.

Even more flexibility is available in the 747-400 Combination. It is two-airplanes-in-one, carrying passengers forward and cargo aft on the main deck. Cargo and passenger loading can be simultaneous. The "Combi" adapts to seasonal variations in passenger and cargo traffic and is ready for changing market demands and charter opportunities. KLM was the first customer to purchase the 747-400 Combi.

THE BOEING 757-200

The Boeing 757-200, member of the popular 757/767 family of medium sized airplanes, is a twin-engine medium-to-long-range jetliner incorporating advanced technology for exceptional fuel efficiency, low noise levels, increased passenger comfort and top operating performance. The 757 offers other virtues as well, including great versatility by reducing airport congestion. It can fly both long- and short-range routes and its broad use effectively lends itself to "hub-and-spoke" planning.

Designed to carry 194 passengers in a typical mixed-class configuration, the 757-200 can accommodate up to 239 passengers in charter service, putting its capacity between that of the Boeing 737-400 or -700 and the 757-300.

The 757-200 brake-release weights range from 220,000 pounds up to a maximum of 255,500 pounds for greater payload or range. A freighter configuration of the 757-200 also is available.

The 757-200 and twin-aisle 767 were developed concurrently, so both share the same technological advancements in propulsion, aerodynamics, avionics, and materials. This commonality reduces training and spares requirements when both are operated in the same fleet. Because of these features, many airline operators operate both 757 and 767 airplanes.

High-bypass-ratio engines combined with the wing design help make the 757 one of the quietest, most fuel-efficient jetliners in the world. The engines have large-diameter fans that move more air outside and around

the hot core, boosting efficiency while reducing noise. Noise containment is further aided by acoustic linings in the engine nacelles. Engines are available from Pratt & Whitney or Rolls-Royce in thrust ratings from 38,200 to 43,100 pounds. When compared to any single-aisle jetliner in service today, the 757 is unsurpassed in fuel efficiency. It consumes up to 43% less fuel per seat than older trijets.

The 757's wing is less swept and is thicker through the center than earlier aircraft, permitting a longer span. Its lower surface is slightly flatter, and the leading edge somewhat sharper. Taken together, these changes improve lift and reduce drag for greater aerodynamic efficiency and lower fuel consumption.

With the improved wing design, less engine power is required for takeoff and landing. Even with full passenger payload, the 757-200 can operate from runways as short as those used by the much smaller 737-200 jetliner—about 5,500 feet for trips up to 2,000 statute miles. In addition, the 757 can reach a higher cruise altitude more quickly than many other jetliners.

These improvements reduce community noise of the already quiet 757-200 engines. In fact, noise levels are significantly lower than the requirements set forth in U.S. Federal Aviation Regulation Part 36, Stage 3, as well as ICAO (International Civil Aviation Organization) Annex 16 Chapter 3.

Lightweight materials contribute to the overall efficiency of the 757 models. Improved aluminum alloys, primarily in the wing skins, save 610 pounds. Advanced composites such as graphite/epoxy are used in control surfaces (including rudder, elevators and ailerons), aerodynamic fairings, engine cowlings and landing gear doors for a weight savings of 1,100 pounds. Another 650 pounds of weight savings is attributable to carbon brakes, which have the added advantage of longer service life than conventional steel brakes.

FLIGHT DECK

The 757-200 flight deck, designed for two-crew member operation, pioneered the use of digital electronics and advanced displays. Those offer increased reliability and advanced features compared to older electro-mechanical instruments.

A fully integrated flight management computer system (FMCS) provides for automatic guidance and control of the 757 from immediately after takeoff to final approach and landing. Linking together digital processors controlling navigation, guidance and engine thrust, the flight management system assures that the aircraft flies the most efficient route and flight profile for reduced fuel consumption, flight time and crew workload.

The precision of global positioning satellite (GPS) system navigation, automated air traffic control functions, and advanced guidance and communications features will be available as part of the new Future Air Navigation System flight management computer, which is scheduled to be introduced in 1998.

The captain and the first officer each has a pair of electronic displays for primary flight instrumentation. The electronic altitude director indicator displays airplane altitude and autopilot guidance cues. The electronic horizontal situation indicator displays a video map of navigation aids, airports, and the planned airplane route. It can display a weather-radar image over these ground features.

The engine indicating and crew alerting system, often called EICAS, monitors and displays engine performance and airplane system status before takeoff. It also provides caution and warning alerts to the flight crew if necessary. EICAS monitoring also aids ground crews by providing maintenance information.

The 757 is available with a wind shear detection system that alerts flight crews and provides flight-path guidance to cope with it. Wind shear, caused by a violent down-burst of air that changes speed and direction as it strikes the ground, can interfere with a normal takeoff and landing.

Flight decks of the 757 and 767 are nearly identical and both aircraft have a common type-rating. Pilots qualified to fly one of the aircraft can also fly the other with only minimal additional familiarization.

Built-in test equipment helps ground crews troubleshoot avionics and airplane systems quickly for easier maintenance than on earlier aircraft. Structural maintenance needs are reduced, owing to new methods of corrosion protection including application of special sealants and enameling of major portions of the fuselage.

INTERIOR

Boeing has developed an attractive and functional interior for the 757's passenger cabin. Sculptured ceiling and sidewall panels made from weight-saving composite materials and accented by recessed lighting provide a spacious look to the interior. Large overhead bins are each 5-feet-long and hold up to 180 pounds of carry-on items. For passenger entertainment, an in-flight video system is available with conveniently positioned overhead monitors. The 757 also can provide in-flight passenger telephone communications services with available air phone and satellite communications.

RANGE CAPABILITY

The demonstrated reliability of the 757 has approval for extended-range twin (engine) operation, or ETOPS. In July 1990, the Federal Aviation Administration granted 180-minute ETOPS certification for 757-200s equipped with both the Rolls-Royce RB211-535E4 and RB211-535C engines. Previously, the FAA had certified the 757-200 equipped with RB211-535E4 engines for 120-minute operation in 1986. In April 1992, the FAA granted 180-minute ETOPS certification for the 757-200 equipped with Pratt & Whitney PW2000-series engines. This followed the FAA's previous certification of Pratt & Whitney PW2000-powered 757-200s for 120-minute operation in April 1990.

For added reliability on ETOPS flights, the 757 is available with extended range features, including a backup hydraulic-motor generator and an auxiliary fan to cool equipment in the electronics bay. High-gross-weight versions of the aircraft can fly 4,500 statute miles nonstop with full passenger payload. These system attributes contribute to the 757's versatility, allowing it to serve more markets.

HISTORY

The first 757-200 rolled out of Boeing's Renton, Wash., plant Jan. 13, 1982, and made its first flight Feb. 19, 1982. The U.S. Federal Aviation Administration certified the aircraft Dec. 21, 1982, after 1,380 hours of flight testing over a 10-month period.

First delivery of a 757-200 took place Dec. 22, 1982, to launch customer Eastern Airlines. Eastern placed the aircraft into service Jan. 1, 1983. On Jan. 14, 1983, the British Civil Aviation Authority certified the 757-200 to fly in the United Kingdom. British Airways, another launch customer for the 757-200, is now a major operator of the twinjet.

Final assembly of the 757-200 and the 757 Freighter are done in the Renton plant. Parts and assemblies for the airplanes are provided by Boeing plants in Auburn and Spokane, Wash.; Portland, Ore.; and Wichita, Kan., as well as by nearly 700 external suppliers.

THE 757 FREIGHTER

The first derivative of the 757 was announced by Boeing Dec. 30, 1985, when United Parcel Service ordered 20. Deliveries of these dedicated cargo airplanes began in Sept. 1987. The basic maximum takeoff weight of the 757F is 250,000 pounds, with an option for 255,500 pounds.

The 757F has no passenger windows or doors and no interior amenities. A large main-deck cargo door is installed in the forward area of the fuselage on the left-hand side. The flight crew boards the aircraft through a single entry door installed immediately aft of the flight deck on the left side of the aircraft.

The interior of the main-deck fuselage has a smooth fiberglass lining. A fixed rigid barrier installed in the front end of the main deck serves as a restraint wall between the cargo and the flight deck. A sliding door in the barrier permits access from the flight deck to the cargo areas.

Up to 15 containers or pallets, each measuring 88 by 125 inches at the base, can be accommodated on the main deck of the 757F. Total main-deck container volume is 6,600 cubic feet and the two lower holds of the airplane provide 1,830 cubic feet for bulk loading. These provide a combined maximum revenue payload capability of 87,500 pounds including container weight. When carrying the maximum load, the 757F has a range of about 2,900 statute miles.

The 757F keeps ton-mile costs to a minimum with its two-person flight deck and twin high-bypass-ratio engines offering excellent fuel economy. This contrasts to older cargo-carrying aircraft in the standard-body class, such as 707s and DC-8s, that have three-person flight crews and are powered by four old-technology engines, which consume considerably more fuel.

BOEING 757-200 SPECIFICATIONS

Wingspan:	124 feet 10 inches
Overall length:	155 feet 3 inches
Tail height:	44 feet 6 inches
Cabin width:	11 feet 7 inches
Lower-hold volume:	1,790 cubic feet
Fuel capacity:	11,276 gallons
Engines and thrust:	Rolls-Royce RB211-535E4 (40,100 pounds) Pratt & Whitney PW2037 (38,200 pounds) Pratt & Whitney PW2040 (41,700 pounds)

STANDARD AND HIGH-GROSS WEIGHT RANGE AND FIELD LENGTH SPECIFICATIONS 757-200 (194 PASSENGERS/TWO CLASS):

Maximum take off weight	Range
220,000 pounds	3,200 statute miles
FAR takeoff field length	5,400 feet
TO	
255,500 pounds	4,520 statute miles
OR:	
255,500 pounds	4,520 statute miles
FAR takeoff field length	6,300 feet

THE BOEING 757-300

The Boeing 757-300, the newest member of the popular 757/767 family of medium-sized airplanes, was launched Sept. 2, 1996, with an order from Condor Flugdienst, a German charter airline.

The 757-300 is a twin-engine medium-to-long-range jetliner offering fuel efficiency, top economic performance and low noise levels.

The 757-300, a stretch version of the 757-200, is 23 feet, 4 inches longer than the 757-200. The extra length allows it to carry 20% more passengers than the 757-200 and increases the available cargo volume by nearly 50%.

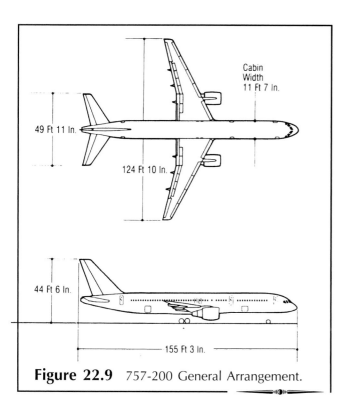

Cabin Width 11 Ft 7 In.

49 Ft 11 In.

124 Ft 10 In.

44 Ft 6 In.

155 Ft 3 In.

Figure 22.9 757-200 General Arrangement.

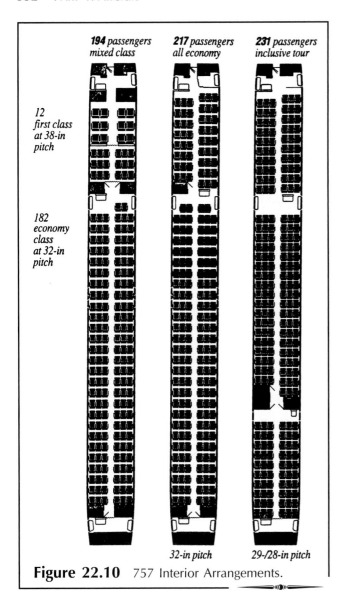

194 passengers
mixed class

217 passengers
all economy

231 passengers
inclusive tour

12 first class at 38-in pitch

182 economy class at 32-in pitch

32-in pitch

29-/28-in pitch

Figure 22.10 757 Interior Arrangements.

vacuum lavatories; new tires, wheels, and brakes; a tail skid; and strengthened wings and landing gear.

The 757 models share many features with the twin-aisle 767, which was developed concurrently with the 757-200. This commonality reduces training and spares requirements when both are operated in the same fleet. Because both 757 models as well as the 767 have a common type-rating, pilots qualified to fly one of the aircraft also can fly the others with only minimal additional familiarization, saving training time and costs. Because of the commonality, many airlines will operate both 757 and 767 airplanes.

INTERIOR FEATURES

The interior of the 757-300 passenger cabin has been redesigned. The interior is the same as that developed for the Next-Generation 737 family. The 737 interior was revised based on the recommendations of airline customers. The new interior is designed to upgrade the overall look and aesthetics of the passenger cabin.

The new overhead stow bins and the new sculptured ceiling have smoother curves, giving the cabin a more open, spacious feeling. A handrail that extends along the bottom of the stow bins as well as a moveable cabin class divider also will be available.

The 757-300 also will be equipped with vacuum lavatories. For airlines, that means reduced service time.

OTHER CHANGES

Other than the interior, most of the changes to the 757-300 were made to accommodate the extended fuselage and increased passenger and cargo load.

The maximum takeoff weight has been increased to 270,000 pounds to preserve the passenger-cargo load capability. The aircraft's wing and landing gear and portions of its fuselage have been strengthened and new wheels, tires, and brakes added to handle the extra weight.

The air control system for the passenger cabin has been modified to accommodate the additional passengers. A new larger precooler, more powerful fans and an additional air control zone have been added.

Because the airplane is longer, several modifications have been made to protect against possible damage from tail strikes during takeoffs and landings. A retractable tail skid similar to that on the 767-300 and 777-300 stretch airplanes has been added. It has a body contact indicator that lets the pilot know if the body has

Designed to carry 243 passengers in a typical mixed-class configuration, the 757-300 can accommodate up to 289 passengers in charter service, putting its capacity between that of the Boeing 757-200 and the 767-300. Because of its additional capacity, it will have about 10% lower seat-mile operating costs than the 757-200, which already has the lowest seat-mile operating cost in its market segment.

As a derivative, the 757-300 will complement the 757-200; it will not be a replacement. Both models will be in production. The 757-300 will retain the simplicity and reliability of the 757-200. Both models will have the same flight deck and operating systems, but some features will change. Besides a lengthened fuselage, changes on the 757-300 will include a new interior with made contact with the ground despite the tail skid. That knowledge helps prevent unnecessary and costly air turn backs.

ENGINES AND WINGS

The 757-300 and 757-200 share many of the same features. Both have high-bypass-ratio engines and a wing design that help make them two of the quietest, most fuel-efficient jetliners in the world. Engines are available from Rolls-Royce or Pratt & Whitney in thrust ratings of 43,100 and 43,850 pounds respectively.

The wing on the 757-300 and 757-200 is less swept and thicker through the center than those on earlier Boeing aircraft, permitting a longer span. The lower wing surface is slightly flatter, and the leading edge somewhat sharper. This improves lift, reduces drag and makes for improved aerodynamic efficiency and low fuel consumption.

The only difference between the 757-300 and the 757-200 wing is that the former will be structurally reinforced to handle the increased load.

THE FLIGHT DECK

The flight deck of the 757-300, like that of the 757-200, is designed for two-crew member operation and furnished with digital electronic displays.

A computerized, fully integrated flight management system (FMS) provides for automatic guidance and control of the airplane from immediately after takeoff to final approach and landing. Linking together digital processors controlling navigation, guidance and engine thrust, the FMS assures that the aircraft flies the most efficient route and flight profile for reduced fuel consumption, flight time and crew workload.

The pilot and the copilot each have a pair of electronic displays for primary flight instrumentation. One display shows an electronic altitude director indicator and the other an electronic horizontal situation indicator.

Two flight deck improvements are being planned for the 757-300 and the 757-200. The Pegasus flight management system and an enhanced engine indication and crew alerting system (EICAS) will be standard on the 757-300. With the Pegasus FMS, operators can choose software options that include elements of the future air navigation system (FANS). FANS function will provide operators with the ability to use advanced systems, such as global positioning system (GPS) sensors and satellite communications, to take full advantage of new communication, navigation and air traffic management systems.

The EICAS upgrade will replace existing computers with enhanced devices that are software loadable. The enhanced EICAS has improved built-in test equipment (BITE) functions that will allow for improved self-diagnosis of faults in a more readable format. On-board software loading will allow operators to use the same EICAS computer as a replacement on any 757 or 767. That reduces the required inventory of spare parts.

THE BOEING 767

The Boeing 767 provides airlines with a profitable, comfortable airliner sized between the standard-body Boeing 757 and the larger, wide-body Boeing 777.

It provides maximum efficiency in the face of rising operational costs, while extending twin-aisle passenger cabin convenience to continental and intercontinental routes.

The 767's design provides excellent fuel efficiency, operational flexibility, low noise levels and an all-digital flight deck. It employs high strength, lightweight aluminum alloys and composite materials.

Its two-aisle passenger cabin follows the tradition of spaciousness established by the Boeing 747, first of the widebody airliners. Extensive passenger research has shown the seven-abreast seating concept is preferred, because 87% of the seats are next to the window or on the aisles. Center seats are only one seat from an aisle. Independent passenger studies also rate the 767 to be one of the most preferred airplanes in all classes of service.

It is estimated that 767s have carried 795 million passengers on more than 4.8 million flights since it first entered service on Sept. 8, 1982. Through June 1997, Boeing had delivered 663 widebody 767 airplanes.

Schedule reliability, in industry measure of departure from the gate within 15 minutes of scheduled time, is nearly 99% for the 767. Fleetwide, daily utilization is more than 10 hours.

BEGAN IN 1978

Production design of the fuel-efficient twinjet began in 1978 when an order for 30 short-to-medium-range 767s was announced by United Airlines. The first 767, still owned by Boeing, was completed and rolled out of the Boeing plant in Everett, WA, Aug. 4, 1981, and made its initial flight Sept. 26.

The 767-300 program got under way in September 1983. This model is longer than the 767-200 by 21 feet

BOEING 757-300 SPECIFICATIONS

Wingspan	124 ft 10 in
Overall length	178 ft. 7 in
Tail height	44 ft 6 in
Body width	12 ft 4 in
Lower cargo hold volume	2,387 cu ft
Fuel capacity	11,490 gal
Engines and thrust	Rolls-Royce RB211-535E4-B (43,100 lb)
	Pratt & Whitney PW2043 (43,850 lb)
Maximum takeoff weight	270,000 lb
Range (240 passengers)	4,000 statute miles
FAR takeoff field length at sea level 86° F (30° C)	9,000 ft

Figure 22.11   Boeing 757-300.

1 inch, has 22% more seating capacity (approximately 40 passengers) and 31% greater cargo volume.

Following the introduction of each model, an extended-range version was presented. To take advantage of their lower ranges and allow long, over-water flights, new features were added—an advanced propulsion system and auxiliary power unit with high-altitude start capability, a fourth hydraulic motor-driven generator, increased cargo compartment fire-suppression capability, and cooling sensors for electronic flight instruments. The 767 now crosses the Atlantic from the United States to Europe more often than any other airplane type.

TECHNICAL IMPROVEMENTS

The wing is thicker, longer and less swept than the wings of earlier Boeing jetliners. This provides excellent takeoff performance and fuel economy. Each 767 is powered by two high-bypass-ratio turbofan engines.

The basic 767-200, at a maximum gross weight of 300,000 pounds, can take off in only 5,600 feet. It can operate non-stop between New York and San Francisco with a two-class load of 224 passengers. Even the higher gross weight 767-200ER (extended range) model with a maximum takeoff weight of 395,000 pounds, can take off in about 9,400 feet. It can reach up to 7,660 statute miles, making possible such non-stop flights as New York to Beirut, Lebanon; London to Bombay, India; and Tokyo to Sydney, Australia with 181 passengers in a three-class configuration.

767-300

The basic 767-300 has a maximum takeoff weight of 345,000 pounds and can carry a two-class load of 269 passengers 4,560 statute miles. The higher gross weight extended range version, at 412,000 pounds maximum takeoff weight, can carry 218 passengers in three-class configuration 7,080 statute miles.

PAYLOAD CAPABILITY

The 767-200 cabin, more than 4 feet wider than the single-aisle Boeing jetliners, seats about 224 passengers in a typical mixed-class configuration (six-abreast in first-class, seven-abreast in tourist class). Many other arrangements are possible, including up to 350 passengers in eight-abreast seating for charter flights in the 300.

The extended-range airplanes typically have three-class seating of 181 to 218 passengers using five-abreast 747-sized first class seats, six-abreast business class and seven-abreast economy class.

Lower-deck volume available for baggage and cargo totals 3,070 cubic feet for the 200 and 4,030 cubic feet for the 300, more than 45% greater than the lower-deck capacity of the 707 and more than any commercial transport in its class.

EXTENDED-RANGE OPERATIONS

In May 1985, the U.S. Federal Aviation Administration (FAA) approved 767s for long-range flights of up to 120 minutes from an alternate airport. In March 1989, the FAA approved the 767 for 180-minute extended twin-engine operation (ETOPS). This allows more direct time-saving trans-Pacific and trans-Atlantic flights from many U.S. gateways.

767-300 FREIGHTER

Boeing announced this derivative of the 767-300ER in January 1993, when United Parcel Service ordered up to 60 airplanes. Deliveries of these dedicated cargo airplanes began in the fourth quarter of 1995. The basic maximum takeoff weight capability of the UPS 767

Freighter is 408,000 pounds, and Boeing offers a payload enhancement up to 412,000 pounds.

The 767 Freighter has no passenger windows or doors and, with the exception of a crew galley and lavatory, no interior amenities. A large main-deck cargo door is installed in the forward area of the fuselage on the left-hand side. The flight crew boards the airplane through a single-entry door installed immediately aft of the flight deck on the left side of the aircraft.

Up to 24 containers or pallets, each measuring 88 inches by 125 inches at the base, can be accommodated on the main deck of the 767 Freighter. Total main deck container volume is 10,080 cubic feet and the two lower holds of the airplane provide 3,157 cubic feet for bulk loading and seven containers.

These provide a combined maximum payload capability of 112,500 pounds, not including container weight. When carrying a near-maximum load of 56 tons, the 767 Freighter has a range of about 3,000 nautical miles. When carrying 45 tons, the 767 Freighter has a range of 4,000 nautical miles.

The interior of the main-deck fuselage has a smooth fiberglass lining. A fixed rigid barrier installed in the front end of the main deck serves as a restraint wall between the cargo and the flight deck. A door in the barrier wall permits access from the flight deck to the cargo area.

The 767 Freighter keeps ton-mile costs to a minimum with its two-person flight deck and twin high-bypass-ration engines offering excellent fuel economy. This contrasts to older cargo-carrying aircraft, such as 707s and DC-8s, which have three-person flight crews and are powered by four engines.

Type commonality with the 757 Freighter further reduces operating and training costs for carriers, such as UPS, who choose to operate both models.

All of the advancement in avionics, aerodynamics, materials and propulsion that were developed for the passenger version of the 767 are incorporated in the freighter.

767-400ER

Boeing launched the 767-400ER in April 1997. This stretched version of the 767-300 addresses the medium-size (250–300 seats) intercontinental market, accommodating growth on routes that don't require the capacity of a 777. It also replaces older airplanes serving transcontinental routes.

The newest 767 features a fuselage that is 21 feet longer than the 767-300, with up to 20% more seats.

767 SPECIFICATIONS

Wing Span	156 feet 1 inch
Overall Length	180 feet 3 inches
Fuselage Length	155 feet
Tail Height	52 feet
Body Width	16.5 feet
Accommodation	218 to 325 passengers
Lower Deck Volume	3,070 cubic feet
Maximum Takeoff Gross Weight	300,000 pounds to 387,000 pounds in extended range version.
Engines	Two Pratt & Whitney PW4000 or General Electric CF6-80C2. Maximum rated thrust per engine: 50,000 pounds up to 62,000 pounds.
Fuel Capacity	16,700 gallons to 24,140 gallons in extended range version.
Range	767-200: 3,850 statute miles
	767-200ER: 7,830 statute miles
Maximum Speed	595 mph at 26,000 feet
Cruising Speed	538 mph at 35,000 feet

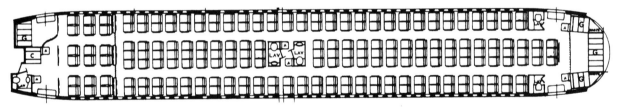

18 First Class – 38 in. Pitch   193 Tourist – 34 in. Pitch

211 Passengers

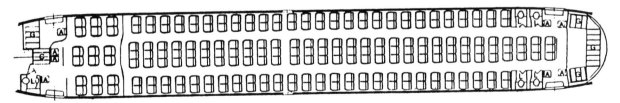

18 First Class – 38 in. Pitch   198 Tourist – 34 in. Pitch

216 Passengers

Figure 22.12   Interior Arrangements—Mixed Class, One Meal Service—767.

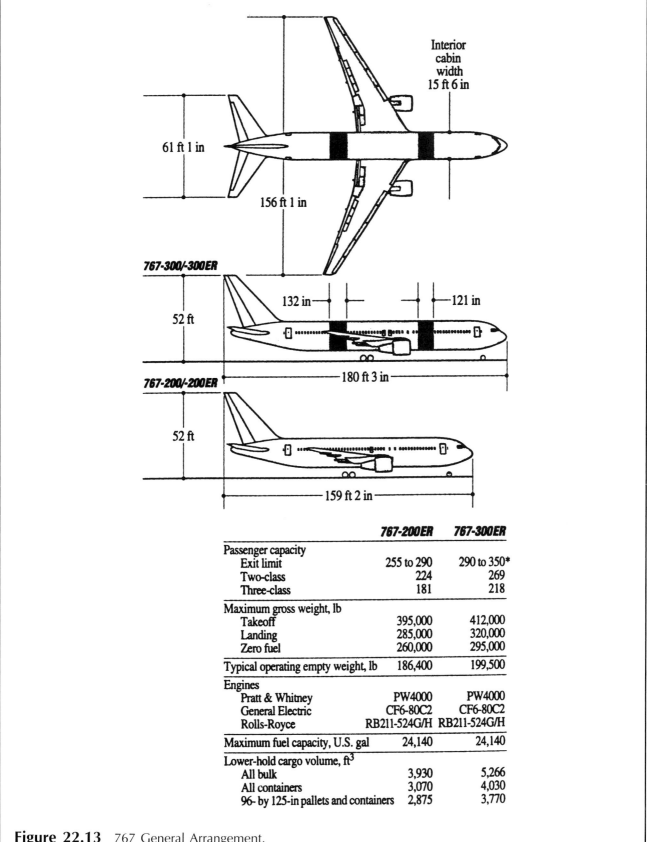

Figure 22.13   767 General Arrangement.

	767-200ER	767-300ER
Passenger capacity		
Exit limit	255 to 290	290 to 350*
Two-class	224	269
Three-class	181	218
Maximum gross weight, lb		
Takeoff	395,000	412,000
Landing	285,000	320,000
Zero fuel	260,000	295,000
Typical operating empty weight, lb	186,400	199,500
Engines		
Pratt & Whitney	PW4000	PW4000
General Electric	CF6-80C2	CF6-80C2
Rolls-Royce	RB211-524G/H	RB211-524G/H
Maximum fuel capacity, U.S. gal	24,140	24,140
Lower-hold cargo volume, ft³		
All bulk	3,930	5,266
All containers	3,070	4,030
96- by 125-in pallets and containers	2,875	3,770

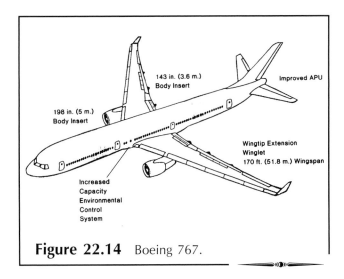

Figure 22.14 Boeing 767.

The additional seats reduce operating costs relative to the 767-300ER, which already offers airlines the lowest operating costs in its class. The 767-400ER will be able to fly 6,470 statute miles, serving all U.S. domestic routes such as Seattle-Miami or Boston-Los Angeles. It also will be able to fly North Atlantic routes such as Atlanta-London, or South American destinations such as New York-Santiago, Chile. Across the Pacific, the 400ER can connect Seattle-Osaka, Japan.

THE BOEING 777

Responding to airline interest in a Boeing airplane that would have a capacity between the 767-300 and 747-400, Boeing Commercial Airplane Group began assessing market preference in late 1986. The four-year effort culminated on October 29, 1990, with the announcement that the Boeing board of directors had formally approved launching the 777 into production. That action followed an Oct. 15 order placed by United Airlines for 34 of the aircraft with options for 34 more. United's initial delivery was scheduled for May 1995. All Nippon Airways on Dec. 19, 1990, became the second launch customer for the new trijet with an order for 18 and options for 7 more. ANA's first delivery was in late 1995.

Initially, United, ANA, British Airways, Japan Airlines and Cathay Pacific were among a number of carriers with whom Boeing held intensive discussions, including many group sessions, to define and evolve the new airplane's configuration. The participating airlines represented a full range of operations in terms of route structure, traffic loads, service frequency and climate. Their input to the design process helped assure that the final product was the broadest possible application to the needs of the world's airlines.

GENERAL DESCRIPTION

The 777's fuselage has a diameter of 20 feet 4 inches, a wider body than any other jetliner except the Boeing 747. The 777's interior cross-section is at least five inches greater than current wide-body trijets, affording more "comfort space" to trade between seat width, aisles and seat pitch. The 777 can be configured in any combination of seating arrangements, ranging from six seats to 10 seats abreast with two aisles.

With an overall length of about 209 feet, the 777 can offer two-class seating for 375 to 400 passengers, or three-class seating for 305 to 328 passengers. In an all-economy configuration, the airplane seats as many as 440.

The airplane has a standard maximum takeoff weight of 506,000 pounds and a range capability of up to 4,660 statute miles. The structural capability of the initial airplane allowed two optional maximum takeoff weights of 515,000 pounds or 535,000 pounds. The first option allows a range of up to 4,950 statute miles; the second option permits a range of up to 5,600 statute miles.

As with other Boeing airplanes, the 777 will be a family of aircraft. A longer-range higher weight version has the same physical dimensions as the initial 777 but is capable of a higher takeoff weight of 580,000 pounds in its standard version and 590,000 pounds as an option, and uses higher engine-thrust ratings and carries more fuel. All of the 777 family members utilize common engines. The longer-range 777 accommodates 305 to 328 passengers in a three-class arrangement on routes of up to 7,600 statute miles.

The 777 family can be developed for still greater capability in the future, including a stretched fuselage for higher passenger capacity. The stretched 777 currently is being studied and is anticipated to be available in 1998.

WING DESIGN

The 777's wing uses the most aerodynamically efficient airfoil ever developed for subsonic commercial aviation. In a further refinement of designs intro-

767—BASIC SPECIFICATIONS

	767-200/-200ER	767-300/-300ER	767-300 Freighter
Wing Span:	156 ft 1 in (47.6 m)	Same	Same
Overall Length:	159 ft 2 in	180 ft 3 in	180 ft 3 in
Engines (two):	**Pratt & Whitney** PW4000 **General Electric** CF6-80C2 **Rolls-Royce** RB211-524G/H. Maximum rated thrust per engine 50,000 pounds to 62,000 pounds	Same	Same
Fuel:	16,700 gal. to 24,140 gal. in extended range version.	Same	Same
Fuselage Length:	155 ft	176 ft 1 in	176 ft 1 in
Tail Height:	52 ft	Same	Same
Body Width:	16.5 ft	Same	Same
Passengers:	181 three-class 224 two-class up to 285 charter	218 three-class 269 two-class up to 350 charter	N/A
Cargo Volume:	3,070 cu ft (86.9 m³)	4,030 cu ft (114.2 m³)	15,252 cu ft (4,322.2 m³)

Interior Seating

767-200 two-class	767-200ER three-class	767-300 two-class	767-300ER three-class	767-300 Freighter
224	181	269	218	N/A

Max Takeoff Weight

Basic

300,000 lb	345,000 lb	345,000 lb	380,000 lb	408,000 lb

Max

335,000 lb	395,000 lb	351,000 lb	412,000 lb	412,000 lb

Max Range (Statute Miles)

5,260 mi	7,660 mi	4,300 mi	6,830 mi	3,760 mi

Figure 22.15 Boeing 767.

duced on the Boeing 757 and 767, the 777's wing features a long span with increased thickness while achieving higher cruise speeds.

This advanced wing enhances the airplane's ability to climb quickly and cruise at higher altitudes than competing airplanes. It also allows the airplane to carry full passenger loads out of many high-elevation, high-temperature airfields.

Fuel volume requirements for the 777 are accommodated entirely within the wing and its structural center section. For the initial airplane, fuel capacity was 31,000 gallons, while the longer-range model can carry up to 44,700 gallons.

Airlines participating in the 777 design effort encouraged Boeing to commit to the performance capabilities of an optimum wing, which has a span of 199 feet 11 inches. However, for ground operations, some of these carriers wanted the 777's wing to take up no more space than the wings of DC-10s, L-1011s and 767s, so that the new airplane could fit into existing gate and taxiway space at crowded airports.

The solution offered was an optional feature that introduced to commercial aviation a concept that has been common on naval aircraft for decades—a hinge and actuation mechanism that enables about 22 feet of each wingtip to fold upward, reducing the wingspan to about 155 feet when the airplane is on the ground.

PROPULSION

The three leading engine manufacturers developed more efficient and quieter turbofans to power the 777, and all three have been selected by 777 customers. United Airlines and ANA selected Pratt & Whitney engines for their 777s, British Airways and Lauda Air chose General Electric engines, and Thai Airways International and Cathay Pacific picked Rolls-Royce engines.

For the initial airplane, these engines were rated in the 71,000- to 74,000-pound thrust class. For the longer-range model, these same engines are capable of thrust ratings in the 82,000- to 85,000-pound category. The engines can be developed to even higher thrust ratings, depending on future payload and range requirements.

All three makes are more powerful than current engines, and offer excellent fuel efficiency while allowing the 777 to be as quiet as a 767, even though the 777 engines will provide 40% more power. Key factors in this performance are new, larger diameter fans with wide-chord fan blade designs and bypass ratios ranging from 6-to-1 to as high as 9-to-1. This compares to the typical .5-to-1 ratio for the engines of today's widebody jets.

Pratt & Whitney is offering the PW4000 series of engines, General Electric is offering its all-new GE90 series and Rolls-Royce is offering the Trent 800 series of engines.

Boeing Commercial Airplane Group applied new initiatives to the entire process of developing the 777 twinjet to support a commitment of delivering a service-ready product that will set the highest standards for quality and reliability.

This effort began with the formation of design/build teams during 1990, following the definition of the basic customer-driven configuration. Under the design/build concept, each team is responsible for a section of airframe or a major system and is staffed by experts from all the diverse disciplines in the airplane development process: engineering, production, procurement, customer support and other specialties. Currently, more than 230 design/build teams, some of which include representatives from suppliers and 777 airline customers, worked on the new airplane's design.

Based at the same location, team members work concurrently, sharing their knowledge with one another rather than applying their skills separately in a sequence of steps. One of the benefits is that structures and systems designs are evaluated from a multidisciplinary perspective to help assure producibility, cost-effectiveness, reliability and maintainability.

The essence of the design/build process is communication, and sophisticated computing technology is enabling team-to-team communication as well as providing a means for the program to develop an integrated design and to eliminate problems early. Powerful digital computer-aided design technology enabled the teams to create the 777's parts and systems as three-dimensional solid images instead of the traditional two-dimensional drawings. Team members shared their designs through a common data base accessed through digital design workstations.

Parts and systems designs were electronically pre-assembled and viewed as solid images on workstation display screens. Any interference or misalignment between parts was readily apparent and corrected before releasing the final design. This greatly reduced the need for costly full-scale mockups of the airplane. Additionally, accuracy and quality were enhanced, the need for engineering changes cut sharply and there was less chance of production problems in the factory.

MATERIALS

New, lightweight, cost-effective structural materials are used in several 777 applications. For example, an improved aluminum alloy is used in the upper wing skin and stringers. Known as 7055, this alloy offers greater compression strength than current alloys, enabling designers to save weight and also improve corrosion and fatigue resistance.

Progress in the development and fabrication of weight-saving advanced composite materials is evident in the 777. Carbon fibers embedded in recently available toughened resins are found in the vertical and horizontal tails. The floor beams of the passenger cabin also are made of these advanced composite materials.

Other composite applications include those on secondary structures such as aerodynamic fairings. Composites, including resins and adhesives, account for 9% of the 777's structural weight, compared to about 3% on other Boeing jets.

FLIGHT DECK AND AIRPLANE SYSTEMS

In response to airline preference expressed during the pre-launch definition phase, the layout of the 777 flight deck is in a horizontal format similar to that of the 747-400. Principal flight, navigation and engine information is presented on six large display screens.

Although these displays resemble conventional cathode ray tube (CRT) screens, they incorporate advanced liquid-crystal display technology. The depth of the new "flat panel displays" are about half that of CRT's. In addition to saving space, the new displays weigh less and require less power. They also generate less heat, which contributes to greater reliability and a longer service life. Another benefit: They do not require the heavy, complex air-conditioning apparatus needed to cool equipment on current flight decks. Pilots appreciate that flat panel displays remain clearly visible in all conditions, even direct sunlight.

CARGO CAPACITY

The fuselage cross-section of the 777 is circular and large enough to accommodate not only a spacious passenger cabin, but excellent capacity in the lower hold. The lower hold mechanized cargo handling system is compatible with all unit load devices (ULD) and pallets. One of the container arrangements utilizes LD-3s loaded side by side. The 777-200 can accommodate a maximum of 32 LD-3 containers plus 600 cubic feet of bulk-loaded cargo for total lower hold volume of 5,656 cubic feet. The 777-300 can accommodate a maximum of 44 LD-3 containers plus the same amount of bulk-loaded cargo as the 200 model for a total lower hold volume of 7,552 cubic feet.

LANDING GEAR

The main landing gear for the 777 is in a standard two-post arrangement but features six-wheel trucks, instead of the conventional four-wheel units. This provides the main landing gear with a total of 12 wheels for better weight distribution on runways and taxi areas, and avoids the need for a supplemental two-wheel gear under the center of the fuselage. Another advantage is that the six-wheel trucks allow for a more economical brake design. The 777 landing gear is the largest ever incorporated into a commercial airplane.

BOEING 777

The 777 is a new wide-body twinjet from Boeing Commercial Airplane Group. The newest member of the Boeing family of jetliners is intended to meet airline demand for a jetliner sized between the company's 767-300 and 747-400.

Length	209 feet 1 inch
Wingspan (with optional wingtips folded)	199 feet 11 inches
Tail Height	60 feet 6 inches
Exterior Fuselage Diameter	20 feet 4 inches
Interior Cross-Section Width	19 feet 3 inches
Weight/Range	Max takeoff weight—Range
Initial model	506,000 lbs 4,660 miles
	Optional
	515,000 lbs 4,950 miles
Longer-range Model	580,000 lbs 7,300 miles
	Optional
	590,000 lbs 7,600 miles
Seating	305–328 three-class
	375–400 two-class
	418–440 all-economy
Interior Configurations	Seating ranges from six to 10 abreast with two aisles.
Cargo Capacity	Up to 32 LD-3 containers plus 600 cubic feet bulk-loaded cargo. Total volume 5,656 cu feet.
Number of Parts	The 777 will have about 132,500 engineered, unique parts. Including rivets, bolts and other fasteners, the airplane will have three million-plus parts.
Program Launched	Oct. 29, 1990
First Flight	June 1994
First Delivery	May 1995 (to United Airlines)

The 777 offers more interior options and greater flexibility than any competing airplane.

- Six-abreast first class—747-size seats and wide aisles.

- Seven-abreast business—comfort level equal to the 747.

- Eight-abreast business—comparable to 767 at six abreast.

- Nine-abreast economy—industry-standard comfort levels.

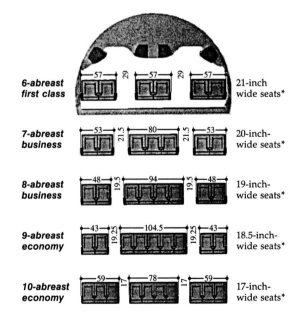

Figure 22.16 777 Interior.

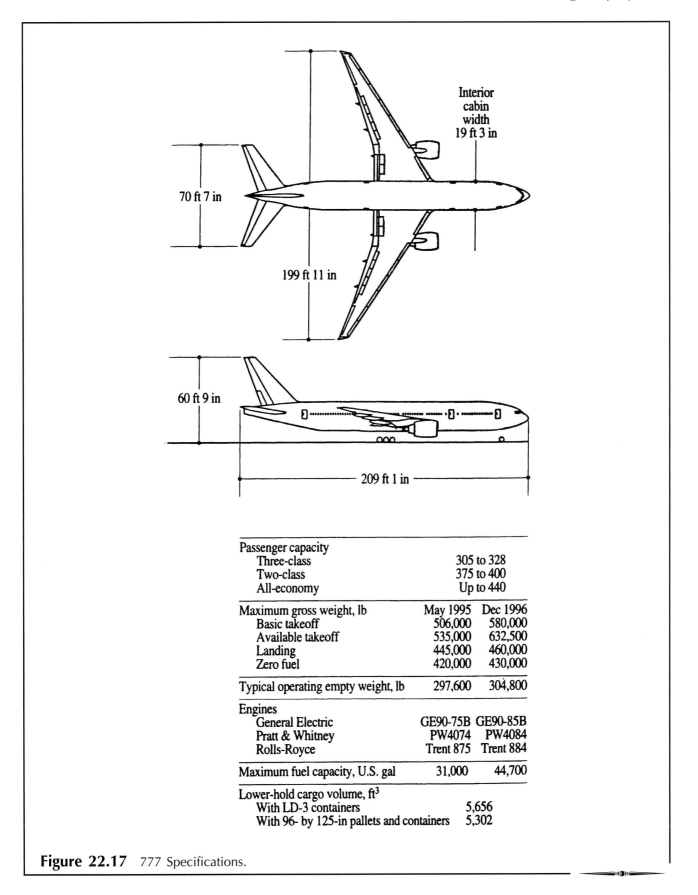

Passenger capacity		
Three-class	305 to 328	
Two-class	375 to 400	
All-economy	Up to 440	
Maximum gross weight, lb	May 1995	Dec 1996
Basic takeoff	506,000	580,000
Available takeoff	535,000	632,500
Landing	445,000	460,000
Zero fuel	420,000	430,000
Typical operating empty weight, lb	297,600	304,800
Engines		
General Electric	GE90-75B	GE90-85B
Pratt & Whitney	PW4074	PW4084
Rolls-Royce	Trent 875	Trent 884
Maximum fuel capacity, U.S. gal	31,000	44,700
Lower-hold cargo volume, ft³		
With LD-3 containers	5,656	
With 96- by 125-in pallets and containers	5,302	

Figure 22.17 777 Specifications.

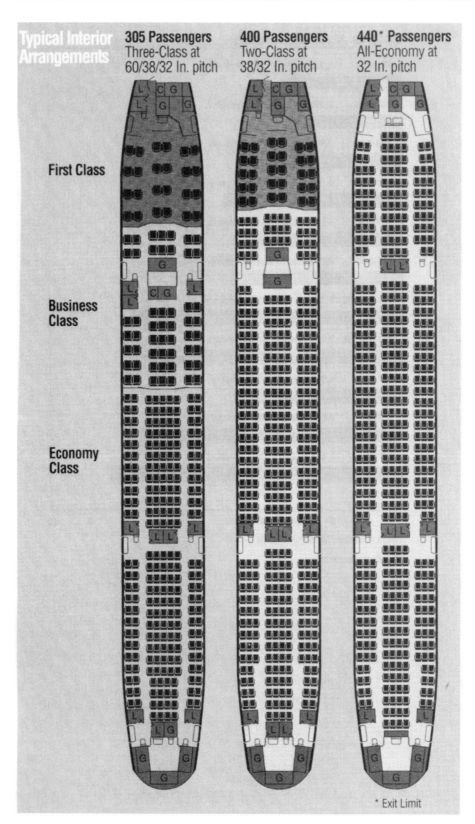

Figure 22.18 777 Interior Arrangements.

Figure 22.19   Boeing 777 Flight Deck.

737-300 2,640 miles/4,250 kilometers

737-400 2,410 miles/3,880 kilometers

737-500 2,760 miles/4,440 kilometers

757-200 4,490 miles/7,220 kilometers

767-200 5,350 miles/8,610 kilometers

767-300 4,630 miles/7,450 kilometers

767-200ER 7,070 miles/12,340 kilometers

767-300ER 7,193 miles/11,576 kilometers

777-200 8,965 miles/13,140 kilometers

777-300 6,057 miles/9,748 kilometers

747-400 8,370 miles/13,470 kilometers

0 1 2 3 4 5 6 7 8 9 10

Range in Statute Miles (thousands)
ER = Extended range

Figure 22.20 Boeing Jetliner Ranges.

BOEING 717

The Boeing 717 twin jet is designed to meet airlines' needs for a cost-effective 100-passenger transport to serve high frequency or low traffic short- to medium-range routes in the growing regional jet market.

Originally launched in October 1995 as the MD-95, the airplane was designated the Boeing 717 following the merger of McDonnell Douglas and The Boeing Company in 1997. AirTran Airlines is the launch customer, and did take delivery of the first airplanes in the summer of 1999.

With a wing span of 93.4 feet and overall length of 124 feet the 717 is similar in size and configuration to the DC-9 Series 30, its highly successful predecessor in regional airline services around the world. Maximum takeoff weight for the 717 will be 114,000 pounds compared to 108,000 pounds for the DC-9 model. Non-stop range will be up to 1,807 statute miles.

Like the DC-9, the 717 features a five-across coach-class seating arrangement. It will incorporate an all new interior with illuminated handrails and larger overhead baggage racks.

The two-crew cockpit incorporates the industry's most modern and proven avionics technology, config-

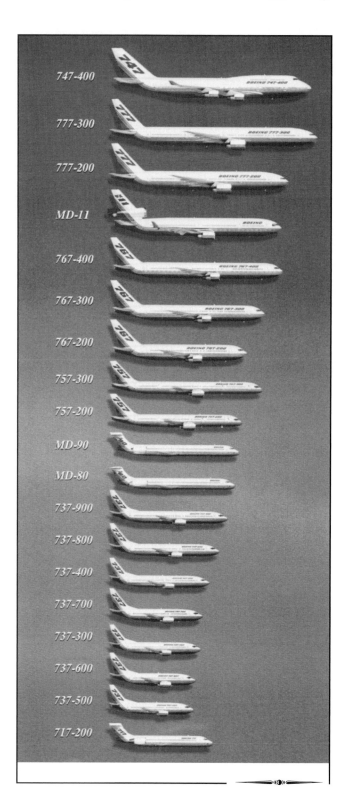

BOEING 717 SPECIFICATIONS

CREW	2, plus cabin attendants
CAPACITY	
Passengers	
Typical, Two Class	106
Cargo Holds	935 ft³
	26.5 m³
DIMENSIONS	
Wingspan	93.4 ft
	28.45 m
Length Overall	124.0 ft
	37.81 m
Height Overall	29 ft 1 in
	8.92 m
WING AREA	
Including Aileron	1,000.7 ft²
	92.97 m²
Sweepback (1/4 chord)	24.5°
AIRPORT NOISE	
(measured against Stage 3/Chapter 3)	
Sideline	–7dB
Takeoff	–7dB
Approach	–6.4dB
ENGINE EMISSIONS	
(measured against ICAO limits)	
Carbon monoxide	–70%
Nitrogen dioxide	–40%
Smoke	–42%
FLAPS	Double Slotted
SLATS	Full span leading edge, 2-position
SPEED BRAKE	Wing mounted spoilers
REVERSERS	Pivot door-type
ENGINES (2)	
Type—BMW/Rolls Royce	BR715
Thrust	18,500 lb
STANDARD DELIVERY DATA	
Design Gross	
Maximum Ramp Weight	115,000 lb
Maximum Takeoff Weight	114,000 lb
Maximum Landing Weight	102,000 lb
Maximum Zero Fuel Weight	96,000 lb
Operator's Empty Weight	68,278 lb
FUEL CAPACITY	
(@ 6.7 lb/gal)	3,673 gal

PERFORMANCE

Space Limited Payload	26,940 lb
Cruise Level Flight Speed	.76 M
	504 mph
FAA Takeoff Field Length	6,200 ft
(MTOW, S.L., Temp = 30°C)	
FAA Landing Field Length	4,740 ft
(MLW, S.L.)	
Desigh range	1,807 st me
(Domestic reserves @	
106 passengers/baggage)	1,570 n mi

ured around six interchangeable liquid crystal display units and advanced Honeywell VIA 2000 computer systems similar to those in other new Boeing jetliners.

Flight deck features in the 717 include an Electronic Instrument System, a dual Flight Management System and a Central Fault Display System. Global Positioning System; Category IIIb automatic landing capability for bad weather operations; and Future Air Navigation Systems are available as optional features.

Two advanced BMW/Rolls-Royce BR715 high-by-pass ratio engines will power the 717. The BR715 engine is rated at 18,500 pounds of takeoff thrust, with lower fuel consumption, reduced exhaust emissions, and significantly lower noise levels than the power plants on comparable airplanes.

The 717 is designed to meet replacement and expansion needs in the 100-seat category, potentially numbering thousands of airplanes. Full-scale development of the new airplane is currently under way.

Boeing has evolved into one of the largest and most successful aircraft manufacturers in the world. Their three major operating organizations are:

• Boeing Commercial Airplane Group.

• Boeing Defense and Space Group.

• Boeing Computer Services.

All are located in Seattle, Washington.

In 1997 the Boeing Company purchased the McDonnell Douglas Corporation for an amount in excess of $13 billion. Boeing anticipated a savings of $1 billion per year under their new organization resulting in a more competitive position. McDonnell Douglas and Airbus Industrie of France were the two rival competi-

tors of Boeing. The three major producers of airline type aircraft were reduced to two by the purchase. Boeing and McDonnell Douglas, the two major defense contractors for military aircraft, were now reduced to one.

The current growth in large aircraft construction and the demand by the airlines of the world for new aircraft, meant that Boeing did not expect that widespread layoffs would occur. The Boeing Company anticipated $48 billion in sales in their first year of operation under the new organization. The St. Louis based McDonnell Douglas facility continued under its name as a major division of Boeing. Boeing's purchase of McDonnell Douglas was generally a surprise; it was not common knowledge that the two companies had been talking about it for three years.

The new combined company operations will be producing aerospace products including commercial aircraft, military aircraft, space satellites, and launch vehicles. There are 200,000 employees in 26 states but the major operation for manufacturing and headquarters will remain in Seattle, Washington. The McDonnell Douglas facility in Long Beach, California, was renamed the Douglas Products Division of Boeing.

Boeing said that the purchase of McDonnell Douglas would meet their strategic objective of creating a better balance of their commercial, defense, and space manufacturing; it was a natural complementary union of the two companies and would preserve the heritage and capabilities of both organizations.

The airline type aircraft being produced by the former McDonnell Douglas Corporation will be made under the Boeing name. The newest aircraft of McDonnell Douglas was the MD 95. This was renamed by Boeing as the 717-200.

Located at Chicago are the headquarters of the Aerospace Company and Commercial Airplane Company. Boeing Engineering and Construction Company, formed in 1974 to provide products and services for energy-related businesses, is located in the Seattle area. So is Boeing Marine Systems, established in 1976 to produce and market hydrofoils. Boeing Military Airplane Company is located primarily in Kansas (with headquarters in both Wichita and Seattle), and the Boeing Vertol Company is in Philadelphia. Among company subsidiaries are Boeing Computer Services Company, Boeing Agri-Industrial Co., BOECON, Boeing Environmental Products, Boeing International Corporation, and Boeing of Canada, Ltd.

From the company's drawing boards have come the military B-17 Flying Fortress, the B-29 and B-50 Superfortresses, the C-97 Stratofreighter, the B-47 Stratojet, the B-52 Stratofortress, the KC-135 jet Stratotanker, and the C-135 jet transport. Boeing's reputation in commercial aviation stands on Stratoliners and Model 314 Flying Boats of the 1930s, the post-war Stratocruisers, and the current line of 707, 727, 737, and 747 jet airliners.

Boeing designated their airline passenger carrying aircraft with a 700 series of numbering. The 707 was the first and the latest is the 777.

In September 2001 the Boeing Company chose to locate its new world headquarters at 100 North Riverside Plaza in Chicago. Boeing announced a series of changes to its corporate structure that included plans for a leaner headquarters located separately from its existing businesses. The headquarters staff, which includes less than 500 people, concentrates on developing global growth opportunities and creating shareholder value. The announcement also elevated to CEO the leaders of the company's three largest business units and gave them broader responsibilities for improving performance and achieving growth objectives.

The cities of Chicago, Dallas-Fort Worth and Denver all were considered as the potential locations for the new world headquarters. The company conducted an extensive site evaluation process that included visits to each of the three metropolitan areas. A company official stated that any one of the three cities would have been adequate, including Seattle, if it were not located in the same area as their other commercial airplane business headquarters. The Chicago location places the company closer to financial organizations and money markets. Other advantages given were Boeing's access to national and international flights, good ground transportation, a favorable business climate and personal life

style issues. A close neighbor is United Airlines, who encouraged Boeing to move to Chicago. United owned Boeing many years ago and is one of its biggest customers. United launched the 777, a very successful airline aircraft.

SONIC CRUISER

The manufacturers of commercial air carrier aircraft appear to be entering a new phase of development. Aircraft will be needed in the coming years that are larger than the current 747. Indications are that the air carrier industry would strongly value an aircraft of this type. The next generation of passenger carrying aircraft will concentrate on higher speed, longer-range, comfort of flight at higher altitudes and quieter takeoffs and landings. Boeing is developing a new aircraft that will satisfy these demands while traveling at a speed approaching the speed of sound. In 1996 the company created a project in its new airplane product development group and designated the aircraft 20XX. The new aircraft has the wings at the rear of the fuselage and small canard wings at the front. A natural taper of the fuselage provides the "area ruling" without intruding upon the cabin. It is anticipated that one advantage of this aircraft would allow flights to go point-to-point instead of using the hub airport system.

Boeing will offer a new Mach 0.95 commercial aircraft that has generated much interest in the air carrier industry which recognizes the potential competitive advantage of speed over size. Airbus Industries is building their giant A380 to carry up to 800 passengers. The Boeing Company is taking a new direction in that it is not going to build a competitive aircraft. Instead they are planning to produce this subsonic aircraft which they believe is needed in the air carrier industry. An air carrier CEO said that the new concept would revolutionize commercial aviation. Due to its high speed an air carrier can make two flights to Europe in one day instead of one flight. Boeing expects the aircraft to save

Figure 22.21   Airbus 380.

Figure 22.22   Sonic Cruiser.

Image by Bob Kane.

an hour on the 3000-mile flight from New York to London, which currently takes 6 hours. The aircraft will carry from 175 to 250 people depending upon its configuration with a 15 to 20 percent increase in performance over other aircraft while having a range of 9000 nautical miles. The new twin engine aircraft is to be named "Sonic Cruiser." Boeing expects to have the aircraft available for commercial service between the years 2006 and 2008. A current fourteen-hour flight to Asia from the United States would result in a three-hour reduction in flight time. This reflects very significant amounts of savings. A United Airlines spokesman said that the new aircraft would fit nicely into United's long-haul routes in the Atlantic and Pacific areas of operation. The success of the aircraft will depend upon its range, payload, noise and operational cost.

BLENDED WING BODY

Boeing's arch rival, Airbus Industrie, a European consortium, will build a double deck aircraft that will carry 600 passengers. Designated the A-380, it will be the world's largest aircraft and it is expected to be in service by the year 2006. This will challenge Boeing's 747 that seats about 420 passengers and has dominated the demand for large aircraft for more than three decades. Boeing proposed a modified version of the 747 that could seat 500–600 passengers but discovered there was insufficient demand to build it.

Boeing's research Laboratory of Advanced Aircraft Technology, the Phantom Works, is working on an air-

craft design that has not been given a formal name. The airplane will be a type of flying wing that resembles a stingray. This Blended Wing Body aircraft will carry as many as 800 passengers in a double deck compartment that is blended into the wing. There is no traditional use of a fuselage or tail fins. Three large engines will be mounted on the upper rear of the aircraft wing. This will provide a high level of quietness inside the cabin area. It may be ten years before the aircraft enters into passenger service. The challenge is not so much of a technical nature but rather that of overcoming potential passenger reluctance to sit inside the wing of an aircraft.

Passengers will be seated in two decks, each with five parallel compartments running the length of the aircraft. Since most of the passengers will not be seated near windows the back of each seat will have a video monitor to provide an outside view similar to display screens found on Boeing 777 aircraft. Several doors in the front of the wing, as well as in the rear, will allow for easy emergence exits.

Intense competition between Boeing and Airbus Industrie has reached a high level recently. Air carriers operating by the present hub-and-spoke concept will probably not find either aircraft to be suitable. Long haul flights over great distances are where these aircraft will be most economically suited.

It will be interesting to see which aircraft will reach the forefront in the years to come. Perhaps each one will find its place in the air transportation world of the future. A photo of the Sonic Cruiser can be found on Boeing's website at www.boeing.com. The Blended Wing Body aircraft can be viewed on Airbus Industrie's website www.airbus.com.

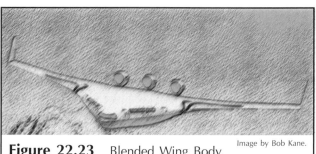

Figure 22.23   Blended Wing Body.

Image by Bob Kane.

CHAPTER 23

The McDonnell Douglas Corporation

I n 1997, the Boeing Company purchased the McDonnell Douglas Corporation for an amount in excess of $13 billion. The McDonnell Douglas facility in Long Beach, California, was renamed the Douglas Products Division of Boeing. See Chapter 22 for more information.

McDonnell Douglas traces its roots back to 1920— just 17 years after the Wright brothers flew for the first time at Kitty Hawk. When the McDonnell Douglas story began, aviation was just emerging from its infancy. Commercial air transportation as we know it did not exist.

During World War I, the airplane had demonstrated some military uses and a potential for further application as an instrument of defense. But military production had ended, and, in the aftermath of the great conflict, the future of America's infant aircraft industry seemed cloudy indeed. Nevertheless, in that environment Donald Douglas determined to pursue a long-held dream. He believed that the future of the airplane rested upon its wide use as a vehicle to serve man by transporting people and cargo through the broad, unconfined highways of the sky, and he wanted to test that belief in his own way. This led him to give up his job as one of the nation's leading aeronautical engineers and go to California, with meager capital, to start a new venture.

On July 22, 1920, Donald Douglas started his business in a tiny office behind a Los Angeles barber shop and began work on a biplane made of wood, wire, and cloth. That biplane, powered by a war surplus engine, was designed for the purpose of being the first to cross America nonstop. Things did not work out as he had planned. Two young Army officers got across the country first. However, that venture brought forth, in time, the famous aircraft series designated DC-Douglas Com-

mercial; and it helped provide the military aircraft which saved the free world during World War II.

It was on the eve of World War II, on July 16, 1939, that James McDonnell founded the McDonnell Aircraft Corporation in St. Louis and provided a new and wider scope for his creativity. When World War II erupted in Europe several weeks later, the United States looked anew at its defenses, and decided that the need of the times was unmistakably for aircraft production.

After a beginning year of struggle, during which few sales and no earnings were achieved, the new company grew rapidly by manufacturing airplane parts, developing the XP-67 bomber destroyer, and producing the AT-21 bomber trainer, contributing substantially to the war effort.

Of greatest significance for the future, however, was McDonnell Aircraft's wartime research on the application of jet propulsion to aircraft, a new concept at that time. The company's impressive progress in this field led to its selection to develop a jet-propelled, carrier-based fighter in January 1943. The historic result was the FH-1 Phantom, the world's first operational carrier-based jet, the first U.S. Navy aircraft to attain a speed of 500 miles per hour, and the progenitor of a long and distinguished line of McDonnell fighter aircraft.

Both men had persistence to match their ambitions, however. Douglas, not long after losing the transcontinental competition, reorganized his company and moved it into what was almost literally a house of dreams—an abandoned movie studio. There he began building torpedo planes for the U.S. Navy, and Douglas Aircraft was on its way to stardom.

McDonnell, his company small enough to fit into the second floor of an office building, found his second

Figure 23.1
McDonnell Douglas Commercial Family

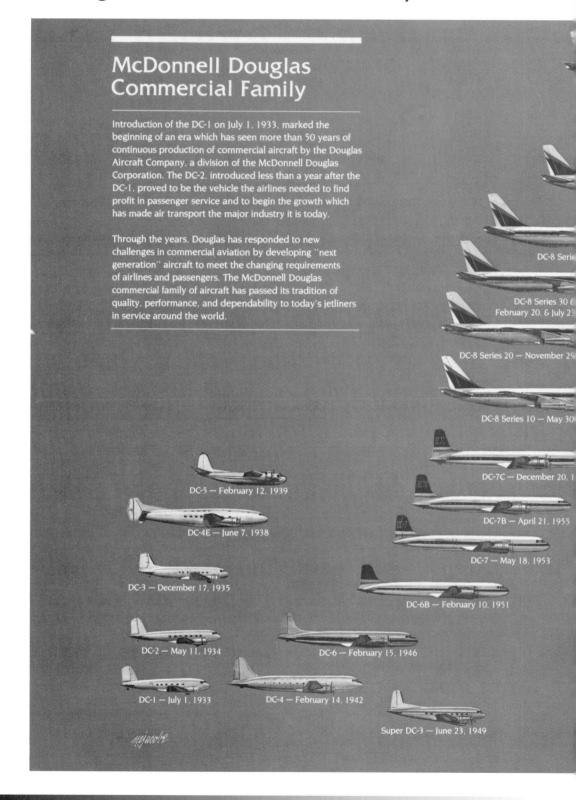

McDonnell Douglas Commercial Family

Introduction of the DC-1 on July 1, 1933, marked the beginning of an era which has seen more than 50 years of continuous production of commercial aircraft by the Douglas Aircraft Company, a division of the McDonnell Douglas Corporation. The DC-2, introduced less than a year after the DC-1, proved to be the vehicle the airlines needed to find profit in passenger service and to begin the growth which has made air transport the major industry it is today.

Through the years, Douglas has responded to new challenges in commercial aviation by developing ''next generation'' aircraft to meet the changing requirements of airlines and passengers. The McDonnell Douglas commercial family of aircraft has passed its tradition of quality, performance, and dependability to today's jetliners in service around the world.

DC-8 Series

DC-8 Series 30 & February 20, & July 23

DC-8 Series 20 — November 29

DC-8 Series 10 — May 30

DC-7C — December 20,

DC-7B — April 21, 1955

DC-7 — May 18, 1953

DC-6B — February 10, 1951

DC-5 — February 12, 1939

DC-4E — June 7, 1938

DC-3 — December 17, 1935

DC-6 — February 15, 1946

DC-2 — May 11, 1934

DC-1 — July 1, 1933

DC-4 — February 14, 1942

Super DC-3 — June 23, 1949

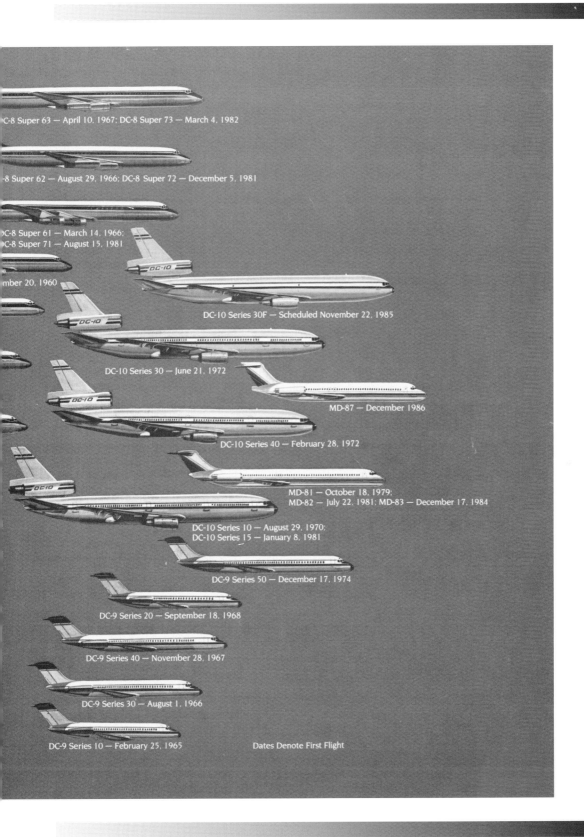

C-8 Super 63 — April 10, 1967; DC-8 Super 73 — March 4, 1982

-8 Super 62 — August 29, 1966; DC-8 Super 72 — December 5, 1981

C-8 Super 61 — March 14, 1966;
C-8 Super 71 — August 15, 1981

mber 20, 1960

DC-10 Series 30F — Scheduled November 22, 1985

DC-10 Series 30 — June 21, 1972

MD-87 — December 1986

DC-10 Series 40 — February 28, 1972

MD-81 — October 18, 1979;
MD-82 — July 22, 1981; MD-83 — December 17, 1984

DC-10 Series 10 — August 29, 1970;
DC-10 Series 15 — January 8, 1981

DC-9 Series 50 — December 17, 1974

DC-9 Series 20 — September 18, 1968

DC-9 Series 40 — November 28, 1967

DC-9 Series 30 — August 1, 1966

DC-9 Series 10 — February 25, 1965   Dates Denote First Flight year better than his first. Orders began to trickle in—orders for ammunition boxes, sections of airplanes, and odds and ends. The trickle grew to a steady flow, and then orders not just for parts, but for whole airplanes began to come in.

Where all this eventually led is a big part of the history of the modern aerospace industry. Donald Douglas, whose first plane made the record books by being the first to lift a useful load exceeding its own weight, went on to design and build commercial airliners that changed the travel habits of the whole world. James McDonnell adopted jet propulsion in its infancy and helped bring it to swift and strong maturity.

Both McDonnell and Douglas were at the forefront in meeting the challenge of the Space Age. Mercury and Gemini spacecraft carried the first American astronauts on a spectacularly successful series of space flights, while the Thor and Delta boosters launched scores of satellites, and S-IVB space vehicles played a significant role in the Saturn/Apollo program that was climaxed by man's first landing on the moon.

The merger of McDonnell and Douglas on April 28, 1967, blended two great heritages into a team of unsurpassed capabilities spanning the full spectrum of aerospace activity. All aircraft produced after the merger are designated MD for McDonnell Douglas.

The one and only *DC-1*—first of the "Douglas Commercial" family, was a low-wing, all-metal monoplane which first flew on July 1, 1933. Two Wright Cyclone 710 hp engines carried 14 passengers at 180 mph.

Before the DC-1 was delivered on September 13, 1933, an order was received for 20 of an improved version, the *DC-2,*—which would cruise at 190 mph. Sales of the DC-2 eventually reached 138.

The immortal *DC-3*—first flew on December 17, 1935. It was a simple, logical evolutionary development of the DC-1 and DC-2. New 1000 hp Pratt & Whitney engines permitted the DC-3 to carry 21 passengers 1480 miles at 195 mph. The world's airlines bought 448 DC-3s, and many times that number of surplus C-47s.

The *DC-4*—carried 144 passengers at more than 200 mph. Its straightforward, four-engine design was laid down in 1938. Roughly three times the size of the DC-3, the DC-4 was commandeered by the U.S. Army Air Forces in 1942, delaying its use in commercial service until 1946. More than 300 eventually were used by the airlines.

The *DC-5*—was a two-engine transport which embodied many DC-3 systems, but it enjoyed limited success and only 12 were built.

The *DC-6*—was to the DC-4 what the DC-3 was to the DC-2. Four Pratt & Whitney R-2800 engines gave the DC-6 8,400 hp and improved its speed to 350 mph from the DC-4's 240 mph. Payload was increased from 11,000 to 14,000 pounds and range extended from 1,750 to 2,600 miles. Cabin pressure was maintained at 5,000 feet while flying at 20,000. The improved *DC-6B* was a great money maker for most airlines. Greater power increased passenger capacity from 58 to 89 and top speed from 350 mph to 380 mph.

The *DC-7*—introduced in May 1953, was powered by four Wright turbo-compound W-3350s. It was the first commercial transport able to fly non-stop westbound across the United States against the prevailing winds. A total of 1,041 of the DC-6/DC-7 series was delivered.

The *DC-8*—powered by four jet turbine engines and capable of speeds of more than 600 mph, first flew on May 30, 1958. As of July 1970, more than 500 DC-8s in all versions had been delivered to the world's airlines. The DC-8 has been produced in eight basic models, with a variety of configurations and power plants. Production is now concentrated in the *Super Sixty* series.

The *DC-8-61*—features a fuselage extension of nearly 37 feet over the original model. In an all-economy passenger configuration, the DC-8-61 can carry 260; the convertible freighter configuration has a cargo volume of 12,535 cubic feet.

The *DC-8-62*—a very-long-range commercial jetliner, can carry 189 passengers or 97,000 pounds of cargo as far as 5000 nautical miles.

All design improvements of the DC-8-61 and -62 are incorporated in the *DC-8-63*. The fuselage extension, aerodynamic improvements to nacelles, pylons, and flaps, plus increased wing span and fuel capacity, combine to provide outstanding payload and range capability.

The *DC-9*—made its first flight on February 25, 1965 and entered airline service in December of the same year. It has been produced in four series and six principal configurations. Recent emphasis has been on the larger DC-9-30 and DC-9-40 versions.

The 90-passenger *DC-9-10*—was expanded into the *DC-9-30,* which first flew on August 1, 1966. The DC-9-30 is 15 feet longer than the DC-9-10. It has a 4-foot increase in wingspan and can carry up to 115 passengers. It was accorded prompt and widespread airline acceptance.

The *DC-9-20*—combines the compact fuselage of the Series 10 with the high-lift wing system of the larger

Series 30. It has proven especially useful for short landing fields.

The *DC-9-40*—accommodating as many as 125 passengers, was introduced in 1968.

The *DC-10*—first flight was on August 29, 1970. It was delivered to American and United Airlines on July 29, 1971. It is a three engine aircraft and can carry up to 380 passengers. The maximum gross weight is 440,000 to 580,000 pounds, depending on the model.

The series *MD-80, -81, -82, -83 and -87*—are twin-engine airplanes. The first model flew on October 18, 1979 and was delivered on September 12, 1980. It can carry up to 172 passengers. The MD-87 first flight was in December 1986 and delivered September 1987. It has a maximum gross weight of 149,500 pounds carrying 130 passengers. After the merger with Boeing in 1997, MD-80 production will cease when outstanding orders for the aircraft are completed.

The *MD-11*—first flew in January 1990 and delivered to the airlines in December 1990. It has three engines of up to 65,000 pounds of thrust each. Its maximum gross weight is 610,000 pounds and can carry 410 passengers.

The *MD-90*—first flew in 1993 and was delivered in 1994. It is a twin-engine aircraft carrying up to 180 passengers with a maximum gross weight of 172,500 pounds.

THE DC-8

In the decade following its maiden flight, the DC-8 established commercial transport world records for speed, altitude, distance, and payload.

From its inception, the jet powered DC-8 embodied advanced aerodynamic and structural concepts, as well as internal systems designed for maximum service reliability, operational convenience, and passenger comfort.

A capacity for improved power, payload, and range capabilities was inherent in the DC-8 design. Four basic models, the Series 10 through 50, in all-passenger, convertible passenger/cargo, and all-cargo versions, and the Super 60 Series 61, Series 62, and Series 63, with freighter models of each—were produced before the last of 556 was delivered on 13 May 1972. This marked the end of 15 years of production, at which time there were 48 DC-8 operators in 28 nations worldwide.

Development of the Super 60 Series in 1965, with increased size capacity, and efficiency, demonstrated the capacity for growth of the DC-8 design. The Super 61 can carry up to 259 passengers on high-density trans-

continental routes. The Super 62, designed for ultra long range operations, carries up to 189 passengers at ranges over 6,000 statute miles. The Super 63, which combined the fuselage extension and payload capacity of the Super 61 with the long-range and aerodynamic and power plant improvements of the Super 62, carries a maximum capacity of 259 passengers and baggage 4,500 statute miles, or lesser loads even greater distances. The DC-8 Super 63F, 63CF is able to carry up to 118,000 pounds of freight, accommodating 18 standard cargo pallets in the main cabin.

The four-engine DC-8 jetliner represented a significant chapter in the evolution of commercial transport design.

McDONNELL DOUGLAS DC-10 JETLINER

A new category of airplane, offering significant advantages over its predecessors, was added to the world's air transportation system with the introduction of the "new dimension" McDonnell Douglas DC-10 into scheduled airline service.

In addition to the luxury and spaciousness inherent in its wide cabin, the three-engine DC-10 incorporates advances in propulsion, aerodynamics, structure, avionics, flight control systems, and environmental compatibility.

The multi-range DC-10 is produced in Long Beach, California, by the Douglas Aircraft Company division of McDonnell Douglas Corporation. Major components and parts are provided by a vast international network of subcontractors and other suppliers.

All versions of the McDonnell Douglas tri-jet transport accommodate from 250 passengers, in a typical mixed first-class and coach arrangement, to 380 passengers in an all-economy configuration.

Engineering design of the new airplane, tenth in a series of commercial transports produced without interruption for more than 40 years, started in January 1968. Manufacturing began with automated machine milling of forged aluminum parts on January 6, 1969, and assembly started June 23, 1969.

The first DC-10 taxied under its own power in a formal debut on July 23, 1970, and made an impressive maiden flight of 3 hours 26 minutes on August 29, 1970.

Five airplanes assigned to the flight test and development program logged more than 1500 hours prior to certification by the Federal Aviation Administration (FAA) for airline service on July 29, 1971. On the same

DC-8 CONFIGURATION AND PERFORMANCE DATA

First Flight

Series 10	May 30, 1958
Series 20	November 29, 1958
Series 30	February 20, 1959
Series 40	July 23, 1959
Series 50	December 20, 1960
Series 54	October 29, 1962
Series 55	January 13, 1964
Series 61	March 14, 1966
Series 62	August 29, 1966
Series 63	April 10, 1967

First Deliveries

Series 10	June 3, 1959 (UAL)
Series 20	January 3, 1960 (EAL)
Series 30	February 7, 1960 (PAA)
Series 40	February 7, 1960 (ACA)
Series 50	April 3, 1961 (KLM)
Series 54	January 30, 1963 (ACA)
Series 55	June 21, 1964 (SBW)
Super 61	January 26, 1967 (UAL)
Super 62	May 3, 1967 (SAS)
Super 63	July 15, 1967 (KLM)
Super 63CF	June 21, 1968 (SBW)

Engines (4)

Series 10
P&W JT3C-6 (13,500 lb thrust)
Series 20
P&W JT4A-9 (16,800 lb thrust)
Series 30
P&W JT4A-11 (17,500 lb thrust)
Series 40
RR Conway R0012 (17,500 lb thrust)
Series 50 and Super 61
P&W JT3D-3 (18,000 lb thrust)
Super 63 and 63CF
P&W JT3D-7 (19,000 lb thrust)

Maximum Gross Weights
123,831 to 161,025 kg (273,000 to 355,000 lb),
depending on model

Maximum Payload
14,243 to 53,408 kg (31,400 to 117,744 lb), depending on model

Passengers
117 to 259

Cargo Space
Passenger—39.34 to 70.98 m^3
(1,390 to 2,508 ft^3); or
Cargo—177.24 to 356.01 m^3 (6,263 to 12,580 ft^3)

Operating Altitude
10,668 m (35,000 ft)

Cruise Speed

Series 10	919 km/hr (496 kn)
Series 20	943 km/hr (509 kn)
Series 30	943 km/hr (509 kn)
Series 40	949 km/hr (512 kn)
Series 50	930 km/hr (502 kn)
Super 61	915 km/hr (494 kn)
Super 62	928 km/hr (501 kn)
Super 63	941 km/hr (508 kn)

Range (maximum fuel)

Series 10	7,686 km (4,150 n mi)
Series 20	8,171 km (4,358 n mi)
Series 30	10,103 km (5,455 n mi)
Series 40	10,881 km (5,875 n mi)
Series 50	12,140 km (6,555 n mi)
Super 61	9,408 km (5,080 n mi)
Super 62	12,445 km (6,720 n mi)
Super 63	11,297 km (6,100 n mi)

Aircraft Dimensions
Length
Std. 45.87 m (150 ft, 6 in.)
Super 61 and 63
57.12 m (187 ft, 5 in.)
Super 62
47.98 m (157 ft, 5 in.)

DC-8 (RETROFITTED)

First Flight

Super 71	August 15, 1981
Super 72	December 12, 1981
Super 73	March 3, 1982

Wing Span
Std and Super 61
43.41 m (142 ft, 5 in.)
Super 62 and 63
45.24 m (148 ft, 5 in.)

Height
(All) 12.90 m (42 ft, 4 in.)

First Deliveries

Super 71	July 15, 1982 (UAL)
Super 72	October 4, 1982 (ZJR)
Super 73	September 1, 1982 (FTL)

Engines (4)
Super 71, 72, and 73
CFM56 (22,000 lb thrust)

Maximum Gross Weights   123,831 to 161,025 kg (273,000 to 355,000 lb), depending on model

Maximum Payload   14,243 to 53,408 kg (31,400 to 117,744 lb), depending on model

Passengers   117 to 259

Cargo Space   Passenger—39.34 to 70.98 m^3 (1,390 to 2,508 ft^3); or Cargo—177.24 to 356.01 m^3 (6,263 to 12,580 ft^3)

Operating Altitude   10,668 m (35,000 ft)

Cruise Speed   Super 71 915 km/hr (494 kn)
Super 72 928 km/hr (501 kn)
Super 73 941 km/hr (508 kn)

Range (maximum fuel)   Super 71 11,538 km (6,230 n mi)
Super 72 14,223 km (7,680 n mi)
Super 73 12,964 km (7,000 n mi)

Aircraft Dimensions
Length   Super 71 and 73
57.12 m (187 ft, 5 in.)
Super 72
47.98 m (157 ft, 5 in.)

Wing Span   Super 71
43.41 m (142 ft, 5 in.)
Super 72 and 73
45.24 m (148 ft, 5 in.)

Height   (All) 12.90 m (42 ft, 4 in.)

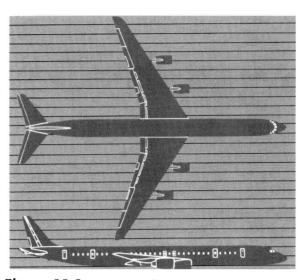

Figure 23.2 McDonnell DC-8.

DC-9 CONFIGURATION AND PERFORMANCE DATA

First Flight

Series 10	February 25, 1965
Series 20	September 18, 1968
Series 30	August 1, 1966
Series 40	November 28, 1967
Series 50	December 17, 1974

First Deliveries

Series 10	September 18, 1965
Series 20	December 11, 1968
Series 30	January 27, 1967
Series 40	February 29, 1968
Series 50	August 14, 1975

Engines (2)

Series 10
P&W JT8D-5 (12,250 lb thrust)
Series 10 and 30
P&W JT8D-1 and -7 (14,000 lb thrust)
Series 20, 30, and 40
P&W JT8D-11 (15,000 lb thrust)
Series 30 and 40
P&W JT8D-9 (14,500 lb thrust)
Series 30 and 40
P&W JT8D-15 (15,500 lb thrust)
Series 50
P&W JT8D-17 (16,000 lb thrust)

Maximum Gross Weights

35,608 to 54,863 kg
(78,500 to 121,000 lb), depending on model

Maximum Payload

8,709 to 17,477 kg
(19,200 to 38,546 lb), depending on model

Passengers

70 to 139

Cargo Space

Passenger—16.98 to 29.26 m³ (600 to 1,034 ft³);
or
Cargo—81.56 to 118.86 m³ (2,882 to 4,200 ft³)

Operating Altitude

10,668 m (35,000 ft)

Cruise Speed

Series 10	895 km/hr (483 kn)
Series 20	891 km/hr (481 kn)
Series 30	882 km/hr (476 kn)
Series 40	
and 50	872 km/hr (471 kn)

Range

Maximum fuel (typical mixed class)

Series 10	2,520 km (1,361 n mi)
Series 20	2,853 km (1,540 n mi)
Series 30	2,592 km (1,400 n mi)
Series 40	2,223 km (1,200 n mi)
Series 50	2,919 km (1,576 n mi)

Aircraft Dimensions

Length

Series 10 and 20
31.80 m (104 ft, 4 in.)
Series 30
36.35 m (119 ft, 3 in.)
Series 40
38.25 m (125 ft, 6 in.)
Series 50
40.69 m (133 ft, 6 in.)

Wing Span

Series 10
27.23 m (89 ft, 4 in.)
Series 20, 30, 40, and 50
28.45 m (93 ft, 4 in.)

Height

Series 10, 20, and 30
8.38 m (27 ft, 6 in.)
Series 40 and 50
8.53 m (28 ft)

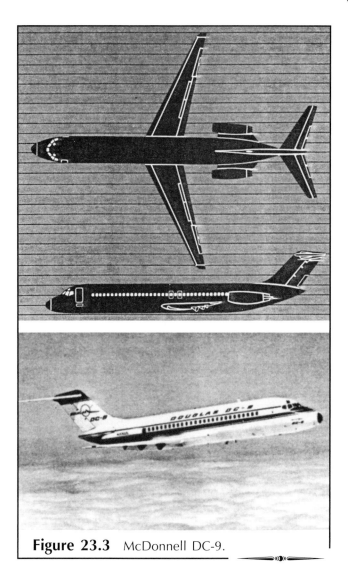

Figure 23.3 McDonnell DC-9.

day, first deliveries were made jointly to American Airlines and to United Air Lines.

Scheduled commercial operation began August 5, 1971, when American Airlines flew its first DC-10 on a Los Angeles-Chicago round trip. United Air Lines inaugurated transcontinental service on August 14, 1971, with a San Francisco-Washington flight.

The first long-range version of the tri-jet, the Series 40, made its debut on February 28, 1972, completing a 4-hour, 10-minute maiden flight. On October 20, 1972, the Series 40 was certified by the FAA for commercial service, and the first of this intercontinental model was delivered to Northwest Orient Airlines on November 10, 1972.

Scheduled commercial operation of the Series 40 was inaugurated on December 13, 1972, by Northwest with a flight from Minneapolis to Milwaukee and Tampa, Florida.

The second long-range model, the Series 30, began its flight test program with a 5-hour, 25-minute first flight on June 21, 1972.

At a joint ceremony on November 21, 1972, Swissair and KLM Royal Dutch Airlines each received a Series 30, marking the first deliveries of this version. Union de Transports Aeriens and Scandinavian Airlines System, the other two members of the KSSU group of airlines, also participated in the delivery program at Long Beach. FAA certification of the Series 30 for airline operation was announced at the ceremony.

First scheduled commercial service with the Series 30 occurred December 15, 1972, with a Swissair flight from Zurich to Montreal.

Performance excellence of the DC-10 was demonstrated during two extended trips during 1972. Starting on July 21 from Long Beach, a Series 10 visited 28 cities in 25 days during a 27,000-mile flight throughout Asia, Europe, and the United States. In October a Series 40 set three nonstop flight records during a 20,000-mile trip to Asia and South America.

The first of the convertible freighter models of the DC-10 completed an impressive maiden flight of 4 hours and 5 minutes on February 28, 1973. A series 30 version, the DC-10CF was painted in the colors of Overseas National Airways (ONA). On April 17, 1973, the first two DC-10CF tri-jets were delivered to ONA and Trans International Airlines. Continental Air Lines received the first Series 10 DC-10CF, taking delivery in February 1974.

A longer-range version of the Series 40 was announced on December 28, 1973, when Japan Air Lines purchased six of the DC-10s. The first of these transports was delivered to JAL on April 9, 1976. The airline inaugurated DC-10 service on July 1, 1976, over its domestic routes.

McDonnell Douglas announced the newest model of the DC-10, the Series 15, in September 1979, with orders from Aeromexico and Mexicana Airlines.

Five models of the DC-10 were produced. The Series 10 model, designed for service on routes of 300 to 4,000 statute miles is powered by General Electric CF6-6 engines, each rated at 40,000 pounds takeoff thrust. This engine was certified by the Federal Aviation Administration on September 16, 1970. The Series 30, an intercontinental version with a range of approximately 5,900 miles, is equipped with advanced General Electric CF6-50 fanjets. The Series 40 model is built in two versions. One, with a range of 5,350 miles, is powered by Pratt & Whitney Aircraft JT9D-20 turbofan engines. The other, equipped with the more powerful

Pratt & Whitney JT9D-59A engines, has a range of approximately 5,800 miles. The fourth model is the DC-10CF (convertible freighter), which can be arranged to carry all passengers, all cargo, or combinations of the two. Available in the basic Series 10, Series 30, or Series 40, the DC-10CF uses either the P&W or G.E. engines. The Series 15 is powered by General Electric CF6-50C2-F engines, each with a takeoff thrust of 46,500 pounds. With greater engine thrust than a Series 10, the Series 15 will operate from hot, high-altitude airports with more passengers and cargo. Range of the Series 15, with full payload, is about 3,600 miles at sea level. Maximum landing weights are 363,500 pounds for the Series 10 and Series 15, and 403,000 pounds for the Series 30 and the Series 40.

All versions of the DC-10CF convertible transport have a total available cargo space of more than 16,000 cubic feet, or as much as four 40-foot-class railroad freight cars. The main cabin will accommodate 30 standard 88 x 108-inch pallets, or 22 88 x 125-inch pallets. A cargo door, $8\frac{1}{2}$ feet x $11\frac{1}{2}$ feet swings upward from the side of the forward fuselage. Time required for complete conversion from an all-passenger to an all-cargo arrangement is 10 hours or less.

Intercontinental models of the DC-10CF will transport up to 155,700 pounds of palletized freight from New York to Frankfurt or from Anchorage to Tokyo. The Series 10 convertible model will haul up to 115,000 pounds of palletized cargo from Los Angeles to Honolulu and 100,000 pounds from New York to London.

The DC-10's General Electric and Pratt & Whitney Aircraft power plants represent significant advances in engine performance and technology. The high-bypass-ratio turbofans yield such improvements as lower specific fuel consumption, lower noise levels, smokeless exhaust, easier maintenance, and design for high reliability. Thrust ratings range from 40,000 to 53,000 pounds.

Two of the engines are mounted conventionally on pylons beneath the wings, and the third is installed above the aft fuselage at the base of the vertical stabilizer. This arrangement offers both aerodynamic and operating advantages. All engines are interchangeable with only minor adjustments; and the installations are designed to provide easy access for inspection and maintenance of all three power plants.

The DC-10 cabin interior is 18 feet 9 inches wide at passenger seat level. A broad ceiling, approximately eight feet high, gives room-like spaciousness. Rapid and easy entrance and exit are provided through eight passenger doors. Six of them, measuring 76 x 42 inches, are wide enough to admit two persons together. The remaining two doors, 76 x 32 inches, are larger than main entrances to first-generation jets.

Two aisles run the length of the cabin, which is separated into three room-like sections. Aisles and seats are wider than those on DC-8 and 707-type transports.

There are three pairs of luxurious lounging chairs per row in the forward first-class section. With four pairs of seats across in the coach section, no passenger is more than one seat from an aisle. If an economy section is specified, seats are arranged in three pairs, plus one set of three.

The DC-10 provides passengers with 30% more window area, in proportion to total size, than any other jetliner. Closed compartments above the window provide storage space for personal effects and carry-on luggage. Baggage racks also can be installed along the centerline of the cabin ceiling.

Airlines have the option of using a lower-deck galley system or a conventional arrangement of galleys in the main cabin to allow more space on the lower deck for cargo.

An advanced air conditioning and cabin pressurization system provides separate automatic temperature controls for the three main cabin sections, the cockpit, and the lower galley, assuring optimum comfort for all passengers regardless of variations in load density in the different areas. Three separate air conditioning systems circulate draft-free fresh air at the rate of 20 cubic feet per minute for each passenger.

The cabin pressurization system maintains sea level pressure in the DC-10 at flight altitudes up to 22,000 feet and a cabin altitude of less than 7,000 feet at flight altitudes up to 40,000 feet. Automatic controls prevent sudden sharp changes in pressure as the aircraft climbs or descends.

The roomy flight deck of the DC-10 has places for a three-person crew and two observers. Prime considerations in cockpit design were simplicity, efficiency, and low crew work-load.

Large windshields provide exceptional visibility, particularly during approaches and landings and for ground maneuvering.

Crew seats, developed by McDonnell Douglas, minimize fatigue on long flights and feature electric-powered adjustment for individual positioning and comfort. The DC-10 has been certified for automatic landing operation under Category IIIA minimum weather conditions, providing capability for operation in near-zero visibility. Many DC-10 features are based on the application of advanced technology to meet airline requirements for operational economy, reliability and maintainability and to provide passengers with higher standards of service.

The airplane is designed specifically to be a "good airport neighbor," operating from existing runways, taxiways, and loading areas. Although each engine produces more than twice as much takeoff thrust as the most powerful engine on first-generation jetliners, the DC-10 power plants are significantly quieter.

The McDonnell Douglas tri-jetliner is the first commercial transport to be certified under the stringent FAA regulations governing sound levels for new aircraft. It also meets sound requirements established by the Port of New York Authority and other airport operators.

In addition, the DC-10 engines are smokeless and do not require dumping of unburned fuel.

Overall length of all DC-10 versions is approximately 182 feet. Wingspan is 155 feet 4 inches on the Series 10 and Series 15 aircraft, and 165 feet 4 inches on the Series 30 and 40. Wings are swept at an angle of 35 degrees.

Gross takeoff weight is 430,000 pounds for the DC-10 Series 10, 455,000 pounds for the Series 15, and 555,000 pounds for the Series 30 and Series 40. Higher takeoff, landing, and zero fuel weights are available in all models.

The DC-10 is a multi-range tri-jet transport designed to answer airline needs in the 1980s and beyond. It can carry up to 380 passengers and is produced in four commercial versions for economical operations on route segments from 300 to 6,500 statute miles.

The DC-10 is powered by advanced-technology, high-bypass-ratio, turbofan engines, which reduce engine noise significantly, and emit no visible smoke. Features include highlift wing devices and a fully automatic landing system for all-weather operation. It is capable of operation from relatively small airports such as New York's La Guardia with a full load bound for Chicago, or from larger airports such as Kennedy International in New York with a full load on non-stop transcontinental or intercontinental flights.

The DC-10's spacious 19-foot diameter fuselage provides luxurious passenger comforts far exceeding those of any first-generation jetliner. Two aisles run the length of the cabin, and no passenger is more than one seat from an aisle. Meals may be prepared in a lower-deck galley and lifted to the passenger cabin by two electric elevators for serving, or served from galleys on the main deck, to free below deck space for additional cargo transport.

The DC-10 began operational service in August 1971, and by December 1979 had been selected by 48 airlines. The DC-10 fleet serves 170 cities worldwide, and averages more than 825 flights and 150,000 passengers daily.

DC-10 CONFIGURATION AND PERFORMANCE DATA

First Flight
Series 10   August 29, 1970
Series 15   January 1981
Series 30   June 21, 1972
Series 30F   November 1985
Series 40   February 28, 1972

First Deliveries
Series 10   July 29, 1971
(AA and UAL)
Series 15   June 15, 1981 (MX)
Series 30   November 21, 1972
(SWA and KLM)
Series 30F   January 1986
Series 40   November 10, 1972
(NWA)
Engines (3)
Series 10
GE CF6-6D (40,000 lb thrust)

Series 15
GE CF6-50C2-F (46,500 lb thrust)
Series 30
GE CF6-50C (51,000 lb thrust)
Series 30F
GE CF6-50C2 (52,500 lb thrust)
Series 40
P&W JT9D-20W (49,400 lb thrust)
P&W JT9D-59A (53,000 lb thrust)

Maximum Gross Weights
199,581 to 262,981 kg
(440,000 to 580,000 lb), depending on model

Maximum Payload
46,820 to 80,254 kg
(103,221 to 177,000 lb), depending on model

Passengers
0 to 380, depending on model

Cargo Space
Passenger—86.17 to 132.16 m³
(3,045 to 4,670 ft³); or
Cargo—413.18 to 500.91 m³
(14,600 to 17,700 ft³)

Operating Altitude
12,801 m (42,000 ft)

Cruise Speed
(All) 945 km/hr (510 kn)

Range (Typical mixed class)
Series 10   6,950 km (3,753 n mi)
Series 15   7,000 km (3,780 n mi)
Series 30   9,950 km (5,373 n mi)
Series 30F with 150,000-lb payload:
                 7,407 km (4,000 n mi)
Series 30F with 170,000-lb payload:
5,926 km (3,200 n mi)
Series 40   8,800 km (4,752 n mi)
Series 40   9,800 km (5,292 n mi)

Aircraft Dimensions
Length
Series 10, 15, and 40
55.55 m (182 ft., 3 in.)
Series 30 and 30F
55.35 m (181 ft, 7 in.)

Wing Span
Series 10 and 15
47.35 m (155 ft, 4 in.)
Series 30, 30F, and 40
50.39 m (165 ft, 4 in.)

Height
(All) 17.53 m (57 ft, 6 in.)

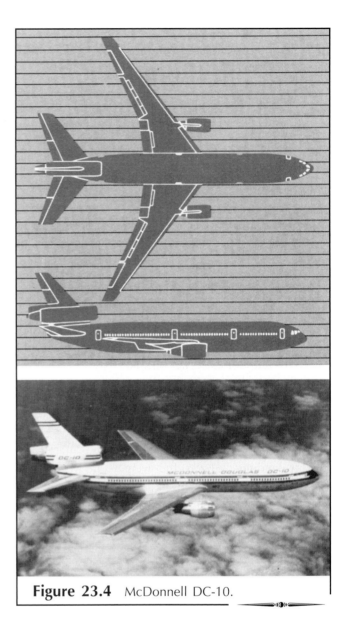

Figure 23.4   McDonnell DC-10.

THE MD-80

The MD-80 is a twin-jet commercial aircraft produced in five versions. Since its introduction in 1981, the versatile MD-80 family has become the fleet mainstay of airlines operating in 40 nations throughout the world.

Advanced Pratt & Whitney JT8D-200 engines and liberal use of sound-suppressing materials allow the MD-80 to meet the most stringent noise regulations. The Pratt & Whitney engines combined with a larger, more efficient wing make the MD-80's operating costs among the lowest in commercial aviation.

Four MD-80 models—the MD-81, MD-82, MD-83, and MD-88, are 147 feet, 10 inches long and accommodate a maximum of 172 passengers. The MD-87 is 130.4 feet in length, with a maximum passenger capacity of 139. Wingspan for all models is 107 feet, 10 inches. Douglas Aircraft Company assembles the MD-80 at Long Beach, California.

Technology advancements in the MD-80 include commercial aviation's first digital flight guidance system. Nonstop range is from 1,750 to 3,260 statute miles, depending on the model. The MD-81's maximum takeoff weight is 140,000 pounds; the MD-82's and the MD88's is 149,500 pounds. The longer range MD-83 has a takeoff weight of 160,000 pounds. The MD-87's maximum takeoff gross weight is 140,000 pounds, with an option to 149,500 pounds.

As of March 1, 1995, orders and other commitments for more than 1200 MD-80s had been received of which over 1,100 had been delivered.

Several factors have contributed to the great success of this program. The flexibility offered by the MD-81, MD-82, MD-83, MD-87, and the newest member of the family, the MD-88, provides a wide spectrum of passenger capacities and aircraft ranges. A high degree of fleet commonality contributes to airline cost savings by reducing training requirements and spare provisions. Thanks to wider seats and aisles, more room for carry-on luggage, a larger number of window and aisle seats, and quieter engines, surveys have consistently shown that passengers prefer to fly aboard MD-80s. Not of least importance is that the MD-80 family evolved from the mature DC-9 and therefore benefits from a proven design while incorporating the latest advances in modern technology.

The MD-83 affords the extra range necessary to perform longer flights in the comfort of five-abreast seating. The smaller MD-87 is well-suited to routes that have lower traffic demands or use shorter airfields. The MD-88 offers such technological advances as electronic flight instruments, a flight management system, and flat panel displays.

The first MD-80 was delivered on September 12, 1980, to Swissair. In little less than 7 years of service, the MD-80 family flew more than 1.1 billion statute miles while carrying more than 205 million passengers. During this time it achieved a near-perfect dispatch rate—98.5%—and proved itself to be the most reliable twin-jet aircraft ever built. What this meant to passengers was the virtual certainty of timely arrival. To airlines, it meant efficient, profitable operation.

The McDonnell Douglas MD-80 family of twin-engine jets helps solve the environmental and economic problems facing airline operators with a blend of new and mature technology, while continuing the highest standards of passenger comfort and efficient cargo transportation over short-to-medium-range routes.

The family includes five models—the MD-81, MD-82, MD-83, MD-87, and MD-88—which offer unmatched passenger appeal and operating reliability. The smaller MD-87 retains a high degree of commonality with the larger MD-80 series to provide a complementary fleet addition for routes of low traffic density.

The MD-88 offers the latest in advanced flight deck technology while retaining flight crew commonality with the basic MD-80.

An intensive program of continued engineering development and product improvement will keep the MD-80 family competitive with any aircraft in its class. Its basic configuration lends itself to incorporation of advanced high-bypass-ratio turbofans or ultra-high-bypass propulsion systems as these are developed. Other technology advances will be incorporated as dictated by market demand.

They have flown more than 20 million revenue hours since beginning service in 1980, covering over 7.7 billion miles, with more than 1.1 billion passengers.

The MD-80 is an advanced-technology successor to the popular DC-9 twin jet, of which 976 were delivered. In service with 82 operators, the worldwide DC-9 fleet provides jet service to 433 cities in 60 nations. Each day this fleet averages over 3,600 flights and carries two million passengers a week. DC-9s have flown more than 17 billion miles, logged over 47 million revenue hours of flight time, and transported 2.9 billion passengers since entering airline service in 1965.

As a result of the merger with Boeing in 1997, MD-80 production will end when current orders for the aircraft are filled.

McDONNELL DOUGLAS MD-80 TECHNICAL SPECIFICATIONS

	MD-81	MD-82/88	MD-83	MD-87
Crew		2, plus cabin attendants		
Capacity				
Passengers				
Typical, Economy	155	155	155	130
Maximum	172	172	172	139
Cargo Holds	1253 ft.³	1253 ft.³	1013 ft.³	937 ft.³
	35.5 m³	35.5 m³	28.7 m³	26.5 m³
Dimensions				
Wingspan	107.8 ft.	107.8 ft.	107.8 ft.	107.8 ft.
	32.8 m	32.8 m	32.8 m	32.8 m

Length Overall	147.8 ft.	147.8 ft.	147.8 ft.	130.4 ft.
	45.1 m	45.1 m	45.1 m	39.7 m
Height Overall	29.6 ft.	29.6 ft.	29.6 ft.	30.5 ft.
	9.05 m	9.05 m	9.05 m	9.3 m

Wing Area

Incl. Aileron	1,209 ft.^{2}	1,209 ft.^{2}	1,209 ft.^{2}	1,209 ft.^{2}
	112 m^2	112 m^2	112 m^2	112 m^2
Sweepback (¼ chord)	24.5°	24.5°	24.5°	24.5°

Landing Gear   Fully retractable tricycle; steerable nose wheel

Tread (Main Wheels)	16.7 ft.	16.7 ft.	16.7 ft.	16.7 ft.
	5.09 m	5.09 m	5.09 m	5.09 m
Wheel Base (Fore & Aft)	72.4 ft.	72.4 ft.	72.4 ft.	62.9 ft.
	22.07 m	22.07 m	22.07 m	19.18 m

Flaps   Double Slotted
Slats   Full span leading edge, 3-position
Speed Brake   Wing mounted spoilers
Reversers   Target, ground operation only
Engines   Two Pratt & Whitney Turbofans

Type	JT8D-209	JT8D-217A/C	JT8D-219	JT8D-217C
Thrust	18,500 lbs	20,000 lbs	21,000 lbs	20,000 lbs
	8,391 kg	9,072 kg	9,525 kg	9,072 kg
Static, sea level (Rev. thrust)	19,250 lbs	20,850 lbs	21,700 lbs	20,850 lbs
	8,731 kg	9,458 kg	9,843 kg	9,458 kg

Standard Delivery Data
Design Gross

Maximum Ramp Weight	141,000 lbs	150,500 lbs	161,000 lbs	141,000 lbs
	63,958 kg	68,267 kg	73,030 kg	63,958 kg
Maximum Takeoff Weight	140,000 lbs	149,500 lbs	160,000 lbs	140,000 lbs
	63,503 kg	67,813 kg	72,576 kg	63,503 kg
				149,500 lbs*
				67,813 kg*
Maximum Landing Weight	128,000 lbs	130,000 lbs	139,500 lbs	128,000 lbs
	58,060 kg	58,968 kg	63,277 kg	58,060 kg
Maximum Zero Fuel Weight	118,000 lbs	122,000 lbs	122,000 lbs	118,000 lbs
	53,524 kg	55,339 kg	55,339 kg	53,524 kg

Fuel Capacity

@ 6.7 lbs./gallon	5,840 gal	5,840 gal	7,000 gal	5,840 gal
	22,106 L	22,106 L	26,495 L	22,106 L
				7,000 gal*
				26,495 L*

Performance

Space Limited Payload	38,105 lbs	38,105 lbs	35,705 lbs	30,820 lbs
	17,284 kg	17,284 kg	16,196 kg	13,980 kg
Maximum Level Flight Speed	.76 M	.76 M	.76 M	.76 M
	504 mph	504 mph	504 mph	504 mph
	811 km/hr	811 km/hr	811 km/hr	811 km/hr
FAA Takeoff Field Length	7,250 ft	7,450 ft	8,375 ft	6,100 ft
(MTOW, S.L., Temp = 30°C)	2,210 m	2,271 m	2,553 m	1,859 m
FAA Landing Field Length	4,850 ft	4,920 ft	5,200 ft	4,690 ft
(MLW, S.L.)	1,478 m	1,500 m	1,585 m	1,430 m
Design Range (FAR Int'l				
reserves)	1,800 st mi**	2,360 st mi**	2,880 st mi**	2,730 st mi***
	1,565 n mi**	2,052 n mi**	2,504 n mi**	2,374 n mi***
	2,897 km**	3,798 km**	4,635 km**	4,395 km***

*With auxiliary fuel tanks.
**MD-81, -82, -83, -88 with 155 passengers and baggage.
***MD-87 with 130 passengers and baggage.

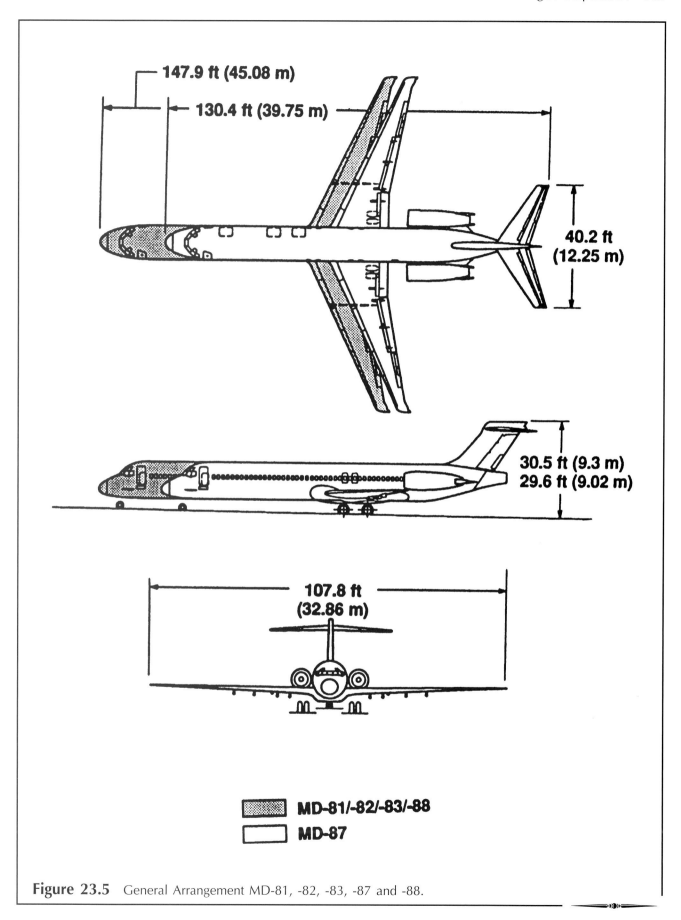

Figure 23.5 General Arrangement MD-81, -82, -83, -87 and -88.

McDONNELL DOUGLAS MD-90 BACKGROUND INFORMATION

The MD-90 series of twin jets is a family of advanced mid-size, medium-range airliners designed to serve the needs of travelers and the airlines in the 1990s and well into the 21st century. McDonnell Douglas launched the MD-90 program in November 1989. First flight of the MD-90 occurred on February 22, 1993, 3 days ahead of the original schedule. FAA certification occurred in late 1994. The first delivery was made to Delta Air Lines in February 1995.

The MD-90 was designed to be technically and economically competitive by incorporating many cost-effective technologies. It offers an advanced flight deck which includes an electronic flight instrument system (EFIS), a full-flight management system (FMS), a state-of-the-art inertial reference system, and LED dot-matrix displays for engine and system monitoring.

The MD-90 is powered by two International Aero Engines V2500 engines designed to be more fuel efficient as well as environmentally friendly by greatly reducing emission levels. The aircraft is the quietest large commercial jetliner in the skies.

The MD-90 retains the popular five-abreast interior arrangement, which offers travelers the best in comfort levels and the lowest interior noise levels of any aircraft in its class. The passenger-pleasing innovation has been a staple of all McDonnell Douglas twin jets, featuring wide seats, fewer center seats and more aisle and window seats.

Other features of the MD-90 include a new look advanced interior design, vacuum lavatories, a variable speed/constant frequency electrical power system, a new auxiliary power unit, an upgraded digital environmental control system, lightweight carbon brakes with digital anti-skid system, and significant improvements to the aircraft hydraulic system.

The MD-90 has an overall length of 152 feet, 7 inches and a wing span of 107 feet, 10 inches. The fuselage provides a cargo volume of 1,300 cubic feet. Long-range cruising speed is Mach 0.76, or approximately 500 mph.

The MD-90-30, with a maximum takeoff gross weight of 156,000 pounds, will carry 153 passengers in a typical mixed-class configuration. Range performance is approximately 2,400 statute miles.

With a takeoff thrust of 25,000 pounds, the MD-90-30's runway lengths are as short as 5,000 feet on a typical 550-statute-mile operation with a full passenger load. At the maximum takeoff gross weight, the MD-90-30 requires only 7,100 feet of runway. A 28,000-pound optional takeoff thrust rating is available for operators in need of special takeoff performance.

Other models of the MD-90 family being considered are the MD-90-50 and the MD-90-55, also powered by the V2500 engine. The MD-90-50 is the extended range variant of the MD-90-30, with a takeoff gross weight of 172,500 pounds and additional fuel. This allows the MD-90-50 to carry 153 passengers over a distance of 3,205 statute miles. The MD-90-55 features additional emergency exits, permitting high density charter configurations of up to 187 passengers.

The MD-90 family is being built on the same assembly line in Long Beach, California, as the current MD-80 jetliners.

Development of a novel modular concept for production of major fuselage sections is the key to operating the joint assembly line. MD-80 and MD-90 fuselages will be built as major subassemblies and introduced as modules on the assembly line.

In addition to providing a more efficient production line to reduce costs and lead times, the new modular approach offers the flexibility to assure incorporation of new technologies and innovations to satisfy customer needs. This procedure will improve the assembly process as well as the quality of MD-80s and MD-90s. The technique will be used throughout the production life of new twin jet series to keep MD-90s fully modern, cost-effective, competitive leaders in the air transport industry for many years to come.

After the merger with Boeing in 1997, MD-90 production will cease when outstanding orders for the aircraft are completed.

McDONNELL DOUGLAS MD-90 TECHNICAL SPECIFICATIONS

		MD-90-30	MD-90-50
Crew		Two plus cabin attendants	
Capacity			
Passengers			
Typical, Mixed Class		153	153
Maximum		172	172
Cargo holds		1,300 ft³	822 ft³*
		36.8 m³	23.3 m³*
Space Limited Payload		38,250 lb	33,500 lb
		17,350 kg	15,195 kg
Dimensions			
Wingspan		107.8 ft	107.8 ft
		32.87 m	32.87 m
Length overall		152.6 ft	152.6 ft
		46.5 m	46.5 m
Height overall		30.6 ft	30.6 ft
		9.4 m	9.4 m
Wing area		1,209 ft²	1,209 ft²
		112 m²	112 m²
Sweep Back at 25% chord		24.5°	24.5°
Landing Gear			
Type		Fully retractable tricycle, steerable nose wheel	
Tread of main wheels		16.7 ft	16.7 ft
		5.09 m	5.09 m
Wheel base—fore & aft		77.2 ft	77.2 ft
		23.52 m	23.52 m
Flaps	Type	Double slotted	
Slats	Type	Full span leading edge, three-position	
Speed Brake	Type	Wing mounted spoilers	
Reversers	Type	Cascade, ground operation only	
Engines	Type	Two International Aero Engines	
Takeoff thrust		V2525-D5	V2528-D5
Static, Sea Level @ 86°F		25,000 lb	28,000 lb
Standard Delivery Data			
Design Gross			
Max Ramp		157,000 lb	173,500 lb
		71,214 kg	78,698 kg
Max Takeoff		156,000 lb	172,500 lb
		70,760 kg	78,245 kg
Max Landing		142,000 lb	150,000 lb
		64,410 kg	68,039 kg
Max Zero Fuel		130,000 lb	135,000 lb

*With optional 1,780 gallon auxiliary fuel tanks installed.

	58,967 kg	61,239 kg
Operators Empty Weight	88,000 lb	91,900 lb
	39,916 kg	41,685 kg

Fuel Capacity

| @ 6.7 lb/gal | 5,840 gal | 7,620 gal |
| | 22,104 L | 28,845 L |

Performance

Cruise Speed	0.76M, 438 n mi/hr,	
(35,000 ft. ISA standard day)	504 st. mi/hr, 812 km/hr	
Design Range (international reserves)	2,400 st. mi	3,205 st. mi
	2,070 n. mi	2,775 n. mi
	3,820 km	5,130 km
FAA Takeoff Field Length	7,105 ft	7,990 ft
at MTOGW, SL Std Day	2,165 m	2,435 m
FAA Landing Field Length	5,250 ft	5,480 ft
at MLW, SL Std Day	1,600 m	1,670 m

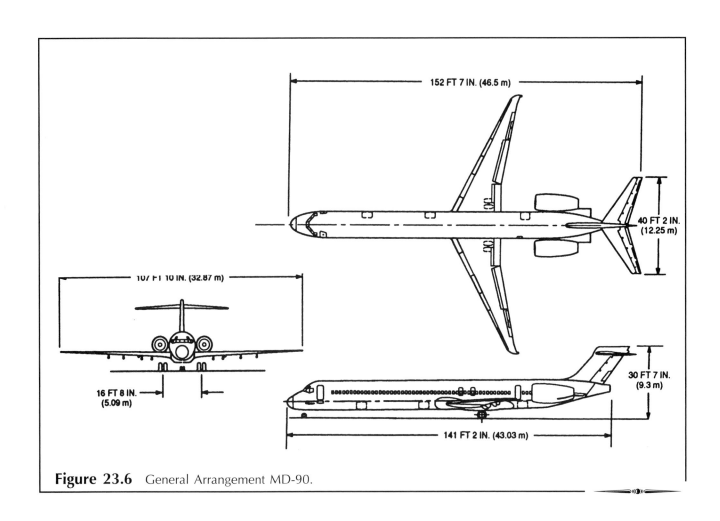

Figure 23.6 General Arrangement MD-90.

McDONNELL DOUGLAS MD-11 BACKGROUND INFORMATION

The MD-11, aviation's largest wide-cabin trijet, is in service with customers in all parts of the world. It is produced in Long Beach, Calif., at the Douglas Aircraft Company division of McDonnell Douglas. A world-wide network of subcontractors and suppliers supports the assembly line.

The MD-11 is available in four models—passenger, all freighter, convertible freighter and "combi," where passengers and freight are carried on the main deck with additional freight carried below the deck. An extended range (ER) feature is available on all versions. A wide variety of interior configurations is available. Seating capacities on the standard airplane vary from 233 in a three-class arrangement to 410 in an all-economy setup. Below the main deck, the MD-11 provides more space for containerized or palletized cargo after passenger bags are loaded than any other airliner, yielding important additional revenue for its operators.

Advances in aerodynamics, propulsion, aircraft systems, cockpit avionics and interior design contribute to the performance and operating economy of all MD-11 models. Aerodynamic improvements include winglets and a redesigned wing trailing edge, a smaller horizontal tail with integral fuel tanks and an extended tail cone. These features reduce drag, save fuel and add range.

The nonstop range of the MD-11 equipped with an auxiliary fuel tank and operating at a maximum takeoff gross weight of 630,500 pounds is approximately 8,300 statute miles with 298 passengers and their bags.

Three engines—General Electric CF6-80C2, Pratt & Whitney 4460, and Pratt & Whitney 4462—are offered to power the MD-11, providing maximum efficiency in their thrust class.

The advanced flight deck features six cathode ray tube displays, digital instrumentation, wind-shear detection and guidance devices, a dual flight management system that helps conserve fuel and a dual digital automatic flight control system (autopilot) with fail operational capability. Computerized system controllers perform automated normal, abnormal and emergency checklist duties for the MD-11's major systems, reducing flight crew requirements from three to two persons.

The MD-11 was launched on Dec. 30, 1986. Assembly of the first unit began March 9, 1988. First flight was on Jan. 10, 1990. Certification occurred Nov. 8, 1990, followed by the first delivery on Dec. 7. For comparison, the MD-11 is 200 feet 10 inches long, 18.6 feet longer than the earlier McDonnell Douglas DC-10 trijet, and carries about 50 more passengers.

As of March 31, 1995, 133 MD-11's had been delivered, and the aircraft was in service with 19 operators. The aircraft are serving more than 100 cities in 54 countries with more than 200 scheduled daily flights. The fleet had compiled a record of nearly 1.2 million revenue flight hours, covering more than 585 million statute miles and carrying over 30 million passengers.

Following the Boeing merger in 1997, it was decided that the MD-11 production will continue depending upon selling enough aircraft to maintain sustained production at an economically feasible rate.

McDONNELL DOUGLAS MD-11 TECHNICAL SPECIFICATIONS— 1996 LEVEL

	Passenger	Freighter	Combi
Capacity			
Passengers	233–410	—	181–214
Cargo Holds			
Main deck	—	17,072/ft.^{3}	6 pallets[a]
	—	473 m^3	
Lower deck[b]	6,850/ft^3	6,850 ft^3	6,850 ft^3
	194 m^3	194 m^3	194 m^3
Dimensions			
Wingspan	169.5 ft	169.5 ft	169.5 ft
	51.7 m	51.7 m	51.7 m
Length Overall	200.8 ft	200.8 ft	200.8 ft
	61.2 m	61.2 m	61.2 m

Height Overall	57.8 ft	57.8 ft	57.8 ft
	17.6 m	17.6 m	17.6 m
Wing Area			
Incl. Aileron	3,648 ft^2	3,648 ft^2	3,648 ft^2
	339 m^2	339 m^2	339 m^2
Sweepback ($^1/_4$ Chord)	35°	35°	35°
Landing Gear			
Tread (Main Wheels)	34.7 ft	34.7 ft	34.7 ft
	10.6 m	10.6 m	10.6 m
Wheel Base (Fore & Aft)	80.8 ft	80.8 ft	80.8 ft
	24.6 m	24.6 m	24.6 m

Engines (3)

Type/Thrust Pratt & Whitney PW4460/60,000 lb (PW4462/62,000 lb optional)
or General Electric CF6-80C2/61,500 lb

Delivery Data

Design Gross

Maximum Takeoff Weight[c]	630,500 lb	630,500 lb	630,500 lb
	285,990 kg	285,990 kg	285,990 kg
Maximum Landing Weight	430,000 lb	481,500 lb[d]	458,000 lb
	195,045 kg	218,405 kg[d]	207,745 kg
Maximum Zero Fuel Weight	400,000 lb	451,300 lb	430,000 lb
	181,437 kg	204,706 kg	195,045 kg
Operator's Empty Weight	285,900 lb	249,200 lb	285,100 lb
	129,683 kg	113,036 kg	129,320 kg
Fuel Capacity (Volume)	38,615 Gal	38,615 Gal	38,615 Gal
	146,174 L	146,174 L	146,174 L
Fuel Capacity (Weight)	258,721 lb	258,721 lb	258,721 lb
	117,354 kg	117,354 kg	117,354 kg

Performance

Weight Limited Payload	114,100 lb	202,100 lb[e]	144,900 lb
	51,764 kg	91,670 kg[e]	65,725 kg
Maximum Level Flight Speed	588 mph/M87	588 mph/M87	588 mph/M87
(31,000 ft.)	945 km/hr	945 km/hr	945 km/hr
FAA Takeoff Field Length[f]	10,450 ft	10,450 ft	10,450 ft
(MTOW, S.L., @ 30°C)	3,115 m	3,115 m	3,115 m
FAA Landing Field Length	6,950 ft.	7,620 ft	7,330 ft
(MLW, S.L.)	2,118 m.	2,323 m	2,234 m
Design Range	7,871 st mi[g]	4,546 st mi[h]	7,733 st mi[i]
(FAR Int'l reserves)	6,840 n mi[g]	3,950 n mi[h]	6,720 n mi[i]
	12,668 km[g]	7,315 kin[h]	12,445 kin[i]
	8,343 st mi[g,j]	—	6,145 st mi[k]
	7,250 n mi[g,j]	—	5,350 n mi[k]
	13,427 km[g,i,j]	—	9,890 km[k]

a. Pallet dimensions: 88" x 125" (223 cm x 318 cm) or 96" x 125" (244 cm x 318 cm).
b. Bulk capacity. Containerized capacity is 32 LD3 containers, or 5566 ft^3 (517 m^3).
c. Optional takeoff weight (standard = 602,500 lb).
d. Optional landing weight (standard = 471,500 lb).
e. Including Tare Weight.
f. Takeoff with optional PW4462 engine with 62,000 lb thrust.
g. 298 passengers with bags, 3-class.
h. Weight limited payload.
i. 183 passengers with bags. 3 class plus 6 main deck pallets of freight.
j. 3,000 US gallon supplemental fuel tank.
k. Space limited payload with 183 passengers.

McDONNELL DOUGLAS MD-11 COMBI, FREIGHTER AND CONVERTIBLE FREIGHTER

BACKGROUND INFORMATION

The advanced MD-11 wide-cabin, three-engine jetliner family being produced by Douglas Aircraft Company includes four models—passenger, combi, all freighter and convertible freighter.

The MD-11 family in all of its versions provides operators worldwide with an economically attractive alternative to four-engine wide-cabin aircraft. Compared to the B747, MD-11 advantages include: lower cost of acquisition; extended intercontinental nonstop range; 29% lower fuel per trip at equivalent seats; increased flexibility for mixed passenger/cargo configurations; equivalent unrestricted overwater operation; and 28% more below-deck revenue pallet or container cargo capacity.

MD-11 COMBI

The MD-11 combi offers outstanding passenger/cargo flexibility. Its overall specifications—wingspan, length, fuel capacity, service doors—are the same as the standard MD-11 passenger version. As a result, the combi can be handled at the same gates and with basically the same ground service equipment as a regular passenger aircraft.

One reason for the MD-11 combi's interior flexibility is the fact that galleys and lavatories can be moved in one-inch increments on the seat tracks. Modular lavatories, galleys and overhead stowage bins, together with a redesigned air conditioning system and a vacuum waste system, accommodate a wide range of configurations.

The MD-11 combi incorporates a newly designed 160-inch wide by 102-inch high main deck cargo door at the rear fuselage. The 160-inch width enables the combi to handle 20-foot long containers.

The combi can be operated in a three-class passenger arrangement together with cargo space for four, six, eight or ten pallets on the upper deck plus containerized and bulk volume of 5,566 cubic feet on the lower deck (including the passengers' baggage).

For the six-pallet arrangement, the combi can be configured for first, business, and economy class passengers, plus 3,340–3,586 cubic feet of cargo on the main deck.

With eight pallets, comparable figures are first, business and economy passengers, plus 4,453–4,781 cubic feet of cargo on the main deck. A three-class arrangement, with four, six, eight or ten pallets on the main deck, carries approximately 150 to 250 passengers. The combi may also be operated as a passenger airplane with no main deck pallets.

Although range varies as a factor of total gross takeoff weight, at a takeoff weight of 630,500 pounds, the MD-11 combi has a range of 7,733 statute miles with 183 passengers and six pallets on the main deck. The MD-11 combi was the first combi transport to meet the FAA's stringent Class C fire and smoke containment requirements in the cargo section.

MD-11 FREIGHTER

McDonnell Douglas has applied its extensive DC-8, DC-10 and KC-10 freighter experience to the design of the MD-11 freighter. In addition to the aerodynamics, cockpit and power plant advances of the basic MD-11, the freighter version also offers higher structural weights, permitting increased cargo payload.

The all-freight MD-11 provides the capacity for 202,100-pound gross payloads and has a 99-inch maximum stack height. Its cargo door, located in the forward fuselage, is 140 inches wide by 102 inches high.

With air cargo needs expected to double by the year 2005, the new MD-11 freighter offers operators superior capacity. The freighter's main cabin will hold up to 17,072 cubic feet of palletized cargo. Its lower compartments will hold an additional 5,566 cubic feet of bulk cargo. All standard industry containers can be accommodated side-by-side in the lower deck.

MD-11 CONVERTIBLE FREIGHTER

The MD-11CF is the newest, most versatile long-haul commercial aircraft available today. It is the only advanced aircraft that provides airlines with the ability to operate in all-passenger or all-freighter configurations.

This conversion capability allows operators to adapt readily to seasonal needs, such as flying passengers in the summer and freight in the winter. Also, it provides them with the capability to respond quickly to airlift requirements resulting from unique world events. Features built into the aircraft allow the operator to convert from passenger to freighter configuration in two days, and from freighter to passenger in three days.

In the freighter mode, the MD-11CF can carry 196,928 pounds of cargo up to a 4,546-statute-mile

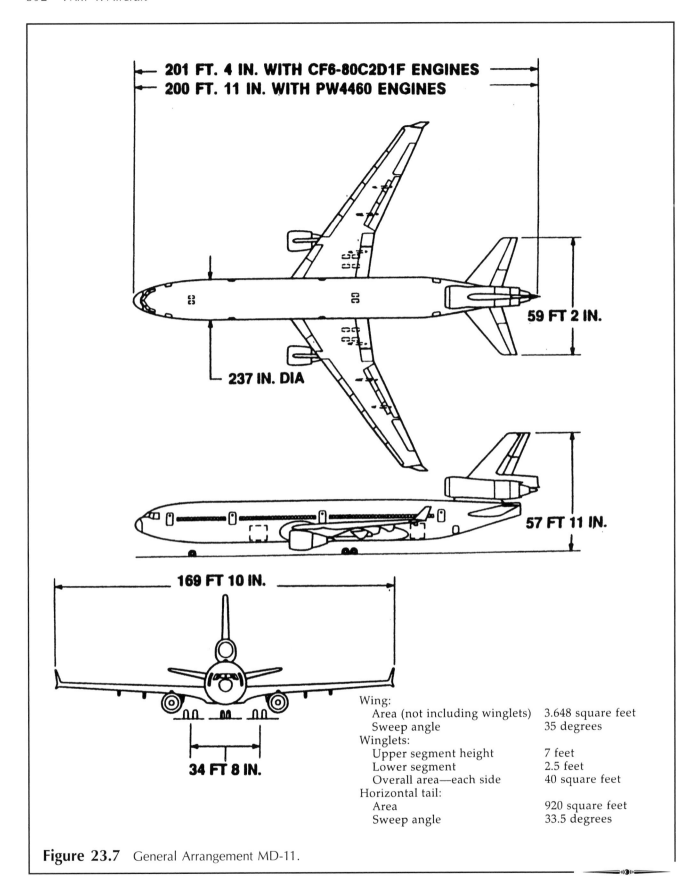

201 FT. 4 IN. WITH CF6-80C2D1F ENGINES
200 FT. 11 IN. WITH PW4460 ENGINES

59 FT 2 IN.

237 IN. DIA

57 FT 11 IN.

169 FT 10 IN.

34 FT 8 IN.

Wing:
   Area (not including winglets)   3.648 square feet
   Sweep angle   35 degrees
Winglets:
   Upper segment height   7 feet
   Lower segment   2.5 feet
   Overall area—each side   40 square feet
Horizontal tail:
   Area   920 square feet
   Sweep angle   33.5 degrees

Figure 23.7   General Arrangement MD-11.

range. The upper deck has 14,508 cubic feet—based on 96-inch pallets—of space available for all sizes of cargo. Another 5,566 cubic feet is available on the lower deck of bulk cargo for a total of more than 20,000 cubic feet.

With the large forward cargo door measuring 140-by-102 inches, the MD-11CF has the flexibility to load either 88- or 96-by-125-inch pallets as well as 10-foot M-1C containers. The stack height is 90.25 inches. The main deck has space for 26 pallets/containers, while the lower deck has room for another 10 pallets or 32 containers.

MD-95

The production of the MD-95 will continue but it has been renumbered the B 717-200 after the merger with Boeing. (Refer to Chapter 22.)

CHAPTER 24

The Lockheed Martin Corporation

In the early 1900s there were three brothers from California named Loughead, Victor and his half brothers Alan and Malcolm. Their name was pronounced Lockheed so they later changed it to that spelling. They said they got tired of hearing it pronounced Loghead. Victor was working in Chicago as an automotive engineer. He helped younger Alan find a job as an automobile mechanic. Alan became interested in aviation and when he returned to San Francisco in 1911, he was a pilot. He understood aircraft design and planned to build an airplane with his brother Malcolm, also an automobile mechanic. They obtained financial support and in 1912 formed their Alco-Hydro Aeroplane Company.

Their design was for a biplane having midwing ailerons. Instead of a conventional rudder and elevator the entire tail assembly moved. The center float gear was built like a sled; on the lower wings were outrigger floats. The airplane was powered by an eighty horsepower water cooled Curtis V-8 engine located in the front of the craft. Alan first flew it on June 15, 1913. He then landed to pick up Malcolm and they flew for twenty minutes over Alcatraz, Angel Island in the bay, and over Nob Hill and Market Street in San Francisco, at a speed of 60 mph.

They decided to use their new aircraft to ferry passengers around the Bay Area for the Panama-Pacific Exposition. For 50 days they carried 600 passengers, at $10.00 each, for a 10 minute ride. This venture netted them $4,000, with which they decided to build another large airplane. They financed their own company and named it the Loughead Aircraft Manufacturing Company and moved to Santa Barbara in 1918.

Their new airplane was a ten passenger twin-engine flying boat and one of the largest seaplanes in the world. It was made of wood and fabric having an upper wing span of 74 feet and a lower wing of 47 feet with pontoons at each tip. The 160 horsepower Hall-Scott water-cooled engines were placed between the wings on each side of the hull.

During the building of this aircraft they hired a twenty-year-old architectural draftsman and auto mechanic. He redesigned the upper wing structure and thus began the career of John K. Northrop.

After World War I they decided to produce a small, inexpensive, single engine, 25 horsepower, water-cooled Sport Biplane. It weighed 800 pounds fully loaded and would fly for an hour on one gallon of fuel. Northrop designed a speed break system for it that would allow for short landings; he got the idea from watching seagulls land. The entire lower wing could be moved almost perpendicular to the airflow during landing, thus creating a huge landing flap. The wings could be folded for storage.

Although an excellent aircraft, timing was against it. In the early 1920s there were surplus World War I aircraft that could be purchased for a small price when compared to the new modern Sport Biplane. The lack of sales forced the company to go out of business in 1921. Malcolm moved to Detroit where he designed a successful hydraulic automobile brake.

In 1926, Alan Loughead formed a new company and Northrop rejoined him as chief engineer. They built an entirely new airplane with many new features. It was an enclosed cockpit and full cantilevered wing. It was named the Vega and set many records flown by the most famous pilots of the era. From this design evolved many successors.

Figure 24.1   The Loughead (Lockheed) Brothers.

In 1929, Northrop left Loughead to start his own company. Alan sold his interest in the company to the Detroit Aircraft Company. The Loughead Aircraft Corporation was organized in 1932 but the stock market crash and the Depression caused the company to cease operating.

The new owners of Lockheed Aircraft Corporation risked their limited funds to develop an all-metal twin-engine transport—the Model 10 Electra. It first flew in 1934 and quickly gained international fame. Following came the Model 12 and Model 14 Electras.

With Europe near war in 1938, Lockheed won a huge order from Britain to build the rugged Hudson bomber—converted from the Model 14 Electra commercial transport—and ultimately delivered 3,000 to the United Kingdom, the U.S., and Allied nations. From the Lockheed plants during World War II, more than 19,000 military aircraft poured out—Hudson bombers, P-38 Lightning fighters, PV-1 Ventura and PV-2 Harpoon antisubmarine planes, Lodestar and Constellation transports, and the Boeing-designed B-17 Flying Fortress—to help smash Nazi-Fascist Axis Forces.

Near the end of World War II, the development of the P-80 (later F-80) Shooting Star, first U.S. operational jet fighter, ushered in the jet age.

After World War II, the graceful Constellation assumed the role it was originally intended to have—a commercial airliner—and became a global Lockheed symbol. In 15 years, some 35 airlines bought 500 Connies in various versions. "Queen of the skies," the Connie advanced air travel to new heights of luxury, speed, and operating efficiency during that era. Other Constellations continued in military service as patrol planes, early warning aircraft, and cargo transports.

In the late 1940s came the P-2 Neptune antisubmarine patrol plane, T-33 T-Bird jet trainer, and the F-94 Starfire jet fighter.

Lockheed's expansion and growth stepped up rapidly in the 1950s with the establishment of a number of new operating divisions: Lockheed-Georgia (1951), Lockheed Missiles & Space (1954), Lockheed Electronics (1959), and Lockheed Shipbuilding and Construction (1959). The original company at Burbank became the Lockheed-California Company. Earlier, Lockheed Air Terminal was formed in 1949, and Lockheed Aircraft Service became a separate division in 1946 (LAS actually began in 1938 as Lockheed's customer service department; it is the oldest aircraft maintenance and modification firm in the U.S.).

Also starting in the mid-1950s was one of the greatest international cooperative ventures in the history of aviation: the Lockheed F-104 Starfighter program in which seven nations on three continents built more than 2,500 of these supersonic fighter aircraft.

Three other Lockheed aircraft born in the 1950s were the T2V SeaStar jet trainer, the L-188 Electra propjet transport, and the 500-mph (800-kph) JetStar I executive transport.

Among the current Lockheed aircraft in recent or present production are the: C-130 and L-100 Hercules propjet cargo carriers (both older and new versions); C-141 StarLifter and C-5 Galaxy (world's largest aircraft) jet transports; L-1011 TriStar jetliner; P-3 Orion and S-3 Viking antisubmarine warfare aircraft; SR-71 strategic reconnaissance aircraft; the U-2 research and reconnaissance aircraft (new version slated); and the JetStar II business transport.

The company is not presently producing transport aircraft for commercial air carrier use.

The stockholders of the Lockheed Corporation and the Martin Marietta Corporation agreed to a merger on March 15, 1995. This resulted in the newest and largest aerospace/defense industry contractor.

L-1011 TRISTAR

Lockheed-California Company's L-1011 TriStar series of jetliners is a family of advanced-technology, wide-bodied commercial transports with a broad range of design options developed to meet airline traffic demands through the rest of the 20th Century.

The L-1011 first flew November 16, 1970, and received its type certificate from U.S. Federal Aviation Administration on April 14, 1972.

The L-1011 has also been officially recognized by the FAA as the quietest of the widebodied jetliners. Powered by three Rolls-Royce RB.211 series engines, the TriStar is from 60 to 75% quieter to the human ear than narrowbodied, four-engine jets, and from 30 to 50% quieter than the small two- and three-engine jetliners.

The Rolls-Royce RB.211-22B engine is a high-bypass-ratio turbofan, rated at 42,000 lbs. of maximum takeoff thrust. Inherent in its design is the capability to produce higher thrust. Through recent advances in RB.211 technology, Rolls-Royce is currently producing a new 50,000-lb.-thrust version, the RB.211-524B.

The Lockheed L-1011 is a three-engine, widebody airliner capable of carrying 240–400 passengers 3,200–6,100 nautical miles.

Lockheed began production on an initial batch of some 300 units, with approximately 45% of the total structure and 65% of the overall aircraft being built by subcontractors. The program was financed through a $400 million line of credit set up with a network of 24 banks, a portion of a $125 billion convertible debenture issue, about $150 million in progress payments from

Specifications

	L-1011-1/-100	L-1011-200	L-1011-500
Length:	177.8ft(54.2m)	177.8ft(54.2m)	164.3ft(50.1m)
Height:	55.3ft(16.9m)	55.3ft(16.9m)	55.3ft(16.9m)
Wing span:	155.3ft(47.3m)	155.3ft(47.3m)	155.3ft(47.3m)
Wing area:	3,456ft^2(320.0m^2)	3,456ft^2(320.0m^2)	—
Cabin length:	135.9ft(41.4m)	135.9ft(41.4m)	—
Cabin width:	18.9ft(5.8m)	18.9ft(5.8m)	—
Cabin height:	7.9ft(2.4m)	7.9ft(2.4m)	—
Cabin volume:	16,000ft^3(453m^3)	16,000ft^3(453m^3)	—
Seating capacity:	256 passengers (mixed class)	256 passengers (mixed class)	256 passengers (mixed class)
Fuel capacity:	23,814 gal (90,140 L)	26,502 gal (100,317 L)	31,642 gal (119,774 L)
Baggage capacity:	3,900ft^3 (110.4m^3)	3,900ft^3 (110.4m^3)	4,200ft^3 (118.9m^3)
Empty Weight:	240,400lbs (109,045kg)[a]	245,800lbs (111,495kg)[b]	240,963lbs (109,298kg)
Gross weight:	430,000lbs (195,045kg)[c]	477,000lbs (216,363kg)	496,000lbs (224,980)[d]
Service ceiling:	42,000ft (12,800m)	42,000ft (12,800m)	42,000ft (12,800m)
Takeoff distance:	7,960ft (2,426m)[e]	8,070ft (2,460m)[f]	9,760ft (2,975m)
Landing distance:	5,690ft (1,734m)	5,800ft (1,768m)[g]	6,420ft (1,957m)
Maximum cruise speed:	599 mph; 520kts[h]; 964km/hr	610mph; 530kts; 982km/hr	605mph; 525kts; 973km/hr[i]
Range:	3,305 miles (5,319km)[j]	4,238 miles (6,820km)[k]	5,998 miles (9,653km)

[a]Empty weight of L-1011-1. Empty weight of L-1011-100 is 244,100 lbs (110,720kg).

[b]Empty weight of L-1011-200. Empty weight of L-1011-250 is 249,054 lbs (112,969kg).

[c]Gross weight of L-1011-1. Gross weight of L-1011-100 is 466,000 lbs (211,375kg).

[d]Gross weight of L-1011-250 also.

[e]T-O distance of L-1011-1. T-O distance of L-1011-100s is 10,640 ft (3,243 m)

[f]T-O distance of L-1011-200. T-O distance of L-1011-250 is 9,310 ft (2,838 m)

[g]Landing distance for L-1011-100/-200/-50 also.

[h]Max speed for L-1011-1. Max cruise for L-1011-100 is 515 kts.

[i]Max speed for L-1011-250 also.

[j]Range of L-1011-1. Range of L-1011-100 is 4,215 miles.

[k]Range of L-1011-200. Range of L-1011-250 is 5,205 miles.

customers, financial assistance from subcontractors, and retained earnings from other programs.

On May 6, 1971, the Administration announced its intention to ask Congress for $250 million to guarantee loans for Lockheed. This came just one day after Eastern Air Lines reaffirmed its order for 50 L-1011s by signing a conditional agreement. Further setting the stage for a Congressional struggle, the British Government, on May 10, approved $240 million for development of the RB.211. Lockheed's loan guarantee legislation squeaked through Congress by a narrow 192–189 margin on August 2 after much heated debate. Lockheed signed new agreements with its banks, its L-1011 customers, and the U.S. government on September 14, 1971.

The L-1011-500 seats 246 passengers in the standard configuration and costs about $40 million. The aircraft was aimed at a developing requirement for transport to fly long thin routes in the 1980s. The L-1011-500 is designed to replace early long-range 707s and DC-8s which are approaching retirement age, are not in compliance with new noise regulations, and are becoming less efficient to operate.

A second major order for the L-1011-500 came in April 1978 when Pan American ordered 12 aircraft and took options on another 14. The deal was valued at $500 million to Lockheed.

In April 1979, Lockheed received FAA type certification for the L-1011-500. Certification by Britain's Civil Aviation Authority (CAA) followed shortly after issuance of the US air-worthiness certificate. Initial deliveries occurred at the end of April, and Lockheed delivered four long-range Tristars to British Airways and two to Delta by the end of 1979.

The fatal crash of an American Airlines DC-10 in May 1979 and the subsequent removal of the aircraft's airworthiness certificate sparked a controversy surrounding the safety of the L-1011's direct competitor, the DC-10. McDonnell Douglas had been enjoying a larger share of the three-engine, medium-long-range airliner market than Lockheed. While Lockheed has not been able to convert any DC-10 users to the L-1011 since most airlines cannot affect major changes in their fleets on short notice, the L-1011 may have gained an edge over the DC-10 in sales to new customers because of the DC-10's tarnished image.

The TriStar family is one of the most versatile commercial transport series ever built, offering economical performance from short- to long-range airline routes. The basic L-1011 aircraft is 177 ft. 8 in. long, with a wing span of 155 ft. 4 in. This version has a maximum gross takeoff weight of 430,000 lbs. and can carry 225 to 400 passengers and cargo over distances of 3,400 statute mi.

Well established for its dependability, quiet operation, advanced features, and passenger comfort, the versatile L-1011 family consists of four versions currently in production:

L-1011-1—Powered by three Rolls-Royce RB.211-22B engines, each rated at 42,000 lbs. (187,000 Newtons) of thrust, the basic L-1011 is designed to carry 225 to 400 passengers and cargo over distances up to 3,400 statute mi. With an overall length of 177 ft. 8 in. and a wing span of 155 ft. 4 in., this version has a maximum gross takeoff weight of 430,000 lbs. The newest Dash One operator is AeroPeru which initiated the first L-1011 service in Latin America in December 1978. Other airlines operating the Dash One include Air Canada, All Nippon Airways, British Airways, Delta Air Lines, Eastern Air Lines, LTU (Federal Republic of Germany), and Trans World Airlines This model has been in service since 1972.

L-1011-100—Utilizing the same airframe and engines as the Dash One, this version carries an additional 18,800 lbs. of fuel, giving it a maximum range of 4,200 statute mi. The Dash 100, in service since 1975, has a maximum gross takeoff weight of 466,000 lbs., an increase of 36,000 lbs. over the basic version.

L-1011-200—The only major difference between this derivative and the Dash 100 is in the propulsion system. Utilizing Rolls-Royce RB.211-524B engines rated at 50,000 lbs. (222,000 Newtons) of thrust, this model is designed for distances up to 4,450 statute mi. This higher-thrust engine provides significantly improved high-altitude takeoff performance, particularly on hot days, and has the same specific fuel consumption at cruise conditions as the basic model. Saudi Arabian Airlines, British Airways, and Delta now operate the Dash 200, and Gulf Air has the model on order. It began service in 1977.

L-1011-500—With a fuselage 13.5 ft. shorter than other L-1011 models, the Dash 500 can carry up to 330 passengers. This newest and longest-range member of the L-1011 family, fitted with the same engines as the Dash 200, is designed to replace aging 707 and DC-8-type aircraft used in relatively low-traffic-density, long-haul markets. With fuel capacity increased to 212,000 lbs., this aircraft can fly up to 6,000 statute mi. nonstop. Maximum gross takeoff weight is increased to 496,000 lbs.

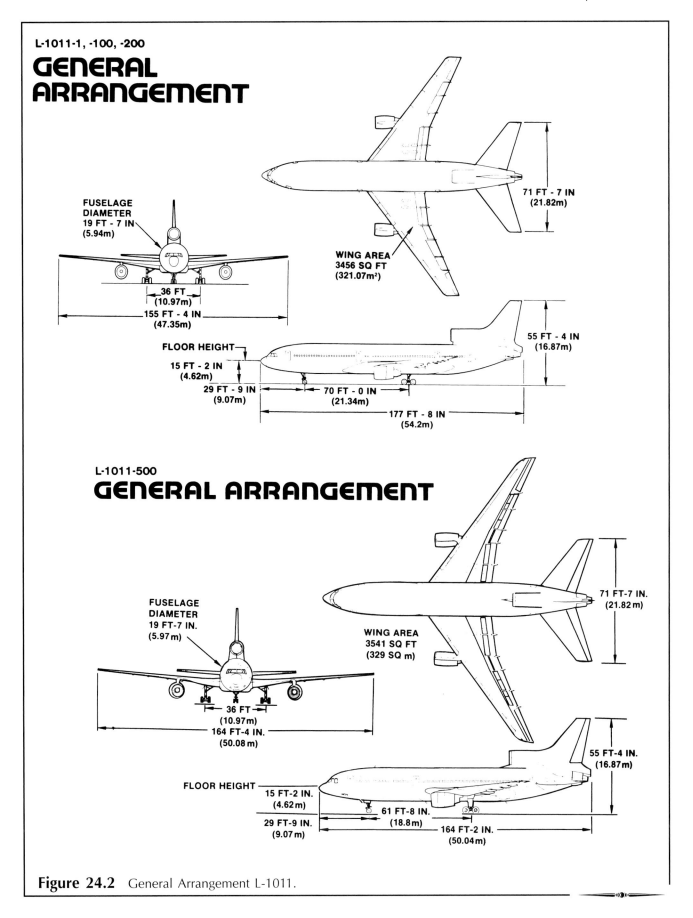

Figure 24.2 General Arrangement L-1011.

THE SKUNK WORKS*

Lockheed's Skunk Works has been a success story in innovation since 1943. The organization has produced a series of technologically advanced aircraft and systems for combat, transport, reconnaissance and research for the U.S. armed forces, intelligence agencies and NASA.

The Skunk Works name came from Al Capp's "Li'l Abner" comic strip, which featured the "Skonk works" where Appalachian hillbillies ground up skunks, old shoes, and other foul-smelling ingredients to brew fearsome drinks and other products. Lockheed engineers identified the secret XP-80 assembly tent, which was also across the street from a malodorous plastics factory, as the place where Kelly was stirring up some kind of potent brew. The nickname stuck, although "skonk" became "skunk" in deference to the non-hillbillies working at the Lockheed facility and because Al Capp objected to anyone else using his unique spelling. Cartoonist Capp and the "Li'l Abner" comic strip departed many years ago, but the Skunk Works—a registered service mark of Lockheed along with the familiar skunk logo—lives on as LADC continues to "brew" the world's most potent aircraft.

The Skunk Works was formally called Advanced Development Projects (ADP) and was a super secret part of the larger Lockheed-California Company. In January 1991 ADP became its own company, the Lockheed Advanced Development Company (LADC).

Although initially shrouded in secrecy, many of the aircraft developed in the Skunk Works have become aviation legends. The Shooting Star was the first aircraft to win an all-jet battle when it downed a Soviet-built MiG-15 during the Korean War. The U-2, operating at more than 70,000 feet is still the world's highest altitude single-engine jet. The record-setting F-104 StarFighter was the first double-sonic aircraft. The SR-71 Blackbird, which initially flew in 1964, still holds the world aircraft marks for speed (more than 2,200 miles per hour) and altitude (85,000 feet-plus). The F-117A Stealth Fighter, the first operational fighter aircraft designed for low observability, won the 1989 Collier Trophy for the Lockheed-Air Force Team.

The Skunk Works began in July 1943 when the U.S. Army Air Corps asked Lockheed to design a fighter around a British deHavilland jet engine in the wake of disturbing news that the Nazis had flown their own swift jet fighter in the skies over Europe. Under an agreement negotiated by Kelly Johnson, the company was to deliver a prototype aircraft within 180 days. Supported by Lockheed President Robert E. Gross, Johnson pirated personnel from other projects, forged a team of 23 engineers and 103 shop mechanics and went to work in a small assembly tent near the Lockheed wind tunnel at Burbank. The Skunk Works completed the prototype XP-80—dubbed Lulu-Belle—in 143 days, 37 days under schedule. The aircraft made its first flight on January 8, 1944, at Muroc Dry Lake (now Edwards Air Force Base), Calif. The XP-80 was the forerunner of the F-80 Shooting Star, America's first operational jet fighter.

Lockheed Advanced Development Company is prepared to satisfy any national need requiring prototyping or specialized technology to produce a rapidly required system of limited quantity in a quick, quiet and cost-effective manner using all the strengths of the corporation.

When the Skunk Works was founded in 1943, Kelly Johnson's philosophy was to use small groups of capable people to produce quick results in a quiet and secure environment. This basic philosophy frequently resulted in products being delivered on or ahead of schedule, under budget, and at costs that were significantly lower than traditional programs.

LADC continues to emphasize streamlined, small project teams staffed with multi-disciplined personnel. Only personnel with a "need-to-know" are accessed to any given program. The bottom-line is that the Skunk Works is cost effective! Because of its quiet culture, they are able to work quickly and deliver quality products on time.

The Quality Assurance and inspection function in no way detracts from the Skunk Works emphasis on doing it right the first time, but rather provides an independent check on engineering and manufacturing. Specialized non-destructive testing and measurement is precisely performed on computerized instrumentation to determine dimensional, electromagnetic, physical, and chemical attributes. Processes are thoroughly monitored and records are generated and maintained from complete raw materials characterization through final product assembly and installation ensuring customer satisfaction and confidence.

---

*From a publication of the Lockheed Advanced Development Company.

U-2 reconnaissance aircraft
First flight - August 1955
World's best-known secret aircraft,
highest-flying single engine jet

A-12 supersonic aircraft
First flight - April 1962
First in the series of the Mach 3
titanium Blackbirds

Have Blue demonstrator
First flight - February 1978
Low observables technology
demonstrated in flight.

F-22 ATF prototype
First flight - September 1990
Lockheed - Boeing - General Dynamics
Advanced Tactical Fighter

Figure 24.3 Lockheed Aircraft.

LADC has full facilities and staff to provide modifications and upgrades for aircraft fleets of one to several hundred. The overhaul and repair capability is unique and adaptable to an ever increasing need.

LADC has a time-tested system of around-the-clock communications and support for World-Wide customers. Skunk Works personnel support depot maintenance and flight operations with provisioning and technical services.

For 50 years the Skunk Works has earned the reputation for being just beyond the leading edge of technology by developing a successful series of prototype and limited production aircraft. Many of these projects were considered incredible, if not impossible, feats of engineering for their time.

LADC blends early prototyping with design refinement to produce advanced systems. The overall result is reduced risk and time to system maturity.

BASIC OPERATING RULES OF THE LOCKHEED SKUNK WORKS

1. The Skunk Works manager must be delegated practically complete control of his program in all aspects. He should report to a division president or higher.

2. Strong but small project offices must be provided both by the military and industry.

3. The number of people having any connection with the project must be restricted in an almost vicious

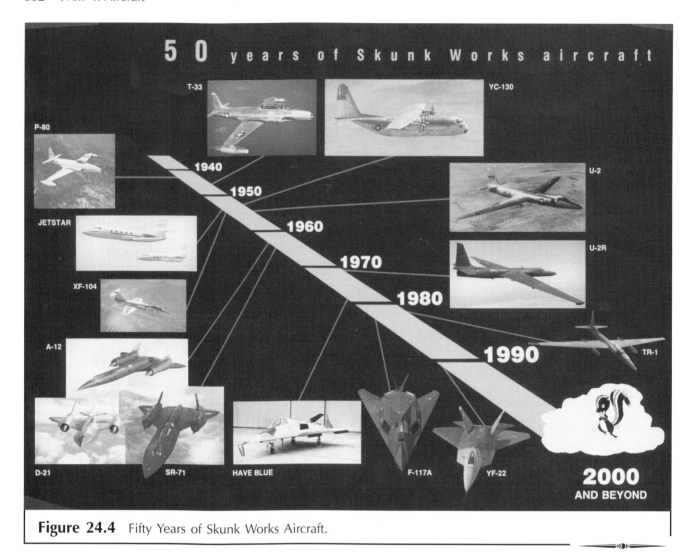

Figure 24.4 Fifty Years of Skunk Works Aircraft.

manner. Use a small number of good people (10% to 25% compared to the so-called normal systems).

4. A very simple drawing and drawing release system with great flexibility for making changes must be provided.

5. There must be a minimum number of reports required, but important work must be recorded thoroughly.

6. There must be a monthly cost review covering not only what has been spent and committed but also projected costs to the conclusion of the program. Don't have the books ninety days late and don't surprise the customer with sudden overruns.

7. The contractor must be delegated and must assume more than normal responsibility to get good vendor bids for subcontract on the project. Commercial bid procedures are very often better than military ones.

8. The inspection system as currently used by ADP, which has been approved by both the Air Force and Navy, meets the intent of existing military requirements and should be used on new projects. Push more basic inspection responsibility back to subcontractors and vendors. Don't duplicate so much inspection.

9. The contractor must be delegated the authority to test his final product in flight. He can and must test it in the initial stages. If he doesn't, he rapidly loses his competency to design other vehicles.

10. The specifications applying to the hardware must be agreed to in advance of contracting. The ADP practice of having a specification section stating clearly which important military specification items will not knowingly be complied with and reasons therefore is highly recommended.

11. Funding a program must be timely so that the contractor doesn't have to keep running to the bank to support government projects.

12. There must be mutual trust between the military project organization and the contractor with very close cooperation and liaison on a day-to-day basis. This cuts down misunderstanding and correspondence to an absolute minimum.

13. Access by outsiders to the project and its personnel must be strictly controlled by appropriate security measures.

14. Because only a few people will be used in engineering and most other areas, ways must be provided to reward good performance by pay not based on the number or personnel supervised.

The famed Skunk Works is a national asset specializing in unique and innovative aircraft designs. Lockheed Martin Skunk Works' unique capability is rapidly prototyping challenging systems. Skunk Works is widely known for such famous aircraft as the SR-71 Blackbird, the world's fastest aircraft, the U-2 recon-

naissance aircraft and the F-117A stealth fighter.

Operated for five decades from Burbank, CA, Skunk Works is now located in facilities in Palmdale, CA. In November 1995, the Aircraft Services Division in Ontario, CA, was combined with the Skunk Works as the maintenance and modification line of business. Aircraft Services specializes in the design, system integration, fabrication and installation of hardware and software systems for special mission aircraft.

LOCKHEED MARTIN F-117A STEALTH FIGHTER

Developed for the U.S. Air Force by the Lockheed Martin Skunk Works, the F-117A Stealth Fighter is the first operational aircraft to exploit low observable stealth technology. Flown by pilots of the 49th Fighter Wing,

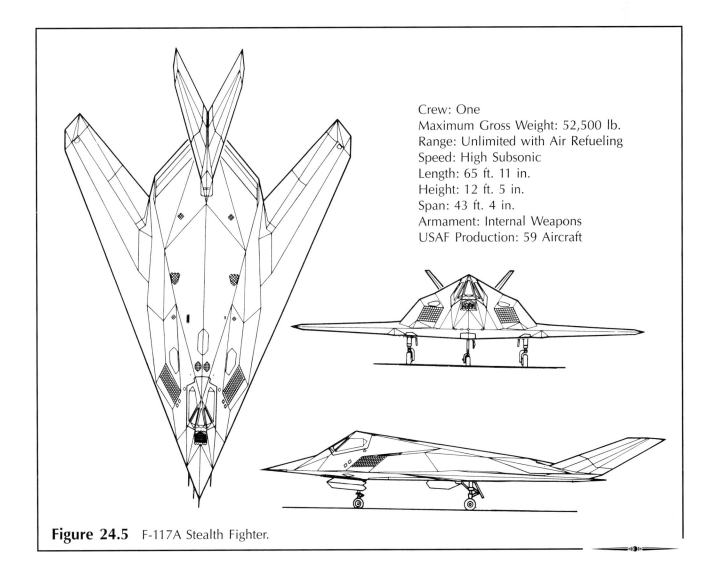

Crew: One
Maximum Gross Weight: 52,500 lb.
Range: Unlimited with Air Refueling
Speed: High Subsonic
Length: 65 ft. 11 in.
Height: 12 ft. 5 in.
Span: 43 ft. 4 in.
Armament: Internal Weapons
USAF Production: 59 Aircraft

Figure 24.5 F-117A Stealth Fighter.

this single-seat fighter is designed to penetrate dense threat environments at night and attack high-value targets with pinpoint accuracy.

The F-117A's combat capabilities greatly contributed to the success of Operation Desert Storm. The F-117A played a key role in destroying Iraq's nuclear/biological/chemical weapons facilities, hardened aircraft shelters, command and control centers, and surface-to-air missile installations, with no combat losses.

Powered by two General Electric F-404 turbofan engines and fly-by-wire flight controls, the F-117A has excellent performance, maneuverability and flying qualities. It is equipped with sophisticated navigation and attack systems integrated into a modern digital avionics suite. A wide variety of tactical weapons can be employed. Detailed planning for missions into target areas is accomplished using an automated mission planning system developed to optimize F-117A capabilities.

The F-117A Stealth Fighter first flew in June 1981, and Lockheed began making production deliveries to the USAF in 1982. With concurrent development and production, the aircraft achieved initial operation capability in October 1983, only five years after go-ahead.

Operational experience has since demonstrated the outstanding quality, reliability and maintainability of the F-117A. Among the laurels associated with this program is the 1989 Collier Trophy, awarded to the Lockheed-USAF F-117A development team for the greatest achievement in aeronautics or astronautics in America.

TWENTY-FIRST CENTURY SPACE TRANSPORTATION SYSTEM X-33 AND VENTURESTAR™

Designed from the ground up to reduce costs in every phase of its operation, the Lockheed Martin team's reusable SSTTO, called VentureStar™, offers a new approach: lifting a body design for efficient launch and cooler re-entry; linear aerospike engines for maximum performance with minimum weight; advanced composite materials for lightweight structures and propellant tanks; a robust thermal protection system; ground operations patterned after aircraft maintenance, with rapid

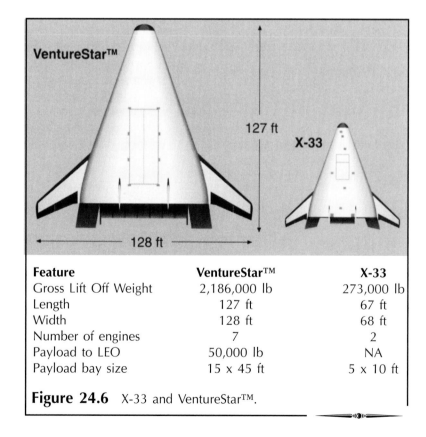

Feature	VentureStar™	X-33
Gross Lift Off Weight	2,186,000 lb	273,000 lb
Length	127 ft	67 ft
Width	128 ft	68 ft
Number of engines	7	2
Payload to LEO	50,000 lb	NA
Payload bay size	15 x 45 ft	5 x 10 ft

Figure 24.6 X-33 and VentureStar™.

turnaround; and a new way of doing business—a cooperative agreement between NASA and the Lockheed Martin team.

In March 2001 the National Aeronautics and Space Administration (NASA) announced that it would no longer fund the $1.3 billion X-33 program. Cost overruns and poor performance were the reasons for the cancellation. This aircraft was to serve as a prototype for the VentureStar™, a space aircraft that would fly from take-off into orbit without using external booster rockets. It was meant to carry people and cargo to the space station and provide transportation to service orbiting satellites.

The X-33 developed problems early. The materials used to build it were too heavy to put into orbit, and its fuel tanks had to be redesigned. A planned flight for the X-33 was delayed from 1999 to the year 2003.

Significant advances were made with the 'aerospike' engine. NASA hopes to salvage some of the X-33 technology including the futuristic linear aerospike engine, lightweight graphic materials and advanced thermal protection. The X-33 was once perceived to be the leading contender to replace the space shuttle.

NASA spent $912 million on developing the X-33 before it was canceled. Lockheed Martin Space Systems spent another $357 million. It is not likely that the company will continue with the X-33 and VentureStar™ programs without government financing.

NASA pledged to spur technology for space travel through the $4.5 billion Space Launch Initiative, which seeks to develop a second-generation reusable launch vehicle.

CHAPTER 25

Airbus Industrie

The largest cooperative venture ever undertaken in the history of European civil aviation was the evolution of the A300 high capacity, widebody, twin engine aircraft which led to the formation of the company known as Airbus Industrie.

The first example of European collaboration was the Caravelle. To save development cost, the airplane utilized the existing nose and flight deck section of the British Comet airplane. It also established a radical rear engine design. Both Comet and Caravelle used Rolls-Royce Avon engines. The Caravelle was not promoted sufficiently to meet European and worldwide needs.

The next British-French effort was the Concorde, a supersonic transport. This aircraft, although successful and still operating, has problems of high noise and operating costs.

In the early 1960s, European governments and airlines met and defined the requirements of a 225 seat "Airbus." By 1966 the French and British governments agreed to a joint development, the outcome of which was the A300. It was agreed that the French would have design leadership on the airframe and the British Rolls Royce have leadership on the engine.

In 1969, the British indicated that they would no longer finance the project and withdrew, however, they did stay as a privileged sub-contractor. Germany then joined the group at this time. Once the A300 program got underway with French and German leadership, other countries joined in contributing parts which amounted to value percentages of France 38, Germany 31, Great Britain 10, Netherlands 3, Spain 2 and the United States 16.

In 1970, the new organization was created when Airbus Industrie was established under French law. The British rejoined the group in 1979 with a 20% share and they became responsible for the wing design and manufacture. The organization has not changed in principle but the shares of the partners have done so. Currently the Airbus Industrie members and their percentage of participation are:

Aerospatiale	France	37.9%
Deutsche Aerospace Airbus	Germany	37.9%
British Aerospace Airbus	U K	20.0%
CASA	Spain	4.2%

In the mid 1970s, discussions took place with U.S. companies about joining the Airbus Industrie group. Due to entrenched interest on both sides no satisfactory joint proposal resulted.

The A310 design incorporated advanced technology for reducing weight and increasing high fuel efficiency. It became an aircraft capable of holding its own against the competitive Boeing 757 and 767 aircraft.

The sales figures for Airbus Industrie aircraft attest to its success with hundreds having been delivered to airline companies worldwide. Eastern Airlines was the first United States air carrier to use the A300 when it purchased 25 airplanes to become the largest Airbus operator at that time. Airbus Industrie is established as the major commercial aircraft manufacturer in Europe. The company's workforce, including their subsidiary Aeroformation, is about 2,000 persons.

Airbus Industrie has demonstrated its ability to compete with the United States large aircraft manufacturers; it has met all technical targets on time, on cost and ahead of competition. It has sold over 1,800 large transport aircraft valued about $100 billion since the first A300 went into service in 1974. The company supports more than 1,000 aircraft in reliable service with

For current information go to the website at: http://www.airbus.com

more than 110 operators worldwide. The operation of the company creates employment for 80,000 highly skilled workers in Europe, including more than 2,000 employees in France. Airbus Industrie has 1,500 suppliers in 27 countries, 30% of whom are in the United States.

Long before entry into service and throughout the operational life of the aircraft, Airbus Industrie customer service helps the airlines get the best out of their aircraft. From first contact, a customer support manager is permanently assigned to oversee the customer's global support requirements. From entry into service, resident customer managers are present in the airline's premises, providing continuous on-site technical support. Focused on airline needs, a comprehensive range of services is offered. With training centers located in Toulouse, Miami, and Beijing, the training division remains close to operators and offers them flexibility and adaptability. To minimize costs, the academic phase of courses can be performed at the customer's base. The Engineering and Technical Division is committed to answering customers' queries in the shortest lead-time and can provide on-site assistance whenever required. To anticipate any possible difficulties all fleet-wide information is shared openly. Technical issues are addressed before they become an issue and in this way Airbus operators achieve excellent aircraft reliability.

The Airbus product line aircraft consists of the A319, A320, A321, A310, A300-600R, A300-600F, A330-200, A330-300, A340-8000, A340-300, A340-500 and the A340-600.

The A300 was Airbus Industrie's first product and the world's first twin-engine, widebody airliner.

It first flew in October 1972 and entered service in May 1974, the European response to an American Airlines specification to which American manufacturers responded with three-engined products because of particular requirements on certain internal US routes.

A twin-engined design has inherent advantages over a tri-jet and proved particularly attractive to fast-growing airlines in South-East Asia as well as in Europe. The economic superiority of the "twin-aisle twin" concept increasingly showed to advantage as fuel prices increased throughout the 1970s and the tri-jet concept was relegated to an ever-smaller niche in the market.

The A300's advanced wing took full advantage of Europe's unmatched length of experience in jetliner wing design. The twin-aisle fuselage cross-section was dimensioned to create minimum drag while providing full widebody, comfort for passengers in all classes. Underfloor cargo compartments accommodated two

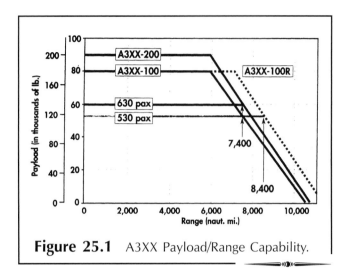

Figure 25.1 A3XX Payload/Range Capability.

LD-3s abreast. These, the standard international containers used on all widebodies, enabled operators to increase revenue with minimum expenditure on ground equipment.

The A300 has been progressively developed as the market and technology have evolved. Improved performance, increased capacity and the introduction of cargo variants broadened its already wide market appeal. Improved systems management technology made it possible for a reduced crew to operate large aircraft safely; the A300 was the first two-person crew widebody to be certificated in 1982.

Airbus Industrie's second product was the A310 launched in July 1978 as the twin-aisle twin concept became increasingly accepted.

The 200-seat A310, 20% smaller than the A300, featured the latest advances in flight instrument and interactive systems monitoring displays and benefited from basic Airbus research into flight crew workload. These were also applied to the A300-600, enabling the airlines to benefit from the economic advantages of a common type-rating between the two aircraft types.

Aerodynamically and structurally, the A310 is one of the world's most advanced aircraft. The high efficiency of its advanced wing design was further enhanced by the addition of drag-reducing wing-tip fences on the A310-300 which entered service in December 1985. This version also incorporated an all-composite vertical fin—the first all-composite item of primary structure to enter service on a civil aircraft—which saves weight and thus reduces fuel consumption. The A310-300 was also the first subsonic civil aircraft to embody automatic in-flight centre-of-gravity control, again to improve efficiency and reduce fuel consumption.

As the twin-aisle twin concept progressively gained ground, operator demand led to its application on longer-distance services. Airlines all over the world became interested in long-range operation of 200–250 seat aircraft in which they could achieve higher load factors with lower cost than the much larger 747. The only available aircraft of this size being twin-engined, the ability of twins to fly long overwater legs came under study.

Airbus research, experiment and operational experience were available as part of the evidence that convinced licensing authorities that such operations could be safely performed. Designed originally for domestic/regional services, the A300 and A310 in their latest form operate regularly on what, not many years ago, would have been regarded as long-haul routes, flying long sectors over water or sparsely inhabited land areas.

With the A300-600 and A310, Airbus Industrie again contributed to a major step forward in airline operation.

By the early 1980s, as Airbus Industrie was achieving recognition in the widebody market, the time was becoming ripe for replacement of the single-aisle designs conceived by the US constructors in the 1960s. It was also the earliest opportunity for the Europeans to re-enter a market in which, acting separately, they had achieved initial success in the early days of jet-powered civil aircraft.

The A320 evolved from the work of several project groups which were gathered into the Airbus fold during the early 1980s and built on the experience gained in programmes such as the Sud Aviation Caravelle and British Aircraft Corporation 1–11. In the meantime, considerable advances in electronics, aerodynamics, structural materials and design had been made and proven by Airbus Industrie, while engine technology had also advanced.

The new project, intended to replace the first-generation 120–150-seaters, was thus backed by decades of experience as well as the growing success of the European partnership.

The A320 was launched in March 1984 and entered service four years later. Its strong marketing features—the widest cabin in its class and a containerised cargo-loading system compatible with widebody cargo systems—combined with cost-efficient technology to produce a hard-to-beat combination of operating economy and revenue-earning capability.

The A320's electronic flight control system is acknowledged as the most advanced in operation or underdevelopment. Electronic flight control ("fly-by-wire") enables design engineers to dispense with highly cumbersome mechanical controls, and leads naturally to a complete reassessment of the relationship between the pilot and his aircraft. This was the subject of a lengthy research and development programme in which practising line pilots were actively involved. It resulted in a flight deck layout which has won enthusiastic acceptance the world over. It also forms the basis of the flight deck and control system for subsequent Airbus products and enables operators to realize the considerable economies of Cross-Crew Qualification across an unprecedented range of aircraft.

In November 1989 a lengthened version designated A321 was launched, seating from 180 to 200 passengers for service from early 1994. The Airbus single-aisle family was completed by the commercial launch in May 1992 of a 120-seat version designated A319. These three aircraft form the most advanced single-aisle range on offer.

At the higher capacity end of the Airbus product line are the twin-engined A330, seating between 300 and 400 passengers, and the four-engined A340. The A340 is built in two versions, the 260-seat A340-200 which has the longest range of any airliner, and the 295-seat A340-300 for service on slightly shorter routes requiring higher capacity.

The A330 and A340 are one single design intended to cover an extremely wide range of service requirements. The twin-engined solution has proved its efficiency over ranges up to 5,000 nm. With lengthening range, four engines show an increasing advantage. The Airbus design team has succeeded in designing a common airframe for two very different tasks, with a common wing—except for items related to the engine—able to accept two or four powerplants.

The A330 is the natural successor to the A300 on domestic trunk routes and such services as US transcontinental or the Pacific Rim routes between Japan, Hong Kong and Singapore. Just over 20% larger than the A300, it caters for the expansion in air travel since the pioneering twin-aisle twin entered service. It also possesses inherent growth potential to maintain its market appeal well into the future.

The A330 first flew in November 1992, for entry into service in the last quarter of 1993.

The A340 first flew in October 1991 and entered service in January 1993, meeting the changing requirements of international travel. Offering three-quarters of the passenger capacity of the 747-400, the A340 enables airlines to achieve higher load factors on routes where competition is severe.

A340 operators can bypass crowded hubs by offering direct point-to-point services which attract the higher

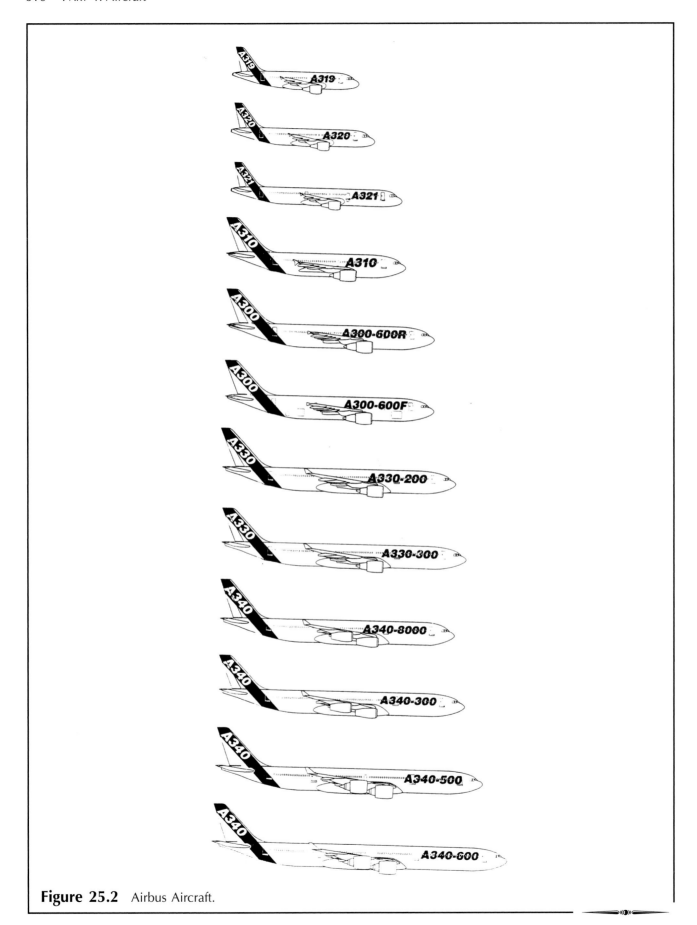

Figure 25.2   Airbus Aircraft.

A319

Airbus Industrie predicts that the world's airlines will require nearly 1,100 aircraft in the "125-seat" category between 1995 and 2009, well over half of this total being required by major airlines. The A319 is aimed at this market.

The A319 is a reduced capacity version of the A320 with 124 seats in a two-class configuration. It offers more range potential and lower operating cost than any competitor in this category.

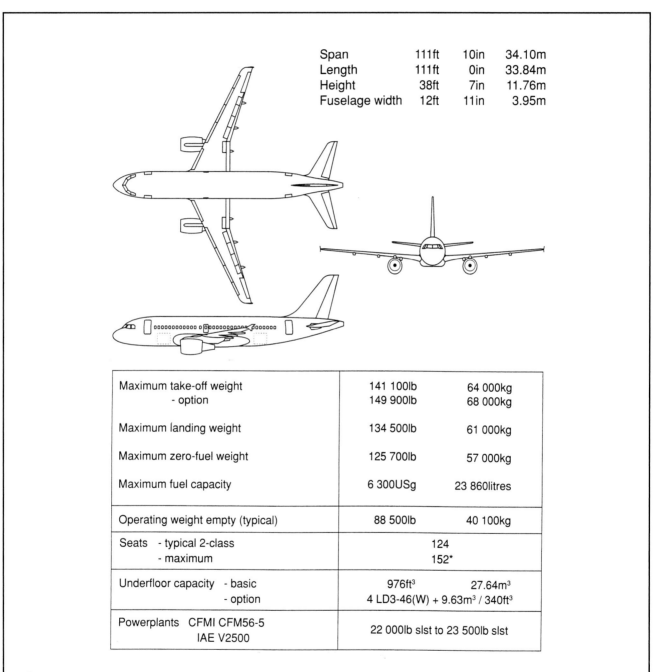

Span	111ft	10in	34.10m
Length	111ft	0in	33.84m
Height	38ft	7in	11.76m
Fuselage width	12ft	11in	3.95m

Maximum take-off weight	141 100lb	64 000kg
- option	149 900lb	68 000kg
Maximum landing weight	134 500lb	61 000kg
Maximum zero-fuel weight	125 700lb	57 000kg
Maximum fuel capacity	6 300USg	23 860litres
Operating weight empty (typical)	88 500lb	40 100kg
Seats - typical 2-class	124	
- maximum	152*	
Underfloor capacity - basic	976ft³	27.64m³
- option	4 LD3-46(W) + 9.63m³ / 340ft³	
Powerplants CFMI CFM56-5	22 000lb slst to 23 500lb slst	
IAE V2500		

Figure 25.3 A319 Airbus Aircraft.

A320

The A320, a 150-seat, single-aisle aircraft, with a second-generation, two-man "glass" cockpit with sidestick controllers, is the first subsonic civil aircraft with fly-by-wire flight controls, giving full flight envelope protection. Being the only non-derivative aircraft in its category, it is able to take full advantage of all advances in avionics, aerodynamics and materials made during the previous decade. Its wider fuselage improves passenger accommodation, gives greater layout flexibility and enables the A320 to offer an optional, standard-based, containerized cargo system for the first time in a single-aisle aircraft.

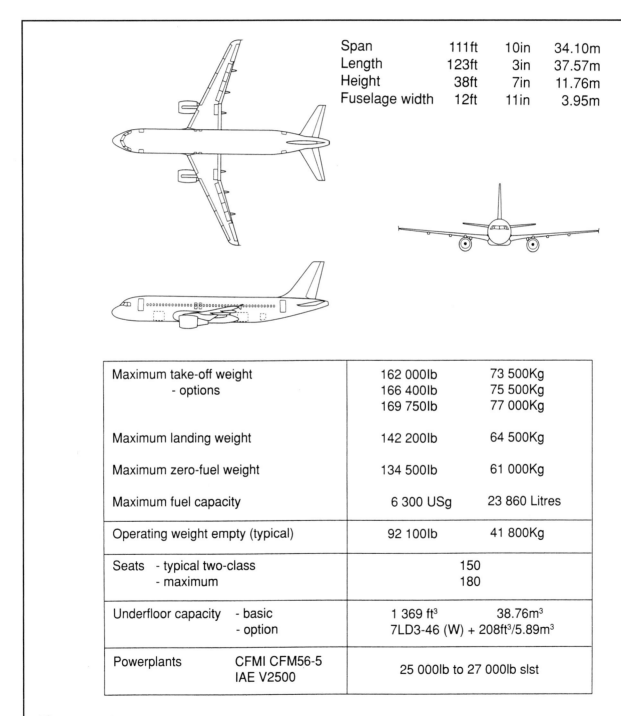

Span	111ft	10in	34.10m
Length	123ft	3in	37.57m
Height	38ft	7in	11.76m
Fuselage width	12ft	11in	3.95m

Maximum take-off weight	162 000lb	73 500Kg
- options	166 400lb	75 500Kg
	169 750lb	77 000Kg
Maximum landing weight	142 200lb	64 500Kg
Maximum zero-fuel weight	134 500lb	61 000Kg
Maximum fuel capacity	6 300 USg	23 860 Litres
Operating weight empty (typical)	92 100lb	41 800Kg
Seats - typical two-class	150	
- maximum	180	
Underfloor capacity - basic	1 369 ft³	38.76m³
- option	7LD3-46 (W) + 208ft³/5.89m³	
Powerplants CFMI CFM56-5	25 000lb to 27 000lb slst	
IAE V2500		

Figure 25.4   A320 Airbus Aircraft.

A321

The A321 is a maximum commonality, minimum change stretch of the A320, produced in response to market demand for an aircraft with the technological efficiency of the A320 to serve on routes with higher traffic densities. The A321 has 40% more underfloor hold volume than the A320 and 25% more seats, giving exceptionally low seat-mile costs.

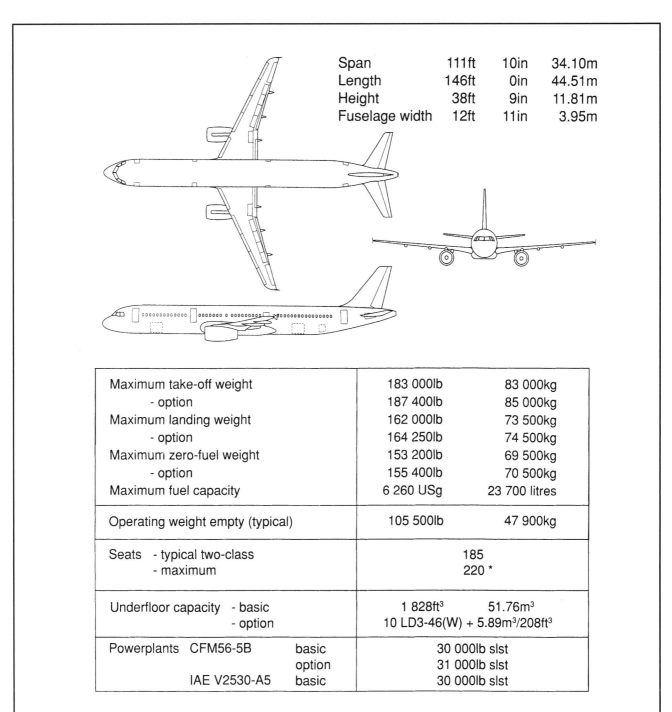

Span	111ft	10in	34.10m
Length	146ft	0in	44.51m
Height	38ft	9in	11.81m
Fuselage width	12ft	11in	3.95m

Maximum take-off weight	183 000lb	83 000kg
- option	187 400lb	85 000kg
Maximum landing weight	162 000lb	73 500kg
- option	164 250lb	74 500kg
Maximum zero-fuel weight	153 200lb	69 500kg
- option	155 400lb	70 500kg
Maximum fuel capacity	6 260 USg	23 700 litres
Operating weight empty (typical)	105 500lb	47 900kg
Seats - typical two-class	185	
- maximum	220 *	
Underfloor capacity - basic	1 828ft³	51.76m³
- option	10 LD3-46(W) + 5.89m³/208ft³	
Powerplants CFM56-5B basic	30 000lb slst	
option	31 000lb slst	
IAE V2530-A5 basic	30 000lb slst	

Figure 25.5 A321 Airbus Aircraft.

A310

The A310 is 20% smaller than the A300 and uses the same fuselage cross-section. The A310 incorporates significant advances in aerodynamics and structure and introduced a new generation of two-man "glass" cockpits with cathode ray tube presentations.

The A310-300 introduced the concept of fuel in the horizontal tail whereby range is increased through increased fuel capacity and through reduced drag, an Airbus Industrie innovation since adopted by other manufacturers. In the course of development, range has been continually increased to well over 5,000 nautical miles.

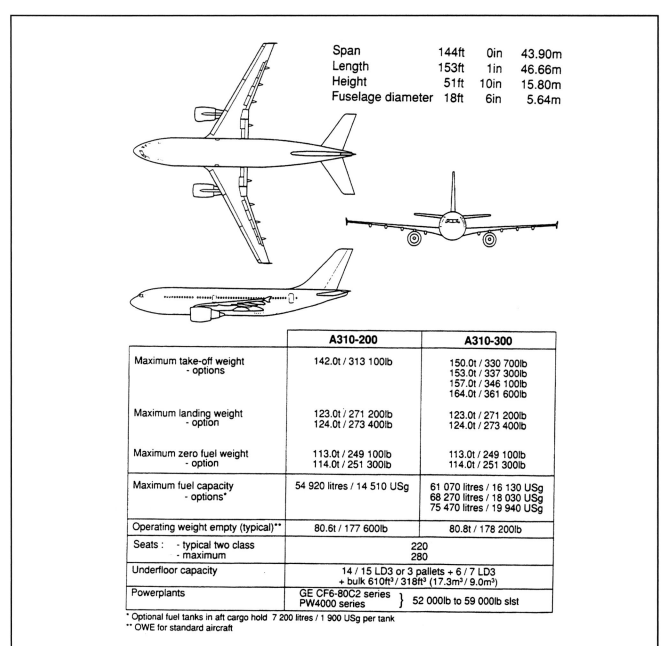

Span	144ft	0in	43.90m
Length	153ft	1in	46.66m
Height	51ft	10in	15.80m
Fuselage diameter	18ft	6in	5.64m

	A310-200	A310-300
Maximum take-off weight - options	142.0t / 313 100lb	150.0t / 330 700lb 153.0t / 337 300lb 157.0t / 346 100lb 164.0t / 361 600lb
Maximum landing weight - option	123.0t / 271 200lb 124.0t / 273 400lb	123.0t / 271 200lb 124.0t / 273 400lb
Maximum zero fuel weight - option	113.0t / 249 100lb 114.0t / 251 300lb	113.0t / 249 100lb 114.0t / 251 300lb
Maximum fuel capacity - options*	54 920 litres / 14 510 USg	61 070 litres / 16 130 USg 68 270 litres / 18 030 USg 75 470 litres / 19 940 USg
Operating weight empty (typical)**	80.6t / 177 600lb	80.8t / 178 200lb
Seats : - typical two class - maximum	220 280	
Underfloor capacity	14 / 15 LD3 or 3 pallets + 6 / 7 LD3 + bulk 610ft³ / 318ft³ (17.3m³ / 9.0m³)	
Powerplants	GE CF6-80C2 series PW4000 series } 52 000lb to 59 000lb slst	

* Optional fuel tanks in aft cargo hold 7 200 litres / 1 900 USg per tank
** OWE for standard aircraft

Figure 25.6 A310 Airbus Aircraft.

A300-600

This aircraft was developed by incorporating A310 systems and technology in the original A300. With a slightly higher passenger and cargo capacity than the A300, the A300-600 benefits from all the advances in technology made during the production lifetime of the original A300. Thus the A310 and A300-600 share a common two-man "glass" cockpit and have extensive systems and engine commonality.

With the same type rating these two aircraft form the basis of the Airbus Industrie widebody family.

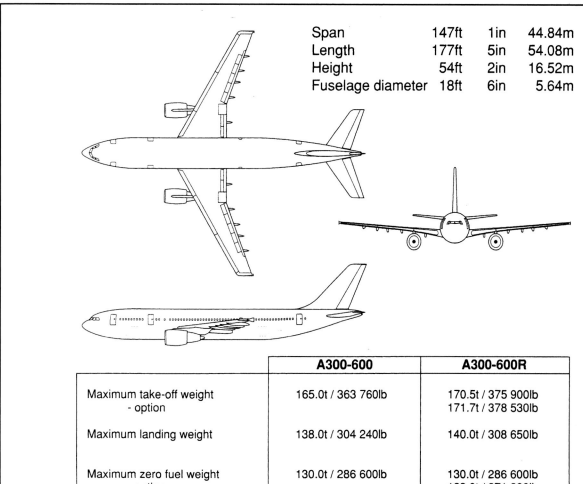

Span	147ft	1in	44.84m
Length	177ft	5in	54.08m
Height	54ft	2in	16.52m
Fuselage diameter	18ft	6in	5.64m

	A300-600	A300-600R
Maximum take-off weight - option	165.0t / 363 760lb	170.5t / 375 900lb 171.7t / 378 530lb
Maximum landing weight	138.0t / 304 240lb	140.0t / 308 650lb
Maximum zero fuel weight - option	130.0t / 286 600lb	130.0t / 286 600lb 123.0t / 271 200lb
Maximum fuel capacity - option*	62 000 litres / 16 380 USg	68 150 litres / 18 000 USg 73 000 litres / 19 280 USg.
Operating weight empty (typical)	90.1t / 198 600lb	90.3t / 199 000lb
Seats - typical two-class - maximum	266 361**	
Underfloor capacity	22 / 23 LD3 or 4 pallets + 10 / 11 LD3 + bulk 610ft³ / 318ft³ (17.3m³ / 9.0m³)	
Powerplants	GE CF6-80C2 series P&W PW4000 series } 56 000lb to 61 500lb slst	

* Optional fuel tank in aft cargo hold
** Current certification limit

Figure 25.7   A300-600 Airbus Aircraft.

A300-600F

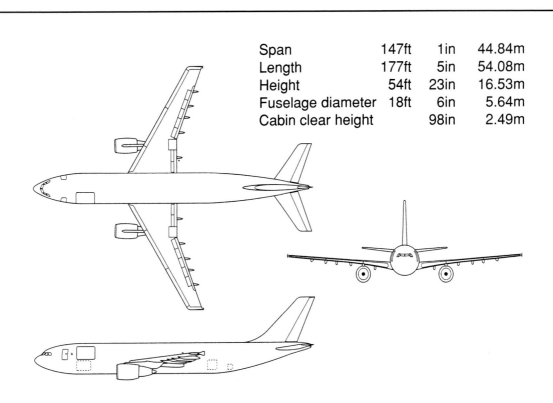

Span	147ft	1in	44.84m
Length	177ft	5in	54.08m
Height	54ft	23in	16.53m
Fuselage diameter	18ft	6in	5.64m
Cabin clear height		98in	2.49m

	Range mode	Optional payload mode
Maximum take-off weight	170.5t / 375 900lb	165.1t / 364 000lb
Maximum landing weight	140.0t / 308 650lb	140.6t / 309 950lb
Maximum zero fuel weight	130.0t / 286 600lb	133.8t / 295 000lb.
Maximum structural payload	51.0t / 112 300lb	54.7t / 120 700lb
Maximum fuel capacity	68 150 litre / 18 000 USg	44 400 litre / 11 730 USg
Operating weight empty (typical)	79.0t / 174 200lb	
Main deck capacity	Nine 88 / 96 x 125 inch + six 88 x 125 inch pallets	
Lower deck capacity	22 / 23 LD3 or 4 pallets + 10 / 11 LD3 + bulk 610ft³ / 318ft³ (17.3m³ / 9.0m³)	
Powerplants	GE CF6-80C2 A5 P&W PW4 158 } 58 000lb to 61 500lb slst	

Figure 25.8   A300-600F Airbus Aircraft.

yield passengers. The smaller very long-range A340-200 also makes it possible to introduce direct services between cities beyond the range of other aircraft.

For the first time, airlines are offered a twin for routes where the twin has advantages and a four-engined aircraft for routes which need a four-engined aircraft, without the penalties normally associated with operating two different aircraft types.

The A330 and A340 retain the proven Airbus twin-aisle cross-section, widely recognized as the most efficient combination of revenue earning space and fuel consumption-reducing slenderness. Both aircraft employ a developed version of the A320's electronic flight control system; their handling qualities are, by design, very similar to those of their smaller relation. Their flight decks are almost identical, except for the number of engine controls. Crews can therefore cross-qualify on the widebodies as well as on their three single-aisle companions—an additional powerful incentive for airlines to invest in the most advanced and efficient family of aircraft on the market.

The benefits of commonality come from reducing the cost of training flight deck, cabin and ground crews, and from increasing flight crew productivity. These benefits can attain levels equivalent to a 10% reduction in fuel burn, or to a 20% reduction in maintenance cost.

A330/A340

The A330/A340, launched in 1987, is one aircraft produced initially in three versions: one twin and two four-engined models. Seating capacity ranges from about 260 to 440. The aircraft share the same airframe, the differences being engines, engine-related systems and fuselage length. Thus, for the first time, airlines are offered a twin for routes where a twin shows advantage and a four-engined aircraft for routes where a four-engined aircraft is needed, without the penalties normally associated with two distinct fleets.

The A330 is a third-generation, twin-engined widebody aircraft with typically 335 seats in a two-class arrangement offering a range of 4,850 nm with a full complement of passengers and baggage. It is ideal as a direct replacement for earlier-generation trijets and as a growth replacement for earlier twinjets.

The four-engined A340 is offered in two sizes, allowing operators to tailor capacity and capability to demand. The larger A340-300 has seat-mile costs on a level with those of the largest four-engined airliner, while the smaller A340-200 has the longest range of any commercial airliner available.

Both the A330 and A340 represent the first steps towards new aircraft families and developments are already foreseen. For the immediate future, market demand is already showing a need for a version of the A340-300 with even greater range capability, a need which will be met by a higher design weight and a higher engine thrust. This "high gross weight" version of the aircraft was available in early 1996.

A330

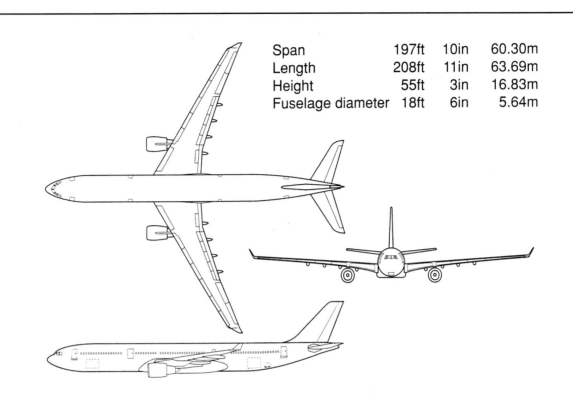

Span	197ft	10in	60.30m
Length	208ft	11in	63.69m
Height	55ft	3in	16.83m
Fuselage diameter	18ft	6in	5.64m

	Basic	**Option**
Maximum take-off weight	212.0t / 467 400lb	217.0t / 478 400lb
Maximum landing weight	174.0t / 383 600lb	179.0t / 394 600lb
- option	177.0t / 390 200lb	
Maximum zero-fuel weight	164.0t / 361 600lb	169.0t / 372 600lb
- option	167.0t / 368 200lb	
Maximum fuel capacity	97 170 litres / 25 670 USg	98 250 litres / 25 950 USg
Operating weight empty (typical)	120.3t / 265 200lb	120.6t / 265 900lb
Seats - typical two-class	335	
- maximum	440	
Underfloor capacity	32/33 LD3 / 11 pallets + bulk 19.7m³ (695ft³)	
Powerplants	CF6-80E 67 500 to 70 000lb slst PW4000 64 000 to 68 000lb slst RR Trent 67 500 to 71 100lb slst	

Figure 25.9   A330 Airbus Aircraft.

A340-200

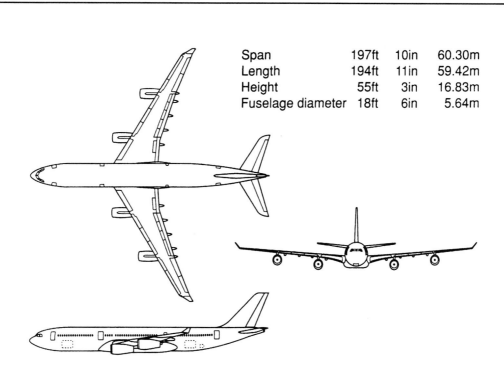

Span	197ft	10in	60.30m
Length	194ft	11in	59.42m
Height	55ft	3in	16.83m
Fuselage diameter	18ft	6in	5.64m

Maximum take-off weight	257.0t / 566 600lb
Maximum landing weight	182.0t / 401 200lb
Maximum zero-fuel weight	170.0t / 374 800lb
Maximum fuel capacity	140 000 litres / 36 980 USg
Operating weight empty (typical)	123.1t / 271 400lb
Seats-typical two-class three-class	300 263
Underfloor capacity	26/27 LD3/9 pallets + Bulk 19.7m³ (695ft³)
Powerplants	CFM56-5C2 31 200lb slst CFM56-5C3 32 500lb slst CFM56-5C4 34 000lb slst

Figure 25.10   A340-200 Airbus Aircraft.

A340-300

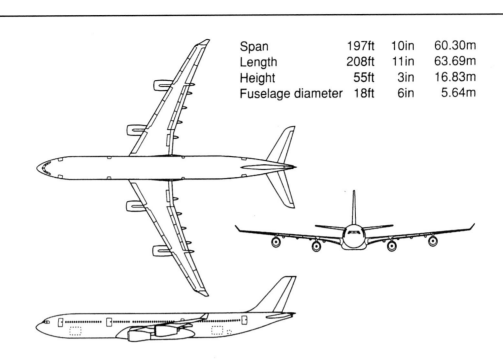

Span	197ft	10in	60.30m
Length	208ft	11in	63.69m
Height	55ft	3in	16.83m
Fuselage diameter	18ft	6in	5.64m

	Basic	**Option**
Maximum take-off weight	257.0t / 566 600lb	271.0t / 597 500lb
Maximum landing weight	187.0t / 412 300lb	190.0t / 418 900lb
Maximum zero-fuel weight	175.0t / 385 800lb	178.0t / 392 400lb
Maximum fuel capacity	140 000 litres / 36 980 USg	141 000 litres / 37 250 USg
Operating weight empty (typical)	126.9t / 279 700lb	129.3t / 285 100lb
Seats-typical - two-class	335	
- three-class	295	
Underfloor capacity	32/33 LD3/11 pallets + Bulk 19.7m³ (695ft³)	
Powerplants	CFM56-5C2 31 200lb slst CFM56-5C3 32 500lb slst CFM56-5C4 34 000lb slst	CFM56-5C4 34 000lb slst

Figure 25.11 A340-300 Airbus Aircraft.

Figure 25.12 A340 Flight Deck.

In the late 1950s space activities with the launching of rockets began. As the size of the rockets grew it became difficult if not impossible to transport these large components from the manufacturing plant to the place of final assembly and launching in Florida and California.

A company was created named Aero Spacelines which modified an existing aircraft, a Boeing 377 transport. The bottom of the fuselage, the wings and tail of the aircraft were utilized. Parts of other aircraft were also used in the modification. The upper part of the airplane was extremely large; the inside measured 20 feet in diameter. The top opened up so that large pieces of cargo, such as a rocket casing, could be loaded. It was named the 'Guppy'; later larger versions were called the 'Pregnant Guppy.' In addition to transporting rocket component parts it was used to transport other large size cargo pieces. It was used to transport DC-10 fuselages from the Convair factory in San Diego to the McDonnell Douglas plant in Long Beach, California.

Airbus Industrie is building a completely new idea of the Guppy. The A300-600ST is the biggest aircraft in the world in terms of volume capacity. The 'Beluga' has a volume capacity of the main deck cargo compartment that is 70% more than the Boeing 747-400F. It is built for efficient loading and unloading by the upward opening of the forward main door allowing easy access to the huge cargo compartment. The aircraft are being used to transport special large cargoes such as helicopters, racing yachts and very large industrial equipment.

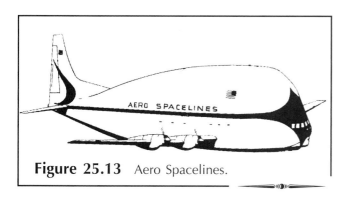

Figure 25.13 Aero Spacelines.

Figure 25.14 A300-600ST Airbus Aircraft.

A380

There appears to be a need for a large air carrier aircraft greater in size than the Boeing 747. Without competition in this market, Boeing would remain a monopoly. To pursue this market Airbus Industrie formed the Large Aircraft Division to develop the A380 aircraft. They worked closely with potential customers to develop the aircraft specifications. Several working groups were formed to cover specific issues. The initial version of the A380 will carry out 555 passengers in a three-class layout over a range of 7,650 nautical miles. It will have a capacity and range growth potential for future development. Seating capacity can increase to 960. The A380 will be compatible with major airports and meet most of the environmental regulations. It will be part of the Airbus Common Flight-deck family. The A380 is planned to make its first flight in 2004 and to enter service in the year 2006. It will cost approximately $198 million. An extended range model will cost up to $220 million.

Airbus considers size to be more important than speed. The A380 will be the largest passenger jet in the world; however, there are more important issues than physical size or maximum take-off weight.

This huge transport aircraft is a symbol of Europe's economic unification and political transformation. The partner nations can develop a world-class aircraft.

The company said the secret is not simply the economics of size. Ingenuity and understanding of new alloys and composites will allow designers to build an aircraft that is stronger and lighter.

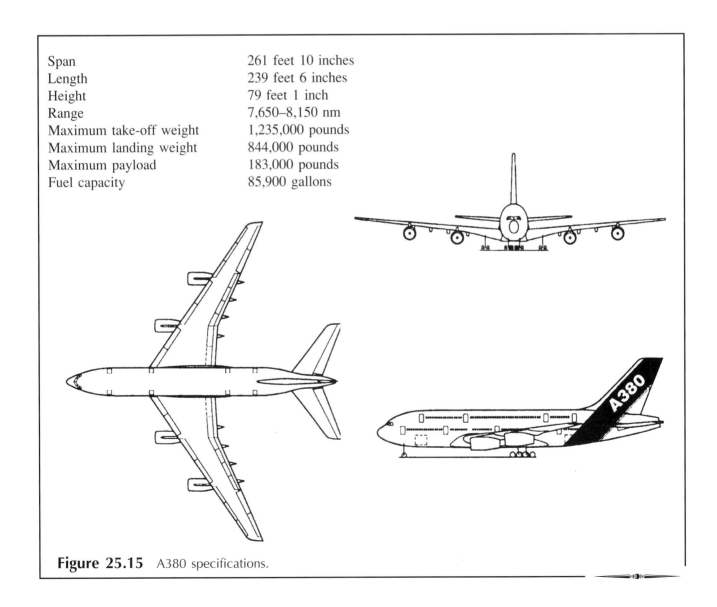

Span	261 feet 10 inches
Length	239 feet 6 inches
Height	79 feet 1 inch
Range	7,650–8,150 nm
Maximum take-off weight	1,235,000 pounds
Maximum landing weight	844,000 pounds
Maximum payload	183,000 pounds
Fuel capacity	85,900 gallons

Figure 25.15   A380 specifications.

A380

CHAPTER 26

Future Aircraft

Mankind progressed through the ages in his quest to fly from mythology to balloons, gliders, and eventually to people carrying controllable powered aircraft. Having reached the goal of flight the next step to be taken was venturing into space. This was accomplished with the Mercury, Gemini, and Apollo orbital spacecraft. Next came the big Saturn rocket carrying men into space and on to the moon.

The Space Shuttle was a combination aircraft and spacecraft. Launched vertically into space and after circling the earth in orbit, it re-entered the earth's atmosphere and landed as an unpowered aircraft.

For many years the desire was for an aircraft that could take off in the conventional manner using its own power, then climbing to outer space and maneuvering in outer space. Finally it would return to earth and land normally.

During the past several years efforts have been made to build such an aircraft. The main problem was in developing the materials for its construction durable enough to survive the extreme demands placed upon it. The matter of building a powerful enough fuel efficient engine was a major obstacle. Scientists using the latest technology have slowly solved these problems. As early as the 1960s a design was created and a half size mock-up was built. However, lacking adequate funding prevented it from being developed.

In the early 1990s, a plane was devised that was sponsored by the United States Air Force through the Hypersonic Systems Technology Program. The vehicle was known as the National Aerospace Plane, the X-30. Contracts were granted to several aircraft industry companies jointly for its development, construction, and testing. It was well underway but unfortunately, after spending millions of dollars, the project was canceled when money was no longer provided. The next effort tried but canceled was the X-33 Venture Star, undertaken by the Lockheed Aircraft Company's Skunk Works at Palmdale, California.

The X-30 was once perceived as the leading contender to replace the space shuttle. However, cost overruns and poor performance prompted NASA to cancel the Lockheed Martin program. NASA pledged to spur technology for space travel through the $4.5 billion Space Launch Initiative which seeks to develop a second generation reusable launch vehicle. NASA hopes to salvage some of the X-33 technology including a futuristic linear aerospike engine, lightweight graphic materials and advanced thermal protection.

An advanced concepts program has been established to create an opportunity to bring together NASA, industry, and university capabilities to develop aeronautical concepts that have potential benefits for the future. This includes the Blended Wing Body technology program to assess the technical and commercial viability of an advanced unconventional aircraft. The Blended Wing Body aircraft will be a very large subsonic aircraft with a payload designed for 800 passengers, a 7000 nautical mile range and a cruise speed of Mach number 0.85. This aircraft combines a rigid wide airfoil shape with a high aspect ratio wing. Because this configuration is such an extremely integrated design, a multidisciplinary process is being utilized to develop a suitable design considering aerodynamics, structures, propulsion and flight mechanics.

An evaluation of this future aircraft design indicates that it will have significant cost and performance benefits over conventional aircraft configurations including an increase in lift-drag ratio, a 20% decrease in fuel consumption and a 10% decrease in operating empty weight.

Considerable effort continues to be made in the development of classical type aircraft carrying passengers such as the Boeing 747 and the Airbus A-340. With

625

the hard to achieve demands for reduction in direct operating cost, environmental issues have been offsetting much of the potential performance gains. The limitations on noise, greenhouse emissions and radiation issues associated with vapor trails producing high altitude cirrus clouds are to be considered.

It is anticipated that the Blended Wing Body aircraft can be achieved and transport aircraft can be produced with which no conventional aircraft would be able to compete. The Blended Wing Body concept presents a number of interesting challenges, any of which can prevent a feasible solution from been achieved. A wide range study is being undertaken at the Cranfield College of Aeronautics that is intended to determine the challenges and/or discover the problems that may occur. It is proposed that these activities will lead to completion of a detailed study of an aircraft with an integrated propulsion system incorporating technologies including laminar flow within a framework which will ensure that it can be successfully manufactured profitably and operated to the benefit of safety and the appeal of the traveling public.

Another project being conducted concerns the National Hypersonics Strategy, which is a joint government-industry undertaking. This aircraft is known as the X-43 and will attain a speed of Mach 7 on its new hydrocarbon ISTAR engine that will cycle from rocket to ramjet to scramjet. Experimental aircraft are being built to gather data and test the propulsion system. Aerojet and Boeing's Rocketdyne are developing the X-43. NASA eventually hopes to have an aircraft that will take off on its own power and then use rocket power to reach a speed of Mach 5 so that the scramjet could then be used along with rockets to propel it into space. NASA anticipates a hypersonic aircraft to replace the space shuttle. It is anticipated that if successful this aircraft will be used by the military and cargo carrying air carriers such as United Parcel Service and Federal Express, two of the largest air freight companies in the world.

Another project announced by the Boeing Company is to build a Blended Wing Body passenger aircraft. Since the Airbus industry has decided to build the giant size double deck A-380 aircraft, it was anticipated that its archrival, Boeing, would build a competitive aircraft. These designs are larger versions of conventional type aircraft having a tube shaped fuselage and swept back wing with the usual type tail and engines of greater power. Boeing could accomplish this by simply building a larger version of its currently successful 747. However, Boeing said that it would abandon plans for the foreseeable fu-

ture in favor of an entirely new airline type aircraft. It is anticipated that this aircraft will carry up to 800 passengers in two decks each with five parallel compartments within the wing. It will not be like traditional aircraft that have a fuselage and tail surfaces. Instead it will be a gigantic flying wing first conceived by Jack Northrop many years ago. Northrop flew conventional propeller engined and jet powered flying wing aircraft successfully shortly after World War II.

Boeing believes the aircraft will compete in speed as well as size. Work at the Boeing research laboratory Phantom Works is developing this new aircraft. It may be a decade before it enters commercial service.

Further details about this aircraft can be found in Chapter 22.

TECHNOLOGY TRANSFER

In 1958, when Congress promulgated the National Aeronautics and Space Administration Act, part of the mission of NASA was to promote domestic technology transfer of technologies and spinoffs from the space program and other NASA research. Studies have shown that the return on NASA's Research and Development has made it an excellent investment, returning $9 of economic benefit for every $1 invested. However, on the average, this return took some 18 years to be realized.

With the domestic technology transfer expectations of the 1950s and 1960s falling short, Congress promulgated further legislation in order to accelerate the process of technology transfer.

THE BAYH-DOLE ACT OF 1980

This Act gave the authority for the government labs to grant exclusive licenses to a commercial firm if doing so was necessary for an invention to reach the commercial market. (Previously, all unclassified inventions resulting from federal funding were placed in the public domain which actually stifled commercialization. Businesses were not anxious to invest product development money when competitors had access to the same government developed results.)

THE STEVENSON-WYDLER ACT OF 1980

Here, Congress specified that domestic technology transfer would actually become part of the federal laboratories' main mission. Specifically, 0.5% of each

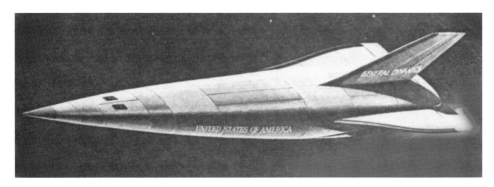

X-30

X-33

X-43

Figure 26.1

Figure 26.2 "Steam Riding Rocket" of the 1830s was the artist's satire of a new steam railway locomotive named the Rocket.

laboratory's R&D budget was to go to an Office of Research and Technology Applications (ORTA).

THE FEDERAL TECHNOLOGY TRANSFER ACT OF 1986

This Act amended the Stevenson-Wydler Act to allow labs to enter into a Cooperative Research and Development Agreement (CRDA) with the private sector. Also, this act allowed for royalty sharing by the government and the individual inventor. In addition, it required regular reporting of technology transfer activities by federal agencies.

EXECUTIVE ORDER 12591

This Order allowed federal agencies to delegate authority to individual labs to enter into cooperative research and development agreements.

DOD REGULATION 3200.12-R-4, 27 DECEMBER 1988 AND USAF REGULATION 80-27, DOMESTIC TECHNOLOGY TRANSFER, 31 JANUARY 1990

These regulations implement the public laws and executive order and provide necessary details for conducting technology transfer activities within DoD and the Air Force.

The objectives of the technology transfer initiative are to maximize the return on the investment for the Research and Development budget through proactive technology transfer; enhance United States international competitiveness through rapid and direct transfer of technologies to the U.S. commercial, civil, and federal sectors; develop, exercise, refine, and rigorize the technology transfer process to provide the most efficient means of transfer.

In fulfilling these objectives, the Program Office intends to utilize, to the extent possible and appropriate, existing technology transfer organizations with their attendant resources and procedures in order to maximize outreach for and eliminate duplication of effort.

There are similar efforts underway by other governments in developing this type of aircraft. If the United States succeeds it will continue to be the leader in aerospace technology and will have the major share of the transportation business of the world. Aerospace is one of the few industries that still produces a trade surplus for the United States.

With all the effort of planning, it is certain that some time about the beginning of the twenty-first century there will fly an aircraft-spacecraft. Hopefully it will be the United States that will lead the way as it did in the development of the airplane in the early years of the twentieth century.

PART 5

GENERAL AVIATION

PART 5

BRIEF OVERVIEW OF CHAPTERS

27. THE GENERAL AVIATION INDUSTRY

- Presents the aspects of general aviation and a presentation of aircraft manufacturers including Piper, Cessna, Mooney and Raytheon-Beech; the General Aviation Manufacturers Association.

CHAPTER 27

The General Aviation Industry

The term general aviation is used to describe a diverse range of aviation activities and includes all segments of the aviation industry except commercial air carriers (including commuter/regional aircraft) and military. Its activities include the training of new pilots, sightseeing, the movement of large heavy loads by helicopter, and flying for corporate/business or personal reasons. Its aircraft range from a one-seat single engine piston aircraft to the long-range corporate jet.

General aviation is an important component of both the aviation industry and our national economy. It provides on-the-spot efficient and direct aviation services that commercial aviation cannot or will not provide. The production and sale of general aviation aircraft, avionics, and other equipment, along with the provision of support services such as flight schools, fixed base operators, finance, and insurance, make the general aviation industry an important contributor to the nation's economy.

General aviation consists of six categories:

- Business
- Air Taxi and Rental
- Special Purpose
- Personal Transportation
- Sport
- Instructional (Figure 27.1.)

BUSINESS FLYING

Business flying is the largest of the aviation categories. There are approximately 176,006 privately owned airplanes, of which many are used partly for business reasons, and approximately 50,000 company-owned airplanes are used exclusively for business. Efficiency and good management are the reasons for their successful use. Business aircraft save companies time and money by flying executives and employees at their convenience. Materials including parts and supplies to keep production lines in operation move continuously via company-owned airplanes on a regular as well as an emergency basis. Most business flying is between cities which are not served by air carriers. The business airplane is a flexible, modern, utilitarian tool providing safety, convenience, and speed in an economical manner.

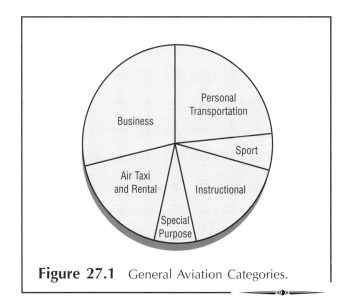

Figure 27.1 General Aviation Categories.

Nearly one-third of all business flights into major metropolitan airports each year connect with scheduled airline flights. The vast majority of general aviation business flights, however, are between communities which lack adequate airline service.

Corporate management and business analysts recognize that corporate aircraft ownership has become an accurate measure of business efficiency, not only on the balance sheet, but also in the use of human resources. For many, the company plane is a practical marketing tool which keeps management face-to-face with customers. The plane permits decentralization without top management losing touch with operations. It gives management flexibility and shortened reaction times in special situations. It cuts overhead costs and provides privacy for in-flight meetings. For many executives, the company airplane is an office on wings.

Surveys of major United States corporations show that the majority of them are reluctant to locate in an area that lacks adequate airport facilities. Many of the top 1,000 U.S. businesses operate their own aircraft because of speed, mobility, flexibility, efficiency, and safety.

AIR TAXI AND RENTAL

Air taxi and rental aircraft provide customized air transportation. Air taxi gives charter service to every community that has an airport, landing strip, or helicopter landing pad. Holders of pilot's licenses rent aircraft from fixed based operators and transport themselves, families, friends, and business associates with the same freedom as with using the automobile.

Time and money are saved by chartering or renting a general aviation airplane. Air taxi companies fly millions of passengers according to their needs.

There are nearly 6,000 airplanes used by air taxi and charter operators.

These small air carriers serve small cities on a regular basis carrying passengers, airmail, and cargo. They are the indispensable link between small town America and the major hub air terminals where passengers have access to the entire world.

SPECIAL PURPOSE

Special purpose aviation is the most diverse. Included is the use of the airplane in conservation of forestry, fish, game, and wildlife; livestock feeding; photography; law enforcement; highway and traffic patrol; transmission; and pipeline inspection to list only a few.

The airplane is an important machine in agriculture; it is used for seeding, fertilizing, and insecticide application on more than 200 million acres of farmland each year. One airplane can cover more acreage in one hour than a tractor can cover in an entire day—and will use only one-ninth the fuel.

PERSONAL TRANSPORTATION

The small airplane is used at the convenience of the pilot for personal use. The small airplane is used in much the same way the family automobile is used except that a greater saving in gas and time is possible. This category includes flying by pilots to maintain their proficiency or further develop their skill as required by the Federal Aviation Administration.

SPORT

Sport flying amounts to 5% of all general aviation activity. These pilots fly for the sheer pleasure, fun, and excitement of leaving the solid ground and "soaring free as a bird." This feeling of freedom has motivated many pilots to seek their certificates and pursue aviation careers.

Many universities and colleges have their own sport flying teams to motivate students and to promote safer flying. The National Intercollegiate Flying Association is an organization composed of these teams. Regional air meets are held throughout the year with the regional winners competing for trophies in an annual national air meet.

INSTRUCTIONAL

Many airline and military pilots learn to fly in general aviation aircraft.

Like most skills, one can never learn all there is to know about flying. The "know-it-all" pilot is dangerous to himself as well as to others. The number of pilot certificates issued has steadily decreased. About 10,000 people are learning to fly each month. The cost of flight training varies considerably depending upon the rating sought, the aircraft flown, and the location. Flight training is usually a bargain when one considers the cost of the aircraft and its maintenance. It is estimated that more than 100,000 new pilots will be certificated in the next ten-year period. Many will continue on to careers in aviation or use their flying skill in connection with their own profession. One out of every four United States airline pilots came from general aviation as well as many military pilots.

While general aviation represents 98% of all aircraft in the United States, it uses only 6% of the aviation fuel. That amounts to only 0.7% of the fuel consumed in all forms of transportation.

Colleges and universities are replacing local airports by providing initial and follow-on flight training. More than 218 U.S. higher learning institutions offer aviation training, most conferring related degrees, according to the University Aviation Association. Of a total aviation-related enrollment of over 41,000, more than 16,000 students are in flight training programs, about 11,000 are taking aviation maintenance courses, 5,500 are specializing in management and approximately 10,000 are learning air traffic control and other areas.

During the 1960s and 1970s, the number of student pilots generally followed changes in economic activity. This pattern, however, has not occurred since 1980. Periods of economic growth that have been accompanied by a resurgence of pilot training. The lack of a GI bill for pilot training may have contributed to the reduced numbers of pilots. A declining population of students and an accelerating attrition rate of private pilots have reduced the total number of private pilots.

Historically, the economic cycle of the general aviation industry has closely paralleled that of the national economy. The theories about the reasons for the decline in sales and pilots are diverse. Some cite high aircraft prices and the availability of low cost alternatives such as ultralights. Others hypothesize that high operating costs and interest rates have been responsible for depressing the industry. Still others allege that the changes in the tax laws and high product liability costs are responsible. Each one of these factors has had some effect. Numerous studies have shown that many of the factors cited above have outweighed the positive effects of a growing economy. This shrinking stock of pilots and the slowing in the expansion of the general aviation fleet has reduced the rate of growth of general aviation.

Although the economics of the industry are important in affecting people's choices, it cannot be overlooked that a fundamental change in the tastes and preferences of the population are taking place. In the long run, this could be as destabilizing to general aviation as the negative economic factors that have plagued the industry over the past years. Changing tastes could upset the fundamental economic equations that have held for many years. If this phenomenon is occurring, then falling prices, operating costs, and real interest rates, accompanied by economic growth, may not be sufficient to revive the market.

Traditional sources of new pilots are drying up in the U.S., which could hurt changes for a prolonged rebound in the general aviation industry. In addition to rising flight training costs, younger persons' incomes have represented a falling percentage of national mean income since 1977. This means the age group most likely to pursue recreational flying has less discretionary income, and increases the appeal of less-expensive substitute activities. Downsizing in the military also has resulted in the shrinking pool of young veterans, the group most likely to use VA flight training benefits.

General aviation consists of hundreds of thousands of people working to bring the advantages of the airplane to every community. It is an important part of America, its present, and its future.

The Federal Government's role is significant. Legislation must be strong but flexible to create conditions that encourage healthy competition and growth in civil aviation. These conditions, which are essential to a strong national economy, result from domestic and international trade and commerce, travel, and transportation. The Federal Government also plays a leading part in safety and economic regulations and in the support given to all aviation interests through research services, air traffic control, airport construction, airmail, weather information, and many other services.

General aviation plays an important role in the aviation industry by providing aviation services that commercial aviation cannot or will not provide. The production and sale of general aviation aircraft, avionics and other equipment, along with provision of support services such as flight schools, fixed base operators, finance and insurance, make the general aviation industry an important contributor to the economy of the nation. Federal rules and policies that apply to general aviation have undergone significant changes in recent years, largely as a result of advances in technology and rapid growth in use of the aviation system. In making these changes, the Federal Government has been propelled by the need to maximize the safety and efficiency of the airport and airway system for all users. It is essential that Federal aviation policies be sensitive to the needs of general aviation, and that continuing efforts be made to accommodate general aviation within the evolving aviation system and work to alleviate special problems such as aircraft product liability. General aviation must continue to accommodate needs required of all users of the aviation system, in the interests of safety, cost-effectiveness, and efficiency.

It is Federal transportation policy to:

1. Continue to fund reliever airports and supporting facilities for use by general aviation.
2. Provide flight services to general aviation in ways that are both cost-effective and responsive to user needs.
3. Make use of advancements in technology to improve general aviation safety and access to airports and airways.
4. Work with the general aviation community in reducing airspace infractions and achieving greater conformity with Federal airspace rules and other aviation requirements.

Perhaps the single most important event for general aviation occurred on August 12, 1994, when President Clinton signed the General Aviation Revitalization Act* which puts an 18-year limitation on product liability for aircraft with a passenger capacity of fewer than 20 passengers. In general, the Act says that, ". . . no civil action for damages for death or injury to persons or damage to property arising out of an accident involving a general aviation aircraft may be brought against the manufacturer . . . if the accident occurred (1) after the applicable limitation period. . . ." There are some exceptions, namely when manufacturers have withheld required performance data from the FAA, for persons killed or injured while on a medical transport flight, for persons killed on the ground, and for suits brought under a written warranty enforceable by law.

The enactment of the legislation represented the culmination of a lengthy industry campaign to revitalize the markets for general aviation products and services and to help restore a once-healthy industry.

Events that have contributed to the downturn in general aviation activity include changes in disposable income; increases in airspace restrictions applied to Visual Flight Rules (VFR) aircraft; reductions in leisure time; shifts in personal preferences for goods, services, and leisure time; and the deregulation of the commercial airline industry.

However, one of the factors that is mentioned most frequently as the cause of the decline in general aviation is the increased cost of owning and operating a general aviation aircraft.

OWNERSHIP COST FACTORS

The cost of owning (maintaining and operating) all classes of general aviation aircraft has been steadily increasing. Although the total nominal cost of owning and operating an aircraft has increased between 4.0 and 4.3% annually since 1978, these costs have largely been inflationary and compare favorably to increases in the consumer price index over the same period.

The nominal cost of purchasing a general aviation aircraft has risen dramatically, far exceeding the rise in inflation. Since 1978, the average cost of purchasing general aviation aircraft has increased. Single engine piston aircraft are up 126%, multi-engine piston aircraft are up 238%, turbo-prop aircraft are up 209%, and turbojet aircraft are up 195%.

Despite relatively low inflation the nominal purchase prices of multi-engine pistons, turboprops, and turbojets have increased significantly.

Increases in produce liability costs are one of the key factors responsible for the large increases in the purchase price of a general aviation aircraft. Annual claims paid by manufacturers have increased from $24 million to over $210 million despite an improved safety record.

Clearly, these ownership cost increases, especially those in the purchase price, have a negative impact on general aviation and are, in large part, responsible for the decline in aircraft purchases over the last several years.

GENERAL AVIATION

By any measure, 2000 was another very good year for general aviation. Unit shipments of general aviation aircraft were on their way to recording a sixth consecutive year of increase. General aviation manufacturers' shipments increased from 928 aircraft in 1994 to 2,525 aircraft in 1999 (up 172 percent) and were up an additional 16.3 percent (2,000 units) during the first three quarters of 2000. Of particular importance is the renewed interest in piston powered aircraft. Shipments of piston powered aircraft have more than tripled between 1994 and 1999 (from 499 to 1,747) and were up an

---

*For a detailed explanation of this Act, refer to Chapter 19.

additional 13.8 percent (1,336 units) during the first nine months of 2000.

Shipments of jet aircraft have increased in each of the past seven years (from 171 in 1992 to 514 in 1999) and are headed toward an eighth consecutive year of increase (352 units, up 15.1 percent) through the first three quarters of 2000. The increased sales of jet aircraft reflects, to a large extent, the relative importance of the rapidly growing fractional ownership programs to the industry's current turnaround and its future growth. While shipments of turboprop aircraft (down 2.6 percent in 1999) have not fared as well as the other two aircraft categories, shipments totaled 233 (up 36.3 percent) during the first 9 months of 2000.

Billings for general aviation aircraft totaled almost $7.9 billion in 1999—an all-time record high. During the first nine months of 2000, the industry reported billings of almost $6.3 billion, up 10.4 percent over the same time period in 1999. The larger increase in shipments relative to billings reflects increased shipments of the lower unit-priced piston aircraft. Export shipments were up 11.3 percent during the first three quarters of 2000. However, billings declined 20.7 percent over the same time period.

Based on the results of the 1999 General Aviation and Air Taxi Activity and Avionics Survey, the active general aviation aircraft fleet and hours flown both increased for a fifth consecutive year, up 7.2 and 13.0 percent, respectively. According to the 1999 survey, the active general aviation fleet totaled 219,464 and flew an estimated 31.8 million hours.

General aviation activity counts at FAA air traffic facilities were mixed in 2000, possibly reflecting the increased price of aviation fuels. In September, the price of jet-A ranged between $2.31 and $2.60 per gallon while the price of avgas ranged between $2.35 and $2.82 per gallon. Operations at combined FAA and contract towers declined 0.5 percent, with itinerant operations down 0.8 percent and local operations basically unchanged from 1999. Conversely, instrument operations at the combined towered airports increased for a fourth consecutive year, up 1.9 percent in 2000 and 17.8 percent over the last four years.

After recording increased activity for eight consecutive years (up 20.3 percent between 1992 and 1999), general aviation activity at FAA en route centers declined by 0.7 percent in 2000. Despite a decline in the number of general aviation aircraft handled in 2000, there were some positive trends that reflect continuing growth in business and corporate flying. Although domestic departures recorded at FAA en route centers were down 1.7 percent, oceanic departures were up 40.4 percent. Additionally, both domestic and oceanic overs at FAA en route centers showed positive gains in 2000, up 2.5 and 16.2 percent, respectively.

Although local operations (generally touch-and-go activity) at FAA and contract towered airports remained unchanged in 2000, local activity was up 17.4 percent during the prior three years. If fuel prices decline as projected, we can expect the turnaround exhibited in recreational and instructional flying over the previous several years to resume once again.

The number of active pilots are estimated to have increased for a third consecutive year in 2000, totaling 645,539. All four of the major pilot categories are estimated to have increased in 2000—student, private, commercial, and airline transport. The number of instrument rated pilots was estimated to increase by nearly 6,000 to 315,100 in 2000, also the third consecutive year of increased numbers.

Although most of the statistics relating to general aviation activity are encouraging, it is the numbers relating to student pilots, one of the key factors impacting the future of the general aviation industry, that are of particular importance to the general aviation industry. The industry has, over the past several years, instituted a number of industry-wide programs, including "BE A PILOT," which are designed to attract new pilots to general aviation. The future direction of the industry will depend, in large part, on the success of these programs.

ACTIVE AIRCRAFT

Based on the results of the 1999 GA Survey, there are an estimated 219,464 active general aviation aircraft. The active fleet has now increased for five consecutive years, up 26.9 percent over this five-year period and up 7.2 percent in 1999.

Single-engine piston aircraft continue to dominate the fleet in 1999, accounting for 68.8 percent of the total active fleet. The next largest groups are multi-engine piston (9.6 percent) and experimental aircraft (9.4 percent). Turboprops, turbojets, and rotorcraft make up relatively small shares of the active fleet, accounting for 2.6, 3.2, and 3.4 percent, respectively. (See Figure 27.2.)

The hours flown chart shows that higher utilization rates provide turboprops, turbojets and rotorcraft a disproportionate share of the total hours flown. These three aircraft categories constitute less than ten percent of the

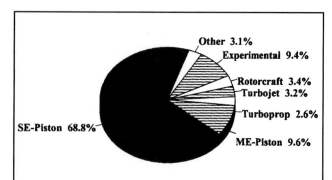

Figure 27.2 Active General Aviation Aircraft Percent by Aircraft Type in 1999.

active fleet but account for nearly 23 percent of total hours flown.

The 1999 GA Survey results for individual aircraft categories are as follows:

1. The number of active fixed-wing piston aircraft totaled 171,923, up 5.5 percent:
   - single-engine piston aircraft increased from 144,234 to 150,886, up 4.6 percent, and
   - multi-engine piston aircraft increased from 18,729 to 21,038 up 12.3 percent.

2. The number of active fixed-wing turbine aircraft totaled 12,799, up 4.6 percent:
   - turboprop aircraft decreased from 6,174 to 5,679, down 8.0 percent, and
   - turbojet aircraft increased from 6,066 to 7,120, up 17.4 percent.

3. The active rotorcraft fleet totaled 7,448, up 0.3 percent:
   - turbine-powered rotorcraft increased from 4,881 to 4,884, and
   - piston-powered rotorcraft increased from 2,545 to 2,564.

4. Active experimental aircraft totaled 20,528, an increase of 24.4 percent:
   - amateur builds increased from 13,189 to 16,858, up 27.89 percent,
   - exhibition aircraft increased from 1,630 to 1,999, up 22.6 percent, and
   - other experimental aircraft decreased from 1,684 to 1,671, down 0.8 percent.

5. The "other aircraft" category increased from 5,580 to 6,765, up 21.2 percent:
   - gliders decreased from 2,105 to 2,041, down 3.0 percent, and
   - lighter-than-air aircraft increased from 3,475 to 4,725, up 36.0 percent.

One explanation for the large percentage growth or declines for individual aircraft categories may be the result of overstated 1997 and 1998 estimates. This is particularly true for the experimental aircraft category, which recorded gains of 24.4 and 12.4 percent in 1999 and 1998, respectively, following a decline of 11.7 percent in 1997.

PRIMARY USE OF AIRCRAFT

A public use category was added to the Survey in 1996. Because of this change in classification of activity, comparisons with 1995 or earlier data should be made with caution. The 1999 survey also included a new use category—Air Medical Services—and eliminated the catchall "Other" category.

Personal (35.6 percent) and instructional flying (18.6 percent) were the two largest uses of general aviation activity in 1999, accounting for 54.2 percent of all hours flown. Personal use flight hours (11.3 million) were up 15.5 percent from 1998 while instructional hours (5.9 million) were up 48.8 percent.

Corporate (11.4 percent) and business (11.3 percent) flying, the third and fourth largest uses for general aviation, were up 6.9 percent in 1999. Corporate hours were up 12.5 percent while business hours increased 2.1 percent. This increase is consistent with the increased numbers of business jets delivered over recent years and is also supported by the increase in the number of turbojet hours in corporate and business use—up 17.3 percent in 1999.

Although air taxi activity (6.0 percent of total hours) declined 21.0 percent in 1999, this category of flying is still up 22.8 percent over the past five years. While this use category has had some fluctuations over the past several years, the estimates appear reasonable, especially considering the rule changes and other issues regarding part 135 operators.

In 1999, hours for aerial observation (1.2 million, 3.9 percent of total hours) were up 53.1 percent, although this use category is still slightly below its 1997 level of 1.3 million hours. Public use, 3.5 percent of all hours flown, decreased by 19.1 percent from 1998, but some of this decline may result from confusion about the definition of the Public Use category.

Aerial application (1.5 million, 4.8 percent of total hours) recorded a 17.5 percent increase in 1999. External load, other work, sightseeing and air tours accounted for a combined 3.5 percent of total hours while the new Air Medical Services category (458,000 hours) accounted for the remaining 1.3 percent of activity. (See Figure 27.3.)

PILOT POPULATION

At the end of 2000, the total pilot population totaled 648,539, over 13,000 more pilots (up 2.1 percent) than a year earlier. All four major groupings—student, private, commercial, and airline transport—registered increases in 2000. These four pilot groupings totaled 630,750 and accounted for 97.3 percent of all pilots in 2000. The three strictly general aviation groupings totaled 491,050 and accounted for 75.7 percent of all pilots.

The estimated number of active student pilots in 2000 was 104,150, up 2.1 percent from the 1999 estimate of 102,000, but less than last year's forecast of 106,100 for 2000.

Industry initiatives are underway to continue the positive growth in student pilots because they are seen as the future of general aviation. The industry's efforts to revive the market for its products and services will, in large part, depend on how successful its programs are in attracting new pilots. The increased supply for student pilots may not only be generated by those seeking private pilot certificates for personal enjoyment, but also for those seeking a career in aviation. Driven by the requirements of commercial air carriers (including regionals/commuters), fractional ownership providers, and corporate flight departments, there is a perceived demand for additional commercial and air transport pilots.

Private pilots totaled 260,700 (up 0.8 percent) in 2000 while the number of commercial pilots totaled 126,200 (up 1.6 percent). The number of airline transport pilots (139,700) was up 1.5 percent in 2000, the 44th consecutive year that this category has posted increased numbers.

The number of helicopter pilots (those holding helicopter certificates only) increased by 3.7 percent to 8,015 in 2000. The number of glider pilots (9,430) increased slightly in 2000 while the number of recreational pilots (344) remained basically unchanged.

The number of instrument-rated pilots (315,100) increased 2.0 percent in 2000. Instrument-rated pilots are currently 57.9 percent of total active pilots (excluding student and recreational pilots), basically the same percentage as in 1999. This represents an increase from the 55.5 percent share in 1995, and reflects the increased sophistication of both aircraft and pilots utilizing the National Airspace System.

HOURS FLOWN

Based on the results of the 1999 GA Survey, the number of hours flown by general aviation aircraft totaled 31.8 million, up 13.0 percent from the 28.1 million reported for 1998. The number of hours flown by general aviation aircraft has increased for five consecutive years, showing an increase of 31.8 percent for the five-year period.

The 1999 Survey results for the individual aircraft categories are as follow:

1. Hours flown by fixed-wing piston aircraft (72.1 percent of total hours flown) totaled 22.9 million, an increase of 12.2 percent:
   - single-engine piston aircraft hours (19.3 million) an increase of 14.9 percent,
   - multi-engine piston aircraft hours (3.6 million) decreased by 0.3 percent.

2. Hours flown by fixed-wing turbine aircraft totaled 4.5 million hours, an increase of 14.0 percent:
   - hours flown by turboprop aircraft were up 2.6 percent, and

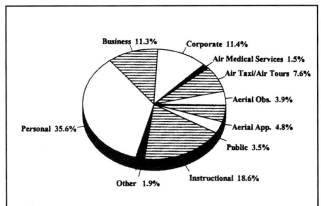

Figure 27.3 General Aviation Aircraft Primary Use in 1999.

- hours flown by turbojet aircraft were up 23.0 percent.

3. Rotorcraft hours flown (2.7 million) were up 17.2 percent from 1998:

   - turbine powered rotorcraft flew 2.2 million hours (up 14.4 percent), and

   - piston-powered rotorcraft flew 0.6 million hours (up 29.3 percent).

4. The number of hours flown by experimental aircraft (1.2 million) increased 16.4 percent over the year, but is still 6.0 percent below the 1997 figure. (See Figure 27.4.)

ACTIVITY AT FAA AIR TRAFFIC FACILITIES

General aviation activity at combined FAA and contract towered airports declined slightly in fiscal year 2000; this following three consecutive years of strong traffic growth—up 13.4 percent over the 1996–1999 period. In 2000, general aviation operations totaled 39.9 million, a decline of 0.5 percent over 1999. Most of the decline occurred in itinerant operations (22.8 million), which were down 0.8 percent. Local operations remained basically flat in 2000 at 17.0 million. Since 1996, local operations are up 17.5 percent and itinerant operations are up 9.7 percent.

In 2000, the top ten general aviation airports, as ranked by operations, accounted for 9.1 percent of general aviation activity at the 459 combined FAA/contract towers, and 5.3 percent of total aircraft activity at towered airports. Of the top 10 airports, three are in

California, two each are in Florida and Texas, and Arizona, Colorado, and Washington each have one. Four of the top ten airports experienced a decline in operations since 1996.

The ten fastest growing general aviation airports, as ranked by the percentage increase in operations, grew from 456,772 general aviation operations in 1996 to almost 1.1 million in 2000, an increase of 130.9 percent. These ten airports account for 2.6 percent of all general aviation activity. The two fastest growing airports during this four-year period were Wilkes-Barre/Scranton, which grew by 191.1 percent (from 33,921 operations to 98,753 operations), and San Antonio/Stinson, which grew by 182.3 percent (from 50,766 to 143,315 operations). (Table 27.1.)

Four of the fastest growing airports, Fresno Yosemite, Pompano Beach, San Antonio/Stinson, and Minneapolis-St. Paul also made the list of top 100 general aviation airports as ranked by operations. They are ranked 39th, 52nd, 83rd, and 100th, respectively. The list of top 10 fastest growing general aviation airports also includes two commercial air carrier hubs—Minneapolis-St. Paul International (MSP) and Covington/Cincinnati International (CVG).

General aviation activity at the 29 large hub airports totaled 1.5 million in 2000, up 0.9 percent over 1999 and 10.1 percent over the four years since 1996. Of the 29 large hubs, 16 have recorded increased general aviation operations over the four-year period. The three major hubs with the largest number of general aviation operations in 2000 were Minneapolis/St. Paul (128,497 operations), Las Vegas/McCarran (119,100 operations), and Phoenix Sky Harbor (116,389 operations). In 2000, general aviation operations as a percent of total operations at these three airports, were 24.5, 22.2, and 18.6 percent, respectively.

General aviation instrument operations at combined FAA and contract tower airports (21.3 million) increased 1.8 percent in 2000, up for the fourth consecutive year. General aviation instrument operations have now increased during six of the last seven years, with activity gains totaling 19.2 percent over the period.

The number of general aviation aircraft handled at en route centers (8.7 million) also declined slightly (0.7 percent) in 2000. This decline came after eight consecutive years of increased activity, a period during which general aviation activity increased 20.3 percent.

While the increases in local operations since 1996 (up 17.5 percent) coincide with the resurgence in the number of student pilots and increased instructional flying, the gains in instrument and en route operations

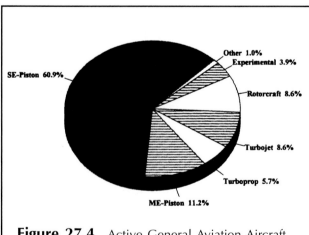

Figure 27.4 Active General Aviation Aircraft Percent Hours Flown in 1999.

Table 27.1 Fastest Growing General Aviation Airports Ranked by % Change in Operations: 1996–2000

Fac. Id.	City/Airport	2000	1996	% Ch. 96–00
AVP	Wilkes-Barre/Scran. Int'l	98,753	33,921	191.1
SSF	San Antonio/Stinson Field	143,315	50,766	182.3
FAT	Fresno Yosemite Int'l.	202,026	80,022	152.5
MSP	Minneapolis-St. Paul Int'l.	128,497	55,004	133.6
CVG	Covington/Cincinnati Int'l.	32,160	14,511	121.6
BTL	Battle Creek/Kellogg	98,194	44,436	121.0
KOA	Kailua/Kona Int'l.	42.244	19,694	114.5
PMP	Pompano Beach Airpark	184,852	92,513	99.8
HLG	Wheeling/OH County	34,059	17,887	90.4
BKL	Cleveland/Burke Lakefront	90,551	48,018	88.6

accompany the expanding fleet of turbojet aircraft and the increase in longer-range business/corporate traffic.

AIRCRAFT SHIPMENTS AND BILLINGS

According to statistics released by the General Aviation Manufacturers Association (GAMA), sales figures show strong gains for both piston and turbojet aircraft in 2000. In the first three quarters of 2000, general aviation aircraft shipments totaled 2000 units—an increase of 16.3 percent over the same period in 1999. This marks the sixth consecutive year of increased demand for general aviation aircraft. Shipments of piston aircraft and jets were up 13.8 and 15.1 percent, respectively. While shipments of turboprop aircraft have been mixed over the past several years (down 2.6 percent in 1999), shipments for this category of aircraft were up 36.3 percent during the first nine months of 2000. (Table 27.2.)

The continued increase in new aircraft sales and deliveries can be attributed to a number of factors: the strength of the U.S. economy; the tremendous success of fractional ownership companies; and an increase in the number of traditional flight departments being operated by corporate America. In addition, there are numerous new product offerings, including the Boeing Business Jet, the Cessna 172 Skyhawk and 182 Skylane, the Cessna Stationair and Turbo Stationair, the Piper

Table 27.2 Annual Shipments of New U.S. Manufactured General Aviation Airplanes

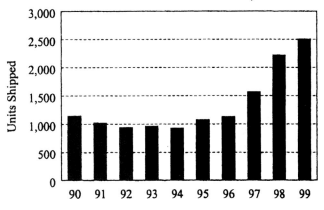

Source: General Aviation Manufacturers Association

Meridian, and the Mooney Eagle. Other recently certificated products include the Cirrus SR20 and the Lancair Columbia 300—which had its first delivery in early 2000.

Billings for general aviation aircraft totaled $6.25 billion for the first nine months of 2000, an increase of 10.4 percent from the corresponding 1999 figure. Over the same period, export shipments are up by 11.3 percent to 444 aircraft. However, export billings decreased by 20.7 percent to $1.44 billion for this nine-month period. Exports represent about 22 percent of all U.S. manufactured aircraft shipped. (Table 27.3.)

Table 27.3   Annual Billings of New U.S. Manufactured General Aviation Airplanes

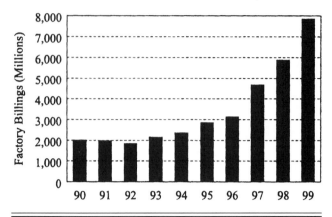

Source: General Aviation Manufacturers Association

REVITALIZATION OF AN INDUSTRY

General aviation continues to be a dominant force in aviation. At year-end 1999 there were 19,098 civil and joint use airports/heliports in operation, with 5,324 available for public use. Of these, 655 airports had commercial service certificates (also used by general aviation). This leaves a total of 18,443 airports/heliports (96.6 percent) used exclusively by general aviation aircraft, with 4,669 available for public use.

General Aviation represents the largest percentage of civil aircraft in the United States and accounts for the majority of operations handled by towered and nontowered U.S. airports, as well as for the majority of certificated pilots in the U.S.

In 1999, there were over 227,000 active civil aircraft in the United States. This includes 219,465 active general aviation aircraft (over 96 percent of the active fleet), nearly 6,000 passenger or cargo jet aircraft air carriers, and over 2,000 regional/commuter aircraft.

Of the 635,472 certificated pilots at the end of 1999, private pilots accounted for more than 40.0 percent of the total. In addition, general aviation itinerant and local operations totaled 39.9 million in 2000, 58.0 percent of the total 68.7 million operations at towered and nontowered U.S. airports.

OPTIMISM IN THE INDUSTRY

August of 2000 marked the sixth year since the passage of the General Aviation Revitalization Act. Since that time, general aviation shipments and billings have more than doubled. The General Aviation Manufacturers Association (GAMA) estimates that more than 25,000 manufacturing jobs have been created in the general aviation industry as a result of the General Aviation Revitalization Act. GAMA also reports increases in general aviation exports, new products as a result of increases in research and development by its members, and an increase in the number of student pilots.

General aviation also came off another record year for billings in 1999, and the year 2000 was likely to set yet another record. Shipments of aircraft were up in all aircraft categories—piston, turboprop, and jet—with all three categories registering double-digit percentage increases through three quarters of 2000. Although turboprop and turbojet shipments were up substantially in 2000, the market continued to be dominated by shipments of piston aircraft.

The strength of general aviation's recovery and the positive outlook throughout the industry can be attributed to a strong U.S. economy and the passage of the General Aviation Revitalization Act, which brought product liability reform to the industry.

From 1994 through 1999, shipments of general aviation aircraft have increased at an average annual rate of over 17.8 percent, from 928 units shipped in 1994, to 2,525 units shipped in 1999. It appeared that 2000 would also show an increase in shipments.

One of the reasons cited for the rise in shipments is the success of the Cessna single-engine piston models introduced in 1997. Cessna has recently announced both plans and orders for four new Citation models, the CJ1, CJ2, Sovereign, and Ultra Encore. Raytheon will begin deliveries of its Premier I, an entry-level jet that features a composite fuselage with metal wings. Raytheon will follow delivery of the Premier I with its Hawker Horizon. Mooney is set to begin deliveries of its new aircraft—the Eagle. The New Piper Aircraft, Inc., recently rolled out its first turbine-powered aircraft, the Malibu Meridian.

Another sign of optimism to the industry is the entry of commercial manufacturers into the general aviation aircraft market. Boeing Business Jets plans to build a larger version of its long-range corporate jet—the BBJ-2. Boeing Business Jets, a joint enterprise of Boeing and General Electric, entered the market with a long-range BBJ based on a hybrid of the B737-700/800 aircraft used in scheduled commercial service. Airbus and Fairchild are also marketing business jets that are based on aircraft originally designed for commercial operations.

Some kit builders are now becoming production companies at the entry level. Cirrus Design Corporation has received a Production Certificate from the FAA for the SR20. This aircraft incorporates the Cirrus Airframe Parachute System (CAPS), a device designed to lower the entire aircraft to the ground in case a catastrophic event eliminates opportunities for control of the aircraft.

Since their start in the 1980s, fractional ownership providers have steadily increased their customer base. According to the National Business Aircraft Association (NBAA), at the end of 2000 there were nearly 2,100 entities involved in fractional ownership of over 500 aircraft. Despite this record growth, it is believed only a small percentage of this market has been developed.

Fractional ownership programs are filling the niche for corporations, celebrities, and business executives that do not generate enough flying to warrant a flight department. Fractional ownership providers offer the customer a more efficient use of his time by providing faster point-to-point travel times and the ability to conduct business while flying. In addition, shareholders of fractional ownerships find the minimum startup concerns and easier exiting options of great benefit.

While the fractional ownership fleet and shareholders have been growing, so too have the turbine business fleet and flight departments of Corporate America. According to the NBAA, the corporate fleet numbers 13,860 and includes 9,195 flight departments. From 1993 to 2000, NBAA estimates that the corporate aircraft fleet grew at an annual rate of 5.4 percent while the number of business flight departments grew at an annual rate of 4.5 percent.

The business aviation community was initially concerned that the success of fractional ownership programs would result in a shutdown of corporate flight departments. These concerns have not come to fruition. Fractional ownership providers generally find their business base to be first-time users of corporate aircraft services, users that traditionally utilized commercial air transportation services. Once introduced to the benefits of corporate flying, some users of fractional programs have found it more cost beneficial to start their own flight departments, instead of incurring the costs of a larger share in a fractional ownership program. As such, the fractional ownership community may be partially responsible for the increase in traditional flight departments since 1993.

Future aircraft production schedules are being increased to meet the expected renewed demand for general aviation aircraft. The Allied Signal *Business Aviation Outlook* forecasts delivery of nearly 6,800 business aircraft over the 2000 to 2010 time period. The increased numbers result from the demand for new and derivative aircraft models entering service with corporate flight departments, the rapidly expanding fractional ownership market, and the projected strong economic growth in the United States, Europe, and Latin America.

The number of amateur-built experimental aircraft in the general aviation fleet has increased consistently for more than a quarter of a century, from 2,100 in 1970 to almost 22,000 today. It is estimated that more than 75 percent of these are active aircraft. According to the industry, about 3,200 kits were sold in 1997 and at least 1,600 were expected to be sold in 1999. The completion rate is about 63 percent (Kit Planes).

The popularity of the amateur-built aircraft results from several factors, including affordability and performance. Amateur-built experimental aircraft represent a test-bed for new technologies that will eventually be introduced in the development and manufacture of the next generation of light general aviation production aircraft. The strength of the used aircraft market and the success of the kit aircraft market demonstrate that demand still exists for affordable aircraft.

The overall general aviation accident rate per 100,000 flying hours has declined over the past 25 years, and is at its lowest rate since 1938—the first year for reporting of accident statistics. The National Transportation Safety Board's (NTSB) preliminary estimate for 1999 is 7.05 general aviation accidents per 100,000 hours flown, down from the 7.12 rate for 1998. This continues the trend for the general aviation accident rate, which has been declining since 1994.

FAA/GOVERNMENT PROGRAMS/INITIATIVES

The partnership between the FAA and the general aviation community is a continuous joint effort aimed at fostering industry improvements and aviation safety.

The FAA Administrator has indicated that the agency intends to support the growth of general aviation while continuing to improve its safety. To this end, a safety program called "Safer Skies" has been established. Together with industry, the FAA will use the latest technology to analyze U.S. and global data to find the root causes of accidents so as to determine the best actions for breaking the chain of events that lead to accidents. For general aviation, this means the FAA will embark on major data improvements, including quality, collection, and analysis.

As part of the "Safer Skies" effort, the General Aviation Joint Steering Committee has chartered a joint government/industry group called the General Aviation

Data Improvement Team (GADIT). The GADIT was established to develop strategies to "increase detail about factors that have contributed to or caused general aviation accidents and incidents;" to "improve the quality and timeliness of estimates of general aviation activity;" and to "suggest alternative and innovative ways to measure the effectiveness of *Safer Skies* interventions for general aviation." The GADIT has been organized to address four areas: activity data, accident data, incident data, and metrics.

The first task—the activity data task—has been organized and several working meetings have already been held. The activity data task team expected to produce its briefing and report during the first quarter of 2001. Due to the sequential nature of the GADIT tasks, the schedule calls for completion of the metrics effort during the second half of 2002.

The FAA, the National Aeronautics and Space Administration (NASA), industry, and other government agencies and universities, are working together to improve the safety and efficiency in our transportation system. To this end, NASA and FAA are planning the Small Aircraft Transportation System (SATS). The National General Aviation Roadmap is a 25-year strategy for developing SATS. It is believed that the SATS can satisfy 21st century transportation demand by relieving pressure on existing ground and air systems, and by creating access to more communities in less time.

The goal of SATS is to provide more rapid transportation to 25 percent of "suburban, rural, and remote communities by 2007 and, to more than 90 percent by 2022." SATS plans to take a "transportation systems approach to safety for small aircraft and landing facilities." By developing an "affordable infrastructure for instrument approaches to ALL runway ends and helipads in the U.S.," SATS is expected to expand opportunities for "air transportation . . . between 5,400 public use landing facilities," with the goal of "safe accessibility by air to 90% more destinations throughout the nation," thereby encouraging "economic development for suburban, rural, and remote America." The infrastructure to support the SATS will be airports that integrate emerging communication, navigation, and surveillance technologies to produce new levels of utility for the Nation's smaller airport infrastructure.

FAA and NASA have also collaborated with the general aviation community in research programs aimed at fostering new technologies in general aviation. Two such programs are AGATE (Advanced General Aviation Transportation Experiments) and GAP (General Aviation Propulsion).

The AGATE Consortium provides a unique partnership between government, industry, and academia. The goal of AGATE is to utilize new technology to produce aircraft that are safer, easier to operate, and more affordable to today's pilot. This will be accomplished through utilization of improved avionics, more crashworthy airframes, and pilot training. NASA's GAP program focuses on development of improved piston and turbine engines.

One of the goals of FAA's Safer Skies initiative is to improve weather and other flight information. The Flight Information Service (FIS) program plans to put real time weather information in the cockpit.

The NASA "Highway in the Sky" project has a goal of putting 21st Century instrumentation into the cockpit—including GPS position and weather displays. Affordable computers will provide an "intuitive pictorial of situational awareness," allowing display of a "Highway" to a preprogrammed destination. The NASA National Aviation Operational Monitoring Service (NAOMS) program has conducted a study of commercial airline pilots to develop "statistically accurate counts of key aviation safety events." This approach to research and data collection is expected to be used to study general aviation and was planned to begin in 2002.

The FAA is also committed to improving navigation through satellite based systems such as the Global Positioning System (GPS) for airport precision approach. The initial 25 Wide Area Augmentation System (WAAS) stations have been installed and certification was expected by year-end 2001. Most IFR aircraft are expected to have GPS/WAAS by 2005. The expected increase in the number of general aviation aircraft equipped with GPS/WAAS and other avionics and communications gear such as Automatic Dependent Surveillance-Broadcast (ADS-B) and 8.33 kHz (radio) channel spacing should be demonstrated in avionics tables included in the GA Survey over the next few years.

MANUFACTURER AND INDUSTRY PROGRAMS/INITIATIVES

The fractional ownership industry was started about 15 years ago and since that time has provided corporate flying services to companies that could not otherwise justify the costs associated with operating a separate flight department. During this time, fractional ownership providers have operated under Federal Aviation Regulation (FAR) Part 91, which governs general aviation. However, there is pressure for fractional ownership providers to operate under Part 135 regulations that govern commercial aircraft such as air carriers, air taxi, and charters. FAR Part 135 providers regard fractional ownership providers as competition that benefits from the right to fly under the less restrictive FAR Part 91 standards.

The FAA has established a formal rulemaking committee, consisting of members from aircraft manufacturers, corporate flight departments, charter operators, fractional owner providers and their customers, and business aircraft management companies. The committee will review current Federal Aviation Regulations regarding fractional ownership activity and propose revisions as may be appropriate. Early last year the committee prepared a draft proposal that would require fractional ownership aircraft to operate under a subpart of Part 91.

It was submitted to the FAA and has undergone analysis to assess the economic impact of the proposed rule. The FAA is now in the process of achieving agency concurrence before notice of proposed rulemaking is issued.

Manufacturers are launching programs to make aircraft ownership easier. The New Piper Aircraft, for example, created Piper Financial Services (PFS). PFS offers competitive interest rates for the purchase and/or leasing of Piper aircraft. The Experimental Aircraft Association (EAA) has entered into an agreement with TFC Textron (formerly Green Tree Aircraft) to finance kit built planes. The general aviation industry is also seeking to increase the number of lending institutions that offer special low, competitive rates for aircraft financing.

As indicated earlier, fractional ownership of turbine powered aircraft has experienced significant growth over the past seven years from about two dozen fractionally owned aircraft in 1993 to nearly 530 in the year 2000. With nearly 3,500 fractional shares and 2,100 fractional owners it is apparent that many fractional owners have shares in more than one aircraft—another testament to the popularity of this option of aircraft ownership.

Over the past several years, the general aviation industry has launched a series of programs and initiatives whose main goals are to promote and assure future growth within the industry. These include the "No Plane, No Gain" program sponsored jointly by GAMA and the NBAA; "Project Pilot" sponsored by the Aircraft Owners and Pilots Association (AOPA); the "Flying Start" program sponsored by EAA; and "BE A PILOT."

"No Plane, No Gain" is an advocacy program created in 1992 by GAMA and NBAA to promote acceptance and increased use of business aviation. The program promotes business aviation as a cost-effective tool for increasing the efficiency, productivity, and profitability of companies.

AOPA's "Project Pilot" promotes the training of new pilots in order to rebuild the pilot population. AOPA believes students that have mentors offering advice and help as training progresses are more likely to complete their training than students who don't have mentors.

The "BE A PILOT" program is jointly sponsored and supported by more than 100 industry organizations. The program, which started in 1996, encourages people of all ages to "Stop Dreaming, and Start Flying." The approach is multi-faceted: (1) create an influx of new pilots; (2) generate flight training leads; (3) encourage improvement in flight school marketing; (4) secure additional funding to expand the effort. "BE A PILOT" started issuing "introductory flight certificates" to interested respondents in May 1997. The certificates can be redeemed for a first flight lesson at a cost of $35.

In the four years since the program started, over 110,000 certificates have been requested. In 2000 there were more than 35,000 requests for "Introductory Flight Certificates—up from 25,000 in past years. The program has over 1,600 participating flight schools and attracts new market entrants via the Internet and cable-television advertising.

The program has been supported by about 100 manufacturers and other aviation businesses and organizations. They have been successful in raising funds for the effort and expected contributions for 2001 to be nearly $2 million. In the latter part of 2000, the "BE A PILOT" moved the program to a higher level of activity and effort by hiring a full-time president and chief executive. As a result the program will be expanded for 2001 to "include new initiatives in media exposure on the benefits of being a pilot for personal, business, and career interests."

Several industry organizations are also targeting young people through the Internet to peak their interest in the world of aviation. The NBAA sponsors "AvKids," a program designed to educate elementary school students about the benefits of business aviation to the community, and career opportunities available to them in business aviation. The National Agricultural Aviation Association is in the process of developing a webpage with information on careers in aerial application. GAMA offers publications, awards, and scholarships to bring education into the nation's classrooms. AOPA's "Apple Program" brings aviation into the classroom, targeting middle and high school students.

GENERAL AVIATION FORECASTS

The general aviation forecasts discussed in the following paragraphs are based on a set of economic assumptions—continuous moderate and sustained economic growth both in the United States and worldwide.

The forecast also assumes that the regulatory environment affecting general aviation will not change dramatically. Specifically, it is assumed that noise and emissions requirements on business turbine aircraft will remain within the bounds prescribed by current rules and regulations. The forecast also assumes that general aviation activity will not be subject to new user-fees or limited access to airports and airspace.

In addition, the forecast assumes that the flight school infrastructure will be improved, and that the industry will be more efficient at keeping consumers interested in aviation through its promotional "learn-to-fly" activities. It is also assumed that announced new products will enter the market and live up to their expectations in regard to price, performance, and availability.

Finally, the forecast assumes that the fractional ownership market will continue to expand and bring new operators and shareholders into business aviation. The forecast further assumes that the fractional ownership community will not by inhibited by certification and regulatory requirements.

To the extent that industry and government programs/initiatives are successful in expanding the market for general aviation products and services, the forecasts discussed in the following pages are likely to be achieved or possibly exceeded. If the industry and government programs are less than fully successful, the active general aviation fleet, hours flown, and pilots could be considerably lower than forecast.

The current forecasts for the general aviation active fleet, hours flown, and fuel consumption use the data obtained from the 1999 survey as the base year. Therefore, the forecast period for the three activity measures extends from 2000 through 2012, and references to average annual growth rates for the forecast period include 13 years. Since final confirmed airmen data for 2000 have not been published, forecasts for certificated pilots are based on actual 1999 data obtained from the official airmen certification records maintained at the FAA Aeronautical Center in Oklahoma City and esti-mated year 2000 data. The forecasts for these series extend from 2000 through 2012, and the average annual growth rates also include 13 years.

ACTIVE FLEET

The forecasts of the active general aviation fleet is based, in large part, on panel discussions at the September 1999 TRB workshop. In any year, the U.S. fleet is assumed to be the sum of new production flowing into the fleet, the fleet size carried over from the previous year, and the attrition of existing aircraft during the current year. Attrition occurs from net exports, retirements, and write-offs. New production depends on economic growth and corporate profitability, new product development and introduction, and the price at which new aircraft are offered for sale.

The active general aviation aircraft fleet is expected to increase at an average annual rate of 0.9 percent over the 13-year forecast period, with the number of active aircraft increasing from 219,464 in 1999 to 245,965 in 2012. The fleet is projected to expand by about 2,200 aircraft annually through 2005 as increased aircraft production and new aircraft products enter the marketplace. The active fleet grows by just under 2,000 aircraft annually over the remaining seven years of the forecast period.

While the production of fixed-wing aircraft is almost double what it was in 1990, even after including kit built, gliders, and lighter-than-air aircraft, it is well below the goal of NASA's program of 10,000 aircraft a year within 10 years, and 20,000 aircraft within 20 years.

The number of single-engine piston active aircraft is projected to increase from 150,886 in 1999 to 164,800 in 2012, an average net addition of just over 1,000 aircraft annually. Many new products have entered the market and recent product developments and ongoing research promise the addition of several new aircraft models over the forecast period.

Because of the current average age of the single-engine piston fleet, large numbers of the older piston aircraft are assumed to be retired throughout the forecast period. If 100LL fuel is eliminated, attrition rates could be higher due to owners retiring their airplane rather than incurring additional costs to keep them flying. Therefore, the net growth in the single-engine piston category is expected to come largely from the introduction of new products from Cessna and Piper, and from full production being achieved by Cirrus and Lancair in the out years of the forecast period.

The size of the active multi-engine piston aircraft fleet is expected to remain basically flat at 21,200 aircraft over the 13-year forecast period. Attrition for the multi-engine piston aircraft is expected to equal production.

The turbine-powered fleet is expected to increase at an average rate of 3.0 percent over the forecast period. Turbojet aircraft are forecast to increase by 4.3 percent annually, from 7,120 in 1999 to 12,280 in 2012. These forecasts are based on the assumption that the turbojet fleet will increase by a net of nearly 400 aircraft annually.

Several factors are responsible for the improved market for business jets. These include a strong U.S. and global economy; the success and rapid growth of the fractional ownership market, new product offerings that have stimulated buyer interests; and a shift from commercial air travel to corporate/business air travel by many business travelers and corporations.

The number of turboprop aircraft is expected to grow from 5,679 in 1999 to 6,600 in 2012, an average annual growth rate of nearly 1.2 percent. These forecasts assume that the turboprop fleet grows by approximately 70 aircraft per year, counting new production and attrition.

The rotorcraft fleet is forecast to grow almost 1.9 percent annually over the 13-year forecast period, from 7,448 in 1999 to 9,460 in 2012. The turbine fleet is projected to grow at an annual rate of 1.5 percent, while the smaller piston fleet size is expected to grow at an annual rate of 2.4 percent.

The number of experimental aircraft is projected to increase from 20,528 in 1999 to 24,080 in 2012, an average annual growth rate of 1.2 percent. Gliders and lighter-than-air aircraft are forecast to increase by 0.8 percent annually, growing from 6,765 in 1999 to 7,545 in 2012.

AIRCRAFT UTILIZATION

It is assumed that the aging of the general aviation fleet is one of the main determinants of declining utilization of general aviation aircraft. Based on results from the 1999 GA survey the average age of aircraft in active general aviation fleet is estimated to be about 27 years, with piston aircraft accounting for the majority of the aging fleet. Data from the1999 GA Survey shows that aircraft utilization peaks at 218 hours for aircraft between 16 and 20 years old and then declines substantially after an aircraft reaches 20 years of age. The aging of the fleet appears to be one of the main causes of

declining utilization of general aviation aircraft during the early and mid-1990s. (Table 27.4.)

While part of the decline in utilization can be attributed to the aging of the general aviation fleet, U.S. economic slowdowns and/or recessions, such as those which occurred in 1990–1991 and 1992 can also impact utilization. The expanding U.S. economy and increased consumer confidence that has prevailed since that time appears to have stabilized or increased utilization rates. New ownership strategies, and other approaches to make flying more affordable should also be positive forces on utilization rates during the forecast period.

For 1999, the utilization rate for single engine piston aircraft is estimated to be approximately 128.1 hours per aircraft. Starting at this base, utilization rates for single-engine piston aircraft are projected to increase to 143.5 hours in 2012, an average annual increase of 0.9 percent.

Growth in the single-engine piston utilization rate is assumed to be the result of two factors. First, utilization rates tend to be higher for newer aircraft and, with approximately 2,000 new aircraft projected to enter the fleet annually, utilization rates should increase for this fact alone. The second factor is the expected increases in the number of student pilots and aircraft that will be required for flight training. The single-engine piston aircraft used for instructional flying tend to have higher utilization rates than those of other aircraft in the same category—375 hours compared to 128 hours. Increased instructional flying will be one of the factors pushing up single engine piston utilization rates over

Table 27.4 1999 Average Flight Hours by Age of Aircraft

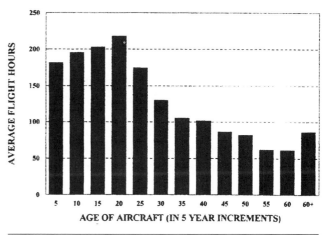

the forecast period.

In 1999, multi-engine piston aircraft utilization rates were estimated to be approximately 169.7 hours per aircraft. The utilization of multi-engine piston aircraft is forecast to grow at an average annual rate of 0.2 percent over the forecast period, reaching 174.5 hours in 2012.

In the turbine fixed-wing fleet, utilization rates for turboprops increased from 285.9 hours in 1998 to 319.0 hours in 1999. Utilization is expected to increase only slightly over the forecast period, reaching an average of 22.7 hours per aircraft in 2012. Turbojet utilization was up 4.8 percent, from an average of 367.0 hours per aircraft in 1998 to 384.6 hours in 1999. Over the forecast period, turbojet utilization is projected to grow at an average annual rate of 2.6 percent.

The increase in utilization rates for turbojets is largely attributable to the increased number of aircraft being operated by fractional ownership providers. While the average corporate jet utilization is about 300 hours per year, it is estimated that utilization for fractional ownership aircraft is about three to four times as much. The expected increase in the percentage of turbojet aircraft operated by fractional ownership providers will push the average turbojet utilization to about 536.2 hours in 2012.

Rotorcraft utilization rates are expected to increase at an average annual rate of 0.4 percent over the 13-year forecast period. Utilization rates for experimental and "other" aircraft are expected to grow by 0.7 and 0.5 percent, respectively, over the same time period.

HOURS FLOWN

Although the active general aviation fleet is forecast to increase by 0.9 percent annually over the 13-year forecast period, the projected annual increase in hours flown is 2.1 percent. General aviation hours flown is projected to increase from 31.8 million in 1999 to 41.7 million in 2012. (Table 27.5.)

Hours flown for single-engine piston aircraft are forecast to increase from 19.3 million in 1999 to 23.7 million in 2012, an average annual increase of 1.6 percent. This is less than the 2.9 percent growth suggested by the Light General Aviation panel at the FAA/TRB Workshop, which was based on the assumption that student pilots would increase by 8.0 percent annually over the 1999 to 2004 period. Based on actual results for 1999 and 2000—the number of student pilots declined from 97,736 in 1998 to 97,359 in 1999 (down 0.4 percent) and then increased 7.0 percent to 104,150

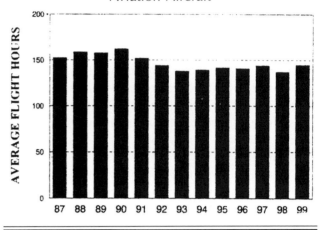

Table 27.5   Average Flight Hours by General Aviation Aircraft

in 2000. Therefore, the panel's projected rates of growth for student pilots and single-engine piston utilization were adjusted accordingly.

Multi-engine piston aircraft hours increase from 3.6 million in 1999 to 3.7 million in 2012, a rate of 0.3 percent annually.

Turboprop aircraft hours flown are projected to increase from 1.8 million in 1999 to 2.1 million in 2012, an annual growth rate of about 1.3 percent. Turbojet hours are expected to increase from 2.7 million in 1999 to almost 6.6 million in 2012, an average annual increase of 7.0 percent.

Rotorcraft hours flown is forecast to increase at an annual rate of 2.3 percent over the 13-year forecast period, from 2.7 to 3.7 million. During the same period, experimental aircraft hours flown are forecast to increase at an annual rate of almost 2.0 percent, reaching 1.6 million in 2012. Hours flown by gliders and lighter-than-air aircraft are projected to increase by 1.4 percent annually.

PILOT POPULATION

The total pilot population is projected to increase from an estimated 648,539 in 2000 to 827,177 by 2012, an annual increase of 2.0 percent over the 13-year forecast period. Annual growth rates for the major general aviation pilot categories are: student pilots, up 2.7 percent annually; private pilots, up 1.4 percent annually; and commercial pilots, up 1.4 percent annually.

While some of the growth of the student pilot population is in response to U.S. economic growth, much of the assumed growth is expected to result from industry-wide programs which are specifically designed to recruit new pilots to general aviation. The growth in numbers of student pilots and certificates issued over the past five years suggest that the programs are having a positive impact. The growth in student pilots also assumes growth in pilot training and flight schools which, in turn, implies future growth in the industry. Based on results from the 1999 GA Survey, the number of hours designated as instructional use is up 34.3 percent since 1994.

The FAA/TRB panel on Light General Aircraft suggested that the student pilot population would grow by eight percent annually during the years 1999–2004. While the student pilot forecasts have been revised downward from last year, the forecast still shows steady increases over the 12-year forecast period—from about 104,000 in 2000 to about 144,000 in 2012. While the projected growth is lower than that suggested by the FAA/TRB panel, it is still meaningful. Higher projected rates for student pilots also result in higher rates for other pilot categories. There is a high correlation between the number of student pilots who move on to the higher pilot classification of private and commercial pilots. AOPA is sponsoring research to develop more rigorous methods for estimating the higher pilot classifications from the numbers of new and renewed student pilot certificates.

Growth rates for the other pilot categories over the 13-year period are: airline transport pilots, up 3.2 percent; recreational, up 1.2 percent; helicopter, up 1.8 percent; and glider, up 0.4 percent.

The number of instrument rated pilots is expected to increase from 315,100 to 2000, to 384,100 in 2012, a 1.7 percent average annual rate of growth. In 2000, it is estimated that 48.6 percent of all active pilots were instrument rated. By 2012, the percentage of instrument rated pilots is projected to decline to 46.4 percent. This is largely the result of new entries into the pilot population, e.g., student pilots who do not require an instrument rating.

GENERAL AVIATION POLICY STATEMENT

General aviation is critically important to the Nation's economy and to the national transportation system. General aviation plays a crucial role in flight training for all segments of aviation and provides unique personal and recreational opportunities. It makes vital contributions to activities ranging from business aviation, to agricultural operations, to Warbird preservation, to glider and balloon flights.

ACCORDINGLY, IT IS THE POLICY OF THE FAA to foster and promote general aviation while continuing to improve its safety record. These goals are neither contradictory nor separable. They are best achieved by cooperating with the aviation community to define mutual concerns and joint efforts to accomplish objectives. We will strive to achieve the goals through voluntary compliance and methods designed to reduce the regulatory burden on general aviation.

The FAA's general aviation programs will focus on:

1. **Safety**
   To protect recent gains and aim for a new threshold.

2. **FAA Services**
   To provide the general aviation community with responsive, customer-driven certification, air traffic, and other services.

3. **Product Innovation and Competitiveness**
   To ensure the technological advancement of general aviation.

4. **System Access and Capacity**
   To maximize general aviation's ability to operate in the National Airspace System.

5. **Affordability**
   To promote economic and efficient general aviation operations, expand participation, and stimulate industry growth.

Advanced Industries, Inc.
P.O. Box 16400
Wichita, KS 67216
(316) 522-0424

Aircraft Modular Products
4000 NW 36th Avenue
Miami, FL 33142
(305) 633-6817

Aircraft Technical Publishers
101 South Hill Drive
Brisbane, CA 94005-1203
(415) 330-9500

Airtechnics, Inc.
230 Ida
Wichita, KS 67211
(316) 267-2849

AlliedSignal Inc.
Electronics and Avionics Systems
400 N. Rogers Road
Olathe, KS 66062
(913) 782-0400

AlliedSignal Inc.
Engines
P.O. Box 52181 MS 67-00/301-22
Phoenix, AZ 85072-2181
(602) 231-1000

Allison Engine Company
P.O. Box 420, Mail Stop UIOA
Indianapolis, IN 46206-0420
(317) 230-2000

Ametek, Inc.
Aerospace Products
900 Clymer Avenue
Sellersville, PA 19860
(215) 257-6531

Boeing Business Jets
P.O. Box 3707, MS IE-77
Seattle, WA 98124
(206) 655-9800

Century Flight Systems, Inc.
P.O. Box 610
Mineral Wells, TX 76067
(940) 325-2517

Cessna Aircraft Company
P.O. Box 7706
Wichita, KS 67277-7706
(316) 941-6000

Commander Aircraft Company
7200 NW 63rd Street
Bethany, OK 73008
(405) 495-8080

Cooper Industries
Champion Aviation Products
900 Upton Avenue
P.O. Box 910
Toledo, OH 43661
(419) 535-2567

Crane Co.
Hydro-Aire Inc.
300 Winona Avenue
Burbank, CA 91504
(818) 842-6121

The Dee Howard Company
P.O. Box 469001
San Antonio, TX 78246
(210) 828-1341

Dowty Aerospace Yakima
P.O. Box 9907
Yakima, WA 98909-9907
(509) 248-5000

DOW-UT Composite Products, Inc.
15 Sterling Drive
Wallingford, CT 06492
(203) 949-5000

Dukes, Inc.
9060 Winnetka Avenue
Northridge, CA 91324
(818) 998-9811

EG&G Pressure Science Inc.
11642 Old Baltimore Pike
Beltsville, MD 20705
(301) 937-4010

Electrosystems, Inc.
P.O. Box 273, Airport Complex
Ft. Deposit, AL 36032
(334) 227-8306

ERDA, Inc.
P.O. Box 129
Peshtigo, WI 54157
(715) 582-4517

FlightSafety International, Inc.
Marine Air Terminal
LaGuardia Airport
New York, NY 11371-1061
(718) 565-4100

GARMIN International, Inc.
1200 East 151st Street
Olathe, KS 66062
(913) 397-8200

GEC-Marconi Aerospace Inc.
110 Algonquin Parkway
Whippany, NJ 07981
(201) 428-9898

BFGoodrich Aerospace
250 N. Cleveland-Massillon Rd.
Akron, OH 44333-2465
(330) 374-2200

Gulfstream Aerospace Corporation
P.O. Box 2206
Savannah, GA 31402
(912) 965-3000

Hartzell Propeller, Inc.
One Propeller Place
Piqua, OH 45356-2634
(937) 778-4200

Honeywell, Inc.
Space and Aviation Control
P.O. Box 29000
Phoenix, AZ 85038-9000
(602) 436-8000

Jeppesen
55 Iverness Drive East
Englewood, CO 80112-5498
(303) 799-9090

Kollsman
Avionics
220 Daniel Webster Highway
Merrimack, NH 03054
(603) 889-2500

Learjet Inc.
P.O. Box 7707
Wichita, KS 67277-7707
(316) 946-2000

Lucas Aerospace
777 Lena Drive
Aurora, OH 44202
(216) 995-1000

Marathon Power Technologies
P.O. Box 8233
Waco, TX 76714-8233
(817) 776-0650

Mooney Aircraft Corporation
Louis Schreiner Field
Kerrville, TX 78028
(210) 896-6000

The Nordam Group
P.O. Box 3365
Tulsa, OK 74101
(918) 587-4105

Northrop Grumman Corporation
Commercial Aircraft Division
P.O. Box 655907
Dallas, TX 75255-5907
(972) 266-2011

Parker Hannifin Corporation
Parker Aerospace
18321 Jamboree Boulevard
Irvine, CA 92715
(714) 833-3000

Penny & Giles Aerospace, Inc.
209 West Main
Valley Center, KS 67147-2298
(316) 755-1223

The New Piper Aircraft, Inc.
2926 Piper Drive
Vero Beach, FL 32960
(561) 567-4361

PPG Industries, Inc.
P.O. Box 2200
Huntsville, AL 35804
(205) 859-2500

Precision Aerospace Corporation
1100 Carillon Point
Kirkland, WA 98033
(425) 739-9997

Raytheon Aircraft Company
P.O. Box 85
Wichita, KS 67201-0085
(316) 676-7111

Rockwell Collins
400 Collins Road, NE
Cedar Rapids, IA 52498
(319) 295-1000

Sabreliner Corporation
7733 Forsyth Boulevard, Suite 1500
St. Louis, MO 63105-1821
(314) 863-6880

SimuFlite Training International
P.O. Box 619119
DFW Airport, TX 75261
(800) 527-2463

Sundstrand Corporation
Sundstrand Aerospace
P.O. Box 7002
Rockford, IL 61125
(815) 226-6512

Teledyne Continental Motors
An Allegheny Teledyne Company
P.O. Box 90
Mobile, AL 36601
(334) 438-3411

Textron, Inc.
Textron Lycoming
652 Oliver Street
Williamsport, PA 17701
(717) 323-6181

Trimble Navigation, Ltd.
2105 Donley Drive
Austin, TX 78746
(512) 432-0400

Unison Industries
7575 Baymeadows Way
Jacksonville, FL 32256
(904) 739-4000

United Technologies Corporation
Pratt & Whitney Canada
1000 Marie-Victorin Boulevard
Longueuil, Quebec Canada
J4G 1A1
(514) 677-9411

Universal Avionics Systems Corporation
3260 E. Lerdo Road
Tucson, AZ 85706
(520) 295-2300

Williams International
P.O. Box 200
Walled Lake, MI 48390-0200
(810) 624-5200

Woodward Governor Company
P.O. Box 7001
Rockford, IL 61125-7001
(815) 877-7442

Figure 27.5   General Aviation Manufacturers Association Members.

Table 27.6   Largest General Aviation Airports Ranked by FY 2000 Aircraft Operations

Facility ID	City/Airport	2000	1996
VNY	Van Nuys	518,682	528,659
LGB	Long Beach/Daughtery Field	392,747	467,412
APA	Denver/Centennial	382,443	361,228
SFB	Orlando/Sanford	363,268	255,923
DAB	Daytona Beach International	358,425	290,438
DVT	Phoenix-Deer Valley Municipal	343,933	373,310
PRC	Prescott/E A Love Field	325,061	298,462
FTW	Fort Worth Meacham	318,566	339,203
SNA	Santa Ana/John Wayne	312,627	299,309
BFI	Seattle/Boeing Field	299,234	280,800
	Operations—Top 10 GA Airports	**3,614,986**	**3,526,343**
	Total GA Operations	**39,723,673**	**35,298,290**

Source: Federal Aviation Administration

Table 27.7   Active Pilot Trends and Forecasts

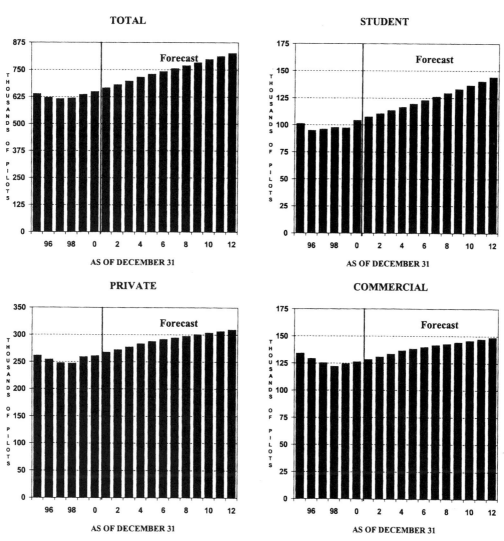

Table 27.8   General Aviation Active Aircraft by Aircraft Type
(In Thousands)

Aircraft Type	1999	1998	1997	1996[1]	1995[1]	1994
Fixed Wing—Total	**184.7**	**175.2**	**166.8**	**163.7**	**162.3**	**150.2**
Piston—Total	**171.9**	**163.0**	**156.1**	**153.6**	**152.8**	**142.2**
One Engine	150.9	144.2	140.0	137.4	137.0	127.4
Two Engine	20.9	18.7	15.9	16.1	15.7	14.8
Other Piston	0.1	0.1	0.1	0.1	0.0	0.1
Turboprop—Total	**5.7**	**6.2**	**5.6**	**5.7**	**5.0**	**4.1**
Single Engine	1.0	1.0	0.7	0.7	0.7	0.5
Two Engine	4.6	5.1	4.9	4.9	4.3	3.6
Other Turboprop	0.0	0.1	0.0	0.1	0.0	0.0
Turbojet—Total	**7.1**	**6.1**	**5.2**	**4.4**	**4.6**	**3.9**
Two Engine	6.4	5.5	4.6	4.1	4.1	3.7
Other Turbojet	0.7	0.6	0.5	0.3	0.5	0.3
Rotocraft—Total	**7.4**	**7.4**	**6.8**	**6.6**	**5.8**	**4.7**
Piston	2.6	2.5	2.3	2.5	1.9	1.6
Turbine	4.9	4.9	4.5	4.1	4.0	3.1
Single-Engine	4.0	4.0	3.8	3.4	3.2	2.5
Multi-engine	0.8	0.8	0.8	0.6	0.7	0.6
Other—Total	**6.8**	**5.6**	**4.1**	**4.2**	**4.7**	**5.9**
Experimental—Total	**20.5**	**16.5**	**14.7**	**16.6**	**15.2**	**12.1**
Total All Aircraft	**219.4**	**204.7**	**192.4**	**191.1**	**188.1**	**172.9**

Source: 1994–1999 General Aviation Activity and Avionics Surveys.

[1] Estimates have been revised to reflect changes in edit and estimation procedures, and may not be comparable to estimates prior to 1995.

Columns may not add to totals due to rounding and estimation procedures

Table 27.9 Total General Aviation Hours Flown by Aircraft Type
(In Thousands)

Aircraft Type	1999	1998	1997	1996[1]	1995[1]	1994
Fixed Wing—Total	**27,444**	**24,392**	**24,111**	**23,402**	**23,196**	**21,203**
Piston—Total	**22,895**	**20,402**	**20,743**	**20,091**	**20,251**	**18,823**
One Engine	19,325	16,823	18,345	17,606	17,831	16,404
Two Engine	3,551	3,567	2,380	2,474	2,416	2,408
Other Piston	18	11	19	11	4	11
Turboprop—Total	**1,811**	**1,765**	**1,655**	**1,768**	**1,490**	**1,142**
Single Engine	357	289	321	328	292	203
Two Engine	1,450	1,459	1,326	1,419	1,181	939
Other Turboprop	4	17	9	22	17	0
Turbojet—Total	**2,738**	**2,226**	**1,713**	**1,543**	**1,455**	**1,238**
Two Engine	2,435	1,995	1,557	1,385	1,352	1,172
Other Turbojet	303	231	155	158	102	66
Rotocraft—Total	**2,744**	**2,342**	**2,084**	**2,122**	**1,961**	**1,777**
Piston	556	430	344	591	337	369
Turbine	2,188	1,912	1,740	1,531	1,624	1,408
Single-Engine	1,744	1,415	1,311	1,282	1,218	1,049
Multi-engine	443	497	429	249	406	359
Other—Total	**318**	**295**	**192**	**227**	**261**	**388**
Experimental—Total	**1,247**	**1,071**	**1,327**	**1,158**	**1,194**	**724**
Total All Aircraft	**31,754**	**28,100**	**27,713**	**26,909**	**26,612**	**24,092**

Source: 1994–1999 General Aviation Activity and Avionics Surveys.

[1] Estimates have been revised to reflect changes in edit and estimation procedures, and may not be comparable to estimates prior to 1995.

Columns may not add to totals due to rounding and estimation procedures

Table 27.10 General Aviation Active Aircraft by Primary Use Category
(In Thousands)

Use Category	1999	1998	1997	1996[1]	1995[1]	1994
Public Use	4.1	4.0	4.1	4.5	N/A	N/A
Corporate	10.8	11.3	10.4	9.9	10.6	9.4
Business	24.5	32.6	27.7	30.7	28.3	26.5
Personal	147.1	124.3	115.6	113.4	113.4	102.5
Instructional	16.1	11.4	14.7	12.7	14.2	15.0
Aerial Application	4.6	4.6	4.9	5.0	5.0	4.3
Aerial Observation	3.2	3.2	3.3	3.0	4.7	5.1
External Load	0.2	0.3	0.2	0.4	0.2	0.1
Other Work	2.4	1.1	0.7	1.0	1.1	1.2
Sightseeing	0.8	0.7	0.7	0.7	0.8	1.3
Air Tours	0.3	0.3	0.2	0.1	0.2	N/A
Air Taxi	4.3	4.9	4.8	4.1	3.8	3.8
Other	N/A	6.0	5.3	5.6	5.9	4.2
Air Medical Services	0.8	N/A	N/A	N/A	N/A	N/A
Total	**219.4**	**204.7**	**192.4**	**191.1**	**188.1**	**172.9**

Source: 1994–1999 General Aviation Activity and Avionics Surveys.

[1] Estimates have been revised to reflect changes in edit and estimation procedures, and may not be comparable to estimates prior to 1995.

N/A = Not applicable

Columns may not add to totals due to rounding and estimation procedures

Table 27.11 Total General Aviation Hours Flown by Use Category
(In Thousands)

Use Category	1999	1998	1997	1996[1]	1995[1]	1994
Public Use	1,111	1,373	1,096	1,047	N/A	N/A
Corporate	3,616	3,213	2,878	2,898	3,069	2,486
Business	3,598	3,523	3,006	3,259	3,335	3,012
Personal	11,294	9,781	9,644	9,037	9,659	8,248
Instructional	5,893	3,961	4,956	4,759	4,410	4,382
Aerial Application	1,535	1,306	1,562	1,713	1,526	1,364
Aerial Observation	1,243	812	1,261	1,057	1,391	1,746
External Load	128	153	112	191	128	135
Other Work	813	286	139	265	280	241
Sightseeing	220	169	127	195	179	309
Air Tours	146	183	114	100	124	N/A
Air Taxi	1,897	2,400	2,008	1,734	1,403	1,545
Other	N/A	940	819	656	1,107	622
Air Medical Services	461	N/A	N/A	N/A	N/A	N/A
Total	**31,755**	**28,100**	**27,713**	**26,909**	**26,612**	**24,092**

Source: 1994–1999 General Aviation Activity and Avionics Surveys.

[1] Estimates have been revised to reflect changes in edit and estimation procedures, and may not be comparable to estimates prior to 1995.

N/A = Not applicable

Columns may not add to totals due to rounding and estimation procedures

PIPER

Piper is one of the best known names in general aviation aircraft manufacturing. These aircraft are used for flight training. It began in the late 1920s when Clarence G. Taylor, born in 1898, started building a light aircraft in Rochester, New York. Taylor's father was a self-taught engineer and Clarence grew up around machinery. At a very young age he dreamed of building his own airplane. A World War I surplus Curtiss Jenny was advertised for sale in a local newspaper. The buyer would be taught to fly it as part of the sale. Taylor purchased the airplane for $750 and spent the next year restoring it. When it was completed in 1926 he made several modifications and design changes. Taylor, with his brother Gordon and another man, then established the North Star Aerial Service Corporation. Taylor had learned to fly and began his career barnstorming throughout New York State. In 1928 the company's name was changed to the Taylor Brothers Aircraft Corporation. Their first airplane was called the *Chummy*. Unfortunately, Gordon Taylor was killed in a crash while flying in an exhibition in Detroit.

Taylor needed larger production facilities. The city of Bradford, Pennsylvania, was seeking companies to locate in their city to increase the local economy. A citizens' committee offered to purchase stock in the company if he would move to Bradford, which he did in 1928. One citizen, an oil man, was William T. Piper, who soon became a member of the board of directors. At the time the *Chummy* was priced at more than four thousand dollars and was not selling well.

Piper, known as the Henry Ford of aviation, was born in New York State in 1881 and was a partner in an oil recovery business in Bradford. He was one of the investors in Taylor's company. He became treasurer of the company and learned to fly the Taylor aircraft.

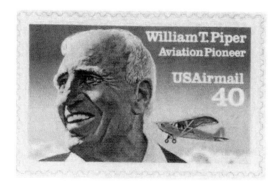

The company was going broke in 1930 due to the depression. The Taylor Brothers Aircraft Corporation entered bankruptcy and closed down for three months. In an effort to save the company, Piper purchased it for $600. He retained Taylor as president. Piper reorganized the company and supplied much of the capital himself. He formed the Taylor Aircraft Company with Taylor as chief engineer. Later that year they produced a single seat sailplane with tubular steel framework, lightweight wings with wire bracing and skids rather than wheels. Piper and Taylor towed it behind an automobile up and down the runway at the airport each weekend. It was eventually sold to a man in Buffalo, New York.

The experience with a glider gave Piper the idea to build a new light aircraft which he expected to be used by flying schools. What he wanted to produce was a simple low powered trainer that would be economical for flight instruction. They had a problem in locating a suitable engine. One which was tried was named the Tiger Kitten. Since this was analogous to a cub, the name seemed to fit the aircraft and that is what it became to be known as. In 1931 the Taylor E-2 was built, the first of its type. It weighed 900 pounds and was a two seater. In the next few years the airplane had many changes influenced by Piper and was designated the J-2. Taylor was not happy with the new design and in 1935 he left the company to form what later became known as the Taylorcraft Company. Taylor built light aircraft for many years. He died at the age of 89 on March 29, 1988, at Houston, Texas. The J-2 was a two place airplane with a wingspan of 35 feet and weighed 932 pounds; named the Taylor Cub.

In March 1937, the factory was totally destroyed by fire including ten aircraft on the production line. Included in the loss were technical drawings, tools and jigs to produce the J-2 model. Piper needed a factory and found one in Lock Haven, Pennsylvania, 80 miles from Bradford. It was formerly a silk mill with a large two story concrete building and 16 acres of space located next to the airport. Production was resumed. In November 1937 the company was changed to the Piper Aircraft Corporation and it went public with a stock offering in 1938.

With few outward changes the E-2 soon became the J-3. The airplane went through several refinements and improvements to be designated the J-3. It was offered for sale as low as $995. A Continental 40 horsepower engine was selected; it was later increased to 65

For current information go to the website at: http://www.newpiper.com

horsepower. The standard color scheme for the J-3 was completely yellow with a black stripe running along the side of the fuselage. A Teddy Bear with the word Cub was painted on the tail. The aircraft gained attention when it made a round-trip nonstop flight between Newark, New Jersey and Miami, Florida, for a total distance of 2,390 miles.

Piper's big success came as a result of Hitler, in Germany, building air power in preparation for World War II. The United States government created the Civil Pilot Training program in 1939. Congress appropriated $4 million to begin the training of ten thousand student pilots attending 460 colleges. The Piper airplane was the appropriate aircraft for this type of training and made up over 75% of the aircraft used in the program.

During the war, Piper built over 6,000 aircraft for use by the military and designated L4 for Liaison. They were used wherever the military operated. There are many events that took place during World War II involving these aircraft. Some were launched from the USS Ranger during the invasion of North Africa in November 1942. Again from a Landing Ship Tank (LST) for the invasion of Sicily. They were used extensively in the Pacific and European theaters of operation.

When the war ended the light aircraft industry rapidly converted to civilian production. Thousands of veterans learned to fly under the GI bill and many did so in the Cub. The production in 1946 was 6,432 J-3 Cubs. The building of the last J-3 airplane was in March 1947. They had produced 20,000 Cubs. Piper introduced its first all metal plane, the Apache, in February of 1954. It was also Piper's first twin engine model and the first in a series to be named after an American Indian tribe (as a salute to Piper's own American Indian heritage).

With the success of the Apache, Piper saw a bright future for General Aviation and expanded its research and development capabilities, as well as its manufacturing base. In 1957 it built a new R&D facility at the old Naval airbase in Vero Beach, Florida. The Sunshine State proved to be an excellent site for experimental flight testing. The first accomplishment of the new facility was the introduction of the PA-25 Pawnee, an agricultural spraying aircraft. This new design broke ground for Piper and also proved to be a huge step toward providing a safer airplane for the world's crop dusters.

William T. Piper worked at the factory until he was taken to the hospital in November 1969; on January 15, 1970, he died—taking that last flight that all pilots must ultimately make.

During the past many years Piper successfully produced several models. Among them were:

Cub Special—1946
Super Cruiser—1946
Family Cruiser—1947
Vagabond—1947
Clipper—1948
Super Cub—1949

> In 1947 two men flew around the world in two Super Cruisers, in four months.

Pacer—1949

> In 1950 a Pacer was flown from Minneapolis to Rome and back.

Tripacer—1950
Apache—1952

> The Apache was the first twin-engined aircraft built by Piper.

Commanche—1956
Aztec—1957
Pawnee—1957
Cherokee—1961
Navajo—1966
Arrow—1967
Warrior—1973
Archer II—1975
Dakota—1978
Tomahawk—1978

Product liability lawsuits throughout the small airplane industry in the 1980s and early 1990s caused many companies to cease production. Others simply went bankrupt. Refer to Chapter 17 for details.

The old Piper Aircraft Corporation no longer exists as a result of Chapter 11 reorganization.

In 1995, a small group of employees took over the Piper Aircraft Corporation and transformed it into the New Piper Aircraft, Inc. During the first year of operation, there were fewer than 100 employees, facing the challenge of putting the Piper name back to the forefront of General Aviation.

To accomplish their goal, engineers had the task of creating an aggressive research and development program to bring new and innovative aircraft to the market. Another crucial area was customer service. Many industries served as models to create the best possible customer service capable of handling world-wide customers. The sales and marketing staffs made it their goal to elevate New Piper as the leader in the owner-flown segment of the General Aviation market as well as the leader in supplying the best training aircraft in the world. The company also concentrated efforts to recruit the best distribution professionals possible.

With this commitment to excellence, the organization has grown to employ more than 1,000 people at its

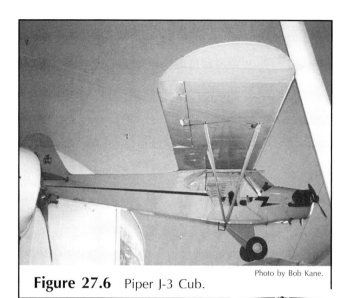

Photo by Bob Kane.

Figure 27.6 Piper J-3 Cub.

headquarters in Vero Beach, Florida. The company once again is a success.

As it has evolved into the current New Piper, the company has introduced new versions of all models. For example, the classic Seneca became the Seneca V. Every model has, of course, been improved because of the newest technology developments. New Piper has also added new models, including a turbo-charged Saratoga called the Saratoga II TC.

In 1997, New Piper began the development of the Malibu Meridian—a single engine turboprop. The first prototype was shown in August 1998, with its first flight a month later. New Piper was delivering new Meridians a mere five years after the company reopened.

The Piper name has flown on more than 20,000 twin engine aircraft in both the training and business sectors since the first Apache rolled onto the runway.

THE ERA OF THE CHEROKEE

Piper expanded its manufacturing facilities in Florida after the new R&D facility was built in Vero Beach in 1957. It soon introduced the PA-28 Cherokee, which was FAA certified in October, 1960. The new aircraft went into production in January, 1961.

The Cherokee design was the frontrunner for many to follow in the next decades. It was a single-engine, four-place, and the Warrior, Archer, Dakota, Arrow, Seneca and Saratoga were all later models based on the innovative Cherokee design.

Such organizations as Saudi Arabian Airlines, the Government of Indonesia, British Aerospace, Flight-

Safety International, Embry-Riddle Aeronautical University, and the University of North Dakota have used the PA-28 line as training aircraft. The list grows as the Cherokee's descendants, including the Archer III, introduced in 1994, are proving themselves in training fleets across the globe.

The Cherokee Six or PA-32 series, introduced in 1965, featured an expanded cabin that could accommodate six people. There was room for luggage to be stowed in a forward baggage compartment, a rear door made it easy for passengers to be seated comfortably, and the passenger cabin was roomier. The PA-32 introduced the Saratoga II TC in 1997, the newest addition to that line.

In 1967, the PA-31 Navajo was introduced, enhancing the twin engine lineup. It was designed to meet the growing demands for expanded business travel. The original spawned a series of aircraft, including the Navajo Chieftain and the Mojave. Later came a lineup of twin turboprops—the Cheyenne I, the Cheyenne II and the Cheyenne IIXL.

The Cheyenne III was introduced in 1979 and later improvements were named the Cheyenne IIIA. These aircraft could seat up to 11 people and could cruise at 300 knots with a range of up to 2,000 statute miles on the thrust of two 720hp Pratt & Whitney engines.

The Cheyenne, though built with the executive market as its target, also worked its way into many training programs and pilots in organizations such as Lufthansa Airlines, Alitalia Airlines, Korean Air, All Nippon Airways, Austrian Airlines, and the Civil Administration of China learned from the Cheyenne.

Many organizations continue to train pilots in Piper aircraft, and others have chosen New Piper to supply both single-engine and twins for their fleets.

Piper excelled in the development of twins, though single engine aircraft was the cornerstone of the company. In 1971 the PA-32 Seneca was introduced. It was a six-place light twin, built around the Cherokee Six frame. The Seneca has worked as an air taxi, a charter aircraft, a trainer for pilots beginning advanced multi-engine classes, and it is popular in the owner-pilot set. The current Seneca V still fits into each of these categories.

Another light twin that has been successful for Piper has been the PA-44 Seminole. It has an Arrow design, but uses a longer fuselage, a T-tail and two counter-rotating 180hp Lycoming engines.

Piper again proved to be an innovator in 1983, ironically at a time when many manufacturers were scaling back or quitting completely. Piper introduced a completely new design—the PA Malibu. It took three years of research to get the first Malibu into the air, but it totally changed personal aviation at a time when the industry needed a boost. The pressurized, six-place, single-engine aircraft offers the comforts and amenities of many small business jets at a fraction of the price and operating cost. Many owner-pilots, especially those who use their own aircraft for business, bought a Malibu. The Malibu Mirage, an upgraded version introduced in 1988, had a 350hp turbo-charged Lycoming engine.

The Piper name has been and will continue to be a frontrunner in the industry, from the first Chummy and Cub aircraft to the newest models of today.

For more history on Piper aircraft, visit the Piper Museum in Lock Haven, Pennsylvania.
http://www.kcnet.org/~piper
http://www.newpiper.com/hist.html

CESSNA

The first generation of aviation pioneers were successful in developing the airplane, to the point of controllable flight, included the Wright brothers, Glenn Curtiss, and others. They were soon followed by the next wave of ingenious builders of aircraft. Each exhibited his own style and technique of aircraft building. They included Walter Beech, Lloyd Stearman, William Piper, Taylor, and others. Perhaps the name best known in building aircraft for general aviation since the 1920s, and still doing so today, was Clyde Cessna. He was born in 1880 in Iowa but moved to Kansas with his family a year later. He developed a rare mechanical ability and kept his father's farm machinery well repaired. By the time that he was a teenager he would go to neighboring farms to repair their equipment. His help was always given freely. A farm machinery dealer, who sold the equipment, realized that he was not being asked to service his products. Upon investigating he discovered that the reason was Clyde Cessna. He quickly hired Cessna to be his service man. The dealer added automobiles to his stock for sale and Cessna became as

adept at auto repair as he was with farm machines. One day when the boss was absent a man came to inquire about the automobile that he was comparing with another make. Cessna knew his auto so well that he had the man on the floor under the car showing him the fine points. He sold the man on the spot, who then drove it away. From then on Cessna became a successful salesman as well as a mechanic. It was not long after that Cessna was made head of an entire agency in Enid, Oklahoma. In his first year he sold over a hundred autos.

In 1911, at the age of 31, Cessna attended an Aerial Circus to see first-hand what these aerial machines looked like and how they performed. After the show he made sketches of a monoplane, along with mental notes, which was owned by a Frenchman and was a copy of the airplane that Louis Bleroit flew across the English Channel.

Upon returning home Cessna rented a garage and started to construct his first airplane. The fuselage was an American made Bleroit that he purchased in New York and had shipped to him. The wing and tail were constructed from his sketches and mental notes. For power he used a four cylinder water cooled marine type engine which produced 60 horsepower. The wings were constructed from spruce wood and covered with the best Irish linen. His brother helped him test fly it. Cessna had not only to test the airplane but also he had to learn to fly while doing so. Before he could get it off the ground on his first try he ground-looped it. On his thirteenth attempt he got off the ground but found himself headed for a grove of trees. Either he did not know how to turn the craft or, if he did, it did not respond. He ended up on the ground against a tree. Two weeks later after more crashes and injuries he succeeded not only in getting into the air but safely making a landing. He exclaimed "I've got it." And he did for many years to come. He soon was putting on one man air shows around his area of Oklahoma for $300 a show. For many it was their first sight of an airplane. For the next few years he spent the winters constructing a new and better aircraft to display the following summer. In 1916, the automobile dealer who gave him the job of running his agency, was building his own brand of automobile. He offered Cessna his auto plant in which to build his airplanes. Thus Wichita, Kansas, became the site of the Cessna company where it still exists today. The second model he built there in 1919, he named "The Comet." Cessna's airplane building stopped when the United States en-

Figure 27.7 Cessna 172.

Photo by Bob Kane.

tered World War I. The next few years he spent farming in Kansas. Little was heard from Cessna until 1925 when Beech and Stearman asked him to join them in a new company in which Cessna would be president. Thus the Travel Air Manufacturing Company began in February, 1925. In 1926, he built a cabin monoplane that was bought by a company to carry mail under the new government contracts. Cessna firmly believed in the single wing monoplane which has continued as the signature of the Cessna company to this day.

In September 1927, Victor Roos invested money in a new company that became known as the Cessna-Roos Aircraft Company. Three months later Roos had an opportunity to become manager of the Swallow Airplane Company and sold his interest in Cessna-Roos to Cessna. The name of the company was changed to Cessna Aircraft Company December 31, 1927; the same name as today.

When the new federal laws were enacted to regulate aviation safety, Cessna was required to demonstrate the strength of his cantilever wing which was new to the industry. The test, in February 1928, involved an inverted wing loaded with the stipulated amount of sand bags. When it held Cessna said "let's see what it will take." After using all the remaining sand bags and six men standing on the wing, for a total of 15,752 pounds, the wing did not break but only sagged until it touched the ground. The strength of the wing was amazing to those who witnessed the test.

Cessna began building his "A" series aircraft. It was a monoplane seating four at a gross weight of 2,260 pounds. The body and tail were made from welded steel tubing and fabric covered. The wing was a wooden structure with fabric covering.

The new company looked forward to a successful business future. It produced three to five aircraft a month and had a small sales department. In early 1929 Cessna was approached by the Curtiss Flying Service who were interested in distributing all of the airplanes that could be built. They promised to sell up to 50 aircraft each month provided Cessna could deliver that quantity. In order to accept the offer it would require a much larger factory. This could only be accomplished by issuing a large amount of stock and straining the financial resources. Construction began on five factory buildings at a cost of $200,000 and a contract was signed. Cessna held the largest share of stock but this was not enough for him to retain control of the company. As soon as the company moved into its new facilities the economy of the nation faltered with the stock market crash on October 28, 1929. Cessna remained optimistic but his Board of Directors closed the factory. This move was probably good because the company never did go bankrupt. No airplanes were built from 1931 through 1933.

The buildings were rented to provide enough income to keep the company alive until manufacturing was resumed after the depression era.

Air races were popular during the 1930s. Several Cessna models won coveted prizes built by Clyde Cessna with his son Eldon. In 1936, at the age of 57, Cessna retired to his farm in Kansas where he spent his time farming and inventing new farm machinery. He had sold his business to his nephews, the Wallace brothers. He died in 1954 at the age of 75 remaining active until the end.

During World War II, the Cessna company built aircraft for the military. One was a twin engine model used for advanced training and nicknamed "the Bamboo Boomer." Many parts for the B-29 were manufactured by the company as well.

After the war, light aircraft soon came into demand for the flying public. Cessna quickly produced two models, the 120, and a deluxe version, the 140. Both were an immediate success; thousands of veterans learned to fly in these airplanes under the GI Bill which paid for the training. A private pilot's license could be obtained for a few hundred dollars. As the years progressed other more modern models were produced. The 170 was a four place airplane; the 180 was larger. All were tail wheel airplanes. Nose wheel models became the 180, 182, and small two place airplanes, the 150 and 152. Many other types were built during the next decades.

During the 1970s and 1980s, product liability lawsuits flourished involving manufacturers of general aviation aircraft. (Refer to Chapter 19.) This resulted in a slow down and eventual cessation of the manufacture of small type airplanes. Cessna did not make any small aircraft for over ten years. With the passage of the General Aviation Revitalization Act of 1994, Cessna announced that it was resuming its former production. A new plant was built in Independence, Kansas, and started production in July, 1996, the first since 1986. This facility consists of a 250,000 square foot main assembly plant with an additional 150,000 square foot separate paint and delivery facility. The first delivery took place in January 1997. Construction continues on the model 172 Skyhawk and the 182 Skylane.

Clyde Cessna would be proud of the aircraft flying today bearing his name.

MOONEY

The Mooney Aircraft Corporation began on July 5, 1946 in a hangar along an airfield in Wichita, Kansas. The brothers Al and Art Mooney joined with businessmen G.C. Yankey and W.L. McMahon as partners and financial backers for their new company. The Mooney Aircraft Corporation certified its first aircraft, the Mooney Mite (M18) just two years later.

The basic aircraft design that Al Mooney created has been on the market for over 50 years and is still in service. The company was outstanding in its production of the highest performance single engine aircraft and in pioneering the performance/value equation. Its trademark forward swept tail is instantly recognized all over the world and helps the aircraft gain speed advantage.

It was announced on March 19, 2002, that Mooney Aircraft Corporation was acquired by Advanced Aerodynamics & Structures, Inc. (AASI) after the U.S. Bankruptcy Court in San Antonio, Texas, gave its approval.

AASI had been operating the Mooney Kerrville, Texas, company since February 2002 under a court approved plan. This was a major step in rebuilding the Mooney product line and a new major general aviation company.

AASI has been renamed the Mooney Aerospace Group, Ltd. It will keep the Kerrville facility as the Mooney Airplane Company. AASI is located in Long Beach, California.

THE EAGLE2 (M20S)

A classic example of an entry level, high performance aircraft is the Mooney Eagle2. It is the leader in performance/value equation in the single engine, piston powered aircraft industry.

The 2001 Eagle2 features a three bladed propeller, which provides a 100 pound useful load increase over the original Eagle. It has a 33 percent improvement in takeoff performance, yet it performs the same as the original Eagle, cruising at 180 KTAS on less than 15gph.

THE OVATION2 (M20R)

The performance/value equation of the Ovation2 is unequaled in the general aviation market. It is the fastest single engine, normally aspirated, piston powered aircraft available. Its unique feature is the McCauley Propeller's ultra thin, two-blade propeller.

The propeller allows a six knots (TAS) increase in cruise speed over its predecessor or 192 KTAS at 8,000 feet, with a weight savings of 12 pounds.

THE BRAVO (M20M)

The flagship of the Mooney fleet, the Mooney M20M Bravo has an inter-cooled Lycoming TIO-540-AF1B and delivers 270hp all the way to 25,000 feet at speeds up to 220 KTAS. It has a complete Garmin avionics stack, yet it still has the Bendix King KFC225 autopilot/flight director.

RAYTHEON (BEECH)

Walter and Olive Ann Beech formed Beech Aircraft in 1932. Their first product was the Beech Staggerwing, a classic cabin biplane design that could cruise at more than 200 miles per hour and carry five passengers in comfort and style.

The Staggerwing established the reputation that has made the Beech name synonymous with reliability and quality for nearly seven decades.

The company grew large by building military training aircraft during World War II. In the post-war era it became a leader in business aviation.

Mr. Beech served as chief executive of the company until his death in 1950. Mrs. Beech succeeded him at the helm, and guided the company until her retirement in 1982. Under her leadership, Beech became a Raytheon Company in 1980. Mrs. Beech died in 1993.

GENERAL AVIATION MANUFACTURERS ASSOCIATION

The General Aviation Manufacturers Association (GAMA) is a national trade association proudly representing over fifty American manufacturers of fixed-wing general aviation aircraft, engines, avionics, and component parts. In addition to building nearly all of the general aviation aircraft flying in the United States, GAMA member companies also operate fleets of aircraft, airport fixed-based operations, and pilot training and maintenance technician training facilities across the nation.

General aviation is one of the nation's most important and dynamic industries, carrying 145 million passengers annually on general aviation aircraft ranging from two-seat training aircraft to intercontinental business jets. General aviation is relied on exclusively by more than 5,400 communities for air transportation needs (scheduled airlines served about 600) and approximately 70 percent of the hours flown by general aviation are for business and commercial purposes.

General aviation is estimated to be a $17 billion industry, generating more than $51 billion annually in economic activity. General aviation exports one-third of its production and leads the world in development of new technology aircraft.

General aviation aircraft fly over 27 million hours—nearly two times the airline flight hours.

Founded in 1970 and headquartered in Washington, DC, GAMA represents the interests of its members before the United States Congress, the Department of Transportation, the Federal Aviation Administration, and other federal and state government agencies directly concerned with the air transportation system. It also maintains close working relationships with other associations representing various facets of the aviation community.

Through public information and education programs, GAMA promotes better understanding of the air transportation environment and the important role general aviation plays in the national economy and in serving America's transportation needs.

Member Companies General Aviation Manufacturers Association

Aircraft Technical Publishers
101 South Hill Drive
Brisbane, CA 94005-1203
(415) 330-9500
www.atp.com

Airtechnics, Inc.
230 Ida
Wichita, KS 67211
(316) 267-2849
www.airtechnics.com

Avidyne Corporation
55 Old Bedford Road
Lincoln, MA 01773
(781) 402-7400
www.avidyne.com

B/E Aerospace, Inc.
4000 NW 36th Ave.
Miami, FL 33142
(305) 633-6817
www.aerospace.com

Boeing Business Jets
P.O. Box 3707
Seattle, WA 98124-2207
(206) 665-9800
www.boeing.com/commercial/bbj

Century Flight Systems, Inc.
Municipal Airport
P.O. Box 610
Mineral Wells, TX 76068
(940) 325-2517
www.centuryflight.com

Cessna Aircraft Company
P.O. Box 7706
Witchita, KS 67277-7706
(316) 517-6000
www.cessna.textron.com

Commander Aircraft Company
7200 NW 63rd Street
Bethany, OK 73008
(405) 495-2255
www.commanderair.com

Crane Aerospace
3000 Winona Avenue
Burbank, CA 91504
(818) 526-2600
www.craneaerospace.com

Curtiss-Wright Corporation
1200 Wall St. W
Lyndhurst, NJ 07071
(201) 896-9811
www.curtiswright.com

Decrane Aircraft Holdings, Inc.
2361 Rosecrans Avenue
Suite 180
El Segundo, CA 90245
(310) 725-9123
www.decraneaircraft.com

Dowty Aerospace Yakima
P.O. Box 9907
Yakima, WA 98909-0907
(509) 248-5000
www.dowty.com

Dukes Aerospace
9060 Winnetka Avenue
Northbridge, CA 91324
(818) 998-9811
www.dukesaerospace.com

Federal Mogul Aviation, Inc.
P.O. Box 686
Liberty, SC 29657-0686
(864) 843-1162
www.federalmogul.com

Flightsafety International, Inc.
Marine Air Terminal
LaGuardia Airport
New York, NY 11371-1061
(718) 565-4100
www.flightsafety.com

Garmin International, Inc.
1200 East 151st Street
Olathe, KS 66062
(913) 397-8200
www.garmin.com/
aviation.html

BFGoodrich Aerospace
Four Coliseum Centre
2730 West Tyvola Road
Charlotte, NC 28217-4578
(704) 423-7000
www.bfgoodrich.com

Gulfstream Aerospace Corporation
P.O. Box 2206
Savannah, GA 31402-2206
(912) 965-3000
www.gulfstream.com

Hamilton Sundstrand Corporation
One Hamilton Road
Windsor Locks, CT 06096
(860) 654-6000
www.hamiltonsundstrandcorp.com

Hartzell Propeller Inc.
One Propeller Place
Piqua, OH 45356-2656
(937) 778-4200
www.hartzellprop.com

Honeywell
P.O. Box 29003
Phoenix, AZ 85038-9003
(602) 231-1000
www.honeywell.com

Jeppesen
55 Inverness Drive East
Englewood, CO 80112-5498
(303) 799-9090
www.jeppesen.com

Kelly Aerospace
P.O. Box 273
Airport Complex
Fort Deposit, AL 36032
(334) 227-8306
www.kellyaerospace.com

Learjet Inc.
P.O. Box 7707
Wichita, KS 67277-7707
(316) 946-2000
www.learjet.com

Meggitt/s-TEC
One S-TEC Way
Municipal Airport
Mineral Wells, TX 76067-9236
(940) 325-9406
www.s-tec.com

Mooney Aircraft Corporation
Louis Schreiner Field
Kerrville, TX 78028
(830) 896-6000
www.mooney.com

The Nordam Group
510 S. Lansing
Tulsa, OK 74120
(918) 587-4105
www.nordam.com

Parker Hannifin Corporation
Parker Aerospace
14300 Alton Parkway
Irvine, CA 92618-1898
(949) 833-3000
www.parker.com

Perkinelmer Fluid Sciences
11642 Old Baltimore Pike
Beltsville, MD 20705
(301) 937-8811
www.perkinelmer.com

The New Piper Aircraft, Inc.
2926 Piper Drive
Vero Beach, FL 32960
(561) 567-4361
www.newpiper.com

PPG Industries, Inc.
5430 San Fernando Road
Glendale, CA 91203
(818) 240-2020
www.ppg.com

**Precision Aerospace
Corporation**
1100 Carillon Point
Kirkland, WA 98033
(425) 739-9997
www.pacpac.com

Raytheon Aircraft Company
P.O. Box 85
Wichita, KS 67201-0085
(316) 676-7111
www.raytheon.com/rac

Rockwell Collins, Inc.
4000 Collins Road, NE
Cedar Rapids, IA 52498-0001
(319) 295-1000
www.collins.rockwell.com

Rolls-Royce
P.O. Box 420
Indianapolis, IN 46206-0420
(317) 230-2000
www.rolls-royce.com

Sabreliner Corporation
Pierre Laclede Center
7733 Forsyth Boulevard
Suite 1500
St. Louis, MO 63105-1821
(314) 863-6880
www.sabreliner.com

**Simuflite Training International,
Inc.**
P.O. Box 619119
DFW Airport, TX 75261
(800) 527-2463
www.simuflite.com

**Smiths Industries Actuation
Systems, Inc.**
110 Algonquin Parkway
Whippany, NJ 07981-1640
(973) 428-9898
www.si-act-sys.com

Spirent Systems Wichita, Inc.
8710 East 32nd Street North
Wichita, KS 67226
(316) 636-2000
www.spirent-systems.com

Teledyne Continental Motors
P.O. Box 90
Mobile, AL 36601-0090
(334) 438-3411
www.tcmlink.com

Textron, Inc.
Textron Lycoming
652 Oliver Street
Williamsport, PA 17701
(570) 323-6181
www.lycoming.textron.com

TRW Aeronautical Systems
1001 Nineteenth Street North
Suite 800
Arlington, VA 22209
(703) 276-5100
www.trw.com

Unison Industries
7575 Baymeadows Way
Jacksonville, FL 32256
(904) 739-4000
www.unisonindustries.com

United Technologies Corporation
Pratt & Whitney Canada
1000 Marie-Victorin Boulevard
Longueuil, QC Canada J4G 1A1
(450) 677-9411
www.pratt-whitney.com

**Universal Avionics Systems
Corp.**
3260 East Universal Way
Tucson, AZ 85706
(520) 295-2300
www.uasc.com

UPS Aviation Technologies, Inc.
2345 Turner Road SE
Salem, OR 97302
(800) 525-6726
www.upsat.com

Williams International
P.O. Box 200
Walled Lake, MI 48390-0200
(248) 624-5200
www.williams-int.com

Woodward Governor Company
P.O. Box 7001
Rockford, IL 61125-7001
(815) 877-7442
www.woodward.com

Table 27.12   General Aviation Airplane Shipment Report
Year End 2000

Make and Model	QI	QII	QIII	QIV	Year End Total
Grand Total					
Civil Shipments	**613**	**704**	**685**	**712**	**2,816**
Grand Total					
Airplane Billings	**$2,071,360,953**	**$2,216,060,548**	**$2,038,084,714**	**$2,217,241,175**	**$8,558,372,390**
American Champion					
Adventurer 7GCAA	4	9	7	3	23
Aurora 7ECA	1	1	1	0	3
Super Decathalon 8KCAB	10	4	5	6	25
Citabria Explorer 7GCBC	4	7	6	5	22
Scout 8GCBC	6	9	5	3	23
Total Units	**25**	**30**	**24**	**17**	**96**
Total Billings	**N/A**	**N/A**	**N/A**	**N/A**	**N/A**
Aviat Aircraft					
A-1A Husky	N/A	N/A	N/A	N/A	4
A-1B Husky	N/A	N/A	N/A	N/A	76
S-2C Pitts	N/A	N/A	N/A	N/A	11
Total Units	**N/A**	**N/A**	**N/A**	**N/A**	**91**
Total Billings	**N/A**	**N/A**	**N/A**	**N/A**	**$13,000,000**
Bellanca					
Super Viking 17-30A	1	0	0	0	1
Total Units	**1**	**0**	**0**	**0**	**1**
Total Billings	**N/A**	**N/A**	**N/A**	**N/A**	**N/A**
Boeing Business Jets[3]					
BBJ	3	5	3	3	14
Total Units	**3**	**5**	**3**	**3**	**14**
Total Billings	**$107,000,000**	**$185,500,000**	**$113,500,000**	**$112,500,000**	**$518,500,000**
Cessna Aircraft					
172 Skyhawk	49	36	34	31	150
172S Skyhawk	59	94	92	95	340
182 Skylane	44	49	90	84	267
206 Stationair	15	11	10	17	53
T206 Stationair	17	17	32	36	102
208 Caravan I	3	7	5	1	16
208B Caravan IB	13	24	17	22	76
525 CJ1	5	18	17	16	56
525A CJ2	0	0	0	8	8
550 Citation Bravo	14	15	13	12	54
560 Citation Encore	0	0	1	5	6
560XL Citation Excel	16	17	26	20	79
650 Citation VII	2	3	4	3	12
750 Citation X	9	7	9	12	37
Total Units	**246**	**298**	**350**	**362**	**1,256**
Total Billings	**$441,546,795**	**$499,750,863**	**$613,055,631**	**$664,632,709**	**$2,218,985,998**

Make and Model	QI	QII	QIII	QIV	Year End Total
Cirrus Design					
Cirrus SR20	15	20	25	35	95
Total Units	**15**	**20**	**25**	**35**	**95**
Total Billings	N/A	N/A	N/A	N/A	N/A
Commander Aircraft					
Commander 114TC	1	0	0	0	1
Commander 115	1	4	1	5	11
Commander 115TC	2	1	4	1	8
Total Units	**4**	**5**	**5**	**6**	**20**
Total Billings	N/A	N/A	N/A	N/A	N/A
Gulfstream					
Gulfstream IV-SP	9	10	9	9	37
Gulfstream V	9	8	8	9	34
Total Units	**18**	**18**	**17**	**18**	**71**
Total Billings	**$639,000,000**	**$629,000,000**	**$598,500,000**	**$656,100,000**	**$2,522,600,000**
Lancair					
Columbia 300 LC-40	N/A	N/A	N/A	N/A	5
Total Units	**N/A**	**N/A**	**N/A**	**N/A**	**5**
Total Billings	N/A	N/A	N/A	N/A	**$1,600,000**
Learjet					
Learjet 31A	11	5	6	5	27
Learjet 45	20	24	18	9	71
Learjet 60	10	8	7	10	35
Total Units	**41**	**37**	**31**	**24**	**133**
Total Billings	**$346,945,100**	**$340,499,160**	**$281,402,515**	**$228,836,750**	**$1,197,683,525**
Maule Air					
M6-235	0	1	0	0	1
MX-7-180C Millennium	0	1	1	0	2
MX-7-180AC	0	0	0	1	1
MXT-7-180	3	2	1	1	7
MXT-7-180A Comet	1	2	2	1	6
MT-7-235 SuperRocket	2	1	1	1	5
MT-7-260	0	0	0	1	1
M-7-235B Super Rocket	0	4	1	2	7
M-7-235C Orion	4	5	6	2	17
M-7-260C	2	3	1	3	9
MT-7-260	0	0	0	1	1
Total Units	**12**	**19**	**13**	**13**	**57**
Total Billings	**$1,290,801**	**$1,956,937**	**$1,374,715**	**$1,367,582**	**$5,990,035**
Micco Aircraft Company					
SP20	N/A	N/A	N/A	N/A	5
SP26	N/A	N/A	N/A	N/A	1
Total Units	**N/A**	**N/A**	**N/A**	**N/A**	**6**
Total Billings	N/A	N/A	N/A	N/A	**$1,025,000**

Make and Model	QI	QII	QIII	QIV	Year End Total
Mooney Aircraft					
M20M Bravo	5	8	8	5	26
M20R Ovation2	14	12	14	15	55
M20S Eagle	5	8	5	1	19
Total Units	**24**	**28**	**27**	**21**	**100**
Total Billings	N/A	N/A	N/A	N/A	N/A
Raytheon Aircraft					
Beech Bonanza A36	22	25	17	21	85
Beech Bonanza B36TC	5	4	4	5	18
Beech Baron 58	13	13	8	16	50
Beech King Air C90B	13	11	13	9	46
Beech King Air B200	24	16	10	9	59
Beech King Air 350	13	12	11	10	46
Beech 1900D Airliner	12	17	12	13	54
Beechjet 400A	13	13	10	15	51
Hawker 800XP	15	19	14	19	67
Total Units	**130**	**130**	**99**	**117**	**476**
Total Billings	**$502,077,000**	**$515,361,000**	**$397,305,000**	**$507,259,000**	**$1,922,002,000**
The New Piper Aircraft					
PA-28-161 Warrior III	14	14	13	2	43
PA-28-181 Archer III	25	26	22	29	102
PA-28R-201 Arrow	6	3	2	7	18
PA-32R-301 Saratoga II HP	4	7	10	7	28
PA-32R-301T Saratoga II TC	12	18	21	19	70
PA-46-350P Malibu Mirage	22	26	15	0	63
PA-46-500TP Meridian	0	0	0	18	18
PA-44-180 Seminole	4	3	0	4	11
PA-34-220T Seneca V	7	17	8	10	42
Total Units	**94**	**114**	**91**	**96**	**395**
Total Billings	**$33,501,257**	**$43,992,588**	**$32,946,853**	**$46,545,134**	**$156,985,832**
Grand Total Civil Shipments	**613**	**704**	**685**	**712**	**2,816**
Grand Total Airplane Billings	**$2,071,360,953**	**$2,216,060,548**	**$2,038,084,714**	**$2,217,241,175**	**$8,558,372,390**

Notes:

1. Billings for American Champion, Bellanca, Cirrus Design, Commander and Mooney are not reported.

2. Aviat Aircraft reports annual totals only.

3. Boeing shipment report revised for 2nd and 3rd quarter.

Shipments By Type

	QI	QII	QIII	QIV	Year-to-Date
Single-Engine Piston	375	432	456	445	1,810
Multi-Engine Piston	24	33	16	30	103
Total Piston	399	465	472	475	1,913
Turboprops	78	87	68	82	315
Turbojets	136	152	145	155	588
Total Turbine	214	239	213	237	903
Grand Total	**613**	**704**	**685**	**712**	**2,816**

2000 Military Airplane Shipments

Make and Model	QI	QII	QIII	QIV	Year-to-Date
Cessna Aircraft					
UC-35A	2	0	0	0	2
Total Units	**2**	**0**	**0**	**0**	**2**
Raytheon Aircraft					
T-6A	7	15	15	12	49
Total Units	**7**	**15**	**15**	**12**	**49**
Grand Total Military					
Shipments	**9**	**15**	**15**	**12**	**51**

Source: General Aviation Manufacturers Association

APPENDICES

A. AVIATION ASSOCIATIONS AND ORGANIZATIONS

B. INTERNATIONAL AIR TRANSPORT ASSOCIATION

C. AIRPORTS COUNCIL INTERNATIONAL MEMBERSHIP

D. INTERNATIONAL AVIATION AUTHORITIES

Due to the inviolability of sufficient information, some of the data may be obsolescent.

Appendix A
Aviation Associations and Organizations ▬▬

Aerospace Education Association
1910 Association Drive
Reston, VA 22091

Aerospace Industries Association
1250 Eye Street, NW
Washington, DC 20005

Aerospace Medical Association
Washington National Airport
Washington DC 20001

Air Canada
Air Canada Center
P.O. Box 14000 Zip 261
Postal Station, St. Laurent
Montreal, Quebec
Canada H4Y 1H4

Airline Pilots Association
535 Herndon Parkway
Herndon, VA 22070

Air Traffic Control Association
2300 Clarendon Blvd. # 711
Arlington, VA 22201

Air Transport Association
1301 Pennsylvania Ave., NW
Washington, DC 20004

Airbus Industrie
Ave Lucien Servanty
F-31707 Blagnac
Toulouse, France

Aircraft Electronics Association
P.O. Box 1963
Independence, MO 64055

Aircraft Owners and Pilots Association (AOPA)
421 Aviation Way
Frederick, MD 21701

Airports Council International
ACI World Headquarters
P.O. Box 125
1215 Geneva 15-Airport
Switzerland

Alaska Airlines
P.O. Box 68900
Seattle, WA 98168

Aloha Airlines
P.O. Box 30038
Honolulu, Hawaii 96820-0028

American Airlines
Box 619616
Dallas-Fort Worth Airport, TX 75261-9616

American Helicopter Society
217 N. Washington Street
Alexandria VA 22314-2538

American Institute of Aeronautics &
   Astronautics
370 L'Enfant Promenade, SW
Washington, DC 20024-2518

Aviation Consumer Protection Division
U.S. Department of Transportation, C-75
400 Seventh Street, SW Room 10405
Washington, DC 20590

Aviation Distributors and Manufacturers
   Association
1900 Arch Street
Philadelphia, PA 19103-1498

Aviation/Space Writers Associations
17 South High Street, Suite 1200
Columbus, OH 43215

Boeing Company
Box 3707
Seattle, WA 98124-2207

Canadian Airlines International
700 Second Street, SW
Calgary, Alberta,
Canada T2P 2W2

Cessna Aircraft company
PO Box 7704
Wichita, KS 67277

Civil Air Patrol
105 South Hansell Street
Maxwell AFB, AL 36112-6332

Continental Airlines
2929 Allen Parkway
Houston, TX 77019

Delta Air Lines
PO Box 20706
Atlanta, GA 30320-6001

Department of the Air Force
The Pentagon
Washington, DC 20330

Department of the Army
The Pentagon
Washington, DC 20310

Department of the Navy
The Pentagon
Washington, DC 20350

Department of Transportation (DOT)
400 Seventh Street, SW
Washington DC 20590

DHL Airways
333 Twin Dolphin Drive
Redwood City, CA 94065-1496

Evergreen International Airlines
1629 K Street, NW
Washington, DC 20006

Experimental Aircraft Association
P.O. Box 3005
Oshkosh, WI 54903-3065

Federal Aviation Administration (FAA)
800 Independence Ave., SW
Washington DC 20591

Federal Express
2005 Corporate Avenue
Memphis, TN 38123-1796

Flight Safety International
3187 Corsair Drive
Atlanta, GA 30341

Future Aviation Professionals of America
4971 Massachusetts Blvd.
Atlanta, GA 30337

General Aviation Manufacturers Association (GAMA)
1400 K Street, NW Suite 801
Washington, DC 20005-2403

Hawaiian Airlines
Honolulu International Airport
Honolulu, Hawaii 96820-0008

Helicopter Association International
1619 Duke Street
Alexandria, VA 22314-4646

International Air Transport Association
2000 Peel Street
Montreal, PQ,
Canada H3A 2R4

International Civil Aviation Organization
1000 Sherbrooke Street West, Suite 327
Montreal, Quebec
Canada H3A 2R2

International Institute of Space Law
3-5 Rue Mario-Nikis, F-75015
Paris, France

Lockheed Corporation
Burbank, CA 91520

McDonnell Douglas Corporation
Box 516
St. Louis, MO 63166

Midway Airlines
5959 South Cicero Avenue
Chicago, IL 60638 3821

National Aeronautics and Space
Administration (NASA)
400 Maryland Ave., SW
Washington, DC 20546

National Aeronautics Association
1815 N. Fort Meyer Drive, Suite 700
Arlington, VA 22209

National Agricultural Aviation Association
1005 E Street, SE
Washington, DC 20003

National Air and Space Museum
6th Street and Independence Avenue, SW
Washington, DC 20560

National Air Transportation Association
4226 King Street
Alexandria, VA 22302

National Association of Air Traffic
Specialists
4780 Corridor Place
Beltsville, MD 20705

National Association of State Aviation Officials
8401 Colesville Road Suite 505A
Silver Spring, MD 20910

National Business Aircraft Association
1200 18th Street, NW Suite 200
Washington, DC 20036

National Intercollegiate Flying Association
Box 3207, Delta State University
Cleveland, MS 38733

National Oceanic and Atmospheric
   Administration
6010 Executive Building
Rockville, MD 20852

National Transportation Safety Board (NTSB)
800 Independence Avenue, SW
Washington, DC 20594

Northwest Airlines
5101 Northwest Drive
St. Paul, MN 55111-3034

Pan American World Airways
200 Park Avenue
New York, NY 10166

Piedmont Airlines
One Piedmont Plaza
Winston-Salem, NC 27156-1000

Piper Aircraft, Inc.
2926 Piper Drive
Vero Beach, FL 32960

Professional Aviation Maintenance
   Association
500 Northwest Plaza, Suite 1016
St. Ann, MO 63074-2209

Soaring Society of America
P.O. Box E
Hobbs, NM 88241-1308

Southwest Airlines
P.O. Box 36611
Dallas, TX 75235-1611

Superintendent of Documents
U.S. Government Printing Office
Washington, DC 20402

The Flying Tiger Line
P.O. Box 92935
Los Angeles, CA 90045-5830

The Ninety-Nines, Inc.
Box 695,
7100 Terminal Drive
Oklahoma City, OK 73159-0965

Trans World Airlines
One City Center
515 North Sixth Street
St. Louis, MO 63101

United Airlines
1200 E. Algonquin Road
Elk Grove Township, IL 60007

United Parcel Service Airlines
1400 North Hurstbourne Parkway
Louisville, KY 40223

United States Pilots Association
11 South Meramec, Suite 810
St. Louis, MO 63105

University Aviation Association
3410 Skyway Drive
Auburn, AL 36830

U.S. Airways
2345 Crystal Drive
Arlington, VA 22227

Women In Aviation International
Morningstar Airport
3647 State Route 503 S.
West Alexandria, OH 45381

Appendix B
International Air Transport Association
Membership List

ADA AIR
Rruga Reshit Collaku, P.5
TIRANA
Albania

ADRIA AIRWAYS
Kuzmiceva 7
LJUBLJANA
61000
Slovenia

AER LINGUS P.L.C.
PO Box 180
Dublin Airport
Dublin
Ireland

AERO ASIA INTERNATIONAL (PVT)
43-J, Block-6
P.E.C.H.S. Karachi
75400
Pakistan

AERO CALIFORNIA S.A. de C.V.
Aguilles Serdan, 1995
Colonia Centro
La Paz
Baja California Sur
23000
Mexico

AEROPERU (Empresa de Transporte Aéreo del Perú)
Av. José Pardo 601
Miraflores
LIMA
Peru

AEROSUR (Comp. Boliviana de Transp. Aéreo Privado S.A.)
Calle Colón Esq. Avenida Irala
C.P. No. 3104
Casilla
Santa Cruz
Bolivia

AEROSWEET AIRLINES
58-A Schevchenka Boulevard
Kiev
25032
Ukraine

AFFRETAIR (PVT) LTD.
P.O. Box 655
HARARE
Zimbabwe

AIR AFRIQUE
13 Avenue Joseph Anoma
Boîte postale 3927
ABIDJAN

AIR CANADA
P.O. Box 14000
Postal Station Saint-Laurent
MONTREAL
Quebec
H4Y 1H4
Canada

AIR CHINA INTERNATIONAL CORP.
Capital International Airport
BEIJING
100621
China, P.R. of

AIR EUROPA (Air Espana, S.A.)
Gran Via Asima 23
Poligono Son Castello
PALMA DE MALLORCA
Baleares
07009
Spain

AERO ZAMBIA Ltd.
1st Floor, Z.N.I.B. House
Dedan Kimathi Road/Private Bag E717
LUSAKA
Zambia

AEROFLOT-RUSSIAN INTERNATIONAL AIRLINES
37 Leningradsky Prospekt
MOSCOW
125167
Russian Federation

AEROLINEAS ARGENTINAS S.A.
Bouchard 547-8
BUENOS AIRES
1106
Argentina

AEROMEXICO
   (Aerovias de Mexico S.A. de C.V.)
Reforma 445-Piso 5
Col. Cauhtemoc
MEXICO D.F.
06500
Mexico

AEROMEXPRESS
Av. Texcoco s/n Esq. Av. Tahel
Col. Penon de Los Banos
MEXICO CITY D.F.
15620
Mexico

AIR ALGERIE (Entr. Nat. d'Expl. de Svcs Aériens)
1, place Maurice Audin
ALGIERS
Algeria

AIR AUSTRAL
BP 611
ST. DENIS CEDEX
97473
Reunion

AIR BALTIC CORPORATION SIA
Riga Airport
RIGA
LV-1053
Latvia

AIR BOTSWANA CORP.
Cycle Mart Building
Lobatse Road, P.O. Box 92
GABORONE
Botswana

AIR CALEDONIE INTERNATIONAL
8, rue Frédéric Surleau
BP 3736
NOUMEA
New Caledonia

AIR INTER EUROPE (Compagnie Air France Euro)
1, Ave. du Marechal Devaux
Paray-Vieille-Poste
PARIS
Cedex
F-91550
France

AIR JAMAICA EXPRESS LIMITED
P.O. Box 34
KINGSTON
10
Jamaica, W.I.

AIR JAMAICA LTD.
72-76 Harbour Street
KINGSTON
Jamaica, W.I.

AIR KORYO
Sunan District
Pyongyang City
Korea, D.P.R. of

AIR LIBERTE S.A.
3, rue du Pont des Halles
RUNGIS Cedex
94656
France

AIR FRANCE
45, rue de Paris
ROISSY C.D.G. Cedex
95747
France

AIR GABON
B.P. 2206
LIBREVILLE
Gabon

AIR LITTORAL
Le Millénaire II
417, rue Samuel Morse
MONTPELLIER Cedex
34961
France

AIR MADAGASCAR
31, avenue de l'Indépendance
ANTANANARIVO
101
Madagascar

AIR MALAWI
Robins Road
P.O. Box 84
BLANTYRE
Malawi

AIR MALDIVES LIMITED
Ameeru Ahmed Magu
MALE
20-05
Maldives, Rep. of

AIR MALTA COMPANY LIMITED
Luqa Airport
LUQA
01
Malta

AIR MARSHALL ISLANDS INC.
P.O. Box 1319
MAJURO
96960
Marshall Islands, Rep. of

AIR MAURITIUS
5 President John Kennedy Street
P.O. Box 441
PORT LOUIS
Mauritius

AIR MOLDOVA INTERNATIONAL
Hotel 4th Floor
Chisinau Airport
Chisinau
MD 2026
Moldova

AIR NAMIBIA
PO Box 731
WINDHOEK
Namibia

AIR NEW ZEALAND LIMITED
Quay Tower, Private Bag 90027
29 Customs Street West
AUCKLAND
1
New Zealand

AIR NIUGINI
Air Niugini House, Jacksons Airport
P.O. Box 7186
BOROKO
Papua New Guinea

AIR NOSTRUM L.A.M.S.A.
Avenida Francisco Valldecabres, 31
VALENCIA, Manises
46940
Spain

AIR PACIFIC LIMITED
Private Mail Bag
NADI Airport
Fiji

AIR SASK AVIATION 1991
Box 320
LA RONGE
Saskatchewan
S0J 1L0
Canada

AIR SEYCHELLES
Victoria House
P.O. Box 386
MAHE
Seychelles

AIR TAHITI
Box 314
Boulevard Pomare
PAPEETE
Tahiti
French Polynesia

AIR TANZANIA CORPORATION
ATC House, Ohio Street
P.O. Box 543
DAR-ES-SALAAM
Tanzania, United Rep. of

AIR U.K. LTD.
Stansted House
STANSTED Airport
Essex
CM24 1AE
United Kingdom

AIR UKRAINE
14, avenue Peremogy
KIEV
252135
Ukraine

AIR UKRAINE INTERNATIONAL
14, Prospekt Peremogy
KIEV
252135
Ukraine

AIR VANUATU (OPERATIONS) LIMITED
P.O. Box 148
PORT VILA
Vanuatu

AIR ZIMBABWE CORPORATION
P.O. Box AP 1
Harare Airport
HARARE
Zimbabwe

AIR-INDIA
Air-India Building, 16th Floor
Nariman Point
BOMBAY
400 021
India

AIRLANKA LTD
Grindlays Bank Building
37, York Street
COLOMBO 1
Sri Lanka

AIRNORTH REGIONAL
General Aviation Area
Darwin Intl Airport, P.O. Box 39548
WINNELLIE
N.T.
0821
Australia

ALASKA AIRLINES, INC.
19300 Pacific Highway South
SEATTLE
Washington
98188
United States of America

ALBANIAN AIRLINES MAK S.H.P.K.
R.R. "Mane Peze" P.Z.
TIRANA
Albania

ALITALIA-LINEE AEREE ITALIANE S.P.A.
Alitalia Centro Direzionale
Viale Alessandro Marchetti, 111
ROMA
00148
Italy

ALLIANCE (African Joint Air Services)
13-15 Kimathi Avenue
P.O. Box 2128
Kampala
Uganda

ALM-ANTILLEAN AIRLINES
Hato Airport
CURACAO
Netherlands Antilles

ALOHA AIRLINES, INC.
Honolulu International Airport
P.O. Box 30028
HONOLULU
Hawaii
96820
United States of America

AMERICA WEST AIRLINES INC.
4000 E. Sky Harbor Boulevard
PHOENIX
Arizona
85034
United States of America

AMERICAN AIRLINES INC.
4333 Amon Carter Boulevard
Fort Worth
DALLAS
Texas
76155
United States of America

ANA (All Nippon Airways Co. Ltd.)
Kasumigaseki Building
2-5 Kasumigaseki 3-chome/Chiyoda-ku
TOKYO
100
Japan

ANSETT AUSTRALIA
P.O. Box 727F
MELBOURNE
Victoria
3001
Australia

ANSETT NEW ZEALAND
50 Grafton Road
P.O. Box 4168
AUCKLAND 1
New Zealand

AOM FRENCH AIRLINES (AOM-Minerve S.A.)
Strategic Orly 108
13-15, rue du Pont des Halles
RUNGIS Cedex
94526
France

ARIANA AFGHAN AIRLINES
P.O. Box 76
KABUL
Afghanistan

ARMENIAN AIRLINES
Zvartnots Airport
YEREVAN
375042
Armenia

AUGSBURG AIRWAYS GmbH
Flughafenstrasse 6
AUGSBURG
86169
Germany

AUSTRAL LINEAS AEREAS S.A.
Av. Leandro N. Alem 1134
BUENOS AIRES
1001
Argentina

AUSTRIAN AIRLINES
Fontanastrasse 1
Postfach 50
VIENNA
1107
Austria

AVENSA (Aerovias Venezolanas, S.A.)
Ave Universidad-Esquina el Chorro
Torre el Chorro, Piso 13, Ap. postal 947
CARACAS
Venezuela

AVIACO (Aviacion y Comercio S.A.)
Maudes No. 51, Edificio Minister
MADRID
E-28003
Spain

AVIANCA (Aerovias Nacionales de Colombia S.A.)
Centro Administrativo
Avenida Eldorado No. 93-30
BOGOTA
Colombia

AVIATECA S.A.
Avenida Hincapie 12-22, Zona 13
Guatemala
Guatemala

AZERBAIJAN AIRLINES (Azerbaijan Hava Yollari)
Prospect Azadlyg, 11
BAKU
370000
Azerbaijan, Rep. of

BALKAN BULGARIAN AIRLINES
Sofia Airport
SOFIA
1540
Bulgaria

BELAVIA-Belarusian Airlines
Nemiga str. 14
Minsk
220004
Belarus, Rep. of

BELLVIEW AIRLINES LTD.
31/37 Toyin Street, Ikeja, PO Box 6571
Water Parks Plaza (2nd Floor)
Lagos
Nigeria

BIMAN BANGLADESH AIRLINES
Motijheel C/A
DHAKA
1000
Bangladesh

BRAATHENS S.A.F.E.
Oksenoyveien 3
P.O. Box 55
OSLO Lufthavn
1330
Norway

BRITISH AIRWAYS Plc
P.O. Box 10, Speedbird House
Heathrow Airport (London)
HOUNSLOW
Middlesex
TW6 2JA
United Kingdom

BRITISH MIDLAND AIRWAYS LIMITED
Donington Hall
CASTLE DONINGTON
Derby
DE74 2SB
United Kingdom

BUSINESS AIR LTD.
Kirkhill Business Hse, Howe Moss Drive
Kirkhill Industrial Estate, Dyce
ABERDEEN
Scotland
AB2 OGL
United Kingdom

BWIA International Airways Ltd.
P.O. Box
604 Golden Grove Road
PIARCO
Trinidad and Tobago

CAMEROON AIRLINES
3, av. du Général de Gaulle
B.P. 4092
DOUALA
Cameroon, Rep. of

CANADIAN AIRLINES INTERNATIONAL LTD
700-2nd Street S.W.
Suite 2800
CALGARY
Alberta
T2P 2W2
Canada

CARGOLUX AIRLINES INTERNATIONAL
Luxembourg
L-2990
Luxembourg

CATHAY PACIFIC AIRWAYS LTD
Swire House, 5th Floor
9, Connaught Road Central
Hong Kong SAR
China, P.R. of

CESKE AEROLINE/CZECH AIRLINES (CSA)
Head Office
Airport Ruzyne
PRAGUE 6
160 08
Czech Republic

CHINA EASTERN AIRLINES
Hongqiao International Airport
SHANGHAI
200335
China, P.R. of

CHINA NORTHERN AIRLINES
3-1 Xiaoheyan Road
Dadong District, Shenyang
Liaoning
110043
China, P.R. of

CHINA NORTHWEST AIRLINES
2 Fenhao Road
Xian Shaanxi
710082
China, P.R. of

CHINA SOUTHERN AIRLINES
Baiyun International Airport
GUANGZHOU City
Guangzhou Province
510405
China, P.R. of

CHINA SOUTHWEST AIRLINES
Shuangliu Airport
CHENGDU
Sichuan
610202
China, P.R. of

CITYJET
The Mezzanine
Terminal Building
DUBLIN Airport
Ireland

COMAIR (PTY.) LTD.
P.O. Box 7015
BONAERO PARK
Transvaal
1622
South Africa

COMPAGNIE AERIENNE CORSE MEDITERRANEE
Aéroport de Campo Dell'Oro
B.P. 505
AJACCIO
20186
France

COMPAGNIE AFRICAINE D'AVIATION-C.A.A.
Edifice du GAP
Boulevard du 30 Juin, Building GAP
KINSHASA
Congo, Dem. Rep. of the

CONTINENTAL AIRLINES INC.
P.O. Box 4607
HOUSTON
Texas
77210-4607
United States of America

CONTINENTAL MICRONESIA, INC.
P.O. Box 8778
TAMUNING
96931
Guam

COPA (Compania Panamena de Aviacion S.A.)
Apartado 1572
Av. Justo Arosemena y Calle 39
PANAMA City
Panama

CROATIA AIRLINES DD
Savska Cesta 41
ZAGREB
10000
Croatia

CROSSAIR, Ltd. Co. (for Reg. Eur. Air Transp.)
for Reg. Eur. Air Transp.
P.O. Box
BASEL
CH-4002
Switzerland

CUBANA (Empresa Consolidada Cubana de Aviacion)
Calle 23 No 64
La Rampa
LA HABANA
10400
Cuba

CYPRUS AIRWAYS LTD
21 Alkeou Street
2404 Engomi
NICOSIA
Cyprus

DELTA AIR LINES, INC.
PO Box 20706
Hartsfield Atlanta Int'l Airport
ATLANTA
Georgia
30320-6001
United States of America

DEUTSCHE BA LUFTFAHRTGESELLSCHAFT GmbH
Wartungsallee 13
München Flughafen
85356
Germany

DRAGONAIR (Hong Kong Dragon Airlines Ltd.)
22nd Floor, Devon House
Taikoo Place, 979 Kings Rd, Quarry Bay
Hong Kong SAR
China, P.R. of

EAGLE AVIATION LTD.
P.O. Box 93926
Mombasa
Kenya

EAST WEST AIRLINES
Sophia Building
18 New Kantwadi Road off Perry Cross Rd
BOMBAY
Bandra (West)
400-050
India

EAT (European Air Transport)
Building 4-5
Brussels National Airport
ZAVENTEM
1930
Belgium

ECUATORIANA (Ecuatoriana de Aviacion S.A.)
Colony Reina Victoria
Torres Almagro, P.O. Box 505
QUITO
Ecuador

EGYPTAIR
Cairo International Airport
CAIRO
Egypt

EL AL ISRAEL AIRLINES LIMITED
P.O. Box 41
Ben-Gurion Intl Airport
TEL AVIV
70 100
Israel

EMIRATES
P.O. Box 686
DUBAI
United Arab Emirates

ESTONIAN AIR
2 Lennujaama Str.
TALLINN
EE0011
Estonia

ETHIOPIAN AIRLINES CORPORATION
P.O. Box 1755
Bole Airport
ADDIS ABABA
Ethiopia

EUROWINGS AG
Flughafenstrasse 21
DORTMUND
44319
Germany

FALCON AVIATION AB
P.O. Box 36
MALMO-STURUP
S-230 32
Sweden

FedEx (Federal Express Corporation)
1980 Nonconnah Boulevards
MEMPHIS
Tennessee
38132
United States of America

FINNAIR OY
Tietotie 11A
Helsinki Airport
HELSINKI
00101
Finland

FLIGHT WEST AIRLINES PTY. LTD.
P.O. Box 1126
EAGLE FARM
Queensland
4007
Australia

GARUDA INDONESIA
Jalan Merdeka Selatan No. 13
P.O. Box 1164
JAKARTA
10110
Indonesia

GB AIRWAYS LTD.
Iain Stewart Centre
Beehive Ring Road
GATWICK Airport
West Sussex
RH6 OPB
United Kingdom

GHANA AIRWAYS CORP.
Ghana Airways House
White Avenue, P.O. Box 1636
ACCRA
Ghana

GILL AVIATION Ltd
New Aviation House
Newcastle Airport
NEWCASTLE
Northumberland
NE13 8BT
United Kingdom

GUJARAT AIRWAYS LTD.
Sapna Shopping Cetre, 1st Floor
20, Vishnas Colony, Alkapuri
Baroda
390 005
India

GULF AIR COMPANY G.S.C.
P.O. Box 138
MANAMA
Bahrain

HAPAG LLOYD FLUG GMBH
Hanover Airport
Flughafenstrasse 10
LANGENHAGEN
30855
Germany

HAZELTON AIRLINES
Orange Road
CUDAL
N.S.W.
2864
Australia

HUNTING CARGO AIRLINES
East Midlands Airport
Building 101
CASTLE DONINGTON
Derbyshire
DE7 2SA
United Kingdom

IBERIA (Líneas Aéreas de España S.A.)
130 Calle Velazquez
MADRID
28006
Spain

ICELANDAIR
Reykjavik Airport
REYKJAVIK
101
Iceland

INDIAN AIRLINES LIMITED
Airlines House
113 Gurdwara Rakabganj Road
NEW DEHLI
110001
India

INTER AIR (Inter Aviation Services (Pty) Ltd.)
Private Bag 8
Johannesburg International Airport
JOHANNESBURG
1627
South Africa

INTERIMPEX-AVIOIMPEX
11 Oktomvri 32
Skopje
91000
Macedonia

IRAN AIR, THE AIRLINE OF THE ISLAMIC
Iran Air Head Office Bldg.
P.O. Box 1395-775, Mehrabad Airport
TEHRAN
Iran

IRAQI AIRWAYS
Saddam Intl Airport
BAGHDAD
Iraq

JAMAHIRIYA LIBYAN ARAB AIRLINES
P.O. Box 2555
Haiti Street
TRIPOLI, Socialist People's
Libyan Arab Jamahiriya

JAPAN AIR SYSTEM COMPANY LTD.
37 Mori Building
3-5-1 Toranomon Minato-Ku
TOKYO
105
Japan

JAPAN AIRLINES COMPANY LTD.
JAL Building, 4-11 Higashi Shinagawa, 2 Chome
Shinagawa-Ku
TOKYO
140
Japan

JAT (Jugoslovenski Aerotransport)
Ho Si Minova 16
NOVI BEOGRAD
YU-11070
Yugoslavia, Fed. Rep. of

JERSEY EUROPEAN AIRWAYS LTD.
Hangar 3
Exeter Airport
DEVONSHIRE
EX5 2BD
United Kingdom

JET AIRWAYS (INDIA) LIMITED
41/42 Maker Chambers III
Nariman Point
BOMBAY
400 021
India

KAZAKSTAN AIRLINES
Zheltoksan St. 59
ALMATY
480004
Kazakstan, Rep. of

KENDELL AIRLINES (Aust.) Pty. Ltd.
86 Baylis Street
P.O. Box 78
WAGGA WAGGA
N.S.W.
2650
Australia

KENYA AIRWAYS LTD.
PO Box 19002
NAIROBI
Kenya

KLM ROYAL DUTCH AIRLINES
Amsterdamseweg 55
AMSTELVEEN
1182 GP
Netherlands

KOREAN AIR
360-1 Gonghang-Dong
Gangseo-Gu
SEOUL
Korea, Republic of

KUWAIT AIRWAYS CORPORATION
P.O. Box 394
Kuwait International Airport
SAFAT
13004
Kuwait

L.B. LIMITED
Princess Tower, West Sunrise
P.O. F207
FREEPORT
Grand Bahama
Bahamas

LAB (Lloyd Aereo Boliviano S.A.)
PO Box 132
Aeropuerto Jorge Wilstermann
COCHABAMBA
Bolivia

LACSA (Lineas Aereas Costarricenses S.A.)
Apartado 1531
SAN JOSE
1000
Costa Rica

LADECO CARGO
Aeropuerto Internacional C.A.M.B.
Casilla 42 Interior, Pudahuel
SANTIAGO
Chile

LADECO S.A.
Avenida Libertador Bernardo O'Higgins, 107
SANTIAGO
Chile

LAM (Linhas Aéreas de Moçambique)
Mavalane Airport
P.O. Box 2060
MAPUTO
Mozambique

LAN-CHILE (Linea Aerea Nacional-Chile S.A.)
Estado 10, Piso 13
P.O. Box 147-D
SANTIAGO
Chile

LANDAIR INTERNATIONAL AIRLINES
Greeneville Municipal Airport
512 Airport Road, P.O. Box 1058
GREENEVILLE
Tennessee
37743
United States of America

LAPA (Lineas Aereas Privadas Argentinas S.A.)
Avenida Santa Fe 1970
2 Piso-CP 1123
BUENOS AIRES
Argentina

LAPSA (Lineas Aereas Paraguayas Sociedad Anonima)
Oliva 455/467
ASUNCION
Paraguay

LAUDA AIR LUFTFAHRT AG.
P.O. Box 56
VIENNA Airport
A-1300
Austria

LESOTHO AIRWAYS CORPORATION
Leabua Jonathan Airport
P.O. Box 861
MASERU
100
Lesotho

LITHUANIAN AIRLINES
A. Gustaicio 4
VILNIUS
2038
Lithuania

LOGANAIR LIMITED
St. Andrews Drive
Glasgow Airport
Paisley
Renfrewshire
PA3 2TG
Scotland

LOT (Polskie Linie Lotnicze)
Al. Jerozolimskie 65/79
WARSAW
00-697
Poland, Republic of

LTU (Lufttransport Unternehmen GmbH & Co.)
Flughafen, Halle 8
DUSSELDORF
D-40474
Germany

LUFTHANSA (Deutsche Lufthansa A.G.)
Von-Gablenz-Strasse 2-6
COLOGNE
50664
Germany

LUFTHANSA CARGO AG
Frachthof 3
FRANKFURT Am Main
6000
Germany

LUFTHANSA CITYLINE GmbH
Am Holzweg 26
Postfach 11 11
KRIFTEL
65825
Germany

LUXAIR (Société Lux. de Navig. Aérienne S.A.)
Aéroport de Luxembourg
LUXEMBOURG
L-2987
Luxembourg

MAERSK AIR A/S
Copenhagen Airport South
DRAGOER
DK-2791
Denmark

MAERSK AIR LTD.
2245-49 Coventry Road
BIRMINGHAM
B26 3NG
United Kingdom

MALAYSIA AIRLINE SYSTEM BERHAD
33rd Floor, Bangunan MAS
Jalan Sultan Ismail
KUALA LUMPUR
50250
Malaysia

MALEV (Hungarian Airlines PLC)
Roosevelt Tèr 2
BUDAPEST J
H-1051
Hungary

MALMO AVIATION SCHEDULE AB
P.O. Box 37
MALMÖ
S-201 20
Sweden

MANX AIRLINES LIMITED
Isle of Man (Ronaldsway) Airport
BALLASALLA
Isle of Man
1M9 2JE
United Kingdom

MEA (Middle East Airlines Airliban)
Beirut International Airport
P.O. Box 206
BEIRUT
Lebanon

MERIDIANA S.p.A.
Zona Industriale A
OLBIA/SS
I-07026
Italy

MERPATI NUSANTARA AIRLINES
Pelni Building
Jalan Angkasa
JAKARTA
10720
Indonesia

MEXICANA (Compania Mexicana de Aviacion SA de CV)
Xola 535, Piso 14
Col del Valle, P.O. Box 12-813
MEXICO D.F.
03100
Mexico

MIAT MONGOLIAN AIRLINES
Airport Buyant Ukhaa
ULAANBAATAR
34
Mongolia

MODILUFT
VIPPS Centre (North Wing), Masjd Moth
2 Commercial Complex, Greater Kailash 11
NEW DELHI
110 048
India

MOUNT COOK GROUP LTD
47 Riccarton Road
P.O. Box 4644
CHRISTCHURCH
New Zealand

NATIONAL AIRLINES CHILE S.A.
Huerfanos 725
Piso 3-B
SANTIAGO
Chile

NEPC Airlines
G.R. Complex
407 & 408 Anna Salai
MADRAS
Nandanam
600 035
India

NIGERIA AIRWAYS LIMITED
Airways House, Muritala Mohammed Airport
P.O. Box 136
LAGOS
Nigeria

NIPPON CARGO AIRLINES (NCA)
Shin-Kasumigaseki Building 10F
3-2, Kasumigaseki 3-chome
TOKYO
Chiyoda-Ku
100
Japan

NORTHWEST AIRLINES INC.
501 Northwest Drive
M.S. B4940
ST. PAUL
Minnesota
55111-3034
United States of America

OLYMPIC AIRWAYS S.A.
96 Syngrou Avenue
ATHENS
GR-117 41
Greece

PACIFIC AIRWAYS CORPORATION
3110 Domestic Airport Road, MIA
PASAY CITY
Metro Manila
1300
Philippines

PACIFIC MIDLAND AIRLINES LTD
PO Box 505
AUCKLAND
New Zealand

PALAIR MACEDONIAN AIRLINES
Kuzman Josifovski Pitu BB
SKOPJE
91000
Macedonia, Former Yug. Rep. of

PAN AM (Pan American World Airways Inc.)
9300 N.W. 36th Street
MIAMI
Florida
33178
United States of America

PHILIPPINE AIRLINES INC.
5th Floor, PAL Building I
Legaspi Street, Legaspi Village
MAKATI, Metro Manila
Philippines

PIA (Pakistan International Airlines Corp.)
PIA Building
Karach Civil Airport
KARACHI
11
Pakistan

PLUNA (Lineas Aereas Uruguayas S.A.)
Puntas de Santiago
C.P. 11500
MONTEVIDEO
1604
Uruguay

POLYNESIAN AIRLINES LTD
P.O. Box 599
APIA
Western Samoa

PORTUGALIA-COMPANHIA PORTUGUESA DE TRA???
Avenida Almirante Gago Coutinho, 88
LISBON
P-1700
Portugal

QANTAS AIRWAYS LIMITED
Level 9, Building A, Qantas Centre
230 Coward Street
Mascot
NSW
2020
Australia

RIGA AIRLINES
1 Melluzu iela 1
RIGA
LV 1067
Latvia

ROYAL AIR MAROC
Aéroport Casablanca-Anfa
CASABLANCA
Morocco

ROYAL BRUNEI AIRLINES
RBI Plaza
Jalan Sultan
BANDAR SERI BEGAWAN 1907
2085
Negara Brunei Darussalam

ROYAL JORDANIAN
P.O. Box 302
AMMAN
Jordan

ROYAL SWAZI NATIONAL AIRWAYS CORP. LTD.
P.O. Box 939
MANZINI
Swaziland

ROYAL TONGAN AIRLINES
Private Bag 9
Post Office
NUKU'ALOFA
Tonga

RYANAIR LIMITED
Corporate Head Office
Dublin Airport
DUBLIN
Co. Dublin
Ireland

SA AIRLINK (PTY) LTD.
P.O. Box 7529
Bonaero Park
JOHANNESBURG
1622
South Africa

SAA (South African Airways)
Airways Towers, Cnr Rissilk & Wolmarans St.
Braamfontein
JOHANNESBURG
2001
South Africa

SABENA
Avenue E. Mounierlaan 2
BRUSSELS
B-1200
Belgium

SAFAIR (PTY) Ltd.
Bonaero Drive
Bonaero Park
KEMPTON PARK
South Africa

SAHARA INDIA AIRLINES
7th Floor, 14 K.G. Marg
NEW DELHI
110 001
India

SAMARA AIRLINES
Samara International Airport
Samara
443025
Russian Federation

SAS (Scandinavian Airlines System)
Frösundaviks Allé 1
SOLNA
Sweden

SATA-AIR ACORES
Avenida Infante D. Henrique, 55-2
PONTA DELGADA
P-9500
Portugal

SAUDI ARABIAN AIRLINES
P.O. Box 620
JEDDAH
21231
Saudi Arabia

SEMPATI AIR
Ground Floor-Terminal Bldg.
Halim Perdana Kusuma Airport
JAKARTA
13610
Indonesia

SIERRA NATIONAL AIRLINES
25 Pultney Street
P.O. Box 285
FREETOWN
Sierra Leone

SINGAPORE AIRLINES LIMITED
8F Airline House
25 Airline Road
SINGAPORE
1781
Singapore, Rep. of

SKYLINE NEPC LTD.
407 & 408 Anna Salai
NANDANAM
Madras
600 035
India

SKYWAYS AB
Box 1537
LINKOPING
S-581 15
Sweden

SOCHI AIRLINES-AVIAPRIMA
Sochi Airport
SOCHI
354355
Russian Federation

SOLOMON AIRLINES
P.O. Box 23
Mendana Avenue
HONIARA-Guadalcanal
Solomon Islands

SPANAIR S.A.
Aeropuerto de Palma, Edificio Spanair
Apdo. de Correos 50086
PALMA DE MALLORCA
07000
Spain

SUDAN AIRWAYS CO. LTD.
SDC Bldg. St 15 New Extension
P.O. Box 253
KHARTOUM
Sudan

SUN AIR (Bop Air (Pty) Ltd.)
P.O. Box 166
Mafikeng
BOPHUTHATSWANA
Johannesburg
1627
South Africa

SUNFLOWER AIRLINES LTD.
Sunflower Hangar
P.O. Box 9452
NADI Airport
Fiji

SURINAM AIRWAYS LTD
Coppenamestraat 136
PARAMARIBO
Suriname

SWISSAIR (Swiss Air Transport Co. Ltd.)
Balsberg
Balz Zimmermann Str.
ZURICH Airport
CH-8058
Switzerland

SYRIAN ARAB AIRLINES
P.O. Box 417
Youssef Alazmeh Square
DAMASCUS
Syrian Arab Republic

T.A.T EUROPEAN AIRLINES
Rue Christiaan Huygens
B.P. 0237
TOURS
F-37002
France

TAAG-Angola Airlines (Linhas Aéreas de Angola)
Rua Missao 123
P.O. Box 79
LUANDA
Angola

TACA INTERNATIONAL AIRLINES, S.A.
Edificio Caribe 2 Piso
SAN SALVADOR
El Salvador

TAESA (Transportes Aereos Ejecutivos S.A. de C.V.)
Aviacion General
Zona de Hangares/C/Numero 27
MEXICO
D.F.
15620
Mexico

TAM-Transportes Aereos Regionais S.A.
Rua General Pantaleao Telles, 210
Sao Paulo-SP
4355-040
Brazil

TAM Transportes Aéreos Meridionais S/A
Rua General Pantaleao Telles, 210
Jardim Aeroporto
SAO PAULO-SP
04355-040
Brazil

TAP-Air Portugal
Bldg 27 10th Floor
P.O. Box 5194
LISBOA
P-1704
Portugal

TAROM (Romanian Air Transport S.A.)
Soseau Bucuresti-Ploesti KM 16.5
OTOPENI Airport
Romania

THAI AIRWAYS INTERNATIONAL PUBLIC CO. LTD.
89 Vibhavadi Rangsit Road
BANGKOK
10900
Thailand

TMA (Trans-Mediterranean Airways S.A.L.)
Beirut International Airport
PO Box 11/3018
BEIRUT
Lebanon

TOWER AIR INC.
Hangar 17
John F. Kennedy Intl Airport
JAMAICA
New York
11430
United States of America

TRANSAERO AIRLINES (Joint Stock Co.)
Gosniiga
Sheremetyevo Airport
MOSCOW
103340
Russian Federation

TRANSAVIA AIRLINES (Transavia Holland B.V.)
Transavia Building
P.O. Box 7777, Havenmeesterweg
SCHIPHOL Airport
NL 1118 ZM
Netherlands

TRANSBRASIL (Transbrasil S.A. Linhas Aereas)
Rua General Pantaleao
Telles 40
SAO PAULO-SP
04355
Brazil

TUNIS AIR
Boulevard 7 November
TUNIS CARTHAGE
1064
Tunisia

TURKISH AIRLINES INC.
Genel Mudurlugu
Atatürk International Airport, Yesilköy
ISTANBUL
34830
Turkey

TWA (Trans World Airlines Inc.)
One City Centre
515 North Sixth Street
ST. LOUIS
Missouri
63101
United States of America

UNITED AIRLINES, INC.
P.O. Box 66100
O'Hare International Airport
CHICAGO
Illinois
60666
United States of America

UPS Airlines
1400 N. Hurstbourne Parkway
LOUISVILLE
Kentucky
40223
United States of America

USAIR INC.
Crystal Park Four
2345 Crystal Drive
ARLINGTON
Virginia
22302
United States of America

VARIG S.A. (Viacao Aerea Rio-Grandense)
Ave. Almte. Silvio de Noronha 365/387
Aeroporto Santos Dumont
RIO DE JANEIRO
ZC
20021-010
Brazil

VASP (Viacao Aerea Sao Paulo S.A.)
Praça Cmte Lineu Gomes S/N0
Edifício Sede-Aeroporto de Congonhas
SAO PAULO-SP
04626-910
Brazil

VIASA (Venezolana Internacional de Aviacion SA)
Apartado de Correos 6857
CARACAS, D.F.
Venezuela

VIRGIN ATLANTIC AIRWAYS LTD.
The Office, Crawley Business Quarter
Manor Royal
CRAWLEY
West Sussex
RH10 2NU
United Kingdom

WIDEROE'S FLYVESELSKAP A/S
P.O. 131
Vollsveien 6
LYSAKER
N-1324
Norway

YEMENIA YEMEN AIRWAYS
P.O. Box 1183
SANA'A
Yemen, Rep. of

ZIMBABWE EXPRESS AIRLINES
89 Nelson Mandela Ave, Kurima House, Ground
P.O. Box 5130
HARARE
Zimbabwe

Appendix C
Airports Council International Membership

Total ACI Membership: 510 Members in 157 Countries/territories.

AFRICA: 49 members in 42 countries/territories.

ALGERIA
ALGIERS   Etablissement de Gestion de Services Aéroportuaires EGSA d'Alger
ANNABA   Etablissement de Gestion de Services Aéroportuaires EGSA d'Annaba
ORAN   Etablissement de Gestion des Services Aéroportuaires-EGSA

BENIN
COTONOU   Aéroport International de Cotonou/Cadjéhoun

BOTSWANA
GABORONE   Department of Civil Aviation

BURKINA FASO
OUAGADOUGOU   Direction de l'Aviation Civile

BURUNDI
BUJUMBURA   Régie des Services Aéronautiques

CAMEROON
YAOUNDE   Aéroports du Cameroun SA

CAPE VERDE
ILHA DO SAL   ASA Empresa Nacional de Aeroportos e Segurança Area E.P.

CENTRAL AFRICAN REPUBLIC
BANGUI   Aéroport de Bangui M'Poko

CHAD
N'DJAMENA   ASECNA-Représentation auprès de la République du Tchad

COMORES
MORONI   Aéroport de Moroni-Hahaya

CONGO (DEM REP)
KINSHASA   Régie des Voies Aérienne

COTE D'IVOIRE
ABIDJAN   SODEXAM (Societé d'Exploitation et de Developpement
                               Aéroportuaire, Aéronautique et Météorologique)
ABIDJAN   Aéroport International Abidjan (AERIA)

DJIBOUTI
DJIBOUTI   Aéroport de Djibouti

EGYPT
CAIRO   Cairo Airport Authority
CAIRO   Civil Aviation Authority

ERITREA
ASMARA   Civil Aviation Authority
ASMARA   Asmara International Airport Management

ETHIOPIA
ADDIS ABABA   Ethiopian Civil Aviation Authority

GABON
LIBREVILLE   Société Anonyme Aéroport de Libreville-ADL

GAMBIA
BANJUL   The Gambia Civil Aviation Authority

GUINEA
CONAKRY   SOGEAC-Aéroport de Conakry G'Bessia

GUINEA-BISSAU
GUINEA   Empresa Nacional de Aeroportos da Guinea-Bissau (ENAG, EP)

KENYA
NAIROBI   Kenya Airports Authority

LA REUNION
SAINT-DENIS   Chambre de Commerce et d'Industrie de la Réunion

LESOTHO
MASERU   Moshoeshoe International Airport

LIBERIA
ROBERTSFIELD   Robertsfield International Airport

MADAGASCAR
ANTANANARIVO   Aéroports de Madagascar-ADEMA

MALAWI
LILONGWE   Airport Developments Limited

MALI
BAMAKO   Aéroports du Mali

MAURITANIA
NOUAKCHOTT   Société Aéroports de Mauritanie

MAURITIUS
PLAISANCE-PLAINE MAGNIEN   SSR International Airport

MOROCCO
CASABLANCA   Office National des Aéroports-ONDA

MOZAMBIQUE
MAPUTO   Aeroportos de Moçambique

NAMIBIA
WINDHOEK   Directorate of Civil Aviation

NIGER
NIAMEY   Aéroport de Niamey

NIGERIA
LAGOS   Federal Airports Authority of Nigeria

RWANDA
KIGALI   Régie des Aéroports du Rwanda-RAR

SENEGAL
DAKAR   Aéroport Léopold Sédar Senghor

SOUTH AFRICA
JOHANNESBURG   Airports Company South Africa (ACSA)
PIETERSBURG   Gateway International Airport

TANZANIA
ZANZIBAR   Zanzibar International Airport
DAR-ES-SALAAM   Directorate of Aerodromes

TOGO
LOME   Société Aéroportuaire de Lomé-Tokoin

TUNISIA
TUNIS   Office des Ports Aériens de Tunisie-OPAT

UGANDA
KAMPALA   Civil Aviation Authority

ZAMBIA
LUSAKA   National Airports Corporation Limited

ASIA: 25 members in 17 countries/territories.

BAHRAIN
BAHRAIN   Civil Aviation Affairs-Bahrain International Airport

BANGLADESH
DHAKA   Civil Aviation Authority of Bangladesh-CAAB

INDIA
NEW DELHI   Airports Authority of India-AAI

JORDAN
AMMAN   Jordan Civil Aviation Authority

KAZAKHSTAN
ALMATY (ALMA-ATA)   Almaty (Alma-Ata) Airport
SHIMKENT   Shimkent Airport

KUWAIT
KUWAIT CITY   Kuwait International Airport

LEBANON
BEIRUT   Directorate General of Civil Aviation

MALDIVES
MALÉ   Maldives Airports Authority

MONGOLIA
ULAN BATOR   Airports Authority of Mongolia

OMAN
MUSCAT   Directorate General of Civil Aviation and Meteorology

PAKISTAN
KARACHI   Civil Aviation Authority

QATAR
DOHA   Doha International Airport

SAUDI ARABIA
JEDDAH   International Airports Projects
JEDDAH   Domestic and Regional Airports

SRI LANKA
COLOMBO   Airport and Aviation Services (SL) Ltd

UNITED ARAB EMIRATES
ABU DHABI	Department of Civil Aviation
DUBAI	Department of Civil Aviation
FUJAIRAH	Department of Civil Aviation
RAS AL KHAIMAH	Civil Aviation Authority
SHARJAH	Sharjah Airport Authority

UZBEKISTAN
NAMANGAN	Namangan Airport
SAMARKAND	Samarkand Airport
TASHKENT	Tashkent Airport

YEMEN
SANA'A	Civil Aviation & Meteorology Authority

EUROPE: 197 members in 44 countries/territories.

ALBANIA
TIRANA	Rinas Airport (Albtransport)

ARMENIA
YEREVAN	Special State Enterprise "Zvartnots" Airport

AUSTRIA
GRAZ	Flughafen Graz Betriebsgesellschaft mbH
INNSBRUCK	Innsbruck Airport
KLAGENFURT	Klagenfurt Wörthersee
LINZ	Linz Airport Authority
SALZBURG	Salzburger Flughafenbetriebsges GmbH
VIENNA	Vienna Airport plc

BELARUS
MINSK	Minsk-2 Airport

BELGIUM
ANTWERP	Internationale Luchthaven Antwerpen
BRUSSELS	Régie des Voies Aériennes-RVA
CHARLEROI	Charleroi Airport
LIEGE	SAB Société de Développement et de Promotion de l'Aéroport de Liège
OSTEND	Luchthaven Oostende
WEVELGEM	Kortrikj-Welvelgem International Airport

BOSNIA HERZEGOVINA
SARAJEVO	Aerodrom Sarajevo

BULGARIA
BOURGAS	Bourgas Airport
SOFIA	Sofia Airport
VARNA	Varna International Airport Ltd

CROATIA
DUBROVNIK	Zracna Luka Dubrovnik-Dubrovnik Airport
PULA	Aerodrom Pula
SPLIT	Split Airport
ZAGREB	Zagreb Airport Ltd

CYPRUS
NICOSIA	Department of Civil Aviation

CZECH REPUBLIC
PRAGUE   Czech Airports Administration

DENMARK
AARHUS   Aarhus Airport, Tirstrup
BILLUND   Billund Airport
COPENHAGEN   Kobenhavns Lufthavne A/S (Copenhagen Airports Ltd)

ESTONIA
TALLINN   SE Estonian Airports

FINLAND
HELSINKI   Civil Aviation Administration

FRANCE
AJACCIO   Chambre de Commerce et d'Industrie d'Ajaccio et de la Corse du Sud
ANGOULEME   Chambre de Commerce et d'Industrie d'Angoulême
AVIGNON   Chambre de Commerce et d'Industrie d'Avignon et de Vaucluse
BASTIA   Chambre de Commerce et d'Industrie de Bastia et de la Haute-Corse
BEAUVAIS   Chambre de Commerce et d'Industrie de l'Oise
BIARRITZ   Syndicat Mixte Aménagement Exploitation Aérodrome Biarritz-
                                  Bayonne-Anglet
BORDEAUX   Chambre de Commerce et d'Industrie de Bordeaux
BREST   Chambre de Commerce et d'Industrie de Brest
CHAMBERY   Chambre de Commerce et d'Industrie de Chambéry et de la Savoie
CHATEAUROUX   Aéroport de Chateauroux-Deols
CLERMONT-FERRAND   Chambre de Commerce et d'Industrie de Clermont-Ferrand Issoire
DIJON   Chambre de Commerce et d'Industrie/Aéroport Dijon-Bourgogne
DOLE   Chambre de Commerce et d'Industrie du Jura
GRENOBLE   Chambre de Commerce et d'Industrie de Grenoble
LE HAVRE   Chambre de Commerce et d'Industrie du Havre
LILLE   Chambre de Commerce et d'Industrie de Lille-Roubaix-Tourcoing
LIMOGES   Chambre de Commerce et d'Industrie de Limoges
LORIENT   Chambre de Commerce et d'Industrie du Morbihan
LYON   Chambre de Commerce et d'Industrie de Lyon
MARSEILLE   Chambre de Commerce et d'Industrie de Marseille
METZ NANCY LORRAINE   Groupement Interconsulaire de Gestion pour l'Aèroport Lorrain (GIGAL)
MONTPELLIER   Chambre de Commerce et d'Industrie de Montpellier
NANTES   Chambre de Commerce et d'Industrie de Nantes
NICE   Chambre de Commerce et d'Industrie Nice-Côte d'Azur
NIMES   Chambre de Commerce et d'Industrie de Nîmes-Uzès Le Vigan
PARIS   Aéroports de Paris
PAU   Chambre de Commerce et d'Industrie de Pau
PERIGUEUX   Chambre de Commerce et d'Industrie de Périgueux
PERPIGNAN   Chambre de Commerce et d'Industrie de Perpignan et des
                                  Pyrénées-Orientales
QUIMPER   Chambre de Commerce et d'Industrie de Quimper
REIMS   Chambre de Commerce et d'Industrie de Reims et d'Epernay
RENNES   Chambre de Commerce et d'Industrie de Rennes
ROUEN   Aéroport Rouen Vallée de Seine
SAINT-ETIENNE   Chambre de Commerce et d'Industrie de Saint-Etienne
STRASBOURG   Chambre de Commerce et d'Industrie de Strasbourg et du Bas-Rhin
TARBES   Chambre de Commerce et d'Industrie de Tarbes et des Hautes-
                                  Pyrénées
TOULOUSE   Chambre de Commerce et d'Industrie de Toulouse

GEORGIA
TBILISI   Tbilisi Airport

GERMANY

AUGSBURG	Augsburger Flughafen GmbH
BADEN-BADEN	Baden Airport GmbH Flughafen Karlsruhe/Baden-Baden
BARTH	Ostsee Flughafen
BERLIN	Berliner Flughafen Gesellschaft mbH-BFG
BREMEN	Flughafen Bremen GmbH
COLOGNE	Flughafen Köln/Bonn GmbH
DORTMUND	Flughafen Dortmund GmbH
DRESDEN	Flughafen Dresden GmbH
DUSSELDORF	Flughafen Düsseldorf GmbH
EGELSBACH	Hessische Flugplatz GmbH Egelsbach
ESSEN/MÜLHEIM	Flughafen Essen/Mülheim
FRANKFURT	Flughafen Frankfurt/Main AG
FRIEDRICHSHAFEN	Flughafen Friedrichshafen GmbH
HAMBURG	Flughafen Hamburg GmbH
HANNOVER	Flughafen Hannover-Langenhagen GmbH
KIRCHBERG	Flughafen Hahn GmbH
LEIPZIG	Flughafen Leipzig/Halle GmbH
LÜBECK	Flughafen Lübeck
MUNICH	Flughafen München GmbH
MÜNSTER	FMO Flughafen Münster/Osnabrück GmbH
NUREMBERG	Flughafen Nürnberg GmbH
ROSTOCK	FRLG Flughafen Rostock-Laage-Güstrow GmbH
SAARBRÜCKEN	Flughafen Saarbrücken GmbH
STUTTGART	Flughafen Stuttgart GmbH

GREECE

ATHENS	Directorate General of Air Transport, Airports Division

HUNGARY

BUDAPEST	Air Traffic and Airport Administration

ICELAND

KEFLAVIK	Civil Aviation Administration

IRELAND

DUBLIN	Aer Rianta-Irish Airports

ISRAEL

TEL-AVIV	Israel Airports Authority

ITALY

BARI	Società Esercizio Aeroporti Puglia (SEAP) Spa
BERGAMO	S.A.C.B.O. S.p.A. Aeroporto di Bergamo
BOLOGNA	SAB Aeroporto G. Marconi di Bologna SpA
CATANZARO	Consorzio Aeroporto "Lamezia Terme"
FLORENCE	Aeroporto di Firenze
GENOA	Aeroporti di Genova SpA
MILAN	SEA-Società SpA Esercizi Aeroportuali
NAPLES	Gestione Servizi Aeroporti Campani SpA-GESAC
PALERMO	GESAP-Società di Gestione dei Servizi Aeroportuali di Palermo
PISA	Società Aeroporto Toscano-SAT
ROME	Aeroporti di Roma
TRIESTE	Consorzio per l'Aeroporto Friuli-Venezia Giulia
TURIN	SAGAT SpA-Società Azionaria Gestione Aeroporto di Torino
VENICE	Società Aeroporto di Venezia Marco Polo SpA-S.A.V.E.
VERONA	Aeroporto Valerio Catullo di Verona Villafranca SpA

LATVIA
RIGA   Riga International Airport

LITHUANIA
KAUNAS   Kaunas Airport
PALANGA   Palanga Airport
SIAULIAI   Siauliai International Airport
VILNIUS   Vilnius Airport

LUXEMBOURG
LUXEMBOURG   Ministère des Transports

MACEDONIA (FORMER YUGOSLAV REP OF)
SKOPJE   Public Enterprise for Airport Services

MALTA
LUQA   Malta International Airport Limited

MOLDOVA
KISHINEV   Kishinev Airport

MONACO
MONACO   Héliport de Monaco

NETHERLANDS
AMSTERDAM   Amsterdam Airport Schiphol
EINDHOVEN   Eindhoven Airport
ENSCHEDE   N.V. Luchthaven Twente (Twente Airport)
GRONINGEN   Groningen Airport Eelde
MAASTRICHT   Maastricht Airport (NV Luchthaven Maastricht)
ROTTERDAM   Rotterdam Airport

NORWAY
OSLO   Civil Aviation Adminisration of Norway

POLAND
BYDGOSZCZ   Bydgoszcz Airport
KATOWICE   Kotowice Airport
WARSAW   "Polish Airports" State Enterprise
WROCLAW   Port Lotniczy Wroclaw SA

PORTUGAL
LISBON   Empresa Publica Aeroportos e Navegaçao Aerea-ANA E.P.
MADEIRA   ANAM, SA Direcçao dos Aeroportos da Madeira

ROMANIA
BAIA MARE   Baie Mare Airport
BUCHAREST   Bucharest Otopeni International Airport RA
BUCHAREST   Bucharest-Baneasa Airport
CLUJ NAPOCA   R.A. Aeroportul Cluj Napoca
CONSTANTA   Constanta International Airport
IASI   R.A. Aeroportul Iasi
SATU MARE   Satu Mare International Airport
TULCEA   Tulcea Airport R.A.
TARGU MURES   Aéroport Vidrasau/Targu Mures
TIMISOARA   Timisoara International Airport

RUSSIAN FEDERATION

ASTRAKHAN	Airport Narmanovo
EKATERINBURG	Koltsovo Airport
IRKUTSK	Irkutsk Airport
KAZAN	Kazan Airport
MAGADAN TOWN	Magadan Airport
MOSCOW I	Domodedovo Airport
MOSCOW II	Moscow Sheremetyevo Airport
MOSCOW III	Stock Company "Vnukovo Airport"
NOVOSIBIRSK	Airport Tolmachovo
PERM	Perm State Unitary Aviation Company
ROSTOV ON DON	Rostov on Don Airport
SAMARA	Samara International Airport
SOCHI	Sochi Airport
ST. PETERSBURG	Pulkovo Airport
STAVROPOL	Mineralye Vody Airport
USINSK	Usinsk Airport
YUZHNO-SAKHALINSK	Yuzhno-Sakhalinsk Airport

SLOVAKIA

BRATISLAVA	Slovak Airports Authority

SLOVENIA

LJUBLJANA	Aerodrom Ljubljana
MARIBOR	Aerodrom Maribor

SPAIN

MADRID	Aeropuertos Españoles y Navegación Aérea (Aena)

SWEDEN

STOCKHOLM	Luftfartsverket-Swedish Civil Aviation Administration
STOCKHOLM	Kommmunala Flygplatsgruppen Svenska Kommunförbundet

SWITZERLAND

BASLE	Basel-Mulhouse Airport
BERNE	Flughafen Bern-Belp
LUGANO	Aeroporto Città di Lugano
GENEVA	Aéroport International de Genève
ZURICH	Zurich Airport Authority

TURKEY

ANKARA	State Airports Authority

UKRAINE

KIEV	Kiev-Borispol Airport
KIEV	Zhulyany International Airport
KRIVIJ RIG	Krivij Rig Airport

UNITED KINGDOM

BIRMINGHAM	Birmingham International Airport plc
BRISTOL	Bristol Airport plc
CARDIFF	Cardiff-Wales Airport Ltd
EXETER	Exeter and Devon Airport Ltd
GUERNSEY	States of Guernsey Board of Administration
HAMPSHIRE	Regional Airports Ltd
HUMBERSIDE	Humberside International Airport Ltd
ISLE OF MAN	Isle of Man Airport
JERSEY	Jersey Airport
LEEDS BRADFORD	Leeds Bradford Airport Ltd
LIVERPOOL	Liverpool Airport plc

LONDON	BAA plc
LONDON CITY	London City Airport Ltd
LONDON LUTON	London Luton Airport Ltd
MANCHESTER	Manchester Airport plc
NEWCASTLE	Newcastle International Airport Ltd.
NORWICH	Norwich Airport Ltd
NOTTINGHAM/DERBY/LEIC/	
BOURNE	National Express Group PLC
PRESTWICK	PIK Limited
SHEFFIELD	Sheffield City Airport Ltd
TEESSIDE	Teesside International Airport Ltd

YUGOSLAVIA
BELGRADE   Enterprise for Airport Services-Aerodrom Beograd

LATIN AMERICA/CARIBBEAN: 36 members in 28 countries/territories.

BELIZE
BELIZE CITY   Philip S.W. Goldson International Airport

BERMUDA
BERMUDA   Bermuda International Airport

BRAZIL
BRASILIA   Empresa Brasileira de Infra-Estrutura Aeroportuaria-INFRAERO

CHILE
SANTIAGO   Dirección General de Aeronáutica Civil

COLOMBIA
BARRANQUILA   Aeropuertos del Caribe S.A.-ACSA
CARTAGENA   Sociedad Aeroportuaria de la Costa S.A.

CUBA
HAVANA   Instituto de Aeronáutica Civil de Cuba

DOMINICAN REPUBLIC
SANTO DOMINGO   Departamento Aeroportuario

DUTCH CARRIBEAN
ARUBA   Aruba Airport Authority

ECUADOR
QUITO   Dirección General de Aviación Civil

EL SALVADOR
SAN SALVADOR   Comisión Ejecutiva Portuaria Autónoma

FRENCH GUIANA
CAYENNE   Chambre de Commerce et d'Industrie de Guyane

GRENADA
ST. GEORGE'S I   Grenada Airports Authority

GUADELOUPE
GRANDE CASE/ST. MARTIN   Aéroport de Grand Case-L'Esperance
POINTE-A-PITRE   Chambre de Commerce et d'Industrie de Pointe-á-Pitre

HAITI
PORT-AU-PRINCE   Autorité Aéroportuaire Nationale

HONDURAS
SAN PEDRO SULA   Doctor Ramon Villeda Morales Airport

JAMAICA
KINGSTON   Airports Authority of Jamaica

MARTINIQUE
FORT-DE-FRANCE   Chambre de Commerce et d'Industrie de la Martinique

MEXICO
MEXICO CITY   Aeropuertos y Servicios Auxiliares (ASA)

NETHERLANDS ANTILLES
BONAIRE   Flamingo Airport
CURAÇAO   Curaçao International Airport N.V.
SINT MAARTEN   Princess Juliana International Airport NV

NICARAGUA
MANAGUA   Aeropuerto Internacional Augusto César Sandino

PANAMA
PANAMA CITY   Dirección de Aeronautica Civil

PUERTO RICO
SAN JUAN   Puerto Rico Ports Authority

SAINT LUCIA
CASTRIES   Saint Lucia Air & Sea Ports Authority

SURINAME
PARAMARIBO   N.V. Lucthaven Beheer

TRINIDAD & TOBAGO
PORT OF SPAIN   Airports Authority of Trinidad & Tobago

URUGUAY
MONTEVIDEO   Dirección General de Infraestructura Aeronáutica

USA
MIAMI, FL   Dade County Aviation Department

VENEZUELA
CARACAS   Instituto Autónomo Aeropuerto Internacional de Maiquetía-IAAIM
CORO   Instituto Autonomo Aeropuertos Estado Falcon
ISLA DE MARGARITA   Consorcio C.V.A.,C.A./Aeropuerto Internacional del Caribe General
                                en Jefe "Santiage Mariño"
MARACAIBO   Direccion General de Aeropuertos del Estado Zulia
MERIDA   Servicio Autonomo del Puerto y Aeropuertos del Estado Merida (SAPAM)

NORTH AMERICA: 142 members in 3 countries/territories.

CANADA
CALGARY   Calgary Airport Authority
EDMONTON   Edmonton Regional Airports Authority
HALIFAX   Halifax International Airport Authority
HAMILTON   Hamilton International Airport
MONTREAL   Aéroports de Montréal
OTTAWA   Ottawa MacDonald-Cartier International Airport Authority
TORONTO   Greater Toronto Airports Authority
WINNIPEG   Winnipeg Airports Authority

USA
ALASKA (BETHEL)   Alaska Department of Transportation and Public Facilities
ALBANY, NY   Albany Airport Authority
ALBUQUERQUE, NM   City of Albuquerque Aviation Department

ALLENTOWN, PA	Lehigh-Northampton Airport Authority
ANCHORAGE, AK	Anchorage International Airport
ATLANTA, GA	City of Atlanta Department of Aviation
ATLANTIC CITY, NJ	Atlantic City International Airport
AUGUSTA, GA	Augusta Airport Authority
AUSTIN, TX	City of Austin Department of Aviation
BAKERSFIELD, CA	Bakersfield/Kern County Department of Airports
BALTIMORE/WASHINGTON	Maryland Aviation Administration
BANGOR, ME	City of Bangor Airport Department
BATON ROUGE, LA	Greater Baton Rouge Airport District
BIRMINGHAM, AL	Birmingham Airport Authority
BLOOMINGTON, IL	Bloomington-Normal Airport
BOISE, ID	Boise Air Terminal
BOSTON, MA	Massachusetts Port Authority
BROWNSVILLE, TX	Brownsville/South Padre Island International Airport
BURBANK, CA	Burbank/Glendale/Pasadena Airport Authority
BURLINGTON, VT	Burlington Airport Commission
CHARLESTON, SC	Charleston County Aviation Authority
CHARLOTTE, NC	Charlotte/Douglas International Airport
CHATTANOOGA, TN	Chattanooga Metropolitan Airport Authority
CHICAGO, IL	City of Chicago-Department of Aviation
CINCINNATI, OH	Kenton County Airport Board
CLEVELAND, OH	City of Cleveland
COLORADO SPRINGS, CO	Colorado Springs Municipal Airport
COLUMBIA, SC	Columbia Metropolitan Airport
COLUMBUS, OH	Columbus Airport Authority
COLUMBUS, OH	Rickenbacker Port Airport
DALLAS, TX	City of Dallas Department of Aviation
DALLAS/FORT WORTH, TX	Dallas/Fort Worth International Airport
DAYTON, OH	City of Dayton Department of Aviation
DAYTONA BEACH, FL	Daytona Beach International Airport
DENVER, CO	City and County of Denver Stapleton International Airport
DES MOINES, IA	City of Des Moines Department of Aviation
DETROIT, MI	Wayne County Division of Airports
DURANGO-LA PLATA, CO	Durango-La Plata County Airport
EL PASO, TX	City of El Paso
EVERETT, WA	Snohomish County Department-Paine Field
FAIRBANKS, AK	Fairbanks International Airport
FAYETTEVILLE, AR	Fayetteville Municipal Airport
FLINT, MI	Bishop International Airport
FORT LAUDERDALE, FL	Broward County Board of Commissioners
FORT MYERS, FL	Southwest Florida International Airport
FORT SMITH, AR	Fort Smith Regional Airport
FORT WAYNE, IN	Fort Wayne-Allen County Airport Authority
FREELAND, MI	Tri-City International Airport Commission
GAINESVILLE, FL	Gainesville-Alachua County Regional Airport Authority
GRAND FORKS, ND	Grand Forks Regional Airport Authority
GRAND RAPIDS, MI	Kent County Aeronautics Board
GREENSBORO, NC	Piedmont Triad International Airport
GULFPORT, MS	Gulfport-Biloxi Regional Airport Authority
HARTFORD, CT	Connecticut Department of Transportation Bureau of Aviation and Ports
HOUSTON, TX	Department of Aviation
HUNTSVILLE, AL	Huntsville-Madison County Airport Authority
INDIANAPOLIS, IN	Indianapolis Airport Authority
JACKSON, MI	Jackson County Airport-Reynolds Field
JACKSON, MS	Jackson Municipal Airport Authority

JACKSONVILLE, FL	Jacksonville Port Authority
KANSAS CITY, MO	Kansas City Aviation Department
KNOXVILLE, TN	Metropolitan Knoxville Airport Authority
LAFAYETTE, LA	Lafayette Airport Commission
LANSING, MI	Capital Region Airport Authority
LAS VEGAS, NV	Clark County Department of Aviation
LEXINGTON, KY	Lexington-Fayette Urban County Airport Board
LINCOLN, NE	City of Lincoln Airport Authority
LOS ANGELES, CA	City of Los Angeles Department of Airports
LOUISVILLE, KY	Regional Airport Authority Louisville & Jefferson County
MCALLEN, TX	McAllen Miller International Airport
MELBOURNE, FL	City of Melbourne Airport Authority
MEMPHIS, TN	Memphis-Shelby County Airport Authority
MILWAUKEE, WI	Milwaukee County Department of Public Works-Airports Division
MINNEAPOLIS/ST PAUL, MN	MSP Metropolitan Airports Commission
MOBILE, AL	Mobile Airport Authority
MOLINE, IL	Metropolitan Airport Authority of Rock Island County
MONTEREY, CA	Monterey Peninsula Airport District
MUSKEGON, MI	Muskegon County Airport
MYRTLE BEACH, SC	Horry County Department of Airports
NASHVILLE, TN	Metropolitan Nashville Airport Authority
NEW ORLEANS, LA	New Orleans Aviation Board
NEW YORK, NY	Port Authority of New York & New Jersey-PANY&NJ
NORFOLK, VA	Norfolk Airport Authority
NORTH PLATTE, NE	North Platte Airport Authority
OAKLAND, CA	Port of Oakland Board of Commissioners
OKLAHOMA CITY, OK	Oklahoma City Airport Trust
OMAHA, NE	Omaha Airport Authority
ORLANDO, FL	Greater Orlando Aviation Authority
PADUCAH, KY	Paducah Airport Corporation
PALM BEACH, FL	Board of County Commissioners Department of Airports
PALM SPRINGS, CA	City of Palm Springs
PASCO, WA	Port of Pasco
PENSACOLA, FL	City of Pensacola
PEORIA, IL	Greater Peoria Airport Authority
PHILADELPHIA, PA	Philadelphia International Airport
PHOENIX, AZ	City of Phoenix Aviation Department
PITTSBURGH, PA	County of Allegheny Department of Aviation
PORTLAND, OR	Port of Portland
RALEIGH-DURHAM, NC	Raleigh-Durham Airport Authority
READING, PA	Reading Regional Airport
REDDING, CA	Redding Municipal Airport
RENO, NV	Airport Authority of Washoe County
RICHMOND, VA	Capital Region Airport Commission
ROANOKE, VA	Roanoke Regional Airport Commission
SACRAMENTO, CA	County of Sacramento Department of Airports
SALINA, KS	Salina Airport Authority
SALT LAKE CITY, UT	Salt Lake City Airport Authority
SAN ANTONIO, TX	City of San Antonio Aviation Department
SAN BERNARDINO, CA	San Bernardino International Airport Authority
SAN DIEGO, CA	San Diego Unified Port District
SAN DIEGO I	County of San Diego
SAN JOSE, CA	City of San Jose Airport Department
SANTA ANA, CA	John Wayne Airport
SARASOTA, FL	Sarasota-Manatee Airport Authority
SAVANNAH, GA	Savannah Airport Commission

SEATTLE, WA	The Port of Seattle Commission
SHREVEPORT, LA	Shreveport Airport Authority
SIOUX CITY, IA	Sioux Gateway Airport Authority
SIOUX FALLS, SD	Sioux Falls Regional Airport Authority
SPOKANE, WA	Spokane Airport Board
SPRINGFIELD, MO	Regional Airport Board City of Springfield
ST. LOUIS, MO	St. Louis Airport Authority
ST. PETERSBURG, FL	St. Petersburg-Clearwater International Airport
TAMPA, FL	Hillsborough County Aviation Authority
TOLEDO, OH	Toledo-Lucas County Port Authority
TOPEKA, KS	Metropolitan Topeka Airport Authority
TUCSON, AZ	Tucson Airport Authority
TULSA, OK	Tulsa Airport Authority
VERO BEACH, FL	Vero Beach Municipal Airport
WASHINGTON, DC	Metropolitan Washington Airports Authority
WHITE PLAINS, NY	Westchester County Department of Transportation
WICHITA, KS	Wichita Airport Authority
YUMA, AZ	Yuma County Airport Authority Inc.

US VIRGIN ISLANDS
ST. THOMAS	Virgin Islands Port Authority

PACIFIC: 61 members in 25 countries/territories.

AMERICAN SAMOA
PAGO PAGO	American Samoa Government, Department of Port Administration

AUSTRALIA
ADELAIDE	Adelaide International Airport
ALICE SPRINGS	Alice Springs Airport
BANKSTOWN	Bankstown Airport
BRISBANE	Archerfield Airport
BRISBANE	Brisbane International Airport
CAIRNS	Cairns Port Authority
CANBERRA	Canberra Airport
GOLD COAST CITY	Coolanga Airport
JANDAKOT	Jandakot Airport
MACKAY	Mackay Port Authority
MELBOURNE	Melbourne International Airport
MELBOURNE	Essendon Airport
MELBOURNE	Moorabbin Airport
NEWCASTLE	Newcastle Airport Limited
PERTH	Perth International Airport, Westralia Airports Corporation Pty Ltd
SUNSHINE COAST	Maroochydore Sunshine Coast Airport
SYDNEY	Sydney International Airport
SYDNEY	Federal Airports Corporation
TOWNSVILLE	Townsville Airport

BRUNEI DARUSSALAM
BANDAR SERI BEGAWAN	Department of Civil Aviation Ministry of Communications

CAMBODIA
PHNOM PENH	Cambodia Airport Management Services Ltd

CANADA
VANCOUVER	Vancouver International Airport Authority

CHINA

BEIJING	Beijing Capital International Airport
GUANGZHOU	Guangzhou Bai Yun International Airport
NANJING	Nanjing Lukou International Airport Co Ltd
SHANGHAI	Shanghai Hongqiao International Airport
SHENZHEN	Shenzhen Airport (Group) Company
XIAMEN	Xiamen International Airport Group Co Ltd

COOK ISLANDS

RAROTONGA	Cook Islands Airport Authority

FIJI

NADI	Civil Aviation Authority of Fiji

FRENCH POLYNESIA

PAPEETE	S.E.T.I.L. Concessionaire Aéroport International de Tahiti-Faa'a

GUAM

AGANA	Guam Airport Authority

HONG KONG, CHINA

HONG KONG	Airport Authority Hong Kong

INDONESIA

JAKARTA	PT (Persero) Angkasa Pura I
JAKARTA	PT (Persero) Angkasa Pura II

JAPAN

CHITOSE	Hokkaido Airport Terminal Co Ltd
FUKUOKA	Fukuoka Airport Building Co Ltd
NAGOYA	Nagoya Airport Terminal Building Co Ltd
OSAKA	Kansai International Airport Company
OSAKA	Kansai (Osaka) International Airport
TOKYO	New Tokyo International Airport Authority
TOKYO	Japan Airport Terminal Co Ltd

KOREA (REP OF)

SEOUL	Korea Airports Authority-KAA

MACAU

MACAU	Macau International Airport Company

MALAYSIA

KUALA LUMPUR	Malaysia Airports Berhad

MARIANAS

SAIPAN	Commonwealth Ports Authority

MICRONESIA

POHNPEI	Pohnpei Port Authority

NEW CALEDONIA

NOUMEA	Chambre de Commerce et d'Industrie de Nouvelle Calédonie

NEW ZEALAND

AUCKLAND	Auckland International Airport Ltd
CHRISTCHURCH	Christchurch International Airport Ltd
DUNEDIN	Dunedin Airport Limited
WELLINGTON	Wellington International Airport Ltd

PHILIPPINES

MANILA	Manila International Airport Authority
SUBIC BAY	Subic Bay International Airport

SINGAPORE
SINGAPORE   Civil Aviation Authority of Singapore

CHINESE TAIPEI
TAIPEI   Civil Aeronautics Administration

THAILAND
BANGKOK   Airports Authority of Thailand

USA
HONOLULU, HI   Hawaii Department of Transportation
SAN FRANCISCO, CA   San Francisco Airports Commission

WESTERN SAMOA
APIA   Western Samoa Airport Authority

Appendix D
International Aviation Authorities ▰

Ministry of Civil Aviation and Tourism
Ansari Watt
P.O. Box 165
Kabul
AFGHANISTAN

Ministère des Transports
Direction Générale de l'Aviation civile
  et de la Météorologie nationale
119, rue Didouche Mourad
Alger
ALGERIE

Direcçao Nacional da Aviaçao Civil
Caixa Postal 569
Luanda
ANGOLA

Directorate of Civil Aviation of Eastern
  Caribbean States
P.O. Box 1130
St. John's
ANTIGUA, West Indies

Comando de Regiones Aéreas
Edificio Condor
Comodoro Pedro Zanni 250
(1104) Buenos Aires
ARGENTINA

Department of Transport and
  Communications
G.P.O. Box 967
Canberra ACT 2600
AUSTRALIA

Federal Ministry for Public Economy
  and Transport
Department of Civil Aviation
Radetzkystrasse 2
A-1030 Wien
AUSTRIA

Director of Civil Aviation
P.O. Box N-975
Nassau-New Providence
BAHAMAS

Director General of Civil Aviation
Government of Bahrain
Bahrain International Airport
P.O. Box 586
STATE OF BAHRAIN

Civil Aviation Authority of Bangladesh
Headquarters Office
Kurmitola, Dhaka 1206
BANGLADESH

Permanent Secretary (Aviation)
International Transport Division
Herbert House, Fontabelle
BARBADOS, West Indies

Administration de l'Aéronautique
Centre Communication Nord, 4ème étage
Rue du Progrès, 80
B-1210 Bruxelles
BELGIQUE

The Chief Civil Aviation Officer
Belize International Airport
P.O. Box 367
Belize City
BELIZE

Direction de l'Aéronautique civile
B.P. 305
Cotonou
RÉPUBLIQUE POPULAIRE DU BÉNIN

The Director
Department of Civil Aviation and Transport
Ministry of Communication
Royal Government of Bhutan
BHUTAN

Dirección General de Aeronáutica Civil
Casilla Postal 9360
La Paz
BOLIVIA

Director of Civil Aviation
P.O. Box 250
Gaborone
BOTSWANA

705

Departamento de Aviaçao Civil
Praça Senador Salgado Filho s/n°
Aeroporto Santos Dumont-4° andar
Ala Sul
20.021 Rio de Janeiro-RJ
BRASIL

Director of Civil Aviation
Ministry of Communications
Brunei International Airport
Bandar Seri Begawan 2015
BRUNEI DARUSSALAM

Ministry of Transport
Levski St. 11
Sofia C
BULGARIA

Direction de l'Aviation civile
01 B.P. 1158
Ouagadougou 01
BURKINA FASO

Ministère des Transports, Postes et
    Télécommunications
B.P. 2000
Bujumbura
RÉPUBLIQUE DU BURUNDI

Ministère des Travaux Publics et du Génie Rural
Direction de l'Aviation Civile
B.P. 86
Phnom-Penh
CAMBODGE

Ministère des Travaux Publics et des
    Transports
Direction de l'Aviation Civile
Yaoundé
RÉPUBLIQUE DU CAMEROUN

Transport Canada
Tower "C", Place de Ville
Ottawa, Ontario
K1A 0N8
CANADA

Minister of Transport, Commerce and Tourism
Cx. P. 74
Praia
Ilha do Santiago
REPUBLICA DE CABO VERDE

Ministère des Transports et de l'Aviation Civile
Direction Générale de l'Aviation civile et de la
    Météorologie
B.P. 941 et 224
Bangui
RÉPUBLIQUE CENTRAFRICAINE

Direction de l'aviation civile
B.P. 96
N'Djaména
RÉPUBLIQUE DU TCHAD

Junta de Aeronáutica Civil
Amunátegui N° 139—7° Piso
SANTIAGO DE CHILE

Director General
Civil Aviation Administration of China
155 Dong-Si Street West
Beijing
PEOPLE'S REPUBLIC OF CHINA

Departamento Administrativo de Aeronautica Civil
    (DAAC)
Aeropuerto Internacional El Dorado
Apartado Aéreo 12307
Bogota, D.E.
COLOMBIA

Direction des Transport Aériens
Secrétariat d'Etat aux Transports et au Tourisme
B.P. 97
Moroni
COMORES

Direction général de l'Agence nationale de l'Aviation
    civile
B.P. 128
Brazzaville
CONGO

Department of Civil Aviation
P.O. Box 329
Rarotonga
COOK ISLANDS

Dirección General de Aviación Civil
Ministerio de Obras Públicas y Transportes
Apartado Postal 5026
San José
COSTA RICA

Direction des Transports
B.P. V 134
Abidjan
RÉPUBLIQUE DU CÔTE D'IVOIRE

Instituto de Aeronaútica Civil de Cuba (IACC)
Dirección de Relaciones Internacionales
Calle 23 No. 64
Municipio Plaza
Apartado Postal 6215
Ciudad de La Habana
CUBA

The Director
Department of Civil Aviation
Government House No. 25
St. George's Hill
Nicosia
CYPRUS

Civil Aviation Administration
Federal Ministry of Transport
Nabrezi Ludvika Svobody 12
110 15 Praha 1
CZECH AND SLOVAK FEDERAL REPUBLIC

Director General
Civil Aviation Administration
Sunan District
Pyongyang
DEMOCRATIC PEOPLE'S REPUBLIC OF KOREA

Ministry of Transport
27, Frederiksholms Kanal
DK-1220 Copenhagen K
DENMARK

Direction de l'Aviation Civile et de la Météorologie
B.P. 204
Djibouti
RÉPUBLIQUE DE DJIBOUTI

Dirección General de Aeronáutica Civil
Edificio "Manuel Fernández Mármol" Novena Planta
Avenida 27 de Febrero
Santo Domingo
REPÚBLICA DOMINICANA

Directorate of Civil Aviation of Eastern
   Caribbean States
P.O. Box 1130
St. John's
ANTIGUA, WEST INDIES

Director General de Aviación Civil
Edificio "Los Andes"
Buenos Aires N° 149 y Av. 10 de Agosto
Quito
ECUADOR

Ministry of Civil Aviation
P.O. Box 52 Cairo Airport Post Office
Heliopolis
Cairo
ARAB REPUBLIC OF EGYPT

Dirección General de Aeronáutica Civil
Aeropuerto de Ilopango
San Salvador
EL SALVADOR, C.A.

The General Manager
Civil Aviation Authority
P.O. Box 978
Addis Ababa
ETHIOPIA

Division of Civil Aviation
Department of Transportation
Kolonia, Pohnpei
P.O. Box 490
Eastern Caroline Islands 96941
THE FEDERATED STATES OF MICRONESIA

Civil Aviation Authority of Fiji
Private Bag
Nadi Airport
FIJI

Civil Aviation Administration
P.O. Box 50
SF-01531 Vantaa
FINLAND

Monsieur le Ministre des Transports
   et de la Mer
Direction Générale de l'Aviation Civile
93 Boulevard du Montparnasse
75270 Paris Cedex 06
FRANCE

Secrétariat Général à l'Aviation Civile et
   Commerciale
B.P. 2.212
Libreville
RÉPUBLIQUE GABONAISE

Director of Civil Aviation
Department of Civil Aviation
Banjul/Yundum International Airport
Yundum
THE GAMBIA, WEST AFRICA

Federal Ministry of Transport
Directorate General for Civil Aviation and Space
   Flight
Robert-Schuman-Platz 1
Postfach 20 01 00
D-5300 Bonn 2
GERMANY

Ghana Civil Aviation Authority
Private Post Bag
Kotoka International Airport
Accra
GHANA

Ministry of Transport and Communications
Civil Aviation Authority
P.O. Box 73751
GR-166 04 Helliniko
GREECE

Permanent Secretary
Ministry of Tourism and Civil Aviation
Young Street
St. George's
GRENADA

Dirección General de Aeronautica Civil
Aeropuerto Internacional "La Aurora"
Zona 13
GUATEMALA, Centro América

Ministère des Transports et des Travaux Publics
Direction nationale de l'Aviation civile
B.P. 95
Conakry
RÉPUBLIQUE DE GUINÉE

Direcçao-Geral Da Aviaçao Civil
Ministério do Equipamento Social
Secretaria de Estado dos Transportes
C.P. 77
Bissau
REPUBLICA DA GUINÉ-BISSAU

Ministerio de Comunicaciones y Transportes
Dirección General de Aviación Civil
Calle 3 de Agosto, No. 45
Malabo
REPÚBLICA DE GUINEA ECUATORIAL

Civil Aviation Department
Ministry of Communications & Works
Oranapai Towers
Wights Lane
Kingston
P.O. Box 1006
Georgetown
GUYANA

Office National de l'Aviation civile
Aéroport International de Port-au-Prince
B.P. 1346
Port-au-Prince
RÉPUBLIQUE D'HAÏTI

Dirección General de Aeronáutica Civil
Aeropuerto International Toncontín
Apartado Postal No. 30145
Tegucigalpa, D.C.
HONDURAS, C.A.

Civil Aviation Department
46/F.,
Queensway Government Offices
66, Queensway
HONG KONG

Ministry of Transport, Communication and Construction
General Directorate of Civil Aviation
H-1400 Budapest Pf. 87
HUNGARY

Civil Aviation Administration
Reykjavic Airport
P.O. Box 350
101 Reykjavik
ICELAND

Office of the Director General of Civil Aviation
East Blocks II & III
R.K. Puram
New Delhi—110066
INDIA

Directorate General of Air Communications
Jl Angkasa I/2—Kemoyaran
Jakarta Pusat
INDONESIA

Civil Aviation Organization
International Affairs & Legal Bureau
P.O. Box 11365—8315
Mehrabad Airport
Tehran
ISLAMIC REPUBLIC OF IRAN

General Establishment of Civil Aviation
Air Transport Department/Organizations Section
P.O. Box 23006
Saddam International Airport
Baghdad
IRAQ

The Librarian
Aeronautical Library
Air Navigation Service Office
Department of Tourism and Transport
Scotch House
Hawkins Street
Dublin 2
IRELAND

Civil Aviation Administration
P.O. Box 8
Ben Gurion International Airport 70 100
ISRAEL

Ministero dei Transporti
Direzione Generale Aviazione Civile
Piazzale degli Archivi, 41
00144 Rome
ITALY

The Director of Civil Aviation
Civil Aviation Department
UDC Building—First Floor
12 Ocean Boulevard
Kingston Mall
Kingston
JAMAICA, WEST INDIES

Civil Aviation Bureau
Ministry of Transport
2-1-3 Kasumigaseki
Chiyoda-ku
Tokyo 100
JAPAN

Civil Aviation Authority
P.O. Box 7547
Amman
JORDAN

Director of Civil Aviation
P.O. Box 30163
Nairobi
KENYA

Director of Civil Aviation
Ministry of Communications
P.O. Box 487
Betio, Tarawa
REPUBLIC OF KIRIBATI

Director General of Civil Aviation
Directorate General of Civil Aviation
P.O. Box 17, Safat
13001 Safat
THE STATE OF KUWAIT
Arabian Gulf

Department of Civil Aviation
2 Pang Kham Street
P.O. Box 119
Vientiane
LAO PEOPLE'S DEMOCRATIC REPUBLIC

Directorate General of Civil Aviation
Beirut International Airport
LEBANON

Director of Civil Aviation
P.O. Box 629
Maseru 100
LESOTHO

Director of Civil Aviation
c/o General Manager
Roberts International Airport
Margibi Country
P.O. Box 1
Robertsfield
LIBERIA

Civil Aviation General Administration
Sharia El-Sadedi
P.O. Box 14399
Tripoli
**THE SOCIALIST PEOPLE'S LIBYAN ARAB
      JAMAHIRIYA**

Ministère des Transports
Direction de l'Aviation civile
19-21 Boulevard Royal
B.P. 590
L-2938
LUXEMBOURG

Ministère des Transports, de la Météorologie et du
      Tourisme
B.P. 921
101—Antananarivo
MADAGASCAR

Chief Civil Aviation Officer
Private Bag 322
Capital City
Lilongwe 3
MALAWI

Director General
Department of Civil Aviation
Terminal 2
Subang—Kuala Lumpur International Airport
Selangor
MALAYSIA

Department of Civil Aviation
Huravve Building
2nd Floor
Malé, 20-05
REPUBLIC OF MALDIVES

Direction Nationale de l'Aviation civile
Ministère des Transports et du Tourisme
B.P. 227
Bamako
RÉPUBLIQUE DU MALI

Director of Civil Aviation
Luqa Airport
Luqa
MALTA

Embassy of the Republic of the
MARSHALL ISLANDS
2433 Massachusetts Avenue N.W.
Washington, D.C. 20008
U.S.A.

Ministère du Commerce et des Transports
Direction de l'Aviation civile
B.P. 91
Nouakchott
RÉPUBLIQUE ISLAMIQUE DE MAURITANIE

The Director of Civil Aviation
Plaisance Airport
Plaine Magnien
MAURITIUS

Dirección General de Aeronáutica Civil
Secretaría de Comunicaciones y Transportes
Providencia No. 807—6° Piso
Colonia des Valle
Codigo Postal 03100
MÉXICO, D.F.

Ministère d'Etat
Place de la Visitation
MC 98000 Monaco Ville
PRINCIPAUTÉ DE MONACO

Director General
Civil Aviation Authority of Mongolia
Ulaan Baatar, Buyant-Ukha Airport
Ulaan Baatar—34
MONGOLIAN PEOPLE'S REPUBLIC

Direction de l'Aéronautique civile
B.P. 1073
Rabat-Principal
MAROC

State Secretary for Civil Aviation
P.O. Box 227
Maputo
MOZAMBIQUE

Department of Civil Aviation
Yangon International Airport Extension Project
  Building
Yangon International Airport
Mingaladon, Yangon
MYANMAR

Director of Civil Aviation
Directorate of Civil Aviation
REPUBLIC OF NAURU
Central Pacific

Department of Civil Aviation
Babar Mahal
Kathmandu
NEPAL

Department of Civil Aviation
Koninginnegracht 19-21
P.O. Box 20903
2500 EX The Hague
THE NETHERLANDS

Civil Aviation Department
Seru Mahuma Z/N
Curaçao
NETHERLANDS ANTILLES

The General Manager
Air Transport Division
Ministry of Transport
Attn: AIPO
P.O. Box 31441
Lower Hutt
NEW ZEALAND

Dirección General de Aeronáutica Civil
Ministerio de Transporte y la Construcción
Apartado Postal 4936
Managua
NICARAGUA

Direction de l'Aviation civile
Ministère des Transports et du Tourisme
B.P. 727
Niamey
RÉPUBLIQUE DU NIGER

Federal Ministry of Civil Aviation
14 Broad Street
Lagos
NIGERIA

Civil Aviation Administration
P.O. Box 8124 Dep.
N-0032 Oslo 1
NORWAY

Directorate General of Civil Aviation
P.O. Box 204
Muscat
SULTANATE OF OMAN

Headquarters, Civil Aviation Authority
19, Liaquat Barracks
Karachi 4
PAKISTAN

Dirección de Aeronáutica Civil
ARP. Marcos A. Gelabert, Vía Israel
Apartados 7501 y 7615
Panamá 5
PANAMA

The Secretary
Department of Civil Aviation
P.O. Box 684
Boroko NCD
PAPUA NEW GUINEA

Dirección General de Aeronáutica Civil (DINAC)
Ministerio de Defensa Nacional—2° Piso
Av. Mcal. Lopez y Vice-Presidente Sánchez
Asunción
PARAGUAY

Dirección General de Transporte Aereo
Ministerio de Transportes y Comunicaciones
Esq. Avdas. 28 de Julio y Garcilaso de la Vega
Lima
PERU

Air Transportation Office
Ninoy Aquino International Airport
Pasay City 1300
PHILIPPINES

General Inspectorate of Civil Aviation
ul. Chalubinskiego 4/6
00-928 Warszawa 67
POLAND

Directorate General of Civil Aviation
Av. da Liberdade, 193
1298, Lisbon CODEX
PORTUGAL

Civil Aviation Department
P.O. Box 3000
Doha
STATE OF QATAR

Civil Aviation Bureau
Ministry of Transportation
Seoul
REPUBLIC OF KOREA

Department of Civil Aviation
Soseaua Bucuresti-Ploiesti Km. 16,5
Bucarest
ROMANIA

Direction générale de l'Aéronautique
B.P. 898
Kigali
RÉPUBLIQUE RWANDAISE

Directorate of Civil Aviation for
SAINT LUCIA
c/o Director of Civil Aviation
P.O. Box 1130
St. John's
Antigua, W.I.

Directorate of Civil Aviation for
SAINT VINCENT AND THE GRENADINES
c/o Director of Civil Aviation
P.O. Box 1130
St. John's
Antigua, W.I.

Administrator of Civil Aviation
P.O. Box 193
Apia
THE INDEPENDENT STATE OF WESTERN SAMOA

Ministry of Communications and Transport
Palazza Turismo
Contrada Omagnano
San Marino 47031
REPUBLIC OF SAN MARINO

Direcçao da Aviaçao Civil
C/P N° 97
Sao Tomé
REPUBLICA DEMOCRATICA DE SAO TOMÉ E PRINCIPE

Presidency of Civil Aviation
P.O. Box 887
Jeddah 21421
SAUDI ARABIA

Direction de l'Aviation civile
B.P. 8184
Aéroport de Dakar-Yoff
SÉNÉGAL

Ministry of Tourism and Transport
Directorate of Civil Aviation
P.O. Box 181
Victoria
Mahe
REPUBLIC OF SEYCHELLES

The Director of Civil Aviation
Ministry of Transport and Communications
Ministerial Office Block
George Street
Freetown
REPUBLIC OF SIERRA LEONE

Civil Aviation Authority of Singapore
P.O. Box 1
Singapore Changi Airport
SINGAPORE 9181

Civil Aviation Division
Ministry of Aviation and Tourism
P.O. Box G20
Honiara
SOLOMON ISLANDS

General Manager
Somalia Civil Aviation Authority
P.O. Box 1737
Mogadishu
SOMALIA

The Director-General: Transport
Directorate Civil Aviation
Private Bag X193
Pretoria 0001
REPUBLIC OF SOUTH AFRICA

Dirección General de Aviácion Civil
c/o Josefa Valcárcel, 52
28027 Madrid
ESPAÑA

Department of Civil Aviation
P.O. Box 535
Lotus Road
Colombo 1
SRI LANKA

Director General of Civil Aviation
Civil Aviation Authority
P.O. Box 430
Blue Nile Avenue
Khartoum
REPUBLIC OF SUDAN

Director of Civil Aviation
P.O. Box 1981
Paramaribo—Zuid
SURINAME

Ministry of Works and Communications
P.O. Box 58
Mbabane
SWAZILAND

Director General
LUFTFARTSVERKET
The Swedish Civil Aviation Administration
S-601 79 Norrkoping
SWEDEN

Office Fédéral de l'Aviation Civile
Inselgasse 1
3003 Berne
SUISSE

Directorate General of Civil Aviation
1 Sahet El-Najmeh
P.O. Box 6257
Damascus
SYRIAN ARAB REPUBLIC

The Director General
Department of Aviation
71 Soi Ngarmdu-Plee
Tungmahamek
Bangkok 10120
THAILAND

Direction de l'Aviation civile
B.P. 2699
Lomé
RÉPUBLIQUE TOGOLAISE

Ministry of Civil Aviation
P.O. Box 845
Queen Salote Road
Nuku'Alofa
TONGA

Director of Civil Aviation
P.O. Box 552
Port of Spain
TRINIDAD AND TOBAGO

Ministère du Transport
Direction Générale de l'Aviation Civile
13, rue no. 8006—Monplaisir
Tunis
TUNISIE

Directorate General of Civil Aviation
Ministry of Communications and Transport
Ulastirma Bakanligi (SHGM)
90. Sokak No:5 (06338)
Emek, Ankara
TURKEY

Director General of Civil Aviation
P.O. Box 5536
Kampala
UGANDA

USSR Ministry of Civil Aviation
Leningradsky Prospekt, 37
Moscow A-167
COMMONWEALTH OF INDEPENDENT STATES

Assistant Under-Secretary for Civil Aviation
Ministry of Communications
P.O. Box 900
Abu Dhabi
UNITED ARAB EMIRATES

Civil Aviation Authority
Department of Transport
2 Marsham Street
London SW1P 3EB
UNITED KINGDOM

Director General of Civil Aviation
P.O. Box 2819
Dar-es-Salaam
UNITED REPUBLIC OF TANZANIA

Federal Aviation Administration
800 Independence Avenue, S.W.
Washington, D.C. 20594
UNITED STATES OF AMERICA

Dirección National de Aviación Civil e Infraestructura
  Aeronáutica
Mercedes 1256
Montevideo
URUGUAY

Director of Civil Aviation
Pacific Building
Port-Vila
VANUATU

Dirección de Aeronáutica Civil
Ministerio de Transporte y Comunicaciones
Torre Este, Piso 32 - Núcleo 3
Parque Central
Avenida Lecuna
Caracas 1010, D.F.
VENEZUELA

Director General
Department of Aviation
Ministry of Transport and Communication
80 Trang Hung Dao Street
Hanoi
THE SOCIALIST REPUBLIC OF VIET NAM

Chairman
Civil Aviation & Met. Authority
Ministry of Communications
P.O. Box 1042
Sana'a
REPUBLIC OF YEMEN

Federal Secretariat for Transport and
  Communications
Air Transport Sector
Bulevar AVNOJ-a 104
11000 Beograd
YUGOSLAVIA

Citoyen Directeur de l'Aéronautique civile
Département des Transports et Communications
B.P. 6514
Kinshasa/N'dolo
RÉPUBLIQUE DU ZAIRE

The Director
Department of Civil Aviation
P.O. Box 50137
Ridgeway
Lusaka
ZAMBIA

Department of Civil Aviation
Sarum House
78 Robert Mugabe Road
P.O. Box 7716
Causeway
Harare
ZIMBABWE

Glossary of Air Transport Terms ▰▬▬▬

The glossary of airline terms has resulted from the need to standardize the various terms and phrases related to air transportation which are in everyday use by the aviation industry in general and the Department of Transportation in particular. The scope of the glossary includes the definitions which are peculiar to air transportation as it relates to general usage. Also included are those terms which have a specialized use although they are non-aviation terms. Terms and phrases which have common usage in areas other than air transportation, such as accounting, business, or law, have been excluded because they are defined in their respective field.

Many of the terms included and their definitions are the responsibility of the Bureau of Accounts and Statistics and are intended for general usage and are neither legal nor binding and do not necessarily reflect the official views or opinions of the Department of Transportation.

A

Abandonment. A voluntary giving up of authority by the carrier to operate or serve a point or points covered in its certificate of public convenience and necessity. Abandonment by a carrier usually requires a public hearing and approval.

Act. The Federal Aviation Act of 1958 as amended.

Administrative law judge. A person appointed in accordance with Civil Service Commission regulations, to conduct hearings. The term also includes presiding officers, individual members, or any other representative assigned to hold a hearing in a proceeding.

Administrator. The administrator of the Federal Aviation Administration.

Aeronautics. The science and art of flight.

Agent, ticket. Any person (other than the air carrier performing the direct air transportation or one of its bona fide regular employees, or an air carrier which subcontracts the performance of charter air transportation which it has contracted to perform) who for compensation or profit: (1) solicits, obtains, receives, or furnishes directly or indirectly passengers or groups of passengers for transportation upon the aircraft of an air carrier, or (2) procures or arranges for air transportation of passengers or groups of passengers upon aircraft of an air carrier by charter, lease, or any other arrangement.

Agent, travel. A person who sells air transportation services to individuals or groups on behalf of, and in the name of, air carriers.

*Agreement, Bermuda. Any bilateral air service or air transport agreement in which capacity may be unilaterally selected by the designated airline(s), but in which tariffs are mutually agreed upon. The first bilateral agreement of its type entered into by two countries. The United States and Great Britain met in Bermuda in 1946 and the two nations granted to each other the five freedoms subject to; government approval of rates, adequate traffic capacity, and review of the carriers' operation in compliance with the principles. The United States made one major concession in that it agreed that the international rates and fares would be subject to agreements that would be made through the International Air Transport Association (IATA). This agreement has been the pattern agreement for all United States bilateral aviation treaties. It serves as a model because of its flexibility.

Agreement. Any agreement between two nations. Generally an air services agreement between two Contracting Parties in which the number of designated airlines and nature of the rights granted are specified, i.e. the routes and traffic freedoms. The agreement frequently also includes provisions for Authorizations, Recognition of Certificates, Application of Laws, Safety, Security, Charges and Duties, Capacity, Statistics, Tariffs, Commercial Operations, Consultations, Amendments, Registration, and the Termination of the agreement. The names of the designated airlines, the types of aircraft and the frequency to be operated are less frequently specified.

Agreement, capacity limitation. An agreement between two or more air carriers stipulating maximum capacity to be offered by each carrier in particular markets, either through the limitation in the number of flights offered by each carrier or the number of seats or cargo space available for sale on each flight, or both.

Agreement, capacity reduction. An agreement between two or more air carriers stipulating a reduction in capacity presently offered by each carrier in particular markets to some agreed level below that presently offered.

Agreement, Five-Freedoms. Formally The International Air Transport Agreement (U.N. Treaty Series 502, Vol. 171 page 387) whereby Parties mutually exchange two technical and three commercial privileges for carrying passengers, mail and freight to and from the other Contracting Parties, as well as beyond to other States. This multilateral agreement is by far the least successful of the group, because it ignores the capacity to be provided, the amount to be charged for the service, and other important issues. See also: Agreement, Two-Freedoms.

Agreement, fuel reduction. An agreement between two or more air carriers adjusting schedules or limiting capacity in an effort to respond to fuel shortages, including periods of mandatory rationing or regulated allocation of fuel.

Agreement, interchange. An agreement under which aircraft of one air carrier are utilized to provide one plane service over its own routes and the routes of other air carriers.

Agreement, multilateral. Any agreement between two or more nations. See also: Convention.

Agreement, Two-Freedoms. Formally The International Air Services Transit Agreement (U.N. Treaty Series 252, Vol. 84 page 389) whereby Contracting States mutually exchange the privileges of overflight and non-commercial landing by *scheduled flights*. It should be noted that the Chicago Convention provides these privileges for non-scheduled flights. See also: Agreement, Five-Freedoms.

Agreement, suspension/substitution. Approval of a carrier's (usually a local service carrier's) suspension of certain services under its operating authority subject to the proviso that the suspended services will be replaced by a substitute air carrier (usually an air taxi operator).

Airbill (air waybill). The non-negotiable shipping document used by domestic air carriers as evidence of an air freight shipment. The document contains shipping instructions, commodity descriptions, and transportation charges applicable to the freight shipped. Sometimes used interchangeably with "air waybill" which is erroneous terminology when the domestic airbill does not meet the uniformity requirements of the air waybill.

Air commerce. The carriage by aircraft of persons or property for compensation or hire, or the carriage of mail by aircraft, or the operation or navigation of aircraft in the conduct or furtherance of a business or vocation.

Air commerce, foreign. The carriage by aircraft persons or property for compensation or hire, or the carriage of mail by aircraft, or the operation or navigation of aircraft in the conduct or furtherance of a business or vocation, in commerce between, a place in the United States and any place outside thereof, whether such commerce moves wholly by aircraft or partly by aircraft and partly by other forms of transportation.

Air commerce, interstate. The carriage by aircraft of persons or property for compensation or hire, or the carriage of mail by aircraft, or the operation or navigation of aircraft in the conduct of furtherance of a business or vocation, in commerce between, a place in any State of the United States, or the District of Columbia, and a place in any other State of the United States, or the District of Columbia; or between places in the same State of the United States through the airspace over any place outside thereof; or between places in the same Territory or possession of the United States, or the District of Columbia, whether such commerce moves wholly by aircraft or partly by aircraft and partly by other forms of transportation.

Air commerce, overseas. The carriage by aircraft of persons or property for compensation or hire, or the carriage of mail by aircraft, or the operation or navigation of aircraft in the conduct or furtherance of a business or vocation, in commerce between, a place in any State of the United States, or the District of Columbia, and any place in a Territory or possession of the United States; or between a place in a Territory or possession of the United States and a place in any other territory or possession of the United States whether such commerce moves wholly by aircraft or partly by aircraft and partly by other forms of transportation.

Aircraft. Any contrivance now known or hereafter invented, used or designed for navigation of or flight in the air.

Aircraft, civil. Any aircraft other than a public aircraft and other than those owned by the United States Government.

Aircraft contacted. Aircraft with which the Flight Service Stations have established radio communications contact. One count is made for each enroute, landing or departing aircraft contacted by Flight Service Station regardless of the number of contacts made with an individual aircraft during the same flight.

Aircraft departure, scheduled. A takeoff scheduled at an airport, as set forth in published schedules.

Aircraft engine, turbine. An engine incorporating as its chief element a turbine rotated by expanding gases. It consists essentially in its most usual form of a rotary air compressor with an air intake, one or more combustion chambers, a turbine, and an exhaust outlet. Aircraft engines of this type have their power applied mainly either as jet thrust (turbojet or turbofan) or as shaft power to rotate a propeller (turboprop).

Aircraft grounding. A voluntary determination by a carrier or carriers, or an order from the Federal Aviation Administration to refrain from flying a particular type of aircraft, as a result of suspected or actual malfunction of such aircraft, until the cause can be determined and appropriate corrective action taken. This term is also used when referring to an occasional inability of an individual aircraft to operate due to weather conditions or minor mechanical reasons, or to a voluntary decision by a carrier to refrain from flying certain aircraft for reasons other than mechanical malfunctions.

Aircraft hour, airborne. The airborne hours of aircraft, computed from the moment an aircraft leaves the ground until it touches the ground at the next point of landing. Often referred to as "wheels-off, wheels-on time."

Aircraft hour, block-to-block. The hours computed from the moment an aircraft first moves under its own power for purposes of flight until it comes to rest at the next point of landing. Block time includes taxi time before takeoff and after landing, takeoff and landing time as well as airborne time. Also referred to as "ramp-to-ramp" hours.

Aircraft hour, revenue. The airborne hours in revenue service, computed from the moment an aircraft leaves the ground until it touches the ground at the next point of landing.

Aircraft hour, revenue per aircraft per day—carrier's equipment. Average hours of productive use per day in revenue service of reporting carrier's equipment determined by dividing (1) aircraft days assigned to carrier's equipment into (2) revenue aircraft hours minus revenue hours on other carrier's interchange equipment plus total hours by others on the carrier's interchange equipment. See Utilization.

Aircraft hour, revenue per aircraft per day—carrier's routes. Average hours of productive use per day in revenue service on reporting carrier's routes determined by dividing (1) aircraft days assigned to service—carrier's routes into (2) revenue aircraft hours.

Aircraft, interchange. An aircraft of one of the partners of an interchange agreement used to provide single-plane service over two or more segments of two or more different carriers. The aircraft flies the entire trip, but the crews are changed so that each carrier flies only over its own segment(s).

Aircraft, large. An aircraft having a maximum passenger capacity of more than 30 seats or a maximum payload capacity of more than 7,500 pounds; except that in connection with operations conducted within the State of Alaska or Hawaii, large aircraft shall mean an aircraft whose maximum certificated takeoff weight is more than 12,500 pounds. When referring to foreign air carriers (Economic Regulations, Part 217), a large aircraft is one having a maximum takeoff weight of more than 18,000 pounds.

Aircraft, leased (rental). Aircraft obtained from (or furnished to) others under lease or rental arrangements. Leased and rented aircraft do not include those used under interchange agreements designed to provide one-plane service over the routes of the air carriers involved.

Aircraft loans guaranteed. Aircraft purchase loans guaranteed by the Federal Government as administered by the Department of Transportation to assist local service, helicopter, intra-Alaska, intra-Hawaii and certain other carriers in obtaining suitable flight equipment.

Aircraft-mile. The distance flown by aircraft in terms of great circle airport-to-airport distance measured in statute miles.

Aircraft-mile flown. The miles (computed in airport-to-airport distances) for each flight stage actually completed, whether or not performed in accordance with the scheduled pattern. For this purpose, operation to a flag stop is a stage completed even though a landing is not actually made. In cases where the inter-airport distances are inapplicable, aircraft miles flown are determined by multiplying the normal cruising speed for the aircraft type by the airborne hours.

Aircraft navigation. The piloting of aircraft.

Aircraft operation. An aircraft arrival or departure from an airport with FAA airport traffic control service. There are two types of operations—local and itinerant.

Aircraft, passenger/cargo. Aircraft configured to accommodate passengers and cargo in the above deck cabin.

Aircraft piracy (hijacking, skyjacking). Any seizure or exercise of control, by force or violence or threat of force or violence, or by any other form of intimidation, and with wrongful intent, of an aircraft.

Aircraft, small. An aircraft having a maximum passenger capacity of 30 seats or less or a maximum payload capacity of 7,500 pounds or less; except that in connection with operations conducted within the State of Alaska or Hawaii, small aircraft shall mean an aircraft whose maximum certificated takeoff weight is 12,500 pounds or less. When referring to foreign air carriers (Economic Regulations, Part 217), a small aircraft is one having a maximum takeoff weight of 18,000 pounds or less.

Aircraft, supersonic transport (SST). A transport aircraft capable of a normal cruising speed greater than the speed of sound (741 mph at sea level).

Aircraft, turbine. Includes aircraft with either turbojet, turbofan, turboprop, or turboshaft engines.

Aircraft, turbofan (fan-jet). An aircraft powered by a turbojet engine(s) whose thrust has been increased by the addition of a low pressure compressor (fan). Sometimes referred to as a "fan-jet" aircraft. The turbofan engine can have an oversized low pressure compressor at the front with part of the flow by-passing the rest of the engine (front fan) or it can have a separate fan driven by a turbine stage (aft-fan).

Aircraft, turbojet. An aircraft powered by a gas-turbine engine(s) incorporating a turbine-driven compressor to take in and compress the air for the combination of fuel, with the gases of combustion (or heated air) being used to both rotate the turbine and to create a thrust producing jet.

Aircraft, turbo-propeller (turboprop, prop-jet). An aircraft powered by a gas-turbine engine(s) in which output is taken as shaft power to drive a propeller via a reduction gear; it also has a small residual jet thrust. Sometimes referred to as a "prop-jet" aircraft.

Aircraft type. A distinctive model as designated by the manufacturer.

Aircraft, vertical/short takeoff and landing (V/STOL). An aircraft capable of taking off and landing vertically or in a short distance.

Aircraft, vertical takeoff and landing (VTOL). A heavier-than-air aircraft that can take off and land vertically.

Aircraft, wide-body. A generic and commonly used term applied to any and all of the newest generation of jet aircraft with a fuselage diameter exceeding 200 inches and whose per engine thrust is greater than 30,000 pounds (i.e., Boeing 747, McDonnell Douglas DC-10, Lockheed L-1011).

Airframe. The structure of an aircraft, excluding engines and accessories. The principal parts of the airframe of an airplane include the fuselage (the body), wings, empennage (the assembly of stabilizing and control surfaces at the tail), landing gear, and nacelles or pods (engine housings).

Air freight forwarder. Any indirect air carrier which, in the ordinary and usual course of its undertaking, (1) assembles and consolidates, or provides for assembling and consolidating, property for shipment by air, or performs or provides for the performance of break-bulk and distributing operations with respect to consolidated shipments, and (2) is responsible for the transportation of property from the point of receipt to the point of destination and utilizes, for the whole or any part of such transportation, the services of a direct air carrier.

Air Cargo. Total volume of freight, mail and express traffic transported by air. Statistics include the following:
Freight & Express Commodities of all kinds—includes small-package counter services, express services and priority reserved freight. **Mail** All classes of mail transported for the U.S. postal Service

Airline (air line). A commonly used corporate name for an air carrier.

Airman. Any individual who engages, as the person in command or as pilot, mechanic, or member of the crew, in the navigation of aircraft while under way; and (except to the extent the Administrator may otherwise provide with respect to individuals employed outside the United States) any individual who is directly in charge of the inspection, maintenance, overhauling, or repair of aircraft, aircraft engines, propellers, or appliances; and any individual who serves in the capacity of aircraft dispatcher or air-traffic controller.

Air navigation facility. Any facility used in, available for use in, or designed for use in, aid of air navigation, including landing areas, lights, any apparatus or equipment for disseminating weather information, for signaling, for radio-directional finding, or for radio or other electrical communication, and any other structure or mechanism having a similar purpose for guiding or controlling flight in the air or the landing and takeoff of aircraft.

Airport. A landing area regularly used by aircraft for receiving or discharging passengers or cargo.

Airport traffic control tower. A central operations facility in the terminal air traffic control system, consisting of a tower cab structure, including an associated IFR room if radar equipped, using air/ground communications and/or radar, visual signaling and other devices, to provide safe and expeditious movement of terminal air traffic.

Air priorities system. A system for assigning air transport priorities to War Air Service Plan traffic (passengers, mail, and cargo), required in time of emergency because of the limitation of available civil aircraft capacity and to assure that such traffic moves in accordance with its degree of urgency. Priorities can be controlled and issued by the air carriers under the provisions of CAB Standby Order ATM-2 or by the Board under the provisions of the CAB War Air Service Program, Air Priorities System.

Air route traffic control center (ARTCC). A central operations facility in the air route traffic control system using air/ground communications and radar, primarily providing enroute separation and safe, expeditious movement of aircraft operating under instrument flight rules within the controlled airspace of that center.

Air taxi operations. Air taxi operations and commuter air carrier operations (takeoffs and landings) carrying passengers, mail or cargo for revenue in accordance with FAR Part 135 or Part 121.

Air taxi operators. Operators of small aircraft "for hire" for specific trips. They operate under CAB Part 298 and FAR 135 which apply to aircraft of 12,500 pounds or less except under special exemption.

Air transport association. The trade association of the U.S. certificated route air carriers.

Air transportation. Interstate, intrastate, overseas, or foreign air transportation.

Air transportation, foreign. The carriage by aircraft of persons or property as a common carrier for compensation or hire or the carriage of mail by aircraft, in commerce between, a place in the United States and any place outside thereof; whether such commerce moves wholly by aircraft or partly by aircraft and partly by other forms of transportation.

Air transportation, interstate. The carriage by aircraft of persons or property as a common carrier for compensation or hire or the carriage of mail by aircraft, in commerce between, a place in any State of the United States, or the District of Columbia, and a place in any other State of the United States, or the District of Columbia; or between places in the same State of the United States through the airspace over any place outside thereof; or between places in the same Territory or possession of the United States, or the District of Columbia, whether such commerce moves wholly by aircraft or partly by aircraft and partly by other forms of transportation.

Air transportation, intrastate. The carriage by aircraft of persons or property as a common carrier for compensation or hire wholly within the same State of the United States.

Air transportation, overseas. The carriage by aircraft of persons or property as a common carrier for compensation or hire or the carriage of mail by aircraft, in commerce between, a place in any State of the United States, or the District of Columbia, and any place in a Territory or possession of the United States; or between a place in a Territory or possession of the United States, and a place in any other Territory or possession of the United States; whether such commerce moves wholly by aircraft or partly by aircraft and partly by other forms of transportation.

Airway. A 10 mile wide path through the navigable airspace equipped with air navigation aids and designated by the Administrator, Federal Aviation Administration, extending from the ground upward to 27,000 feet. At and above 27,000 feet the high altitude jet route system is used.

Airway, federal. A portion of the navigable airspace of the United States designated by the Administrator as a Federal airway.

Air waybill. The non-negotiable uniform shipping document used in air freight transportation (especially in international transportation), by air carriers as evidence of a shipment. The document contains shipping instructions, commodity description, and transportation charges applicable to the freight shipped. While the document is standardized for international shipments by the Warsaw Convention the term is sometimes used interchangeably with "airbill" a largely domestic document which may or may not have uniformity within a country.

Airworthiness (airworthy). When applied to a particular aircraft or component part, it denotes the ability of such aircraft or component part to perform its function satisfactorily through a range of operations determined by the Federal Aviation Administration.

All cargo carrier. One of a class of air carriers holding certificates of public convenience and necessity issued by the CAB, authorizing the performance of scheduled air freight, express, and mail transportation over specified routes, as well as the conduct of nonscheduled operations, which may include passengers.

American society of travel agents (ASTA). A trade association of the travel agency industry.

Appliance. Instruments, equipment, apparatus, parts, appurtenances, or accessories, of whatever description, which are used, or are capable of being used, in the navigation, operation, or control or aircraft in flight (including parachutes and including communication equipment and any other mechanism or mechanisms installed in or attached to aircraft during flight), and which are not a part or parts of aircraft, aircraft engines, or propellers.

Appointment, agency. The process whereby travel agents are designated by each airline to represent and sell air travel services of that airline. Agents are usually appointed automatically by the airline members of ATC and IATA after those organizations have approved them.

Approach control facility. A terminal air traffic control facility providing approach control service.

Assets. The items on the balance sheet of a business showing the value of its total investments.

Available seat-miles (ASM's). The aircraft miles flown in each flight stage multiplied by the number of seats available on that stage for revenue passenger use.

Available seat mile. One seat transported one mile.

Available Ton Mile. One ton of capacity (passenger and/or cargo) transported one mile.

B

Baggage, excess. Passenger baggage in excess of a free allowance and subject to a charge for its transportation.

Balance sheet. A statement of assets, liabilities, and stockholder equity (or equivalent interest of individual proprietors or partners) as at a particular date.

Business transportation. Any use of an aircraft not for compensation or hire by an individual for the purpose of transportation required by a business in which he is engaged.

C

Cabotage. The carriage of air traffic which originates and terminates within the boundaries of a given country by an air carrier of another country. Sometimes called the Eighth Freedom, rights to such traffic are often specifically excluded in bilaterals. Cabotage is recognized in the Chicago Convention but when granted cabotage is usually severely restricted.

Capacity, maximum payload. The maximum certificated takeoff weight of an aircraft, less the empty weight, less all justifiable aircraft equipment, and less the operating load (consisting of minimum fuel load, oil, flight crew, stewards' supplies, etc.). The allowance for the weight of the crew, oil, and fuel is as follows: (a) crew—200 pounds per crew member required under FAA regulations, (b) oil—350 pounds, (c) fuel—the minimum weight of fuel required under FAA regulations for a flight between domestic points 200 miles apart; provided, however, that in the case of aircraft for which a maximum zero fuel weight is prescribed by the FAA, maximum payload capacity means the maximum zero fuel weight, less the empty weight, less all justifiable aircraft equipment, and less the operating load (consisting of minimum flight crew, stewards' supplies, etc., but not including, disposable fuel or oil).

Cargo, air. In the United States, this term refers to the total volume of freight, mail, and express traffic which is transported by air. U.S. air cargo consists of the following classes of service: Priority mail—air mail and air parcel post; nonpriority mail—aircraft of first class mail on a space available basis; foreign mail-mail destined to or from foreign countries; air express—priority movement of packages generally under 50 pounds; air freight—the airlift of commodities of all kinds.

Carrier, air. Any person who undertakes, whether directly or indirectly or by a lease or any other arrangement, to engage in air transportation.

Carrier, certificated air. One of a class of air carriers holding certificates of public convenience and necessity, issued by the Board, authorizing the holder to engage in air transportation.

Carrier, certificated route air. One of a class of air carriers performing scheduled air transportation over specified routes and a limited amount of nonscheduled operations. Certificated route air carriers often are referred to as "scheduled carriers," although they also perform nonscheduled service.

Carrier, common air. An air transportation business that holds out its services for public hire.

Carrier, commuter air. An air taxi operator which (1) performs at least five round trips per week between two or more points and publishes flight schedules which specify the times, days of the week, and places between which such flights are performed, or (2) transports mail by air pursuant to a current contract with the United States Postal Service.

Carrier, designated air. The carrier, a national of one country which is a party to a bilateral agreement, chosen by that country to operate service over a specific route or routes (or charter service under a charter agreement) and specifically named by diplomatic note to the other party.

Carrier, direct air. Any air carrier directly engaged in the operation of aircraft, pursuant to a certificate of public convenience and necessity issued under Section 401 of the Federal Aviation Act of 1958, as amended, or under the authority conferred by any applicable regulation or order of the Board.

Carrier, domestic air. A carrier operating primarily within and between the 50 States of the United States and the District of Columbia.

Carrier, foreign air. Any person, not a citizen of the United States, who undertakes, whether directly or indirectly or by lease or any other arrangement, to engage in foreign air transportation.

Carrier, foreign flag air. An air carrier other than a U.S. flag air carrier engaged in international air transportation. "Foreign air carrier" is a more all-inclusive term than "foreign-flag air carrier," presumably including those non-U.S. air carriers operating solely within their own domestic boundaries, but in practice the two terms are used interchangeably.

Carrier, helicopter air. Domestic certificated route air carriers employing helicopter aircraft for their primary operations.

Carrier, indirect air. Any citizen of the United States who engages indirectly in air transportation including air freight forwarders, persons authorized by the Board to transport by air used household goods of personnel of the Department of Defense, tour operators, study group charterers, overseas military personnel charter operators, and travel group charter organizers.

Carrier, international and territorial air. In the strictest sense, an air carrier conducting international and territorial operations only. This term, however, is often used when referring to any air carrier which performs, in addition to its domestic operations, international and territorial operations.

Carrier, intrastate air. Any citizen of the United States who undertakes whether directly or indirectly or by lease or any other arrangement, to engage solely in intrastate air transportation.

Carrier local service air. A group of air carriers originally established in the late 1940s to foster and provide air service to small and medium communities on relatively low density routes to large air traffic hubs. A subsidy payment program was instituted for these carriers since their authorization by the Board was of an experimental basis and operating losses were projected for the first years of the carriers' operations. These carriers have since evolved from their "feeder" airlines origination into "regional" carriers with only certain of their operations subsidy eligible.

Carrier, supplemental air. An air carrier holding a certificate issued under section 401(d)(3) of the Federal Aviation Act of 1958, as amended, or a special operating authorization issued under section 417 of the Act, or operating authority issued pursuant to section 7 or 9 of Public Law 87-528. Such carrier is authorized to operate charter flights, supplementing scheduled service.

Carrier, trunk air. A class of certificated route air carriers receiving original certification under the "grandfather clause" of the Civil Aeronautics Act (August 22, 1938) and whose primary operations are in domestic scheduled passenger service between relatively medium and large air traffic hubs. In addition, these carriers may have certificated authority for scheduled all-cargo, scheduled international passenger and/or cargo, and nonscheduled service.

Carrier, United States flag air. A citizen of the United States engaged in air transportation between the United States (and/ or its possessions and territories) and one or more foreign countries, pursuant to a certificate of public convenience and, necessity or other operating authorization issued and approved by the President.

Certificate of public convenience and necessity. A certificate issued to an air carrier under Section 401 of the Federal Aviation Act of 1958 authorizing the carrier to engage in air transportation. The certificate may contain certain designated routes and certain designated points or geographical areas to be served and any limitations and restrictions imposed on such service as the Board may specify.

Certificated. Holding a currently valid certificate of public convenience and necessity.

Certificated route air carrier. An air carrier holding a certificate of public convenience and necessity to conduct scheduled services over specified routes. Certain nonscheduled or charter operations may also be conducted by these carriers.

Charter, advanced booking (ABC). The charter of the entire capacity of an aircraft or at least 40 seats by a charter operator. The charter is required to be a round trip with a minimum duration of seven days in international charters. The charter organizers acts independent of the direct air carrier and must receive full payment from the charter participants at least sixty days prior to departure in the case of European charters and thirty days in the case of all other charters. Foreign originating ABC's are organized in compliance with the applicable rules of the originating country and operated pursuant to an intergovernmental agreement providing for its acceptance by the United States.

Charter, inclusive tour (ITC). The charter of the entire capacity of an aircraft or at least 40 seats (providing the remaining capacity of the aircraft is chartered by a person or persons authorized to charter aircraft) by a tour operator. The inclusive tour charter is required to be a round trip with a minimum of three stops other than the point of origin, to be a minimum of seven days in duration and the cost of which must include all accommodations and surface transportation. Such cost shall not be less than 110 percent of any available fare or fares, embodied in a tariff on file with the Board, charged by a route carrier, or combination of such carriers (including charge for stopovers) for individually ticketed service on the circle route beginning at the point of origin, to the various points where stopovers are made, and return to the point of origin.

Charter, one-stop inclusive tour. The charter of the entire capacity of an aircraft or at least 40 seats (providing the remaining capacity of the aircraft is chartered by a person or persons authorized to charter aircraft) which is arranged and sponsored by a tour operator organizer for a group. The charter must be on a round-trip basis with a minimum duration of four (4) days in the case of North American charters, seven (7) days in the case of all other charters. The total cost of the tour to each participant shall include the cost of ground accommodations and services and shall be an amount not less than the aggregate of the charter price of the participants seat (i.e., the charter price specified in the charter contract divided by the number of seats specified in the charter contract) and a sum representing ground services for each night of the tour.

Chosen instrument. A nation's flag air carrier possessing, by its government's design or choice, sole international operating authority. Sometimes an air carrier controlled by a government.

Civil aeronautics board. An independent U.S. Government agency established under the Civil Aeronautics Act of 1938 (52 Stat. 973), which has broad responsibility for the encouragement and development of an air transportation system properly adapted to the present and future needs of the foreign and domestic commerce of the United States, of the Postal Service, and of the national defense. It is vested with economic regulatory powers over civil aviation within the United States, and between the United States and foreign countries. Among its powers, the Board issues certificates of public convenience and necessity to air carriers and has jurisdiction over the tariffs for air transportation.

Civil reserve air fleet (CRAF). A group of commercial aircraft with crews, which are allocated in times of emergency for exclusive military use in both international and domestic service. The CRAF aircraft are allocated to the Department of Defense, by type and registration number, by the Department of Transportation for use under stated conditions.

Commission, travel agent. The payment by airlines to a travel agent of specified amounts of money in return for the agent's sales of air transportation. Travel agent's commissions are usually set by ATC and IATA resolutions, as approved by the Board, and are usually expressed and paid by each carrier as a percentage of the value of the air transportation sold on that air carrier.

Commuter operator. Operators of small aircraft of a maximum size of 60 seats who perform at least five scheduled round trips per week between two or more points or carry mail. They operate under CAB Part 298, FAR 135, and at times FAR 121.

Competitive market. Any city pair or pair of geographical areas served by more than one air carrier. For the purposes of the Origin and Destination Survey, a competitive market exists where two or more air carriers offer service between the city pairs or geographical areas and at least two air carriers control in excess of 10 percent of the traffic each. For the purposes of Part 298 (air taxi operators), a competitive market is a pair of points between which an air carrier, holding a certificate of public convenience and necessity pursuant to Section 401(d)(1) or (2) of the Act, has authority to serve by reason of such certificate, and such authority has not been suspended, or has authority to serve by reason of an exemption authorization issued pursuant to Section 416(b)(1) of the Act.

Contract operator. An air carrier operating on a private for-hire basis, as distinguished from a public or common air carrier, holding a commercial operator certificate (issued by the FAA under FAR 121) authorizing the carrier to operate aircraft over 12,500 pounds for the transportation of goods or passengers for compensation or hire.

Conference, Chicago. A conference in 1944, of fifty-two allied and neutral nations resulting in: (1) Bilateral Agreement Rules, a framework upon which bilateral negotiations are to be conducted between two nations; (2) The International Civil Aviation Organization (ICAO); (3) International Air Transit Agreement; and (4) International Air Transport Agreement. The term Chicago Convention is normally applied only to the Convention on International Civil Aviation; (United Nations—Treaty Series #102, Volume 15, page 295) which established rules of Air Navigation, ICAO and International Air Transport. The International Air Services Transit Agreement; (United Nations #252, Volume 84, page 389) and the International Air Transport Agreement (United Nations #502, Volume 171, page 387) were also products of the Chicago Conference, but are not normally referred to as a part of the Convention.

Conference. A gathering of delegates from several nations to deal with a specific subject. The subject may be quite focused, such as Hijacking, or quite complicated, such as organizing the administration of all international civil aviation following a great world war, such as the Paris Conference of 1919 or the Chicago Conference of 1944. See also: Convention.

Convention. A multilateral agreement, i.e. document, which is the result of a conference called to deal with a specific subject. The document might be quite focused, such as dealing only with Hijacking, or quite complicated, such as the administration of international civil aviation. See also: Conference.

Convention, Chicago. The multilateral agreement developed at Chicago in 1944 which established ICAO, the International Civil Aviation Organization. Formally the Convention on International Civil Aviation, (U.N. Treaty Series 102, Vol. 15 page 295).

Convention, Havana. The multilateral agreement developed at Havana in 1928. Formally the Convention on Commercial Aviation (U.N. Treaty Series 2963, Vol. 129 Page 223). Similar to the Paris Convention which recognized that every country has complete and exclusive sovereignty over the air space above its territory and territorial waters. Signed by twenty-one countries including the United States.

Convention, Paris. The International Convention for Air Navigation held in Paris in 1919, recognizing that each nation has complete and exclusive control of the air space above its territory. It was ratified by twenty-six countries and serves as the document for international air transportation outside the Western Hemisphere. Signed by the United States but not ratified because the convention was associated with the League of Nations. Its main accomplishment was the establishment of Sovereignty of Air Space Theory.

Convention, Warsaw. The Convention for the Unification of Certain Rules Relating to the International Carriage by Air, signed at Warsaw, October 12, 1929. This convention came into force on February 13, 1933, and most countries have now become parties, including the United States as of October 29, 1934. The rules in the convention provide liability for damage for death or injury to passengers, destruction, loss, or damage to baggage and goods, and loss resulting from delay in transporting passengers, baggage, and merchandise. Further, it establishes the monetary limits for the above described loss, damage and delay. This convention was modified by the Hague Protocol on September 28, 1955, and entered into force on August 1, 1963. However, the Hague Protocol does not apply on transportation from/to the United States as it has not been ratified by the United States.

D

Decision, initial. The decision of the presiding officer(s), following a hearing initially deciding the case. The initial decision becomes the decision without further proceedings unless there is an appeal to, or review on motion of, within time provided by rule.

Decision, recommended. The decision of the presiding officer(s), following a hearing recommending a disposition of the case. The entire record of the hearing, including the recommended decision, either in specific cases or by general rule thereafter is certified for decision. All cases involving foreign air transportation, with decisions subject to the approval of the President, are submitted through recommended decisions.

Denied boarding compensation. Compensation paid to a passenger holding confirmed reserved space, who presents himself for carriage at the appropriate time and place, and the flight for which the passenger holds confirmed reserved space is unable to accommodate the passenger and departs without him. The passenger must have complied fully with the carrier's requirements as to ticketing, check-in, and reconfirmation procedures and be acceptable for transportation under the carrier's tariff.

Department of transportation. An executive department of the U.S. Government established by the Department of Transportation Act of 1966 (80 Stat. 931), for the purpose of developing national transportation policies and programs conducive to the provision of fast, safe, efficient and convenient transportation at the lowest cost consistent therewith. The Department consists of the Secretary, the Under Secretary, and the heads of the operating agencies, which include the United States Coast Guard, the Federal Aviation Administration, the Federal Railroad Administration, and several other administrative units.

Depreciation, flight equipment. Charges to expense for depreciation of airframes, aircraft engines, airframe and engine parts, and other flight equipment.

Distance, airport-to-airport. The great-circle distance, measured in statute miles, between airports as listed in the book of Official Airline Route Maps and Airport-to-Airport Mileages, published by Airline Tariff Publishers, Inc.

Distance, great-circle. The distance on a course along a great circle of the globe, the shortest distance between two points on the earth's surface.

Docket. A record of the principal matters pertaining to a specific Board proceeding or case, including a transcript of the hearings, exhibits, and correspondence. Such a case file is open to public inspection.

Domestic passenger fare investigation. A major investigation and hearing, from 1970 through 1974, on the various phases in the regulatory components of passenger air fares in the 48 contiguous States (Alaska and Hawaii excluded). Phase 1 examined new standards for the depreciation of aircraft for ratemaking purposes. Phase 2 adopted principles for the treatment of aircraft leasing in the computation of regulatory expenses and investment. Phase 3 investigated the treatment of deferred Federal Income Taxes in the regulatory investment. Phase 4 examined the legalities of joint fares. Phase 5 investigated the relationship of discount fares to the normal fares. Phase 6 was centered on methodological standards of load factor and seating configurations to be used in regulatory ratemaking. Phase 7 was concerned with the methods of allocating costs for ratemaking purposes and the fare level. Phase 8 examined the allowable rate of return on investment and the debt/equity relationship of that investment. Phase 9 investigated the fare structure and the methods of its calculation.

E

Executive transportation. Any use of an aircraft by a corporation, company or other organization for the purposes of transporting its employees and/or property not for compensation or hire and employing professional pilots for the operation of the aircraft.

Exemption. Temporary authorization pursuant to Section 416(b) of the Act permitting: (1) an air carrier to engage in air transportation in a manner otherwise prohibited by its certificate of public convenience and necessity; or (2) an air carrier or class of air carriers to engage in air transportation in a manner otherwise prohibited by the Federal Aviation Act.

Expense, aircraft and traffic servicing. Compensation of ground personnel and other expenses incurred on the ground to protect and control the in-flight movement of aircraft; schedule and prepare aircraft operational crew for flight assignment; handle and service aircraft while in line operation; service and handle aircraft on the ground after issuance of documents establishing the air carrier's responsibility to provide air transportation; and in-flight expenses of handling and protecting all nonpassenger traffic including passenger baggage.

Expense, flying operations. Expenses incurred directly in the in-flight operation of aircraft and expenses attached to the holding of aircraft and aircraft operational personnel in readiness for assignment to an in-flight status.

Expense, passenger service. Expenses of activities contributing to the comfort, safety and convenience of passengers while in flight and when flights are interrupted. Includes salaries and expenses of cabin attendants and passenger food expense.

Expense, traffic. Those expenses that are related to and vary with the traffic (passengers and/or cargo) actually transported. It includes such cost elements as traffic servicing expenses, reservations and sales expense, and advertising and publicity expense.

Expense, transport-related. Expenses incurred for providing air transportation facilities associated with the performance of services which emanate from and are incidental to air transportation services performed by the carrier (i.e., in-flight services of food, beverage, and entertainment which are sold; air cargo pick-up and delivery expenses; ground restaurant and food services and; mutual aid payments).

Express. Property transported by air under published air express tariffs. Originally, express referred to the priority movement of parcel shipments moving on aircraft in conjunction with an agreement between the various air carriers and REA Express, Inc. With the cessation of operations by REA Express, Inc. in 1976, this term refers to the replacement services offered by the various air carriers.

F

Fare. The amount per passenger or group of persons stated in the applicable tariff for the transportation thereof and includes baggage unless the context otherwise requires.

Fare, coach (tourist). The fare applicable to the transportation of a passenger or passengers at a quality of service below that of first-class service, but higher than or superior to the level of economy service.

Fare, discount. A reduced fare designed to stimulate traffic volume. Such fares are subject to one or more travel restrictions, and are typically calculated as a percentage reduction from the normal full fare.

Fare, economy. A charge for domestic air transportation at a level of service below that of coach service. The significant difference between coach and economy service is that the coach passenger receives a complementary meal while the economy passenger has an option of purchasing a meal. Seating density in the economy area may be higher than in the coach service area. In international air transportation, economy fare applies to second class service, or service just below that of first-class. It is synonymous with the term coach fare within the U.S.

Fare, excursion. A type of discount fare.

Fare, first-class. The fare applicable to the transportation of a passenger or passengers for whom premium quality services are provided.

Fare, joint. A fare published as a single factor that applies to transportation over the joint lines or routes of two or more carriers and which is made and published by arrangements or agreement between such carriers evidenced by concurrence or power of attorney.

Fare, promotional. A type of discount fare.

Fare structure. The particular fares charged for trips of varying distances and the relationship between coach fares and fares for the other classes of service. The manner in which the fare level should be distributed to, and recouped from, the passenger transport services operated by the air carriers. Used most often in regulatory ratemaking.

Federal Aviation Act. The Federal Aviation Act of 1958 as amended Public Law 85-726, 85th Congress, S. 3880. An Act to continue the Civil Aeronautics Board as an agency of the United States, to create a Federal Aviation Agency (Administration), to provide for the regulation and promotion of civil aviation in such manner as to best foster its development and safety, and to provide for the safe and efficient use of the airspace by both civil and military aircraft.

Federal Aviation Administration. Formerly the Federal Aviation Agency, became part of the Department of Transportation in 1967 as a result of the Department of Transportation Act (1966, 80 STAT. 932). The FAA is charged with: regulating air commerce to promote its safety and development; achieving the efficient use of the navigable airspace of the United States; promoting, encouraging and developing civil aviation; developing and operating a common system of air traffic control and air navigation for both civilian and military aircraft; and promoting the development of a national system of airports.

Flight. Of or related to the airborne movement of an aircraft. Commonly used as an abbreviated form of scheduled flight.

Flight equipment. Airframes, aircraft engines, aircraft propellers, aircraft communications and navigational equipment, miscellaneous equipment used in the operation of the aircraft, and improvements to leased flight equipment.

Flight plan. Specified information relating to the intended flight of an aircraft that is filed orally or in writing with a flight service station or an air traffic control facility.

Flight, scheduled. Any aircraft itinerary periodically operated between terminal points that is separately designated, by flight number or otherwise, in the published schedules of an air carrier.

Flight service station (FSS). Air Traffic Service facilities within the National Airspace System which provides preflight pilot briefing and enroute communications with VFR flights assist lost IFR/VFR aircraft, assist aircraft having emergencies, relay ATC clearances, originate, classify, and disseminate Notices to Airmen, broadcast aviation weather and NAS information receive and close flight plans, monitor radio NAVAIDS, notify search and rescue units of missing VFR aircraft, and operate the National weather teletypewriter systems.

Foreign air carrier permit. A permit issued to a foreign air carrier authorizing it to conduct air transport operations between foreign countries and cities in the United States, either in accordance with the terms of a bilateral air transport agreement, or nonscheduled air service agreement, or under conditions of comity and reciprocity.

Foreign-flag air carrier. An air carrier other than a U.S. flag air carrier in international air transportation. "Foreign air carrier" is a more inclusive term than "foreign-flag air carrier," presumably including those non-U.S. air carriers operating solely within their own domestic boundaries; but in practice the two terms are used interchangeably.

Form 41. The various financial and traffic forms and reports required to be filed with the Board pursuant to Part 241 (Hence "41") of the Civil Aeronautics Board's Economic Regulations comprising the Uniform System of Accounts and Reports for Certificated Air Carriers.

Freedom, air. The privilege granted by one nation to an airline of another nation to operate over or within its territory.

Freedoms, the First Freedom of the Air. The privilege of non-government aircraft to fly over a Contracting Party's territory usually granted bilaterally but also frequently granted multilaterally. See also: Agreement, Two-Freedoms.

Freedoms, the Second Freedom of the Air. The privilege of non-government aircraft to land in a Contracting Party's territory for non-commercial purposes, i.e. technical landings. Usually granted bilaterally, but also frequently granted multilaterally. See also: Agreement, Two-Freedoms.

Freedoms, the Third Freedom of the Air. The privilege of carrying revenue passengers, cargo, and mail from the carrier's own territory (outbound) and off loading them in the territory of another Contracting Party. Usually granted bilaterally. See also: Agreement, Five-Freedoms.

Freedoms, the Fourth Freedom of the Air. The privilege of carrying revenue passengers, cargo, and mail from another Contracting Party's territory (in bound) to the home territory of the airline. Usually granted bilaterally. See also: Agreement, Five Freedoms.

Freedoms, the Fifth Freedom of the Air. The privilege of carrying revenue passengers, cargo, and mail between another Contracting Party's territory and the territory of a third nation. Frequently granted bilaterally, but occasionally withheld. See also: Agreement, Five-Freedoms.

Freedoms, the Sixth Freedom of the Air. The linkage of the Fourth Freedom privilege from one nation to the Third Freedom privilege of another nation, permitting an airline to carry commercial between two distant points *by passing through* its home country. Example: Airline "n" has rights to serve countries "a" and "z". By selling to the same person in "z" two tickets, one "z to n" and another "n to a" the airline can carry that person as Sixth Freedom traffic from "z" to "a" via country "n." Note: airline "n" does not have any official right to carry traffic from "z" to "a." Sixth Freedom is not officially recognized in the Chicago Convention, and is occasionally specifically prohibited in bilateral Air Service Agreements.

Freedoms, the Seventh Freedom of the Air. The linkage of the Fifth Freedom from one route to the Fifth Freedom of another route at a common Fourth Freedom point, permitting an airline to carry commercial traffic between two points *without passing through* the airline's home country. Example: Airline "n" has rights to serve country "p" via route 1 and also via route 2, and to continue on to "y" via route "1" and to continue on to "z" via route "2." By selling the same person in "z" two tickets, one "z to p" and another "p to y" the airline can carry that person as Seventh Freedom traffic from "z" to "y" via point "p" without touching "n." Note: airline 'n' does not have any official right to carry traffic from "z" to "y." Seventh Freedom is not officially recognized in the Chicago Convention.

Freedoms, the Eighth Freedom of the Air. See: Cabotage.

Freight. Property, other than express, mail, and excess passenger baggage, transported by air under published air freight tariffs.

G

"Grandfather rights." The automatic granting of a certificate of public convenience and necessity to those air carriers which had been in continuous operation, and in possession of an air mail contract, for a period of 90 days prior to the passage of the Civil Aeronautics Act of 1938 (Grandfather Clause, Section 401e). Automatic granting of operational authority to a common carrier which has regularly and continuously served the public prior to its subjection to regulation.

General and administrative expenses. Expenses of a general corporate nature and expenses incurred in performing activities which contribute to more than a single operating function such as general financial accounting activities, purchasing activities, representation at law, and other general operational administration not directly applicable to a particular function.

General aviation. Consists of aviation other than military and commercial common carriage and includes business flying, instructional flying, personal flying, and commercial flying such as agricultural spraying and aerial photography.

H

Hearing. Rulemaking, licensing or adjudicatory proceeding for the taking of evidence, in the form of testimony or documents, and the presentation of arguments. Hearings may be presided over by one or more members of the body which comprises the Board, or one or more administrative law judges.

Holding out. The practice of presenting or offering products or services (in this case, air transportation) for sale to the general public.

Hub. A highly populated area consisting of one or more airport cities which the air carriers use as a terminus for routes; a point of concentrating arrivals and departures for passenger access to other flights. Analogous to a wheel with spokes and the hub as the central point.

I

Incidental revenues, net. Revenues less related expenses from services incidental to air transportation, such as sales of service, supplies, and parts, and rental of operating property and equipment.

Income statement. A statement of revenues and expenses and resulting net income or loss covering a stated period of time.

Instrument flight rules (IFR). Rules specified by qualified authority (FAA) for flight under weather conditions such that visual reference cannot be made to the ground and the pilot must rely on instruments to fly and navigate.

International and territorial operations. Operators of aircraft flying between the 50 States of the United States and foreign points, between the 50 States and U.S. possessions or territories, and between foreign points. Includes both the combination passenger/cargo and the all cargo carriers engaged in international and territorial operations.

International air transport association. A voluntary organization open to any scheduled air carrier whose home country is a member (or eligible to be) of the International Civil Aviation Organization (ICAO). Its main function is the economic regulation of international air transportation, in particular, international rates and fares, that are set by one of seven Regional or Joint Traffic Conferences and subject to unanimous resolutions of the carriers and provided that the countries do not object.

International civil aviation organization. A specialized agency of the United Nations composed of contracting states to develop the principles and techniques of international air navigation and to foster the planning and development of international air transport.

Intra-Alaska operations. The granting of statehood to Alaska and Hawaii requires the inclusion of their intra-state operations with the domestic group even for the years prior to 1959. In early CAB publications, intra-Hawaii operations were included with domestic, and later treated separately as a territorial group. When intra-Alaska data became available, both intra-Hawaii and intra-Alaska were grouped, and continued to be treated, separately, as territorial operations until 1959, when they were included with domestic.

Intra-Hawaii operations. The granting of statehood to Alaska and Hawaii requires the inclusion of their intrastate operations with the domestic group. However, this *Handbook* includes such operations with the domestic group even for the years prior to 1959. In early CAB publications, intra-Hawaii operations were included with domestic, and later treated separately as a territorial group. When intra-Alaska data became available, both intra-Hawaii and intra-Alaska were grouped, and continued to be treated, separately, as territorial operations until 1959, when they were included with domestic.

Intrastate. Existing or occurring within a single state. Within one state of the United States.

L

Landing area. Any locality, either of land or water, including airports and intermediate landing fields, which is used, or intended to be used, for the landing and take-off of aircraft, whether or not facilities are provided for the shelter, servicing, or repair of aircraft, or for receiving or discharging passengers or cargo.

Large regionals. Certificated air carriers with annual operating revenues of between $10,000,000 and $75,000,000.

Load factor, revenue passenger. The percent that revenue passenger-miles are of available seat-miles in revenue passenger services, representing the proportion of aircraft seating capacity that is actually sold and utilized.

$$\text{Load Factor} = \frac{\text{Revenue passenger miles}}{\text{Available seat miles}}$$

M

Mail, nonpriority. Mail moving at surface transportation rates lower than those established for mail bearing postage established specifically for air mail service.

Mail priority. Mail bearing postage at rates established specifically for air mail service or mail moving at service transportation rates equivalent to those established for air mail service.

Majors. Certificated air carriers with annual operating revenues of $1,000,000,000 or more.

Medium regionals. Certificated air carriers with annual operating revenues of less than $10,000,000.

Merger. The acquisition of one airline by another, either through purchase of stock or direct purchase of assets, and the merging of operations.

Military airlift command (MAC). A major command organization of the United States Air Force which provides air transportation for personnel and cargo for *all* military services on a worldwide basis. MAC is the contractor for the U.S. Air Force's Logair and the U.S. Navy's Quicktrans.

Mutual aid pact. A voluntary agreement among several air carriers (originally trunk carriers only, now may include local service carriers) providing for mutual assistance in the event any party's flight operations are shut down by a strike called before exhaustion of the procedures of the Railway Labor Act, or under other special conditions. If a strike fulfilling the requirements of the agreement should occur, the parties remaining in operation pay to the strike-bound carrier their increased "windfall" revenues during the term of, and attributable to, the strike less applicable added direct costs. The actual formulation of these payments is complex, but basically provides that the "windfall" payments to the struck carrier cover a percentage (declining, by 5% per week from 50% for the first two weeks of the strike, to 35% for the fifth and any additional weeks of the strike) of the struck carrier's normal air transport operating expenses for the flight operations shut down. Should "windfall" payments fail to meet the required percentage of the struck carrier's operating expenses then "supplemental" payments must be made by all participating carriers, whether liable for "windfall" payments or not, to meet the deficit between "windfall" payments and the operating expenses to be reimbursed. The maximum annual obligation of a participating carrier to contribute to "supplemental" payments is 1% of the paying carrier's air transport operating revenue in the preceding calendar year.

N

Nationals. Certificated air carriers with annual operating revenues of between $100 million and $1,000,000,000.

National Aeronautics and Space Administration (NASA). A U.S. Government organization established by the National Aeronautics and Space Act of 1958 (72 Stat. 426; 42 U.S.C. 2451) with the principal statutory functions to: conduct research for the solution of problems of flight within and outside the earth's atmosphere, and develop, construct, test and operate aeronautical and space vehicles; conduct activities required for the exploration of space with manned and unmanned vehicles, and arrange for the most effective utilization of the scientific and engineering resources of the United States with other nations engaged in aeronautical and space activities for peaceful purposes. Many of NASA's research programs have led to findings and developments which are applicable to today's conventional air transportation.

National Transportation Safety Board (NTSB). An autonomous agency established as such in 1975, by the Independent Safety Board Act. The Board seeks to assure that all types of transportation in the United States are conducted safely. The Board investigates accidents and makes recommendations to Government agencies, the transportation industry, and others on safety measures and practices.

Navigable airspace. The airspace above the minimum altitudes of flight prescribed by regulations issued under the FAA Act, and shall include airspace needed to insure safety in takeoff and landing of aircraft.

Net profit margin. Net profit after interest and after taxes as percent of operating revenues.

Nonscheduled. Of or relating to air transport services or operations performed pursuant to chartering of aircraft or other activities not constituting an integral part of services performed pursuant to published schedules and related nonrevenue operations.

Nonstop. Service between two points on a single flight with no scheduled stops between the points. Authority granted, in a certificate of public convenience and necessity, to a carrier to service two points without additional scheduled stops.

No show. A person who books a reservation, or books a reservation and purchases a ticket for a flight, and fails to use the reservation or ticket and also fails to notify the carrier of that intent prior to the flight's departure.

O

Official airline guide (OAG). A bimonthly publication of the scheduled operations and service of the air carriers. Printed in a format to show service and fares to one city from all other cities where direct or simple connecting service is available, with separate editions for North America, Worldwide, and Air-cargo services. (Note: Not considered the same as the "published schedule" as filed by a carrier with the Board. However, a carrier's schedule, fare, and service information printed in the OAG except that which is for air transportation wholly between foreign points, must be contained in the published schedules and tariffs filed at the Board).

Operating expenses. Expenses incurred in the performance of air transportation. Includes direct aircraft operating expenses and ground and indirect operating expenses.

Operating profit or loss. The profit or loss from performance of air transportation, based on over-all operating revenues and over-all operating expenses. Does not include nonoperating income and expenses or special items and is before income taxes.

Operating Profit Margin. Operating profit (operating revenues minus operating expenses) as percent of operating revenues.

Operating revenues. Revenues from the performance of air transportation and related incidental services. Includes (1) transport revenues from the carriage of all classes of traffic in scheduled and nonscheduled services including the performance of aircraft charters and (2) nontransport revenues consisting of Federal subsidy (where applicable) and the net amount of revenues less related expenses from services incidental to air transportation.

Operation(s), aircraft. The use of aircraft, for the purpose of air navigation and includes the navigation of aircraft. Any person who causes or authorizes the operation of aircraft, whether with or without the right of legal control (in the capacity of owner, lessee, or otherwise) of the aircraft, shall be deemed to be engaged in the operation of aircraft within the meaning of the Federal Aviation Act.

Operation(s), domestic. Flight stages within the 50 States of the United States and the District of Columbia including operation between States separated by foreign territory or major expanses of international waters. Currently includes; the domestic operations of the certificated trunk carriers and Pan American, the operations of the local service, helicopter, Alaskan, Hawaiian, domestic all-cargo and "other carriers." The "other carriers" classification contains the operations of Aspen Airways and Wright Airlines. In addition, any trans-border Canadian operations conducted on the domestic route segments of U.S. air carriers are shown as domestic operations.

Operation(s), international. Flight stages with one or both terminals outside of territory under U.S. jurisdiction.

Operation(s), international/territorial. Flight stages with one or both terminals outside the 50 States of the United States and the District of Columbia.

Operation(s), overseas/foreign. Applies to all operations other than domestic; including but not limited to overseas operations between a place in a State, or the District of Columbia and any place in a Territory or possession of the U.S., or between a place in a Territory or a possession of the U.S., and a place in any other Territory or possession of the U.S. and foreign operations between a place in the U.S. and any place outside thereof.

Operation(s), territorial. Flight stages with both terminals within territory under U.S. jurisdiction where at least one of the terminals is not within a State or the District of Columbia.

Operator, air taxi. A classification of air carriers which directly engage in the air transportation of persons or property or mail in any combination of such transportation and which: (1) do not, directly or indirectly, utilize large aircraft; (2) do not hold a certificate of public convenience and necessity or other economic authority other than that provided in Part 298 of the Board's Economic Regulations; and (3) have and maintain in effect liability insurance coverage in compliance with Board requirements.

Operator, commercial. One of a class of air carriers operating on a private for-hire basis, as distinguished from a public or common air carrier, holding a commercial operator certificate, issued by the Administrator of the Federal Aviation Administration (pursuant to Part 45 of the Civil Air Regulations) authorizing it to operate aircraft in air commerce for the transportation of goods or passengers for compensation or hire.

Operator, fixed-base. One who conducts a business operation at an airport or airfield, involving the selling and/or servicing of aircraft, giving flying instruction, making charter flights, etc.

Opinion. An order, in whole or in part; an initial decision.

Order. The whole or part of a final disposition, whether affirmative, negative, injunctive or declaratory in form in a matter other than rulemaking but including licensing.

Origin and destination survey. An abbreviated form for Domestic (also International), Origin-Destination Survey of Airline Passenger Traffic, a 10% sample of passengers' origins and destinations in air transportation based on an analysis of selected flight coupons.

Overflight. A scheduled flight which does not stop at an intermediate point in its scheduled route because: (a) the point is certified as a flag stop, and there is no traffic to be deplaned or enplaned; (b) the carrier has received authority to temporarily suspend service to that point; (c) weather conditions or other safety and technical reasons do not permit landing; or (d) for any other reason. The aircraft need not fly directly over the point.

Oversale. The sale of (or the acceptance of reservations for) more space (passenger seats) than is actually available on a flight. A practice which is used sometimes by the air carriers as an allowance for that historical percentage of passengers who fail, for some reason, to utilize the space they have reserved on a flight. In those cases where the actual number of passengers with purchased tickets exceed the available space for a flight, the carrier is liable for denied boarding compensation to those passengers not accommodated on the flight or on comparable air transportation (subject to Part 250 of Economic Regulations).

P

Passenger-mile. One passenger transported one mile. Passenger-miles are computed by multiplying the aircraft miles flown on each flight stage by the number of passengers transported on that stage.

Passenger-mile, nonrevenue. One nonrevenue passenger transported one mile.

Passenger-mile, revenue. One revenue passenger transported one mile in revenue service.

Passenger, revenue. A person receiving air transportation from the air carrier for which remuneration is received by the air carrier. Air carrier employees or others receiving air transportation against whom token charges are levied are considered nonrevenue passengers. Infants for whom a token fare is charged are not counted as passengers.

Passenger, revenue per aircraft. The average number of passengers carried per aircraft in revenue passenger services, derived by dividing the total revenue passenger-miles by the total aircraft miles flown in revenue passenger services.

Payload. The actual or potential revenue-producing portion of an aircraft's takeoff weight, in passengers, free baggage, excess baggage, freight, express, and mail.

Pooling. An agreement between two or more air carriers to share revenues in particular markets in some predetermined ratio regardless of traffic carried by each individual carrier. Unlawful without prior approval.

Prehearing conference. A conference held before an administrative law judge prior to the actual hearing. At a prehearing conference, administrative and procedural guidelines are adopted and issues of the particular case are defined.

Productivity. Average total number of employees divided into the indicated traffic and financial measures for the year.

Promotion and sales expenses. Costs incurred in promoting the use of air transportation generally and creating a public preference for the services of particular air carriers. Includes the functions of selling, advertising and publicity, space reservations, and developing tariffs and flight schedules for publication.

Public service revenues (subsidy). Payments by the federal government which provide for air service to communities in the United States where traffic levels are such that air service could not otherwise be supported.

R

Rate of return, corporate (return on investment and ROI). An overall rate of return on investment representing a return on the air carrier's (corporation's) total operations including nontransport ventures. In developing such a return, no adjustment is made to the data reported in financial statements submitted in Form 41. The corporate rate of return is developed by dividing, (a) the net income after taxes plus interest expenses on debt by, (b) the total investment in the carrier. This rate of return is calculated on a recurrent basis for presentation of the financial performance of the carrier and differs from the regulatory rate of return used for rate making and subsidy purposes.

$$\text{Return on Investment} = \frac{\text{Net Profit}}{\text{Assets}}$$

Rate of return, regulatory (return on investment and ROI). A rate of return on a carrier's (carrier group's or industry's) recognized investment calculated and used by the Board as a "fair and reasonable return" in determining the fare level in the regulatory rate-making process and in determining the subsidy need for a carrier (carrier group or industry). Differs from corporate rate of return which includes all corporate operations and ventures while regulatory rate of return essentially includes only those elements found used and useful to the operation of certificated route air transportation.

Rate, general commodity. A rate which is published to apply on all articles or commodities except those which will not be accepted for transportation under the terms of the tariff containing such rate or of governing tariffs.

Rate, joint. A rate, published as a single factor, that applies to transportation over the lines or routes of two or more carriers and which is made and published by arrangement or agreement between such carriers, evidenced by concurrence or power of attorney.

Rate, specific commodity. A rate which is published to apply only on a specific commodity or commodities which are specifically named or described in the item naming such rate or in an item specifically referred to by such rate in the manner prescribed by Part 221.75 of Economic Regulations.

Rebate. The practice of charging, demanding, collecting, or receiving less compensation for air transportation, or for any service in connection therewith, than the rates, fares, or charges specified in the air carrier's then currently effective tariffs on file with the Board; or refunding or remitting, in any manner or by any device, directly or indirectly, or through any agent, or broker, or otherwise, any portion of the rates, fares, or charges so specified, or extending to any person any privileges or facilities, with respect to matters required by the Board to be specified in tariffs or agreements except those specified therein.

Return on investment. Net profits plus interest expense (on long-term debt) divided by long-term debt plus stockholder's equity (net worth).

Revenue. Compensation or remuneration received by the carrier.

Revenue, charter. Revenue from nonscheduled air transport services where the party or parties receiving the transportation obtains exclusive use of the aircraft at published tariff rates and the remuneration paid by such party accrues directly to, and the responsibility for providing transportation is that of, the accounting air carrier. Passenger charter revenues are from charter flights carrying only passengers and their personal baggage. Freight charter revenues are from charter flights carrying either freight only, or passengers and freight simultaneously.

Revenue, foreign mail. Revenues from the transportation by air of mail outside the United States by U.S. flag carriers for a foreign government.

Revenue, passenger. Revenues from the transportation of passengers by air. These revenues are predominantly from individually ticketed passengers carried in scheduled service.

Revenue passenger enplanements. The count of the total number of passengers boarding aircraft. This includes both originating and connecting passengers.

Revenue passenger load factor. Revenue passenger miles as a percent of available seat miles in revenue passenger services, representing the proportion of aircraft seating capacity that is actually sold and utilized.

Revenue passenger mile. One fare-paying passenger transported one mile in revenue service.

Revenue ton mile. One ton of revenue traffic (passenger and/or cargo) transported one mile.

Revenue, transport. Revenues from the transportation by air of all classes of traffic in scheduled and nonscheduled services, including the performance of charters.

Revenue, transport-related. Remuneration received for providing air transportation facilities associated with the performance of services which emanate from and are incidental to air transportation services performed by the air carrier (i.e., in-flight services of food, beverage and entertainment; air cargo pick-up and delivery charges; ground restaurant and food services; and amounts received from mutual aid benefits).

Route. A system of points to be served by an air carrier as indicated in its certificate of public convenience and necessity. A route may include all points on a carrier's system or may represent only a systematic portion of all of the points within a carrier's total system.

Route, certificated. A listing of points to which an air carrier is authorized to provide air transportation, subject to the terms, conditions, and limitations prescribed in a carrier's certificate of public convenience and necessity issued pursuant to Section 401(d)(1) or (2) of the Act.

S

Scheduled airlines. Carriers certificated by the Federal Government under Section 401 of the Federal Aviation Act permitting the operation of large aircraft larger than 60 seats.

Schedule, published. An official schedule of an air carrier showing the points between which the air carrier is authorized to engage in air transportation, all aircraft that will be operated by the air carrier between such points, and the time of arrival and departure at each point.

Scheduled service. Transport service operated over the routes of a U.S. scheduled airline, based on published flight schedules, including extra sections.

Seat-mile. One passenger seat transported one statute mile. Used to report available passenger carrying capacity on an aircraft, however, when the seat is occupied by a revenue passenger, the measurement unit is referred to as a revenue passenger-mile (RPM).

Seat-mile, available. The aircraft miles flown on each flight stage multiplied by the number of seats available for revenue use on that stage.

Service, coach (tourist). The basic transport service specifically established for the carriage of passengers at fares that are predicated on both the operation of specifically designated aircraft space and a quality of service regularly and ordinarily provided by the trunk air carriers.

Service, economy. Domestically, transport service established for the carriage of passengers at fares and quality of service below each service. Internationally, synonymous with coach service.

Service, first-class. Transport service established for the carriage of passengers at premium fares that are predicated on both the operation of specifically designated aircraft space and a quality of service above that which is regularly and ordinarily provided.

Service, mixed. Transport service for the carriage in any combination of first-class, coach (tourist), and/or economy (thrift) passengers on the same aircraft. May include freight, express, and/or mail, but excludes all-first-class, all-coach and all-economy service.

Service, nonscheduled. Includes transport service between points not covered by certificates of public convenience and necessity issued to the air carrier; services pursuant to the charter or hiring of aircraft; other revenue services not constituting an integral part of the services performed pursuant to published schedules; and related nonrevenue flights.

Service, scheduled. Transport service operated over an air carrier's certificated routes pursuant to published flight schedules, including extra sections and related nonrevenue flights.

Service, shuttle. A relatively low-fare, no-reservation no-frill service. The lower fare is based on the cost savings of high density seating, no reservations, and no meal or beverage service. This service is usually only offered in high traffic markets and may also require the passenger to carry his own baggage to the boarding gate.

Service, tourist (coach). In international operations, "tourist" is the generally used term for coach service.

Show cause order. More properly, but rather uncommon, "order to show cause." An order directing the respondent to show cause why the Board should not adopt the findings and conclusions specified in the order.

Space available. A term applied to passengers who, for lack of reservations and/or for reduced-rate charges, must await the boarding of other passengers, and will not themselves be boarded unless there is additional space available on board the aircraft.

Speed, block-to-block (block speed). The average speed in statute miles per hour, of an aircraft between the time the aircraft first moves under its own power for purposes of flight, until it comes to rest at the next point of landing. Since this speed is from airport ramp to airport ramp, it includes taxi time before takeoff and after landing, takeoff and landing time as well as airborne time. It is calculated by dividing the sum of airport-to-airport distances, in statute miles, by the number of block hours.

Stage, flight. The operation of an aircraft from takeoff to landing.

Stage length, average (overall flight stage length). The average distance covered per aircraft hop in revenue service, from take-off to landing. Derived by dividing the total aircraft miles flown in revenue services by the number of revenue aircraft departures performed.

Stop, flag. A point on an air carrier's certificated route that is scheduled to be served only when traffic is to be picked up or discharged.

Stop, intermediate. A scheduled stop for traffic or technical purposes, made at a point in a scheduled route or flight other than the terminal points.

Subsidy. Compensation paid pursuant to Section 406 of the Federal Aviation Act, to air carriers to enable them to maintain and continue the development of needed air services. In recent years, subsidy has been paid only to local service carriers and Alaskan carriers with the objective of assuring continued air service to small communities which do not generate sufficient traffic to support viable commercial operations. Trunkline carriers retain statutory eligibility for subsidy but no subsidy has been paid to trunklines since the 1950's.

Supplemental air carrier. One of a class of air carriers holding certificates, authorizing them to perform passenger and cargo charter services supplementing the scheduled service of the certificated route air carriers. They are sometimes referred to as nonscheduled carriers.

T

Tariff. The notice of fares and rates applicable to the transportation of persons or property, and the rules relating to or affecting such fares and rates or transportation.

Tariff, published. A publication containing rates applicable to the transportation of persons or cargo and rules relating to or affecting such rates or transportation.

Ticket. A printed document that serves as evidence of payment of the fare for air transportation. Generally, this takes the form of the standard Air Traffic Conference ticket which is composed of an auditor's coupon, agent's coupon, flight coupon(s), and passenger's coupon. It authorizes carriage between the points and via the routing indicated, and also shows the passenger's name, class of service, carrier(s), flight number(s), date of travel and all conditions of the contract of carriage.

Ton-mile. One ton transported one mile. Ton-miles are computed by multiplying the aircraft miles flown on each flight stage by the number of tons transported on that stage.

Ton-mile, available. The total number of tons available for the transportation of passengers, freight and mail multiplied by the number of miles which this capacity is flown.

Ton-mile, mail. One ton of U.S. and/or foreign mail transported one mile.

Ton-mile, passenger. One ton of passenger weight (including all baggage) transported one mile.

Ton-mile, revenue. One ton of revenue traffic transported one statute mile. Revenue ton-miles are computed by multiplying tons of revenue traffic (passengers, freight, mail, and express) by the miles that this traffic is flown.

Tour, inclusive. A round-trip tour which combines air transportation (pursuant to an inclusive tour charter or group or individual inclusive tour tariffs in scheduled service) and land services, and which meets additional requirements of minimum days accommodations, and other land services to be included in the price of the tour.

Tour package. A joint service that gives a traveler a significantly lower price for a combination of services than could be obtained if each had to be purchased separately by the traveler. Thus, the total price of a package tour might include a roundtrip plane ticket, hotel accommodations, meals, several sight-seeing bus tours, and theater tickets.

Tour wholesaler. A person who contracts with hotels, sight-seeing and other ground components to provide ground packages, for sale to individuals, through travel agents and direct air carriers, to be used in conjunction with scheduled air transportation.

Traffic, air. The passengers and cargo (freight, express and mail) transported on any aircraft movement.

Traffic density. The total amount or units of traffic traveling or carried; between two points; over a route, over a route segment; on a flight.

Traffic, interline. Traffic (passengers and/or cargo) transported over the lines or routes of two or more carriers as a single movement with an interline connection.

Traffic, revenue. Passengers and cargo transported by air for which remuneration is received by the air carrier. Passengers (including air carrier employees) and cargo carried for token service charges are not considered revenue traffic.

Trip. In common speech, the term "trip" tends to include both the going and returning portions of a journey. In airline usage, it is important to distinguish between whether "trip" is used in a one-way or round-trip sense. Published statistics on average length of air trips are almost always one-way distances since it is virtually impossible to determine from reported data what the round-trip distance is. Fares, on the other hand, are sometimes quoted as one-way prices and, at other times as round-trip prices; the round-trip price is not always equal to twice the one-way price.

U

United States, citizen of. Refers to: (1) an individual who is a citizen of the United States or of one of its possessions; or (2) a partnership of which each member is such an individual; or (3) a corporation or association created or organized under the laws of the United States or any State, Territory, or possession of the United States, of which the president and two-thirds or more of the Board of Directors and other managing officers thereof are such individuals and in which at least 75 percent of the voting interest is owned or controlled by persons who are citizens of the United States or of one of its possessions.

United States, continental. The 48 contiguous States, and the District of Columbia.

United States Territory. For statistical reporting purposes: areas or places under the possession and jurisdiction of the United States outside the 50 States of the United States and the District of Columbia (e.g., Guam, Puerto Rico, and the Virgin Islands).

Use-it-or-lose-it policy. A basic policy of affording the advantages of air transportation to as many persons as practicable. The Board has substantially expanded the services of subsidized local carriers and has given many small cities, with marginal or unknown traffic potentialities, a chance to demonstrate that they will use and can support new or improved air services adapted to their specific needs. The Board expects the cities awarded local air service to make a determined effort to generate the traffic forecast in the certification proceedings. Unless adequate use is made of subsidized air services, the cost to the Government is unjustified and the service will be terminated.

U.S. Scheduled Airlines. Carriers certificated by the federal government under Section 401 of the Federal Aviation Act permitting the operation of large aircraft with sixty seats or more.

U.S. flag carriers or American flag carrier. One of a class of air carriers holding a certificate of public convenience and necessity approved by the President, authorizing scheduled operations over specified route between the United States (and/or its territories) and one or more foreign countries.

Utilization. Average daily use of aircraft for a period of time, usually monthly or yearly, obtained by dividing the total hours flown by the number of aircraft; then divide the result by the number of days for the time period.

$$\text{Utilization} = \frac{\dfrac{\text{Hours flown}}{\text{Number of aircraft}}}{\text{Number of days}}$$

V

Visual flight rules (VFR). Rules specified by qualified authority establishing minimum flying altitudes and limits of visibility to govern visual flight.

W

War air service program (WASP). The program designed, pursuant to Executive Order 12490, to provide in time of national emergency for the maintenance of essential civil air routes and services, and to provide for the distribution and redistribution of air carrier aircraft among civil air transport carriers after withdrawal of aircraft allocated to the Civil Reserve Air Fleet.

Weight, allowable gross. The maximum gross weight (of the aircraft and its contents) which an air-craft is licensed to carry into the air on each flight stage.

Weight, maximum certificated takeoff. The maximum takeoff weight authorized by the terms of the aircraft airworthiness certificate. (This is found in the airplane operating record or in the airplane flight manual which is incorporated by regulation into the airworthiness certificate.)

Weight, maximum gross takeoff. The maximum permissible weight of an aircraft and its contents at takeoff. Includes the empty weight of the aircraft, accessories, fuel, crew and payload.

Weight, passenger. A standard weight of 200 lbs. per passenger (including all baggage), used for all civil operations and classes of service.

Y

Yield. The air transport revenue per unit of traffic carried in air transportation. May be calculated and presented several ways (*e.g.,* passenger revenue per passenger-mile, per aircraft-mile, per passenger ton-mile and per passenger).

$$\text{Yield} = \frac{\text{Passenger revenue}}{\text{Revenue passenger miles}}$$

Index

A

Abbas ibn-Firnas, 30
Accessories and aviation/aerospace industry, 7
Accidents. *See also* National Transportation Safety Board (NTSB); Safety/security
  Air Transport International flight 805, 265
  American Airlines DC-10 flight 102, 270
  American Airlines McDonnell Douglas DC-10 (May 1979), 260–261
  categories of, 281
  Cessna 177-B (April 1996), 271–272
  Cessna Model 172K (XP) (Feb. 1980), 263
  China Eastern Airlines MD-11, 269
  classification of, 255–256
  Continental Airlines (COA) flight 1943, Douglas DC-9-32 (Feb. 1996), 272–274
  Delta Flight 191 (Aug. 1985), 264
  Douglas DC-9-32 (May, 1996), 277–278
  information sources for, 281–282
  International Civil Aviation Organization (ICAO) and, 257–258
  International Transportation Safety Association and, 398
  leading causes of, 282
  Lockerbie, Scotland, (Dec. 21, 1988), 148
  Mitsubishi MU-sB/Piper PA-32 Saratoga collision (1992), 268–269
  National Technical Information Service (NTIS) and, 259
  National Transportation Safety Board (NTSB) and, 250–253
  overall general aviation rate of, 641
  statistics (1982–2000), 293–301
  statistics (2000), 284–286, 288–292, 302
  Trans World Airlines B-727 (4-79), 262–263
  Trans World Airlines flight 843, 267
  Trans World Airlines (TWA) flight 800, Boeing 747–131 (July 1996), 278–280
  United Airlines B-737 (1991), 265–266
  United Airlines flight 232, DC-10-10, 270–271
  United Express flight 5925, Beechcraft 1900C/Beechcraft King Air A90 collision (Nov. 1996), 275–276
  Wings West Airlines Beech C-99/Rockwell Commander (Aug. 1984), 261–262
  World Trade Center bombings, (Sept. 11, 2001), 10–11, 280–281
Accountability and Free Flight Phase I, 214–215
Accounting, 447–459
Achenbach, 46
Adams, Brock, 147
Ader, Clement, 45, 48, 62
Administration, 160, 199–203. *See also individual departments, i.e.* Office of Budget
Administrative Law Judges (accident information source), 282
Admiralty laws, 471–472
Advance Land Acquisition Loans, 176
Advanced Automation System Facility, 231
Advanced Development Projects (ADP), 600
Advanced General Aviation Transportation Experiments (AGATE), 642
Advertising and commercial blimps, 39
Aerial applications, 637, 643
Aerial Carriage of Sir George Cayley, 41–42
Aerial Experiment Association, 67
Aerial observation, 636–637
Aerocurvo Ponzelli, 71
Aerodrome, 57, 59
Aeromedical (segment) of Civil Reserve Air Fleet (CRAF), 18–20
Aeronautical Society of Great Britain, 44
Aeronautics and Space federal regulations, 483–487
Aerospace Industries Association (AIA), 520–527
Aerospatiale, 607
Agencies of DOT
  Bureau of Transportation Statistics, 182, 184
  Federal Aviation Administration (FAA), 165–166
  Federal Highway Administration (FHWA), 166–170
  Federal Motor Carrier Safety Administration (FMCSA), 185–187
  Federal Railroad Administration (FRA), 170–173
  Federal Transit Administration (FTA), 176–178
  Maritime Administration (MARAD), 179–181
  National Highway Traffic Safety Administration, 173–175
  Research and Special Programs Administration (RSPA), 182–183
  Saint Lawrence Seaway Development Corporation, 178–180
  United States Coast Guard, 161–165
Aids to Navigation (U.S. Coast Guard), 163
Air Agency Rating Certificate, 234, 237
Air cargo. *See* Cargo
Air carrier all-cargo certificate, 309
Air carrier economic regulations. *See* Economic regulations
Air carrier fleet, 515
Air carrier management/organization
  economics and, 425–428
  engineering department and, 433
  finance department and, 431
  flight operations department and, 432
  geographic distribution and, 424
  ground operations department and, 432
  industrial relations department and, 430
  interdependence of functions, 423–424
  legal department and, 430
  line department and, 431
  Load Factors and, 417
  maintenance department and, 433
  obsolescence/technological change and, 424
  organization (flowchart), 428–430
  overhaul department and, 432–433
  planning department and, 431
  principles of, 418–421
  public relations and, 430
  purchasing department and, 431
  sales/marketing and, 431–432
  scheduling department and, 431
  staff departments, 430
  subcontractors and, 433
Air carrier marketing
  activities/research and, 436–437
  definition/functions, 435
  fleet planning and, 514
  place and, 436–440
  price and, 436, 441–449
  product and, 436–437
  promotion and, 436, 440–441
Air Carrier Operating Certificates, 234, 236–237